ACCOUNTING PRINCIPLES, VOLUME 1

A Wiley Canada Custom Publication for

Kwantlen Polytechnic University

ACCT 1110

WILEY

Wiley Canada Custom Services

JOHN WILEY & SONS CANADA, LTD.

Cover Design: Natalia Burobina

Marketing Manager: Aida Krneta
Custom Coordinator: Sara Tinteri

Printed and bound in Canada

John Wiley & Sons Canada, Ltd
6045 Freemont Blvd.
Mississauga, Ontario
L5R 4J3
WILEY   Visit our website at: www.wiley.ca

CONTENTS – VOLUME 1

ACCOUNTING PRINCIPLES

ACCOUNTING PRINCIPLES

FIFTH CANADIAN EDITION

→ Jerry J. Weygandt *Ph.D., C.P.A.*
University of Wisconsin—Madison

→ Donald E. Kieso *Ph.D., C.P.A.*
Northern Illinois University

→ Paul D. Kimmel *Ph.D., C.P.A.*
University of Wisconsin—Milwaukee

→ Barbara Trenholm *M.B.A., F.C.A.*
University of New Brunswick—Fredericton

→ Valerie A. Kinnear *M.Sc. (Bus. Admin.), C.A.*
Mount Royal University

In collaboration with
Joan Barlow, Mount Royal University
Brad Witt, Humber Institute of Technology & Advanced Learning

WILEY

John Wiley & Sons Canada, Ltd.

To our students—past, present, and future

Library and Archives Canada Cataloguing in Publication

Accounting principles / Jerry J. Weygandt... [et al.]. --

5th Canadian ed.

ISBN 978-0-470-16079-4 (pt. 1)

1. Accounting--Textbooks. I. Weygandt, Jerry J.

HF5636.A33 2009a   657'.044   C2009-903891-9

Production Credits

Acquisitions Editor: Zoë Craig
Vice President & Publisher: Veronica Visentin
Vice President, Publishing Services: Karen Bryan
Creative Director, Publishing Services: Ian Koo
Director, Market Development: Carolyn Wells
Marketing Manager: Aida Krneta
Editorial Manager: Karen Staudinger
Developmental Editor: Daleara Jamasji Hirjikaka
Media Editor: Channade Fenandoe
Editorial Assistant: Laura Hwee
Design & Typesetting: OrangeSprocket Communications
Cover Design: Natalia Burobina
Printing & Binding: World Color Press Inc.

Printed and bound in the United States
1 2 3 4 5 WC 14 13 12 11 10

John Wiley & Sons Canada, Ltd.
6045 Freemont Blvd.
Mississauga, Ontario L5R 4J3
Visit our website at: www.wiley.ca

Fifth Canadian Edition

Barbara Trenholm, MBA, FCA, is a professor emerita at the University of New Brunswick, for which she continues to teach locally and internationally on a part-time basis. Her teaching and educational leadership has been widely recognized. She is a recipient of the Leaders in Management Education Award, the Global Teaching Excellence Award, and the University of New Brunswick's Merit Award and Dr. Allan P. Stuart Award for Excellence in Teaching.

Barbara Trenholm is an active member of the Board of Directors of Atomic Energy of Canada Limited and Plazacorp Retail Properties Ltd. She is a past member, and co-chair, of the University of New Brunswick Pension Board of Trustees and a past member of the Canadian Institute of Chartered Accountants (CICA) Board of Directors. She is a past president of the New Brunswick Institute of Chartered Accountants, and has served as a member of the Atlantic School of Chartered Accountancy Board of Governors, the CICA Qualifications Committee, the International Qualifications Appraisal Board, the Education Reeingineering Task Force, and the American Accounting Association's Globalization Initiatives Task Force. She has chaired and been a member of numerous other education committees at both the provincial and national levels of the profession.

She has presented at many conferences and published widely in the field of accounting education and standard-setting in journals including *Accounting Horizons, Journal of the Academy of Business Education, CAmagazine, CGA Magazine,* and *CMA Magazine*. She is also the Canadian author of Kimmel, Weygandt, Kieso, and Trenholm, *Financial Accounting: Tools for Business Decision-Making*, published by John Wiley & Sons Canada, Ltd.

Valerie Kinnear, M.Sc. (Bus. Admin.), CA, is an associate professor of accounting in the Bissett School of Business, Mount Royal University, in Calgary, Alberta. She has a wide range of teaching experience, including introductory, intermediate, and advanced financial accounting as well as introductory managerial accounting and finance courses. She has been nominated for the Distinguished Faculty Award at Mount Royal for her teaching expertise. Professor Kinnear has chaired and served on numerous faculty and university committees and held a variety of administrative positions at Mount Royal, including acting dean of the School of Business and acting director of Business Education and Training in the Faculty of Continuing Education & Extension. She is currently chair of the Management, Marketing, and Human Resources Academic Unit and has previously been chair of a variety of business programs, including Accounting, Financial Services, Supply Chain Management, and Insurance.

She has also been active in the accounting profession. She participated in the Institute of Chartered Accountants of Alberta student education program in a variety of roles, including as an instructor, marker, author, and member of the Alberta Institute's Examinations Committee. She has also served as a member of the Professional Services Policy Board of the Canadian Institute of Chartered Accountants, as a board member of the Canadian Accounting Academic Association, and as treasurer for many volunteer community organizations in Calgary.

Professor Kinnear has a Bachelor of Social Work from the University of Calgary, a Master of Science in Business Administration from the University of British Columbia, and professional accounting experience with PricewaterhouseCoopers, Farvolden and Company Chartered Accountants, and Kinnear & Smistad Chartered Accountants.

U.S. Edition

Jerry J. Weygandt, PhD, CPA, is the Arthur Andersen Alumni Professor of Accounting at the University of Wisconsin—Madison. He holds a PhD in accounting from the University of Illinois. His articles have appeared in *Accounting Review, Journal of Accounting Research, Accounting Horizons, Journal of Accountancy*, and other academic and professional journals. Professor Weygandt is the author of other accounting and financial reporting books and is a member of the American Accounting Association, the American Institute of Certified Public Accountants, and the Wisconsin Society of Certified Public Accountants. He is the recipient of the Wisconsin Institute of CPAs' Outstanding Educator's Award and the Lifetime Achievement Award. In 2001 he received the American Accounting Association's Outstanding Accounting Educator Award.

Donald E. Kieso, PhD, CPA, received his bachelor's degree from Aurora University and his doctorate in accounting from the University of Illinois. He has served as chairman of the Department of Accountancy and is currently the KPMG Emeritus Professor of Accounting at Northern Illinois University. He has public accounting experience with PricewaterhouseCoopers (San Francisco and Chicago) and Arthur Andersen & Co. (Chicago) and research experience with the Research Division of the American Institute of Certified Public Accountants (New York). He has done post-doctoral work as a Visiting Scholar at the University of California at Berkeley and is a recipient of NIU's Teaching Excellence Award and four Golden Apple Teaching Awards. Professor Kieso is the author of other accounting and business books and is a member of the American Accounting Association, the American Institute of Certified Public Accountants, and the Illinois CPA Society. He is the recipient of the Outstanding Accounting Educator Award from the Illinois CPA Society, the FSA's Joseph A. Silvoso Award of Merit, the NIU Foundation's Humanitarian Award for Service to Higher Education, the Distinguished Service Award from the Illinois CPA Society, and in 2003 an honorary doctorate from Aurora University.

Paul D. Kimmel, PhD, CPA, received his bachelor's degree from the University of Minnesota and his doctorate in accounting from the University of Wisconsin. He is an Associate Professor at the University of Wisconsin—Milwaukee, and has public accounting experience with Deloitte (Minneapolis). He was the recipient of the UWM School of Business Advisory Council Teaching Award and the Reggie Taite Excellence in Teaching Award, and is a three-time winner of the Outstanding Teaching Assistant Award at the University of Wisconsin. He is also a recipient of the Elijah Watts Sells Award for Honorary Distinction for his results on the CPA exam. He is a member of the American Accounting Association and the Institute of Management Accountants and has published articles in *Accounting Review, Accounting Horizons, Advances in Management Accounting, Managerial Finance, Issues in Accounting Education*, and *Journal of Accounting Education*, as well as other journals. His research interests include accounting for financial instruments and innovation in accounting education. He has published papers and given numerous talks on incorporating critical thinking into accounting education, and helped prepare a catalogue of critical thinking resources for the Federated Schools of Accountancy.

How to Use the Study Aids in this Book

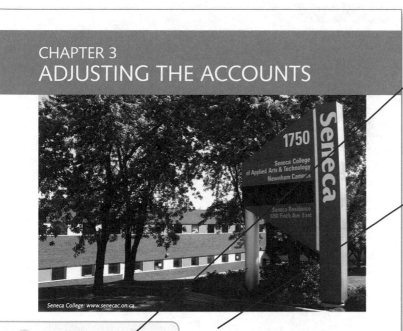

CHAPTER 3
ADJUSTING THE ACCOUNTS

Seneca College: www.senecac.on.ca

The Navigator is a learning system designed to guide you through each chapter and help you succeed in learning the material. It consists of (1) a checklist at the beginning of each chapter, which outlines text features and study skills you will need, and (2) a series of check boxes that prompts you to use the learning aids in the chapter and set priorities as you study.

Concepts for Review, listed at the beginning of each chapter, are the accounting concepts you learned in previous chapters that you will need to know in order to understand the topics you are about to cover. Page references are provided for your review before reading the chapter.

✓ THE NAVIGATOR

- ☐ Understand *Concepts for Review*
- ☐ Read *Feature Story*
- ☐ Scan *Study Objectives*
- ☐ Read *Chapter Preview*
- ☐ Read text and answer *Before You Go On*
- ☐ Work *Demonstration Problem*
- ☐ Review *Summary of Study Objectives*
- ☐ Answer *Self-Study Questions*
- ☐ Complete assignments

CONCEPTS FOR REVIEW:

Before studying this chapter, you should understand or, if necessary, review:

a. The double-entry system

b. How to increase and dec____ and owner's equity acco____ procedures. (Ch. 2, pp. 5___

c. How to journalize transa___

d. How to post transactions___ pp. 67–68)

e. How to prepare a trial ba___

Fiscal Year Ends, But Classes Move On

TORONTO, Ont.—In accounting, as in comedy, timing is everything. An organization's fiscal year end is like a punch line—everything leads up to it. And once it's done, you start all over again.

At Seneca College's 14 locations in the Greater Toronto Area, as at most schools, the majority of students arrive in September and leave in April or May. But the college's fiscal year ends on March 31, rather than at the end of the academic year. "The reason goes back to 1967 and the provincial act establishing community colleges in Ontario," explains Ron Currie, Seneca's Vice-President of Finance and Administration. "That's the government's year end."

If Seneca's fiscal year end were a different date, however, one thing would remain the same. Seneca must apply revenues to the fiscal period when the service is performed in order to correctly follow revenue recognition criteria. For example, Seneca might collect tuition for the summer term in one accounting period, but provide teaching services in the following accounting period. "Typically," says Mr. Currie, "students pay in March for a summer semester course, so those prepayments get deferred on our balance sheet. Same with the student activity fees."

Seneca's main sources of funding for its post-secondary programs are provincial grants and student tuition fees. Private and corporate training, however, is funded on a fee-for-service basis. Still, the principles are the same. "Let's say XYZ Corporation came along and gave us $30,000 to run a program in March, April, and May," Mr. Currie elaborates. "We would defer two-thirds of it to the next [fiscal] year."

Expenses, too, must be recorded in the year when they are incurred. "Our utility bills and invoices for legal fees for the last month or two of the fiscal year tend to come in after our year end," Mr. Currie continues. "In order to record the expenses in the proper year, we accrue them based on an estimate."

For things like course study guides, which are usually prepared by staff in one fiscal year but sold to students the following year, it's the other way around. "In that case, we take the costs associated with developing the materials and categorize them as a prepaid expense in one fiscal year and record it as an expense when recording the corresponding revenue in the next fiscal year."

Recording revenues and expenses in the correct period is a challenge, but one that must be met to properly reflect the school's activity in each period.

The Navigator

The **Feature Story** helps you picture how the chapter topic relates to the real world of accounting and business. Throughout the chapter, references to the Feature Story will help you put new ideas in context, organize them, and remember them.

Study Objectives at the beginning of each chapter provide you with a framework for learning the specific concepts and procedures covered in the chapter. Each study objective reappears at the point within the chapter where the concept is discussed. You can review all the study objectives in the **Summary of Study Objectives** at the end of the chapter. End-of-chapter material is keyed to study objectives.

STUDY OBJECTIVES:

After studying this chapter, you should be able to:

1. Explain the accrual basis of accounting, and revenue and expense recognition criteria.
2. Prepare adjusting entries for prepayments.
3. Prepare adjusting entries for accruals.
4. Describe the nature and purpose of an adjusted trial balance, and prepare one.
5. Prepare adjusting entries for the alternative treatment of prepayments (Appendix 3A).

The Navigator

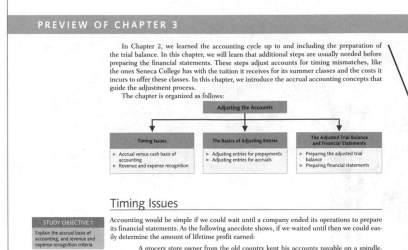

PREVIEW OF CHAPTER 3

In Chapter 2, we learned the accounting cycle up to and including the preparation of the trial balance. In this chapter, we will learn that additional steps are usually needed before preparing the financial statements. These steps adjust accounts for timing mismatches, like the ones Seneca College has with the tuition it receives for its summer classes and the costs it incurs to offer these classes. In this chapter, we introduce the accrual accounting concepts that guide the adjustment process.

The chapter is organized as follows:

Adjusting the Accounts

Timing Issues	The Basics of Adjusting Entries	The Adjusted Trial Balance and Financial Statements
► Accrual versus cash basis of accounting	► Adjusting entries for prepayments	► Preparing the adjusted trial balance
► Revenue and expense recognition	► Adjusting entries for accruals	► Preparing financial statements

The **Preview** graphically outlines the major topics and subtopics that will be discussed. This narrative and visual preview gives you a mental framework upon which to arrange the new information you are about to learn.

Timing Issues

STUDY OBJECTIVE 1

Explain the accrual basis of accounting, and revenue and expense recognition criteria.

Accounting would be simple if we could wait until a company ended its operations to prepare its financial statements. As the following anecdote shows, if we waited until then we could easily determine the amount of lifetime profit earned:

A grocery store owner from the old country kept his accounts payable on a spindle, accounts receivable on a notepad, and cash in a shoebox. His daughter, a CGA, chided her father: "I don't understand how you can run your business this way. How do you know what you've earned?"

"Well," her father replied, "when I arrived in Canada 40 years ago, I had nothing but the pants I was wearing. Today, your brother is a doctor, your sister is a teacher, and you are a CGA. Your mother and I have a nice car, a well-furnished house, and a home by the lake. We have a good business and everything is paid for. So, you add all that together, subtract the pants, and there's your profit."

Although the grocer may be correct in his evaluation about how to calculate his profit over his lifetime, most companies need more immediate feedback on how they are doing. For example, management usually wants monthly financial statements. Investors want to view the results of publicly traded companies at least quarterly. The Canada Revenue Agency requires financial statements to be filed with annual income tax returns.

Consequently, accountants divide the life of a business into [...] month, a three-month quarter, or a year. Time periods of less th [...] periods.

An accounting time period that is one year long is called [...] period used by many businesses is the same as the calendar yea [...] However, it can be different. Seneca College's fiscal year is April [...] typical of many colleges, universities, and governments. Some r [...] period for their fiscal year. The Forzani Group does this, and [...] January (some years the first Sunday in February) as its fiscal ye [...]

Because the life of a business is divided into accounting ti [...] to record transactions is important. Many business transactions [...] ing time period. For example, computer equipment purchased [...] still being used today. We also saw in the feature story that som [...]

---

130 CHAPTER 3 | Adjusting the Accounts

In October, Pioneer Advertising Agency earned $200 in fees for advertising services that were not billed to clients until November. Because these services have not been billed, they have not been recorded. The following adjusting entry is made on October 31:

A	=	L	+	OE
+200				+200

Cash flows: no effect

Oct. 31	Accounts Receivable	200	
	Service Revenue		200
	To accrue revenue earned but not billed or collected.		

After the adjusting entry is posted, the accounts show the following:

Accounts Receivable					Service Revenue		
Oct. 21	10,000	Oct. 31	9,000		Oct. 21	10,000	
31 Adj.	200				25	800	
Oct. 31 Bal.	1,200				31 Adj.	400	
					31 Adj.	200	
					Oct. 31 Adj.	11,400	

The asset Accounts Receivable shows that $1,200 is owed by clients at the balance sheet date. The balance of $11,400 in Service Revenue represents the total revenue earned during the month. If the adjusting entry is not made, assets and owner's equity on the balance sheet, and revenues and profit on the income statement, will all be understated.

On November 10, Pioneer receives $200 cash for the services performed in October. The following entry is made:

A	=	L	+	OE
+200				
−200				

↑ Cash flows: +200

Nov. 10	Cash	200	
	Accounts Receivable		200
	To record cash collected on account.		

Accrued Expenses

Alternative terminology
Accrued expenses are also called *accrued liabilities*.

Expenses incurred but not yet paid or recorded at the statement date are called accrued expenses. Interest, rent, property taxes, and salaries can be accrued expenses. Accrued expenses result from the same causes as accrued revenues. In fact, an accrued expense on the books of one company is an accrued revenue for another company. For example, the $200 accrual of revenue by Pioneer is an accrued expense for the client that received the service.

Adjustments for accrued expenses are needed for two purposes: (1) to record the obligations that exist at the balance sheet date, and (2) to recognize the expenses that apply to the current accounting period. Before adjustment, both liabilities and expenses are understated. Profit and owner's equity are overstated. An adjusting entry for accrued expenses results in an increase (debit) to an expense account and an increase (credit) to a liability account, as follows:

Accrued Expenses

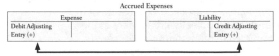

Expense		Liability	
Debit Adjusting Entry (+)			Credit Adjusting Entry (+)

Helpful hint To make the illustration easier to understand, a simplified method for calculating interest is used. In reality, interest is calculated using the exact number of days in the interest period and year.

Interest. On October 2, Pioneer Advertising Agency signed a $5,000, three-month note payable, due January 2, 2012. The note requires interest to be paid at an annual rate of 6%. The amount of interest that has accumulated is determined by three factors: (1) the face value, or principal amount, of the note; (2) the interest rate, which is always expressed as an annual rate; and (3) the length of time that the note is outstanding (unpaid).

Interest is sometimes due monthly, and sometimes when the principal is due. For Pioneer, the total interest due on the $5,000 note at its due date three months later is $75 ($5,000 × 6% × $\frac{3}{12}$ months). Interest rates are always expressed as an annual rate. Because the interest rate is for one year, the time period must be adjusted for the fraction of the year that the note is outstanding.

The **Accounting Equation** has been inserted in the margin next to journal entries throughout the text. This feature helps you understand the impact of each accounting transaction on the financial position and cash flows.

Alternative Terminology familiarizes you with other commonly used terms.

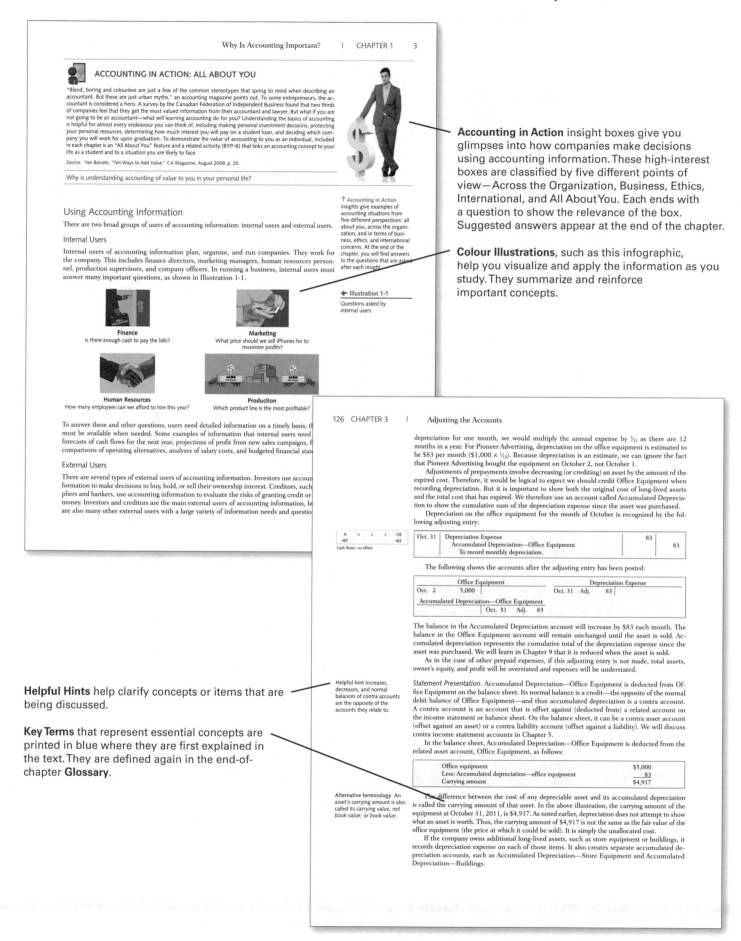

Accounting in Action insight boxes give you glimpses into how companies make decisions using accounting information. These high-interest boxes are classified by five different points of view—Across the Organization, Business, Ethics, International, and All About You. Each ends with a question to show the relevance of the box. Suggested answers appear at the end of the chapter.

Colour Illustrations, such as this infographic, help you visualize and apply the information as you study. They summarize and reinforce important concepts.

Helpful Hints help clarify concepts or items that are being discussed.

Key Terms that represent essential concepts are printed in blue where they are first explained in the text. They are defined again in the end-of-chapter **Glossary**.

Within the textbook page images:

Why Is Accounting Important? | CHAPTER 1   3

ACCOUNTING IN ACTION: ALL ABOUT YOU

"Bland, boring and colourless are just a few of the common stereotypes that spring to mind when describing an accountant. But these are just urban myths," an accounting magazine points out. To some entrepreneurs, the accountant is considered a hero. A survey by the Canadian Federation of Independent Business found that two thirds of companies feel that they get the most valued information from their accountant and lawyer. But what if you are not going to be an accountant—what will learning accounting do for you? Understanding the basics of accounting is helpful for almost every endeavour you can think of, including making personal investment decisions, protecting your personal resources, determining how much interest you will pay on a student loan, and deciding which company you will work for upon graduation. To demonstrate the value of accounting to you as an individual, included in each chapter is an "All About You" feature and a related activity (BYP-6) that links an accounting concept to your life as a student and to a situation you are likely to face.

Source: Yan Barcelo, "Ten Ways to Add Value," *CA Magazine*, August 2009, p. 20.

Why is understanding accounting of value to you in your personal life?

Using Accounting Information

There are two broad groups of users of accounting information: internal users and external users.

Internal Users

Internal users of accounting information plan, organize, and run companies. They work for the company. This includes finance directors, marketing managers, human resources personnel, production supervisors, and company officers. In running a business, internal users must answer many important questions, as shown in Illustration 1-1.

↑ Accounting in Action insights give examples of accounting situations from five different perspectives: all about you, across the organization, and in terms of business, ethics, and international concerns. At the end of the chapter, you will find answers to the questions that are asked after each insight

← Illustration 1-1
Questions asked by internal users

Finance
Is there enough cash to pay the bills?

Marketing
What price should we sell iPhones for to maximize profits?

Human Resources
How many employees can we afford to hire this year?

Production
Which product line is the most profitable?

To answer these and other questions, users need detailed information on a timely basis; th[...] must be available when needed. Some examples of information that internal users need [...] forecasts of cash flows for the next year, projections of profit from new sales campaigns, f[...] comparisons of operating alternatives, analyses of salary costs, and budgeted financial stat[...]

External Users

There are several types of external users of accounting information. Investors use accoun[...] formation to make decisions to buy, hold, or sell their ownership interest. Creditors, such [...] pliers and bankers, use accounting information to evaluate the risks of granting credit or [...] money. Investors and creditors are the main external users of accounting information, b[...] are also many other external users with a large variety of information needs and questi[...]

---

126   CHAPTER 3 | Adjusting the Accounts

depreciation for one month, we would multiply the annual expense by $\frac{1}{12}$ as there are 12 months in a year. For Pioneer Advertising, depreciation on the office equipment is estimated to be $83 per month ($1,000 × $\frac{1}{12}$). Because depreciation is an estimate, we can ignore the fact that Pioneer Advertising bought the equipment on October 2, not October 1.

Adjustments of prepayments involve decreasing (or crediting) an asset by the amount of the expired cost. Therefore, it would be logical to expect we should credit Office Equipment when recording depreciation. But it is important to show both the original cost of long-lived assets and the total cost that has expired. We therefore use an account called Accumulated Depreciation to show the cumulative sum of the depreciation expense since the asset was purchased.

Depreciation on the office equipment for the month of October is recognized by the following adjusting entry:

A	=	L	+	OE
−83				−83

Cash flows: no effect

Oct. 31	Depreciation Expense	83	
	Accumulated Depreciation—Office Equipment		83
	To record monthly depreciation.		

The following shows the accounts after the adjusting entry has been posted:

Office Equipment		Depreciation Expense	
Oct. 2 5,000		Oct. 31 Adj. 83	

Accumulated Depreciation—Office Equipment
Oct. 31   Adj.   83

The balance in the Accumulated Depreciation account will increase by $83 each month. The balance in the Office Equipment account will remain unchanged until the asset is sold. Accumulated depreciation represents the cumulative total of the depreciation expense since the asset was purchased. We will learn in Chapter 9 that it is reduced when the asset is sold.

As in the case of other prepaid expenses, if this adjusting entry is not made, total assets, owner's equity, and profit will be overstated and expenses will be understated.

Statement Presentation. Accumulated Depreciation—Office Equipment is deducted from Office Equipment on the balance sheet. Its normal balance is a credit—the opposite of the normal debit balance of Office Equipment—and thus accumulated depreciation is a contra account. A contra account is an account that is offset against (deducted from) a related account on the income statement or balance sheet. On the balance sheet, it can be a contra asset account (offset against an asset) or a contra liability account (offset against a liability). We will discuss contra income statement accounts in Chapter 5.

In the balance sheet, Accumulated Depreciation—Office Equipment is deducted from the related asset account, Office Equipment, as follows:

Office equipment	$5,000
Less: Accumulated depreciation—office equipment	83
Carrying amount	$4,917

Helpful hint Increases, decreases, and normal balances of contra accounts are the opposite of the accounts they relate to.

Alternative terminology An asset's carrying amount is also called its *carrying value, net book value,* or *book value.*

The difference between the cost of any depreciable asset and its accumulated depreciation is called the carrying amount of that asset. In the above illustration, the carrying amount of the equipment at October 31, 2011, is $4,917. As noted earlier, depreciation does not attempt to show what an asset is worth. Thus, the carrying amount of $4,917 is not the same as the fair value of the office equipment (the price at which it could be sold). It is simply the unallocated cost.

If the company owns additional long-lived assets, such as store equipment or buildings, it records depreciation expense on each of those items. It also creates separate accumulated depreciation accounts, such as Accumulated Depreciation—Store Equipment and Accumulated Depreciation—Buildings.

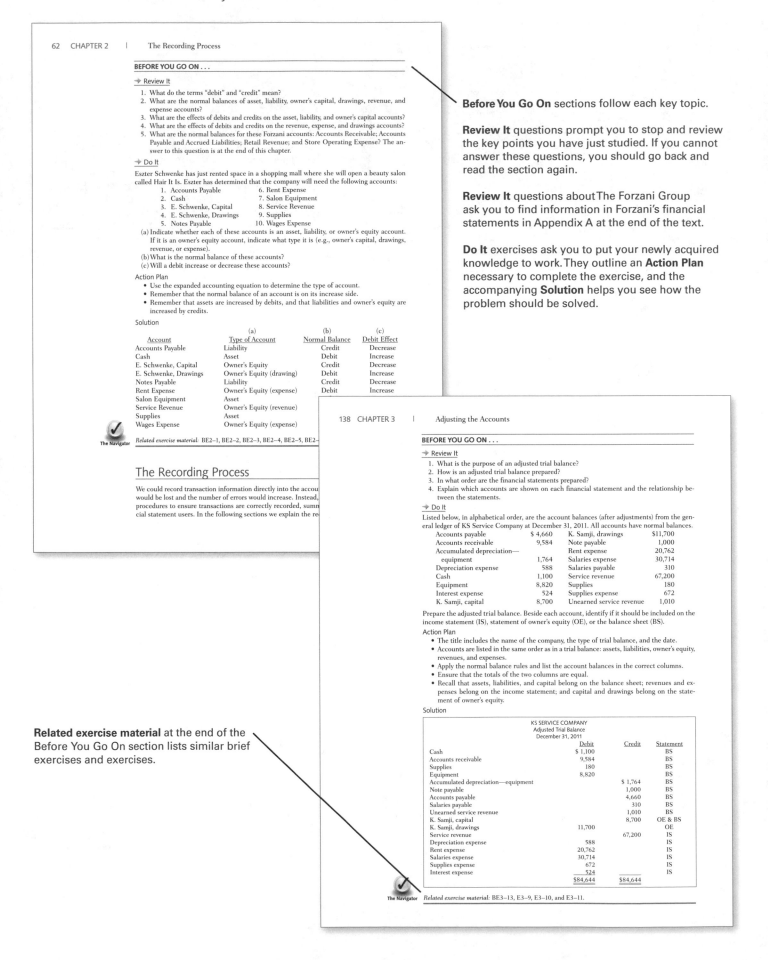

BEFORE YOU GO ON . . .

→ Review It

1. What do the terms "debit" and "credit" mean?
2. What are the normal balances of asset, liability, owner's capital, drawings, revenue, and expense accounts?
3. What are the effects of debits and credits on the asset, liability, and owner's capital accounts?
4. What are the effects of debits and credits on the revenue, expense, and drawings accounts?
5. What are the normal balances for these Forzani accounts: Accounts Receivable; Accounts Payable and Accrued Liabilities; Retail Revenue; and Store Operating Expense? The answer to this question is at the end of this chapter.

→ Do It

Eszter Schwenke has just rented space in a shopping mall where she will open a beauty salon called Hair It Is. Eszter has determined that the company will need the following accounts:

1. Accounts Payable   6. Rent Expense
2. Cash   7. Salon Equipment
3. E. Schwenke, Capital   8. Service Revenue
4. E. Schwenke, Drawings   9. Supplies
5. Notes Payable   10. Wages Expense

(a) Indicate whether each of these accounts is an asset, liability, or owner's equity account. If it is an owner's equity account, indicate what type it is (e.g., owner's capital, drawings, revenue, or expense).
(b) What is the normal balance of these accounts?
(c) Will a debit increase or decrease these accounts?

Action Plan

- Use the expanded accounting equation to determine the type of account.
- Remember that the normal balance of an account is on its increase side.
- Remember that assets are increased by debits, and that liabilities and owner's equity are increased by credits.

Solution

		(a)	(b)	(c)
Account		Type of Account	Normal Balance	Debit Effect
Accounts Payable		Liability	Credit	Decrease
Cash		Asset	Debit	Increase
E. Schwenke, Capital		Owner's Equity	Credit	Decrease
E. Schwenke, Drawings		Owner's Equity (drawing)	Debit	Increase
Notes Payable		Liability	Credit	Decrease
Rent Expense		Owner's Equity (expense)	Debit	Increase
Salon Equipment		Asset		
Service Revenue		Owner's Equity (revenue)		
Supplies		Asset		
Wages Expense		Owner's Equity (expense)		

Related exercise material: BE2–1, BE2–2, BE2–3, BE2–4, BE2–5, BE2–

The Navigator

The Recording Process

We could record transaction information directly into the accou[ ]
would be lost and the number of errors would increase. Instead,
procedures to ensure transactions are correctly recorded, summ[ ]
cial statement users. In the following sections we explain the re[ ]

BEFORE YOU GO ON . . .

→ Review It

1. What is the purpose of an adjusted trial balance?
2. How is an adjusted trial balance prepared?
3. In what order are the financial statements prepared?
4. Explain which accounts are shown on each financial statement and the relationship between the statements.

→ Do It

Listed below, in alphabetical order, are the account balances (after adjustments) from the general ledger of KS Service Company at December 31, 2011. All accounts have normal balances.

Accounts payable	$ 4,660	K. Samji, drawings	$11,700
Accounts receivable	9,584	Note payable	1,000
Accumulated depreciation—		Rent expense	20,762
equipment	1,764	Salaries expense	30,714
Depreciation expense	588	Salaries payable	310
Cash	1,100	Service revenue	67,200
Equipment	8,820	Supplies	180
Interest expense	524	Supplies expense	672
K. Samji, capital	8,700	Unearned service revenue	1,010

Prepare the adjusted trial balance. Beside each account, identify if it should be included on the income statement (IS), statement of owner's equity (OE), or the balance sheet (BS).

Action Plan

- The title includes the name of the company, the type of trial balance, and the date.
- Accounts are listed in the same order as in a trial balance: assets, liabilities, owner's equity, revenues, and expenses.
- Apply the normal balance rules and list the account balances in the correct columns.
- Ensure that the totals of the two columns are equal.
- Recall that assets, liabilities, and capital belong on the balance sheet; revenues and expenses belong on the income statement; and capital and drawings belong on the statement of owner's equity.

Solution

KS SERVICE COMPANY Adjusted Trial Balance December 31, 2011			
	Debit	Credit	Statement
Cash	$ 1,100		BS
Accounts receivable	9,584		BS
Supplies	180		BS
Equipment	8,820		BS
Accumulated depreciation—equipment		$ 1,764	BS
Note payable		1,000	BS
Accounts payable		4,660	BS
Salaries payable		310	BS
Unearned service revenue		1,010	BS
K. Samji, capital		8,700	OE & BS
K. Samji, drawings	11,700		OE
Service revenue		67,200	IS
Depreciation expense	588		IS
Rent expense	20,762		IS
Salaries expense	30,714		IS
Supplies expense	672		IS
Interest expense	524		IS
	$84,644	$84,644	

The Navigator   *Related exercise material:* BE3–13, E3–9, E3–10, and E3–11.

Before You Go On sections follow each key topic.

Review It questions prompt you to stop and review the key points you have just studied. If you cannot answer these questions, you should go back and read the section again.

Review It questions about The Forzani Group ask you to find information in Forzani's financial statements in Appendix A at the end of the text.

Do It exercises ask you to put your newly acquired knowledge to work. They outline an **Action Plan** necessary to complete the exercise, and the accompanying **Solution** helps you see how the problem should be solved.

Related exercise material at the end of the Before You Go On section lists similar brief exercises and exercises.

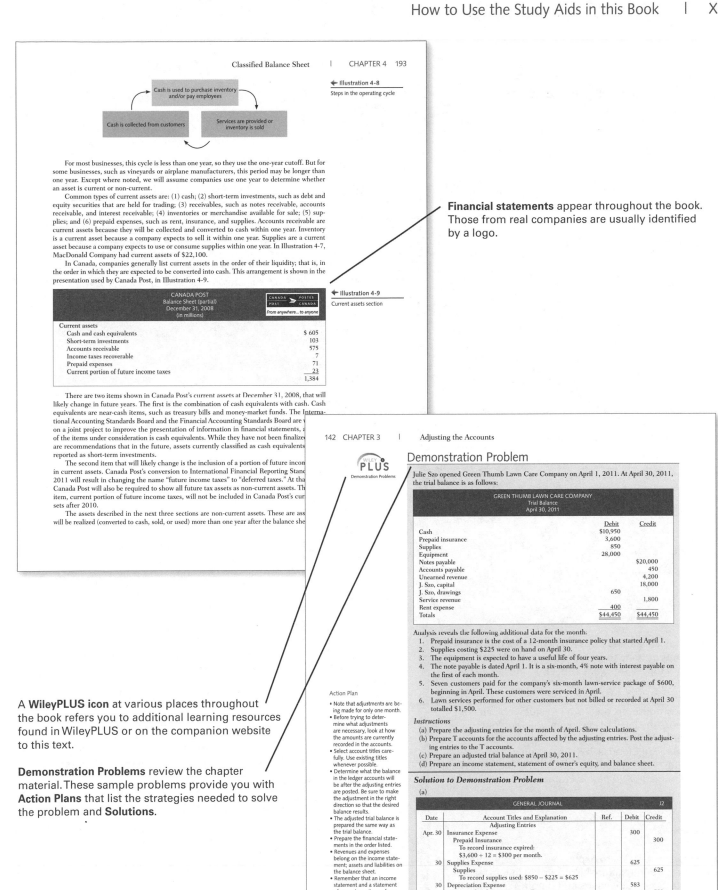

Classified Balance Sheet | CHAPTER 4 193

← Illustration 4-8
Steps in the operating cycle

Cash is used to purchase inventory and/or pay employees

Cash is collected from customers

Services are provided or inventory is sold

For most businesses, this cycle is less than one year, so they use the one-year cutoff. But for some businesses, such as vineyards or airplane manufacturers, this period may be longer than one year. Except where noted, we will assume companies use one year to determine whether an asset is current or non-current.

Common types of current assets are: (1) cash; (2) short-term investments, such as debt and equity securities that are held for trading; (3) receivables, such as notes receivable, accounts receivable, and interest receivable; (4) inventories or merchandise available for sale; (5) supplies; and (6) prepaid expenses, such as rent, insurance, and supplies. Accounts receivable are current assets because they will be collected and converted to cash within one year. Inventory is a current asset because a company expects to sell it within one year. Supplies are a current asset because a company expects to use or consume supplies within one year. In Illustration 4-7, MacDonald Company had current assets of $22,100.

In Canada, companies generally list current assets in the order of their liquidity; that is, in the order in which they are expected to be converted into cash. This arrangement is shown in the presentation used by Canada Post, in Illustration 4-9.

← Illustration 4-9
Current assets section

CANADA POST
Balance Sheet (partial)
December 31, 2008
(in millions)

CANADA POST POSTES CANADA
From anywhere...to anyone

Current assets	
Cash and cash equivalents	$ 605
Short-term investments	103
Accounts receivable	575
Income taxes recoverable	7
Prepaid expenses	71
Current portion of future income taxes	23
	1,384

There are two items shown in Canada Post's current assets at December 31, 2008, that will likely change in future years. The first is the combination of cash equivalents with cash. Cash equivalents are near-cash items, such as treasury bills and money-market funds. The International Accounting Standards Board and the Financial Accounting Standards Board are [...] on a joint project to improve the presentation of information in financial statements, a [...] of the items under consideration is cash equivalents. While they have not been finalize[...] are recommendations that in the future, assets currently classified as cash equivalents [...] reported as short-term investments.

The second item that will likely change is the inclusion of a portion of future incom[...] in current assets. Canada Post's conversion to International Financial Reporting Stan[...] 2011 will result in changing the name "future income taxes" to "deferred taxes." At tha[...] Canada Post will also be required to show all future tax assets as non-current assets. Th[...] item, current portion of future income taxes, will not be included in Canada Post's cur[...] sets after 2010.

The assets described in the next three sections are non-current assets. These are ass[...] will be realized (converted to cash, sold, or used) more than one year after the balance she[...]

Financial statements appear throughout the book. Those from real companies are usually identified by a logo.

---

142 CHAPTER 3 | Adjusting the Accounts

WILEY PLUS
Demonstration Problems

Demonstration Problem

Julie Szo opened Green Thumb Lawn Care Company on April 1, 2011. At April 30, 2011, the trial balance is as follows:

GREEN THUMB LAWN CARE COMPANY Trial Balance April 30, 2011		
	Debit	**Credit**
Cash	$10,950	
Prepaid insurance	3,600	
Supplies	850	
Equipment	28,000	
Notes payable		$20,000
Accounts payable		450
Unearned revenue		4,200
J. Szo, capital		18,000
J. Szo, drawings	650	
Service revenue		1,800
Rent expense	400	
Totals	$44,450	$44,450

Analysis reveals the following additional data for the month.
1. Prepaid insurance is the cost of a 12-month insurance policy that started April 1.
2. Supplies costing $225 were on hand on April 30.
3. The equipment is expected to have a useful life of four years.
4. The note payable is dated April 1. It is a six-month, 4% note with interest payable on the first of each month.
5. Seven customers paid for the company's six-month lawn-service package of $600, beginning in April. These customers were serviced in April.
6. Lawn services performed for other customers but not billed or recorded at April 30 totalled $1,500.

Instructions
(a) Prepare the adjusting entries for the month of April. Show calculations.
(b) Prepare T accounts for the accounts affected by the adjusting entries. Post the adjusting entries to the T accounts.
(c) Prepare an adjusted trial balance at April 30, 2011.
(d) Prepare an income statement, statement of owner's equity, and balance sheet.

Action Plan
- Note that adjustments are being made for only one month.
- Before trying to determine what adjustments are necessary, look at how the amounts are currently recorded in the accounts.
- Select account titles carefully. Use existing titles whenever possible.
- Determine what the balance in the ledger accounts will be after the adjusting entries are posted. Be sure to make the adjustment in the right direction so that the desired balance results.
- The adjusted trial balance is prepared the same way as the trial balance.
- Prepare the financial statements in the order listed.
- Revenues and expenses belong on the income statement; assets and liabilities on the balance sheet.
- Remember that an income statement and a statement of owner's equity are for a period of time; the balance sheet is at the end of the accounting period.

Solution to Demonstration Problem
(a)

GENERAL JOURNAL				J2
Date	Account Titles and Explanation	Ref.	Debit	Credit
	Adjusting Entries			
Apr. 30	Insurance Expense		300	
	Prepaid Insurance			300
	To record insurance expired: $3,600 ÷ 12 = $300 per month.			
30	Supplies Expense		625	
	Supplies			625
	To record supplies used: $850 − $225 = $625			
30	Depreciation Expense		583	
	Accumulated Depreciation—Equipment			583
	To record monthly depreciation: $28,000 ÷ 4 = $7,000 × 1/12 = $583 per month.			

A **WileyPLUS icon** at various places throughout the book refers you to additional learning resources found in WileyPLUS or on the companion website to this text.

Demonstration Problems review the chapter material. These sample problems provide you with **Action Plans** that list the strategies needed to solve the problem and **Solutions**.

Summary of Study Objectives

1. Explain the accrual basis of accounting, and revenue and expense recognition criteria. In order to provide timely information, accountants divide the life of a business into specific time periods. Therefore it is important to record transactions in the correct time period. Under the accrual basis of accounting, events that change a company's financial statements are recorded in the periods in which the events occur, rather than in the periods in which the company receives or pays cash. Revenue and expense recognition criteria are necessary to ensure that the accrual basis of accounting is properly followed. Revenue is recognized (recorded) in the period when there is a related increase in assets or decrease in liabilities. Expenses should be recognized (recorded) when there is a related decrease in assets or an increase in liabilities. Expenses are recorded in the same period as revenue is recognized, if there is a direct association between the revenues and expenses. If there is no association between revenues and expenses, expenses are recorded in the period they are incurred.

2. Prepare adjusting entries for prepayments. Prepayments are either prepaid expenses or unearned revenues. Adjusting entries for prepayments record the portion of the prepayment that applies to the expense or revenue of the current accounting period. The adjusting entry for prepaid expenses debits (increases) an expense account and credits (decreases) an asset account. For a long-lived asset, the contra asset account Accumulated Depreciation is used instead of crediting the asset account directly. The adjusting entry for unearned revenues debits (decreases) a liability account and credits (increases) a revenue account.

3. Prepare adjusting entries for accruals. Accruals are either accrued revenues or accrued expenses. Adjusting entries for accruals record revenues and expenses that

apply to the current accounting period and that have not yet been recognized through daily journal entries. The adjusting entry for accrued revenue debits (increases) a receivable account and credits (increases) a revenue account. The adjusting entry for an accrued expense debits (increases) an expense account and credits (increases) a liability account.

4. Describe the nature and purpose of an adjusted trial balance, and prepare one. An adjusted trial balance shows the balances of all accounts, including those that have been adjusted, at the end of an accounting period. It proves that the total of the accounts with debit balances is still equal to the total of the accounts with credit balances after the adjustments have been posted. Financial statements are prepared from an adjusted trial balance in the following order: (1) income statement, (2) statement of owner's equity, and (3) balance sheet.

5. Prepare adjusting entries for the alternative treatment of prepayments (Appendix 3A). Prepayments may initially be debited (increased) to an expense account. Unearned revenues may initially be credited (increased) to a revenue account. At the end of the period, these accounts may be overstated. The adjusting entries for prepaid expenses is a debit (increase) to an asset account and a credit (decrease) to an expense account. Adjusting entries for unearned revenues are a debit (decrease) to a revenue account and a credit (increase) to a liability account. It does not matter which alternative is used to record and adjust prepayments, as the ending account balances should be the same with both methods.

The Navigator

Glossary

Accrual basis of accounting A basis for accounting in which revenues are recorded when earned and expenses are recorded when incurred. (p. 119)

Accrued expenses Expenses incurred but not yet paid in cash or recorded. (p. 123 and 130)

Accrued revenues Revenues earned but not yet received in cash or recorded. (p. 123 and 129)

Adjusted trial balance A list of accounts and their balances after all adjustments have been posted. (p. 135)

Adjusting entries Entries [...] counting period to ensure [...] recognition criteria are foll[...]

Carrying amount The di[...] a depreciable asset and its [...] other words, it is the unallo[...] the depreciable asset's cost[...]

Cash basis of accounting [...] which revenue is recorded [...] expense is recorded when c[...]

WILEY PLUS
Glossary
Key Term Matching Acti[...]

The **Summary of Study Objectives** relates the study objectives to the key points in the chapter. It gives you another opportunity to review, as well as to see how all the key topics within the chapter are related.

The **Glossary** defines all the terms and concepts introduced in the chapter. Page references help you find any terms you need to study further. The **WileyPLUS icon** tells you that there is a searchable, comprehensive glossary, as well as a Key Term Matching Activity available on the companion website and in WileyPLUS.

Self-Study Questions

WILEY PLUS Quizzes

Answers are at the end of the chapter.

(SO 4) K **1.** Which of the following statements about an account is true?
 (a) The left side of an account is the credit or decrease side.
 (b) An account is an individual accounting record of increases and decreases in specific asset, liability, and owner's equity items.
 (c) There are separate accounts for specific assets and liabilities but only one account for owner's equity items.
 (d) The right side of an account is the debit or increase side.

(SO 1) K **2.** Debits:
 (a) increase both assets and liabilities.
 (b) decrease both assets and liabilities.
 (c) increase assets and decrease liabilities.
 (d) decrease assets and increase liabilities.

(SO 1) K **3.** A revenue account:
 (a) is increased by debits.
 (b) is decreased by credits.
 (c) has a normal balance of a debit.
 (d) is increased by credits.

(SO 1) K **4.** Accounts that normally have debit balances are:
 (a) assets, expenses, and revenues.
 (b) assets, expenses, and owner's capital.
 (c) assets, liabilities, and drawings.
 (d) assets, drawings, and expenses.

(SO 2) K **5.** What is the correct sequence of steps in the recording process?
 (a) Analyzing transactions; preparing a trial balance
 (b) Analyzing transactions; entering transactions in a journal; posting transactions
 (c) Entering transactions in a journal; posting transactions; preparing a trial balance
 (d) Entering transactions in a journal; posting transactions; analyzing transactions

(SO 3) K **6.** Which of these statements about a journal is false?
 (a) It is not a book of original entry.
 (b) It provides a chronological record of transactions.
 (c) It helps to locate errors because the debit and credit amounts for each entry can be easily compared.
 (d) It shows in one place the complete effect of a transaction.

(SO 4) K **7.** A ledger:
 (a) contains only asset and liability accounts.
 (b) should show accounts in alphabetical order.
 (c) is a collection of the entire group of accounts maintained by a company.
 (d) is a book of original entry.

(SO 4) K **8.** Posting:
 (a) is normally done before journalizing.
 (b) transfers ledger transaction data to the journal.
 (c) is an optional step in the recording process.
 (d) transfers journal entries to ledger accounts.

(SO 5) K **9.** A trial balance:
 (a) is a list of accounts with their balances at a specific time.
 (b) proves that journalized transactions are accurate.
 (c) will not balance if a correct journal entry is posted twice.
 (d) proves that all transactions have been recorded.

(SO 5) AP **10.** A trial balance will not balance if:
 (a) the collection of an account receivable is posted twice.
 (b) the purchase of supplies on account is debited to Supplies and credited to Cash.
 (c) a $100 cash drawing by the owner is debited to Drawings for $1,000 and credited to Cash for $100.
 (d) a $450 payment on account is debited to Accounts Payable for $45 and credited to Cash for $45.

The Navigator

Questions

(SO 1) C **1.** What is an account? Will a company need more than one account? Explain.

(SO 1) K **2.** What is debiting an account? What is crediting an account?

(SO 1) C **3.** Jos Arcelus, a fellow student, says that the double-entry system means each transaction is recorded in two places: the journal and the ledger. Is Jos correct? Explain.

Self-Study Questions form a practice test that gives you an opportunity to check your knowledge of important topics. Answers appear on the last page of the chapter.

Self-study questions are keyed to study objectives. In addition, the level of cognitive skill required to solve the question has been classified with a letter code following Bloom's Taxonomy. You will find more information about Bloom's and this coding system on page XVII of this Preface.

The **WileyPLUS icon** tells you that there are quizzes on the website that can further help you master this material.

Questions allow you to explain your understanding of concepts and relationships covered in the chapter. (Keyed to Study Objectives and Bloom's Taxonomy.)

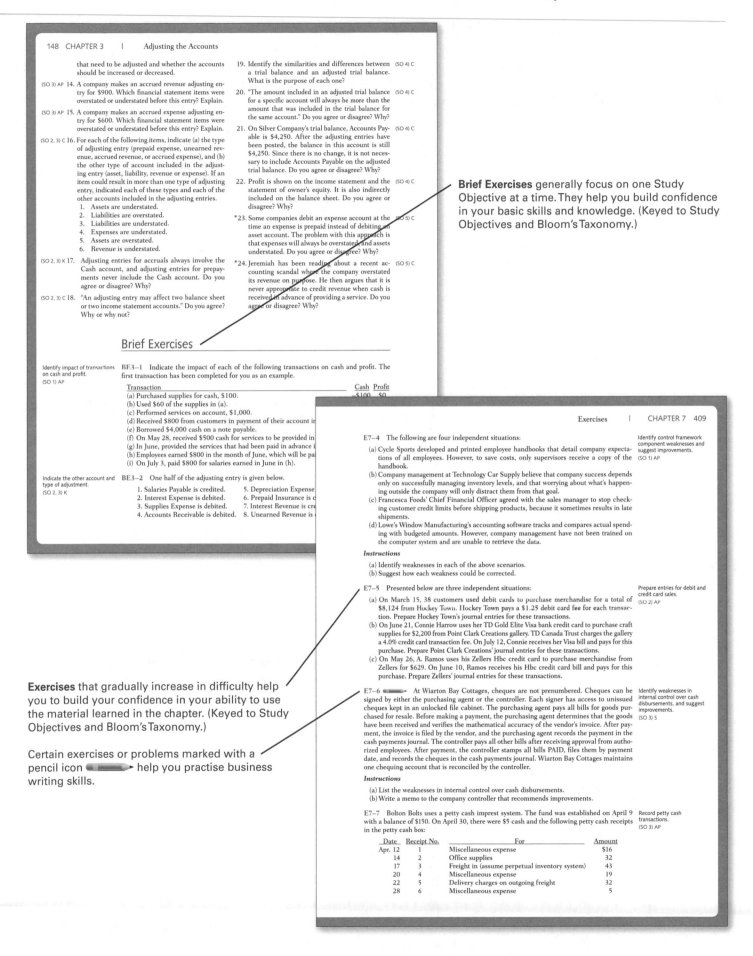

148 CHAPTER 3 | Adjusting the Accounts

that need to be adjusted and whether the accounts should be increased or decreased.

(SO 3) AP 14. A company makes an accrued revenue adjusting entry for $900. Which financial statement items were overstated or understated before this entry? Explain.

(SO 3) AP 15. A company makes an accrued expense adjusting entry for $600. Which financial statement items were overstated or understated before this entry? Explain.

(SO 2, 3) C 16. For each of the following items, indicate (a) the type of adjusting entry (prepaid expense, unearned revenue, accrued revenue, or accrued expense), and (b) the other type of account included in the adjusting entry (asset, liability, revenue or expense). If an item could result in more than one type of adjusting entry, indicated each of these types and each of the other accounts included in the adjusting entries.
  1. Assets are understated.
  2. Liabilities are overstated.
  3. Liabilities are understated.
  4. Expenses are understated.
  5. Assets are overstated.
  6. Revenue is understated.

(SO 2, 3) K 17. Adjusting entries for accruals always involve the Cash account, and adjusting entries for prepayments never include the Cash account. Do you agree or disagree? Why?

(SO 2, 3) C 18. "An adjusting entry may affect two balance sheet or two income statement accounts." Do you agree? Why or why not?

19. Identify the similarities and differences between (SO 4) C a trial balance and an adjusted trial balance. What is the purpose of each one?

20. "The amount included in an adjusted trial balance (SO 4) C for a specific account will always be more than the amount that was included in the trial balance for the same account." Do you agree or disagree? Why?

21. On Silver Company's trial balance, Accounts Payable is $4,250. After the adjusting entries have (SO 4) C been posted, the balance in this account is still $4,250. Since there is no change, it is not necessary to include Accounts Payable on the adjusted trial balance. Do you agree or disagree? Why?

22. Profit is shown on the income statement and the (SO 4) C statement of owner's equity. It is also indirectly included on the balance sheet. Do you agree or disagree? Why?

*23. Some companies debit an expense account at the (SO 5) C time an expense is prepaid instead of debiting an asset account. The problem with this approach is that expenses will always be overstated and assets understated. Do you agree or disagree? Why?

*24. Jeremiah has been reading about a recent accounting scandal where the company overstated (SO 5) C its revenue on purpose. He then argues that it is never appropriate to credit revenue when cash is received in advance of providing a service. Do you agree or disagree? Why?

Brief Exercises generally focus on one Study Objective at a time. They help you build confidence in your basic skills and knowledge. (Keyed to Study Objectives and Bloom's Taxonomy.)

Brief Exercises

Identify impact of transactions on cash and profit. (SO 1) AP

BE3–1 Indicate the impact of each of the following transactions on cash and profit. The first transaction has been completed for you as an example.

Transaction	Cash	Profit
(a) Purchased supplies for cash, $100.	–$100	$0
(b) Used $60 of the supplies in (a).		
(c) Performed services on account, $1,000.		
(d) Received $800 from customers in payment of their account in		
(e) Borrowed $4,000 cash on a note payable.		
(f) On May 28, received $500 cash for services to be provided in		
(g) In June, provided the services that had been paid in advance i		
(h) Employees earned $800 in the month of June, which will be pai		
(i) On July 3, paid $800 for salaries earned in June in (h).		

Indicate the other account and type of adjustment. (SO 2, 3) K

BE3–2 One half of the adjusting entry is given below.

1. Salaries Payable is credited.   5. Depreciation Expense
2. Interest Expense is debited.   6. Prepaid Insurance is c
3. Supplies Expense is debited.   7. Interest Revenue is cre
4. Accounts Receivable is debited.   8. Unearned Revenue is

Exercises that gradually increase in difficulty help you to build your confidence in your ability to use the material learned in the chapter. (Keyed to Study Objectives and Bloom's Taxonomy.)

Certain exercises or problems marked with a pencil icon help you practise business writing skills.

Exercises | CHAPTER 7 409

E7–4 The following are four independent situations:

Identify control framework component weaknesses and suggest improvements. (SO 1) AP

(a) Cycle Sports developed and printed employee handbooks that detail company expectations of all employees. However, to save costs, only supervisors receive a copy of the handbook.
(b) Company management at Technology Car Supply believe that company success depends only on successfully managing inventory levels, and that worrying about what's happening outside the company will only distract them from that goal.
(c) Francesca Foods' Chief Financial Officer agreed with the sales manager to stop checking customer credit limits before shipping products, because it sometimes results in late shipments.
(d) Lowe's Window Manufacturing's accounting software tracks and compares actual spending with budgeted amounts. However, company management have not been trained on the computer system and are unable to retrieve the data.

Instructions

(a) Identify weaknesses in each of the above scenarios.
(b) Suggest how each weakness could be corrected.

E7–5 Presented below are three independent situations:

Prepare entries for debit and credit card sales. (SO 2) AP

(a) On March 15, 38 customers used debit cards to purchase merchandise for a total of $8,124 from Hockey Town. Hockey Town pays a $1.25 debit card fee for each transaction. Prepare Hockey Town's journal entries for these transactions.
(b) On June 21, Connie Harrow uses her TD Gold Elite Visa bank credit card to purchase craft supplies for $2,200 from Point Clark Creations gallery. TD Canada Trust charges the gallery a 4.0% credit card transaction fee. On July 12, Connie receives her Visa bill and pays for this purchase. Prepare Point Clark Creations' journal entries for these transactions.
(c) On May 26, A. Ramos uses his Zellers Hbc credit card to purchase merchandise from Zellers for $629. On June 10, Ramos receives his Hbc credit card bill and pays for this purchase. Prepare Zellers' journal entries for these transactions.

E7–6 At Wiarton Bay Cottages, cheques are not prenumbered. Cheques can be signed by either the purchasing agent or the controller. Each signer has access to unissued cheques kept in an unlocked file cabinet. The purchasing agent pays all bills for goods purchased for resale. Before making a payment, the purchasing agent determines that the goods have been received and verifies the mathematical accuracy of the vendor's invoice. After payment, the invoice is filed by the vendor, and the purchasing agent records the payment in the cash payments journal. The controller pays all other bills after receiving approval from authorized employees. After payment, the controller stamps all bills PAID, files them by payment date, and records the cheques in the cash payments journal. Wiarton Bay Cottages maintains one chequing account that is reconciled by the controller.

Identify weaknesses in internal control over cash disbursements, and suggest improvements. (SO 3) S

Instructions

(a) List the weaknesses in internal control over cash disbursements.
(b) Write a memo to the company controller that recommends improvements.

E7–7 Bolton Bolts uses a petty cash imprest system. The fund was established on April 9 with a balance of $150. On April 30, there were $5 cash and the following petty cash receipts in the petty cash box:

Record petty cash transactions. (SO 3) AP

Date	Receipt No.	For	Amount
Apr. 12	1	Miscellaneous expense	$16
14	2	Office supplies	32
17	3	Freight in (assume perpetual inventory system)	43
20	4	Miscellaneous expense	19
22	5	Delivery charges on outgoing freight	32
28	6	Miscellaneous expense	5

---

156 CHAPTER 3 | Adjusting the Accounts

Prepare and post transaction and adjusting entries for prepayments.
(SO 2, 5) AP

*E3–13 At Sabo Company, the following select transactions occurred in January, the company's first month of operations:

Jan. 2 Paid $1,320 for a one-year insurance policy.
15 Paid $1,400 for supplies.
25 Received $3,750 cash for services to be performed in the future.

On January 31, it is determined that $1,900 of the service revenue has been earned and that there is $450 of supplies on hand.

Instructions

(a) Assume Sabo records all prepaid costs as assets and all revenue collected in advance as liabilities. Journalize and post the January transactions and adjustments at January 31. Use T accounts. (*Note:* Posting to the Cash account is not necessary.)
(b) Assume Sabo records all prepaid costs as expenses, and all revenue collected in advance as revenue. Journalize and post the January transactions and adjustments at January 31. (*Note:* Posting to the Cash account is not necessary.)
(c) Compare the balances in the T accounts from (a) to those obtained in (b).

Problems: Set A

Determine profit on cash and accrual bases; recommend method.
(SO 1) AP

P3–1A Your examination of the records of Southlake Co. shows the company collected $85,500 cash from customers and paid $48,400 cash for operating costs during 2011. If Southlake followed the accrual basis of accounting, it would report the following year-end balances:

	2011	2010
Accounts payable	$ 1,500	$ 1,250
Accounts receivable	4,200	2,700
Accumulated depreciation	11,300	10,000
Prepaid insurance	1,500	1,300
Supplies	750	400
Unearned revenues	1,200	1,500

Instructions

(a) Determine Southlake's profit on a cash basis for 2011.
(b) Determine Southlake's profit on an accrual basis for 2011.

Taking It Further Which method do you recommend Southlake use? Why?

Prepare and post transaction and adjusting entries for prepayments.
(SO 2) AP

P3–2A Ouellette & Associates began operations on January 1, 2011. Its fiscal year end is December 31 and it prepares financial statements and adjusts its accounts annually. Ouellette records all prepaid costs as assets and all revenue collected in adva[...] transactions for 2011 follow:

1. On January 10, bought office supplies for $3,400 cash. A physi[...] 2011, revealed $925 of supplies still on hand.
2. On March 31, purchased equipment for $21,000 cash. The eq[...] seven-year useful life.
3. Paid cash for a $3,780, one-year insurance policy on April 1, 2[...] effect on this date.
4. Leased a truck on September 1 for a one-year period for $500[...] lease cost of $6,000 in cash.
5. On October 15, received a $1,600 advance cash payment fro[...] services expected to be provided in the future. As at Decembe[...] services had not been performed.
6. On December 1, rented out unneeded office space for a six-mo[...] date, and received a $1,620 cheque for the first three months'[...]

Each **Problem** helps you pull together and apply several concepts of the chapter. Two sets of problems—Set A and Set B—are usually keyed to the same study objectives and cognitive level. These provide additional opportunities to apply concepts learned in the chapter.

Taking It Further is an extra question at the end of each problem designed to challenge you to think beyond the basic concepts covered in the problem, and to provide written explanations. Your instructor may assign problems with or without this extra element.

---

608 CHAPTER 10 | Current Liabilities and Payroll

Continuing Cookie Chronicle

(*Note:* This is a continuation of the Cookie Chronicle from Chapters 1 through 9.)

Recall that Cookie Creations borrowed $2,000 on November 16, 2010, from Natalie's grandmother. Interest on the note is 3% per year and the note plus interest was to be repaid in 12 months.

Natalie is considering paying back her grandmother before the note becomes due in November 2011.

Instructions

(a) Calculate the total interest expense recorded in 2010. Calculate total interest expense to be incurred in 2011 if the loan is repaid on its due date.
(b) If Natalie's grandmother's loan were to be repaid at the end of August 2011, calculate Cookie Creations' cash savings.
(c) Identify to Natalie some of the advantages and disadvantages of repaying the loan before it becomes due.
(d) Prepare the journal entry to record the loan repayment at the end of August 2011. Recall that a monthly adjusting journal entry was prepared for the months of November 2010 (half month), December 2010, and January 2011.

Cumulative Coverage—Chapters 3 to 10

The unadjusted trial balance of LeBrun Company at its year end, July 31, 2011, is as follows:

LEBRUN COMPANY
Trial Balance
July 31, 2011

	Debit	Credit
Cash	$ 17,400	
Petty cash	200	
Accounts receivable	38,500	
Allowance for doubtful accounts		$ 2,000
Note receivable (due December 31, 2011)	10,000	
Merchandise inventory	40,900	
Prepaid expenses	16,000	
Land	50,000	
Building	155,000	
Accumulated depreciation—building		10,800
Equipment	25,000	
Accumulated depreciation—equipment		12,200
Patent	75,000	
Accumulated amortization—patent		15,000
Accounts payable		78,900
Mortgage payable (due August 1, 2026)		124,200
S. LeBrun, capital		127,690
S. LeBrun, drawings	54,000	
Sales		750,000
Cost of goods sold	450,000	
Operating expenses	181,220	
Interest revenue		400
Interest expense	7,970	
Totals	$1,121,190	$1,121,190

The **Continuing Cookie Chronicle** is a serial problem found in each chapter. It follows the operations of a hypothetical small company, Cookie Creations. The company is owned by a student and the purpose of the serial problem is to reinforce the application of accounting to the type of business a student could operate.

In selected chapters, a **Cumulative Coverage Problem** follows the Continuing Cookie Chronicle. The cumulative coverage problem pulls together, and uses, topics you have learned over several chapters.

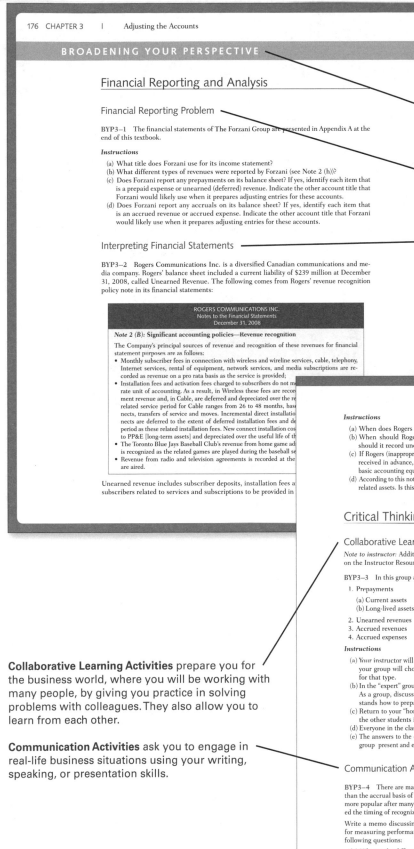

BROADENING YOUR PERSPECTIVE

Financial Reporting and Analysis

Financial Reporting Problem

BYP3–1   The financial statements of The Forzani Group are presented in Appendix A at the end of this textbook.

Instructions

(a) What title does Forzani use for its income statement?
(b) What different types of revenues were reported by Forzani (see Note 2 (h))?
(c) Does Forzani report any prepayments on its balance sheet? If yes, identify each item that is a prepaid expense or unearned (deferred) revenue. Indicate the other account title that Forzani would likely use when it prepares adjusting entries for these accounts.
(d) Does Forzani report any accruals on its balance sheet? If yes, identify each item that is an accrued revenue or accrued expense. Indicate the other account title that Forzani would likely use when it prepares adjusting entries for these accounts.

Interpreting Financial Statements

BYP3–2   Rogers Communications Inc. is a diversified Canadian communications and media company. Rogers' balance sheet included a current liability of $239 million at December 31, 2008, called Unearned Revenue. The following comes from Rogers' revenue recognition policy note in its financial statements:

ROGERS COMMUNICATIONS INC.
Notes to the Financial Statements
December 31, 2008

Note 2 (B): Significant accounting policies—Revenue recognition

The Company's principal sources of revenue and recognition of these revenues for financial statement purposes are as follows:
- Monthly subscriber fees in connection with wireless and wireline services, cable, telephony, Internet services, rental of equipment, network services, and media subscriptions are recorded as revenue on a pro rata basis as the service is provided;
- Installation fees and activation fees charged to subscribers do not me... rate unit of accounting. As a result, in Wireless these fees are recor... ment revenue and, in Cable, are deferred and depreciated over the re... related service period for Cable ranges from 26 to 48 months, bas... nects, transfers of service and moves. Incremental direct installatio... nects are deferred to the extent of deferred installation fees and de... period as these related installation fees. New connect installation cos... to PP&E [long-term assets] and depreciated over the useful life of th...
- The Toronto Blue Jays Baseball Club's revenue from home game ad... is recognized as the related games are played during the baseball se...
- Revenue from radio and television agreements is recorded at the ... are aired.

Unearned revenue includes subscriber deposits, installation fees a... subscribers related to services and subscriptions to be provided in...

Instructions

(a) When does Rogers recognize its revenue from monthly subscriber fees?
(b) When should Rogers record unearned revenue from its subscription services? When should it record unearned revenue for its Blue Jays home game admission revenue?
(c) If Rogers (inappropriately) recorded these unearned revenues as revenue when the cash was received in advance, what would be the effect on the company's financial position? (Use the basic accounting equation and explain what elements would be overstated or understated.)
(d) According to this note, Rogers' new installation costs are depreciated over the useful life of the related assets. Is this an appropriate method of expense recognition for these costs? Explain.

Critical Thinking

Collaborative Learning Activity

Note to instructor: Additional instructions and material for this group activity can be found on the Instructor Resource Site.

BYP3–3   In this group activity, you will review the following types of adjusting entries:

1. Prepayments
   (a) Current assets
   (b) Long-lived assets
2. Unearned revenues
3. Accrued revenues
4. Accrued expenses

Instructions

(a) Your instructor will divide the class into "home" groups of five students. Each member of your group will choose one type of adjusting entry and then move to the "expert" group for that type.
(b) In the "expert" group, you will be given a handout explaining your type of adjusting entry. As a group, discuss the handout and ensure that each group member thoroughly understands how to prepare that entry.
(c) Return to your "home" group and explain how to prepare your type of adjusting entry to the other students in the group.
(d) Everyone in the class will write a short quiz on the four types of adjusting journal entries.
(e) The answers to the quiz will be reviewed in class by having one member from each "expert" group present and explain the correct adjusting entry for that group's type of adjusting entry.

WILEY PLUS
Working in Groups

Communication Activity

BYP3–4   There are many people today who believe that the cash basis of accounting is better than the accrual basis of accounting in predicting a company's future success. This idea became more popular after many reports of corporate financial scandals where management manipulated the timing of recognizing expenses and revenues in accrual accounting to influence profit.

Write a memo discussing whether you believe the cash basis of accounting is more reliable for measuring performance than the accrual basis. Include in your memo the answers to the following questions:

(a) What is the difference in calculating profit using the accrual basis of accounting versus the cash basis of accounting?

WILEY PLUS
Writing Handbook

The Broadening Your Perspective section helps you pull together various concepts covered in the chapter and apply them to real-life business and personal decisions.

Financial Reporting Problems familiarize you with the format, content, and uses of financial statements prepared by The Forzani Group Ltd., which are presented in Appendix A at the end of the text.

Interpreting Financial Statements asks you to apply the concepts you have learned to specific situations faced by actual companies.

Collaborative Learning Activities prepare you for the business world, where you will be working with many people, by giving you practice in solving problems with colleagues. They also allow you to learn from each other.

Communication Activities ask you to engage in real-life business situations using your writing, speaking, or presentation skills.

178 CHAPTER 3 | Adjusting the Accounts

(b) Do you believe that it is possible for management to manipulate profit using the accrual basis of accounting? If yes, identify one way that management might be able to increase profit by manipulating the timing of revenue or expense recognition.
(c) Do you believe that it is possible for management to manipulate profit using the cash basis of accounting? If yes, identify one way that management might be able to increase profit when using the cash basis of accounting.

Ethics Case

BYP3–5 Die Hard Company is a pesticide manufacturer. Its sales dropped a lot this year because of new legislation that outlawed the sale of many of Die Hard's chemical pesticides. In the coming year, Die Hard will have new, environmentally safe chemicals to replace these discontinued products. Sales in the next year are expected to be much higher than sales of any previous year. The drop in sales and profits appears to be a one-year exception.

Still, the company president is afraid that a large drop in the current year's profits could cause a significant drop in the market price of Die Hard's shares, and could make the company a takeover target. To avoid this possibility, the company president urges Carole Chiasson, the controller, to accrue all possible revenues and to defer as many expenses as possible when preparing this period's December 31 year-end adjusting entries. He says to Carole, "We need the revenues this year, and next year we can easily absorb expenses deferred from this year." Carole did not record the adjusting entries until January 17, but she dated the entries December 31 as if they were recorded then. Carole also did everything possible to follow the president's request.

Instructions

(a) Who are the stakeholders in this situation?
(b) What are the ethical considerations of (1) the president's request, and (2) Carole's decision to date the adjusting entries December 31?
(c) Can Carole aggressively accrue revenues and defer expenses and still be ethical?

"All About You" Activity

BYP3–6 A critical issue for accountants is the decision whether an expenditure should be recorded as an asset or an expense. The distinction between asset and expense is not always clear. In certain instances, businesses have been forced to restate their financial statements because management has recorded an asset when an expense should be recorded. The All About You feature indicates that post-secondary education results in higher earnings over an adult's working life and thus the money you are spending on your education today should be of significant future benefit. The question is then whether your education would meet the accounting definition of an asset or an expense.

Instructions

(a) Consider the nature of the cost of your education. What factor[s] considered an asset? What factors suggest that it should be co[...]
(b) Do you think the nature of the program you're taking should your education should be considered an asset or an expense?
(c) Economic theory suggests that people will always consider t[he] expenditure and only incur the cost if the expected benefit is g[...] that every expenditure would meet the definition of an asset cost of a vacation to Hawaii to be as valuable as a year of colleg[e] both as assets on a personal balance sheet? Why or why not?
(d) If you were applying for a loan, what might the potential effec[...] application if you understated your assets? What might be t[...] bank if your assets are overstated and expenses understated?

Through **Ethics Cases**, you will reflect on ethical situations an accountant typically confronts.

The **WileyPLUS icon** indicates that online resources accompany these Broadening Your Perspective activities.

All About You Activities ask you questions about the All About You feature in the chapter, helping you apply accounting principles to your personal finances and to a variety of other circumstances that you can relate to on a personal level.

Answers to Chapter Questions | CHAPTER 3 179

ANSWERS TO CHAPTER QUESTIONS

Answers to Accounting in Action Insight Questions

All About You, p. 121

Q: How should you account for the cost of your post-secondary education? Should you be recognizing the cost as an expense each year or should you recognize it as an asset?
A: Expenses are recognized when there has been a decrease in an asset or an increase in a liability. Paying for an education will reduce assets such as cash and may also increase liabilities if you have to take out student loans. Therefore, most accountants would tell you that you should record the cost of your education as an expense as you incur those costs. On the other hand, it could be argued that your education is creating an asset—your increased future earning power. But then you would have to estimate the value of this asset. As with many situations in accounting, it is not easy to determine the correct answer.

Business Insight, p. 128

Q: If a business collects cash when the gift card is sold, how can gift card sales in December result in revenues in January?
A: Gift cards sales are simply another example of unearned revenues. At the time the gift card is sold, the business must record unearned revenue, which is a liability. When a customer redeems the gift card by making a purchase, then the company will reduce the liability and record revenue.

Ethics Insight, p. 134

Q: How could an adjusting entry be used to overstate profit?
A: If the adjusting entry reduces or eliminates an expense that should be recorded, profit will be overstated. For example, if the company uses unrealistically long useful lives in its depreciation calculations, the depreciation expense will be too low, and profit too high. Or if, for example, revenues are recognized before they have been earned, then profit may be overstated.

Answer to Forzani Review It Question 4, p. 128

Forzani reported depreciation expense of $47,613 thousand and $44,468 thousand in fiscal 2009 and 2008, respectively.

Answers to Self-Study Questions

1. b 2. d 3. d 4. c 5. d 6. a 7. b 8. a 9. c *10. a

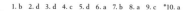

Remember to go back to the beginning of the chapter to check off your completed work! ←

Answers to Chapter Questions offer suggested answers for questions that appear in the chapter's **Accounting in Action** insight boxes, **Review It** questions based on The Forzani Group's financial statements, and **Self-Study Questions**.

After you complete your assignments, it's a good idea to go back to **The Navigator** checklist at the start of the chapter to see if you have used all the study aids of the chapter.

The Use of Bloom's Taxonomy

Bloom's Taxonomy is a classification framework that you can use to develop your skills from the most basic to the most advanced competence levels: knowledge, comprehension, application, analysis, synthesis, and evaluation. These levels are hierarchical in nature in that performance at each level requires mastery of all prior levels.

Questions, exercises, and problems at the end of each chapter of this text have been classified by the knowledge level required in answering each one. Below you will learn what your role is in each of the six skill levels and how you can demonstrate mastery at each level. Key word clues will help you recognize the skill level required for a particular question.

(K) Knowledge (Remembering)

Student's role: "I read, listen, watch, or observe; I take notes and am able to recall information; ask and respond to questions."
Student demonstrates knowledge by stating who, what, when, why, and how in the same form in which they learned it.
Key word clues: define, identify, label, name, etc.

(C) Comprehension (Understanding)

Student's role: "I understand the information or skill. I can recognize it in other forms and I can explain it to others and make use of it."
Student demonstrates comprehension by giving an example of how the information would be used.
Key word clues: describe, distinguish, give example, compare, differentiate, explain, etc.

(AP) Application (Solving the Problem)

Student's role: "I can apply my prior knowledge and understanding to new situations."
Student demonstrates knowledge by solving problems independently, recognizing when the information or skill is needed and using it to solve new problems or complete tasks.
Key word clues: calculate, illustrate, prepare, complete, use, produce, etc.

(AN) Analysis (Detecting)

Student's role: "I can break down the information into simpler parts and understand how these parts are related."
Student demonstrates knowledge by recognizing patterns and hidden meanings, filling in missing information, correcting errors, identifying components and effects.
Key word clues: analyze, break down, compare, contrast, deduce, differentiate, etc.

(S) Synthesis (Creating)

Student's role: "I use all knowledge, understanding, and skills to create alternatives. I can convey this information to others effectively."
Student demonstrates knowledge by acting as a guide to others, designing, creating.
Key word clues: relate, tell, write, categorize, devise, formulate, generalize, create, design, etc.

(E) Evaluation (Appraisal)

Student's role: "I am open to and appreciative of the value of ideas, procedures, and methods and can make well-supported judgements, backed up by knowledge, understanding, and skills."
Student demonstrates knowledge by formulating and presenting well-supported judgement, displaying consideration of others, examining personal options, making wise choices.
Key word clues: appraise, assess, criticize, critique, decide, evaluate, judge, justify, recommend, etc.

How Do You Learn Best?

This questionnaire aims to find out something about your preferences for the way you work with information. You will have a preferred learning style. One part of that learning style is your preference for the intake and the output of ideas and information.

Circle the letter of the answer that best explains your preference. Circle more than one if a single answer does not match your perception. Leave blank any question that does not apply.

1. You are helping someone who wants to go to your airport, town centre, or railway station. You would:
   V) draw, or give her a map.
   A) tell her the directions.
   R) write down the directions (without a map).
   K) go with her.

2. You are not sure whether a word should be spelled "dependent" or "dependant." You would:
   V) see the words in your mind and choose by the way they look.
   A) think about how each word sounds and choose one.
   R) find it in a dictionary.
   K) write both words on paper and choose one.

3. You are planning a holiday for a group. You want some feedback from them about the plan. You would:
   V) use a map or website to show them the places.
   A) phone, text, or e-mail them.
   R) give them a copy of the printed itinerary.
   K) describe some of the highlights.

4. You are going to cook something as a special treat for your family. You would:
   V) look through the cookbook for ideas from the pictures.
   A) ask friends for suggestions.
   R) use a cookbook where you know there is a good recipe.
   K) cook something you know without the need for instructions.

5. A group of tourists wants to learn about the parks and wildlife reserves in your area. You would:
   V) show them Internet pictures, photographs, or picture books.
   A) talk about or arrange a talk for them to learn about parks or wildlife reserves.
   R) give them a book or pamphlets about the parks or wildlife reserves.
   K) take them to a park or wildlife reserve and walk with them.

6. You are about to purchase a digital camera or mobile phone. Other than price, what would most influence your decision?
   V) It is a modern design and looks good.
   A) The salesperson telling me about its features.
   R) Reading the details about its features.
   K) Trying or testing it.

7. Remember a time when you learned how to do something new. Try to avoid choosing a physical skill, such as riding a bike. You learned best by:
   V) diagrams and charts—visual clues.
   A) listening to somebody explaining it and asking questions.
   R) written instructions—e.g., a manual or textbook.
   K) watching a demonstration.

8. You have a problem with your knee. You would prefer that the doctor:
   V) showed you a diagram of what was wrong.
   A) described what was wrong.
   R) gave you a web address or something to read about it.
   K) used a plastic model of a knee to show what was wrong.

9. You want to learn a new program, skill, or game on a computer. You would:
   V) follow the diagrams in the book that came with it.
   A) talk with people who know about the program.
   R) read the written instructions that came with the program.
   K) use the controls or keyboard.

10. I like websites that have:
    V) interesting design and visual features.
    A) audio where I can listen to music or news.
    R) interesting written descriptions, lists, and explanations.
    K) things I can click on, shift, or try.

11. Other than price, what would most influence your decision to buy a new, non-fiction book?
    V) The way it looks is appealing.
    A) A friend talks about it and recommends it.
    R) Quickly reading parts of it.
    K) It has real-life stories, experiences, and examples.

12. You are using a book or website to learn how to take photos with your new digital camera. You would like to have:
    V) diagrams showing the camera and what each part does.
    A) a chance to ask questions and talk about the camera and its features.
    R) clear written instructions with lists and bullet points about what to do.
    K) many examples of good and poor photos and how to improve them.

13. Do you prefer an instructor who likes to use
    V) diagrams, charts, or graphs?
    A) question and answer, talk, group discussions, or guest speakers?
    R) handouts, books, or readings?
    K) demonstrations, models, or practical sessions?

14. You have finished a competition or test and would like some feedback. You would like to have feedback:
    V) using graphs showing you what you had achieved.
    A) from somebody who talks it through with you.
    R) using a written description of your results.
    K) using examples from what you have done.

15. You are going to choose food at a restaurant or café. You would:
    V) look at what others are eating or look at pictures of each dish.
    A) listen to the waiter or ask friends to recommend choices.
    R) choose from descriptions on the menu.
    K) choose something that you have had there before.

16. You have to make an important speech at a conference or special occasion. You would:
    V) make diagrams or get graphs to help explain things.

    A) write a few key words and practise saying your speech over and over.
    R) write your speech and learn from reading it over several times.
    K) gather many examples and stories to make the talk real and practical.

Count your choices: ☐   ☐   ☐   ☐
                 V   A   R   K

Determine whether your learning style is primarily visual (V), aural (A), reading/writing (R), or kinesthetic (K). You may have more than one learning style preference—many people do. This is known as a multimodal style. Look at the learning styles chart below and on the next page to determine what will help you learn the best.

Learning Styles Chart

 ## Visual

WHAT TO DO IN CLASS	WHAT TO DO WHEN STUDYING	TEXT FEATURES THAT MAY HELP YOU	WHAT TO DO PRIOR TO EXAMS
• Pay close attention to charts, drawings, and handouts your instructor uses. • Underline and highlight. • Use different colours. • Use symbols, flow charts, graphs, different arrangements on the page, white space.	Convert your lecture notes into "page pictures." To do this: • Use the "What to do in class" strategies. • Reconstruct images in different ways. • Redraw pages from memory. • Replace words with symbols and initials. • Look at your pages.	• The Navigator • Feature Story • Preview • Infographics/Illustrations • Photos • Accounting in Action insight boxes • Accounting Equation Analyses in margins • Key Terms in blue • Words in bold or italics • Demonstration Problem/Action Plan • Questions/Exercises/Problems • Financial Reporting and Analysis	• Recall your "page pictures." • Draw diagrams where appropriate. • Practise turning your visuals back into words.

Aural

WHAT TO DO IN CLASS	WHAT TO DO WHEN STUDYING	TEXT FEATURES THAT MAY HELP YOU	WHAT TO DO PRIOR TO EXAMS
• Attend lectures and tutorials. • Discuss topics with students and instructors. • Explain new ideas to other people. • Leave spaces in your lecture notes for later recall. • Describe overheads, pictures, and visuals to somebody who was not in class.	You may take poor notes because you prefer to listen. Therefore: • Expand your notes by talking with others and with information from your textbook. • Record summarized notes and listen. • Read summarized notes out loud. • Explain your notes to another "aural" person.	• Preview • Infographics/Illustrations • Accounting in Action insight boxes • Review It/Do It/Action Plan • Summary of Study Objectives • Glossary • Demonstration Problem/Action Plan • Self-Study Questions • Questions/Exercises/Problems • Financial Reporting and Analysis • Critical Thinking, particularly the Collaborative Learning Activities	• Talk with the instructor. • Spend time in quiet places recalling the ideas. • Practise writing answers to old exam questions. • Say your answers out loud.

Reading/Writing

WHAT TO DO IN CLASS	WHAT TO DO WHEN STUDYING	TEXT FEATURES THAT MAY HELP YOU	WHAT TO DO PRIOR TO EXAMS
• Use lists and headings. • Use dictionaries, glossaries, and definitions. • Read handouts, textbooks, and supplemental library readings. • Use lecture notes.	• Write out words again and again. • Reread notes silently. • Rewrite ideas and principles into other words. • Turn charts, diagrams, and other illustrations into statements.	• The Navigator • Feature Story • Study Objectives • Preview • Accounting Equation Analysis in margins • Review It/Do It/Action Plan • Summary of Study Objectives • Glossary • Self-Study Questions • Questions/Exercises/Problems/ Taking It Further • Writing Problems • Financial Reporting and Analysis • Critical Thinking, particularly the Communication activities and the Collaborative Learning activities	• Write exam answers. • Practise with multiple-choice questions. • Write paragraphs, beginnings, and endings. • Write your lists in outline form. • Arrange your words into hierarchies and points.

Kinesthetic

WHAT TO DO IN CLASS	WHAT TO DO WHEN STUDYING	TEXT FEATURES THAT MAY HELP YOU	WHAT TO DO PRIOR TO EXAMS
• Use all your senses. • Go to labs, take field trips. • Listen to real-life examples. • Pay attention to applications. • Use hands-on approaches. • Use trial-and-error methods.	You may take poor notes because topics do not seem concrete or relevant. Therefore: • Put examples in your summaries. • Use case studies and applications to help with principles and abstract concepts. • Talk about your notes with another "kinesthetic" person. • Use pictures and photographs that illustrate an idea.	• The Navigator • Feature Story • Preview • Infographics/Illustrations • Review It/Do It/Action Plan • Summary of Study Objectives • Demonstration Problem/Action Plan • Self-Study Questions • Questions/Exercises/Problems • Financial Reporting and Analysis • Critical Thinking, particularly the All About You activities and the Collaborative Learning a ctivities	• Write practice answers. • Role-play the exam situation

For all learning styles: Be sure to use the learning aids on the companion website to enhance your understanding of the concepts and procedures of the text. In particular, use the tutorials, study aids (including the searchable glossary, PowerPoint presentations, and problem-solving techniques), and practice tools (including additional demonstration problems, key term matching activities, and quizzes).

To the Instructor

Student-Focused and Instructor-Friendly—
The Solution for Your Accounting Principles Class!

We are entering the new world of not only IFRS but multiple GAAP with Canadian GAAP for Private Enterprises. The teaching of introductory accounting has never involved so much change!

Our approach to this edition has been to keep in mind when it will be used, starting on the eve of IFRS and Canadian GAAP for Private Enterprises and continuing in the early years of their implementation. And since this is an introductory accounting text, we have not compared what is in place now versus what was in place. We have taken the attitude that students starting their accounting studies really don't care about the way things used to be. Therefore, there are only a few places where we thought it was important to tie in the new standards with the old.

While a lot has changed, from an introductory accounting point of view, much is still the same. Where companies switching to IFRS have the choice, experience has shown that they will continue to follow the legacy methods and stay with the balance sheet and the traditional presentation. Therefore, the focus for introductory students continues to be the fundamental principles.

As with previous editions of *Accounting Principles*, the goal has been to create a book about accounting that makes the subject clear and fascinating to students. Even in the new world of IFRS, that is still our passion: to empower students to succeed by giving them the tools and the motivation they need to excel in their accounting courses and their future careers. We are confident that this new edition, with its strong pedagogical foundations, continuing currency and accuracy of the material, and exciting new features, is the best edition yet.

Welcome to the fifth Canadian edition of *Accounting Principles*—the solution to make **all business students excited about accounting regardless of their future career path!**

Pedagogical Effectiveness

This text is part of a complete learning package that includes the constantly evolving system, *WileyPLUS*. This system provides students of *all learning styles* with numerous opportunities to connect theory to practice in an engaging and interactive manner. A virtual Teaching Assistant to instructors and Study Peer to students, *WileyPLUS* enables instructors to spend more quality time on teaching and less time on grading and administering the course, and helps students learn more efficiently and succeed beyond the classroom. Our Learning Styles model, incorporated in previous editions, is part of the entire package, including *WileyPLUS*, enabling students with different learning approaches to better understand the material.

Study objectives have been designed to facilitate learning, and stepped-out pedagogy was used to break down complex topics, making the material more manageable for students. Bloom's Taxonomy, which underlies the structure of *Accounting Principles*, continues to facilitate progressive learning by categorizing material in a building block fashion. Before You Go On feedback sections at the end of each major study objective and Demonstration Problems were augmented in number, coverage, and level of difficulty to facilitate student understanding.

We continue to recognize the increasing diversity found within today's classrooms. The text material has been thoroughly reviewed by an instructor of English as a Second Language to ensure that *Accounting Principles* offers students an unprecedented level of clarity and readability.

Relevance for Users

It has always been our goal to motivate non-accounting students to learn accounting. In order to illustrate the importance of financial accounting to non-accounting majors, we started Chapter 1 with a section about why accounting is important to everyone, not just accountants. We consistently emphasize this point throughout the text and have added a new type of Accounting in Action insight box in this edition called All About You. These boxes demonstrate how learning accounting is useful for students in managing their own financial affairs. We also kept the Accounting in Action insight box Across the Organization, which was introduced in the fourth edition. These clearly demonstrate how accounting is used to address issues in marketing, finance, management, and other functions. It is our sincere hope that non-accounting majors have the opportunity to appreciate accounting both personally and professionally.

This edition continues, and expands, the inclusion of user-oriented material to demonstrate the relevance of accounting to all students, no matter what their area of study. Our focus company is again The Forzani Group—the largest sporting goods retailer in Canada. Forzani was chosen because its stores have a high name recognition with students, it operates in a single industry, and it has relatively simple financial statements. References to Forzani have been included throughout the chapter, including Review It questions, ratio analysis, end-of-chapter assignments, and in Forzani's financial statements in Appendix A at the end of the textbook.

This edition was also subject to a comprehensive updating to ensure that it continues to be relevant and fresh. All real-world examples were updated, or replaced, in the text as appropriate, including the chapter-opening feature stories, the Accounting in Action insight boxes, and references to real-world examples in the text and end-of-chapter material.

XXII | To the Instructor

Our textbook includes references to over 200 real-world companies. In addition, 61% of the chapter-opening feature stories were replaced with new stories, 81% of the Accounting in Action insight boxes are new, and all the Review It questions relating to Forzani are new, using information from Forzani's 2009 financial statements.

We continue to feature problem material that allows students to tie the concepts they are learning together and place them in context. Central to this is the Continuing Cookie Chronicle. This serial problem allows students to apply chapter topics in an ongoing scenario where a young entrepreneur builds her small business.

Expanded Topical Coverage

Additional topical coverage was requested by instructors to help them better prepare students for the complexities of today's world of accounting. As always, these topics had to pass a strict test to warrant their inclusion: they were added only if they represented a major concept, issue, or procedure that a beginning student should understand. Some of the more significant additions include the following:

- Chapter 1: Accounting in Action was expanded to include information on the two new sets of accounting standards, International Financial Reporting Standards (IFRS) and Canadian GAAP for Private Enterprises. The concepts of recognition and measurement are introduced. Charts illustrating the characteristics of the different forms of business organization and the accounting differences by type of business organization were included.
- Chapter 2: The Recording Process now introduces the accounting cycle and relates the steps in the recording process to the accounting cycle.
- Chapter 3: Adjusting the Accounts now also links the material in the chapter with the accounting cycle. A "Do It" exercise has been added to the appendix (regarding alternative treatment of prepaid expenses and unearned revenues). The end-of-chapter demonstration problem has been expanded by including posting and preparing an adjusted trial balance, and financial statements.
- Chapter 4: Completion of the Accounting Cycle was expanded to illustrate how IFRS affects the presentation of the balance sheet. The acid-test ratio was added as another measure of liquidity. A "Do It" exercise was added to each of the appendices and the demonstration problem was expanded to include a post-closing trial balance.
- Chapter 5: Accounting for Merchandising Operations also contains information on the impact of IFRS on the income statement. A "Do It" exercise was added to the appendix on the periodic inventory system, as well as a second demonstration problem on journal entries in the perpetual inventory system.

- Chapter 6: Inventory Costing has been updated to reflect the new accounting standards on inventory cost determination methods and lower of cost or net realizable value. A "Do It" exercise has been added to each of the appendices. A second demonstration problem has been included to provide material on inventory costing with both the perpetual and periodic inventory systems.
- Chapter 7: Internal Control and Cash expanded the definition of internal control to include primary components, with a focus on control activities. Descriptions of control activities have been updated and revised.
- Chapter 8: Accounting for Receivables now includes an illustration of a promissory note.
- Chapter 9: Long-Lived Assets has been updated with terminology that is consistent with IFRS. The impact of IFRS on long-lived assets was included throughout the chapter.
- Chapter 10: Current Liabilities and Payroll was expanded to include a discussion on the definition of a liability. Accounting for customer loyalty programs and gift cards was added. The material on contingencies was expanded to include the perspective of both IFRS and Canadian GAAP for Private Enterprises. Material on payroll was significantly expanded including calculation of payroll deductions.
- Chapter 11: Financial Reporting Concepts was updated to include the six components of the IFRS conceptual framework. The discussion of the qualitative characteristics was expanded to show the fundamental characteristics and enhancing characteristics. In addition, material was added to reflect new revenue recognition guidance. The zero profit method of recognizing revenue was added to replace the completed contract method. A section on different measurements (cost, fair value, and amortized cost) was added.
- Chapter 14: Corporations: Income and Equity Reporting includes an expanded discussion of the statement of comprehensive income. Intra-period income tax concepts have been applied to discontinued operations and other comprehensive income. The statement of changes in shareholders' equity has been added. The difference in income and equity reporting between IFRS and Canadian GAAP for Private Enterprises is illustrated.
- Chapter 15: Long-Term Liabilities features new material on leases under IFRS and compares that with Canadian GAAP for Private Enterprises.
- Chapter 16: Investments was substantially rewritten to incorporate new material on trading securities, investments reported at amortized cost, strategic investments reported at fair value, and equity accounting for strategic investments with significant influence.
- Chapter 17: The Cash Flow Statement demonstration problem was expanded to a full analysis including comparative balance sheets as well as the income statement and additional information.
- Chapter 18: Financial Statement Analysis now includes additional commentary in the ratio analysis sections to aid in interpretation.

Organizational Changes

Changes to the text's organization were made to simplify chapters or to provide instructors with greater flexibility of coverage. Some of the areas most affected are as follows:

- Chapter 3: Adjusting the Accounts moved the material on accrual versus cash basis of accounting before the discussion of revenue and expense recognition to illustrate that the accrual basis of accounting requires standards for determining when to recognize revenues and expenses.
- Chapter 4: Completion of the Accounting Cycle now includes a discussion of the operating cycle, material previously included in Chapter 5.
- Chapter 5: Accounting for Merchandising Operations repositioned the single-step income statement before the multiple-step income statement. Material on the operating cycle was moved to Chapter 4.
- Chapter 6: Inventory Costing now shows the perpetual inventory system in the chapter and the periodic system in the appendix to improve consistency with Chapter 5. LIFO was deleted, factors affecting choice of cost formula were updated, and the section on lower of cost or net realizable value was rewritten to incorporate new standards.
- Chapter 8: Accounting for Receivables moves the percentage of receivables approach before the percentage of sales approach because of the increasing emphasis on proper balance sheet valuations.
- Chapter 9: Long-Lived Assets shows the revisions to accounting for impairments and exchanges under IFRS.
- Chapter 10: Current Liabilities and Payroll now has a separate section on payroll accounting in the chapter that combines material previously included under determinable liabilities and in the appendix, eliminating the overlap. The appendix on payroll is now devoted to new material on calculating payroll deductions.
- Chapter 13: Corporations: Organization and Share Capital Transactions now introduces the journal entry for recording cash dividends, which was previously introduced in Chapter 14.
- Chapter 14: Corporations: Income and Equity Reporting now includes material on discontinued operations. This material was previously found in Chapter 18: Financial Statement Analysis.
- Chapter 15: Long-Term Liabilities now records and reports bonds net of premiums and discounts. The lease section was reorganized to explain finance leases first and then operating leases, consistent with IFRS.
- Chapter 16: Investments was entirely restructured by purpose of the investment as follows: (1) trading securities; (2) debt held to earn interest, reported at amortized cost; (3) strategic equity investments without significant influence, reported at fair value; and (4) strategic equity investments with significant influence using the equity method.
- Chapter 18: Financial Statement Analysis integrates the comprehensive illustration of ratio analysis previously included in the appendix with the chapter material on the

ratios. The illustrations of the comparative ratio analyses were restructured to emphasize the three different comparisons.

Unparalleled End-of-Chapter Material

The fifth Canadian edition continues to have a complete range of end-of-chapter material to satisfy all courses. This material guides students through the basic levels of cognitive understanding—knowledge, comprehension, application, analysis, synthesis, and evaluation—in a step-by-step process, starting first with questions, followed by brief exercises, exercises, problems, and finally, integrative cases to broaden a student's perspective.

Instructors told us they wanted more breadth and depth within each of these groupings to give them more flexibility in assigning end-of-chapter material. Using Bloom's Taxonomy of Learning, all of the end-of-chapter material was carefully reviewed. Topical gaps were identified and additional material added as required to facilitate progressive learning. Complexities were added to the Before You Go On, Self-Study Questions, and selected end-of-chapter material to increase the range and difficulty level of material available to test critical problem-solving skills.

A Taking It Further question has been added to the end of every problem. All of these questions were designed to help you determine how far your students have taken their understanding of the material. To ensure maximum flexibility, problems can also be assigned with or without the Taking It Further question.

The Continuing Cookie Chronicle, a serial problem following the life of a simulated student-owned company in each chapter, has been updated and given more conceptual material that attempts to integrate real-life experience and examples to the changing demands of financial accounting and reporting requirements.

The Collaborative Learning Activities reflect true group activities and not just problems that could be done in groups. These activities have been updated and revised to make it easier for instructors to use a portion of the activities. The quizzes provided for instructors for many of the Collaborative Learning Activities can be used as either a "classroom assessment tool" or for marks, as fits your situation. The instructor's resource material includes tips on how to use these activities in class, as well as suggestions for changing the level of difficulty depending on the current class composition.

The All About You boxes mentioned earlier are mirrored in the Broadening Your Perspective section. New All About You activities have been designed to help students appreciate that learning accounting is helpful for everyone, regardless of their current and future career plans.

In total, we have 1633 different end-of-chapter items for students to test their understanding of accounting. We have added 471 new questions, brief exercises, exercises, problems, and cases to the end-of-chapter material. That means that over 28% of the end-of-chapter material is new! The remaining material was substantially updated and revised, as required.

Special Student Supplements

Accounting Principles is accompanied by special student supplements to help students master the material and achieve success in their studies.

The **Student Study Guide**, a comprehensive review of accounting and a powerful tool for students, is a workbook containing a summary of key points of each chapter along with practice exercises and solutions. **Working Papers** are partially completed accounting forms for the end-of-chapter material, so that students can redirect limited time to important accounting concepts rather than formatting. The **City Cycle Practice Set** exposes students to a real-world simulation of maintaining a complete set of accounting records for a business.

Acknowledgements

During the course of developing *Accounting Principles*, Fifth Canadian Edition, the authors benefited from the feedback from instructors and students of accounting principles courses throughout the country, including many users of the previous editions of this text. The constructive suggestions and innovative ideas helped focus this revision on motivating students to want to learn accounting. In addition, the input and advice of the ancillary authors, contributors, and proofreaders provided valuable feedback throughout the development of this edition.

"Ensuring Student Success in Principles of Accounting" Workshop Participants

These Workshops were set up to allow instructors to meet, discuss, and share ideas. They allowed us to better understand your challenges as you endeavour to bring accounting to life for your students. They also gave us a vision, not just for the text, but for the entire package.

Participants in Workshops held for the current edition include:

Joan Barlow, *Mount Royal University*
Maria Belanger, *Algonquin College*
Lisa Boynton, *triOS College*
Andrea Chance, *George Brown College, University of Guelph*
David Ferries, *Algonquin College*
David Fleming, *George Brown College*
Ramona Girdauskas, *Seneca College*
Robert Harvey, *Algonquin College*
David Inhaber, *SAIT Polytechnic*
Barbara Katz, *Kwantlen Polytechnic University*
Gerry La Rocca, *Vanier College*
Cécile Laurin, *Algonquin College*
Thomas Leung, *Sprott-Shaw Community College*
Sally Mitzel, *Sheridan College*
Karen Murkar, *Seneca College*
Keri Norrie, *Camosun College*
Clifton Philpott, *Kwantlen Polytechnic University*
Regina Plateo, *Centennial College*
Steven Plateo, *George Brown College*
David Sale, *Kwantlen Polytechnic University*

Pina Salvaggio, *Dawson College*
Marie Sinnott, *College of New Caledonia*
Norman Douglas Stephenson, *Seneca College*
Carol Stewart, *Kwantlen Polytechnic University*
Helen Vallee, *Kwantlen Polytechnic University*
Brad Witt, *Humber College*
Julie Wong, *Dawson College*
Jerry P. Zdril, *Grant MacEwan University*

Reviewers

Peter Alpaugh, *George Brown College*
Glenn Ankrom, *CDI College*
Vida Barker, *Centennial College*
Margo Burtch, *Seneca College*
Meredith Delaney, *Seneca College*
Dave Fleming, *George Brown College*
Robert Greco, *CDI College*
Amy Greene, *triOS College*
Kenneth Hartford, *St. Clair College*
Robert Holland, *Nova Scotia Community College*
Yvonne Jacobs, *College of the North Atlantic*
Jeremy Jarvis, *Kwantlen Polytechnic University*
Lesley Johnson, *Sheridan College*
Cécile Laurin, *Algonquin College*
Barb Lee, *College of New Caledonia*
Lori MacIsaac, *College of the North Atlantic*
Pat Margeson, *New Brunswick Community College*
Fiaz Merani, *SAIT Polytechnic*
Debbie Musil, *Kwantlen Polytechnic University*
Joe Pidutti, *Durham College*
David Sale, *Kwantlen Polytechnic University*
Pina Salvaggio, *Dawson College*
John Shepherd, *College of New Caledonia*
Don Smith, *Georgian College*
Sophia Stewart, *Sheridan College*
Rod Tilley, *Mount Saint Vincent University*
Barrie Tober, *Niagara College*
Helen Vallee, *Kwantlen Polytechnic University*
Joan Wallwork, *Kwantlen Polytechnic University*
Dan Wong, *SAIT Polytechnic*
Julie Wong, *Dawson College*

Textbook Contributors

Peter Alpaugh, *George Brown College*
Sally Anderson, *Mount Royal University*
Joan Barlow, *Mount Royal University*
Cécile Laurin, *Algonquin College*
Brad Witt, *Humber College*
Julie Wong, *Dawson College*

Supplement Contributors

Vida Barker, *Centennial College*
Maria Belanger, *Algonquin College*
Carole Bowman, *Sheridan College*
Cynthia Brown, *Bow Valley College*
Shelley Coyle
Laura Cumming, *Dalhousie University*
Angela Davis, *University of Winnipeg*
Meredith Delaney, *Seneca College*
Robert Ducharme, *University of Waterloo*
Cynthia Duncan, *Seneca College*
Susan Fisher, *Algonquin College*
Gerry La Rocca, *Vanier College*
Cécile Laurin, *Algonquin College*
Debbie Musil, *Kwantlen Polytechnic University*
Jeff Power, *St. Mary's University*
Carole Reid Clyne, *Centennial College*
John Shepherd, *Kwantlen Polytechnic University*
Marie Sinnott, *College of New Caledonia*
Helen Vallee, *Kwantlen Polytechnic University*
Jerry P. Zdril, *Grant MacEwan University*
Patricia Zima, *Mohawk College*

Through their editorial contributions, the following people added to the real-world flavour of the text and its clarity:

Alison Arnot
Laurel Hyatt
Zofia Laubitz

Accuracy

We have made every effort to ensure that this text is error-free. *Accounting Principles* has been extensively reviewed and proofed at more than five different production stages prior to publication. In addition, the end-of-chapter material has been independently solved and then checked by at least three individuals, in addition to the authors, prior to publication of the text. We would like to express our sincere gratitude to everyone who spent countless hours ensuring the accuracy of this text and the solutions to the end-of-chapter material.

Publications

We would like to thank The Forzani Group Ltd. for allowing us to reproduce its 2009 financial statements in Appendix A. We would also like to acknowledge the co-operation of the many Canadian and international companies that allowed us to include extracts from their financial statements in the text and end-of-chapter material.

A Final Note of Thanks

I consider it a privilege to be trusted to continue with the excellent work and high standards established by Barbara Trenholm in previous Canadian editions of *Accounting Principles*. I am also very thankful for her generosity in sharing her perspective and expertise throughout the writing of this edition. I am extremely grateful for her mentorship.

I am indebted to Joan Barlow, of Mount Royal University, and Brad Witt, of Humber College, for their contributions to the textbook and for their thoughtful reading of the text and problems. This textbook has greatly benefited from the chapters and features that they have contributed to the text.

I appreciate the exemplary support and professional commitment given me by the talented team in the Wiley Canada higher education division. I wish to also thank Wiley's dedicated sales representatives who work tirelessly to serve your needs.

It would not have been possible to write this text without the understanding of my employer, colleagues, students, family, and friends. Together, they provided a creative and supportive environment for my work.

Suggestions and comments from all users—instructors and students alike—of this textbook and its supplements are encouraged and appreciated.

Valerie Kinnear
vkinnear@mtroyal.ca
Calgary, Alberta

November 2009

CHAPTER 1
ACCOUNTING IN ACTION

forzanigroup.com

The **Navigator** learning system encourages you to use the learning aids in the chapter and set priorities as you study.

Concepts for Review highlight concepts from your earlier reading that you need to understand before starting the new chapter.

THE NAVIGATOR

- ☐ Understand *Concepts for Review*
- ☐ Read *Feature Story*
- ☐ Scan *Study Objectives*
- ☐ Read *Chapter Preview*
- ☐ Read text and answer *Before You Go On*
- ☐ Work *Demonstration Problem*
- ☐ Review *Summary of Study Objectives*
- ☐ Answer *Self-Study Questions*
- ☐ Complete assignments

CONCEPTS FOR REVIEW:

Before studying this chapter, you should understand or, if necessary, review:

a. How to use the study aids in this book. (pp. vii–xvi)

b. What the Bloom's Taxonomy classifications (K, C, AP, AN, S, and E) mean. (p. xvii)

c. How you learn best. (pp. xviii–xx)

d. The student supplements that accompany this text. (p. xxiv)

Making the Right Moves

CALGARY, Alta.—When it comes to football, everyone knows you need to "keep your eye on the ball" if you want to stay in the game. In business, as in sports, an organization needs to keep a careful eye on its financial accounting information if it wants to succeed and thrive. Consider the story of Calgary-based Forzani Group Ltd., Canada's "largest and only national sporting goods retailer."

The company kicked off in 1974 when Calgary Stampeder John Forzani and three of his teammates launched Forzani's Locker Room, a small retail operation that sold athletic footwear. Gradually, the business expanded to include clothing and sports equipment. In 1988, it launched RnR, its Relaxed and Rugged banner, specializing in leisure and recreational apparel.

Five years later, in 1993, the company went public and its shares began trading on the Toronto Stock Exchange. Expansion then continued with a series of acquisitions including Sports Experts in 1994, Coast Mountain Sports in 2000, Sport Mart in 2001, Gen-X Sports and Nevada Bob's Golf in 2004, National Sports in 2005, Fitness Source in 2006, and Athletes World in 2007. In addition, the company launched Hockey Experts and Pegasus in 2006.

Today, The Forzani Group offers a comprehensive assortment of brand-name and private-brand products, operating stores from coast to coast, under the following corporate and franchise banners: Sport Chek, Coast Mountain Sports, Sport Mart, National Sports, Athletes World, Sports Experts, Intersport, Econosports,

Atmosphere, Tech Shop, Pegasus, Nevada Bob's Golf, Hockey Experts, S3, and The Fitness Source. At the end of the third quarter of its 2009 fiscal year, the company operated 335 corporate and 226 franchise stores. It also retails online at www.sportmart.ca and provides a sporting goods information site at www.sportchek.ca. For its 2009 fiscal year end, the company scored retail system sales of more than $1.3 billion and profit of almost $29.3 million.

These are rather impressive numbers for a company that started out as a single retail outlet! In fact, the spectacular growth is the result of countless decisions made along the way. Does a particular acquisition make sense financially? Should the company operate its stores under separate banners? Is e-commerce worth pursuing? While many factors have no doubt contributed to The Forzani Group's success, one thing is certain: to make these strategic decisions and others, the company's management relied on accounting information.

They're not the only ones. Over the years, other parties have used The Forzani Group's financial information, too. Its shareholders and potential investors have used it to make investment decisions, and its creditors have analyzed it to determine whether to issue loans or other forms of credit.

In short, sound accounting information lets The Forzani Group and all interested parties know exactly how the business is doing at all times—an essential part of any winning strategy!

The Navigator

STUDY OBJECTIVES:

After studying this chapter, you should be able to:

1. Identify the use and users of accounting.
2. Explain Canadian accounting standards and apply basic accounting concepts.
3. Use the accounting equation and explain the meaning of assets, liabilities, and owner's equity.
4. Analyze the effects of business transactions on the accounting equation.
5. Prepare financial statements.

The Navigator

The **Chapter Preview** outlines the major topics and subtopics you will see in the chapter.

The feature story about The Forzani Group highlights the importance of having good financial information to make good business decisions. This applies not just to companies but also to individuals. You cannot earn a living, spend money, buy on credit, make an investment, or pay taxes without receiving, using, or giving financial information. Good decision-making for companies and individuals depends on good information.

This chapter shows you that accounting is the system that produces useful financial information for decision-making. The chapter is organized as follows:

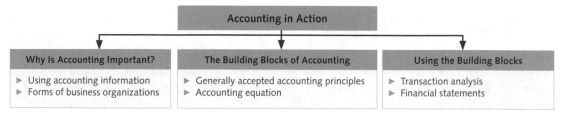

Why Is Accounting Important?

STUDY OBJECTIVE 1

Identify the use and users of accounting.

Essential terms are printed in blue when they first appear, and are defined in the end-of-chapter glossary.

Accounting is the information system that identifies, records, and communicates the economic events of an organization to a wide variety of interested users. The world's economic systems depend on highly transparent, relevant, understandable, and reliable financial reporting. When that does not happen, it can have disastrous results. Individuals such as financial advisers Bernard Madoff in New York and Earl Jones in Quebec concealed fraudulent investment operations, resulting in huge losses to investors, by hiding financial information regarding what was actually happening to the amounts invested by others.

A vital part of communicating economic events is the accountant's ability and responsibility to analyze and interpret the reported information. In analysis, accountants use ratios, percentages, graphs, and charts to highlight significant financial trends and relationships. In interpretation, they explain the uses, meaning, and limitations of the reported data. Accounting has long been labelled the "language of business" and has consistently ranked as one of the top career opportunities in business.

You might think this is all well and good for students who want to become accountants, but what about someone who has plans to be anything *but* an accountant?

Understanding the basics of accounting is helpful for almost every endeavour you can think of. By studying accounting, you will learn how the world of business—large and small—actually works. Whether you plan to own your own business in the future, work for someone else in their business, or invest in a business, learning how to read and interpret financial information will give you a valuable set of skills.

When you study accounting, you will also learn a lot about management, finance, and marketing, which will give you a solid foundation for your future studies. For example, you will learn how making a sale is meaningless unless it is a profitable sale and the money can eventually be collected from the customer. Marketing managers must also be able to decide pricing strategies based on costs. Accounting is what quantifies these costs and explains why a product or service costs what it does. So think of this textbook as your introduction to accounting across the organization.

It doesn't matter if you plan to become a doctor, lawyer, social worker, teacher, engineer, architect, or entrepreneur—whatever you choose, a working knowledge of accounting will be relevant and useful. Accounting is all about you. Make the most of this course—it will serve you for a lifetime in ways you cannot now imagine.

On the companion website to this text, there is more information about why accounting is important and what potential career opportunities exist. In addition, there are profiles of business people who use accounting information.

The **Web Icon** tells you about additional resources on the companion website that expand on the topic being discussed.

WILEY
PLUS
Career Paths

ACCOUNTING IN ACTION: ALL ABOUT YOU

"Bland, boring and colourless are just a few of the common stereotypes that spring to mind when describing an accountant. But these are just urban myths," an accounting magazine points out. To some entrepreneurs, the accountant is considered a hero. A survey by the Canadian Federation of Independent Business found that two thirds of companies feel that they get the most valued information from their accountant and lawyer. But what if you are not going to be an accountant—what will learning accounting do for you? Understanding the basics of accounting is helpful for almost every endeavour you can think of, including making personal investment decisions, protecting your personal resources, determining how much interest you will pay on a student loan, and deciding which company you will work for upon graduation. To demonstrate the value of accounting to you as an individual, included in each chapter is an "All About You" feature and a related activity (BYP-6) that links an accounting concept to your life as a student and to a situation you are likely to face.

Source: Yan Barcelo, "Ten Ways to Add Value," *CA Magazine*, August 2009, p. 20.

Why is understanding accounting of value to you in your personal life?

Using Accounting Information

There are two broad groups of users of accounting information: internal users and external users.

Internal Users

Internal users of accounting information plan, organize, and run companies. They work for the company. This includes finance directors, marketing managers, human resources personnel, production supervisors, and company officers. In running a business, internal users must answer many important questions, as shown in Illustration 1-1.

↑ **Accounting in Action** insights give examples of accounting situations from five different perspectives: all about you, across the organization, and in terms of business, ethics, and international concerns. At the end of the chapter, you will find answers to the questions that are asked after each insight.

← **Illustration 1-1**

Questions asked by internal users

Finance
Is there enough cash to pay the bills?

Marketing
What price should we sell iPhones for to maximize profits?

Human Resources
How many employees can we afford to hire this year?

Production
Which product line is the most profitable?

To answer these and other questions, users need detailed information on a timely basis; that is, it must be available when needed. Some examples of information that internal users need include forecasts of cash flows for the next year, projections of profit from new sales campaigns, financial comparisons of operating alternatives, analyses of salary costs, and budgeted financial statements.

External Users

There are several types of external users of accounting information. Investors use accounting information to make decisions to buy, hold, or sell their ownership interest. Creditors, such as suppliers and bankers, use accounting information to evaluate the risks of granting credit or lending money. Investors and creditors are the main external users of accounting information, but there are also many other external users with a large variety of information needs and questions.

For example, labour unions want to know whether the owners can afford to pay increased wages and benefits. Customers are interested in whether a company will continue to honour its product warranties and support its product lines. Taxing authorities, such as Canada Revenue Agency, want to know whether the company respects the tax laws. Regulatory agencies, such as provincial securities commissions that regulate companies that sell shares to the public, want to know whether the company is respecting established rules. And economic planners use accounting information to forecast economic activity.

Some questions that external users may ask about a company are shown in Illustration 1-2.

➜ **Illustration 1-2**

Questions asked by external users

Investors
Is the company earning enough to give me a return on my investment?

Creditors
Will the company be able to pay its debts as they come due?

Labour Unions
Can the company afford the pay raise we are asking for?

Customers
Will the company stay in business long enough to service the products I buy from it?

ACCOUNTING IN ACTION: ACROSS THE ORGANIZATION INSIGHT

The Great Little Box Company, based in Vancouver, involves its employees in the company's success by regularly sharing information and acknowledging employee contributions. Every month, the company shares its corporate and financial information with all employees. These meetings ensure that everyone knows how the company is doing and what could be done to improve things. They also provide a forum for employee input and for recognizing and rewarding employees for their efforts. The company also shares 15% of its profits with employees on a monthly basis; divided equally among all eligible part-time and full-time employees. When there is a profit, the share for each employee is included in their paycheque following the monthly meeting.

Source: Industry Canada, Managing for Business Success: Great Little Box Company: A Team Approach to Success, Part 1, available at: http://www.ic.gc.ca/eic/site/mfbs-gprea.nsf/eng/lu00055.html [accessed on July 27, 2009]

What is the value of providing all of a company's employees with financial information about the company?

Ethics in Financial Reporting

In order for financial information to have value for its users, whether internal or external, it must be prepared by individuals with high standards of ethical behaviour. Ethics in accounting is of the utmost importance to accountants and decision-makers who rely on the financial information they produce.

Fortunately, most individuals in business are ethical. Their actions are both legal and responsible. They consider the organization's interests when they make decisions. Accountants and other professionals have extensive rules of conduct to guide their behaviour with each other and the public. In addition, many companies today have codes of conduct, or statements of corporate values, that outline their commitment to ethical behaviour in their internal and external relationships. The behaviour of management is critical for creating the appropriate tone from the top of the organization.

Throughout this textbook, ethical considerations will be presented to highlight the importance of ethics in financial reporting. Every chapter includes an Ethics Case in the end-of-chapter material that simulates a business situation and asks you to put yourself in the position of a key decision-maker. When you analyze these ethical situations, you should follow the steps outlined in Illustration 1-3.

Ethics in Accounting

1. Recognize an ethical situation and the ethical issues involved.
Use your personal ethics or an organization's code of ethics to identify ethical situations and issues. Some business and professional organizations provide written codes of ethics for guidance in common business situations.

2. Identify and analyze the main elements in the situation.
Identify the *stakeholders*—persons or groups who may be harmed or benefited. Ask the question: What are the responsibilities and obligations of the parties involved?

3. Identify the alternatives, and weigh the impact of each alternative on various stakeholders.
Select the most ethical alternative, considering all the consequences. Sometimes there will be one right answer. Other situations involve more than one possible solution. These situations require an evaluation of each alternative and the selection of the best one.

The companion website to this text includes a discussion of ethics and ethical issues that involve accounting and financial reporting.

↑ Illustration 1-3

Steps used to analyze ethics cases and situations

Forms of Business Organization

As we have seen, businesses rely on accounting information to operate. Businesses can be organized in different ways. The most common examples are the proprietorship, partnership, and corporation. Illustration 1-4 compares some of the characteristics of these forms.

	Proprietorship	Partnership	Corporation
Owners	Proprietor: one	Partners: two or more	Shareholders: one or more
Owner's liability	Unlimited	Unlimited	Limited
Private or public	Private	Usually private	Private or public
Taxation of profits	Paid by the owner	Paid by the partners	Paid by the corporation
Life of organization	Limited	Limited	Indefinite

← Illustration 1-4

Characteristics of business organizations

Proprietorship

A business owned by one person is a **proprietorship**. The owner is usually the operator of the business. Small service businesses (hair stylists, plumbers, and mechanics), farms, and small retail stores (antique shops, corner grocery stores, and independent bookstores) are often proprietorships.

Often only a relatively small amount of money (capital) is needed to start in business as a proprietorship. The owner (the proprietor) receives any profits, suffers any losses, and is personally liable (responsible) for all debts of the business. This is known as **unlimited liability**.

There is no legal distinction between the business as an economic unit and the owner. Thus the life of a proprietorship is limited to the life of the owner. However, the records of the business activities must be kept separate from the personal records and activities of the owner. The profits of the business are reported and taxed on the owner's personal income tax return.

Many businesses in Canada are proprietorships, but they earn only a small percentage of the revenue earned by Canadian businesses as a whole. In this textbook, we start with proprietorships because many students organize their first business this way.

Partnership

A business owned by two or more persons who are associated as partners is a **partnership**. In most aspects, a partnership is similar to a proprietorship, except that there is more than one owner. Partnerships are often used to organize service-type businesses, including professional practices (lawyers, doctors, architects, and accountants).

Typically, a partnership agreement (written or oral) defines the initial investments of each partner, the duties of each partner, how profit (or loss) will be divided, and what the settlement will be if a partner dies or withdraws. As in a proprietorship, for accounting purposes the partnership activities must be kept separate from the personal activities of each partner. The partners' share of the profit must be reported and taxed on the partners' income tax return.

Each partner generally has unlimited liability for all debts of the partnership, even if one of the other partners created the debt. This means that any of the partners can be forced to give up his or her personal assets in order to repay the partnership debt, just as can happen to an owner in a proprietorship. We will learn more about partnerships in Chapter 12.

Corporation

A business that is organized (incorporated) as a separate legal entity under federal or provincial corporate law is a **corporation**. A corporation is responsible for its debts and paying taxes on its profit. A corporation's ownership is divided into transferable shares. The corporation's separate legal status provides the owners of the shares (shareholders) with **limited liability** as they risk losing only the amount that they have invested in the company's shares. They are not personally liable for the debts of the corporate entity. Shareholders may sell all or part of their shares to other investors at any time. Easy changes of ownership are part of what makes it attractive to invest in a corporation. Because ownership can be transferred through the sale of shares and without dissolving the corporation, the corporation enjoys an unlimited life.

Although there are many more proprietorships and partnerships than corporations in Canada, the revenue produced by corporations is far greater. Most of the largest companies in Canada—for example, Bombardier, EnCana, Imperial Oil, Loblaw, and Magna—are corporations.

Corporations such as these are publicly traded. That is, their shares are listed on Canadian stock exchanges. Public corporations commonly distribute their financial statements to shareholders, creditors, other interested parties, and the general public upon request. Forzani is a public corporation. You can access its financial statements on its website, which is given in our feature story, as well as in Appendix A at the back of this textbook.

Other companies are private corporations, as they do not issue publicly traded shares. Some of the largest private companies in Canada include the Jim Pattison Group, the Irving Group, and McCain Foods. Like proprietorships and partnerships, these companies almost never distribute their financial statements publicly. We will discuss the corporate form of organization in Chapters 13 and 14.

BEFORE YOU GO ON . . .

→ **Review It**

1. Why is good accounting important?
2. How can the study of accounting benefit you?
3. Who uses accounting information? Name some specific internal and external users of accounting information?
4. Why is ethics important in terms of accounting information?
5. What are the differences between a proprietorship, partnership, and corporation?

Related exercise material: BE1–1, BE1–2, BE1–3, and E1–1.

↓ **Helpful hints** help clarify concepts or items that are being discussed.

Helpful hint You can usually tell if a company is a corporation by looking at its name. The words *Limited (Ltd.)*, *Incorporated (Inc.)*, or *Corporation (Corp.)* usually follow its name.

Before You Go On questions at the end of major text sections are an opportunity to stop and re-examine the key points you have studied. *Related exercise material* tells you which Brief Exercises (BE) and Exercises (E) at the end of the chapter have similar study objectives.

The Navigator

The Building Blocks of Accounting

Financial information is communicated in accounting reports, and the most common reports are financial statements. We have included Forzani's financial statements for the year ended February 1, 2009, in Appendix A of this textbook as an example. We will refer to these statements throughout the textbook.

To make the information in financial statements meaningful, accountants have to prepare the reports in a standardized way. Every profession develops a body of theory based on principles and assumptions. Accounting is no exception.

Generally Accepted Accounting Principles

The accounting profession has developed a set of standards that are generally accepted and universally practised. This common set of standards, called **generally accepted accounting principles (GAAP)**, includes broad principles and practices, as well as rules and procedures. These standards indicate how to report economic events.

In Canada, the Accounting Standards Board (AcSB), an independent standard-setting body created by the Canadian Institute of Chartered Accountants (CICA), has the main responsibility for developing GAAP. The AcSB's most important criterion for accounting principles is this: the principle should lead to external users having the most useful financial information possible when they are making business decisions. In other words, the basic objective of financial reporting is to communicate information that is useful to investors, creditors, and other users when they make decisions.

It is important to understand that GAAP is not static and that it changes over time. The AcSB creates new standards and modifies GAAP after a long process of consultation with organizations and individuals that are interested in, or affected by, the principles. This process ensures that the main purpose of financial statements—providing information that is relevant to decision-making—continues to be met.

A recent and very dramatic change in Canadian GAAP is the implementation of two sets of standards: International Financial Reporting Standards, and Canadian GAAP for Private Enterprises.

International Financial Reporting Standards and Canadian GAAP for Private Enterprises

In its Strategic Plan, issued in January 2006, the AcSB noted that "one size does not necessarily fit all" and decided to pursue separate strategies for publicly accountable enterprises and for private enterprises. Effective January 1, 2011, all Canadian publicly accountable enterprises must follow International Financial Reporting Standards (IFRS), a set of global standards developed by the International Accounting Standards Board (IASB). **Publicly accountable enterprises** include publicly traded companies, as well as securities brokers and dealers, banks, and credit unions whose role is to hold assets for the public as part of their primary business.

Traditionally, accounting standards differed from country to country, making it difficult for investors, creditors, and others to make informed decisions about companies doing business in today's increasingly global environment. The IASB has worked, and continues to do so, with accounting standard setters across the globe to harmonize accounting standards where possible. IFRS are used as the main basis of financial reporting in more than 100 countries, including Australia, Russia, members of the European Union, and China. India and Japan, along with Canada, join in 2011. The United States is working on a convergence project with the IASB but at the time of writing had not yet set a specific date for adopting IFRS.

In Canada, the decision to adopt IFRS was made in order to enhance Canadian public companies' ability to compete in an increasingly global marketplace. When IFRS are used, the financial statements of Canadian public companies will be understood by investors and creditors throughout the world. Using IFRS will also help Canadian companies that operate in multiple countries, by allowing them to produce one set of financial statements rather than multiple sets with different accounting principles.

STUDY OBJECTIVE 2

Explain Canadian accounting standards and apply basic accounting concepts.

↯ **Alternative terminology** notes give synonyms that you may hear or see in the workplace, in companies' financial statements, and occasionally in this textbook.

Alternative terminology The words *standard* and *principle* mean the same thing in accounting.

Helpful hint Accounting standards use the word "enterprise" as it is a broader term than "company" or "business." The word "enterprise" means that the accounting standard applies to the different forms of business organizations, as well as specific projects. Throughout this text, instead of using the word "enterprise," we will frequently use the words "company" or "business," as they are more common terms.

On the other hand, for many years critics have argued that traditional Canadian GAAP had too many complex standards that were not relevant for private companies. Since IFRS has even more requirements than traditional Canadian GAAP, the AcSB decided that all private companies, regardless of size, should have the choice of either adopting IFRS or following a new set of standards called Canadian GAAP for Private Enterprises.

The new Canadian GAAP for Private Enterprises requires considerably less information in financial statements than was required by traditional Canadian GAAP. A main reason for this change is that users of a private company's financial statements generally have the ability to obtain additional information from the company if required, and because these users typically require less information.

Given the differences between IFRS and GAAP for Private Enterprises, and the fact that private companies will have a choice, financial statement users will need to know which standards the company is following. Companies will be required to report this in their financial statements. In this textbook, as we proceed through the material, we will point out where there are differences in the two sets of standards. However, the two sets of standards have a great deal in common in the type of material covered in an introductory accounting textbook.

Both IFRS and Canadian GAAP for Private Enterprises are considered "principles-based" as opposed to "rules-based" standards. Principles-based standards are designed to encourage the use of professional judgement in applying basic accounting principles. As you learn more about accounting, you will see that we will frequently refer to basic principles, as opposed to detailed rules, when deciding how to account for specific events. In the following sections, we introduce a few of these basic principles and concepts.

ACCOUNTING IN ACTION: BUSINESS INSIGHT

The new reporting requirements under International Financial Reporting Standards have made some smaller public companies consider going private. Take, for example, Calgary-based Humpty's Restaurants International Inc., which, after 19 years on the public market, decided that being private would be less costly and make the company more competitive. Humpty's estimated being private would have saved $80,000 in 2009 and the savings in 2010 would be about $120,000. This is a significant amount, considering that the restaurants' 2008 revenue was about $7 million and profit was just $503,000. Humpty's has not relied on equity financing or issued shares to raise capital or complete acquisitions for many years. It has six corporate stores and 44 franchises in Western Canada and has no plans for operational changes, though it will continue to explore franchise expansion opportunities.

Source: Dan Healing, "Humpty's Gets Cracking on Going Private," *Calgary Herald*, July 17, 2009.

Why will it be less expensive for a company like Humpty's Restaurants to use Canadian GAAP for Private Enterprises than IFRS?

Going Concern

The **going concern assumption** is the assumption that a company will continue to operate in the foreseeable future. Although some businesses fail, most companies continue operating for a long time. The going concern assumption presumes that the company will operate long enough to use its assets for their intended purpose and to complete the company's commitments.

This assumption is one of the most important assumptions in GAAP as it has implications regarding what information is useful for decision-makers and affects many of the accounting standards you will learn. If a company is a going concern, then financial statement users will find it useful for the company to report certain assets, such as land, at their cost. Land is acquired so a company can use it, not so it can be resold. Therefore, what matters is the amount the company gave up to acquire the land, not an estimate of its current worth. If a company is not a going concern, and the land is going to be sold, then financial statement users will be more interested in the land's current value.

If a company is not regarded as a going concern, or if there are significant doubts about its ability to continue as a going concern, then this must be stated in the financial statements, along with the reason why the company is not regarded as a going concern. Otherwise you can assume that the company is a going concern—even though this is not explicitly stated.

Economic Entity

The **economic entity assumption** (or entity concept) requires that an entity's business activities be kept separate and distinct from the activities of its owner and all other economic entities. An economic entity can be any organization or unit in society. It may be a company (such as The Forzani Group Ltd.), a governmental unit (such as the Province of Manitoba), a municipality (such as the Ville de Montréal), a native band council (such as the Kingsclear Indian Band), a school board (such as the Burnaby School Board), a club (such as the Melfort Rotary Club), or a proprietorship (such as Ellen's Boutique).

To illustrate, if Ellen Gélinas, owner of Ellen's Boutique, charges any of her personal living costs as expenses of Ellen's Boutique, then the economic entity assumption is being violated. This example also illustrates that an economic entity is not the same thing as a legal entity. You will recall from our earlier discussion that a proprietorship is not a separate legal entity from its owner. But the owner and the proprietorship are economically separate and must be accounted for as such.

Recognition and Measurement

Recognition is the process of recording a transaction in the accounting records. Once a transaction has been recognized or recorded, it will be included in the financial statements. **Measurement** is the process of determining the amount that should be recognized. At the time something is acquired, the transaction is first measured at the amount of cash that was paid or at the value exchanged. For example, if the Gjoa Company purchased land for $100,000, the land is recorded in Gjoa's records at $100,000. This amount is referred to as the asset's historical cost.

But what should Gjoa Company do if, by the end of the next year, the land's fair value has increased to $120,000? Under both IFRS and Canadian GAAP for Private Enterprises, historical cost is the primary basis used in financial statements, which means that Gjoa Company would continue to report the land at its historical cost of $100,000. This is often called the **cost principle**.

Alternative terminology
The cost principle is also known as the *historical cost principle*.

Cost has an important advantage over other valuations. It is reliable. Cost is definite and verifiable. The values exchanged at the time something is acquired can be objectively measured. Users can therefore rely on the information that is supplied, as they know it is based on fact.

However, critics argue that cost is often not relevant. They believe fair values provide more useful information. **Fair value** is the amount of the consideration that would be agreed upon in an arm's-length transaction between knowledgeable, willing parties who are under no compulsion to act. Fair value is not the amount that an entity would receive or pay in a forced transaction, involuntary liquidation, or distress sale.

At the time of acquisition, cost and fair value are the same. In later periods, cost and fair value differ, but the cost amount continues to be used for accounting in most circumstances. There are some exceptions that we will learn about in later chapters, and we will see that IFRS either allow or require fair value in more circumstances than Canadian GAAP for Private Enterprises.

Fundamental to this discussion is that only transactions that can be expressed as an amount of money can be included in the accounting records. This has been known as the **monetary unit assumption**. This assumption makes it possible for accounting to quantify (measure) economic events. In Canada, we mainly use the Canadian dollar to record these transactions. However, some companies report their results in U.S. dollars. In Europe, the euro (€) is used; in China, the yuan (CNY) is used; and so on.

The monetary unit assumption allows us to ignore the impact of inflation. Although inflation can be a significant accounting issue in some countries, Canada's inflation policy—set out by the federal government and the Bank of Canada—is to keep inflation at between 1% and 3% per year. Consequently, inflation is not considered an issue for accounting in Canada.

The monetary unit assumption does prevent some relevant information from being included in the accounting records. For example, the health of the owner, the quality of service, and the morale of employees would not be included, because they cannot be quantified in monetary amounts.

Other Financial Reporting Concepts

We have barely scratched the surface in terms of learning about financial reporting concepts and generally accepted accounting principles. Many other concepts and principles will be introduced as we move forward through the text. For example, in later chapters we will introduce the revenue and expense recognition criteria, the cost-benefit and materiality constraints, and concepts such as full disclosure, consistency, and comparability. Chapter 11 explores these principles in greater detail, and introduces the conceptual framework of accounting, a system that guides the development and application of accounting principles, including the relationships and hierarchy of these concepts. A conceptual framework is also important for companies to refer to when exercising professional judgement about how to apply GAAP to their specific circumstances.

BEFORE YOU GO ON . . .

→ Review It

1. What are generally accepted accounting principles?
2. What generally accepted accounting principles do companies in Canada use?
3. Explain the going concern and economic entity assumptions.
4. What is meant by recognition and measurement in accounting?
5. Explain the cost principle and the monetary unit assumptions.
6. What is the difference between cost and fair value?

The Navigator

Related exercise material: BE1–4, BE1–5, and E1–2.

Accounting Equation

STUDY OBJECTIVE 3

Use the accounting equation and explain the meaning of assets, liabilities, and owner's equity.

The categories that are used for classifying economic events are also essential building blocks of accounting. The two basic elements of a business are what it owns and what it owes. Assets are the resources owned by a business. Forzani has total assets of $689 million at February 1, 2009. Liabilities and owner's equity are the rights or claims against these resources. The claims of those who are owed money or other obligations (the creditors) are called liabilities. The claims of owners are called owner's equity. Forzani has liabilities of $356 million and owner's equity of $333 million. Illustration 1-5 shows how the relationship between assets, liabilities, and owner's equity is expressed as an equation.

→ **Illustration 1-5**

Accounting equation

Resources		Claims Against the Resources		
Assets	=	Liabilities	+	Owner's Equity
$689 million	=	$356 million	+	$333 million

Alternative terminology
The accounting equation is sometimes referred to as the *balance sheet equation.*

This equation is called the **accounting equation**. Assets must equal the sum of liabilities and owner's equity. Liabilities are shown before owner's equity in the accounting equation because creditors' claims are paid before ownership claims if a business is liquidated.

The accounting equation is the same for all economic entities regardless of their size, nature of business, or form of business organization. It applies to a small proprietorship such as a corner grocery store as much as it does to a large corporation such as The Forzani Group Ltd. This equation is the basis for recording and summarizing the economic events of a company.

Let's look at the categories in the accounting equation in more detail.

Assets

As noted earlier, **assets** are the resources owned by a business. They are used to carry out activities such as the production and distribution of merchandise. Every asset is capable of providing future services or benefits. In a company, that service potential or future economic benefit eventually results in cash inflows (receipts).

For example, imagine that a local pizza parlour, called Campus Pizza, owns a delivery truck. This truck provides economic benefits because it is used to deliver pizzas. Campus Pizza also owns other assets such as tables, chairs, a sound system, a cash register, an oven, dishes, supplies, and, of course, cash. Other common examples of assets include merchandise inventory held for resale, investments, land, buildings, equipment, patents, and copyrights. **Accounts receivable** is the asset created when a company sells services or products to customers who promise to pay cash in the future.

Liabilities

Liabilities are current obligations, arising from past events, to make a future payment of assets or services. That is, liabilities are present debts and obligations. For example, businesses of all sizes usually borrow money and purchase merchandise inventory and supplies on credit. Campus Pizza, for instance, purchases pizza ingredients and beverages on credit from suppliers. These obligations to pay cash to the supplier in the future are called **accounts payable**. Campus Pizza also has a note payable to the Bank of Montreal for the money it borrowed to purchase its delivery truck. A **note payable** is supported by a written promise to pay a specific amount, at a specific time, in the future. Campus Pizza may also have wages payable to employees, Goods and Services Taxes (GST) payable and Provincial Sales Taxes (PST) payable to the federal and provincial governments, and property taxes payable to the municipality. All of these persons or entities that Campus Pizza owes money to are called its **creditors**.

A creditor who is not paid after a certain length of time has the legal right to force the liquidation of a business. In that case, the law requires that creditor claims be paid before ownership claims are paid.

Owner's Equity

The owner's claim on the assets of the company is known as **owner's equity**. It is equal to total assets minus total liabilities. Here is why: As shown in the accounting equation, assets are resources that can be claimed by either creditors or owners. To find out what belongs to owners, we subtract creditors' claims (the liabilities) from assets. The remainder—owner's equity—is the owner's claim on the assets of the business. This amount is also called **net assets**. Since the claims of creditors must be paid before ownership claims, the owner's equity is often called residual equity. If the equity is negative—that is, if total liabilities are more than total assets— the term "owner's deficiency" (or deficit) describes the shortage.

In a proprietorship, owner's equity is increased by investments made by the owner and decreased by withdrawals made by the owner. Owner's equity is also increased when a company generates a profit from business activities. Let's look at each of these equity components in more detail.

Investments. Investments by the owner are recorded as increases to what is known as the owner's capital account. Investments may be cash or other assets (e.g., a vehicle or computer) that are contributed by the owner. Accordingly, investments such as these result in an increase in an asset and an increase in owner's equity.

Drawings. An owner may withdraw cash (or other assets) for personal use. These drawings could be recorded as a direct decrease of owner's equity. However, it is generally considered better to use a separate account classification called **drawings** so that the total withdrawals for the accounting period can be determined. Drawings result in a decrease in an asset and a decrease in owner's equity.

Alternative terminology
Profit is also sometimes called *net income* or *earnings* or *net earnings*.

Profit. Revenues increase owner's equity, and expenses decrease owner's equity. **Profit** results when revenues are greater than expenses. Owner's equity then increases correspondingly. Conversely, if expenses are greater than revenues, a **loss** results and owner's equity decreases.

Revenues. **Revenues** result from business activities that are done to earn profit. Generally, revenues result from performing services, selling merchandise inventory, renting property, and lending money.

Revenues result in an increase in an asset (or a decrease in a liability when a customer has paid in advance) and an increase in owner's equity. They come from different sources and are given different names, depending on the type of business. Campus Pizza, for instance, has two categories of revenues: pizza sales and beverage sales. Common sources of revenue include sales, fees, services, commissions, interest, and rent.

Expenses. **Expenses** are the costs of assets that are consumed and services that are used in a company's ordinary business activities. Expenses result in a decrease in owner's equity and a corresponding decrease in an asset or an increase in a liability. Like revenues, there are many kinds of expenses and they are identified by various names, depending on the type of asset consumed or service used. For example, Campus Pizza recognizes (records) the following expenses: cost of ingredients (meat, flour, cheese, tomato paste, mushrooms, etc.), cost of beverages, wages expense, utility expense (electricity, gas, and water expense), telephone expense, delivery expense (gasoline, repairs, licences, insurance, etc.), supplies expense (napkins, detergents, aprons, etc.), rent expense, insurance expense, and interest expense.

Illustration 1-6 summarizes the transactions that change owner's equity.

➤ Illustration 1-6

Transactions that increase and decrease owner's equity

Increases in owner's equity	Decreases in owner's equity
Investments by the owner	Drawings by the owner
Revenues	Expenses

In Illustration 1-7, we have expanded the basic accounting equation in Illustration 1-5 to show the different parts of owner's equity. This illustration shows the relationship between revenues, expenses, profit (or loss), and owner's equity.

➤ Illustration 1-7

Expanded accounting equation

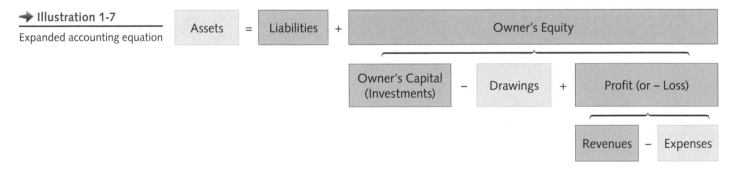

Accounting Differences by Type of Business Organization

Previously, you were introduced to different forms of business organizations: the proprietorship, partnership, and corporation. In the early chapters of this text, we focus mostly on proprietorships. Partnerships and corporations will be discussed in more detail in later chapters. Until that time, you need only a general understanding of the accounting distinctions between these types of organization.

Accounting for assets, liabilities, revenues, and expenses is the same, regardless of the form of business organization. The main distinction between the forms of organizations is found in (1) the terminology that is used to name the equity section, and (2) the accounting and reporting of the owner's investments and withdrawals. In Illustration 1-8, we summarize these differences.

	Proprietorship	Partnership	Corporation
Equity section called:	Owner's equity	Partners' equity	Shareholders' equity
Investments by owners added to:	Owner's capital	Partners' capital	Share capital
Profits added to:	Owner's capital	Partners' capital	Retained earnings
Withdrawals by owners called:	Drawings	Drawings	Dividends
Withdrawals deducted from:	Owner's capital	Partners' capital	Retained earnings

← **Illustration 1-8**

Accounting differences by type of business organization

In a proprietorship, equity is summarized and reported in a one-line capital account. In a partnership, equity is summarized and reported in separate one-line capital accounts for each partner. In a corporation, investments by all of the shareholders are grouped together and called *share capital*. In a corporation, regardless of the number of shareholders, one account called Retained Earnings is used to record the accumulated profit (or earnings) of the company that have been retained (i.e., not paid out to shareholders) in the company.

In Illustration 1-5, when the assets, liabilities, and equity were reported for The Forzani Group, the equity was identified as owner's equity to keep the illustration simpler. Technically, since Forzani is a corporation, this equity should have been called *shareholders' equity*, as shown in Illustration 1-8.

BEFORE YOU GO ON . . .

→ Review It

1. What is the accounting equation?
2. What are assets, liabilities, and owner's equity?
3. Identify some of the assets that you own personally and some of the liabilities that you owe.
4. What are the different types of equity reported by each form of business organization?

→ Do It

Classify the following items as assets, liabilities, or owner's equity: (1) cash, (2) service revenue, (3) drawings, (4) accounts receivable, (5) accounts payable, and (6) salaries expense. For any items that affect owner's equity, please indicate whether these items increase or decrease equity.

Action Plan
- Understand that assets are resources owned by a business.
- Understand that liabilities are amounts owed by a business.
- Understand the items that affect owner's equity. Investments and revenues increase owner's equity. Drawings and expenses decrease owner's equity.

Solution
1. Cash is classified as an asset.
2. Service revenue is classified as revenue, which increases profit and ultimately owner's equity.
3. Drawings decrease owner's equity.
4. Accounts receivable are amounts that are due from customers, and are classified as an asset.
5. Accounts payable are amounts that are owed to creditors, and are classified as a liability.
6. Salaries expense is classified as an expense, which decreases profit and ultimately owner's equity.

Related exercise material: BE1–6, BE1–7, BE1–8, BE1–9, E1–3, E1–4, E1–5, E1–6, and E1–7.

Sometimes **Review It** questions are alone; other times they come with practice exercises. The **Do It** exercises like the one here ask you to put your new knowledge to work. They also outline an Action Plan you need to follow to do the exercise.

The Navigator

Using the Building Blocks

Transaction Analysis

We began the chapter by telling you that accounting is the information system that identifies, records, and communicates the economic events of an organization. The first step in accounting is to determine what the company should record. Not all events are recorded and reported as accounting transactions. Only events that cause changes in assets, liabilities, or owner's equity should be recorded. For example, suppose a new employee is hired. Should this event be recorded in the company's accounting records? The answer is no. While the hiring of an employee will lead to future accounting transactions (e.g., the payment of a salary after the work has been completed), no accounting transaction has occurred at the time of hiring.

An **accounting transaction** occurs when assets, liabilities, or owner's equity items change as the result of some economic event. Illustration 1-9 summarizes the process that is used to decide whether or not to record an event.

→ Illustration 1-9

Transaction identification process

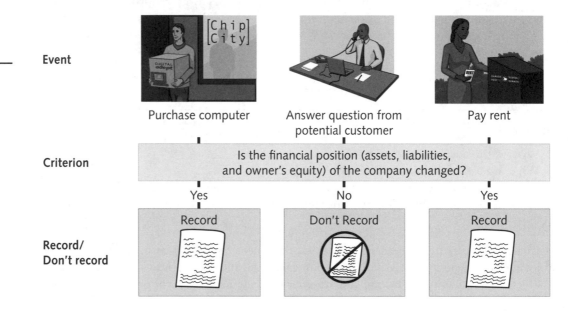

Event	Purchase computer	Answer question from potential customer	Pay rent
Criterion	Is the financial position (assets, liabilities, and owner's equity) of the company changed?		
	Yes	No	Yes
Record/ Don't record	Record	Don't Record	Record

Once a transaction has been identified, it must be analyzed for its effect on the components of the accounting equation before it can be recorded. This analysis must identify the specific items that are affected and the amount of change in each item.

Each transaction must have a dual effect on the equation for the two sides of the accounting equation to be equal. For example, if an asset is increased, there must be a corresponding

1. decrease in another asset, or
2. increase in a liability, or
3. increase in owner's equity.

Two or more items could be affected when an asset is increased. For example, as one asset is increased by $10,000, another asset could decrease by $6,000, and a liability could increase by $4,000. Any change in a liability or owner's equity item also has to be analyzed like this.

As a general example, we will now look at transactions incurred by a computer programming business during its first month of operations. You should study these transactions until you are sure you understand them. They are not difficult, but they are important to your success in this course. Being able to analyze how transactions affect the accounting equation is essential for understanding accounting.

Transaction (1): Investment by Owner. Marc Doucet decides to open a computer programming business, which he names Softbyte. On September 1, 2011, he invests $15,000 cash in the business, which he deposits in a bank account opened under the name of Softbyte. This transaction results in an equal increase in both assets and owner's equity for Softbyte. In this case, there is an increase in the asset account, Cash, $15,000, and an equal increase in the owner's equity account, M. Doucet, Capital, $15,000. The effect of this transaction on the basic equation is:

	Assets	=	Liabilities + Owner's Equity
			M. Doucet,
	Cash	=	Capital
(1)	+$15,000	=	+$15,000

> When a specific **account title** is used, the account name is capitalized. The exception to this is in financial statements (introduced in the next section).

Notice that the two sides of the basic equation remain equal. Note also that investments by an owner are **not** revenues. The increase therefore has to be recorded as an investment in the owner's capital account rather than as revenue from operations.

Transaction (2): Purchase of Equipment for Cash. Softbyte purchases computer equipment for $7,000 cash. This transaction results in an equal increase and decrease in total assets, though the composition of assets changes. Cash is decreased by $7,000, and the asset account Equipment is increased by $7,000. The specific effect of this transaction and the cumulative effect of the first two transactions are:

		Assets		=	Liabilities	+	Owner's Equity
		Cash	+	Equipment	=			M. Doucet, Capital
	Old Balances	$15,000			=			$15,000
(2)		−7,000		+$7,000				
	New Balances	$ 8,000	+	$7,000	=			$15,000
			$15,000				$15,000	

Notice that total assets are still $15,000, and that Doucet's equity also remains at $15,000, the amount of his original investment.

Transaction (3): Purchase of Supplies on Credit. Softbyte purchases $1,600 of computer paper and other supplies that are expected to last several months from the Chuah Supply Company. Chuah Supply agrees to allow Softbyte to pay this bill next month (in October). This transaction is referred to as a purchase on account, or a credit purchase. Assets are increased because of the expected future benefits of using the paper and supplies. Liabilities are increased by the amount that is due to Chuah Supply Company. So, the asset Supplies is increased by $1,600 and the liability Accounts Payable is increased by the same amount. The effect on the equation is:

			Assets			=	Liabilities	+	Owner's Equity
							Accounts		M. Doucet,
		Cash	+ Supplies +	Equipment	=	Payable	+	Capital
	Old Balances	$8,000	+	$7,000	=			$15,000
(3)			+$1,600			+$1,600		
	New Balances	$8,000 +	$1,600 +	$7,000	=	$1,600	+	$15,000
			$16,600				$16,600	

Total assets are now $16,600. This total is matched by a $1,600 creditor's claim and a $15,000 ownership claim.

Transaction (4): Services Provided for Cash. Softbyte receives $1,200 cash from customers for programming services it has provided. This transaction is Softbyte's main revenue-producing activity. Remember that revenue increases profit, which then increases owner's equity. Cash is increased by $1,200, and Service Revenue is increased by $1,200. We don't have room to give details for each individual revenue and expense account in this illustration, so revenues (and expenses when we get to them) will be summarized under one column heading for Revenues and one for Expenses. However, it is important to keep track of the account titles that are affected (e.g., Service Revenue), as they will be needed when financial statements are prepared in the next section. The new balances in the equation are:

		Assets			=	Liabilities +	Owner's Equity	
							M. Doucet,	
		Cash	+ Supplies	+ Equipment	=	Accounts Payable	+ Capital	+ Revenues
	Old Balances	$8,000 +	$1,600 +	$7,000	=	$1,600	+ $15,000	
(4)		+1,200						+$1,200
	New Balances	$9,200 +	$1,600 +	$7,000	=	$1,600	+ $15,000	+ $1,200
			$17,800				$17,800	

The two sides of the equation balance at $17,800.

Transaction (5): Purchase of Advertising on Credit. Softbyte receives a bill for $250 from the local newspaper for advertising the opening of its business. It postpones payment of the bill until a later date. This transaction results in an increase in liabilities, through the Accounts Payable account, and a decrease in owner's equity, through the Advertising Expense account. The cost of advertising is an expense, and not an asset, because the benefits have already been used.

Note that owner's equity decreases because an expense is incurred, which in turn reduces profit and owner's equity. Here is the effect on the accounting equation:

		Assets			= Liabilities +		Owner's Equity		
						M. Doucet,			
		Cash	+ Supplies	+ Equipment =	Accounts Payable	+ Capital	+ Revenues	− Expenses	
	Old Balances	$9,200 +	$1,600 +	$7,000 =	$1,600	+ $15,000	+ $1,200		
(5)					+$250			−$250	
	New Balances	$9,200 +	$1,600 +	$7,000 =	$1,850	+ $15,000	+ $1,200	− $250	
			$17,800				$17,800		

The two sides of the equation still balance at $17,800.

Expenses do not have to be paid in cash at the time they are incurred. When payment is made on the later date, the liability Accounts Payable will be decreased and the asset Cash will also be decreased [see transaction (8)].

Transaction (6): Services Provided for Cash and Credit. Softbyte provides $3,500 of programming services for customers. Cash of $1,500 is received from customers, and the balance of $2,000 is billed to customers on account. This transaction results in an equal increase in assets and owner's equity. Three specific items are affected: Cash is increased by $1,500; Accounts Receivable is increased by $2,000; and Service Revenue is increased by $3,500. The new balances are as follows:

		Assets				= Liabilities +		Owner's Equity		
			Accounts			Accounts	M. Doucet,			
		Cash	+ Receivable	+ Supplies	+ Equipment =	Payable	+ Capital	+ Revenues	− Expenses	
	Old Balances	$ 9,200		+ $1,600 +	$7,000 =	$1,850	+ $15,000	+ $1,200	− $250	
(6)		+1,500	+$2,000					+3,500		
	New Balances	$10,700 +	$2,000	+ $1,600 +	$7,000 =	$1,850	+ $15,000	+ $4,700	− $250	
			$21,300					$21,300		

You might wonder why owner's equity is increased by $3,500 when only $1,500 has been collected. The reason is that the assets from earning revenues do not have to be in cash. Owner's equity is increased when revenues are earned. In Softbyte's case, revenues are earned when the service is provided. When collections on account are received at a later date, Cash will be increased and Accounts Receivable will be decreased [see transaction (9)].

Transaction (7): Payment of Expenses. The expenses paid in cash for September are store rent, $600; salaries of employees, $900; and utilities, $200. These payments result in an equal decrease in assets and owner's equity. Cash is decreased by $1,700 in total ($600 + $900 + $200) and expense accounts are increased by the same amount, which then decreases owner's equity. Here is the effect of these payments on the equation:

	Assets				=	Liabilities +		Owner's Equity		
	Cash +	Accounts Receivable +	Supplies +	Equipment =		Accounts Payable +	M. Doucet, Capital +	Revenues −	Expenses
Old Balances	$10,700 +	$2,000 +	$1,600 +	$7,000 =		$1,850 +	$15,000 +	$4,700 −	$ 250
(7)	−600								−600
	−900								−900
	−200								−200
New Balances	$ 9,000 +	$2,000 +	$1,600 +	$7,000 =		$1,850 +	$15,000 +	$4,700 −	$1,950

$19,600 $19,600

The two sides of the equation now balance at $19,600. Three lines are now needed in the analysis in order to show the different types of expenses that have been paid.

Transaction (8): Payment of Accounts Payable. Softbyte pays its $250 advertising bill in cash. Remember that the bill was previously recorded in transaction (5) as an increase in Accounts Payable and a decrease in owner's equity. This payment on account decreases the asset Cash by $250 and also decreases the liability Accounts Payable. The effect of this transaction on the equation is:

	Assets				=	Liabilities +		Owner's Equity		
	Cash +	Accounts Receivable +	Supplies +	Equipment =		Accounts Payable +	M. Doucet, Capital +	Revenues −	Expenses
Old Balances	$9,000 +	$2,000 +	$1,600 +	$7,000 =		$1,850 +	$15,000 +	$4,700 −	$1,950
(8)	−250					−250			
New Balances	$8,750 +	$2,000 +	$1,600 +	$7,000 =		$1,600 +	$15,000 +	$4,700 −	$1,950

$19,350 $19,350

Notice that the payment of a liability for an expense that has previously been recorded does not affect owner's equity. This expense was recorded in transaction (5) and should not be recorded again.

Transaction (9): Receipt of Cash on Account. The sum of $600 in cash is received from some customers who were billed for services in transaction (6). This transaction does not change total assets, but it does change the composition of those assets. Cash is increased by $600, and Accounts Receivable is decreased by $600. The new balances are:

	Assets				=	Liabilities +		Owner's Equity		
	Cash +	Accounts Receivable +	Supplies +	Equipment =		Accounts Payable +	M. Doucet, Capital +	Revenues −	Expenses
Old Balances	$8,750 +	$2,000 +	$1,600 +	$7,000 =		$1,600 +	$15,000 +	$4,700 −	$1,950
(9)	+600	−600							
New Balances	$9,350 +	$1,400 +	$1,600 +	$7,000 =		$1,600 +	$15,000 +	$4,700 −	$1,950

$19,350 $19,350

Note that a collection on account for services that were billed and recorded earlier does not affect owner's equity. Revenue was already recorded in transaction (6) and must not be recorded again.

Transaction (10): Signed Contract to Rent Equipment in October. Marc Doucet and an equipment supplier sign a contract for Softbyte to rent equipment for the months of October and November at the rate of $250 per month. Softbyte is to pay each month's rent at the start of the month. There is no effect on the accounting equation because the assets, liabilities, and owner's equity have not changed. An accounting transaction has not occurred. At this point Softbyte has not paid for anything, nor has it used the equipment and therefore has not incurred any expenses.

		Assets			=	Liabilities +		Owner's Equity		
	Cash	+ Accounts Receivable	+ Supplies	+ Equipment	=	Accounts Payable	+ M. Doucet, Capital	+ Revenues	− Expenses
Old Balances	$9,350 +	$1,400 +	$1,600 +	$7,000	=	$1,600 +	$15,000	+ $4,700	− $1,950
(10) No entry									
New Balances	$9,350 +	$1,400 +	$1,600 +	$7,000	=	$1,600 +	$15,000	+ $4,700	− $1,950
			$19,350					$19,350	

Note that the new balances are all identical to the old balances as nothing has changed.

Transaction (11): Withdrawal of Cash by Owner. Marc Doucet withdraws $1,300 in cash from the business for his personal use. This transaction results in an equal decrease in assets and owner's equity. The asset Cash is decreased by $1,300, and Drawings is increased by $1,300, which then decreases owner's equity, as follows:

		Assets			=	Liabilities +		Owner's Equity			
	Cash	+ Accounts Receivable	+ Supplies	+ Equipment	=	Accounts Payable	+ M. Doucet, Capital	− M. Doucet, Drawings	+ Revenues	− Expenses
Old Balances	$9,350 +	$1,400 +	$1,600 +	$7,000	=	$1,600 +	$15,000		+ $4,700	− $1,950
(11)	−1,300							−$1,300		
New Balances	$8,050 +	$1,400 +	$1,600 +	$7,000	=	$1,600 +	$15,000	− $1,300	+ $4,700	− $1,950
			$18,050					$18,050		

Note that both drawings and expenses reduce owner's equity, as shown in the accounting equation above. However, an owner's drawings are not expenses. Expenses are incurred for the purpose of earning revenue. Drawings do not generate revenue. They are a *disinvestment*; that is, the effect of an owner's cash withdrawal is the opposite of the effect of an owner's investment. Like owner's investments, drawings are not included when profit is determined.

Summary of Transactions

Softbyte's transactions are summarized in Illustration 1-10 to show their cumulative effect on the accounting equation. The transaction number and the specific effects of each transaction are indicated.

	Assets				=	Liabilities +		Owner's Equity			
		Accounts				Accounts	M. Doucet,	M. Doucet,			
	Cash	+ Receivable	+ Supplies	+ Equipment	=	Payable	+ Capital	– Drawings	+ Revenues	– Expenses
(1)	+$15,000						+$15,000			
(2)	–7,000			+$7,000						
(3)			+$1,600			+$1,600				
(4)	+1,200								+$1,200	
(5)						+250				–$ 250
(6)	+1,500	+$2,000							+3,500	
(7)	–600									–600
	–900									–900
	–200									–200
(8)	–250					–250				
(9)	+600	–600								
(10)	No entry									
(11)	–1,300							–$1,300		
	$ 8,050 +	$1,400 +	$1,600 +	$7,000	=	$1,600 +	$15,000 –	$1,300 +	$4,700 –	$1,950
			$18,050					$18,050		

The illustration demonstrates some significant facts.

↑ **Illustration 1-10**

Tabular summary of Softbyte transactions

1. Each transaction must be analyzed for its effects on:
   (a) the three components (assets, liabilities, and owner's equity) of the accounting equation, and
   (b) specific items within each component.
2. The two sides of the equation must always be equal.

This section on transaction analysis is not the formal method of recording transactions. We will start illustrating that in Chapter 2. But understanding how transactions change assets, liabilities, and owner's equity is fundamental to understanding accounting and also business in general. No matter what area of an organization you work in, you will need to understand the impact of transactions on the organization if you want to move into more senior positions.

BEFORE YOU GO ON . . .

➔ Review It

1. Provide examples of two kinds of transactions: (a) an economic event that should be recorded; and (b) an event that should not be recorded.
2. If an asset increases, what are the three possible effects on the accounting equation? What are the possible effects if a liability increases?

➔ Do It

Transactions for the month of August by Verma & Co., a public accounting firm, are shown below. Prepare a tabular analysis (i.e., make a table) that shows the effects of these transactions on the accounting equation, like what is shown in Illustration 1-10.

1. The owner, Anil Verma, invested $25,000 of cash in the business.
2. Office equipment was purchased on credit, $7,000.
3. Services were performed for customers for $8,000. Of this amount, $2,000 was received in cash and $6,000 is due on account.
4. Rent of $850 was paid for the month.
5. Customers on account paid $4,000 (see transaction 3).
6. The owner withdrew $1,000 of cash for personal use.

Action Plan
  • Analyze the effects of each transaction on the accounting equation.
  • Use appropriate account names for the account titles (not descriptions).
  • Keep the accounting equation in balance.

Solution

		Assets		=	Liabilities +		Owner's Equity			
	Cash	+ Accounts Receivable +	Office Equipment	=	Accounts Payable +	A. Verma, Capital −	A. Verma, Drawings +	Revenues −	Expenses
1.	+$25,000					+$25,000			
2.			+$7,000		+$7,000				
3.	+2,000	+$6,000						+$8,000	
4.	−850								−$850
5.	+4,000	−4,000							
6.	−1,000						−$1,000		
	$29,150 +	$2,000 +	$7,000	=	$7,000 +	$25,000 −	$1,000 +	$8,000 −	$850
		$38,150					$38,150		

The Navigator

Related exercise material: BE1–10, BE1–11, E1–8, E1–9, E1–10, and E1–11.

Financial Statements

Helpful hint The income statement, statement of owner's equity and cash flow statement all report information for a period of time. The balance sheet reports information at a point in time.

The next step in accounting is to communicate the information that has been identified, recorded, and summarized. The information from the summarized accounting data is communicated in four financial statements:

1. Income statement. An **income statement** presents the revenues and expenses, and the resulting profit or loss for a specific period of time.
2. Statement of owner's equity. A **statement of owner's equity** summarizes the changes in owner's equity for a specific period of time.
3. Balance sheet. A **balance sheet** reports the assets, liabilities, and owner's equity at a specific date.
4. Cash flow statement. A **cash flow statement** summarizes information about the cash inflows (receipts) and outflows (payments) for a specific period of time.

Each statement gives management, owners, and other interested parties relevant financial data.
The financial statements of Softbyte and how they relate to each other are shown in Illustration 1-11. You will see that the statements are interrelated: (1) Profit of $2,750 shown on the income statement is added to the beginning balance of owner's capital in the statement of owner's equity. (2) Owner's capital of $16,450 at the end of the reporting period in the statement of owner's equity is also reported on the balance sheet. (3) Cash of $8,050 on the balance sheet is also reported on the cash flow statement.

← **Illustration 1-11**

Financial statements and their interrelationships

SOFTBYTE
Income Statement
Month Ended September 30, 2011

Revenues		
Service revenue		$4,700
Expenses		
Advertising expense	$250	
Rent expense	600	
Salaries expense	900	
Utilities expense	200	
Total expenses		1,950
Profit		$2,750

SOFTBYTE
Statement of Owner's Equity
Month Ended September 30, 2011

M. Doucet, capital, September 1, 2011		$ 0
Add: Investments	$15,000	
Profit	2,750	17,750
		17,750
Less: Drawings		1,300
M. Doucet, capital, September 30, 2011		$16,450

SOFTBYTE
Balance Sheet
September 30, 2011

Assets	
Cash	$ 8,050
Accounts receivable	1,400
Supplies	1,600
Equipment	7,000
Total assets	$18,050
Liabilities and Owner's Equity	
Liabilities	
Accounts payable	$ 1,600
Owner's equity	
M. Doucet, capital	16,450
Total liabilities and owner's equity	$18,050

①

②

③

SOFTBYTE
Cash Flow Statement
Month Ended September 30, 2011

Operating activities		
Cash receipts from customers	$ 3,300	
Cash payments for operating expenses	(1,950)	
Net cash provided by operating activities		$ 1,350
Investing activities		
Purchase of equipment	$ (7,000)	
Net cash used by investing activities		(7,000)
Financing activities		
Investments by owner	$15,000	
Drawings by owner	(1,300)	
Net cash provided by financing activities		13,700
Net increase in cash		8,050
Cash, September 1, 2011		0
Cash, September 30, 2011		$ 8,050

Helpful hint 1. Profit is calculated first and is needed to determine the ending balance in owner's capital. 2. The ending balance in owner's capital is needed for preparing the balance sheet. 3. The cash shown on the balance sheet is needed for preparing the cash flow statement.

To keep it simple, we did not include cents in the dollar amounts we recorded in the Softbyte example in the previous section of the chapter. In reality, it is important to understand that cents should be, and are, used when transactions are recorded in a company's internal accounting records. The situation is different for financial reporting purposes, however. Financial statement amounts are normally rounded to the nearest dollar, thousand dollars, or million dollars, depending on the size of the company. Forzani rounds its numbers to the nearest thousand dollars. This is done to remove unimportant detail and make the information easier for the reader to understand.

The essential features of Softbyte's four financial statements are briefly described in the following sections.

Income Statement

Alternative terminology
The income statement is sometimes called the *statement of earnings* or *statement of operations*.

Softbyte's income statement reports the revenues and expenses for a specific period of time. The income statement is prepared from the data in the owner's equity columns (specifically the Revenues and Expenses columns) of Illustration 1-10. The statement's heading names the company and type of statement, and shows the time period covered by the statement. The main purpose of the income statement is to report the profitability of the company's operations over a specified period of time (a month, quarter, or year). To indicate that it applies to a period of time, the income statement date names the time period. For Softbyte, this appears as Month Ended September 30, 2011, which means the statement is for a one-month period.

On the income statement, revenues are listed first, followed by expenses. Finally, profit (or loss) is determined. Note that investment and withdrawal transactions between the owner and the business are not included in the measurement of profit.

Statement of Owner's Equity

Softbyte's statement of owner's equity reports the changes in owner's equity for the same period of time as the income statement. Data for preparing the statement of owner's equity are taken from the owner's equity columns (specifically the Capital and Drawings columns) of the tabular summary (Illustration 1-10) and from the income statement. The heading of this statement names the company and type of statement, and shows the time period covered by the statement. As the time period is the same as it is for the income statement, it is also dated Month Ended September 30, 2011. The beginning owner's equity amount is shown on the first line of the statement. Normally, zero balances are not shown. We have included one here because, unless it is the first period of operations, companies normally have a beginning balance. Then the owner's investments, the profit, and the drawings are identified. The information in this statement indicates why owner's equity has increased or decreased during the period.

What if Softbyte reported a loss in its first month? The loss would reduce owner's capital. Instead of adding profit, the loss would be deducted in the same section as owner's drawings.

Balance Sheet

Alternative terminology
The balance sheet is sometimes called the *statement of financial position*.

Softbyte's balance sheet reports the assets, liabilities, and owner's equity at a specific date. The balance sheet is prepared from the Assets and Liabilities column headings and the month-end data shown in the last line of the tabular summary (Illustration 1-10). The heading of a balance sheet must identify the company, statement, and date. The balance sheet is like a snapshot of the company's financial condition at a specific moment in time (usually the end of a month, quarter, or year). To indicate that the balance sheet is at a specific point in time, the date only mentions the point in time (there is no indication of a time period). For Softbyte, the date is September 30, 2011. Sometimes, the words "as at" precede the balance sheet date. Notice that the assets are listed at the top, followed by liabilities and owner's equity. Total assets must equal total liabilities and owner's equity. In other words, the balance sheet must balance.

Cash Flow Statement

Softbyte's cash flow statement gives information about the cash receipts and cash payments for a specific period of time. To help investors, creditors, and others analyze a company's cash, the cash flow statement reports the following: (1) the cash effects of the company's operating activities during a period; (2) the cash inflows and outflows from investing transactions (e.g., the purchase and sale of land, buildings, and equipment); (3) the cash inflows and outflows from financing transactions (e.g., borrowing and repayments of debt, and investments and withdrawals by the owner); (4) the net increase or decrease in cash during the period; and (5) the cash amount at the end of the period.

Alternative terminology
The cash flow statement is sometimes called the *statement of cash flows*.

Reporting the sources, uses, and change in cash is useful because investors, creditors, and others want to know what is happening to a company's most liquid resource, its money. The cash flow statement gives answers to the following simple but important questions:

1. Where did the cash come from during the period?
2. What was the cash used for during the period?
3. What was the change in the cash balance during the period?

Softbyte's cash flow statement, shown in Illustration 1-11, is for the same period of time as the income statement and the statement of owner's equity. Note that the positive numbers indicate cash inflows or increases. Numbers in parentheses indicate cash outflows or decreases. Parentheses are often used in financial statements to indicate negative, or opposite, numbers. As shown in the statement, cash increased by $8,050 during the month. Operating activities increased cash by $1,350. Investing activities decreased cash by $7,000. Financing activities increased cash by $13,700. At this time, you do not need to know how these amounts are determined. In Chapter 17 we will look at the cash flow statement in detail.

Using the Information in the Financial Statements

Illustration 1-11 introduced the financial statements for Softbyte. Every set of financial statements also has explanatory notes and supporting schedules that are an essential part of the statements. For example, as previously mentioned, at the very least a company will have to indicate if it is following IFRS or Canadian GAAP for Private Enterprises.

Public corporations issue their financial statements and supplementary materials in an annual report. The **annual report** is a document that includes useful non-financial information about the company, as well as financial information.

Non-financial information may include a management discussion of the company's mission, goals, and objectives; market position; and the people involved in the company. Financial information may include a review of current operations and a historical summary of key financial figures and ratios, in addition to comparative financial statements. Public company financial statements are audited and include the auditors' report. There is also a statement of management responsibility for the statements.

Now is a good time to go to Appendix A at the end of this textbook, where you will find The Forzani Group Ltd.'s financial statements taken from its annual report. Carefully examine the format and content of each financial statement outlined earlier in Illustration 1-11. What similarities can you find between the financial statements in Illustration 1-11 and the more complicated financial statements for Forzani?

You will see that The Forzani Group's transactions have been accumulated for the year ended February 1, 2009, and grouped together in categories. When similar transactions are grouped together, they are being reported in aggregate. By presenting recorded data in aggregate, the accounting information system simplifies a large number of transactions. As a result, the company's activities are easier to understand and are more meaningful. This simplification does mean less detail, however. The Forzani Group's financial statements are highly condensed and some critics would argue that the statements are too simple. Still, Forzani is not the only organization that reports in this way. Most companies report condensed information for two reasons: it's simpler, and it also avoids revealing significant details to competitors.

We will ask you to look at Forzani's statements at different times throughout the text. At this point, they will probably look complex and confusing to you. By the end of this course, however, you'll be surprised at your ability to understand and interpret them.

For **Review It** questions about The Forzani Group, you need to use Forzani's financial statements in Appendix A at the end of this textbook.

BEFORE YOU GO ON . . .

→ Review It

1. Describe the income statement, statement of owner's equity, balance sheet, and cash flow statement.
2. Why does it matter in which order the financial statements are prepared?
3. Explain how Forzani's financial statements are interrelated: identify specific accounts and amounts. The answer to this question is given at the end of the chapter.
4. What information is normally found in an annual report?

The Navigator

Related exercise material: BE1–12, BE1–13, BE1–14, BE1–15, BE1–16, BE1–17, BE1–18, E1–12, E1–13, E1–14, E1–15, and E1–16.

Demonstration Problem

Demonstration Problems

The **Demonstration Problem** is a final review before you work on the assignment material. The problem-solving strategies in the margins give you tips about how to approach the problem. The solutions show both the form and the content of complete answers.

Raman Balakra opens his own law office on July 1, 2011. During the first month of operations, the following transactions occurred:

1. Invested $11,000 in cash in the law practice.
2. Hired a legal assistant to work part-time for $500 per month.
3. Paid $800 for July rent on office space.
4. Purchased office equipment on account, $3,000.
5. Provided legal services to clients for cash, $1,500.
6. Borrowed $700 cash from a bank on a note payable.
7. Provided legal services to a client on account, $2,000.
8. Collected $500 of the amount owed by a client on account (see transaction 7).
9. Paid monthly expenses: salaries, $500; utilities, $300; and telephone, $100.
10. Withdrew $1,000 cash for personal use.

Action Plan

- Make sure that assets equal liabilities plus owner's equity in each transaction.
- Investments and revenues increase owner's equity. Withdrawals and expenses decrease owner's equity.

Instructions

(a) Prepare a tabular analysis of the transactions.
(b) Prepare the income statement, statement of owner's equity, and balance sheet for Raman Balakra, Barrister & Solicitor.

Solution to Demonstration Problem

(a)

Transaction	Cash	+ Accounts Receivable	+ Equipment	= Note Payable	+ Accounts Payable	+ R. Balakra, Capital	− R. Balakra, Drawings	+ Revenues	− Expenses
(1)	+$11,000					+$11,000			
(2) No Entry									
(3)	−800								−$800
(4)			+$3,000		+$3,000				
(5)	+1,500							+$1,500	
(6)	+700			+$700					
(7)		+$2,000						+2,000	
(8)	+500	−500							
(9)	−500								−500
	−300								−300
	−100								−100
(10)	−1,000						−$1,000		
	$11,000 +	$1,500 +	$3,000 =	$700 +	$3,000 +	$11,000 −	$1,000 +	$3,500 −	$1,700

$15,500 $15,500

Assets = **Liabilities** + **Owner's Equity**

(b)

RAMAN BALAKRA, BARRISTER & SOLICITOR
Income Statement
Month Ended July 31, 2011

Revenues		
Fees earned		$3,500
Expenses		
Rent expense	$800	
Salaries expense	500	
Utilities expense	300	
Telephone expense	100	
Total expenses		1,700
Profit		$1,800

RAMAN BALAKRA, BARRISTER & SOLICITOR
Statement of Owner's Equity
Month Ended July 31, 2011

R. Balakra, capital, July 1, 2011		$ 0
Add: Investments	$11,000	
Profit	1,800	12,800
		12,800
Less: Drawings		1,000
R. Balakra, capital, July 31, 2011		$11,800

RAMAN BALAKRA, BARRISTER & SOLICITOR
Balance Sheet
July 31, 2011

Assets	
Cash	$11,000
Accounts receivable	1,500
Equipment	3,000
Total assets	$15,500

Liabilities and Owner's Equity	
Liabilities	
Note payable	$ 700
Accounts payable	3,000
Total liabilities	3,700
Owner's equity	
R. Balakra, capital	11,800
Total liabilities and owner's equity	$15,500

Action Plan (continued)

- Prepare the financial statements in the order listed.
- The income statement shows revenues and expenses for a period of time.
- Profit (or loss) is calculated on the income statement and carried forward to the statement of owner's equity.
- The statement of owner's equity shows the changes in owner's equity for the same period of time as the income statement.
- The owner's capital at the end of the period is carried forward from the statement of owner's equity to the balance sheet.
- The balance sheet reports assets, liabilities, and owner's equity at a specific date.

The Navigator

Summary of Study Objectives

1. *Identify the use and users of accounting.* Accounting is the information system that identifies, records, and communicates the economic events of an organization to a wide variety of interested users. Good accounting is important to people both inside and outside the organization. Internal users, such as management, use accounting information to plan, control, and evaluate business operations. External users include investors and creditors, among others. Accounting data are used by investors (owners) to decide whether to buy, hold, or sell their financial interests. Creditors (suppliers and bankers) evaluate the risks of granting credit or lending money based on the accounting information. Other groups that use accounting information are taxing authorities, regulatory agencies, customers, labour unions, and economic planners. For our economic system to function smoothly, reliable and ethical accounting and financial reporting are critical. The most common examples of business organizations are proprietorship, partnership, and corporation.

2. *Explain Canadian accounting standards and apply basic accounting concepts.* Generally accepted accounting principles are a common set of guidelines that are used to prepare and report accounting information. In Canada, as of 2011 there are two sets of standards or GAAP. Publicly accountable enterprises follow International Financial Reporting Standards (IFRS) and private enterprises have the choice of following IFRS or Canadian GAAP for Private Enterprises.

The going concern assumption presumes that a business will continue operations for enough time to use its assets for their intended purpose and to complete its commitments. The economic entity assumption requires the activities of each economic entity to be kept separate from the activities of its owner and other economic entities. Recognition is the process of recording items and measurement is the process of determining the amount that should be recognized. The cost principle states that assets should be recorded at their historical (original) cost. The monetary unit assumption requires that only transaction data that can be expressed as an amount of money be included in the accounting records, and it assumes that the monetary unit is stable.

3. *Use the accounting equation and explain the meaning of assets, liabilities, and owner's equity.* The accounting equation is: Assets = Liabilities + Owner's Equity. Assets are resources owned by a business that are capable of providing future services or benefits.

Liabilities are current obligations arising from past events to make future payments of assets or services. Owner's equity is the owner's claim on the company's assets and is equal to total assets minus total liabilities. Owner's equity is increased by investments by the owner and by revenues. It is decreased by drawings and expenses. Revenues are the increase in assets, or decrease in liabilities, that result from business activities that are done to earn profit. Expenses are the cost of assets consumed or services used in a company's ordinary business activities. Drawings are withdrawals of cash or other assets from the business for the owner's personal use.

4. *Analyze the effects of business transactions on the accounting equation.* Each business transaction must have a dual effect on the accounting equation. For example, if an individual asset is increased, there must be a corresponding (1) decrease in another asset, (2) increase in a liability, and/or (3) increase in owner's equity.

5. *Prepare financial statements.* An income statement presents the revenues and expenses, and the resulting profit or loss, of a company for a specific period of time. A statement of owner's equity summarizes the changes in owner's equity that have occurred for a specific period of time. A balance sheet reports the assets, liabilities, and owner's equity of a business at a specific date. A cash flow statement summarizes information about the cash inflows (receipts) and outflows (payments) for a specific period of time.

The Navigator

Glossary

WILEY **PLUS** Glossary
Key Term Matching Activity

Accounting   The information system that identifies, records, and communicates the economic events of an organization to a wide variety of interested users. (p. 2)

Accounting equation   Assets = Liabilities + Owner's Equity. (p. 10)

Accounting transaction   An economic event that is recorded in the accounting records because it changed the assets, liabilities, or owner's equity items of the organization. (p. 14)

Accounts payable   A liability created by buying services or products on credit. It is an obligation to pay cash to a supplier in the future. (p. 11)

Accounts receivable   An asset created when selling services or products to customers who promise to pay cash in the future. (p. 11)

Annual report   Information that a company gives each year to its shareholders and other interested parties about its operations and financial position. It includes the

financial statements and auditors' report, in addition to information and reports by management. (p. 23)

Assets   Resources owned by a business that are capable of providing future services or benefits. (p. 11)

Balance sheet   A financial statement that reports the assets, liabilities, and owner's equity at a specific date. (p. 20)

Cash flow statement   A financial statement that provides information about the cash inflows (receipts) and cash outflows (payments) for a specific period of time. (p. 20)

Corporation   A business organized as a separate legal entity under corporation law, with ownership divided into transferable shares. (p. 6)

Cost principle   An accounting principle that states that assets should be recorded at their historical (original) cost. (p. 9)

Creditors   All of the persons or entities that a company owes money to. (p. 11)

Drawings Withdrawals of cash or other assets from an unincorporated business for the owner's personal use. Drawings reduce owner's equity. (p. 11)

Economic entity assumption An assumption that requires the activities of the entity to be kept separate and distinct from the activities of its owner and of all other economic entities. (p. 9)

Expenses The cost of assets consumed or services used in a company's ordinary business activities. Expenses result in a reduction of owner's equity. (p. 12)

Fair value The amount of the consideration that would be agreed upon in an arm's-length transaction between knowledgeable, willing parties who are under no compulsion to act. (p. 9)

Generally accepted accounting principles (GAAP) An accepted set of accounting standards that includes broad principles, practices, as well as rules and procedures. These standards indicate how to report economic events. (p. 7)

Going concern assumption An assumption that a company will continue to operate in the foreseeable future. (p. 8)

Income statement A financial statement that presents the revenues and expenses and resulting profit (or loss) for a specific period of time. (p. 20)

Investments by the owner The increase in owner's equity that results from assets put into the business by the owner. (p. 11)

Liabilities Current obligations, arising from past events, to make future payments of assets or services. (p. 11)

Limited liability The legal principle that the owners' liability for the debts of the business is limited to the amount they invested in the business. (p. 6)

Loss The amount by which expenses are greater than revenues. A loss decreases owner's equity. (p. 12)

Measurement The process of determining the amount that should be recognized. (p. 9)

Monetary unit assumption An assumption that states that only transaction data that can be expressed as an amount of money may be included in the accounting records. It is also assumed that the monetary unit is stable. (p. 9)

Net assets Total assets minus total liabilities; equal to owner's equity. (p. 11)

Note payable A liability supported by a written promise to pay a specific amount, at a specific time, in the future. (p. 11)

Owner's equity The owner's claim on the assets of the company, which is equal to total assets minus total liabilities. (p. 11)

Partnership An association of two or more persons to carry on as co-owners of a business for profit. (p. 6)

Profit The amount by which revenues are greater than expenses. Profit increases owner's equity. (p. 12)

Proprietorship A small business owned by one person. (p. 5)

Publicly accountable enterprises Publicly traded companies as well as securities brokers and dealers, banks, and credit unions whose role is to hold assets for the public as part of their primary business. (p. 7)

Recognition The process of recording a transaction in the accounting records. (p. 9)

Revenues The increase in assets, or decrease in liabilities, that results from business activities that are done to earn profit. (p. 12)

Statement of owner's equity A financial statement that summarizes the changes in owner's equity for a specific period of time. (p. 20)

Unlimited liability The principle that the owners of a business are personally liable (responsible) for all debts of the business. (p. 5)

Self-Study Questions

WILEY PLUS Quizzes

Answers are at the end of the chapter.

(SO 1) K 1. Which of the following statements about users of accounting information is incorrect?
(a) Management is an internal user.
(b) Taxing authorities are external users.
(c) Creditors are external users.
(d) Regulatory authorities are internal users.

2. Which of the following characteristics are related (SO 1) K to corporations as opposed to partnerships and proprietorships?
(a) Simple to form, unlimited legal liability, limited life
(b) Limited legal liability, limited life, income taxes on profit paid by the organization
(c) More than one owner, income taxes on profit paid by the owners, unlimited legal liability
(d) Income taxes paid by the organization, limited legal liability, indefinite life

(SO 2) K   3. Which of the following statements about International Financial Reporting Standards (IFRS) is correct?
  (a) Canada is following the lead of the United States in adopting IFRS.
  (b) Under IFRS, companies that operate in more than one country must produce separate financial statements for each of those countries.
  (c) All Canadian publicly accountable enterprises must use IFRS effective January 1, 2011.
  (d) Canadian private enterprises are not allowed to use IFRS. They must use Canadian GAAP for Private Enterprises.

(SO 2) C   4. Which of the following statements is incorrect?
  (a) Under the going concern assumption, it is assumed that a company ends its operations once a year for reporting purposes.
  (b) The economic entity assumption states that the activities of the entity should be kept separate from those of its owner and other entities.
  (c) Under the cost principle, assets continue to be recorded at their historical (original) cost, even if the fair value has increased.
  (d) An important part of the monetary unit assumption is that the monetary unit is assumed to remain stable.

(SO 3) AP   5. As at December 31, after its first year of operations, Stoneland Company has assets of $8,500; revenues of $6,000; expenses of $3,500; owner's capital of $5,000; and drawings of $500. What are the liabilities for Stoneland Company as at December 31?
  (a) $1,500
  (b) $2,500
  (c) $500
  (d) $3,500

(SO 3) C   6. Profit will result during a time period when:
  (a) assets are greater than liabilities.
  (b) assets are greater than revenues.
  (c) expenses are greater than revenues.
  (d) revenues are greater than expenses.

(SO 4) AP   7. The effects on the accounting equation of performing services on account are:
  (a) increased assets and decreased owner's equity.
  (b) increased assets and increased owner's equity.
  (c) increased assets and increased liabilities.
  (d) increased liabilities and increased owner's equity.

(SO 5) AP   8. Genesis Company buys a $10,000 machine on credit. Initially, this transaction will only affect the:
  (a) income statement.
  (b) balance sheet.
  (c) income statement and statement of owner's equity.
  (d) income statement, statement of owner's equity, and balance sheet.

(SO 5) K   9. The financial statement that reports assets, liabilities, and owner's equity is the:
  (a) income statement.
  (b) statement of owner's equity.
  (c) balance sheet.
  (d) cash flow statement.

(SO 5) C   10. Which of the following items is *not* reported on the statement of owner's equity?
  (a) Investments by the owner
  (b) Drawings
  (c) Profit
  (d) Cash flow from operating activities

The Navigator

Questions

(SO 1) C   1. "Accounting is ingrained in our society and it is vital to our economic system." Do you agree? Explain.

(SO 1) C   2. Why should everyone study accounting whether they are going to be an accountant or not?

(SO 1) C   3. (a) Distinguish between internal and external users of accounting data. (b) How does accounting provide relevant data for these users?

(SO 1) C   4. Why is ethics important to the accounting profession? To statement users?

(SO 1) C   5. Explain the differences between the following forms of business organization: (a) proprietorship, (b) partnership, (c) public corporation, and (d) private corporation.

(SO 2) C   6. Veronica argues that all Canadian companies should follow the same set of generally accepted accounting principles. Explain to Veronica why there are two sets of standards in Canada and how she can tell what standards the company is using.

(SO 2) C   7. Explain the going concern assumption and how a user of financial statements can tell if the company is a going concern or not.

(SO 2) C   8. How does the going concern assumption support the cost principle?

(SO 2) K   9. What is the economic entity assumption?

(SO 2) C 10. What is the monetary unit assumption? What type of information is not included in the financial statements because of this assumption?

(SO 3) K 11. What is the accounting equation? What is the expanded accounting equation?

(SO 3) K 12. (a) Define assets, liabilities, and owner's equity. (b) What items increase and decrease owner's equity?

(SO 3) K 13. What is the difference between Accounts Payable and Accounts Receivable? Between Accounts Payable and Notes Payable?

(SO 3) K 14. Explain the difference in accounting for the three forms of a business organization: (a) a proprietorship, (b) a partnership, and (c) a corporation.

(SO 4) C 15. Are the following events recorded in the accounting records? Explain your answer in each case.
(a) The owner of the company dies.
(b) Supplies are purchased on account.
(c) An employee is terminated.
(d) The company wins an award as one of the top 50 companies in Canada to work for.

(SO 4) C 16. Can a business have a transaction in which only the left (assets) side of the accounting equation is affected? If yes, give an example.

(SO 4) AP 17. Explain how the following transactions affect the accounting equation:
(a) Paid cash for employees' salaries.
(b) Purchased equipment and signed a note payable for the amount owing.

(c) Owner withdrew cash from the business.
(d) Performed services on account.
(e) Collected amount owing from a customer for services previously provided.

18. Paul Dumas withdrew $10,000 from his business, (SO 4) AP Dumas Pharmacy, which is organized as a proprietorship. Dumas' accountant recorded this withdrawal as an increase in an expense and a decrease in cash. Is this treatment correct? Why or why not?

19. A company's profit appears directly on the income (SO 5) C statement and the statement of owner's equity. It is also included indirectly in the company's balance sheet. Do you agree or disagree? Explain.

20. Explain how the following pairs of financial state- (SO 5) C ments are interrelated: (a) income statement and statement of owner's equity, (b) statement of owner's equity and balance sheet, and (c) balance sheet and cash flow statement.

21. André is puzzled as he reads **Forzani's** financial (SO 5) C statements. He notices that the numbers have all been rounded to the nearest thousand. He thought financial statements were supposed to be accurate and he is now wondering what happened to the rest of the money. Respond to André's concern.

22. **Forzani's** year end is not a fixed date; rather, it can (SO 5) C vary slightly from one year to the next. What possible problems does this create for financial statement users?

When the financial results of real companies are used in the end-of-chapter material, the company's name is shown in red.

Brief Exercises

BE1–1 A list of decisions made by different users of accounting information follows:

1. Decide whether the company pays fair wages.
2. Decide whether the company can pay its obligations.
3. Decide whether a marketing proposal will be cost-effective.
4. Decide whether the company's profit will permit an increase in drawings.
5. Decide how the company should finance its operations.

Identify users of accounting information.
(SO 1) K

The different users are identified in the table that follows. (a) Insert the number (1–5) of the kind of decision described above that each user would likely make. (b) Indicate whether the user is internal or external.

User	(a) Kind of Decision	(b) Internal or External User
Owner		
Marketing manager		
Creditor		
Chief financial officer		
Labour union		

Discuss ethical issues.
(SO 1) AN

BE1–2 Imagine and describe an ethical dilemma that each of the following individuals might encounter:

1. A student in an introductory accounting course
2. A production supervisor
3. A salesperson
4. A banker
5. The prime minister of Canada

Identify forms of business organization.
(SO 1) C

BE1–3 Match each of the following forms of business organization with the correct set of characteristics: proprietorship (PP), partnership (P), and corporation (C).

(a) ___ Shared control; combined skills and resources
(b) ___ Easier to transfer ownership and raise funds; no personal liability; entity pays income tax
(c) ___ Simple to set up; founder keeps control

Identify application of IFRS and Canadian GAAP for Private Enterprises.
(SO 2) C

BE1–4 For each of the following statements related to International Financial Reporting Standards (IFRS) and/or Canadian GAAP for Private Enterprises, indicate whether the statement is true or false by placing a T or an F in the blank at the start of each statement.

(a) ___ All publicly accountable enterprises must follow IFRS as of 2011.
(b) ___ All private enterprises must follow Canadian GAAP for Private Enterprises as of 2011.
(c) ___ Under both IFRS and Canadian GAAP for Private Enterprises, there are more requirements to provide information in the financial statements than there were under traditional Canadian GAAP.
(d) ___ Private companies that are larger than the prescribed threshold will have to use IFRS.
(e) ___ Companies will be required to include a note in their financial statements stating if they are using IFRS or Canadian GAAP for Private Enterprises
(f) ___ Using IFRS may help Canadian public companies attract investors from around the globe.

Identify GAAP concepts.
(SO 2) C

BE1–5 Match each of the following terms with the best description below:

1. Generally accepted accounting principles
2. Going concern assumption
3. Economic entity assumption
4. Cost principle
5. Monetary unit assumption

(a) ___ Transactions are recorded in terms of units of money.
(b) ___ Transactions are recorded based on the actual amount received or paid.
(c) ___ Accounting for a business excludes any personal transactions of the owner and the transactions of any other entity.
(d) ___ These are the broad principles and practices, as well as rules and procedures, that indicate how to report economic events.
(e) ___ Businesses are expected to continue operating indefinitely.

Solve accounting equation.
(SO 3) AP

BE1–6 Presented below is the accounting equation. Determine the missing amounts:

Assets	=	Liabilities	+	Owner's Equity
$95,000		$54,000		(a)
(b)		$120,000		$71,000
$49,000		(c)		$22,000

Solve accounting equation.
(SO 3) AP

BE1–7 Use the accounting equation to answer each of the following questions:

(a) Cai Company has liabilities of $220,000. The balance in M. Cai, Capital is $100,000; in drawings, $40,000; revenues, $440,000; and expenses, $330,000. What is the amount of Cai Company's total assets?

(b) Pereira Company has total assets of $80,000. The balance in Karen Pereira's Capital is $30,000; in drawings, $7,000; revenues, $55,000; and expenses, $45,000. What is the amount of the company's total liabilities?

(c) Yellow Co. has total assets of $800,000 and its liabilities are equal to one quarter of its total assets. What is the amount of Yellow Co.'s owner's equity?

BE1–8 At the beginning of the year, Lam Company had total assets of $750,000 and total liabilities of $500,000. Answer each of the following independent questions:

Solve accounting equation. (SO 3) AP

(a) If total assets increased by $120,000 during the year and total liabilities decreased by $90,000, what is the amount of owner's equity at the end of the year?

(b) During the year, total liabilities decreased by $85,000. The company incurred a loss of $50,000. Lifei Lam made an additional investment of $100,000 and made no withdrawals. What is the amount of total assets at the end of the year?

(c) Total assets increased by $90,000 during the year. Profit was $175,000. There were no additional owner's investments, but Lifei Lam withdrew $60,000. What is the amount of total liabilities at the end of the year?

(d) Total assets increased by $25,000, and total liabilities decreased by $50,000. There were no additional owner's investments, and Lifei Lam withdrew $40,000. What is the amount of profit or loss for the year?

BE1–9 Indicate whether each of the following items is an asset (A), a liability (L), or part of owner's equity (OE):

Identify assets, liabilities, and owner's equity. (SO 3) AP

(a) ___ Cash
(b) ___ Accounts payable
(c) ___ Drawings
(d) ___ Accounts receivable
(e) ___ Supplies
(f) ___ Equipment
(g) ___ E. Johnston, drawings
(h) ___ Salaries payable
(i) ___ Service revenue
(j) ___ E. Johnston, capital
(k) ___ Rent expense
(l) ___ Note payable

BE1–10 Presented below are eight business transactions. Indicate whether the transactions increased (+), decreased (–), or had no effect (NE) on each element of the accounting equation.

Determine effects of transactions on accounting equation. (SO 4) AP

1. Purchased $250 of supplies on account.
2. Performed $500 of services on account.
3. Paid $300 of operating expenses.
4. Paid $250 cash on account for the supplies purchased in item 1 above.
5. Invested $1,000 cash in the business.
6. Owner withdrew $400 cash.
7. Hired an employee to start working the following month.
8. Received $500 from a customer who had been billed previously in item 2 above.

Use the following format, in which the first one has been done for you as an example:

Transaction	Assets	Liabilities	Owner's Equity			
			Capital	Drawings	Revenues	Expenses
1.	+$250	+$250	NE	NE	NE	NE

BE1–11 Classify each of the following items as owner's investments (I), drawings (D), revenue (R), expenses (E), or as having no effect on owner's equity (NE):

Determine effects of transactions on owner's equity. (SO 4) AP

(a) ___ Costs incurred for advertising

(b) ___ Commission earnings
(c) ___ Equipment received from the company owner
(d) ___ Amounts paid to employees
(e) ___ Cash paid to purchase equipment
(f) ___ Services performed on account
(g) ___ Rent received
(h) ___ Utilities incurred
(i) ___ Cash distributed to company owner
(j) ___ Collection of an account receivable

Classify accounts.
(SO 3, 5) C

BE1–12   Below are some items found in the financial statements of Kaustev Sen, M.D. Indicate (a) whether each of the following items is an asset (A), liability (L), or part of owner's equity (OE); and (b) which financial statement—income statement (IS), statement of owner's equity (OE), or balance sheet (BS)—it would be reported on. The first one has been done for you as an example.

	(a)	(b)
1. Accounts receivable	A	BS
2. Wages payable	___	___
3. Wages expense	___	___
4. Office supplies	___	___
5. Supplies expense	___	___
6. K. Sen, capital (opening balance)	___	___
7. K. Sen, capital (ending balance)	___	___
8. Service revenue	___	___
9. Equipment	___	___
10. Note payable	___	___
11. Cash	___	___
12. K. Sen, drawings	___	___

Determine missing items in owner's equity.
(SO 3, 5) AP

BE1–13   Presented below is information from the statements of owner's equity for Kirkham Consulting for the first three years of operation. Determine the missing amounts:

	2010	2011	2012
P. Kirkham, capital, January 1	$ 0	$63,000	(c)
Investment in the year	50,000	0	20,000
Profit (loss) for the year	25,000	(b)	17,000
Drawings in the year	(a)	25,000	12,000
P. Kirkham, capital, December 31	63,000	53,000	(d)

Identify elements of financial statements.
(SO 5) C

BE1–14   The Calgary Exhibition and Stampede Limited has the following selected accounts in its corporate financial statements. In each case, identify whether the item would appear on the balance sheet (BS) or income statement (IS).

(a) ___ Accounts receivable
(b) ___ Inventory
(c) ___ Interest expense
(d) ___ Share capital
(e) ___ Equipment
(f) ___ Stampede revenue
(g) ___ Agricultural activities revenue
(h) ___ Accounts payable and accrued liabilities
(i) ___ Cash and short-term deposits
(j) ___ Administration, marketing, and park services expenses
(k) ___ Food and beverage revenue

BE1–15 Schwinghamer Enterprises had a capital balance of $125,000 at the beginning of the period. At the end of the accounting period, the capital balance was $150,000.

Calculate profit.
(SO 5) AP

(a) If there were no additional investments or withdrawals, what is the profit for the period?

(b) Assuming there was an additional investment of $5,000 but no withdrawals, what is the profit for the period?

(c) Assuming there was an additional investment of $10,000 and a withdrawal of $7,000, what is the profit for the period?

BE1–16 Portage Company is owned and operated by Nate Hudson. In alphabetical order below are the financial statement items for Portage Company. Using the appropriate items, prepare an income statement for the month ended August 31, 2011.

Prepare an income statement.
(SO 5) AP

Accounts payable	$90,000	N. Hudson, capital, August 1, 2011	$26,000
Accounts receivable	72,500	N. Hudson, drawings	3,000
Advertising expense	1,200	Rent expense	1,300
Cash	49,000	Service revenue	11,000

BE1–17 Refer to the data in BE1–16. Using these data and the information from Portage's income statement, prepare a statement of owner's equity.

Prepare a statement of owner's equity.
(SO 5) AP

BE1–18 Refer to the data in BE1–16. Using these data and the information from Portage's statement of owner's equity prepared in BE1–17, prepare a balance sheet for Portage Company.

Prepare a balance sheet.
(SO 5) AP

Exercises

E1–1 Roots Canada Ltd. is known around the world for its clothing and accessories. It has more than 120 stores in Canada and the United States, and more than 60 locations in Asia.

Identify users and uses of accounting information.
(SO 1) C

Instructions

(a) Identify two internal users of Roots' accounting information. Write a question that each user might try to answer by using accounting information.

(b) Identify two external users of Roots' accounting information. Write a question that each user might try to answer by using accounting information.

E1–2 Marietta Company, a proprietorship, had the following selected business transactions during the year:

Identify GAAP.
(SO 2) C

(a) Land with a cost of $208,000 was reported at its fair value of $260,000.

(b) A lease agreement to rent equipment from an equipment supplier starting next year was signed. The rent is $500 per month and the lease is for two years. Payments are due at the start of each month. Nothing was recorded in Marietta Company's accounting records when the lease was signed.

(c) Marietta paid the rent for an apartment for the owner's personal use and charged it to Rent Expense.

(d) Marietta wanted to make its profit look worse than it really was, so it adjusted its expenses upward to include the effects of inflation.

(e) Marietta included a note in its financial statements stating the company was a going concern and is following GAAP for Private Enterprises.

Instructions

(a) In each situation, identify whether the accounting treatment is correct or not, and why.

(b) If it is incorrect, state what should have been done.

Match words with
descriptions.
(SO 1, 2, 3) K

E1–3   Here are some terms from the chapter:

1. Accounts payable
2. Expenses
3. Creditor
4. International Financial Reporting Standards (IFRS)
5. Profit
6. Assets
7. Corporation
8. Generally accepted accounting principles
9. Accounts receivable
10. Owner's equity

Instructions

Match each term with the best description that follows:

(a) ___ A company that raises money by issuing shares
(b) ___ An accepted set of accounting standards that includes broad principles, practices, rules, and procedures
(c) ___ Obligations to suppliers of goods
(d) ___ Amounts due from customers
(e) ___ Equal to net assets
(f) ___ A party that a company owes money to
(g) ___ Resources owned by a business that have the ability to provide a future benefit
(h) ___ The set of accounting standards that all publicly accountable enterprises in Canada have to follow
(i) ___ Results when revenues exceed expenses
(j) ___ The cost of assets consumed or services used in a company's ordinary business activities

Relate concepts to forms of
business organization.
(SO 1, 3) C

E1–4   Listed below are several statements regarding different forms of business organization.

Instructions

For each statement, indicate if that statement is true or false for each of the forms of business organizations by placing a T or an F in each column.

	Proprietorship	Partnership	Corporation
1. Owners have limited liability	___	___	___
2. Withdrawals of assets by owners are called drawings	___	___	___
3. Ownership claim on assets is called partners' equity	___	___	___
4. Entity pays income taxes on its profits	___	___	___
5. Withdrawals of assets by owners reduce Retained Earnings	___	___	___
6. Owners are called shareholders	___	___	___
7. Need to have a minimum of two owners	___	___	___
8. Entity has a limited life	___	___	___
9. The entity has a separate legal existence from its owners	___	___	___

Classify accounts and prepare
accounting equation.
(SO 3) AP

E1–5   The following items (in U.S. millions) were taken from a recent balance sheet of Nike, Inc. Nike is the largest seller of athletic apparel and footwear in the world.

Accounts payable	$1,031.9	Notes payable	$ 812.1
Accounts receivable	2,883.9	Other assets	2,595.9
Cash	2,291.1	Other liabilities	2,712.5
Inventories	2,357.0	Retained earnings	5,451.4
Investments	1,164.0	Share capital	3,241.7
Land, buildings, and equipment	1,957.7		

Instructions

(a) Classify each of the above items as an asset (A), liability (L), or shareholders' (owner's) equity (SE) item.
(b) Show the amounts in Nike's accounting equation by calculating the value of Nike's total assets, total liabilities, and total shareholders' equity.

E1–6   The summaries of balance sheet and income statement data for three proprietorships follow. Three items are missing from each summary.

Determine missing items. (SO 3) AP

	Wyatt Company	Maxim Enterprises	Distasi Services
Beginning of year:			
Total assets	$ 85,000	$134,000	(g)
Total liabilities	62,000	(d)	$30,000
Total owner's equity	(a)	52,000	33,000
End of year:			
Total assets	110,000	(e)	79,000
Total liabilities	(b)	61,000	42,000
Total owner's equity	60,000	44,000	(h)
Changes during year in owner's equity:			
Investments by owner	(c)	0	5,000
Drawings	18,000	(f)	25,000
Total revenues	175,000	99,000	85,000
Total expenses	140,000	48,000	(i)

Instructions

Determine the missing amounts.

E1–7   The Depeau Company had the following assets and liabilities on the dates indicated:

Calculate profit (or loss). (SO 3) AP

December 31	Total Assets	Total Liabilities
2009	$350,000	$200,000
2010	420,000	265,000
2011	510,000	330,000

Don Depeau began business on January 1, 2009, with an investment of $100,000.

Instructions

Use the accounting equation and the change in owner's equity during the year to calculate the profit (or loss) for:

(a) 2009, assuming Don Depeau's drawings were $60,000 for the year.
(b) 2010, assuming Don Depeau made an additional investment of $50,000 and had no drawings in 2010.
(c) 2011, assuming Don Depeau made an additional investment of $10,000 and his drawings were $40,000 for the year.

E1–8   A list of effects on the accounting equation follows. For each effect, give an example of a transaction that would cause it.

Give examples of transactions. (SO 4) C

1. Increases an asset and increases a liability.
2. Increases an asset and increases owner's equity.
3. Decreases an asset and decreases a liability.
4. Decreases owner's equity and decreases an asset.
5. Increases a liability and decreases owner's equity.
6. Increases one asset and decreases another asset.

Analyze effects of transactions for new company.
(SO 4) AP

E1–9   Here are the transactions for Lush Lawn Care during its first month of operations:

1. Rudy Holland, the owner, made a $15,000 cash investment to start business.
2. Paid monthly rent, $600.
3. Purchased equipment for $5,000. Paid $1,000 cash and signed a note for the balance.
4. Purchased supplies for cash, $500.
5. Billed customers for services performed, $2,500.
6. Rudy Holland withdrew cash for his personal use, $1,000.
7. Received $1,500 from customers billed in transaction 5.
8. Incurred advertising expense on account, $500.
9. Received $1,000 cash from customers for services performed.
10. Paid $300 on account for advertising expense incurred in transaction 8.

Instructions

Prepare a tabular analysis of the above transactions, as shown in Illustration 1-10 in the text.

Analyze effects of transactions for an existing company.
(SO 4) AP

E1–10   Paterson Computer Company had Cash of $8,000, Accounts Receivable of $20,000, Accounts Payable of $3,000, and B. Paterson, Capital of $25,000 at the beginning of May. During the month of May, the following transactions occurred:

1. Purchased computer equipment for $19,000 from Digital Equipment. Paid $2,000 cash and signed a note payable for the balance.
2. Received $5,000 from customers for contracts billed in April.
3. Paid $4,000 for May rent of office space.
4. Paid $2,000 of the amounts owing to suppliers at the beginning of May.
5. Provided computer services to Brieske Construction Company for $3,000 cash.
6. Paid NB Power $1,000 for energy used in May.
7. Ms. Paterson invested an additional $10,000 in the business.
8. Paid Digital Equipment $1,100 on account of the note payable issued for the computer equipment purchased in transaction 1. Of this, $100 was for interest expense.
9. Hired an employee to start working in June.
10. Incurred advertising expense on account for May, $2,000.

Instructions

Prepare a tabular analysis of the above transactions, as shown in Illustration 1-10 in the text. The first row is the amounts the company had at the beginning of May.

Analyze transactions. Calculate profit and increase in owner's equity.
(SO 4) AP

E1–11   An analysis of the transactions for Bnita & Co., a public accounting firm, for its first month of operation s, August 2011, follows:

	Cash	+	Accounts Receivable	+	Supplies	+	Office Equipment	−	Accounts Payable	+	B. Bnita, Capital	−	B. Bnita, Drawings	+	Revenues	−	Expenses
1.	+$10,000						+$5,000				+$15,000						
2.	−2,000						+5,000		+$3,000								
3.					+$750				+750								
4.	+2,700		+$3,400												+$6,100		
5.	−1,500								−1,500								
6.	−2,200												−$2,200				
7.	−750																−750 Rent
8.	+1,450		−1,450														
9.	−2,900																−2,900 Salaries
10.									+550								−550 Utilities

Instructions

(a) Describe each transaction that occurred in the month.
(b) Calculate the increase in owner's equity for the month.
(c) Calculate the amount of profit for the month.

E1–12   Below are some items found in the financial statements of Petr Zizler, Orthodontist. Indicate (a) whether each of the following items is an asset (A), liability (L), or part of owner's equity (OE); and (b) which financial statement—income statement (IS), statement of owner's equity (OE), or balance sheet (BS)—it would be reported on. The first one has been done for you as an example.

Classify accounts.
(SO 3, 5) C

	(a)	(b)
1. Accounts payable	L	BS
2. Accounts receivable	——	——
3. Cash	——	——
4. Dental equipment	——	——
5. Furniture and fixtures	——	——
6. Interest payable	——	——
7. Interest revenue	——	——
8. Interest expense	——	——
9. Investment by the owner	——	——
10. Orthodontist fees earned	——	——
11. P. Zizler, capital (opening balance)	——	——
12. P. Zizler, drawings	——	——
13. Salaries expense	——	——
14. Supplies	——	——
15. Supplies expense	——	——

E1–13   An analysis of transactions for Bnita & Co. for August 2011 was presented in E1–11.

Prepare financial statements.
(SO 5) AP

Instructions

Prepare an income statement and statement of owner's equity for August and a balance sheet at August 31.

E1–14   Atlantic Cruise Co. is owned by Irina Sail. The following information is an alphabetical listing of financial statement items for the company for the year ended July 31, 2011:

Prepare income statement and statement of owner's equity.
(SO 5) AP

Accounts payable	$ 50,000	Interest expense	$ 20,000
Accounts receivable	42,000	Investments by owner	5,000
Advertising expense	3,500	Maintenance expense	83,000
Cash	27,000	Notes payable	400,000
Equipment	120,000	Salaries expense	128,000
Food, fuel, and other expenses	65,500	Ships	550,000
I. Sail, capital, August 1, 2010	279,000	Supplies	15,000
I. Sail, drawings	35,000	Ticket revenue	355,000

Instructions

Prepare an income statement and a statement of owner's equity for the year.

E1–15   Refer to the financial information in E1–14 for the Atlantic Cruise Company at July 31, 2011.

Prepare balance sheet.
(SO 5) AP

Instructions

Prepare the balance sheet.

E1–16   Judy Cumby is the sole owner of Deer Park, a public camping ground near Gros Morne National Park. Judy has gathered the following financial information for the year ended December 31, 2011:

Calculate profit and owner's equity and prepare balance sheet.
(SO 5) AP

Revenues—camping fees	$160,000	Revenues—general store	$ 40,000
Operating expenses	150,000	Cash on hand	10,000
Supplies on hand	2,500	Original cost of equipment	110,000

Fair value of equipment	$125,000	Notes payable	$70,000
Accounts payable	11,500	J. Cumby, capital, January 1	17,000
Accounts receivable	21,000	J. Cumby, drawings	5,000

Instructions

(a) Calculate Deer Park's profit for the year.
(b) Calculate Judy's owner's equity at December 31.
(c) Prepare a balance sheet at December 31.

Problems: Set A

Identify financial statements
for decision-making.
(SO 1) S

P1–1A   Financial decisions often depend more on one type of financial statement than others. Consider the following independent, hypothetical situations:

1. The South Face Co. is thinking about extending credit to a new customer. The terms of credit would require the customer to pay within 45 days of receipt of the goods.
2. An investor is considering purchasing a company called Music Online Co. The investor plans on owning the company for at least five years.
3. The president of Tech Toy Limited is trying to determine whether the company is generating enough cash to increase the amount of dividends paid to shareholders and still have enough cash to buy additional equipment when needed.
4. Caisse d'Économie Base Montréal is thinking about extending a loan to a small company. The company would be required to make interest payments at the end of each year for five years, and to repay the loan at the end of the fifth year.

Taking It Further is an extra
question at the end of each
problem designed to challenge
students to think beyond the
basics concepts covered in the
problem, and to provide written explanations. Your instructor may assign problems with
or without this extra element.

Instructions

In each situation, state whether the individual making the decision would depend mostly on information in the income statement, balance sheet, or cash flow statement. Briefly justify your choice.

Taking It Further   Why is it important to users of financial statements to know that the statements have been prepared by individuals who have high standards of ethical behaviour?

Determine forms of business
organization.
(SO 1) AP

P1–2A   Five independent situations follow:

1. Dawn Addington, a student looking for summer employment, opened a vegetable stand along a busy local highway. She buys produce from local farmers each morning and then sells it in the afternoon as people return home from work.
2. Joseph Counsell and Sabra Surkis each own a bike shop. They have decided to combine their businesses and try to expand their operations to include snowboards. They expect that in the coming year they will need funds to expand their operations.
3. Three chemistry professors have formed a business that uses bacteria to clean up toxic waste sites. Each has contributed an equal amount of cash and knowledge to the venture. The use of bacteria in this situation is experimental, and legal obligations could result.
4. Abdur Rahim has run a successful but small organic food store for over five years. The increased sales at his store have made him believe the time is right to open a chain of organic food stores across the country. Of course, this will require a substantial investment for inventory and store equipment, as well as for employees and other resources. Abdur has minimal personal savings.
5. Mary Emery, Richard Goedde, and Jigme Tshering have law degrees and recently passed their bar exams. They have decided to start a law practice in their hometown.

Instructions

In each case, explain what form of organization the business is likely to take: proprietorship, partnership, or corporation. Give reasons for your choice.

Taking It Further Frequently, individuals start a business as a proprietorship and later incorporate the business. What are some of the advantages of doing this?

P1–3A Five independent situations follow:

Assess accounting treatment. (SO 2) C

1. Human Solutions Incorporated believes its people are its most significant asset. It estimates and records their value on its balance sheet.
2. Barton Co. is carrying equipment at its current fair value of $100,000. The equipment had an original cost of $75,000.
3. Steph Wolfson, owner of the Sound Effects Company, bought a computer for her personal use. She paid for the computer with company funds and debited the Computers account.
4. West Spirit Oil Corp. is a very small oil and gas company that is listed on the Alberta Stock Exchange. The president asked each of the shareholders to approve using Canadian GAAP for Private Enterprises instead of IFRS to reduce expenses for accounting services. He received 100% approval and has advised the company accountant to prepare the 2011 financial statements accordingly.
5. White Wall Tire Company is potentially on the verge of bankruptcy and the accountant is preparing its financial statements. The accountant advises the owner that it will be necessary to include a note to this effect in the financial statements.

Instructions

(a) For each of the above situations, determine if the accounting treatment of the situation is correct or incorrect. Explain why.
(b) If the accounting treatment is incorrect, explain what should be done.

Taking It Further Why is it important for companies to follow generally accepted accounting principles when preparing their financial statements?

P1–4A The following selected data are for Jaroslawsky Trading Company for its first three years of operations:

Determine missing items. (SO 3, 4) AP

January 1:	2010	2011	2012
Total assets	$ 40,000	$ (f)	$ (j)
Total liabilities	0	45,000	(k)
Total owner's equity	(a)	65,000	(l)
December 31:			
Total assets	(b)	140,000	155,000
Total liabilities	45,000	(g)	85,000
Total owner's equity	(c)	75,000	(m)
Changes during year in owner's equity:			
Investments by owner during the year	9,000	0	(n)
Drawings by owner during the year	12,000	(h)	36,000
Profit or loss for the year	(d)	40,000	(o)
Total revenues for the year	125,000	(i)	155,000
Total expenses for the year	(e)	105,000	126,000

Instructions

Determine the missing amounts.

Taking It Further What information does the owner of a company need in order to decide whether he or she is able to withdraw cash from the business?

P1–5A On April 1, Angela Loken established the Loken Travel Agency. The following transactions are for her first month of operations:

Analyze transactions and calculate owner's equity. (SO 3, 4) AP

Apr. 1 Deposited $12,000 in the agency's bank account at the CIBC.
    2 Paid rent for the month, $1,100.

Apr. 2 Purchased office equipment for $7,500, paying $2,000 cash and signing a note payable for the balance.

7 Incurred $300 of advertising costs, on account.

8 Paid $725 for office supplies.

11 Earned $9,000 for services provided, with $1,000 paid in cash and the remainder on account.

17 Paid the amount due in the April 7 transaction.

25 Withdrew $500 for personal use.

30 Paid employee salaries, $3,500.

30 Received a bill for utilities for the month, $400.

30 Received $5,000 from customers who were billed in the April 11 transaction.

Instructions

(a) Prepare a tabular analysis of the effects of the above transactions on the accounting equation.

(b) From an analysis of the owner's equity, calculate the account balance in A. Loken, Capital, at April 30.

Taking It Further   Assume that on April 28, Loken Travel Agency received a $500 advance cash payment from a customer for services to be provided in May. Should this be recorded as revenue in April when the cash is received? Why or why not?

Classify accounts and prepare accounting equation.
(SO 3, 5) AP

P1–6A   Listed in alphabetical order, the following selected items (in thousands) were taken from Capital Aviation's December 31 financial statements:

1.	L BS	Accounts payable	$1,197	11.	___ ___	Notes payable	$2,536
2.	___ ___	Accounts receivable	547	12.	___ ___	Other assets	1,270
3.	___ ___	Aircraft fuel expense	432	13.	___ ___	Other expenses	650
4.	___ ___	Airport fee expense	309	14.	___ ___	Other liabilities	1,436
5.	___ ___	Cargo revenues	161	15.	___ ___	Other revenue	230
6.	___ ___	Cash	632	16.	___ ___	Passenger revenues	1,681
7.	___ ___	C. Chung, capital, January 1	1,160	17.	___ ___	Property and equipment	3,561
8.	___ ___	C. Chung, drawings	14	18.	___ ___	Salaries expense	596
9.	___ ___	Interest expense	75	19.	___ ___	Spare parts and supplies	237
10.	___ ___	Maintenance expense	78				

Instructions

(a) In each case, identify on the blank line in the first column whether the item is an asset (A), liability (L), capital (C), drawings (D), revenue (R), or expense (E) item. The first one has been done for you as an example.

(b) Indicate on the blank line in the second column which financial statement—income statement (IS), statement of owner's equity (OE), or balance sheet (BS)—each item would be reported on. The first one has been done for you as an example.

(c) Show the amounts in Capital Aviation's accounting equation by calculating the value of total assets, total liabilities, and total owner's equity at December 31.

Taking It Further   Is it important for Capital Aviation to keep track of its different types of revenues as separate items? Explain.

Analyze transactions and prepare balance sheet.
(SO 4, 5) AP

P1–7A   The following events concern Anita LeTourneau, a Manitoba law school graduate, for March 2011:

1. On March 4, she spent $10 on a lottery ticket.

2. On March 7, she won $250,000 in the lottery and immediatcly quit her job as a junior lawyer.

3. On March 10, she decided to open her own law practice, and deposited $40,000 of her winnings in a business chequing account.

4. On March 14, she purchased a new condominium with a down payment of $100,000 from her personal funds plus a home mortgage of $200,000.

5. On March 15, Ms. LeTourneau signed a rental agreement for her law office space for $1,000 a month, starting March 15. She paid the first month's rent, as it is due on the 15th of each month.

6. On March 19, she hired a receptionist. He will be paid $500 a week and will begin working on March 24.

7. On March 20, she purchased office furniture for her law practice from a company that had just declared bankruptcy. The furniture was worth at least $12,000 but Anita was able to buy it for only $8,000.

8. On March 21, she purchased $500 of office supplies on account.

9. On March 24, she purchased $6,500 of computer and other equipment for her law practice for $2,000 plus a $4,500 note payable due in six months.

10. On March 31, she performed $3,000 of legal services on account.

11. On March 31, she paid her receptionist $500 for the week.

12. On March 31, she paid $300 for the supplies purchased on account on March 21.

Instructions

(a) Prepare a tabular analysis of the effects of the above transactions on the accounting equation.

(b) Calculate profit and owner's equity for the month ended March 31.

(c) Prepare a balance sheet at March 31.

Taking It Further   How should Anita determine which transactions should be recorded and which ones should not be recorded?

P1–8A   Tony Tiberio opens a law office under the name Tony Tiberio, Barrister & Solicitor, on July 1, 2011. On July 31, the balance sheet showed Cash $4,000; Accounts Receivable $1,900; Supplies $500; Office Equipment $5,000; Accounts Payable $5,500; and T. Tiberio, Capital $5,900. During August, the following transactions occurred:

Analyze transactions and prepare financial statements. (SO 4, 5) AP

Aug. 4   Collected $1,200 of accounts receivable.

5   Earned fees of $6,500, of which $3,000 was collected from clients and the remainder was on account.

7   Paid $2,100 on accounts payable.

12   Purchased additional office equipment for $1,600, paying $400 cash and leaving the balance on account.

15   Paid salaries, $3,500; rent for August, $1,100; and advertising expenses, $275.

18   Collected the balance of the accounts receivable from July 31.

20   Withdrew $500 for personal use.

26   Borrowed $2,000 from the Bank of Montreal on a note payable.

28   Signed a contract to provide legal services to a client in September for $4,500. The client will pay the amount owing after the work has been completed.

29   Received telephone bill for August, $275.

30   Billed a client $1,000 for services provided in August.

Instructions

(a) Beginning with the July 31 balances, prepare a tabular analysis of the effects of the August transactions on the accounting equation.

(b) Prepare an income statement and statement of owner's equity for August, and a balance sheet at August 31.

Taking It Further   What are the differences between purchasing an item on account and signing a note payable for the amount owing?

Prepare financial statements.
(SO 5) AP

P1–9A   Bennett's Home Renovations was started in 2005 by Jim Bennett. Jim operates the business from an office in his home. Listed below, in alphabetical order, are the company's assets and liabilities as at December 31, 2011, and the revenues, expenses, and drawings for the year ended December 31, 2011:

Accounts payable	$ 9,240	Note payable	$ 30,800
Accounts receivable	10,080	Office supplies	595
Cash	7,700	Office supplies expense	2,975
Equipment	29,400	Renovation fee revenue	154,700
Insurance expense	3,375	Salaries expense	87,430
Interest expense	1,190	Truck	42,000
J. Bennett, drawings	44,800	Truck operating expenses	19,545

Jim's capital at the beginning of 2011 was $54,350. He made no investments during the year.

Instructions

Prepare an income statement, statement of owner's equity, and balance sheet.

Taking It Further   Why is it necessary to prepare the income statement first, then the statement of owner's equity, and the balance sheet last?

Determine missing amounts, and comment.

(SO 5) AN

The **pencil icon** means that you have to write a detailed answer.

P1–10A   Here are incomplete financial statements for Wu Company:

WU COMPANY
Balance Sheet
January 31, 2011

Assets		Liabilities and Owner's Equity	
Cash	$10,000	Liabilities	
Accounts receivable	(i)	Notes payable	$ (iii)
Land	15,000	Accounts payable	18,500
Building and equipment	45,000	Total liabilities	45,000
Total assets	$ (ii)	W. Wu, capital	(iv)
		Total liabilities and owner's equity	$85,000

WU COMPANY
Income Statement
Year Ended January 31, 2011

Revenues		
Fees earned		$75,000
Expenses		
Salaries expense	$30,000	
Other expenses	28,000	
Supplies expense	(v)	
Total expenses		64,000
Profit		$ (vi)

WU COMPANY
Statement of Owner's Equity
Year Ended January 31, 2011

W. Wu, capital, February 1, 2010	$14,000
Add: Investments	(vii)
Profit	(viii)
	40,000
Less: W. Wu, drawings	(ix)
W. Wu, capital, January 31, 2011	$ (x)

Instructions

(a) Calculate the missing amounts (i) to (x).

(b) Write a memo explaining (1) the sequence for preparing the financial statements, and (2) the interrelationships between the income statement, statement of owner's equity, and balance sheet.

Taking It Further   Why isn't the balance sheet dated the same way as the income statement and statement of owner's equity: "Year Ended January 31, 2011"?

P1–11A   The balance sheet of Confucius Book Shop at April 30, 2011, is as follows:

Discuss errors and prepare corrected balance sheet.
(SO 2, 3, 5) AP

CONFUCIUS BOOK SHOP Balance Sheet April 30, 2011			
Assets		**Liabilities and Owner's Equity**	
Building	$110,000	Accounts payable	$ 15,000
C. Cai, capital	85,000	Accounts receivable	37,000
Cash	10,000	Equipment and furnishings	58,000
Land	50,000	Supplies	4,000
Notes payable	120,000	"Plug"	261,000
	$375,000		$375,000

Cenhai Cai, the owner of the book shop, willingly admits that he is not an accountant. In fact, he couldn't get the balance sheet to balance without "plugging" the numbers (making up numbers to give the desired result). He gives you the following additional information:

1. A professional real estate appraiser estimated the value of the land at $50,000. The actual cost of the land was $36,000.

2. Accounts receivable includes amounts due from customers in China for 35,000 yuan, which is about $5,000 Canadian. Cenhai didn't know how to convert the currency for reporting purposes so he added the 35,000 yuan to the $2,000 due from Canadian customers. He thought it more important to know how much he was owed by each customer in the currency they would likely pay him with anyway. Cenhai also believes that Accounts Receivable is a liability. He sees it as bad for the business that he doesn't have the cash from his customers yet.

3. Cenhai reasons that equipment and furnishings are a liability because it will cost him money in the future to maintain these items.

4. Cenhai reasons that the note payable must be an asset because getting the loan was good for the business. If he had not obtained the loan, he would not have been able to purchase the land and buildings.

5. Cenhai believes that his capital account is also an asset. He has invested in the business, and investments are assets; therefore his capital account is an asset.

Instructions

(a) Identify any corrections that should be made to the balance sheet, and explain why by referring to the appropriate accounting concept.

(b) Prepare a corrected balance sheet for Confucius Book Shop at April 30. (*Hint*: The capital account may need to be adjusted in order to balance.)

Taking It Further   Explain to Cenhai why all transactions affect at least two financial statement items.

Problems: Set B

Identify financial statements for decision-making.
(SO 1) S

P1–1B   Financial decisions often depend more on one type of financial statement than on others. Consider the following independent, hypothetical situations:

1. An Ontario investor is considering purchasing a company called Fight Flab Co., which operates a chain of 13 fitness centres in the greater Toronto area. The investor plans on owning the company for a minimum of five years.
2. The Backroads Company is considering extending credit to a new customer. The terms of credit would require the customer to pay within 45 days of receipt of the goods.
3. The senior partner of Private Label Enterprises is trying to determine if the company is generating enough cash to increase the partners' drawings and still ensure the company has enough cash for the company to expand its operations.
4. Laurentian Bank is thinking about extending a loan to a small company. The company would be required to make interest payments at the end of each year for three years, and to repay the loan at the end of the third year.

Instructions

In each situation, state whether the individual making the decision would depend mostly on information in the income statement, balance sheet, or cash flow statement. Briefly justify your choice.

Taking It Further   Why is it important to users of financial statements to know that the statements have been prepared by individuals who have high standards of ethical behaviour?

Determine forms of business organization.
(SO 1) AP

P1–2B   Five independent situations follow:

1. Three computer science professors have formed a business to sell software to reduce and control spam e-mail. Each has contributed an equal amount of cash and knowledge to the venture. While their software looks promising, they are concerned about the legal liabilities that their business might confront.
2. Joseph LeBlanc, a student looking for summer employment, opened a bait shop in a small shed on a local fishing dock.
3. Robert Steven and Tom Cheng each own a snowboard manufacturing business and have now decided to combine their businesses. They expect that in the next year they will need funds to expand their operations.
4. Darcy Becker, Ellen Sweet, and Meg Dwyer recently graduated with marketing degrees. Friends since childhood, they have decided to start a consulting business that focuses on branding strategies for small and medium-sized businesses.
5. Hervé Gaudet wants to rent DVD players and DVDs in airports across the country. His idea is that customers will be able to rent equipment and DVDs at one airport, watch the DVDs on their flights and return the equipment and DVDs at their destination airport. Of course, this will require a substantial investment for equipment and DVDs, as well as employees and space in each airport.

Instructions

In each case, explain what form of organization the business is likely to take: proprietorship, partnership, or corporation. Give reasons for your choice.

Taking It Further   What are the advantages of two individuals first forming a partnership to run a business, and later incorporating?

P1–3B Five independent situations follow:

Assess accounting treatment. (SO 2) C

1. In preparing its financial statements, Karim Company estimated and recorded the impact of the recent death of its president.
2. Paradis Company recently purchased a powerboat. It plans on inviting clients for outings occasionally, so the boat was paid for with company funds and recorded in the company's records. Marc Paradis' family will use the boat whenever it is not being used to entertain clients. It is estimated that the boat will be used by the family about 75% of the time.
3. Because of a "flood sale," equipment worth $300,000 was purchased by Montigny Company for only $200,000. The equipment was recorded at $300,000 on Montigny's books.
4. Vertical Lines Company was on the verge of filing for bankruptcy, but a turnaround in the economy has resulted in the company being very healthy financially. The company president insists that the accountant put a note in the financial statements that states the company is a real going concern now.
5. Three Green Thumbs is a landscaping business operated as a partnership. The partners plan on incorporating and going public in three years. They agree that the company should use International Financial Reporting Standards (IFRS) and also agree that they do not need to put that information in the financial statements as they are currently a private company.

Instructions

(a) For each of the above situations, determine if the accounting treatment of the situation is correct or incorrect. Explain why.
(b) If the accounting treatment is incorrect, explain what should be done.

Taking It Further Why is it important for private and public companies to follow generally accepted accounting principles when preparing their financial statements?

P1–4B The following selected data are for Siksika Trading Company for its first three years of operations:

Determine missing items. (SO 3, 4) AP

	2010	2011	2012
January 1:			
Total assets	$ (a)	$ 80,000	$135,000
Total liabilities	0	(e)	(k)
Total owner's equity	50,000	(f)	(l)
December 31:			
Total assets	80,000	(g)	170,000
Total liabilities	(b)	75,000	(m)
Total owner's equity	40,000	(h)	80,000
Changes during year in owner's equity:			
Investments by owner during the year	5,000	(i)	0
Drawings by owner during the year	0	10,000	(n)
Profit or loss for the year	(c)	25,000	60,000
Total revenues for the year	(d)	(j)	155,000
Total expenses for the year	110,000	105,000	(o)

Instructions

Determine the missing amounts.

Taking It Further What information does the owner of a company need in order to decide whether he or she needs to invest additional cash in the business?

Analyze transactions and
calculate owner's equity.
(SO 3, 4) AP

P1–5B   Jaeger's Repair Shop was started on May 1 by R. Jaeger. A summary of the May transactions follows:

May 1   Invested $15,000 to start the repair shop.
  2   Purchased equipment for $8,000, paying $2,000 cash and signing a note payable for the balance.
  5   Paid rent for the month, $940.
  7   Purchased $850 of supplies on account.
  9   Received $2,100 in cash from customers for repair services.
 16   Provided repair services on account to customers, $1,800.
 26   Collected $500 on account for services billed on May 16.
 27   Paid for supplies purchased on May 7.
 28   Paid $220 for advertising.
 30   Withdrew $500 for personal use.
 31   Received May telephone bill, $100.
 31   Paid part-time employee salaries, $1,000.
 31   Billed a customer $350 for repair services.

Instructions

(a) Prepare a tabular analysis of the effects of the above transactions on the accounting equation.
(b) From an analysis of the owner's equity, calculate the account balance in R. Jaeger, Capital at May 31.

Taking It Further   Assume that on May 28, Jaeger Repair Shop received a $500 advance cash payment from a customer for work to be performed in June. Should this be recorded as revenue in May? Why or why not?

Classify accounts and prepare
accounting equation.
(SO 3, 5) AP

P1–6B   Listed in alphabetical order, the following selected items (in thousands) were taken from Happy Valley Hotel & Resorts' December 31 financial statements:

1.	_L_ _BS_	Accounts payable	$ 159	9.	___ ___	Operating expenses	$661
2.	___ ___	Accounts receivable	90	10.	___ ___	Other assets	512
3.	___ ___	Cash	100	11.	___ ___	Other liabilities	256
4.	___ ___	Hotel real estate and		12.	___ ___	Other revenue	37
		equipment	1,435	13.	___ ___	Revenues from	
5.	___ ___	Interest expense	33			hotel operations	841
6.	___ ___	Investments	150	14.	___ ___	Salaries payable	35
7.	___ ___	Non-hotel real estate	100	15.	___ ___	T. Waye, capital, January 1	966
8.	___ ___	Notes payable	802	16.	___ ___	T. Waye, drawings	15

Instructions

(a) In each case, identify on the blank line, in the first column, whether the item is an asset (A), liability (L), capital (C), drawings (D), revenue (R), or expense (E) item. The first one has been done for you as an example.
(b) Indicate on the blank line, in the second column, which financial statement—income statement (IS), statement of owner's equity (OE), or balance sheet (BS)—each item would be reported on. The first one has been done for you as an example.
(c) Show the amounts in Happy Valley Hotel & Resorts' accounting equation by calculating the value of total assets, total liabilities, and total owner's equity at December 31.

Taking it Further   Is it important for Happy Valley Hotel & Resorts to keep track of its different types of expenses as separate items? Explain.

Analyze transactions and
prepare balance sheet.
(SO 4, 5) AP

P1–7B   Lynn Barry started her own consulting firm, Barry Consulting, on June 1, 2011. The following transactions occurred during the month of June:

June 1 Barry sold her shares in Big Country Airlines for $5,000, which she deposited in her personal bank account.

1 Barry transferred $4,500 from her personal account to a business account in the name of Barry Consulting.

2 Paid $750 for office rent for the month.

3 Purchased $475 of supplies on account.

5 Paid $80 to advertise in the *County News*.

9 Received $2,175 for services provided.

12 Withdrew $400 for personal use.

15 Performed $3,000 of services on account.

17 Paid $1,500 for employee salaries.

21 Received $2,400 for services provided on account on June 15.

22 Paid for the supplies purchased on account on June 3.

25 Signed a contract to provide consulting services to a client for $5,500. Services will be performed and paid for in July.

26 Borrowed $4,000 from the bank and signed a note payable.

29 Used part of the cash borrowed from the bank on June 26 to purchase office equipment for $1,650.

30 Paid $150 for telephone service for the month.

Instructions

(a) Prepare a tabular analysis of the effects of the above transactions on the accounting equation.

(b) Calculate profit and owner's equity for the month ended June 30.

(c) Prepare a balance sheet at June 30.

Taking It Further   How should Lynn determine which transactions should be recorded and which ones should not be recorded?

P1–8B   Brian Fraser opened the Fraser Veterinary Clinic in Regina on August 1, 2011. On August 31, the balance sheet showed Cash $4,500; Accounts Receivable $1,800; Supplies $400; Office Equipment $6,500; Accounts Payable $3,200; and B. Fraser, Capital $10,000. During September, the following transactions occurred:

Analyze transactions and prepare financial statements. (SO 4, 5) AP

Sept. 1 Paid $2,800 of the accounts payable.

1 Paid $800 rent for September.

4 Collected $1,450 of the accounts receivable.

5 Hired a part-time office assistant at $75 per day to start work the following week.

8 Purchased additional office equipment for $5,000, paying $1,000 cash and signing a note payable for the balance.

14 Performed $500 of veterinary services on account.

15 Paid $200 for advertising.

18 Collected $500 from customers who received services on September 14.

20 Paid $250 for Brian's daughter and friends to go horseback riding on her birthday.

25 Borrowed $7,500 from the Western Bank on a note payable.

26 Sent a statement reminding a customer that he still owed the company money from August.

28 Earned revenue of $4,300, of which $2,900 was paid in cash and the balance was due in October.

29 Paid the part-time office assistant $675 for working nine days in September.

30 Received the telephone bill for the month, $175.

30 Withdrew $750 cash for personal expenses.

Instructions

(a) Beginning with the August 31 balances, prepare a tabular analysis of the effects of the September transactions on the accounting equation.

(b) Prepare an income statement and statement of owner's equity for September, and a balance sheet at September 30.

Taking It Further   Explain the correct accounting treatment of the transaction on August 20.

Prepare financial statements.
(SO 5) AP

P1–9B   Judy Johansen operates an interior design business, Johansen Designs. Listed below, in alphabetical order, are the company's assets and liabilities as at December 31, 2011, and the revenues, expenses, and drawings for the year ended December 31, 2011:

Accounts payable	$ 5,840	J. Johansen, drawings	$35,000
Accounts receivable	7,645	Note payable	5,950
Cash	10,390	Office supplies	525
Computer equipment	8,050	Office supplies expense	2,625
Design fee revenue	122,395	Rent expense	16,800
Furniture	11,730	Salaries expense	66,360
Interest expense	315	Telephone expense	5,320

Judy's capital at the beginning of 2011 was $30,575. She made no investments during the year.

Instructions

Prepare an income statement, statement of owner's equity, and balance sheet.

Taking It Further   Why is the balance sheet prepared after the statement of owner's equity?

Determine missing amounts, and comment.
(SO 5) AN

P1–10B   Here are incomplete financial statements for Baxter Company:

BAXTER COMPANY
Balance Sheet
November 30, 2011

Assets		Liabilities and Owner's Equity	
Cash	$ 5,000	Liabilities	
Accounts receivable	10,000	Notes payable	$59,600
Land	(i)	Accounts payable	(ii)
Building and equipment	45,000	Total liabilities	66,500
Total assets	$110,000	Owner's equity	
		B. Baxter, capital	(iii)
		Total liabilities and owner's equity	$ (iv)

BAXTER COMPANY
Income Statement
Year Ended November 30, 2011

Revenues		
Fees earned		$80,000
Expenses		
Salaries expense	$37,500	
Other expenses	(v)	
Supplies expense	6,000	
Total expenses		62,500
Profit		$ (vi)

BAXTER COMPANY Statement of Owner's Equity Year Ended November 30, 2011	
B. Baxter, capital, December 1, 2010	$35,000
Add: Investments	(vii)
Profit	(viii)
	57,500
Less: B. Baxter, drawings	(ix)
B. Baxter, capital, November 30, 2011	$ (x)

Instructions

(a) Calculate the missing amounts (i) to (x).

(b) Write a memo explaining (1) the sequence for preparing the financial statements, and (2) the interrelationships between the income statement, statement of owner's equity, and balance sheet.

Taking It Further Why aren't the income statement and the statement of owner's equity dated the same way as the balance sheet: "November 30, 2011"?

P1–11B GG Company was formed on January 1, 2011. On December 31, Guy Gélinas, the owner, prepared a balance sheet:

Discuss errors and prepare corrected balance sheet.
(SO 2, 5) AP

GG COMPANY Balance Sheet December 31, 2011			
Assets		**Liabilities and Owner's Equity**	
Cash	$ 15,000	Accounts and notes payable	$ 45,000
Accounts receivable	55,000	Boat loan payable	13,000
Supplies	20,000	G. Gélinas, capital	25,000
Boat	18,000	Profit for 2011	25,000
	$108,000		$108,000

Guy willingly admits that he is not an accountant by training. He is concerned that his balance sheet might not be correct. He gives you the following additional information:

1. The boat actually belongs to Guy Gélinas, not to GG Company. However, because he thinks he might take customers out on the boat occasionally, he decided to list it as an asset of the company. To be consistent, he also listed as a liability of the company the personal bank loan that he took out to buy the boat.

2. Guy spent $15,000 to purchase more supplies than he usually does, because he heard that the price of the supplies was expected to increase. It did, and the supplies are now worth $20,000. He thought it best to record the supplies at $20,000, as that is what it would have cost him to buy them today.

3. Guy has signed a contract to purchase equipment in January 2012. The company will have to pay $5,000 cash for the equipment when it arrives and the balance will be payable in 30 days. Guy has already reduced Cash by $5,000 because he is committed to paying this amount.

4. The balance in G. Gélinas, Capital is equal to the amount Guy originally invested in the company when he started it on January 1, 2011.

5. Guy combined notes payable of $15,000 with accounts payable of $30,000 as he thought this was more efficient.

6. Guy knows that a balance sheet needs to balance but on his first attempt he had $108,000 of assets and $83,000 of liabilities and owner's equity. He reasoned that the difference was the amount of profit the company earned this year and added that to the balance sheet as part of owner's equity.

Instructions

(a) Identify any corrections that should be made to the balance sheet, and explain why by referring to the appropriate accounting concepts, assumption or principle.
(b) Prepare a corrected balance sheet for GG Company. (*Hint*: To get the balance sheet to balance, adjust owner's equity.)

Taking It Further   Assume that Guy did not make any withdrawals from the company in 2011, nor any investments other than his initial investment of $25,000. What was the actual profit for the year?

Continuing Cookie Chronicle

The **Continuing Cookie Chronicle** starts in this chapter and continues in every chapter throughout the book. This feature chronicles the growth of a hypothetical small business to show how the concepts you learn in each chapter can be applied in the real world.

Natalie Koebel spent much of her childhood learning the art of cookie-making from her grandmother. They passed many happy hours mastering every type of cookie imaginable and later creating new recipes that were both healthy and delicious. Now at the start of her second year in college, Natalie is investigating various possibilities for starting her own business as part of the requirements of the Entrepreneurship program she is taking. A long-time friend insists that Natalie has to somehow include cookies in her business plan and, after a series of brainstorming sessions, Natalie settles on the idea of operating a cookie-making school. She will start on a part-time basis and offer her services in peoples' homes. Now that she has started thinking about it, the possibilities seem endless. During the fall, she will concentrate on Christmas cookies. She will offer group sessions (which will probably be more entertainment than education for the participants) and individual lessons. Natalie also decides to include children in her target market. The first difficult decision is coming up with the perfect name for her business. In the end, she settles on "Cookie Creations" and then moves on to more important issues.

Instructions

(a) What form of business organization—proprietorship, partnership, or corporation—do you recommend that Natalie use for her business? Discuss the benefits and weaknesses of each form and give the reasons for your choice.
(b) Will Natalie need accounting information? If yes, what information will she need and why? How often will she need this information?
(c) In addition to Natalie, who do you anticipate to be the users of Natalie's accounting information? What information will these identified users need and why?
(d) Which set of accounting standards will Natalie likely adopt when compiling her accounting information? Why?
(e) Identify specific asset, liability, and equity accounts that Cookie Creations will likely use to record its business transactions.
(f) Should Natalie open a separate bank account for the business? Why or why not?

Financial Reporting and Analysis

Financial Reporting Problem

BYP1–1 The Forzani Group Ltd.'s financial statements have been reproduced in Appendix A at the back of the textbook.

Instructions

(a) How many notes to the financial statements are presented for The Forzani Group? How many pages of the financial statement package do these notes use? How many pages do the financial statements themselves use?

(b) Notice that the dates on the financial statements are February 1, 2009, and February 3, 2008. What is The Forzani Group's fiscal year end? (See note 2 (j) to the financial statements.)

(c) What were The Forzani Group's total assets as at February 1, 2009? As at February 3, 2008?

(d) What is the amount of change in The Forzani Group's profit (Forzani calls this "net earnings") from 2008 to 2009?

(e) What amount of cash did The Forzani Group have on February 1, 2009? On February 3, 2008?

(f) In the notes to the financial statements (note 2), the company highlights a number of accounting policies. At the end of this note, it also discusses its planned change to International Financial Reporting Standards (IFRS). When is the company required to change to IFRS? Will it show a comparative prior year based on prior Canadian GAAP or based on IFRS? For Forzani, which year ends will be shown in its first report under IFRS?

Interpreting Financial Statements

BYP1–2 Research In Motion Limited (RIM) is a Canadian company that designs, manufactures, and markets mobile communications solutions. RIM's award-winning products include the BlackBerry wireless platform, software development tools, and software/hardware licensing agreements. In the assets section of its 2009 balance sheet, the following data were presented:

RESEARCH IN MOTION LIMITED.
Balance Sheet (partial)
February 28, 2009
(in U.S. thousands)

RIM

Assets	2009	2008
Cash	$ 835,546	$1,184,398
Short term investments	682,666	420,709
Trade receivables	2,112,117	1,174,692
Other receivables	157,728	74,689
Inventory	682,400	396,267
Other current assets	187,257	135,849
Deferred income tax asset—current	183,872	90,750
Long term investments	720,635	738,889
Capital assets	1,334,648	705,955
Intangible assets	1,066,527	469,988
Goodwill	137,572	114,455
Deferred income tax asset—non-current	404	4,546
Total assets	$8,101,372	$5,511,187

Instructions

(a) For a company such as RIM, what do you think its most important economic resources (assets) would be? Where are these recorded on the balance sheet? At what value (if any) should they be shown?

(b) Does the balance sheet tell you what RIM is worth? What information does the balance sheet give you about the company's value?

(c) Why do you think a Canadian company such as RIM would prepare its financial statements in U.S. dollars?

Critical Thinking

Collaborative Learning Activity

WILEY
PLUS

Working in Groups

Note to instructor: Additional instructions and material for this group activity can be found on the Instructor Resource Site.

BYP1–3   In this group activity, you will analyze and record the transactions for a service company.

Instructions

(a) Complete the transaction table supplied by your instructor without consulting your classmates.

(b) Your instructor will divide the class into groups. One member of your group will take on the role of recorder as the group completes a new transaction table. You can refer to your individual transaction table for answers during the group activity but you should not change your individual answers. When your answers differ, you must explain your reasoning to the other members of the group.

(c) Each group will hand in the group transaction table along with the individual transaction tables of each member.

Communication Activity

BYP1-4 Robert Joote is the owner of Peak Company. Robert has prepared the following balance sheet:

PEAK COMPANY Balance Sheet Month Ended December 31, 2011	
Assets	
Equipment	$20,500
Cash	10,500
Supplies	2,000
Accounts payable	(5,000)
Total assets	$28,000
Liabilities and Owner's Equity	
R. Joote, capital	$21,000
Accounts receivable	(3,000)
R. Joote, drawings	(2,000)
Notes payable	12,000
Total liabilities and owner's equity	$28,000

Robert didn't know how to determine the balance for his capital account so he just "plugged" the number (he made up a number that would give him the result that he wanted). He had heard somewhere that assets had to equal the total of liabilities and owner's equity so he made up a number for capital so that these would be equal.

Instructions

In a memo, explain to Robert (a) how to determine the balance for his capital account, (b) why his balance sheet is incorrect, and (c) what he should do to correct it. Include in your explanation how the financial statements are interrelated, and why the order of preparation is important.

Ethics Case

BYP1-5 Chief executive officers (CEOs) and chief financial officers (CFOs) of publicly traded companies must personally certify that their companies' financial statements and other financial information contain no untrue statements and do not leave out any important facts. After many corporate scandals, the certification requirement was introduced as a way to hold top executives personally responsible for the integrity of their company's financial information.

Khan Corporation just hired a new management team, and its members say they are too new to the company to know whether the most recent financial reports are accurate or not. They refuse to sign the certification.

Instructions

(a) Who are the stakeholders in this situation?
(b) Should the CEO and CFO sign the certification? Explain why or why not.
(c) What are the CEO's and CFO's alternatives?

"All About You" Activity

BYP1–6   In the "All About You" feature, we introduced the idea that having a background in accounting is of value not just to accountants but to you as an individual. Accounting is all about providing and using information for decisions that you face either as a student or after graduation. Following are three such decisions.

1. You have $5,000 to invest and you are trying to decide if you should invest in Company A or Company B.
2. You will be graduating this year and have received job offers from Company C and Company D. You are deciding which company you should work for and you want to accept a position in a company that is financially stable and has growth potential.
3. Your brother owns his own landscaping business that has been operating for two years. He wants to buy some more equipment for the business and asked you to loan him $5,000.

Instructions

(a) For each decision, indicate what information you would want to have in order to make an optimal decision.
(b) Based on what you have learned in Chapter 1, how will learning about accounting help you with the above decisions?

ANSWERS TO CHAPTER QUESTIONS

Answers to Accounting in Action Insight Questions

All About You Insight, p. 3

Q: Why is understanding accounting of value to you in your personal life?
A: How do you make sure that the balance shown by the bank is the right amount in your bank account? Learning accounting will provide you with tools that will help you track your transactions and ensure that the bank balance is correct. You will learn how to calculate how much your paycheque should be. Examining your potential employer's financial statements will help you predict if the company will have enough cash to pay you now and if the company has growth potential. Stay tuned to the "All About You" features and related activities for more!

Across the Organization Insight, p. 4

Q: What is the value of providing all of a company's employees with financial information about the company?
A: Financial information shows the results of the employees' work. When employees are provided with this information, it increases their understanding of how the business functions and what their role is in the company's success or failure. Sharing financial information can assist in educating employees, managing costs and relationships, building team spirit, and setting goals, among other things.

Business Insight, p. 8

Q: Why will it be less expensive for a company like Humpty's Restaurants to use Canadian GAAP for Private Enterprises than IFRS?

A: IFRS requires significantly more financial information in financial statements than Canadian GAAP for Private Enterprises. Researching and reporting this information is a significant time commitment, which means a company needs more employees working in accounting. Also, these individuals must be able to deal with more complex reporting requirements and thus are likely to be relatively well paid, increasing the company's salary costs.

Answer to Forzani Review It Question 3, p. 24

The net earnings amount of $29,325 thousand (also known as *profit*) on the statement of operations (also known as the *income statement*) is included on the statement of retained earnings to determine the ending balance in retained earnings of $178,754 thousand. A statement of retained earnings is prepared by corporations, and is similar to the statement of owner's equity prepared by proprietorships.

The ending retained earnings balance of $178,754 thousand on Forzani's statement of retained earnings is also reported on the balance sheet. Finally, the $3,474 thousand ending cash balance reported as an asset on the balance sheet is explained on the statement of cash flows (also known as the cash flow statement), which ends with this same ending cash balance.

Answers to Self-Study Questions

1. d   2. d   3. c   4. a   5. a   6. d   7. b   8. b   9. c   10. d

Remember to go back to the beginning of the chapter to check off your completed work!

←

CHAPTER 2
THE RECORDING PROCESS

✓ THE NAVIGATOR

- ☐ Understand *Concepts for Review*
- ☐ Read *Feature Story*
- ☐ Scan *Study Objectives*
- ☐ Read *Chapter Preview*
- ☐ Read text and answer *Before You Go On*
- ☐ Work *Demonstration Problem*
- ☐ Review *Summary of Study Objectives*
- ☐ Answer *Self-Study Questions*
- ☐ Complete assignments

CONCEPTS FOR REVIEW:

Before studying this chapter, you should understand or, if necessary, review:

a. Why assets equal liabilities plus owner's equity. (Ch. 1, p. 10)

b. What assets, liabilities, owner's capital, drawings, revenues, and expenses are. (Ch. 1, pp. 11–12)

c. What transactions are, and how they affect the basic accounting equation. (Ch. 1, pp. 14–19)

Dancing to Her Own Business Tune

CALGARY, Alta.—At the Prestige Dance Academy, tiny pink ballerinas admire themselves before the mirrors. Their energetic teacher, Amanda Hunsley, dances along with them, encouraging them to express themselves through music.

Even when she was a young child taking dance lessons, Ms. Hunsley knew she wanted to run her own business. At just 19, while in her second year of studies at Mount Royal College, she opened her own dance school. Seven years later, the Prestige Dance Academy has a part-time staff of nine teaching some 800 students tap, jazz, ballet, creative performing arts, lyrical, preschool, mom and me, hip-hop, and intensive dance.

"I combined my love for kids and for business," she says. "I get to come to work every day and have this place that is mine and teach the kids what I love."

Ms. Hunsley takes care of hiring and scheduling the staff, registrations and any other administrative work, and advertising and marketing. To ensure the business's finances don't fall through the cracks, a bookkeeper helps with her record keeping.

While the dance academy provides birthday parties and summer camps, the bulk of the business is weekly dance lessons that run from September to June. Parents register their children in the fall, providing postdated cheques or a lump-sum payment for the entire year. Ms. Hunsley recently began accepting credit or debit cards for the lump-sum payments.

Using QuickBooks accounting software, Ms. Hunsley creates an account for each student registered and tracks their payments. Not surprisingly, September is the busiest time for creating new accounts and entering the initial monthly payments, as well as the lump-sum payments. At the beginning of each month, Ms. Hunsley records the payment of the postdated cheques then deposits the money in the bank. Expenses, such as lease payments (including heat, light, and water), phone and Internet bills, and staff salaries, are also entered into the system.

When she receives her bank statement at month end, Ms. Hunsley reconciles it with her own records. Her bookkeeper then produces three reports—an income statement, statement of retained earnings, and a balance sheet—so she can see how the business is doing. The bookkeeper also files quarterly sales tax reports and produces the T4s. At year end, Ms. Hunsley saves her QuickBooks file to disk and passes it on to her accountant, who looks for any problems and produces a final set of financial statements.

"I don't think you could run a business properly without being so on top of the finances," she stresses. "That's why I have a bookkeeper… You can't put some of that stuff off."

Good record keeping also allows Ms. Hunsley more time for what she enjoys most. Despite the tremendous growth of the business, she still taught about 15 hours a week while expecting a baby girl. Though she didn't plan to teach immediately after the baby was born, she would continue running the business, and planned to return to teaching within a few months. "Teaching and working with kids is my favourite part," she says.

The Navigator

The Navigator

In Chapter 1, we used the accounting equation to analyze transactions. The combined effects of these transactions were presented in a tabular form. This method could work for small companies like Softbyte (the fictitious company discussed in Chapter 1) because they have relatively few transactions. But imagine Prestige Dance in the feature story using the same tabular format as Softbyte. With 800 students, the dance academy has too many transactions to record each one this way. Instead, a set of procedures and records are used to keep track of transaction data more easily.

This chapter introduces and illustrates the basic procedures and records. It is organized as follows:

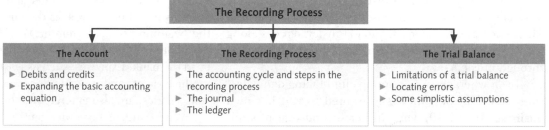

The Account

STUDY OBJECTIVE 1

Define debits and credits and illustrate how they are used to record business transactions.

An **account** is an individual accounting record of increases and decreases in a specific asset, liability, or owner's equity item. For example, Softbyte has separate accounts called Cash, Accounts Receivable, Accounts Payable, Service Revenue, Salaries Expense, and so on.

In its simplest form, an account has three parts: (1) the title of the account, (2) a left or a debit side, and (3) a right or a credit side. Because these parts of an account are positioned like the letter T, it is called a **T account**. The basic form of an account is shown in Illustration 2-1.

Illustration 2-1 ➡

Basic form of T account

The actual form that is used in real life is more complex than the above T, which account that will be explained later in the chapter. The T account format is a learning tool that will be used throughout the book to explain basic accounting relationships. It is also a form used by professional accountants for analytical purposes.

Debits and Credits

WILEY PLUS

Tutorials:
Accounting Cycle Tutorial

The term **debit** means left. The term **credit** means right. These terms are often abbreviated Dr. for debit and Cr. for credit. Debit and credit are simply directional signals that describe where entries are made in the accounts. Entering an amount on the left side of an account is called debiting the account. Entering an amount on the right side is called crediting the account.

When the totals of the two sides are compared, an account will have a debit balance if the total of the debit amounts exceeds the credits. On the other hand, an account will have a credit balance if the credit amounts are more than the debits.

The recording of debits and credits in an account is shown below for Softbyte's cash transactions. The data are taken from the Cash column of the tabular summary in Illustration 1-10.

Tabular Summary	Account Form		
Cash	**Cash**		
	(Debits)	(Credits)	
+$15,000			
−7,000	15,000	7,000	
+1,200	1,200	600	
+1,500	1,500	900	
−600	600	200	
−900		250	
−200		1,300	
−250	Balance 8,050		
+600			
−1,300			
$ 8,050			

In the tabular summary, every positive item is a receipt of cash. Every negative amount is a payment of cash. Notice that in the account format the increases in cash are recorded as debits, and the decreases in cash are recorded as credits. The account balance, a debit of $8,050, indicates that Softbyte had $8,050 more increases than decreases in cash. We will learn in the next section why debits and credits are used in this way.

Debit and Credit Procedure

In Chapter 1, you learned that each transaction must affect two or more accounts to keep the basic accounting equation in balance. We will also see that, for each transaction, debits must equal credits. The equality of debits and credits is the basis for the double-entry system of recording transactions.

In the **double-entry system**, the dual (two-sided) effect of each transaction is recorded in the appropriate accounts. This system is used all over the world and gives a logical method for recording transactions and ensuring the amounts are recorded accurately. If every transaction is recorded with equal debits and credits, then the sum of all the debits to the accounts must equal the sum of all the credits.

Assets and Liabilities. In the Softbyte illustration, increases in Cash—an asset account—were entered on the left side, and decreases in Cash were entered on the right side. Why did we do this instead of the opposite? First, we know that in the basic accounting equation (assets = liabilities + owner's equity), assets are on the left or debit side of the equation. So, to be consistent, when the double-entry system was created, it was decided that the normal balance of asset accounts should also be on the left side. Second, there are usually more increases in asset accounts than decreases. Logically, then, for the balance in an asset account to be on the debit side, increases also need to be recorded on that side. This is why asset accounts normally show debit balances.

So remember this: increases in assets must be entered on the left or debit side, and decreases in assets must be entered on the right or credit side.

Similarly, because liabilities are on the right or credit side of the accounting equation, liability accounts normally show credit balances. Credits to a liability account should be more than the debits to that account. Increases in liabilities must be entered on the right or credit side, and decreases in liabilities must be entered on the left or debit side.

To summarize, because assets are on the opposite side of the accounting equation from liabilities, increases and decreases in assets are recorded opposite from increases and decreases in liabilities. In this way, the total amount of debits always equals the total amount of credits and the equation stays in balance. The effects that debits and credits have on assets and liabilities and the normal balances are as follows:

Helpful hint Debits must equal credits for each transaction.

Helpful hint Increases in accounts are always on the same side as the normal balance for that account.

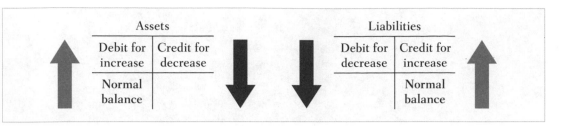

Knowing the normal balance in an account may also help you find errors. In automated systems, the computer is programmed to find these normal balance exceptions and to print out error or exception reports. In manual systems, a careful inspection of the accounts has to be done to find balances that are not normal. For example, a credit balance in an asset account such as Land or a debit balance in a liability account such as Wages Payable probably means there was a recording error. Occasionally, an abnormal balance may be correct. The Cash account, for example, will have a credit balance when a company has overdrawn its bank balance.

Owner's Equity. As explained in Chapter 1, owner's equity is increased by owner's investments and revenues. It is decreased by owner's drawings and expenses. Separate accounts are kept for each of these types of transactions.

Owner's Capital. Investments by owners are credited to the owner's capital account. Like liability accounts, the owner's capital account is increased by credits and decreased by debits. For example, when cash is invested in the business, the Cash account is debited and Owner's Capital is credited.

The rules of debit and credit for the Owner's Capital account and the normal balance are as follows:

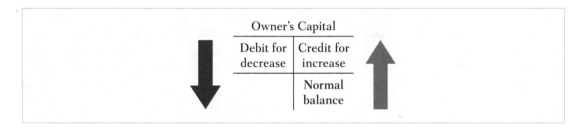

As liabilities and owner's equity are on the same side of the accounting equation, the rules of debit and credit are the same for these two types of accounts.

Owner's Drawings. An owner may withdraw cash or other assets for personal use. Withdrawals should be recorded as debits because withdrawals decrease owner's equity. Withdrawals could be debited directly to Owner's Capital. However, it is better to have a separate account, called Drawings, as we did in Chapter 1. The separate account makes it easier to add up the total withdrawals for the accounting period and to prepare the statement of owner's equity. Because the drawings account decreases owner's equity, the account has a normal debit balance. Note that increases and decreases are recorded opposite to how they are recorded in Owner's Capital, which increases owner's equity. Credits to an owner's drawings account are unusual, but might be used to correct a withdrawal recorded in error, for example.

The rules of debit and credit for the Drawings account and the normal balance are as follows:

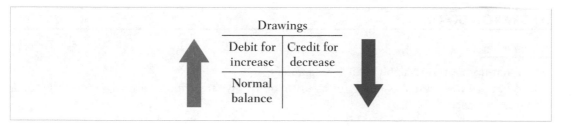

Revenues and Expenses. When revenues are earned, owner's equity is increased. Accordingly, the effect of debits and credits on revenue accounts is the same as their effect on Owner's Capital. Revenue accounts are increased by credits and decreased by debits.

Expenses have the opposite effect: expenses decrease owner's equity. As a result, expenses are recorded as debits because debits decrease owner's equity. Since expenses are the negative factor in calculating profit, and revenues are the positive factor, it is logical that the increase and decrease sides of expense accounts should be the reverse of revenue accounts. Thus, expense accounts are increased by debits and decreased by credits.

Credits to revenue accounts should exceed the debits. Debits to expense accounts should exceed the credits. Thus, revenue accounts normally show credit balances. Expense accounts normally show debit balances.

The effect of debits and credits on revenues and expenses and the normal balances are as follows:

Expanding the Basic Accounting Equation

You have already learned the basic accounting equation. Illustration 2-2 expands this equation to show the accounts that form owner's equity. In addition, the debit/credit rules and effects on each type of account are shown. Study this diagram carefully. It will help you to understand the basics of the double-entry system. Like the basic equation, the expanded basic equation must always be in balance (total debits must equal total credits).

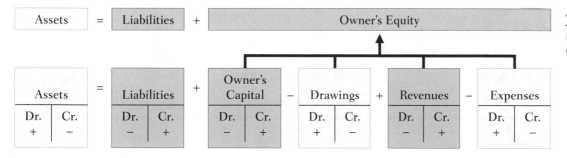

← Illustration 2-2

Expanded basic equation and debit/credit rules and effects

Remember, the normal balance of each account is on its increase side. So assets, drawings, and expense accounts have a normal debit balance, while liabilities, owner's capital, and revenue accounts have a normal credit balance.

BEFORE YOU GO ON . . .

→ Review It

1. What do the terms "debit" and "credit" mean?
2. What are the normal balances of asset, liability, owner's capital, drawings, revenue, and expense accounts?
3. What are the effects of debits and credits on the asset, liability, and owner's capital accounts?
4. What are the effects of debits and credits on the revenue, expense, and drawings accounts?
5. What are the normal balances for these Forzani accounts: Accounts Receivable; Accounts Payable and Accrued Liabilities; Retail Revenue; and Store Operating Expense? The answer to this question is at the end of this chapter.

→ Do It

Eszter Schwenke has just rented space in a shopping mall where she will open a beauty salon called Hair It Is. Eszter has determined that the company will need the following accounts:

1. Accounts Payable	6. Rent Expense
2. Cash	7. Salon Equipment
3. E. Schwenke, Capital	8. Service Revenue
4. E. Schwenke, Drawings	9. Supplies
5. Notes Payable	10. Wages Expense

(a) Indicate whether each of these accounts is an asset, liability, or owner's equity account. If it is an owner's equity account, indicate what type it is (e.g., owner's capital, drawings, revenue, or expense).
(b) What is the normal balance of these accounts?
(c) Will a debit increase or decrease these accounts?

Action Plan

- Use the expanded accounting equation to determine the type of account.
- Remember that the normal balance of an account is on its increase side.
- Remember that assets are increased by debits, and that liabilities and owner's equity are increased by credits.

Solution

Account	(a) Type of Account	(b) Normal Balance	(c) Debit Effect
Accounts Payable	Liability	Credit	Decrease
Cash	Asset	Debit	Increase
E. Schwenke, Capital	Owner's Equity	Credit	Decrease
E. Schwenke, Drawings	Owner's Equity (drawing)	Debit	Increase
Notes Payable	Liability	Credit	Decrease
Rent Expense	Owner's Equity (expense)	Debit	Increase
Salon Equipment	Asset	Debit	Increase
Service Revenue	Owner's Equity (revenue)	Credit	Decrease
Supplies	Asset	Debit	Increase
Wages Expense	Owner's Equity (expense)	Debit	Increase

The Navigator

Related exercise material: BE2–1, BE2–2, BE2–3, BE2–4, BE2–5, BE2–6, BE2–7, E2–2, E2–3, and E2–4.

The Recording Process

We could record transaction information directly into the accounts, but important information would be lost and the number of errors would increase. Instead, accountants follow systematic procedures to ensure transactions are correctly recorded, summarized, and reported to financial statement users. In the following sections we explain the recording process.

The Accounting Cycle and Steps in the Recording Process

The procedures used in recording transaction information is part of a series of steps, called the **accounting cycle**, which accountants follow in preparing financial statements as shown in Illustration 2-3.

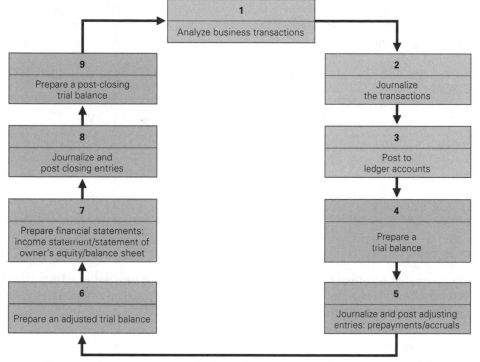

← Illustration 2-3

The accounting cycle

The steps in the recording process are the first three steps in the accounting cycle:

1. Analyze each transaction for its effects on the accounts.
2. Record the transaction in a journal (book of original entry).
3. Transfer the journal information to the correct accounts in the ledger (book of accounts).

The fourth step will be discussed later in the chapter. The remaining steps, 5 through 9, will be discussed in the next two chapters.

The recording process begins with analyzing the transaction. Deciding what to record is the most critical point in the accounting cycle. Recall from Chapter 1 that a transaction is recorded only if it causes the company's financial position (assets, liabilities, and owner's equity) to change.

Documents, such as a sales slip, cheque, bill, cash register tape, or bank statement, are analyzed to determine the effects of the transaction on specific accounts. Ms. Hunsley's Prestige Dance Academy in the feature story uses customers' payments and the company's cheques written for expenses to begin its recording process.

Then the transaction is entered in the journal. After that, the information in the journal entry is transferred to the correct accounts in the ledger. The sequence of events in the recording process is shown in Illustration 2-4.

← Illustration 2-4

The recording process

Analyze each transaction   Record transaction in a journal   Transfer journal information to ledger accounts

The steps in the recording process are repeated again and again in every company, whether a computerized or manual accounting system is used. However, the first two steps—the analysis and entering of each transaction—must be done by a person even when a computerized system is used. The major difference between a computerized and a manual accounting system is in transferring information from the journal to the ledger. In computerized systems, this is done automatically by the computer, which substantially reduces the possibility of making mistakes. In order to understand how computerized systems do this, we need to understand the manual way of processing accounting data. We will focus on the manual approach in this chapter.

BEFORE YOU GO ON . . .

→ Review It

1. What is the accounting cycle?
2. What are the three steps in the recording process?
3. What is the main advantage of a computerized accounting system?

The Navigator

Related exercise material: BE2-8

The Journal

STUDY OBJECTIVE 3

Explain what a journal is, and journalize transactions.

Transactions are first recorded in chronological (date) order in a **journal** and then transferred to the accounts. For this reason, the journal is referred to as the book of original entry. For each transaction, the journal shows the debit and credit effects on specific accounts. Companies can use various kinds of journals, but every company has the most basic form of journal, a **general journal**. Whenever we use the term "journal" in this textbook without a description of it, we mean the general journal.

The journal makes some important contributions to the recording process:
- It discloses the complete effect of a transaction in one place.
- It provides a chronological record of transactions.
- It helps to prevent and locate errors, because the debit and credit amounts for each entry can be easily compared.
- It gives an explanation of the transaction and, if there is one, identifies the source document.

Journalizing

The second step in the accounting cycle, entering transaction data in the journal, is known as **journalizing**. A separate journal entry is made for each transaction. A complete entry consists of the following: (1) the date of the transaction, (2) the accounts and amounts to be debited and credited, and (3) a brief explanation of the transaction.

To illustrate the technique of journalizing, let's look at the first two transactions of Softbyte from Chapter 1. These transactions were (1) September 1, Marc Doucet invested $15,000 cash in the business, and (2) computer equipment was purchased for $7,000 cash (we will assume that this transaction also occurred on September 1). In tabular form, these transactions appeared in Chapter 1 as follows:

| | Assets | | = Liabilities + | Owner's Equity |
	Cash +	Equipment		M. Doucet, Capital
(1)	+$15,000			+$15,000
(2)	−7,000	+$7,000		

In journal form, these transactions would appear as follows:

GENERAL JOURNAL					J1
Date	Account Titles and Explanation	Ref.	Debit	Credit	
2011 Sept. 1	Cash		15,000		
	M. Doucet, Capital			15,000	
	Invested cash in business.				
1	Equipment		7,000		
	Cash			7,000	
	Purchased equipment for cash.				

Since this is the first page of Softbyte's general journal, it is numbered J1. As illustrated in the previous illustration, the standard form and content of journal entries are as follows:

1. The date of the transaction is entered in the Date column.
2. The account to be debited is entered first at the left margin of the column headed Account Titles and Explanation. The account to be credited is then entered on the next line and indented from the left margin. The indentation visually separates the accounts to be debited and credited, so there is less chance of switching the debits and credits.
3. The amounts for the debits are recorded in the Debit (left) column and the amounts for the credits are recorded in the Credit (right) column.
4. A brief explanation of the transaction is given on the line below the credit account title. To simplify the illustrations in this textbook, journal entry explanations are often left out. Remember, however, that in real life, explanations are essential for every journal entry.
5. A blank row can be left between journal entries. This makes the journal easier to read.
6. The column titled Ref. (which stands for "reference") is left blank when the journal entry is made. This column is used later, when the journal entries are transferred to the ledger accounts. At that time, the ledger account number is placed in the Reference column to indicate where the amount in the journal entry was transferred to.

Students often find it difficult to decide what account title to use. To make the decision easier, the main thing to consider is that each title has to accurately describe the account's content. For example, the account title used for the computer equipment purchased by Softbyte may be Equipment, Computer Equipment, Computers, or Office Equipment. However, once a company chooses the specific title to use, all transactions for the account should be recorded under that account title.

When you complete the assignments in this text, if specific account titles are given, you should use those. If account titles are not given, you should create account titles that identify the nature and content of each account. The account titles used in journalizing should not contain explanations (such as Cash Paid or Cash Received).

If an entry affects only two accounts, one debit and one credit, it is considered a simple journal entry. Some transactions, however, involve more than two accounts. When three or more accounts are required in one journal entry, the entry is called a **compound entry**. To illustrate, recall from Chapter 1 that Softbyte provided $3,500 of programming services to customers (assume this was on September 9). It received $1,500 cash from the customers for these services. The balance, $2,000, was owed on account. The compound entry to record this transaction is as follows:

GENERAL JOURNAL					J1
Date	Account Titles and Explanation	Ref.	Debit	Credit	
2011 Sept. 9	Cash		1,500		
	Accounts Receivable		2,000		
	Service Revenue			3,500	
	Performed services for cash and credit.				

A	=	L	+	OE
+1,500				+3,500
+2,000				

↑ Cash flows: +1,500

In a compound entry, just as in a simple entry, the total debit and credit amounts must be equal. Also, all of the debits are listed before the credits are listed.

ACCOUNTING IN ACTION: BUSINESS INSIGHT

As Mississauga, Ontario–based Magellan Aerospace has recently experienced, incorrect and unrecorded transactions can have a serious impact on profit. The company launched an internal investigation of one of its divisions after overvalued accounts receivable were found on the company's books during bill collection. The investigation found unsupported and unrecorded transactions—accounting irregularities that increased the aircraft parts company's 2007 loss to $11.3 million. Correcting the misstatements, which took place from 2003 to 2007, resulted in pre-tax losses of $5.8 million after estimated insurance recoveries. The losses occurred "as the overstated carrying values of the assets were written down to their appropriate values," the company said.

Source: CBC News, "After fixing bad accounting, Magellan loses $11.3 million" (April 1, 2008), < http://www.cbc.ca/money/story/2008/04/01/magellan-loss.html> (accessed on February 9, 2009).

How can unrecorded accounts receivable transactions increase a loss on the income statement?

BEFORE YOU GO ON . . .

→ Review It

1. What is the purpose of the journal in the recording process?
2. What is the standard form and content of a journal entry in the general journal?
3. What is a compound journal entry and what are the debit and credit rules for compound entries?

→ Do It

In starting her beauty salon, Hair It Is, Eszter Schwenke did the following:

May 1   Opened a bank account in the name of Hair It Is and deposited $20,000 of her own money in this account as her initial investment.

   3   Purchased equipment on account (to be paid in 30 days), for a total cost of $4,800.

   7   Hired a stylist and agreed to pay her $500 per week.

(a) In what form (type of record) should Eszter first record these three activities?
(b) Prepare the entries to record the transactions.

Action Plan

• Understand which activities need to be recorded and which do not.
• Analyze the effects of the transactions on asset, liability, and owner's equity accounts.
• Apply the debit and credit rules.
• Record the transactions in the general journal following the formatting rules.

Solution

(a) Each transaction that is recorded is entered in the general journal.
(b)

May 1	Cash	20,000	
	E. Schwenke, Capital		20,000
	Invested cash in the business.		
3	Equipment	4,800	
	Accounts Payable		4,800
	Purchased equipment on account.		
7	No entry because no transaction has occurred.		

The Navigator

Related exercise material: BE2–9, BE2–10, E2–4, E2–5, and E2–6.

The Ledger

The entire group of accounts maintained by a company is called the ledger. The **ledger** keeps all the information about changes in each account in one place.

Companies can use different kinds of ledgers, but every company has a **general ledger**. A general ledger contains all the asset, liability, and owner's equity accounts. Whenever we use the term "ledger" on its own in this textbook, we mean the general ledger.

A business can use a loose-leaf binder or card file for the ledger, with each account kept on a separate sheet or card. However, most companies use a computerized accounting system that keeps each account in a separate file. In a computerized system, such as the QuickBooks accounting software used by Prestige Dance Academy in the feature story, each account is numbered so that it is easier to identify.

The ledger should be arranged in the same order that is used to present the accounts in the financial statements, beginning with the balance sheet accounts. The asset accounts come first, followed by liability accounts, owner's capital, drawings, revenues, and expenses. The ledger gives the balance in each account. The ledger will also show all of the increases and decreases that have been made to each account.

STUDY OBJECTIVE 4

Explain what a ledger is, and post journal entries.

Standard Form of Account

The simple T account form used in accounting textbooks is often very useful for illustrations and for learning accounting. In reality, however, the account forms that are used in ledgers are designed to include additional information. A very popular form in both manual and computerized systems, using the data (and assumed dates) from Softbyte's Cash account, follows:

GENERAL LEDGER					
CASH					
Date	Explanation	Ref.	Debit	Credit	Balance
2011					
Sept. 1			15,000		15,000
1				7,000	8,000
3			1,200		9,200
9			1,500		10,700
17				600	10,100
17				900	9,200
20				200	9,000
25				250	8,750
30			600		9,350
30				1,300	8,050

This form is often called the three-column form of account because it has three money columns: debit, credit, and balance. The balance in the account is determined after each transaction. Note that the explanation space and reference columns make it possible to give information about the transaction. In manual accounting systems, the explanation space is usually left blank because it is too time-consuming to copy explanations from the general journal. Computerized accounting systems will automatically include in the ledger the explanation that was originally recorded in the journal entry.

Posting

The procedure of transferring journal entries to the ledger accounts is called **posting**. It is the third step in the accounting cycle. Posting has the following steps:

1. General Ledger. In the ledger, enter the date, journal page, and debit or credit amount shown in the journal in the correct columns of each affected account.
2. General Journal. In the reference column of the journal, write the account numbers to which the debit and credit amounts were posted in the ledger.

Illustration 2-5 ➜

Posting a journal entry

These steps are shown in Illustration 2-5 using Softbyte's first journal entry.

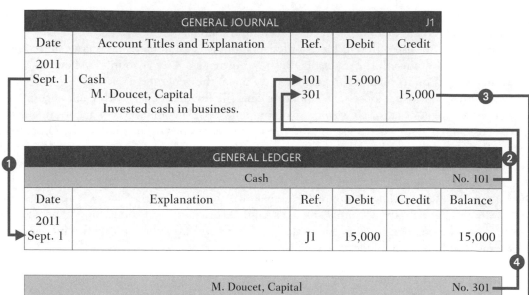

1. Post to debit account: enter date, journal page number, and amount.
2. Enter debit account number in journal reference column.
3. Post to credit account: enter date, journal page number, and amount.
4. Enter credit account number in journal reference column.

The reference column in the journal has several purposes. The numbers in this column indicate the entries that have been posted. After the last entry has been posted, this column should be looked at carefully to see that all postings have been made. The references also show the account numbers to which the amounts have been posted. The reference column of a ledger account indicates the journal page where the transaction was posted from.

Posting should be done in chronological order. That is, all the debits and credits of one journal entry should be posted before going to the next journal entry. Postings should be made on a timely basis—normally monthly—to keep the ledger up to date. In a computerized accounting system, posting usually occurs automatically right after each journal entry is prepared.

Chart of Accounts

The first step in designing an accounting system—whether computerized or manual—is to create a **chart of accounts**. The chart of accounts is the framework for the entire database of accounting information. It lists the account names and numbers of all the accounts in the ledger. The numbering system that is used to identify the accounts usually starts with the balance sheet accounts. The income statement accounts come next.

Because each company is different, the types of accounts they have and how many they have are also different. The number of accounts depends on the amount of detail that management wants. The management of one company may want one account for all types of utility expense. Another company may keep separate expense accounts for each type of utility expense, such as gas, electricity, and water.

ACCOUNTING IN ACTION: ACROSS THE ORGANIZATION

The numbering system used to identify accounts can be quite sophisticated or relatively simple. For example, Goodyear Canada Inc. uses an eight-digit system. The first three digits identify the account classification as follows:

100–199 Assets	300–399 Revenues
200–299 Liabilities and Owner's Equity	400–599 Expenses

The balance of the numbering system can be used to describe location, but is usually used to facilitate reporting requirements (at a more detailed level) or to segregate activities in order to ensure that account reconciliations can be done efficiently.

In contrast, a small company, Beanz Espresso Bar in Charlottetown, uses the basic four-digit numbering system set up by its accounting software, Simply Accounting. There is no need for other digits describing location as there is only one store and the basic system provides all the detail that the owner needs.

When deciding how to create a chart of accounts, whom should an accountant consult with?

In this and the next two chapters, we will show the accounting cycle for a service company named Pioneer Advertising Agency. Accounts 100–199 indicate asset accounts; 200–299 indicate liabilities; 300–399 indicate owner's equity accounts; 400–499, revenues; and 500–999, expenses. The chart of accounts for Pioneer Advertising Agency, owned by Clarence Byrd, is shown in Illustration 2-6.

Accounts shown in red are used in this chapter; accounts shown in black are explained in later chapters. From your study of transaction analysis in Chapter 1, you will be familiar with all of the accounts shown in red except for Unearned Revenue and Prepaid Insurance. These two new accounts will be introduced in the next section in Transactions 3 and 5, respectively.

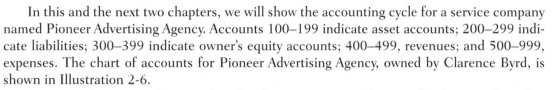

← Illustration 2-6

Chart of accounts

PIONEER ADVERTISING AGENCY
Chart of Accounts

Assets		Owner's Equity	
101.	Cash	301.	C. Byrd, Capital
112.	Accounts Receivable	306.	C. Byrd, Drawings
129.	Advertising Supplies	350.	Income Summary
130.	Prepaid Insurance		
151.	Office Equipment		**Revenues**
152.	Accumulated Depreciation—	400.	Service Revenue
	Office Equipment		
			Expenses
Liabilities		611.	Advertising Supplies Expense
200.	Notes Payable	711.	Depreciation Expense
201.	Accounts Payable	722.	Insurance Expense
209.	Unearned Revenue	726.	Salaries Expense
212.	Salaries Payable	729.	Rent Expense
230.	Interest Payable	905.	Interest Expense

You will notice that there are gaps in the numbering system of the chart of accounts for Pioneer Advertising. Gaps make it possible to insert new accounts whenever they are needed.

WILEY PLUS

Chart of Accounts

The Recording Process Illustrated

In the following section, we show the basic steps in analyzing and recording the October 2011 transactions of the Pioneer Advertising Agency. The agency's accounting period is one month. A basic analysis and a debit/credit analysis are done before each transaction is journalized and posted. For simplicity, the illustrations show the T account form instead of the standard account form.

Study these transaction analyses carefully. The purpose of transaction analysis is to identify (1) the type of account involved, (2) whether the account is increased or decreased, and (3) whether the account needs to be debited or credited. You should always do this analysis before preparing a journal entry. It will help you understand the journal entries discussed in this chapter, as well as more complex journal entries in later chapters.

Transaction (1) →

Investment of cash by owner

Transaction (2) →

Purchase of office equipment

Transaction (3) →

Receipt of cash in advance from customer

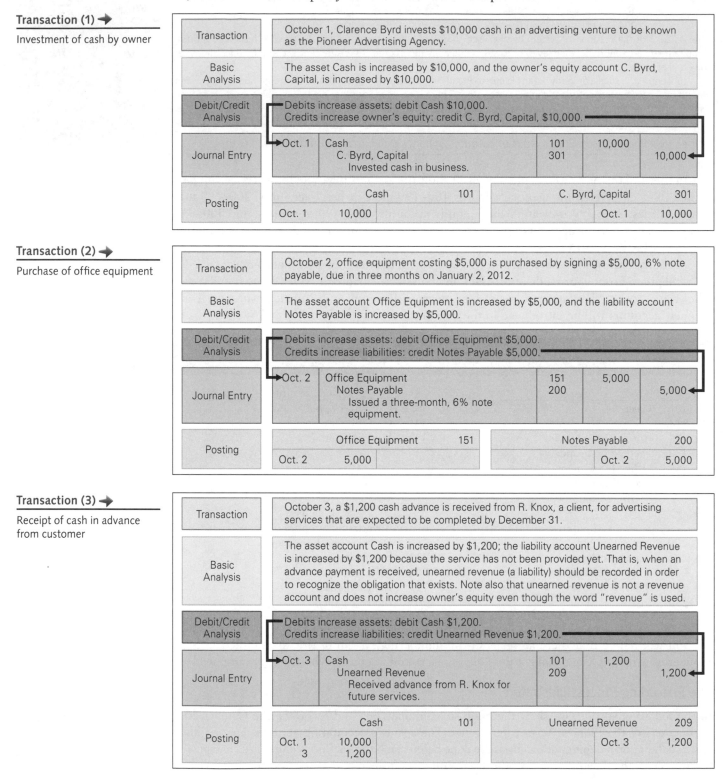

Transaction (4)

Payment of monthly rent

Transaction	October 3, office rent for October is paid in cash, $900.
Basic Analysis	The expense account Rent Expense is increased by $900 because the payment is only for the current month. Note that expenses are recorded as debits because debits decrease owner's equity. The asset account Cash is decreased by $900.
Debit/Credit Analysis	Debits increase expenses: debit Rent Expense $900. Credits decrease assets: credit Cash $900.

Journal Entry

Oct. 3	Rent Expense	729	900	
	Cash	101		900
	Paid October rent.			

Posting

Cash			101		Rent Expense		729
Oct. 1	10,000	Oct. 3	900	Oct. 3	900		
3	1,200						

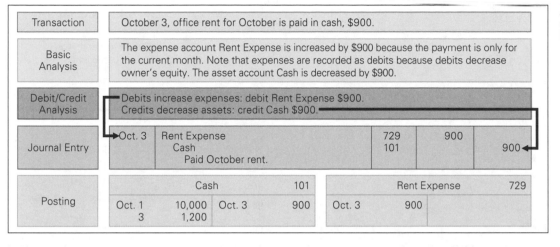

Transaction (5)

Payment of insurance

Transaction	October 3, $600 is paid for a one-year insurance policy, which will expire next year on September 30.
Basic Analysis	The asset account Prepaid Insurance is increased by $600 because the payment is for more than the current month. The asset account Cash is decreased by $600. Note that costs that will benefit more than one accounting period are identified as prepaid expenses or prepayments. When a prepayment is made, an asset account is debited in order to show the service or benefit that will be received in the future.
Debit/Credit Analysis	Debits increase assets: debit Prepaid Insurance $600. Credits decrease assets: credit Cash $600.

Journal Entry

Oct. 3	Prepaid Insurance	130	600	
	Cash	101		600
	Paid one-year policy, expiring on September 30, 2012.			

Posting

Cash			101		Prepaid Insurance		130
Oct. 1	10,000	Oct. 3	900	Oct. 3	600		
3	1,200	3	600				

Transaction (6)

Purchase of supplies on credit

Transaction	October 4, an estimated three-month supply of advertising materials is purchased on account from Aero Supply for $2,500.
Basic Analysis	The asset account Advertising Supplies is increased by $2,500. The liability account Accounts Payable is increased by $2,500.
Debit/Credit Analysis	Debits increase assets: debit Advertising Supplies $2,500. Credits increase liabilities: credit Accounts Payable $2,500.

Journal Entry

Oct. 4	Advertising Supplies	129	2,500	
	Accounts Payable	201		2,500
	Purchased supplies on account from Aero Supply.			

Posting

Advertising Supplies		129		Accounts Payable		201
Oct. 4	2,500				Oct. 4	2,500

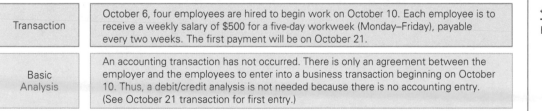

Transaction (7)

Hiring of employees

Transaction	October 6, four employees are hired to begin work on October 10. Each employee is to receive a weekly salary of $500 for a five-day workweek (Monday–Friday), payable every two weeks. The first payment will be on October 21.
Basic Analysis	An accounting transaction has not occurred. There is only an agreement between the employer and the employees to enter into a business transaction beginning on October 10. Thus, a debit/credit analysis is not needed because there is no accounting entry. (See October 21 transaction for first entry.)

Transaction (8) →

Withdrawal of cash by owner

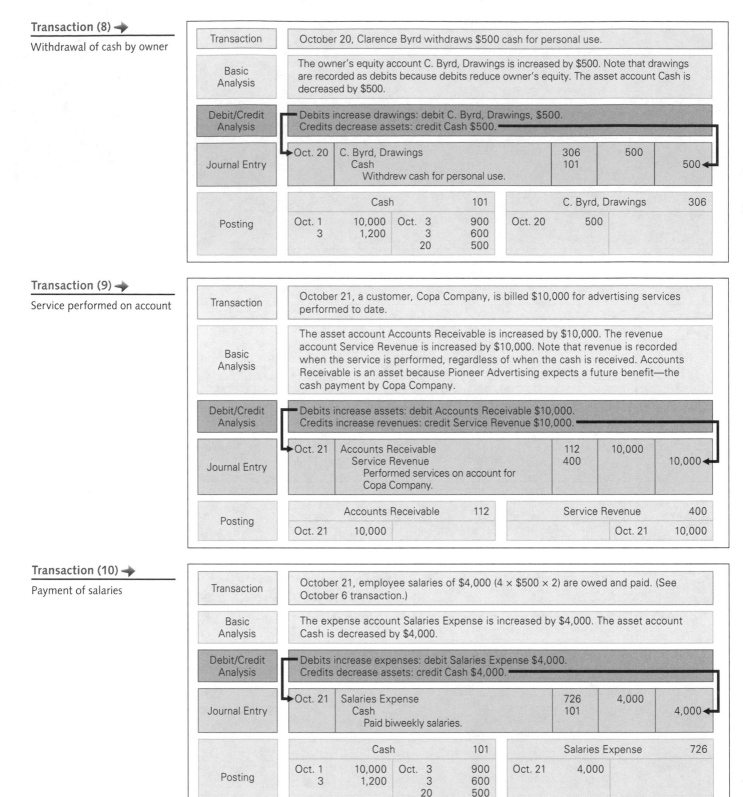

Transaction	October 20, Clarence Byrd withdraws $500 cash for personal use.
Basic Analysis	The owner's equity account C. Byrd, Drawings is increased by $500. Note that drawings are recorded as debits because debits reduce owner's equity. The asset account Cash is decreased by $500.
Debit/Credit Analysis	Debits increase drawings: debit C. Byrd, Drawings, $500. Credits decrease assets: credit Cash $500.

Journal Entry

Oct. 20	C. Byrd, Drawings	306	500	
	Cash	101		500
	Withdrew cash for personal use.			

Posting

	Cash		101		C. Byrd, Drawings		306
Oct. 1	10,000	Oct. 3	900	Oct. 20	500		
3	1,200	3	600				
		20	500				

Transaction (9) →

Service performed on account

Transaction	October 21, a customer, Copa Company, is billed $10,000 for advertising services performed to date.
Basic Analysis	The asset account Accounts Receivable is increased by $10,000. The revenue account Service Revenue is increased by $10,000. Note that revenue is recorded when the service is performed, regardless of when the cash is received. Accounts Receivable is an asset because Pioneer Advertising expects a future benefit—the cash payment by Copa Company.
Debit/Credit Analysis	Debits increase assets: debit Accounts Receivable $10,000. Credits increase revenues: credit Service Revenue $10,000.

Journal Entry

Oct. 21	Accounts Receivable	112	10,000	
	Service Revenue	400		10,000
	Performed services on account for Copa Company.			

Posting

	Accounts Receivable	112		Service Revenue		400
Oct. 21	10,000				Oct. 21	10,000

Transaction (10) →

Payment of salaries

Transaction	October 21, employee salaries of $4,000 (4 × $500 × 2) are owed and paid. (See October 6 transaction.)
Basic Analysis	The expense account Salaries Expense is increased by $4,000. The asset account Cash is decreased by $4,000.
Debit/Credit Analysis	Debits increase expenses: debit Salaries Expense $4,000. Credits decrease assets: credit Cash $4,000.

Journal Entry

Oct. 21	Salaries Expense	726	4,000	
	Cash	101		4,000
	Paid biweekly salaries.			

Posting

	Cash		101		Salaries Expense		726
Oct. 1	10,000	Oct. 3	900	Oct. 21	4,000		
3	1,200	3	600				
		20	500				
		21	4,000				

← Transaction (11)

Receipt of cash for services provided

Transaction	October 25, services were provided to a customer and $800 cash was received immediately.
Basic Analysis	The asset account Cash is increased by $800. The revenue account Service Revenue is increased by $800.
Debit/Credit Analysis	Debits increase assets: debit Cash $800. Credits increase revenues: credit Service Revenue $800
Journal Entry	Oct. 25	Cash	101	800	
		Service Revenue	400		800
		Collected cash for services provided.			

Posting

	Cash	101			Service Revenue	400
Oct. 1	10,000	Oct. 3	900		Oct. 21	10,000
3	1,200	3	600		25	800
25	800	20	500			
		21	4,000			

← Transaction (12)

Receipt of cash from collecting part of an account receivable

Transaction	October 31, received $9,000 cash from Copa Company in payment of part of its account. (See October 21 transaction.)
Basic Analysis	The asset account Cash is increased by $9,000. The asset account Accounts Receivable is decreased by $9,000. Note that service revenue is not recorded here; it was recorded on October 21 when the service was performed.
Debit/Credit Analysis	Debits increase assets: debit Cash $9,000. Credits decrease assets: credit Accounts Receivable $9,000.
Journal Entry	Oct. 31	Cash	101	9,000	
		Accounts Receivable	112		9,000
		Received cash on account from			
		Copa Company.			

Posting

	Cash	101			Accounts Receivable	112	
Oct. 1	10,000	Oct. 3	900	Oct. 21	10,000	Oct. 31	9,000
3	1,200	3	600				
25	800	20	500				
31	9,000	21	4,000				

← Transaction (13)

Partial payment of account payable

Transaction	October 31, paid Aero Supply $750 as partial payment of its account payable. (See October 4 transaction.)
Basic Analysis	The liability account Accounts Payable is decreased by $750. The asset Cash is decreased by $750.
Debit/Credit Analysis	Debits decrease liabilities: debit Accounts Payable $750. Credits decrease assets: credit Cash $750.
Journal Entry	Oct. 31	Accounts Payable	201	750	
		Cash	101		750
		Paid cash on account to Aero Supply.			

Posting

	Cash	101			Accounts Payable	201	
Oct. 1	10,000	Oct. 3	900	Oct. 31	750	Oct. 4	2,500
3	1,200	3	600				
25	800	20	500				
31	9,000	21	4,000				
		31	750				

Summary Illustration of Journalizing and Posting

The general journal and general ledger for Pioneer Advertising Agency for October follow:

Date	Account Titles and Explanation	Ref.	Debit	Credit
2011				
Oct. 1	Cash	101	10,000	
	C. Byrd, Capital	301		10,000
	Invested cash in business.			
2	Office Equipment	151	5,000	
	Notes Payable	200		5,000
	Issued three-month, 6% note for office equipment.			
3	Cash	101	1,200	
	Unearned Revenue	209		1,200
	Received advance from R. Knox for future services.			
3	Rent Expense	729	900	
	Cash	101		900
	Paid October rent.			
3	Prepaid Insurance	130	600	
	Cash	101		600
	Paid one-year policy, expiring on September 30, 2012.			
4	Advertising Supplies	129	2,500	
	Accounts Payable	201		2,500
	Purchased supplies on account from Aero Supply.			
20	C. Byrd, Drawings	306	500	
	Cash	101		500
	Withdrew cash for personal use.			
21	Accounts Receivable	112	10,000	
	Service Revenue	400		10,000
	Performed services on account for Copa Company.			
21	Salaries Expense	726	4,000	
	Cash	101		4,000
	Paid biweekly salaries.			
25	Cash	101	800	
	Service Revenue	400		800
	Collected cash for services provided.			
31	Cash	101	9,000	
	Accounts Receivable	112		9,000
	Received cash on account from Copa Company.			
31	Accounts Payable	201	750	
	Cash	101		750
	Paid cash on account to Aero Supply.			

GENERAL JOURNAL   J1

GENERAL LEDGER							

Cash 101

Oct. 1	10,000	Oct. 3	900
3	1,200	3	600
25	800	20	500
31	9,000	21	4,000
		31	750
Bal.	14,250		

Accounts payable 201

Oct. 31	750	Oct. 4	2,500
		Bal.	1,750

Unearned Revenue 209

		Oct. 3	1,200
		Bal.	1,200

Accounts Receivable 112

Oct. 21	10,000	Oct. 31	9,000
Bal.	1,000		

C. Byrd, Capital 301

		Oct. 1	10,000
		Bal.	10,000

Advertising Supplies 129

Oct. 4	2,500		
Bal.	2,500		

C. Byrd, Drawings 306

Oct. 20	500		
Bal.	500		

Prepaid Insurance 130

Oct. 3	600		
Bal.	600		

Service Revenue 400

		Oct. 21	10,000
		25	800
		Bal.	10,800

Office Equipment 151

Oct. 2	5,000		
Bal.	5,000		

Salaries Expense 726

Oct. 21	4,000		
Bal.	4,000		

Notes Payable 200

		Oct. 2	5,000
		Bal.	5,000

Rent Expense 729

Oct. 3	900		
Bal.	900		

BEFORE YOU GO ON . . .

→ Review It

1. What is the difference between journalizing and posting?
2. What is the purpose of (a) the ledger, and (b) a chart of accounts?

→ Do It

The following events occurred during the second week of business of Hair It Is, a beauty salon owned by Eszter Schwenke.

May 13 Paid $92 for utilities.
    14 Performed $1,280 of hairstyling services ($1,000 was collected in cash and $280 was on account).
    15 Paid $500 in wages to the stylist hired on May 7.

The opening balance in the Cash account was $20,000.
(a) Record these transactions in the general journal.
(b) Post the journal entries to the general ledger.

Action Plan

- Analyze the transactions. Determine the accounts affected and whether the transaction increases or decreases the account.
- Record the transaction in the general journal using debits and credits. Remember that the name of the account to be credited is indented and the amount is recorded in the right-hand column.
- Posting involves transferring the journalized debits and credits to specific accounts in the ledger.
- Determine the ending balances by netting (calculating the difference between) the total debits and credits.

Solution

(a)

May 13	Utilities Expense		92	
	Cash			92
	Paid utilities.			
14	Cash		1,000	
	Accounts Receivable		280	
	Hairstyling Service Revenue			1,280
	Performed services for cash and on account.			
15	Wages Expense		500	
	Cash			500
	Paid employee.			

(b)

Cash		Accounts Receivable		Hairstyling Service Revenue		Wages Expense		Utilities Expense	
20,000	92	280			1,280	500		92	
1,000	500								
20,408									

The Navigator

Related exercise material: BE2–11, BE2–12, E2–7, and E2–8.

The Trial Balance

A **trial balance** is a list of accounts and their balances at a specific time. The preparation of the trial balance is the fourth step in the accounting cycle, as shown in Illustration 2-3. It is prepared monthly if the company is preparing monthly financial statements. Since companies must prepare annual financial statements, the trial balance must be prepared at least once a year.

In the trial balance, the accounts are listed in the same order as they are in the ledger, with debit balances in the left column and credit balances in the right column. The totals of the two columns must be equal.

The main purpose of a trial balance is to prove (check) that the debits equal the credits after posting. That is, the sum of the debit account balances must equal the sum of the credit account balances. If the totals are not the same, this means an error was made in journalizing or posting the transactions. For example, the trial balance will not balance if an incorrect amount is posted in the ledger. If the trial balance does not balance, then the error must be located and corrected before proceeding.

A trial balance is also useful in preparing financial statements, as will be explained in the next two chapters. The procedure for preparing a trial balance is as follows:

1. List the account titles and their balances in the same order as the chart of accounts. Debit balances are entered in the debit column and credit balances are entered in the credit column.
2. Total the debit and credit columns.
3. Ensure that the totals of the two columns are equal.

Illustration 2-7 is the trial balance prepared from the ledger of Pioneer Advertising Agency shown earlier in the chapter. Note that the total of the debit accounts, $28,750, is equal to the total of the credit accounts, $28,750. If any accounts have a zero balance, they can be omitted from the trial balance.

← **Illustration 2-7**

Pioneer Advertising Agency trial balance

PIONEER ADVERTISING AGENCY Trial Balance October 31, 2011		
	Debit	Credit
Cash	$14,250	
Accounts receivable	1,000	
Advertising supplies	2,500	
Prepaid insurance	600	
Office equipment	5,000	
Notes payable		$ 5,000
Accounts payable		1,750
Unearned revenue		1,200
C. Byrd, capital		10,000
C. Byrd, drawings	500	
Service revenue		10,800
Salaries expense	4,000	
Rent expense	900	
Totals	$28,750	$28,750

Limitations of a Trial Balance

Although a trial balance can reveal many types of bookkeeping errors, it does not prove that all transactions have been recorded or that the ledger is correct. There can be many errors even when the trial balance columns agree. For example, the trial balance may balance in the following cases: (1) a transaction is not journalized, (2) a correct journal entry is not posted, (3) a journal entry is posted twice, (4) incorrect accounts are used in journalizing or posting, or (5) offsetting errors (errors that hide each other) are made in recording the amount of a transaction. In other words, as long as equal debits and credits are posted, even to the wrong account or in the wrong amount, the total debits will equal the total credits when the trial balance is prepared.

Locating Errors

The procedure for preparing a trial balance is quite simple. However, if the trial balance does not balance, locating an error in a manual accounting system can be time-consuming, tiring, and frustrating. Errors generally result from mathematical mistakes, incorrect postings, or simply recopying data incorrectly. In a computerized system, the trial balance is usually balanced because most computerized systems will not let you enter an unbalanced journal entry, and because there are rarely software errors in posting or the preparation of the trial balance.

What do you do if you have a manual trial balance that does not balance? First determine the amount of the difference between the two columns of the trial balance. After you know this amount, try the following steps:

1. If the error is an amount such as $1, $100, or $1,000, re-add the trial balance columns. Recalculate the account balances.
2. If the error can be evenly divided by two, scan the trial balance to see if a balance equal to half the error has been entered in the wrong column.
3. If the error can be evenly divided by nine, retrace the account balances on the trial balance to see whether they are incorrectly copied from the ledger. For example, if a balance was $12 but was listed as $21, a $9 error has been made. Reversing the order of numbers is called a transposition error.

4. If the error cannot be evenly divided by two or nine, scan the ledger to see whether an account balance in the amount of the error has been omitted from the trial balance. Scan the journal to see whether a posting in the amount of the error has been omitted. Check your additions.

Of course, if there is more than one error, these steps may not work.

ACCOUNTING IN ACTION: ALL ABOUT YOU

The double-entry accounting system used by many businesses today is in fact more than 500 years old. An Italian friar, Luca Pacioli, is considered to be the "Father of Accounting." His book, *Summa de Arithmetica, Geometria, Proportioni et Proportionalita (Everything about Arithmetic, Geometry, and Proportions)*, published in 1494, included a section on accounting. However, Pacioli didn't invent double-entry accounting; he simply described a method that Venetian merchants used during the Italian Renaissance. Pacioli's chapters on accounting, entitled "De Computis et Scripturis" (Of Reckonings and Writings), included most of the accounting cycle known today. They described journals and ledgers, assets (including receivables and inventories), liabilities, capital, revenue, and expense accounts. The book demonstrated year-end closing entries and proposed using a trial balance to prove a balanced ledger. The details of the bookkeeping method Pacioli presented have been followed in accounting texts and the profession for centuries.

Source: L. Murphy Smith, "Luca Pacioli: The Father of Accounting" (revised October 1, 2008), <http://acct.tamu.edu/smith/ethics/pacioli.htm> (accessed February 9, 2009).

Pacioli also wrote "a person should not go to sleep at night until the debits equalled the credits." Is this still good advice over 500 years later?

Some Simplistic Assumptions

To keep things simple, we have made some assumptions in the material in this textbook. These include not using cents and sales taxes in the transaction data.

Use of Dollars and Cents

We have not included cents in the amounts we record in journal entries, general ledger accounts, and trial balances. Excluding cents from entries will save you time and effort and you will still understand the accounting process. In reality, it is important to remember that cents are used in the formal accounting records.

Dollar signs are not used in the journals or ledgers. Dollar signs are used only in the trial balance and the financial statements. Generally, a dollar sign is shown only for the first item in the column, and for the total of that column. A single line is placed under the column of figures to be added or subtracted. The total amount is double-underlined to indicate the final sum.

Sales Taxes

Sales taxes in Canada include the Goods and Services Tax (GST) and the Provincial Sales Tax (PST). In British Columbia, Ontario, New Brunswick, Nova Scotia, and Newfoundland and Labrador, GST and PST have been combined into one tax, called the Harmonized Sales Tax (HST).

In general, a company pays sales taxes on the goods and services it purchases, and collects sales taxes on the goods that it sells and the services it provides. The company then remits the sales taxes, or portions of them, to the government. However, accounting for sales taxes is complicated and there are many exceptions. For example, not only do provincial sales tax rates vary across the country, but the method of calculating this tax can also vary. In addition, not all companies and their goods are taxable.

Although sales taxes are an important part of business, accounting transactions are presented in this textbook without the added complexity of these taxes. If you would like to learn more about this topic, sales taxes are discussed in more detail in Appendix B at the end of this textbook.

BEFORE YOU GO ON . . .

→ Review It

1. What is a trial balance, and what is its main purpose?
2. How is a trial balance prepared?
3. What are the limitations of a trial balance?

→ Do It

Koizumi Kollections has the following alphabetical list of accounts and balances at July 31, 2011:

Account	Amount	Account	Amount
Accounts payable	$33,700	Land	$ 51,000
Accounts receivable	71,200	Machinery and equipment	35,700
Building	86,500	Notes payable	49,500
Cash	3,200	Operating expenses	105,100
J. Koizumi, capital	99,400	Service revenue	171,100
J. Koizumi, drawings	4,000	Unearned service revenue	3,000

Each of the above accounts has a normal balance. Prepare a trial balance with the accounts in the same order as they would be in the ledger (in other words, in financial statement order).

Action Plan

- Reorder the accounts as they would normally be in the general ledger: balance sheet accounts are listed first (assets, liabilities, and equity) followed by income statement accounts (revenues and expenses).
- Determine whether each account has a normal debit or credit balance.
- List the amounts in the appropriate debit or credit column.
- Total the trial balance columns. Total debits must equal total credits or a mistake has been made.

Solution

		KOIZUMI KOLLECTIONS Trial Balance July 31, 2011		
			Debit	Credit
Cash			$ 3,200	
Accounts receivable			71,200	
Land			51,000	
Building			86,500	
Machinery and equipment			35,700	
Accounts payable				$ 33,700
Unearned service revenue				3,000
Notes payable				49,500
J. Koizumi, capital				99,400
J. Koizumi, drawings			4,000	
Service revenue				171,100
Operating expenses			105,100	
Totals			$356,700	$356,700

Related exercise material: BE2–13, BE2–14, E2–1, E2–9, E2–10, E2–11, E2–12, and E2–13.

The Navigator

Demonstration Problems

Demonstration Problem

Nge Aung opened the Campus Laundromat on September 1, 2011. During the first month of operations, the following transactions occurred:

Sept. 1 Invested $15,000 cash and laundry equipment worth $5,000 in the business.

2 Paid $1,000 cash for store rent for the month of September.

3 Borrowed $15,000 cash from the bank and signed a $15,000, 6-month, 5% note payable.

3 Purchased washers and dryers for $20,000 cash.

6 Paid $1,200 for a one-year insurance policy.

10 Received a bill from *The Daily News* for advertising the opening of the laundromat, $300.

15 Billed a nearby restaurant $500 for laundry services performed on account.

20 Withdrew $700 cash for personal use.

25 Received $300 cash from the restaurant billed on September 15. The balance of the account will be collected in October.

29 Received $400 cash advance from the college residence for services to be performed in October.

30 Cash receipts for laundry services performed for the month were $6,200.

30 Paid employee salaries of $1,600.

30 Paid *The Daily News* $200 of the amount owed from the bill received September 10.

The chart of accounts for the company is the same as the one for Pioneer Advertising Agency in Illustration 2-6 except for the following: No. 153 Laundry Equipment and No. 610 Advertising Expense.

Instructions

(a) Journalize the September transactions.

(b) Open ledger accounts and post the September transactions.

(c) Prepare a trial balance at September 30, 2011.

(d) Prepare an income statement, statement of owner's equity, and balance sheet for Campus Laundromat.

Action Plan

- Determine if the transaction should be recorded or not.
- In journalizing, use specific account titles taken from the chart of accounts.
- In journalizing, use the debit and credit rules and make sure debits equal credits.
- Give an appropriate description of each journal entry.
- Arrange the ledger in statement order, beginning with the balance sheet accounts.
- Post in chronological order.
- Put account numbers in the reference column to indicate the amount has been posted.
- Ensure the trial balance lists accounts in the same order as in the ledger.
- List debit balances in the left column of the trial balance and credit balances in the right column.

Solution to Demonstration Problem

(a)

	GENERAL JOURNAL			J1
Date	Account Titles and Explanation	Ref.	Debit	Credit
2011				
Sept. 1	Cash	101	15,000	
	Laundry Equipment	153	5,000	
	N. Aung, Capital	301		20,000
	Invested cash and equipment in business.			
2	Rent Expense	729	1,000	
	Cash	101		1,000
	Paid September rent.			
3	Cash	101	15,000	
	Notes Payable	200		15,000
	Borrowed from bank and signed a 6-month, 5% note payable.			
3	Laundry Equipment	153	20,000	
	Cash	101		20,000
	Purchased laundry equipment for cash.			
6	Prepaid Insurance	130	1,200	
	Cash	101		1,200
	Paid one-year insurance policy.			

10	Advertising Expense		610	300	
	Accounts Payable		201		300
	Received bill from *The Daily News* for advertising.				
15	Accounts Receivable		112	500	
	Service Revenue		400		500
	Performed laundry services on account.				
20	N. Aung, Drawings		306	700	
	Cash		101		700
	Withdrew cash for personal use.				
25	Cash		101	300	
	Accounts Receivable		112		300
	Received cash on account.				
29	Cash		101	400	
	Unearned Revenue		209		400
	Received cash in advance from customer.				
30	Cash		101	6,200	
	Service Revenue		400		6,200
	Received cash for laundry services.				
30	Salaries Expense		726	1,600	
	Cash		101		1,600
	Paid employee salaries.				
30	Accounts Payable		201	200	
	Cash		101		200
	Made a partial payment to *The Daily News*.				

(b)

GENERAL LEDGER

Cash				101
Sept. 1	15,000	Sept. 2	1,000	
3	15,000	3	20,000	
25	300	6	1,200	
29	400	20	700	
30	6,200	30	1,600	
		30	200	
Bal.	12,200			

Unearned Revenue				209
		Sept. 29	400	
		Bal.	400	

N. Aung, Capital				301
		Sept. 1	20,000	
		Bal.	20,000	

Accounts Receivable				112
Sept. 15	500	Sept. 25	300	
Bal.	200			

N. Aung, Drawings				306
Sept. 20	700			
Bal.	700			

Prepaid Insurance				130
Sept. 6	1,200			
Bal.	1,200			

Service Revenue				400
		Sept. 15	500	
		30	6,200	
		Bal.	6,700	

Laundry Equipment				153
Sept. 1	5,000			
3	20,000			
Bal.	25,000			

Advertising Expense				610
Sept. 10	300			
Bal.	300			

Notes Payable				200
		Sept. 3	15,000	
		Bal.	15,000	

Salaries Expense				726
Sept. 30	1,600			
Bal.	1,600			

Accounts Payable				201
Sept. 30	200	Sept. 10	300	
		Bal.	100	

Rent Expense				729
Sept. 2	1,000			
Bal.	1,000			

(c)

CAMPUS LAUNDROMAT
Trial Balance
September 30, 2011

	Debit	Credit
Cash	$12,200	
Accounts receivable	200	
Prepaid insurance	1,200	
Laundry equipment	25,000	
Notes payable		$15,000
Accounts payable		100
Unearned revenue		400
N. Aung, capital		20,000
N. Aung, drawings	700	
Service revenue		6,700
Advertising expense	300	
Salaries expense	1,600	
Rent expense	1,000	
Totals	$42,200	$42,200

(d)

CAMPUS LAUNDROMAT
Income Statement
Month Ended September 30, 2011

Revenues		
Service revenue		$6,700
Expenses		
Advertising expense	$ 300	
Salaries expense	1,600	
Rent expense	1,000	2,900
Profit		$3,800

CAMPUS LAUNDROMAT
Statement of Owner's Equity
Month Ended September 30, 2011

N. Aung, capital, September 1		$ 0
Add: Investments	$20,000	
Profit	3,800	23,800
Less: Drawings		700
N. Aung, capital, September 30		$23,100

CAMPUS LAUNDROMAT
Balance Sheet
September 30, 2011

Assets		
Cash		$12,200
Accounts receivable		200
Prepaid insurance		1,200
Laundry equipment		25,000
Total assets		$38,600
Liabilities and Owner's Equity		
Liabilities		
Notes payable	$15,000	
Accounts payable	100	
Unearned service revenue	400	$15,500
Owner's equity		
N. Aung, capital		23,100
Total liabilities and owner's equity		$38,600

The Navigator

Summary of Study Objectives

1. Define debits and credits and illustrate how they are used to record transactions. Debit means left and credit means right. The normal balance of an asset is a debit because assets are on the left side of the accounting equation. Assets are increased by debits and decreased by credits. The normal balance of liabilities and owner's capital is a credit because they are on the right side of the accounting equation. Liabilities and owner's capital are increased by credits and decreased by debits. Revenues are recorded as credits because credits increase owner's equity. Credits increase revenues and debits decrease revenues. Expenses and drawings are recorded as debits because debits decrease owner's equity. Expenses and drawings are increased by debits and decreased by credits.

2. Describe the accounting cycle and the steps in the recording process. The accounting cycle is a series of steps followed by accountants in preparing financial statements. The steps in the recording process are the first three steps in the accounting cycle. These steps: (a) analyze each transaction for its effect on the accounts, (b) record the transaction in a journal, and (c) transfer the journal information to the correct accounts in the ledger.

3. Explain what a journal is, and journalize transactions. A journal (a) discloses the complete effect of a transaction in one place, (b) provides a chronological record of transactions, (c) helps to prevent and locate errors because the debit and credit amounts for each entry can be easily compared, and (d) explains the transaction and, if there is one, identifies the source document.

4. Explain what a ledger is, and post journal entries. The entire group of accounts maintained by a company is called the ledger. The ledger keeps in one place all the information about changes in each of the specific account balances. Posting is the procedure of transferring journal entries to the ledger accounts. This part of the recording process brings together in each account the effects of journalized transactions.

5. Explain the purpose of a trial balance, and prepare one. A trial balance is a list of accounts and their balances at a specific time. Its main purpose is to prove that debits and credits are equal after posting. A trial balance uncovers certain types of errors in journalizing and posting, and is useful in preparing financial statements. Preparing a trial balance is the fourth step in the accounting cycle.

The Navigator

Glossary

WILEY PLUS — Glossary Key Term Matching Activity

Account A record of increases and decreases in a specific asset, liability, or owner's equity item. (p. 58)

Accounting cycle A series of steps followed by accountants in preparing financial statements. (p. 63)

Chart of accounts A list of accounts and the account numbers that identify where the accounts are in the ledger. (p. 68)

Compound entry An entry that affects three or more accounts. (p. 65)

Credit The right side of an account. (p. 58)

Debit The left side of an account. (p. 58)

Double-entry system A system that records the dual (two-sided) effect of each transaction in appropriate accounts. (p. 59)

General journal The book of original entry in which transactions are recorded when they are not recorded in other specialized journals. (p. 64)

General ledger A ledger that contains accounts for all assets, liabilities, equities, revenues, and expenses. (p. 67)

Journal An accounting record where transactions are recorded in chronological (date) order. (p. 64)

Journalizing The entering of transaction data in the journal. (p. 64)

Ledger A record that contains all of a company's accounts. (p. 67)

Posting The procedure of transferring journal entries to the ledger accounts. (p. 67)

T account A form of account that looks like the letter T. It has the title above the horizontal line. Debits are shown to the left of the vertical line, credits to the right. (p. 58)

Trial balance A list of accounts and their balances at a specific time, usually at the end of the accounting period. (p. 76)

Self-Study Questions

WILEY **PLUS** Quizzes

Answers are at the end of the chapter.

(SO 1) K 1. Which of the following statements about an account is true?
   (a) The left side of an account is the credit or decrease side.
   (b) An account is an individual accounting record of increases and decreases in specific asset, liability, and owner's equity items.
   (c) There are separate accounts for specific assets and liabilities but only one account for owner's equity items.
   (d) The right side of an account is the debit or increase side.

(SO 1) K 2. Debits:
   (a) increase both assets and liabilities.
   (b) decrease both assets and liabilities.
   (c) increase assets and decrease liabilities.
   (d) decrease assets and increase liabilities.

(SO 1) K 3. A revenue account:
   (a) is increased by debits.
   (b) is decreased by credits.
   (c) has a normal balance of a debit.
   (d) is increased by credits.

(SO 1) K 4. Accounts that normally have debit balances are:
   (a) assets, expenses, and revenues.
   (b) assets, expenses, and owner's capital.
   (c) assets, liabilities, and drawings.
   (d) assets, drawings, and expenses.

(SO 2) K 5. What is the correct sequence of steps in the recording process?
   (a) Analyzing transactions; preparing a trial balance
   (b) Analyzing transactions; entering transactions in a journal; posting transactions
   (c) Entering transactions in a journal; posting transactions; preparing a trial balance
   (d) Entering transactions in a journal; posting transactions; analyzing transactions

(SO 3) K 6. Which of these statements about a journal is false?
   (a) It is not a book of original entry.
   (b) It provides a chronological record of transactions.
   (c) It helps to locate errors because the debit and credit amounts for each entry can be easily compared.
   (d) It shows in one place the complete effect of a transaction.

(SO 4) K 7. A ledger:
   (a) contains only asset and liability accounts.
   (b) should show accounts in alphabetical order.
   (c) is a collection of the entire group of accounts maintained by a company.
   (d) is a book of original entry.

(SO 4) K 8. Posting:
   (a) is normally done before journalizing.
   (b) transfers ledger transaction data to the journal.
   (c) is an optional step in the recording process.
   (d) transfers journal entries to ledger accounts.

(SO 5) K 9. A trial balance:
   (a) is a list of accounts with their balances at a specific time.
   (b) proves that journalized transactions are accurate.
   (c) will not balance if a correct journal entry is posted twice.
   (d) proves that all transactions have been recorded.

(SO 5) AP 10. A trial balance will not balance if:
   (a) the collection of an account receivable is posted twice.
   (b) the purchase of supplies on account is debited to Supplies and credited to Cash.
   (c) a $100 cash drawing by the owner is debited to Drawings for $1,000 and credited to Cash for $100.
   (d) a $450 payment on account is debited to Accounts Payable for $45 and credited to Cash for $45.

The Navigator

Questions

(SO 1) C 1. What is an account? Will a company need more than one account? Explain.

(SO 1) K 2. What is debiting an account? What is crediting an account?

(SO 1) C 3. Jos Arcelus, a fellow student, says that the double-entry system means each transaction is recorded in two places: the journal and the ledger. Is Jos correct? Explain.

(SO 1) K 4. Explain the relationship between the normal balance in each type of account and the basic accounting equation.

(SO 1) K 5. Identify the normal balance for (a) asset accounts, (b) liability accounts, and (c) owner's equity accounts: (1) capital, (2) drawings, (3) revenue, and (4) expense. State the effect of debits and credits on each of these.

(SO 1) C 6. Kim Nguyen, a beginning accounting student, believes credit balances are favourable and debit balances are unfavourable. Is Kim correct? Discuss.

(SO 1) C 7. Why are increases to drawings and expenses recorded as debits?

(SO 1) C 8. Indicate whether the following accounts generally will have (a) debit entries only, (b) credit entries only, or (c) both debit and credit entries:
(a) Accounts Payable
(b) Accounts Receivable
(c) Cash
(d) Drawings
(e) Rent Expense
(f) Service Revenue

(SO 2) K 9. What is the accounting cycle? Describe the first three steps.

(SO 2) K 10. Jessica Gillies doesn't understand how to decide if a transaction should be recorded or not. Explain.

(SO 2) K 11. Give two examples of business documents that are analyzed when journal entries are being prepared.

(SO 2) K 12. Ben Benoit, a fellow student, is unclear about similarities and differences between using a manual system or a computerized system in the recording process. Briefly explain, including the benefit of a computerized system.

(SO 3) C 13. What is the difference between a simple and a compound journal entry? What rule must be followed when recording a compound entry so the accounting equation remains balanced?

(SO 3) C 14. A company receives cash from a customer. List three different accounts that could be credited and the circumstances under which each of these accounts are credited.

15. Amber Rose believes that accounting would be more efficient if transactions were recorded directly in the ledger accounts. Explain to Amber the advantages of first recording transactions in the journal, and then posting them to the ledger. (SO 3, 4) AP

16. Explain the differences between the format of a T account and the standard form of accounts. In your explanation, include the benefits of each format, and when each format is typically used. (SO 4) AP

17. What are the differences between a ledger and a chart of accounts? (SO 4) AP

18. What is a trial balance? What are its purposes? (SO 5) AP

19. Kap Shin is confused about how accounting information moves through the accounting system. He believes the flow of information is as follows: (SO 3, 4, 5) AP
(a) Debits and credits are posted to the ledger.
(b) The business transaction occurs.
(c) Information is entered in the journal.
(d) Financial statements are prepared.
(e) A trial balance is prepared.

Show Kap the correct flow of information.

20. Two students are discussing the use of a trial balance. They wonder if the following errors in different companies would prevent a trial balance from balancing. For each error, what would you tell the students? (SO 5) AN
(a) The bookkeeper debited Supplies for $750 and debited Accounts Payable for $750 for the purchase of supplies on account.
(b) Cash collected on account was debited to Cash for $1,000 and credited to Service Revenue for $1,000.
(c) A journal entry recording the payment of rent expense was posted to the general ledger as a $650 debit to rent expense and a $560 credit to Cash.

21. Jamal Nazari is doing the accounting for a company that has a December 31 year end. He is wondering if the heading on its trial balance should read "Year Ended December 31" or just "December 31." Which one is correct? Explain why. (SO 5) C

Brief Exercises

Calculate account balances.
(SO 1) AP

BE2–1   For the two accounts that follow, calculate the balance and indicate whether it is a debit or credit balance:

Accounts Receivable		Accounts Payable	
8,000	5,210	220	390
6,340	2,750	560	710
	2,390	175	850
		355	

Indicate type of account, financial statement classification and normal balance.
(SO 1) K

BE2–2   For each the following accounts, indicate (a) if the account is an asset, liability, or owner's equity account; (b) on which financial statement the account appears (balance sheet, income statement, or statement of owner's equity); and (c) whether the account would have a normal debit or credit balance.

1. Accounts Receivable
2. Accounts Payable
3. Equipment
4. Rent Expense
5. B. Damji, Drawings
6. Supplies
7. Unearned Revenue
8. Cash
9. Service Revenue
10. Prepaid Insurance

Indicate debit and credit effects and normal balance.
(SO 1) K

BE2–3   For each of the following accounts, indicate (a) the effect of a debit on the account, (b) the effect of a credit on the account, and (c) the normal balance:

1. Accounts Payable
2. Accounts Receivable
3. Cash
4. Office Equipment
5. J. Takamoto, Capital
6. J. Takamoto, Drawings
7. Notes Payable
8. Prepaid Rent
9. Insurance Expense
10. Salaries Expense
11. Service Revenue
12. Unearned Revenue

Indicate when to use debits and credits.
(SO 1) K

BE2–4   Indicate whether you would use a debit or credit to record the following changes:

1. Decrease in Accounts Receivable
2. Increase in Cash
3. Increase in Notes Payable
4. Increase in Salaries Expense
5. Increase in Drawings
6. Decrease in Equipment
7. Decrease in Accounts Payable
8. Increase in Service Revenue

Identify accounts to be debited and credited.
(SO 1) C

BE2–5   The following is a list of transactions. (a) Indicate the account debited and the account credited. (b) For each account, identify whether it is an asset, liability, or owner's equity account. For owner's equity accounts, state whether it is capital, drawings, revenue, or an expense.

1. Equipment is purchased on account.
2. Cash is received for services to be provided in the next month.
3. The current month's utility bill is paid in cash.
4. Cash is paid for office supplies.
5. Cash is received for services provided that day.
6. Customer is billed for services provided that day.
7. Joan Parker, the company's owner withdraws cash from the company's bank account for personal use.
8. Cash is paid to employees for the current month's wages.

Identify accounts to be debited and credited.
(SO 1) C

BE2–6   Ing Welding Company had the following transactions for June. Identify the accounts to be debited and credited for each transaction.

June 1 D. Ing invests $5,500 cash in a small welding business.
2 Buys equipment on account for $3,000.
3 Pays $500 to a landlord for June rent.
4 Pays $800 for a one-year insurance policy.
12 Bills T. Sargeant $350 for welding work done.
22 Receives $350 cash from T. Sargeant for worked billed on June 12.
25 Hires an employee to start work on July 2.
29 Pays for equipment purchased on June 2.

BE2–7 Fischer's Financial Consulting has the following transactions during August.

Identify accounts and basic debit/credit analysis. (SO 1) C

Aug. 1 Received $17,000 cash from the company's owner, Jim Fischer.
4 Paid rent in advance for three months, $3,600.
5 Purchased $440 of office supplies on account.
6 Received $950 from clients for services provided.
17 Billed clients $1,500 for services provided.
27 Paid secretary $750 salary.
29 Paid the company's owner, Jim Fischer, $500 cash for personal use.

For each transaction, indicate (a) the basic type of account to be debited and credited (asset, liability, owner's equity); (b) the specific accounts to debit and credit (for example, Cash, Service Revenue, Accounts Payable); and (c) whether each account is increased (+) or decreased (–), and by what amount. Use the following format, in which the first one has been done for you as an example:

	Account Debited			Account Credited		
	(a)	(b)	(c)	(a)	(b)	(c)
Transaction	Basic Type	Specific Account	Effect	Basic Type	Specific Account	Effect
Aug. 1	Asset	Cash	+ $17,000	Owner's Equity	J. Fischer, Capital	+ $17,000

BE2–8 Princess Printing Company had the following transactions with a customer during January: (1) performed services, such as printing flyers, and billed the customer; (2) collected cash on account from the customer; and (3) sent a statement at the end of the month, showing the balance owing, to the customer. Analyze each of these transactions and determine if they should be recorded or not. Explain why or why not for each transaction.

Analyze transactions. (SO 2) AP

BE2–9 Using the data in BE2–6 for Ing Welding Company, journalize the transactions.

Record transactions. (SO 3) AP

BE2–10 Using the data in BE2–7 for Fischer's Financial Consulting, journalize the transactions.

Record transactions. (SO 3) AP

BE2–11 Using T accounts, post the journal entries from BE2–10 to the general ledger.

Post journal entries. (SO 4) AP

BE2–12 Using T accounts, post the following journal entries to the general ledger.

Post journal entries. (SO 4) AP

GENERAL JOURNAL			
Date	Account title and explanation	Debit	Credit
Sept. 2	Cash	875	
	Service Revenue		875
4	Furniture	750	
	Accounts Payable		750
10	Accounts Receivable	1,200	
	Service Revenue		1,200
15	Salaries Expense	250	
	Cash		250
28	Cash	300	
	Accounts Receivable		300
30	Accounts Payable	550	
	Cash		550

Prepare trial balance.
(SO 5) AP

BE2–13   Use the ledger balances that follow to prepare a trial balance for the Pettipas Company at April 30, 2011. All account balances are normal.

Accounts payable	$ 3,900	Prepaid insurance	$1,500
Accounts receivable	3,000	Rent expense	800
C. Pettipas, capital	22,000	Salaries expense	4,000
C. Pettipas, drawings	1,200	Service revenue	8,100
Cash	8,400	Supplies	650
Equipment	14,600	Unearned revenue	150

Identify errors in trial balance.
(SO 5) AP

BE2–14   There are two errors in the following trial balance: (1) one account has been placed in the wrong column, and (2) there is a transposition error. Identify the two errors.

BOURQUE COMPANY Trial Balance December 31, 2010		
	Debit	Credit
Cash	$15,000	
Accounts receivable	1,800	
Prepaid insurance		$3,500
Accounts payable		2,000
Unearned revenue		2,200
L. Bourque, capital		15,400
L. Bourque, drawings	4,900	
Service revenue		27,500
Salaries expense	18,600	
Rent expense	2,400	
Totals	$42,700	$50,600

Exercises

Match concepts with
descriptions.
(SO 1, 2, 3, 4, 5) K

E2–1   Here are some of the concepts discussed in the chapter:

1. Account
2. Analyzing transactions
3. Chart of accounts
4. Credit
5. Debit
6. Journal
7. Journalizing
8. Ledger
9. Posting
10. Trial balance

Instructions

Match each concept with the best description below. Each concept may be used more than once, or may not be used at all.

(a) ___ The normal balance for liabilities
(b) ___ The first step in the recording process
(c) ___ The procedure of transferring journal entries to the ledger accounts
(d) ___ A record of increases and decreases in a specific asset, liability, or owner's equity item
(e) ___ The left side of an account
(f) ___ The entering of transaction data in the journal
(g) ___ A list of accounts and their balances at a specific time
(h) ___ Used to decrease the balance in an asset account
(i) ___ A list of all of a company's accounts
(j) ___ An accounting record where transactions are recorded in chronological (date) order

E2–2 Kobayashi Company has the following accounts:

Account	(a) Type of Account	(b) Financial Statement	(c) Normal Balance
1. Cash	Asset	Balance sheet	Debit
2. M. Kobayashi, Capital			
3. Accounts Payable			
4. Building			
5. Consulting Fee Revenue			
6. Insurance Expense			
7. Interest Earned			
8. Notes Receivable			
9. Prepaid Insurance			
10. Rent Expense			
11. Supplies			

Instructions

Complete the table. Identify (a) the type of account (e.g., asset, liability, owner's capital, drawings, revenue, expense); (b) what financial statement it is presented on; and (c) the normal balance of the account. The first one is done for you as an example.

E2–3 In the first month of business, Visser Interior Design Company had the following transactions:

Mar. 3 The owner, Lynne Visser, invested $10,000 cash in the business.
 6 Purchased a used car for $6,500 cash, for use in the business.
 7 Purchased supplies on account for $500.
 12 Billed customers $2,100 for services performed.
 21 Paid $225 cash for advertising the launch of the business.
 25 Received $1,200 cash from customers billed on March 12.
 28 Paid for the supplies purchased on March 7.
 30 Received $750 cash from a customer for services to be performed in April.
 31 Paid Lynne Visser $600 cash for her personal use.

Instructions

For each transaction indicate:
 (a) The basic type of account debited and credited (asset, liability, owner's equity)
 (b) The specific account debited and credited (Cash, Rent Expense, Service Revenue, etc.)
 (c) Whether each account is increased (+) or decreased (–), and by what amount
Use the following format, in which the first transaction is given as an example:

	Account Debited			Account Credited		
Transaction	(a) Basic Type	(b) Specific Account	(c) Effect	(a) Basic Type	(b) Specific Account	(c) Effect
Mar. 3	Asset	Cash	+$10,000	Owner's Equity	L. Visser, Capital	+$10,000

E2–4 Data for Visser Interior Design are presented in E2–3.

Instructions

Journalize the transactions.

Record transactions.
(SO 3) AP

E2–5 Selected transactions for Gardiner Real Estate Agency during its first month of business follow:

Oct. 1 Samuel Gardiner opens Gardiner Real Estate Agency with an investment of $14,000 cash and $3,000 of office equipment.

    2 Hired an administrative assistant at an annual salary of $24,000.

    3 Purchased additional office equipment for $4,450, paying $850 cash and signing a note payable for the balance.

  10 Received $350 cash as a fee for renting an apartment.

  16 Sold a house and lot to B. Rollins. The commission due from Rollins is $7,500 (it is not paid by Rollins at this time).

  27 Paid $700 for advertising costs during October.

  29 Received a $95 bill for telephone service during the month of October (the bill is paid in November).

  30 Paid the administrative assistant $2,000 in salary for October.

  31 Received $7,500 cash from B. Rollins for the October 16 transaction.

Instructions

Journalize the transactions.

Record revenue and expense transactions.
(SO 3) AP

E2–6 Selected transactions for Chaloux Group Company are presented below:

1. Shelly Chaloux, the owner, invested $7,500 cash in the company.
2. Provided services to a client and billed the client $1,600.
3. Collected $1,600 from the client billed in transaction 2.
4. Provided services to a client and received $875 cash.
5. Received $15,000 cash from the bank and signed a one-year, 5% note payable.
6. Received $500 cash from a client for services to be provided next year.
7. Paid $625 for the current month's rent.
8. Purchased $440 of office supplies on account.
9. Paid $1,640 for a one-year insurance policy.
10. Purchased $5,000 office equipment for cash.
11. Paid $800 cash for legal services to be received the following year.
12. Paid for the office supplies purchased on account in transaction 8.
13. Shelly Chaloux, the owner, withdrew $900 cash for personal use.
14. Paid the current month's telephone bill, $220.

Instructions

(a) Identify the transactions that created revenue for the Chaloux Group and journalize those transactions.
(b) Identify the transactions that created expenses for the Chaloux Group and journalize those transactions.
(c) Explain why the other transactions did not create either revenues or expenses.

Post journal entries.
(SO 4) AP

E2–7 Journal entries for Gardiner Real Estate Agency's transactions were prepared in E2–5.

Instructions

Post the journal entries to the general ledger, using T accounts.

E2–8 Csilla Revesz has prepared the following list of statements about the general ledger.

1. The general ledger contains all the asset and liability accounts, but no owner's equity accounts.
2. The general ledger is sometimes referred to as simply the ledger.
3. The accounts in the general ledger are arranged in alphabetical order.
4. Each account in the general ledger must be numbered.
5. The general ledger is a book of original entry.
6. The ledger shows all of the increases and decreases to each account.

Correct statements about the ledger.
(SO 4) K

Instructions

Identify each statement as true or false. If false, correct the statement.

E2–9 Fortin Co.'s ledger is as follows:

Record transactions and prepare trial balance.
(SO 3, 5) AP

Cash				
Oct. 1	1,200	Oct. 3	400
10	650	12	500
15	3,000	30	600
20	800	31	250
25	2,000	31	500

Accounts Receivable			
Oct. 6	1,000	Oct. 20	800
20	940		

Supplies	
Oct. 4	800

Equipment	
Oct. 3	5,400

Notes Payable		
	Oct. 3	5,000

Accounts Payable			
Oct. 12	500	Oct. 4	800
		28	400

A. Fortin, Capital		
	Oct. 1	1,200
	25	2,000

A. Fortin, Drawings	
Oct. 30	600

Service Revenue		
	Oct. 6	1,000
	10	650
	15	3,000
	20	940

Advertising Expense	
Oct. 28	400

Rent Expense	
Oct. 31	250

Store Expense	
Oct. 31	500

Instructions

(a) Journalize the October transactions, and give explanations for each entry.
(b) Determine the October 31, 2011, balance for each account. Prepare a trial balance at October 31, 2011.

E2–10 On July 31, 2011, Lee Meche, MD, had the following balances in the ledger for his medical practice: Cash $8,800; Accounts Receivable $2,750; Supplies $585; Equipment $15,550; Notes Payable $10,000; Accounts Payable $850; L. Meche, Capital $15,000; L. Meche, Drawings $5,125; Medical Fee Revenue $10,410; Rent Expense $1,200; and Salaries Expense $2,250. Selected transactions during August 2011 follow:

Post journal entries and prepare trial balance.
(SO 4, 5) AP

GENERAL JOURNAL					
Date	Account Titles and Explanation	Ref.	Debit	Credit
2011				
Aug. 1	Rent Expense		1,200	
	Cash			1,200
10	Accounts Payable		420	
	Cash			420
12	Cash		2,400	
	Accounts Receivable			2,400
25	Salaries Expense		2,250	
	Cash			2,250
30	Notes Payable		500	
	Interest Expense		40	
	Cash			540
31	Cash		5,910	
	Accounts Receivable		2,550	
	Medical Fee Revenue			8,460
31	L. Meche, Drawings		4,770	
	Cash			4,770

Instructions

(a) Create T accounts and enter the July 31 balances.

(b) Post the transactions to the T accounts. Create new T accounts if needed.

(c) Prepare a trial balance at August 31.

Analyze errors and their effect on the trial balance.
(SO 5) AN

E2–11   The accountant for Smistad Guitar Repair Company made a number of errors in journalizing and posting, as described below:

1. A credit posting of $400 to Accounts Receivable was omitted.
2. A debit posting of $750 for Prepaid Insurance was debited to Insurance Expense.
3. A collection on account of $100 was journalized and posted as a $100 debit to Cash and a $100 credit to Service Revenue.
4. A credit posting of $500 to Salaries Payable was made twice.
5. A cash purchase of supplies for $250 was journalized and posted as a $25 debit to Supplies and a $25 credit to cash.
6. A debit of $475 to Advertising Expense was posted as $457.

Instructions

Considering each error separately, indicate the following using the format below where error number 1 is given as an example.

(a) Will the trial balance be in balance?

(b) What is the amount of the error if the trial balance will not balance?

(c) Which trial balance column will have the larger total?

	(a)	(b)	(c)
Error	In Balance	Difference	Larger Column
1.	No	$400	Debit

Prepare corrected trial balance.
(SO 5) AP

E2–12   Terry Zelinski, the owner of Royal Mountain Tours, prepared the following trial balance at March 31, 2011.

Cash	$12,800	
Accounts receivable	4,090	
Supplies	840	
Equipment	7,350	
Accounts payable		$ 2,500
T. Zelinski, capital		24,000
T. Zelinski, drawings		3,650

Service revenue		6,750
Advertising expense	3,700	
Salaries expense	400	
Totals	$29,180	$36,900

A review shows that Terry made the following errors in the accounting records:
1. A purchase of $400 of supplies on account was recorded as a credit to cash. The debit entry was correct.
2. A $100 credit to accounts receivable was posted as $1,000.
3. A journal entry to record service revenue of $620 earned on account was not prepared or posted.
4. A journal entry to record the payment of $240 for an advertising expense was correctly prepared but the credit to cash was posted as a debit. The debit to advertising expense was properly posted.

Instructions

Prepare the correct trial balance at March 31, 2011, using the format shown in the chapter. (*Hint*: You should also make sure that the account balances are recorded in the correct columns on the trial balance.)

E2–13   The trial balance of O'Callaghan's Counselling Services, at its year end July 31, 2011, is presented below with the accounts in alphabetical order.

Prepare financial statements. (SO 5) AP

Accounts	Debit	Credit
Accounts payable		$ 4,515
Accounts receivable	$ 3,670	
C. O'Callaghan, capital		34,670
C. O'Callaghan, drawings	28,990	
Cash	2,895	
Equipment	29,450	
Insurance expense	1,020	
Prepaid insurance	340	
Rent expense	5,440	
Salaries expense	22,770	
Service revenue		58,090
Supplies	395	
Supplies expense	2,980	
Unearned revenue		675
	$97,950	$97,950

Instructions

Prepare an income statement, statement of owner's equity, and balance sheet.

Problems: Set A

P2–1A   Miranda Brock, Lawyer, has the following accounts:

Identify type of account, financial statement, normal balances, and debits and credits.
(SO 1) K

Accounts Payable	Land	Rent Revenue
Accounts Receivable	Legal Fees Earned	Salaries Expense
Building	M. Brock, Capital	Salaries Payable
Cash	M. Brock, Drawings	Supplies
Equipment	Notes Receivable	Supplies Expense
Insurance Expense	Prepaid Insurance	Unearned Legal Fees
Interest Earned	Rent Expense	

Instructions

For each of these accounts, identify (a) the type of account (e.g., asset, liability, owner's capital, drawings, revenue, expense); (b) what financial statement it is presented on; (c) the normal balance of the account; (d) whether the account is increased by a debit or credit; and (e) whether the account is decreased by a debit or credit. Use the following format, in which the first one is done for you as an example.

	(a)	(b)	(c)	(d)	(e)
Account	Type of Account	Financial Statement	Normal Balance	Increase	Decrease
Accounts payable	Liability	Balance sheet	Credit	Credit	Debit

Taking It Further   Explain the relationship between the normal balance in each type of account and the basic accounting equation.

Perform transaction analysis and journalize transactions.
(SO 1, 2, 3) AP

P2–2A   JB Paint Designs began operations on April 1, 2011. The company completed the following transactions in its first month:

Apr. 1 The owner, Jay Butterfield, invested $13,500 cash in the company.
      2 Purchased a one-year insurance policy effective April 1, and paid the first month's premium of $115.
      2 Purchased painting equipment for $3,000 cash.
      3 Purchased $375 of supplies on account.
      7 Paid cash for $870 of advertising expenses.
      8 Finished a painting project for Maya Angelina and billed her $750.
     10 Received a $1,500 contract from a customer, SUB Terrain Inc., to paint its new office space. SUB Terrain will pay when the project is complete.
     25 Completed the contract with SUB Terrain Inc. from April 10 and collected the amount owing.
     27 Collected the amount owing from April 8.
     28 The owner, Jay Butterfield, withdrew $870 cash for his personal use.
     30 Paid for the supplies purchased on account on April 3.

Instructions

(a) For each transaction, indicate: (1) the basic type of account debited and credited (asset, liability, or owner's equity); (2) the specific account debited and credited (Cash, Rent Expense, Service Revenue, etc.); and (3) whether each account is increased (+) or decreased (−), and by what amount. Use the following format, in which the first transaction is given as an example:

	Account Debited			Account Credited		
	(1)	(2)	(3)	(1)	(2)	(3)
	Basic	Specific		Basic	Specific	
Transaction	Type	Account	Effect	Type	Account	Effect
Apr. 1	Asset	Cash	+$13,500	Owner's Equity	J. Butterfield, Capital	+$13,500

(b) Prepare a journal entry for each transaction.

Taking It Further   Jay doesn't understand why a debit increases the cash account and yet a credit to J. Butterfield, Capital increases that account. He reasons that debits and credits cannot both increase account balances. Explain to Jay why he is wrong.

P2–3A Bucket Club Miniature Golf and Driving Range was opened on May 1. The following events and transactions are for May:

Journalize transactions. (SO 3) AP

May 1 Amin Mawani, the owner, invested $70,000 cash in the business.

3 Purchased Lee's Golf Land for $210,000. The price consists of land, $100,000; building, $70,000; and equipment, $40,000. Paid $60,000 cash and signed a note payable for the balance.

4 Purchased golf clubs and other equipment for $6,000 from Woods Company on account.

5 Advertised the opening of Bucket Club Miniature Golf and Driving Range, paying $1,800.

6 Paid $2,760 cash for a one-year insurance policy.

15 Collected $2,500 cash from customers for golf fees earned.

19 Paid Woods Company $5,000 for the items purchased on May 4.

20 Billed a customer, Deer Fern Inc., $500 for golf fees earned. Deer Fern Inc. agreed to pay the amount owing in 10 days.

30 Paid salaries of $2,445.

30 Received $500 from Deer Fern Inc. for the May 20 transaction.

31 Collected $4,000 cash from customers for golf fees earned.

31 Paid $750 of interest on the note payable.

31 Paid Amin Mawani $1,750 for his personal use.

The company's chart of accounts includes the following accounts: Cash; Accounts Receivable; Prepaid Insurance; Land; Buildings; Equipment; Accounts Payable; Notes Payable; A. Mawani, Capital; A. Mawani, Drawings; Golf Fees Earned; Advertising Expense; Salaries Expense; and Interest Expense.

Instructions

Journalize the May transactions.

Taking It Further After Amin has reviewed the journal entries, he complains that they don't seem to be very useful. Explain to Amin the purpose of the journal entries and the next step in the accounting cycle. Include in your answer whether or not Amin will find any useful information after the next step is completed.

P2–4A Francesca Virmani, a licensed architect, formed a company called Virmani Architects on April 1, 2011. The following events and transactions occurred in the first month:

Journalize transactions, post, and prepare trial balance. (SO 3, 4, 5) AP

Apr. 1 Francesca invested $15,000 cash and $6,000 of office equipment in the company.

2 Hired a secretary-receptionist at a salary of $1,900 monthly.

3 Paid office rent for the month, $950.

3 Purchased architectural supplies on account from Halo Company, $1,750.

10 Completed blueprints on garage for Pro-Built Construction and billed them $975.

20 Received $1,200 cash for services performed for a client, P. Donahue.

21 Received $800 cash from Pro-Built Construction for work completed on April 10.

23 Received a $1,000 cash advance from R. Sherstabetoff for the design of a new home.

28 Paid $900 to Halo Company on account.

29 Paid secretary-receptionist for the month, $1,900.

29 Paid Francesca $1,500 for her personal use.

30 The telephone bill for April was $155. The company will pay it in May.

Virmani Architects uses the following chart of accounts: No. 101 Cash; No. 112 Accounts Receivable; No. 126 Supplies; No. 151 Office Equipment; No. 201 Accounts Payable; No. 209 Unearned Revenue; No. 301 F. Virmani, Capital; No. 306 F. Virmani , Drawings; No. 400 Service Revenue; No. 726 Rent Expense; No. 729 Salaries Expense; and No. 737 Telephone Expense.

Instructions

(a) Journalize the transactions.
(b) Post to the ledger accounts. Use the standard form of account.
(c) Prepare a trial balance as at April 30, 2011.

Taking It Further   Francesca asks how to decide whether a transaction should be recorded or not. Provide her with a general rule and include specific reference to the May 2 and May 30 transactions in your answer.

Journalize transactions, post, and prepare trial balance.
(SO 3, 4, 5) AP

P2–5A   Abramson Financial Services was formed on May 1, 2011. The following events and transactions are from its first month:

May	1	Jacob Abramson invested $40,000 cash and office equipment worth $10,000 in the company.
	1	Hired one employee to work in the office for a salary of $2,475 per month.
	2	Paid $3,300 cash for a one-year insurance policy.
	5	Signed a two-year rental agreement on an office and paid $4,800 cash. Half was for the May 2011 rent and the other half was for the final month's rent. (*Hint*: The portion for the final month is considered prepaid rent.)
	8	Purchased additional office equipment costing $17,000. A cash payment of $7,000 was made immediately. Signed a note payable for the balance.
	9	Purchased office supplies for $500 cash.
	15	Purchased more office supplies for $750 on account.
	17	Completed a contract for a client for $3,000 on account.
	22	Paid $250 for May's telephone bill.
	25	Completed services for a client and immediately collected $1,100.
	26	Paid Jacob Abramson $1,600 cash for his personal use.
	28	Collected $2,500 from the client billed on May 17.
	30	Paid for the office supplies purchased on account on May 15.
	30	Paid $50 interest expense on the note payable.
	31	Received a cash advance of $500 for services to be completed in June.
	31	Paid the employee's monthly salary, $2,475.

Instructions

(a) Prepare journal entries to record the transactions.
(b) Post the journal entries to ledger accounts. Use T accounts.
(c) Prepare a trial balance as at May 31, 2011.

Taking It Further   Jacob asks if the change in his cash account balance, from the beginning to the end of the month, is equal to his profit or loss for the month. Explain to Jacob whether or not this is true and why.

Journalize transactions, post, and prepare trial balance.
(SO 3, 4, 5) AP

P2–6A   Vista Theatre, owned by Nadiya Fedkovych, is unique as it only shows movies that are part of a theme with two or more sequels. As at May 31, 2011, the ledger of Vista Theatre showed the following: Cash, $15,000; Land, $85,000; Buildings, $70,000; Equipment, $20,000; Accounts Payable, $5,000; Mortgage Payable, $118,000; and N. Fedkovych, Capital, $67,000. In June, the following events and transactions occurred:

| Jun. | 2 | Rented three *Batman* movies, to be shown in the first three weeks of June. The film rental was $22,000. Of that amount, $10,000 was paid in cash and the balance will be paid on June 10. |

2 Hired M. Brewer to operate the concession stand. Brewer agreed to pay Vista Theatre 18% of gross concession receipts, on the last day of each month, for the right to operate the concession stand.

3 Ordered three *Shrek* movies, to be shown the last 10 days of June. The film rental will cost $900 per night.

9 Received $16,300 cash from customers for admissions.

10 Paid the balance due on the *Batman* rental.

10 Paid the accounts payable owing at the end of May.

11 Paid advertising expenses, $950.

20 Received $16,600 cash from admissions.

21 Received the *Shrek* movies and paid one half of the $9,000 ($900 × 10 nights) rental fee. The balance is to be paid on July 1.

29 Paid salaries of $4,200.

30 Received statement from Brewer showing gross receipts from concessions of $8,500 and the balance due to Vista Theatre of $1,530 ($8,500 × 18%) for March. Brewer paid one half the balance due and will pay the rest on July 5.

30 Received $18,400 cash from admissions.

30 Made a $1,725 mortgage payment. Of this amount, $1,250 is a principal payment, and $475 is interest on the mortgage.

In addition to the accounts identified above, Vista Theatre's ledger includes the following: Accounts Receivable; Admission Revenue; Concession Revenue; Advertising Expense; Film Rental Expense; Interest Expense; and Salaries Expense.

Instructions

(a) Journalize the June transactions.
(b) Enter the beginning balances in the ledger as at June 1. Use the standard form of account.
(c) Post the June journal entries to the ledger.
(d) Prepare a trial balance at the end of June.

Taking It Further A friend of yours is considering buying Vista Theatre from the current owner. Using the information in the trial balance, comment on whether or not this may be a sound company for your friend to purchase.

P2–7A Collegiate Laundry has a December 31 year end. The company's trial balance on November 30, 2011, is as follows:

Journalize transactions, post, and prepare trial balance.
(SO 3, 4, 5) AP

COLLEGIATE LAUNDRY		
Trial Balance		
November 30, 2011		
	Debit	Credit
Cash	$ 2,800	
Accounts receivable	6,800	
Supplies	1,100	
Laundry equipment	21,000	
Accounts payable		$ 5,765
Unearned revenue		1,300
J. Cochrane, capital		19,500
J. Cochrane, drawings	33,000	
Laundry revenue		69,900
Insurance expense	4,015	
Rent expense	9,350	
Salaries expense	11,525	
Utilities expense	6,875	
	$96,465	$96,465

The December transactions were as follows:

Dec. 1 Borrowed $5,000 cash from the First Financial Bank and signed a note payable.
2 Purchased a used pressing machine for $5,500 cash from another company. The machine was probably worth $7,000, but the other company needed the cash and was anxious to sell it.
2 Paid December rent, $850.
4 Received $5,550 cash from customers in payment of their accounts.
7 Paid the $365 monthly insurance premium.
9 Paid $2,900 to creditors on account.
10 Performed $800 of services for customers who had paid in advance in November.
11 Received $1,350 cash from customers for services provided.
15 Purchased $400 of supplies on account.
20 Billed customers $5,750 for services provided.
22 Paid employee salaries of $1,450 (includes a year-end bonus of $300).
24 Owner withdrew $3,000 for personal use.
29 Received $425 cash from a customer for services to be provided in January.
30 Paid the bank $525. Of this amount, $25 is interest and the remainder is a principal payment.
31 The bill for December utilities was $615. The bill will be paid in January.

Instructions

(a) Journalize the December transactions.
(b) Enter the November 30 balances in ledger accounts. Use T accounts.
(c) Post the December journal entries to the T accounts. You may need to add new accounts for some of the transactions.
(d) Prepare a trial balance at December 31, 2011.

Taking It Further   Comment on the company's cash balance. What concerns or suggestions do you have for the company to consider in January?

Prepare financial statements.
(SO 5) AP

P2–8A   Refer to the trial balance for Abramson Financial Services prepared in P2–5A part (c).

Instructions

(a) Prepare an income statement for May.
(b) Prepare a statement of owner's equity for May.
(c) Prepare a balance sheet at the end of May 2011.

Taking It Further   Discuss how well the company performed in its first month of operations.

Journalize transactions, post, and prepare trial balance.
(SO 3, 4, 5) AP

P2–9A   Leo Mataruka owns and manages a computer repair service. It had the following trial balance on December 31, 2010 (its fiscal year end):

CYBERDYNE REPAIR SERVICE
Trial Balance
December 31, 2010

	Debit	Credit
Cash	$ 2,000	
Accounts receivable	16,500	
Repair parts inventory	16,000	
Shop equipment	28,000	
Accounts payable		$23,000
Unearned revenue		2,000
L. Mataruka, capital		37,500
Totals	$62,500	$62,500

A summary of transactions for January 2011 follows:

Jan.   2 Leo went to his bank and got a personal loan of $6,000 by signing a note payable.

   3 Leo transferred $5,000 from his personal bank account into Cyberdyne's bank account.

   4 Purchased additional repair parts inventory on account, $5,200.

   6 Miscellaneous expenses were paid in cash, $1,300.

   10 Collected $7,200 cash from customers on account.

   15 Cash was paid to creditors on account, $6,500.

   19 Advertising costs were paid in cash, $600.

   20 Purchased additional equipment for $4,800 cash.

   29 Repair services done in January were for $5,000 cash and $15,000 on account.

   30 Wages for January were paid in cash, $2,900.

   30 Paid January and February's rent, for a total of $1,800.

   31 Leo withdrew $500 cash. He used the cash to make a payment on his personal loan.

   31 A total of $4,500 of the repair parts inventory was used in the month. (*Hint*: Debit this to Repair Parts Expense.)

Instructions

(a) Prepare journal entries to record each of Cyberdyne's January transactions.

(b) Open ledger accounts for each of the accounts listed in the trial balance, and enter the December 31, 2010, balances. Use T accounts.

(c) Post the journal entries to the accounts in the ledger.

(d) Prepare a trial balance as at January 31, 2011.

Taking It Further   Is the purchase of the repair parts inventory a debit to an asset or an expense? Explain.

P2–10A   Refer to the trial balance prepared in part (d) of P2–9A for Cyberdyne Repair Service.

Prepare financial statements. (SO 5) AP

Instructions

Use the trial balance to do the following:

(a) Prepare an income statement for Cyberdyne Repair Service.

(b) Prepare a statement of owner's equity.

(c) Prepare a balance sheet.

Taking It Further   Leo does not understand (1) why even though his business is profitable, he still has to invest additional cash; and (2) why he was able to withdraw only $500 cash. Based on your review of the financial statements, what explanations can you give him?

P2–11A   The ledger of Super Delivery Service has the following account balances at the company's year end, August 31, 2011:

Prepare trial balance and financial statements. (SO 5) AP

Accounts Payable	$ 3,235	Repair Expense	1,580
Accounts Receivable	4,275	Salaries Expense	5,665
Cash	?	Salaries Payable	925
Delivery Equipment	49,720	Service Revenue	37,780
Gas and Oil Expense	12,145	Supplies	265
Insurance Expense	2,020	Supplies Expense	2,650
Interest Expense	975	J. Rowe, Capital	48,750
Notes Payable	19,500	J. Rowe, Drawings	24,400
Prepaid Insurance	405	Unearned Revenue	675

Instructions

(a) Prepare a trial balance, with the accounts arranged in ledger (financial statement) order, as illustrated in the chapter, and determine the missing amount for Cash.

(b) Prepare an income statement, statement of owner's equity, and balance sheet.

Taking It Further   The owner, Jan Rowe, is not sure how much cash she can withdraw from the company each year. After reviewing the financial statements, comment on the amount she withdrew this year.

Analyze errors and effects on trial balance.
(SO 5) AN

P2–12A   A co-op student, working for Insidz Co., recorded the company's transactions for the month. At the end of the month, the owner of Insidz Co. reviewed the student's work and had some questions about the following transactions:

1. Insidz Co. received $255 cash from a customer on account, which was recorded as a debit to Cash of $255 and a credit to Accounts Receivable of $552.
2. A service provided for cash was posted as a debit to Cash of $2,000 and a credit to Accounts Receivable of $2,000.
3. A credit of $750 for interest earned was neither recorded nor posted. The debit was recorded and posted correctly.
4. The debit to record $1,000 of drawings was posted to the Salary Expense account. The credit was posted correctly.
5. Services of $325 were provided to a customer on account. The co-op student debited Accounts Receivable $325 and credited Service Revenue $325.
6. A purchase of supplies for $2,500 on account was recorded as a debit to Supplies and a debit to Accounts Payable.
7. Insidz Co. received a cash advance of $500 from a customer for work to be done next month. Cash was debited $500 but there was no credit because the co-op student was not sure what to credit.
8. A cash payment of $495 for salaries was recorded as a debit to Salaries Expense and a credit to Salaries Payable.
9. Insidz Co. purchased $2,600 of equipment on account and made a $6,200 debit to Equipment and a $6,200 credit to Accounts Payable.
10. A $650 utility bill for the month was received at the end of the month. It was not recorded because it had not been paid.

Instructions

(a) Indicate which transactions are correct and which are incorrect.

(b) For each error identified in (a), answer the following:

1. Will the trial balance be in balance?
2. Which account(s) will be incorrectly stated because of the error?
3. For each account you identified in (2) as being incorrect, is the account overstated or understated? By how much?
4. Is the debit column total of the trial balance stated correctly? If not, does correcting the errors increase or decrease the total and by how much?
5. Is the credit column total of the trial balance stated correctly? If not, does correcting the errors increase or decrease the total and by how much?

Taking It Further Your best friend thinks it is a waste of time to correct all of the above errors. Your friend reasons that as long as the trial balance is balanced, then there is no need to correct an error. Do you agree or disagree with your friend? Explain, using at least two of the above errors to make your points.

P2–13A The trial balance of Winter Co. does not balance:

Prepare correct trial balance. (SO 4, 5) AN

WINTER CO.
Trial Balance
June 30, 2011

	Debit	Credit
Cash		$ 2,635
Accounts receivable	$ 1,942	
Supplies	500	
Equipment	6,400	
Accounts payable		2,200
Unearned fees	1,765	
F. Winter, capital		11,231
F. Winter, drawings	800	
Fees earned		2,680
Salaries expense	3,000	
Office expense	1,010	
	$15,417	$18,746

Your review of the ledger reveals that each account has a normal balance. You also discover the following errors:

1. Cash received from a customer on account was debited to Cash for $750 and Accounts Receivable was credited for the same amount. The actual collection was $570.
2. The purchase of supplies on account for $360 was recorded as a debit to Equipment for $360 and a credit to Accounts Payable for $360.
3. Services of $890 were performed on account for a client. Accounts Receivable was debited for $89 and Fees Earned was credited for $890.
4. A debit posting to Office Expense of $700 was not done.
5. A payment on account for $205 was credited to Cash for $205 and debited to Accounts Payable for $502.
6. The withdrawal of $400 cash for Winter's personal use was debited to Salaries Expense for $400 and credited to Cash for $400.
7. A transposition error (reversal of digits) was made when copying the balance in the Fees Earned to the trial balance. The correct balance recorded in the account was $2,860.
8. The general ledger contained a Prepaid Insurance account with a debit balance of $565.

Instructions

Prepare a correct trial balance.

Taking It Further After the trial balance is corrected for the above errors, could there still be errors? Explain why or why not.

Problems: Set B

Identify type of account, financial statement, normal balances, and debits and credits.
(SO 1) K

P2–1B Walter Isaacson, Medical Practice, has the following accounts:

Wages Payable	Office Equipment
Wages Expense	Notes Payable
W. Isaacson, Drawings	Medical Fees Earned
W. Isaacson, Capital	Interest Expense
Unearned Medical Fees	Insurance Expense
Rent Revenue	Furniture
Rent Expense	Computer
Prepaid Rent	Cash
Office Supplies Expense	Accounts Receivable
Office Supplies	Accounts Payable

Instructions

For each of these accounts, identify (a) the type of account (e.g., asset, liability, owner's capital, drawings, revenue, expense); (b) what financial statement it is presented on; (c) the normal balance of the account; (d) whether the account is increased by a debit or credit; and (e) whether the account is decreased by a debit or credit. Use the following format, in which the first one is done for you as an example.

Account	(a) Type of Account	(b) Financial Statement	(c) Normal Balance	(d) Increase	(e) Decrease
Wages payable	Liability	Balance sheet	Credit	Credit	Debit

Taking It Further Explain the relationship between the normal balance in each type of account and the basic accounting equation.

Perform transaction analysis and journalize transactions.
(SO 1, 2, 3) AP

P2–2B Battistella Couture & Design Co. began operations in 2009. During February 2011, the company had the following transactions:

Feb. 1 Paid February rent, $475.

2 Purchased sewing supplies for $250 on account.

6 Finished sewing a suit, delivered it to the customer, and collected $750 cash.

7 Received an order from another customer to design and sew a leather jacket for $885.

10 Agreed to sew a wedding dress for a customer. Received $250 cash from the customer as a down payment.

12 The owner of the company, Karen Battistella, withdrew $700 cash for personal use.

15 Finished sewing the leather jacket (see February 7 transaction) and billed the customer.

25 Paid for the supplies purchased on February 2.

27 The customer billed on February 15 paid the amount owing.

28 Borrowed $2,000 cash from the bank and signed a note payable for the amount owing.

28 Purchased a new sewing machine for $2,500 cash.

Instructions

(a) For each transaction, indicate: (1) the basic type of account debited and credited (asset, liability, or owner's equity); (2) the specific account debited and credited (Cash, Rent Expense, Service Revenue, etc.); and (3) whether each account is increased (+) or decreased (−), and by what amount. Use the following format, in which the first transaction is given as an example:

	Account Debited			Account Credited		
	Basic	Specific		Basic	Specific	
Transaction	Type	Account	Effect	Type	Account	Effect
Feb. 1	Owner's Equity	Rent Expense	+ $475	Asset	Cash	− $475

(b) Prepare a journal entry for each transaction.

Taking It Further   Karen is confused about why debits are used to record expenses and why credits are used to decrease cash. Explain.

P2–3B   Mountain Adventure Biking Park was started on April 1 by Dustin Tanner. The following events and transactions are for June:

Journalize transactions.
(SO 3) AP

Apr.   1   Tanner invested $50,000 cash in the business.

3   Purchased an out-of-use ski hill for $320,000, paying $25,000 cash and signing a note payable for the balance. The $320,000 purchase price consisted of land, $175,000; building, $80,000; and equipment, $65,000.

8   Incurred advertising expenses of $2,800 on account.

13   Paid $5,500 cash for a one-year insurance policy.

15   Received $2,700 cash from customers for admission fees.

16   Paid salaries to employees, $1,800.

20   Billed a customer, Celtic Fern Ltd., $1,500 for admission fees for exclusive use of the park that day. Celtic Fern Ltd. agreed to pay the amount owing within 10 days.

22   Hired a park manager at a salary of $4,000 per month, effective May 1.

29   Received $1,500 cash from Celtic Fern Ltd. for the April 20 transaction.

30   Received $5,900 cash for admission fees.

30   Paid $1,650 on account for advertising expenses incurred on April 8.

30   Paid $1,250 interest expense on the note payable.

30   Paid Dustin Tanner $600 cash for his personal use.

The company's chart of accounts includes the following accounts: Cash; Accounts Receivable; Prepaid Insurance; Land; Building; Equipment; Accounts Payable; Notes Payable; D. Tanner, Capital; D. Tanner, Drawings; Admissions Revenue; Advertising Expense; Salaries Expense; and Interest Expense.

Instructions

Journalize the April transactions.

Taking It Further   After Dustin has reviewed the journal entries, he complains that they don't seem to be very useful. Explain to Dustin the purpose of the journal entries and the next step in the accounting cycle. Include in your answer whether or not Dustin will find any useful information after the next step is completed.

Journalize transactions, post, and prepare trial balance.
(SO 3, 4, 5) AP

P2–4B   Ghita Mancini, a CGA, opened an accounting practice, Mancini Accounting Services, on May 1, 2011. The following events and transactions occurred in the first month of operations.

May	1	Ghita invested $20,000 cash and office equipment worth $8,500 in the business.
	1	Paid $950 for office rent for May.
	2	Hired a secretary-receptionist at a salary of $2,400 per month.
	3	Purchased $950 of office supplies on account from Read Supply Company.
	11	Completed a tax assignment and billed Arnold Co. $2,275 for services rendered.
	17	Completed accounting services and collected $1,350 cash from the client.
	21	Received $1,200 cash from Arnold Co. for the May 11 transaction.
	22	Received a $3,500 cash advance on a management consulting engagement with Arch Co.
	23	Paid 60% of the balance due to Read Supply Company.
	30	The May telephone bill was $215. It will be paid in June.
	31	Paid the secretary-receptionist $2,400 salary for the month.
	31	Paid Ghita $925 cash for her personal use.

Mancini Accounting Services uses the following chart of accounts: No. 101 Cash; No. 112 Accounts Receivable; No. 126 Office Supplies; No. 151 Office Equipment; No. 201 Accounts Payable; No. 209 Unearned Accounting Fees; No. 301 G. Mancini, Capital; No. 306 G. Mancini, Drawings; No. 400 Accounting Fees Earned; No. 726 Rent Expense; No. 729 Salaries Expense; and No. 737 Telephone Expense.

Instructions

(a) Journalize the transactions.
(b) Post to the ledger accounts. Use the standard form of account.
(c) Prepare a trial balance at May 31, 2011.

Taking It Further   Ghita asks how to decide whether a transaction should be recorded or not. Provide her with a general rule and include specific reference to the May 2 and May 30 transactions in your answer.

Journalize transactions, post, and prepare trial balance.
(SO 3, 4, 5) AP

P2–5B   Kiersted Financial Services was formed on November 1, 2011. During the month of November, the following events and transactions occurred:

Nov.	1	Haakon Kiersted, the owner, invested $35,000 cash and office equipment in the company. The equipment had originally cost Haakon $25,000 but was currently worth $12,000.
	2	Hired one employee to work in the office for a monthly salary of $2,825.
	3	Signed a three-year contract to lease office space for $2,140 per month. Paid the first and last month's rent in cash. (*Hint*: The payment for the final month's rent should be considered an asset and be recorded in Prepaid Rent.)
	4	Purchased a one-year insurance policy for $4,740 to be paid in monthly instalments on the fourth day of each month. Paid the first month's premium.
	5	Purchased additional office equipment for $18,000. Paid $6,000 cash and signed a note payable for the balance.
	6	Purchased supplies for $1,550 on account.
	7	Purchased additional supplies for $475 cash.
	16	Completed services for a customer and immediately collected $990.
	20	Completed services for two customers and billed them a total of $4,500.
	26	Paid $1,000 for the office supplies purchased on account on November 6.
	27	The telephone bill for November was $220. It will be paid in December.
	27	Received a $750 cash advance from a customer for services to be provided in December.

29 Collected $2,800 from one of the customers billed on November 20.
30 Paid $60 interest on the note payable.
30 Paid the employee's monthly salary, $2,825.
30 Paid Haakon Kiersted $700 for his personal use.
30 Paid Sony Ltd. for a new sound system for Haakon's home, $1,150 cash.

Instructions

(a) Prepare journal entries to record the transactions.
(b) Post the journal entries to T accounts.
(c) Prepare a trial balance as at November 30, 2011.

Taking It Further   Haakon asks if the change in his cash account balance from the beginning to the end of the month is equal to his profit or loss for the month. Explain to Haakon whether or not this is true and why.

P2–6B   Highland Theatre is owned by Finnean Ferguson. At June 30, 2011, the ledger showed the following: Cash $6,000; Land $90,000; Buildings $80,000; Equipment $25,000; Accounts Payable $5,000; Mortgage Payable $125,000; and F. Ferguson, Capital $71,000. During July, the following events and transactions occurred:

Journalize transactions, post, and prepare trial balance.
(SO 3, 4, 5) AP

July   2 Paid film rental of $800 on first movie to run in July.
2 Paid advertising expenses, $625.
3 Ordered two additional films at $750 each.
5 Highland Theatre contracted with Seibert Company to operate a concession stand. Seibert agrees to pay Highland Theatre 20% of gross concession receipts, payable monthly, for the right to operate the concession stand.
10 Received $1,950 cash from admissions.
11 Made $2,000 principal payment on mortgage. Also paid $500 interest on the mortgage.
12 Paid $350 cash to have the projection equipment repaired.
15 Received one of the films ordered on July 3 and was billed $750. The film will be shown in July.
25 Received $5,500 cash from customers for admissions.
26 Paid $3,200 of the accounts payable.
28 Prepaid a $700 rental on a special film to be shown in August.
30 Paid Finnean Ferguson $1,200 for his personal use.
31 Received a statement from Seibert: it shows gross concession receipts of $2,600 and a balance due to Highland Theatre of $520 ($2,600 × 20%) for July. Seibert paid one half of the balance due and will pay the rest on August 5.
31 Paid salaries, $1,900.

In addition to the accounts identified above, Highland Theatre's ledger includes the following: Accounts Receivable; Prepaid Rentals; F. Ferguson, Drawings; Admission Revenue; Concession Revenue; Advertising Expense; Film Rental Expense; Repairs Expense; Salaries Expense; and Interest Expense.

Instructions

(a) Journalize the July transactions.
(b) Enter the beginning balances in the ledger as at June 30. Use the standard form of account.
(c) Post the July journal entries to the ledger.
(d) Prepare a trial balance at the end of July 2011.

Taking It Further   A friend of yours is considering buying Highland Theatre from the current owner. Using the information in the trial balance, comment on whether or not this may be a sound company for your friend to purchase.

Journalize transactions, post, and prepare trial balance. (SO 3, 4, 5) AP

P2–7B Brisebois Dry Cleaners has a July 31 year end. The company's trial balance on June 30, 2011, is as follows:

BRISEBOIS DRY CLEANERS Trial Balance June 30, 2011		
	Debit	Credit
Cash	$ 11,660	
Note receivable	5,000	
Accounts receivable	5,845	
Supplies	3,975	
Equipment	31,480	
Accounts payable		$ 13,090
Unearned revenue		1,920
E. Brisebois, capital		55,920
E. Brisebois, drawings	37,050	
Dry cleaning revenue		109,455
Salaries expense	57,750	
Rent expense	11,385	
Repair expense	1,720	
Utilities expense	14,520	
Totals	$180,385	$180,385

The July transactions were as follows:

July 2 Paid July rent, $1,035.
   3 Purchased new equipment with a suggested manufacturer's price of $5,500. After much negotiating, paid $1,500 cash and signed a note payable for $3,600.
   5 Collected $3,285 cash on the June 30 accounts receivable.
  10 Performed $1,920 of services for customers who paid in advance in June.
  11 Received $4,730 cash from customers for services performed.
  13 Paid $9,742 to creditors on account.
  14 Purchased supplies for $495 on account.
  24 Billed customers $5,950 for services performed.
  25 Collected the $5,000 note receivable plus interest of $200.
  26 Signed a contract with a nursing home to provide laundry services at a rate of $1,650 per month starting in August. The first payment will be collected on August 1.
  27 Received $650 cash from a customer for services to be provided in August.
  28 The utility bill for July is $1,320. This bill will be paid in August.
  29 Paid employee salaries of $5,250.
  31 Paid the owner, E. Brisebois, $3,370 cash for personal use.
  31 Paid $300 of the note payable plus $20 interest.

Instructions

(a) Journalize the transactions.
(b) Enter the June 30 balances in T accounts.
(c) Post the July journal entries to the T accounts. You may need to add new accounts for some of the transactions.
(d) Prepare a trial balance at July 31, 2011.

Prepare financial statements. (SO 5) AP

Taking It Further   Comment on the company's cash balance. What concerns and suggestions do you have for the company to consider in August?

P2–8B   Refer to the trial balance prepared for Kiersted Financial Services in P2–5B part (c).

Instructions

(a) Prepare an income statement.
(b) Prepare a statement of owner's equity.
(c) Prepare a balance sheet.

Taking It Further Discuss how well the company did in its first month of operations.

P2–9B Gary Hobson owns and manages Soft-Q Repair Service, which fixes computers. Soft-Q had the following trial balance at March 31, 2011 (its year end):

Journalize transactions, post, and prepare trial balance.
(SO 3, 4, 5) AP

SOFT-Q REPAIR SERVICE Trial Balance March 31, 2011		
	Debit	Credit
Cash	$ 2,600	
Accounts receivable	14,400	
Repair parts inventory	17,400	
Shop equipment	30,100	
Accounts payable		$23,750
G. Hobson, capital		40,750
Totals	$64,500	$64,500

A summary of Soft-Q's transactions for April 2011 follows:

Apr. 1 Borrowed $12,000 cash from the bank, signing a note payable.
2 Paid $11,000 to creditors on account.
3 Purchased additional repair parts inventory on account, $4,700.
10 Gary invested $3,000 of his own cash in the business.
11 Miscellaneous expenses were paid in cash, $2,050.
13 Advertising costs were paid in cash, $750.
16 Cash was collected from customers on account, $6,000.
29 Repair services provided in April were for $3,000 cash and $7,000 on account.
30 Wages for April were paid in cash, $4,450.
30 Gary withdrew $1,000 cash for personal use.
30 Paid the bank $555 on the note payable, of which $55 is interest and $500 is a partial payment of the note.
30 Paid April's rent, $1,650.
30 A total of $3,705 of repair parts were used in the month. (*Hint*: Debit this to Repair Parts Expense.)

Instructions

(a) Prepare journal entries to record each of the April transactions.
(b) Open ledger accounts for each of the accounts listed in the trial balance, and enter the March 31, 2011, balances. Use T accounts.
(c) Post the journal entries to the accounts in the ledger.
(d) Prepare a trial balance as at the end of April.

Taking It Further Is the purchase of the repair parts inventory a debit to an asset or an expense? Explain.

P2–10B Refer to the trial balance prepared in part (d) of P2–9B for Soft-Q Repair Service.

Prepare financial statements.
(SO 5) AP

Instructions

Use the trial balance to do the following:
(a) Prepare an income statement.
(b) Prepare a statement of owner's equity.
(c) Prepare a balance sheet.

Taking It Further   Gary is considering selling the business. Based on your review of the financial statements, would you be interested in buying the business or do you have concerns? Discuss.

P2–11B   The ledger of Lazdowski Marketing Services has the following account balances at the company's year end, October 31, 2011:

Accounts payable	$ 4,430	Marketing fees earned	$?
Accounts receivable	6,010	Notes payable	48,850
Advertising expense	14,970	Office furniture	56,685
Cash	4,930	Office supplies	1,240
Computer equipment	25,970	Office supplies expense	5,000
D. Lazdowski, capital	57,410	Prepaid rent	975
D. Lazdowski, drawings	75,775	Rent expense	11,700
Insurance expense	2,020	Unearned marketing fees	3,555
Interest expense	2,445	Wages expense	20,545

Instructions

(a) Prepare a trial balance, with the accounts arranged in ledger (financial statement) order, as illustrated in the chapter, and determine the missing amount for Marketing fees earned.
(b) Prepare an income statement, statement of owner's equity, and balance sheet.

Taking It Further   The owner, Donna Lazdowski, is not sure how much cash she can withdraw from the company each year. After reviewing the financial statements, comment on the amount she withdrew this year.

P2–12B   The bookkeeper for Shigeru's Dance Studio did the following in journalizing and posting:

1. A debit posting to Prepaid Insurance of $3,600 was not done.
2. A debit posting of $500 to Accounts Receivable was debited to Accounts Payable.
3. A purchase of supplies on account of $850 was debited to Supplies for $580 and credited to Accounts Payable for $580.
4. A credit to Wages Payable for $1,200 was posted as a credit to Cash.
5. A debit posting of $250 to Cash was posted twice.
6. A debit side of the entry to record the payment of $1,200 for drawings was posted to Wages Expense.
7. A credit to Service Revenue for $400 was posted as a credit to Unearned Service Revenue.
8. A debit to Accounts Payable of $250 was posted as a credit to Accounts Payable.
9. A purchase of equipment on account for $6,400 was posted as a $4,600 debit to Equipment and a $4,600 credit to Cash.
10. The provision of $950 of services on account was not recorded because the customer did not pay cash until the following month.

Instructions

(a) Indicate which of the above transactions are correct and which are incorrect.
(b) For each error identified in (a), answer the following:

1. Will the trial balance be in balance?
2. Which account(s) will be incorrectly stated because of the error?
3. For each account identified in (2) as being incorrect, is the account overstated or understated and by how much?
4. Is the debit column total of the trial balance stated correctly? If not, does correcting the errors increase or decrease the total and by how much?
5. Is the credit column total of the trial balance stated correctly? If not, does correcting the errors increase or decrease the total and by how much?

Taking It Further Your best friend thinks it is a waste of time to correct all of the above errors. Your friend reasons that as long as the trial balance is balanced, then there is no need to correct an error. Do you agree or disagree with your friend? Explain using at least two of the above errors to make your points.

P2–13B The trial balance that follows for Shawnee Slopes Company does not balance: Prepare correct trial balance. (SO 4, 5) AN

SHAWNEE SLOPES COMPANY Trial Balance June 30, 2011		
	Debit	Credit
Cash	$ 5,875	
Accounts receivable		$ 3,120
Prepaid insurance	500	
Equipment	14,200	
Accounts payable		5,140
Property taxes payable	500	
A. Shawnee, capital		17,900
Service revenue	6,847	
Advertising expense		1,132
Property tax expense	1,100	
Salaries expense	4,150	
Totals	$33,172	$27,292

Your review of the ledger reveals that each account has a normal balance. You also discover the following errors:

1. Prepaid Insurance and Property Tax Expense were each understated by $300.
2. A $410 credit to Service Revenue was incorrectly posted as a $140 credit.
3. A debit posting to Salaries Expense of $350 was not done.
4. A $750 cash withdrawal by the owner was debited to A. Shawnee, Capital, for $750 and credited to Cash for $750.
5. A $650 purchase of supplies on account was debited to Equipment for $650 and credited to Cash for $650.
6. A cash payment of $320 for advertising was debited to Advertising Expense for $230 and credited to Cash for $230.
7. A $275 collection from a customer was debited to Cash for $275 and debited to Accounts Receivable for $275.
8. A cash payment on account for $90 was recorded as a $90 credit to Cash and a $90 credit to Accounts Payable.
9. A $2,000 note payable was issued to purchase equipment. The transaction was neither journalized nor posted.

Instructions

Prepare a correct trial balance. (*Note*: You may need to add new accounts.)

Taking It Further After the trial balance is corrected for the above errors, could there still be errors? Explain why or why not.

Continuing Cookie Chronicle

(*Note:* The Continuing Cookie began in Chapter 1 and will continue in each chapter.)

After researching the different forms of business organization, Natalie Koebel decides to operate "Cookie Creations" as a proprietorship. She then starts the process of getting the business running. In November 2010, the following activities take place:

Nov. 8 Natalie cashes her Canada Savings Bonds and receives $520, which she deposits in her personal bank account.

8 She opens a bank account under the name "Cookie Creations" and transfers $500 from her personal account to the new account.

10 Natalie pays $175 to have advertising brochures and posters printed. She plans to distribute these as opportunities arise.

12 She buys baking supplies, such as flour, sugar, butter, and chocolate chips, for $135 cash.

15 Natalie starts to gather some baking equipment to take with her when teaching the cookie classes. She has an excellent top-of-the-line food processor and mixer that originally cost her $750. Natalie decides to start using it only in her new business. She estimates that the equipment is currently worth $500.

16 Natalie realizes that her initial cash investment is not enough. Her grandmother lends her $2,000 cash, for which Natalie signs a one-year 3% note payable in the name of the business. Natalie deposits the money in the business bank account.

17 She buys more baking equipment for $900 cash.

20 She teaches her first class and collects $125 cash.

25 Natalie books a second class for December 4 for $125. She receives $25 cash in advance as a down payment.

26 Natalie teaches a group of Grade 2 students how to make sugar cookies. At the end of the class, Natalie leaves an invoice for $250 with the school principal. The principal says she will pass the invoice along to school board administration and the invoice will be paid sometime in December.

30 A $75 invoice is received for the use of Natalie's cell phone. The cell phone is used exclusively for Cookie Creations' business. The invoice is for services provided in November and is due on December 15, 2010.

Instructions

(a) Prepare journal entries to record the November transactions.
(b) Post the journal entries to ledger accounts.
(c) Prepare a trial balance at November 30, 2010.

Financial Reporting and Analysis

Financial Reporting Problem

BYP2–1   The financial statements of The Forzani Group for 2009 are shown in Appendix A at the back of this textbook. They contain the following selected accounts (in thousands):

Accounts payable and accrued liabilities	$277,820
Accounts receivable	84,455
Cash	3,474
Retail revenue	994,043
Inventory	291,497
Interest expense	5,175
Prepaid expenses	2,827

Instructions

(a) Answer the following questions:

1. What is the increase side (i.e., debit or credit) and decrease side for each of the above accounts?
2. What is the normal balance for each of these accounts?

(b) Identify the other account that is most commonly involved in the transaction, and the effect on that account, when:

1. Accounts receivable are decreased.
2. Accounts receivable are increased.
3. Retail revenue is increased.
4. Inventory is increased.
5. Interest expense is increased.
6. Prepaid expenses are increased.

Interpreting Financial Statements

BYP2–2   Viterra Inc. is one of Canada's leading agri-businesses. The following list of accounts and amounts was taken from Viterra Inc.'s 2008 financial statements:

VITERRA INC. List of Accounts October 31, 2008 (in thousands)	
Accounts payable and accrued liabilities	$ 928,596
Accounts receivable	773,830
Bank indebtedness and short-term debt	18,424
Cash	183,536
Cost of sales expense	5,750,735
Depreciation expense	106,832
Future income taxes—assets	61,875
Future income taxes—liabilities	166,476
Gain on disposal of assets	1,263

Goodwill and intangible assets	$ 322,254
Income tax expense	89,702
Interest expense	37,785
Inventories	837,943
Investments	7,645
Long-term debt	610,088
Operating, general, and administrative expenses	494,227
Other assets	69,238
Other expenses	11,266
Other liabilities	64,183
Prepaid expenses and deposits	91,183
Property, plant, and equipment	1,154,859
Sales and operating revenues	6,777,566
Shareholders' (owner's) equity, November 1, 2007	1,912,443
Short-term investments	486,129

Instructions

(a) Prepare a trial balance for Viterra Inc., with the accounts in financial statement order.
(b) Present the accounts and balances of Viterra Inc. in the form of the accounting equation: Assets = Liabilities + Shareholders' (Owner's) Equity.

Critical Thinking

Collaborative Learning Activity

Working in Groups

Note to instructor: Additional instructions and material for this group activity can be found on the Instructor Resource Site.

BYP2–3   In this group activity, you will work with a partner to complete five transactions using the handout from your teacher.

Instructions

(a) Your instructor will divide the class into pairs.
(b) Each pair will complete the transactions on the paper handed out by the instructor.
(c) This exercise is followed by a brief quiz based on the above collaborative activity.

Communication Activity

Writing Handbook

BYP2–4   White Glove Company offers home cleaning services. Two common transactions for the company are billing customers for services performed and paying employee salaries. For example, on March 15, bills that totalled $6,000 were sent to customers, and $2,000 in salaries was paid to employees.

Instructions

Write a memo to your instructor that explains how these transactions are recorded in the double-entry system. Include in your memo (1) how the debit and credit rules are applied to these transactions, and (2) an explanation of what the normal balances are in the accounts affected by the transactions.

Ethics Case

Ethics in Accounting

BYP2–5   Vu Hung is the assistant chief accountant at Lim Company, a manufacturer of computer chips and cellular phones. The company currently has total sales of $20 million. It is the end of the first quarter. Vu is hurriedly trying to prepare a general ledger trial balance so that quarterly financial statements can be prepared and released to management and regulatory agencies. The credits on the trial balance add up to $1,000 more than the debits.

In order to meet the 4:00 p.m. deadline, Vu decides to force the debits and credits into balance by adding the amount of the difference to the Equipment account. She chose Equipment because it is one of the larger account balances. Proportionally, it will be the least misstated. She believes that the difference will not affect anyone's decisions. She wishes that she had more time to find the error, but realizes that the financial statements are already late.

Instructions

(a) Who are the stakeholders in this situation?
(b) What are the ethical issues involved?
(c) What are Vu's alternatives?

"All About You" Activity

BYP2–6   The "All About You" feature indicates that Pacioli, who described the double-entry accounting system used over 500 years ago, wrote "a person should not go to sleep at night until the debits equalled the credits."

In the double-entry system, debits and credits are used to record the dual effect of each transaction in the appropriate accounts and to keep the basic accounting equation in balance. For each transaction, the debits must equal the credits; therefore, the total debits and credits for all of the accounts should be equal. If the total debits do not equal the credits, there is an error in the accounting records.

You are a first-year university student and very excited about moving away from home to go to university. Your parents have given you $4,000 and you have a $13,000 student loan. Your parents have told you that $4,000 is all you get for the school year and you are not to phone home for more money.

At September 1, you had $17,000 cash ($4,000 + $13,000), $1,000 worth of clothes, and a cell phone that cost $100. You have kept all of the receipts for all of your expenditures between September 1 and December 15. The following is a complete list of your receipts.

Receipts	Amount
Rent on furnished apartment	$1,600
Groceries	1,200
Tuition for September to December	2,800
Textbooks	600
Entertainment (movies, beverages, restaurants)	1,500
New clothes	1,500
Cell phone bill	200
Cable TV and Internet bill	250
Computer	1,000
Bus fare	175
Airfare to go home at Christmas	450

You are enrolled in an accounting course and you have set up an accounting system to track your expenditures. On December 15, you prepared the following trial balance from your accounting records:

Personal Trial Balance December 15, 2010		
Account	Debit	Credit
Cash	$ 6,175	
Clothes	2,500	
Cell phone	100	
Computer	100	
Student loan		13,000
Personal equity		5,100
Rent expense	1,600	
Groceries		1,200
Tuition for September to December	2,800	
Textbooks for September to December	600	
Entertainment	1,500	
Cell phone expense	200	
Cable TV and Internet expense	250	
Bus fare	175	
Airfare	540	
	$16,540	$19,300

On December 15, you checked the balance in your bank account and you only have $5,725 cash. You can't sleep, because you know there are some errors in your accounting records and that you will probably have to ask your parents for more money for the next semester.

Instructions

(a) Calculate your personal equity (deficit) at September 1, 2010.

(b) Prepare a corrected trial balance at December 15, 2010. For each error identified, describe the error.

(c) Calculate your personal equity (deficit) at December 15, 2010.

(d) Will it be necessary for you to ask you parents for more money for the next semester? Explain.

ANSWERS TO CHAPTER QUESTIONS

Answers to Accounting in Action Insight Questions

Business Insight, p. 66

Q: How can unrecorded accounts receivable transactions increase a loss on the income statement?

A: One possibility is that the problem was caused by company employees keeping payments from customers for themselves, and not recording the cash receipt transaction in the company's records. This would result in a larger accounts receivable balance than the amounts owed to the company by customers. When the problem is discovered, the company must reduce the accounts receivable balance to the correct amount. The other side of the journal entry is a debit to an expense on the income statement, and thus a smaller profit or larger loss.

Across the Organization, p. 69

Q: When deciding how to create a chart of accounts, whom should an accountant consult with?

A: When designing a chart of accounts, an accountant should consult with anyone who will need information from the accounting system. The more information required, the more complex the chart of accounts. For example, at Goodyear, there are different product lines and different regions so, a result, many accounts are required. The accountant (or accounting department) will need to consult with the different managers to determine what level of detail is required. They will then design the chart of accounts so the accounting system can provide the required level of detail.

At a small company like Beanz, typically only the manager or owner would be consulted to find out how much information they need. But if Beanz has bank loans, then the accountant may want to talk to the bank to ensure that the chart of accounts is designed to meet the lender's information needs.

All About You, p. 78

Q: Pacioli also wrote "a person should not go to sleep at night until the debits equalled the credits." Is this still good advice over 500 years later?

A: Perseverance can be a very useful attribute for an accounting student. Sometimes it can be difficult and time-consuming to find an error and correct it. Many students find this very frustrating and give up too soon and thus miss the opportunity to learn and increase their confidence. On the other hand, sleep is very important and can provide you with a fresh perspective the next day.

Answer to Forzani Review It Question 5, p. 62

Normal balances: Accounts Receivable (asset)—debit; Accounts Payable and Accrued Liabilities (liability)—credit; Retail Revenue (revenue)—credit; and Store Operating Expense (expense)—debit.

Answers to Self-Study Questions

1. b   2. c   3. d   4. d   5. b   6. a   7. c   8. d   9. a   10. c

Remember to go back to the beginning of the chapter to check off your completed work!

←

CHAPTER 3
ADJUSTING THE ACCOUNTS

senecac.on.ca

✔ THE NAVIGATOR

- ☐ Understand *Concepts for Review*
- ☐ Read *Feature Story*
- ☐ Scan *Study Objectives*
- ☐ Read *Chapter Preview*
- ☐ Read text and answer *Before You Go On*
- ☐ Work *Demonstration Problem*
- ☐ Review *Summary of Study Objectives*
- ☐ Answer *Self-Study Questions*
- ☐ Complete assignments

CONCEPTS FOR REVIEW:

Before studying this chapter, you should understand or, if necessary, review:

a. The double-entry system. (Ch. 2, p. 59)

b. How to increase and decrease assets, liabilities, and owner's equity accounts using debit and credit procedures. (Ch. 2, pp. 59–61)

c. How to journalize transactions. (Ch. 2, pp. 64–66)

d. How to post transactions to the general ledger. (Ch. 2, pp. 67–68)

e. How to prepare a trial balance. (Ch. 2, pp. 76–78)

Fiscal Year Ends, But Classes Move On

TORONTO, Ont.—In accounting, as in comedy, timing is everything. An organization's fiscal year end is like a punch line—everything leads up to it. And once it's done, you start all over again.

At Seneca College's 14 locations in the Greater Toronto Area, as at most schools, the majority of students arrive in September and leave in April or May. But the college's fiscal year ends on March 31, rather than at the end of the academic year. "The reason goes back to 1967 and the provincial act establishing community colleges in Ontario," explains Ron Currie, Seneca's Vice-President of Finance and Administration. "That's the government's year end."

If Seneca's fiscal year end were a different date, however, one thing would remain the same. Seneca must apply revenues to the fiscal period when the service is performed in order to correctly follow revenue recognition criteria. For example, Seneca might collect tuition for the summer term in one accounting period, but provide teaching services in the following accounting period. "Typically," says Mr. Currie, "students pay in March for a summer semester course, so those prepayments get deferred on our balance sheet. Same with the student activity fees."

Seneca's main sources of funding for its post-secondary programs are provincial grants and student tuition fees. Private and corporate training, however, is funded on a fee-for-service basis. Still, the principles are the same. "Let's say XYZ Corporation came along and gave us $30,000 to run a program in March, April, and May," Mr. Currie elaborates. "We would defer two-thirds of it to the next [fiscal] year."

Expenses, too, must be recorded in the year when they are incurred. "Our utility bills and invoices for legal fees for the last month or two of the fiscal year tend to come in after our year end," Mr. Currie continues. "In order to record the expenses in the proper year, we accrue them based on an estimate."

For things like course study guides, which are usually prepared by staff in one fiscal year but sold to students the following year, it's the other way around. "In that case, we take the costs associated with developing the materials and categorize them as a prepaid expense in one fiscal year and record it as an expense when recording the corresponding revenue in the next fiscal year."

Recording revenues and expenses in the correct period is a challenge, but one that must be met to properly reflect the school's activity in each period.

The Navigator

STUDY OBJECTIVES:

After studying this chapter, you should be able to:

1. Explain the accrual basis of accounting, and revenue and expense recognition criteria.
2. Prepare adjusting entries for prepayments.
3. Prepare adjusting entries for accruals.
4. Describe the nature and purpose of an adjusted trial balance, and prepare one.
5. Prepare adjusting entries for the alternative treatment of prepayments (Appendix 3A).

The Navigator

In Chapter 2, we learned the accounting cycle up to and including the preparation of the trial balance. In this chapter, we will learn that additional steps are usually needed before preparing the financial statements. These steps adjust accounts for timing mismatches, like the ones Seneca College has with the tuition it receives for its summer classes and the costs it incurs to offer these classes. In this chapter, we introduce the accrual accounting concepts that guide the adjustment process.

The chapter is organized as follows:

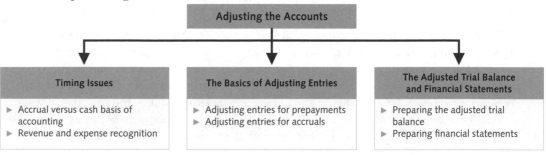

Timing Issues

STUDY OBJECTIVE 1

Explain the accrual basis of accounting, and revenue and expense recognition criteria.

Accounting would be simple if we could wait until a company ended its operations to prepare its financial statements. As the following anecdote shows, if we waited until then we could easily determine the amount of lifetime profit earned:

> A grocery store owner from the old country kept his accounts payable on a spindle, accounts receivable on a notepad, and cash in a shoebox. His daughter, a CGA, chided her father: "I don't understand how you can run your business this way. How do you know what you've earned?"
>
> "Well," her father replied, "when I arrived in Canada 40 years ago, I had nothing but the pants I was wearing. Today, your brother is a doctor, your sister is a teacher, and you are a CGA. Your mother and I have a nice car, a well-furnished house, and a home by the lake. We have a good business and everything is paid for. So, you add all that together, subtract the pants, and there's your profit."

Although the grocer may be correct in his evaluation about how to calculate his profit over his lifetime, most companies need more immediate feedback on how they are doing. For example, management usually wants monthly financial statements. Investors want to view the results of publicly traded companies at least quarterly. The Canada Revenue Agency requires financial statements to be filed with annual income tax returns.

Consequently, accountants divide the life of a business into specific time periods, such as a month, a three-month quarter, or a year. Time periods of less than one year are called **interim periods**.

An accounting time period that is one year long is called a **fiscal year**. The accounting period used by many businesses is the same as the calendar year (January 1 to December 31). However, it can be different. Seneca College's fiscal year is April 1 through March 31, which is typical of many colleges, universities, and governments. Some retail companies use a 52-week period for their fiscal year. The Forzani Group does this, and has chosen the last Sunday in January (some years the first Sunday in February) as its fiscal year end.

Because the life of a business is divided into accounting time periods, determining when to record transactions is important. Many business transactions affect more than one accounting time period. For example, computer equipment purchased by Seneca College last year is still being used today. We also saw in the feature story that sometimes Seneca College collects tuition fees in one fiscal year and then teaches the course in the next fiscal year. In the following section, we will see that deciding when to recognize revenues and expenses will have a significant impact on the usefulness of financial statements.

Accrual versus Cash Basis of Accounting

There are two ways of deciding when to recognize or record revenues and expenses:

1. With the **accrual basis of accounting**, transactions and other events are recorded in the period when they occur, and not when the cash is paid or received. For example, service revenue is recognized when the service is performed, rather than when the cash is received. Expenses are recognized when services (e.g., salaries) or goods (e.g., supplies) are used or consumed, rather than when the cash is paid.

2. Under the **cash basis of accounting**, revenue is recorded when cash is received, and expenses are recorded when cash is paid.

Which one provides better information for users when they make decisions about companies? To answer that question, consider this simple example. Suppose you own a painting company and you paint a large building during year 1. In year 1, you pay $50,000 cash for the cost of the paint and your employees' salaries. Assume that you bill your customer $80,000 at the end of year 1, and that you receive the cash from your customer in year 2.

On an accrual basis, the revenue is reported during the period when the service is performed—year 1. Expenses, such as employees' salaries and the paint used, are recorded in the period in which the employees provide their services and the paint is used—year 1. Thus, your profit for year 1 is $30,000. No revenue or expense from this project is reported in year 2.

If, instead, you were reporting on a cash basis, you would report expenses of $50,000 in year 1 because you paid for them in year 1. Revenues of $80,000 would be recorded in year 2 because you received cash from the customer in year 2. For year 1, you would report a loss of $50,000. For year 2, you would report a profit of $80,000.

Illustration 3-1 summarizes this information and shows the differences between the accrual-based numbers and cash-based numbers.

	Year 1		Year 2	
Activity				
	Purchased paint, painted building, paid employees		Received payment for work done in year 1	
Accrual basis	Revenue	$80,000	Revenue	$ 0
	Expenses	50,000	Expenses	0
	Profit	$30,000	Profit	$ 0
Cash basis	Revenue	$ 0	Revenue	$80,000
	Expenses	50,000	Expenses	0
	Loss	$(50,000)	Profit	$80,000

Illustration 3-1

Accrual versus cash basis accounting

Note that the total profit for years 1 and 2 is $30,000 for both the accrual and cash bases. However, the difference in when the revenue and expense are recognized causes a difference in the amount of profit or loss each year. Which basis provides better information about how profitable your efforts were each year? It's the accrual basis, because it shows the profit earned on the job in the same year as when the work was performed.

Thus, the accrual basis of accounting is widely recognized as being significantly more useful for decision-making than the cash basis of accounting. In fact, it has become an underlying assumption that all financial statements are prepared using the accrual basis of accounting. This means there is no need to report that the accrual basis has been used. The basis of accounting (cash or accrual) will need to be explicitly stated only in the rare cases where the cash basis is used.

While the accrual basis of accounting provides better information, it is more complex than the cash basis of accounting. It is easy to determine when to recognize revenues or expenses if the only determining factor is when the cash is received or paid. But when using the accrual basis, it is necessary to have standards about when to record revenues and expenses.

Revenue and Expense Recognition

Canada's conversion to International Financial Reporting Standards (IFRS) has resulted in new standards for revenue and expense recognition for public Canadian companies. And to make things more complicated, at the time this book was written, the International Accounting Standards Board, along with U.S. standard setters, were working on a joint project to revise the IFRS revenue and expense recognition standards. Because these deliberations were not anticipated to be completed in the near future, in this chapter we describe the IFRS standards in effect at that time.

According to IFRS standards, revenue is recognized when there is an increase in assets or a decrease in liabilities as the result of a contract with a customer. In general, this simply means that the revenue must be recognized in the period when it is earned. That is, revenue is recognized when the service has been performed or the goods have been sold and delivered. We need to ensure that revenue recognition is restricted to situations where revenue can be reliably measured, and collection is reasonably certain.

To illustrate, assume that a dry-cleaning business cleans clothing on June 30, and customers do not claim and pay for their clothes until the first week of July. Following the revenue recognition criteria, revenue is considered earned in June when the service is performed, rather than in July when the cash is received. So at June 30, the dry cleaner would report a receivable on its balance sheet and revenue on its income statement for the service performed.

Expenses, on the other hand, are recognized when there is a decrease in assets or an increase in liabilities, excluding transactions with the owner. Expense recognition is tied to revenue recognition when there is a direct association between costs incurred and the earning of revenue. For example, in the dry-cleaning business in the previous paragraph, the salary expense for the cleaning on June 30 should be reported in the income statement for the same period in which the service revenue is recognized. This process is commonly referred to as matching.

Sometimes, however, there is no direct relationship between expenses and revenue. For example, we will see in the next section that long-lived assets may be used to help generate revenue over many years, but the use of the asset is not directly related to earning specific revenue. In these cases, we will see that expenses are recognized in the income statement over the life of the asset.

In other cases, the benefit from the expenditure is fully used in the current period, or there is a great deal of uncertainty about whether or not there is a future benefit. In these situations, the costs are reported as expenses in the period in which they occur.

For the types of businesses and transactions you will encounter in introductory accounting, Canadian GAAP for Private Enterprises has effectively the same revenue and expense recognition criteria as described above. Therefore, in this textbook, we will not need to determine which standards a company is following when recognizing revenues and expenses.

ACCOUNTING IN ACTION: ALL ABOUT YOU

You are probably paying a lot for your education. According to the education information website CanLearn.ca, a student attending CEGEP, trade school, college, or university full-time can expect to pay anywhere between $2,500 and $8,000 per year for tuition. If the cost of books, supplies, student fees, transportation, housing, and other expenses is factored in, that amount can rise substantially—to $15,000 a year or more to cover a year of post-secondary education expenses, or about $60,000 for a four-year program.

That is the cost, but what is the future value of your education? The U.S. Commerce Department's Census Bureau recently published a report indicating that, over an adult's working life, high school graduates can expect, on average, to earn US$1.2 million. Meanwhile, those with a bachelor's degree will earn US$2.1 million, people with a master's degree will earn US$2.5 million, those with a doctorate will make US$3.4 million, and people with a professional degree will garner US$4.4 million. When you consider those numbers, the money you're spending now on your education should be a significant benefit to you in the future.

Sources: CanLearn.ca, www.canlearn.ca/eng/postsec/cost/index.shtml [accessed on March 26, 2009]; About.com, "US Government Info," usgovinfo.about.com/library/weekly/aa072602a.htm [accessed on March 26, 2009].

How should you account for the cost of your post-secondary education? Should you be recognizing the cost as an expense each year or should you recognize it as an asset?

BEFORE YOU GO ON . . .

→ Review It

1. Why do we need to divide the life of a company into specific time periods?
2. What are the differences between the cash and accrual bases of accounting?
3. What are the criteria for recognizing revenue and expenses?

→ Do It

On January 1, 2011, customers owed Jomerans $30,000 for services provided before December 31, 2010. During 2011, Jomerans Co. received $125,000 cash from customers. On December 31, 2011, customers owed Jomerans $19,500 for services provided before December 31, 2011. Calculate revenue for 2011 using (a) the cash basis of accounting, and (b) the accrual basis of accounting.

Action Plan

- For the cash basis of accounting, revenue is equal to the cash received.
- For the accrual basis of accounting, revenue is recognized in the period in which it is earned, not when it is collected.
- Under the accrual basis of accounting, cash collected in 2011 for revenue earned in 2010 should not be included in the 2011 revenue.
- Under the accrual basis of accounting, amounts receivable at the end of 2011, for services provided in 2011, should be included in the 2011 revenue.

Solution

(a) Revenue for 2011, using the cash basis of accounting $125,000

(b) Cash received from customers in 2011 $125,000
     Deduct: Collection of 2010 receivables   (30,000)
     Add: Amounts receivable at December 31, 2011   19,500
     Revenue for 2011, using the accrual basis of accounting $114,500

Related exercise material: BE3–1, E3–1, and E3–2.

The Navigator

The Basics of Adjusting Entries

For revenues to be recorded in the correct period, adjusting entries are made at the end of the accounting period. **Adjusting entries** are needed to ensure that revenue and expense recognition criteria are followed. Adjusting entries also make it possible to report the correct amounts for assets, liabilities, and owner's equity on the balance sheet.

Adjusting entries are needed every time financial statements are prepared. In Chapter 2, you saw examples of preparing financial statements from a trial balance, without adjusting entries. Those examples are included to provide students with opportunities to practise preparing financial statements. But in reality, adjusting entries are almost always necessary to prepare financial statements on an accrual basis.

Adjusting entries are part of the accounting cycle introduced in Chapter 2. You will recall that we learned the first four steps of the accounting cycle in Chapter 2. In this chapter, we will learn the adjusting process, which consists of steps 5 and 6 in the cycle. From this point on, we will follow correct accounting procedures and prepare financial statements from adjusted trial balances, never from trial balances prepared before adjusting entries (also known as unadjusted trial balances).

The final two steps in the cycle will be covered in Chapter 4. The diagram of the accounting cycle, highlighting the steps learned in this chapter, is shown again in Illustration 3-2 for your reference.

Tutorials:
Accounting Cycle Tutorial

Illustration 3-2 ➔

The accounting cycle

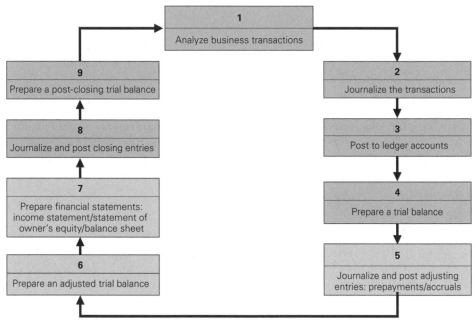

There are some common reasons why the trial balance—from step 4 in the accounting cycle—may not contain complete and up-to-date data.

1. Some events are not recorded daily because it is not efficient to do so. For example, companies do not record the daily use of supplies or the earning of wages by employees.

2. Some costs are not recorded during the accounting period because they expire with the passage of time rather than through daily transactions. Examples are rent and insurance.

3. Some items may be unrecorded. An example is a utility bill for services in the current accounting period that the company will not receive until the next accounting period.

Therefore, we must analyze each account in the trial balance to see if it is complete and up to date. The analysis requires a full understanding of the company's operations and the interrelationship of accounts. Preparing adjusting entries is often a long process. For example, to accumulate the adjustment data, a company may need to count its remaining supplies. It may also need to prepare supporting schedules of insurance policies, rental agreements, and other contractual commitments.

Adjustment data are often not available until after the end of the period. For example, telephone and other bills will not be received until after the month end or year end. In such cases, the data are gathered as soon as possible after the end of the period and adjusting entries are made but they are still dated as at the balance sheet date.

Types of Adjusting Entries

Adjusting entries can be classified as prepayments or accruals, as follows:

PREPAYMENTS	ACCRUALS
1. **Prepaid Expenses** Expenses paid in cash and recorded as assets before they are used or consumed. 2. **Unearned Revenues** Cash received and recorded as a liability before revenue is earned.	1. **Accrued Expenses** Expenses incurred but not yet paid in cash or recorded. 2. **Accrued Revenues** Revenues earned but not yet received in cash or recorded.

Examples and explanations of each type of adjustment are given on the following pages. Each example is based on the October 31 trial balance of Pioneer Advertising Agency from Chapter 2, reproduced here in Illustration 3-3.

← Illustration 3-3

Trial balance

PIONEER ADVERTISING AGENCY
Trial Balance
October 31, 2011

	Debit	Credit
Cash	$14,250	
Accounts receivable	1,000	
Advertising supplies	2,500	
Prepaid insurance	600	
Office equipment	5,000	
Notes payable		$ 5,000
Accounts payable		1,750
Unearned revenue		1,200
C. Byrd, capital		10,000
C. Byrd, drawings	500	
Service revenue		10,800
Salaries expense	4,000	
Rent expense	900	
Totals	$28,750	$28,750

For illustration purposes, we assume that Pioneer Advertising uses an accounting period of one month. Thus, monthly adjusting entries will be made and they will be dated October 31.

Adjusting Entries for Prepayments

Prepayments are either prepaid expenses or unearned revenues. Adjusting entries are used to record the portion of the prepayment that has expired in the current accounting period and to reduce the asset account where the prepaid expense was originally recorded. This type of adjustment is necessary because the prepayment no longer has future benefit and consequently is no longer an asset—it has been used.

For unearned revenues, the adjusting entry records the revenue earned in the current period and reduces the liability account where the unearned revenue was originally recorded. This type of adjustment is necessary because the unearned revenue is no longer owed and so is no longer a liability—the service has been provided and the revenue earned.

STUDY OBJECTIVE 2

Prepare adjusting entries for prepayments.

Prepaid Expenses

As we saw in Chapter 2, costs paid in cash before they are used or consumed are called prepaid expenses. When such a cost is incurred, an asset (prepaid) account is debited to show the service or benefit that will be received in the future and cash is credited. Prepayments often occur for insurance, supplies, advertising, and rent.

Prepaid expenses are assets that expire either with the passage of time (e.g., rent and insurance) or as the asset is used up (e.g., office supplies). The cost of the portion of the asset that has expired or been used up is an expense. It is not practical to record the expiration of these assets daily. Instead, they are recorded when financial statements are prepared. At each statement date, companies make adjusting entries: (1) to record the expenses that apply to the current accounting period, and (2) to show the unexpired costs in the asset accounts.

Before the prepaid expenses are adjusted, assets are overstated and expenses are understated. Therefore, as shown below, an adjusting entry for prepaid expenses results in an increase (debit) to an expense account and a decrease (credit) to an asset account.

Prepaid Expenses

Asset		Expense	
Unadjusted Balance	Credit Adjusting Entry (−) ⟶	Debit Adjusting Entry (+)	

Supplies. The purchase of supplies, such as pens and paper, generally results in an increase (debit) to an asset account. During daily operations, supplies are used up. Rather than recording journal entries as the supplies are used, supplies expense is recorded at the end of the accounting period as an adjustment. At that point, the remaining supplies are counted (a physical inventory of supplies is taken). The difference between the balance in the supplies (asset) account and the cost of supplies actually remaining gives the supplies used (the expense) for the period.

Pioneer Advertising Agency purchased advertising supplies costing $2,500 on October 4. A debit (increase) was made to the asset account Advertising Supplies. This account shows a balance of $2,500 in the October 31 trial balance. An inventory count at the close of business on October 31 reveals that only $1,000 of supplies remains. That means $1,500 ($2,500 − $1,000) of the supplies have been used and the following adjusting entry is made:

A	=	L	+	OE
−1,500				−1,500

Cash flows: no effect

Oct. 31	Advertising Supplies Expense	1,500	
	Advertising Supplies		1,500
	To record supplies used.		

After the adjusting entry is posted, the two advertising supplies accounts are as follows:

Advertising Supplies				Advertising Supplies Expense		
Oct. 4	2,500	Oct. 31	Adj. 1,500	Oct. 31 Adj. 1,500		
Oct. 31 Bal.	1,000					

The asset account Advertising Supplies now shows a balance of $1,000, which is equal to the cost of supplies remaining at the statement date. Advertising Supplies Expense shows a balance of $1,500, which is the cost of supplies used in October. If the adjusting entry is not made, October expenses will be understated and profit overstated by $1,500. Also, both assets and owner's equity will be overstated by $1,500 on the October 31 balance sheet.

Insurance. Companies purchase insurance to protect themselves from losses caused by fire, theft, and unforeseen accidents. Insurance must be paid in advance and the term of coverage is usually one year. Insurance payments (premiums) made in advance are normally charged to the asset account Prepaid Insurance when they are paid. At the financial statement date, it is necessary to make an adjustment to debit (increase) Insurance Expense and credit (decrease) Prepaid Insurance for the cost that has expired during the period.

On October 3, Pioneer Advertising Agency paid $600 for a one-year fire insurance policy. The starting date for the coverage was October 1. The premium was charged to Prepaid Insurance when it was paid. This account shows a balance of $600 in the October 31 trial balance. An analysis of the policy reveals that $50 ($600 ÷ 12) of insurance expires each month. Thus, the following adjusting entry is made:

Oct. 31	Insurance Expense	50	
	Prepaid Insurance		50
	To record insurance expired.		

A	=	L	+	OE
−50				−50

Cash flows: no effect

After the adjusting entry is posted, the accounts are as follows:

Prepaid Insurance						Insurance Expense		
Oct. 3		600	Oct. 31	Adj.	50	Oct. 31	Adj.	50
Oct. 31	Bal.	550						

The asset Prepaid Insurance shows a balance of $550. This amount represents the unexpired cost for the remaining 11 months of coverage (11 × $50). The $50 balance in Insurance Expense is equal to the insurance cost that has expired in October. If this adjustment is not made, October expenses will be understated by $50 and profit overstated by $50. Also, both assets and owner's equity will be overstated by $50 on the October 31 balance sheet.

Depreciation. A business usually owns a variety of long-lived assets such as land, buildings, equipment, and vehicles. These long-lived assets provide service for a number of years. Thus, each is recorded as an asset, rather than as an expense, in the year it is acquired. The length of service is called the **useful life**.

From an accounting perspective, the purchase of a long-lived asset is basically a long-term prepayment for services. Similar to other prepaid expenses, it is necessary to recognize the cost that has been used up (the expense) during the period, and report the unused cost (the asset) at the end of the period. **Depreciation** is the process of allocating the cost of long-lived assets to expense over their useful lives in a systematic and rational manner. Only assets with specified useful lives are depreciated. When an asset such as land has an unlimited useful life, it is not depreciated.

It is important to note that depreciation is an allocation concept. The portion of the long-lived asset that is used up or expires in each period must be reported as an expense. Depreciation is not an attempt to recognize the change in the value of the long-lived asset. Depreciation simply allocates the cost of a long-lived asset over its useful life.

Calculation of Depreciation. A common procedure for calculating depreciation expense is to divide the cost of the asset by its useful life. This is called the **straight-line depreciation method**. The useful life must be estimated because, at the time an asset is acquired, the company does not know exactly how long the asset will be used. Thus, depreciation is an estimate rather than a factual measurement of the expired cost.

Pioneer Advertising purchased office equipment that cost $5,000 on October 2. If its useful life is expected to be five years, annual depreciation is $1,000 ($5,000 ÷ 5). Illustration 3-4 shows the formula to calculate annual depreciation expense in its simplest form.

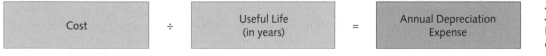

← Illustration 3-4

Formula for straight-line depreciation

Of course, if you are calculating depreciation for partial periods, the annual expense amount must be adjusted for the relevant portion of the year. For example, if we want to determine the depreciation for one month, we would multiply the annual expense by $\frac{1}{12}$ as there are 12 months in a year. For Pioneer Advertising, depreciation on the office equipment is estimated to be $83 per month ($1,000 × ¹⁄₁₂). Because depreciation is an estimate, we can ignore the fact that Pioneer Advertising bought the equipment on October 2, not October 1.

Adjustments of prepayments involve decreasing (or crediting) an asset by the amount of the expired cost. Therefore, it would be logical to expect we should credit Office Equipment when recording depreciation. But it is important to show both the original cost of long-lived assets and the total cost that has expired. We therefore use an account called Accumulated Depreciation to show the cumulative sum of the depreciation expense since the asset was purchased.

Depreciation on the office equipment for the month of October is recognized by the following adjusting entry:

A	=	L	+	OE
−83				−83

Cash flows: no effect

Oct. 31	Depreciation Expense	83	
	Accumulated Depreciation—Office Equipment		83
	To record monthly depreciation.		

The following shows the accounts after the adjusting entry has been posted:

Office Equipment		Depreciation Expense	
Oct. 2 5,000		Oct. 31 Adj. 83	

Accumulated Depreciation—Office Equipment	
	Oct. 31 Adj. 83

The balance in the Accumulated Depreciation account will increase by $83 each month. The balance in the Office Equipment account will remain unchanged until the asset is sold. Accumulated depreciation represents the cumulative total of the depreciation expense since the asset was purchased. We will learn in Chapter 9 that it is reduced when the asset is sold.

As in the case of other prepaid expenses, if this adjusting entry is not made, total assets, owner's equity, and profit will be overstated and expenses will be understated.

Helpful hint Increases, decreases, and normal balances of contra accounts are the opposite of the accounts they relate to.

Statement Presentation. Accumulated Depreciation—Office Equipment is deducted from Office Equipment on the balance sheet. Its normal balance is a credit—the opposite of the normal debit balance of Office Equipment—and thus accumulated depreciation is a contra account. A **contra account** is an account that is offset against (deducted from) a related account on the income statement or balance sheet. On the balance sheet, it can be a contra asset account (offset against an asset) or a contra liability account (offset against a liability). We will discuss contra income statement accounts in Chapter 5.

In the balance sheet, Accumulated Depreciation—Office Equipment is deducted from the related asset account, Office Equipment, as follows:

Office equipment	$5,000
Less: Accumulated depreciation—office equipment	83
Carrying amount	$4,917

Alternative terminology An asset's carrying amount is also called its *carrying value, net book value,* or *book value.*

The difference between the cost of any depreciable asset and its accumulated depreciation is called the **carrying amount** of that asset. In the above illustration, the carrying amount of the equipment at October 31, 2011, is $4,917. As noted earlier, depreciation does not attempt to show what an asset is worth. Thus, the carrying amount of $4,917 is not the same as the fair value of the office equipment (the price at which it could be sold). It is simply the unallocated cost.

If the company owns additional long-lived assets, such as store equipment or buildings, it records depreciation expense on each of those items. It also creates separate accumulated depreciation accounts, such as Accumulated Depreciation—Store Equipment and Accumulated Depreciation—Buildings.

Unearned Revenues

Cash received before revenue is earned is recorded by increasing (crediting) a liability account for unearned revenues. Examples are rent, magazine subscriptions, and customer deposits for future services. Airlines such as Air Canada treat receipts from the sale of tickets as unearned revenue until the flight service is provided. Similarly, tuition fees that are received prior to the start of an academic session, as in the feature story about the summer session at Seneca College, are considered unearned revenue.

Unearned revenues are the opposite of prepaid expenses. Indeed, unearned revenue on the books of one company is likely to be a prepayment on the books of the company that has made the advance payment. For example, your landlord will have unearned rent revenue when you (the tenant) have prepaid rent.

As shown in Chapter 2, when a payment is received for services that will be provided in a future accounting period, Cash is debited (increased) and an unearned revenue account (a liability) should be credited (increased) to recognize the obligation that exists. Unearned revenues become earned when the service is provided to the customer.

It may not be practical to make daily journal entries as the revenue is earned. Instead, recognition of earned revenue is normally delayed until the end of the accounting period. Then an adjusting entry is made to record the revenue that has been earned and to show the liability that remains at the end of the accounting period. Before adjustment, liabilities are overstated and revenues are understated. If revenues are understated, then profit and owner's equity will also be understated. As shown below, the adjusting entry for unearned revenues results in a decrease (debit) to a liability account and an increase (credit) to a revenue account.

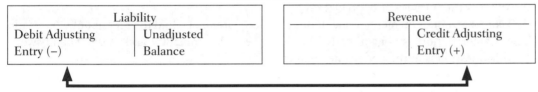

Unearned Revenue

Liability		Revenue	
Debit Adjusting Entry (−)	Unadjusted Balance		Credit Adjusting Entry (+)

Pioneer Advertising Agency received $1,200 on October 3 from R. Knox for advertising services that will be completed by December 31. The payment was originally credited to Unearned Revenue, and this account shows a balance of $1,200 in the October 31 trial balance. An evaluation of work performed by Pioneer for Knox during October shows that $400 of work was done. This also means that the liability has been reduced. The following adjusting entry is made:

Oct. 31	Unearned Revenue	400	
	Service Revenue		400
	To record revenue for services provided.		

A	=	L	+	OE
		−400		+400

Cash flows: no effect

After the adjusting entry is posted, the accounts show:

Unearned Revenue				Service Revenue		
Oct. 31 Adj. 400	Oct. 4	1,200			Oct. 21	10,000
	Oct. 31 Bal.	800			25	800
					31 Adj.	400
					Oct. 31 Bal.	11,200

The liability Unearned Revenue now shows a balance of $800. This amount represents the remaining advertising services that will be performed in the future. At the same time, Service Revenue shows additional revenue of $400 earned in October. If this adjustment is not made, revenues and profit will be understated by $400 in the income statement. As well, liabilities will be overstated by $400 and owner's equity understated by that amount on the October 31 balance sheet.

ACCOUNTING IN ACTION: BUSINESS INSIGHT

Gift cards have become popular holiday gifts. And with recent legislation in Ontario, Alberta, British Columbia, and other provinces eliminating the use of expiry dates on the cards, their benefits to the consumer have increased. But what is the benefit to businesses? Many have discovered that gift card sales in December give their revenues in the new year a boost. A large chunk of gift cards sold in December are used in January or February. In fact, Statistics Canada has found that the usual drop in sales from December to January has started to moderate, which it attributes in part to the redemption of gift cards in January. The recognition of December gift card sales as revenue in January gives the start of the next year a significant boost to profit in a traditionally slow time.

Sources: Tamara Gignac, "Province bans gift card expiry dates and fees," *Calgary Herald*, September 11, 2008, Ontario Ministry of Government Services, "Backgrounder: Eliminating Gift Card Expiry Dates," May 29, 2007, www.gov.on.ca/mgs/en/News/133713.html> [accessed on March 26, 2009].

If a business collects cash when the gift card is sold, how can gift card sales in December result in revenues in January?

BEFORE YOU GO ON . . .

→ Review It

1. What are the purposes of adjusting entries?
2. What is the effect on assets, owner's equity, expenses, and profit if a prepaid expense adjusting entry is not made?
3. What is the purpose of depreciation?
4. Using Forzani's statement of operations (income statement), find the amount of depreciation (or amortization as Forzani calls it) expense recorded for 2009 and 2008. The answer to this question is at the end of the chapter.
5. What is the effect on liabilities, owner's equity, revenues, and profit if an unearned revenue adjusting entry is not made?

→ Do It

The trial balance of Panos Co. on March 31, 2011, includes the following selected accounts before adjusting entries:

	Debit	Credit
Prepaid Insurance	$ 1,200	
Office Supplies	2,800	
Office Equipment	24,000	
Accumulated Depreciation—Office Equipment		$2,200
Unearned Revenue		9,300

An analysis of the accounts shows the following:
1. The one-year insurance policy was purchased on March 1, 2011.
2. Office supplies on hand at March 31 total $800.
3. Office equipment was purchased on April 1, 2010, and has an estimated useful life of ten years.
4. One-third of the unearned revenue was earned in March.

Prepare the adjusting entries for the month of March.

Action Plan
- Make sure you prepare adjustments for the correct time period.
- Adjusting entries for prepaid expenses require a debit to an expense account and a credit to an asset or contra asset account.
- Adjusting entries for unearned revenues require a debit to a liability account and a credit to a revenue account.

Solution

1. Mar. 31	Insurance Expense		100	
	Prepaid Insurance			100
	To record insurance expired: $1,200 \div 12$.			
2. 31	Office Supplies Expense		2,000	
	Office Supplies			2,000
	To record supplies used: $2,800 previously on hand − $800 currently on hand = $2,000 used.			
3. 31	Depreciation Expense		200	
	Accumulated Depreciation—Office Equipment			200
	To record monthly depreciation: $24,000 \div 10 \times \frac{1}{12}$.			
4. 31	Unearned Revenue		3,100	
	Service Revenue			3,100
	To record revenue earned: $9,300 \times \frac{1}{3} = $3,100 earned.			

Related exercise material: BE3–3, BE3–4, BE3–5, BE3–6, BE–7, E3–4, and E3–5.

The Navigator

Adjusting Entries for Accruals

STUDY OBJECTIVE 3

Prepare adjusting entries for accruals.

The second category of adjusting entries is accruals. Unlike prepayments, which have already been recorded in the accounts, accruals are not recognized through daily entries and thus are not included in the accounts. Accruals are required in situations where cash will be paid or received after the end of the accounting period.

Until an accrual adjustment is made, the revenue account (and the related asset account) is understated for accrued revenues. Similarly, the expense account (and the related liability account) is understated for accrued expenses. Thus, adjusting entries for accruals increase both a balance sheet account and an income statement account. We now look at each type of adjusting entry for accruals—accrued revenues and accrued expenses—in more detail.

Accrued Revenues

Revenues earned but not yet received in cash or recorded at the statement date are accrued revenues. Accrued revenues may accumulate (accrue) with the passage of time, as happens with interest revenue and rent revenue. Or they may result when services have been performed but the payment has not been billed or received, as can happen with commissions and fees. The former are unrecorded because the earning of interest and rent does not involve daily transactions. The latter may be unrecorded because only a portion of the total service has been provided or the bill has not been prepared.

Alternative terminology
Accrued revenues are also called *accrued receivables.*

An adjusting entry is required for two purposes: (1) to show the receivable that exists at the balance sheet date, and (2) to record the revenue that has been earned during the period. Before the adjustment is recorded, both assets and revenues are understated. Accordingly, as shown below, an adjusting entry for accrued revenues results in an increase (debit) to an asset account and an increase (credit) to a revenue account.

Accrued Revenues

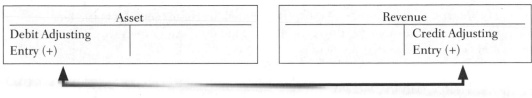

Asset		Revenue	
Debit Adjusting Entry (+)			Credit Adjusting Entry (+)

In October, Pioneer Advertising Agency earned $200 in fees for advertising services that were not billed to clients until November. Because these services have not been billed, they have not been recorded. The following adjusting entry is made on October 31:

A	=	L	+	OE
+200				+200

Cash flows: no effect

Oct. 31	Accounts Receivable	200	
	Service Revenue		200
	To accrue revenue earned but not billed or collected.		

After the adjusting entry is posted, the accounts show the following:

Accounts Receivable				Service Revenue			
Oct. 21	10,000	Oct. 31	9,000			Oct. 21	10,000
31 Adj.	200					25	800
Oct. 31 Bal.	1,200					31 Adj.	400
						31 Adj.	200
						Oct. 31 Adj.	11,400

The asset Accounts Receivable shows that $1,200 is owed by clients at the balance sheet date. The balance of $11,400 in Service Revenue represents the total revenue earned during the month. If the adjusting entry is not made, assets and owner's equity on the balance sheet, and revenues and profit on the income statement, will all be understated.

On November 10, Pioneer receives $200 cash for the services performed in October. The following entry is made:

A	=	L	+	OE
+200				
−200				

⬆ Cash flows: +200

Nov. 10	Cash	200	
	Accounts Receivable		200
	To record cash collected on account.		

Accrued Expenses

Expenses incurred but not yet paid or recorded at the statement date are called accrued expenses. Interest, rent, property taxes, and salaries can be accrued expenses. Accrued expenses result from the same causes as accrued revenues. In fact, an accrued expense on the books of one company is an accrued revenue for another company. For example, the $200 accrual of revenue by Pioneer is an accrued expense for the client that received the service.

Adjustments for accrued expenses are needed for two purposes: (1) to record the obligations that exist at the balance sheet date, and (2) to recognize the expenses that apply to the current accounting period. Before adjustment, both liabilities and expenses are understated. Profit and owner's equity are overstated. An adjusting entry for accrued expenses results in an increase (debit) to an expense account and an increase (credit) to a liability account, as follows.

Accrued Expenses

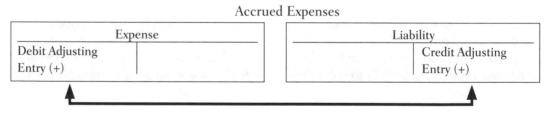

Helpful hint To make the illustration easier to understand, a simplified method for calculating interest is used. In reality, interest is calculated using the exact number of days in the interest period and year.

Interest. On October 2, Pioneer Advertising Agency signed a $5,000, three-month note payable, due January 2, 2012. The note requires interest to be paid at an annual rate of 6%. The amount of interest that has accumulated is determined by three factors: (1) the face value, or principal amount, of the note; (2) the interest rate, which is always expressed as an annual rate; and (3) the length of time that the note is outstanding (unpaid).

Interest is sometimes due monthly, and sometimes when the principal is due. For Pioneer, the total interest due on the $5,000 note at its due date three months later is $75 ($5,000 × 6% × $\frac{3}{12}$ months). Interest rates are always expressed as an annual rate. Because the interest rate is for one year, the time period must be adjusted for the fraction of the year that the note is outstanding.

The formula for calculating interest and how it applies to Pioneer Advertising Agency for the month of October are shown in Illustration 3-5.

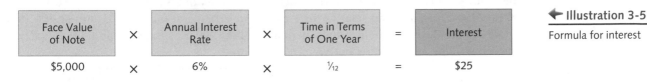

The accrued expense adjusting entry at October 31 is as follows:

Oct. 31	Interest Expense	25	
	Interest Payable		25
	To accrue interest on note payable.		

A	=	L	+	OE
		+25		−25

Cash flows: no effect

After this adjusting entry is posted, the accounts show:

Interest Expense		Interest Payable	
Oct. 31 Adj. 25			Oct. 31 Adj. 25

Interest Expense shows the interest charges for the month of October. The amount of interest owed at the statement date is shown in Interest Payable. It will not be paid until the note comes due, on January 2, 2012. The Interest Payable account is used instead of crediting Notes Payable in order to show the two types of obligations (interest and principal) in the accounts and statements. If this adjusting entry is not made, liabilities and expenses will be understated, and profit and owner's equity will be overstated.

Since this is a three-month note, Pioneer Advertising will also need to make identical adjustments at the end of November and at the end of December to accrue for interest expense incurred in each of these months. After the three adjusting entries have been posted, the balance in Interest Payable is $75 ($25 × 3). The following entry is made on January 2, 2012, when the note and interest are paid:

Jan. 2	Interest Payable	75	
	Note Payable	5,000	
	Cash		5,075
	To record payment of note and interest.		

A	=	L	+	OE
−5,075		−75		
		−5,000		

↓ Cash flows: −5,075

This entry does two things: (1) it eliminates the liability for Interest Payable that was recorded in the October 31, November 30, and December 31 adjusting entries; and (2) it eliminates the note payable. Notice also that the Interest Expense account is not included in this entry, because the full amount of interest incurred was accrued in previous months.

Salaries. Some types of expenses, such as employee salaries and commissions, are paid after the work has been performed. At Pioneer Advertising, employees began work on October 10. They are paid every two weeks and were last paid on October 21. The next payment of salaries will not occur until November 4. As shown on the calendar, in Illustration 3-6, there are six working days that remain unpaid at October 31 (October 24–28 and 31).

OCTOBER 2011							NOVEMBER 2011						
S	M	Tu	W	Th	F	S	S	M	Tu	W	Th	F	S
						1			1	2	3	4	5
2	3	4	5	6	7	8	6	7	8	9	10	11	12
9	10	11	12	13	14	15	13	14	15	16	17	18	19
16	17	18	19	20	21	22	20	21	22	23	24	25	26
23	24	25	26	27	28	29	27	28	29	30			
30	31												

Start of pay period → 10

Adjustment period

Payday

Payday

Helpful hint Recognition of an accrued expense does not mean that a company is slow or bad at paying its debts. The accrued liability may not be payable until after the balance sheet date.

A	=	L	+	OE
		+2,400		−2,400

Cash flows: no effect

At October 31, the salaries for the last six working days (Monday, October 24, to Friday, October 28, and Monday, October 31) represent an accrued expense and a related liability for Pioneer Advertising. The four employees each earn a salary of $500 for a five-day workweek, or $100 per day. Thus, accrued salaries for Pioneer Advertising at October 31 are $2,400 ($100 × 6 days × 4 employees). The accrual will increase both Salaries Expense and Salaries Payable through the following adjusting entry:

Oct. 31	Salaries Expense	2,400	
	Salaries Payable		2,400
	To record accrued salaries.		

After this adjusting entry is posted, the accounts show the following:

Salaries Expense		Salaries Payable	
Oct. 21	4,000		Oct. 31 Adj. 2,400
31 Adj. 2,400			
Oct. 31 Bal. 6,400			

After this adjustment, the balance in Salaries Expense of $6,400 ($100 × 16 days × 4 employees) is the actual salary expense for October (the employees started work on October 10). The balance in Salaries Payable of $2,400 is the amount of the liability for salaries owed as at October 31. If the $2,400 adjustment for salaries is not recorded, Pioneer's expenses and liabilities will be understated by $2,400. Profit and owner's equity will be overstated by $2,400.

At Pioneer Advertising, salaries are payable every two weeks. The next payday is November 4, when total salaries of $4,000 will again be paid. The payment consists of $2,400 of salaries payable at October 31 plus $1,600 of salaries expense for November ($100 × 4 working days [for the period November 1–4] × 4 employees). The following entry is therefore made on November 4:

A	=	L	+	OE
−4,000		−2,400		−1,600

Cash flows: −4,000

Nov. 4	Salaries Payable	2,400	
	Salaries Expense	1,600	
	Cash		4,000
	To record November 4 payroll.		

This entry does two things: (1) it eliminates the liability for salaries payable that was recorded in the October 31 adjusting entry, and (2) it records the proper amount of salaries expense for the period between Tuesday, November 1, and Friday, November 4.

BEFORE YOU GO ON . . .

→ Review It

1. If an accrued revenue adjusting entry is not made, what is the effect on assets, owner's equity, revenues, and profit?
2. If an accrued expense adjusting entry is not made, what is the effect on liabilities, owner's equity, expenses, and profit?

→ Do It

Alvin Hobbs is the owner of the new company Micro Computer Services. At the end of August 2011, the first month of business, Alvin is trying to prepare monthly financial statements. The following information is for August:

1. At August 31, Micro Computer Services owed its employees $800 in salaries that will be paid on September 2.
2. On August 1, Micro Computer Services borrowed $30,000 from a local bank on a five-year term loan. The annual interest rate is 5% and interest is paid monthly on the first of each month.
3. Service revenue earned in August but not yet billed or recorded at August 31 totalled $1,100.

Prepare the adjusting entries needed at August 31, 2011.

Action Plan

- Remember that accruals are entries that were not previously recorded; therefore, the adjustment pattern is different from the pattern for prepayments.
- Adjusting entries for accrued revenues require a debit to a receivable account and a credit to a revenue account.
- Adjusting entries for accrued expenses require a debit to an expense account and a credit to a liability account.

Solution

1. Aug. 31	Salaries Expense		800	
		Salaries Payable		800
		To record accrued salaries.		
2.	31	Interest Expense	125	
		Interest Payable		125
		To record accrued interest: $30,000 × 5% × ¹⁄₁₂ = $125		
3.	31	Accounts Receivable	1,100	
		Service Revenue		1,100
		To accrue revenue earned but not billed or collected.		

Related exercise material: BE3–2, BE3–8, BE3–9, BE3–10, BE3–11, BE3–12, E3–3, E3–6, E3–7, and E3–8.

 The Navigator

Summary of Basic Relationships

The two basic types of adjusting entries are summarized below. Take some time to study and analyze the adjusting entries in the summary. Be sure to note that each adjusting entry affects one balance sheet account and one income statement account.

	Type of Adjustment	Reason for Adjustment	Accounts before Adjustment	Adjusting Entry
Prepayments	Prepaid expenses	Prepaid expenses, originally recorded in asset accounts, have been used.	Assets overstated; expenses understated	Dr. Expense Cr. Asset
	Unearned revenues	Unearned revenues, originally recorded in liability accounts, have been earned.	Liabilities overstated; revenues understated	Dr. Liability Cr. Revenue
Accruals	Accrued revenues	Revenues have been earned but not yet received in cash or recorded.	Assets understated; revenues understated	Dr. Asset Cr. Revenue
	Accrued expenses	Expenses have been incurred but not yet paid in cash or recorded.	Expenses understated; liabilities understated	Dr. Expense Cr. Liability

It is important to understand that adjusting entries never involve the Cash account (except for bank reconciliations, which we will study in Chapter 7). In the case of prepayments, cash has already been received or paid, and was already recorded in the original journal entry. The adjusting entry reallocates or adjusts amounts between a balance sheet account (e.g., prepaid assets or unearned revenues) and an income statement account (e.g., expenses or revenues). In the case of accruals, cash will be received or paid in the future and recorded then. The adjusting entry records the receivable or payable and the related revenue or expense.

ACCOUNTING IN ACTION: ETHICS INSIGHT

In the wake of financial scandals that are still making an impression, the Canadian Securities Administrators introduced requirements for management to evaluate the reliability of a company's accounting system and controls. This includes a review of the procedures that are used to record recurring and nonrecurring adjusting entries.

This review will include asking such questions as the following: How are the adjustments developed, authorized, and checked? What principles does the accounting department use to make adjusting entries? Do the accounting estimates and judgements reflect any biases that would consistently overstate or understate key amounts? Are the proper people involved in the year-end decision making? All of these and similar questions are designed to improve the quality and reliability of the financial statements.

How could an adjusting entry be used to overstate profit?

Pioneer Advertising Agency Illustration

The journalizing and posting of adjusting entries for Pioneer Advertising Agency on October 31 are shown below and on the following two pages. The title "Adjusting Entries" may be inserted in the general journal between the last transaction entry from Chapter 2 and the first adjusting entry so that the adjusting entries are clearly identified. As you review the general ledger, note that the adjustments are highlighted in colour.

GENERAL JOURNAL					J2
Date	Account Titles and Explanation	Ref.	Debit		Credit
2011	*Adjusting Entries*				
Oct. 31	Advertising Supplies Expense	611	1,500		
	Advertising Supplies	129			1,500
	To record supplies used.				
31	Insurance Expense	722	50		
	Prepaid Insurance	130			50
	To record insurance expired.				
31	Depreciation Expense	711	83		
	Accumulated Depreciation—Office Equipment	152			83
	To record monthly depreciation.				
31	Unearned Revenue	209	400		
	Service Revenue	400			400
	To record revenue for services provided.				
31	Accounts Receivable	112	200		
	Service Revenue	400			200
	To accrue revenue earned but not billed or collected.				
31	Interest Expense	905	25		
	Interest Payable	230			25
	To accrue interest on note payable.				
31	Salaries Expense	726	2,400		
	Salaries Payable	212			2,400
	To record accrued salaries.				

GENERAL LEDGER

		Cash			101				Interest Payable		230
Oct.	1	10,000	Oct.	3	900				Oct.	31 Adj.	25
	3	1,200		3	600					Bal.	25
	25	800		20	500						
	31	9,000		21	4,000			C. Byrd, Capital			301
				31	750				Oct.	1	10,000
	Bal.	14,250								Bal.	10,000

		Accounts Receivable			112				C. Byrd, Drawings		306
Oct.	21	10,000	Oct.	31	9,000	Oct.	20	500			
	31 Adj.	200					Bal.	500			
	Bal.	1,200									

		Advertising Supplies			129				Service Revenue		400
Oct.	4	2,500	Oct.	31 Adj.	1,500				Oct.	21	10,000
	Bal.	1,000								25	800
										31 Adj.	400
		Prepaid Insurance			130					31 Adj.	200
Oct.	3	600	Oct.	31 Adj.	50					Bal.	11,400
	Bal.	550									

		Office Equipment			151				Advertising Supplies Expense		611
Oct.	2	5,000				Oct.	31 Adj.	1,500			
	Bal.	5,000					Bal.	1,500			

	Accumulated Depreciation—								Depreciation Expense		711
		Office Equipment			152	Oct.	31 Adj.	83			
			Oct.	31 Adj.	83		Bal.	83			
				Bal.	83						

		Notes Payable			200				Insurance Expense		722
			Oct.	2	5,000	Oct.	31 Adj.	50			
				Bal.	5,000		Bal.	50			

		Accounts Payable			201				Salaries Expense		726
Oct.	31	750	Oct.	4	2,500	Oct.	21	4,000			
				Bal.	1,750		31 Adj.	2,400			
								6,400			

		Unearned Revenue			209				Rent Expense		729
Oct.	31 Adj.	400	Oct.	3	1,200	Oct.	3	900			
				Bal.	800		Bal.	900			

		Salaries Payable			212				Interest Expense		905
			Oct.	31 Adj.	2,400	Oct.	31 Adj.	25			
				Bal.	2,400		Bal.	25			

The Adjusted Trial Balance and Financial Statements

After all adjusting entries have been journalized and posted, another trial balance is prepared from the general ledger accounts. This is called an **adjusted trial balance**. If you refer back to Illustration 3-2, you will see that this is step 6 of the accounting cycle.

STUDY OBJECTIVE 4

Describe the nature and purpose of an adjusted trial balance, and prepare one.

Preparing the Adjusted Trial Balance

The procedures for preparing an adjusted trial balance are the same as those described in Chapter 2 for preparing a trial balance. An adjusted trial balance, like a trial balance, only proves that the ledger is mathematically accurate. As discussed in Chapter 2, it does not prove that there are no mistakes in the ledger.

An adjusted trial balance proves that the total debit balances and the total credit balances in the ledger are equal after all adjustments have been made. The adjusted trial balance gives all data that are needed for preparing financial statements.

The adjusted trial balance for Pioneer Advertising Agency is presented in Illustration 3-7. It has been prepared from the ledger accounts shown in the previous section. The amounts affected by the adjusting entries are highlighted in colour in the adjusted trial balance columns. Compare these amounts to those in the unadjusted trial balance in Illustration 3-3.

Illustration 3-7 ➜

Adjusted trial balance

PIONEER ADVERTISING AGENCY Adjusted Trial Balance October 31, 2011		
	Debit	Credit
Cash	$14,250	
Accounts receivable	1,200	
Advertising supplies	1,000	
Prepaid insurance	550	
Office equipment	5,000	
Accumulated depreciation—office equipment		$ 83
Notes payable		5,000
Accounts payable		1,750
Unearned revenue		800
Salaries payable		2,400
Interest payable		25
C. Byrd, capital		10,000
C. Byrd, drawings	500	
Service revenue		11,400
Advertising supplies expense	1,500	
Depreciation expense	83	
Insurance expense	50	
Salaries expense	6,400	
Rent expense	900	
Interest expense	25	
	$31,458	$31,458

Preparing Financial Statements

Preparing financial statements is the seventh step in the accounting cycle. Financial statements can be prepared directly from the adjusted trial balance. The preparation of financial statements from the adjusted trial balance of Pioneer Advertising Agency and the interrelationships of the data are shown in Illustrations 3-8 and 3-9.

As Illustration 3-8 shows, companies first prepare the income statement from the revenue and expense accounts. Next, the statement of owner's equity is prepared from the owner's capital and drawings accounts, and from the profit (or loss) shown in the income statement. As Illustration 3-9 shows, companies then prepare the balance sheet from the asset and liability accounts and the ending owner's capital balance that is reported in the statement of owner's equity.

Illustration 3-8 ↓

Preparation of the income statement and statement of owner's equity from the adjusted trial balance

PIONEER ADVERTISING AGENCY
Adjusted Trial Balance
October 31, 2011

	Debit	Credit
Cash	$14,250	
Accounts receivable	1,200	
Advertising supplies	1,000	
Prepaid insurance	550	
Office equipment	5,000	
Accumulated depreciation—		
office equipment		$ 83
Notes payable		5,000
Accounts payable		1,750
Unearned revenue		800
Salaries payable		2,400
Interest payable		25
C. Byrd, capital		10,000
C. Byrd, drawings	500	
Service revenue		11,400
Advertising supplies expense	1,500	
Depreciation expense	83	
Insurance expense	50	
Salaries expense	6,400	
Rent expense	900	
Interest expense	25	
	$31,458	$31,458

PIONEER ADVERTISING AGENCY
Income Statement
Month Ended October 31, 2011

Revenues		
Service revenue		$11,400
Expenses		
Advertising supplies expense	$1,500	
Depreciation expense	83	
Insurance expense	50	
Salaries expense	6,400	
Rent expense	900	
Interest expense	25	
Total expenses		8,958
Profit		$ 2,442

PIONEER ADVERTISING AGENCY
Statement of Owner's Equity
Month Ended October 31, 2011

C. Byrd, capital, October 1		$ 0
Add: Investments		10,000
Profit		2,442
		12,442
Less: Drawings		500
C. Byrd, capital, October 31		$11,942

Illustration 3-9 ↓

Preparation of the balance sheet from the adjusted trial balance

PIONEER ADVERTISING AGENCY
Adjusted Trial Balance
October 31, 2011

	Debit	Credit
Cash	$14,250	
Accounts receivable	1,200	
Advertising supplies	1,000	
Prepaid insurance	550	
Office equipment	5,000	
Accumulated depreciation—		
office equipment		$ 83
Notes payable		5,000
Accounts payable		1,750
Unearned revenue		800
Salaries payable		2,400
Interest payable		25
C. Byrd, capital		10,000
C. Byrd, drawings	500	
Service revenue		11,400
Advertising supplies expense	1,500	
Depreciation expense	83	
Insurance expense	50	
Salaries expense	6,400	
Rent expense	900	
Interest expense	25	
	$31,458	$31,458

PIONEER ADVERTISING AGENCY
Balance Sheet
October 31, 2011

Assets		
Cash		$14,250
Accounts receivable		1,200
Advertising supplies		1,000
Prepaid insurance		550
Office equipment	$5,000	
Less: Accumulated depreciation	83	4,917
Total assets		$21,917

Liabilities and Owner's Equity		
Liabilities		
Notes payable		$ 5,000
Accounts payable		1,750
Unearned revenue		800
Salaries payable		2,400
Interest payable		25
Total liabilities		9,975
Owner's equity		
C. Byrd, capital		11,942
Total liabilities and owner's equity		$21,917

BEFORE YOU GO ON . . .

➜ Review It

1. What is the purpose of an adjusted trial balance?
2. How is an adjusted trial balance prepared?
3. In what order are the financial statements prepared?
4. Explain which accounts are shown on each financial statement and the relationship between the statements.

➜ Do It

Listed below, in alphabetical order, are the account balances (after adjustments) from the general ledger of KS Service Company at December 31, 2011. All accounts have normal balances.

Accounts payable	$ 4,660	K. Samji, drawings	$11,700
Accounts receivable	9,584	Note payable	1,000
Accumulated depreciation—		Rent expense	20,762
equipment	1,764	Salaries expense	30,714
Depreciation expense	588	Salaries payable	310
Cash	1,100	Service revenue	67,200
Equipment	8,820	Supplies	180
Interest expense	524	Supplies expense	672
K. Samji, capital	8,700	Unearned service revenue	1,010

Prepare the adjusted trial balance. Beside each account, identify if it should be included on the income statement (IS), statement of owner's equity (OE), or the balance sheet (BS).

Action Plan

• The title includes the name of the company, the type of trial balance, and the date.
• Accounts are listed in the same order as in a trial balance: assets, liabilities, owner's equity, revenues, and expenses.
• Apply the normal balance rules and list the account balances in the correct columns.
• Ensure that the totals of the two columns are equal.
• Recall that assets, liabilities, and capital belong on the balance sheet; revenues and expenses belong on the income statement; and capital and drawings belong on the statement of owner's equity.

Solution

KS SERVICE COMPANY Adjusted Trial Balance December 31, 2011			
	Debit	Credit	Statement
Cash	$ 1,100		BS
Accounts receivable	9,584		BS
Supplies	180		BS
Equipment	8,820		BS
Accumulated depreciation—equipment		$ 1,764	BS
Note payable		1,000	BS
Accounts payable		4,660	BS
Salaries payable		310	BS
Unearned service revenue		1,010	BS
K. Samji, capital		8,700	OE & BS
K. Samji, drawings	11,700		OE
Service revenue		67,200	IS
Depreciation expense	588		IS
Rent expense	20,762		IS
Salaries expense	30,714		IS
Supplies expense	672		IS
Interest expense	524		IS
	$84,644	$84,644	

The Navigator   *Related exercise material:* BE3–13, E3–9, E3–10, and E3–11.

APPENDIX 3A ▶ ALTERNATIVE TREATMENT OF PREPAID EXPENSES AND UNEARNED REVENUES

In our discussion of adjusting entries for prepaid expenses and unearned revenues, we illustrated transactions that already had entries in balance sheet accounts. In the case of prepaid expenses, the prepayment was debited to an asset account. In the case of unearned revenue, the cash received was credited to a liability account. Recording transactions in a balance sheet account improves internal control over assets and it imitates the real flow of costs (i.e., from asset to expense).

> **STUDY OBJECTIVE 5**
> Prepare adjusting entries for the alternative treatment of prepayments.

Some businesses use an alternative treatment of recording transactions, which is also acceptable. At the time an expense is prepaid, an expense account is debited (increased) and Cash is credited (decreased). At the time of a receipt for future services, Cash is debited (increased) and a revenue account is credited (increased). The following sections describe the circumstances that justify such entries and the different adjusting entries that may be needed.

Prepaid Expenses

Prepaid expenses become expired costs either as time passes, as with insurance, or as they are used up, as with advertising supplies. If, when it makes a purchase, the company expects to consume the supplies before the next financial statement date, it may be more convenient to first debit (increase) an expense account rather than an asset account.

Assume that Pioneer Advertising expects that all of the supplies purchased on October 4 will be used before the end of the month. A debit of $2,500 to Advertising Supplies Expense on October 4, rather than to the asset account Advertising Supplies, will eliminate the need for an adjusting entry on October 31, if all the supplies are used. At October 31, the Advertising Supplies Expense account will show a balance of $2,500, which is the cost of supplies purchased between October 4 and October 31.

But what if the company does not use all the supplies and an inventory of $1,000 of advertising supplies remains on October 31? Obviously, an adjusting entry is needed. The following adjusting entry is then made:

Oct. 31	Advertising Supplies	1,000	
	Advertising Supplies Expense		1,000
	To record supply inventory.		

A	=	L	+	OE
+1,000				+1,000

Cash flows: no effect

After posting of the adjusting entry, the accounts show the following:

Advertising Supplies		Advertising Supplies Expense	
Oct. 31 Adj. 1,000		Oct. 4 2,500	Oct. 31 Adj. 1,000
		Oct. 31 Bal. 1,500	

After adjustment, the asset account Advertising Supplies shows a balance of $1,000, which is equal to the cost of supplies on hand at October 31. In addition, Advertising Supplies Expense shows a balance of $1,500, which is equal to the cost of supplies used between October 4 and October 31. If the adjusting entry is not made, expenses will be overstated and profit will be understated by $1,000 in the October income statement. Also, both assets and owner's equity will be understated by $1,000 on the October 31 balance sheet.

A comparison of the entries and accounts for advertising supplies in the chapter and here in the appendix follows:

Prepayment Debited to Asset Account (as in chapter)				Prepayment Debited to Expense Account (as in appendix)		
Oct. 4	Advertising Supplies	2,500		Oct. 4	Advertising Supplies Expense	2,500	
	Accounts Payable		2,500		Accounts Payable		2,500
31	Advertising Supplies Expense	1,500		31	Advertising Supplies	1,000	
	Advertising Supplies		1,500		Advertising Supplies Expense		1,000

After posting of the entries, the accounts appear as follows:

Prepayment Debited to Asset Account (as in chapter)	Prepayment Debited to Expense Account (as in appendix)
Advertising Supplies	**Advertising Supplies**
Oct. 4 2,500 | Oct. 31 Adj. 1,500	Oct. 31 Adj. 1,000 |
Oct. 31 Bal. 1,000 |	
Advertising Supplies Expense	**Advertising Supplies Expense**
Oct. 31 Adj. 1,500 |	Oct. 4 2,500 | Oct. 31 Adj. 1,000
	Oct. 31 Bal. 1,500 |

Note that the account balances under each alternative are the same at October 31 (Advertising Supplies $1,000, and Advertising Supplies Expense $1,500).

Unearned Revenues

Unearned revenues are earned either as time passes, as with unearned rent, or by providing the service, as with unearned fees. Rather than first crediting (increasing) an unearned revenue (liability) account, a revenue account may be credited (increased) when cash is received for future services. Then a different adjusting entry may be necessary.

To illustrate, assume that when Pioneer Advertising received $1,200 for future services on October 3, the services were expected to be performed before October 31. In such a case, Service Revenue would be credited. If all the revenue is in fact earned before October 31, no adjustment is needed. However, if at the statement date $800 of the services have not been provided, an adjusting entry is needed. The following adjusting entry is made:

A	=	L	+	OE
		+800		−800

Cash flows: no effect

Oct. 31	Service Revenue	800	
	Unearned Revenue		800
	To record unearned revenue.		

After posting of the adjusting entry, the accounts show:

Unearned Revenue		Service Revenue		
	Oct. 31 Adj. 800	Oct. 31 Adj. 800	Oct. 3 1,200	
			Oct. 31 Bal. 400	

The liability account Unearned Revenue shows a balance of $800, which is equal to the services that will be provided in the future. In addition, the balance in Service Revenue equals the services provided in October. If the adjusting entry is not made, both revenues and profit will be overstated by $800 in the October income statement. On the October 31 balance sheet, liabilities will also be understated by $800, and owner's equity will be overstated by $800.

A comparison of the entries and accounts for service revenue and unearned revenue in the chapter and here in the appendix follows:

Unearned Revenue Credited to Liability Account (as in chapter)				Unearned Revenue Credited to Revenue Account (as in appendix)		
Oct. 3	Cash	1,200		Oct. 3	Cash	1,200	
	Unearned Revenue		1,200		Service Revenue		1,200
31	Unearned Revenue	400		31	Service Revenue	800	
	Service Revenue		400		Unearned Revenue		800

After posting the entries, the accounts will show:

Unearned Revenue Credited to Liability Account (as in chapter)				Unearned Revenue Credited to Revenue Account (as in appendix)			
Unearned Revenue				**Unearned Revenue**			
Oct. 31 Adj.	400	Oct. 3	1,200			Oct. 31 Adj.	800
		Oct. 31 Bal.	800				
Service Revenue				**Service Revenue**			
		Oct. 31 Adj.	400	Oct. 31 Adj.	800	Oct. 3	1,200
						Oct. 31 Bal.	400

Note that the balances in the accounts are the same under the two alternatives (Unearned Revenue $800, and Service Revenue $400).

There is no method of alternative adjusting entries for accruals or estimates, because no entries occur before these types of adjusting entries are made.

BEFORE YOU GO ON . . .

→ Do It

Mansell Consulting records prepayments as expenses and cash received in advance of providing services as revenue. During February, the following transactions occurred:

Feb. 4 Paid $950 for office supplies.

10 Received $2,350 from a client for services to be performed in the future.

On February 28, it determined that $1,750 of the service revenue had been earned and that there was $750 of office supplies on hand.

(a) Journalize the February transactions.

(b) Journalize the adjusting entries at February 28.

Action Plan

- Expenses are recorded as debits and revenues as credits.
- If a prepayment is recorded as an expense, an adjustment will be required at the end of the period if an asset exists.
- If cash received in advance of providing services is recorded as revenue, an adjustment will be required at the end of the period if an obligation to provide the service exists.

Solution

(a) Feb. 4	Office Supplies Expense		950	
	Cash			950
	To record purchase of office supplies.			
10	Cash		2,350	
	Service Revenue			2,350
	To record cash received for services to be provided.			
(b) 28	Office Supplies		750	
	Office Supplies Expense			750
	To record supplies on hand as an asset.			
28	Service Revenue		600	
	Unearned Revenue			600
	To record the obligation to provide services in the future ($2,350 – $1,750).			

Related exercise material: *BE3–14, *BE3–15, *E3–12, and *E3–13.

The Navigator

Demonstration Problem

Julie Szo opened Green Thumb Lawn Care Company on April 1, 2011. At April 30, 2011, the trial balance is as follows:

GREEN THUMB LAWN CARE COMPANY Trial Balance April 30, 2011		
	Debit	Credit
Cash	$10,950	
Prepaid insurance	3,600	
Supplies	850	
Equipment	28,000	
Notes payable		$20,000
Accounts payable		450
Unearned revenue		4,200
J. Szo, capital		18,000
J. Szo, drawings	650	
Service revenue		1,800
Rent expense	400	
Totals	$44,450	$44,450

Analysis reveals the following additional data for the month:

1. Prepaid insurance is the cost of a 12-month insurance policy that started April 1.
2. Supplies costing $225 were on hand on April 30.
3. The equipment is expected to have a useful life of four years.
4. The note payable is dated April 1. It is a six-month, 4% note with interest payable on the first of each month.
5. Seven customers paid for the company's six-month lawn-service package of $600, beginning in April. These customers were serviced in April.
6. Lawn services performed for other customers but not billed or recorded at April 30 totalled $1,500.

Instructions

(a) Prepare the adjusting entries for the month of April. Show calculations.
(b) Prepare T accounts for the accounts affected by the adjusting entries. Post the adjusting entries to the T accounts.
(c) Prepare an adjusted trial balance at April 30, 2011.
(d) Prepare an income statement, statement of owner's equity, and balance sheet.

Solution to Demonstration Problem

(a)

GENERAL JOURNAL				J2
Date	Account Titles and Explanation	Ref.	Debit	Credit
	Adjusting Entries			
Apr. 30	Insurance Expense		300	
	Prepaid Insurance			300
	To record insurance expired:			
	$3,600 ÷ 12 = $300 per month.			
30	Supplies Expense		625	
	Supplies			625
	To record supplies used: $850 − $225 = $625			
30	Depreciation Expense		583	
	Accumulated Depreciation—Equipment			583
	To record monthly depreciation:			
	$28,000 ÷ 4 = $7,000 × 1/12 = $583 per month.			

Action Plan

- Note that adjustments are being made for only one month.
- Before trying to determine what adjustments are necessary, look at how the amounts are currently recorded in the accounts.
- Select account titles carefully. Use existing titles whenever possible.
- Determine what the balance in the ledger accounts will be after the adjusting entries are posted. Be sure to make the adjustment in the right direction so that the desired balance results.
- The adjusted trial balance is prepared the same way as the trial balance.
- Prepare the financial statements in the order listed.
- Revenues and expenses belong on the income statement; assets and liabilities on the balance sheet.
- Remember that an income statement and a statement of owner's equity are for a period of time; the balance sheet is at the end of the accounting period.

		Debit	Credit
30	Interest Expense	67	
	Interest Payable		67
	To accrue interest on note payable:		
	$\$20,000 \times 4\% \times \frac{1}{12} = \$67$.		
30	Unearned Revenue	700	
	Service Revenue		700
	To record service revenue:		
	$\$600 \div 6$ months $= \$100$ per month;		
	$\$100$ per month $\times 7$ customers $= \$700$.		
30	Accounts Receivable	1,500	
	Service Revenue		1,500
	To accrue revenue earned but not billed or collected.		

(b)

GENERAL LEDGER

Accounts Receivable

Apr. 30 Adj.	1,500	
Apr. 30 Bal.	1,500	

Prepaid Insurance

Apr. 30 Bal.	3,600	Apr. 30 Adj.	300
Apr. 30 Bal.	3,300		

Supplies

Apr. 30 Bal.	850	Apr. 30 Adj.	625
Apr. 30 Bal.	225		

Accumulated Depreciation—Equipment

		Apr. 30 Adj.	583
		Apr. 30 Bal.	583

Interest Payable

		Apr. 30 Adj.	67
		Apr. 30 Bal.	67

Unearned Revenue

Apr. 30 Adj.	700	Apr. 30 Bal.	4,200
		Apr. 30 Bal.	3,500

Service Revenue

		Apr. 30 Bal.	1,800
		30 Adj.	700
		30 Adj.	1,500
		Apr. 30 Bal.	4,000

Depreciation Expense

Apr. 30 Adj.	583	
Apr. 30 Bal.	583	

Insurance Expense

Apr. 30 Adj.	300	
Apr. 30 Bal.	300	

Supplies Expense

Apr. 30 Adj.	625	
Apr. 30 Bal.	625	

Interest Expense

Apr. 30 Adj.	67	
Apr. 30 Bal.	67	

(c)

GREEN THUMB LAWN CARE COMPANY
Adjusted Trial Balance
April 30, 2011

	Debit	Credit
Cash	$10,950	
Accounts receivable	1,500	
Prepaid insurance	3,300	
Supplies	225	
Equipment	28,000	
Accumulated depreciation–equipment		$ 583
Notes payable		20,000
Accounts payable		450
Interest payable		67
Unearned revenue		3,500
J. Szo, capital		18,000
J. Szo, drawings	650	
Service revenue		4,000
Depreciation expense	583	
Insurance expense	300	
Interest expense	67	
Rent expense	400	
Supplies expense	625	
Totals	$46,600	$46,600

(d)

GREEN THUMB LAWN CARE COMPANY
Income Statement
Month Ended April 30, 2011

Revenues		
Service revenue		$4,000
Expenses		
Depreciation expense	$ 583	
Insurance expense	300	
Interest expense	67	
Rent expense	400	
Supplies expense	625	1,975
Profit		$2,025

GREEN THUMB LAWN CARE COMPANY
Statement of Owner's Equity
Month Ended April 30, 2011

J. Szo, capital, April 1		$ 0
Add: Investments	$18,000	
Profit	2,025	20,025
Less: Drawings		650
J. Szo, capital, April 30		$19,375

GREEN THUMB LAWN CARE COMPANY
Balance Sheet
April 30, 2011

Assets		
Cash		$10,950
Accounts receivable		1,500
Prepaid insurance		3,300
Supplies		225
Lawn care equipment	$28,000	
Less: Accumulated depreciation	583	27,417
Total assets		$43,392

Liabilities and Owner's Equity		
Liabilities		
Notes payable		$20,000
Accounts payable		450
Interest payable		67
Unearned service revenue		3,500
Total liabilities		24,017
Owner's equity		
J. Szo, capital		19,375
Total liabilities and owner's equity		$43,392

The Navigator

Summary of Study Objectives

1. *Explain the accrual basis of accounting, and revenue and expense recognition criteria.* In order to provide timely information, accountants divide the life of a business into specific time periods. Therefore it is important to record transactions in the correct time period. Under the accrual basis of accounting, events that change a company's financial statements are recorded in the periods in which the events occur, rather than in the periods in which the company receives or pays cash. Revenue and expense recognition criteria are necessary to ensure that the accrual basis of accounting is properly followed. Revenue is recognized (recorded) in the period when there is a related increase in assets or decrease in liabilities. Expenses should be recognized (recorded) when there is a related decrease in assets or an increase in liabilities. Expenses are recorded in the same period as revenue is recognized, if there is a direct association between the revenues and expenses. If there is no association between revenues and expenses, expenses are recorded in the period they are incurred.

2. *Prepare adjusting entries for prepayments.* Prepayments are either prepaid expenses or unearned revenues. Adjusting entries for prepayments record the portion of the prepayment that applies to the expense or revenue of the current accounting period. The adjusting entry for prepaid expenses debits (increases) an expense account and credits (decreases) an asset account. For a long-lived asset, the contra asset account Accumulated Depreciation is used instead of crediting the asset account directly. The adjusting entry for unearned revenues debits (decreases) a liability account and credits (increases) a revenue account.

3. *Prepare adjusting entries for accruals.* Accruals are either accrued revenues or accrued expenses. Adjusting entries for accruals record revenues and expenses that apply to the current accounting period and that have not yet been recognized through daily journal entries. The adjusting entry for accrued revenue debits (increases) a receivable account and credits (increases) a revenue account. The adjusting entry for an accrued expense debits (increases) an expense account and credits (increases) a liability account.

4. *Describe the nature and purpose of an adjusted trial balance, and prepare one.* An adjusted trial balance shows the balances of all accounts, including those that have been adjusted, at the end of an accounting period. It proves that the total of the accounts with debit balances is still equal to the total of the accounts with credit balances after the adjustments have been posted. Financial statements are prepared from an adjusted trial balance in the following order: (1) income statement, (2) statement of owner's equity, and (3) balance sheet.

5. *Prepare adjusting entries for the alternative treatment of prepayments (Appendix 3A).* Prepayments may initially be debited (increased) to an expense account. Unearned revenues may initially be credited (increased) to a revenue account. At the end of the period, these accounts may be overstated. The adjusting entries for prepaid expenses are a debit (increase) to an asset account and a credit (decrease) to an expense account. Adjusting entries for unearned revenues are a debit (decrease) to a revenue account and a credit (increase) to a liability account. It does not matter which alternative is used to record and adjust prepayments, as the ending account balances should be the same with both methods.

The Navigator

Glossary

WILEY PLUS
Glossary
Key Term Matching Activity

Accrual basis of accounting   A basis for accounting in which revenues are recorded when earned and expenses are recorded when incurred. (p. 119)

Accrued expenses   Expenses incurred but not yet paid in cash or recorded. (p. 123)

Accrued revenues   Revenues earned but not yet received in cash or recorded. (p. 123)

Adjusted trial balance   A list of accounts and their balances after all adjustments have been posted. (p. 135)

Adjusting entries   Entries made at the end of an accounting period to ensure that the revenue and expense recognition criteria are followed. (p. 122)

Carrying amount   The difference between the cost of a depreciable asset and its accumulated depreciation; in other words, it is the unallocated or unexpired portion of the depreciable asset's cost. (p. 126)

Cash basis of accounting   A basis for accounting in which revenue is recorded when cash is received and an expense is recorded when cash is paid. (p. 119)

Contra account An account that is offset against another account on the income statement or balance sheet. (p. 126)

Depreciation The allocation of the cost of a long-lived asset to expense over its useful life in a rational and systematic manner. (p. 125)

Fiscal year An accounting period that is one year long. It does not need to start and end on the same days as the calendar year. (p. 118)

Interim periods Accounting time periods that are less than one year long. (p. 118)

Prepaid expenses Costs paid in cash and recorded as assets before they are used or consumed. (p. 123)

Straight-line depreciation method A depreciation method in which depreciation expense is calculated as the cost divided by the useful life. (p. 125)

Unearned revenues Revenues received in cash and recorded as liabilities before they are earned. (p. 123)

Useful life The length of service of a depreciable asset. (p. 125)

Note: All questions, exercises, and problems below with an asterisk (*) relate to material in Appendix 3A

Self-Study Questions

WILEY PLUS Quizzes

Answers are at the end of the chapter.

(SO 1) C 1. The accrual basis of accounting is considered superior to the cash basis of accounting because:
 (a) it is easier to use.
 (b) it provides better information about the activities of the business.
 (c) it records events in the period in which the cash is paid.
 (d) All of the above.

(SO 1) K 2. Revenue should be recognized when:
 (a) it is earned.
 (b) there is an increase in assets or decrease in liabilities as the result of a contract with a customer.
 (c) the service is provided or the goods are sold and delivered.
 (d) All of the above.

(SO 1) K 3. Adjusting entries are made to ensure that:
 (a) revenues and expenses are recorded in the correct accounting period.
 (b) the accrual basis of accounting is used.
 (c) assets and liabilities have up-to-date balances at the end of an accounting period.
 (d) All of the above.

(SO 2) AP 4. The trial balance shows Supplies $1,350 and Supplies Expense $0. If $600 of supplies are on hand at the end of the period, the adjusting entry is:

(a) Supplies	600	
Supplies Expense		600
(b) Supplies	750	
Supplies Expense		750
(c) Supplies Expense	750	
Supplies		750
(d) Supplies Expense	600	
Supplies		600

5. Accumulated Depreciation is: (SO 2) K
 (a) an expense account.
 (b) an owner's equity account.
 (c) a liability account.
 (d) a contra asset account.

6. On February 1, Magazine City received $600 for (SO 2) AP ten, 12-month subscriptions to *Outdoor Magazine* and credited the Unearned Subscription Revenue account. February is the first month of the subscription. What adjusting entry should Magazine City make on February 28?

(a) Unearned Subscription Revenue	50	
Subscription Revenue		50
(b) Subscription Revenue	50	
Unearned Subscription Revenue		50
(c) Subscription Revenue	550	
Unearned Subscription Revenue		550
(d) Unearned Subscription Revenue	550	
Subscription Revenue		550

7. A bank has a three-month, $6,000 note receivable, (SO 3) AP issued on November 1 at an interest rate of 4%. Interest is due at maturity. What adjusting entry should the bank record on November 30?

(a) Cash	20	
Interest Revenue		20
(b) Interest Receivable	20	
Interest Revenue		20
(c) Note Receivable	60	
Unearned Interest Revenue		60
(d) Interest Receivable	60	
Interest Revenue		60

(SO 3) AP 8. Kathy Kiska earned a salary of $400 for the last week of September. She will be paid in October. The adjusting entry for Kathy's employer at September 30 is:

(a) Salaries Expense	400	
Salaries Payable		400
(b) Salaries Expense	400	
Cash		400
(c) Salaries Payable	400	
Cash		400
(d) No entry is required.		

(SO 4) C 9. Which of the following statements about the adjusted trial balance is *incorrect*?

(a) An adjusted trial balance proves that the total debit balances and the total credit balances in the ledger are equal after all adjustments are made.

(b) The adjusted trial balance is the main basis for preparing financial statements.

(c) The adjusted trial balance lists the account balances divided into assets and liabilities.

(d) The adjusted trial balance is prepared after the adjusting entries have been journalized and posted.

*10. The trial balance shows Supplies $0 and Supplies   (SO 5) AP
Expense $1,350. If $600 of supplies are on hand at the end of the period, the adjusting entry is:

(a) Supplies	600	
Supplies Expense		600
(b) Supplies Expense	750	
Supplies		750
(c) Supplies	750	
Supplies Expense		750
(d) Supplies Expense	600	
Supplies		600

Questions

(SO 1) K 1. (a) Why do accountants divide the life of a business into specific time periods? (b) What are "interim periods" and "fiscal years"?

(SO 1) C 2. How does the accrual basis of accounting differ from the cash basis of accounting? Which method gives decision makers more useful information about the company? Why?

(SO 1) C 3. The Higher Education College collects tuition for the fall term from registered students in August. The fall term runs from September to December. In what month(s) should the college recognize the revenue earned from tuition fees? Explain your reasoning.

(SO 1) C 4. Pierce Dussault, a lawyer, accepts a legal engagement in March, does the work in April, and is paid in May. If Dussault's law firm prepares monthly financial statements, when should it recognize revenue from this engagement? Why?

(SO 1) C 5. In completing the engagement in question 4, Dussault incurred $500 of salary expenses in March that are specifically related to this engagement, $2,500 in April, and none in May. How much expense should be deducted from revenue in the month(s) when the revenue is recognized? Why?

(SO 1) C 6. Why are adjusting entries needed? Include in your explanation some of the reasons why the trial balance may not include complete and up-to-date data.

(SO 2) C 7. The name Prepaid Expense suggests that this account is an expense and belongs on an income statement. Instead the account appears on the balance sheet as an asset. Explain why this is appropri-

ate and why prepaid expenses need to be adjusted at the end of each period.

8. "Depreciation is a process of valuation that results   (SO 2) C
in the reporting of the fair value of the asset." Do you agree? Explain.

9. Explain the difference between (a) depreciation ex-   (SO 2) K
pense and accumulated depreciation, and (b) cost and carrying amount.

10. What is a contra account? Why do we use a con-   (SO 2) C
tra account to record accumulated depreciation instead of directly reducing the long-lived asset?

11. The name Unearned Revenue suggests that this   (SO 2) C
type of account is a revenue account and belongs on the income statement. Instead the account appears on the balance sheet as a liability. Explain why this is appropriate and why unearned revenues require adjustment at the end of the period.

12. Waiparous Hotel bills and collects cash from cus-   (SO 3) C
tomers at the end of their stay. On March 31, there are customers who have already stayed at the hotel for several days and will not be checking out until later in the week. Is it necessary to make an adjusting entry on March 31? Why or why not? If yes, specify the name and type of accounts that need to be adjusted and whether the accounts should be increased or decreased.

13. On February 4, ARU Company receives and pays a   (SO 3) C
utility bill for the month of January. Is it necessary to make an adjusting entry for January? Why or why not? If yes, specify the name and type of accounts

that need to be adjusted and whether the accounts should be increased or decreased.

(SO 3) AP 14. A company makes an accrued revenue adjusting entry for $900. Which financial statement items were overstated or understated before this entry? Explain.

(SO 3) AP 15. A company makes an accrued expense adjusting entry for $600. Which financial statement items were overstated or understated before this entry? Explain.

(SO 2, 3) C 16. For each of the following items, indicate (a) the type of adjusting entry (prepaid expense, unearned revenue, accrued revenue, or accrued expense), and (b) the other type of account included in the adjusting entry (asset, liability, revenue or expense). If an item could result in more than one type of adjusting entry, indicated each of these types and each of the other accounts included in the adjusting entries.
1. Assets are understated.
2. Liabilities are overstated.
3. Liabilities are understated.
4. Expenses are understated.
5. Assets are overstated.
6. Revenue is understated.

(SO 2, 3) K 17. Adjusting entries for accruals always involve the Cash account, and adjusting entries for prepayments never include the Cash account. Do you agree or disagree? Why?

(SO 2, 3) C 18. "An adjusting entry may affect two balance sheet or two income statement accounts." Do you agree? Why or why not?

19. Identify the similarities and differences between (SO 4) C a trial balance and an adjusted trial balance. What is the purpose of each one?

20. "The amount included in an adjusted trial balance (SO 4) C for a specific account will always be more than the amount that was included in the trial balance for the same account." Do you agree or disagree? Why?

21. On Silver Company's trial balance, Accounts Payable is $4,250. After the adjusting entries have been posted, the balance in this account is still $4,250. Since there is no change, it is not necessary to include Accounts Payable on the adjusted trial balance. Do you agree or disagree? Why? (SO 4) C

22. Profit is shown on the income statement and the (SO 4) C statement of owner's equity. It is also indirectly included on the balance sheet. Do you agree or disagree? Why?

*23. Some companies debit an expense account at the (SO 5) C time an expense is prepaid instead of debiting an asset account. The problem with this approach is that expenses will always be overstated, and assets understated. Do you agree or disagree? Why?

*24. Jeremiah has been reading about a recent ac- (SO 5) C counting scandal where the company overstated its revenue on purpose. He then argues that it is never appropriate to credit revenue when cash is received in advance of providing a service. Do you agree or disagree? Why?

Brief Exercises

Identify impact of transactions on cash and profit.
(SO 1) AP

BE3–1 Indicate the impact of each of the following transactions on cash and profit. The first transaction has been completed for you as an example.

Transaction	Cash	Profit
(a) Purchased supplies for cash, $100.	–$100	$0
(b) Used $60 of the supplies in (a).		
(c) Performed services on account, $1,000.		
(d) Received $800 from customers in payment of their account in (c).		
(e) Borrowed $4,000 cash on a note payable.		
(f) On May 28, received $500 cash for services to be provided in June.		
(g) In June, provided the services that had been paid in advance in (f).		
(h) Employees earned $800 in the month of June, which will be paid on July 3.		
(i) On July 3, paid $800 for salaries earned in June in (h).		

Indicate the other account and type of adjustment.
(SO 2, 3) K

BE3–2 One half of the adjusting entry is given below.
1. Salaries Payable is credited.
2. Interest Expense is debited.
3. Supplies Expense is debited.
4. Accounts Receivable is debited.
5. Depreciation Expense is debited.
6. Prepaid Insurance is credited.
7. Interest Revenue is credited.
8. Unearned Revenue is debited.

(a) Indicate the account title, and if the account will be debited or credited, for the other half of the entry.

(b) For each of the above, describe the nature of the adjustment.

BE3–3 Calculate the missing information in each of the following independent situations:

	A Co.	B Co.
Supplies on hand, May 31, 2010	$ 875	$1,515
Supplies purchased during the year	3,230	2,970
Supplies on hand, May 31, 2011	1,295	?
Supplies used during the year	?	3,275

Calculate missing data for supplies.
(SO 2) AP

BE3–4 Spahn Cleaning Company had $475 of cleaning supplies on hand on January 1, 2011. On March 2, 2011, it purchased additional cleaning supplies for $1,695 on credit. On December 31, 2011, a count showed $250 of cleaning supplies on hand.

(a) Prepare the journal entry to record the purchase of supplies on March 2, 2011.

(b) Calculate the amount of cleaning supplies used during the year.

(c) Prepare the adjusting entry required at December 31, 2011.

(d) Using T accounts, enter the January 1, 2011, balance in Cleaning Supplies and Cleaning Supplies Expense, post the two journal entries, and indicate the adjusted balance in each account.

Prepare and post transaction and adjusting entries for supplies.
(SO 2) AP

BE3–5 On June 1, 2010, Bere Co. paid $3,900 to Sting Insurance Company for a one-year insurance policy. Bere Co. has a December 31 fiscal year end and adjusts accounts annually. Complete the following for Bere Co.

(a) Prepare the June 1, 2010, journal entry.

(b) Calculate the amount of insurance that expired during 2010 and the unexpired cost at December 31, 2010.

(c) Prepare the adjusting entry required at December 31, 2010.

(d) Using T accounts, post the journal entries in (a) and (c) above, and indicate the adjusted balance in each account.

Prepare and post transaction and adjusting entries for insurance.
(SO 2) AP

BE3–6 On January 1, 2010, Creed Co. purchased a delivery truck for $42,000. It estimates the truck will have a seven-year useful life. Creed Co. has a December 31 fiscal year end.

(a) Prepare the journal entry to record the purchase of the delivery truck on January 1, 2010.

(b) Prepare the adjusting entries required on December 31, 2010 and 2011.

(c) Indicate the balance sheet presentation of the delivery truck at December 31, 2010 and 2011, and the amount of depreciation expense in the 2010 and 2011 income statements.

Prepare transaction and adjusting entries for depreciation; show statement presentation.
(SO 2) AP

BE3–7 On June 1, 2010, Sting Insurance Co. received $3,900 cash from Bere Co. for a one-year insurance policy. Sting Insurance Co. has an October 31 fiscal year end and adjusts accounts annually. Complete the following for Sting Insurance Co.

(a) Prepare the June 1, 2010, journal entry.

(b) Calculate the amount of revenue earned during 2010 and the amount unearned at October 31, 2010.

(c) Prepare the adjusting entry required on October 31, 2010.

(d) Using T accounts, post the entries for (a) and (c) above and indicate the adjusted balance in each account.

Prepare and post transaction and adjusting entries for unearned revenue.
(SO 2) AP

BE3–8 Ullmann Maintenance Co. has a $595 monthly contract with the sports store Rackets Plus for general maintenance services. Ullmann invoices Rackets Plus on the first of the month for the previous month's services provided. Rackets Plus must then pay for the previous month's services by the 10th of the following month.

(a) Ullmann has a November 30 fiscal year end. Why will it need to prepare an adjusting entry on November 30?

Prepare transaction and adjusting entries for accrued revenue.
(SO 3) AP

(b) Prepare Ullmann's November 30 adjusting entry.
(c) Will Ullmann need to record a journal entry on December 1 when it invoices Rackets Plus? Why or why not?
(d) Ullmann receives $595 from Rackets Plus on December 9 for services provided in November. Prepare Ullmann's journal entry.

Prepare transaction and adjusting entries for salaries.
(SO 3) AP

BE3–9 The total payroll for Classic Autos Co. is $5,000 every Friday ($1,000 per day) for employee salaries earned during a five-day week (Monday through Friday, inclusive). Salaries were last paid on Friday, May 27. This year, the company's fiscal year end, May 31, falls on a Tuesday. Salaries will be paid next on Friday, June 3, at which time employees will receive pay for the five-day workweek. Prepare the journal entries to record the following:

(a) The payment of salaries on May 27
(b) The adjusting journal entry to accrue salaries at May 31
(c) The payment of salaries on June 3

Prepare transaction and adjusting entries for interest.
(SO 3) AP

BE3–10 On July 31, 2010, a company purchased a truck for use in the business for $40,000, paying $18,000 cash and signing a 6% note payable for the remainder. The interest and principal of the note are due on January 31, 2011. Prepare the journal entry to record the following:

(a) The purchase of the truck on July 31, 2010
(b) The accrual of the interest at year end, December 31, 2010, assuming interest has not previously been accrued
(c) The repayment of the interest and note on January 31, 2011

Prepare transaction and adjusting entries for accrued expenses.
(SO 3) AP

BE3–11 Refer to BE3–8. Assume that Rackets Plus adjusts its accounts on a monthly basis.

(a) Will Rackets Plus need to prepare an adjusting entry on November 30? If so, prepare the entry.
(b) Will Rackets Plus need to record a journal entry on December 1 when it receives the invoice from Ullmann Maintenance for November's services? If so, prepare the journal entry.
(c) Prepare Racket Plus's journal entry on December 9 when it pays Ullmann $595.

Identify effect of adjustment on elements of financial statements.
(SO 2, 3) C

BE3–12 For each type of adjustment, indicate the effect of the adjustment on the elements of the financial statements, by completing the table. Use (I) for an increase, (D) for a decrease, and (NE) for no effect.

Type of Adjustment	Assets	Liabilities	Owner's Equity	Revenue	Expenses	Profit
Prepaid expenses						
Unearned revenues						
Accrued revenues						
Accrued expenses						

Prepare adjusted trial balance and identify financial statement.
(SO 4) AP

BE3–13 The account balances (after adjustments) from the general ledger of Winterholt Company at September 30, 2011, follow in alphabetical order. All accounts have normal balances.

Accounts payable	$ 3,570	Equipment	$28,900
Accounts receivable	6,730	Insurance expense	1,560
Accumulated depreciation—		Prepaid insurance	780
equipment	6,200	Salaries expense	12,215
Depreciation expense	3,100	Salaries payable	875
C. Winterholt, capital	15,450	Service revenue	48,450
C. Winterholt, drawings	21,000	Unearned service revenue	840
Cash	1,100		

(a) Prepare the adjusted trial balance.
(b) Beside each account, identify whether it is an asset (A), liability (L), capital (C), drawing (D), revenue (R), or expense (E).
(c) Beside each account, identify whether it should be included on the income statement (IS), statement of owner's equity (OE), or balance sheet (BS).

*BE3–14 Refer to BE3–4. Assume that instead of debiting purchases of cleaning supplies to the Cleaning Supplies account, Spahn Cleaning debits them to the Cleaning Supplies Expense account. Spahn's trial balance at December 31 shows Cleaning Supplies $475 and Cleaning Supplies Expense $1,695. On December 31, there is $250 of supplies on hand.

Prepare and post adjusting entry for supplies.
(SO 5) AP

(a) Prepare the adjusting entry at December 31. Using T accounts, enter the balances in the accounts, post the adjusting entry, and indicate the adjusted balance in each account.
(b) Compare the adjusted balances in BE3–4, where an asset account was originally debited, with the adjusted balances you determined here in (a), where an expense account was originally debited. Does it matter whether an original entry is recorded to an asset account or an expense account? Explain.

*BE3–15 Refer to BE3–7. Assume that instead of crediting Unearned Revenue for the $3,900, one-year insurance policy, Sting Insurance Co. credits Insurance Revenue on June 1, 2010.

Prepare and post adjusting entry for unearned revenue.
(SO 5) AP

(a) Prepare the adjusting entry at October 31, 2010. Using T accounts, enter the balances in the accounts, post the adjusting entry, and indicate the adjusted balance in each account.
(b) Compare the adjusted balances in BE3–7, where a liability account was originally credited, with the adjusted balances you determined here in (a), where a revenue account was originally credited. Does it matter whether an original entry is recorded to a liability account or a revenue account? Explain.

Exercises

E3–1 Toth Company began operations on January 1, 2011. During the year, the company earned $32,000 in service revenue. Of this amount, $22,000 was received in cash in 2011. The remainder was collected in 2012.

Determine profit using cash and accrual bases. Comment on usefulness.
(SO 1) AP

The company paid $16,550 cash for operating expenses in 2011. This included $2,000 for a one-year insurance policy effective April 1, 2011, and $800 for supplies. At December 31, 2011, the company owed $2,425 for operating expenses incurred in 2011, and had $550 of supplies on hand.

Instructions

(a) Calculate profit for 2011 under the cash basis of accounting.
(b) Calculate profit for 2011 under the accrual basis of accounting.
(c) Which basis of accounting (cash or accrual) gives the most useful information for decision-makers? Explain.

E3–2 For the following independent situations, use professional judgement to determine when the company should recognize revenue from the transactions:

Identify when revenue is recognized.
(SO 1) AP

(a) WestJet Airlines sells you a nonrefundable airline ticket in September for your flight home at Christmas.
(b) Leon's Furniture sells you a home theatre in January on a "no money down, no interest, and no payments for one year" promotional deal.
(c) The Toronto Blue Jays sell season tickets to games in the Rogers Centre on-line. Fans can purchase the tickets at any time, although the season does not officially begin until April. It runs from April through October.
(d) The RBC Financial Group loans you money at the beginning of August. The loan and the interest are repayable in full at the end of November.
(e) In August, you order a sweater from Sears using its on-line catalogue. Sears ships the sweater to you in September and you charge it to your Sears credit card. In October, you receive your Sears bill and pay it.
(f) You pay for a one-year subscription to *Canadian Business* magazine in May.
(g) You purchase a gift card in December from iTunes to give to your friend for Christmas. Your friend uses the gift card in January.

Instructions

Identify when revenue should be recognized in each of the above situations.

Identify accounts affected by and the impact of adjusting entries.
(SO 2, 3) C

E3–3 Adjusting entries are used to ensure that revenues, expenses, assets, and liabilities are correctly recorded on the income statement and balance sheet. Listed below are eight examples where adjusting entries are required.

1. To record interest accrued on a note payable.
2. To record interest accrued on a note receivable.
3. To allocate the cost of a depreciable asset over its useful life.
4. To record revenue earned but not billed or collected.
5. To record revenue earned that was previously received in advance.
6. To record insurance that has expired.
7. To record salaries owed.
8. To record supplies used.

Instructions

Assuming a company records all prepaid costs as assets and all revenue collected in advance as liabilities, for each of these examples, indicate the following:
   (a) The type (revenue or expense) and name of the income statement account that will be affected by the adjusting entry and whether the adjustment will increase or decrease that account.
   (b) Whether the adjusting entry will increase, decrease, or have no effect on amount of profit reported on the income statement.
   (c) The type (asset, contra asset, or liability) and name of the balance sheet account that will be affected by the adjusting entry and whether the adjustment will increase or decrease that account.
   (d) Whether the adjusting entry will increase, decrease, or have no effect on the owner's equity balance on the balance sheet.

The first one has been done for you as an example:

| | Income Statement | | | | Balance Sheet | | | |
Example	Type of Account	Account Name	Increase or Decrease	Impact on Profit	Type of Account	Account Name	Increase or Decrease	Impact on Owner's Equity
1.	Expense	Interest Expense	Increase	Decrease	Liability	Interest Payable	Increase	Decrease

Prepare and post transaction and adjusting entries for prepayments.
(SO 2) AP

E3–4 Action Quest Games initially records all prepaid costs as assets and all revenue collected in advance as liabilities, and adjusts its accounts annually. The following information is available for the year ended December 31, 2011:

1. Purchased a one-year insurance policy on April 1, 2011, for $4,740 cash.
2. On September 25, 2011, received $3,600 cash from a corporation that sponsors games for the most improved students attending a nearby school. The $3,600 was for 10 games, worth $360 each, that are played on the first Friday of each month. The first month was October. (Use the account Unearned Game Revenue.)
3. On November 1, 2011, paid $5,850 for three months' rent in advance.
4. Signed a contract for cleaning services starting December 1, 2011, for $1,050 per month. Paid for the first two months on December 1.
5. Sold $1,350 of gift certificates in 2011. On December 31, 2011, determined that $475 of these gift certificates had not yet been redeemed. (Use the account Unearned Gift Certificate Sales.)

Instructions

   (a) For each transaction, prepare a journal entry to record the initial transaction.
   (b) For each transaction, prepare the adjusting journal entry required on December 31, 2011.
   (c) Post each of these entries to T accounts and calculate the final balance in each account. (*Note:* Posting to the Cash account is not necessary.)

E3–5 Action Quest Games owns the following long-lived assets:

Prepare adjusting entries for depreciation; calculate accumulated depreciation and carrying amount.
(SO 2) AP

Asset	Date Purchased	Cost	Estimated Useful Life
Furniture	January 1, 2011	$ 8,800	4 years
Lighting equipment	December 31, 2008	28,000	7 years
Computer equipment	July 1, 2009	12,600	3 years

Instructions

(a) Prepare depreciation adjusting entries for Action Quest Games for the year ended December 31, 2011.

(b) For each asset, calculate its accumulated depreciation and carrying amount at December 31, 2011.

E3–6 Action Quest Games records adjusting entries on an annual basis. The company has the following information available on accruals that must be recorded for the year ended December 31, 2011:

Prepare adjusting and related transaction entries for accruals.
(SO 3) AP

1. The December utility bill for $425 was unrecorded on December 31. Action Quest paid the bill on January 17, 2012.
2. Action Quest is open seven days a week and employees are paid a total of $3,500 every Monday for a seven-day (Monday–Sunday) workweek. December 31, 2011, is a Saturday, so employees will have worked six days (Monday–Saturday) since their last payday. Employees will be paid next on January 2, 2012.
3. Action Quest has a 5% note payable with its bank for $45,000. Interest is payable on a monthly basis on the first of the month.
4. Action Quest receives a commission from Pizza Shop next door for all pizzas sold to customers using Action Quest's facility. The amount owing for December is $490, which Pizza Shop will pay on January 5, 2012.
5. Action Quest sold some equipment on November 1, 2011, in exchange for a $6,000, 6% note receivable. The principal and interest are due on February 1, 2012.

Instructions

(a) For each of the above, prepare the adjusting entry required at December 31, 2011.
(b) For each of the above, prepare the journal entry to record the related cash transaction in 2012. Assume all payments and receipts are made as indicated.

E3–7 Nile Company had the following trial balance at June 30, 2011 (its year end):

Prepare transaction and adjusting entries.
(SO 2, 3) AP

	Debit	Credit
Cash	$ 5,840	
Accounts receivable	850	
Supplies	1,100	
Equipment	9,360	
Accumulated depreciation—equipment		$ 3,900
Unearned service revenue		1,500
R. Nile, capital		11,750
Totals	$17,150	$17,150

During the month of July the following selected transactions took place:

July 2 Paid $750 cash for rent for July, August, and September.
  10 Purchased $200 of supplies for cash.
  14 Collected the full balance of accounts receivable.
  20 Received $700 cash from a customer for services to be provided in August.
  25 Provided $1,300 of services for a customer and immediately collected cash.

Additional information:
1. At July 31, the company had provided $800 of services for a client that it had not billed or recorded.

2. Supplies on hand at July 31, $800.
3. The equipment has a six-year useful life.
4. As at July 31, the company had earned $900 of revenue that had been paid in advance.

Instructions

(a) Record the July transactions.
(b) Prepare monthly adjusting entries at July 31.

Prepare adjusting entries.
(SO 2, 3) AP

E3–8   The ledger of Bourque Rental Agency on March 31, 2011, includes the following selected accounts before preparing quarterly adjusting entries:

	Debit	Credit
Supplies	$ 2,800	
Prepaid insurance	3,600	
Equipment	21,600	
Accumulated depreciation—equipment		$ 9,450
Unearned rent revenue		9,300
Notes payable		20,000
Rent revenue		60,000
Wages expense	14,000	

An analysis of the accounts shows the following:
1. The equipment has a four-year useful life.
2. One-quarter of the unearned rent is still unearned on March 31, 2011.
3. The note payable has an interest rate of 6%. Interest is paid every June 30 and December 31.
4. Supplies on hand at March 31 total $850.
5. The one-year insurance policy was purchased on January 1, 2011.
6. As at March 31, a tenant owed Bourque $700 for the month of March.

Instructions

Prepare the quarterly adjusting entries required at March 31, 2011.

Analyze adjusted data.
(SO 2, 3, 4) AN

E3–9   Thietke Company's fiscal year end is December 31. On January 31, 2011, the company's partial adjusted trial balance shows the following:

THIETKE COMPANY Adjusted Trial Balance (Partial) January 31, 2011		
	Debit	Credit
Supplies	$ 700	
Prepaid insurance	2,400	
Equipment	7,680	
Accumulated depreciation—equipment		$4,800
Salaries payable		800
Unearned revenue		750
Service revenue		2,000
Depreciation expense	80	
Insurance expense	400	
Salaries expense	1,900	
Supplies expense	950	

Instructions

(a) If the amount in Supplies Expense is the January 31 adjusting entry, and the balance in Supplies on January 1 was $800, what was the amount of supplies purchased in January?
(b) If the amount in Insurance Expense is the January 31 adjusting entry, and the original insurance premium was for one year, what was the total premium, and when was the policy purchased?

(c) If the amount in Depreciation Expense is the depreciation for one month, when was the equipment purchased?

(d) If the balance in Salaries Payable on January 1, 2011, was $1,200, what was the amount of salaries paid in cash during January?

(e) If $1,700 was received in January for services performed in January, what was the balance in Unearned Revenue at December 31, 2010?

E3–10 The trial balances before and after adjustment for Lim Company at the end of its fiscal year are as follows:

Prepare adjusting entries from analysis of trial balances.

(SO 2, 3, 4) AP

LIM COMPANY
Trial Balances
August 31, 2011

	Before Adjustment Debit	Before Adjustment Credit	After Adjustment Debit	After Adjustment Credit
Cash	$ 9,583		$ 9,583	
Accounts receivable	8,700		9,230	
Office supplies	2,450		710	
Prepaid insurance	3,775		2,525	
Office equipment	14,100		14,100	
Accumulated depreciation—office equipment		$ 3,525		$ 4,700
Accounts payable		5,800		5,800
Notes payable		20,000		20,000
Salaries payable		0		1,125
Interest payable		0		83
Unearned service revenue		1,600		900
E. Lim, capital		5,600		5,600
E. Lim, drawings	10,000		10,000	
Service revenue		45,000		46,230
Salaries expense	17,000		18,125	
Rent expense	15,000		15,000	
Interest expense	917		1,000	
Office supplies expense	0		1,740	
Insurance expense	0		1,250	
Depreciation expense	0		1,175	
Totals	$81,525	$81,525	$84,438	$84,438

Instructions

Prepare the adjusting entries that were made.

E3–11 The adjusted trial balance for Lim Company is given in E3–10.

Prepare financial statements from adjusted trial balance.

(SO 4) AP

Instructions

Prepare Lim Company's income statement, statement of owner's equity, and balance sheet.

***E3–12** Refer to the information provided in E3–4 for Action Quest Games.

Prepare and post transaction and adjusting entries for prepayments.

(SO 5) AP

Instructions

(a) For each transaction in E3–4, prepare a journal entry, assuming that Action Quest records all prepaid costs as expenses and all revenue collected in advance as revenues.

(b) For each transaction, prepare the adjusting journal entry on December 31, 2011, assuming prepaid costs are recorded as expenses and revenues collected in advance are recorded as revenues.

(c) Post each of the entries in (a) and (b) to T accounts and calculate the final balance in each account. (*Note*: Posting to the Cash account is not necessary.)

(d) Compare your balances in (c) above to those obtained in E3–4 part (c). Comment on your findings.

Prepare and post transaction
and adjusting entries for
prepayments.
(SO 2, 5) AP

*E3–13   At Sabo Company, the following select transactions occurred in January, the company's first month of operations:

Jan. 2 Paid $1,320 for a one-year insurance policy.
    15 Paid $1,400 for supplies.
    25 Received $3,750 cash for services to be performed in the future.

On January 31, it is determined that $1,900 of the service revenue has been earned and that there is $450 of supplies on hand.

Instructions

(a) Assume Sabo records all prepaid costs as assets and all revenue collected in advance as liabilities. Journalize and post the January transactions and adjustments at January 31. Use T accounts. (*Note*: Posting to the Cash account is not necessary.)
(b) Assume Sabo records all prepaid costs as expenses, and all revenue collected in advance as revenue. Journalize and post the January transactions and adjustments at January 31. (*Note*: Posting to the Cash account is not necessary.)
(c) Compare the balances in the T accounts from (a) to those obtained in (b).

Problems: Set A

Determine profit on cash and
accrual bases; recommend
method.
(SO 1) AP

P3–1A   Your examination of the records of Southlake Co. shows the company collected $85,500 cash from customers and paid $48,400 cash for operating costs during 2011. If Southlake followed the accrual basis of accounting, it would report the following year-end balances:

	2011	2010
Accounts payable	$ 1,500	$ 2,250
Accounts receivable	4,200	2,700
Accumulated depreciation	11,300	10,000
Prepaid insurance	1,500	1,300
Supplies	750	400
Unearned revenues	1,200	1,500

Instructions

(a) Determine Southlake's profit on a cash basis for 2011.
(b) Determine Southlake's profit on an accrual basis for 2011.

Taking It Further   Which method do you recommend Southlake use? Why?

Prepare and post transaction
and adjusting entries for
prepayments.
(SO 2) AP

P3–2A   Ouellette & Associates began operations on January 1, 2011. Its fiscal year end is December 31 and it prepares financial statements and adjusts its accounts annually. Ouellette records all prepaid costs as assets and all revenue collected in advance as liabilities. Selected transactions for 2011 follow:

1. On January 10, bought office supplies for $3,400 cash. A physical count at December 31, 2011, revealed $925 of supplies still on hand.
2. On March 31, purchased equipment for $21,000 cash. The equipment has an estimated seven-year useful life.
3. Paid cash for a $3,780, one-year insurance policy on April 1, 2011. The policy came into effect on this date.
4. Leased a truck on September 1 for a one-year period for $500 per month. Paid the full lease cost of $6,000 in cash.
5. On October 15, received a $1,600 advance cash payment from a client for accounting services expected to be provided in the future. As at December 31, one-quarter of these services had not been performed.
6. On December 1, rented out unneeded office space for a six-month period starting on this date, and received a $1,620 cheque for the first three months' rent.

Instructions

(a) For each of items 1 through 6, do the following:
   1. Prepare a journal entry to record the original transaction.
   2. Indicate which elements in financial statements (assets, liabilities, owner's equity, revenue, expenses, and profit) are either understated or overstated at December 31, 2011, before adjusting entries are prepared and posted.
   3. Prepare the adjusting journal entry required on December 31, 2011.
(b) Post each of these entries to T accounts and calculate the final balance in each account. (*Note:* Posting to the Cash account is not necessary.)

Taking It Further   Could Ouellette & Associates avoid the need to record adjusting entries by originally recording items 1 through 4 as expenses, and items 5 and 6 as revenues? Explain.

P3–3A   Ouellette & Associates records adjusting entries on an annual basis. The company has the following information available on accruals that must be recorded for the year ended December 31, 2011:

Prepare entries for adjustments and subsequent entries for accruals.
(SO 3) AP

1. Ouellette has a $30,000, 5% note payable. Interest is paid every six months, on October 31 and March 31. Assume that Ouellette made the correct interest payment on October 31, 2011, and March 31, 2012.
2. Ouellette pays its employees a total of $6,500 every second Thursday. Employees work a five-day week, Monday to Friday, and are paid for all statutory holidays. December 31, 2011, is a Saturday. Employees were paid on Thursday, December 22, 2011, (for the pay period starting Friday, December 9 ending Thursday, December 22) and will be paid again on Thursday, January 5, 2012 (for the pay period starting on Friday December 23, ending on Thursday January 5).
3. Ouellette has a $10,000, 8% note receivable with a customer. Interest is receivable on a monthly basis on the first of the month. Assume the customer paid the correct amount on December 1, 2011.
4. Ouellette has a contract with a customer where it provides services prior to billing the customer. On December 31, 2011, this customer owed Ouellette $3,750. Ouellette billed the customer on January 5, 2012, and collected the full amount on January 18, 2012.
5. Ouellette received the $550 December utility bill on January 7, 2012. The bill was paid on its due date, January 15, 2012.

Instructions

For each of the above items, do the following:
  (a) Prepare the adjusting journal entries required on December 31, 2011.
  (b) Prepare the journal entry to record the related cash transaction in 2012. Assume all payments and receipts are made as indicated.

Taking It Further   Indicate which elements in the financial statements (assets, liabilities, owner's equity, revenue, expenses, and profit) would be either understated or overstated at December 31, 2011, if the accounts were not adjusted.

P3–4A   The following independent items for Last Planet Theatre during the year ended December 31, 2010, may require a transaction journal entry, an adjusting entry, or both. The company records all prepaid costs as assets and all unearned revenues as liabilities and adjusts accounts annually.

Prepare transaction and adjusting entries.
(SO 2, 3) AP

1. Office supplies on hand amounted to $595 on December 31, 2009. On July 10, 2010, additional office supplies were purchased for $1,070 cash. On December 31, 2010, a physical count showed that supplies on hand amounted to $780.
2. On June 1, 2010, the theatre borrowed $25,000 from BMO at an annual interest rate of 5.25% The principal and interest are to be repaid on March 1, 2011.
3. Purchased theatre equipment on June 2, 2010, for $23,500 cash. The equipment was estimated to have a useful life of 10 years.

4. Last Planet Theatre puts on eight plays each season. Season tickets sell for $160 each and 250 sold in September for the upcoming 2010–2011 season, which begins in October 2010 and ends in May 2011 (one play per month). Last Planet Theatre credited Unearned Season Ticket Revenue for the full amount received.

5. Every Tuesday, the total payroll is $4,200 for wages earned during the previous six-day workweek (Tuesday to Sunday). Wages were last paid on Tuesday, December 28. This year, December 31 falls on a Friday.

6. Last Planet Theatre rents the theatre to a local children's choir, which uses the space for rehearsals twice a week at a rate of $500 per month. The choir was short of cash at the beginning of December and sent Last Planet Theatre a cheque for $350 on December 5, and a promise to pay the balance in January. On January 7, 2011, Last Planet Theatre received a cheque for the balance owing from December plus all of January's rent.

7. Upon reviewing its books on December 31, 2010, the theatre noted that the telephone bill for the month of December had not yet been received. A call to the phone company determined that the December telephone bill was $275. The bill was paid on January 10.

Instructions

(a) Prepare the journal entries to record the 2010 transactions for items 1 though 6.
(b) Prepare the year-end adjusting entry for items 1 through 7.
(c) Prepare the journal entries to record:
   1. the payment of wages on Tuesday, January 4 (item 5).
   2. the receipt of the cheque from the children's choir on January 7 (item 6)
   3. the payment of the utility bill on January 10 (item 7)
   4. the payment of the note and interest on March 1, 2011 (item 2)

Taking It Further   There are three basic reasons why an unadjusted trial balance may not contain complete or up-to-date data. List these reasons and provide examples of each one using items 1 to 7 to illustrate your explanation.

Prepare adjusting entries.
(SO 2, 3) AP

P3–5A   Melody Lane Co. provides music lessons to many clients across the city. The following information is available to be used in recording annual adjusting entries at the company's September 30, 2011, year end:

1. On October 1, 2010, the company had a balance of $2,000 in its supplies account. Additional supplies were purchased during the year totalling $1,800. The supplies inventory on September 30, 2011, amounts to $750.

2. On November 1, 2010, Melody Lane purchased a one-year insurance policy for $3,200.

3. On February 28, 2011, Melody Lane borrowed $20,000 from the bank and signed a 10-month, 6% note payable. Interest and principal are to be paid at maturity.

4. On March 1, 2011, Melody Lane purchased a grand piano (to be used in music lessons) for $24,000. The piano's estimated useful life is 15 years.

5. On June 1, 2011, a client paid $1,500 for six months of lessons starting June 1, 2011. Melody Lane recorded this cash receipt as Unearned Revenue.

6. On July 15, 2011, the company paid $9,000 to Pinnacle Holdings to rent additional studio space for nine months starting August 1. Melody Lane recorded the full payment as Prepaid Rent.

7. On September 1, 2011, Melody Lane signed a contract with a neighbourhood school to provide weekly piano lessons to some of its students for a fee of $2,000 per month. The contract calls for lessons to start on October 1, 2011.

8. Music lessons were provided to a local church group for $1,500 on September 28, 2011. Melody Lane has not yet invoiced the group or recorded the transaction.

9. Melody Lane's instructors have earned wages of $2,900 for the last week of September, 2011. This amount will be paid to the instructors on the next payday: October 5, 2011.

10. In early October 2011, Melody Lane received an invoice for $475 from the utilities company for September utilities. The amount has not yet been recorded or paid.

Instructions

Prepare the adjusting journal entries.

Taking It Further   Is it better to prepare monthly adjusting entries or annual adjusting entries as Melody Lane does? Why?

P3–6A   A review of the ledger of Greenberg Company at December 31, 2010, produces the following important data for the preparation of annual adjusting entries:

Prepare adjusting entries. (SO 2, 3) AP

1. Prepaid Advertising, December 31 unadjusted balance, $14,160: This balance consists of payments on two advertising contracts for monthly advertising in two trade magazines. The first advertisement runs in the month in which the contract is signed. The terms of the contracts are as follows:

Contract	Signing Date	Amount	Number of Magazine Issues
A650	March 1	$ 6,240	12
B974	July 1	7,920	24
		$14,160	

2. Delivery trucks, December 31 unadjusted balance, $72,000: The company owns two delivery trucks. The first, purchased for $32,000 on January 2, 2007, has an estimated six-year useful life. The second, purchased for $40,000 on June 1, 2009, has an estimated five-year useful life.
3. Notes Payable, December 31 unadjusted balance, $85,000: This consists of a 10-month, 7% note, dated June 1. Interest is payable at maturity.
4. Salaries Payable, December 31 unadjusted balance, $0: There are nine salaried employees. Salaries are paid every Saturday for a six-day workweek (Monday–Saturday). Six employees receive a salary of $750 per week, and three employees earn $600 per week. December 31 is a Friday.
5. Unearned Rent Revenue, December 31 unadjusted balance, $288,000: Greenberg began subleasing office space to tenants in its new building on November 1. At December 31, Greenberg had the following rental contracts that were paid in full for the entire term of the lease:

Date	Term (in months)	Monthly Rent	Number of Leases	Total Rent Paid
Nov. 1	6	$4,000	5	$120,000
Dec. 1	6	7,000	4	168,000
				$288,000

Instructions

(a) Prepare the adjusting entries at December 31, 2010. Show all your calculations.
(b) For item 2, calculate the accumulated depreciation and carrying amount of each truck on December 31, 2010.

Taking It Further   What is the purpose of recording depreciation? Why is land not depreciated?

P3–7A   During the first week of January 2011, Chisata Moritaka began an interior design business, Exotic Designs. She kept no formal accounting records; however, she did keep a list of cash receipts and payments. At the end of 2011, she approached her bank for a loan, and was asked to submit financial statements prepared on an accrual basis.

Prepare accrual-based financial statements from cash-based information. (SO 1, 2, 3, 4) AP

The following information is available for the year ended December 31, 2011:

	Cash Receipts	Cash Payments
Investment by owner	$28,500	
Equipment		$18,000
Supplies		8,200
Rent payments		9,800
Insurance premium		1,980
Advertising		3,400

Salaries		19,850
Telephone		1,020
Drawings by owner		24,000
Design service revenue	60,350	
Total	$88,850	$86,250

Additional information:

1. The equipment has an estimated six-year useful life and was purchased at the beginning of 2011.
2. There was $850 of supplies on hand on December 31, 2011.
3. Rent payments included a $750 monthly payment and an $800 deposit that is refundable at the end of the two-year lease.
4. The insurance premium was for a one-year period and expires on March 1, 2012.
5. The December telephone bill of $200 will be paid in January 2012.
6. Salaries earned in the last week in December and to be paid in January 2012 amounted to $550.
7. Design revenue earned but not yet collected by December 31, 2011, amounted to $5,200.

Instructions

(a) Calculate the cash balance at December 31, 2011.
(b) Prepare an accrual-based income statement, statement of owner's equity, and balance sheet for the year ended December 31, 2011.

Taking It Further   Why are total expenses on the income statement not the same amount as total cash payments?

Prepare and post adjusting entries, and prepare adjusted trial balance.
(SO 2, 3, 4) AP

P3–8A Alpine Tours has a July 31 fiscal year end and prepares adjustments on an annual basis. The following trial balance was prepared before recording the year-end adjustments:

ALPINE TOURS Trial Balance July 31, 2011	Debit	Credit
Cash	$ 3,000	
Accounts receivable	2,360	
Prepaid insurance	6,100	
Supplies	860	
Office equipment	13,440	
Accumulated depreciation—office equipment		$ 8,400
Buses	140,400	
Accumulated depreciation—buses		58,500
Accounts payable		1,900
Notes payable		54,000
Unearned fees		14,000
F. Rosenthal, capital		25,000
F. Rosenthal, drawings	47,000	
Fees earned		110,600
Advertising expense	820	
Gas and oil expense	7,170	
Interest expense	1,575	
Rent expense	2,175	
Salaries expense	46,875	
Supplies expense	625	
	$272,400	$272,400

Other data:

1. The insurance policy has a one-year term that began on November 1, 2010.

2. The office equipment has an estimated useful life of eight years. The buses have an estimated useful life of 12 years.
3. A physical count shows $210 of supplies on hand at July 31.
4. The note payable has an annual interest rate of 7%. Interest is paid at the start of each month.
5. Deposits of $1,400 each were received for advance tour reservations from 10 school groups. At July 31, three of these deposits have been earned.
6. Bus drivers are paid a combined total of $425 per day. At July 31, five days of salaries are unpaid.
7. A senior citizens' organization that had not made an advance deposit took a Coastal Tour on July 31 for $1,150. This group was not billed for the tour until August 2.
8. Additional advertising costs of $620 have been incurred but not recorded. (Use the Accounts Payable account.)

Instructions

(a) Journalize the annual adjusting entries at July 31, 2011.
(b) Prepare a ledger. Enter the trial balance amounts and post the adjusting entries.
(c) Prepare an adjusted trial balance at July 31, 2011.

Taking It Further As at July 31, 2011, approximately how old are the buses and office equipment?

P3–9A The Highland Cove Resort has an August 31 fiscal year end and prepares adjusting entries on a monthly basis. The following trial balance was prepared before recording the August 31 month-end adjustments:

Prepare and post adjusting entries, and prepare adjusted trial balance and financial statements.
(SO 2, 3, 4) AP

HIGHLAND COVE RESORT Trial Balance August 31, 2011		
	Debit	Credit
Cash	$ 18,900	
Prepaid insurance	5,300	
Supplies	995	
Land	35,000	
Cottages	150,000	
Accumulated depreciation—cottages		$ 44,750
Furniture	33,000	
Accumulated depreciation—furniture		12,925
Accounts payable		6,500
Unearned rent revenue		15,500
Mortgage payable		96,000
K. MacPhail, capital		85,000
K. MacPhail, drawings	42,735	
Rent revenue		249,150
Depreciation expense	5,775	
Insurance expense	5,830	
Interest expense	4,840	
Repair expense	14,400	
Salaries expense	153,000	
Supplies expense	2,450	
Utilities expense	37,600	
	$509,825	$509,825

Other data:
1. The company pays $6,360 for its annual insurance policy on May 31 of each year.

2. A count shows $690 of supplies on hand on August 31, 2011.
3. The cottages have an estimated useful life of 50 years.
4. The furniture has an estimated useful life of 10 years.
5. Customers must pay a $100 deposit if they want to book a cottage during peak times. An analysis of these bookings indicates that 155 deposits were received (all credited to Unearned Rent Revenue) and only 45 of the deposits have not yet been earned by August 31, 2011.
6. The mortgage interest rate is 6.5% per year. Interest has been paid to August 1, 2011.
7. Salaries accrued to the end of August were $840.
8. The August utility bill of $1,560 is unrecorded and unpaid.
9. On August 25, a local business contracted with Highland Cove to rent one of the cottages for six months starting October 1 at a rate of $1,500 per month. An advance payment equal to two months of rent is to be paid on September 5.
10. On August 31, Highland Cove has earned $1,350 of rent revenue from customers who are currently using the cottages but will not pay the amount owing until they check out in September. This amount is in addition to any deposits earned in item (5) above.

Instructions

(a) Prepare the monthly adjusting journal entries on August 31.
(b) Prepare a ledger, enter the trial balance amounts, and post the adjusting entries.
(c) Prepare an adjusted trial balance at August 31.
(d) Prepare an income statement and a statement of owner's equity for the year ended August 31, and a balance sheet as at August 31, 2011.

Taking It Further   Is the owner's capital account on the August 31, 2011, adjusted trial balance the same amount as shown in the August 31, 2011, balance sheet? Why or why not?

Prepare adjusting entries and financial statements.
(SO 2, 3, 4) AP

P3–10A   The unadjusted and adjusted trial balances of the Queen Street Advertising Agency as at November 30, 2011, follow:

	Unadjusted		Adjusted	
	Debit	Credit	Debit	Credit
	QUEEN STREET ADVERTISING AGENCY			
	Trial Balance			
	November 30, 2011			
Accounts payable		$ 4,200		$ 4,800
Accounts receivable	$ 13,650		$ 14,750	
Accumulated depreciation—printing equipment		28,500		34,000
Advertising revenue		58,750		60,750
Art supplies	7,200		1,265	
Art supplies expense	0		5,935	
Cash	9,000		9,000	
Depreciation expense	0		5,500	
Insurance expense	0		1,600	
Interest expense	875		1,000	
Interest payable		0		125
Note payable		30,000		30,000
Prepaid insurance	2,400		800	
Printing equipment	66,000		66,000	
Rent expense	7,150		7,750	
S. Dufferin, capital		17,800		17,800
S. Dufferin, drawings	27,200		27,200	
Salaries expense	12,875		14,350	
Salaries payable		0		1,475
Unearned advertising revenue		7,100		6,200
	$146,350	$146,350	$155,150	$155,150

Instructions

(a) Prepare the adjusting entries that were made.

(b) Prepare an income statement and a statement of owner's equity for the year ended November 30, 2011, and a balance sheet at November 30.

(c) Calculate the annual interest rate on the note. The note payable has been outstanding for eight months. Interest is paid on a monthly basis at the beginning of each month.

(d) Determine the balance in Salaries Payable on November 30, 2010. The company paid $15,250 in salaries in 2011.

Taking It Further A friend of yours is considering purchasing the company from Sally Dufferin and asks you to comment on the company's results of operations and its financial position. Is the company performing well or not? Does the financial position appear healthy or weak? Use specific information from the financial statements to support your answer.

P3–11A Here is an alphabetical list of Scholz Consulting Co.'s accounts at its fiscal year end of March 31, 2011, before adjustments. All accounts have normal balances.

Prepare adjusting entries, adjusted trial balance, and financial statements.

(SO 2, 3, 4) AP

Accounts payable	$ 3,495	Furniture	$ 8,780
Accounts receivable	7,270	Note payable	5,500
Accumulated depreciation—		Prepaid insurance	1,980
computer equipment	2,465	R. Scholz, capital	9,160
Accumulated depreciation—		R. Scholz, drawings	59,500
furniture	4,390	Rent expense	9,625
Cash	2,485	Salaries expense	33,475
Computer equipment	7,395	Supplies	3,290
Consulting fees earned	106,750	Telephone expense	1,700
		Unearned consulting fees	3,740

Other data:

1. A one-year insurance policy was purchased on July 1, 2010.

2. On March 31, 2010, there was $845 of supplies on hand. During the year, $2,445 of additional supplies were purchased. A count of supplies on March 31, 2011, shows $710 of supplies on hand.

3. The computer equipment has an estimated useful life of three years.

4. The furniture has an estimated useful life of 10 years.

5. As at March 31, 2011, an analysis shows $1,825 of the unearned consulting fees were still unearned.

6. The nine-month, 6% note was issued on November 1, 2010. Interest and principal are due on the maturity date.

7. Salaries accrued to March 31 were $655.

8. On March 15, the company signed a contract to provide consulting services to Xendor Inc., starting April 1, 2011. The contract is for three months at a rate of $4,100 per month. Payment is due at the start of each month.

9. On March 31, 2011, the company had earned but not billed or recorded consulting revenue of $2,675.

10. The telephone bill for March 2011 was $155. It has not been recorded or paid.

Instructions

(a) Prepare adjusting journal entries for the year ended March 31, 2011, as required.

(b) Prepare an adjusted trial balance in proper account order.

(c) Prepare an income statement and statement of owner's equity for the year ended March 31, 2011, and a balance sheet at March 31, 2011.

Taking It Further Comment on the company's results of operations and its financial position. In your analysis, refer to specific items in the financial statements.

Prepare and post transaction
and adjusting entries for
prepayments.
(SO 2, 5) AP

*P3–12A   Horowitz Piano Co. began operations on January 1, 2011. Its fiscal year end is December 31. It prepares financial statements and adjusts its accounts annually. Selected transactions for 2011 follow:

1. On January 15, 2011, bought supplies for $960 cash. A physical count on December 31, 2011, revealed $245 of supplies still on hand.
2. Bought a $3,090, one-year insurance policy for cash on April 1, 2011. The policy came into effect on this date.
3. On November 1, received a $1,750 advance cash payment from five clients ($350 each) for services expected to be provided in the future. As at December 31, services had still not been performed for two of the clients.

Instructions

(a) Assume that Horowitz Piano Co. records all prepaid costs as assets and all revenues collected in advance as liabilities.
   1. Prepare the journal entries for the original transactions.
   2. Prepare the adjusting journal entries at December 31, 2011.
   3. Post these journal entries to T accounts and calculate the balance in each account after adjustments. You do not need to post to the Cash account.
(b) Assume instead that Horowitz Piano Co. records all prepaid costs as expenses and all revenues collected in advance as revenues.
   1. Prepare the journal entries for the original transactions.
   2. Prepare the adjusting journal entries at December 31, 2011.
   3. Post these journal entries to T accounts and calculate the balance in each account after adjustments. You do not need to post to the Cash account.

Taking It Further   Compare the balance in each account calculated under (a) above with the balances calculated in (b). Comment on your findings.

Prepare adjusting entries,
adjusted trial balance, and
financial statements.
(SO 3, 4, 5) AP

*P3–13A   The Global Graphics Company was organized on January 1, 2011, by Betty Batke. Global Graphics records all prepayments in income statement accounts. At the end of the first six months of operations, the trial balance had the following accounts:

GLOBAL GRAPHICS COMPANY Trial Balance June 30, 2011		
	Debit	Credit
Cash	$ 8,300	
Accounts receivable	13,000	
Equipment	42,800	
Accounts payable		$ 7,480
Note payable		22,000
B. Batke, capital		35,000
B. Batke, drawings	20,000	
Graphic design revenue		60,700
Insurance expense	2,880	
Rent expense	3,500	
Salaries expense	29,950	
Supplies expense	2,950	
Utilities expense	1,800	
	$125,180	$125,180

Analysis reveals the following additional data:
1. At June 30, there was $825 of supplies on hand.
2. The six-month, 5% note payable was issued on March 1. Interest and principal are payable on the maturity date.
3. On February 1, 2011, the company purchased a one-year insurance policy for $2,880.

4. At June 30, graphic design revenue of $1,250 was unearned.
5. Graphic design revenue earned but unbilled and unrecorded at June 30 totalled $1,975.
6. The equipment was purchased on February 1, 2011, and has an estimated useful life of eight years.
7. July rent of $500 was paid on June 30 and is included in Rent Expense.

Instructions

(a) Journalize the adjusting entries at June 30. (Adjustments are recorded every six months.)
(b) Prepare an adjusted trial balance.
(c) Prepare an income statement and statement of owner's equity for the six months ended June 30, and a balance sheet at June 30, 2011.

Taking It Further   If Global Graphics recorded all prepayments in balance sheet accounts, would this result in different numbers in the financial statements than in (c)?

Problems: Set B

P3–1B Your examination of the records of Northland Co. shows the company collected $136,200 cash from customers and paid $108,700 cash for operating costs in 2011. If Northland followed the accrual basis of accounting, it would report the following year-end balances:

Determine profit on cash and accrual bases; recommend method.
(SO 1) AP

	2011	2010
Accounts payable	$ 3,990	$ 1,460
Accounts receivable	6,100	13,200
Accumulated depreciation	18,250	15,000
Prepaid insurance	620	1,530
Supplies	550	2,350
Unearned revenues	7,400	1,560

Instructions

(a) Determine Northland's profit on a cash basis for 2011.
(b) Determine Northland's profit on an accrual basis for 2011.

Taking It Further   Which method do you recommend Northland use? Why?

P3–2B Burke Bros. began operations on January 1, 2011. Its fiscal year end is December 31 and it prepares financial statements and adjusts its accounts annually. Burke Bros. records all prepaid costs as assets and all revenue collected in advance as liabilities. Selected transactions from 2011 follow:

Prepare and post transaction and adjusting entries for prepayments.
(SO 2) AP

1. On January 9, bought office supplies for $2,950 cash. A physical count on December 31, 2011, revealed $770 of supplies still on hand.
2. Purchased a $5,040, one-year insurance policy for cash on February 1. The policy came into effect on this date.
3. On June 1, purchased equipment for $30,800 cash. The equipment has an estimated seven-year useful life.
4. Rented equipment from Abe's Rentals for a six-month period effective September 1, 2011, for $250 per month and paid cash for the full amount.
5. Rented unused office space to Dawn Clarke for an eight-month period effective August 1, 2011, for $350 per month and collected cash from Dawn for the full amount.
6. On November 15, received a $1,425 advance cash payment from three clients for services to be provided in the future. As at December 31, services had been performed for two of the clients ($475 each).

Instructions

(a) For each of items 1 through 6, do the following:

1. Prepare a journal entry to record the original transaction.
2. Indicate which elements in financial statements (assets, liabilities, owner's equity, revenue, expenses, and profit) are either understated or overstated at December 31, 2011, before adjusting entries are prepared and posted.
3. Prepare the adjusting journal entry required on December 31, 2011.

(b) Post each of these entries to T accounts and calculate the final balance in each account. (*Note*: Posting to the Cash account is not necessary.)

Taking It Further   Could Burke Bros. avoid the need to record adjusting entries by originally recording items 1 through 6 as expenses, and items 5 and 6 as revenues? Explain.

Prepare entries for adjustments and subsequent transactions for accruals.
(SO 3) AP

P3–3B   Burke Bros. records adjusting entries on an annual basis. The company has the following information available on accruals that must be recorded for the year ended December 31, 2011:

1. Burke Bros. has a $40,000, 5% note payable. Interest is payable on a monthly basis on the first of the month. Assume that Burke Bros. made the correct interest payment on December 1, 2011, and January 1, 2012.
2. Burke Bros. pays its employees a total of $7,500 every second Monday for work completed the two preceding weeks. Employees work a five-day week, Monday to Friday, and are paid for all statutory holidays. December 31, 2011, is a Saturday. Employees were paid on Monday, December 19, 2011, and will be paid again on Monday, January 2, 2012.
3. Burke Bros. has a $10,000, 7% note receivable with a customer. Interest is receivable every six months on October 31 and April 30. Assume the customer makes the correct payment to Burke Bros. on October 31, 2011, and April 30, 2012.
4. Burke Bros. owns drilling equipment, which it rents to customers for $1,200 per day. On December 31, 2011, a customer has had the equipment for 10 days. Burke Bros. billed the customer for 14 days when the equipment was returned on January 4, 2012. The customer paid the full amount that day.
5. Burke Bros. received the $255 December telephone bill on January 5, 2012. The bill was paid on January 10, 2012.

Instructions

For each of the above items, do the following:

(a) Prepare the adjusting journal entry required on December 31, 2011.
(b) Prepare the journal entry to record the related cash transaction in 2012. Assume all payments and receipts are made as indicated.

Taking It Further   Indicate which elements in the financial statements (assets, liabilities, owner's equity, revenue, expenses, and profit) would be either understated or overstated at December 31, 2011, if the accounts were not adjusted.

Prepare transaction and adjusting entries.
(SO 2, 3) AP

P3–4B   The following independent items for Théâtre Dupuis during the year ended November 30, 2010, may require a transaction journal entry, an adjusting entry, or both. The company records all prepaid costs as assets and all unearned revenues as liabilities and adjusts accounts annually.

1. Office supplies on hand amounted to $550 on November 30, 2009. On February 17, 2010, additional office supplies were purchased for $1,770 cash. On November 30, 2010, a physical count showed that supplies on hand amounted to $440.
2. On June 1, 2010, borrowed $7,000 from La caisse populaire Desjardins at an annual interest rate of 5.5%. The principal and interest are to be repaid on February 1, 2011.
3. Théâtre Dupuis puts on 10 plays each season. Season tickets sell for $210 each and 150 were sold in August for the upcoming 2010–2011 season, which starts in September 2010 and ends in June 2011 (one play per month). Théâtre Dupuis credited Unearned Season Ticket Revenue for the full amount received.

4. The total payroll for the theatre is $4,500 every Wednesday for employee wages earned during the previous five-day week (Wednesday through Sunday). Wages were last paid (and recorded) on Wednesday, November 24. This year, November 30 falls on a Tuesday.

5. Théâtre Dupuis rents the theatre to a local seniors' choir, which uses the space for rehearsals twice a week at a rate of $450 per month. The new treasurer of the choir accidentally sent a cheque for $100 on November 1. The treasurer promised to send a cheque in December for the balance when she returns from her vacation. On December 4, Théâtre Dupuis received a cheque for the balance owing from November plus all of December's rent.

6. Upon reviewing the books on November 30, 2010, it was noted that the utility bill for the month of November had not yet been received. A call to Hydro-Québec determined that the utility bill was for $935. The bill was paid on December 10.

7. Owned a truck during the year that had originally been purchased on December 1, 2007, for $39,000. The truck's estimated useful life is six years.

Instructions

(a) Prepare the journal entries to record the original transactions for items 1 through 5.
(b) Prepare the year-end adjusting entry for items 1 through 7.
(c) Prepare the journal entry to record:
    1. the payment of wages on Wednesday, December 1 (item 4).
    2. the receipt of the cheque from the seniors' choir on December 4 (item 5).
    3. the payment of the utility bill on December 10 (item 6).
    4. the payment of the note and interest on February 1, 2011 (item 2)

Taking It Further There are three basic reasons why an unadjusted trial balance may not contain complete or up-to-date data. List these reasons and provide examples of each one using items 1 to 7 to illustrate your explanation.

P3–5B Best First Aid offers first aid training to individuals and groups across the city. The following information is available to be used in recording annual adjusting entries for the company's October 31, 2011, year end:

Prepare adjusting entries.
(SO 2, 3) AP

1. Best First Aid purchased equipment on November 1, 2006, for $9,000. The equipment was estimated to have a useful life of six years.

2. On November 1, 2010, the company had a balance of $1,000 in its supplies account. Additional supplies were purchased during the year totalling $2,500. The supplies inventory on October 31, 2011, amounts to $980.

3. The company paid a premium of $3,600 for a one-year insurance policy starting on May 31, 2011. Best First Aid recorded the payment as prepaid insurance.

4. On July 1, 2011, Best First Aid borrowed $28,000 and signed a nine-month, 6% note payable. Interest and principal are payable at maturity.

5. On October 1, 2011, Best First Aid moved to new offices. Rent is $800 per month. Best First Aid paid the first three months' rent that day.

6. Best First Aid requires a $200 deposit from clients as an advance payment for first aid training courses when they are booked. As at October 31, 2011, Best First Aid has deposits for 14 training courses recorded as unearned revenue. A review of the company's records shows that the company has provided all but three of the 14 training courses.

7. On October 1, 2011, Best First Aid signed a contract with UC Company to provide seven days of first aid training to UC employees, starting in November, at a rate of $1,500 per day. The contract calls for UC to pay for the amount owed by December 31, 2011.

8. On October 28, 2011, Best First Aid provided a first aid training course to MRC employees. Best First Aid was too busy to invoice MRC that day. Instead, it prepared the $1,550 invoice on November 2, 2011. MRC agreed to pay this amount on November 15, 2011.

9. Best First Aid has two employees, who are each paid $125 per day. On October 31, 2011, these employees had each worked three days since they were last paid.

10. In early November, Best First Aid received an invoice for $360 from Telus for October telephone charges. The amount has not yet been recorded or paid.

Instructions

Prepare the adjusting journal entries.

Taking It Further   Is it better to prepare monthly adjusting entries or annual adjusting entries as Best First Aid does? Why?

Prepare adjusting entries.
(SO 2, 3) AP

P3–6B   A review of the ledger of Hashmi Company at December 31, 2010, produces the following data for the preparation of annual adjusting entries:

1. Notes Receivable, December 31, 2010, unadjusted balance, $25,000. Hashmi has a 7% note receivable issued on October 1, 2010, maturing on June 1, 2011. Interest and principal are to be paid in full on the maturity date.
2. Prepaid Insurance, December 31, 2010, unadjusted balance, $14,200. The company has separate insurance policies on its buildings and its motor vehicles. Policy B4564 on the buildings was purchased on September 1, 2009, for $10,200. The policy has a term of two years. Policy A2958 on the vehicles was purchased on January 1, 2010, for $5,700. This policy also has a term of two years.
3. Buildings, December 31, 2010, unadjusted balance, $291,500. The first, purchased for $127,500 on September 1, 1998, has an estimated 30-year useful life. The second, purchased for $164,000 on May 1, 2003, has an estimated 40-year useful life.
4. Unearned Subscription Revenue, December 31, 2010, unadjusted balance, $54,000. The company began selling magazine subscriptions in 2010. The selling price of a subscription is $40 for 12 monthly issues. Customers start receiving the magazine in the month the subscription is purchased. A review of subscription contracts that customers have paid for prior to December 31 reveals the following:

Subscription Date	Number of Subscriptions
October 1	325
November 1	450
December 1	575
	1,350

5. Salaries Payable, December 31, 2010, unadjusted balance, $0. There are nine salaried employees, each of whom is paid every Monday for the previous week (Monday to Friday). Six employees receive a salary of $625 each per week, and three employees earn $750 each per week. December 31 is a Friday.

Instructions

(a) Prepare calculations to show why the balance (before adjustments) in the Prepaid Insurance account is $14,200 and why the balance (before adjustments) in the Unearned Subscription Revenue account is $54,000.
(b) Prepare the adjusting entries at December 31, 2010. Show all your calculations.
(c) For item 3, calculate the accumulated depreciation and carrying amount of each building on December 31, 2010.

Taking It Further   What is the purpose of recording depreciation? Why is land not depreciated?

Prepare accrual-based
financial statements from
cash-based information.
(SO 1, 2, 3, 4) AP

P3–7B   During the first week of November 2010, Danielle Charron opened a ski and snowboard repair shop, The Radical Edge, on a busy ski hill. She did not do any bookkeeping, but she kept careful track of all her cash receipts and cash payments. She gives you the following information at the end of the ski season, April 30, 2011:

	Cash Receipts	Cash Payments
Investment by owner	$30,000	
Ski and snowboard repair services	33,250	
Repair equipment		$24,000
Insurance		1,800
Rent		2,275

Supplies		2,700
Newspaper advertising		475
Utility bills		950
Drawings by owner		6,000
Part-time employee wages		3,600
Totals	$63,250	$41,800

Additional information:

1. The repair equipment was purchased at the beginning of November and has an estimated useful life of eight years.
2. The one-year insurance policy expires on October 31, 2011.
3. On November 1, 2010, the company began renting space at a cost of $325 per month on a one-year lease. As required by the lease contract, Danielle has paid the last month's rent in advance.
4. The part-time employee is owed $120 at April 30, 2011, for unpaid wages.
5. At April 30, 2011, customers owe The Radical Edge $720 for services they have received but have not paid for.
6. There was $450 of supplies on hand on April 30, 2011.

Instructions

(a) Calculate the cash balance at April 30, 2011.
(b) Prepare an accrual-based income statement, statement of owner's equity, and balance sheet for the six months ended April 30, 2011.

Taking It Further   Why are total expenses on the income statement not the same amount as total cash payments?

P3–8B   Okeke Limo Service has prepared the following trial balance before preparing its year-end adjusting entries:

Prepare and post adjusting entries, and prepare adjusted trial balance.
(SO 2, 3, 4) AP

OKEKE LIMO SERVICE
Trial Balance
December 31, 2011

	Debit	Credit
Cash	$ 12,100	
Accounts receivable	3,200	
Prepaid insurance	3,840	
Prepaid rent	1,150	
Supplies	2,550	
Automobiles	60,000	
Accumulated depreciation—automobiles		$ 12,000
Office furniture	16,000	
Accumulated depreciation—office furniture		10,400
Notes payable		46,000
Unearned revenue		3,000
B. Okeke, capital		41,000
B. Okeke, drawings	30,100	
Service revenue		116,600
Salaries expense	57,500	
Interest expense	2,415	
Rent expense	13,800	
Repair expense	6,000	
Gas and oil expense	20,345	
	$229,000	$229,000

Other data:

1. Service revenue earned but not billed or recorded at December 31, 2011, was $1,750.
2. The one-year insurance policy of $3,840 was paid on March 1, 2011.
3. A physical count of supplies at December 31, 2011, shows $525 of supplies on hand.
4. The automobiles have an estimated useful life of five years.
5. The office furniture has an estimated useful life of 10 years.
6. Interest on the 7% note payable is paid on the first day of each quarter (January 1, April 1, July 1, and October 1).
7. Employees' salaries total $230 per day. At December 31, three days of salaries are unpaid.
8. One of Okeke's customers paid in advance for a six-month contract at a rate of $500 per month. The contract began on September 1, 2011, and Okeke credited Unearned Revenue at the time.
9. On December 28, 2011, Okeke paid $1,150 for January 2012 rent.

Instructions

(a) Journalize the annual adjusting entries at December 31, 2011.
(b) Prepare a ledger. Enter the trial balance amounts and post the adjusting entries.
(c) Prepare an adjusted trial balance at December 31, 2011.

Taking It Further   As at December 31, 2011, approximately how old are the automobiles and office furniture?

Prepare and post adjusting entries, and prepare adjusted trial balance and financial statements.
(SO 2, 3, 4) AP

P3–9B   Mountain Best Lodge has a May 31 fiscal year end and prepares adjusting entries on a monthly basis. The following trial balance was prepared before recording the May 31 month-end adjustments:

MOUNTAIN BEST LODGE Trial Balance May 31, 2011		
	Debit	Credit
Cash	$ 2,365	
Prepaid insurance	2,275	
Supplies	975	
Land	80,000	
Lodge	180,000	
Accumulated depreciation—lodge		$ 62,625
Furniture	18,000	
Accumulated depreciation—furniture		14,100
Accounts payable		4,700
Unearned rent revenue		8,750
Mortgage payable		146,400
M. Rundle, capital		60,880
M. Rundle, drawings	28,055	
Rent revenue		102,100
Advertising expense	500	
Depreciation expense	7,425	
Salaries expense	49,350	
Supplies expense	2,240	
Interest expense	10,065	
Insurance expense	5,005	
Utilities expense	13,300	
	$399,555	$399,555

Other data:

1. The company pays $5,460 for its annual insurance policy on September 30 of each year.
2. A count of supplies on May 31 shows $760 of supplies on hand.
3. The lodge was purchased on May 31, 1997, and has an estimated useful life of 40 years.

4. The furniture was purchased on June 1, 2007, and has an estimated useful life of five years.

5. Customers must pay a $50 deposit if they want to book a room in advance during peak times. An analysis of these bookings indicates that 175 deposits were received (all credited to Unearned Rent Revenue) and 60 of the deposits have been earned by May 31, 2011.

6. The mortgage interest rate is 7.5% per year. Interest has been paid to May 1, 2011. The next payment is due on June 1.

7. Salaries accrued to the end of May were $975.

8. The May utility bill of $1,525 is unrecorded and unpaid.

9. On May 28, a local business contracted with Mountain Best Lodge to rent one of the rooms for four months starting June 1 at a rate of $1,400 per month. An advance payment equal to two months of rent is to be paid on June 1.

10. On May 31, Mountain Best Lodge has earned $950 of rent revenue from customers who are currently using the rooms but will not pay the amount owing until they check out in June. This amount is in addition to any deposits earned in item (5) above.

Instructions

(a) Journalize the monthly adjusting entries on May 31.
(b) Prepare a ledger. Enter the trial balance amounts and post the adjusting entries.
(c) Prepare an adjusted trial balance at May 31.
(d) Prepare an income statement and statement of owner's equity for the year ended May 31, and a balance sheet at May 31.

Taking It Further   Is the owner's capital account on the May 31, 2011, adjusted trial balance the same amount as shown in the May 31, 2011, balance sheet? Why or why not?

P3–10B   The unadjusted and adjusted trial balances of Sainte-Catherine Interior Design Co. as at September 30, 2011, follow:

Prepare adjusting entries and financial statements.

(SO 2, 3, 4) AP

	Unadjusted Debit	Unadjusted Credit	Adjusted Debit	Adjusted Credit
	SAINTE-CATHERINE INTERIOR DESIGN CO. Trial Balance September 30, 2011			
Accounts payable		$ 4,350		$ 4,660
Accounts receivable	$ 6,335		$ 7,435	
Accumulated depreciation—equipment		4,500		5,000
C. Larocque, capital		10,000		10,000
C. Larocque, drawings	2,700		2,700	
Cash	3,250		3,250	
Commission revenue		14,420		15,845
Depreciation expense	0		500	
Equipment	16,000		16,000	
Interest expense	50		100	
Interest payable		0		50
Notes payable		12,000		12,000
Prepaid rent	2,400		1,050	
Rent expense	0		1,350	
Salaries expense	13,050		13,990	
Salaries payable		0		940
Supplies	1,750		1,075	
Supplies expense	0		675	
Unearned revenue		875		550
Utilities expense	610		920	
	$46,145	$46,145	$49,045	$49,045

Instructions

(a) Prepare the adjusting journal entries that were made for the quarter.

(b) Prepare an income statement and a statement of owner's equity for the three months ending September 30 and a balance sheet at September 30.

(c) If the note bears interest at 5%, how many months has it been outstanding? Interest is payable at the beginning of the month.

Taking It Further   A friend of yours is considering purchasing the company from Catherine Larocque and asks you to comment on the company's results of operations and its financial position. Is the company performing well or not? Does the financial position appear healthy or weak? Use specific information from the financial statements to support your answer.

Prepare adjusting entries, adjusted trial balance, and financial statements.
(SO 2, 3, 4) AP

P3–11B   Here is an alphabetical list of Mahadeo Consulting Co.'s accounts at its fiscal year end of May 31, 2011, before adjustments. All accounts have normal balances.

Accounts payable	$ 21,470	M. Mahadeo, capital	$18,752
Accounts receivable	3,760	M. Mahadeo, drawings	82,140
Accumulated depreciation—		Note receivable	7,500
computer equipment	1,275	Prepaid insurance	1,890
Accumulated depreciation—		Rent expense	10,120
furniture	8,838	Salaries expense	32,950
Cash	2,825	Supplies	2,930
Computer equipment	7,650	Telephone expense	1,560
Consulting fees earned	117,350	Unearned consulting fees	5,280
Furniture	19,640		

Other data:

1. A one-year insurance policy was purchased on September 30, 2010.
2. On May 31, 2010, there was $525 of supplies on hand. During the year, $2,405 of additional supplies was purchased. A count of supplies on May 31, 2011, shows $475 of supplies on hand.
3. The computer equipment has an estimated useful life of three years.
4. The furniture has an estimated useful life of 10 years.
5. An analysis shows that $3,650 of the unearned consulting fees was earned by May 31, 2011.
6. The note receivable, issued on April 1, 2011, bears an annual interest rate of 5.5%. Interest and principal are receivable in full on the December 1, 2011, maturity date.
7. Salaries accrued to May 31 were $890.
8. On May 21, the company signed a contract to provide consulting services to Mawani Inc., starting June 1, 2011. The contract is for three months at a rate of $3,600 per month. Payment is due at the start of each month.
9. On May 31, 2011, the company had earned but not billed or received consulting revenue of $2,925.
10. The telephone bill for May 2011 was for $155. It has not been recorded or paid.

Instructions

(a) Prepare adjusting journal entries for the year ended May 31, 2011, as required.

(b) Prepare an adjusted trial balance in proper account order.

(c) Prepare an income statement, statement of owner's equity, and a balance sheet for the year ended May 31, 2011.

Taking It Further   Comment on the company's results of operations and financial position. In your analysis, refer to specific items in the financial statements.

*P3–12B   Garrett Bass Co. began operations on January 1, 2011. Its fiscal year end is December 31. It prepares financial statements and adjusts its accounts annually. Selected transactions for 2011 follow:

Prepare and post transaction and adjusting entries for prepayments.
(SO 2, 5) AP

1. On January 1, 2011, bought supplies for $1,250 cash. A physical count at December 31, 2011, revealed $375 of supplies still on hand.
2. Bought a $2,820, one-year insurance policy for cash on February 1, 2011. The policy came into effect on this date.
3. On December 1, Garrett received a $1,200 advance cash payment from four clients ($300 each) for services expected to be provided in the future. As at December 31, services had been performed for only one of the clients.

Instructions

(a) Assume that Garrett Bass Co. records all prepaid costs as assets and all revenues collected in advance as liabilities.
   1. Prepare the journal entries for the original transactions.
   2. Prepare the adjusting journal entries at December 31, 2011.
   3. Post these journal entries to T accounts and calculate the balance in each account after adjustments. You do not need to post to the Cash account.

(b) Assume instead that Garrett Bass Co. records all prepaid costs as expenses and all revenues collected in advance as revenues.
   1. Prepare the journal entries for the original transactions.
   2. Prepare the adjusting journal entries at December 31, 2011.
   3. Post these journal entries to T accounts and calculate the balance in each account after adjustments. You do not need to post to the Cash account.

Taking It Further   Compare the balances in each account calculated under (a) above with those calculated in (b). Comment on your findings.

*P3–13B   Royal Graphics Company was organized on July 1, 2011, by Jan Bejar. Royal Graphics records all prepayments in income statement accounts. At the end of the first six months of operations, the trial balance had the following accounts:

Prepare adjusting entries, adjusted trial balance, and financial statements.
(SO 3, 4, 5) AP

ROYAL GRAPHICS COMPANY
Trial Balance
December 31, 2011

	Debit	Credit
Cash	$ 7,250	
Accounts receivable	7,450	
Equipment	46,500	
Accounts payable		$ 6,190
Note payable		25,000
J. Bejar, capital		34,500
J. Bejar, drawings	17,400	
Graphics fees earned		62,525
Insurance expense	2,220	
Rent expense	4,025	
Salaries expense	38,280	
Supplies expense	3,350	
Utilities expense	1,740	
	$128,215	$128,215

Analysis reveals the following additional data:

1. At December 31, $585 of supplies was on hand.
2. The three-month, 6% note payable was issued November 1. Interest and principal are payable at maturity.

3. On August 1, 2011, the company purchased a one-year insurance policy for $2,220.
4. During the first six months of operations, Royal Graphics collected $6,500 cash from customers before providing services to them. At December 31, $5,100 of this amount has been earned.
5. Equipment was purchased on August 1, 2011, and has an estimated useful life of 12 years.
6. Utilities of $225 are owed at December 31.
7. January 2012 rent of $575 was paid on December 31, 2011, and is included in Rent Expense.

Instructions

(a) Journalize the adjusting entries at December 31. (Adjustments are recorded every six months.)
(b) Prepare an adjusted trial balance.
(c) Prepare an income statement and statement of owner's equity for the six months ended December 31, and a balance sheet at December 31, 2011.

Taking It Further   If Royal Graphics recorded all prepayments in balance sheet accounts, would this result in different numbers in the financial statements than in (c)?

Continuing Cookie Chronicle

(*Note:* This is a continuation of the Cookie Chronicle from Chapters 1 and 2. Use the information from the previous chapters and follow the instructions below using the ledger accounts you have already prepared.)

It is the end of November and Natalie has been in touch with her grandmother. Her grandmother asked her how well things went in her first month of business. Natalie, too, would like to know if she has been profitable or not during November. Natalie realizes that, in order to determine Cookie Creations' profit, she must first make adjustments. Natalie puts together the following additional information:

1. A count reveals that $75 of brochures and posters remained at the end of November.
2. A count reveals that $35 of baking supplies were used during November.
3. Natalie estimates that all of her baking equipment will have a useful life of three years, or 36 months. (Assume Natalie decides to record a full month's worth of depreciation, regardless of when the equipment was obtained by the business.)
4. Recall that Natalie's grandmother has decided to charge interest of 3% on the note payable extended on November 16. The loan plus interest is to be repaid in 12 months. (Assume that half a month of interest accrued during November.)

Instructions

Using the information that you have gathered through Chapter 2, and based on the new information above, do the following:
(a) Prepare and post the adjusting journal entries.
(b) Prepare an adjusted trial balance.
(c) Prepare an income statement.
(d) Was Cookie Creations profitable in November? Why is it better for Cookie Creations to measure profitability after adjusting journal entries have been prepared and posted instead of before?

Cumulative Coverage—Chapters 1 to 3

On August 31, 2011, the account balances of Pitre Equipment Repair were as follows:

PITRE EQUIPMENT REPAIR Trial Balance August 31, 2011	Debit	Credit
Cash	$ 1,880	
Accounts receivable	3,720	
Supplies	800	
Store equipment	15,000	
Accumulated depreciation—store equipment		$ 1,500
Accounts payable		3,100
Unearned service revenue		400
Salaries payable		700
R. Pitre, capital		15,700
	$21,400	$21,400

During September, the following transactions were completed:

Sept. 1 Borrowed $10,000 from the bank and signed a two-year, 5% note payable.
8 Paid $1,100 for employees' salaries, of which $400 is for September and $700 for August.
10 Received $1,200 cash from customers on account.
12 Received $3,400 cash for services performed in September.
17 Purchased additional supplies on account, $1,500.
20 Paid creditors $4,500 on account.
22 Paid September rent, $500.
25 Paid salaries, $1,200.
27 Performed services on account and billed customers for services provided, $900.
29 Received $700 from customers for future services.
30 Purchased additional store equipment on account, $3,000.

The company adjusts its accounts on a monthly basis. Adjustment data consist of the following:

1. Supplies on hand at September 30 cost $1,280.
2. Accrued salaries payable at September 30 total $775.
3. Store equipment has an expected useful life of five years.
4. Unearned service revenue of $450 is still not earned at September 30.
5. Interest is payable on the first of each month.

Instructions

(a) Enter the August 31 balances in general ledger accounts.
(b) Journalize the September transactions.
(c) Post to the ledger accounts.
(d) Prepare a trial balance at September 30.
(e) Journalize and post adjusting entries.
(f) Prepare an adjusted trial balance.
(g) Prepare an income statement and a statement of owner's equity for September, and a balance sheet at September 30, 2011.

BROADENING YOUR PERSPECTIVE

Financial Reporting and Analysis

Financial Reporting Problem

BYP3–1   The financial statements of The Forzani Group are presented in Appendix A at the end of this textbook.

Instructions

(a) What title does Forzani use for its income statement?

(b) What different types of revenues were reported by Forzani (see Note 2 (h))?

(c) Does Forzani report any prepayments on its balance sheet? If yes, identify each item that is a prepaid expense or unearned (deferred) revenue. Indicate the other account title that Forzani would likely use when it prepares adjusting entries for these accounts.

(d) Does Forzani report any accruals on its balance sheet? If yes, identify each item that is an accrued revenue or accrued expense. Indicate the other account title that Forzani would likely use when it prepares adjusting entries for these accounts.

Interpreting Financial Statements

BYP3–2   Rogers Communications Inc. is a diversified Canadian communications and media company. Rogers' balance sheet included a current liability of $239 million at December 31, 2008, called Unearned Revenue. The following comes from Rogers' revenue recognition policy note in its financial statements:

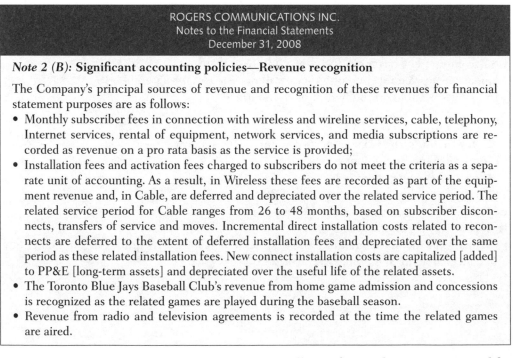

ROGERS COMMUNICATIONS INC.
Notes to the Financial Statements
December 31, 2008

Note 2 (B): **Significant accounting policies—Revenue recognition**

The Company's principal sources of revenue and recognition of these revenues for financial statement purposes are as follows:

- Monthly subscriber fees in connection with wireless and wireline services, cable, telephony, Internet services, rental of equipment, network services, and media subscriptions are recorded as revenue on a pro rata basis as the service is provided;

- Installation fees and activation fees charged to subscribers do not meet the criteria as a separate unit of accounting. As a result, in Wireless these fees are recorded as part of the equipment revenue and, in Cable, are deferred and depreciated over the related service period. The related service period for Cable ranges from 26 to 48 months, based on subscriber disconnects, transfers of service and moves. Incremental direct installation costs related to reconnects are deferred to the extent of deferred installation fees and depreciated over the same period as these related installation fees. New connect installation costs are capitalized [added] to PP&E [long-term assets] and depreciated over the useful life of the related assets.

- The Toronto Blue Jays Baseball Club's revenue from home game admission and concessions is recognized as the related games are played during the baseball season.

- Revenue from radio and television agreements is recorded at the time the related games are aired.

Unearned revenue includes subscriber deposits, installation fees and amounts received from subscribers related to services and subscriptions to be provided in future periods.

Instructions

(a) When does Rogers recognize its revenue from monthly subscriber fees?
(b) When should Rogers record unearned revenue from its subscription services? When should it record unearned revenue for its Blue Jays home game admission revenue?
(c) If Rogers (inappropriately) recorded these unearned revenues as revenue when the cash was received in advance, what would be the effect on the company's financial position? (Use the basic accounting equation and explain what elements would be overstated or understated.)
(d) According to this note, Rogers' new installation costs are depreciated over the useful life of the related assets. Is this an appropriate method of expense recognition for these costs? Explain.

Critical Thinking

Collaborative Learning Activity

Note to instructor: Additional instructions and material for this group activity can be found on the Instructor Resource Site.

BYP3–3 In this group activity, you will review the following types of adjusting entries:

1. Prepayments

    (a) Current assets
    (b) Long-lived assets

2. Unearned revenues
3. Accrued revenues
4. Accrued expenses

Instructions

(a) Your instructor will divide the class into "home" groups of five students. Each member of your group will choose one type of adjusting entry and then move to the "expert" group for that type.
(b) In the "expert" group, you will be given a handout explaining your type of adjusting entry. As a group, discuss the handout and ensure that each group member thoroughly understands how to prepare that entry.
(c) Return to your "home" group and explain how to prepare your type of adjusting entry to the other students in the group.
(d) Everyone in the class will write a short quiz on the four types of adjusting journal entries.
(e) The answers to the quiz will be reviewed in class by having one member from each "expert" group present and explain the correct adjusting entry for that group's type of adjusting entry.

Communication Activity

BYP3–4 There are many people today who believe that the cash basis of accounting is better than the accrual basis of accounting in predicting a company's future success. This idea became more popular after many reports of corporate financial scandals where management manipulated the timing of recognizing expenses and revenues in accrual accounting to influence profit.

Write a memo discussing whether you believe the cash basis of accounting is more reliable for measuring performance than the accrual basis. Include in your memo the answers to the following questions:

(a) What is the difference in calculating profit using the accrual basis of accounting versus the cash basis of accounting?

(b) Do you believe that it is possible for management to manipulate profit using the accrual basis of accounting? If yes, identify one way that management might be able to increase profit by manipulating the timing of revenue or expense recognition.

(c) Do you believe that it is possible for management to manipulate profit using the cash basis of accounting? If yes, identify one way that management might be able to increase profit when using the cash basis of accounting.

Ethics Case

WILEY PLUS

Ethics in Accounting

BYP3–5 Die Hard Company is a pesticide manufacturer. Its sales dropped a lot this year because of new legislation that outlawed the sale of many of Die Hard's chemical pesticides. In the coming year, Die Hard will have new, environmentally safe chemicals to replace these discontinued products. Sales in the next year are expected to be much higher than sales of any previous year. The drop in sales and profits appears to be a one-year exception.

Still, the company president is afraid that a large drop in the current year's profits could cause a significant drop in the market price of Die Hard's shares, and could make the company a takeover target. To avoid this possibility, the company president urges Carole Chiasson, the controller, to accrue all possible revenues and to defer as many expenses as possible when preparing this period's December 31 year-end adjusting entries. He says to Carole, "We need the revenues this year, and next year we can easily absorb expenses deferred from this year." Carole did not record the adjusting entries until January 17, but she dated the entries December 31 as if they were recorded then. Carole also did everything possible to follow the president's request.

Instructions

(a) Who are the stakeholders in this situation?

(b) What are the ethical considerations of (1) the president's request, and (2) Carole's decision to date the adjusting entries December 31?

(c) Can Carole aggressively accrue revenues and defer expenses and still be ethical?

"All About You" Activity

BYP3–6 A critical issue for accountants is the decision whether an expenditure should be recorded as an asset or an expense. The distinction between asset and expense is not always clear. In certain instances, businesses have been forced to restate their financial statements because management has recorded an asset when an expense should be recorded. The "All About You" feature indicates that post-secondary education results in higher earnings over an adult's working life and thus the money you are spending on your education today should be of significant future benefit. The question is then whether your education would meet the accounting definition of an asset or an expense.

Instructions

(a) Consider the nature of the cost of your education. What factors suggest that it should be considered an asset? What factors suggest that it should be considered an expense?

(b) Do you think the nature of the program you're taking should affect whether the cost of your education should be considered an asset or an expense? Explain.

(c) Economic theory suggests that people will always consider the benefit and cost of any expenditure and only incur the cost if the expected benefit is greater. Wouldn't this mean that every expenditure would meet the definition of an asset? Would you consider the cost of a vacation to Hawaii to be as valuable as a year of college? Would you record them both as assets on a personal balance sheet? Why or why not?

(d) If you were applying for a loan, what might the potential effect be on the success of your application if you understated your assets? What might be the potential effect on the bank if your assets are overstated and expenses understated?

ANSWERS TO CHAPTER QUESTIONS

Answers to Accounting in Action Insight Questions

All About You, p. 121

Q: How should you account for the cost of your post-secondary education? Should you be recognizing the cost as an expense each year or should you recognize it as an asset?

A: Expenses are recognized when there has been a decrease in an asset or an increase in a liability. Paying for an education will reduce assets such as cash and may also increase liabilities if you have to take out student loans. Therefore, most accountants would tell you that you should record the cost of your education as an expense as you incur those costs. On the other hand, it could be argued that your education is creating an asset—your increased future earning power. But then you would have to estimate the value of this asset. As with many situations in accounting, it is not easy to determine the correct answer.

Business Insight, p. 128

Q: If a business collects cash when the gift card is sold, how can gift card sales in December result in revenues in January?

A: Gift cards sales are simply another example of unearned revenues. At the time the gift card is sold, the business must record unearned revenue, which is a liability. When a customer redeems the gift card by making a purchase, then the company will reduce the liability and record revenue.

Ethics Insight, p. 134

Q: How could an adjusting entry be used to overstate profit?

A: If the adjusting entry reduces or eliminates an expense that should be recorded, profit will be overstated. For example, if the company uses unrealistically long useful lives in its depreciation calculations, the depreciation expense will be too low, and profit too high. Or if, for example, revenues are recognized before they have been earned, then profit may be overstated.

Answer to Forzani Review It Question 4, p. 128

Forzani reported depreciation expense of $47,613 thousand and $44,468 thousand in fiscal 2009 and 2008, respectively.

Answers to Self-Study Questions

1. b   2. d   3. d   4. c   5. d   6. a   7. b   8. a   9. c   *10. a

Remember to go back to the beginning of the chapter to check off your completed work!

←

CHAPTER 4
COMPLETION OF THE ACCOUNTING CYCLE

moulestores.com

 THE NAVIGATOR

- [ ] Understand *Concepts for Review*
- [ ] Read *Feature Story*
- [ ] Scan *Study Objectives*
- [ ] Read *Chapter Preview*
- [ ] Read text and answer *Before You Go On*
- [ ] Work *Demonstration Problem*
- [ ] Review *Summary of Study Objectives*
- [ ] Answer *Self-Study Questions*
- [ ] Complete assignments

CONCEPTS FOR REVIEW:

Before studying this chapter, you should understand or, if necessary, review:

a. When to recognize revenues and expenses. (Ch. 3, p. 120)

b. How to make adjusting entries. (Ch. 3, pp. 122–135)

c. How to prepare an adjusted trial balance. (Ch. 3, pp. 135–138)

d. How the balance sheet, income statement, and statement of owner's equity are connected. (Ch. 3, p. 137)

Breezing through the Month End with Style

WINNIPEG, Man.—Owned and operated by the Gorenstein family of Winnipeg, Moulé has four gallery-style retail stores in Vancouver, Winnipeg, and Portland, Oregon. Each one features gifts, jewellery, and other treasures from around the world. The items have been crafted by talented artists working in glass, ceramics, metal, and other media. Founded in 1987, Moulé also designs and manufactures a signature line of soft, feminine, and sophisticated women's apparel. The clothing is sold in Moulé stores and distributed across North America and as far away as Japan, and was recently featured in the movie *Sex and the City*.

Month end finds Moulé's chief operations officer, Laurie Gorenstein, running off extra reports for things like sales, GST and PST, commissions, and inventory on the CYBEX POS computer software he uses for most of the company's accounting. (He tracks payables on QuickBooks.) "Basically, I receive all the invoices from the stores at month end, do a second count, and check it against the figures in the computer. Then I run the general ledger and the trial balance."

"My accountant checks them, and we make any updates or corrections necessary—such as a cheque posted to the wrong account—with an adjusting or correcting entry," he continues. By checking things monthly, "it usually comes out pretty smoothly." Monthly financial statements then follow.

"So it really is pretty easy," says Mr. Gorenstein. Once a year, the load gets a little heavier when the books are closed—as with many businesses, Moulé's fiscal year ends December 31—and the year's financial statements are prepared. At this point, he's very glad of the care taken to find discrepancies and to make adjustments at month end. If errors are left undetected, "then they come back to haunt you months later and you can spend forever trying to sort them out."

Moulé has an "open-to-buy" system, which allows the store to use past sales data to predict future sales. By inputting merchandise sales margins daily and analyzing this information monthly, Mr. Gorenstein can track what sells best when, which leads to better planning and purchasing decisions. "The 'open-to-buy system' is specific to 20 different categories of merchandise, so we know what month is best for each," he explains. And tracking the merchandise so closely also significantly reduces the potential for error on the financial side.

The Navigator

STUDY OBJECTIVES:

After studying this chapter, you should be able to:

1. Prepare closing entries and a post-closing trial balance.
2. Explain the steps in the accounting cycle including optional steps.
3. Prepare correcting entries.
4. Prepare a classified balance sheet.
5. Illustrate measures used to evaluate liquidity.
6. Prepare a work sheet (Appendix 4A).
7. Prepare reversing entries (Appendix 4B).

The Navigator

In Chapter 3, we learned about the adjusting process and how to prepare financial statements directly from the adjusted trial balance. In this chapter, we will explain the remaining steps in the accounting cycle—the closing process. Once again, we will use the Pioneer Advertising Agency as an example.

After that we will look at correcting entries. As Laurie Gorenstein of Moulé notes in the feature story, locating and correcting errors on a regular basis is very important. We end by discussing the classification and use of balance sheets. The chapter is organized as follows:

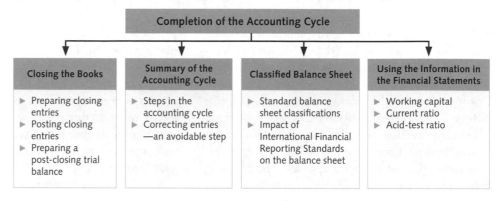

Closing the Books

STUDY OBJECTIVE 1

Prepare closing entries and a post-closing trial balance.

At the end of the accounting period, the accounts are made ready for the next period. This is called **closing the books**. When closing the books, it is important to know the difference between temporary and permanent accounts.

In previous chapters, you learned that all income statement accounts (revenue and expenses) and the owner's drawings account are components of the owner's capital account. They are considered **temporary accounts** because they contain data for only a single accounting period and are closed at the end of the period.

In contrast, all balance sheet accounts are considered **permanent accounts** because their balances are carried forward into the next accounting period. This means that permanent accounts are not closed. Illustration 4-1 identifies the accounts in each category.

Illustration 4-1 ➜

Temporary versus permanent accounts

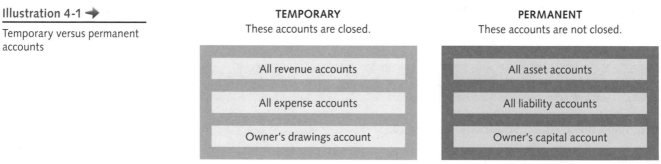

Preparing Closing Entries

At the end of the accounting period, **closing entries** are used to transfer the temporary account balances (revenues, expenses, and drawings) to the permanent owner's capital account. Closing entries formally record in the ledger the transfer of profit (or loss) and the owner's drawings to the owner's capital account.

WILEY PLUS

Tutorials: (Accounting Cycle)

This updates the owner's capital balance to its balance at the end of the period, as shown on the statement of owner's equity and the balance sheet. These entries also result in a zero balance in each temporary account. The temporary accounts are then ready to collect data in the next accounting period.

Journalizing and posting closing entries is a required step in the accounting cycle. This step is done after financial statements have been prepared. Closing entries are generally journalized and posted only at the end of a company's annual accounting period. Moulé, introduced in the feature story, closes its books once a year.

When closing entries are prepared, each income statement account could be closed directly to the owner's capital account. However, to do so would result in an excessive amount of detail in the owner's capital account. Instead, companies first close the revenue and expense accounts to another temporary account, **Income Summary**, and then they transfer the resulting profit or loss from this account to owner's capital. Illustration 4-2 shows the closing process.

Helpful hint After the revenue and expense accounts have been closed, the balance in the Income Summary account should be equal to the profit or loss for the period.

◄ Illustration 4-2

Closing process

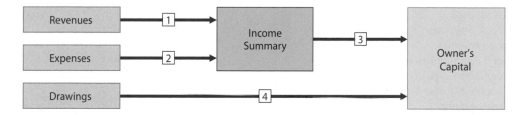

The four steps in Illustration 4-2 represent four closing entries:

1. **Close revenue accounts.** Debit each individual revenue account for its balance, and credit Income Summary for total revenues.
2. **Close expense accounts.** Debit Income Summary for total expenses, and credit each individual expense account for its balance.
3. **Close Income Summary.** Debit Income Summary for its balance (or credit it if there is a loss) and credit (debit) the owner's capital account.
4. **Close drawings.** Debit the owner's capital account and credit the owner's drawings account for the balance in drawings.

Companies record closing entries in the general journal. The heading "Closing Entries," inserted in the journal between the last adjusting entry and the first closing entry, identifies these entries. Then the company posts the closing entries to the ledger accounts.

Closing Entries Illustrated

To illustrate the journalizing and posting of closing entries, we will continue using the example of Pioneer Advertising Agency introduced in Chapters 2 and 3. In practice, companies generally prepare closing entries only at the end of the annual accounting period. However, to illustrate the process, we will assume that Pioneer Advertising Agency closes its books monthly.

Pioneer Advertising's adjusted trial balance on October 31, first shown in Chapter 3 (Illustration 3-7), is shown again here in Illustration 4-3. The temporary accounts have been highlighted in red. C. Byrd, Capital is not a temporary account, but it has also been highlighted because it is used in the closing process.

Remember that the capital account balance in the trial balance is the opening balance (plus any investments made by the owner during the period)—it is not the ending balance that appears in the statement of owner's equity and balance sheet. This permanent account is updated to its ending balance by transferring the profit (loss) and drawings for the period from the temporary accounts.

The closing entries at October 31 follow Illustration 4-3.

Illustration 4-3 ➜

Adjusted trial balance

PIONEER ADVERTISING AGENCY
Adjusted Trial Balance
October 31, 2011

	Debit	Credit
Cash	$14,250	
Accounts receivable	1,200	
Advertising supplies	1,000	
Prepaid insurance	550	
Office equipment	5,000	
Accumulated depreciation—office equipment		$ 83
Notes payable		5,000
Accounts payable		1,750
Unearned revenue		800
Salaries payable		2,400
Interest payable		25
C. Byrd, capital		10,000
C. Byrd, drawings	500	
Service revenue		11,400
Advertising supplies expense	1,500	
Depreciation expense	83	
Insurance expense	50	
Salaries expense	6,400	
Rent expense	900	
Interest expense	25	
	$31,458	$31,458

GENERAL JOURNAL					J3
Date	Account Titles and Explanation		Ref.	Debit	Credit
	Closing Entries				
2011	(1)				
Oct. 31	Service Revenue		400	11,400	
	Income Summary		350		11,400
	To close revenue account.				
	(2)				
31	Income Summary		350	8,958	
	Advertising Supplies Expense		611		1,500
	Depreciation Expense		711		83
	Insurance Expense		722		50
	Salaries Expense		726		6,400
	Rent Expense		729		900
	Interest Expense		905		25
	To close expense accounts.				
	(3)				
31	Income Summary		350	2,442	
	C. Byrd, Capital		301		2,442
	To close profit.				
	(4)				
31	C. Byrd, Capital		301	500	
	C. Byrd, Drawings		306		500
	To close drawings account.				

Be careful when you prepare closing entries: (1) Remember that the reason for making closing entries is to bring the temporary accounts to zero balances. Do not make the mistake of doubling the revenue, expense, drawings, and income summary account balances, rather than bringing them to zero. (2) Do not close owner's drawings with the expenses. The drawings that an owner makes are not an expense, so they are not a factor in determining profit.

Posting Closing Entries

The posting of the closing entries ("Clos.") is as follows:

GENERAL LEDGER

Cash   101

Oct.	1	10,000	Oct.	3	900
	3	1,200		3	600
	25	800		20	500
	31	9,000		24	4,000
				31	750
Oct.	31 Bal.	14,250			

Accounts Receivable   112

Oct.	21	10,000	Oct.	31	9,000
	31 Adj.	200			
Oct.	31 Bal.	1,200			

Advertising Supplies   129

Oct.	4	2,500	Oct.	31 Adj.	1,500
Oct.	31 Bal.	1,000			

Prepaid Insurance   130

Oct.	4	600	Oct.	31 Adj.	50
Oct.	31 Bal.	550			

Office Equipment   151

Oct.	2	5,000	
Oct.	31 Bal.	5,000	

Accumulated Depreciation— Office Equipment   152

			Oct.	31 Adj.	83
			Oct.	31 Bal.	83

Notes Payable   200

			Oct.	2	5,000
			Oct.	31 Bal.	5,000

Accounts Payable   201

Oct.	31	750	Oct.	4	2,500
			Oct.	31 Bal.	1,750

Unearned Revenue   209

Oct.	31 Adj.	400	Oct.	3	1,200
			Oct.	31 Bal.	800

Salaries Payable   212

			Oct.	31 Adj.	2,400
			Oct.	31 Bal.	2,400

Interest Payable   230

			Oct.	31 Adj.	25
			Oct.	31 Bal.	25

C. Byrd, Capital   301

			Oct.	1	10,000
Oct.	31 Clos.	500		31 Clos.	2,442
			Oct.	31 Bal.	11,942

C. Byrd, Drawings   306

Oct.	20	500	Oct.	31 Clos.	500
Oct.	31 Bal.	0			

Income Summary   350

Oct.	31 Clos.	8,958	Oct.	31 Clos.	11,400
			Oct.	31 Bal.	2,442
Oct.	31 Clos.	2,442			
			Oct.	31 Bal.	0

Service Revenue   400

			Oct.	21	10,000
				25	800
				31 Adj.	400
Oct.	31 Clos.	11,400		31 Adj.	200
			Oct.	31 Bal.	0

Advertising Supplies Expense   611

Oct.	31 Adj.	1,500	Oct.	31 Clos.	1,500
Oct.	31 Bal.	0			

Depreciation Expense   711

Oct.	31 Adj.	83	Oct.	31 Clos.	83
Oct.	31 Bal.	0			

Insurance Expense   722

Oct.	31 Adj.	50	Oct.	31 Clos.	50
Oct.	31 Bal.	0			

Salaries Expense   726

Oct.	21	4,000			
Oct.	31 Adj.	2,400	Oct.	31 Clos.	6,400
Oct.	31 Bal.	0			

Rent Expense   729

Oct.	3	900	Oct.	31 Clos.	900
Oct.	31 Bal.	0			

Interest Expense   905

Oct.	31 Adj.	25	Oct.	31 Clos.	25
Oct.	31 Bal.	0			

Stop and check your work after the closing entries are posted:
1. The balance in Income Summary, immediately before the final closing entry to transfer the balance to the owner's capital account, should equal the profit (or loss) reported in the income statement (see Illustration 3-8 in Chapter 3).
2. All temporary accounts (revenues, expenses, owner's drawings, and Income Summary) should have zero balances.
3. The balance in the capital account should equal the ending balance reported in the statement of owner's equity and balance sheet (see Illustrations 3-8 and 3-9 in Chapter 3).

ACCOUNTING IN ACTION: ACROSS THE ORGANIZATION

Ever since the first finance benchmarking studies in the 1980s, chief financial officers (CFOs) have been very interested in information that allows them to compare their companies with other companies. A 2007 study by UK consulting firms BPM International and the Paragon Consulting Group compared the close times of 530 of the world's largest companies in the United States, Britain, and continental Europe over the previous four years. It found that European firms were speeding up their close times, while British firms remained stagnant and U.S. firms slowed down. Although U.S. companies remain the world's fastest at closing their books, European companies may take the lead within a decade.

Source: Alan Rappaport, "Running a Close Race," CFO.com, October 19, 2007.

Why are CFOs interested in knowing how long it takes for companies to close their books?

Preparing a Post-Closing Trial Balance

Helpful hint Total debits in a post-closing trial balance will not equal total assets on the balance sheet if contra accounts, such as accumulated depreciation, are present. Accumulated depreciation is deducted from assets on the balance sheet but added to the credit column in a trial balance.

After all closing entries have been journalized and posted, another trial balance is prepared from the ledger. It is called a **post-closing trial balance**. The post- (or after-) closing trial balance lists permanent accounts and their balances after closing entries have been journalized and posted. The purpose of this trial balance is to prove the equality of the permanent account balances that are carried forward into the next accounting period. Since all temporary accounts have zero balances after closing, the post-closing trial balance contains only permanent—balance sheet—accounts.

The post-closing trial balance for Pioneer Advertising Agency is shown in Illustration 4-4. Note that the account balances are the same as the ones in the company's balance sheet (Pioneer Advertising's balance sheet is shown in Chapter 3, Illustration 3-9).

Illustration 4-4 ➡

Post-closing trial balance

PIONEER ADVERTISING AGENCY Post-Closing Trial Balance October 31, 2011		
	Debit	Credit
Cash	$ 14,250	
Accounts receivable	1,200	
Advertising supplies	1,000	
Prepaid insurance	550	
Office equipment	5,000	
Accumulated depreciation—office equipment		$ 83
Notes payable		5,000
Accounts payable		1,750
Unearned revenue		800
Salaries payable		2,400
Interest payable		25
C. Byrd, capital		11,942
	$22,000	$22,000

A post-closing trial balance provides evidence that the journalizing and posting of closing entries has been completed properly. It also shows that the accounting equation is in balance at the end of the accounting period and the beginning of the next accounting period.

As in the case of the trial balance, the post-closing trial balance does not prove that all transactions have been recorded or that the ledger is correct. For example, the post-closing trial balance will still balance if a transaction is not journalized and posted, or if a transaction is journalized and posted twice. This is why it is so important, as Laurie Gorenstein of Moulé says in the feature story, to find and correct all errors before the books are closed.

BEFORE YOU GO ON . . .

→ Review It

1. How do permanent accounts differ from temporary accounts?
2. Describe the four entries used to close the books.
3. After closing entries are posted, what amounts on what financial statements should the balance in the owner's capital account agree with?
4. What are the differences between a trial balance, adjusted trial balance, and post-closing trial balance?

→ Do It

The adjusted trial balance for the Nguyen Company shows the following: H. Nguyen, Drawings $5,000; H. Nguyen, Capital $42,000; Service Revenue $18,000; Rent Expense $2,000; Supplies Expense $500; and Wages Expense $7,500. Nguyen Company's statement of owner's equity for the year showed a profit of $8,000 and closing owner's capital of $45,000. (a) Prepare the closing entries at December 31. (b) Create T accounts for Income Summary and H. Nguyen, Capital, and post the closing entries to these accounts.

Action Plan

- Debit each individual revenue account for its balance and credit the total to Income Summary.
- Credit each individual expense account for its balance and debit the total to Income Summary.
- Stop and check your work: Does the balance in Income Summary equal the reported profit?
- Debit the balance in Income Summary and credit the amount to the owner's capital account (do the opposite if the company had a loss).
- Credit the balance in the drawings account and debit the amount to the owner's capital account. Do not close drawings with the expenses.
- Stop and check your work: Do the temporary accounts have zero balances? Does the ending balance in the owner's capital account equal the closing owner's capital reported on the statement of owner's equity?

Solution

Dec. 31	Service Revenue	18,000	
	Income Summary		18,000
	To close revenue account.		
31	Income Summary	10,000	
	Rent Expense		2,000
	Supplies Expense		500
	Wages Expense		7,500
	To close expense accounts.		
31	Income Summary	8,000	
	H. Nguyen, Capital		8,000
	To close Income Summary.		
31	H. Nguyen, Capital	5,000	
	H. Nguyen, Drawings		5,000
	To close drawings.		

Income Summary				H. Nguyen, Capital			
Clos.	10,000	Clos.	18,000			Bal.	42,000
		Bal.	8,000*	Clos.	5,000	Clos.	8,000
Clos.	8,000					Bal.	45,000**
		Bal.	0				

* Check if this equals profit.   ** Check if this equals closing owner's capital.

The Navigator

Related exercise material: BE4–1, BE4–2, BE4–3, BE4–4, E4–1, E4–2, E4–3, and E4–4.

WILEY
PLUS

Tutorials: (Accounting Cycle)

Summary of the Accounting Cycle

In Chapters 2 and 3 and in the first part of Chapter 4, you have been learning the steps in the accounting cycle. In the following section we review these steps and discuss optional steps.

Steps in the Accounting Cycle

As introduced in Chapter 2, the cycle begins with the analysis and recording of business transactions. Chapter 3 covers the adjustment process. Chapter 4 covers the final steps of the accounting cycle—the closing process. The steps in the accounting cycle are reproduced here in Illustration 4-5.

Illustration 4-5 ➜

Steps in the accounting cycle

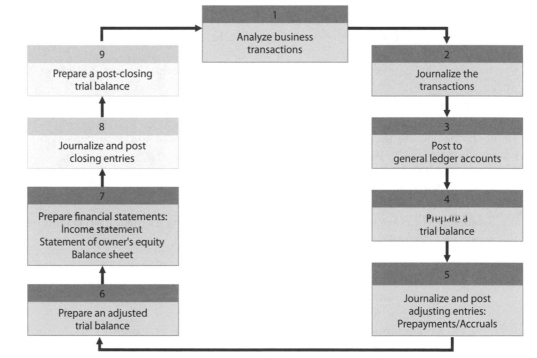

Optional steps: If a work sheet is prepared, steps 4, 5, and 6 are done in the work sheet, and adjusting entries are journalized and posted after step 7. If reversing entries are prepared, they occur between steps 9 and 1.

The steps in the cycle are done in sequence and are repeated in each accounting period. Steps 1 and 2 can occur every day during the accounting period, as explained in Chapter 2. Steps 3 through 7 are done periodically, such as monthly, quarterly, or annually. Steps 8 and 9, closing entries and a post-closing trial balance, are usually done only at the end of a company's annual accounting period.

There are also two optional steps in the accounting cycle: work sheets and reversing entries. These optional steps are explained in the following two sections.

Work Sheets—An Optional Step

Some accountants like to use an optional multiple-column form known as a **work sheet** to help them prepare adjusting entries and the financial statements. As its name suggests, the work sheet is a working tool. It is not a permanent accounting record; it is neither a journal nor a part of the general ledger. Companies generally computerize work sheets using an electronic spreadsheet program such as Excel.

Although using a work sheet is optional, it is useful. For example, a work sheet makes it easier to prepare interim (e.g., monthly or quarterly) financial information. The monthly or quarterly adjusting entries can be entered in the work sheet, and interim financial statements can then be easily developed.

As the preparation of a work sheet is optional, its basic form and the procedure for preparing it are explained in Appendix 4A at the end of the chapter.

Reversing Entries—An Optional Step

Some accountants prefer to reverse certain adjusting entries by making a reversing entry at the beginning of the next accounting period. A **reversing entry** is the exact opposite of the adjusting entry made in the previous period. Use of reversing entries is an optional bookkeeping procedure; it is not a required step in the accounting cycle. We have therefore chosen to explain this topic in Appendix 4B at the end of the chapter.

BEFORE YOU GO ON . . .

→ Review It

1. What are the required steps in the accounting cycle?
2. What are the optional steps in the accounting cycle?
3. What are the differences between transaction, adjusting, closing, and reversing journal entries?

Related exercise material: BE4–5, BE4–6, E4–5.

The Navigator

Correcting Entries—An Avoidable Step

Unfortunately, errors may happen in the recording process. The accounting cycle does not include a specific step for correcting errors because this step is not needed if the accounting records have no errors. But if errors exist, they should be corrected as soon as they are discovered by journalizing and posting **correcting entries**. If the accounting records have no errors, no correcting entries are needed.

You should understand several differences between correcting entries and adjusting entries. First, adjusting entries are an integral part of the accounting cycle. Correcting entries, on the other hand, are unnecessary if the records have no errors. Second, adjustments are journalized and posted only at the end of an accounting period. In contrast, correcting entries are made whenever an error is discovered. Finally, adjusting entries always affect at least one balance sheet account (not Cash) and one income statement account. In contrast, correcting entries can involve any combination of accounts that need to be corrected. Adjusting and correcting entries do have one thing in common, however: in both cases, they must be journalized and posted before closing entries.

To determine the correcting entry, it is useful to compare the incorrect entry with the entry that should have been made. Doing this helps identify the accounts and amounts that should—and should not—be corrected. After comparison, a correcting entry is made to correct the accounts. This approach is shown in the following two cases.

STUDY OBJECTIVE 3

Prepare correcting entries.

Case 1. On May 10, a $50 cash collection on account from a customer is journalized and posted as a debit to Cash $50 and as a credit to Service Revenue $50. The error is discovered on May 20 when the customer pays the remaining balance in full.

INCORRECT ENTRY (MAY 10)		
Cash	50	
Service Revenue		50

CORRECT ENTRY (MAY 10)		
Cash	50	
Accounts Receivable		50

Comparison of the incorrect entry with the correct entry that should have been made (but was not) reveals that the debit to Cash of $50 is correct. However, the $50 credit to Service Revenue should have been credited to Accounts Receivable. As a result, both Service Revenue and Accounts Receivable are overstated in the ledger. The following correcting entry is needed:

A	=	L	+	OE
−50				−50

Cash flows: no effect

Correcting Entry		
May 20	Service Revenue	50	
Accounts Receivable		50
To correct entry of May 10.		

Case 2. On May 18, office equipment that costs $450 is purchased on account. The transaction is journalized and posted as a debit to Delivery Equipment $45 and as a credit to Accounts Payable $45. The error is discovered on June 3 when the monthly statement for May is received from the creditor.

INCORRECT ENTRY (MAY 18)		
Delivery Equipment	45	
Accounts Payable		45

CORRECT ENTRY (MAY 18)		
Office Equipment	450	
Accounts Payable		450

A comparison of the two entries shows that three accounts are incorrect. Delivery Equipment is overstated by $45; Office Equipment is understated by $450; and Accounts Payable is understated by $405 ($450 − $45). The correcting entry is as follows:

A	=	L	+	OE
+450		+405		
−45				

Cash flows: no effect

Correcting Entry		
June 3	Office Equipment	450	
Delivery Equipment		45
Accounts Payable		405
To correct May 18 entry.		

Alternative Approach. Instead of preparing a correcting entry, many accountants simply reverse the incorrect entry and then record the correct entry. This approach will result in more entries and postings, but it is often easier and more logical.

Sometimes errors are not found until after the temporary accounts have been closed. A correcting entry that fixes an error from a previous accounting year is called a prior period adjustment. These correcting entries can be very complex, and will be covered in a later chapter.

ACCOUNTING IN ACTION: BUSINESS INSIGHT

Canadian telecom equipment maker Nortel Networks' name has become synonymous with accounting woes in recent years. The company filed for bankruptcy protection in January 2009 after losing almost $7 billion since 2005. Nortel has had to restate its financial statements several times. The most recent restatements affected the financials for 2004, 2005, and the first nine months of 2006, as well as adjustments to periods before 2004. The revision to the previously reported first nine months of 2006 were expected to increase revenues and net earnings by about $24 million and $15 million, respectively; while revisions to its previously reported 2005 and 2004 financial results reduced revenue by approximately $87 million and $42 million, respectively. As for the financial results before 2004, the negative impacts were expected to be approximately $27 million on revenue, and $5 million on net earnings.

Sources: Joe Schneider, "Pensioners seek payments from Nortel," *The Globe and Mail*, April 16, 2009; Nortel Networks news release, March 1, 2007.

Nortel filed for bankruptcy protection in January 2009. Is it possible there is a link between the need to correct all of these accounting errors and that fact?

BEFORE YOU GO ON . . .

➜ **Review It**

1. What are the differences between adjusting journal entries and correcting journal entries?
2. What is the advantage of reversing an incorrect journal entry and then preparing the correct journal entry, instead of making one compound correcting journal entry?

➜ **Do It**

The Chip 'N Dough Company made the following adjusting journal entry to record $5,200 of depreciation expense on a delivery truck at year end:

Feb. 28	Depreciation Expense	520	
	Cash		520
	To record depreciation on delivery truck.		

Prepare the required correcting entry.

Action Plan

• Determine the correct entry that should have been made.
• Compare it with the incorrect entry made and make the required corrections.
• **Or** use the alternative approach of reversing the incorrect journal entry and recording the correct journal entry.

Solution

Feb. 28	Cash	520	
	Depreciation Expense	4,680	
	Accumulated Depreciation—Truck		5,200
	To correct depreciation adjustment.		

Depreciation expense is understated by $4,680 ($5,200 – $520).

OR

Feb. 28	Cash	520	
	Depreciation Expense		520
	To reverse incorrect depreciation adjustment.		
28	Depreciation Expense	5,200	
	Accumulated Depreciation—Truck		5,200
	To record the correct depreciation entry.		

Related exercise material: BE4–7, BE4–8, E4–6, and E4–7.

The Navigator

Classified Balance Sheet

The balance sheet presents a snapshot of a company's financial position at a point in time. The balance sheets that we have seen so far have all been very basic, with items classified simply as assets, liabilities, or owner's equity. To improve users' understanding of a company's financial position, companies often group similar assets and similar liabilities together.

STUDY OBJECTIVE 4

Prepare a classified balance sheet.

Alternative terminology
The balance sheet is also known as the statement of financial position.

Standard Balance Sheet Classifications

A **classified balance sheet** generally has the classifications listed in Illustration 4-6.

Assets	Liabilities and Owner's Equity
Current assets	Current liabilities
Long-term investments	Long-term (non-current) liabilities
Property, plant, and equipment	Owner's (Shareholders') equity
Intangible assets	

◄ **Illustration 4-6**

Standard balance sheet classifications

These groupings help readers determine such things as (1) whether the company has enough assets to pay its debts as they come due, and (2) the claims of short- and long-term creditors on total assets. These classifications are shown in the balance sheet of MacDonald Company in Illustration 4-7. In the sections that follow, we explain each of these groupings.

Illustration 4-7 ➜

Classified balance sheet

MACDONALD COMPANY Balance Sheet November 30, 2011			
Assets			
Current assets			
Cash		$ 6,600	
Short-term investments		2,000	
Accounts receivable		7,000	
Inventories		4,000	
Supplies		2,100	
Prepaid insurance		400	
Total current assets			$ 22,100
Long-term investments			
Equity investment		$ 5,200	
Debt investment		2,000	
Total long-term investments			7,200
Property, plant, and equipment			
Land		$40,000	
Building	$75,000		
Less: Accumulated depreciation	15,000	60,000	
Office equipment	$24,000		
Less: Accumulated depreciation	5,000	19,000	
Total property, plant, and equipment			119,000
Goodwill			3,100
Total assets			$151,400
Liabilities and Owner's Equity			
Current liabilities			
Notes payable		$11,000	
Accounts payable		2,100	
Unearned revenue		900	
Salaries payable		1,600	
Interest payable		450	
Current portion of notes payable		1,000	
Total current liabilities			$ 17,050
Long-term liabilities			
Mortgage payable		$ 9,000	
Notes payable		1,300	
Total long-term liabilities			10,300
Total liabilities			27,350
Owner's equity			
J. MacDonald, capital			124,050
Total liabilities and owner's equity			$151,400

Current Assets

Current assets are normally cash and other assets that will be converted to cash, sold, or used up in one year from the balance sheet date. Some companies use a period longer than one year to classify assets as current because they have an operating cycle that is longer than one year.

The **operating cycle** of a company is the time it takes to go from starting with cash to ending with cash in producing revenues. Illustration 4-8 shows the basic steps involved in an operating cycle.

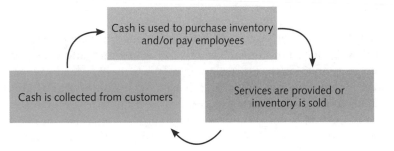

← Illustration 4-8

Steps in the operating cycle

For most businesses, this cycle is less than one year, so they use the one-year cutoff. But for some businesses, such as vineyards or airplane manufacturers, this period may be longer than one year. Except where noted, we will assume companies use one year to determine whether an asset is current or non-current.

Common types of current assets are: (1) cash; (2) short-term investments, such as debt and equity securities that are held for trading; (3) receivables, such as notes receivable, accounts receivable, and interest receivable; (4) inventories or merchandise available for sale; (5) supplies; and (6) prepaid expenses, such as rent, insurance, and supplies. Accounts receivable are current assets because they will be collected and converted to cash within one year. Inventory is a current asset because a company expects to sell it within one year. Supplies are a current asset because a company expects to use or consume supplies within one year. In Illustration 4-7, MacDonald Company had current assets of $22,100.

In Canada, companies generally list current assets in the order of their liquidity; that is, in the order in which they are expected to be converted into cash. This arrangement is shown in the presentation used by Canada Post, in Illustration 4-9.

← Illustration 4-9

Current assets section

CANADA POST Balance Sheet (partial) December 31, 2008 (in millions)	CANADA POST ➤ POSTES CANADA From anywhere... to anyone
Current assets	
Cash and cash equivalents	$ 605
Short-term investments	103
Accounts receivable	575
Income taxes recoverable	7
Prepaid expenses	71
Current portion of future income taxes	23
	1,384

There are two items shown in Canada Post's current assets at December 31, 2008, that will likely change in future years. The first is the combination of cash equivalents with cash. Cash equivalents are near-cash items, such as treasury bills and money-market funds. The International Accounting Standards Board and the Financial Accounting Standards Board are working on a joint project to improve the presentation of information in financial statements, and one of the items under consideration is cash equivalents. While they have not been finalized, there are recommendations that in the future, assets currently classified as cash equivalents will be reported as short-term investments.

The second item that will likely change is the inclusion of a portion of future income taxes in current assets. Canada Post's conversion to International Financial Reporting Standards in 2011 will result in changing the name "future income taxes" to "deferred taxes." At that point, Canada Post will also be required to show all future tax assets as non-current assets. Thus, this item, current portion of future income taxes, will not be included in Canada Post's current assets after 2010.

The assets described in the next three sections are non-current assets. These are assets that will be realized (converted to cash, sold, or used) more than one year after the balance sheet date.

Long-Term Investments

Long-term investments are generally investments in long-term debt (for example, loans, notes, bonds, or mortgages) that management intends to hold to earn interest or equity (for example, shares) of other corporations that management plans to hold for many years for strategic reasons. They also include investments in long-lived assets such as real estate if the asset is not being used as part of the company's operating activities. These assets are classified as long-term because they are not readily marketable or expected to be converted into cash within one year. In Illustration 4-7, MacDonald Company reported long-term investments of $7,200 on its balance sheet.

Some companies have only one line on the balance sheet showing total long-term investments, and provide all of the details in the notes to the financial statements. If an item is simply called an "investment," without specifying if it is a short- or long-term investment, you should always assume it is a long-term investment.

Investments that are accounted for using the equity method must be shown separately. Equity accounting is used when a company owns enough of another company to have a significant influence over its operations. This will be discussed further in Chapter 16.

Empire Company Limited (shown in the partial balance sheet in Illustration 4-10), has three lines for long-term investments on its balance sheet. Additional information on these investments is included in notes 5 and 6. A total for long-term investments is not included in Illustration 4-10, as Empire does not show a subtotal for all of its long-term investments on the balance sheet.

Illustration 4-10 ➡

Long-term investments section

EMPIRE COMPANY LIMITED
Balance Sheet (partial)
May 2, 2009
(in millions)

EMPIRE
COMPANY LIMITED

Investments (realizable value $1.1)	$ 1.1
Investments, at equity (realizable value $254.4) (Note 5)	18.8
Loans and other receivables (Note 6)	75.3

Alternative terminology
Property, plant, and equipment are sometimes called *capital assets* or *fixed assets*.

Property, Plant, and Equipment

Property, plant, and equipment are long-lived, tangible assets that are used in the business and are not intended for sale. This category includes land, buildings, equipment, and furniture. In Illustration 4-7, MacDonald Company reported property, plant, and equipment of $119,000.

Although the order of property, plant, and equipment on the balance sheet can vary among companies, in Canada these assets have traditionally been listed in their order of permanency. Land is usually listed first, because it has an indefinite life, and is followed by the asset with the next longest useful life (normally buildings), and so on.

Since property, plant, and equipment benefit future periods, their cost is allocated to expense over their useful lives through depreciation, as we learned in Chapter 3. Assets that are depreciated are reported at their carrying amount (cost minus accumulated depreciation).

Danier Leather Inc. reported the total carrying amount (or "net book value" as Danier calls it) of $19,339 thousand for its property, plant, and equipment on its balance sheet. Danier reports the cost, accumulated depreciation (or "accumulated amortization" as Danier calls it), and net book value of each category of property, plant, and equipment in a note to the financial statements, as shown in Illustration 4-11. This practice is very common for public companies to keep the balance sheet from looking too cluttered.

Note that, except for land (which has an unlimited useful life), all other property, plant, and equipment items are depreciated. This includes leasehold improvements, which are long-lived additions or renovations made to leased property.

← Illustration 4-11

Property, plant, and equipment section

DANIER LEATHER INC.
Notes to the Financial Statements
June 27, 2009
(in thousands)

DANIER
LEAVE ORDINARY BEHIND™

Note 5. Property and Equipment

	Cost	Accumulated Amortization	Net Book Value
Land	$ 1,000	$ –	$ 1,000
Building	7,064	2,185	4,879
Leasehold improvements	23,539	15,949	7,590
Furniture and equipment	8,786	5,884	2,902
Computer hardware and software	7,302	4,334	2,968
	$47,691	$28,352	$19,339

Intangible Assets

Intangible assets are long-lived assets that do not have physical substance. They give a company rights and privileges and include such things as goodwill, patents, copyrights, trademarks, trade names, and licences. Goodwill results from the acquisition of another company when the price paid for the company is higher than the fair value of the purchased company's net assets. In Illustration 4-7, MacDonald Company reported $3,100 of goodwill.

Intangible assets are normally divided into two groups for accounting purposes: those with definite lives and those with indefinite lives. Similar to buildings and equipment, intangible assets with definite useful lives are amortized. Similar to land, intangible assets with indefinite lives are not amortized.

Note that while the term "depreciation" is normally used for the allocation of cost over the useful lives of property, plant, and equipment, the term "amortization" is used for the allocation of the cost of intangible assets. We will learn more about intangible assets in Chapter 9.

Illustration 4-12 shows how Shaw Communications reported intangible assets in its balance sheet. As shown in Shaw's balance sheet, goodwill is reported separately from other intangible assets. All of Shaw Communications' intangible assets have indefinite lives, so they are not amortized.

← Illustration 4-12

Intangible assets section

SHAW COMMUNICATIONS INC.
Balance Sheet (partial)
November 30, 2008
(in thousands)

SHAW)

Intangible assets	
Broadcast licences	$4,776,114
Goodwill	88,111
	4,864,225

Current Liabilities

Current liabilities are obligations that are expected to be settled within one year from the balance sheet date or in the company's normal operating cycle. As with current assets, companies use a period longer than one year if their operating cycle is longer than one year.

Common examples of current liabilities are notes payable, accounts payable, salaries payable, interest payable, sales taxes payable, unearned revenues, and current maturities of long-term liabilities (payments to be made within the next year on long-term debt). Corporations may also have income taxes payable included in the current liabilities section of the balance sheet. In Illustration 4-7, MacDonald Company reported six different types of current liabilities, for a total of $17,050.

Similar to current assets, current liabilities are often listed in order of liquidity. That is, the liabilities that will be due first are listed first. However, many companies simply list the items in their current liabilities section according to a company tradition. The current liabilities section from Sears Canada's balance sheet is shown in Illustration 4-13.

Illustration 4-13 ➡

Current liabilities section

SEARS CANADA INC. Balance Sheet (partial) January 31, 2009 (in millions)	**Sears**
Current liabilities	
Accounts payable	$ 640.9
Accrued liabilities	383.6
Income and other taxes payable	39.4
Principal payments on long-term obligations due within one year (Note 7)	32.1
Future income tax liabilities (Note 3)	2.5
	1,098.5

Users of financial statements look closely at the relationship between current assets and current liabilities. This relationship is important in evaluating a company's ability to pay its current liabilities. We will talk more about this later in the chapter when we learn how to use the information in the financial statements.

Long-Term Liabilities

Alternative terminology
Long-term liabilities are sometimes called *non-current liabilities, long-term obligations,* or *long-term debt.*

Obligations that are expected to be paid after one year or longer are classified as **long-term liabilities**. Liabilities in this category can include bonds payable, mortgages payable, notes payable, lease liabilities, and deferred income taxes (income taxes payable after more than one year), among others. In Illustration 4-7, MacDonald Company reported long-term liabilities of $10,300.

Illustration 4-14 shows the long-term liabilities that Tim Hortons Inc. reported on a recent balance sheet.

Illustration 4-14 ➡

Long-term liabilities section

TIM HORTONS INC. Balance Sheet (partial) December 31, 2008 (in thousands)	
Long-term obligations	
Term debt (note 14)	$332,506
Advertising fund restricted debt (notes 9 and 14)	6,929
Capital leases (note 17)	59,052
Deferred income taxes (note 7)	13,604
Other long-term liabilities	74,072
	486,163

Notes 7, 9, 14, and 17 contain additional details about the debt, including how much must be paid during each of the next five years. The notes also contain information about restrictions placed on Tim Hortons as a result of these obligations.

Equity

Alternative terminology
Share capital is also commonly known as *capital stock.*

The content of the equity section varies with the form of business organization. In a proprietorship, there is one capital account under the heading "Owner's equity." In a partnership, there is a capital account for each partner under the heading "Partners' equity."

For a corporation, shareholders' equity always includes two parts: share capital and retained earnings. Amounts that are invested in the business by the shareholders are recorded as share capital. Profit that is kept for use in the business is recorded in the retained earnings account.

Some corporations may have other parts to the equity section, such as contributed surplus, which arises from the sale of shares, and accumulated other comprehensive income. We will learn more about corporation equity accounts in later chapters.

Illustration 4-15 shows how WestJet Airlines Ltd., a corporation, reported its shareholders' equity section in its balance sheet.

WESTJET AIRLINES LTD. Balance Sheet (partial) December 31, 2008 (in thousands)	
Shareholders' equity	
Share capital (note 8(b))	$ 452,885
Contributed surplus	60,193
Accumulated other comprehensive loss (note 12(c))	(38,112)
Retained earnings	611,171
	1,086,137

← Illustration 4-15

Shareholders' equity section

Impact of International Financial Reporting Standards on Balance Sheet Presentation

It is important to note that, when it comes to balance sheet presentation, International Financial Reporting Standards (IFRS) allow for some choices. Experience has shown that where choices exist, companies have continued to follow the practices they used prior to adopting IFRS. Thus, the differences in balance sheet presentation when following IFRS compared with following Canadian accounting standards may not be as significant as some people originally expected. In the following sections, we will look at the basic differences that could arise.

Statement Name

Under IFRS, the balance sheet is called the statement of financial position. Canadian accounting standards have always allowed companies to use either of these titles. Companies will continue to have the choice under IFRS. While "statement of financial position" more accurately describes the content of the statement, "balance sheet" has been much more widely used. As many Canadian companies will continue to use balance sheet, we also use that term in this textbook.

Classification of Balance Sheet Items

The IFRS state that companies are to present current and non-current assets, and current and non-current liabilities, as separate classifications on the balance sheet. The criteria for deciding if an asset, or a liability, is current or non-current were described earlier in this chapter.

IFRS also require companies to separately show property, plant, and equipment, intangible assets, and long-term investments on the balance sheet, in the same way as illustrated earlier in the chapter. The standards are designed to ensure separate presentation on the face of the balance sheet for items that are different in nature or function.

In practice, companies following IFRS typically include the heading *non-current assets* on the balance sheet, and group property, plant, and equipment, intangible assets, and long-term investments under this heading. We did not use this heading earlier in the chapter because it is not typically used by Canadian companies. While the use of the heading will likely increase over time, it is not required. Therefore, we do not use it in illustrations in this textbook.

Many companies following IFRS use the term "non-current liabilities," as opposed to "long-term liabilities," as we have used earlier in this chapter. IFRS do not prohibit the use of alternative descriptions as long as the meaning is clear. As the term "long-term liabilities" is acceptable, and it is more widely used in Canada, we use this term in this textbook.

Order of Items

IFRS do not lay down the order or format in which items are to be presented in the balance sheet, except where a presentation based on liquidity provides information that is more relevant than classifying items as current and non-current. (Financial institutions are examples of companies that might more appropriately use the liquidity basis of presentation.) Companies are allowed to choose how to order items, depending on the nature of the company and its transactions, to provide information that is relevant to understanding the company's financial position.

The result is that there is more variation in the ordering of items in the balance sheet than was previously the practice under Canadian accounting standards. Some companies put non-current assets before current assets. Some companies show current assets in order of increasing liquidity, not in order of decreasing liquidity, as we have shown in this textbook. When companies show non-current assets before current assets, they also show non-current liabilities before current liabilities. Also, owner's equity can be listed before or after liabilities.

International Financial Reporting Standards Illustrated

In order to help you understand some of the potential differences in the balance sheet when IFRS are followed, we have created a balance sheet for a hypothetical company, International MacDonald Limited. The information is based on the balance sheet for MacDonald Company, shown earlier in Illustration 4-7.

In Illustration 4-16, we have assumed the business is an incorporated company, not a proprietorship as in Illustration 4-7, in order to show the differences in the equity section. As MacDonald Company is a private company, it does not have to follow IFRS. If International MacDonald Limited is a public company, it will have to follow IFRS.

In Illustration 4-16, we show how the balance sheet would look if the company decides to follow the differences discussed in the previous sections. Notice the different statement name, the different classifications, and the different order of items in the statement. But total assets, and total liabilities and equity, are still the same amounts.

Illustration 4-16 ➡

IFRS sample statement of financial position

INTERNATIONAL MACDONALD LIMITED
Statement of Financial Position
November 30, 2011

Assets

Non-current assets			
Property, plant, and equipment			
Land		$40,000	
Building	$75,000		
Less: Accumulated depreciation	15,000	60,000	
Office equipment	$24,000		
Less: Accumulated depreciation	5,000	19,000	
Total property, plant, and equipment			$119,000
Long-term investments			
Equity investment		$ 5,200	
Debt investment		2,000	
Total long-term investments			7,200
Goodwill			3,100
Total non-current assets			129,300
Current assets			
Prepaid insurance		$ 400	
Supplies		2,100	
Inventories		4,000	
Accounts receivable		7,000	
Short-term investments		2,000	
Cash		6,600	
Total current assets			22,100
Total assets			$151,400

Equity and Liabilities

Shareholders' equity			
Share capital		$74,000	
Retained earnings		50,050	
Total shareholders' equity			$124,050
Non-current liabilities			
Mortgage payable		$ 9,000	
Notes payable		1,300	
Total long-term liabilities			10,300

Current liabilities		
Notes payable	$11,000	
Accounts payable	2,100	
Unearned revenue	900	
Salaries payable	1,600	
Interest payable	450	
Current portion of notes payable	1,000	
Total current liabilities		17,050
Total liabilities		27,350
Total equity and liabilities		$151,400

 ## ACCOUNTING IN ACTION: ALL ABOUT YOU

Similar to a company's balance sheet, a personal balance sheet reports what you own and what you owe. What are the items of value that you own—your personal assets? Some of your assets are liquid—such as cash or short-term savings. Others, such as vehicles, real estate, and some types of investments, are less liquid. Some assets, such as real estate and investments, tend to increase in value, thereby increasing your personal equity. Other assets, such as vehicles and furniture, tend to fall in value, thereby decreasing your personal equity.

What are the amounts that you owe—your personal liabilities? Student loans, credit cards? These liabilities may be either current or long-term. Your personal equity is the difference between your total assets and total liabilities. Financial planners call this your *net worth* or *personal equity*.

In Canada, household debt, in the form of consumer credit and mortgages, continued to rise faster than equity in 2008. Canadian stock prices fell significantly during the third quarter of 2008, resulting in a 3.2% drop in household net worth, or a total of $191 billion. There was also slower growth in residential real estate values and household borrowing continued. Total household assets fell 2.2% in the third quarter of 2008. Meanwhile, the amount of household debt relative to net worth, continued to grow, though at a slower pace than in the past. Households had 20.9 cents of debt for every dollar of net worth.

But age is the biggest single factor in determining where you stand in the race for wealth. Most of us spend our 20s, 30s, and 40s paying off student loans, mortgages, and raising children. It is only in our 50s that we begin to accumulate wealth.

Source: Statistics Canada, "National balance sheet accounts," *The Daily*, Tuesday, December 16, 2008.

Should you prepare a personal balance sheet each year?

BEFORE YOU GO ON . . .

➜ Review It

1. What are the major sections in a classified balance sheet?
2. What factors determine whether assets should be classified as current or non-current?
3. How should accounts be ordered in the (a) current assets; (b) property, plant, and equipment; and (c) current liabilities sections of the balance sheet?
4. Using Forzani's balance sheet, identify the components of its current assets and current liabilities at February 1, 2009. Can you tell if current assets and current liabilities are listed in order of liquidity, or in some other order? The answers to these questions are at the end of the chapter.

➜ Do It

Canadian Tire Corporation, Limited has the following selected accounts listed in a recent balance sheet:

Accounts payable and other	Long-term debt
Accounts receivable	Long-term receivables
Bank indebtedness	Merchandise inventories
Current portion of long-term debt	Other long-term liabilities
Goodwill	Prepaid expenses and deposits
Intangibles	Property and equipment

Classify each of the above accounts as current assets, non-current assets, current liabilities, or non-current liabilities.

Action Plan

- Current assets include all assets that will be realized within one year.
- Current liabilities are obligations that are expected to be paid within one year.
- Non-current assets are all assets that will be realized in more than one year.
- Obligations that are due after more than one year are classified as non-current liabilities.

Solution

Account	Balance Sheet Classification
Accounts payable and other	Current liabilities
Accounts receivable	Current assets
Bank indebtedness	Current liabilities
Current portion of long-term debt	Current liabilities
Goodwill	Non-current assets
Income taxes payable	Current liabilities
Intangibles	Non-current assets
Long-term debt	Non-current liabilities
Merchandise inventories	Current assets
Other long-term liabilities	Non-current liabilities
Prepaid expenses and deposits	Current assets
Property and equipment	Non-current assets

The Navigator

Related exercise material: BE4–9, BE4–10, E4–8, and E4–9.

Using the Information in the Financial Statements

In Chapter 1, we briefly discussed how the financial statements give information about a company's performance and financial position. In this chapter, we will begin to learn about a tool, called ratio analysis, that can be used to analyze financial statements in order to make a more meaningful evaluation of a company. Ratio analysis expresses the relationships between selected items in the financial statements.

As you study the chapters of this book, you will learn about three general types of ratios that are used to analyze financial statements: liquidity, profitability, and solvency ratios. Liquidity ratios measure a company's **liquidity**—the company's ability to pay its obligations as they come due within the next year and to meet unexpected needs for cash. As the name suggests, profitability ratios measure a company's profit or operating success for a specific period of time. Solvency ratios measure a company's ability to pay its total liabilities and survive over a long period of time. In this chapter, we introduce three liquidity ratios: working capital, the current ratio, and the acid-test ratio.

Working Capital

When liquidity is being evaluated, an important relationship is the one between current assets and current liabilities. The difference between current assets and current liabilities is called **working capital**. Working capital is important because it shows a company's ability to pay its short-term debts. When current assets are more than current liabilities at the balance sheet date, the company will likely be able to pay its liabilities. When the reverse is true, short-term creditors may not be paid.

Forzani's working capital is $79,802 thousand, as shown in Illustration 4-17, where amounts are in thousands.

Illustration 4-17 ➜

Working capital

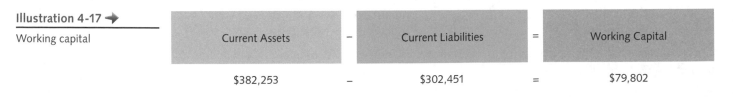

Current Assets	–	Current Liabilities	=	Working Capital
$382,253	–	$302,451	=	$79,802

Current Ratio

A second measure of short-term debt-paying ability is the **current ratio**, which is calculated by dividing current assets by current liabilities. The current ratio is a more dependable indicator of liquidity measures than working capital. Two companies with the same amount of working capital may have very different current ratios.

Illustration 4-18 shows the current ratio for Forzani at February 1, 2009 (in thousands of dollars):

← Illustration 4-18

Current ratio

Current Assets	÷	Current Liabilities	=	Current Ratio
$382,253	÷	$302,451	=	1.26:1

This ratio tells us that on February 1, 2009, Forzani had $1.26 of current assets for every dollar of current liabilities. As a general rule, a higher current ratio indicates better liquidity.

The current ratio is useful, but it does not take into account the composition of the current assets. For example, a satisfactory current ratio does not disclose the fact that a portion of current assets may be tied up in slow-moving inventory.

Acid-Test Ratio

The **acid-test ratio** is a measure of the company's immediate short-term liquidity. The ratio is calculated by dividing the sum of cash, short-term investments, and receivables by current liabilities. These assets are highly liquid compared with inventory and prepaid expenses. The inventory may not be readily saleable, and the prepaid expenses may not be transferable to others.

Alternative terminology
The acid-test ratio is also known as the *quick ratio*.

Illustration 4-19 shows the acid-test ratio for Forzani at February 1, 2009 (in thousands of dollars):

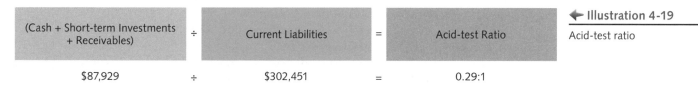

← Illustration 4-19

Acid-test ratio

(Cash + Short-term Investments + Receivables)	÷	Current Liabilities	=	Acid-test Ratio
$87,929	÷	$302,451	=	0.29:1

This ratio tells us that on February 1, 2009, Forzani had $0.29 of highly liquid assets for every dollar of current liabilities. As with the current ratio, a higher acid-test ratio generally indicates better liquidity.

Ratios should never be interpreted without considering certain factors: (1) general economic and industry conditions, (2) other specific financial information about the company over time, and (3) comparison with ratios for other companies in the same or related industries. We will have a longer discussion about how to interpret ratios in Chapter 18.

BEFORE YOU GO ON . . .

➡ Review It

1. What is working capital? How can it be expressed as a ratio?
2. How can two companies with the same amount of working capital have different current ratios?
3. Why is the acid-test ratio a better measure of immediate liquidity than the current ratio?

Related exercise material: BE4–11, BE4–12, E4–10, and E4–11.

The Navigator

APPENDIX 4A ▶ WORK SHEETS

As discussed in the chapter, a work sheet is a multiple-column form that may be used in the adjustment process and in preparing financial statements. The five steps for preparing a work sheet are described in the next section. They must be done in the order they are presented in.

Steps in Preparing a Work Sheet

We will use the October 31 trial balance and adjustment data for Pioneer Advertising Agency from Chapter 3 to show how to prepare a work sheet. Each step of the process is described below and shown in Illustration 4A-1.

Tutorials:
Work Sheet Walkthrough

Step 1. Prepare a Trial Balance on the Work Sheet. Enter all ledger accounts with balances in the account title space. Debit and credit amounts from the ledger are entered in the trial balance columns.

Step 2. Enter the Adjustments in the Adjustment Columns. When a work sheet is used, all adjustments are entered in the adjustment columns. In entering the adjustments, relevant trial balance accounts should be used. If additional accounts are needed, they should be inserted on the lines immediately below the trial balance totals. A different letter identifies the debit and credit for each adjusting entry.

Year-end adjustments must still be recorded in the journal, but not until after the work sheet is completed and the financial statements have been prepared.

The adjustments on Pioneer Advertising Agency's work sheet are the same as the adjustments shown on pages 123 to 133 of Chapter 3. They are recorded in the adjustment columns of the work sheet as follows:

(a) Debit Advertising Supplies Expense (an additional account) $1,500 for the cost of supplies used, and credit Advertising Supplies $1,500.

(b) Debit Insurance Expense (an additional account) $50 for the insurance that has expired, and credit Prepaid Insurance $50.

(c) Debit Unearned Revenue $400 for fees previously collected and now earned, and credit Service Revenue $400.

(d) Debit Accounts Receivable $200 for fees earned but not billed, and credit Service Revenue $200.

(e) Two additional accounts relating to interest are needed. Debit Interest Expense $25 for accrued interest, and credit Interest Payable $25.

(f) Debit Salaries Expense $2,400 for accrued salaries, and credit Salaries Payable (an additional account) $2,400.

(g) Two additional accounts are needed. Debit Depreciation Expense $83 for the month's depreciation, and credit Accumulated Depreciation—Office Equipment $83.

Note in the illustration that, after all the adjustments have been entered, the adjustment columns are totalled to prove the equality of the two adjustment column totals.

Step 3. Enter the Adjusted Balances in the Adjusted Trial Balance Columns. The adjusted balance of an account is calculated by combining the amounts entered in the first four columns of the work sheet for each account. For example, the Prepaid Insurance account in the trial balance columns has a $600 debit balance and a $50 credit in the adjustment columns. These two amounts combine to result in a $550 debit balance in the adjusted trial balance columns. For each account on the work sheet, the amount in the adjusted trial balance columns is equal to the account balance that will appear in the ledger after the adjusting entries have been journalized and posted. The balances in these columns are the same as those in the adjusted trial balance in Illustration 4-3.

After all account balances have been entered in the adjusted trial balance columns, the columns are totalled to prove the equality of the two columns. If these columns do not agree, the financial statement columns will not balance and the financial statements will be incorrect. The total of each of these two columns in Illustration 4A-1 is $31,458.

Step 4. Enter the Adjusted Trial Balance Amounts in the Correct Financial Statement Columns. The fourth step is to enter adjusted trial balance amounts in the income statement or balance sheet columns of the work sheet. Balance sheet accounts are entered in the correct balance sheet debit and credit columns. For instance, Cash is entered in the balance sheet debit column and Notes Payable is entered in the credit column. Accumulated Depreciation is entered in the credit column because it has a credit balance.

Helpful hint Every adjusted trial balance amount must appear in one of the four statement columns.

Because the work sheet does not have columns for the statement of owner's equity, the balance in owner's capital is entered in the balance sheet credit column. In addition, the balance in the owner's drawings account is entered in the balance sheet debit column because it is an owner's equity account with a debit balance.

The amounts in revenue and expense accounts such as Service Revenue and Salaries Expense are entered in the correct income statement columns. The last four columns of Illustration 4A-1 show where each account is entered.

Step 5. Total the Statement Columns, Calculate the Profit (or Loss), and Complete the Work Sheet. Each of the financial statement columns must be totalled. The profit or loss for the period is then found by calculating the difference between the totals of the two income statement columns. If total credits are more than total debits, profit has resulted. In such a case, as shown in Illustration 4A-1, the word "Profit" is inserted in the account title space. The amount is then entered in the income statement debit column so that the totals of the two income statement columns are equal.

The profit or loss must also be entered in the balance sheet columns. If there is a profit, as is the case for Pioneer Agency, the amount is entered in the balance sheet credit column. The credit column is used because profit increases owner's equity. It is also necessary to enter the same amount in the credit column of the balance sheet as was entered in the debit column of the income statement so the financial statement columns will balance.

Conversely, if total debits in the income statement columns are more than total credits, a loss has occurred. In such a case, the amount of the loss is entered in the income statement credit column (to balance the income statement columns) and the balance sheet debit column (because a loss decreases owner's equity).

After the profit or loss has been entered, new column totals are determined. The totals shown in the debit and credit income statement columns will now match. The totals shown in the debit and credit balance sheet columns will also match. If either the income statement columns or the balance sheet columns are not equal after the profit or loss has been entered, there is an error in the work sheet.

Illustration 4A-1
Preparing a work sheet—Steps 1–5

Pioneer Advertising Agency
Worksheet
Month Ended October 31, 2011

Account Titles	Unadjusted Trial Balance Dr.	Unadjusted Trial Balance Cr.	Adjustments Dr.	Adjustments Cr.	Adjusted Trial Balance Dr.	Adjusted Trial Balance Cr.	Income Statement Dr.	Income Statement Cr.	Balance Sheet Dr.	Balance Sheet Cr.
Cash	14,250				14,250				14,250	
Accounts receivable	1,000		(d) 200		1,200				1,200	
Advertising supplies	2,500			(a) 1,500	1,000				1,000	
Prepaid insurance	600			(b) 50	550				550	
Office equipment	5,000				5,000				5,000	
Notes payable		5,000				5,000				5,000
Accounts payable		1,750				1,750				1,750
Unearned revenue		1,200	(c) 400			800				800
C. Byrd, capital		10,000				10,000				10,000
C. Byrd, drawings	500				500				500	
Service revenue		10,800		(c) 400 (d) 200		11,400		11,400		
Salaries expense	4,000		(f) 2,400		6,400		6,400			
Advertising supplies expense			(a) 1,500		1,500		1,500			
Rent expense	900				900		900			
Insurance expense			(b) 50		50		50			
Interest expense			(e) 25		25		25			
Interest payable				(e) 25		25				25
Salaries payable				(f) 2,400		2,400				2,400
Depreciation expense			(g) 83		83		83			
Accumulated depreciation				(g) 83		83				83
Totals	28,750	28,750	4,658	4,658	31,458	31,458	8,958	11,400	22,500	20,058
Profit					-		2,442			2,442
							11,400	11,400	22,500	22,500

1. Prepare a trial balance on the work sheet.

2. Enter adjustment data.

3. Enter adjusted balances.

4. Enter adjusted balances in appropriate statement columns.

5. Total the statement columns, calculate profit (or loss), and complete the work sheet.

Preparing Financial Statements from a Work Sheet

After a work sheet has been completed, all the data required to prepare the financial statements are at hand. The income statement is prepared from the income statement columns. The balance sheet and statement of owner's equity are prepared from the balance sheet columns.

Note that the amount shown for owner's capital in the work sheet is the account balance before considering drawings and profit (loss). When there have been no additional investments of capital by the owner during the period, this amount is the balance at the beginning of the period.

Using a work sheet, accountants can prepare financial statements before adjusting entries have been journalized and posted. However, the completed work sheet is not a substitute for formal financial statements. Data in the financial statement columns of the work sheet are not properly arranged for statement purposes. Also, as noted earlier, the financial statement presentation for some accounts differs from their statement columns on the work sheet. A work sheet is basically an accountant's working tool. It is not given to management or other parties.

BEFORE YOU GO ON . . .

→ Do It

Susan Elbe is preparing a work sheet. Explain to Susan how she should extend the following adjusted trial balance accounts to the financial statement columns of the work sheet.

Accumulated Depreciation—Equipment
B. Sykes, Drawings
Cash
Equipment
Salaries Expense
Salaries Payable
Service Revenue

Action Plan

- Assets and drawings belong in the balance sheet debit column
- Liabilities, capital, and contra assets belong in the balance sheet credit column
- Revenues belong in the income statement credit column
- Expenses belong in the income statement debit column

Solution

Account	Work Sheet Column
Accumulated Depreciation—Equipment	Balance sheet credit column
B. Sykes, Drawings	Balance sheet debit column
Cash	Balance sheet debit column
Equipment	Balance sheet debit column
Salaries Expense	Income statement debit column
Salaries Payable	Balance sheet credit column
Service Revenue	Income statement credit column

Related exercise material: *BE4–13, *BE4–14, and *E4–12.

The Navigator

APPENDIX 4B ▶ REVERSING ENTRIES

STUDY OBJECTIVE 7

Prepare reversing entries.

After the financial statements are prepared and the books are closed, it can be helpful to reverse some of the adjusting entries before recording the regular transactions of the next period. Such entries are called reversing entries. A reversing entry is made at the beginning of the next accounting period and is the exact opposite of the adjusting entry that was made in the previous period. The recording of reversing entries is an optional step in the accounting cycle.

The purpose of reversing entries is to simplify the recording of future transactions that are related to an adjusting entry. As you may recall from Chapter 3, the payment of salaries on November 4 after an adjusting entry resulted in two debits: one to Salaries Payable and the other to Salaries Expense. With reversing entries, the entire later payment can be debited to Salaries Expense. You do not have to remember what has gone on before. The use of reversing entries does not change the amounts reported in the financial statements. It simply makes it easier to record transactions in the next accounting period.

Accounting with and without Reversing Entries

Reversing entries are used to reverse two types of adjusting entries: accrued revenues and accrued expenses. To illustrate the optional use of reversing entries for accrued expenses, we will use the salaries expense transactions for Pioneer Advertising Agency as shown in Chapters 2, 3, and 4. The transaction and adjustment data were as follows:

1. October 21 (initial salary entry): Salaries of $4,000 earned between October 10 and October 21 are paid.
2. October 31 (adjusting entry): Salaries earned between October 24 and October 31 are $2,400. The company will pay the employees this amount in the November 4 payroll.
3. November 4 (subsequent salary entry): Salaries paid are $4,000. Of this amount, $2,400 applies to accrued salaries payable and $1,600 was earned between November 1 and November 4.

The comparative entries with and without reversing entries are as follows.

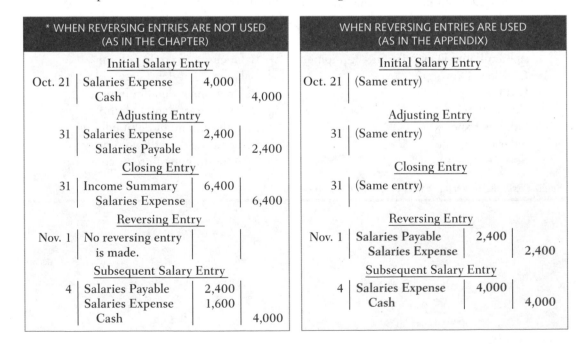

* WHEN REVERSING ENTRIES ARE NOT USED (AS IN THE CHAPTER)				WHEN REVERSING ENTRIES ARE USED (AS IN THE APPENDIX)			
Initial Salary Entry				**Initial Salary Entry**			
Oct. 21	Salaries Expense	4,000		Oct. 21	(Same entry)		
	Cash		4,000				
Adjusting Entry				**Adjusting Entry**			
31	Salaries Expense	2,400		31	(Same entry)		
	Salaries Payable		2,400				
Closing Entry				**Closing Entry**			
31	Income Summary	6,400		31	(Same entry)		
	Salaries Expense		6,400				
Reversing Entry				**Reversing Entry**			
Nov. 1	No reversing entry is made.			Nov. 1	Salaries Payable	2,400	
					Salaries Expense		2,400
Subsequent Salary Entry				**Subsequent Salary Entry**			
4	Salaries Payable	2,400		4	Salaries Expense	4,000	
	Salaries Expense	1,600			Cash		4,000
	Cash		4,000				

The first three entries are the same whether or not reversing entries are used. The last two entries are different. The November 1 reversing entry eliminates the $2,400 balance in Salaries Payable that was created by the October 31 adjusting entry. The reversing entry also creates a $2,400 credit balance in the Salaries Expense account. As you know, it is unusual for an expense account to have a credit balance. The balance is correct in this instance, though, because it anticipates that the entire amount of the first salary payment in the new accounting period will be debited to Salaries Expense. This debit will eliminate the credit balance, and the resulting debit balance in the expense account will equal the actual salaries expense in the new accounting period ($1,600 in this example).

When reversing entries are made, all cash payments of expenses can be debited to the expense account. This means that on November 4 (and every payday) Salaries Expense can be debited for the amount paid without regard to any accrued salaries payable. Being able to make the same entry each time simplifies the recording process: future transactions can be recorded as if the related adjusting entry had never been made.

The posting of the entries with reversing entries is as follows, using T accounts.

Salaries Expense				Salaries Payable			
Oct. 21 Paid	4,000			Nov. 1 Rev.	2,400	Oct. 31 Adj.	2,400
31 Adj.	2,400					Nov. 1 Bal.	0
Oct. 31 Bal.	6,400	Oct. 31 Clos.	6,400				
Oct. 31 Bal.	0	Nov. 1 Rev.	2,400				
Nov. 4 Paid	4,000						
Nov. 7 Bal.	1,600						

Pioneer Agency could also have used reversing entries for accrued revenues. Recall that Pioneer had accrued revenues of $200, which were recorded by a debit to Accounts Receivable and credit to Service Revenue. Thus, the reversing entry on November 1 is:

Nov. 1	Service Revenue	200	
	Accounts Receivable		200
	To reverse Oct. 31 accrued revenue adjusting entry.		

A	=	L	+	OE
−200				−200

Cash flows: no effect

Later in November, when Pioneer collects the accrued revenue, it debits Cash and credits Service Revenue for the full amount collected. There would be no need to refer back to the October 31 adjusting entries to see how much relates to the prior month. Thus, as shown in the previous example with accrued expenses, the recording process is simplified.

BEFORE YOU GO ON . . .

→ Do It

Pelican Company has a note receivable with a customer. On March 31, Pelican recorded an adjusting entry to accrue $300 of interest earned on the note. On April 30, Pelican collected $400 cash from the customer for interest earned from January 1 to April 30. Record Pelican's (a) March 31 adjusting entry, (b) April 1 reversing entry, and (c) April 30 entry.

Action Plan

• Adjusting entries for accrued revenues are required when revenue has been earned but not yet received in cash or recorded.
• A reversing entry is the exact opposite of the adjusting entry.
• When a reversing entry has been recorded, it is not necessary to refer to the previous adjustment when recording the subsequent receipt of cash.

Solution

			Debit	Credit
(a)	Mar. 31	Interest Receivable	300	
		Interest Earned		300
		To record accrued interest.		
(b)	Apr. 1	Interest Earned	300	
		Interest Receivable		300
		To reverse Mar. 31 adjusting entry.		
(c)	Apr. 30	Cash	400	
		Interest Earned		400
		To record interest collected.		

The Navigator

Related exercise material: *BE4–15, *BE4–16, *E4-13, and *E4–14.

Demonstration Problem

WILEY PLUS

Demonstration Problems

At the end of its first month of operations, Paquet Answering Service has the following unadjusted trial balance, with the accounts presented in alphabetical order rather than in financial statement order:

PAQUET ANSWERING SERVICE Trial Balance August 31, 2011		
	Debit	Credit
Accounts payable		$ 2,400
Accounts receivable	$ 2,800	
Accumulated depreciation—building		500
Accumulated depreciation—equipment		1,000
Advertising expense	400	
Depreciation expense	1,500	
Building	150,000	
Cash	5,400	
Equipment	60,000	
Insurance expense	200	
Interest expense	350	
Interest payable		1,350
Land	50,000	
Long-term debt investments	15,000	
Long-term equity investments	7,000	
Mortgage payable		140,000
Prepaid insurance	2,200	
R. Paquet, capital		155,000
R. Paquet, drawings	1,000	
Salaries expense	3,200	
Service revenue		5,700
Short-term investments	4,800	
Supplies	1,000	
Supplies expense	300	
Utilities expense	800	
Totals	$305,950	$305,950

Instructions

(a) Calculate the profit or loss for the month.

(b) Calculate owner's equity at August 31, 2011.

(c) Prepare a classified balance sheet for Paquet Answering Service at August 31, 2011. Assume that $5,000 of the mortgage payable is due over the next year.

(d) Journalize the closing entries.

(e) Create T accounts for Income Summary and R. Paquet, Capital, and post the closing entries.

(f) Prepare a post-closing trial balance.

Solution to Demonstration Problem

(a) Profit (loss) = Revenue − expenses

$$= \$5,700 - \$400 - \$1,500 - \$200 - \$350 - \$3,200 - \$300 - \$800$$
$$= \$(1,050)$$

(b) Owner's equity August 31, 2011 = Opening capital − loss − drawings

$$= \$155,000 - \$1,050 - \$1,000$$
$$= \$152,950$$

(c)

PAQUET ANSWERING SERVICE
Balance Sheet
August 31, 2011

Assets

Current assets			
Cash			$ 5,400
Short-term investments			4,800
Accounts receivable			2,800
Prepaid insurance			2,200
Supplies			1,000
Total current assets			16,200
Long-term investments			
Equity investments		$ 7,000	
Debt investments		15,000	
Total long-term investments			22,000
Property, plant, and equipment			
Land		$ 50,000	
Building	$150,000		
Less: Accumulated depreciation	500	149,500	
Equipment	$ 60,000		
Less: Accumulated depreciation	1,000	59,000	258,500
Total assets			$296,700

Liabilities and Owner's Equity

Current liabilities		
Accounts payable		$ 2,400
Interest payable		1,350
Current portion of mortgage payable		5,000
Total current liabilities		8,750
Long-term liabilities		
Mortgage payable		135,000
Total liabilities		143,750
Owner's equity		
R. Paquet, capital		152,950
Total liabilities and owner's equity		$296,700

Action Plan

- Identify which accounts are balance sheet accounts and which are income statement accounts.
- If revenues are more than expenses, this results in a profit; if expenses are more than revenues, this results in a loss.
- In preparing a classified balance sheet, know the contents of each of the sections.
- In journalizing closing entries, remember that there are four entries. Revenues and expenses are closed to the Income Summary account; the Income Summary account and the drawings account are closed to owner's capital.
- Always check your work. Make sure the balance in Income Summary equals profit before closing the Income Summary account. Make sure that the balance in the owner's capital account after posting the closing entries equals the amount reported on the balance sheet.
- In preparing a post-closing trial balance, put the accounts in financial statement order. Remember that all temporary accounts will have a zero balance and do not need to be included.

(d)

			Debit	Credit
Aug. 31	Service Revenue		5,700	
		Income Summary		5,700
		To close revenue account.		
31	Income Summary		6,750	
		Advertising Expense		400
		Depreciation Expense		1,500
		Insurance Expense		200
		Interest Expense		350
		Salaries Expense		3,200
		Supplies Expense		300
		Utilities Expense		800
		To close expense accounts.		
31	R. Paquet, Capital		1,050	
		Income Summary		1,050
		To close Income Summary.		
31	R. Paquet, Capital		1,000	
		R. Paquet, Drawings		1,000
		To close drawings.		

(e)

Income Summary			
Clos.	6,750	Clos.	5,700
Bal.	1,050		
		Clos.	1,050
		Bal.	0

R. Paquet, Capital			
		Bal.	155,000
Clos.	1,050		
Clos.	1,000		
		Bal.	152,950

(f)

PAQUET ANSWERING SERVICE
Post-Closing Trial Balance
August 31, 2011

	Debit	Credit
Cash	$ 5,400	
Short-term investments	4,800	
Accounts receivable	2,800	
Prepaid insurance	2,200	
Supplies	1,000	
Long-term equity investments	7,000	
Long-term debt investments	15,000	
Land	50,000	
Building	150,000	
Accumulated depreciation—building		$ 500
Equipment	60,000	
Accumulated depreciation—equipment		1,000
Accounts payable		2,400
Interest payable		1,350
Mortgage payable		140,000
R. Paquet, capital		152,950
Totals	$298,200	$298,200

The Navigator

Summary of Study Objectives

1. **Prepare closing entries and a post-closing trial balance.** At the end of an accounting period, the temporary account balances (revenue, expense, income summary, and owner's drawings) are transferred to the owner's capital account by journalizing and posting closing entries. Separate entries are made to close revenues and expenses to Income Summary; then Income Summary to owner's capital; and, finally, owner's drawings to owner's capital. The temporary accounts begin the new period with a zero balance and the owner's capital account is updated to show its end-of-period balance. A post-closing trial balance has the balances in permanent accounts (i.e., balance sheet accounts) that are carried forward to the next accounting period. The purpose of this balance, as with other trial balances, is to prove the equality of these account balances.

2. **Explain the steps in the accounting cycle including optional steps.** The steps in the accounting cycle are (1) analyze business transactions, (2) journalize the transactions, (3) post to ledger accounts, (4) prepare a trial balance, (5) journalize and post adjusting entries, (6) prepare an adjusted trial balance, (7) prepare financial statements, (8) journalize and post closing entries, and (9) prepare a post-closing trial balance.

3. **Prepare correcting entries.** Correcting entries are recorded whenever an error (an incorrect journal entry) is found. A correcting entry can be determined by comparing the incorrect entry with the journal entry that should have been recorded (the correct entry). The comparison will show which accounts need to be corrected and by how much. The correcting entry will correct the accounts. An equally acceptable alternative is to reverse the incorrect entry and then record the correct entry.

4. **Prepare a classified balance sheet.** In a classified balance sheet, assets are classified as current assets; long-term investments; property, plant, and equipment; and in-tangible assets. Liabilities are classified as either current or long-term (non-current). Current assets are assets that will be realized within one year of the balance sheet date. Current liabilities are liabilities that must be paid from current assets within one year of the balance sheet date. The classified balance also includes an equity section, which varies with the form of business organization.

5. **Illustrate measures used to evaluate liquidity.** One of the measures used to evaluate a company's short-term liquidity is its working capital, which is the excess of current assets over current liabilities. This can also be expressed as the current ratio (current assets ÷ current liabilities). The acid-test ratio is a measure of the company's immediate short-term liquidity and is calculated by dividing the sum of cash, short-term investments, and receivables by current liabilities.

6. **Prepare a work sheet (Appendix 4A).** A work sheet is an optional multi-column form, used to assist in preparing adjusting entries and financial statements. The steps in preparing a work sheet are (1) prepare a trial balance on the work sheet, (2) enter the adjustments in the adjustment columns, (3) enter adjusted balances in the adjusted trial balance columns, (4) enter adjusted trial balance amounts in correct financial statement columns, and (5) total the statement columns, calculate profit (or loss), and complete the work sheet.

7. **Prepare reversing entries (Appendix 4B).** Reversing entries are optional entries used to simplify bookkeeping. They are made at the beginning of the new accounting period and are the direct opposite of the adjusting entry made in the preceding period. Only accrual adjusting entries are reversed. If reversing entries are used, then subsequent cash transactions can be recorded without referring to the adjusting entries prepared at the end of the previous period.

The Navigator

Glossary

WILEY **PLUS** Glossary
Key Term Matching Activity

Acid-test ratio A measure of the company's immediate short-term liquidity. (p. 201)

Classified balance sheet A balance sheet that has several classifications or sections. (p. 191)

Closing entries Entries made at the end of an accounting period to transfer the balances of temporary accounts (revenues, expenses, income summary, and drawings) to the permanent owner's equity account, owner's capital. (p. 182)

Closing the books The process of journalizing and posting closing entries to update the capital account and prepare the temporary accounts for the next period's postings. (p. 182)

Correcting entries Entries to correct errors that were made when transactions were recorded. (p. 189)

Current assets Cash and other assets that will be converted to cash, sold, or used up in one year from the balance sheet date or in the company's normal operating cycle. (p. 192)

Current liabilities   Obligations that are expected to be settled within one year from the balance sheet date or in the company's normal operating cycle. (p. 195)

Current ratio   A measure of short-term debt-paying ability that is determined by dividing current assets by current liabilities. (p. 201)

Income summary   A temporary account that is used in closing revenue and expense accounts. (p. 183)

Intangible assets   Long-lived assets that do not have physical substance and are rights and privileges that result from ownership. They include goodwill, patents, copyrights, trademarks, trade names, and licences. (p. 195)

Liquidity   The ability of a company to pay obligations as they come due within the next year and to meet unexpected needs for cash. (p. 200)

Long-term investments   Investments in long-term debts that management intends to hold to earn interest or in equity of other companies that management plans to hold for many years as a strategic investment. (p. 194)

Long-term liabilities   Obligations that are expected to be paid after one year or longer. (p. 196)

Operating cycle   The time it takes to go from starting with cash to ending with cash in producing revenues. (p. 192)

Permanent accounts   Balance sheet accounts, whose balances are carried forward to the next accounting period. (p. 182)

Post-closing trial balance   A list of debit and credit balances of the permanent (balance sheet) accounts after closing entries have been journalized and posted. (p. 186)

Property, plant, and equipment   Long-lived tangible assets that are used in the operations of the business and are not intended for sale. They include land, buildings, equipment, and furniture. (p. 194)

Reversing entry   An entry made at the beginning of the next accounting period that is the exact opposite of the adjusting entry made in the previous period. (p. 189)

Temporary accounts   Revenue, expense, income summary, and drawings accounts, whose balances are transferred to owner's capital at the end of an accounting period. (p. 182)

Working capital   The difference between current assets and current liabilities. (p. 200)

Work sheet   A multiple-column form that may be used in the adjustment process and in preparing financial statements. (p. 189)

Note: All questions, exercises, and problems below with an asterisk (*) relate to material in Appendices 4A and 4B.

Self-Study Questions

WILEY
PLUS Quizzes

Answers are at the end of the chapter.

(SO 1) K   1. When a loss has occurred, Income Summary is:
    (a) debited, and owner's capital is credited.
    (b) credited, and owner's capital is debited.
    (c) debited, and owner's drawings is credited.
    (d) credited, and owner's drawings is debited.

(SO 1) K   2. After the closing entries have been posted, the balance in the owner's capital account should equal:
    (a) the profit or loss reported on the income statement.
    (b) the opening capital balance reported on the statement of owner's equity.
    (c) the ending capital balance reported on the statement of owner's equity and balance sheet.
    (d) the opening capital balance plus any investments made by the owner during the period.

(SO 1) K   3. Which types of accounts will appear in the post-closing trial balance?
    (a) Permanent accounts
    (b) Temporary accounts
    (c) Income statement accounts
    (d) All accounts

4. Which of the following is an optional step in the accounting cycle?   (SO 2) K
    (a) Journalizing and posting closing entries
    (b) Preparing an adjusted trial balance
    (c) Preparing a post-closing trial balance
    (d) Journalizing reversing entries

5. Cash of $250 is received at the time a service is provided. The transaction is journalized and posted as a debit to Cash of $250 and a credit to Accounts Receivable of $250. The correcting entry is: (SO 3) AP

(a) Service Revenue	250	
Accounts Receivable		250
(b) Accounts Receivable	250	
Service Revenue		250
(c) Cash	250	
Service Revenue		250
(d) Accounts Receivable	250	
Cash		250

(SO 4) K 6. Which of the following statements about current assets is *incorrect*?
  (a) Current assets normally are cash and other assets that will be converted to cash, sold, or used up in one year from the balance sheet date.
  (b) Supplies are not current assets and should be included as part of property, plant, and equipment on the balance sheet.
  (c) Some companies use a period longer than one year to classify assets as current because they have an operating cycle that is longer than one year.
  (d) Prepaid expenses are considered current assets because they will be used or will expire within one year.

(SO 4) K 7. Long-term liabilities:
  (a) are obligations that are expected to be paid before one year from the balance sheet date.
  (b) cannot be called non-current liabilities.
  (c) are sometimes listed on the balance sheet before current liabilities, if the company is following International Financial Reporting Standards.
  (d) include accounts payable, salaries payable, and interest payable.

(SO 5) AP 8. A company reports current assets of $10,000 and current liabilities of $8,000. Its current ratio is:
  (a) $2,000.
  (b) 80%.
  (c) 1.25:1.
  (d) unknown without information about the amount of cash, short-term investments, and receivables, which is needed to calculate the ratio.

*9. In a work sheet, profit is entered in the following columns: (SO 6) K
  (a) income statement (Dr.) and balance sheet (Dr.).
  (b) income statement (Cr.) and balance sheet (Dr.).
  (c) income statement (Dr.) and balance sheet (Cr.).
  (d) income statement (Cr.) and balance sheet (Cr.).

*10. On December 31, 2011, Mott Company correctly made an adjusting entry to recognize $2,000 of accrued salaries payable. On January 8, 2012, total salaries of $3,400 were paid. Assuming the correct reversing entry was made on January 1, 2012, the entry on January 8, 2012, will result in a credit to Cash of $3,400, and the following debit(s): (SO 7) AP
  (a) Salaries Payable $1,400, and Salaries Expense $2,000.
  (b) Salaries Payable $2,000, and Salaries Expense $1,400.
  (c) Salaries Expense $3,400.
  (d) Salaries Payable $3,400.

Questions

(SO 1) C 1. What are permanent and temporary accounts? What is the relationship between them?

(SO 1) C 2. What are the two reasons for recording closing entries?

(SO 1) C 3. What is the purpose of using an income summary account? If an income summary account was not used, how would the closing entries change?

(SO 1) C 4. Why is the owner's drawings account not closed with the expense accounts? Why is a separate entry required to close this account?

(SO 1) C 5. Brenda has been told that, after the closing entries have been posted, she should stop and check her work. Explain to Brenda what she should be checking for.

(SO 1) K 6. What is the content and purpose of a post-closing trial balance?

(SO 2) K 7. Which steps in the accounting cycle may be done daily, which steps are done on a periodic basis (monthly, quarterly, or annually), and which steps are usually done only at the company's fiscal year end?

(SO 2) K 8. What three steps in the accounting cycle involve preparing a trial balance, and in what order are they prepared?

9. Although using a work sheet is optional, it is useful. Do you agree? Explain. (SO 2) C

10. How do correcting entries differ from adjusting entries? (SO 3) C

11. Describe how to determine which accounts, and what amounts, to include in a correcting entry. (SO 3) C

12. What is the purpose of classifying assets and liabilities into categories on the balance sheet? (SO 4) C

13. What is meant by the term "operating cycle"? (SO 4) C

14. Define "current assets." In what order are current assets recorded for most Canadian companies? What other order can be used and in what circumstances? (SO 4) C

15. What are the differences between the three categories of non-current assets: long-term investments; property, plant, and equipment; and intangible assets? (SO 4) C

16. How are current liabilities different from long-term liabilities? (SO 4) C

17. Describe the differences in balance sheet presentation that may arise between companies that follow International Financial Reporting Standards and those that follow traditional Canadian standards. (SO 4) K

(SO 5) C   18. What is liquidity? Identify one measure of liquidity.

(SO 5) C   19. What factors need to be considered when interpreting ratios?

(SO 5) C   20. What are the differences between the current ratio and the acid-test ratio?

(SO 6) C *21. How is profit or loss calculated on a work sheet? How is this number entered on the work sheet if the company has profit? How is it entered if the company has a loss?

*22. Why is it necessary to journalize and post adjusting entries if they have already been entered on the work sheet?   (SO 6) C

*23. What are the differences between a reversing entry and an adjusting entry? Are reversing entries required?   (SO 7) C

*24. When and how is it helpful to use reversing entries? Describe when reversing entries should not be used.   (SO 7) C

Brief Exercises

Identify temporary and permanent accounts.
(SO 1) K

BE4–1   In the blank space, identify each of the following accounts as either a temporary (T) or a permanent (P) account.

_____ Accounts payable
_____ Accounts receivable
_____ Depreciation expense
_____ General and operating expenses
_____ Property taxes payable
_____ Interest on long-term debt expense
_____ S. Young, capital

_____ Long-term debt
_____ Other revenues
_____ Prepaid expenses
_____ Equipment
_____ S. Young, drawings
_____ Accumulated depreciation
_____ Short-term investments

Prepare closing entries and calculate capital account balance.
(SO 1) AP

BE4–2   Willis Company has the following year-end account balances on September 30, 2011: Service Revenue $53,800; Salaries Expense $15,400; Rent Expense $12,000; Supplies Expense $3,500; B. Willis, Capital $67,000; and B. Willis, Drawings $22,000.

(a) Prepare the closing entries.
(b) Calculate the balance in B. Willis, Capital after the closing entries have been posted.

Prepare and post closing entries.
(SO 1) AP

BE4–3   The adjusted trial balance for Mosquera Golf Club at its October 31, 2011, year end included the following:

	Debit	Credit
Cash	$ 5,500	
Prepaid expenses	3,000	
Equipment	85,000	
Accumulated depreciation—equipment		$ 15,000
Accounts payable		12,000
Unearned golf fees		1,500
N. Mosquera, capital		75,000
N. Mosquera, drawings	45,000	
Golf fees earned		150,000
Maintenance expense	23,000	
Rent expense	10,000	
Salaries expense	82,000	

(a) Prepare closing entries.
(b) Using T accounts, post the closing entries and calculate the balance in each account.

Prepare post-closing trial balance.
(SO 1) AP

BE4–4   Refer to the information in BE4–3 for Mosquera Golf Club. Prepare a post-closing trial balance.

BE4–5 The required steps in the accounting cycle are listed below in random order. List the steps in the correct order by writing the numbers 1 to 9 in the blank spaces.

List steps in accounting cycle.
(SO 2) K

(a) ___ Prepare a post-closing trial balance.
(b) ___ Prepare an adjusted trial balance.
(c) ___ Analyze business transactions.
(d) ___ Prepare a trial balance.
(e) ___ Journalize the transactions.
(f) ___ Journalize and post the closing entries.
(g) ___ Prepare the financial statements.
(h) ___ Journalize and post the adjusting entries.
(i) ___ Post to the ledger accounts.

BE4–6 Fern Company opened for business on March 1 and purchased supplies on March 2 for $750 cash. On March 31, the company's year end, it had $200 of supplies on hand. Complete the following steps in the accounting cycle with regard to the supplies:

Apply the steps in accounting cycle to the purchase and use of supplies.
(SO 2) AP

(a) Journalize the transaction.
(b) Post to the ledger accounts. (Use T accounts; ignore the Cash account.)
(c) Journalize and post any required adjusting entries.
(d) Assuming the company closes its books monthly, journalize and post required closing entries.

BE4–7 At Hébert Company, the following errors were discovered after the transactions had been journalized and posted:

Identify impact of error.
(SO 3) AP

1. A collection of cash on account from a customer for $980 was recorded as a debit to Service Revenue of $980 and a credit to Accounts Receivable of $980.
2. An invoice to a customer for $600 of services on account was recorded as a $600 debit to Accounts Receivable and a $600 credit to Unearned Service Revenue.
3. A $500 cash payment to the owner, Roch Hébert, was recorded as a debit to Salary Expense of $500 and a credit to Cash of $500.
4. The purchase of office supplies on account for $1,850 was recorded as a debit to Equipment of $1,580 and a credit to Accounts Payable of $1,580.
5. The payment of cash to a creditor of $270 was recorded as a $720 debit to Accounts Payable and a $720 credit to Cash.

Indicate the impact of each error on the balance sheet and income statement by stating whether assets, liabilities, owner's equity, revenues, expenses, and profit are understated (U), overstated (O), or if there is no effect (NE). Use the following format, in which the answer for the first error is given as an example:

	Balance Sheet			Income Statement		
Error	Assets	Liabilities	Owner's Equity	Revenues	Expenses	Profit
1.	U	NE	U	U	NE	U

BE4–8 Refer to the information in BE4–7 for Hébert Company. Prepare the correcting journal entries.

Prepare correcting entries.
(SO 3) AP

BE4–9 The standard balance sheet classifications for assets and liabilities are as follows:

Classify balance sheet accounts.
(SO 4) K

1. Current assets
2. Long-term investments
3. Property, plant, and equipment
4. Intangible assets
5. Current liabilities
6. Long-term liabilities

Match the classifications above with the accounts below by writing the correct number in the blank spaces:

(a)____ Supplies
(b)____ Accounts Payable
(c)____ Building
(d)____ Prepaid Insurance
(e)____ Note Payable (due in 5 years)
(f) ____ Goodwill
(g) ____ Unearned Revenue
(h) ____ Accounts Receivable
(i) ____ Accumulated Depreciation—Building
(j) ____ Patents
(k) ____ Note Receivable (due in 3 years)
(l) ____ Salaries Payable

Prepare current assets section of balance sheet.
(SO 4) AP

BE4–10   The adjusted trial balance of Reuben Company includes the following accounts: Accounts Receivable $13,700; Accounts Payable $9,250; Prepaid Insurance $3,900; Cash $19,300; Supplies $5,200; and Short-Term Investments $8,200. Prepare the current assets section of the balance sheet as at December 31, 2011, with the accounts in order of decreasing liquidity.

Calculate working capital and current ratio and compare liquidity ratio measures.
(SO 5) K

BE4–11   On December 31, 2011, Big Company had $1 million of current assets and $900,000 of current liabilities. On the same day, Small Company had $200,000 of current assets and $100,000 of current liabilities. Calculate the working capital and current ratio for both companies and compare the results. Which liquidity measure is more relevant?

Calculate working capital, current ratio, and acid-test ratio, and comment on liquidity.
(SO 5) AP

BE4–12   Cool Delight Company specializes in creating novelty ice cream desserts. It reported current assets of $175,200 and current liabilities of $136,750 at August 31, 2011. Included in current assets are Cash $10,500; Short-Term Investments $7,600; and Accounts Receivable $27,200. Calculate Cool Delight's working capital, current ratio, and acid-test ratio. Comment on Cool Delight's liquidity.

Complete work sheet.
(SO 6) AP

*****BE4–13**   The accountant for Coulombe Company is almost finished preparing the work sheet for the year ended July 31, 2011. The totals of the accounts in the income statement and balance sheet columns are presented below. Calculate the profit or loss, write this number in the proper columns, and calculate the final totals for these columns. Clearly indicate whether the company had a profit or a loss.

	Income Statement		Balance Sheet	
	Dr.	Cr.	Dr.	Cr.
Totals	37,250	28,950	37,050	45,350
Profit or loss				
Totals				

Complete work sheet.
(SO 6) AP

*****BE4–14**   The accountant for Orange Line Company is almost finished preparing the work sheet for the year ended August 31, 2011. The totals of the accounts in the income statement and balance sheet columns are presented below. Calculate the profit or loss, write this in the proper columns, and calculate the final totals for these columns. Clearly indicate whether the company had a profit or loss.

	Income Statement		Balance Sheet	
	Dr.	Cr.	Dr.	Cr.
Totals	33,300	45,400	71,800	59,700
Profit or loss				
Totals				

Prepare and post reversing and subsequent entries.
(SO 7) AP

*****BE4–15**   At October 31, Orlaida Company made an accrued expense adjusting entry of $1,200 for salaries. On November 6, it paid salaries of $3,000: $1,200 for October salaries and $1,800 for November salaries. (a) Prepare the November 1 reversing entry and the November 6 journal entry to record the payment of salaries. (b) Indicate the balances in Salaries Payable and Salaries Expense after posting the two entries.

Prepare and post reversing and subsequent entries.
(SO 7) AP

*****BE4–16**   At October 31, Orlaida Company also had interest receivable of $5,600. On November 10, interest of $6,000 was received. (a) Prepare the November 1 reversing entry and the November 10 journal entry. (b) Indicate the balances in Interest Receivable and Interest Earned after posting the two entries.

Exercises

E4–1   Selected T accounts for Rothwell Designs follow. All June 30 postings are from closing entries.

Prepare closing entries.
(SO 1) AP

Salaries Expense			
June 1	4,000	June 30	9,500
28	5,500		
June 30 Bal.	0		

J. Rothwell, Capital			
		June 1 Bal.	11,000
June 30	2,650	30	2,375
		June 30 Bal.	10,725

Utilities Expense			
June 10	550	June 30	1,225
24	675		
June 30 Bal.	0		

J. Rothwell, Drawings			
June 13	900	June 30	2,650
25	1,750		
June 30 Bal.	0		

Service Revenue			
June 30	15,800	June 15	6,500
		24	9,300
		June 30 Bal.	0

Rent Expense			
June 1	2,700	June 30	2,700
June 30 Bal.	0		

Instructions

(a) Prepare the closing entries that were made.
(b) Post the closing entries to the Income Summary.
(c) What should the ending balance of the account J. Rothwell, Capital, agree with and in which financial statement(s)?

E4–2   Selected T accounts for Victoire Esthetics to May 31, 2011, follow.

Prepare a statement of owner's equity and closing entries.
(SO 1) AP

B. Victoire, Capital			
		May 1 Bal.	7,500
		10	5,000
		May 31 Bal.	12,500

B. Victoire, Drawings			
May 5	1,000		
15	1,100		
25	1,150		
May 31 Bal.	3,250		

Income Summary			
May 31	6,000	May 31	10,000
		May 31 Bal.	4,000

Instructions

(a) Prepare a statement of owner's equity for May 2011.
(b) Prepare and post entries to close the income summary and drawings accounts.

Prepare and post closing
entries and prepare post-
closing trial balance.
(SO 1) AP

E4–3   At the end of its fiscal year, the adjusted trial balance of Donatello Company is as follows:

DONATELLO COMPANY
Adjusted Trial Balance
July 31, 2011

	Debit	Credit
Cash	$ 5,840	
Accounts receivable	11,440	
Prepaid expenses	1,620	
Supplies	470	
Equipment	17,600	
Accumulated depreciation—equipment		$ 5,400
Accounts payable		4,245
Interest payable		525
Unearned service revenue		2,750
Notes payable (due on July 1, 2013)		15,000
B. Donatello, capital		31,200
B. Donatello, drawings	16,500	
Service revenue		71,700
Depreciation expense	2,700	
Salaries expense	36,050	
Interest expense	1,350	
Rent expense	16,400	
Supplies expense	20,850	
	$130,820	$130,820

Instructions

(a) Prepare the closing entries and post them to the correct accounts.

(b) Prepare a post-closing trial balance at July 31, 2011.

Prepare and post closing
entries and prepare post-
closing trial balance.
(SO 1) AP

E4–4   An alphabetical list of the adjusted account balances (all accounts have normal balances) at August 31, 2011, for Alpine Bowling Lanes is as follows:

Accounts payable	$ 12,300	Interest expense	$ 4,800
Accounts receivable	10,780	Interest payable	400
Accumulated depreciation—building	30,900	Investment in bonds	10,000
Accumulated depreciation—equipment	24,960	Land	64,000
Depreciation expense	9,300	Mortgage payable	99,780
Bowling revenues	35,900	Prepaid insurance	4,590
Building	128,800	Supplies	740
Cash	17,940	T. Williams, capital	125,000
Equipment	62,400	T. Williams, drawings	16,000
Insurance expense	870	Unearned bowling revenue	980

Instructions

(a) Prepare the closing entries at August 31.

(b) Prepare T accounts for the accounts affected by the closing entries. Post the closing entries.

(c) Prepare a post-closing trial balance at August 31, 2011.

Apply the steps in accounting
cycle.
(SO 2) AP

E4–5   Tim Sasse started Sasse Roof Repairs on April 2, 2011, by investing $4,000 cash in the business. During April, the following transactions occurred:

Apr.   6   Purchased supplies for $1,500 cash.
     15   Repaired a roof for a customer and collected $600 cash.
     25   Received $1,200 cash in advance from a customer for roof repairs to his house and garage.

On April 30, 2011, the following information was available:

1. There is $1,100 of supplies on hand.
2. Of the $1,200 received on April 25, the company has earned $400 by completing repairs to the garage roof.
3. Earned but unbilled revenue at April 30 was $500.

Instructions

(a) Journalize the transactions.
(b) Post to the ledger accounts. (Use T accounts.)
(c) Journalize and post any required adjusting entries.
(d) Prepare an adjusted trial balance.
(e) Assuming the company closes its books on a monthly basis, journalize and post closing entries.

E4–6   Choi Company has an inexperienced accountant. During the first two weeks on the job, the accountant made the following errors in journalizing transactions. All incorrect entries were posted.

Prepare correcting entries and analyze impact of error. (SO 3) AP

1. A payment on account of $920 to a creditor was debited $290 to Accounts Payable and credited $290 to Cash.
2. The purchase of supplies on account for $560 was debited $56 to Equipment and credited $56 to Accounts Payable.
3. A $400 withdrawal of cash for L. Choi's personal use was debited $400 to Salaries Expense and credited $400 to Cash.
4. Received $700 cash from a customer on account. Cash was debited $700 and Service Revenue was credited $700.
5. A customer was billed $175 for services provided. Accounts Receivable was debited $175 and Unearned Service Revenue was credited $175.

Instructions

(a) Prepare the correcting entries.
(b) Indicate the impact of each error on the balance sheet and income statement by stating whether total assets, liabilities, owner's equity, revenues, expenses, and profit are understated (U), overstated (O), or if there is no effect (NE). Use the following format, in which the answer for the first error is given as an example:

| | Balance Sheet | | | | Income Statement | | |
Error	Assets	Liabilities	Owner's Equity		Revenues	Expenses	Profit
1.	O	O	NE		NE	NE	NE

E4–7   The owner of D'Addario Company has been doing all of the company's bookkeeping. When the accountant arrived to do the year-end adjusting entries, she found the following errors:

Prepare correcting entries. (SO 3) AP

1. A payment of salaries of $625 was debited to Supplies and credited to Cash, both for $625.
2. The investment of cash of $2,000 by the owner, Toni D'Addario, was debited to Short-Term Investments and credited to Cash, both for $2,000.
3. The collection of an accounts receivable of $780 was debited to Cash and credited to Accounts Receivable, both for $870.
4. The company had purchased $440 of supplies on account. This entry was correctly recorded. When the account was paid, Supplies was debited $440 and Cash was credited $440.
5. Equipment costing $3,500 was purchased by signing a six-month note payable. Equipment Expense was debited and Accounts Payable was credited, both for $3,500.

Instructions

(a) Correct the errors by reversing the incorrect entry and preparing the correct entry.
(b) Correct the errors without reversing the incorrect entry.

Identify accounts and balance sheet classifications.
(SO 4) K

E4–8 The Jean Coutu Group (PJC) Inc. has the following selected accounts included in its recent financial statements:

Accounts payable and accrued liabilities	Income taxes expense
Accounts receivable	Income taxes payable
Accumulated other comprehensive loss	Income taxes receivable
Capital assets	Inventories
Capital stock	Investments
Cash and cash equivalents	Long-term debt
Contributed surplus	Long-term debt due within one year
Current portion of long-term debt	Long-term lease obligation
Employee future benefit obligation	Mortgages and loans receivable
Financing expenses	Other revenues
General and operating expenses	Prepaid expenses
Goodwill	Retained earnings

Instructions

(a) Identify if the account belongs on the balance sheet (BS) or income statement (IS).
(b) For each account that belongs on the balance sheet, identify its classification.

Prepare financial statements.
(SO 4) AP

E4–9 The adjusted trial balance for Donatello Company is presented in E4–3.

Instructions

(a) Prepare an income statement and statement of owner's equity for the year. Mr. Donatello invested $5,000 cash in the business during the year.
(b) Prepare a classified balance sheet at July 31, 2011.

Prepare financial statements and comment on liquidity.
(SO 4, 5) AN

E4–10 Refer to the list of adjusted account balances presented in E4–4 for Alpine Bowling Lanes at August 31, 2011.

Instructions

(a) Prepare an income statement and statement of owner's equity for the year ended August 31, 2011, and a classified balance sheet at August 31, 2011. Assume the following: (1) $12,750 of the mortgage payable will be paid before August 31, 2012; and (2) the company intends to keep its investment in bonds until the bonds mature in 2020.
(b) Calculate working capital, the current ratio, and the acid-test ratio.
(c) Comment on the company's liquidity.

Calculate working capital, current ratio, and acid-test ratio, and comment on liquidity.
(SO 5) AN

E4–11 Shoppers Drug Mart Corporation is Canada's largest retail pharmacy, with stores in each province (including Pharmaprix in Quebec) and two territories. The following data (in thousands) were taken from Shoppers' financial statements:

	Jan. 3, 2009	Dec. 29, 2007	Dec. 30, 2006
Cash	$ 36,567	$ 27,588	$ 62,865
Accounts receivable	448,476	372,206	307,779
Current assets	2,384,464	2,172,199	1,821,423
Current liabilities	1,843,860	2,159,045	1,577,784

Instructions

(a) Calculate the working capital, current ratio, and acid-test ratio for each year.
(b) Discuss Shoppers Drug Mart's liquidity on January 3, 2009, compared with the two previous years.

Prepare work sheet.
(SO 6) AP

*E4–12   The unadjusted trial balance for Garden Designs at its month end, April 30, 2011, is as follows:

	Debit	Credit
GARDEN DESIGNS		
Trial Balance		
April 30, 2011		
Cash	$14,840	
Accounts receivable	8,780	
Prepaid rent	4,875	
Equipment	18,900	
Accumulated depreciation—equipment		$ 4,725
Accounts payable		5,670
Notes payable		11,600
T. Hibiscus, capital		25,960
T. Hibiscus, drawings	3,650	
Service revenue		12,930
Salaries expense	9,840	
	$60,885	$60,885

Other data:
1. Revenuc of $720 was earned but unrecorded as at April 30, 2011.
2. On April 1, the company paid $4,875 rent in advance for April 1 to August 31.
3. The equipment has an estimated useful life of eight years.
4. Interest on the note payable is due on the first day of each month for the previous month's interest. The note payable has a 6% annual interest rate.

Instructions

Prepare the work sheet for the month ended April 30, 2011.

Prepare and post adjusting, closing, reversing, and subsequent entries.
(SO 1, 7) AP

*E4–13   On December 31, the unadjusted trial balance of Masterson Employment Agency shows the following selected data:

Accounts receivable	$24,000	Cash	$7,600
Interest expense	7,800	Commission revenue	$92,000
I. Masterson, capital	48,000	Interest payable	0

Analysis shows that adjusting entries are required to (1) accrue $4,400 of commission revenue, and (2) accrue $1,500 of interest expense.

Instructions

(a) Prepare and post (1) the adjusting entries and (2) the closing entries for the temporary accounts at December 31.
(b) Prepare and post reversing entries on January 1.
(c) Prepare and post the entries to record (1) the collection of $6,200 of commissions (including the accrued commission from December 31) on January 10, and (2) the payment of $2,235 interest on January 31 (consisting of the accrued interest from December 31 plus January's interest).

Prepare adjusting, reversing, and subsequent entries.
(SO 7) AP

*E4–14   Rosborough Company provides property management services to a variety of companies. At its fiscal year end on April 30, 2011, adjustments were required for the following items:

1. Property management revenue of $600 was earned but not recorded.
2. Of the balance in the Unearned Property Management Revenue account, $250 had been earned.

3. Depreciation expense for the year ended April 30, 2011, was $4,850.
4. Interest of $545 on a note payable had accrued.
5. Prepaid insurance of $385 had expired.
6. Property taxes for the calendar year payable every year on June 30. The company estimated property taxes for 2011 to be $3,912.

Instructions

(a) Identify the adjustments for which it could be useful to prepare reversing entries.
(b) Prepare these reversing entries on May 1, 2011.
(c) Explain why and how the reversing entries are useful for these adjustments but not for the other adjustments.

Problems: Set A

Analyze account data, prepare closing entries and post-closing trial balance, and discuss.

(SO 1) AN

P4–1A   LeCoure Consulting is in the middle of preparing and posting closing entries at its September 30, 2011, year end. The following T accounts show the balances before the accounts were closed and the closing entries that were posted to them:

Cash			Accumulated Depreciation	
20,000				10,000

Equipment			Accounts Payable	
60,000				5,000

Professional Fees Earned			Other Expenses	
275,000	275,000		20,000	20,000

J. LeCoure, Drawings			Operating Expenses	
125,000	125,000		145,000	145,000

J. LeCoure, Capital			Other Revenue	
125,000	60,000		20,000	20,000
	130,000			

Income Summary	
?	?

Instructions

(a) Reconstruct, in general journal format, the closing entries that were journalized and posted to the above T accounts. (*Hint*: Notice that some of the amounts in the T accounts are repeated several times. Think about which ones are related to each other in terms of the closing entries.)
(b) Post the closing entries to the Income Summary account.
(c) Prepare a post-closing trial balance.
(d) Will the total debits on the post-closing trial balance equal total assets at September 30, 2011? Explain.

Taking It Further   Explain why all accounts are not closed.

P4–2A The adjusted trial balance for Toronto Tennis Park is as follows:

Prepare financial statements, closing entries, and post-closing trial balance.
(SO 1, 4) AP

TORONTO TENNIS PARK
Adjusted Trial Balance
December 31, 2011

	Debit	Credit
Cash	$ 6,185	
Accounts receivable	13,500	
Prepaid insurance	8,400	
Supplies	1,140	
Investments	25,000	
Land	46,800	
Building	187,580	
Accumulated depreciation—building		$ 37,520
Equipment	26,000	
Accumulated depreciation—equipment		5,600
Accounts payable		13,220
Salaries payable		3,000
Interest payable		350
Unearned revenue		2,190
Notes payable ($7,500 must be paid in 2012)		63,925
T. Fichman, capital		165,000
T. Fichman, drawings	59,200	
Service revenue		139,800
Advertising expense	2,400	
Depreciation expense	10,300	
Utilities expense	2,175	
Interest expense	4,155	
Insurance expense	3,500	
Salaries expense	32,100	
Supplies expense	2,170	
	$430,605	$430,605

Instructions

(a) Prepare an income statement, statement of owner's equity, and classified balance sheet. The owner, Tara Fichman, invested $2,500 cash in the business during the year.
(b) Prepare the closing entries.
(c) Use T accounts to post the closing entries and calculate the balance in each account. (Ignore the accounts not affected by the closing entries.)
(d) Prepare a post-closing trial balance.

Taking It Further Describe how the classified balance sheet of this company might look different if it followed International Financial Reporting Standards.

P4–3A   The following is Elbow Cycle Repair Shop's trial balance at January 31, 2011, the company's fiscal year end:

ELBOW CYCLE REPAIR SHOP Trial Balance January 31, 2011		
	Debit	Credit
Cash	$ 3,200	
Accounts receivable	6,630	
Prepaid insurance	6,420	
Supplies	5,240	
Land	50,000	
Building	90,000	
Accumulated depreciation—building		$ 11,000
Equipment	27,000	
Accumulated depreciation—equipment		4,500
Accounts payable		6,400
Unearned revenue		1,950
Mortgage payable		102,000
H. Dude, capital		61,000
H. Dude, drawings	101,100	
Service revenue		235,550
Salaries expense	115,200	
Utilities expense	12,000	
Interest expense	5,610	
	$422,400	$422,400

Other data:

1. Service revenue earned but not recorded at January 31, 2011, was $1,550.
2. The 12-month insurance policy was purchased on March 1, 2010.
3. A physical count of supplies shows $580 on hand on January 31, 2011.
4. The building has an estimated useful life of 45 years. The equipment has an estimated useful life of 15 years.
5. Salaries of $1,520 are accrued and unpaid at January 31, 2011.
6. The mortgage payable has a 6% interest rate. Interest is paid on the first day of each month for the previous month's interest.
7. By January 31, 2011, $850 of the unearned revenue has been earned.
8. During the next fiscal year, $4,500 of the mortgage payable is to be paid.

Instructions

(a) Prepare the adjusting entries.
(b) Prepare an adjusted trial balance.
(c) Prepare an income statement, statement of owner's equity, and classified balance sheet. The owner, Henry Dude, invested $5,000 cash in the business on November 17, 2010.
(d) Prepare the closing entries.

Taking It Further   Henry Dude is concerned that he had to invest cash into the business this year. Based on the information in the financial statements, what do you suggest to Henry?

P4–4A   Lee Chang opened Lee's Window Washing on July 1, 2011. In July, the following transactions were completed:

July   1   Chang invested $20,000 cash in the business.
     1   Purchased a used truck for $25,000, paying $5,000 cash and signing a note payable for the balance.
     3   Purchased cleaning supplies for $2,100 on account.
     5   Paid $1,800 on a one-year insurance policy, effective July 1.

12 Billed customers $4,500 for cleaning services.
18 Paid $1,400 of amount owed on cleaning supplies.
20 Paid $2,000 for employee salaries.
21 Collected $3,400 from customers billed on July 12.
25 Billed customers $9,000 for cleaning services.
31 Paid gas and oil for the month on the truck, $550.
31 Withdrew $1,600 cash for personal use.

Instructions

(a) Journalize and post the July transactions.
(b) Prepare a trial balance at July 31.
(c) Journalize and post the following adjustments:
   1. Earned but unbilled fees at July 31 were $1,500.
   2. The truck has an estimated useful life of four years.
   3. One twelfth of the insurance expired.
   4. An inventory count shows $700 of cleaning supplies on hand at July 31.
   5. Accrued but unpaid employee salaries were $800.
   6. The note payable has a 5.5% annual interest rate.
(d) Prepare an adjusted trial balance.
(e) Prepare the income statement and statement of owner's equity for July, and a classified balance sheet at July 31, 2011. Of the note payable, $5,000 must be paid by July 1, 2012.
(f) Journalize and post the closing entries.
(g) Prepare a post-closing trial balance at July 31.

Taking It Further   Does the company need to make adjusting and closing entries at the end of every month?

P4–5A   Bob Hibberd, CGA, was hired by Edgemont Entertainment Installations to prepare its financial statements for April 2011. Using all the ledger balances in the owner's records, Hibberd put together the following trial balance:

Analyze errors and prepare corrections.
(SO 3) AP

EDGEMONT ENTERTAINMENT INSTALLATIONS Trial Balance April 30, 2011		
	Debit	Credit
Cash	$ 4,960	
Accounts receivable	3,200	
Supplies	3,800	
Equipment	11,220	
Accumulated depreciation—equipment		$ 2,387
Accounts payable		2,275
Salaries payable		500
Unearned revenue		590
S. Morris, capital		17,700
Service revenue		7,950
Salaries expense	7,000	
Advertising expense	445	
Miscellaneous expense	490	
Depreciation expense	187	
Repair expense	100	
Totals	$31,402	$31,402

Hibberd reviewed the records and found the following errors:

1. The first salary payment made in April was for $1,900, which included $500 of salaries payable on March 31. The payment was recorded as a debit to Salaries Expense of $1,900 and a credit to Cash of $1,900. (No reversing entries were made on April 1.)

2. The owner, Stuart Morris, paid himself $2,200 and recorded this as salary expense.
3. April rent of $950 was paid on April 26. The company has not recorded this transaction.
4. Cash received from a customer on account was recorded as $690 instead of $960.
5. A payment of $145 for a miscellaneous expense was entered as a debit to Advertising Expense of $45 and a credit to Cash of $45.
6. A cash payment for a repair expense on equipment of $220 was recorded as a debit to Equipment of $220 and a credit to Cash of $220.
7. The purchase on account of equipment that cost $3,400 was recorded as a debit to supplies and a credit to accounts payable for $3,400.
8. The depreciation expense of $187 for the month of April was calculated using the balance in the equipment account of $11,220. All of the company's equipment is expected to have a five-year useful life. (*Note:* Assume the equipment in error 7 was purchased on April 1, 2011.)

Instructions

(a) Prepare an analysis of each error that shows (1) the incorrect entry, (2) the correct entry, and (3) the correcting entry.
(b) Prepare a correct trial balance.

Taking It Further   Explain how the company's financial statements would be incorrect if error 2 was not corrected and why it is important to correct this error.

Determine impact of errors on financial statements, and correct.
(SO 3) AP

P4–6A   The following accounting errors were found in the journal of Crossé Company:

1. The payment of the current month's rent for $500 was recorded as a debit to Rent Payable and a credit to Cash, both for $500. (*Note:* This had not been previously accrued.)
2. The collection of an account receivable for $400 was debited to Cash and credited to Service Revenue, both for $400.
3. A payment for Utilities Expense of $230 was recorded as a debit to Utilities Expense and a credit to Cash, both for $320.
4. A customer was billed $850 for services provided on account. Accounts Receivable was debited and Unearned Service Revenue was credited, both for $850.
5. A $600 accrual of Interest Earned was recorded as a debit to Interest Earned and a credit to Interest Receivable, both for $600.
6. A payment of a $250 account payable was recorded as debit to Accounts Payable and a credit to Cash, both for $250.
7. A $300 advance from a customer was recorded as a debit to Unearned Service Revenue and a credit to Service Revenue, both for $300.
8. The purchase of $350 of supplies on account was recorded as a debit to Salaries Expense and a credit to Accounts Payable, both for $530.

Instructions

(a) For each item, indicate the effect and amount of the error—understatement (U), overstatement (O), or no effect (NE)—on the income statement and balance sheet components. Use the following format, where the first one has been done for you as an example.

	Income Statement			Balance Sheet		
Item	Revenue	Expenses	Profit	Assets	Liabilities	Owner's Equity
1.	NE	U $500	O $500	NE	U $500	O $500

(b) Correct each error by reversing the incorrect entry and then recording the correct entry.

Taking It Further   Explain why it is incorrect to record billing a customer for services provided on account, as described in error 4.

P4–7A Below is an alphabetical list of the adjusted accounts of Dunder Tour Company at its year end, December 31, 2011. All accounts have normal balances.

Calculate capital account balance; prepare classified balance sheet and liquidity ratios.

(SO 1, 4, 5) AP

Accounts payable	$ 7,300	Note receivable	$18,400
Accounts receivable	3,500	Equipment	50,000
Accumulated depreciation—equipment	15,000	F. Dunder, capital	17,300
Depreciation expense	10,000	F. Dunder, drawings	33,000
Cash	4,500	Patent	15,000
Insurance expense	1,500	Prepaid insurance	2,800
Interest expense	2,800	Service revenue	65,000
Interest payable	700	Short-term investments	2,800
Interest receivable	100	Supplies	3,100
Interest revenue	1,100	Supplies expense	2,400
Note payable	40,000	Unearned revenue	3,500

Other data:
1. In 2012, $3,000 of the notes payable becomes due.
2. The note receivable is due in 2013.
3. On July 18, 2011, Fred Dunder invested $3,200 cash in the business.

Instructions

(a) Calculate the post-closing balance in F. Dunder, Capital on December 31, 2011.
(b) Prepare a classified balance sheet.
(c) On December 31, 2010, Dunder Tour Company had current assets of $17,400 and current liabilities of $22,300. Calculate the company's working capital and current ratio on December 31, 2010, and December 31, 2011.
(d) On December 31, 2010, the total of Dunder Tour Company's cash, short-term investments, and current receivables was $15,600. Calculate the company's acid-test ratio on December 31, 2010, and December 31, 2011.

Taking It Further Has the company's ability to pay its debts improved or weakened over the year?

P4–8A Danier Leather Inc. is one of the largest publicly traded specialty apparel leather retailers in the world. The follow information can be found on its recent balance sheets (all amounts in thousands):

Calculate working capital, current ratio, and acid-test ratio; and comment on liquidity.

(SO 5) AN

	June 27, 2009	June 28, 2008	June 30, 2007
Cash	$24,628	$19,882	$20,579
Accounts receivable	351	755	724
Total current assets	48,056	49,853	56,422
Total current liabilities	10,967	11,205	30,275

The company did not have any short-term investments on these balance sheets.

Instructions

(a) Calculate Danier Leather's working capital, current ratio, and acid-test ratio for each year.
(b) What does each of the measures calculated in (a) show? Comment on Danier's liquidity.

Taking It Further A company will almost always have a larger current ratio than its acid-test ratio. Why? Would you expect this difference to be larger in a company like Danier Leather than in a company like WestJet Airlines? Why or why not?

*P4–9A The unadjusted trial balance and adjustment data for Elbow Cycle Repair Shop are presented in P4–3A.

Prepare work sheet.

(SO 6) AP

Instructions

Prepare a work sheet for the year ended January 31, 2011.

Taking It Further   Is it still necessary to record the adjusting entries in the journal and post them to the ledger accounts when using a worksheet?

Prepare work sheet, classified balance sheet, adjusting and closing entries, and post-closing trial balance.
(SO 1, 4, 6) AP

P4–10A   Water World Park's year end is September 30. The company's trial balance prior to adjustments follows:

WATER WORLD PARK
Trial Balance
September 30, 2011

	Debit	Credit
Cash	$ 11,770	
Accounts receivable	0	
Supplies	18,600	
Prepaid insurance	33,000	
Land	80,000	
Building	480,000	
Accumulated depreciation—building		$ 96,000
Equipment	120,000	
Accumulated depreciation—equipment		48,000
Accounts payable		23,600
Wages payable		
Interest payable		
Unearned admission revenue		3,700
Mortgage payable		350,000
M. Berge, capital		175,450
M. Berge, drawings	14,000	
Admission revenue		250,065
Concession revenue		16,720
Wages expense	123,000	
Repairs expense	30,500	
Advertising expense	9,660	
Utilities expense	16,900	
Insurance expense	5,500	
Interest expense	20,605	
Depreciation expense	0	
Supplies expense	0	
	$963,535	$963,535

Other data:

1. The concession is operated by another company that pays Water World Park a percentage of its revenues. As at September 30, 2011, this company owed Water World Park $1,175. This amount will be paid on October 10, 2011.
2. A physical count showed $1,350 of supplies on hand at September 30, 2011.
3. The building has an expected useful life of 30 years. The equipment's expected useful life is 10 years.
4. A one-year insurance policy was purchased on December 1, 2010, for $33,000.
5. Accrued wages payable at September 30, 2011, were $2,950.
6. The mortgage payable has an annual interest rate of 6%. The last payment was on September 1, 2011.
7. As at September 30, 2011, there was $700 of revenue received in advance that was still unearned.
8. A utility bill for September of $950 has not been paid or recorded.

Instructions

(a) Prepare a work sheet, using the information provided above.
(b) Prepare a classified balance sheet. (*Note*: In the next fiscal year, $50,000 of the mortgage payable is due for payment.)
(c) Journalize the adjusting entries.

(d) Journalize the closing entries.

(e) Prepare a post-closing trial balance.

Taking It Further Explain why preparing a work sheet is an optional step in the accounting cycle.

*P4–11A Farid Company had the following balances on its December 31, 2010, balance sheet:

Interest receivable	$1,020	Wages payable	$56,250
Prepaid insurance	5,000	Unearned service revenue	25,000

Prepare and post transaction entries, with and without reversing entries.
(SO 7) AP

During 2011, the following transactions occurred:

1. On February 1, $1,530 cash was collected for interest on a note receivable for the period November 1, 2010, to February 1, 2011.
2. On January 7, $75,000 was paid to employees for wages earned between December 8, 2010, and January 7, 2011.
3. On May 1, the company's insurance policy expired and the company paid $15,000 for a one-year policy.
4. Services of $200,000 provided in 2011 included $185,000 of services for cash and $15,000 of services to customers who had made advance payments during 2010.

Instructions

(a) Assuming that the company does not use reversing entries:
   1. Prepare journal entries to record the transactions above for 2011.
   2. Post your entries to T accounts, and calculate the balance in each account. (Ignore the cash account.)

(b) Assuming that Farid uses reversing entries:
   1. Prepare reversing entries as appropriate on January 1, 2011.
   2. Prepare journal entries to record the transactions above for 2011.
   3. Post your entries to T accounts, and calculate the balance in each account. (Ignore the cash account.)

(c) Compare the account balances in (a) with those in (b).

Taking It Further Comment on the usefulness of reversing entries.

*P4–12A The unadjusted trial balance for Veda's Video Arcade at its fiscal year end of May 31, 2011, is as follows:

Prepare adjusting, reversing, and subsequent cash entries.
(SO 7) AP

VEDA'S VIDEO ARCADE Trial Balance May 31, 2011		
	Debit	Credit
Cash	$ 6,420	
Accounts receivable	0	
Supplies	2,950	
Equipment	128,000	
Accumulated depreciation—equipment		$ 57,600
Wages payable		0
Interest payable		0
Note payable		60,000
Unearned game fee revenue		1,500
V. Gupta, capital		30,000
V. Gupta, drawings	34,400	
Game fee revenue		82,545
Rent expense	13,600	
Wages expense	43,800	
Supplies expense	0	
Depreciation expense	0	
Interest expense	2,475	
	$231,645	$231,645

Other data:

1. On May 31, 2011, Veda's Video Arcade had earned but not collected or recorded $750 of game fee revenue. On June 19, it collected this amount plus an additional $1,150 for game fee revenue earned in June.
2. There was $875 of supplies on hand on May 31, 2011.
3. The equipment has an estimated useful life of 10 years.
4. Accrued salaries to May 31 were $1,390. The next payday is June 3 and the employees will be paid a total of $1,980 that day.
5. The note payable has a 6.5% annual interest rate. Interest is paid quarterly. Interest was last paid on March 1, 2011. The next payment is due on June 1, 2011.
6. As at May 31, 2011, there was $700 of game fee revenue that had not been earned.

Instructions

(a) Prepare adjusting journal entries for the year ended May 31, 2011, as required.
(b) Prepare reversing entries where appropriate.
(c) Prepare journal entries to record the June 2011 cash transactions.
(d) Now assume reversing entries were not prepared as in (b) above. Prepare journal entries to record the June 2011 cash transactions.

Taking It Further   Why is it not appropriate to use reversing entries for all of the adjusting entries?

Problems: Set B

Analyze account data, prepare closing entries and post-closing trial balance, and discuss.
(SO 1) AN

P4–1B   LaPorte Repair Company is in the middle of preparing and posting closing entries at its October 31, 2011, year end. The following T accounts show the balances before the accounts were closed and the closing entries that were posted to them:

Cash			Accumulated Depreciation		
30,000					35,000

Equipment			Accounts Payable		
85,000					10,000

Repair Service Revenue			Other Expenses		
180,000		180,000	30,000		30,000

R. LaPorte, Drawings			Repair Service Expense		
50,000		50,000	125,000		125,000

R. LaPorte, Capital			Other Revenue		
50,000		60,000	35,000		35,000
		60,000			

Income Summary		
?		?

Instructions

(a) Reconstruct, in general journal format, the closing entries that were journalized and posted to the above T accounts. (*Hint*: Notice that some of the amounts in the T accounts are repeated several times. Think about which ones are related to each other in terms of the closing entries.)
(b) Post the closing entries to the Income Summary account.
(c) Prepare a post-closing trial balance.
(d) Will the total debits on the post-closing trial balance equal total assets at September 30, 2011? Explain.

Taking It Further Explain the purpose of closing entries and the post-closing trial balance.

P4–2B The adjusted trial balance for Arctic River Golf Dome is as follows:

Prepare financial statements, closing entries, and post-closing trial balance.
(SO 1, 4) AP

ARCTIC RIVER GOLF DOME Adjusted Trial Balance December 31, 2011	Debit	Credit
Cash	$ 8,400	
Accounts receivable	7,500	
Prepaid insurance	1,200	
Supplies	570	
Investments	15,000	
Land	102,500	
Building	150,000	
Accumulated depreciation—building		$ 24,000
Equipment	28,000	
Accumulated depreciation—equipment		8,400
Accounts payable		12,740
Salaries payable		2,850
Interest payable		1,400
Unearned revenue		2,190
Mortgage payable ($3,000 is payable in 2012)		198,000
A. Putyuk, capital		73,500
A. Putyuk, drawings	7,200	
Service revenue		73,500
Salaries expense	47,040	
Depreciation expense	5,800	
Utilities expense	5,280	
Interest expense	12,870	
Insurance expense	1,800	
Supplies expense	3,420	
	$396,580	$396,580

Instructions

(a) Prepare an income statement, statement of owner's equity, and classified balance sheet. The owner, Annie Putyuk, invested $3,300 cash in the business during 2011.
(b) Prepare the closing entries.
(c) Using T accounts, post the closing entries and calculate the balance in each account. (Ignore the accounts that are not affected by the closing entries.)
(d) Prepare a post-closing trial balance.

Taking It Further Describe how the classified balance sheet of this company might look different if it used International Financial Reporting Standards.

P4–3B Some data relating to Edge Sports Repair Shop appear below.

Other data:

1. Service revenue earned but not recorded at September 30, 2011, was $1,150.
2. The 12-month insurance policy was purchased on December 1, 2010.
3. A physical count of supplies shows $960 on hand on September 30, 2011.
4. The building has an estimated useful life of 40 years. The equipment has an estimated useful life of eight years.
5. Salaries of $975 are accrued and unpaid at September 30, 2011.
6. The mortgage payable has a 5.5% interest rate. Interest is paid on the first day of each month for the previous month's interest.
7. On September 30, 2011, one quarter of the unearned revenue was still unearned.
8. During the next fiscal year, $5,400 of the mortgage payable is to be paid.

Prepare adjusting entries, adjusted trial balance, financial statements, and closing entries.
(SO 1, 4) AP

The following is Edge Sports Repair Shop's trial balance at September 30, 2011, the company's fiscal year end:

EDGE SPORTS REPAIR SHOP Trial Balance September 30, 2011	Debit	Credit
Cash	$ 6,750	
Accounts receivable	11,540	
Prepaid insurance	4,140	
Supplies	3,780	
Land	55,000	
Building	98,000	
Accumulated depreciation—building		$ 17,150
Equipment	38,000	
Accumulated depreciation—equipment		9,500
Accounts payable		8,550
Unearned revenue		3,300
Mortgage payable		125,000
R. Brachman, capital		60,000
R. Brachman, drawings	103,525	
Service revenue		189,550
Salaries expense	75,900	
Utilities expense	10,113	
Interest expense	6,302	
	$413,050	$413,050

Instructions

(a) Prepare the adjusting entries.

(b) Prepare an adjusted trial balance.

(c) Prepare an income statement, statement of owner's equity, and classified balance sheet. The owner, Ralph Brachman, invested $4,000 cash in the business on November 21, 2010.

(d) Prepare the closing entries.

Taking It Further   Ralph Brachman is concerned that he had to invest $4,000 cash into the business this year. Based on the information in the financial statements, what are your recommendations to Ralph?

Complete all steps in accounting cycle.
(SO 2) AP

P4–4B   Laura Eddy opened Eddy's Carpet Cleaners on March 1, 2011. In March, the following transactions were completed:

Mar.   1   Laura invested $10,000 cash in the business.
       1   Purchased a used truck for $6,500, paying $1,500 cash and signing a note payable for the balance.
      3   Purchased cleaning supplies for $1,200 on account.
      5   Paid $1,200 on a one-year insurance policy, effective March 1.
    12   Billed customers $4,800 for cleaning services.
    18   Paid $500 of amount owed on cleaning supplies.
    20   Paid $1,800 for employee salaries.
    21   Collected $1,400 from customers billed on March 12.
    25   Billed customers $2,500 for cleaning services.
    31   Paid gas and oil for the month on the truck, $375.
    31   Withdrew $900 cash for personal use.

Instructions

(a) Journalize and post the March transactions.

(b) Prepare a trial balance at March 31.

(c) Journalize and post the following adjustments:
 1. The truck has an estimated useful life of five years.
 2. One-twelfth of the insurance expired.
 3. An inventory count shows $400 of cleaning supplies on hand at March 31.
 4. Accrued but unpaid employee salaries were $500.
 5. The note payable has a 4.5% annual interest rate.
 6. Earned but unbilled fees at March 31 were $1,500.
(d) Prepare an adjusted trial balance.
(e) Prepare the income statement and statement of owner's equity for March, and a classified balance sheet at March 31, 2011. Of the note payable, $2,000 must be paid by March 1, 2012.
(f) Journalize and post the closing entries.
(g) Prepare a post-closing trial balance at March 31.

Taking It Further Does the company need to make adjusting and closing entries at the end of every month?

P4–5B Ian Mathers, CGA, was hired by Interactive Computer Installations to prepare its financial statements for March 2011. Using all the ledger balances in the owner's records, Mathers put together the following trial balance:

Analyze errors and prepare corrections.
(SO 3) AP

INTERACTIVE COMPUTER INSTALLATIONS Trial Balance March 31, 2011		
	Debit	Credit
Cash	$ 7,150	
Accounts receivable	3,850	
Supplies	3,100	
Equipment	11,460	
Accumulated depreciation—equipment		$ 4,631
Accounts payable		3,500
Salaries payable		750
Unearned revenue		955
M. Hubert, capital		15,375
Service revenue		7,800
Salaries expense	6,300	
Advertising expense	600	
Miscellaneous expense	210	
Depreciation expense	191	
Repair expense	150	
Totals	$33,011	$33,011

Mathers then reviewed the records and found the following errors:

1. The purchase on account of equipment for $2,100 on March 1 was recorded as a debit to Supplies and a credit to Accounts Payable, both for $1,200.
2. March rent of $1,150 was paid on March 2. The company has not recorded this transaction.
3. Cash received from a customer on account was recorded as $870 instead of $780.
4. A payment of a $575 account payable was entered as a debit to Cash and a credit to Accounts Receivable, both for $575.
5. The first salary payment made in March was for $2,000, which included $750 of salaries payable on February 28. The payment was recorded as a debit to Salaries Expense of $2,000 and a credit to Cash of $2,000. (No reversing entries were made on March 1.)
6. A $360 cash payment for a repair expense on equipment was recorded as a debit to Equipment and a credit to Accounts Payable, both for $360.
7. The owner, Maurice Hubert, paid himself $1,800 and recorded this as salary expense.
8. The depreciation expense of $191 for the month of March was calculated using the balance in the equipment account of $11,460. All of the company's equipment is expected to have a five-year useful life.

Instructions

(a) Prepare an analysis of each error that shows (1) the incorrect entry, (2) the correct entry, and (3) the correcting entry.

(b) Prepare a correct trial balance.

Taking It Further   Explain how the company's financial statements would be incorrect if error 6 was not corrected and why it is important to correct this error.

Determine impact of errors on financial statements, and correct.

(SO 3) AP

P4–6B   Fu Company is owned and operated by Jeremy Fu. The following errors were found in the journal of the company:

1. The purchase of $700 of supplies on account was recorded as a debit to Supplies Expense and a credit to accounts payable, both for $700. (*Note:* The company records prepayments as assets.)
2. A $600 payment of an account payable was recorded as a debit to Cash and a credit to Accounts Payable, both for $600.
3. A cash advance of $350 from a customer was recorded as a debit to Unearned Service Revenue and a credit to Service Revenue, both for $350.
4. The depreciation adjusting entry was incorrectly recorded as $850. The amount should have been $580.
5. A customer was billed $650 for services provided on account. Unearned Service Revenue was debited and Service Revenue was credited, both for $650.
6. The accrual of $750 of interest expense was recorded as a debit to Interest Expense and a credit to Cash, both for $750.
7. A $500 collection of cash from a customer on account was recorded as a debit to Accounts Receivable and a credit to cash, both for $500.
8. The purchase of equipment for $2,300 was recorded as a debit to Repairs Expense and a credit to Cash, both for $3,200.
9. A $950 payment for rent for Jason Fu's (the company's owner) apartment was debited to Rent Expense and credited to Cash, both for $950.

Instructions

(a) For each item, indicate the effect and amount of the error—understatement (U), overstatement (O), or no effect (NE)—on the income statement and balance sheet components. Use the following format, where the first one has been done for you as an example.

	Income Statement				Balance Sheet		
Item	Revenue	Expenses	Profit		Assets	Liabilities	Owner's Equity
1.	NE	O $700	U $700		U $700	NE	U $700

(b) Correct each error by reversing the incorrect entry and then recording the correct entry.

Taking It Further   Why it is incorrect to record the payment of the company owner's apartment rent as an expense, as described in error 9?

Calculate capital account balance; prepare classified balance sheet and liquidity ratios.

(SO 1, 4, 5) AP

P4–7B   Below is an alphabetical list of the adjusted accounts of Matrix Consulting Services at its year end, March 31, 2011. All accounts have normal balances.

Accounts payable	$11,650	Interest revenue	$ 400
Accounts receivable	4,700	N. Anderson, capital	36,500
Accumulated depreciation—		N. Anderson, drawings	57,700
computer equipment	20,000	Note payable	30,000
Advertising expense	12,000	Note receivable	10,000
Depreciation expense	8,000	Patent	16,000
Cash	3,900	Prepaid insurance	4,400
Computer equipment	48,000	Service revenue	79,800
Insurance expense	4,000	Short-term investments	3,000

Interest expense	1,800	Supplies	2,300
Interest payable	150	Supplies expense	3,700
Interest receivable	200	Unearned revenue	1,200

Other data:
1. Of the notes payable, $10,000 becomes due on July 1, 2011, and the rest on July 1, 2012.
2. The note receivable is due on June 1, 2013.
3. On September 20, 2010, Neo Anderson, the owner, invested $3,800 cash in the business.

Instructions

(a) Calculate the post-closing balance in N. Anderson, Capital, on March 31, 2011.
(b) Prepare a classified balance sheet.
(c) On March 31, 2010, Matrix Consulting Services had current assets of $30,700 and current liabilities of $15,950. Calculate the company's working capital and current ratio on March 31, 2010, and March 31, 2011.
(d) On March 31, 2010, the total of Matrix Consulting Services' cash, short-term investments, and current receivables was $25,500. Calculate the company's acid-test ratio on March 31, 2010, and March 31, 2011.

Taking It Further   Has the company's short-term ability to pay its debts improved or weakened over the year?

P4–8B   Big Rock Brewery creates and sells premium natural unpasteurized beer. Its 2008 balance sheet showed current assets of $6,683,416, and current liabilities of $4,675,236. The 2007 balance sheet reported current assets of $5,598,289 and current liabilities of $5,511,611. The 2006 balance sheet had current assets of $11,554,028 and current liabilities of $4,376,683. The company's cash plus receivables total $2,634,544 at December 31, 2008; $2,440,159 at December 31, 2007; and $7,570,501 at December 31, 2006. *Note:* Big Rock Brewery did not have short-term investments on its balance sheet.

Calculate working capital and current ratio, and comment on liquidity.
(SO 5) AN

Instructions

(a) Calculate Big Rock's working capital, current ratio, and acid-test ratio for each year.
(b) What does each of the measures calculated in (a) show? Comment on Big Rock's liquidity.

Taking It Further   At a specific point in time, a company will always have a larger current ratio than its acid-test ratio. Why? Would you expect this difference to be larger in a company like Big Rock Brewery than in a company like WestJet Airlines? Why or why not?

*P4–9B   The unadjusted trial balance and adjustment data for Edge Sports Repair Shop are presented in P4–3B.

Prepare work sheet.
(SO 6) AP

Instructions

Prepare a work sheet for the year ended September 30, 2011.

Taking It Further   Is it still necessary to record the adjusting entries in the journal and post them to the ledger accounts?

*P4–10B   Kumar Management Services manages condominiums for owners (service revenue) and rents space in its own office building (rent revenue). Some data relating to Kumar Management Servcies appear below.

Prepare work sheet, classified balance sheet, adjusting and closing entries, and post-closing trial balance.
(SO 1, 4, 6) AP

1. As at December 31, 2011, the company has earned $1,750 of service revenue that has not been collected or recorded.
2. A physical count showed $645 of supplies on hand at December 31, 2011.
3. The building has an expected useful life of 45 years. The equipment's expected useful life is 12 years.
4. A one-year insurance policy was purchased on April 1, 2011, for $3,100.

5. A utility bill for December of $725 has not been paid or recorded.
6. Accrued wages payable at December 31, 2011, were $950.
7. The mortgage payable has an annual interest rate of 6%. The last payment was on December 1, 2011.
8. As at December 31, 2011, $1,900 of the unearned rent had been earned.

The trial balance, prior to recording journal entries, at the end of the fiscal year is as follows:

KUMAR MANAGEMENT SERVICES
Trial Balance
December 31, 2011

	Debit	Credit
Cash	$ 11,800	
Accounts receivable	23,600	
Supplies	3,150	
Prepaid insurance	3,100	
Land	58,000	
Building	112,500	
Accumulated depreciation—building		$ 22,500
Equipment	51,000	
Accumulated depreciation—equipment		17,000
Accounts payable		10,750
Salaries payable		0
Interest payable		0
Unearned rent revenue		5,000
Mortgage payable		100,000
M. Kumar, capital		112,150
M. Kumar, drawings	28,500	
Service revenue		66,100
Rent revenue		24,000
Salaries expense	38,675	
Utilities expense	15,800	
Property tax expense	5,375	
Insurance expense	775	
Interest expense	5,225	
Depreciation expense	0	
Supplies expense	0	
	$357,500	$357,500

Instructions

(a) Prepare a work sheet, using the information provided above.
(b) Prepare a classified balance sheet. (*Note:* In the next year, $10,000 of the mortgage payable is due for payment.)
(c) Journalize the adjusting entries.
(d) Journalize the closing entries.
(e) Prepare a post-closing trial balance.

Taking It Further   Explain why preparing a work sheet is an optional step in the accounting cycle.

Prepare and post transaction entries, with and without reversing entries.
(SO 7) AP

*P4–11B   Southwood Property Company had the following balances on its November 30, 2010, balance sheet:

Rent receivable	$4,360	Property taxes payable	$ 4,000
Prepaid insurance	8,250	Unearned service revenue	20,000

After November 30, 2010, the following transactions occurred:

1. On December 4, 2010, rent for October, November, and December 2010, totalling $6,540 cash, was collected.

2. On June 30, 2011, property tax of $9,600 was paid.

3. On October 31, 2011, the company's insurance policy expired and a new one-year policy was purchased for $9,000.

4. Services of $400,000, provided between December 1, 2010, and November 30, 2011, included $380,000 of services for cash and $20,000 of services to customers who had made advance payments before November 30, 2010.

Instructions

(a) Assuming that the company does not use reversing entries:
1. Prepare journal entries to record the above transactions.
2. Post your entries to T accounts and calculate the balance in each account.

(b) Assuming that the company uses reversing entries:
1. Prepare reversing entries where appropriate for December 1, 2010.
2. Prepare journal entries to record the above transactions.
3. Post your entries to T accounts and calculate the balance in each account.

(c) Compare the account balances in (a) with those in (b).

Taking It Further   Comment on the usefulness of reversing entries.

P4–12B   The unadjusted trial balance for Laurie's Laser Games at its fiscal year end of April 30, 2011, is as follows:

Prepare adjusting, reversing, and subsequent cash entries. (SO 7) AP

LAURIE'S LASER GAMES Trial Balance April 30, 2011		
	Debit	Credit
Cash	$ 5,300	
Accounts receivable	0	
Supplies	3,825	
Equipment	140,000	
Accumulated depreciation—equipment		$ 49,000
Wages payable		0
Interest payable		0
Note payable		96,000
Unearned game fee revenue		1,875
L. Glans, capital		32,800
L. Glans, drawings	28,500	
Game fee revenue		70,000
Rent expense	14,400	
Wages expense	53,250	
Supplies expense	0	
Depreciation expense	0	
Interest expense	4,400	
	$249,675	$249,675

Other data:

1. On April 30, 2011, Laurie's Laser Games had earned but not collected or recorded $250 of game fee revenue. On May 21, 2011, Laurie's Laser Games collected this amount plus an additional $1,250 for game fee revenue earned in May.

2. There was $540 of supplies on hand on April 30, 2011.

3. The equipment has an estimated useful life of 10 years.

4. On April 30, salaries earned but not paid or recorded were $1,950. The next payday is May 5 and the employees will be paid a total of $2,785 that day.

5. The note payable has a 5% annual interest rate. Interest is paid quarterly. Interest was last paid on April 1, 2011. The next payment is due on July 1, 2011.

6. On April 30, $1,475 of the unearned game fee revenue had been earned.

Instructions

(a) Prepare adjusting journal entries for the year ended April 30, 2011, as required.
(b) Prepare reversing entries where appropriate.
(c) Prepare journal entries to record the May and June 2011 cash transactions.
(d) Now assume reversing entries were not prepared as in (b) above. Prepare journal entries to record the May and June 2011 cash transactions.

Taking It Further   Why is it not appropriate to use reversing entries for all of the adjusting entries?

Continuing Cookie Chronicle

(*Note:* This is a continuation of the Cookie Chronicle from Chapters 1 through 3.)

Natalie had a very busy December. At the end of the month, after Natalie has journalized and posted her December transactions and adjusting entries, her company has the following adjusted trial balance:

	Debit	Credit
COOKIE CREATIONS		
Adjusted Trial Balance		
December 31, 2010		
Cash	$1,130	
Accounts receivable	875	
Baking supplies	450	
Prepaid insurance	1,100	
Baking equipment	1,400	
Accumulated depreciation—baking equipment		$ 78
Accounts payable		75
Salaries payable		56
Unearned revenue		300
Interest payable		8
Note payable, 3%, principal and interest due November 16, 2010		2,000
N. Koebel, capital		1,000
N. Koebel, drawings	500	
Teaching revenue		4,305
Salaries expense	856	
Telephone expense	125	
Advertising supplies expense	175	
Baking supplies expense	1,025	
Depreciation expense	78	
Insurance expense	100	
Interest expense	8	
	$7,822	$7,822

Instructions

Using the information in the adjusted trial balance, do the following:

(a) Prepare an income statement and a statement of owner's equity for the two months ended December 31, 2010, and a classified balance sheet at December 31, 2010.
(b) Calculate Cookie Creations' working capital, current ratio, and acid-test ratio. Comment on Cookie Creations' liquidity.
(c) Natalie has decided that her year end will be December 31, 2010. Prepare closing entries.
(d) Prepare a post-closing trial balance.

Cumulative Coverage—Chapters 2 to 4

Alou Equipment Repair has a September 30 year end. The company adjusts and closes its accounts on an annual basis. On August 31, 2011, the account balances of Alou Equipment Repair were as follows:

ALOU EQUIPMENT REPAIR Trial Balance August 31, 2011		
	Debit	Credit
Cash	$ 2,790	
Accounts receivable	7,910	
Supplies	8,500	
Equipment	9,000	
Accumulated depreciation—equipment		$ 1,800
Accounts payable		3,100
Unearned service revenue		400
J. Alou, capital		21,200
J. Alou, drawings	15,600	
Service revenue		49,600
Rent expense	5,500	
Salaries expense	24,570	
Telephone expense	2,230	
	$76,130	$76,130

During September, the following transactions were completed:

Sept. 1 Borrowed $10,000 from the bank and signed a two-year, 5% note payable.
    2 Paid September rent, $500.
    8 Paid employee salaries, $1,050.
   12 Received $1,500 cash from customers on account.
   15 Received $5,700 cash for services performed in September.
   17 Purchased additional supplies on account, $1,300.
   20 Paid creditors $2,300 on account.
   21 Paid September telephone bill, $200.
   22 Paid employee salaries, $1,050.
   27 Performed services on account and billed customers for services provided, $900.
   29 Received $550 from customers for services to be provided in the future.
   30 Paid J. Alou $800 cash for personal use.

Adjustment data consist of the following:
1. Supplies on hand at September 30 cost $1,000.
2. Accrued salaries payable at September 30 total $630.
3. The equipment has an expected useful life of five years.
4. Unearned service revenue of $450 is still not earned at September 30.
5. Interest is payable on the first of each month.

Instructions

(a) Prepare T accounts and enter the August 31 balances.
(b) Journalize the September transactions.
(c) Post to T accounts.
(d) Prepare a trial balance at September 30.
(e) Journalize and post adjusting entries.
(f) Prepare an adjusted trial balance at September 30.
(g) Prepare an income statement and a statement of owner's equity, and a classified balance sheet.
(h) Prepare and post closing entries.
(i) Prepare post-closing trial balance at September 30.

BROADENING YOUR PERSPECTIVE

Financial Reporting and Analysis

Financial Reporting Problem

BYP4–1   The financial statements and accompanying notes of The Forzani Group are presented in Appendix A at the end of this book.

Instructions

(a) How is Forzani's balance sheet classified? What classifications does it use?

(b) How are Forzani's assets and liabilities ordered (e.g., in order of liquidity, permanency, etc.)?

(c) When Forzani starts following International Financial Reporting Standards in 2011, what other alternatives will it have for ordering its assets and liabilities in the balance sheet?

(d) Forzani's working capital, current ratio, and acid-test ratio for the fiscal year 2009 are calculated in the chapter. Calculate its working capital, current ratio, and acid-test ratio for the fiscal year 2008. Compare the 2009 figures with the 2008 results and comment on the differences.

Interpreting Financial Statements

BYP4–2   The Gap, Inc. reports its financial results for 52-week fiscal periods ending on a Saturday around the end of January each year. The following information ($ in US millions) was included in recent annual reports:

	Jan. 31, 2009	Feb. 2, 2008	Feb. 3, 2007	Jan. 28, 2006	Jan. 29, 2005
Total assets	$7,564	$7,838	$8,544	$8,821	$10,048
Working capital	$1,847	$1,653	$2,757	$3,297	$4,062
Current ratio	1.86:1	1.68:1	2.21:1	2.70:1	2.81:1
Cash	$1,715	$1,724	$2,030	$2,035	$2,245
Current liabilities	$2,158	$2,433	$2,272	$1,942	$2,242

Instructions

(a) By what percentage did The Gap's total assets increase or decrease overall from 2005 to 2009? What was the change in each year?

(b) Comment on the change in The Gap's liquidity. Which measure seems to give a better indication of its liquidity: working capital or the current ratio? What could the reason be for the change in The Gap's liquidity during the period?

(c) Do you believe that The Gap's creditors should be concerned about its liquidity?

(d) If you were a creditor of The Gap and you were concerned about the decrease in the current ratio from 2005 to 2008, what additional information could you ask for to help you assess its liquidity?

Critical Thinking

Collaborative Learning Activity

Note to instructor: Additional instructions and material for this group activity can be found on the Instructor Resource Site.

BYP4–3   In this group activity, you will classify and define accounts.

Working in Groups

Instructions

(a) Your instructor will divide the class into groups and provide each group with an envelope filled with account names. As a group, identify each account's normal balance and whether it is a permanent or a temporary account on the sheet provided. Calculate total debits and total credits.

(b) Using the second handout, place each account in the proper financial statement classification and calculate the accounting equation.

Hint: Net income must be added and withdrawals deducted from equity to balance the accounting equation.

Communication Activity

BYP4–4   Your best friend is thinking about opening a business. He has never studied accounting and has no idea about the steps that must be followed in order to produce financial statements for his business.

Writing Handbook

Instructions

Write a memo to your friend that lists and explains each of the steps in the accounting cycle in the order in which they should be completed. Include information on when each of these steps should be done and explain the purpose of the different types of journal entries and trial balances. Your memo should also discuss the optional steps in the accounting cycle.

Ethics Case

BYP4–5   As the controller of Breathless Perfume Company, you discover a significant misstatement that overstated profit in the previous year's financial statements. The misleading financial statements are in the company's annual report, which was issued to banks and other creditors less than a month ago.

Ethics in Accounting

After much thought about the consequences of telling the president, Eddy Lieman, about this misstatement, you gather your courage to inform him. Eddy says, "Hey! What they don't know won't hurt them. But, just so we set the record straight, we'll adjust this year's financial statements for last year's misstatement. We can absorb that misstatement better this year than last year anyway! Just don't make that kind of mistake again."

Instructions

(a) Who are the stakeholders in this situation?

(b) What are the ethical issues in this situation?

(c) As the controller, what would you do in this situation?

"All About You" Activity

BYP4–6　As discussed in the "All About You" feature, in order to evaluate your personal financial position, you need to prepare a personal balance sheet. Assume that you have gathered the following information about your current personal finances.

Amount owed on student loan (long-term)	$10,000
Balance in chequing account	1,200
Automobile	8,000
Balance on automobile loan (short-term)	2,400
Balance on automobile loan (long-term)	3,600
Computer and accessories	1,200
Clothes and furniture	4,000
Balance owed on credit cards	1,000

Instructions

(a) Prepare a personal balance sheet using the format you have learned for a balance sheet for a proprietorship. For the Capital account, use Personal Equity (Deficit).

(b) Assume that you borrow an additional $5,000 in student loans to cover the cost of tuition for the upcoming school year. What is the impact on your Personal Equity (Deficit) if the cost of tuition is considered an expense? What is the impact on your Personal Equity (Deficit) if the cost of tuition is considered an asset?

(c) Assume instead of borrowing to cover the cost of tuition, you earn $8,000 working during the summer and that after paying for your tuition you have $2,000 in your chequing account. What is the impact on your Personal Equity (Deficit) if the cost of the tuition is considered an expense?

(d) Assume that you make a $600 payment from your chequing account on your automobile loan. What is the impact on your Personal Equity (Deficit)?

ANSWERS TO CHAPTER QUESTIONS

Answers to Accounting in Action Insight Questions

Across the Organization Insight, p. 186

Q: Why are CFOs interested in knowing how long it takes for companies to close their books?

A: There are two basic reasons: (1) the more time a company needs to close its books, the more it costs the company; and (2) accounting information must be timely to be useful. Therefore, a CFO would be interested in comparing his or her company to others to determine if improvement is needed or not.

Business Insight, p. 190

Q: Nortel filed for bankruptcy protection in January 2009. Is it possible there is a link between the need to correct all of these accounting errors and the fact that Nortel filed for bankruptcy protection?

A: When a company has as many problems with accounting errors as Nortel had, investors and creditors become less confident that the company is well run. This may result in creditors demanding earlier payment on loans. When this happens, the company has less cash to run its operations and may run into financial difficulty. Filing for bankruptcy gives a company like Nortel time to reorganize its operations without having to pay its debts.

All About You, p. 199

 Q: Should you prepare a personal balance sheet each year?
 A: In order to attain your financial objectives, you need to set goals early. A personal balance sheet provides a benchmark that allows you to measure your progress towards your financial goals.

Answer to Forzani Review It Question 4, p. 199

Forzani's current assets include Cash, $3,474; Accounts Receivable, $84,455; Inventory, $291,497; and Prepaid Expenses, $2,827. Its current liabilities include Indebtedness under revolving credit facility, $17,130; Accounts Payable and Accrued Liabilities, $277,820; and the Current Portion of Long-Term Debt, $7,501. All amounts are listed in thousands. Forzani's current assets and current liabilities appear to be listed in order of liquidity, with the most current or liquid account listed first.

Answers to Self-Study Questions

1. b   2. c   3. a   4. d   5. b   6. b   7. c   8. c   *9. c   *10. c

Remember to go back to the beginning of the chapter to check off your completed work!

←

CHAPTER 5
ACCOUNTING FOR MERCHANDISING OPERATION

coastmountain.com

✓ THE NAVIGATOR

- ☐ Understand *Concepts for Review*
- ☐ Read *Feature Story*
- ☐ Scan *Study Objectives*
- ☐ Read *Chapter Preview*
- ☐ Read text and answer *Before You Go On*
- ☐ Work *Demonstration Problems*
- ☐ Review *Summary of Study Objectives*
- ☐ Answer *Self-Study Questions*
- ☐ Complete assignments

CONCEPTS FOR REVIEW:

Before studying this chapter, you should understand or, if necessary, review:

a. How to close revenue, expense, and drawings accounts. (Ch. 4, pp. 182–188)

b. The steps in the accounting cycle. (Ch. 4, p. 188)

c. How to prepare an income statement (Ch. 3, p. 137)

d. How to prepare a classified balance sheet (Ch. 4, pp. 191–200)

Mountainous Inventory Management

The outdoor-lifestyle store Coast Mountain Sports is part of the Forzani Group Ltd. chain of sporting goods retailers. Its focus is on equipment, clothing, and footwear for backcountry adventures, week-long backpacking trips, camping weekends, or simply a walk in a park. When Forzani acquired Coast Mountain Sports in June 2000, it consisted of five stores, typically 6,000 square feet (about 550 square metres) in size. By May 2009, there were 23 stores ranging in size up to 25,000 square feet (approximately 2,300 square metres). They're big stores that hold a lot of inventory—on average 1.2 units per square foot, or 20,000 stock-keeping units (SKUs)—which requires strict inventory management.

The merchandising team, which includes planners, buyers, and allocators, keeps track of the on-hand inventory at each store. They use historical trends and future market trends to determine what to buy and what to stock in each store. Inventory is replenished at the stores through twice-weekly deliveries.

All the inventory purchased is shipped to a central warehouse, which distributes it to each store, explains Mike Kreuger, controller at the Forzani Group. The store's point of sale system (WinDSS) manages the store register, and a back office inventory system manages the receipt of product transfers from the central distribution centre. Stores receive cartons shipped from the distribution centre by scanning a label on the carton that indicates the store number and information about the product inside. This increases the stores' on-hand inventory.

All store transactions from WinDSS are entered nightly in the company's central inventory management system, called the Portfolio Merchandise Management (PMM) System. Forzani uses the PMM System to purchase, receive, distribute, and maintain inventory. The distribution centre's warehouse management system (WMS) links with the PMM to record all distribution centre transactions including receipts, transfers, and adjustments.

Invoices are matched to receiving done by the warehouse. If there is a price difference between the purchase order or receipt and the vendor invoice, the correct price is confirmed with the head office buyer. If the supplier is correct, then a cost adjustment is done. If the supplier invoice is wrong and the supplier overcharged, then the supplier would be notified and a chargeback processed to its account.

Sales and returns are processed through each store's WinDSS point of sale system. Every night, the stores' sales information is uploaded to the PMM System at head office, which adjusts its records of the on-hand inventory for each store, explains Kreuger. As well, the sales information is uploaded into Audit Works, which verifies and analyzes all sales transactions. The information is then merged with the general ledger in the corporation's financial system at month end.

Needless to say, inventory management at a large retailer like Coast Mountain Sports requires a number of essential systems and complex processes, without which it would be impossible to manage inventory efficiently and effectively.

The Navigator

STUDY OBJECTIVES:

After studying this chapter, you should be able to:

1. Describe the differences between service and merchandising companies.
2. Prepare entries for purchases under a perpetual inventory system.
3. Prepare entries for sales under a perpetual inventory system.
4. Perform the steps in the accounting cycle for a merchandising company.
5. Prepare single-step and multiple-step income statements.
6. Calculate the gross profit margin and profit margin.
7. Prepare the entries for purchases and sales under a periodic inventory system and calculate cost of goods sold (Appendix 5A).

The Navigator

The first four chapters of this text focused mostly on service companies, like the fictional Pioneer Advertising. Other examples of service companies include Air Canada, Canada Post, College Pro Painters, and Scotiabank. Coast Mountain Sports, as indicated in the feature story, buys and sells goods instead of performing services to earn a profit. Merchandising companies that purchase and sell directly to consumers—such as Coast Mountain Sports and the other stores in the Forzani Group, Canadian Tire, Mountain Equipment Co-op, and Toys "R" Us— are called retailers.

The chapter is organized as follows:

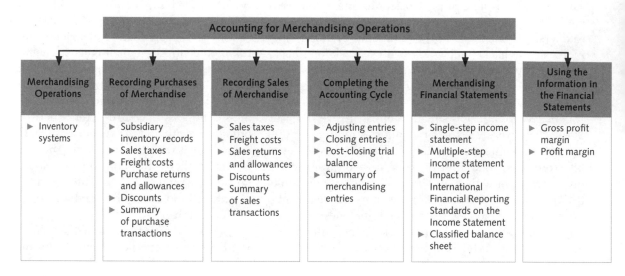

Merchandising Operations

STUDY OBJECTIVE 1

Describe the differences between service and merchandising companies.

Merchandising involves purchasing products—also called merchandise inventory or just inventory—to resell to customers. The steps in the accounting cycle for a merchandising company are the same as the steps for a service company. However, merchandising companies need additional accounts and entries in order to record merchandising transactions.

Measuring profit for a merchandising company is basically the same as for a service company. That is, profit (or loss) is equal to revenues less expenses. In a merchandising company, the main source of revenues is the sale of merchandise. These revenues are called **sales revenue**, or simply sales. Expenses for a merchandising company are divided into two categories: (1) cost of goods sold, and (2) operating expenses. A service company does not have a cost of goods sold because it provides services, not goods.

The **cost of goods sold** is the total cost of merchandise sold during the period. This expense is directly related to the revenue earned from the sale of the goods. Sales revenue less cost of goods sold is called **gross profit**. For example, when a calculator that costs $15 is sold for $25, the gross profit is $10. Merchandisers report gross profit earned on sales in the income statement.

After gross profit is calculated, operating expenses are deducted to determine profit (or loss). **Operating expenses** are expenses that are incurred in the process of earning sales revenue or service revenue. The operating expenses of a merchandising company include the same basic expenses found in a service company, such as salaries, advertising, insurance, rent, and depreciation.

The calculations of profit for both a service and a merchandising company are shown in Illustration 5-1. As you can see, the items in the two blue boxes are used only by a merchandising company because service companies do not sell goods.

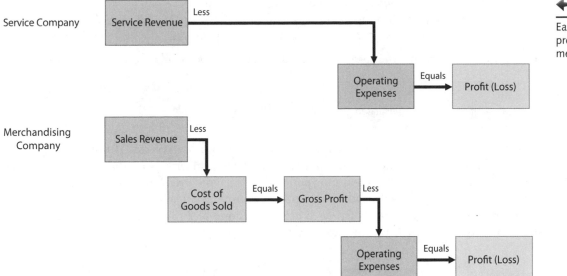

← Illustration 5-1

Earnings measurement process for a service and a merchandising company

In addition, you will recall from Chapter 4 that the operating cycle—the time it takes to go from cash to cash in producing revenues—is usually longer in a merchandising company than in a service company. The purchase of merchandise inventory and the lapse of time until it is sold lengthen the cycle. We will learn more about measuring the length of the operating cycle in later chapters.

Inventory Systems

A merchandising company must keep track of its inventory to determine what is available for sale (inventory) and what has been sold (cost of goods sold). The inventory is reported as a current asset on the balance sheet. The cost of goods sold is an expense on the income statement.

There are two kinds of systems used to account for inventory and cost of goods sold: a perpetual inventory system and a periodic inventory system.

Perpetual Inventory System

In a **perpetual inventory system**, the company keeps detailed records of each inventory purchase and sale. This system continuously—perpetually—shows the quantity and cost of the inventory that should be on hand for every item. Coast Mountain Sports in our feature story uses its perpetual inventory system to prepare monthly reports of items in stock and total inventory value. With the use of bar codes, optical scanners, and point-of-sale software, a store can keep a running record of every item that it buys and sells.

When inventory items are sold under a perpetual inventory system, the cost of the goods sold (the original purchase cost of the merchandise) is obtained from the inventory records. This cost is transferred from the Merchandise Inventory account (an asset) to the Cost of Goods Sold account (an expense). Under a perpetual inventory system, the company determines and records the cost of goods sold and the reduction in inventory each time a sale occurs.

Periodic Inventory System

In a **periodic inventory system**, companies do not keep detailed inventory records of the goods on hand throughout the period. Instead, the cost of goods sold is determined only at the end of the accounting period; that is, periodically. At that point, the company takes a physical inventory count to determine the quantity and cost of the goods on hand.

To determine the cost of goods sold in a periodic inventory system, the following steps are necessary:

1. Start with beginning inventory—the cost of goods on hand at the beginning of the accounting period. (This is the same amount as the previous period's ending inventory.)

2. Add the cost of goods purchased during the period.
3. Subtract ending inventory—the cost of goods on hand at the end of the accounting period as determined from the physical inventory count.

Illustration 5-2 presents the formula to calculate cost of goods sold.

This calculation is, in fact, also used in a perpetual inventory system. However, the cost of goods sold is determined and recorded at the point of each sale in a perpetual inventory system, and totalled at the end of the accounting period. In a periodic inventory system, one calculation to find the total cost of goods sold for that period is done at the end of the accounting period.

Illustration 5-3 compares when each activity is done and the timing of the cost of goods sold calculation under the two inventory systems.

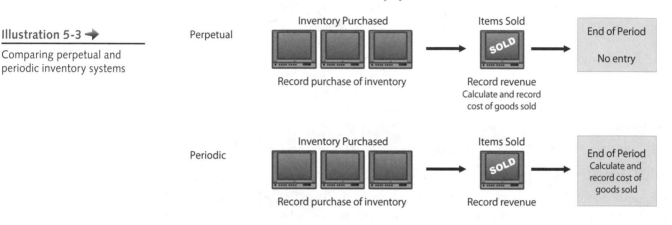

Choosing an Inventory System

How do companies decide which inventory system to use? They compare the cost of the detailed record keeping that is required for a perpetual inventory system to the benefits of having the additional information about, and control over, their inventory. Traditionally, only companies that sold merchandise with high unit values—such as automobiles or major home appliances—used the perpetual inventory system. However, the reduced cost of computers and electronic scanners has enabled many more companies to install perpetual inventory systems.

A perpetual inventory system gives better control over inventories. Since the inventory records show the quantities that should be on hand, the goods can be counted at any time to see whether the amount of goods actually on hand agrees with the inventory records. Any shortages that are uncovered can be immediately investigated.

A perpetual inventory system also makes it easier to answer questions from customers about merchandise availability. Management can also maintain optimum inventory levels and avoid running out of stock. As discussed in the feature story, Coast Mountain Sport uses its perpetual inventory system to keep track of inventory on-hand at each store. This helps the planners, and buyers to determine what to buy and stock at each store.

Some businesses find it unnecessary or uneconomical to invest in a computerized perpetual inventory system. Many small businesses, in particular, find that a perpetual inventory system costs more than it is worth. Managers of these businesses can control merchandise and manage day-to-day operations using a periodic inventory system.

A complete physical inventory count is always taken at least once a year under both the perpetual and periodic inventory systems. Companies using a periodic inventory system must count their merchandise to determine quantities on hand and establish the cost of the goods sold and the ending inventory for accounting purposes. In a perpetual inventory system, they must count their merchandise to verify that the accounting records are correct. We will learn more about how to determine the quantity and cost of inventory later in this chapter and in the next chapter.

Because the perpetual inventory system is widely used, we illustrate it in this chapter. The periodic system is described in Appendix 5A.

 ACCOUNTING IN ACTION: ACROSS THE ORGANIZATION

Bonnie Brooks, President and CEO of the Bay is trying to capture a new type of shopper during recessionary times—the pragmatist; someone who spends $1,900 per year on clothing and looks for timeless pieces priced in the mid-range. Now more than ever, the store's focus is on fashion. It has doubled its stock of higher-end lines, while also expanding its mid-priced labels. It dropped half of its brands, worth more than $1 billion in annual retail sales, for more contemporary labels. Store productivity, measured in sales per square foot, had fallen to $165 in 2005, the last year public documents for the now-private company were available. The aim is to raise that figure to $200, which would be less than half the productivity of Wal-Mart Canada or some US luxury department stores. The average US department store has a sales productivity of $180. To boost productivity, the Bay will devote more space to faster-selling categories of apparel, shoes, handbags, and cosmetics, and reduce the space devoted to slower-moving items like appliances, furniture, and home decor. The goal is to trim total inventory by 10 percent.

Source: Marina Strauss, "The pragmatic fashionista: Bonnie Brooks," *The Globe and Mail*, April 23, 2009

Why are retail managers concerned with sales dollars per square foot?

BEFORE YOU GO ON . . .

→ Review It

1. How is the measurement of profit in a merchandising company different from measuring profit in a service company?
2. How does a perpetual inventory system differ from a periodic inventory system?
3. What are the benefits of a perpetual inventory system?

Related exercise material: BE5–1.

The Navigator

Recording Purchases of Merchandise

Companies purchase inventory using either cash or credit (on account). They normally record purchases when the goods are received from the seller. Every purchase should be supported by a document that provides written evidence of the transaction.

For example, there should be a cash receipt that indicates the items purchased and the amounts paid for each cash purchase. Cash purchases are recorded by an increase in Merchandise Inventory and a decrease in Cash.

Credit purchases should be supported by a purchase invoice showing the total purchase price and other relevant information. The purchaser uses a copy of the sales invoice sent by the seller as a purchase invoice. For example, in Illustration 5-4, Chelsea Electronics (the buyer) uses as a purchase invoice the sales invoice prepared by Highpoint Audio & TV Supply (the seller).

STUDY OBJECTIVE 2

Prepare entries for purchases under a perpetual inventory system.

Illustration 5-4 ➜

Sales/purchase invoice

		INVOICE NO. 731

Highpoint Audio & TV Supply

277 Wellington Street, West
Toronto, Ontario, M5V 3H2

▼

S O L D   T O

Firm name:	Chelsea Electronics
Attention of:	James Hoover, Purchasing Agent
Address:	21 King Street West

Hamilton	Ontario	L8P 4W7
City	Province	Postal Code

Date: May 4, 2011	Salesperson: Malone	Terms 2/10, n/30	FOB shipping point

Catalogue No.	Description	Quantity	Price	Amount
X572Y9820	65" Flat-panel LCD HDTV	1	2,300	$2,300
A2547Z45	High Definition PVR Cable Box	5	300	1,500

IMPORTANT: ALL RETURNS MUST BE MADE WITHIN 10 DAYS	TOTAL	$3,800

The buyer, Chelsea Electronics, makes the following entry to record the purchase of merchandise from Highpoint Audio & TV Supply. The entry increases Merchandise Inventory and increases Accounts Payable.

A	=	L	+	OE
+3,800		+3,800		

Cash flows: no effect

May 4	Merchandise Inventory	3,800	
	Accounts Payable		3,800
	To record goods purchased on account per invoice #731, terms 2/10, n/30.		

Only the goods purchased to sell to customers are recorded in the Merchandise Inventory account. As we learned in Chapter 2, purchases of assets to use in the business—such as supplies or equipment—should be debited to the specific asset accounts.

Subsidiary Inventory Records

Imagine an organization like Coast Mountain Sport recording purchases and sales of its 20,000 inventory items in only one general ledger account—Merchandise Inventory. It would be almost impossible to determine the balance remaining of any particular inventory item at any specific time.

Instead, under a perpetual inventory system, a subsidiary ledger is used to organize and track individual inventory items. A **subsidiary ledger** is a group of accounts that share a common characteristic (for example, all inventory accounts). The subsidiary ledger frees the general ledger from the details of individual balances. In addition to having one for inventory, it is common to have subsidiary ledgers for accounts receivable (to track individual customer balances), accounts payable (to track individual creditor balances), and payroll (to track individual employee pay records).

A subsidiary ledger is an addition to, and an expansion of, the general ledger, as Illustration 5-5 shows.

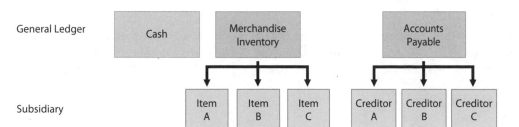

Relationship of general ledger and subsidiary ledgers

The general ledger account that summarizes the subsidiary ledger data is called a **control account**. In this illustration, the general ledger accounts Merchandise Inventory and Accounts Payable are control accounts with subsidiary ledgers. Cash is not a control account because there is no subsidiary ledger for this account.

Purchases and sales of each item of merchandise are recorded and posted to the individual inventory subsidiary ledger account. At any point in time, the inventory subsidiary ledger shows detailed information about the quantity and cost of each inventory item.

The detailed individual data from the inventory subsidiary ledger are summarized in the Merchandise Inventory control account in the general ledger. At all times, the control account balance must equal the total of all the individual inventory account balances.

Additional information about how to record and balance subsidiary and control account transactions can be found in Appendix C at the end of this textbook.

Sales Taxes

Sales taxes include the federal Goods and Services Tax (GST), the Provincial Sales Tax (PST), and in several provinces, the Harmonized Sales Tax (HST), which is a combination of GST and PST. GST or HST are paid by merchandising companies on the goods they purchase for resale. However, this cost is not part of the cost of the merchandise, because companies can get back any GST or HST they pay on purchases by offsetting it against the GST or HST they collect from customers.

PST is not paid by a merchandiser—it is paid only by the final consumer. Therefore, retail businesses do not have to pay PST on any merchandise they purchase for resale.

As mentioned in Chapter 2, the accounting transactions described in this textbook are presented without the added complexity of sales taxes. That is why Invoice No. 731 shown in Illustration 5-4 did not include GST, which would normally be added to the invoice price. Sales taxes are discussed in more detail in Appendix B at the end of this textbook.

Freight Costs

The sales/purchase invoice should indicate when ownership of the goods transfers from the seller to the buyer. The company that owns the goods while they are being transported to the buyer's place of business pays the transportation charges and is responsible for any damage to the merchandise during transit. The point where ownership is transferred is called the FOB point and may be expressed as either "FOB destination" or "FOB shipping point." The letters FOB mean "free on board."

Alternative terminology
Other common shipping terms include FCA (free carrier), CIF (cost, insurance, freight), FAS (free alongside), and CPT (carriage paid to).

FOB shipping point means:
1. Ownership changes from the seller to the buyer when the goods are placed on the carrier by the seller—the "shipping point."
2. The buyer pays the freight costs and is responsible for damages.

FOB destination means:
1. Ownership changes from the seller to the buyer when the goods are delivered by the carrier to the buyer's place of business— the "destination."
2. The seller pays the freight and is responsible for damages.

For example, the purchase invoice in Illustration 5-4 indicates that freight is FOB shipping point. The buyer (Chelsea Electronics) therefore pays the freight charges. Illustration 5-6 demonstrates these shipping terms.

Illustration 5-6 ➡

Terms of shipping

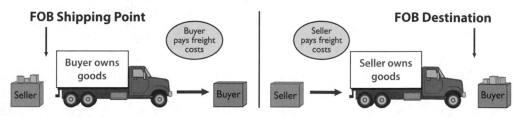

When the buyer pays for the freight costs, Merchandise Inventory is debited for the cost of the transportation. Why? Freight is just another part of the cost of purchasing the goods.

For example, if upon delivery of the goods to Chelsea Electronics on May 4, Chelsea pays Public Carrier Co. $150 for freight charges, the entry on Chelsea Electronics' books is:

A	=	L	+	OE
+150				
−150				

⬇ Cash flows: −150

May 4	Merchandise Inventory	150	
	Cash		150
	To record payment of freight on goods purchased.		

Thus, any freight costs incurred by the buyer are included in the cost of the merchandise.

But if the seller pays freight costs on outgoing merchandise, these costs are an operating expense to the seller. Costs incurred to earn revenue are recorded as expenses. These costs increase an expense account titled Delivery Expense or Freight Out. If the freight terms on the invoice in Illustration 5-4 had been FOB destination, then Highpoint Audio & TV Supply would have paid the delivery charge and recorded the following journal entry:

A	=	L	+	OE
−150				−150

⬇ Cash flows: −150

May 4	Delivery Expense (or Freight Out)	150	
	Cash		150
	To record payment of freight on goods sold.		

When the seller pays the freight charges, it will usually establish a higher invoice price for the goods to cover the shipping expense.

Purchase Returns and Allowances

A purchaser may be dissatisfied with the merchandise received if the goods are damaged or defective or of inferior quality, or if the goods do not meet the purchaser's specifications. In such cases, the purchaser may return the goods to the seller. This transaction is known as a **purchase return**. Alternatively, the purchaser may choose to keep the merchandise if the seller is willing to grant an allowance (deduction) from the purchase price. This transaction is known as a **purchase allowance**.

Assume that Chelsea Electronics returned goods costing $300 to Highpoint Audio & TV Supply on May 9. Highpoint will issue Chelsea a credit, which allows Chelsea to reduce its accounts payable. The entry by Chelsea Electronics for the returned merchandise is as follows:

A	=	L	+	OE
−300		−300		

Cash flows: no effect

May 9	Accounts Payable	300	
	Merchandise Inventory		300
	To record return of goods to Highpoint Audio & TV Supply.		

Because Chelsea Electronics increased Merchandise Inventory when the goods were purchased, Merchandise Inventory is decreased when Chelsea Electronics returns the goods (or when it is granted an allowance).

Discounts

Some events do not require a separate journal entry. For example, the terms of a credit purchase may include an offer of a **quantity discount** for a bulk purchase. A quantity discount gives a reduction in price according to the volume of the purchase—in other words, the larger the number of items purchased, the better the discount. Quantity discounts are not recorded or accounted for separately.

Quantity discounts are not the same as **purchase discounts**, which are offered to customers for early payment of the balance due. This incentive offers advantages to both parties: the purchaser saves money and the seller shortens its operating cycle by more quickly converting accounts receivable to cash.

Purchase discounts are noted on the invoice by the use of credit terms that specify the amount and time period for the purchase discount. They also indicate the length of time the buyer has to pay the full invoice price. In the sales invoice in Illustration 5-4, credit terms are 2/10, n/30 (read "two ten, net thirty"). This means that a 2% cash discount may be taken on the invoice price (less any returns or allowances) if payment is made within 10 days of the invoice date (the discount period). Otherwise, the invoice price, less any returns or allowances, is due 30 days from the invoice date.

Although purchase discounts are common in certain industries, not every seller offers them. When the seller chooses not to offer a discount for early payment, credit terms will specify only the maximum time period for paying the balance due. For example, the time period may be stated as n/30, meaning that the net amount must be paid in 30 days.

In contrast to quantity discounts, purchase discounts are recorded separately. When an invoice is paid within the discount period, the Merchandise Inventory account will be reduced by the amount of the discount because inventory is recorded at cost. By paying within the discount period, a company reduces the cost of its inventory.

To illustrate, assume that Chelsea Electronics pays the balance owing to Highpoint Audio & TV Supply of $3,500 (gross invoice price of $3,800 less purchase returns and allowances of $300) on May 14, the last day of the discount period. The discount is $70 ($3,500 × 2%), and the amount of cash paid by Chelsea Electronics to Highpoint Audio & TV Supply is $3,430 ($3,500 − $70). Chelsea Electronics' entry to record its May 14 payment to Highpoint Audio & TV Supply is:

May 14	Accounts Payable	3,500	
	Merchandise Inventory		70
	Cash		3,430
	To record payment of invoice #731 within discount period.		

A = L + OE
−70   −3,500
−3,430

↓ Cash flows: −3,430

As a general rule, a company should usually take all available discounts. Not taking a discount is viewed as paying interest for use of the money not yet paid to the seller. For example, if Chelsea Electronics passed up the discount, it would have paid 2 percent for the use of $3,500 for 20 days. This equals an annual interest rate of 36.5% (2% × 365 ÷ 20). Obviously, it would be better for Chelsea Electronics to borrow at bank interest rates than to lose the purchase discount.

If, contrary to best practices, Chelsea Electronics did not take advantage of the purchase discount and instead made full payment of $3,500 on June 3, the journal entry to record this payment would be:

June 3	Accounts Payable	3,500	
	Cash		3,500
	To record payment of invoice #731 with no discount taken.		

A = L + OE
−3,500   −3,500

↓ Cash flows: −3,500

Summary of Purchase Transactions

The following T account (with transaction descriptions in parentheses) gives a summary of the effects of the transactions on Merchandise Inventory. Chelsea Electronics originally purchased $3,800 worth of inventory for resale. It paid $150 in freight charges. It then returned $300 worth of goods. And Chelsea Electronics received a discount of $70 by paying Highpoint Audio & TV Supply in the discount period. This results in a balance in Merchandise Inventory of $3,580.

		Merchandise Inventory			
(Purchase)	May 4	3,800	May 9	300	(Purchase return)
(Freight)	4	150	14	70	(Purchase discount)
	Bal.	3,580			

BEFORE YOU GO ON ...

➡ Review It

1. What do the terms "FOB shipping point" and "FOB destination" mean?
2. Under the perpetual inventory system, what entries are made to record purchases, freight costs paid by the purchaser, purchase returns and allowances, and purchase discounts?
3. Why is the merchandise inventory account reduced if the company receives a purchase allowance or a purchase discount?

➡ Do It

On September 4, New Idea Company buys merchandise on account from Junot Company for $1,500, terms 2/10, n/30, FOB shipping point. The correct company pays freight charges of $75 on September 5. On September 8, New Idea Company returns $200 of the merchandise to Junot Company. On September 14, New Idea Company pays the total amount owing. Record the transactions on New Idea Company's books.

Action Plan
- Purchases of goods for resale are recorded in the asset account Merchandise Inventory.
- Examine freight terms to determine which company pays the freight charges.
- Freight charges paid by the purchaser increase the cost of the merchandise inventory.
- The Merchandise Inventory account is reduced by the cost of merchandise returned.
- Calculate purchase discounts using the net amount owing.
- Reduce the Merchandise Inventory account by the amount of the purchase discount.

Solution

New Idea Company (buyer)

Sept. 4	Merchandise Inventory	1,500	
	Accounts Payable		1,500
	To record goods purchased on account.		
5	Merchandise Inventory	75	
	Cash		75
	To record freight paid on goods purchased.		
8	Accounts Payable	200	
	Merchandise Inventory		200
	To record return of goods.		
14	Accounts Payable ($1,500 − $200)	1,300	
	Merchandise Inventory ($1,300 × 2%)		26
	Cash ($1,300 − $26)		1,274
	To record cash payment within the discount period.		

The Navigator

Related exercise material: BE5–2, BE5–3, BE5–4, BE5–5, and BE5–6.

Recording Sales of Merchandise

Sales revenue, like service revenue, is recorded when there is an increase in assets (typically cash or accounts receivable) as the result of a contract with a customer. For merchandising companies, this means that sales revenue is recorded (recognized) when the ownership of the goods is transferred from the seller to the buyer. At this point, the sales transaction is completed and the sale price has been established. Alternatively, if the customer has paid in advance, a merchandiser may decrease a liability (unearned sales revenue) when the sales transaction is completed.

STUDY OBJECTIVE 3

Prepare entries for sales under a perpetual inventory system.

Sales of merchandise may be made on credit or for cash. Every sales transaction should be supported by a business document that gives written evidence of the sale. Cash register tapes provide evidence of cash sales. A sales invoice, like the one shown in Illustration 5-4, provides support for a credit or cash sale. The seller prepares the invoice and gives a copy to the buyer.

Two entries are made for each sale in a perpetual inventory system:

1. The first entry records the sales revenue: Cash (or Accounts Receivable, if it is a credit sale) is increased by a debit, and the revenue account Sales is increased by a credit for the selling (invoice) price of the goods.
2. The second entry records the cost of the merchandise sold: the expense account Cost of Goods Sold is increased by a debit, and the asset account Merchandise Inventory is decreased by a credit for the cost of the goods. This entry ensures that the Merchandise Inventory account will always show the amount of inventory that should be on hand.

To illustrate a credit sales transaction, we will use the sales invoice shown in Illustration 5-4. Assuming that the merchandise cost Highpoint $2,400 when it purchased the merchandise, Highpoint Audio & TV Supply's $3,800 sale to Chelsea Electronics on May 4 is recorded as follows:

May 4	Accounts Receivable	3,800	
	Sales		3,800
	To record credit sale to Chelsea Electronics per invoice #731.		
4	Cost of Goods Sold	2,400	
	Merchandise Inventory		2,400
	To record cost of merchandise sold to Chelsea Electronics per invoice #731.		

A	=	L	+	OE
+3,800				+3,800

Cash flows: no effect

A	=	L	+	OE
−2,400				−2,400

Cash flows: no effect

For internal decision-making purposes, merchandisers may use more than one sales account, just as they use more than one inventory account. For example, Highpoint Audio & TV Supply may keep separate sales accounts for its televisions, DVD players/recorders, cable boxes, and home theatre systems. By using separate sales accounts for major product lines, company management can monitor sales trends more closely and respond more strategically to changes in sales patterns. For example, if home theatre system sales are increasing while DVD player/recorder sales are decreasing, the company can re-evaluate its advertising and pricing policies on each of these items.

However, on the income statement shown to outside investors, a merchandiser would normally give only a single sales figure—the sum of all of its individual sales accounts. This is done for two reasons. First, giving details on individual sales accounts would add too much length to the income statement and possibly make it less understandable. Second, companies do not want their competitors to know the details of their operating results.

Sales Taxes

Sales taxes are collected by merchandising companies on the goods that they sell. When a company collects sales taxes on the sale of a good or service, these sales taxes are not recorded as revenue. The sales taxes are collected for the federal and provincial governments, and are owed to these collecting authorities. Sales taxes that are collected on the sale of a good or service are recorded as a liability until they are paid to the governments. As stated earlier, accounting for sales taxes is complicated and is explained in Appendix B at the end of this textbook.

Freight Costs

As discussed earlier in the chapter, freight terms—FOB destination and FOB shipping point—on the sales invoice indicate when ownership is transferred, and they therefore indicate who is responsible for shipping costs. If the term is FOB destination, the seller is responsible for getting the goods to their intended destination. As explained earlier, freight costs paid by the seller on merchandise sold are an operating expense to the seller and are debited to a Freight Out or Delivery Expense account.

In Highpoint Audio & TV Supply's sale of electronic equipment to Chelsea Electronics, the freight terms (FOB shipping point) indicate that the purchaser, Chelsea Electronics, must pay the cost of shipping the goods from Highpoint Audio & TV Supply's location in Toronto to Chelsea Electronics' location in Hamilton. Highpoint Audio & TV Supply, the seller, makes no journal entry to record the cost of shipping, since this is Chelsea's cost.

Sales Returns and Allowances

We now look at the "flipside" of purchase returns and allowances, which the seller records as **sales returns and allowances**. When customers (purchasers) return goods, or are given price reductions, the seller will either return cash to the buyer, or reduce the buyer's account receivable if the goods were originally purchased on credit.

The seller will need to record the reduction in cash or accounts receivable as well as the reduction in sales. But it is important for management to know about the amount of sales returns and allowances. If there is a large amount of returns and allowances, this suggests that there is inferior merchandise, inefficiencies in filling orders, errors in billing customers, and/or mistakes in the delivery or shipment of goods. In order to provide information on sales returns and allowances to management, a **contra revenue account** called Sales Returns and Allowances is used. By using a contra account, management can keep track of both the original sales and the amount of sales returns and allowances.

Helpful hint Remember that the increases, decreases, and normal balances of contra accounts are the opposite of the accounts they correspond to.

To illustrate, Highpoint Audio & TV Supply will record the following entry to record the goods returned on May 9 by Chelsea Electronics for a credit of $300:

A	=	L	+	OE
−300				−300

Cash flows: no effect

May 9	Sales Returns and Allowances	300	
	Accounts Receivable		300
	To record credit granted to Chelsea Electronics for returned goods.		

If the merchandise is not damaged and can be sold again, the seller will also need to record a second entry when goods are returned. Assuming this is the case with the goods returned by Chelsea, and assuming that the goods originally cost Highpoint $140, Highpoint Audio & TV Supply will record a second entry as follows:

A	=	L	+	OE
+140				+140

Cash flows: no effect

May 9	Merchandise Inventory	140	
	Cost of Goods Sold		140
	To record cost of returned goods.		

Notice that these two entries are basically the reverse of the entries recorded when the sale was originally made. Since the customer is reversing the original sale, it should make sense that the journal entries reflect this reversal.

If the goods are damaged or defective and can no longer be sold, the second entry is not prepared. The second entry is also not required when the seller gives the buyer an allowance. If the goods have not been returned, or are defective and cannot be resold, the seller cannot increase its Merchandise Inventory and the original cost of goods sold recorded is still the correct amount. Giving a customer a sales allowance, or letting them return defective goods, does not change the original cost of the goods sold.

ACCOUNTING IN ACTION: BUSINESS INSIGHT

Returned goods can put a dent in a business's profits. When a customer returns a product, the business has to decide whether to scrap, liquidate, refurbish, return to seller, or return to stock. Calgary-based Liquidation World, the largest liquidator in Canada, has made a successful venture out of offering companies an opportunity to get some value out of unwanted products by liquidating them. It buys merchandise from companies in Canada, the United States, the Caribbean, and the Far East and sells it in outlets in Canada and the United States at prices 30 to 70 percent below normal. It's essentially a win-win situation for businesses and consumers: consumers get good value on a variety of quality goods, while manufacturers, wholesalers, and retailers have a place to dispose of unwanted merchandise.

What accounting information would help a manager decide what to do with returned goods?

Discounts

Sales are recorded at invoice price—whether it is the full retail price, a sales price, or a volume discount price. No separate entry is made to record a quantity discount, or to show that the goods were sold at a special sales price.

Another type of discount, as discussed earlier in the chapter, is a cash discount for the early payment of the balance due. A seller may offer this to a customer to provide an incentive to pay early. From the seller's point of view, this is called a **sales discount**.

Basically, a sales discount is a reduction in the selling price that a customer may or may not take advantage of. At the point of sale, it is not known if the customer will use the discount, so the revenue recorded at the point of sale is the full invoice price. If the customer subsequently decides to take advantage of the discount, then the seller must record the fact that revenue has been reduced.

As with sales returns and allowances, management will want to monitor if customers are taking advantage of the sales discounts. Thus, a second contra revenue account, Sales Discounts, is used instead of directly reducing the Sales account. To determine net sales, the balances in Sales Discounts and in Sales Returns and Allowances are both subtracted from the balance in Sales.

The entry by Highpoint Audio & TV Supply to record the cash receipt from Chelsea Electronics on May 14 (within the discount period) is:

May 14	Cash	3,430	
	Sales Discounts	70	
	Accounts Receivable		3,500
	To record collection of invoice #731 within discount period.		

A	=	L	+	OE
+3,430				−70
−3,500				

↑ Cash flows: +3,430

If the discount is not taken, Highpoint Audio & TV Supply increases Cash and decreases Accounts Receivable by $3,500 at the date of collection. In this case, there is no need to adjust revenue, as the original amount recorded is the amount earned.

Summary of Sales Transactions

A summary of the effects of Highpoint's sales transactions is shown in the following T accounts. Highpoint Audio & TV Supply sold merchandise for $3,800, with $300 of it later returned. A sales discount of $70 was given because the invoice was paid within the discount period. In contrast to the purchase transactions shown on page 254, which affected only one account, Merchandise Inventory, sales transactions are recorded in several accounts. In addition, cost of goods sold is calculated and recorded at the time of each sale transaction in a perpetual inventory system.

Sales				Sales Returns and Allowances		
	May 4	3,800		May 9	300	
Sales Discounts				**Cost of Goods Sold**		
May 14	70			May 4	2,400	May 9	140
				Bal. 2,260		

Highpoint Audio & TV Supply's gross profit on these transactions with Chelsea Electronics is $1,170 ($3,800 − $300 − $70 − $2,260).

BEFORE YOU GO ON . . .

→ Review It

1. Under a perpetual inventory system, what are the two entries that must be recorded at the time of each sale?
2. What journal entries (if any) are recorded by the seller when the shipping terms are FOB destination? FOB shipping point?
3. When goods are returned or payment is received within a discount payment period, why is it important to use the contra revenue accounts Sales Returns and Allowances and Sales Discounts, rather than simply to reduce the Sales account?

→ Do It

On September 4, Junot Company sells merchandise for $1,500 on account to New Idea Company, terms 2/10, n/30, FOB shipping point. The original cost of the merchandise to Junot Company was $800. Per the terms of sale, the correct company pays freight charges of $75 on September 5. On September 8, goods with a selling price of $200 and a cost of $80 are returned and restored to inventory. On September 14, Junot Company receives the correct payment from New Idea Company. Record the transaction on the books of Junot Company.

Action Plan
- Record both the sale and the cost of goods sold at the time of the sale.
- Freight costs are paid by the seller only when the freight terms are FOB destination.
- Record sales returns in the contra account Sales Returns and Allowances and reduce Cost of Goods Sold when merchandise is returned to inventory.
- Calculate sales discounts using the net amount owing.
- Record sales discounts in the contra account Sales Discounts.

Solution

Junot Company (seller)

Sept. 4	Accounts Receivable		1,500	
	Sales			1,500
	To record credit sale.			
4	Cost of Goods Sold		800	
	Merchandise Inventory			800
	To record cost of goods sold.			
8	Sales Returns and Allowances		200	
	Accounts Receivable			200
	To record credit given for receipt of returned goods.			
8	Merchandise Inventory		80	
	Cost of Goods Sold			80
	To record cost of goods returned.			
14	Cash ($1,300 − $26)		1,274	
	Sales Discounts ($1,300 × 2%)		26	
	Accounts Receivable ($1,500 − $200)			1,300
	To record cash receipt within the discount period.			

The Navigator

Related exercise material: BE5–7, BE5–8, BE5–9, E5–2, E5–3, and E5–4.

Completing the Accounting Cycle

Up to this point, we have shown the basic entries for recording transactions for purchases and sales in a perpetual inventory system. Now, it is time to consider the remaining steps in the accounting cycle for a merchandising company. All of the steps in the accounting cycle for a service company are also used for a merchandising company.

STUDY OBJECTIVE 4

Perform the steps in the accounting cycle for a merchandising company.

Adjusting Entries

A merchandising company generally has the same types of adjusting entries as a service company. But a merchandiser that uses a perpetual inventory system may need one additional adjustment to make the accounting inventory records the same as the actual inventory on hand. This is necessary if errors in the accounting records have occurred, or if inventory has been stolen or damaged. Even though the Merchandise Inventory account gives a record of the inventory on hand, it only indicates what *should* be there, not necessarily what actually *is* there.

How does a company know if an adjustment is needed? The company will need to do a physical count of inventory on hand. As mentioned earlier in the chapter, a company must do a physical inventory count at least once a year.

Taking a physical inventory involves the following:

1. Counting the units on hand for each item of inventory.
2. Applying unit costs to the total units on hand for each item of inventory.
3. Totalling the costs for each item of inventory to determine the total cost of goods on hand.

If Highpoint Audio & TV Supply's accounting records show an ending inventory balance of $40,500 at the end of May and a physical inventory count indicates only $40,000 on hand, the following adjusting journal entry should be prepared.

May 31	Cost of Goods Sold	500	
	Merchandise Inventory		500
	To record difference between inventory records and physical units on hand.		

A	=	L	+	OE
−500				−500

Cash flows: no effect

The non-existent inventory is removed from the Merchandise Inventory account so that the balance stays accurate and performance measures that are based on inventory are not distorted. Inventory shortages are recorded in the Cost of Goods Sold account. Although this inventory has not been sold, inventory losses are considered part of the cost of the selling goods.

ACCOUNTING IN ACTION: ALL ABOUT YOU

We've all had a sales clerk in the fitting room hand us a card indicating the number of items we're taking in. It's pretty clear this is to prevent theft—that is, inventory shrinkage. But is this practice effective in preventing theft?

Apparently not enough for Le Chateau, whose biggest store in Montreal has 20 fitting rooms and a big problem with inventory shrinkage due to theft of low-ticket items. The store's shrinkage rates were 4.6%, compared with the industry average of 1.6%. Le Chateau was the first retailer in Canada to implement a new touchscreen/barcode combination technology. Rather than counting hangars and issuing number cards, attendants scan each tag and the information on the items—including colour and size—is automatically captured on the touchscreen. Within eight months of using the system, shrinkage at the store had been reduced by $30,000.

Sources: Denise Deveau, "Out of Fitting Rooms, into the Profits," *Canadian Retailer*, September/October 2007.

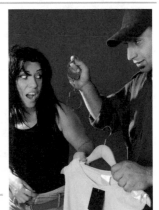

Are there advantages to you as a customer when retailers increase theft prevention measures?

Closing Entries

Using assumed data, an adjusted trial balance follows in Illustration 5–7 for Highpoint Audio & TV Supply at May 31, the company's year end. The accounts that are only used by a merchandising company are highlighted in red.

Illustration 5-7 ➜

Adjusted trial balance

HIGHPOINT AUDIO & TV SUPPLY Adjusted Trial Balance May 31, 2011	Debit	Credit
Cash	$ 9,500	
Notes receivable	10,000	
Accounts receivable	6,100	
Merchandise inventory	40,000	
Prepaid insurance	1,800	
Store equipment	80,000	
Accumulated depreciation–store equipment		$ 24,000
Accounts payable		20,800
Salaries payable		5,000
Notes payable		36,000
R. Lamb, capital		45,000
R. Lamb, drawings	15,000	
Sales		480,000
Sales returns and allowances	16,700	
Sales discounts	4,300	
Cost of goods sold	315,000	
Salaries expense	45,000	
Rent expense	19,000	
Utilities expense	17,000	
Advertising expense	16,000	
Depreciation expense	8,000	
Freight out	7,000	
Insurance expense	2,000	
Interest revenue		1,000
Rent revenue		2,400
Interest expense	1,800	
Totals	$614,200	$614,200

A merchandising company, like a service company, closes all accounts that affect profit to income summary. In journalizing, the company credits all temporary accounts with debit balances, and debits all temporary accounts with credit balances, as shown below for Highpoint Audio & TV Supply.

Helpful hint A merchandising company has more temporary accounts than a service company. Remember that Sales Returns and Allowances, Sales Discounts, and Cost of Goods Sold are temporary accounts and must be closed to Income Summary.

May 31	Sales	480,000	
	Interest Revenue	1,000	
	Rent Revenue	2,400	
	Income Summary		483,400
	To close income statement accounts with credit balances.		
31	Income Summary	451,800	
	Sales Returns and Allowances		16,700
	Sales Discounts		4,300
	Cost of Goods Sold		315,000
	Salaries Expense		45,000
	Rent Expense		19,000
	Utilities Expense		17,000
	Advertising Expense		16,000
	Depreciation Expense		8,000
	Freight Out		7,000
	Insurance Expense		2,000
	Interest Expense		1,800
	To close income statement accounts with debit balances.		

31	Income Summary	31,600	
	R. Lamb, Capital		31,600
	To close income summary to capital.		
31	R. Lamb, Capital	15,000	
	R. Lamb, Drawings		15,000
	To close drawings to capital.		

Post-Closing Trial Balance

After the closing entries are posted, all temporary accounts have zero balances. The R. Lamb, Capital account will have the same balance as is reported on the statement of owner's equity and balance sheet, and will be carried over to the next period. As with a service company, the final step in the accounting cycle is to prepare a post-closing trial balance. You will recall that the purpose of this trial balance is to ensure that debits equal credits in the permanent (balance sheet) accounts after all temporary accounts have been closed.

The only new account in the post-closing trial balance of a merchandising company is the current asset account Merchandise Inventory. The post-closing trial balance is prepared in the same way as described in Chapter 4 and is not shown again here.

Summary of Merchandising Entries

Illustration 5-8 summarizes the entries for the merchandising accounts using a perpetual inventory system.

	Transactions	Daily Recurring Entries	Debit	Credit
Purchases	Purchasing merchandise for resale.	Merchandise Inventory	XX	
		Cash or Accounts Payable		XX
	Paying freight costs on merchandise purchases, FOB shipping point.	Merchandise Inventory	XX	
		Cash		XX
	Receiving purchase returns or allowances from suppliers.	Cash or Accounts Payable	XX	
		Merchandise Inventory		XX
	Paying creditors on account within discount period.	Accounts Payable	XX	
		Merchandise Inventory		XX
		Cash		XX
	Paying creditors on account after the discount period.	Accounts Payable	XX	
		Cash		XX
Sales	Selling merchandise to customers.	Cash or Accounts Receivable	XX	
		Sales		XX
		Cost of Goods Sold	XX	
		Merchandise Inventory		XX
	Giving sales returns or allowances to customers.	Sales Returns and Allowances	XX	
		Cash or Accounts Receivable		XX
		Merchandise Inventory	XX	
		Cost of Goods Sold		XX
	Paying freight costs on sales, FOB destination	Freight Out	XX	
		Cash		XX
	Receiving payment on account from customers within discount period.	Cash	XX	
		Sales Discounts	XX	
		Accounts Receivable		XX
	Receiving payment on account from customers after discount period.	Cash	XX	
		Accounts Receivable		XX

← Illustration 5-8

Daily recurring and adjusting and closing entries

Illustration 5-8 (cont.) →

Daily recurring and adjusting and closing entries

	Events	Adjusting and Closing Entries	Debit	Credit
Adjusting Entries	Determining, after a physical count, that inventory in general ledger is higher than inventory actually on hand.	Cost of Goods Sold Merchandise Inventory	XX	XX
Closing Entries	Closing temporary accounts with credit balances.	Sales Other Revenues Income Summary	XX XX	XX

	Closing temporary accounts with debit balances.	Income Summary
		   Sales Returns and Allowances
		   Sales Discounts
		   Cost of Goods Sold
		   Freight Out
		   Other expenses
			XX	XX
				XX
				XX
				XX
				XX

BEFORE YOU GO ON . . .

→ Review It

1. Why is an adjustment to the Merchandise Inventory account sometimes necessary?
2. How are closing entries for a merchandising company different from closing entries for a service company?
3. What merchandising account(s) will appear in the post-closing trial balance?

→ Do It

The trial balance of Yee Clothing Company at December 31 shows Merchandise Inventory $25,000; J. Yee, Capital $12,000; Sales $162,400; Sales Returns and Allowances $4,800; Sales Discounts $950; Cost of Goods Sold $110,000; Rental Revenue $6,000; Freight Out $1,800; Rent Expense $8,800; Salaries Expense $22,000; and J. Yee, Drawings $3,600. Yee Clothing Company's statement of owner's equity for the year showed profit of $20,050 and closing owner's capital of $28,450. Prepare the closing entries for the above accounts. Create T accounts for Income Summary and J. Yee, Capital, and post the closing entries to these accounts.

Action Plan
- Debit each temporary account with a credit balance and credit the total to the Income Summary account.
- Credit each temporary account with a debit balance and debit the total to the Income Summary account.
- Stop and check your work: Does the balance in the Income Summary account equal the reported profit?
- Debit the balance in the Income Summary account and credit the amount to the owner's capital account. (Do the opposite if the company had a loss.)
- Credit the balance in the drawings account and debit the amount to the owner's capital account. Do not close drawings with the expenses.
- Stop and check your work: Does the balance in the owner's capital account equal the ending balance reported in the statement of owner's equity?

Solution

Dec. 31	Sales	162,400	
	Rental Revenue	6,000	
	Income Summary		168,400
	To close income statement accounts with credit balances.		
31	Income Summary	148,350	
	Sales Returns and Allowances		4,800

		Sales Discounts			950
		Cost of Goods Sold			110,000
		Freight Out			1,800
		Rent Expense			8,800
		Salaries Expense			22,000
		To close income statement accounts with debit balances.			
	31	Income Summary		20,050	
		J. Yee, Capital			20,050
		To close Income Summary account.			
	31	J. Yee, Capital		3,600	
		J. Yee, Drawings			3,600
		To close drawings account.			

Income Summary					J. Yee, Capital			
Clos.	148,350	Clos.	168,400				Bal.	12,000
		Bal.	20,050*	Clos.	3,600	Clos.		20,050
Clos.	20,050						Bal.	28,450**
		Bal.	0					

* Check = Profit   ** Check = Closing Owner's capital

Related exercise material: BE5–10, BE5–11, E5–5, and E5–6.

The Navigator

Merchandising Financial Statements

Merchandisers widely use the classified balance sheet introduced in Chapter 4 and one of two forms of income statements. This section explains the use of these financial statements by merchandisers.

STUDY OBJECTIVE 5

Prepare single-step and multiple-step income statements.

Single-Step Income Statement

The income statement form used in previous chapters of this textbook is the **single-step income statement.** The statement is so named because only one step—subtracting total expenses from total revenues—is required in determining profit.

In a single-step income statement, all data are classified under two categories: (1) revenues and (2) expenses. A condensed single-step income statement for Highpoint Audio & TV Supply, using the data from the adjusted trial balance in Illustration 5-7, is shown in Illustration 5-9.

◄ **Illustration 5-9**

Single-step income statement

HIGHPOINT AUDIO & TV SUPPLY Income Statement Year Ended May 31, 2011		
Revenues		
Net sales		$459,000
Interest revenue		1,000
Rent revenue		2,400
Total revenues		462,400
Expenses		
Cost of goods sold	$315,000	
Operating expenses	114,000	
Interest expense	1,800	
Total expenses		430,800
Profit		$ 31,600

This is called a condensed income statement because it shows totals for net sales and for operating expenses, but not the details of how these numbers were calculated. There are two main reasons for using the single-step format: (1) a company does not realize any profit until total revenues exceed total expenses, so it makes sense to divide the statement into these two categories; and (2) the single-step format is simple and easy to read.

Multiple-Step Income Statement

The **multiple-step income statement** is so named because it shows several steps in determining profit (or loss). This form is often considered more useful than a single-step income statement because the steps give additional information about a company's profitability. A multiple-step income statement is consistent with International Financial Reporting Standards (IFRS), which require a company to include additional line items, headings, and subtotals in the income statement when it helps to understand the company's financial performance.

Net Sales

The multiple-step income statement for a merchandising company begins by presenting sales revenue, the company's main revenue-producing activity. The contra revenue accounts Sales Returns and Allowances and Sales Discounts are deducted from Sales to arrive at **net sales**. The sales revenue section for Highpoint Audio & TV Supply (using data from the adjusted trial balance in Illustration 5-7) is as follows:

Sales revenue		
Sales		$480,000
Less: Sales returns and allowances	$16,700	
Sales discounts	4,300	21,000
Net sales		459,000

Many companies condense this information and report only the net sales figure in their income statement. This alternative was shown in the single-step income statement in Illustration 5-9.

Gross Profit

The next step is the calculation of gross profit. In Illustration 5-1, you learned that cost of goods sold is deducted from sales revenue to determine gross profit. For this calculation, companies use net sales as the amount of sales revenue. Based on the sales data above and the cost of goods sold in the adjusted trial balance in Illustration 5-7, the gross profit for Highpoint Audio & TV Supply is $144,000, calculated as follows:

Net sales	$459,000
Cost of goods sold	315,000
Gross profit	144,000

Operating Expenses

Operating expenses are the next component in measuring profit for a merchandising company. They are the recurring expenses associated with the central operations of the company—other than cost of goods sold—which are incurred in the process of earning sales revenue. These expenses are similar in service and merchandising companies.

Highpoint Audio & TV Supply would classify the following items in its adjusted trial balance (as shown in Illustration 5-7) as operating expenses: Salaries expense, $45,000; Rent expense, $19,000; Utilities expense, $17,000; Advertising expense, $16,000; Depreciation expense, $8,000; Freight out, $7,000; and Insurance expense $2,000. This results in total operating expenses of $114,000.

Sometimes operating expenses are subdivided into selling expenses and administrative expenses. Selling expenses are associated with making sales. They include expenses for sales promotion, as well as the expenses of completing the sale (e.g., freight costs). Administrative expenses relate to general operating activities such as management, accounting, and legal costs.

Profit from Operations

Profit from operations, or the results of the company's normal operating activities, is determined by subtracting operating expenses from gross profit:

Gross profit	$144,000
Operating expenses	114,000
Profit from operations	30,000

The purpose of showing profit from operations as a separate number from overall profit is to assist users of financial statements in understanding the company's main operations. The additional information helps users in making projections of future financial performance.

Non-Operating Activities

Non-operating activities are other revenues and expenses not related to the company's main operations. Examples of other revenues include interest revenue, rental revenue (if earned from renting assets not needed for operations), and investment income. Examples of other expenses include interest expense.

Based on the data in Highpoint Audio & TV Supply's adjusted trial balance shown in Illustration 5-7, the company will show the following non-operating activities in its multiple-step income statement:

Other revenues	
Interest revenue	$1,000
Rent revenue	2,400
Total non-operating revenues	3,400
Other expenses	
Interest expense	1,800
Net non-operating revenues	1,600

It is also common for companies to combine the two non-operating sections—other revenues and other expenses—into a single "Other Revenues and Expenses" section.

Profit

Profit is the final outcome of all the company's operating and non-operating activities. Highpoint's profit is $31,600 after adding its net non-operating revenue of $1,600 to profit from operations as follows:

Profit from operations	$30,000
Net non-operating revenues	1,600
Profit	$31,600

If there are no non-operating activities, the company's profit from operations becomes its profit—or "bottom line."

In Illustration 5-10, we bring together all the above steps in a comprehensive multiple-step income statement for Highpoint Audio & TV Supply.

Illustration 5-10 ➜

Multiple-step income statement

HIGHPOINT AUDIO & TV SUPPLY Income Statement Year Ended May 31, 2011			
Calculation of net sales and gross profit	Sales revenue		
	Sales		$480,000
	Less: Sales returns and allowances	$16,700	
	Sales discounts	4,300	21,000
	Net sales		459,000
	Cost of goods sold		315,000
	Gross profit		144,000
Calculation of operating expenses and profit from operations	Operating expenses		
	Salaries expense	$45,000	
	Rent expense	19,000	
	Utilities expense	17,000	
	Advertising expense	16,000	
	Depreciation expense	8,000	
	Freight out	7,000	
	Insurance expense	2,000	
	Total operating expenses		114,000
	Profit from operations		30,000
Calculation of non-operating activities and profit	Other revenues		
	Interest revenue	$ 1,000	
	Rent revenue	2,400	
	Total non-operating revenues	3,400	
	Other expenses		
	Interest expense	1,800	
	Net non-operating revenues		1,600
	Profit		$ 31,600

Note that the profit amounts in Illustrations 5-9 (single-step) and 5-10 (multiple-step) are the same. The only differences between the two forms of income statements are the amount of detail shown and the order of presentation.

Impact of International Financial Reporting Standards on the Income Statement

Similar to the discussion in Chapter 4 on the balance sheet, converting to IFRS may have an impact on the presentation of information in the income statement. However, a small company like Highpoint TV & Audio Supply would likely follow Canadian GAAP for Private Enterprises and would not be affected by the IFRS rules. For the most part, companies that follow IFRS will be corporations. Issues specific to corporations will be addressed later in Part 3 of this textbook. Some IFRS-related issues are beyond the scope of an introductory accounting course and are not included in this textbook. In the following sections, we will discuss the parts of IFRS that might affect the income statements of companies like Highpoint.

Terminology

One difference between IFRS and Canadian accounting standards is in the use of the words "income" and "profit." Canadian terminology uses "income" as the equivalent of "profit." IFRS uses "income" as the equivalent of "revenue," and "profit" as the difference between "income" and expenses. Throughout this edition of the textbook, we have partially adopted IFRS terminology by using the terms "profit" and "loss" instead of "net income" and "net loss". We believe that "profit" is a more understandable term to introductory accounting students than "net income."

However, it should be noted that IFRS still allows the use of the term "net income" to describe profit, as long as the meaning is clear. And it is not anticipated that Canadian companies will change their own terminology preferences with regard to the adoption of IFRS.

Classification of Expenses

While IFRS does not dictate the exact form of the income statement it does encourage companies to classify operating and other expenses based on either the nature of the expenses or their function within the company. The nature of an expense method classifies expenses based on what the resources were spent on (e.g., depreciation, employee costs, transportation, and advertising). The function of an expense method classifies expenses based on which business function the resources were spent on (e.g., costs of sales, administration, and selling).

Under Canadian accounting standards, companies have primarily classified expenses according to function and they will likely continue to do this under IFRS. But the IFRS recommendation to report information on the nature of expenses, even when the function basis has been used, would increase the informational value of the financial statements.

Headings and Subtotals

In general, IFRS are concerned with making sure that the appropriate information relevant to understanding a company's financial performance is included in the income statement. Thus, requirements to include relevant line items, headings, and subtotals in the income statement helps to prevent companies from concealing important information by combining together several accounts and reporting only the total amount.

Some Canadian accounting standards were revised to incorporate IFRS standards during the period of time leading up to the full transition to IFRS. Standards related to inventory and income statement presentation were modified in 2008. Prior to that, many Canadian companies combined the cost of goods sold and operating expenses into one number in the income statement. Effective in 2008, companies were required to report cost of goods sold separately. Now it will be possible to calculate the gross profit sub-total for all Canadian companies, not just those companies that provided the information on a voluntary basis.

The headings, totals, and subtotals that should be reported in the income statement will evolve as accounting standard setters continue to study this issue.

Small merchandising companies, such as Highpoint Audio & TV Supply, will continue to use the format of the multiple-step income statement shown in Illustration 5-10. A small company like Highpoint could decide to separate its operating expenses into selling expenses and administrative expenses. But as this separation is not required for companies like Highpoint, we will not include it in the illustrations in this textbook.

Classified Balance Sheet

Recall from Chapter 4 that merchandise inventory is a current asset because we expect to sell it within one year of the balance sheet date. Also recall from Chapter 4 that items are typically listed under current assets in their order of liquidity. Merchandise inventory is less liquid than accounts receivable because the goods must first be sold before revenue can be collected from the customer. Thus, in the balance sheet, merchandise inventory is reported as a current asset immediately below accounts receivable. Illustration 5-11 presents the assets section of a classified balance sheet for Highpoint Audio & TV Supply.

HIGHPOINT AUDIO & TV SUPPLY Balance Sheet (partial) May 31, 2011		
Assets		
Current assets		
Cash		$ 9,500
Notes receivable		10,000
Accounts receivable		6,100
Merchandise inventory		40,000
Prepaid insurance		1,800
Total current assets		67,400
Property, plant, and equipment		
Store equipment	$80,000	
Less: Accumulated depreciation	24,000	56,000
Total assets		$123,400

← **Illustration 5-11**

Assets section of a classified balance sheet

Helpful hint The $40,000 is the cost of the inventory on hand, not its expected selling price.

The remaining two financial statements, the statement of owner's equity and cash flow statement (to be discussed in Chapter 17), are the same as those of a service company. They are not shown in this chapter.

BEFORE YOU GO ON . . .

➜ **Review It**

1. How is a single-step income statement different from a multiple-step income statement?
2. What are non-operating activities and how are they reported in a single-step income statement and in a multiple-step income statement?

➜ **Do It**

Silver Store reported the following information: Sales $620,000; Sales Returns and Allowances $32,000; Sales Discounts $10,200; Cost of Goods Sold $422,000; Depreciation Expense $10,000; Insurance Expense $5,000; Interest Expense $1,700; Rent Expense $15,000 and Salaries Expense $80,000. Calculate the following amounts: (a) net sales, (b) gross profit, (c) total operating expenses, (d) profit from operations, and (e) profit.

Action Plan
- Deduct Sales Returns and Allowances and Sales Discounts from Sales to arrive at net sales.
- Deduct Cost of Goods Sold from net sales to arrive at gross profit.
- Identify which expenses are operating expenses and which are non-operating expenses.
- Deduct operating expenses from gross profit to arrive at profit from operations.
- Deduct any non-operating expenses from (and add any non-operating revenues to) profit from operations to arrive at profit.

Solution

(a) Net sales: $620,000 − $32,000 − $10,200 = $577,800
(b) Gross profit: $577,800 − $422,000 = $155,800
(c) Total operating expenses: $10,000 + $5,000 + $15,000 + $80,000 = $110,000
(d) Profit from operations: $155,800 − $110,000 = $45,800
(e) Profit: $45,800 − $1,700 = $44,100

The Navigator

Related exercise material: BE5–12, BE5–13, E5–7, E5–8, and E5–9.

Using the Information in the Financial Statements

STUDY OBJECTIVE 6

Calculate the gross profit margin and profit margin.

In Chapter 4, we introduced a tool called ratio analysis that investors and creditors use to determine additional information about how a company is performing. In this chapter, we introduce two **profitability ratios**. Profitability ratios measure a company's profit or operating success for a specific period of time. The two profitability ratios we examine in this chapter are the gross profit margin and profit margin.

Gross Profit Margin

A company's gross profit may be expressed as a percentage, called the **gross profit margin**. This is done by dividing the amount of gross profit by net sales. For Highpoint Audio & TV Supply, the gross profit margin is 31.4%, as calculated in Illustration 5-12.

Gross profit margin

Gross Profit	÷	Net Sales	=	Gross Profit Margin
$144,000	÷	$459,000	=	31.4%

The gross profit margin is generally considered to be more useful than the gross profit amount because the margin shows the relative relationship between net sales and gross profit. For example, a gross profit amount of $1 million may sound impressive. But, if it is the result of a gross profit margin of only 7%, it is not so impressive.

The amount and trend of gross profit are closely watched by management and other interested parties. They compare current gross profit with amounts reported in past periods. They also compare the company's gross profit margin with the margin of competitors and with industry averages. Such comparisons give information about the effectiveness of a company's purchasing and the soundness of its pricing policies. In general, a higher gross profit margin is seen as being more favourable than a lower gross profit margin.

Gross profit is important because inventory has a significant effect on a company's profitability. Cost of goods sold is usually the largest expense on the income statement. Gross profit represents a company's merchandising profit. It is not a measure of the overall profitability, because operating expenses have not been deducted.

Profit Margin

Overall profitability is measured by examining profit. Profit is often expressed as a percentage of sales, similar to the gross profit margin. The **profit margin** measures the percentage of each dollar of sales that results in profit. It is calculated by dividing profit by net sales. Highpoint Audio & TV Supply's profit margin of 6.9% is calculated in Illustration 5-13.

Profit margin

Profit	÷	Net Sales	=	Profit Margin
$31,600	÷	$459,000	=	6.9%

How do the gross profit margin and profit margin differ? The gross profit margin measures how much more the selling price is than the cost of goods sold. The profit margin measures by how much the selling price covers all expenses (including the cost of goods sold). A company can improve its profit margin by increasing its gross profit margin, or by controlling its operating expenses (and non-operating activities), or by doing both.

BEFORE YOU GO ON . . .

→ Review It

1. Explain the difference between the gross profit margin and profit margin.
2. Calculate The Forzani Group Ltd.'s gross profit margin and profit margin for fiscal 2009 and 2008 using the financial information found in Appendix A of this textbook. Indicate whether these ratios improved or weakened in 2009. The answers to these questions are at the end of the chapter.

Related exercise material: BE5–14, E5–1, E5–10, and E5–11.

The Navigator

APPENDIX 5A ▶ PERIODIC INVENTORY SYSTEM

STUDY OBJECTIVE 7

Prepare the entries for purchases and sales under a periodic inventory system and calculate cost of goods sold.

As described in this chapter, there are two basic systems of accounting for inventories: (1) the perpetual inventory system, and (2) the periodic inventory system. In the chapter, we focused on the characteristics of the perpetual inventory system. In this appendix, we discuss and illustrate the periodic inventory system.

One key difference between the two inventory systems is the timing for calculating the cost of goods sold. In a periodic inventory system, the cost of the merchandise sold is not recorded on the date of sale. Instead, the cost of goods sold during the period is calculated by taking a physical inventory count at the end of the period, and deducting the cost of this inventory from the cost of the merchandise available for sale during the period.

There are other differences between the perpetual and periodic inventory systems. Under a periodic inventory system, purchases of merchandise are recorded in the Purchases expense account, rather than the Merchandise Inventory asset account. Also, under a periodic system, it is customary to record in separate accounts purchase returns and allowances, purchase discounts, and freight in. That way, accumulated amounts are known for each.

To illustrate the recording of merchandise transactions under a periodic inventory system, we will use the purchase/sale transactions between Highpoint Audio & TV Supply (the seller) and Chelsea Electronics (the buyer) from earlier in this chapter.

Recording Purchases of Merchandise

Based on the sales invoice (Illustration 5-4) and receipt of the merchandise ordered from Highpoint Audio & TV Supply, Chelsea Electronics records the $3,800 purchase as follows:

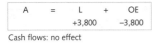

A   =   L   +   OE
         +3,800   −3,800
Cash flows: no effect

May 4	Purchases	3,800	
	Accounts Payable		3,800
	To record goods purchased on account per invoice #731, terms 2/10, n/30.		

Purchases is a temporary expense account whose normal balance is a debit.

Freight Costs

When the buyer pays for the freight costs, the account Freight In is debited. For example, Chelsea pays Public Carrier Co. $150 for freight charges on its purchase from Highpoint Audio & TV Supply. The entry on Chelsea's books is as follows:

A   =   L   +   OE
−150   −150
⬇ Cash flows: −150

May 4	Freight In	150	
	Cash		150
	To record payment of freight on goods purchased.		

Like Purchases, Freight In is a temporary expense account whose normal balance is a debit. Just as freight was a part of the cost of the merchandise inventory in a perpetual inventory system, freight in is part of the cost of goods purchased in a periodic inventory system. The cost of goods purchased should include any freight charges for transporting the goods to the buyer.

Purchase Returns and Allowances

Chelsea Electronics returns $300 worth of goods and prepares the following entry to recognize the return:

A   =   L   +   OE
         −300   +300
Cash flows: no effect

May 9	Accounts Payable	300	
	Purchase Returns and Allowances		300
	To record return of goods to Highpoint Audio & TV Supply.		

Purchase Returns and Allowances is a temporary account whose normal balance is a credit. It is a contra account whose balance is deducted from the balance in Purchases.

Purchase Discounts

Recall that the invoice terms were 2/10, n/30. On May 14, Chelsea Electronics pays the balance owing to Highpoint Audio & TV Supply of $3,500 ($3,800 less return of $300) less the 2% discount for payment within 10 days. Chelsea Electronics records the following entry:

May 14	Accounts Payable	3,500	
	Purchase Discounts ($3,500 × 2%)		70
	Cash ($3,500 − $70)		3,430
	To record payment of invoice #731 within discount period.		

A = L + OE
−3,430 = −3,500 + 70

↓ Cash flows: −3,430

Purchase Discounts is a temporary account whose normal balance is a credit. It is a contra account subtracted from the Purchases account.

In each of the above transactions, a temporary expense account was used to record purchases of merchandise rather than the Merchandise Inventory account that is used in a perpetual inventory system. A comparison of purchase transactions under the two inventory systems is shown later in the appendix.

Recording Sales of Merchandise

The seller, Highpoint Audio & TV Supply, records the sale of $3,800 of merchandise to Chelsea Electronics on May 4 (sales invoice in Illustration 5-4) as follows:

May 4	Accounts Receivable	3,800	
	Sales		3,800
	To record credit sale to Chelsea Electronics per invoice #731.		

A = L + OE
+3,800 +3,800

Cash flows: no effect

As previously explained, in a periodic inventory system, there is no entry to record the cost of goods sold and reduction of inventory at the point of sale.

Freight Costs

There is no difference between the accounting for freight costs by the seller in a perpetual and a periodic inventory system. In both systems, freight costs paid by the seller are debited to Freight Out or Delivery Expense, which are both operating expense accounts. Recall that in this example the freight terms were FOB shipping point, so Highpoint did not incur freight costs.

Sales Returns and Allowances

The $300 return of goods on May 9 is recorded by Highpoint Audio & TV Supply as follows:

May 9	Sales Returns and Allowances	300	
	Accounts Receivable		300
	To record credit given to Chelsea Electronics for returned goods.		

A = L + OE
−300 −300

Cash flows: no effect

Just as there is only one entry needed when sales are recorded in a periodic inventory system, one entry is also all that is needed to record a return. Different from the perpetual system, it doesn't matter if the inventory is damaged and discarded, or returned to inventory; no entry is needed in the periodic inventory system.

Sales Discounts

On May 14, Highpoint Audio & TV Supply receives a payment of $3,430 on account from Chelsea Electronics. Highpoint records this payment as follows:

A	=	L	+	OE
+3,430				−70
−3,500				

↑ Cash flows: +3,430

May 14	Cash	3,430	
	Sales Discounts ($3,500 × 2%)	70	
	Accounts Receivable		3,500
	To record collection of invoice #731 within discount period.		

Comparison of Entries—Perpetual vs. Periodic

Illustration 5A-1 ↓

Comparison of journal entries under perpetual and periodic inventory systems

Illustration 5A-1 summarizes the periodic inventory entries shown in this appendix and compares them with the perpetual inventory entries shown earlier in the chapter. Entries that are different in the two systems are shown in colour.

ENTRIES ON CHELSEA ELECTRONICS' BOOKS (BUYER)

	Transaction	Perpetual Inventory System			Periodic Inventory System		
May 4	Purchase of merchandise on credit.	Merchandise Inventory	3,800		Purchases	3,800	
		Accounts Payable		3,800	Accounts Payable		3,800
4	Freight cost on purchases.	Merchandise Inventory	150		Freight In	150	
		Cash		150	Cash		150
9	Purchase returns and allowances.	Accounts Payable	300		Accounts Payable	300	
		Merchandise Inventory		300	Purchase Returns and Allowances		300
14	Payment on account with a discount.	Accounts Payable	3,500		Accounts Payable	3,500	
		Merchandise Inventory		70	Purchase Discounts		70
		Cash		3,430	Cash		3,430

ENTRIES ON HIGHPOINT AUDIO & TV SUPPLY'S BOOKS (SELLER)

	Transaction	Perpetual Inventory System			Periodic Inventory System		
May 4	Sale of merchandise on credit.	Accounts Receivable	3,800		Accounts Receivable	3,800	
		Sales		3,800	Sales		3,800
		Cost of Goods Sold	2,400		No entry for cost of		
		Merchandise Inventory		2,400	goods sold		
9	Return of merchandise sold.	Sales Returns and Allowances	300		Sales Returns and Allowances	300	
		Accounts Receivable		300	Accounts Receivable		300
		Merchandise Inventory	140		No entry for cost of		
		Cost of Goods Sold		140	goods sold		
14	Cash received on account with a discount.	Cash	3,430		Cash	3,430	
		Sales Discounts	70		Sales Discounts	70	
		Accounts Receivable		3,500	Accounts Receivable		3,500

Calculating Cost of Goods Sold

In a periodic inventory system, the Merchandise Inventory account is not continuously updated for each purchase and sale. As we saw in the entries above, temporary accounts are used instead to accumulate the cost of the goods purchased throughout the period, and no entries are made to accumulate the cost of goods sold. Thus, the dollar amount of merchandise on hand at the end of the period and the cost of goods sold for the period are not known by looking at the general ledger accounts.

Instead, these amounts will have to be determined at the end of the accounting period in a periodic inventory system. Recall from Illustration 5-2, shown earlier in the chapter, that the basic equation to calculate cost of goods sold is: Beginning Inventory + Cost of Goods Purchased = Cost of Goods Available for Sale − Ending Inventory = Cost of Goods Sold.

To illustrate the calculation of cost of goods sold, we will use assumed data for Highpoint Audio & TV Supply so we can compare the results with its cost of goods sold under the perpetual inventory system shown in the chapter. Assume that Highpoint Audio & TV Supply's general ledger, under the periodic inventory system, shows the following balances at its year end on May 31, 2011:

- Merchandise Inventory $ 35,000
- Purchases 325,000
- Purchase Returns and Allowances 10,400
- Purchase Discounts 6,800
- Freight In 12,200

Beginning Inventory

If Highpoint Audio & TV Supply uses the periodic inventory system, it will not record any transactions in the Merchandise Inventory account during the period, and the balance in this account will not have changed since the beginning of the year. Thus the $35,000 balance in the general ledger—as shown above—is equal to beginning inventory.

Cost of Goods Purchased

In a periodic inventory system, four accounts—Purchases, Purchase Returns and Allowances, Purchase Discounts, and Freight In—are used to record the purchase of inventory. These four accounts are combined as follows to calculate the cost of goods purchased.

First, **net purchases** is calculated by subtracting the balances in the Purchase Returns and Allowances and Purchase Discounts accounts from the balance in the Purchases account. Highpoint's net purchases for the year ended May 31, 2011 is $307,800 ($325,000 − $10,400 − $6,800).

Then the **cost of goods purchased** is calculated by adding the balance in the Freight In account to net purchases. Highpoint's cost of goods purchased is $320,000 ($307,800 + $12,200).

Cost of Goods Available for Sale

As shown earlier in the chapter, in Illustration 5-2, the **cost of goods available for sale** is equal to the cost of the goods on hand at the beginning of the period (beginning inventory) plus the cost of goods purchased during the period. This is the total amount that the company could have sold during the period. Highpoint's cost of goods available for sale for the year ended May 31, 2011, is $355,000 ($35,000 + $320,000).

Ending Inventory

To determine the cost of the inventory on hand on May 31, 2011, Highpoint Audio & TV Supply must take a physical inventory. You will recall from earlier in this chapter that Highpoint determined its cost of goods on hand on May 31, 2011 (ending inventory) is $40,000. The inventory on hand is the same regardless of the inventory system used. But with a periodic inventory system, Highpoint will have no way of knowing if there are inventory shortages or not.

You will learn later in this appendix that the balance in the Merchandise Inventory account is adjusted from the beginning balance of $35,000 to the ending balance of $40,000 as part of the closing process.

Cost of Goods Sold

Once the ending inventory is determined, the cost of goods sold is calculated by subtracting the ending inventory from the cost of goods available for sale. Highpoint's cost of goods sold is $315,000 ($355,000 − $40,000).

Multiple-Step Income Statement—Periodic

The only reporting difference in a multiple-step income statement is that the cost of goods sold section has more detail in a periodic inventory system—as shown in Illustration 5A-2—than in a perpetual inventory system, where only one line is reported for the cost of goods sold. Note that cost of goods sold and profit are the same amounts as shown in Illustration 5-10 in the chapter.

Illustration 5A-2 ➡

Multiple-step income statement

HIGHPOINT AUDIO & TV SUPPLY			
Income Statement			
Year Ended May 31, 2011			
Sales revenue			
Sales			$480,000
Less: Sales returns and allowances		$16,700	
Sales discounts		4,300	21,000
Net sales			459,000
Cost of goods sold			
Inventory, June 1, 2010		$ 35,000	
Purchases	$325,000		
Less: Purchase returns and allowances	$10,400		
Purchase discounts	6,800	17,200	
Net purchases	307,800		
Add: Freight in	12,200		
Cost of goods purchased		320,000	
Cost of goods available for sale		355,000	
Inventory, May 31, 2011		40,000	
Cost of goods sold			315,000
Gross profit			144,000
Operating expenses			
Salaries expense		$ 45,000	
Rent expense		19,000	
Utilities expense		17,000	
Advertising expense		16,000	
Depreciation expense		8,000	
Freight out		7,000	
Insurance expense		2,000	
Total operating expenses			114,000
Profit from operations			30,000
Other revenues			
Interest revenue		$ 1,000	
Rent revenue		2,400	
Total non-operating revenues		3,400	
Other expenses			
Interest expense		1,800	
Net non-operating revenues			1,600
Profit			$ 31,600

Using the periodic inventory system does not affect the content of the balance sheet. As in the perpetual system, merchandise inventory is reported in the current assets section, and at the same amount.

Completing the Accounting Cycle

After preparing the financial statements, closing entries and a post-closing trial balance complete the accounting cycle. For a merchandising company, as for a service company, all accounts that affect the determination of profit are closed to the owner's capital account, whether a perpetual or periodic inventory system is used.

In a periodic inventory system, the closing entries are the same as those we previously learned about, with one exception: the treatment of Merchandise Inventory. As we saw in the previous section, the balance reported for inventory in the adjusted trial balance is its beginning balance, not its ending balance.

Two closing journal entries are used to update the Merchandise Inventory account from the beginning balance of $35,000 to the ending balance of $40,000. These two entries for Highpoint Audio & TV Supply are as follows:

May 31	Income Summary	35,000	
	Merchandise Inventory		35,000
	To close beginning inventory.		
31	Merchandise Inventory	40,000	
	Income Summary		40,000
	To record ending inventory.		

A	=	L	+	OE
−35,000				−35,000

Cash flows: no effect

A	=	L	+	OE
+40,000				+40,000

Cash flows: no effect

After the closing entries are posted, the Merchandise Inventory account will show the following:

Merchandise Inventory			
June 1, 2010 Bal.	35,000	May 31, 2011 Clos.	35,000
May 31, 2011 Clos.	40,000		
May 31, 2011 Bal.	40,000		

The effect of the two closing journal entries on the Merchandise Inventory account is similar to the effect that the closing process has on the owner's capital account. The ending inventory and capital balances must be updated to agree with the balance sheet at the end of the period. The balance sheet reports these ending balances, not the amounts in the adjusted trial balance. The ending balance in Merchandise Inventory now becomes the beginning inventory amount for the next period.

The remaining closing entries are as we saw in prior chapters and are not shown here. The only difference between a merchandising company using the periodic inventory system and a service company is that there are several additional temporary accounts that must be closed.

Temporary accounts with credit balances include the Sales, Purchase Returns and Allowances, and Purchase Discounts accounts. These will need to be debited for their individual account balances and the total is credited to the Income Summary account. Temporary accounts with debit balances include the Sales Returns and Allowances, Sales Discounts, Purchases, and Freight In accounts. These will need to be credited for their individual account balances and the total is debited to the Income Summary account.

After the closing entries are posted, a post-closing trial balance is prepared. The post-closing trial balance is prepared in the same way as described in earlier chapters and is not explained again here.

BEFORE YOU GO ON . . .

→ Do It

On August 1, White Company buys merchandise on account from Red Company for $1,000, terms 2/10, n/30, FOB destination. The correct company pays freight charges of $70 on August 1. On August 3, White Company returns $150 of the merchandise to Red Company. On August 10, White Company pays the total amount owing.

(a) Record White Company's transactions assuming the company uses a periodic inventory system.
(b) Record Red Company's transactions assuming the company uses a periodic inventory system.

Action Plan
• In a periodic system, purchases of inventory are recorded in the Purchases account.
• Examine freight terms to determine which company pays the freight charges.
• Calculate purchase discounts using the net amount owing and record in a Purchase Discounts account.

- In a period system, the cost of goods sold is not recorded at the time of the sale.
- In a periodic system, inventory is not adjusted for returned merchandise.
- Calculate sales discounts using the net amount owing and record in a Sales Discounts account.

Solution

(a) White Company (buyer)

Aug. 1	Purchases	1,000	
	Accounts Payable		1,000
	To record goods purchased on account.		
1	No entry – seller pays for freight		
3	Accounts Payable	150	
	Purchase Returns and Allowances		150
	To record return of goods.		
10	Accounts Payable ($1,000 − $150)	850	
	Purchase Discounts ($850 × 2%)		17
	Cash ($850 − $17)		833
	To record cash payment within the discount period.		

(b) Red Company (seller)

Aug. 1	Accounts Receivable	1,000	
	Sales		1,000
	To record credit sale.		
1	Delivery Expense	70	
	Cash		70
	To record payment of freight costs for goods sold.		
3	Sales Returns and Allowances	150	
	Accounts Receivable		150
	To record credit given for receipt of returned goods.		
10	Cash ($850 − $17)	833	
	Sales Discounts ($850 × 2%)	17	
	Accounts Receivable ($1,000 − $150)		850
	To record cash receipt within the discount period.		

The Navigator

Related exercise material: *BE5–15, *BE5–16, *BE5–17, *E5–12, *E5–13, *E5–14, *E5–15, and *E5–16.

Demonstration Problem 1

WILEY PLUS

Demonstration Problems

The following information is for Cappelio Distributors. The company uses the perpetual inventory system.

June 1 Purchased merchandise inventory for resale from AP Manufacturers for $7,000. Terms of purchase were 2/10, n/30, FOB shipping point.

   2 The correct company paid $225 cash for freight charges.

   3 Noted that there was some damage on the goods. AP Manufacturers granted Cappelio a $500 allowance.

  10 Paid AP Manufacturers the amount owing.

  15 Sold the entire merchandise inventory purchased on June 1 to Seaside Motor Inn for $10,700, terms 2/10, n/30, FOB destination.

  16 The appropriate party paid $200 freight for the delivery of the goods sold to Seaside Motor Inn on June 15.

  18 Credited the account of Seaside Motor Inn $600 as the merchandise did not meet all of Seaside Motor Inn's specifications. (*Note:* None of the merchandise was returned.)

  25 Received a cheque from Seaside Motor Inn for full payment of its account.

Instructions

Journalize the June transactions for Cappelio Distributors.

Solution to Demonstration Problem 1

		GENERAL JOURNAL		
Date		Account Titles and Explanation	Debit	Credit
June	1	Merchandise Inventory	7,000	
		Accounts Payable		7,000
		Purchased merchandise on account.		
	2	Merchandise Inventory	225	
		Cash		225
		Paid freight charges on purchase of goods.		
	3	Accounts Payable	500	
		Merchandise Inventory		500
		Received an allowance on goods purchased.		
	10	Accounts Payable ($7,000 − $500)	6,500	
		Merchandise Inventory ($6,500 × 2%)		130
		Cash ($6,500 − $130)		6,370
		Paid for merchandise in discount period.		
	15	Accounts Receivable	10,700	
		Sales		10,700
		Cost of Goods Sold ($7,000 + $225 − $500 − $130)	6,595	
		Merchandise Inventory		6,595
		Sold merchandise on account.		
	16	Delivery Expense	200	
		Cash		200
		Paid freight charges on sale of goods.		
	18	Sales Returns and Allowances	600	
		Accounts Receivable		600
		Granted Seaside Motor Inn an allowance.		
	25	Cash ($10,100 − $202)	9,898	
		Sales Discounts ($10,100 × 2%)	202	
		Accounts Receivable ($10,700 − $600)		10,100
		Received payment from customer in the discount period.		

Action Plan

- Merchandise Inventory account is used for all transactions that affect the cost of the goods purchased.
- Cost of goods sold must be calculated and recorded at point of sale in a perpetual inventory system.
- A contra account is used for sales allowances given to customers.
- A contra account is used for sales discounts taken by customers.

Demonstration Problem 2

The adjusted trial balance data for the year ended December 31, 2011, for Dykstra Company are as follows:

WILEY
PLUS

Demonstration Problems

DYKSTRA COMPANY Adjusted Trial Balance December 31, 2011		
	Debit	Credit
Cash	$ 14,500	
Accounts receivable	15,100	
Merchandise inventory	29,000	
Prepaid insurance	2,500	
Land	150,000	
Building	500,000	
Accumulated depreciation—building		$ 40,000
Equipment	95,000	
Accumulated depreciation—equipment		18,000
Accounts payable		10,600

Property taxes payable		4,000
Mortgage payable—due before December 31, 2012		25,000
Mortgage payable—long-term		530,000
G. Dykstra, capital		81,000
G. Dykstra, drawings	12,000	
Sales		627,200
Sales returns and allowances	5,700	
Sales discounts	1,000	
Cost of goods sold	353,800	
Advertising expense	12,000	
Depreciation expense	29,000	
Freight out	7,600	
Insurance expense	4,500	
Property tax expense	24,000	
Salaries expense	61,000	
Utilities expense	18,000	
Interest revenue		2,500
Interest expense	3,600	
Totals	$1,338,300	$1,338,300

Instructions

(a) Prepare a multiple-step income statement for the year ended December 31, 2011.

(b) Prepare a statement of owner's equity for Dykstra Company for the year ended December 31, 2011. No additional investments were made by Mr. Dykstra during the year.

(c) Prepare a classified balance sheet as at December 31, 2011.

(d) Prepare closing entries.

Solution to Demonstration Problem

Action Plan

- Remember that the major subtotal headings in the income statement are net sales, gross profit, profit from operations, and profit (loss).
- Prepare the income statement in steps:
  1. Sales less sales returns and allowances and sales discounts equals net sales.
  2. Net sales less cost of goods sold equals gross profit
  3. Gross profit less operating expenses equals profit from operations.
  4. Profit from operations plus or minus non-operating revenue or expense items equals profit.
- Merchandise Inventory is a current asset in the classified balance sheet.
- Sales Returns and Allowances, Sales Discounts, and Cost of Goods Sold are all temporary accounts that must be closed.

(a)

DYKSTRA COMPANY Income Statement Year Ended December 31, 2011		
Sales revenues		
Sales		$627,200
Less: Sales returns and allowances	$ 5,700	
Sales discounts	1,000	6,700
Net sales		620,500
Cost of goods sold		353,800
Gross profit		266,700
Operating expenses		
Advertising expense	$ 12,000	
Depreciation expense	29,000	
Freight out	7,600	
Insurance expense	4,500	
Property tax expense	24,000	
Salaries expense	61,000	
Utilities expense	18,000	
Total operating expenses		156,100
Profit from operations		110,600
Other revenues and expenses		
Interest revenue	$ 2,500	
Interest expense	3,600	(1,100)
Profit		$109,500

(b)

DYKSTRA COMPANY Statement of Owner's Equity Year Ended December 31, 2011	
G. Dykstra, capital, January 1, 2011	$ 81,000
Add: Profit	109,500
	190,500
Deduct: Drawings	12,000
G. Dykstra, capital, December 31, 2011	$178,500

(c)

DYKSTRA COMPANY Balance Sheet December 31, 2011		
Assets		
Current assets		
Cash		$ 14,500
Accounts receivable		15,100
Merchandise inventory		29,000
Prepaid insurance		2,500
Total current assets		61,100
Property, plant, and equipment		
Land		150,000
Building	$500,000	
Less: Accumulated depreciation	40,000	460,000
Equipment	$ 95,000	
Less: Accumulated depreciation	18,000	77,000
Total property, plant, and equipment		687,000
Total assets		$748,100
Liabilities and Owner's Equity		
Current liabilities		
Accounts payable		$ 10,600
Property taxes payable		4,000
Current portion of mortgage payable		25,000
Total current liabilities		39,600
Long-term liabilities		
Mortgage payable		530,000
Total liabilities		569,600
Owner's equity		
G. Dykstra, capital		178,500
Total liabilities and owner's equity		$748,100

(d)

Dec. 31	Sales	627,200	
	Interest Revenue	2,500	
	Income Summary		629,700
	To close revenue accounts.		
31	Income Summary	520,200	
	Sales Returns and Allowances		5,700
	Sales Discounts		1,000
	Cost of Goods Sold		353,800
	Advertising Expense		12,000
	Depreciation Expense		29,000
	Freight Out		7,600
	Insurance Expense		4,500

	Property Tax Expense		24,000
	Salaries Expense		61,000
	Utilities Expense		18,000
	Interest Expense		3,600
	To close expense accounts.		
31	Income Summary	109,500	
	G. Dykstra, Capital		109,500
	To close Income Summary.		
31	G. Dykstra, Capital	12,000	
	G. Dykstra, Drawings		12,000
	To close drawings.		

The Navigator

Summary of Study Objectives

1. **Describe the differences between service and merchandising companies.** A service company performs services. It has service or fee revenue and operating expenses. A merchandising company sells goods. It has sales revenue, cost of goods sold, gross profit, and operating expenses.

2. **Prepare entries for purchases under a perpetual inventory system.** The Merchandise Inventory account is debited for all purchases of merchandise and freight, if freight is paid by the buyer. It is credited for purchase returns and allowances and purchase discounts. Purchase discounts are cash reductions to the net invoice price for early payment.

3. **Prepare entries for sales under a perpetual inventory system.** When inventory is sold, two entries are required: (1) Accounts Receivable (or Cash) is debited and Sales is credited for the selling price of the merchandise. (2) Cost of Goods Sold is debited and Merchandise Inventory is credited for the cost of the inventory items sold. Contra revenue accounts are used to record sales returns and allowances and sales discounts. Two entries are also required to record sales returns when the returned merchandise can be sold again in the future. Freight costs paid by the seller are recorded as an operating expense.

4. **Perform the steps in the accounting cycle for a merchandising company.** Each of the required steps in the accounting cycle for a service company is also done for a merchandising company. An additional adjusting journal entry may be required under a perpetual inventory system. The Merchandise Inventory account must be adjusted to agree with the physical inventory count if there is a difference in the amounts. Merchandising companies have additional temporary accounts that must also be closed at the end of the accounting year.

5. **Prepare single-step and multiple-step income statements.** In a single-step income statement, all data are classified under two categories (revenues or expenses), and profit is determined by one step. A multiple-step income statement shows several steps in determining profit. Net sales is calculated by deducting sales returns and allowances and sales discounts from sales. Next, gross profit is calculated by deducting the cost of goods sold from net sales. Profit (loss) from operations is then calculated by deducting operating expenses from gross profit. Total non-operating activities are added to (or deducted from) profit from operations to determine profit.

6. **Calculate the gross profit margin and profit margin.** The gross profit margin, calculated by dividing gross profit by net sales, measures the gross profit earned for each dollar of sales. The profit margin, calculated by dividing profit by net sales, measures the profit (total profit) earned for each dollar of sales. Both are measures of profitability that are closely watched by management and other interested parties.

7. **Prepare the entries for purchases and sales under a periodic inventory system and calculate cost of goods sold (Appendix 5A).** In a periodic inventory system, separate temporary accounts are used to record (a) purchases, (b) purchase returns and allowances, (c) purchase discounts, and (d) freight costs paid by the buyer. Purchases – purchase returns and allowances – purchase discounts = net purchases. Net purchases + freight in = cost of goods purchased.

In a periodic inventory system, only one journal entry is made to record a sale of merchandise. Cost of goods sold is not recorded at the time of the sale. Instead, it is calculated as follows at the end of the period: Beginning inventory + cost of goods purchased = cost of goods available for sale. Cost of goods available for sale – ending inventory = cost of goods sold.

Glossary

Contra revenue account   An account that is offset against (deducted from) a revenue account on the income statement. (p. 256)

Control account   An account in the general ledger that summarizes the detail for a subsidiary ledger and controls it. (p. 251)

Cost of goods available for sale   The cost of the goods on hand at the beginning of the period (beginning inventory) plus the cost of goods purchased during the period. (p. 273)

Cost of goods purchased   Net purchases (purchases minus purchase returns and allowances and purchase discounts) plus freight in. (p. 273)

Cost of goods sold   The total cost of merchandise sold during the period. In a perpetual inventory system, it is calculated and recorded for each sale. In a periodic inventory system, the total cost of goods sold for the period is calculated at the end of the accounting period by deducting ending inventory from the cost of goods available for sale. (p. 246)

FOB destination   A freight term indicating that the buyer accepts ownership when the goods are delivered to the buyer's place of business. The seller pays the shipping costs and is responsible for damages to the goods during transit. (p. 251)

FOB shipping point   A freight term indicating that the buyer accepts ownership when the goods are placed on the carrier by the seller. The buyer pays freight costs from the shipping point to the destination and is responsible for damages. (p. 251)

Gross profit   Sales revenue (net sales) less cost of goods sold. (p. 246)

Gross profit margin   Gross profit expressed as a percentage of net sales. It is calculated by dividing gross profit by net sales. (p. 268)

Multiple-step income statement   An income statement that shows several steps to determine profit or loss. (p. 264)

Net purchases   Purchases minus purchase returns and allowances and purchase discounts. (p. 273)

Net sales   Sales less sales returns and allowances and sales discounts. (p. 264)

Non-operating activities   Other revenues and expenses that are unrelated to the company's main operations. (p. 265)

Operating expenses   Expenses incurred in the process of earning sales revenues. They are deducted from gross profit in the income statement. (p. 246)

Periodic inventory system   An inventory system where detailed inventory records are not updated whenever a transaction occurs. The cost of goods sold is determined only at the end of the accounting period. (p. 247)

Perpetual inventory system   An inventory system where detailed records, showing the quantity and cost of each inventory item, are updated whenever a transaction occurs. The records continuously show the inventory that should be on hand. (p. 247)

Profit from operations   Profit from a company's main operating activity, determined by subtracting operating expenses from gross profit. (p. 265)

Profit margin   Profit expressed as a percentage of net sales. It is calculated by dividing profit by net sales. (p. 269)

Profitability ratios   Measures of a company's profit or operating success (or shortcomings) for a specific period of time. (p. 268)

Purchase discount   A discount, based on the invoice price less any returns and allowances, given to a buyer for early payment of a balance due. (p. 253)

Purchase returns (allowances)   The return, or reduction in price, of unsatisfactory merchandise that was purchased. It results in a debit to Cash or Accounts Payable. (p. 252)

Quantity discount   A cash discount that reduces the invoice price and is given to the buyer for volume purchases. (p. 253)

Sales discount   A reduction, based on the invoice price less any returns and allowances, given by a seller for early payment of a credit sale. (p. 257)

Sales returns (allowances)   The return, or reduction in price, of unsatisfactory merchandise that was sold. It results in a credit to Cash or Accounts Receivable. (p. 256)

Sales revenue   The main source of revenue in a merchandising company. (p. 246)

Single-step income statement   An income statement that shows only one step (revenues less expenses) in determining profit (or loss). (p. 263)

Subsidiary ledger   A group of accounts that give details for a control account in the general ledger. (p. 250)

Note: All questions, exercises, and problems below with an asterisk (*) relate to material in Appendix 5A.

Self-Study Questions

WILEY
PLUS Quizzes

Answers are at the end of the chapter.

(SO 1) K **1.** Which of the following statements about the perpetual inventory system is false?
  (a) The cost of goods sold is calculated and recorded with each sale.
  (b) The perpetual inventory system continuously shows the quantity and cost of inventory on hand.
  (c) It is not necessary to do a physical count of the inventory if the perpetual inventory system is used.
  (d) A perpetual inventory system results in more clerical work and additional costs compared with the periodic inventory system.

(SO 2) K **2.** When goods are shipped with the freight terms FOB shipping point:
  (a) the buyer pays the freight costs and debits Merchandise Inventory.
  (b) the buyer pays the freight costs and debits Freight Expense.
  (c) the seller pays the freight costs and debits Delivery Expense.
  (d) the seller pays the freight costs and debits Cost of Goods Sold.

(SO 2) AP **3.** A $750 purchase of merchandise inventory is made on June 13, terms 2/10, n/30. On June 16, merchandise costing $50 is returned. What amount will be paid as payment in full on June 22?
  (a) $686
  (b) $700
  (c) $735
  (d) $750

(SO 3) K **4.** To record the sale of goods for cash in a perpetual inventory system:
  (a) only one journal entry is necessary to record the cost of goods sold and reduction of inventory.
  (b) only one journal entry is necessary to record the receipt of cash and the sales revenue.
  (c) two journal entries are necessary: one to record the receipt of cash and sales revenue, and one to record the cost of the goods sold and reduction of inventory.
  (d) two journal entries are necessary: one to record the receipt of cash and reduction of inventory, and one to record the cost of the goods sold and sales revenue.

(SO 3) K **5.** Which of the following is a contra sales account that normally has a debit balance?
  (a) Sales Returns and Allowances
  (b) Sales

  (c) Freight Out
  (d) Cost of Goods Sold

(SO 4) K **6.** The steps in the accounting cycle for a merchandising company using the perpetual inventory system are the same as those for a service company *except*:
  (a) an additional adjusting journal entry for inventory may be needed in a merchandising company.
  (b) closing journal entries are not required for a merchandising company.
  (c) a post-closing trial balance is not required for a merchandising company.
  (d) a multiple-step income statement is required for a merchandising company.

(SO 5) K **7.** Which of the following appears on both a single-step and a multiple-step income statement?
  (a) Merchandise inventory
  (b) Gross profit
  (c) Profit from operations
  (d) Cost of goods sold

(SO 6) AP **8.** Net sales are $400,000, cost of goods sold is $310,000, operating expenses are $60,000, and other revenues are $5,000. What are the gross profit margin and profit margin?
  (a) 7.5% and 8.8%
  (b) 22.5% and 7.4%
  (c) 22.5% and 8.8%
  (d) 77.5% and 8.8%

(SO 7) K *9. When goods are purchased for resale by a company using a periodic inventory system:
  (a) purchases are debited to Merchandise Inventory.
  (b) purchases are debited to Purchases.
  (c) purchase returns are debited to Purchase Returns and Allowances.
  (d) freight costs are debited to Purchases.

(SO 7) AP *10. If beginning inventory is $60,000, purchases are $400,000, purchase returns and allowances are $25,000, freight in is $5,000, and ending inventory is $50,000, what is the cost of goods sold?
  (a) $385,000
  (b) $390,000
  (c) $410,000
  (d) $430,000

Questions

(SO 1) C 1. What components of revenues and expenses are different for a merchandising company and a service company?

(SO 1) C 2. Why is the normal operating cycle for a merchandising company likely to be longer than the operating cycle for a service company?

(SO 1) C 3. Explain the differences between a perpetual and a periodic inventory system. Include in your explanation why the words "perpetual" and "periodic" are used for the two systems.

(SO 1) C 4. Suppose you are starting a company that sells used clothes. What factors would you consider in determining whether to use a perpetual or a periodic inventory system?

(SO 1) C 5. Song Yee wonders why a physical inventory count is necessary in a perpetual inventory system. After all, the accounting records show how much inventory is on hand. Explain why a physical inventory count is required in a perpetual inventory system.

(SO 1) C 6. Describe the costs and the benefits of a perpetual inventory system compared with a periodic inventory system.

(SO 2) C 7. What is the purpose of an inventory subsidiary ledger? What are the advantages of using one?

(SO 2) C 8. What is the relationship between the inventory subsidiary ledger and the Merchandise Inventory account in the general ledger?

(SO 2) C 9. What are the differences between FOB shipping point and FOB destination? Explain the differences between how freight costs are recorded for inventory purchases as opposed to inventory sales.

(SO 2) C 10. Fukushima Company received an invoice for $16,000, terms 1/10, n/30. It will have to borrow from its bank in order to pay the invoice in 10 days. The interest rate Fukushima pays on its bank loans is 7.25%. Should it take advantage of the cash discount offered or not? Support your answer with calculations.

(SO 3) C 11. Wiley Book Company sells a book that cost $50 for $75 cash. The accountant prepares a journal entry with a debit to Cash for $75, a credit to Inventory for $50, and a credit to Gross Profit for $25. What part of this is incorrect and why is it important to use the correct accounts? The company uses a perpetual inventory system.

(SO 2, 3) C 12. Explain the difference between a quantity discount, a purchase discount, and a sales discount. Explain how each of them is recorded.

13. Inventory was purchased on credit in April and (SO 2, 3) C paid for in May. It was sold on credit in June. Cash was collected from the customer in July. In which month should the company record cost of the inventory as an expense and in which month should it record the revenue from the sale? Why?

14. Why are sales returns recorded in a contra revenue account and not debited directly to the Sales account? (SO 3) C

15. When the seller records a sales return or a sales allowance, sometimes they also adjust cost of goods sold and inventory, and sometimes they do not. Explain when it is necessary to also record an entry in the cost of goods sold and inventory accounts, what is debited and credited, and what amount is used. (SO 3) C

16. "The steps in the accounting cycle for a merchandising company are different from those in the accounting cycle for a service company." Do you agree or disagree? Explain. (SO 4) C

17. Snow Co. uses a perpetual inventory system. Will the company ever need to record an adjustment to the Merchandise Inventory account when recording other adjusting journal entries? What may have caused the need for an adjustment and how will the company know if one is required? (SO 4) C

18. Compared with a service company, what additional accounts must be closed for a merchandising company using a perpetual inventory system? Include in your answer if the account should be debited or credited to close it. (SO 4) C

19. Explain the differences between a single-step and a multiple-step income statement. (SO 5) K

20. Explain the terms "net sales," "gross profit," "profit from operations," and "profit". Are these terms used only by merchandising companies or are they used by service companies also? (SO 5) C

21. Why is interest expense reported as a non-operating expense instead of as an operating expense on a multiple-step income statement? (SO 5) C

22. What is the difference between gross profit and gross profit margin? Why is it useful to calculate a company's gross profit margin? (SO 6) C

23. How is the gross profit margin different from the profit margin? (SO 6) C

*24. Explain the differences between how inventory purchases are recorded in a periodic system compared with a perpetual system. Also explain the differences in recording sales in a periodic system compared with a perpetual system. (SO 7) K

(SO 7) K *25. Renata purchases merchandise at garage sales and later sells these goods at a flea market. Assuming Renata uses a periodic inventory system, how would she calculate her cost of goods sold and gross profit?

*26. In a periodic inventory system, closing entries are posted to the Merchandise Inventory account. What is the purpose of these entries? (SO 7) C

Brief Exercises

Calculate missing amounts in determining profit.
(SO 1) AP

BE5–1 The components in the income statements of companies A, B, C, and D follow. Determine the missing amounts.

	Sales	Cost of Goods Sold	Gross Profit	Operating Expenses	Profit
Company A	$250,000	$150,000	$ (a)	$60,000	$ (b)
Company B	118,000	70,000	(c)	(d)	25,500
Company C	75,000	(e)	32,500	(f)	11,000
Company D	(g)	71,900	78,500	39,500	(h)

Calculate balance in inventory control account.
(SO 2) AP

BE5–2 Old Fashioned Candy Company sells three types of candies. The company uses a perpetual inventory system and a subsidiary ledger to keep track of its inventory. Determine the balance in the inventory control account in the general ledger if the company had the following items on hand on March 31:

Inventory Item	Packages on Hand	Cost per Package
Jelly beans	300	$1.65
Licorice sticks	500	2.20
Bubble gum	275	1.20

Calculate inventory balances.
(SO 2) AP

BE5–3 Old Fashioned Candy Company (see BE5–2) has decided to expand its sales to include Canada Mints. It purchases 600 packages from its supplier at a cost of $12.50 per package, terms 2/10, n/30, FOB shipping point. The freight charges are $120. Old Fashioned Candy Company pays for the merchandise within the discount period. What are the total cost and cost per package of this inventory item, and the balance in the Merchandise Inventory control account in the general ledger after these transactions?

Identify effect of purchase transactions on elements of financial statements.
(SO 2) C

BE5–4 Allied Company uses a perpetual inventory system. The company had the following transactions in February.

Feb. 5 Allied purchased $10,000 of merchandise from NW Wholesale, terms 2/10, n/30, FOB shipping point.

6 The correct company paid freight costs of $125.

8 Allied returned $1,200 of the merchandise purchased on February 5.

11 Allied paid the balance due to NW Wholesale.

For each transaction: (a) determine the type and name of the accounts that are affected, whether the account is increased or decreased, and by how much; (b) indicate the effect of the transaction on profit and owner's equity. Write (NE) if there is no effect. Use the following format. If the transaction affects two accounts of the same type, use two rows for that transaction. The first one has been done for you as an example.

Date	Assets	Liabilities	Owner's Equity	Revenue	Expenses	Profit
Feb. 5	Inventory + 10,000	Accounts Payable + 10,000	NE			NE

Record purchase transactions—perpetual system.
(SO 2) AP

BE5–5 Prepare the journal entries to record the following purchase transactions in Xiaoyan Company's books. Xiaoyan uses a perpetual inventory system.

Jan. 2 Xiaoyan purchased $10,000 of merchandise from Feng Company, terms n/30, FOB destination.

4 The correct company paid freight costs of $135.

6 Xiaoyan returned $1,000 of the merchandise purchased on January 2 because it was not needed.

12 Xiaoyan paid the balance owing to Feng.

BE5–6 Prepare the journal entries to record the following purchase transactions in Jarek Company's books. Jarek uses a perpetual inventory system.

Mar. 12 Jarek purchased $15,000 of merchandise from Dalibor Company, terms 2/10, n/30, FOB shipping point.

13 The correct company paid freight costs of $155.

14 Jarek returned $3,000 of the merchandise purchased on March 12 because it was damaged.

22 Jarek paid the balance owing to Dalibor.

Record purchase transactions with a purchase discount—perpetual system. (SO 2) AP

BE5–7 NW Wholesale Company uses a perpetual inventory system. The company had the following transactions in February.

Feb. 5 NW Wholesale sells $10,000 of merchandise to Allied Company, terms 2/10, n/30, FOB shipping point. The merchandise had cost NW Wholesale $5,500.

6 The correct company paid freight costs of $135.

8 Allied returned $1,200 of the merchandise purchased on February 5. The inventory is not damaged and can be resold. NW Wholesale restores it to inventory. The cost of the merchandise was $660.

11 NW Wholesale collects the balance due from Allied.

Identify effect of sales transactions on elements of financial statements. (SO 3) C

For each transaction: (a) determine the type and name of the accounts that are affected, if the account is increased or decreased, and by how much; and (b) indicate the effect of the transaction on profit and owner's equity. Write (NE) if there is no effect. Use the following format. If the transaction affects two accounts of the same type, use two rows for that transaction. See BE5–4 for an example.

Date	Assets	Liabilities	Owner's Equity	Revenue	Expenses	Profit

BE5–8 Prepare journal entries to record the following sales transactions in Feng Company's books. Feng uses a perpetual inventory system.

Jan. 2 Feng sold $10,000 of merchandise to Xiaoyan Company, terms n/30, FOB destination. The cost of the merchandise sold was $6,300.

4 The correct company paid freight costs of $155.

6 Xiaoyan returned $1,000 of the merchandise purchased on January 2 because it was not needed. The cost of the merchandise returned was $840, and it was restored to inventory.

12 Feng received the balance due from Xiaoyan.

Record sales transactions—perpetual system. (SO 3) AP

BE5–9 Prepare journal entries to record the following sales transactions in Dalibor Company's books. Dalibor uses a perpetual inventory system.

Mar. 12 Dalibor sold $15,000 of merchandise to Jarek Company, terms 2/10, n/30, FOB shipping point. The cost of the merchandise sold was $8,500.

13 The correct company paid freight costs of $155.

14 Jarek returned $3,000 of the merchandise purchased on March 12 because it was damaged. The cost of the merchandise returned was $1,700. Dalibor examined the merchandise, decided it was no longer saleable, and discarded it.

22 Dalibor received the balance due from Jarek.

Record sales transactions—perpetual system. (SO 3) AP

Prepare adjusting entry.
(SO 4) AP

BE5–10 At its April 30 year end, the inventory records of Pajewski Company showed merchandise inventory of $98,000. Through a physical count, the company determined that its actual inventory on hand was $96,500. Record the necessary adjusting entry.

Prepare closing entries.
(SO 4) AP

BE5–11 Prasad Company has the following merchandise account balances at its July 31 year end: Sales $175,000; Sales Returns and Allowances $2,500; Sales Discounts $750; Cost of Goods Sold $100,000; Merchandise Inventory $48,000; and Freight Out $1,500. Prepare the entries to close the appropriate accounts to the Income Summary account.

Calculate net sales, gross profit, profit from operations, and profit.
(SO 5) AP

BE5–12 Crisp Crunchy Company has the following account balances: Sales $510,000; Interest Revenue $8,000; Sales Returns and Allowances $15,000; Sales Discounts $5,000; Cost of Goods Sold $350,000; Depreciation Expense $12,000; Insurance Expense $3,000; Interest Expense $10,000; Rent Expense $40,000; and Salaries Expense $50,000. Assuming Crisp Crunchy Company uses a multiple-step income statement, calculate the following: (a) net sales, (b) gross profit, (c) profit from operations, and (d) profit.

Identify placement of items on income statements.
(SO 5) AP

BE5–13 Explain where each of the following items would appear on (a) a single-step income statement and (b) a multiple-step income statement: depreciation expense, cost of goods sold, freight out, insurance expense, interest expense, interest revenue, rent revenue, sales discounts, and sales returns and allowances.

Calculate profitability ratios and comment.
(SO 6) AP

BE5–14 In 2011, Red River Company reported net sales of $550,000, cost of goods sold of $300,000, and operating expenses of $200,000. In 2010, Red River Company reported net sales of $600,000, cost of goods sold of $350,000, and operating expenses of $225,000. Calculate the gross profit margin and profit margin for both 2010 and 2011. Comment on Red River Company's changing profitability.

Record purchase transactions—periodic system.
(SO 7) AP

*BE5–15 Prepare the journal entries to record these transactions on Allied Company's books. Allied Company uses a periodic inventory system.

Feb. 5 Allied purchased $10,000 of merchandise from NW Wholesale Company, terms 2/10, n/30, FOB shipping point.
6 The correct company paid freight costs of $135.
8 Allied returned $1,200 of the merchandise purchased on February 5.
11 Allied paid the balance due to NW Wholesale.

Record sales transactions—periodic system.
(SO 7) AP

*BE5–16 Prepare the journal entries to record these transactions on NW Wholesale Company's books. NW Wholesale Company uses a periodic inventory system.

Feb. 5 NW Wholesale sells $10,000 of merchandise to Allied, terms 2/10, n/30, FOB shipping point.
6 The correct company paid freight costs of $135.
8 Allied returned $1,200 of the merchandise purchased on February 5. The inventory is not damaged and can be resold. NW Wholesale restores it to inventory.
11 NW Wholesale collects the balance due from Allied.

Calculate net purchases, cost of goods purchased, cost of goods sold, and gross profit.
(SO 7) AP

*BE5–17 Treble Company uses a periodic inventory system and reports the following information: net sales $625,000; purchases $400,000; purchase returns and allowances $11,000; purchase discounts $8,000; freight in $16,000; beginning inventory $60,000; ending inventory $80,000; and freight out $12,500. Calculate (a) net purchases, (b) cost of goods purchased, (c) cost of goods available for sale, (d) cost of goods sold, and (e) gross profit.

Exercises

E5–1   Here are some of the terms discussed in the chapter:

Match concepts with descriptions.
(SO 1, 2, 3, 4, 5, 6) K

1. Gross profit	9. Sales discounts
2. Perpetual inventory system	10. FOB destination
3. Cost of goods sold	11. Sales allowance
4. Purchase returns	12. Non-operating activities
5. Freight out	13. Profit margin
6. FOB shipping point	14. Contra revenue account
7. Periodic inventory system	15. Merchandise inventory
8. Subsidiary ledger	16. Purchase discounts

Instructions

Match each term with the best description below. Each term may be used more than once, or may not be used at all.

(a) ___ An expense account that shows the cost of merchandise sold

(b) ___ A group of accounts that share a common characteristic, such as all inventory accounts

(c) ___ An account, such as Sales Discounts, that is deducted from a revenue account on the income statement

(d) ___ The return of unsatisfactory purchased merchandise

(e) ___ Freight terms where the seller will pay for the cost of shipping the goods

(f) ___ An inventory system where the inventory records need to be updated at year end to show the inventory on hand

(g) ___ A reduction in price given for unsatisfactory inventory

(h) ___ Sales revenue less cost of goods sold

(i) ___ Revenues, expenses, gains, and losses that are not part of the company's main operations

(j) ___ Freight terms where the buyer will pay for the cost of shipping the goods

(k) ___ An inventory system where the cost of goods sold is calculated and recorded with every sales transaction

(l) ___ An asset that shows goods purchased for resale

(m) ___ Profit divided by net sales

(n) ___ A price reduction given by a seller for early payment on a credit sale

E5–2   Merchandising companies have several types of transactions involving the purchase and sale of merchandise inventory. Listed below are examples of these transactions.

Identify accounts affected by and the impact of inventory transactions.
(SO 2, 3) C

1. Purchasing merchandise on account.
2. Paying cash for freight on merchandise purchase.
3. Returning purchases to seller for credit on account.
4. Paying the amount owing for merchandise purchases within the discount period.
5. Selling merchandise on account.
6. Paying cash for freight on sales.
7. Allowing a customer to return merchandise for credit and restoring the merchandise to inventory.
8. Receiving payment from the customer within the discount period.

Instructions

Assuming a perpetual inventory system is used, indicate the following for each of these inventory transactions:

(a) The type (asset or liability) and name of the balance sheet account(s) that will be affected by the transaction and whether the transaction will increase or decrease that account.

(b) Does the transaction increase, decrease, or have no effect on the owner's equity balance on the balance sheet?

(c) The type (revenue or expense) and name of the income statement account(s) that will be affected by the merchandising transaction and whether the transaction will increase or decrease that account. Write (NE) if the transaction does not affect any income statement accounts.

(d) Does the transaction increase, decrease, or have no effect on amount of profit reported on the income statement?

Use two rows if more than one balance sheet or income statement account is affected by the transaction. The first one has been done for you as an example:

		Balance Sheet				Income Statement		
Inventory Transaction	Type of Account	Account Name	Increase or Decrease	Impact on Owner's Equity	Type of Account	Account Name	Increase or Decrease	Impact on Profit
1.	Asset	Inventory	Increase	NE	NE			NE
	Liability	Accounts Payable	Increase					

Record purchase and sales transactions—perpetual system.
(SO 2, 3) AP

E5–3 The following transactions occurred in April and May. Both companies use a perpetual inventory system.

Apr. 5 Olaf Company purchased merchandise from DeVito Company for $15,000, terms 2/10, n/30, FOB destination. DeVito had paid $10,500 for the merchandise.

6 The correct company paid freight costs of $500.

8 Olaf Company returned damaged merchandise to DeVito Company and was given a purchase allowance of $2,500. DeVito determined the merchandise could not be repaired and sent it to the recyclers. The merchandise had cost DeVito $1,750.

May 2 Olaf paid the amount due to DeVito Company in full.

Instructions

(a) Prepare the journal entries to record the above transactions on the books of Olaf Company.

(b) Prepare the journal entries to record the above transactions on the books of DeVito Company.

Record purchase and sales transactions—perpetual system.
(SO 2, 3) AP

E5–4 The following merchandise transactions occurred in December. Both companies use a perpetual inventory system.

Dec. 3 Pippen Company sold merchandise to Thomas Co. for $48,000, terms 2/10, n/30, FOB shipping point. This merchandise cost Pippen Company $32,000.

4 The correct company paid freight charges of $750.

8 Thomas Co. returned unwanted merchandise to Pippen. The returned merchandise had a sales price of $2,400 and a cost of $1,600. It was restored to inventory.

13 Pippen Company received the balance due from Thomas Co.

Instructions

(a) Prepare the journal entries to record these transactions on the books of Pippen Company.

(b) Prepare the journal entries to record these transactions on the books of Thomas Co.

(c) Calculate the gross profit earned by Pippen on the above transactions.

Record inventory transactions and closing entries—perpetual system.
(SO 2, 3, 4) AP

E5–5 The following transactions occurred in June and July. Pele Company uses a perpetual inventory system.

June 10 Pele Company purchased $5,000 of merchandise from Duvall Company, terms 2/10, n/30, FOB shipping point.

11 The correct company paid $275 of freight costs to Hoyt Movers.
12 Damaged goods totalling $500 were returned to Duvall for credit.
20 Pele paid Duvall Company in full.
July 15 Pele sold all of the remaining merchandise purchased from Duvall for $9,500 cash.
15 Pele paid $250 of freight costs to AAA Transit to deliver the goods to the customer.
17 Pele gave its customer a $300 cash sales allowance for damaged goods. Pele uses a perpetual inventory system.

Instructions

(a) Record each of the above transactions on the books of Pele Company.
(b) Prepare closing entries on July 31 for the temporary accounts.

E5–6 Collegiate Office Supply sells various office furniture items and uses a perpetual inventory system. At the beginning of October, it had no office chairs in stock. On October 3, Collegiate purchased 100 office chairs from Katts Ltd. for $8,300, terms n/30, FOB shipping point. Collegiate also paid $300 of freight costs to Freight Company for the delivery of the chairs. On October 9, Collegiate sold 30 chairs to Butler Inc. for $165 each on credit, terms 2/10, n/30, FOB destination. On that same date, Collegiate paid $30 cash to Freight Company for the delivery of the chairs to Butler Inc. On October 11, Butler Inc. returned five chairs. Collegiate credited Butler's account and the chairs were returned to inventory. Collegiate received the amount owing from Butler Inc. on October 19.

October 31 is Collegiate's year end. The chairs were counted as part of the annual inventory count and it was determined that there were 74 chairs on hand. Collegiate paid Katts Ltd. on November 5 for the chairs purchased on October 6.

Record and post inventory transactions and adjusting entries—perpetual system. (SO 2, 3, 4) AP

Instructions

(a) Calculate the total cost of the goods (chairs) available for sale and the average cost per chair.
(b) Calculated the net sales, cost of goods sold, and gross profit earned as a result of the above transactions and events.
(c) Calculate the balance in the merchandise inventory account on October 31, before and after any necessary adjustments. Assume the balance was zero on October 1.

E5–7 Financial information follows for three different companies:

Calculate missing amounts. (SO 5) AP

	Natural Cosmetics	Mattar Grocery	SE Footware
Sales	$195,000	$ (e)	$158,000
Sales returns and allowances	(a)	5,000	14,000
Net sales	179,000	105,000	(i)
Cost of goods sold	87,000	(f)	(j)
Gross profit	(b)	38,000	24,000
Operating expenses	45,000	(g)	18,000
Profit from operations	(c)	(h)	(k)
Other expenses	4,000	6,000	(l)
Profit	(d)	10,000	4,000

Instructions

Determine the missing amounts.

E5–8 The following information from Chevalier Company's general ledger is presented for the year ended December 31, 2011:

Prepare single-step and multiple-step income statements and closing entries—perpetual system. (SO 4, 5) AP

Advertising expense	$ 55,000	Interest revenue	$ 30,000
Depreciation expense	125,000	Merchandise inventory	67,000
Cost of goods sold	985,000	Rent revenue	24,000
Delivery expense	25,000	Salaries expense	875,000

G. Chevalier, capital	$535,000	Sales	$2,400,000
G. Chevalier, drawings	150,000	Sales discounts	8,500
Insurance expense	15,000	Sales returns and allowances	41,000
Interest expense	70,000	Unearned sales revenue	8,000

Instructions

(a) Prepare a single-step income statement.
(b) Prepare a multiple-step income statement.
(c) Prepare closing entries.

Classify accounts of merchandising company.
(SO 5) K

E5–9   You are given the following list of accounts from the adjusted trial balance of Swirsky Company:

Accounts payable	Land
Accounts receivable	Merchandise inventory
Accumulated depreciation—office building	Mortgage payable
Advertising expense	Note receivable (due in six months)
Depreciation expense	Office building
B. Swirsky, capital	Prepaid insurance
B. Swirsky, drawings	Property tax payable
Cash	Salaries expense
Freight out	Salaries payable
Insurance expense	Sales
Interest expense	Sales discounts
Interest payable	Sales returns and allowances
Interest revenue	Unearned sales revenue

Instructions

For each account, identify whether it should be reported on the balance sheet, statement of owner's equity, or income statement. Assuming Swirsky Company prepares a classified balance sheet and a multiple-step income statement, specify how the account should be classified. For example, Accounts Payable would be classified under current liabilities on the balance sheet.

Prepare financial statements and calculate ratios— perpetual system.
(SO 5, 6) AP

E5–10   An alphabetical list of Rikard's adjusted accounts at its fiscal year end, August 31, 2011, follows. All accounts have normal balances.

Accounts payable	$ 18,035	Office furniture	$ 28,500
Accounts receivable	2,570	Prepaid insurance	1,575
Accumulated depreciation—		R. Smistad, capital	71,950
office furniture	7,400	R. Smistad, drawings	85,000
Accumulated depreciation—		Rent expense	24,000
store equipment	13,040	Salaries expense	55,000
Depreciation expense	6,110	Salaries payable	2,250
Cash	5,640	Sales	458,300
Cost of goods sold	273,360	Sales discounts	2,275
Insurance expense	2,205	Sales returns and allowances	14,555
Interest expense	1,925	Store equipment	32,600
Interest payable	450	Supplies	1,680
Merchandise inventory	70,350	Supplies expense	5,040
Note payable	38,500	Unearned sales revenue	2,460

Other data:
1. Of the notes payable, $5,000 becomes due on February 17, 2012. The balance is due in 2013.
2. On July 18, 2011, Rikard invested $3,500 cash in the business.

Instructions

(a) Prepare a multiple-step income statement, statement of owner's equity, and classified balance sheet.
(b) Calculate the gross profit margin and profit margin.

E5–11 Best Buy Co., Inc. reported the following information for three recent fiscal years (in U.S. millions):

Calculate profitability ratios. (SO 6) AN

	2009	2008	2007
Sales	$27,433	$40,023	$35,934
Cost of goods sold	20,938	30,477	27,165
Profit from operations	1,442	2,161	1,999
Profit	984	1,407	1,377

Instructions

(a) Calculate the gross profit margin and profit margin for Best Buy for each of the three years.
(b) Recalculate profit margin using profit from operations as opposed to profit.
(c) Comment on whether the ratios improved or weakened over the three years.

*E5–12 Data for Pippen Company and Thomas Co. are presented in E5–4.

Record purchase and sales transaction entries—periodic system. (SO 7) AP

Instructions

(a) Prepare the journal entries to record these transactions on the books of Pippen Company assuming a periodic inventory system is used instead of a perpetual system.
(b) Prepare the journal entries to record these transactions on the books of Thomas Co. assuming a periodic inventory system is used instead of a perpetual system.

*E5–13 The Furano Company had the following merchandise transactions in May:

Record purchase and sales transaction entries—perpetual and periodic systems. (SO 2, 3, 7) AP

May 2 Purchased $1,200 of merchandise from Digital Suppliers, terms 2/10, n/30, FOB shipping point.
  2 The correct company paid $100 freight costs.
  3 Returned $200 of the merchandise to Digital as it did not meet specifications.
  9 Paid Digital the balance owing.
  12 Sold three-quarters of the remaining merchandise to SunDial Company for $1,500, terms 2/10, n/30.
  14 SunDial returned part of the merchandise. Furano gave SunDial a credit of $180 and returned the merchandise to inventory. The merchandise had a cost of $100.
  22 Received the correct balance owing from SunDial.

Instructions

(a) Prepare journal entries for Furano Company assuming it uses a perpetual inventory system.
(b) Prepare journal entries for Furano Company assuming it uses a periodic inventory system.

*E5–14 Memories Company commenced operations on July 1. Memories Company uses a periodic inventory system. During July, Memories Company was involved in the following transactions and events:

Record inventory transactions and calculate gross profit— periodic system. (SO 7) AP

July 2 Purchased $20,000 of merchandise from Suppliers Inc. on account, terms 2/10, n/30, FOB shipping point.
  5 Paid $500 of freight costs on July 2 shipment.
  8 Sold merchandise for $1,000 cash.

11 Paid Suppliers Inc. the full amount owing.
15 Sold merchandise for $5,000 on account, 1/10, n/30, FOB shipping point.
25 Received full payment for the merchandise sold on July 15.
31 Memories did a physical count and determined there was $16,500 of inventory on hand.

Instructions

(a) Record the transactions in Memories Company's books.
(b) What was Memories' gross profit for July?

Determine missing amounts
for cost of goods sold section–
periodic system.
(SO 7) AP

*E5–15   Below are the cost of goods sold sections for the two most recent years for two companies using a periodic inventory system:

	Company 1		Company 2	
	Year 1	Year 2	Year 1	Year 2
Beginning inventory	$ 250	$ (e)	$1,000	$ (n)
Purchases	1,500	(f)	(j)	9,550
Purchase returns and allowances	50	100	300	400
Purchase discounts	30	50	150	100
Net purchases	(a)	1,850	7,210	(o)
Freight in	110	(g)	(k)	550
Cost of goods purchased	(b)	(h)	7,900	(p)
Cost of goods available for sale	(c)	2,300	(l)	(q)
Ending inventory	(d)	400	1,450	1,250
Cost of goods sold	1,480	(i)	(m)	(r)

Instructions

Fill in the missing amounts to complete the cost of goods sold sections.

Prepare multiple-step income
statement and closing entries–
periodic system.
(SO 7) AP

*E5–16   The following selected information is for Okanagan Company for the year ended January 31, 2011:

Freight in	$ 10,000	Purchase discounts	$ 2,000
Freight out	7,000	Purchase returns and allowances	6,000
Insurance expense	12,000	Rent expense	20,000
Interest expense	6,000	Salaries expense	61,000
Merchandise inventory, beginning	61,000	Salaries payable	2,500
Merchandise inventory, ending	42,000	Sales	315,000
O. G. Pogo, capital	105,000	Sales discounts	4,000
O. G. Pogo, drawings	42,000	Sales returns and allowances	13,000
Purchases	200,000	Unearned sales revenue	4,500

Instructions

(a) Prepare a multiple-step income statement.
(b) Prepare closing entries.

Problems: Set A

Identify problems and
recommend inventory system.
(SO 1) C

P5–1A   AAA Dog 'n Cat Shop sells a variety of merchandise for the pet owner, including pet food, grooming supplies, toys, and kennels. Most customers use the option to purchase on account and take 60 days, on average, to pay their accounts. The owner of AAA Dog 'n Cat Shop, Adam Fleming, has decided the company needs a bank loan because the accounts payable need to be paid in 30 days. Adam estimates that it takes 45 days, on average, to sell merchandise from the time it arrives at his store. Since the company earns a good profit every year, the bank manager is willing to give AAA Dog 'n Cat Shop a loan but wants monthly financial statements.

Adam has also noticed that, while some of the merchandise sells very quickly, other items do not. Sometimes he wonders just how long he has had some of those older items. He has also noticed that he regularly seems to run out of some merchandise items. Adam is also concerned about preparing monthly financial statements. The company uses a periodic inventory system and Adam counts inventory once a year. He is wondering how he is going to calculate the cost of goods sold for the month without counting the inventory at the end of every month. He has come to you for help.

Instructions

(a) Explain to Adam what an operating cycle is and why he is having problems paying the bills.

(a) Explain to Adam how the periodic inventory system is contributing to his problems.

Taking It Further Make a recommendation about what inventory system the company should use and why.

P5–2A At the beginning of the current tennis season, on April 1, 2011, Kicked-Back Tennis Shop's inventory consisted of 55 tennis racquets at a cost of $50 each. Kicked-Back uses a perpetual inventory system. The following transactions occurred in April:

Record and post inventory transactions—perpetual system. Calculate net sales and gross profit.
(SO 2, 3) AP

Apr. 2 Purchased 170 additional racquets from Roberts Inc. for $8,500, terms n/30.

4 Received credit from Roberts for the five returned damaged racquets purchased on April 2.

5 Sold 45 racquets to Tennis Dome for $95 each, terms n/30.

6 Tennis Dome returned 15 of the racquets after determining it had purchased more racquets than it needed. Kicked-Back gave Tennis Dome a credit on its account and returned the racquets to inventory.

10 Sold 40 rackets at $95 each to cash customers.

12 Ten of these racquets were returned for cash. The customers claimed they never play tennis and had no idea why they had been talked into purchasing the racquets. Refunded cash to these customers and returned the racquets to inventory.

17 An additional 10 of the racquets sold on April 10 were returned because the rackets were damaged. The customers were refunded cash and the racquets were sent to a local children's club as a gift.

25 Sold 60 racquets to the Summer Club for $95 each, terms n/30.

29 Summer Club returned 25 of the racquets after the tennis pro had examined the racquets and determined that these racquets were of inferior quality. Kicked-Back gave Summer Club a credit and decided to return the racquets to inventory with plans to sell them for the reduced price of $75 each.

Instructions

(a) Record the transactions for the month of April for Kicked-Back.

(b) Create T accounts for sales, sales returns, cost of goods sold, and merchandise inventory. Post the opening balance and April's transactions, and calculate the April 30 balances.

(c) Calculate net sales and gross profit.

Taking It Further Assume that the owner of Kicked-Back hired an employee to run the store and is not involved in operating the business. The owner wants to know the amount of net sales and gross profit for the month. Will the owner be missing any important information, by requesting only these two numbers? Explain.

Record inventory transactions
and post to inventory
account—perpetual system.
(SO 2, 3) AP

P5–3A Travel Warehouse distributes suitcases to retail stores and extends credit terms of n/30 to all of its customers. Travel Warehouse uses a perpetual inventory system and at the end of June its inventory consisted of 25 suitcases purchased at $30 each. During the month of July, the following merchandising transactions occurred:

July 1 Purchased 50 suitcases on account for $30 each from Trunk Manufacturers, terms n/30, FOB destination.

2 The correct company paid $125 freight on the July 1 purchase.

4 Received $150 credit for five suitcases returned to Trunk Manufacturers because they were damaged.

10 Sold 45 suitcases on account to Satchel World for $55 each.

12 Issued a $275 credit for five suitcases returned by Satchel World because they were the wrong colour. The suitcases were returned to inventory.

15 Purchased 60 additional suitcases from Trunk Manufacturers for $27.50 each, terms, n/30, FOB shipping point.

18 Paid $150 freight to AA Trucking Company for merchandise purchased from Trunk Manufacturers.

21 Sold 54 suitcases on account to Fly-By-Night for $55 each.

23 Gave Fly-By-Night a $110 credit for two returned suitcases. The suitcases had been damaged and were sent to the recyclers.

30 Paid Trunk Manufacturers for the July 1 purchase.

31 Received balance owing from Satchel World.

Instructions

(a) Record the transactions for the month of July for Travel Warehouse.

(b) Create a T account for merchandise inventory. Post the opening balance and July's transactions, and calculate the July 31 balance.

(c) Determine the number of suitcases on hand at the end of the month and calculate the average cost per suitcase of the inventory on hand.

Taking It Further Explain how freight terms can affect the selling price, and the cost, of merchandise. Use the transactions on July 1 and 15 between Travel Warehouse and Trunk Manufacturer as part of your explanation.

Record inventory
transactions—perpetual
system.
(SO 2, 3) AP

P5–4A Presented below are selected transactions for Norlan Company during September and October of the current year. Norlan uses a perpetual inventory system.

Sept. 1 Purchased merchandise on account from Hillary Company at a cost of $65,000, FOB shipping point, terms 1/15, n/30.

2 The correct company paid $2,000 of freight charges to Trucking Company on the September 1 merchandise purchase.

5 Returned for credit $7,000 of damaged goods purchased from Hillary Company on September 1.

15 Sold the remaining merchandise purchased from Hillary Company to Irvine Company for $90,000, terms 2/10, n/30, FOB destination.

16 The correct company paid $3,000 of freight charges on the September 15 sale of merchandise.

17 Issued Irvine Company a credit of $4,000 for returned goods. These goods had cost Norlan Company $2,400 and were returned to inventory.

25 Received the balance owing from Irvine Company for the September 15 sale.

30 Paid Hillary Company the balance owing for the September 1 purchase.

Oct. 1 Purchased merchandise on account from Kimmel Company at a cost of $50,000, terms 2/10, n/30, FOB destination.

2 The correct company paid freight costs of $1,200 on the October 1 purchase.

3 Obtained a purchase allowance of $2,000 from Kimmel Company to compensate for some minor damage to goods purchased on October 1.

10 Paid Kimmel Company the amount owing on the October 1 purchase.

11 Sold all of the merchandise purchased from Kimmel Company to Kieso Company for $80,000, terms 2/10, n/30, FOB shipping point.

12 The correct company paid $800 freight costs on the October 11 sale.

17 Issued Kieso Company a sales allowance of $1,500 because some of the goods did not meet Kieso's exact specifications.

31 Received a cheque from Kieso Company for the balance owing on the October 11 sale.

Instructions

Prepare journal entries to record the above transactions for Norlan Company.

Taking It Further   Explain why companies should always take advantage of purchase discounts even if they have to borrow from the bank. Refer to the two purchases made by Norlan Company in your answer.

P5–5A   Nisson Distributing Company had the following merchandising transactions in the month of April 2011. At the beginning of April, Nisson's ledger showed Cash $14,000, Merchandise Inventory, $3,000, and M. Nisson, Capital, $17,000.

Record and post inventory transactions—perpetual system. Prepare partial income statement.
(SO 2, 3, 5) AP

Apr. 2 Purchased merchandise from Kai Supply Co. for $8,900, terms 1/15, n/30, FOB shipping point.

3 The correct company paid $300 cash for freight charges on the April 2 purchase.

4 Sold merchandise on account to Kananaskis Distributors for $11,600, terms 2/10, n/30, FOB destination. The cost of the merchandise was $7,300.

5 The correct company paid $250 freight on the April 4 sale.

6 Issued a $700 credit for merchandise returned by Kananaskis. The merchandise originally cost $425 and was returned to inventory.

8 Purchased merchandise from Testa Distributors for $4,500, terms 2/10, n/30, FOB destination.

9 The correct company paid $110 freight costs on the April 8 purchase.

10 Received a $300 credit from Testa for returned merchandise.

15 Paid Kai Supply Co. the amount due.

18 Paid Testa the balance owing from the April 8 purchase.

23 Sold merchandise for $7,500 cash. The cost of this merchandise was $4,500.

24 Purchased merchandise from Pigeon Distributors for $2,800 cash.

25 Made a $230 cash refund to a cash customer for merchandise returned. The returned merchandise had a cost of $140. The merchandise was damaged and could not be resold.

26 Received a $500 refund from Pigeon Distributors for returned goods on the cash purchase of April 24.

28 Collected the balance owing from Kananaskis.

30 Sold merchandise to Bower Company for $3,800, terms n/30, FOB shipping point. Nisson's cost for this merchandise was $2,200.

Instructions

(a) Record the transactions assuming Nisson uses a perpetual inventory system.

(b) Set up general ledger accounts, enter the beginning cash, merchandise inventory, and capital balances, and post the transactions.

(c) Prepare a partial multiple-step income statement, up to gross profit, for the month of April 2011.

Taking It Further   Assume that on May 2 Bower Company returns all of the merchandise it had purchased on April 30 and is given a full refund. Should this affect Nisson's gross profit earned in April, as calculated in (c) above? Why or why not?

Prepare adjusting and closing entries, and single-step and multiple-step income statements—perpetual system.
(SO 4, 5) AP

P5–6A An alphabetical list of Scarboro Wholesale Centre's account balances at its fiscal year end, July 31, 2011, follows. All accounts have normal balances.

Accounts payable	$ 37,500		Interest receivable	$ 300
Accumulated depreciation—			Interest revenue	1,200
equipment	33,400			
Cash	15,655		Merchandise inventory	71,800
Cost of goods sold	712,100		Note payable	45,000
Depreciation expense	8,350		Notes receivable	40,000
E. Martel, capital	90,850		Rent expense	20,000
E. Martel, drawings	75,800		Salaries expense	69,800
Equipment	83,500		Sales	916,700
Freight out	5,900		Sales discounts	4,625
Insurance expense	3,620		Sales returns and allowances	18,050
Interest expense	2,700		Unearned revenue	7,550

All adjustments have been recorded and posted except for the inventory adjustment. Merchandise inventory actually on hand at July 31, 2011, is $68,900.

Instructions

(a) Prepare the adjusting entry.
(b) Prepare a single-step income statement.
(c) Prepare a multiple-step income statement.
(d) Prepare the closing entries. Post to the Income Summary account. Check that the balance in the Income Summary account before closing it is equal to profit.

Taking It Further Compare the two income statements and comment on the usefulness of each one.

Prepare adjusting and closing entries and financial statements—perpetual system. Calculate ratios.
(SO 4, 5, 6) AP

P5–7A The unadjusted trial balance of World Enterprises for the year ending December 31, 2011, follows:

WORLD ENTERPRISES
Trial Balance
December 31, 2011

	Debit	Credit
Cash	$ 12,000	
Accounts receivable	19,200	
Merchandise inventory	27,050	
Supplies	2,940	
Land	30,000	
Building	150,000	
Accumulated depreciation—building		$ 24,000
Equipment	45,000	
Accumulated depreciation—equipment		18,000
Accounts payable		35,600
Unearned sales revenue		4,000
Mortgage payable		147,100
S. Kim, capital		46,415
S. Kim, drawings	25,170	
Sales		263,770
Sales returns and allowances	2,500	
Sales discounts	3,275	
Cost of goods sold	171,225	
Interest expense	9,975	
Salaries expense	35,450	
Utilities expense	5,100	
	$538,885	$538,885

Other data:

1. There is $750 of supplies on hand on December 31, 2011.
2. Depreciation expense for the year is $6,600 for the building and $4,500 for the equipment.
3. Accrued interest expense at December 31, 2011, is $1,000.
4. Unearned sales revenue of $975 is still unearned at December 31, 2011. On the sales that were earned, cost of goods sold was $2,000.
5. A physical count of merchandise inventory indicates $23,800 on hand on December 31, 2011.
6. Of the mortgage payable, $9,800 is to be paid in 2012.
7. Seok Kim invested $5,000 cash in the business on July 19, 2011.
8. Last year, the company had a current ratio of 1.45 to 1, acid-test ratio of 1.10 to 1, gross profit margin of 35%, and profit margin of 10%.

Instructions

(a) Prepare the adjusting journal entries assuming they are prepared annually.
(b) Prepare a multiple-step income statement, statement of owner's equity, and classified balance sheet.
(c) Prepare the closing entries.
(d) Calculate the current ratio, acid-test ratio, gross profit margin, and profit margin for 2011.

Taking It Further Compare the 2011 ratios with the 2010 ratios and comment on any trends in the company's liquidity and profitability.

P5–8A Magna International Inc. is a leading global supplier of technologically advanced automotive components, systems, and modules. Selected financial information (in U.S. millions) follows:

Calculate ratios and comment.
(SO 6) AN

	2008	2007	2006
Sales	$23,704	$26,067	$24,180
Cost of goods sold	20,982	22,599	21,211
Profit	71	663	528
Current assets	7,371	8,770	7,060
Current liabilities	5,093	5,658	4,783

Instructions

Calculate the gross profit margin, profit margin, and current ratio for each year.

Taking It Further Evaluate Magna International's performance over the three-year period.

*P5–9A Data for Travel Warehouse are presented in P5–3A.

Record inventory transactions—periodic system.
(SO 7) AP

Instructions

Record the July transactions for Travel Warehouse, assuming a periodic inventory system is used instead of a perpetual inventory system.

Taking It Further What are the costs and benefits for Travel Warehouse of using a perpetual, as opposed to a periodic, system?

*P5–10A Data for Norlan Company are presented in P5–4A.

Record inventory transactions—periodic system.
(SO 7) AP

Instructions

Record the September and October transactions for Norlan Company, assuming a periodic inventory system is used instead of a perpetual inventory system.

Taking It Further Why might a periodic system be better than a perpetual system for Norlan Company?

Record and post inventory
transactions—periodic
system. Prepare partial income
statement.
(SO 7) AP

*P5–11A   Data for Nisson Distributing Company are presented in P5–5A. A physical inventory count shows $4,952 of inventory on hand on April 30, 2011.

Instructions

(a) Record the transactions assuming Nisson uses a periodic inventory system.
(b) Set up general ledger accounts, enter all beginning balances, and post the transactions.
(c) Prepare a partial multiple-step income statement, up to gross profit, for the month of April 2011.

Taking It Further   Will gross profit be higher, lower, or the same amount, if using a periodic inventory system instead of a perpetual inventory system? Explain.

Prepare financial statements
and closing entries—periodic
system.
(SO 7) AP

*P5–12A   The following is an alphabetical list of Bud's Bakery's adjusted account balances at the end of the company's fiscal year on November 30, 2011:

Accounts payable	$ 32,310	Inventory, December 1, 2010	$ 34,360
Accounts receivable	13,770	Land	85,000
Accumulated depreciation—		Mortgage payable	106,000
building	61,200	Prepaid insurance	4,500
Accumulated depreciation—		Property tax expense	3,500
equipment	19,880	Purchases	634,700
Building	175,000	Purchase discounts	6,300
B. Hachey, capital	104,480	Purchase returns and allowances	13,315
B. Hachey, drawings	12,000	Rent revenue	2,800
Cash	8,500	Salaries expense	122,000
Depreciation expense	14,000	Salaries payable	8,500
Equipment	57,000	Sales	872,000
Freight in	5,060	Sales discounts	8,250
Freight out	8,200	Sales returns and allowances	9,845
Insurance expense	9,000	Unearned sales revenue	3,000
Interest expense	5,300	Utilities expense	19,800

Additional facts:

1. Bud's Bakery uses a periodic inventory system.
2. Of the mortgage payable, $8,500 is due in the next year.
3. A physical count determined that merchandise inventory on hand at November 30, 2011, was $37,350.

Instructions

(a) Prepare a multiple-step income statement, statement of owner's equity, and classified balance sheet.
(b) Prepare the closing journal entries.
(c) Post closing entries to the inventory and capital accounts. Check that the balances in these accounts are the same as the amounts on the balance sheet.

Taking It Further   If you had not been told that Bud's Bakery uses a periodic inventory system, how could you have determined that? What information is available in a periodic inventory system that is not available in a perpetual inventory system?

Problems: Set B

P5–1B Home Décor Company sells a variety of home decorating merchandise, including pictures, small furniture items, dishes, candles, and area rugs. The company uses a periodic inventory system and counts inventory once a year. Most customers use the option to purchase on account and many take more than a month to pay. The owner of Home Décor, Rebecca Sherstabetoff, has decided that the company needs a bank loan because the accounts payable need to be paid long before the accounts receivable are collected. The bank manager is willing to give Home Décor a loan but wants monthly financial statements.

Identify problems and recommend inventory system.
(SO 1) C

Rebecca has also noticed that, while some of her merchandise sells very quickly, other items do not. Sometimes she wonders just how long she has had some of those older items. She has also noticed that she regularly seems to run out of some merchandise. And she is wondering how she is going to find time to count the inventory every month so she can prepare the monthly financial statements for the bank. She has come to you for help.

Instructions

(a) Explain to Rebecca what an operating cycle is and why she is having problems paying her bills.
(b) Explain to Rebecca how her inventory system is contributing to her problems.

Taking It Further Make a recommendation about what inventory system she should use and why.

P5–2B At the beginning of the current golf season, on April 1, 2011, Swing-Town Golf Shop's inventory included 25 specialty hybrid golf clubs at a cost of $150 each. Swing-Town uses a perpetual inventory system. The following transactions occurred in April:

Record and post inventory transactions—perpetual system. Calculate net sales and gross profit.
(SO 2, 3) AP

Apr. 2 Purchased 100 additional clubs from Weir Inc. for $15,000, terms n/30.
      4 Received credit from Weir for the four returned damaged clubs purchased on April 2.
      5 Sold 18 clubs to Big Golf Practice Range for $250 each, terms n/30.
      6 Big Golf Practice Range returned eight of the clubs after determining it had purchased more clubs than it needed. Swing-Town gave Big Golf Practice Range a credit on its account and returned the clubs to inventory.
     10 Sold 30 clubs at $250 each to cash customers.
     12 Ten of these clubs were returned for cash. The customers claimed they never play golf and had no idea why they had been talked into purchasing the clubs. Refunded cash to these customers and returned the clubs to inventory.
     17 An additional 10 of the clubs sold on April 10 were returned because the clubs were damaged. The customers were refunded cash and the clubs were sent to a local Seniors' Club as a gift.
     25 Sold 40 clubs to Pro-Shop for $250 each, terms n/30.
     29 Pro-Shop returned 25 of the clubs after the golf pro had examined the clubs and determined that these clubs were of inferior quality. Swing-Town gave Pro-Shop a credit and decided to return the clubs to inventory with plans to sell them for the reduced price of $175 each.

Instructions

(a) Record the transactions for the month of April for Swing-Town Golf.
(b) Create T accounts for sales, sales returns, cost of goods sold, and merchandise inventory. Post the opening balance and April's transactions, and calculate the April 30 balances.
(c) Calculate net sales and gross profit.

Taking It Further   Swing-Town's owner thinks that it is a waste of time and effort for the bookkeeper to use a sales returns and allowances account and thinks that the bookkeeper should just reduce the sales account for any sales returns or allowances. Explain to Swing-Town's owner how he would benefit from using a sales returns and allowances account.

Record inventory transactions and post to inventory account—perpetual system.
(SO 2, 3) AP

P5–3B   Phantom Book Warehouse distributes hardcover books to retail stores and extends credit terms of n/30 to all of its customers. Phantom uses a perpetual inventory system and at the end of May had an inventory of 230 books purchased at $6 each. During the month of June, the following merchandise transactions occurred:

June 1   Purchased 170 books on account for $6 each from Reader's World Publishers, terms n/30, FOB destination.
   2   The correct company paid $85 freight on the June 1 purchase.
   3   Sold 190 books on account to Book Nook for $10 each.
   6   Received $60 credit for 10 books returned to Reader's World Publishers.
  18   Issued a $40 credit to Book Nook for the return of four damaged books. The books were determined to be no longer saleable and were destroyed.
  20   Purchased 140 books on account for $5.50 each from Reader's World Publishers, terms n/30, FOB shipping point.
  21   The correct company paid $70 freight for the July 20 purchase.
  27   Sold 100 books on account to Readers Bookstore for $10 each.
  28   Granted Readers Bookstore a $150 credit for 15 returned books. These books were restored to inventory.
  30   Paid Reader's World Publishers for the June 1 purchase.
  30   Received the balance owing from Book Nook.

Instructions

(a) Record the transactions for the month of June for Phantom Book Warehouse.
(b) Create a T account for merchandise inventory. Post the opening balance and June's transactions, and calculate the June 30 balance.
(c) Determine the number of books on hand at the end of the month and calculate the average cost per book of the inventory on hand at June 30.

Taking It Further   Explain how freight terms can affect the selling price, and the cost, of merchandise. Use the transactions on June 1 and 20 between Phantom Book Warehouse and Reader's World Publishers as part of your explanation.

Record inventory transactions—perpetual system.
(SO 2, 3) AP

P5–4B   Transactions follow for Leeland Company during October and November of the current year. Leeland uses a perpetual inventory system.

Oct. 2   Purchased merchandise on account from Gregory Company at a cost of $35,000, terms 2/10, n/30, FOB destination.
   4   The correct company paid freight charges of $900 to Rail Company for shipping the merchandise purchased on October 2.
   5   Returned damaged goods having a gross invoice cost of $6,000 to Gregory Company. Received a credit for this.
  11   Paid Gregory Company the balance owing for the October 2 purchase.
  17   Sold the remaining merchandise purchased from Gregory Company to Kurji Company for $62,500, terms 2/10, n/30, FOB shipping point.
  18   The correct company paid Intermodal Co. $800 freight costs for the October 17 sale.
  19   Issued Kurji Company a sales allowance of $2,500 because some of the goods did not meet Kurji's exact specifications.
  27   Received the balance owing from Kurji Company for the October 17 sale.
Nov. 1   Purchased merchandise on account from Romeo Company at a cost of $60,000, terms 1/15, n/30, FOB shipping point.

2 The correct company paid freight charges of $4,000.

5 Sold the merchandise purchased from Romeo Company to Barlow Company for $110,500, terms 2/10, n/30, FOB destination.

6 The correct company paid freight charges of $2,600.

7 Issued Barlow a credit of $7,000 for returned goods. These goods had cost Leeland $4,050 and were returned to inventory.

29 Received a cheque from Barlow Company for the balance owing on the November 5 sale.

30 Paid Romeo Company the amount owing on the November 1 purchase.

Instructions

Prepare journal entries to record the above transactions for Leeland Company.

Taking It Further Explain why companies should always take advantage of purchase discounts even if they have to borrow from the bank. Refer to the two purchases made by Leeland Company in your answer.

P5–5B Copple Hardware Store had the following merchandising transactions in May 2011. At the beginning of May, Copple's ledger showed Cash $10,000, Merchandise Inventory $5,000, and B. Copple, Capital, $15,000.

Record and post inventory transactions—perpetual system. Prepare partial income statement.

(SO 2, 3, 5) AP

May 1 Purchased merchandise from Lathrop Wholesale Supply Co. for $5,800, terms 1/10, n/30, FOB destination.

3 The correct company paid $200 cash for freight charges on the May 1 merchandise purchase.

4 Sold merchandise for $3,700, terms 1/10, n/30, FOB destination. The cost of the merchandise was $2,250.

5 The correct company paid $100 freight on the May 4 sale.

8 Purchased supplies for $900 cash.

9 Purchased merchandise from Harlow Distributors for $2,000, terms 1/10, n/30, FOB shipping point.

10 The correct company paid $300 freight on the May 9 purchase.

12 Received $200 credit from Harlow Distributors for returned merchandise.

14 Received the amount due from the customer billed on May 4.

19 Paid Harlow Distributors for the balance owing.

21 Sold merchandise for $2,600 cash. The merchandise sold had a cost of $1,590.

28 Made cash refunds to customers for returned merchandise, $100. The returned merchandise had a cost of $65 and was restored to inventory.

29 Received a $230 refund from a supplier for poor-quality merchandise purchased with cash.

31 Paid Lathrop Wholesale Supply for the balance owing.

31 Sold merchandise to Bower Company for $1,900, terms n/30, FOB shipping point. The cost of the merchandise sold was $1,150.

Instructions

(a) Record the transactions assuming Copple uses a perpetual inventory system.

(b) Set up general ledger accounts, enter the beginning cash, merchandise inventory, and capital balances, and post the transactions.

(c) Prepare a partial multiple-step income statement, up to gross profit, for May 2011.

Taking It Further Assume that on June 2 Bower Company returns all of the merchandise it had purchased on May 31 and is given a full refund. Should this affect the amount of gross profit reported in Copple's income statement for the month of May, as calculated in (c) above? Why or why not?

Prepare adjusting and closing entries, and single-step and multiple-step income statements—perpetual system.

(SO 4, 5) AP

P5–6B An alphabetical list of Mississauga Wholesale Centre's account balances at its fiscal year end, March 31, 2011, follows. All accounts have normal balances.

Accounts payable	$ 38,500	K. Martinson, drawings	$ 16,800
Accumulated depreciation—		Merchandise inventory	46,500
equipment	24,000		
Advertising expense	29,850	Notes payable	22,000
Cash	22,800	Notes receivable	25,000
Cost of goods sold	497,300	Rent expense	36,000
Depreciation expense	6,400	Rent revenue	3,450
Equipment	68,000	Salaries expense	136,630
Freight out	16,700	Sales	765,750
Insurance expense	3,500	Sales discounts	3,750
Interest expense	1,320	Sales returns and allowances	12,400
Interest revenue	1,750	Supplies expense	6,500
K. Martinson, capital	71,000	Unearned sales revenue	3,000

All adjustments have been recorded and posted except for the inventory adjustment. Merchandise inventory actually on hand at March 31, 2011, is $43,900.

Instructions

(a) Prepare the inventory adjusting entry.
(b) Prepare a single-step income statement.
(c) Prepare a multiple-step income statement.
(d) Prepare the closing entries. Post to the Income Summary account. Check that the balance in Income Summary before closing it is equal to profit.

Taking It Further Compare the two income statements and comment on the usefulness of each one.

Prepare adjusting and closing entries and financial statements—perpetual system. Calculate ratios.

(SO 4, 5, 6) AP

P5–7B The unadjusted trial balance of Global Enterprises for the year ending December 31, 2011, follows:

GLOBAL ENTERPRISES
Trial Balance
December 31, 2011

	Debit	Credit
Cash	$ 14,000	
Accounts receivable	15,700	
Short-term investments	17,000	
Merchandise inventory	37,500	
Supplies	1,650	
Furniture and equipment	26,800	
Accumulated depreciation—furniture and equipment		$ 10,720
Leasehold improvements	42,000	
Accumulated depreciation—leasehold improvements		8,400
Accounts payable		26,850
Unearned sales revenue		3,000
Note payable		35,000
I. Rochefort, capital		45,500
I. Rochefort, drawings	35,500	
Sales		238,500
Sales returns and allowances	4,520	
Sales discounts	4,600	
Cost of goods sold	129,200	
Insurance expense	1,800	
Rent expense	6,100	
Salaries expense	31,600	
	$367,970	$367,970

Other data:
1. There was $950 of supplies on hand on December 31, 2011.
2. Depreciation expense for the year is $5,360 on the furniture and equipment, and $4,200 on the leasehold improvements.
3. Accrued interest expense at December 31, 2011, is $1,200.
4. Accrued interest revenue at December 31, 2011, is $850.
5. Of the unearned sales revenue, $1,600 is still unearned at December 31, 2011. On the sales that were earned, the cost of goods sold was $525.
6. A physical count of merchandise inventory indicates $35,675 on hand on December 31, 2011.
7. Of the note payable, $5,000 is to be paid in 2012.
8. Ingrid Rochefort invested $7,500 cash in the business on May 21, 2011.
9. Last year, the company had a current ratio of 2.1 to 1, acid-test ratio of 1.1 to 1, gross profit margin of 40%, and profit margin of 25%.

Instructions

(a) Prepare the adjusting journal entries assuming they are prepared annually.
(b) Prepare a multiple-step income statement, statement of owner's equity, and classified balance sheet.
(c) Prepare the closing entries.
(d) Calculate the current ratio, acid-test ratio, gross profit margin, and profit margin for 2011.

Taking It Further Compare the 2011 ratios with the 2010 ratios and comment on any trends in the company's liquidity and profitability.

P5–8B The following information (in thousands) is for Danier Leather Inc.:

Calculate ratios and comment.
(SO 6) AN

	2008	2007	2006
Current assets	$ 49,853	$ 56,422	$ 48,623
Current liabilities	11,205	30,275	12,243
Net sales	163,550	158,099	148,351
Cost of goods sold	87,365	79,565	76,953
Profit	12,895	1,653	(5,503)

Instructions

Calculate the gross profit margin, profit margin, and current ratio for Danier Leather for 2008, 2007, and 2006.

Taking It Further Evaluate Danier Leather's performance over the three-year period.

*P5–9B Data for Phantom Book Warehouse are presented in P5–3B.

Record inventory transactions—periodic system.
(SO 7) AP

Instructions

Record the June transactions for Phantom Book Warehouse, assuming a periodic inventory system is used instead of a perpetual inventory system.

Taking It Further What are the costs and benefits for Phantom Book Warehouse of using a perpetual, as opposed to a periodic, system?

*P5–10B Data for Leeland Company are presented in P5–4B.

Record inventory transactions—periodic system.
(SO 7) AP

Instructions

Record the October and November transactions for Leeland Company, assuming a periodic inventory system is used instead of a perpetual inventory system.

Taking It Further Why might a periodic system be better than a perpetual system for Leeland Company?

Record and post inventory
transactions—periodic
system. Prepare partial income
statement.
(SO 7) AP

*P5–11B Data for Copple Hardware Store are presented in P5–5B. A physical inventory count shows the company has $7,727 of inventory on hand at May 31, 2011.

Instructions

(a) Record the transactions assuming Copple uses a periodic inventory system.

(b) Set up general ledger accounts, enter the beginning cash, merchandise inventory, and capital balances, and post the transactions.

(c) Prepare a partial multiple-step income statement, up to gross profit, for the month of May 2011.

Taking It Further   Will gross profit be higher, lower, or the same amount, if using a periodic inventory system instead of a perpetual inventory system? Explain.

Prepare financial statements
and closing entries—periodic
system.
(SO 7) AP

*P5–12B The following is an alphabetical list of Tse's Tater Tots' adjusted account balances at the end of the company's fiscal year on December 31, 2011:

Accounts payable	$ 86,300	Interest revenue	$ 1,050
Accounts receivable	44,200	Inventory, Jan. 1, 2011	40,500
Accumulated depreciation—			
building	51,800	Land	75,000
Accumulated depreciation—			
equipment	42,900	Mortgage payable	155,000
Building	190,000	Property tax expense	4,800
Cash	17,000	Purchases	441,600
Depreciation expense	23,400	Purchase discounts	8,830
Equipment	110,000	Purchase returns and allowances	20,070
Freight in	5,600	Salaries expense	127,500
Freight out	7,500	Salaries payable	3,500
H. Tse, capital	143,600	Sales	642,800
H. Tse, drawings	14,450	Sales discounts	12,700
Insurance expense	9,600	Sales returns and allowances	11,900
Interest expense	11,345	Unearned sales revenue	8,300
Interest payable	945	Utilities expense	18,000

Additional facts:

1. Tse's Tater Tots uses a periodic inventory system.

2. A physical inventory count determined that merchandise inventory on December 31, 2011, was $34,600.

3. Of the mortgage payable, $17,000 is to be paid during the next year.

Instructions

(a) Prepare a multiple-step income statement, a statement of owner's equity, and a classified balance sheet.

(b) Prepare the closing journal entries.

(c) Post the closing entries to the inventory and capital accounts. Check that the balances in these accounts are the same as the amounts on the balance sheet.

Taking It Further   If you had not been told that Tse's Tater Tots uses a periodic inventory system, how could you have determined that? What information is available in a periodic inventory system that is not available in a perpetual inventory system?

Continuing Cookie Chronicle

(*Note:* This is a continuation of the Cookie Chronicle from Chapters 1 through 4. From the information gathered in the previous chapters, follow the instructions below using the ledger account balances from Chapter 4.)

Because Natalie has had such a successful first few months, she is considering other opportunities to develop her business. One opportunity is the sale of fine European mixers. The owner of Kzinski Supply Co. has approached Natalie to become the exclusive Canadian distributor of these fine mixers. The current cost of a mixer is approximately $525 Canadian, and Natalie would sell each one for $1,050. Natalie comes to you for advice on how to account for these mixers. Each appliance has a serial number and can be easily identified.

Natalie asks you the following questions:

1. Would you consider these mixers to be inventory? Or should they be classified as supplies or equipment?
2. I've learned a little about keeping track of inventory using both the perpetual and the periodic systems of accounting for inventory. Which system do you think is better? Which one would you recommend for the type of inventory that I want to sell?
3. How often do I need to count inventory if I maintain it using the perpetual system? Do I need to count inventory at all?

In the end, Natalie decides to use the perpetual inventory system. The following transactions happen during the month of January 2011:

Jan. 4 Bought five deluxe mixers on account from Kzinski Supply Co. for $2,625, FOB shipping point, terms n/30.
6 Paid $100 freight on the January 4 purchase.
7 Returned one of the mixers to Kzinski because it was damaged during shipping. Kzinski issues Cookie Creations a credit note for the cost of the mixer plus $20 for the cost of freight that was paid on January 6 for one mixer.
8 Collected $875 of the accounts receivable from December 2009.
12 Three deluxe mixers are sold on account for $3,150, FOB destination, terms n/30.
14 Paid the $75 of delivery charges for the three mixers that were sold on January 12.
14 Bought four deluxe mixers on account from Kzinski Supply Co. for $2,100, FOB shipping point, terms n/30.
18 Natalie was concerned that there was not enough cash available to pay for all of the mixers purchased. She invested an additional $1,000 cash in Cookie Creations.
19 Paid $80 freight on the January 14 purchase.
20 Sold two deluxe mixers for $2,100 cash.
28 Natalie issued a cheque to her assistant for all the help the assistant has given her during the month. Her assistant worked 20 hours in January and was also paid the $56 owing at December 31, 2009. (Recall that Natalie's assistant earns $8 an hour.)
29 Paid a $145 cell phone bill ($75 for the December 2009 account payable and $70 for the month of January). (Recall that the cell phone is only used for business purposes.)
29 Paid Kzinski all amounts due.

As at January 31, 2011, the following adjusting entry data are available:

1. A count of baking supplies reveals that none were used in January.
2. Another month's worth of depreciation needs to be recorded on the baking equipment bought in November. (Recall that the baking equipment cost $1,400 and has a useful life of three years or 36 months.)

3. An additional month's worth of interest on her grandmother's loan needs to be accrued. (Recall Cookie Creations borrowed $2,000 and the interest rate is 3%.)

4. During the month, $100 of insurance has expired.

5. An analysis of the unearned revenue account reveals that no lessons have been taught this month because Natalie has been so busy selling mixers. As a result, there is no change to the unearned revenue account. Natalie hopes to book the outstanding lessons in February.

6. An inventory count of mixers at the end of January reveals that Natalie has three mixers remaining.

Instructions

Using the information from previous chapters and the new information above, do the following:

(a) Answer Natalie's questions.
(b) Prepare and post the January 2011 transactions.
(c) Prepare a trial balance.
(d) Prepare and post the adjusting journal entries required.
(e) Prepare an adjusted trial balance.
(f) Prepare a multiple-step income statement for the month ended January 31, 2011.
(g) Calculate gross profit margin and profit margin.
(h) Natalie is concerned that she had to invest more of her own cash during the month. Comment on the relationship between Cookie Creations' profitability and the balance in the company's cash account at month end.

Cumulative Coverage—Chapters 2 to 5

The Board Shop, owned by Andrew John, sells skateboards in the summer and snowboards in the winter. The shop has an August 31 fiscal year end and uses a perpetual inventory system. On August 1, 2011, the company had the following balances in its general ledger:

Cash	$ 19,985	A. John, drawings	$ 43,300
Inventory	112,700	Sales	758,500
Prepaid insurance	4,140	Rent revenue	1,200
Store equipment	53,800	Sales returns and allowances	11,420
Accumulated depreciation—		Cost of goods sold	520,340
store equipment	13,450	Salaries expense	92,900
Accounts payable	18,620	Rent expense	17,050
Unearned sales revenue	4,820	Advertising expense	9,625
Notes payable	36,000	Interest expense	1,980
A. John, capital	54,650		

During August, the last month of the fiscal year, the company had the following transactions:

Aug. 1   Paid $1,550 for August's rent.
   2   Paid $4,500 on account.
   4   Sold merchandise costing $8,500 for $12,250 cash.
   5   Purchased merchandise on account from Orange Line Co., FOB shipping point, for $24,500.
   5   Paid freight charges of $500 on merchandise purchased from Orange Line Co.
   8   Purchased store supplies on account for $345.
   9   Refunded a customer $425 cash for returned merchandise. The merchandise had cost $290 and was returned to inventory.
   10   Sold merchandise on account to Spider Company for $16,750, terms 2/10, n/30, FOB shipping point. The merchandise had a cost of $11,340.
   11   Paid Orange Line Co. for half of the merchandise purchased on August 5.
   12   Spider Company returned $750 of the merchandise it purchased. Board Shop issued Spider a credit memo. The merchandise had a cost of $510 and was returned to inventory.

15 Paid salaries, $4,200.

19 Spider Company paid the amount owing.

21 Purchased $9,900 of merchandise from Rainbow Option Co. on account, terms 2/10, n/30, FOB destination.

23 Returned $800 of the merchandise to Rainbow Option Co. and received a credit memo.

24 Received $525 cash in advance from customers for merchandise to be delivered in September.

29 Paid $1,200 for advertising.

30 Paid Rainbow Option Co. the amount owing.

31 Andrew John withdrew $3,800 cash.

Instructions

(a) Create a general ledger account for each of the above accounts and enter the August 1 balances.

(b) Record and post the August transactions.

(c) Prepare a trial balance at August 31.

(d) Record and post the following adjustments:

1. Four months of the 12-month insurance policy have expired.

2. The store equipment has an estimated eight-year useful life.

3. Of the notes payable, $6,000 must be paid on September 1 each year.

4. An analysis of the Unearned Sales Revenue account shows that $3,570 has been earned by August 31. A corresponding $2,430 for Cost of Goods Sold will also need to be recorded for these sales.

5. Interest accrued on the note payable to August 31 was $180.

6. A count of the merchandise inventory on August 31 shows $126,720 of inventory on hand.

(e) Prepare an adjusted trial balance at August 31.

(f) Prepare a multiple-step income statement, statement of owner's equity, and classified balance sheet.

(g) Record and post closing entries.

(h) Prepare a post-closing trial balance at August 31.

BROADENING YOUR PERSPECTIVE

Financial Reporting and Analysis

Financial Reporting Problem

BYP5–1 The financial statements for The Forzani Group Ltd. are reproduced in Appendix A at the end of this text.

Instructions

(a) Is The Forzani Group a service company or a merchandising company?

(b) Significant accounting policies are identified in Note 2 to the consolidated financial statements. In regard to Note 2 (b), does The Forzani Group recognize any volume rebates and/or supplier discounts? If yes, how are they recognized?

(c) Does The Forzani Group show the amount of sales returns? If yes, why do you think it does this?

(d) Does The Forzani Group use a single-step or multiple-step income statement format?

(e) Are any non-operating revenues and non-operating expenses included in The Forzani Group's income statement?

(f) Determine the following values:
1. Percentage change in revenue from 2008 to 2009
2. Percentage change in "operating earnings before undernoted items" from 2008 to 2009
3. Gross profit margin for each of the 2008 and 2009 fiscal years
4. Profit margin for each of the 2008 and 2009 fiscal years

(g) Based on the data in part (f) above, what conclusions can be drawn about Forzani's profitability in 2008 compared with 2009?

Interpreting Financial Statements

BYP5–2   Selected information from Big Rock Brewery Income Trust's income statements for three recent years follows (in thousands):

	2008	2007	2006
Net revenue	$37,633	$36,450	$38,700
Cost of goods sold	14,905	14,207	13,773
Operating expense	18,126	16,960	16,182
Interest expense	178	—	—
Income tax expense (recovery)	(531)	(169)	365

Instructions

(a) Calculate gross profit and profit for each of the three years.

(b) Calculate the percentage change in net revenue and profit from 2006 to 2008.

(c) Calculate the gross profit margin for each of the three years. Comment on any trend in this percentage.

(d) Calculate the profit margin for each of the three years. Comment on any trend in this percentage.

(e) How well has the company managed its operating expenses over the three-year period?

Critical Thinking

Collaborative Learning Activity

Note to instructor: Additional instructions and material for this group activity can be found on the Instructor Resource Site.

BYP5–3   In this group activity, you will journalize merchandising transactions.

The Academic Bookstore (the buyer) started its business on the first day of this month and purchased books from Evergreen Publishing (the seller). Each transaction between the two companies generates a journal entry in the books of each company.

Instructions

(a) Your instructor will divide the class into groups. Each group will split into two sub-groups: buyers and sellers.

(b) In your smaller groups, journalize the transactions given to you by your instructor. Record the entries once everyone is in agreement.

(c) Form a pair with a student from the other sub-group. Review the entries of the buyer and the seller with your partner and identify and understand the differences from the two points of view.

(d) You may be asked by your instructor to write a short quiz on this topic.

Communication Activity

BYP5–4 Consider the following events listed in chronological order:

1. Dexter Maersk decides to buy a custom-made snowboard and calls The Great Canadian Snowboard Company to inquire about its products.
2. Dexter asks The Great Canadian Snowboard Company to manufacture a custom board for him.
3. The company sends Dexter a purchase order to fill out, which he immediately completes, signs, and sends back with the required 25% down payment.
4. The Great Canadian Snowboard Company receives Dexter's purchase order and down payment, and begins working on the board.
5. The Great Canadian Snowboard Company has its fiscal year end. At this time, Dexter's board is 75% completed.
6. The company completes the snowboard for Dexter and notifies him that he can take the snowboard home.
7. Dexter picks up his snowboard from the company and takes it home.
8. Dexter tries the snowboard out and likes it so much that he carves his initials in it.
9. The Great Canadian Snowboard Company bills Dexter for the cost of the snowboard, less the 25% down payment.
10. The company receives partial payment from Dexter.
11. The company receives payment of the balance due from Dexter.

Instructions

In a memo to the president of The Great Canadian Snowboard Company, answer these questions:

(a) When should The Great Canadian Snowboard Company record the revenue and expense related to the snowboard? Refer to the revenue and expense recognition criteria in your answer.

(b) Suppose that, with his purchase order, Dexter was not required to make a down payment. Would that change your answer to part (a)?

Ethics Case

BYP5–5 Rita Pelzer was just hired as the assistant controller of Liu Stores. The company is a specialty chain store with nine retail stores concentrated in one metropolitan area. Among other things, the payment of all invoices is centralized in one of the departments Rita will manage. Her main responsibilities are to maintain the company's high credit rating by paying all bills when they are due and to take advantage of all cash discounts.

Jamie Caterino, the former assistant controller, who has now been promoted to controller, is training Rita in her new duties. He instructs Rita to continue the practice of preparing all cheques for the amount due less the discount and to date the cheques the last day of the discount period. "But," Jamie continues, "we always hold the cheques at least four days beyond the discount period before mailing them. That way we get another four days of interest on our money. Most of our creditors need our business and don't complain. And, if they scream about our missing the discount period, we blame it on Canada Post. I think everybody does it. By the way, welcome to our team!"

Instructions

(a) What are the ethical considerations in this case?
(b) Which stakeholders are harmed or benefited?
(c) Should Rita continue the practice started by Jamie? Does she have any choice?

"All About You" Activity

BYP5–6   In the "All About You" feature, you learned about inventory theft and a relatively new technology to help prevent theft. You have recently accepted a part-time sales position at a clothing store called College Fashions. The owner-manager of the store knows that you are enrolled in a business program and seeks your advice on preventing inventory shrinkage due to theft. The owner-manager is aware that the industry average shrinkage rates are 1.6% of revenues but does not know College Fashions' shrinkage rate.

Instructions

(a) Assume the store uses a perpetual inventory system. Explain to the owner-manager how she can determine the amount of inventory shrinkage.
(b) The owner-manager wants to know if she should implement touchscreen and barcode technology in the store. What would you want to know before making this technology expenditure?
(c) Assume that College Fashions' sales revenues are $400,000 and the shrinkage rate is 4%. What is the dollar amount that College Fashions loses due to shrinkage?
(d) Go to the Retail Council of Canada website at **http://www.retailcouncil.org** and search for the document "Chapter 10 – Loss Prevention."

  1. Identify the primary control factor in reducing shrinkage.
  2. Explain why great customer service is the best defence against shoplifting.
  3. Identify the other controls, procedures, and tools that will help to reduce customer shoplifting.
  4. The document states that "In the last 10 years, employee theft has almost equalled customer theft as the greatest cause of shrinkage." Identify the controls that will help reduce employee theft.

ANSWERS TO CHAPTER QUESTIONS

Answers to Accounting in Action Insight Questions

Across the Organization Insight, p. 249

Q: Why are retail managers concerned with sales dollars per square foot?
A: Sales dollars per square foot is a common measurement of efficiency for retail stores. Most retailer stores rent space from a landlord where the rent charges are based on the number of square feet in the store so it is very useful to also know the sales dollars per square foot. This also allows retail managers to compare different size stores, or different product lines to help determine sales mix, just at the Bay is doing.

Business Insight, p. 257

Q: What accounting information would help a manager decide what to do with returned goods?

A: The manager would need to know the potential revenues and expenses for each alternative. For example, returning goods to stock and selling them again may provide the highest revenue but the cost of getting the goods ready for resale may also be high. The revenue earned from liquidating the returned goods may be much lower but the cost of doing this may also be very low. The manager should compare the estimated profit --not just the revenue earned --of each alternative when deciding what to do.

All About You Insight, p. 259

Q: Are there advantages to you as a customer when retailers increase theft prevention measures?

A: Many customers see theft prevention measures, such as locked fitting rooms, or having a store employee track the items they are taking into a fitting room, as a very annoying personal inconvenience. But there are benefits to the customers as well as the stores. Retailers have to be able to pass all of their costs on to customers in order to remain in business. When inventory theft increases, the selling price will also have to increase or the store will not be profitable. If customers are not willing to pay the increased prices then the store may have to go out of business resulting in less choice for consumers, and fewer jobs. Inconveniences in using the fitting rooms may be a far smaller price to pay than the alternatives.

Answer to Forzani Review It Question 2, p. 269

Forzani's gross profit margin for 2008 is 35.94% ($478,401 ÷ $1,331,009). The company's gross profit margin weakened slightly in 2009, to 35.90% ($483,519 ÷ $1,346,758). Forzani's profit margin for 2008 is 3.57% ($47,451 ÷ $1,331,009). The profit margin weakened in 2009, to 2.18% ($29,325 ÷ $1,346,758). All dollar amounts are given in thousands.

Answers to Self-Study Questions

1. c   2. a   3. a   4. c   5. a   6. a   7. d   8. c   *9. b   *10. b

Remember to go back to the beginning of the chapter to check off your completed work!

←

CHAPTER 6
INVENTORY COSTING

sportchek.ca

✓ THE NAVIGATOR

☐ Understand *Concepts for Review*

☐ Read *Feature Story*

☐ Scan *Study Objectives*

☐ Read *Chapter Preview*

☐ Read text and answer *Before You Go On*

☐ Work *Demonstration Problem*

☐ Review *Summary of Study Objectives*

☐ Answer *Self-Study Questions*

☐ Complete assignments

CONCEPTS FOR REVIEW:

Before studying this chapter, you should understand or, if necessary, review:

a. The cost principle (Ch. 1, p. 9) and expense recognition criteria (Ch. 3, p. 120).

b. The difference between calculating cost of goods sold in a perpetual inventory system and in a periodic inventory system. (Ch. 5, pp. 255–258 and 272–273)

c. How to journalize inventory transactions in perpetual and periodic inventory systems. (Ch. 5, pp. 250–258 and 270–272)

d. How to prepare financial statements for a merchandising company. (Ch. 5, pp. 263–267)

Inventory Check: A Big Job for Sport Chek

Sport Chek is Forzani Group Ltd.'s superstore. It is the only national big box sporting goods retailer in Canada, providing a variety of sporting goods all under one roof. As of May 2009, there were 127 Sport Chek stores from coast to coast.

The inventory in each store is physically counted at least once a year. A third party, along with store staff, does the physical count to ensure an unbiased count. The company's external and internal auditors are also present during some counts. All counts are blind counts, meaning the counter does not know the number of items that have been recorded in inventory, and each item is scanned individually from the item ticket. Store staff also perform random spot checks of the third-party counts to ensure the accuracy and completeness of the count.

Goods in transit are not included in the inventory count; instead, Forzani's Portfolio Merchandise Management (PMM) System creates a file called a "freeze file" that includes a count of on-hand inventory only. The company compares this freeze file with the third-party count file, which is loaded into the system after count night.

Preliminary count results are provided to the store manager and store operations manager to review significant gains and losses. Once the store manager and store operations manager have signed off on the counts, the shrinkage results are posted to the stock ledger in the PMM System and the company's general ledger.

Inventory turnover is watched very closely on a store-by-store basis by the merchandising department, finance department, and senior management. Another key metric watched closely is sales per square foot, which is managed on a store basis and across the entire Sport Chek banner.

Although retail pricing may differ by province, depending on regional promotions, inventory costing is the same for the entire banner. The cost to purchase products from suppliers may also vary from season to season; however, since Forzani values inventory using the average cost formula, these cost changes are accounted for. And since Sport Chek doesn't sell specialized products to specific customers, but rather makes its goods available to any consumer visiting the store, the company can use the average cost formula for its entire inventory.

Like all Forzani stores, Sport Chek uses the perpetual inventory method to track inventory. When the Sport Chek warehouse receives a product, it uses the number of units received at the purchase order cost, together with the on-hand quantity recorded in the PMM System and its current average cost, to determine the new average cost.

Inventory is valued at the lower of cost and net realizable value. Cost includes invoice cost, duties, freight, and distribution costs. Net realizable value is defined as the expected selling price. Included within the cost of sales for a specific period are charges to inventory made throughout the year, including the disposal of obsolete and damaged products, inventory shrinkage, and markdowns to net realizable values.

The Navigator

STUDY OBJECTIVES:

After studying this chapter, you should be able to:

1. Describe the steps in determining inventory quantities.

2. Calculate cost of goods sold and ending inventory in a perpetual inventory system using the specific identification, FIFO, and average methods of cost determination.

3. Determine the financial statement effects of inventory cost determination methods and of inventory errors.

4. Demonstrate the presentation and analysis of inventory.

5. Calculate ending inventory and cost of goods sold in a periodic inventory system using FIFO and average inventory cost formulas (Appendix 6A).

6. Estimate ending inventory using the gross profit and retail inventory methods (Appendix 6B).

The Navigator

In the previous chapter, we discussed accounting for merchandise transactions. In this chapter, we first explain the procedures for determining inventory quantities. We then discuss the three methods for determining the cost of goods sold and the cost of inventory on hand: the specific identification method and the two cost formulas, FIFO and average. Next we see the effects of cost determination methods and inventory errors on a company's financial statements. We end by illustrating methods of reporting and analyzing inventory.

The chapter is organized as follows:

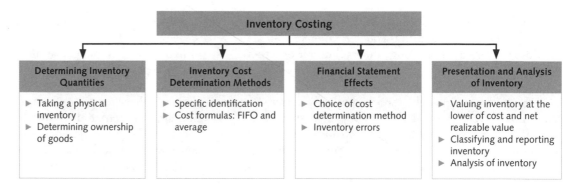

Determining Inventory Quantities

All companies need to count their entire inventory at least once a year, whether they are using a perpetual or periodic inventory system. This is called taking a physical inventory. Companies using a perpetual inventory system such as Sport Chek in our feature story, use this information to check the accuracy of their perpetual inventory records. Recall from Chapter 5 that in a perpetual inventory system the accounting records continuously—perpetually—show the amount of inventory that should be on hand, not necessarily the amount that actually is on hand. An adjusting entry is required if the physical inventory count does not match what was recorded in the general ledger.

In a periodic inventory system, inventory quantities are not continuously updated. Companies using a periodic inventory system must take a physical inventory to determine the amount on hand at the end of the accounting period. Once the ending inventory amount is known, this amount is then used to calculate the cost of goods sold for the period and to update the Merchandise Inventory account in the general ledger.

Inventory quantities are determined in two steps: (1) by taking a physical inventory of goods on hand, and (2) by determining the ownership of goods.

Taking a Physical Inventory

Taking a physical inventory involves actually counting, weighing, or measuring each kind of inventory on hand. Taking an inventory can be an enormous task for many companies, especially for retail stores such as Sport Chek, which has thousands of inventory items. An inventory count is generally more accurate when goods are not being sold or received during the counting. This is why companies often count their inventory when they are closed or when business is slow.

To make fewer errors in taking the inventory, a company should ensure that it has a good system of internal control. Internal control is the process designed and implemented by management to help their organization achieve reliable financial reporting, effective and efficient operations, and compliance with relevant laws and regulations. Some of the internal control procedures for counting inventory are as follows:

1. The counting should be done by employees who are not responsible for either custody of the inventory or keeping inventory records.
2. Each counter should establish that each inventory item actually exists, how many there are of it, and what condition each item is in. For example, does each box actually contain what it is supposed to contain?
3. There should be a second count by another employee or auditor. Counting should be done in teams of two.
4. Prenumbered inventory tags should be used to ensure that all inventory items are counted and that no items are counted more than once.

In our feature story we saw how Sport Chek incorporates many of these controls into its inventory count. We will learn more about internal controls in Chapter 7.

After the physical inventory is taken, the quantity of each kind of inventory item is listed on inventory summary sheets. To ensure accuracy, the listing should be verified by a second employee or an auditor. Unit costs are then applied to the quantities in order to determine the total cost of the inventory; this will be explained later in the chapter, when we discuss inventory costing.

Determining Ownership of Goods

When we take a physical inventory, we need to consider the ownership of goods. To determine ownership of the goods, two questions must be answered: Do all of the goods included in the count belong to the company? Does the company own any goods that were not included in the count?

Goods in Transit

A complication in determining ownership is goods in transit (on board a public carrier such as a railway, airline, truck, or ship) at the end of the accounting period. The problem is determining who should include the goods in its inventory: the purchaser or the seller.

Goods in transit should be included in the inventory of the company that has ownership (legal title) of the goods. We learned in Chapter 5 that ownership is determined by the terms of sale, as shown in Illustration 6-1 and described below:

← Illustration 6-1

Terms of sale

1. When the terms are FOB (free on board) shipping point, ownership (legal title) of the goods passes to the buyer when the public carrier accepts the goods from the seller.
2. When the terms are FOB destination, ownership (legal title) of the goods remains with the seller until the goods reach the buyer.

Inventory quantities may be seriously miscounted if goods in transit at the statement date are ignored. The company may have purchased goods that have not yet been received, or it may have sold goods that have not yet been delivered. For example, assume that Hill Company has 20,000 units of inventory in its warehouse on December 31. It also has the following goods in transit: (1) sales of 1,500 units shipped December 31, FOB destination, and (2) purchases of 2,500 units shipped FOB shipping point by the seller on December 31. Hill has legal title to both the units sold and the units purchased. If units in transit are ignored, inventory quantities would be understated by 4,000 units (1,500 + 2,500).

As we will see later in this chapter, inaccurate inventory quantities not only affect the inventory amount on the balance sheet, they also affect the cost of goods sold reported in the income statement.

Consigned Goods

In some lines of business, it is customary to hold goods belonging to other parties and to sell them, for a fee, without ever taking ownership of the goods. These are called **consigned goods**.

For example, artists often display their paintings and other works of art on consignment at galleries. In such cases, the art gallery (the consignee) does not take ownership of the art—it still belongs to the artist (the consignor). Therefore, if an inventory count is taken, any art on consignment should not be included in the art gallery's inventory.

When a consigned good sells, the consignee then takes a commission and pays the consignor the remainder. Many craft stores, second-hand clothing and sporting goods stores, and antique dealers sell goods on consignment to keep their inventory costs down and to avoid the risk of purchasing an item they will not be able to sell. Some manufacturers may also make consignment agreements with their suppliers in order to keep their inventory levels low.

Other Situations

Sometimes goods are not physically present at a company because they have been taken home *on approval* by a customer. Goods on approval should be added to the physical inventory count because they still belong to the seller. The customer will either return the item or decide to buy it.

In other cases, goods are sold but the seller is holding them for alteration, or until they are picked up or delivered to the customer. These goods should not be included in the physical count, because legal title to ownership has passed to the customer. Damaged or unsaleable goods should be separated from the physical count and any loss should be recorded.

ACCOUNTING IN ACTION: ALL ABOUT YOU INSIGHT

Downturns in the economy can cut a giant hole in the clothing budget. But luckily for you, there is an alternative to paying full price in an upscale boutique: the consignment store. During the recent economic downturn, sales in second-hand stores increased across Canada. And consignment shopping is no longer just for women. Although they've been slow to embrace used clothes, men are starting to try them on for size. Some of the shoppers at Off The Cuff in Toronto came in to sell their expensive designer suits from former jobs on Bay Street, but found themselves taking advantage of the great deals, such as a $6,000 leather jacket going for $600 and an overcoat with a list price of $2,300 for $800.

Still, sales at consignment stores in the United States haven't been as rosy. Since the financial meltdown in the fall of 2008, many have been hurt not only by people shopping less but because those who remain are taking advantage of discounts of up to 80 percent at the mall.

Source: Deirdre Kelly, "When the going gets tough, tough guys get thrifty," *The Globe and Mail*, June 25, 2009.
Anne Di'Innocenzio, "Resale shops are latest casualty of bad economy," *Associated Press*, April 9, 2009.

What is one disadvantage of buying items on consignment?

BEFORE YOU GO ON . . .

→ Review It

1. What are the steps for determining inventory quantities?
2. How is ownership determined for goods in transit?
3. Who has title to consigned goods?

→ Do It

Too Good to Be Threw Company completed its inventory count on June 30. It arrived at a total inventory value of $200,000, counting everything currently on hand in its warehouse. You have been given the information listed below. How will the following information affect the inventory count and cost?

1. Goods costing $15,000 that are being held on consignment for another company were included in the inventory.
2. Goods purchased for $10,000 and in transit at June 30 (terms FOB shipping point) and not included in the count.
3. Inventory sold for $18,000 that cost $12,000 when purchased and was in transit at June 30 (terms FOB destination) and not included in the count.

Action Plan

Apply the rules of ownership to goods held on consignment:

- Goods held on consignment for another company are not included in inventory.
- Goods held on consignment by another company are included in inventory.

Apply the rules of ownership to goods in transit:

- FOB shipping point: Goods sold or purchased and shipped FOB shipping point belong to the buyer when in transit.
- FOB destination: Goods sold or purchased and shipped FOB destination belong to the seller until they reach their destination.

Solution

1. The goods held on consignment for another company should be deducted from Too Good to Be Threw's inventory count.
2. The goods in transit on June 30 purchased FOB shipping point should be added to the company's inventory count.
3. The $12,000 of goods in transit on June 30 sold FOB destination should be added to the company's inventory count.

The correct inventory cost is $207,000 ($200,000 − $15,000 + $10,000 + $12,000), not $200,000 as originally calculated.

Related exercise material: BE6–1, BE6–2, E6–1, and E6–2.

The Navigator

Inventory Cost Determination Methods

The physical inventory count we described in the last section determines the quantities on hand, but does not determine their cost. Before comparing with the perpetual inventory records, costs will need to be assigned to the inventory items. Costs must also be assigned to inventory items, in a perpetual inventory system, when calculating the cost of goods sold each time a sale is recorded.

When all identical inventory items have been purchased at the same unit cost, the calculations are simple. However, when identical items have been purchased at different costs during the period, it is difficult to decide what the unit costs are of the items that have been sold and what the unit costs are of the items that remain in inventory.

In Chapter 5, you did not have this problem because you were either told the cost of goods sold, or it was assumed for simplicity that all identical inventory items had the same unit cost. In Chapter 6, we build on what you learned in Chapter 5. In this chapter, identical items will not be purchased for the same cost and you will have to determine the cost of the goods sold and the cost of the ending inventory.

In the next section, we will examine three methods of determining cost of goods sold and the cost of inventory. One method—specific identification—uses the actual physical flow of goods to determine cost. We will look at this method first.

STUDY OBJECTIVE 2

Calculate cost of goods sold and ending inventory in a perpetual inventory system using the specific identification, FIFO, and average methods of cost determination.

Tutorials:
Inventory Cost Determination Methods

Specific Identification

The **specific identification** method tracks the actual physical flow (movement) of the goods in a perpetual inventory system. Each item of inventory is marked, tagged, or coded with its specific unit cost so that, at any point in time, the cost of the goods sold and the cost of the ending inventory can be determined.

Assume, for example, that in December Fraser Valley Electronics buys three identical LCD HDTVs at costs of $700, $750, and $800. During the month, the two HDTVs costing $700 and $800 are sold at a selling price of $1,200 each. At December 31, the $750 LCD HDTV is still on hand. The cost of goods sold for the month is $1,500 ($700 + $800) and ending inventory is $750. It is possible to determine this when the physical flow of the specific items can be tracked.

Illustration 6-2 →

Specific identification

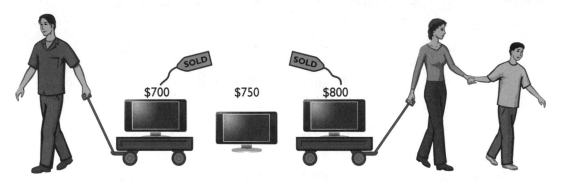

In theory, specific identification is the ideal method for determining cost. This method matches the actual cost of goods sold against sales revenue and reports ending inventory at actual cost. But this method is not practical in many situations. While bar coding is often used to identify an inventory item—such as the specific type of LCD HDTVs in Illustration 6-2—it is rare to use bar codes to identify whether the specific LCD HDTV sold was the one purchased for $700, $750, or $800.

Even if more advanced technology would allow companies to specifically identify each of the LCD HDTVs, the main problem with the specific identification method, in this situation, is that it may allow management to manipulate profit. For example, assume that Fraser Valley Electronics wants to maximize its profit just before year end. When selling one of the three LCD HDTVs referred to earlier, management could choose the TV with the lowest cost ($700) to match against revenues ($1,200). Or, it could minimize profit by selecting the TV with the highest cost ($800).

Therefore, Canadian and international accounting standards do not allow companies to use specific identification when goods are interchangeable as is the case in the LCD HDTV example. The standards also specify that if the goods are not ordinarily interchangeable or if the goods are produced for a specific purpose, then specific identification must be used. Sport Chek, in our feature, is an example of a company that cannot use specific identification because it doesn't sell specialized goods.

Automobiles are a good example of a type of inventory where specific identification is used. Automobiles can be individually identified by serial number. Also, each automobile often has slightly different characteristics, which means one automobile may not be interchangeable with another.

Cost Formulas: FIFO and Average

Because the specific identification method is only suitable for certain kinds of inventories, other methods of cost determination, known as cost formulas, are used. The two inventory cost formulas used in Canada and internationally are:

1. First-in, first-out (FIFO), where the cost of the first item purchased is considered to be the cost of the first item sold

2. Average, where the cost is determined using an average of the cost of the items purchased

FIFO and average are known as "cost formulas" because they assume a flow of costs that may not be the same as the actual physical flow of goods, unlike the specific identification method.

While specific identification is normally used only in a perpetual inventory system, FIFO and average can be used in both the perpetual and periodic inventory systems. Recall from Chapter 5 that the two systems differ in determining when the cost of goods sold is calculated and recorded.

Under a perpetual inventory system, the cost of goods sold is determined as each item is sold. Under a periodic inventory system, the cost of goods available for sale (beginning inventory plus the cost of goods purchased) is allocated to ending inventory and cost of goods sold at the end of the period. Recall that in a periodic system, the cost of goods sold is calculated by deducting the ending inventory from the cost of goods available for sale.

Canadian and international accounting standards allow the use of both the perpetual and the periodic inventory systems. However, the cost determination methods are limited to specific identification, FIFO, and average. Another method, last-in, first-out (LIFO), is used by about 10% of companies in the United States. As LIFO is not permitted in Canada or internationally, it is not discussed in this textbook.

Similar to the structure in Chapter 5, the perpetual inventory system will be used in this chapter to illustrate FIFO and average inventory formulas. Appendix 6A explains the use of FIFO and average inventory formulas under a periodic inventory system.

To illustrate the application of the FIFO and average cost formulas, we will assume that Fraser Valley Electronics has the information shown in Illustration 6-3 for one of its products, a Z202 Astro Condenser.

FRASER VALLEY ELECTRONICS Z202 Astro Condensers					
Date	Explanation	Units	Unit Cost	Total Cost	Total Units in Inventory
Jan. 1	Beginning inventory	100	$10	$ 1,000	100
Apr. 15	Purchase	200	11	2,200	300
May 1	Sales	150			150
Aug. 24	Purchase	300	12	3,600	450
Sept. 1	Sales	400			50
Nov. 27	Purchase	400	13	5,200	450
				$12,000	

Illustration 6-3

Inventory purchases, sales, and units on hand

Perpetual Inventory System—First-In, First-Out (FIFO)

The **first-in, first-out (FIFO) cost formula** assumes that the earliest (oldest) goods purchased are the first ones to be sold. This does not necessarily mean that the oldest units are in fact sold first; only that the cost of the oldest units is used first to calculate cost of goods sold. Although the cost formula chosen by a company does not have to match the actual physical movement of the inventory, it should correspond as closely as possible. FIFO often does match the actual physical flow of merchandise, because it generally is good business practice to sell the oldest units first.

We will use the information for Fraser Valley's Z202 Astro Condenser, in Illustration 6-3, to prepare a perpetual inventory schedule with the FIFO cost formula. Perpetual inventory schedules are organized to show how the cost of goods sold for each sale is calculated. They also show the cost and number of units of inventory on hand throughout the year.

A perpetual inventory schedule starts with the inventory on hand at the beginning of the year. Purchases and sales are then added to the schedule in chronological order. When using FIFO, the number of units at each different cost must be tracked.

Illustration 6-4 shows how to record the beginning inventory of 100 units costing $10 each and the April 15 purchase of 200 units costing $11 each. Notice that the $10 units are shown separately from the $11 units in the balance columns and that the total cost of $3,200 is equal to 100 units × $10/unit + 200 units × $11/unit.

Illustration 6-4 →

Perpetual inventory schedule—FIFO (Calculation as at April 15)

	PURCHASES			COST OF GOODS SOLD			BALANCE		
Date	Units	Cost	Total	Units	Cost	Total	Units	Cost	Total
Jan. 1							100	$10	$1,000
Apr. 15	200	$11	$2,200				100	10	} 3,200
							200	11	

The next transaction is the May 1 sale of 150 units. Remember that in a perpetual inventory system the cost of the goods sold is calculated every time a sale is made. Therefore, on May 1, we apply FIFO to determine if the 150 units that were sold cost $10, $11, or a mix of both amounts.

Under FIFO, the cost of the oldest goods on hand before the sale is allocated to the cost of goods sold. Accordingly, we start with the beginning inventory of 100 units costing $10 each. Since 150 units were sold on May 1, this means they sold the entire beginning inventory, and 50 of the $11 units. This leaves 150 (200 − 50) of the $11 units on hand after the sale is recorded. In Illustration 6-5, we have added this information to the perpetual inventory schedule started in Illustration 6-4.

Illustration 6-5 →

Perpetual inventory schedule—FIFO (Calculation as at May 1)

	PURCHASES			COST OF GOODS SOLD			BALANCE		
Date	Units	Cost	Total	Units	Cost	Total	Units	Cost	Total
Jan. 1							100	$10	$1,000
Apr. 15	200	$11	$2,200				100	10	} 3,200
							200	11	
May 1				100	$10	} $1,550			
				50	11		150	11	1,650

After additional purchases are made on August 24, the inventory on hand now consists of 150 units at $11 and 300 units at $12, which totals 450 units at $5,250, as shown in Illustration 6-6.

Illustration 6-6 →

Perpetual inventory schedule—FIFO (Calculation as at August 24)

	PURCHASES			COST OF GOODS SOLD			BALANCE		
Date	Units	Cost	Total	Units	Cost	Total	Units	Cost	Total
Jan. 1							100	$10	$1,000
Apr. 15	200	$11	$2,200				100	10	} 3,200
							200	11	
May 1				100	$10	} $1,550			
				50	11		150	11	1,650
Aug. 24	300	12	3,600				150	11	} 5,250
							300	12	

On September 1, when 400 units are sold, the cost of goods sold is assumed to consist of the remaining $11 units purchased on April 15 (150 units), and 250 of the $12 units purchased on August 24. This leaves 50 of the $12 units in inventory, or $600 in total.

After a purchase of 400 units on November 27, the inventory consists of 450 units, of which there are 50 of the $12 units from the August 24 purchase and 400 of the $13 units purchased on November 27. These two transactions are shown in Illustration 6-7, to complete the perpetual inventory schedule started in Illustration 6-4.

	PURCHASES			COST OF GOODS SOLD			BALANCE		
Date	Units	Cost	Total	Units	Cost	Total	Units	Cost	Total
Jan. 1							100	$10	$1,000
Apr. 15	200	$11	$2,200				100	10	} 3,200
							200	11	
May 1				100	$10	} $1,550			
				50	11		150	11	1,650
Aug. 24	300	12	3,600				150	11	} 5,250
							300	12	
Sept. 1				150	11	} 4,650			
				250	12		50	12	600
Nov. 27	400	13	5,200				50	12	} 5,800
							400	13	
	900		$11,000	550		$6,200			

← Illustration 6-7

Perpetual inventory schedule—FIFO (Calculation as at November 27)

Note that beginning inventory is $1,000, total purchases are $11,000, total cost of goods sold is $6,200, and ending inventory is $5,800. These numbers can be used to check the calculations in the perpetual inventory schedule. Remember that beginning inventory plus purchases minus cost of goods sold equals ending inventory. In this case we see that the schedule is balanced because $1,000 + $11,000 − $6,200 = $5,800.

Whether a perpetual or periodic inventory system is used, FIFO will always result in the same cost of goods sold and ending inventory amounts. Under both inventory systems, the first costs are the ones assigned to cost of goods sold regardless of when the sales actually happened. The periodic inventory system using the FIFO cost formula will be illustrated in Appendix 6A.

Perpetual Inventory System—Average

The **average cost formula** recognizes that it is not possible to measure a specific physical flow of inventory when the goods available for sale are homogeneous and non-distinguishable. It is used by a variety of companies including Sport Chek in our feature story. Under this cost formula, the allocation of the cost of goods available for sale is based on the weighted average unit cost. The formula of the **weighted average unit cost** is presented in Illustration 6-8.

Cost of Goods Available for Sale ÷ Total Units Available for Sale = Weighted Average Unit Cost

← Illustration 6-8

Calculation of weighted average unit cost

Note that the weighted average unit cost is **not** calculated by taking a simple average of the costs of each purchase. Rather, it is calculated by weighting the quantities purchased at each unit cost. This is done by dividing the cost of goods available for sale by the units available for sale at the date of each purchase.

We will again use the information for Fraser Valley's Z202 Astro Condenser, in Illustration 6-3, to prepare a perpetual inventory schedule with the average cost formula so you can compare the similarities and differences between the average and FIFO methods. In Illustration 6-9, notice that the beginning inventory of $1,000 and the April 15 purchase of $2,200 are combined to show a total cost of goods available for sale of $3,200. Using the formula in Illustration 6-8, the weighted average unit cost on April 15 is $10.67 ($3,200.00 ÷ 300).

	PURCHASES			COST OF GOODS SOLD			BALANCE		
Date	Units	Cost	Total	Units	Cost	Total	Units	Cost	Total
Jan. 1							100	$10.00	$1,00.00
Apr. 15	200	$11.00	$2,200.00				300	10.67	3,200.00

← Illustration 6-9

Perpetual inventory schedule—Average (Calculation as at April 15)

On May 1, the cost of goods sold is calculated using the $10.67 weighted average unit cost. The cost of the remaining 150 units of inventory on hand is also calculated using the same unit cost.

On August 24, when 300 units costing $12 each are purchased, it is necessary to calculate a new weighted average unit cost. After adding the total cost of the August 24 purchase to the May 1 ending balance, the total cost of the goods available for sale is $5,200 ($3,600.00 + $1,600.00). There are 450 total units available for sale, calculated by adding the 300 units purchased on August 24 to the 150 units in inventory. The new weighted average unit cost is $11.56 ($5,200 ÷ 450).

These two transactions have been added to the perpetual inventory schedule as shown in Illustration 6-10.

Illustration 6-10 ➔

Perpetual inventory schedule—Average (Calculation as at August 24)

Date		PURCHASES			COST OF GOODS SOLD			BALANCE		
Date	Units	Cost	Total	Units	Cost	Total	Units	Cost	Total
Jan. 1							100	$10.00	$1,000.00
Apr. 15	200	$11,00	$2,200.00				300	10.67	3,200.00
May 1				150	$10.67	$1,600.00	150	10.67	1,600.00
Aug. 24	300	12.00	3,600.00				450	11.56	5,200.00

Notice that the May 1 sale did not change the average unit cost. But the August 24 purchase did change the average unit cost. This pattern is repeated with the September 1 sale and the November 27 purchase. The cost of goods sold and ending inventory on September 1 are calculated using the $11.56 average unit cost calculated on August 24. On November 27, after purchasing 400 units at $13 each, a new weighted average unit cost of $12.84 is determined ($5,777.88 ÷ 450). The August 24 and November 27 transactions are shown in Illustration 6-11, to complete the perpetual inventory schedule started in Illustration 6-9.

Illustration 6-11 ➔

Perpetual inventory schedule—Average (Calculation as at November 27)

Date		PURCHASES			COST OF GOODS SOLD			BALANCE		
Date	Units	Cost	Total	Units	Cost	Total	Units	Cost	Total
Jan. 1							100	$10.00	$1,000.00
Apr. 15	200	$11.00	$2,200.00				300	10.67	3,200.00
May 1				150	$10.67	$1,600.00	150	10.67	1,600.00
Aug. 24	300	12.00	3,600.00				450	11.56	5,200.00
Sept. 1				400	11.56	4,622.22	50	11.56	577.78
Nov. 27	400	13.00	5,200.00				450	12.84	5,777.78
	900		$11,000.00	550		$6,222.22			

As with FIFO, it is important to check that beginning inventory + purchases − cost of goods sold = ending inventory. Once again we can see that the perpetual inventory schedule is balanced because $1,000.00 + $11,000.00 − $6,222.22 = $5,777.78.

🔍 ACCOUNTING IN ACTION: INTERNATIONAL INSIGHT

What happened to last-in, first-out (LIFO)? Until January 1, 2008, LIFO was permitted in Canada. Even though it was allowed, because it was not permitted for income tax purposes, few companies actually used it in Canada. The few that did were subsidiaries of U.S. companies, where the use of LIFO is permitted for income tax purposes.

Both international and Canadian standard setters have eliminated the use of the LIFO cost formula. The reasons were many, including the following: (1) assigning the oldest (earliest) costs to the ending inventory did not represent the physical inventory flows for most goods, and (2) because the oldest costs were assigned to ending inventory under LIFO, the cost of ending inventory did not provide a fair representation of the recent cost of inventories on hand.

What types of inventories are physically moved on a LIFO basis? Should companies that use this physical movement still be allowed to use LIFO for accounting purposes?

In practice, these average unit costs may be rounded to the nearest cent, or even to the nearest dollar. In the calculations in Illustrations 6-9 to 6-11, the exact unit cost amounts were used, along with a computerized schedule. But for presentation purposes, the unit costs have been rounded to the nearest two digits. However, it is important to remember that this is a method of allocating costs and not a method to track actual costs. Using four digits, or even cents, may suggest a false level of accuracy but it will reduce rounding errors in the perpetual inventory schedules.

In summary, this cost formula uses the average unit cost of the goods that are available for sale to determine the cost of goods sold and ending inventory. When a perpetual inventory system is used, an updated average unit cost is determined after each purchase. This amount is then used to record the cost of goods sold on subsequent sales until another purchase is made and a new average unit cost is calculated. Because the average unit cost changes with each purchase, this cost formula is sometimes called the moving average cost formula.

BEFORE YOU GO ON . . .

→ Review It

1. When must the specific identification method be used to determine the cost of goods sold and the cost of ending inventory?
2. What are the differences between the FIFO and average cost formulas?
3. Which method of cost determination does The Forzani Group Ltd. use? The answer to this question is at the end of the chapter.

→ Do It

The accounting records of Wynneck Sports Company show the following:

Date	Explanation	Units	Unit Cost	Total Cost
Mar. 1	Beginning inventory	4,000	$3	$12,000
10	Purchase	6,000	4	24,000
19	Sales	8,000		
22	Purchase	5,000	5	25,000
28	Sales	5,500		
				$61,000

Determine the cost of goods sold and ending inventory under a perpetual inventory system using the (a) FIFO and (b) average cost formulas.

Action Plan

- For FIFO, allocate the first costs to the cost of goods sold at the date of each sale. The latest costs will be allocated to the goods on hand (ending inventory).
- For average, determine the weighted average unit cost (cost of goods available for sale ÷ number of units available for sale) after each purchase. Multiply this cost by the number of units sold to determine the cost of goods sold and by the number of units on hand to determine the cost of the ending inventory.
- Prove that beginning inventory + purchases − cost of goods sold = ending inventory.

Solution

(a) FIFO—Perpetual

	PURCHASES			COST OF GOODS SOLD			BALANCE		
Date	Units	Cost	Total	Units	Cost	Total	Units	Cost	Total
Mar. 1							4,000	$3	$12,000
10	6,000	$4	$24,000				4,000 / 6,000	3 / 4 }	36,000
19				4,000 / 4,000	$3 / 4 }	$28,000	2,000	4	8,000
22	5,000	5	25,000				2,000 / 5,000	4 / 5 }	33,000
28				2,000 / 3,500	4 / 5 }	25,500	1,500	5	7,500
	11,000		$49,000	13,500		$53,500			

Check: $12,000 + $49,000 − $53,500 = $7,500

(b) Average—Perpetual

Date	PURCHASES			COST OF GOODS SOLD			BALANCE		
	Units	Cost	Total	Units	Cost	Total	Units	Cost	Total
Mar. 1							4,000	$3.00	$12,000
10	6,000	$4	$24,000				10,000	3.60	36,000
19				8,000	$3.60	$28,000	2,000	3.60	7,200
22	5,000	5	25,000				7,000	4.60	32,200
28				5,500	4.60	25,300	1,500	4.60	6,900
	11,000		$49,000	13,500		$54,100			

The Navigator

Check: $12,000 + $49,000 − $54,100 = $6,900

Related exercise material: BE6–3, BE6–4, BE6–5, BE6–6, BE6–7, E6–3, E6–4, and E6–5.

Financial Statement Effects

STUDY OBJECTIVE 3

Determine the financial statement effects of inventory cost determination methods and of inventory errors.

Inventory affects both the income statement and the balance sheet. The ending inventory is included as a current asset on the balance sheet and cost of goods sold is an expense on the income statement. Cost of goods sold will affect profit, which in turn will affect owner's equity on the balance sheet. Thus, the choice of cost determination method can have a significant impact on the financial statements.

Errors can also occur when a physical inventory is being taken or when the cost of the inventory is being determined. The effects of these errors on financial statements can be major. We will address these topics in the next two sections.

Choice of Cost Determination Method

If companies have goods that are not ordinarily interchangeable, or goods that have been produced for specific projects, they must use the specific identification method to determine the cost of their inventory. Otherwise, they must use either FIFO or average.

We learned in our feature story that Sport Chek uses average. How should a company such as Sport Chek choose between FIFO and average? It should consider the following objectives in determining the correct method:

1. Choose the method that corresponds as closely as possible to the physical flow of goods.
2. Report an inventory cost on the balance sheet that is close to the inventory's recent costs.
3. Use the same method for all inventories having a similar nature and use in the company.

After a company chooses a method of determining the cost of its inventory, this method should be used consistently from one period to the next. Consistency is what makes it possible to compare financial statements from one period to the next. Using FIFO in one year and average in the next year would make it difficult to compare the profits for the two years.

This is not to say that a company can never change from one method to another. However, a change in the method of cost determination can only occur if the physical flow of inventory changes and a different method would result in more relevant information in the financial statements. Such changes and their effect on profit should be disclosed in the financial statements. Where possible, companies must also go back and restate the prior years' financial statements using the new method. This respects the **full disclosure** requirement, in which all relevant information is to be disclosed. Full disclosure is discussed more in Chapter 11.

Income Statement Effects

To understand the impact of the FIFO and average cost formulas on the income statement, we will now compare the effects on Fraser Valley Electronics. The condensed income statements in Illustration 6-12 assume that Fraser Valley sold its 550 units for $11,500 and that its operating expenses were $2,000.

FRASER VALLEY ELECTRONICS Condensed Income Statements	FIFO	Average
Sales	$11,500	$11,500
Cost of goods sold	6,200	6,222
Gross profit	5,300	5,278
Operating expenses	2,000	2,000
Profit	$ 3,300	$ 3,278

← Illustration 6-12

Comparative effects of inventory cost formulas

The sales and the operating expense are the same under both FIFO and average. But the cost of goods sold amounts are different. This difference is the result of how the unit costs are allocated under each cost formula. Each dollar of difference in cost of goods sold results in a corresponding dollar difference in profit. For Fraser Valley, there is a $22 difference in cost of goods sold and in profit between FIFO and average.

In periods of changing prices, the choice of inventory cost formula can have a significant impact on profit. In a period of rising prices, as is the case here, FIFO produces a higher profit. This happens because the expenses matched against revenues are the lower unit costs of the first units purchased. As shown in Illustration 6-12, FIFO reports the higher profit ($3,300) and average the lower ($3,278).

If prices are falling, the results from the use of FIFO and average are reversed. FIFO will report the lower profit and average the higher. If prices are stable, both cost formulas will report the same results.

Compared with FIFO, average will result in more recent costs being reflected in cost of goods sold. This will better match current costs with current revenues and provide a better income statement valuation. But better matching is not critical in the choice of inventory cost determination methods. It is more important to use the cost formula that best approximates the physical flow of goods or represents recent costs on the balance sheet.

Balance Sheet Effects

One advantage of FIFO is that the costs allocated to ending inventory will approximate the inventory item's current (replacement) cost. For example, for Fraser Valley, 400 of the 450 units in the ending inventory are costed at the November 27 unit cost of $13. Since management needs to replace inventory after it is sold, a valuation that is closer to the replacement cost is helpful for decision-making.

By extension, a limitation of average is that in a period of inflation the costs allocated to inventory may be understated in terms of the current cost of the inventory. That is, the average cost formula results in older costs being included in inventory. This is true for Fraser Valley Electronics. The cost of the ending inventory includes the $10 unit cost of the beginning inventory. This understatement becomes even larger if the inventory includes goods that were purchased in one or more prior accounting periods.

Summary of Effects

The key differences that result from the three methods of determining cost during a period of rising prices are summarized in Illustration 6-13. The effects will be reversed if prices are falling. When prices are constant, the cost of goods sold and ending inventory will be the same for all three cost determination methods.

Income statement	Specific Identification	FIFO	Average
Cost of goods sold	Variable	Lower	Higher
Gross profit and profit	Variable	Higher	Lower
Balance sheet			
Cash flow	Same	Same	Same
Ending inventory	Variable	Higher	Lower
Owner's equity	Variable	Higher	Lower

← Illustration 6-13

A summary of the financial statement effects of cost determination methods and a comparison of FIFO and Average

We have seen that both inventory on the balance sheet and profit on the income statement are higher when FIFO is used in a period of rising prices. Do not confuse this with cash flow. All three methods of cost determination—specific identification, FIFO, and average—produce exactly the same cash flow. Sales and purchases are not affected by the methods of cost determination. The only thing that is affected is the allocation between ending inventory and cost of goods sold, which does not involve cash.

It is also worth remembering that all three cost determination methods will give exactly the same results over the life cycle of the business or its product. That is, the allocation between cost of goods sold and ending inventory may vary within a period, but will produce the same cumulative results over time. Although much has been written about the impact of the choice of inventory cost determination method on a variety of performance measures, in reality there is little real economic distinction among them *over time*.

Inventory Errors

Some inventory errors are caused by mistakes in counting or pricing the inventory. Other inventory errors are because of mistakes in recognizing the timing of the transfer of legal title for goods in transit. These mistakes result in three basic types of inventory errors:

1. Errors in determining beginning inventory
2. Errors in determining and recording the cost of goods purchased
3. Errors in determining ending inventory

These inventory errors can also cause an error in cost of goods sold. Recall that beginning inventory plus cost of goods purchased minus cost of goods sold must equal ending inventory. Therefore, if there is an error in any one of these four components, this will cause an error in another. This relationship is shown in the flow of costs through the Merchandise Inventory and Cost of Goods Sold T accounts below:

Merchandise Inventory		Cost of Goods Sold	
Beginning inventory			
Cost of goods purchased	Cost of goods sold	➔ Cost of goods sold	
Ending inventory			

Errors in cost of goods sold will affect the income statement, and errors in ending inventory will affect the balance sheet (both ending inventory and owner's capital). In the following sections, we will illustrate these effects.

Income Statement Effects

Cost of goods sold will be incorrect if there is an error in any one of beginning inventory, cost of goods purchased, or ending inventory, but the other two are correct. This can more easily be seen if we rearrange these components, as shown in the Merchandise Inventory account above, to: Beginning Inventory + Cost of Goods Purchased − Ending Inventory = Cost of Goods Sold.

The impact on cost of goods sold of an overstatement or understatement in one of beginning inventory, cost of goods purchased, or ending inventory can be shown by using the cost of goods sold formula in Illustration 6-14.

⬇ Illustration 6-14

Effects of inventory errors on cost of goods sold

Impact on Cost of Goods Sold	Error in Beginning Inventory		Error in Cost of Goods Purchased		Error in Ending Inventory	
Beginning Inventory	Overstated	Understated				
+ Cost of Goods Purchased			Overstated	Understated		
− Ending Inventory					Overstated	Understated
= Cost of Goods Sold	**Overstated**	**Understated**	**Overstated**	**Understated**	**Understated**	**Overstated**

Notice that if beginning inventory or cost of goods purchased is understated, cost of goods sold will be understated (assuming that there are no other offsetting errors). On the other hand, an understatement of ending inventory results in an overstatement of cost of goods sold, because ending inventory is deducted when determining cost of goods sold.

Note that these errors can occur in either a perpetual or a periodic inventory system and that regardless of which system is used, these types of errors have the same impact on cost of goods sold. But one of the major benefits of a perpetual inventory system is that these errors are much more likely to be caught and corrected before the financial statements are prepared. For example, if cost of goods purchased is overstated, this means that the Inventory account is overstated because it is debited when inventory is purchased. When the inventory is physically counted, the error will be noticed. The overstatement will be investigated and often the error in cost of goods purchased is found and corrected. But if the error in cost of goods purchased is not found, an adjustment will be made to the inventory account. Recall from chapter 5 that this adjustment will result in a debit to Cost of Goods Sold and a credit to Inventory. The result is ending inventory is correctly stated but cost of goods sold is overstated.

Once the impact of the error on cost of goods sold is determined, then we can determine the effect of this error on the income statement by using the income statement formula. These results are summarized below in Illustration 6-15. U stands for understatement, O for overstatement, and NE for no effect.

Nature of Error	Net Sales	–	Cost of Goods Sold	=	Gross Profit	–	Operating Expenses	=	Profit
Overstate beginning inventory	NE	–	O	=	U	–	NE	=	U
Understate beginning inventory	NE	–	U	=	O	–	NE	=	O
Overstate cost of goods purchased	NE	–	O	=	U	–	NE	=	U
Understate cost of goods purchased	NE	–	U	=	O	–	NE	=	O
Overstate ending inventory	NE	–	U	=	O	–	NE	=	O
Understate ending inventory	NE	–	O	=	U	–	NE	=	U

Illustration 6-15

Effects of inventory errors on income statement

Notice that an overstatement in cost of goods sold produces an understatement in gross profit and profit. An understatement in cost of goods sold produces an overstatement in gross profit and profit. This is because cost of goods sold is deducted from net sales when calculating gross profit.

Since the ending inventory of one period becomes the beginning inventory of the next period, an error in ending inventory of the current period will have a reverse effect on the profit of the next period. This is shown in Illustration 6-16. Note that the $3,000 understatement of ending inventory in 2010 will result in an overstatement of cost of goods sold and an understatement of profit. It also results in an understatement of beginning inventory in 2011, an understatement of cost of goods sold, and an overstatement of profit of the same amount.

	2010		2011	
	Incorrect	Correct	Incorrect	Correct
Sales	$80,000	$80,000	$90,000	$90,000
Cost of goods sold	48,000	45,000	57,000	60,000
Gross profit	32,000	35,000	33,000	30,000
Operating expenses	10,000	10,000	20,000	20,000
Profit	$22,000	$25,000	$13,000	$10,000

$(3,000)
Profit understated

$3,000
Profit overstated

The combined profit for two years is correct because the errors cancel each other out.

Illustration 6-16

Effects of inventory errors on income statements of two successive years

Over the two years, total profit is correct. The errors offset one another. Notice that total income using incorrect data is $35,000 ($22,000 + $13,000). This is the same as the total income of $35,000 ($25,000 + $10,000) using correct data. Nevertheless, the distortion of the year-by-year results can have a serious impact on financial analysis and management decisions.

Note that an error in the beginning inventory does not result in a corresponding error in the ending inventory. The accuracy of the ending inventory depends entirely on correctly taking and costing the inventory at the balance sheet date.

Balance Sheet Effects

The effects of inventory errors on the balance sheet can be determined by using the basic accounting equation: assets = liabilities + owner's equity. In the following table, U is for understatement, O is for overstatement, and NE is for no effect.

Nature of Error	Assets	=	Liabilities	+	Owner's Equity
Understate ending inventory	U	=	NE	+	U
Overstate ending inventory	O	=	NE	+	O

Errors in beginning inventory have no impact on the balance sheet if ending inventory is correctly calculated in the current period. Understating ending inventory (assuming there are no other offsetting errors) will understate profit. If profit is understated, then owner's equity will be understated, because profit is part of owner's equity.

The effect of an error in ending inventory on the next period was shown in Illustration 6-16. If the error is not corrected, total profit for the two periods would be correct. Thus, total assets and owner's equity reported on the balance sheet at the end of 2011 will also be correct.

Errors in the cost of goods purchased may also have an effect on the balance sheet. For example, if a company records a purchase of inventory on account in 2011, that should have been recorded in 2012, accounts payable will be overstated at December 31, 2011. And in this situation, owner's equity at December 31, 2011 will be understated because profit for 2011 is understated. Thus, the balance sheet will still balance even though it is incorrect.

Regardless of the nature of the error (and there are many possible combinations of errors), using the cost of goods sold, income statement, and balance sheet equations will help ensure that you catch the total effect of inventory errors.

BEFORE YOU GO ON . . .

→ Review It

1. Which inventory cost formula gives the higher profit in a period of rising prices? The higher balance sheet valuation? The higher cash flow?
2. What factors should management consider when it chooses a method of determining inventory cost?
3. How do inventory errors affect the income statement? The balance sheet?

→ Do It

On December 31, Silas Company counted and recorded $600,000 of inventory. This count did not include $90,000 of goods in transit, shipped to Silas on December 29, FOB shipping point. Silas recorded the purchase on January 3 when the goods were received. (a) Determine the correct December 31 inventory balance. (b) Identify any accounts that are in error, and state the amount and direction (i.e., overstatement or understatement) of the error.

Action Plan
- Use the cost of goods sold and income statement relationships to determine the impact of an error on the income statement.
- Use the accounting equation to determine the impact of an error on the balance sheet.

Solution

(a) The correct inventory count should have been $690,000 ($600,000 + $90,000).

(b) *Income statement accounts*: Because the purchase had not been recorded, the cost of goods purchased is understated (U) by $90,000. And because the inventory had not been included in the inventory count, the ending inventory is also understated. Thus, as shown below, the two errors cancel each other out, and the cost of goods sold and profit will be correct.

Beginning inventory	No effect
Plus: Cost of goods purchased	<u>U $90,000</u>
Cost of goods available for sale	U $90,000
Less: Ending inventory	<u>U $90,000</u>
Cost of goods sold	No effect because the errors cancel each other out

Balance sheet accounts: Merchandise Inventory and Accounts Payable are both understated (U) by $90,000. The accounting equation shows the impact:

Assets	=	Liabilities	+	Owner's equity
U $90,000	=	U $90,000	+	no effect

Related exercise material: BE6–8, BE6–9, BE6–10, BE6–11, E6–6, E6–7, and E6–8.

The Navigator

Presentation and Analysis of Inventory

Presenting inventory on the financial statements is important because inventory is usually the largest current asset (merchandise inventory) on the balance sheet and the largest expense (cost of goods sold) on the income statement. In addition, these reported numbers are critical for analyzing how well a company manages its inventory. In the next sections, we will discuss the presentation and analysis of inventory.

STUDY OBJECTIVE 4

Demonstrate the presentation and analysis of inventory.

Valuing Inventory at the Lower of Cost and Net Realizable Value

Before reporting inventory on the financial statements, we must first ensure that it is properly valued. The value of inventory items sometimes falls due to changes in technology or style. For example, suppose you manage a retail store that sells computers, and at the end of the year the computers' value has dropped almost 25%. Do you think inventory should be stated at cost, in accordance with the cost principle, or at its lower value?

As you probably reasoned, this situation requires an exception to following the cost basis of accounting. When the value of inventory is lower than its cost, the inventory is written down to its net realizable value at the end of the period. This is called the **lower of cost and net realizable value (LCNRV) rule**. **Net realizable value (NRV)** is the selling price less any costs required to make the goods ready for sale. Sport Chek uses expected selling price as its measure of net realizable value. This is common for retail companies because their goods are ready for sale without incurring any further costs.

The lower of cost or NRV rule is applied to the items in inventory at the end of the accounting period. To apply this rule, four steps are followed:

1. Determine the cost of the items in ending inventory using the appropriate cost determination method: specific identification, FIFO, or average.
2. Determine the net realizable value of the items in ending inventory.
3. Compare the values determined in steps 1 and 2.
4. Use the lower value to report inventory on the balance sheet.

To illustrate, assume that on March 31, 2010, Wacky World has the following lines of merchandise with costs and net realizable values as indicated. The lower of cost and NRV produces the following results:

	Cost	NRV	Lower of Cost and NRV
Television sets			
LCD	$ 60,000	$ 55,000	$ 55,000
Plasma	45,000	52,000	45,000
	105,000	107,000	100,000
Car video and audio equipment			
LCD media package	48,000	45,000	45,000
Global positioning system	15,000	14,000	14,000
	63,000	59,000	59,000
Total inventory	$168,000	$166,000	$159,000

This means Wacky World will report $159,000 for merchandise inventory on its balance sheet. The lower of cost and net realizable value rule is applied to individual inventory items, not total inventory. In some cases, it can be applied to groups of similar items. For instance, in the above example, all of the company's different types of LCD televisions were grouped together and we compared the cost of the LCD televisions with their total net realizable value.

If Wacky World uses a perpetual inventory system, the entry to adjust inventory from cost to net realizable value would be the following:

A   =   L   +   OE
-9,000   -9,000

Cash flows: no effect

Mar. 31	Cost of Goods Sold	9,000	
	Merchandise Inventory		9,000
	To record decline in inventory value from original cost of $168,000 to net realizable value of $159,000.		

Companies need to report this loss in value in the notes to the financial statements. Thus, some companies may choose to debit a separate expense account to make it easier to keep track of the amount. But since this loss is recorded in an adjusting journal entry, almost all companies are able to determine and report the amount without using a special account. Since almost all companies debit cost of goods sold when recording the decline in value, we will also follow that method in this textbook.

When there is clear evidence of an increase in net realizable value because of changed economic circumstances, the amount of the writedown is reversed. The evidence required for this reversal would generally be an increase in selling prices. If the item of inventory that had been previously written down has been sold, there is no need to record a reversal. If the item of inventory that was previously written down to net realizable value is still on hand, and the selling price has increased, then the reversal is recorded. The reversing entry will consist of a debit to merchandise inventory and a credit to cost of goods sold.

It is not usual for reversals to happen. Most companies will sell their inventory at a reduced price, instead of waiting for the price to recover. Thus, it is not that often that a company will still have the inventory on hand a year later, and the selling price will have increased. While reversals are relatively rare, the amount of any such reversal must be reported in the notes to the financial statements.

If there is a recovery in the value of the inventory, the write-up can never be larger than the original writedown. The lower of cost or net realizable value rule will still be applied to the inventory. This ensures that the inventory is never reported at an amount greater than its original cost.

Classifying and Reporting Inventory

How a company classifies its inventory depends on whether the company is a merchandiser or a manufacturer. A merchandiser *buys* its inventory. A manufacturer *produces* its inventory. In a merchandising company, inventory consists of many different items. Textbooks, paper, and pens, for example, are just a few of the inventory items on hand in a bookstore. These items have two common characteristics: (1) they are owned by the company, and (2) they are in a form ready for sale to customers. Only one inventory classification, merchandise inventory, is needed to describe the many different items that make up the total inventory.

In a manufacturing company, some goods may not yet be ready for sale. As a result, inventory is usually classified into three categories: raw materials, work in process, and finished goods. For example, Bombardier classifies the steel, fibreglass, upholstery material, and other components that are on hand waiting to be used in production as raw materials. Motorized consumer products such as Ski-Doos and Sea-Doos that are on the assembly line in various stages of production are classified as work in process. Ski-Doos and Sea-Doos that are completed and ready for sale are identified as finished goods.

As discussed in the previous section, inventory is reported on the balance sheet at the lower of cost or net realizable value. Inventory is typically recorded as a current asset because management expects to sell it within the next year. But if part of the inventory will not be sold for more than a year, this inventory should be reported as a non-current asset. For example, if inventory is being stockpiled because of concerns about future prices, then it may be appropriate to classify this inventory as a non-current asset.

In the notes to a company's financial statements, the following information should be included: (1) the major inventory classifications; (2) the cost determination method (specific identification, FIFO, or average); (3) the value of inventory reported at net realizable value; (4) the cost of goods sold; and (5) the amount of any writedown to net realizable value or reversals of previous writedowns, including the reason why the writedown was reversed.

Forzani reported inventory of $291,497 thousand under current assets in its 2009 balance sheet. It reported cost of sales (another term for cost of goods sold) of $863,239 thousand in its income statement. Note 2(b) to Forzani's financial statements, reproduced in Appendix A at the end of this textbook, discloses that inventory is valued at the lower of cost and net realizable value. Cost is determined using the average cost formula, as you saw when you answered the Review It question about Forzani earlier in the chapter. Forzani also reported that it made an adjustment to its beginning inventory because of new Canadian accounting standards for inventories that no longer permit companies to include storage costs in the cost of inventory. You will learn more about these types of adjustments later in this textbook.

It should be noted that Canadian accounting standards for inventories were changed effective January 1, 2008 to be the same as the International Financial Reporting Standards (IFRS) for inventories. The conversion to IFRS, and to Canadian GAAP for Private Enterprises, effective January 1, 2011, will not result in further changes in accounting for inventories. Accounting for inventory is the same under both sets of GAAP.

Analysis of Inventory

A delicate balance must be kept between having too little inventory and too much inventory. On one hand, management wants to have a variety and quantity of merchandise available so that customers will find a wide selection of items in stock. But having too much inventory on hand can cost the company money in storage costs, interest costs (on money tied up in inventory), and costs due to hi-tech goods becoming obsolete, or changing fashions. On the other hand, low inventory levels can result in stockouts, lost sales, and unhappy customers.

How quickly a company sells its inventory, or turns it over, is one way to determine whether the company has too much or too little inventory. We can also use this information to evaluate a company's liquidity, or its ability to pay obligations that are expected to come due in the next year. In Chapter 4, we introduced the current and acid-test ratios, which are also measures of liquidity. Inventory is a significant component of the current ratio and a high level of inventory will result in a high current ratio. But if the inventory is not turning over very quickly, this may be a problem. In this section, we add another liquidity ratio that is commonly used to evaluate inventory levels: the inventory turnover ratio. We also present a related measure: the average days to sell the inventory.

Inventory Turnover

The **inventory turnover** ratio measures the number of times, on average, inventory is sold (turned over) during the period. It is calculated by dividing the cost of goods sold by average inventory.

Whenever a ratio compares a balance sheet figure (e.g., inventory) with an income statement figure (e.g., cost of goods sold), the balance sheet figure must be averaged. Average balance sheet figures are determined by adding beginning and ending balances together and dividing by two. Averages are used to ensure that the balance sheet figures (which represent end-of-period amounts) cover the same period of time as the income statement figures (which represent amounts for the entire period). Illustration 6-17 shows the formula for calculating the inventory turnover ratio for The Forzani Group Ltd. for fiscal 2009 (dollars in thousands).

Illustration 6-17 ➡

Inventory turnover

Cost of Goods Sold	÷	Average Inventory	=	Inventory Turnover
$863,239	÷	$\dfrac{\$291,497 + \$319,445}{2}$	=	2.8 times

Generally, the more times that inventory turns over each year, the more efficiently sales are being made.

Days Sales in Inventory

The inventory turnover ratio is complemented by the **days sales in inventory** ratio. It converts the inventory turnover ratio into a measure of the average age of the inventory on hand. This ratio is calculated by dividing 365 days by the inventory turnover ratio, as in Illustration 6-18.

Illustration 6-18 ➡

Days sales in inventory

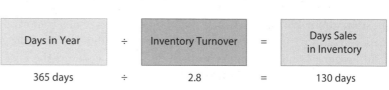

Days in Year	÷	Inventory Turnover	=	Days Sales in Inventory
365 days	÷	2.8	=	130 days

This means that Forzani's inventory, on average, is in stock for 130 days. This ratio must be interpreted carefully: it should be compared with the company's ratio in previous years, and with the industry average. However, you must recognize that this average will be different for each type of inventory item (e.g., sneakers vs. bicycles). What we see here is a total average only.

We learned in our feature story that Forzani also monitors sales per square foot for each Sport Chek store. This type of information cannot be calculated from the financial statements and so is not illustrated in this textbook. It is an example of the type of information that is available to internal users of financial information, but not external users.

ACCOUNTING IN ACTION: ACROSS THE ORGANIZATION

Let's talk inventory—BIG inventory. The world's largest dump truck, the Caterpillar 797B, is as tall as a three-storey building and has a 380-tonne capacity. Manufactured by Illinois-based Caterpillar Inc., the Cat 797B costs millions of dollars and requires one heck of a big garage for storage. Obviously, Caterpillar needs to avoid having too much of this kind of inventory sitting around tying up its resources. Conversely, it has to have enough inventory to meet customers' demands. Part of Caterpillar's success is its effective inventory management. Over a 10-year period, Caterpillar's sales increased by more than 97%, while its inventory increased by only 49%. Items spent an average 76 days in inventory instead of 87. To achieve this reduction in the amount of resources tied up in inventory, Caterpillar vastly improved its distribution system. It can now ship products to job sites in nearly 200 countries in less than 24 hours more than 99.7% of the time. In fact, Caterpillar is so well known for its parts distribution expertise, it formed a wholly owned subsidiary—Caterpillar Logistics Services—to market integrated supply chain solutions to other companies.

Source: "How Many Dump Trucks Did You Want?" Kimmel et al. *Financial Accounting: Tools of Business Decision Making.* Toronto: John Wiley & Sons Canada Ltd., 2009. p. 280.

How can an efficient distribution system reduce expenses by reducing the number of days sales in inventory?

BEFORE YOU GO ON . . .

→ Review It

1. When should inventory be reported at an amount different from cost?
2. What inventory information should be disclosed in the financial statements?
3. How can you tell if a company has too much or too little inventory on hand?

→ Do It

Westwood Hockey Company uses a perpetual inventory system and has the following items in its inventory at December 31, 2011:

Product	Quantity	Per Unit Cost	Per Unit Net Realizable Value
Jerseys	95	$50	$45
Socks	155	5	6

(a) What amount for inventory should Westwood Hockey Company report on its balance sheet?
(b) Record any necessary adjustments.

Action Plan
- Calculate the cost of the inventory.
- Calculate the net realizable value of the inventory.
- For each inventory item, determine which number is lower—cost or net realizable value.
- Record a journal entry to adjust the inventory account to net realizable value if required.

Solution

(a)

	Cost		Net Realizable Value		Lower of Cost and Net Realizable Value
Jerseys	(95 × $50)	$4,750	(95 × $45)	$4,275	$4,275
Socks	(155 × $5)	775	(155 × $6)	930	775
Total inventory		$5,525		$5,205	$5,050

(b)

Dec. 31	Cost of Goods Sold ($5,525 − $5,050)	475	
	Merchandise Inventory		475
	To record decline in inventory value from its cost of $5,525 to net realizable value of $5,050.		

Related exercise material: BE6–12, BE6–13, BE6–14, E6–9, and E6–10.

The Navigator

APPENDIX 6A ▶ INVENTORY COST FORMULAS IN PERIODIC SYSTEMS

STUDY OBJECTIVE 5

Calculate ending inventory and cost of goods sold in a periodic inventory system using FIFO and average inventory cost formulas.

Both of the inventory cost formulas described in the chapter for a perpetual inventory system can be used in a periodic inventory system. To show how to use FIFO and average in a periodic system, we will use the data below for Fraser Valley Electronics' Astro Condensers.

FRASER VALLEY ELECTRONICS Z202 Astro Condensers				
Date	Explanation	Units	Unit Cost	Total Cost
Jan. 1	Beginning inventory	100	$10	$ 1,000
Apr. 15	Purchase	200	11	2,200
Aug. 24	Purchase	300	12	3,600
Nov. 27	Purchase	400	13	5,200
Total		1,000		$12,000

These data are the same as those shown earlier in the chapter, except that the sales information has been omitted. In the periodic inventory system, we don't keep track of the number or cost of units sold during the year. Instead we wait until the end of the period to allocate the cost of goods available for sale to ending inventory and cost of goods sold.

Fraser Valley Electronics had a total of 1,000 units available for sale during the year. The total cost of these units was $12,000. A physical inventory count at the end of the year determined that 450 units remained on hand. Using these data, Illustration 6A-1 shows the formula for calculating cost of goods sold that we first learned in Chapter 5.

Illustration 6A-1 →

Formula for cost of goods sold

Beginning Inventory	+	Cost of Goods Purchased	=	Cost of Goods Available for Sale	−	Ending Inventory	=	Cost of Goods Sold
100 units $1,000	+	900 units $11,000	=	1,000 units $12,000	−	450 units ?	=	550 units ?

If we apply this formula to the unit numbers, we can determine that 550 units must have been sold during the year. The total cost (or "pool of costs") of the 1,000 units available for sale was $12,000. We will demonstrate the allocation of this pool of costs using FIFO and average in the next sections. In a periodic system, the cost formulas are applied to the ending inventory, which is then deducted from the cost of goods available for sale to calculate the cost of goods sold.

Periodic System—First-In, First-Out (FIFO)

Similar to perpetual FIFO, the cost of the oldest goods on hand is allocated to the cost of goods sold. This means that the cost of the most recent purchases is assumed to remain in ending inventory. The allocation of the cost of goods available for sale at Fraser Valley Electronics under FIFO is shown in Illustration 6A-2.

Illustration 6A-2 →

Periodic system—FIFO

COST OF GOODS AVAILABLE FOR SALE				
Date	Explanation	Units	Unit Cost	Total Cost
Jan. 1	Beginning inventory	100	$10	$ 1,000
Apr. 15	Purchase	200	11	2,200
Aug. 24	Purchase	300	12	3,600
Nov. 27	Purchase	400	13	5,200
	Total	1,000		$12,000

Step 1: Ending Inventory				Step 2: Cost of Goods Sold	
Date	Units	Unit Cost	Total Cost		
Nov. 27	400	$13	$5,200	Cost of goods available for sale	$12,000
Aug. 24	50	12	600	Less: Ending inventory	5,800
Total	450		$5,800	Cost of goods sold	$ 6,200

◄ Illustration 6A-2 (cont.)

Periodic system—FIFO

The cost of the ending inventory is determined by taking the unit cost of the most recent purchase and working backward until all units of inventory have been costed. In this example, the 450 units of ending inventory must be costed using the November 27 and August 24 purchase costs. The last purchase was 400 units at $13 on November 27. The remaining 50 units (450 – 400) are costed at the price of the second most recent purchase, $12 on August 24.

Once the cost of the ending inventory is determined, the cost of goods sold is calculated by subtracting the cost of the ending inventory (the cost of the goods not sold) from the cost of the goods available for sale (the pool of costs).

The cost of goods sold can also be separately calculated or proven as shown below. To determine the cost of goods sold using FIFO, simply start at the first item of beginning inventory and count forward until the total number of units sold (550) is reached. Note that of the 300 units purchased on August 24, only 250 units are assumed to be sold. This agrees with our calculation of ending inventory, where 50 of these units were assumed to be unsold and included in our ending inventory.

Date	Units	Unit Cost	Cost of Goods Sold
Jan. 1	100	$10	$1,000
Apr. 15	200	11	2,200
Aug. 24	250	12	3,000
Total	550		$6,200

Because of the potential for calculation errors, we recommend that you calculate the cost of goods sold both ways in your assignments. It is also helpful to check that the total of the cost of goods sold and ending inventory is equal to the cost of goods available for sale ($6,200 + $5,800 = $12,000).

Periodic System—Average

The weighted average unit cost is calculated in the same manner as we calculated it in a perpetual inventory system: by dividing the cost of the goods available for sale by the units available for sale. The key difference between this calculation in a periodic system and in a perpetual system is that this calculation is done after every purchase in a perpetual system. In a periodic system, it is done only at the end of the period, as shown in Illustration 6A-3.

◄ Illustration 6A-3

Calculation of weighted average unit cost

The weighted average unit cost, $12 in this case, is then applied to the units on hand to determine the cost of the ending inventory. The allocation of the cost of goods available for sale at Fraser Valley Electronics using the average cost formula is shown in Illustration 6A-4.

COST OF GOODS AVAILABLE FOR SALE				
Date	Explanation	Units	Unit Cost	Total Cost
Jan. 1	Beginning inventory	100	$10	$ 1,000
Apr. 15	Purchase	200	11	2,200
Aug. 24	Purchase	300	12	3,600
Nov. 27	Purchase	400	13	5,200
	Total	1,000		$12,000

Step 1: Ending Inventory	Step 2: Cost of Goods Sold
Calculate unit cost: $12,000 ÷ 1,000 = $12 Units × Unit Cost = Total Cost 450 $12 $5,400	Cost of goods available for sale $12,000 Less: Ending inventory 5,400 Cost of goods sold $ 6,600

We can prove our calculation of the cost of goods sold under the average cost formula by multiplying the units sold by the weighted average unit cost (550 × $12 = $6,600). And, again, we can prove our calculations by ensuring that the total of the ending inventory and the cost of goods sold equals the cost of goods available for sale ($5,400 + $6,600 = $12,000).

The results of applying the average cost formula under the periodic inventory system should be compared with Illustration 6-11 shown earlier in the chapter, which represents the results of applying the average cost formula under a perpetual inventory system. Notice that under a periodic inventory system, the ending inventory of $5,400 and the cost of goods sold of $6,600 are **not** the same as the values calculated under a perpetual inventory system even though the average cost formula was used for both systems. This is because in a perpetual inventory system, a new (moving) average is calculated with each purchase; in a periodic inventory system, the same weighted average is used to calculate the cost of goods sold for all the units sold during the period.

BEFORE YOU GO ON . . .

→ **Do It**

The accounting records of Cookie Cutters Company show the following data:

Beginning inventory	4,000 units at $3
Purchases	6,000 units at $4
Sales	8,000 units at $8

Determine the cost of goods sold and ending inventory under a periodic inventory system using (a) FIFO, and (b) average.

Action Plan
- Ignore the selling price in allocating cost.
- Calculate the number of units available for sale, the cost of goods available for sale, and the ending inventory in units.
- Determine the cost of ending inventory first. Calculate cost of goods sold by subtracting ending inventory from the cost of goods available for sale.
- For FIFO, allocate the latest costs to the goods on hand. (The first costs will be allocated to the cost of goods sold.)
- For average, determine the weighted average unit cost (cost of goods available for sale ÷ number of units available for sale). Multiply this cost by the number of units on hand.
- Prove your work: Calculate the cost of goods sold separately and then check that ending inventory + cost of goods sold = cost of goods available for sale.

Solution

Total units available for sale = 4,000 + 6,000 = 10,000

Cost of goods available for sale = (4,000 × $3) + (6,000 × $4) = $36,000

Ending inventory = 4,000 + 6,000 − 8,000 = 2,000 units

   (a) FIFO ending inventory: 2,000 × $4 = $8,000

      FIFO cost of goods sold: $36,000 − $8,000 = $28,000

      Cost of goods sold (COGS) proof: (4,000 × $3) + (4,000 × $4) = $28,000

      Check: $28,000 + $8,000 = $36,000

   (b) Weighted average unit cost: $36,000 ÷ 10,000 = $3.60

      Average ending inventory: 2,000 × $3.60 = $7,200

      Average cost of goods sold: $36,000 − $7,200 = $28,800

      COGS proof: 8,000 × $3.60 = $28,800

      Check: $28,800 + $7,200 = $36,000

Related exercise material: BE6–15, BE6–16, E6–11, E6–12, E6–13, and E6–14.

The Navigator

APPENDIX 6B ▶ ESTIMATING INVENTORIES

When a company uses a periodic inventory system, it must be able to do a physical count of its inventory in order to determine the cost of its ending inventory and the cost of goods sold. But what if a company cannot do a physical count? It may be impractical or impossible to count the inventory. Fortunately, it is possible to do an estimate.

STUDY OBJECTIVE 6

Estimate ending inventory using the gross profit and retail inventory methods.

There are two reasons for sometimes needing to estimate inventories. First, management may want monthly or quarterly financial statements but does not have the time for, or want the expense of, doing a physical inventory count every month or quarter. Second, a casualty such as a fire or flood may make it impossible to take a physical inventory.

Companies that use a perpetual inventory system are less likely to need inventory estimates since the perpetual inventory system keeps detailed inventory records continuously. Inventory estimates are usually associated with the periodic system.

There are two widely used methods of estimating inventories: (1) the gross profit method, and (2) the retail inventory method.

Gross Profit Method

The **gross profit method** estimates the cost of ending inventory by applying the gross profit margin to net sales. It is commonly used to prepare interim (e.g., monthly) financial statements in a periodic inventory system. This method is relatively simple but effective.

To use this method, a company needs to know its net sales, cost of goods available for sale (beginning inventory + cost of goods purchased), and gross profit margin. Gross profit for the period is estimated by multiplying net sales by the gross profit margin. The estimated gross profit is then used to calculate the estimated cost of goods sold and the estimated ending inventory.

The formulas for using the gross profit method are given in Illustration 6B-1.

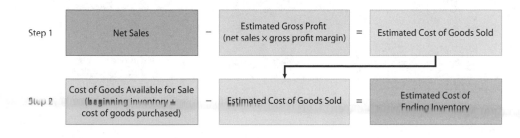

◀ **Illustration 6B-1**

Gross profit method formulas

To illustrate, assume that Lalonde Company wants to prepare an income statement for the month of January. Its records show net sales of $200,000, beginning inventory of $40,000, and cost of goods purchased of $120,000. In the preceding year, the company had a 30% gross profit margin. It expects to earn the same margin this year. Given these facts and assumptions, Lalonde can calculate the estimated cost of the ending inventory at January 31 under the gross profit method as follows:

Step 1:	Net sales	$200,000
	Less: Estimated gross profit ($200,000 × 30%)	60,000
	Estimated cost of goods sold	$140,000
Step 2:	Beginning inventory	$ 40,000
	Cost of goods purchased	120,000
	Cost of goods available for sale	160,000
	Less: Estimated cost of goods sold	140,000
	Estimated cost of ending inventory	$ 20,000

The gross profit method is based on the assumption that the gross profit margin will remain constant from one year to the next. But it may not remain constant, because of a change in merchandising policies or in market conditions. In such cases, the margin should be adjusted to reflect the current operating conditions. In some cases, a better estimate can be had by applying this method to a department or product line as a whole.

The gross profit method should not be used in preparing a company's financial statements at the end of the year. These statements should be based on a physical inventory count. Accountants and managers often use the gross profit method to test the reasonableness of the ending inventory amount, however.

Retail Inventory Method

Helpful hint In determining inventory at retail, selling prices on the unit are used. Tracing actual unit costs to invoices is unnecessary.

A retail store, such as The Forzani Group's Sport Chek, has thousands of types of merchandise. In such cases, determining the cost of each type of merchandise can be difficult and time-consuming if the company has used a periodic inventory system. For these retail companies, it can be easier to calculate the selling price, or retail price of the total inventory, than to look at the purchase invoices to find the cost of each individual inventory item. Most retail businesses can establish a relationship between cost and selling price—called the cost-to-retail percentage or ratio. The cost-to-retail percentage is then applied to the ending inventory at retail prices to determine the estimated cost of the inventory. This is called the **retail inventory method** of estimating the cost of inventory.

To use the retail inventory method, a company's records must show both the cost and the retail value of the goods available for sale. The formulas for using the retail inventory method are given in Illustration 6B-2.

Illustration 6B-2 ➔

Retail inventory method formulas

The logic of the retail method can be demonstrated by using unit-cost data. Assume that 10 units purchased at $7 each ($70 in total) are priced to sell for $10 per unit ($100 in total). The cost-to-retail ratio is 70% ($70 ÷ $100). If four units remain unsold, their retail value is $40 and their cost is $28 ($40 × 70%). This amount agrees with the total cost of goods on hand on a per-unit basis (4 × $7).

The following example shows how to apply the retail method, using assumed data for Zboyovsky Co.:

	At Cost	At Retail
Beginning inventory	$14,000	$ 21,500
Goods purchased	61,000	78,500
Goods available for sale	$75,000	100,000
Net sales		70,000
Step 1: Ending inventory at retail		$ 30,000
Step 2: Cost-to-retail ratio = $75,000 ÷ $100,000 = 75%		
Step 3: Estimated cost of ending inventory $30,000 × 75% =	$22,500	

Using the retail inventory method also makes it easier to take a physical inventory at the end of the year. The goods on hand can be valued at the prices marked on the merchandise. The cost-to-retail ratio is then applied to the goods on hand at retail to determine the ending inventory at cost. This value can be used for reporting purposes in the year-end financial statements if the results are similar to using cost.

The retail inventory method is also useful for estimating the amount of shrinkage due to breakage, loss, or theft. For example, assume that the retail value of Zboyovsky's physical inventory count is $29,400. When this amount is compared with the estimated retail value of $30,000 that was calculated above, it reveals a $600 estimated inventory shortage at retail. The estimated inventory shortage at cost is $450 ($600 × 75%).

The major disadvantage of the retail method is that it is an averaging technique. It may produce an incorrect inventory valuation if the mix of the ending inventory is not representative of the mix in the goods available for sale. Assume, for example, that the cost-to-retail ratio of 75% in the Zboyovsky Co. illustration consists of equal proportions of inventory items that have cost-to-retail ratios of 70%, 75%, and 80%, respectively. If the ending inventory contains only items with a 70% ratio, an incorrect inventory cost will result. This problem can be lessened by applying the retail method to a department or product line as a whole.

BEFORE YOU GO ON . . .

➔ Do It

At May 31, Purcell Company has net sales of $330,000 and cost of goods available for sale of $230,000. Last year, the company had a gross profit margin of 35%. Calculate the estimated cost of the ending inventory.

Action Plan
- Calculate the estimated cost of goods sold.
- Deduct the estimated cost of goods sold from cost of goods available for sale.

Solution

Net sales	$330,000
Less: Estimated gross profit ($330,000 × 35%)	115,500
Estimated cost of goods sold	$214,500
Cost of goods available for sale	$230,000
Less: Estimated cost of goods sold	214,500
Estimated cost of ending inventory	$ 15,500

The Navigator

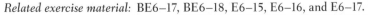
Related exercise material: BE6–17, BE6–18, E6–15, E6–16, and E6–17.

Demonstration Problem 1 (Perpetual Inventory System)

Englehart Company uses a perpetual inventory system. The company has the following inventory data for the month of March:

Date	Explanation	Units	Unit Cost	Total Cost
Mar. 1	Beginning inventory	200	$4.30	$ 860
10	Purchase	500	4.50	2,250
15	Sales	(500)		
20	Purchase	400	4.75	1,900
25	Sales	(400)		
30	Purchase	300	5.00	1,500
		500		$6,510

Instructions

Determine the cost of ending inventory at March 31 and cost of goods sold for March under (a) FIFO, and (b) average.

Solution to Demonstration Problem 1

(a) FIFO—Perpetual

Action Plan

• In a perpetual inventory system, cost of goods sold is calculated for each sale and a running balance of the ending inventory on hand is maintained.

• For FIFO, allocate the first costs to the cost of goods sold at the date of each sale. The latest costs will be allocated to the goods on hand (ending inventory).

• For average, determine the weighted average unit cost (cost of goods available for sale ÷ number of units available for sale) after each purchase. Multiply this cost by the number of units sold to determine the cost of goods sold and by the number of units on hand to determine the cost of the ending inventory.

• Check that beginning inventory + purchases – cost of goods sold = ending inventory.

	PURCHASES			COST OF GOODS SOLD			BALANCE		
Date	Units	Cost	Total	Units	Cost	Total	Units	Cost	Total
Mar. 1							200	$4.30	$ 860
10	500	$4.50	$2,250				200	4.30	} 3,110
							500	4.50	
15				200	$4.30	} $2,210	200	4.50	900
				300	4.50				
20	400	4.75	1,900				200	4.50	} 2,800
							400	4.75	
25				200	4.50	} 1,850	200	4.75	950
				200	4.75				
30	300	5.00	1,500				200	4.75	} 2,450
							300	5.00	
	1,200		$5,650			$4,060			

Check: $860 + $5,650 – $4,060 = $2,450

(b) Average—Perpetual

	PURCHASES			COST OF GOODS SOLD			BALANCE		
Date	Units	Cost	Total	Units	Cost	Total	Units	Cost	Total
Mar. 1							200	$4.30	$ 860
10	500	$4.50	$2,250				700	4.44	3,110
15				500	$4.44	$2,220	200	4.44	890
20	400	4.75	1,900				600	4.65	2,790
25				400	4.65	1,860	200	4.65	930
30	300	5.00	1,500				500	4.86	2,430
	1,200		$5,650	900		$4,080			

Check: $860 + $5,650 – $4,080 = $2,430

Demonstration Problem 2 (Periodic Inventory System)

Englehart Company uses a periodic inventory system. The company has the following inventory data for the month of March:

Inventory,	March 1	200 units @ $4.30	$ 860
Purchases,	March 10	500 units @ $4.50	2,250
	20	400 units @ $4.75	1,900
	30	300 units @ $5.00	1,500

The physical inventory count on March 31 shows 500 units on hand.

Instructions

Determine the cost of ending inventory at March 31 and cost of goods sold for March under (a) FIFO, and (b) average.

Solution to Demonstration Problem 2

The cost of goods available for sale is $6,510, calculated as follows:

Inventory,	March 1	200	units @ $4.30	$ 860
Purchases,	March 10	500	units @ $4.50	2,250
	20	400	units @ $4.75	1,900
	30	300	units @ $5.00	1,500
		1,400		$6,510

The physical inventory count on March 31 shows 500 units on hand.

The number of units sold is 900 (1,400 units available for sale – 500 units on hand).

(a) FIFO—Periodic

Ending inventory:	Date	Units	Unit Cost	Total Cost
	Mar. 30	300	$5.00	$1,500
	20	200	4.75	950
		500		$2,450

Cost of goods sold: $6,510 – $2,450 = $4,060

Proof of cost of goods sold:	Date	Units	Unit Cost	Total Cost
	Mar. 1	200	$4.30	$ 860
	10	500	4.50	2,250
	20	200	4.75	950
		900		$4,060

Check: $4,060 + $2,450 = $6,510

(b) Average—Periodic

Weighted average unit cost:	$6,510 ÷ 1,400 units = $4.65 per unit
Ending inventory:	500 units × $4.65 = $2,325
Cost of goods sold:	$6,510 – $2,325 = $4,185
Proof of cost of goods sold:	900 units × $4.65 = $4,185
Check:	$4,185 + $2,325 = $6,510

Action Plan

- In a periodic system, cost of ending inventory and cost of goods sold are determined at the end of the period.
- Allocate costs to ending inventory. Subtract ending inventory from the cost of goods available for sale to determine the cost of goods sold for each cost formula.
- For FIFO, allocate the latest costs to the goods on hand. (The first costs will be allocated to the cost of goods sold.)
- For average, calculate the weighted average unit cost (cost of goods available for sale divided by the total units available for sale). Multiply this cost by the number of units on hand.
- Check your work: do an independent calculation of cost of goods sold and check that cost of goods sold + ending inventory = cost of goods available for sale.

The Navigator

Summary of Study Objectives

1. ***Describe the steps in determining inventory quantities.*** The steps in determining inventory quantities are (1) taking a physical inventory of goods on hand, and (2) determining the ownership of goods in transit, on consignment, and in similar situations.

2. ***Calculate cost of goods sold and ending inventory in a perpetual inventory system using the specific identification, FIFO, and average methods of cost determination.*** Costs are allocated to the cost of goods sold account each time a sale occurs in a perpetual inventory system. The cost is determined by specific identification or by one of two cost formulas: FIFO (first-in, first-out) and average.

Specific identification is used for goods that are not ordinarily interchangeable. This method tracks the actual physical flow of goods, allocating the exact cost of each merchandise item to cost of goods sold and ending inventory.

The FIFO cost formula assumes a first-in, first-out cost flow for sales. Cost of goods sold consists of the cost of the earliest goods purchased. Ending inventory is determined by allocating the cost of the most recent purchases to the units on hand.

The average cost formula is used for goods that are homogeneous or non-distinguishable. Under average, a new weighted (moving) average unit cost is calculated after each purchase and applied to the number of units sold and the number of units remaining in inventory.

3. ***Determine the financial statement effects of inventory cost determination methods and of inventory errors.*** Specific identification results in the best match of costs and revenues on the income statement. When prices are rising, average results in a higher cost of goods sold and lower profit than FIFO. Average results in a better match on the income statement of more current costs with current revenues than does FIFO. On the balance sheet, FIFO results in an ending inventory that is closest to the current (replacement) value and the best balance sheet valuation. All three methods result in the same cash flow.

An error in beginning inventory will have a reverse effect on profit in the current year (e.g., an overstatement of beginning inventory results in an overstatement of cost of goods sold and an understatement of profit). An error in the cost of goods purchased will have a reverse effect on profit (e.g., an overstatement of purchases results in an overstatement of cost of goods sold and an understatement of profit). An error in ending inventory will have a similar effect on profit (e.g., an overstatement of ending inventory results in an understatement of cost of goods sold and an overstatement of profit). If ending inventory errors are not corrected in the following period, their effect on profit for the second period is reversed and total profit for the two years will be correct. On the balance sheet, ending inventory errors will have the same effects on total assets and total owner's equity, and no effect on liabilities.

4. ***Demonstrate the presentation and analysis of inventory.*** Inventory is valued at the lower of cost and net realizable value, which results in an increase in cost of goods sold, and a reduction in inventory when the net realizable value is less than cost. The writedown is reversed if the net realizable value of the inventory increases, but the value of the inventory can never be higher than its original cost.

Ending inventory is reported as a current asset on the balance sheet at the lower of cost and net realizable value. Cost of goods sold is reported as an expense on the income statement. Additional disclosures include the method of cost determination.

The inventory turnover ratio is a measure of liquidity. It is calculated by dividing the cost of goods sold by average inventory. It can be converted to days in inventory by dividing 365 days by the inventory turnover ratio.

5. ***Calculate ending inventory and cost of goods sold in a periodic inventory system using FIFO and average inventory cost formulas (Appendix 6A).*** Under the FIFO cost formula, the cost of the most recent goods purchased is allocated to ending inventory. The cost of the earliest goods on hand is allocated to cost of goods sold. Under the average cost formula, the total cost available for sale is divided by the total units available to calculate a weighted average unit cost. The weighted average unit cost is applied to the number of units on hand at the end of the period to determine ending inventory. Cost of goods sold is calculated by subtracting ending inventory from the cost of goods available for sale.

The main difference between applying cost formulas in a periodic inventory system and applying cost formulas in a perpetual inventory system is the timing of the calculations. In a periodic inventory system, the cost formula is applied at the end of the period. In a perpetual inventory system, the cost formula is applied at the date of each sale to determine the cost of goods sold.

6. ***Estimate ending inventory using the gross profit and retail inventory methods (Appendix 6B).*** Two methods of estimating inventories are the gross profit method and the retail inventory method. Under the gross profit method, the gross profit margin is applied to net sales to determine the estimated cost of goods sold. The estimated cost of goods sold is subtracted from the cost of goods available for sale to determine the estimated cost of the ending inventory. Under the retail inventory method, a cost-to-retail ratio is calculated by dividing the cost of goods available for sale by the retail value of the goods available for sale. This ratio is then applied to the ending inventory at retail to determine the estimated cost of the ending inventory.

Glossary

Average cost formula An inventory cost formula that assumes that the goods available for sale are homogeneous or non-distinguishable. The cost of goods sold and the ending inventory are determined using an average cost, calculated by dividing the cost of the goods available for sale by the units available for sale. (p. 321)

Consigned goods Goods held for sale that belong to another party. The party holding the goods is called the consignee, and the party that owns the goods is called the consignor. (p. 316)

Days sales in inventory A liquidity measure of the average number of days that inventory is held. It is calculated as 365 days divided by the inventory turnover ratio. (p. 332)

First-in, first-out (FIFO) cost formula An inventory cost formula that assumes that the costs of the earliest (oldest) goods purchased are the first to be recognized as the cost of goods sold. The costs of the latest goods purchased are assumed to remain in ending inventory. (p. 319)

Full disclosure The requirement that all information that is relevant for decision-making be disclosed. (p. 324)

Gross profit method A method for estimating the cost of the ending inventory by applying the gross profit margin to net sales. (p. 337)

Inventory turnover A liquidity measure of the number of times, on average, that inventory is sold during the period. It is calculated by dividing cost of goods sold by average inventory. Average inventory is calculated by adding beginning inventory and ending inventory balances and dividing the result by two. (p. 332)

Lower of cost and net realizable value (LCNRV) A basis for stating inventory at the lower of its original cost and the net realizable value at the end of the period. (p. 329)

Net realizable value (NRV) The selling price of an inventory item, less any estimated costs required to make the item saleable. (p. 329)

Retail inventory method A method for estimating the cost of the ending inventory by applying a cost-to-retail ratio to the ending inventory at retail prices. (p. 338)

Specific identification An inventory costing method used when goods are distinguishable and not ordinarily interchangeable. It follows the actual physical flow of goods and items are specifically costed to arrive at the cost of goods sold and the cost of the ending inventory. (p. 318)

Weighted average unit cost The average cost of inventory weighted by the number of units purchased at each unit cost. It is calculated by dividing the cost of goods available for sale by the number of units available for sale. (p. 321)

Note: All questions, exercises, and problems below with an asterisk (*) relate to material in Appendices 6A and 6B.

Self-Study Questions

Answers are at the end of the chapter.

(SO 1) K   1. Which of the following should not be included in a company's physical inventory?
     (a) Goods held on consignment from another company
     (b) Goods shipped on consignment to another company
     (c) Goods in transit that were purchased from a supplier and shipped FOB shipping point
     (d) Goods in transit that were sold to a customer and shipped FOB destination

(SO 2) AP   2. Fine Wine Company uses a perpetual inventory system and has the following opening inventory, purchases, and sales of inventory in April:

	Units	Unit Cost	Total Cost
Inventory, Apr. 1	8,000	$11	$ 88,000
Purchase, Apr. 9	12,000	12	144,000
Sale, Apr. 12	15,000	?	
Purchase, Apr. 18	5,000	13	65,000

What was the average unit cost after the last purchase on April 18?
     (a) $11.60
     (b) $12.00
     (c) $11.88
     (d) $12.30

(SO 2) AP   3. Using the data in question 2 above, the cost of goods sold under FIFO is:
     (a) $174,000.
     (b) $172,000.
     (c) $185,000.
     (d) $177,000.

(SO 3) C   4. In periods of rising prices, the average cost formula will produce:
     (a) higher profit than FIFO.
     (b) the same inventory as FIFO.
     (c) lower profit than FIFO.
     (d) higher inventory than FIFO.

(SO 3) C 5. In Fran Company, ending inventory is understated by $4,000. The effects of this error on the current year's cost of goods sold and profit, respectively, are:
(a) understated, overstated.
(b) overstated, understated.
(c) overstated, overstated.
(d) understated, understated.

(SO 4) K 6. Rickety Company purchased 1,000 units of inventory at a cost of $91 each. There are 200 units left in ending inventory. The net realizable value of these units is $80 each. The ending inventory under the lower of cost and net realizable value rule is:
(a) $16,000.
(b) $18,200.
(c) $2,200.
(d) $80,000.

(SO 4) AP 7. If a company's cost of goods sold is $120,000, its beginning inventory is $15,000, and its ending inventory is $25,000, what are its inventory turnover and days sales in inventory?
(a) 0.2 times and 1,825 days.
(b) 4.8 times and 76 days.
(c) 6 times and 61 days.
(d) 8 times and 46 days.

(SO 5) AP *8. Kam Company uses a periodic inventory system and has the following:

	Units	Unit Cost	Total Cost
Inventory, Jan. 1	8,000	$11	$ 88,000
Purchase, June 19	13,000	12	156,000
Purchase, Nov. 8	5,000	13	65,000
	26,000		$309,000

If 9,000 units are on hand at December 31, the cost of the goods sold under average is:
(a) $106,962.
(b) $108,000.
(c) $180,000.
(d) $202,038.

*9. Somers Company has sales of $150,000 and a cost (SO 6) AP
of goods available for sale of $135,000. If the gross profit margin is 30%, the estimated cost of the ending inventory under the gross profit method is:
(a) $15,000.
(b) $30,000.
(c) $40,500.
(d) $105,000.

*10. Retail Home Company reports the following select- (SO 6) AP
ed information: cost of goods available for sale at cost, $60,000; at retail, $100,000; and net sales at retail, $80,000. What is the estimated cost of Retail Home Company's ending inventory under the retail method?
(a) $12,000
(b) $20,000
(c) $40,000
(d) $60,000

Questions

(SO 1) C 1. Your friend Tom Wetzel has been hired to help take the physical inventory in Kikujiro's Hardware Store. Explain to Tom what this job will involve.

(SO 1) C 2. Explain to Janine Company whether the buyer or the seller should include goods in transit in their inventory. Also explain when the seller should record the sale.

(SO 1) C 3. What are consigned goods? Which company, the consignee or the consignor, should include consigned goods in its inventory balance? Explain why.

(SO 1) C 4. Your friend, the assistant store manager at Southside Boutique, wants to know if the following items should be included in the store's inventory count: (1) items on hold for customers who promised to return and purchase the items within the next week; (2) items left for alterations by customers; and (3) items taken on approval by customers. If you need to make any assumptions to answer your friend, include that in your explanation.

5. Dave Wier believes that the allocation of the cost of (SO 2) C
goods available for sale should be based on the actual physical flow of the goods. Explain to Dave why this may be both impractical and inappropriate.

6. Explain circumstances in which the specific identi- (SO 2) C
fication method is used.

7. Distinguish between the three methods of deter- (SO 2) C
mining cost for inventories: specific identification, FIFO, and average. Include the advantages of each in your answer.

8. Is it possible to use the specific identification meth- (SO 2) C
od in both perpetual and periodic inventory systems? Explain.

9. Compare the financial statement effects of using (SO 3) C
the FIFO and average cost formulas during a period of declining prices on (a) cash, (b) ending inventory, (c) cost of goods sold, and (d) profit.

(SO 3) C 10. Which inventory cost formula—FIFO or average—provides the better income statement valuation? The best balance sheet valuation? Explain.

(SO 3) C 11. What factors should a company consider when it is choosing between the two inventory cost formulas—FIFO and average?

(SO 3) C 12. Mila Company discovers in 2011 that its ending inventory at December 31, 2010, was understated by $5,000. What effect will this error have on (a) 2010 profit, (b) 2011 profit, and (c) the combined profit for the two years?

(SO 3) C 13. If an error in ending inventory in one year will have the reverse effect in the following year, does this error need to be corrected when it is discovered?

(SO 4) C 14. Lucy Ritter is studying for the next accounting exam. What should Lucy know about (a) when not to use the cost basis of accounting for inventories, and (b) the meaning of "net realizable value" in the lower of cost and net realizable value method?

(SO 4) C 15. "The key to successful business operations is effective inventory management." Do you agree? Explain.

(SO 4) AN 16. What problems may occur if a company's inventory turnover ratio is too high or too low?

(SO 4) AN 17. If a company's days sales in inventory ratio increases from one year to the next, would this be viewed as a sign that the company's inventory management has improved or deteriorated? Explain.

(SO 4) K 18. Wabanaki Company's balance sheet shows inventories of $162,800. What additional disclosures should be made?

*19. Vance is studying for his next accounting quiz. (SO 5) C He argues that the earliest costs should be used when calculating ending inventory using FIFO in a periodic inventory system because they are the first costs. Is he correct? Why or why not?

*20. Explain why ending inventory and cost of goods (SO 5) C sold under the FIFO cost formula are the same amounts whether a company uses a perpetual or periodic inventory system. Since this is the case, why would a company bother using a perpetual inventory system?

*21. Explain why ending inventory and cost of goods (SO 5) C sold under the average cost formula are not the same amounts in a perpetual system as they are in a periodic inventory system.

*22. How is the average cost formula different when it (SO 5) K is used in a periodic inventory system and in a perpetual inventory system?

*23. When is it necessary to estimate inventories? (SO 6) K

*24. Since a company's gross profit margin remains (SO 6) C constant from year to year, a company can use this method to determine its ending inventory, instead of doing an inventory count, for the year-end financial statements. Do you agree or disagree? Explain.

*25. Both the gross profit method and the retail inven- (SO 6) C tory method are based on averages. For each method, describe the average used, how it is determined, and how it is applied.

*26. Explain the major weakness of the retail method (SO 6) C and when it is not appropriate to use it.

Brief Exercises

BE6–1   Helgeson Company has identified the following items to include or exclude when it takes its physical inventory. Indicate whether each item should be included or excluded.

Identify items in inventory. (SO 1) K

(a) Goods shipped on consignment by Helgeson to another company
(b) Goods in transit to Helgeson from a supplier, shipped FOB destination
(c) Goods sold to a customer but being held for delivery
(d) Goods from another company held on consignment by Helgeson
(e) Goods in transit to a customer, shipped FOB shipping point

BE6–2   Mary Ann's Hat Shop counted the entire inventory in the store on August 31 and arrived at a total inventory cost of $68,000. The count included $5,000 of inventory held on consignment for a local designer; $600 of inventory that was being held for customers who were deciding if they actually wanted to purchase the merchandise; and $950 of inventory that had been sold to customers but was being held for alterations. There were two shipments of inventory received on September 1. The first shipment cost $6,000. It had been shipped on August 29, terms FOB destination, and the freight charges were $240. The second shipment cost $4,520. It had been shipped on August 28, terms FOB shipping point, and the freight charges were $180. Neither of these shipments was included in the August 31 count. Calculate the correct cost of the inventory on August 31.

Calculate inventory cost. (SO 1) AP

Apply specific identification
cost determination method.
(SO 2) AP

BE6–3   On January 3, Piano Company purchased three electronic pianos, model EBS, for $1,000 each. On January 20, it purchased two additional model EBS electronic pianos for $1,200 each. During the month, it sold two pianos; one that had been purchased on January 3, and one that had been purchased on January 20. Calculate the cost of goods sold for the month and ending inventory on January 31 using specific identification.

Recommend cost
determination method.
(SO 2) AP

BE6–4   The following are three inventory cost determination methods:

  1. Specific identification
  2. FIFO
  3. Average

Below is a list of different types of companies and their main inventory item. Beside each one, insert the number of the inventory cost determination method above that the company would most likely use.

  (a) ___ Grocery store (food)
  (b) ___ Brewing company (hops)
  (c) ___ Car dealership (automobiles)
  (d) ___ Gas station (fuel)
  (e) ___ Clothing store (clothing)

Apply perpetual FIFO.
(SO 2) AP

BE6–5   First Choice Company uses the FIFO cost formula in a perpetual inventory system. Fill in the missing amounts for items (a) through (k) in the following perpetual inventory schedule:

Date	PURCHASES			COST OF GOODS SOLD			BALANCE		
	Units	Cost	Total	Units	Cost	Total	Units	Cost	Total
June 1							200	$6.00	$1,200.00
7	400	$7.35	$2,940.00				(a)	(b)	(c)
18				350	(d)	(e)	(f)	(g)	(h)
26	375	$7.90	2,962.50				(i)	(j)	(k)

Apply perpetual average.
(SO 2) AP

BE6–6   Average Joe Company uses the average cost formula in a perpetual inventory system. Fill in the missing amounts for items (a) through (k) in the following perpetual inventory schedule:

Date	PURCHASES			COST OF GOODS SOLD			BALANCE		
	Units	Cost	Total	Units	Cost	Total	Units	Cost	Total
June 1							200	$6.00	$1,200.00
7	400	$7.35	$2,940.00				(a)	(b)	(c)
18				350	(d)	(e)	(f)	(g)	(h)
26	375	$7.90	2,962.50				(i)	(j)	(k)

Apply perpetual FIFO and
average.
(SO 2) AP

BE6–7   Yip Company uses a perpetual inventory system. The following data are available for its first month of operations:

  May 2   Purchased 250 units for $6 each.
      3   Purchased 400 units for $7 each.
     10   Sold 275 units for $10 each.
     15   Purchased 350 units for $8 each.
     25   Sold 325 units for $12 each.

Calculate the cost of goods sold and ending inventory under (a) FIFO and (b) average. (*Hint*: Round the average cost per unit to three decimal places.)

BE6–8 For each statement that follows, identify the inventory cost formula that best fits the description, assuming a period of rising prices:

(a) It results in a balance sheet inventory amount that is closer to the replacement cost.
(b) It does a better job of matching recent costs against revenue.
(c) It understates the value of the inventory on the balance sheet.
(d) It may overstate gross profit.

Identify inventory cost formula.
(SO 3) C

BE6–9 Interactive.com just started business and is trying to decide which inventory cost formula to use. Assuming prices are falling, as they often do in the information technology sector, answer the following questions for Interactive.com:

(a) Which formula will result in the higher ending inventory? Explain.
(b) Which formula will result in the higher cost of goods sold? Explain.
(c) Which formula will result in the higher cash flow? Explain.
(d) What factors are important for Interactive.com to consider as it tries to choose the most appropriate inventory cost formula?

Compare impact of inventory cost formulas.
(SO 3) C

BE6–10 Johal Company incorrectly included $25,000 of goods held on consignment for Hajol Company in Johal's beginning inventory for the year ended December 31, 2010. The ending inventory for 2010 was correctly counted. What is the impact on the 2010 financial statements? On the 2011 financial statements?

Determine effect of beginning inventory error.
(SO 3) AN

BE6–11 Creole Company reported profit of $90,000 in 2010. The company forgot to include items stored in a separate room in the warehouse. As a result, ending inventory was understated by $7,000.

(a) What is the correct profit for 2010?
(b) What effect, if any, will this error have on total assets and owner's equity reported on the balance sheet at December 31, 2010?
(c) Assuming the inventory is correctly counted on December 31, 2011, will this error have any impact on the 2011 financial statements?

Determine effects of inventory error over two years.
(SO 3) AN

BE6–12 Svenska Electronic Centre accumulates the following cost and net realizable value data at December 31:

Inventory Categories	Cost	Net Realizable Value
Cameras	$12,000	$11,200
Cell phones	9,000	9,500
DVD players	14,000	10,600

(a) Calculate the lower of cost and net realizable value valuation.
(b) What adjustment should Svenska record if it uses a perpetual inventory system?

Determine LCNRV valuation and prepare adjustment.
(SO 4) AP

BE6–13 Piper Specialty Music Equipment uses a perpetual inventory system and determines cost using the specific identification cost determination method. The company has the following information available regarding its inventory at its year end:

Inventory Categories	Cost	Net Realizable Value
Cameras	$12,000	$11,200
Cell phones	9,000	9,500

Cost of goods sold for the year was $285,400.

(a) What is the correct ending inventory and cost of goods sold that should be reported in the financial statements?
(b) What must be disclosed in the notes to the financial statements?

Determine inventory disclosures.
(SO 4) AP

Calculate inventory ratios.
(SO 4) AP

BE6–14   Ry Company reported net sales of $550,000; cost of goods purchased of $300,000; beginning inventory of $22,250; and ending inventory of $27,750. Calculate the inventory turnover and days sales in inventory ratios.

Apply periodic cost FIFO and average.
(SO 5) AP

*BE6–15   In its first month of operations, Quilt Company made three purchases of merchandise in the following sequence: 250 units at $6; 400 units at $7; and 350 units at $8. There are 400 units on hand at the end of the period. Quilt uses a periodic inventory system. Calculate the cost to be allocated to ending inventory and cost of goods sold under (a) FIFO, and (b) average.

Record transactions in periodic and perpetual inventory systems.
(SO 2, 5) AP

*BE6–16   At the beginning of the year, Seller Company had 700 units with a cost of $3 per unit in its beginning inventory. The following inventory transactions occurred during the month of January:

> Jan. 3   Sold 500 units on account for $5 each.
> 9   Purchased 1,000 units on account for $4 per unit.
> 15   Sold 800 units for cash for $8 each.

Prepare journal entries assuming that Seller Company uses FIFO under (a) the periodic inventory system and (b) the perpetual inventory system.

Apply gross profit method.
(SO 6) AP

*BE6–17   Jansen Company had beginning inventory of $60,000; net sales of $350,000; and cost of goods purchased of $250,000. In the previous year, the company had a gross profit margin of 40%. Calculate the estimated cost of the ending inventory using the gross profit method.

Apply retail inventory method.
(SO 6) AP

*BE6–18   On June 30, Fabric Villa has the following data related to the retail inventory method: Goods available for sale at cost $35,000; at retail $50,000; and net sales of $40,000. Calculate the estimated cost of the ending inventory using the retail inventory method.

Exercises

Identify items in inventory.
(SO 1) K

E6–1   Shippers Company had the following inventory situations to consider at January 31, its year end:

1. Goods held on consignment for MailBoxes Etc. since December 22
2. Goods shipped on consignment to Rinehart Holdings on January 5
3. Goods that are still in transit and were shipped to a customer, FOB destination, on January 28
4. Goods that are still in transit and were shipped to a customer, FOB shipping point, on January 27
5. Goods that are still in transit and were purchased from a supplier, FOB destination, on January 25
6. Goods that are still in transit and were purchased from a supplier, FOB shipping point, on January 29
7. Freight costs due on goods in transit from item 6 above
8. Freight costs due on goods in transit from item 3 above
9. Office supplies on hand at January 31

Instructions

Identify which of the above items should be included in inventory. If the item should not be included in inventory, state where it should be recorded.

E6–2 First Bank is considering giving Moghul Company a loan. First, however, it decides that it would be a good idea to have further discussions with Moghul's accountant. One area of particular concern is the inventory account, which has a year-end balance of $281,000. Discussions with the accountant reveal the following:

Determine correct inventory amount.
(SO 1) AP

1. Moghul sold goods that cost $35,000 to Novotna Company, FOB destination, on December 28. The goods are not expected to arrive at their destination in India until January 12. The goods were not included in the physical inventory because they were not in the warehouse.
2. The physical count of the inventory did not include goods that cost $95,000 that were shipped to Moghul, FOB shipping point, on December 27 and were still in transit at year end.
3. Moghul received goods that cost $28,000 on January 2. The goods were shipped FOB shipping point on December 26 by Cellar Co. The goods were not included in the physical count.
4. Moghul sold goods that cost $49,000 to Sterling of Canada, FOB shipping point, on December 30. The goods were received by Sterling on January 8. They were not included in Moghul's physical inventory.
5. Moghul received goods that cost $44,000 on January 2 that were shipped, FOB destination, on December 29. The shipment was a rush order that was supposed to arrive on December 31. This purchase was not included in the ending inventory of $281,000.
6. On December 31, Board Company had $30,500 of goods held on consignment for Moghul. The goods were not included in Moghul's ending inventory balance.

Instructions
Determine the correct inventory amount at December 31.

E6–3 On December 1, Discount Electronics has three identical LCD TVs in inventory. The purchase dates, serial numbers, and cost of each of the three items are as follows:

Apply specific identification.
(SO 2) AP

Date	Serial Number	Cost
June 1	#1012	$500
September 1	#1045	450
November 30	#1056	400

All three LCD TVs are priced to sell at $750. At December 31, one TV remained in inventory. Discount Electronics uses a periodic inventory system.

Instructions

(a) Explain how Discount Electronics would use specific identification to determine the cost of the ending inventory and cost of goods sold in December.
(b) If Discount Electronics used the specific identification method, how might it manipulate its income? What would Discount's cost of goods sold and gross profit be if the company wanted to maximize income? What would Discount's cost of goods sold and gross profit be if the company wanted to minimize income?
(c) Should Discount Electronics use specific identification or one of the two cost formulas (FIFO or average) instead? Explain.

E6–4 Outdoor Experience Company uses a perpetual inventory system and, as at June 1, has a beginning inventory of 200 tents. This consists of 50 tents at a cost of $200 and 150 tents at a cost of $225. During June, the company had the following purchases and sales of tents:

Apply perpetual FIFO, record journal entries, and calculate gross profit.
(SO 2) AP

	Purchases		Sales	
	Units	Unit Cost	Units	Unit Price
June 9			120	$320
12	300	$205		
16			280	320
21	400	210		
24			350	330

Instructions

(a) Calculate the cost of goods sold and ending inventory using FIFO.
(b) Prepare journal entries to record the purchases and sales. Assume all purchases and sales are made on account.
(c) Calculate gross profit for June.

Apply perpetual average, record journal entries, and calculate gross profit.
(SO 2) AP

E6–5 Basic Furniture Company uses a perpetual inventory system and has beginning inventory, as at June 1, of 500 bookcases at a cost of $125 each. During June, the company had the following purchases and sales of bookcases:

	Purchases		Sales	
	Units	Unit Cost	Units	Unit Price
June 6	1,500	$127		
10			1,000	$200
14	1,200	128		
16			1,600	205
26	1,100	129		

Instructions

(a) Calculate the cost of goods sold and ending inventory using average. (*Hint*: Round the average cost per unit to three decimal places.)
(b) Prepare journal entries to record the purchases and sales. Assume all purchases and sales are made on account.
(c) Calculate gross profit for June.

Apply perpetual FIFO and average. Answer questions about results.
(SO 2, 3) AP

E6–6 Dene Company uses a perpetual inventory system and reports the following inventory transactions for the month of July:

		Units	Unit Cost	Total Cost
July 1	Inventory	150	$5	$ 750
12	Purchases	230	6	1,380
15	Sale	250		
16	Purchases	490	7	3,430
23	Purchases	175	8	1,400
27	Sale	570		

Instructions

(a) Calculate the cost of goods sold and ending inventory under (1) FIFO and (2) average. (*Hint*: Round the average cost per unit to three decimal places.)
(b) Which cost formula gives the higher ending inventory? Why?
(c) Which cost formula results in the higher cost of goods sold? Why?
(d) Which cost formula results in the higher cash flow? Why?

Determine effects of inventory errors.
(SO 3) AN

E6–7 Glacier Fishing Gear reported the following amounts for its cost of goods sold and ending inventory:

	2011	2010
Cost of goods sold	$170,000	$175,000
Ending inventory	30,000	30,000

Glacier made two errors: (1) 2010 ending inventory was overstated by $3,000, and (2) 2011 ending inventory was understated by $4,000.

Instructions

(a) Calculate the correct cost of goods sold and ending inventory for each year.
(b) Describe the impact of the errors on profit for 2010 and 2011 and on owner's equity at the end of 2010 and 2011.
(c) Explain why it is important that Glacier Fishing Gear correct these errors as soon as they are discovered.

E6–8 <!-- arrow --> Marrakesh Company reported the following income statement data for the years ended December 31:

Correct partial income statements and comment.
(SO 3) AN

	2011	2010
Sales	$530,000	$500,000
Cost of goods sold	410,000	410,000
Gross profit	$120,000	$ 90,000

The inventories at January 1, 2010, and December 31, 2011, are correct. However, the ending inventory at December 31, 2010, was understated by $20,000.

Instructions

(a) Prepare the correct income statement up to gross profit for the two years.
(b) What is the combined effect of the inventory error on total gross profit for the two years?
(c) Calculate the gross profit margin for each of the two years, before and after the correction.
(d) In a letter to the president of Marrakesh Company, explain what has happened: discuss the nature of the error and its effect on the financial statements.

E6–9   Cody Camera Shop is determining the lower of cost and net realizable value of its inventory. The following data are available at December 31:

Determine LCNRV valuation.
(SO 4) AP

		Units	Unit Cost	Net Realizable Value
Cameras:	Minolta	5	$175	$160
	Canon	7	140	142
Light Meters:	Vivitar	12	135	129
	Kodak	10	115	120

Instructions

(a) Determine the lower of cost and net realizable value of the ending inventory.
(b) Prepare the journal entry required, if any, to record the adjustment from cost to net realizable value assuming Cody Camera Shop uses a perpetual inventory system.
(c) What information regarding its inventory will Cody Camera Shop need to report in the notes to its financial statements?

E6–10   The following information is available for Danier Leather Inc. for three recent years (in thousands):

Calculate inventory turnover, days sales in inventory, and gross profit margin.
(SO 4) AP

	2008	2007	2006
Inventory	$ 27,404	$ 28,561	$ 32,348
Sales	163,550	158,099	148,351
Cost of goods sold	87,365	79,565	76,953

Instructions

Calculate the inventory turnover, days sales in inventory, and gross profit margin for Danier Leather Inc. for 2008 and 2007. Comment on any trends.

*E6–11   Dene Company uses a periodic inventory system and reports the following inventory transactions for the month of July:

Apply periodic FIFO and average.
(SO 5) AP

		Units	Unit Cost	Total Cost
July 1	Inventory	150	$5	$ 750
12	Purchases	230	6	1,380
16	Purchases	490	7	3,430
23	Purchases	175	8	1,400

A physical inventory count determined that 225 units were on hand at July 31.

Instructions

(a) Calculate the ending inventory and the cost of goods sold under (1) FIFO and (2) average.
(b) For part 2 of instruction (a), explain why the average unit cost is not $6.50.
(c) How do the results for instruction (a) differ from E6–6 where the same information was used in a perpetual inventory system?

Apply periodic FIFO and
average.
(SO 5) AP

*E6–12 Zambia Company uses a periodic inventory system. Its records show the following for the month of May, with 25 units on hand at May 31:

		Units	Unit Cost	Total Cost
May 1	Inventory	30	$ 8	$240
15	Purchases	45	11	495
24	Purchases	15	12	180
	Total	90		$915

Instructions

Calculate the ending inventory and cost of goods sold at May 31 using the FIFO and average cost formula. Prove the cost of goods sold calculations.

Apply periodic and perpetual
FIFO and average.
(SO 2, 5) AP

*E6–13 Powder Co. sells an Xpert snowboard that is popular with snowboard enthusiasts. Information follows for Powder's purchases and sales of Xpert snowboards during November:

Date	Transaction	Units	Unit Purchase Price	Unit Sales Price
Nov. 1	Beginning inventory	25	$295	
5	Purchase	30	300	
12	Sale	(42)		$450
19	Purchase	35	305	
22	Sale	(45)		460
25	Purchase	20	310	

Instructions

(a) Calculate the cost of goods sold and the ending inventory using FIFO and average, assuming Powder Co. uses a perpetual inventory system. (*Hint*: Round the average cost per unit to three decimal places.)

(b) What would be the ending inventory and cost of goods sold if Powder Co. used FIFO and average in a periodic inventory system? (*Hint*: Round the average cost per unit to three decimal places.)

Record transactions in
perpetual and periodic
inventory systems.
(SO 2, 5) AP

*E6–14 Refer to the data for Powder Co. in E6–13. Assume that all of Powder's sales are for cash and all of its purchases are on account.

Instructions

(a) Record the purchases and sales for Powder Co. in a perpetual inventory system under (1) FIFO and (2) average.

(b) Record the purchases and sales for Powder Co. in a periodic inventory system under (1) FIFO and (2) average.

Estimate inventory loss using
gross profit method.
(SO 6) AP

*E6–15 The inventory of Farhad Company was destroyed by fire on March 1. From an examination of the accounting records, the following data for the first two months of the year are obtained: Sales $55,000; Sales Returns and Allowances $1,000; Sales Discounts $500; Freight Out $1,500; Purchases $31,200; Freight In $1,200; Purchase Returns and Allowances $1,400; and Purchase Discounts $300.

Instructions

Determine the inventory lost by fire, assuming a beginning inventory of $23,000 and a gross profit margin of 40%.

Estimate cost of ending
inventory using retail method.
(SO 6) AP

*E6–16 Agnew Shoe Store uses the retail inventory method for its two departments: men's shoes and women's shoes. The following information is obtained for each department:

Item	Men's Shoes	Women's Shoes
Beginning inventory at cost	$ 36,000	$ 45,000
Beginning inventory at retail	58,050	95,750
Cost of goods purchased	216,000	315,000
Retail price of goods purchased	348,400	670,200
Net sales	365,000	635,000

Instructions

Calculate the estimated cost of the ending inventory for each shoe department under the retail inventory method.

*E6–17 Nancy's Running Store has two departments: running shoes and running clothes. The selling price of running clothes is 1.7 times their cost; the selling price of running shoes is double their cost. During the previous year, the company had an overall gross profit margin of 45%. The information for the first six months of the current year is as follows:

Estimate ending inventory using gross profit and retail methods. Compare results. (SO 6) AN

	Running Shoes	Running Clothes
Beginning inventory at cost	$ 48,000	$ 35,000
Sales for the six months	288,600	242,000
Purchases at cost	145,000	132,500

Instructions

(a) Estimate the cost of the ending inventory using the gross profit method.
(b) Estimate the cost of the ending inventory using the retail method.
(c) Do the two methods give the same estimate? Why or why not? Which method would you recommend in this situation?

Problems: Set A

P6–1A Kananaskis Country Company is trying to determine the value of its ending inventory as at February 28, 2011, the company's year end. The accountant counted everything that was in the warehouse as at February 28, which resulted in an ending inventory valuation of $65,000. However, he was not sure how to treat the following transactions, so he did not include them in inventory:

Identify items in inventory. (SO 1) AP

1. Kananaskis shipped $875 of inventory on consignment to Banff Company on February 20. By February 28, Banff Company had sold $365 of this inventory for Kananaskis.
2. On February 28, Kananaskis was holding merchandise that had been sold to a customer on February 25 but needed some minor alterations before the customer would take possession. The customer has paid for the goods and will pick them up on March 3 after the alterations are complete. This inventory cost $490 and was sold for $880.
3. On February 27, Kananaskis shipped goods costing $950 to a customer and charged the customer $1,300. The goods were shipped FOB destination and the receiving report indicates that the customer received the goods on March 3.
4. On February 26, Seller Company shipped goods to Kananaskis, FOB shipping point. The invoice price was $375 plus $30 for freight. The receiving report indicates that the goods were received by Kananaskis on March 2.
5. Kananaskis had $630 of inventory put aside in the warehouse. The inventory is for a customer who has asked that the goods be shipped on March 10.
6. Also in Kananaskis' warehouse is $400 of inventory that Craft Producers shipped to Kananaskis on consignment.
7. On February 26, Kananaskis issued a purchase order to acquire goods costing $750. The goods were shipped FOB destination. The receiving report indicates that Kananaskis received the goods on March 2.
8. On February 26, Kananaskis shipped goods to a customer, FOB shipping point. The invoice price was $350 plus $25 for freight. The cost of the items was $280. The receiving report indicates that the goods were received by the customer on March 4.

Instructions

(a) For each of the above transactions, specify whether the item should be included in ending inventory, and if so, at what amount. Explain your reasoning.
(b) What is the revised ending inventory valuation?

Taking It Further   If the accountant of Kananaskis Company is paid a bonus based on profit, which of these errors might he consider overlooking and not correct? Explain.

Apply specific identification.
(SO 2) AP

P6–2A   Village Sales, a Ford dealership, has provided you with the following information with respect to its vehicle inventory for the month of October. The company uses the specific identification method.

Date	Explanation	Model	Serial #	Unit Cost	Unit Selling Price
Oct. 1	Inventory	Focus	C63825	$14,000	
		Focus	C81362	19,000	
		Mustang	G62313	25,000	
		Escape	E11396	23,000	
		Flex	X3892	26,000	
		F-150	F1883	21,000	
		F-150	F1921	24,000	
8	Sales	Focus	C81362		$21,000
		Mustang	G62313		27,000
12	Purchases	Mustang	G71811	26,000	
		Mustang	G71891	24,000	
		Flex	X4212	27,000	
		Flex	X4214	30,000	
		Escape	E21202	25,000	
18	Sales	Mustang	G71891		26,000
		Flex	X3892		28,000
		F-150	F1921		26,000
		Escape	E21202		27,000
23	Purchases	F-150	F2182	22,000	
		Mustang	G72166	29,000	
		Escape	E28268	25,000	

Instructions

(a) Determine the cost of goods sold and the ending inventory for the month of October.
(b) Determine the gross profit for the month of October.

Taking It Further   Discuss whether Village Sales should use the specific identification method or one of the cost formulas.

Apply perpetual FIFO.
Record sales and inventory
adjustment, and calculate
gross profit.
(SO 2) AP

P6–3A   You are given the following information for Lahti Company for the month ended November 30, 2011:

Date	Description	Units	Unit Price
Nov. 1	Beginning inventory	60	$50
9	Purchase	100	46
15	Sale	120	
22	Purchase	150	44
29	Sale	160	
30	Purchase	45	42

Lahti Company uses a perpetual inventory system.

Instructions

(a) Calculate the cost of goods sold and the ending inventory using FIFO.
(b) Assume the sales price was $66 per unit for the goods sold on November 15, and $60 per unit for the sale on November 29. Prepare journal entries to record these transactions.
(c) Calculate gross profit for November.
(d) Assume that at the end of November, the company counted its inventory. There are 73 units on hand. What journal entry, if any, should the company make to record the shortage? What is gross profit after this shortage is recorded?

Taking It Further   What might Lahti do to reduce or eliminate inventory shortages in the future?

P6-4A   Information for Lahti Company is presented in P6-3A. Assume the same inventory data and that the company uses a perpetual inventory system. Ignore the inventory shortage in P6-3A (d).

Apply perpetual average and answer questions.
(SO 2, 3) AP

Instructions

(a) Calculate the cost of goods sold and the ending inventory using average. (*Hint*: Round the average cost per unit to two decimal places.)

(b) Assume that Lahti Company wants to change to the FIFO cost formula. What factors must it consider before making this change?

(c) If the company does change to FIFO and prices continue to fall, would you expect the cost of goods sold and ending inventory amounts to be higher or lower than these amounts under average?

Taking It Further   Which inventory cost formula—FIFO or average—will provide Lahti with the better income statement valuation? The better balance sheet valuation? Explain.

P6-5A   Reliable Camera Mart sells a wide variety of special digital cameras and uses a perpetual inventory system. On May 1, 2011, Reliable had five Model 10 digital cameras on hand at a unit cost of $95. During May and June, the company had the following purchases and sales for this camera (all for cash):

Apply perpetual FIFO and average. Answer questions about financial statement effects.
(SO 2, 3) AP

	Purchases		Sales	
	Units	Unit Cost	Units	Unit Price
May 4			2	$200
18	5	$105		
31			6	225
June 5	5	110		
12			3	245
25			2	245

Instructions

(a) Determine the cost of goods sold and ending inventory under a perpetual inventory system using (1) FIFO and (2) average. (*Hint*: Round the average cost per unit to two decimal places.)

(b) Calculate gross profit using (1) FIFO and (2) average.

(c) Which cost formula produces the higher cash flow?

Taking It Further   What factors should the owner of Reliable Camera Mart consider when choosing a cost formula?

P6-6A   You are given the following information for Amelia Company. All transactions are settled in cash. Returns are usually not damaged and are restored immediately to inventory for resale. Amelia uses a perpetual inventory system and the average cost formula. Increased competition has reduced the price of the product.

Record transactions using perpetual average. Apply LCNRV.
(SO 2, 4) AP

Date	Transaction	Units	Unit Price
July 1	Beginning inventory	25	$10
5	Purchase	55	9
8	Sale	70	15
10	Sale return	15	15
15	Purchase	50	8
16	Purchase return	10	8
20	Sale	55	12
25	Purchase	10	7

Instructions

(a) Prepare the required journal entries for the month of July for Amelia Company. (*Hint*: Round the average cost per unit to two decimal places.)

(b) Determine the ending inventory for Amelia.

(c) On July 31, Amelia Company learns that the product has a net realizable value of $8 per unit. What amount should the ending inventory be valued at on the July 31 balance sheet?

(d) What amount should the cost of goods sold be valued at on the July income statement? Prepare the journal entry, if required, to recognize the decrease in value of this product.

Taking It Further What if Amelia had used FIFO instead of average? How would this affect the July 31 ending inventory on the balance sheet compared with average?

Determine effects of inventory errors.
(SO 1, 3) AN

P6–7A The records of Gillies Company show the following amounts in its December 31 financial statements:

	2011	2010	2009
Total assets	$925,000	$900,000	$850,000
Owner's equity	750,000	700,000	650,000
Cost of goods sold	550,000	550,000	500,000
Profit	90,000	80,000	70,000

Gillies made the following errors in determining its ending inventory:

1. The ending inventory account balance at December 31, 2009, did not include $20,000 of goods held on consignment by Leblanc Company.

2. The ending inventory account balance at December 31, 2010, included goods sold and shipped on December 30, 2010, FOB shipping point. The selling price of these goods was $40,000 and the cost of these goods was $32,000. The goods arrived at the destination on January 4, 2011.

All purchases and sales of inventory were recorded in the correct fiscal year.

Instructions

(a) Calculate the correct amount for each of the following for 2009, 2010, and 2011:
   1. Total assets
   2. Owner's equity
   3. Cost of goods sold
   4. Profit

(b) Indicate the effect of these errors (overstated, understated, or no effect) on cash at the end of 2009, 2010, and 2011.

Taking It Further If the merchandise inventory balance is correct as at December 31, 2011, is it necessary to correct the errors in the previous years' financial statements? Explain.

Determine effects of inventory errors. Calculate inventory turnover.
(SO 3, 4) AN

P6–8A The records of Alyssa Company show the following data:

	2011	2010	2009
Income statement:			
Sales	$340,000	$320,000	$300,000
Cost of goods sold	235,000	225,000	215,000
Operating expenses	66,000	66,000	66,000
Balance sheet:			
Merchandise inventory	45,000	35,000	25,000

After its July 31, 2011, year end, Alyssa discovered two errors:

1. Merchandise inventory at July 31, 2010, was actually $45,000, not $35,000. Alyssa had goods held on consignment at another company that were not included in the physical count.

2. In July 2010, Alyssa recorded a $15,000 inventory purchase on account that should have been recorded in August 2010.

Instructions

(a) Prepare incorrect and corrected income statements for Alyssa for the years ended July 31, 2009, 2010, and 2011.

(b) What is the impact of these errors on the owner's equity at July 31, 2011?

(c) Calculate the correct and incorrect inventory turnover ratios for 2010 and 2011.

Taking It Further Compare the trends in the incorrectly calculated annual profits with the trends in the correctly calculated annual profits. Does it appear that management may have deliberately made these errors, or do they appear to be honest errors? Explain.

P6–9A You have been provided with the following financial information regarding R-Steel Co.'s inventory for March and April.

Apply LCNRV and prepare adjustment. (SO 4) AP

	Steel Inventory (in tonnes)	Cost/Tonne	NRV/Tonne
March 31	3,000	$705	$740
April 30	2,500	735	720

Instructions

(a) Calculate the cost, the net realizable value, and the amount to be reported on the balance sheet for R-Steel's inventory at (1) March 31 and (2) April 30.

(b) Prepare any journal entries required to record the LCNRV of the steel inventory at (1) March 31 and (2) April 30. R-Steel uses a perpetual inventory system.

(c) Assume that during the month of May the company did not purchase or sell any steel inventory and that the NRV/tonne was $730 on May 31. Is an adjusting entry required at May 31? Explain. If so, prepare the adjusting entry.

(d) What will have to be disclosed in R-Steel's notes to the financial statements with regard to its steel inventory?

Taking It Further Why is it important to report inventory at the LCNRV on the balance sheet?

P6–10A The following financial information (in US$ millions) is for two major corporations for the three years ended December 31:

Calculate ratios. (SO 4) AN

PepsiCo Inc.	2008	2007	2006
Net sales	$43,251	$39,474	$35,137
Cost of sales	20,351	18,038	15,762
Profit	5,142	5,658	5,642
Cash and short-term investments	2,277	2,481	2,822
Accounts receivable	4,683	4,389	3,725
Inventory	2,522	2,290	1,926
Prepaid expenses and other current assets	1,324	991	657
Current liabilities	8,787	7,753	6,860

Coca-Cola Company			
Net sales	$31,944	$28,857	$24,088
Cost of sales	11,374	10,406	8,164
Profit	5,807	5,981	5.080
Cash and short-term investments	4,979	4,308	2,590
Accounts receivable	3,090	3,317	2,587
Inventory	2,187	2,220	1,641
Prepaid expenses and other current assets	1,920	2,260	1,623
Current liabilities	12,988	13,225	8,890

Instructions

Calculate the inventory turnover, days sales in inventory, current ratio, acid-test ratio, gross profit margin, and profit margin for each company for 2008 and 2007.

Taking It Further Comment on each company's profitability and liquidity.

Apply periodic FIFO
and average.
(SO 5) AP

*P6–11A Ng Company had a beginning inventory on January 1 of 250 units of Product SXL at a cost of $16 per unit. During the year, the following purchases were made:

	Units	Unit Cost
Mar. 15	700	$15
July 20	500	14
Sept. 4	450	13
Dec. 2	100	12

At the end of the year, there were 300 units on hand. Ng Company uses a periodic inventory system.

Instructions

(a) Determine the cost of goods available for sale.
(b) Determine the cost of the ending inventory and the cost of goods sold using (1) FIFO and (2) average. (*Hint*: Round the average cost per unit to two decimal places.)
(c) During the year Ng Company sold Product SXL for $32 per unit. Calculate gross profit using (1) FIFO and (2) average.

Taking It Further The owner of Ng Company would like to minimize his income taxes. Last year, prices were rising and Ng Company used the average cost formula. Should Ng Company continue to use average or change to FIFO? Explain.

Apply periodic and
perpetual FIFO.
(SO 2, 5) AP

*P6–12A You are given the following information about Réal Novelty's inventory for the month of May.

Date	Description	Units	Unit Cost
May 1	Beginning inventory	25,000	$2.25
2	Sale	10,000	
6	Purchase	30,000	2.30
10	Sale	25,000	
15	Sale	5,000	
19	Purchase	35,000	2.50
24	Sale	40,000	
28	Purchase	45,000	2.75

Instructions

(a) Calculate the cost of ending inventory and cost of the goods sold using FIFO in (1) a periodic inventory system and (2) a perpetual inventory system.
(b) Compare your results for parts 1 and 2 of instruction (a), and comment on the differences between the two systems.

Taking It Further Companies are required to disclose their inventory cost determination method. Should they also be required to disclose if they are using a periodic or a perpetual inventory system? Explain.

Apply periodic and
perpetual average.
(SO 2, 5) AP

*P6–13A You are given the following information for Yuan Company for January 2011:

Date	Description	Units	Unit Price
Jan. 1	Beginning inventory	250	$28
8	Purchase	110	32
10	Sale	175	60
15	Purchase	100	36
25	Sale	120	65
26	Purchase	110	40
27	Purchase return	6	40

Instructions

(a) Calculate the ending inventory and cost of goods sold using average in (1) a periodic inventory system and (2) a perpetual inventory system. (*Hint*: Round the average cost per unit to two decimal places.)

(b) Compare the ending inventory and cost of goods sold using the average cost formula in a perpetual system and in a periodic system.

Taking It Further Discuss the differences and similarities between the two systems when using average.

P6–14A Chung Company lost all of its inventory in a fire on December 28, 2011. The accounting records showed the following gross profit data for November and December:

(right margin) Determine inventory loss using gross profit method. (SO 6) AP

	November	December (to Dec. 28)
Sales	$450,000	$600,000
Sales returns and allowances	10,000	12,000
Sales discounts	4,500	5,400
Purchases	275,745	355,235
Purchase returns and allowances	11,700	12,900
Purchase discounts	2,950	3,500
Freight in	4,573	4,100
Beginning inventory	22,700	26,270
Ending inventory	26,270	?

Chung is fully insured for fire losses but must prepare a report for the insurance company.

Instructions

Determine the amount of inventory lost by Chung as a result of the fire.

Taking It Further The insurance adjustor is concerned that this method of calculating the cost of the inventory destroyed might not be accurate. What factors contribute to the accuracy of the ending inventory amount when using the gross profit method?

P6–15A Varocher's Movie Gallery uses the retail inventory method to estimate its monthly ending inventories. The following information is available at October 31, 2011:

(right margin) Determine ending inventory using retail method. (SO 6) AP

	Video Games		DVDs	
	Cost	Retail	Cost	Retail
Beginning inventory	$ 275,000	$ 423,000	$ 190,000	$ 322,000
Purchases	1,180,000	1,800,000	1,045,000	1,771,000
Purchase returns and allowances	23,600	36,000	20,900	35,400
Purchase discounts	5,900		5,100	
Freight in	5,000		6,200	
Sales		1,825,000		1,650,000
Sales returns and allowances		27,000		24,000

At October 31, Varocher's Movie Gallery takes a physical inventory count at retail. The actual retail values of the inventories in each department on October 31, 2011, are as follows: Video Games $381,250, and DVDs $426,100.

Instructions

Determine the estimated cost of the ending inventory at October 31, 2011, using the retail inventory method.

Taking It Further Calculate the store's loss on October 31, 2011, from theft and other causes, at retail and at cost.

Problems: Set B

Identify items in inventory.
(SO 1) AP

P6–1B Banff Company is trying to determine the value of its ending inventory as at February 28, 2011, the company's year end. The accountant counted everything that was in the warehouse as at February 28, which resulted in an ending inventory cost of $56,000. However, she was not sure how to treat the following transactions, so she did not include them in inventory:

1. On February 20, Banff Company had received $875 of inventory on consignment from Kananaskis Company. By February 28, Banff Company had sold $365 of this inventory for Kananaskis.
2. On February 25, Banff ordered goods costing $750. The goods were shipped FOB shipping point on February 27. The receiving report indicates that Banff received the goods on March 1.
3. On February 26, Banff shipped goods costing $800 to a customer. The goods were shipped FOB shipping point. The receiving report indicates that the customer received the goods on March 1.
4. On February 27, Wah Company shipped goods to Banff, FOB destination. The invoice price was $350 plus $25 for freight. The receiving report indicates that the goods were received by Banff on March 2.
5. On February 28, Banff packaged goods and moved them to the shipping department for shipping to a customer, FOB destination. The invoice price was $425 plus $20 for freight. The cost of the items was $360. The receiving report indicates that the goods were received by the customer on March 2.
6. Banff had damaged goods set aside in the warehouse because they were not saleable. These goods originally cost $400. Banff had expected to sell these items for $600 before they were damaged.
7. On February 28, Banff was holding merchandise that had been sold to a customer on February 25 but needed some engraving done before the customer would pick it up. The customer has paid for the goods and will pick them up on March 3 after the engraving is finished. This inventory cost $940 and was sold for $1,340.
8. Banff had $570 of inventory on consignment at a craft shop.
9. Banff had $620 of inventory at a customer's warehouse "on approval." The customer was going to let Banff know whether it wanted the merchandise by the end of the week, March 7.

Instructions

(a) For each of the above transactions, specify whether the item in question should be included in ending inventory, and if so, at what amount. Explain your reasoning.
(b) What is the revised ending inventory cost?

Taking It Further If the owner of Banff Company wants to minimize the amount of income taxes he or she will have to pay, what errors might the owner tell the accountant to not correct? Explain.

Apply specific identification.
(SO 2) AP

P6–2B Irene Best Piano Sales has provided you with the following information with respect to its piano inventory for the month of August. The company uses the specific identification method.

Date	Explanation	Model	Serial #	Unit Cost	Unit Selling Price
Aug. 1	Inventory	Yamaha	YH6318	$1,500	
		Suzuki	SZ5716	1,100	
		Suzuki	SZ5824	1,700	
		Suzuki	SZ5828	1,600	
		Kawai	KG1239	900	
		Kawai	KG1268	1,500	
		Kawai	KG1520	600	
		Steinway	ST0815	1,200	
		Steinway	ST8411	2,600	

Date	Explanation	Model	Serial #	Unit Cost	Unit Selling Price
		Steinway	ST0944	$2,200	
10	Sales	Suzuki	SZ5828		$2,700
		Kawai	KG1520		1,400
15	Purchases	Yamaha	YH4418	1,300	
		Yamaha	YH5632	1,600	
18	Sales	Yamaha	YH4418		2,100
		Steinway	ST0944		3,700
		Kawai	KG1239		1,400
		Suzuki	SZ5824		2,850
22	Purchases	Suzuki	SZ6132	1,800	
		Suzuki	SZ6148	1,600	
26	Sales	Suzuki	SZ6132		2,900
		Steinway	ST0815		2,000
		Yamaha	YH6318		2,500
		Yamaha	YH5632		2,600

Instructions

(a) Determine the cost of goods sold and the ending inventory for the month of August.
(b) Determine the gross profit for the month of August.

Taking It Further   Discuss whether Irene Best Piano Sales should use the specific identification method or one of the cost formulas.

P6–3B   You are given the following information for Danielle Company for the month ended June 30, 2011:

Apply perpetual average. Record sales and inventory adjustment and calculate gross profit.

(SO 2) AP

Date	Description	Units	Unit Price
June 1	Beginning inventory	20	$50
4	Purchase	85	55
10	Sale	90	
18	Purchase	35	58
25	Sale	30	
28	Purchase	15	60

Danielle Company uses a perpetual inventory system.

Instructions

(a) Calculate the cost of goods sold and the ending inventory using average. (*Hint*: Round the average cost per unit to two decimal places.)
(b) Assume the sales price was $90 per unit for the goods sold on June 10, and $95 per unit for the sale on June 25. Prepare journal entries to record these transactions.
(c) Calculate gross profit for June.
(d) At the end of June, the company counted its inventory. There were 36 units on hand. What journal entry, if any, should the company make to record the difference? What is gross profit after this difference is recorded?

Taking It Further   Explain what might have caused the difference between the perpetual inventory records and the inventory count.

P6–4B   Information for Danielle Company is presented in P6–3B. Assume the same inventory data and that the company uses a perpetual inventory system. Ignore the inventory difference from P6-3B (d).

Apply perpetual FIFO and answer questions.

(SO 2, 3) AP

Instructions

(a) Calculate the cost of goods sold and the ending inventory using FIFO.
(b) Assume that Danielle Company wants to change to the average cost formula. What factors must it consider before making this change?

(c) If the company does change to average and prices continue to rise, would you expect the cost of goods sold and ending inventory amounts to be higher or lower than these amounts under FIFO?

Taking It Further Which inventory cost formula—FIFO or average—will provide Danielle with the best income statement valuation? The best balance sheet valuation? Explain.

Apply perpetual FIFO and average. Answer questions about financial statement effects.
(SO 2, 3) AP

P6–5B Grinder Company sells a variety of skateboards and accessories. Information follows for Grinder's purchases and sales during April and May 2011 of GrindKing, one of its top brands of skateboards:

	Purchases		Sales	
	Units	Unit Cost	Units	Unit Price
Apr. 8			18	$320
23	50	$202		
26			50	300
May 9	24	198		
21			32	290

Grinder uses a perpetual inventory system. On April 1, Grinder had 36 units on hand at a cost of $210 each. All purchases and sales during April and May were on account.

Instructions

(a) Determine the cost of goods sold and ending inventory under a perpetual inventory system using (1) FIFO and (2) average. (*Hint*: Round the average cost per unit to three decimal places.)
(b) Calculate gross profit using (1) FIFO and (2) average.
(c) Which cost formula produces the higher cash flow?

Taking It Further What factors should Grinder's owner consider when choosing a cost formula?

Record transactions using perpetual FIFO. Apply LCNRV.
(SO 2, 4) AP

P6–6B You are given the following information for transactions by Schwinghamer Co. All transactions are settled in cash. Returns are normally not damaged and are restored immediately to inventory for resale. Schwinghamer uses a perpetual inventory system and the FIFO cost formula.

Date	Transaction	Units	Unit Price
Oct. 1	Beginning inventory	60	$14
5	Purchase	110	13
8	Sale	140	20
10	Sale return	25	20
15	Purchase	35	12
16	Purchase return	5	12
20	Sale	70	16
25	Purchase	15	11

Instructions

(a) Prepare the required journal entries for the month of October for Schwinghamer Co.
(b) Determine the ending inventory for Schwinghamer.
(c) On October 31, Schwinghamer Co. learns that the product has a net realizable value of $10 per unit. What amount should ending inventory be valued at on the October 31 balance sheet?
(d) What amount should cost of goods sold be valued at on the October income statement? Prepare the journal entry, if required, to recognize the decrease in value of this product.

Taking It Further What if Schwinghamer had used average instead of FIFO? How would this affect the October 31 ending inventory on the balance sheet compared with FIFO?

P6–7B The records of Leblanc Company show the following amounts in its December 31 financial statements:

Determine effects of inventory errors.
(SO 1, 3) AN

	2011	2010	2009
Total assets	$600,000	$575,000	$525000
Owner's equity	280,000	275,000	250,000
Cost of goods sold	315,000	335,000	300,000
Profit	60,000	50,000	40,000

Leblanc made the following errors in determining its ending inventory:

1. The ending inventory account balance at December 31, 2009, included $20,000 of goods held on consignment for Gillies Company.
2. The ending inventory account balance at December 31, 2010, did not include goods that were purchased for $30,000 and shipped on December 30, 2010, FOB shipping point.

All purchases and sales of inventory were correctly recorded each year.

Instructions

(a) Calculate the correct amount for each of the following for 2009, 2010, and 2011:
   1. Total assets
   2. Owner's equity
   3. Cost of goods sold
   4. Profit
(b) Indicate the effect of these errors (overstated, understated, or no effect) on cash at the end of 2009, 2010, and 2011.

Taking It Further   If the merchandise inventory balance is correct as at December 31, 2011, is it necessary to correct the errors in the previous years' financial statements? Explain.

P6–8B The records of Pelletier Company show the following data:

Determine effects of inventory errors. Calculate inventory turnover.
(SO 3, 4) AN

	2011	2010	2009
Income statement:			
Sales	$324,000	$312,000	$300,000
Cost of goods sold	270,000	255,000	240,000
Operating expenses	50,000	50,000	50,000
Balance sheet:			
Merchandise inventory	20,000	30,000	35,000

After its July 31, 2011, year end, Pelletier discovered two errors:

1. Ending inventory in 2010 was overstated by $10,000. Pelletier included goods held on consignment for another company in the physical count.
2. In August 2009, Pelletier recorded a $15,000 inventory purchase on account for goods that had been received in July 2009. The physical inventory account correctly included this inventory, and $35,000 is the correct amount of inventory at July 31, 2009.

Instructions

(a) Prepare incorrect and corrected income statements for the years ended July 31, 2009, 2010, and 2011.
(b) What is the combined effect of the errors on owner's equity at July 31, 2011, before correction?
(c) Calculate the correct and incorrect inventory turnover ratios for each of the years 2010 and 2011.

Taking It Further   Compare the trends in the incorrectly calculated annual profits with the trends in the correctly calculated annual profits. Does it appear that management may have deliberately made these errors, or do they appear to be honest errors? Explain.

P6–9B You have been provided with the following financial information regarding Love Paper Co.'s inventory for June and July.

Apply LCNRV and prepare adjustment.
(SO 4) AP

	Paper Inventory (in tonnes)	Cost/Tonne	NRV/Tonne
June 30	5,000	$760	$850
July 31	6,700	880	815

Instructions

(a) Calculate the cost, the net realizable value, and the amount to be reported on the balance sheet for Love Paper's inventory at (1) June 30 and (2) July 31.

(b) Prepare any journal entries required to record the LCNRV of the paper inventory at (1) June 30 and (2) July 31. Love Paper uses a perpetual inventory system.

(c) Assume that during the month of August the company did not purchase any additional paper inventory and that on August 31 it had 5,500 tonnes in inventory and the NRV/tonne was $820. Is an adjusting entry required at August 31? Explain. If so, prepare the adjusting entry.

(d) What is Love Paper required to disclose in its notes to the financial statements with regards to LCNRV?

Taking It Further Why is it important to report inventory at the LCNRV on the balance sheet?

Calculate ratios.
(SO 4) AN

P6–10B The following financial information (in US$ millions) is for two major corporations for the three fiscal years ending as follows:

Home Depot, Inc.	February 1, 2008	February 3, 2007	January 28, 2006
Net sales	$71,288	$77,349	$79,022
Cost of sales	47,298	51,352	52,476
Profit	2,260	4,395	5,761
Cash and short-term investments	525	457	614
Accounts receivable	972	1,259	3,223
Inventory	10,673	11,731	12,822
Other current assets	1,192	1,227	1,341
Current liabilities	11,153	12,706	12,931
Lowe's Companies, Inc.			
Net sales	$48,230	$48,283	$46,927
Cost of sales	31,729	31,556	30,729
Profit	2,195	2,809	3,105
Cash and short-term investments	661	530	796
Inventory	8,209	7,611	7,144
Other current assets	381	545	374
Current liabilities	8,022	7,751	6,539

Instructions

Calculate the inventory turnover, days sales in inventory, current ratio, acid-test ratio, gross profit margin, and profit margin for each company for 2009 and 2008.

Taking It Further Comment on each company's profitability and liquidity.

Apply periodic FIFO and average.
(SO 5) AP

*P6–11B Savita Company had a beginning inventory on January 1, 2011, of 100 units of product E2-D2 at a cost of $30 per unit. During the year, purchases were as follows:

	Units	Unit Cost
Feb. 20	600	$32
May 5	300	36
Oct. 12	200	42
Nov. 8	150	44

Savita uses a periodic inventory system. At the end of the year, there were 225 units on hand.

Instructions

(a) Determine the cost of goods available for sale.

(b) Determine the ending inventory and the cost of goods sold using (1) FIFO and (2) average.

(c) During the year, Savita Company sold product E2-D2 for $70 per unit. Calculate gross profit using FIFO and average.

Taking It Further The owner of Savita Company would like to minimize her income taxes. Last year, prices were falling and Savita Company used FIFO. Should Savita Company continue to use FIFO or change to average? Explain.

*P6–12B You are given the following information about Tumatoe Company's inventory for the month of August.

Date	Description	Units	Unit Cost
Aug. 1	Beginning inventory	15,000	$3.75
2	Sale	10,000	
6	Purchase	40,000	4.00
10	Sale	30,000	
15	Sale	4,500	
19	Purchase	45,000	4.25
24	Sale	50,000	
28	Purchase	20,000	4.50

Instructions

(a) Calculate the cost of ending inventory and cost of the goods sold using average in (1) a periodic system and (2) a perpetual system. (*Hint*: Round the average cost per unit to four decimal places.)

(b) Compare your results for parts 1 and 2 of instruction (a), and comment on the differences between the two systems.

Taking It Further Companies are required to disclose their inventory cost determination method. Should they also be required to disclose if they are using a periodic or a perpetual inventory system? Explain.

*P6–13B You are given the following information for Armadillo Company for January 2011:

Date	Description	Units	Unit Price
Jan. 1	Beginning inventory	35	$60
5	Purchase	125	64
7	Sale	110	90
14	Purchase	30	68
20	Sale	60	95
21	Sale return	5	95
25	Purchase	20	70

Instructions

(a) Calculate the ending inventory and cost of goods sold using the FIFO cost formula in (1) a perpetual inventory system, and (2) a periodic inventory system.

(b) Compare the ending inventory and cost of goods sold amounts using FIFO in a perpetual system and FIFO in a periodic system.

Taking It Further Discuss the differences or similarities between the two inventory systems when using FIFO.

Determine inventory loss
using gross profit method.
(SO 6) AP

*P6–14B   Thierry Company lost 80% of its inventory in a fire on March 23, 2011. The accounting records showed the following gross profit data for February and March:

	February	March (to Mar. 23)
Sales	$309,000	$292,500
Sales returns and allowances	6,000	5,800
Sales discounts	3,000	2,700
Purchases	203,000	196,000
Purchase returns and allowances	4,300	3,940
Purchase discounts	2,000	1,950
Freight in	3,000	2,940
Beginning inventory	17,500	25,200
Ending inventory	25,200	?

Thierry is fully insured for fire losses but must prepare a report for the insurance company.

Instructions

Determine both the estimated total inventory and the inventory lost in the March fire.

Taking It Further   The insurance adjustor is concerned that this method of calculating the cost of the inventory destroyed might not be accurate. What factors contribute to the accuracy of the ending inventory amount when using the gross profit method?

Determine ending inventory
using retail method.
(SO 6) AP

*P6–15B   Abbotsford Department Store uses the retail inventory method to estimate its monthly ending inventories. The following information is available for two of its departments at August 31, 2011:

	Clothing		Jewellery and Cosmetics	
	Cost	Retail	Cost	Retail
Sales		$1,375,000		$895,000
Sales returns and allowances		27,000		5,400
Purchases	$770,000	1,440,000	$560,000	918,000
Purchase returns and allowances	36,000	65,500	12,200	19,700
Purchase discounts	5,000		2,800	
Freight in	7,900		5,700	
Beginning inventory	50,600	92,000	29,000	48,000

On August 31, Abbotsford Department Store takes a physical inventory count at retail. The actual retail values of the inventories in each department on August 31, 2011, are as follows: Clothing $112,750, and Jewellery and Cosmetics $53,300.

Instructions

Determine the estimated cost of the ending inventory for each department on August 31, 2011, using the retail inventory method.

Taking It Further   Calculate the store's loss on August 31, 2011, from theft and other causes, at retail and at cost.

Continuing Cookie Chronicle

(*Note:* This is a continuation of the Cookie Chronicle from Chapters 1 through 5.)

Natalie is busy establishing both divisions of her business (cookie classes and mixer sales) and completing her business diploma. Her goals for the next 11 months are to sell one mixer per month and to give two to three classes per week.

The cost of the fine European mixers is expected to increase. Natalie has just negotiated new terms with Kzinski that include shipping costs in the negotiated purchase price (mixers will be shipped FOB destination).

Recall that Natalie has three mixers in inventory: Mixer #1—serial number 12459, Mixer #2—serial number 23568, and Mixer #3—serial number 36994. Inventory cost for each of these units is $545.

The following mixer purchase and sale transactions occur in February and March 2011:

Feb. 2   Natalie buys two deluxe mixers on account from Kzinski Supply Co. for $1,100 ($550 each), FOB destination, terms n/30. Mixer #4—serial number 49295 and Mixer #5—serial number 56204 are added to inventory.

   16   She sells one deluxe mixer, Mixer #4, for $1,050 cash.

Mar. 2   She buys two deluxe mixers on account from Kzinski Supply Co. for $1,134, FOB destination, terms n/30. Mixer #6—serial number 193896 and Mixer #7—serial number 72531 are added to inventory.

    4   She returns one deluxe mixer, Mixer # 6, received on March 2, to Kzinski Supply Co. The mixer is not the one she had ordered.

   30   Natalie sells two deluxe mixers, Mixer #5 and Mixer #7, for a total of $2,100 cash.

All of the mixers Natalie has purchased and sold, with the exception of Mixer #6, are identical. Natalie has accounted for all of these transactions by mixer number to ensure that she does not lose track of mixers on hand and mixers that have been sold. Natalie wonders if she is accounting for the costs of these mixers correctly.

Instructions

(a) Given that Natalie has accounted for all of these transactions by mixer number, what is the total cost of goods sold for February and March, and the inventory balance at the end of March in Cookie Creations' accounting records?

(b) Answer Natalie's concern–has she been accounting for these transactions correctly? Why or why not? What are the other alternatives that Natalie could use in accounting for her mixer inventory?

(c) Using the average cost formula in a perpetual inventory system, prepare a schedule to track the purchases and sales, and the balance of the mixer inventory account. Use the format from Illustration 6-11.

(d) Prepare a journal entry to correct the March 31 inventory balance from the amount calculated in (a) above, to the ending inventory balance determined using the average cost formula in (c).

BROADENING YOUR PERSPECTIVE

Financial Reporting and Analysis

Financial Reporting Problem

BYP6–1   Refer to the financial statements and Notes to Consolidated Financial Statements for The Forzani Group Ltd. in Appendix A.

Instructions

(a) How does Forzani value its inventory?

(b) Which inventory cost formula does Forzani use? Is this cost formula applied in a perpetual or periodic inventory system?

(c) Do you think that using a different cost formula than the one identified in (b) above would have a material effect on Forzani's results? Explain.

(d) Would using the specific identification cost determination method be appropriate for a Canadian mass market retailer like Forzani? Explain.

(e) For 2009 and 2008, calculate Forzani's inventory as a percentage of current assets and its cost of sales as a percentage of total revenue. Comment on the results.

(f) Forzani's inventory turnover and days sales in inventory were calculated for fiscal 2009 in this chapter in Illustrations 6-17 and 6-18. Calculate these same two ratios for fiscal 2008 (Forzani's inventory at the end of fiscal 2007 was $302,207 thousand). Comment on whether Forzani's management of its inventory improved or weakened in 2009.

Interpreting Financial Statements

BYP6–2 The following information was taken from the management discussion and analysis section of Indigo Books & Music Inc.'s March 28, 2009, annual report (in thousands):

	2009	2008	2007
Cost of sales (cost of goods sold)	$530,300	$524,700	$493,900
Inventories	$221,767	$206,259	$224,059

Additional information from the company's annual report:

1. Inventories are valued at the lower of cost, determined using a moving average cost formula, and market, being net realizable value. Under this method, inventory is recorded at the level of the individual article (stock keeping unit or SKU).

2. Costs include all direct and reasonable expenditures that are incurred in bringing inventories to their present location and condition. Vendor rebates are recorded as a reduction in the price of the products and corresponding inventory is recorded net of vendor rebates.

3. The average cost of an article is continually updated based on the cost of each purchase recorded into inventory. When the company permanently reduces the retail price of an item, there is a corresponding reduction in inventory recognized in the period if the markdown incurred brings the retail price below the cost of the item.

4. The amount of inventory writedowns as a result of net realizable value lower than cost was $1.7 million in fiscal 2009, and there were no reversals of inventory writedowns that were recognized in prior periods. The amount of inventory with net realizable value equal to cost was $1.9 million.

Instructions

(a) Calculate the company's inventory turnover and days sales in inventory ratios for 2009 and 2008. Comment on whether Indigo's management of its inventory improved or weakened in 2009.

(b) Indigo combines the cost of sales with selling and administrative expenses in its income statements. However, cost of sales information is given in Note 3 to the financial statements and in the management discussion and analysis section of the annual report. Is it appropriate for Indigo to do this? Why might Indigo not report cost of sales separately in its income statement?

(c) Does Indigo use a periodic or perpetual inventory system? Explain.

(d) Does Indigo follow the lower of cost or net realizable value rule? Did the application of this rule have any effect on 2009 results? Explain.

(e) Indigo uses the average cost formula to account for its inventories. A major competitor, Amazon.com, Inc., uses the FIFO cost formula to account for its inventories. What difficulties would this create in comparing Indigo's financial results with those of Amazon.com? Explain.

(f) Barnes & Noble, Inc., based in the United States, was the world's largest bookseller in 2009 (according to its website) and was using the retail inventory method to value its inventories. Indigo changed in fiscal 2005 from using the retail inventory method to using the moving average cost formula. Why might Indigo have decided to make this change? Include in your answer a discussion of the costs and benefits of both methods.

Critical Thinking

Collaborative Learning Activity

Note to instructor: Additional instructions and material for this group activity can be found on the Instructor Resource Site.

Working in Groups

BYP6–3 In this group activity, you will review two inventory cost formulas using a perpetual inventory system:

Instructions

(a) Your instructor will divide the class into pairs. Each partner will select one of the above cost formulas and join the "expert" group for that cost formula.

(b) In your "expert" group, you will be given material explaining the inventory cost formula you have chosen. You will work together to

1. calculate ending inventory, cost of goods sold, and gross profit, and

2. illustrate the income statement and balance sheet presentation for your cost formula. Ensure that each group member thoroughly understands the cost formula.

(c) Return to your original partner and explain the cost formula to your partner. Compare the differences between the various formulas.

(d) You may be asked by your instructor to write a short quiz on this topic.

Communication Activity

Writing Handbook

BYP6–4 You are the controller of Small Toys. Mutahir Kazmi, the president, recently mentioned to you that he found an error in the 2010 financial statements that he believes has now corrected itself. In discussions with the Purchasing Department, Mutahir determined that the 2010 ending inventory was understated by $1 million. However, the 2011 ending inventory is correct. Mutahir assumes that 2011 profit is correct and comments to you, "What happened has happened—there's no point in worrying about it now."

Instructions

You conclude that Mutahir is wrong. Write a brief, tactful memo to him that clarifies the situation.

Ethics Case

Ethics in Accounting

BYP6–5 Discount Diamonds carries only one brand and size of diamond—all are identical. Each batch of diamonds that is purchased is carefully coded and marked with its purchase cost. The cost of a diamond can fluctuate significantly from day to day in the marketplace. The company president says she wants to know the profit on each diamond the company sells. You are given the following data from March:

Mar. 1	Beginning inventory was 140 diamonds at a cost of $300 per diamond.
3	Purchased 200 diamonds at a cost of $340 each.
5	Sold 170 diamonds for $600 each.
10	Purchased 340 diamonds at a cost of $370 each.
25	Sold 500 diamonds for $650 each.

Instructions

(a) The president is suggesting the use of specific identification to determine cost of goods sold and the cost of the ending inventory.

1. If specific identification was used, show how Discount Diamonds could *maximize* its gross profit for the month by choosing which diamonds to sell on March 5 and March 25. Calculate the *maximum* gross profit.

2. If specific identification was used, show how Discount Diamonds could *minimize* its gross profit for the month by choosing which diamonds to sell on March 5 and March 25. Calculate the *minimum* gross profit.

(b) Assume that Discount Diamonds uses the average cost formula and a perpetual inventory system. How much gross profit would Discount Diamonds report under this cost formula?

(c) Who are the stakeholders in this situation? Is specific identification cost determination appropriate for this type of business? Why?

(d) Which inventory cost determination method should Discount Diamonds choose? Explain.

"All About You" Activity

BYP6–6 In the "All About You" feature, you read about consignment shops and how they provide an alternative to paying full price for quality goods. As a student living on a tight budget, you have decided to sell some of your textbooks. You are considering two options: selling the textbooks yourself or taking them to the second-hand bookstore that sells used textbooks on consignment.

Instructions

(a) What is selling on consignment? If you sell your books on consignment, will you be the consignor or the consignee?

(b) What are the advantages and disadvantages of selling your textbooks on consignment?

(c) It is suggested that there should be a written agreement between the consignor and consignee. If you decide to sell your textbooks on consignment, what should be agreed to in writing?

(d) Should you keep your accounting textbook forever?

ANSWERS TO CHAPTER QUESTIONS

Answers to Accounting in Action Insight Questions

All About You Insight, p. 316

Q: What is one disadvantage of buying items on consignment?

A: Consignment stores do not typically allow you to return goods, so you need to be very careful when purchasing items.

International Insight, p. 322

Q: What types of inventories are physically moved on a LIFO basis? Should companies that use this physical movement still be allowed to use LIFO for accounting purposes?

A: Inventories that are stockpiled, such as gravel or coal, are physically moved on a LIFO basis. These companies should still follow Canadian and international accounting standards and use either the FIFO or average cost formula. It is more important that the cost formula provide useful information than that it match the physical flow. Under international accounting standards, there is a greater emphasis on correct balance sheet valuation. LIFO, which uses the oldest costs on the balance sheet, provides the least relevant information regarding the value of the inventory on hand.

Across the Organization Insight, p. 333

Q: How can an efficient distribution system reduce expenses by reducing the number of days sales in inventory?

A: Companies like Caterpillar cannot expect their customers to wait for long periods of time when they need to purchase equipment or parts. Previously, in order to make sure the company could meet its customers' needs, Caterpillar would have to keep a large selection of items on hand. Now that the distribution system is more efficient, the company doesn't need to have as many items in inventory even though sales have increased. Even distribution departments can play a large role in making a company profitable.

Answer to Forzani Review It Question 3, p. 323

In Note 2(b) to its financial statements, Forzani discloses that it uses the average cost formula to determine the cost of its inventories.

Answers to Self-Study Questions

1. a   2. d   3. d   4. c   5. b   6. a   7. c   *8. d   *9. b   *10. a

Remember to go back to the beginning of the chapter to check off your completed work!

←

CHAPTER 7
INTERNAL CONTROL AND CASH

beanzespressobar.com

 THE NAVIGATOR

CONCEPTS FOR REVIEW:

Before studying this chapter, you should understand or, if necessary, review:

a. The role of ethics in financial reporting. (Ch. 1, pp. 4–5)

b. How cash transactions are recorded. (Ch. 2, pp. 70–73)

c. How cash is classified on a balance sheet. (Ch. 4, pp. 192–193)

d. What internal control is. (Ch. 6, p. 314)

Keeping Track of the Cash

CHARLOTTETOWN, P.E.I.—Located right in the heart of downtown Charlottetown, Beanz Espresso Bar is bustling with activity on weekdays. On average, 1,200 customers stop by each day for its selection of specialty coffees, homemade soups, sandwiches, and baked goods. "Our back door leads into a federal government building, so we get a lot of office workers coming through," says owner Lori Kays, who launched the business with her husband and business partner, Doug Hurry, back in 1995. "But we really cater to every age group since we're open seven days a week."

Lunch is the busiest time for Beanz, which seats 65 on the main floor plus an additional 45 on its deck. The two cash registers are shared by the six staff members working behind the counter on any given shift. "In an ideal situation, one or two people would be designated to ring in orders, but when we get swamped, we all have to work together to keep things running smoothly," says Ms. Kays.

The prices of most items are pre-programmed in the machines, which reduces the chances of entry errors. Each register generates a sales report at the end of the day. Ms. Kays checks the day's cash receipts against the report to make sure they match. She also verifies the closing balances for the two floats—$250 for each till. "I tend to allow a few dollars' leeway since we round down amounts here and there when customers are short a few cents."

If the difference is larger, she goes through the register's internal tape to trace the source. "I will backtrack and try to make sure there weren't any payouts for which a receipt should have been turned in—we often make a run to the grocery store for something we need using cash from the till," she explains. For these petty cash items, staff use the Paid Out button on the till and have a receipt/invoice to match the payout. "A lot of times it's just an item that's been rung in improperly," she says.

Ms. Kays does all of her bookkeeping herself using Simply Accounting software. "I post my sales totals each day and reconcile everything with my bank statements once a month," she says. "At the end of every year, I do everything except the last few adjusting entries before sending things off to the accountants." Careful cash control throughout the year helps ensure that everything adds up every time!

The Navigator

STUDY OBJECTIVES:

After studying this chapter, you should be able to:

1. Explain the activities that help achieve internal control.
2. Apply control activities to cash receipts.
3. Apply control activities to cash disbursements including petty cash.
4. Describe the control features of a bank account.
5. Prepare a bank reconciliation.
6. Report cash on the balance sheet.

The Navigator

As the feature story about Beanz Espresso Bar shows, control of cash is important. Business owners and managers are responsible for safeguarding cash and other assets and for making sure that financial information is reliable. In this chapter, we explain the important features of an internal control system and describe how these controls apply to cash receipts and disbursements, including the use of a petty cash fund. Then we describe the use of a bank and explain how cash is reported on the balance sheet.

The chapter is organized as follows:

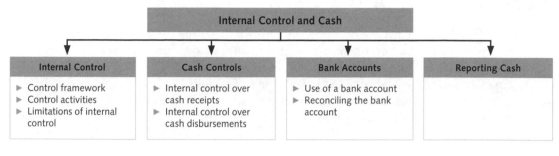

Internal Control

STUDY OBJECTIVE 1

Explain the activities that help achieve internal control.

Could there be dishonest employees where you work? Unfortunately, the answer sometimes is "Yes." The following real occurrences show this well:

- A trusted bookkeeper stole almost $1 million from 21 non-profit daycare centres.
- The controller of a Canadian manufacturing company paid himself $2 million more than his normal pay level by writing unauthorized cheques on the company's payroll account. He got rid of the cancelled cheques when they were returned from the bank and then he altered the books.
- An assistant bank manager stole more than $10 million from a Toronto bank by making loans to fictitious companies.
- A high-level executive of a Canadian newspaper empire was sentenced to more than six years in prison for his role in the misappropriation of millions of dollars.

Helpful hint Errors are unintentional mistakes. Irregularities are intentional mistakes and misrepresentations.

These situations, as well as the possibility of honest errors, emphasize that a good system of internal control is necessary.

Internal control is the process that management designs and implements to help an organization achieve:

1. Reliable financial reporting
2. Effective and efficient operations
3. Compliance with relevant laws and regulations

Internal control has received increased attention in recent years. For example, the *Sarbanes-Oxley Act* governing publicly traded companies was created in the United States to help restore confidence in financial reporting. In Canada, similar legislation requires senior executives, such as CFOs and CEOs, of publicly traded companies to formally certify the effectiveness of their company's internal controls. Several control frameworks have been created to help managers and auditors design and evaluate internal controls (e.g., CICA's Canadian Criteria of Control and measures from the Committee of Sponsoring Organizations of the Treadway Commission, or COSO).

Control Framework

An effective control framework is likely to have the following components:

- Control environment
- Risk assessment
- Control activities
- Information and communication
- Monitoring

Control Environment

Internal control is the responsibility of management. In order to create a strong and sustainable control environment, management must create a corporate culture that values clear rules—and expect everyone to stick to those rules. Management can contribute to a strong control environment in many ways, such as by creating a corporate code of conduct, supporting a rigorous internal control program, establishing a hotline for anonymous reporting, and consistently disciplining employees who break the established rules.

Risk Assessment

To assess risk, management evaluates internal vulnerabilities and how they are connected with changes in the external environment. Risk may be related to financial reporting, operations, or compliance with laws and regulations. Understanding potential risks is the first step in designing an effective control framework.

Control Activities

Control activities are the policies and procedures that help ensure that management's directions are followed. They are the actions that must be taken to respond to risks that threaten reliable financial reporting, effective and efficient operations, and compliance with relevant laws and regulations. The specific control activities that are used depend on the size and type of business, and on management's control philosophy. Control activities are explored in greater detail in the next section.

Information and Communication

Relevant information must be identified, collected, and communicated. The daily sales report generated by cash registers at Beanz Espresso Bar in the feature story is an example of information and communication being used as a form of internal control.

Monitoring

Monitoring involves identifying problems and reporting them to appropriate levels of the organization where action can be taken. To be effective, problems must be communicated to employees who have the authority to act on the information. In the feature story, the small size of the Beanz Espresso Bar makes monitoring much easier. Ms. Kays, the owner, personally oversees the day-to-day activities. For larger organizations, ongoing management activities help monitor the control systems.

Control Activities

While each component of the internal control framework is important, we will focus here on just one: control activities. Control activities that apply to most companies include:

- Establishment of responsibility
- Physical and IT controls
- Segregation of duties
- Independent checks of performance
- Documentation procedures
- Human resource controls

Each of these control activities is explained in the following sections.

Establishment of Responsibility

An essential control activity is to make specific employees responsible for specific tasks. Control is most effective when only one person is responsible for a task. To illustrate, assume that the cash in the cash register at the end of the day at Beanz Espresso Bar in the feature story is $50 less than it should be according to the tape in the cash register. If only one person at the restaurant has operated the register, that person is probably responsible for the shortage. If two or more individuals have worked the register, however, as happens at Beanz Espresso Bar when the restaurant is busy, it may be impossible to determine who is responsible for the error.

Internal control would be strengthened at Beanz Espresso Bar if all staff members had their own cash drawers. On the other hand, the owner, Lori Kays, has a procedure to reduce the problems that may result from having more than one person using the same cash drawer. Ms. Kays is able to quickly identify any shortages at Beanz Espresso Bar by checking the cash receipts against the cash register sales report at the end of each day.

Responsibility for authorizing and approving transactions must also be given to the correct person. For example, the vice-president of finance—not the vice-president of sales—should establish policies for making credit sales.

Segregation of Duties

Segregation of duties is essential in a system of internal control. As long as it does not double how much effort is needed, the work of one employee should be a reliable basis for monitoring the work of another employee. In other words, duties should be divided up so that one person cannot both commit a fraud and cover it up. There are two common ways of applying this control activity:

1. The responsibility for related activities should be assigned to different individuals.
2. The responsibility for accounting for an asset should be separate from the responsibility for physical custody of that asset.

Related Activities. When one person is responsible for all related activities, the potential for errors and irregularities increases. To show how this can be a problem, we will look at the related activities in purchasing and selling merchandise.

Related purchasing activities include ordering merchandise, receiving the goods, and paying (or authorizing payment) for the merchandise. How could someone commit a fraud if he or she is responsible for all—or even two—of these activities? Here are some examples. If the same person is responsible for ordering and for receiving, he can arrange to have an order sent to his home and pretend the goods were received by the company. Or if the same person is responsible for ordering and paying for the merchandise, she can place orders with friends or with suppliers who give kickbacks. When a second person is not needed to authorize the payment, it can happen that no one notices that the company may be paying too much for its purchases of merchandise. Or, even worse, fictitious invoices might be approved for payment. When the responsibility for ordering, receiving, and paying is given to different individuals, there is less risk of such abuses.

Similarly, related sales activities should be done by different individuals. Related selling activities include making a sale, shipping (or delivering) the goods to the customer, and billing the customer. When one person handles related sales transactions, he or she can make sales at unauthorized prices to increase sales commissions, ship goods to him- or herself, or understate the amount that is billed in sales to friends and relatives. These abuses are reduced by dividing the sales tasks: salespersons make the sale, shipping department employees ship the goods based on the sales order, and billing department employees prepare the sales invoice after comparing the sales order with the report of goods shipped.

It is also important to segregate selling duties in small businesses such as Beanz Espresso Bar in our feature story. For the reasons mentioned above, the same person should not take and fill an order, and then collect payment from the customer. Since segregation of selling duties in a small business can be difficult, because there are fewer people, it is useful to have the sales prices of items pre-programmed into the cash registers—as they are at Beanz Espresso Bar. This decreases the risk of an employee undercharging a friend on purpose.

Custody of Assets. If the same person has physical custody of an asset and keeps the accounting records for that asset, then errors or theft could be hidden by altering the accounting records. When the employee who keeps the records of an asset is a different person from the employee who keeps the asset itself (the custodian), the employee who keeps the asset is unlikely to use it dishonestly. The separation of accounting responsibility from the custody of assets is especially important for cash and inventories because these assets are vulnerable to unauthorized use or theft.

Documentation Procedures

Documents give evidence that transactions and events have happened. At Beanz Espresso Bar, the cash register sales report and internal tape is the restaurant's documentation for a sale and the amount of cash received. Similarly, a shipping document indicates that goods have been shipped, and a sales invoice indicates that the customer has been billed for the goods. By adding signatures (or initials) to a document, it also becomes possible to identify the individual(s) responsible for the transaction or event.

Procedures should be established for documents. First, whenever possible, documents should be prenumbered and all documents should be accounted for. Prenumbering helps to prevent a transaction from being recorded more than once, or not at all. Second, source documents (such as original receipts) for accounting entries should be promptly sent to the accounting department to help the transaction be recorded in a timely way. This control helps make the accounting records accurate and reliable.

Documentation as a control procedure also includes ensuring that all controls are written down and kept updated. Well-maintained documentation procedures ensure that the control activities are not forgotten and can make it easier to train new employees.

Physical and IT Controls

Physical and information technology (IT) controls include mechanical and electronic controls to safeguard (protect) assets and improve the accuracy and reliability of the accounting records.

Companies will take many approaches to protecting their information systems. One such approach is **encryption**, which is a way of rearranging messages so that they cannot be read by anyone who does not know the scrambling process. **Firewalls**, or systems designed to prevent unauthorized access to a private network connected to the Internet, are also used. Information security is an area of growing importance to companies, as computers continue to become an integral part of every business.

Examples of these controls are shown in Illustration 7-1.

◀ **Illustration 7-1**

Physical and IT controls

Safes, vaults, and safety deposit boxes for cash and business papers

Locked warehouses and storage cabinets for inventories and records

Computer facilities with password (or biometric, encryption technology, or firewalls) access

Alarms to prevent break-ins

Television monitors and garment sensors to discourage theft

Time clocks to record time worked

Independent Checks of Performance

Most internal control systems include independent internal and/or external reviews of performance and records. This means having an independent person verify that the company's control activities are being correctly followed. To get the most from a performance review:

1. The review should be done periodically or by surprise.
2. The review should be done by someone who is independent of the employee who is responsible for the information.
3. Discrepancies and exceptions should be reported to a management level that can do whatever is necessary to correct the situation.

Internal Review. Segregating the physical custody of assets from accounting record keeping is not enough to ensure that nothing has been stolen. An independent review still needs to be done. In such a review, the accounting records are compared with existing assets or with external sources of information. The reconciliation of the cash register sales report with the cash in the register by Beanz Espresso Bar owner Lori Kays in the feature story is an example of comparing records with assets. When the person who does the review works for the organization, we call this an internal review.

In large companies, control activities, including independent internal reviews, are often monitored by internal auditors. **Internal auditors** are company employees who evaluate the effectiveness of the company's system of internal control. They periodically review the activities of departments and individuals to determine whether the correct control activities are being followed. But an internal audit is effective only when the audit results are reported to senior management and/or the company's owners.

Internal control over financial reporting is so important to users of financial statements today that the Canadian Securities Administrators now require the chief executive officer and chief financial officer to certify that they have evaluated the effectiveness of the company's internal control over financial reporting. Their conclusions must be included in the company's management discussion and analysis section of the annual report and they must describe the evaluation process that they used.

External Review. It is useful to contrast independent *internal* reviews with independent *external* reviews. **External auditors**, in contrast to internal auditors, are independent of the company. They are professional accountants hired by a company to report on whether or not the company's financial statements fairly present the company's financial position and results of operations.

All public companies, including The Forzani Group Ltd., are required to have an external audit. A copy of Forzani's auditors' report is included in Appendix A. As you will see in the report, external auditors plan and perform an audit that will allow them to be reasonably sure that the financial statements do not contain any significant errors. In the following section on the limitations of internal control, the concept of reasonable assurance is discussed further.

While external auditors need to understand a company's internal controls, they are not required to test how effective the controls are or to give any kind of assurance about a company's internal control. In Canada, this is the responsibility of company management.

Human Resource Controls

Human resource control measures can include the following:

1. Bonding of employees who handle cash. Bonding means getting insurance protection—called **fidelity insurance**—against the theft of assets by dishonest employees. If an employer has fidelity insurance, the insurance company will compensate the employer for losses incurred as a result of the dishonesty of an employee. This measure also helps safeguard cash in two ways: First, the insurance company carefully screens all individuals before adding them to the policy and may reject risky applicants. Second, bonded employees know that the insurance company will prosecute all offenders.
2. Rotating employees' duties and requiring employees to take vacations. These measures discourage employees from attempting any thefts since they will not be able to permanently hide their improper actions. Many bank embezzlements, for example, have been discovered when the guilty employee was on vacation or assigned to a new position.

Limitations of Internal Control

No matter how well it is designed and operated, a company's system of internal control can only give reasonable assurance that assets are properly safeguarded and that accounting records are reliable. The concept of reasonable assurance is based on the belief that the cost of control activities should not be more than their expected benefit.

To illustrate, consider shoplifting losses in retail stores. Such losses could be eliminated by having a security guard stop and search customers as they leave the store. Store managers have concluded, however, that the negative effects of doing this cannot be justified. Instead, stores have tried to control shoplifting losses by using less costly and intrusive procedures such as posting signs that state "We reserve the right to inspect all packages" and "All shoplifters will be prosecuted," using hidden TV cameras and store detectives to watch customer activity, and using sensor equipment at exits.

The human factor is an important limit in every system of internal control. A good system can become ineffective as a result of employee fatigue, carelessness, indifference, or lack of proper training. For example, a receiving clerk may not bother to count goods received, or may alter or "fudge" the counts.

Occasionally, two or more individuals may work together to get around controls, which eliminates the protection offered by segregating duties. If a supervisor and a cashier collaborate to understate cash receipts, the system of internal control may be beaten (at least in the short run). This is often referred to as collusion.

The size of the business may also limit internal control. As mentioned earlier, in small companies it may be difficult to segregate duties or have independent checks of performance. As shown in our feature story, in small companies the owner needs to be responsible for independent checks of performance and may have to oversee functions that should not be done by the same person, such as authorizations over assets and access to the assets, if it is not possible to segregate these duties.

ACCOUNTING IN ACTION: ALL ABOUT YOU

Protect your identity. Personal information, such as your name, date of birth, address, credit card number, and social insurance number (SIN), can be used to steal money from your bank account, make purchases, or even get a job. Are you a victim?

According to a 2008 survey of Canadian consumers, conducted by the McMaster eBusiness Research Centre, almost 1.7 million Canadian adults were the victim of some kind of identity fraud in the last year. The victims spent over 20 million hours and more than $150 million to resolve the problems associated with the frauds. More than half of these frauds involved the unauthorized use of credit cards. In addition to the fraud victims, another 2.7% of Canadian adults indicated that their personal data had been accessed by unauthorized people as part of a data breach, thus another 700,000 Canadian adults became at risk for identity fraud.

Source: **Susan Sproule and Norm Archer**, "Measuring Identity Theft in Canada: 2008 Consumer Survey,"
Working Paper 23, McMaster eBusiness Research Centre, available at:
http://www.merc-mcmaster.ca/working-papers/measuring-identity-theft-in-canada-2008-consumer-survey/

Whose responsibility is it for losses due to unauthorized credit card use?

BEFORE YOU GO ON . . .

→ Review It

1. What are the three things that internal control helps an organization achieve?
2. Identify and describe the five main components of an effective control framework.
3. What are the limitations of internal control?

→ Do It

In each of the following situations, identify the appropriate control activity and state whether it has been supported or violated:

(a) The purchasing department orders, receives, and pays for merchandise.
(b) All cheques are prenumbered and accounted for.
(c) The internal auditor performs surprise cash account checks.
(d) Extra cash is kept locked in a safe that can only be accessed by the head cashier.
(e) Each cashier has his or her own cash drawer.
(f) The company's controller received a plaque for distinguished service because he had not taken a vacation in five years.

Action Plan

- Understand each of the control activities: establishment of responsibility, segregation of duties, documentation procedures, physical and IT controls, independent checks of performance, and human resource controls.

Solution

(a) Violation of segregation of duties.
(b) Support of documentation procedures.
(c) Support of independent checks of performance.
(d) Support of physical and IT controls.
(e) Support of establishment of responsibility.
(f) Violation of human resource controls (employees should take vacations).

The Navigator

Related exercise material: BE7–1, E7–1, E7–2, E7–3, and E7–4.

Cash Controls

Just as cash is the beginning of a company's operating cycle, it is also usually the starting point for a company's system of internal control. Cash is easily concealed and transported, lacks owner identification, and is highly desirable. In addition, because of the large volume of cash transactions, errors may easily happen when handling and recording cash.

To safeguard cash and ensure the accuracy of the accounting records, effective internal control over cash is essential. In the following sections, we explain the application of control activities to cash receipts and disbursements.

Internal Control over Cash Receipts

STUDY OBJECTIVE 2

Apply control activities to cash receipts.

Cash receipts come from a variety of sources: cash sales; collections on account from customers; the receipt of interest, dividends, and rents; investments by owners; bank loans; and proceeds from the sale of property, plant, and equipment. Generally, internal control over cash receipts is more effective when all cash receipts are deposited intact in the bank account every day. Illustration 7-2 shows how the control activities explained earlier apply to cash receipt transactions.

Illustration 7-2 ➜

Application of control activities to cash receipts

Control Activities over Cash Receipts

Establishment of Responsibility

Only designated personnel (cashiers) are authorized to handle cash receipts.

Physical and IT Controls

Store cash in safes and bank vaults; limit access to storage areas; use cash registers; deposit all cash in a bank daily.

Segregation of Duties

Different individuals receive cash, record cash receipts, and hold the cash.

Independant Checks of Performance

Supervisors count cash receipts daily; controller's office compares total receipts with bank deposits daily.

Documentation Procedures

Use remittance advices (mail receipts), cash register tapes, and deposit slips.

Human Resource Controls

Bond personnel who handle cash; require employees to take vacations.

As might be expected, companies vary considerably in how they apply these principles. To illustrate internal control over cash receipts, we will discuss useful control activities for a retail store with over-the-counter, mail-in, and electronic receipts.

Over-the-Counter Receipts

Control of over-the-counter receipts in retail businesses is centred on cash registers that customers can see. A cash sale should be "rung up" on a cash register with the amount clearly visible to the customer. This measure prevents the cashier from entering a lower amount and keeping the extra cash. The customer is given a cash register receipt and, if paying with cash, is expected to count the change that is received.

Receipts for cash sales—paid by coins and paper currency—are becoming rarer. Most customers pay by debit or bank credit card. Although banks charge retailers when these cards are used, there are many advantages for retailers that accept these forms of payment. As they are convenient for customers, the business may get more sales. They also improve internal control because employees handle less cash. There is more information on debit and credit card transactions in the following sections.

Most companies use point-of-sale cash registers that separate daily sales on the cash register tape according to each type of payment: cash, debit card, credit card, or cheque. The cash register tape shows each transaction, totals for each payment type, and an overall total. Cash register tapes should be locked into the register and removed by a supervisor or manager—never by the cashier.

At the end of his or her shift, the cashier should count the cash in the register, record the amount, and turn over the cash and the record of the amount to either a supervisor or the person responsible for making the bank deposit. The procedures will be different in every company, but the basic principles should be the same. The person or persons who handle the cash and make the bank deposit should not have access to the cash register tapes or the accounting records. The cash register tapes should be used in creating the journal entries in the accounting records. An independent person who does not handle the cash should make sure that the amount deposited at the bank agrees with the cash register tapes and the accounting records.

Companies with recurring cash transactions often use a special journal, called a **cash receipts journal**, to record all their receipts of cash. A **special journal** is used to record similar types of transactions. The types of special journals that are used depend largely on the types of transactions that happen frequently. Special journals are shown in Appendix C at the end of this textbook.

Debit Card Transactions   Sales using debit cards are considered cash transactions. Debit cards allow customers to spend only what is in their bank account. When a debit card sale occurs, the bank immediately deducts the cost of the purchase from the customer's bank account. The retailer has a choice about how often the proceeds from debit card transactions are electronically transferred into the retailer's bank account. Some retailers ask the bank to make one deposit at the end of each business day; other retailers wait and have several days of transactions deposited together. Banks usually charge the retailer a transaction fee for each debit card transaction and deduct this fee from the amount deposited in the retailer's bank account.

In many ways, accepting a debit card payment is similar to accepting a personal cheque from a customer. Both are ways for customers to spend the money in their bank accounts. But the major advantage of debit cards is that the retailer knows immediately if the customer has enough money in the bank to pay for the purchase. When a cheque is accepted, it takes several days for the retailer to find out whether the customer had sufficient funds. Most businesses are willing to pay a fee to the bank when customers use debit cards because there is no uncertainty about whether the customer has enough money in their bank account to pay for the purchase.

To illustrate, suppose that on March 21, 10 customers use debit cards to purchase merchandise totalling $800 from Lee Company. Assuming the bank charges Lee Company $0.50 per debit card transaction, the entry made to record these transactions by Lee Company is as follows:

A	=	L	+	OE
+795				−5
				+800

↑ Cash flows: +795

Mar. 21	Cash		795	
	Debit Card Expense (10 × $0.50)		5	
	Sales			800
	To record debit card sales.			

In addition to the service charge for each transaction, Lee Company will also pay a monthly rental charge for the point-of-sale equipment that it uses for debit and credit card transactions.

Bank Credit Card Transactions   Sales using credit cards issued by banks, such as Visa and MasterCard, are considered cash sales by the retailer. A credit card gives customers access to money made available by a bank or other financial institution (essentially a short-term loan that has to be repaid). When a customer uses a bank credit card, the bank transfers the amount of the sale to the retailer's bank, less a service fee. Banks generally charge the retailer a fee that averages 3.5% of the credit card sale. Retailers with a high number of transactions usually get a lower rate; those with a small number of transactions often have a higher rate. Similar to debit card transactions, the retailer's bank will wait until the end of the day and make one deposit for the full day's credit card transactions to the retailer's bank account; there is also the option of having one deposit every few days.

The fees for bank credit cards are generally higher than debit card fees. Why? With a debit card, the bank is charging only for transferring the customer's money to the retailer. With a credit card, the bank is taking the risk that the customer may never repay it for the loan. As we will see in Chapter 8, sometimes companies are not able to collect their receivables. Bank credit cards help retailers avoid this problem. Except for the higher bank charges, recording a bank credit card sale is very similar to recording a debit card sale.

To illustrate, suppose that on March 21, Lee Company sells $800 of merchandise to customers who use bank credit cards. The banks charge Lee Company a service fee of 3.5% for credit card sales. The entry made to record these transactions by Lee Company is:

A	=	L	+	OE
+772				−28
				+800

↑ Cash flows: +772

Mar. 21	Cash		772	
	Credit Card Expense ($800 × 3.5%)		28	
	Sales			800
	To record bank credit card sales.			

In addition to accepting bank credit cards, many large department stores and gasoline companies have their own credit cards. Sales using the retailer's own credit cards are credit sales; they result in accounts receivable, not cash, at the point of sale.

Mail-In Receipts

Helpful hint When billing customers, many companies state "Pay by cheque; do not send cash through the mail." This is done to reduce the risk of cash receipts being misappropriated when they are received.

As an individual customer, you may be more familiar with over-the-counter receipts than with mail-in receipts. However, many companies receive payment from their customers through the mail. Think, for example, of the number of cheques received through the mail each day by companies such as Rogers, Telus, or Bell Mobility.

All mail-in receipts should be opened in the presence of two mail clerks. These receipts are generally in the form of cheques. Each cheque should promptly be stamped "For Deposit Only." This restrictive endorsement reduces the chances that an employee could take the cheque and use it personally. With this type of endorsement, banks will not give cash to an individual.

A list of the cheques that are received each day should be prepared in duplicate. This list shows the name of the issuer of the cheque, the purpose of the payment, and the amount of the cheque. Each mail clerk should sign the list to establish responsibility for the data. The original copy of the list, along with the cheques and remittance advices, is then sent to the cashier's department, where the daily bank deposit is prepared. A copy of the list is sent to the accounting department, where a journal entry to debit Cash and credit Accounts Receivable, or the appropriate account as required, is recorded. The accounting department will also compare the copy of the list with a copy of the bank deposit to make sure that all mail receipts were included in the bank deposit. In a small company, where it is not possible to have the necessary segregation of duties, the owner should be responsible for cash receipts.

Electronic Receipts

Electronic funds transfer (EFT) systems transfer funds between parties without the use of paper (e.g., deposits, cheques). Debit and bank credit cards, discussed earlier in this chapter, are examples of electronic funds transfers.

Another type of EFT receipt happens when customers use on-line banking to pay their accounts. When a customer pays his or her account, the cash is instantly transferred from the customer's bank account to the company's bank account. These transactions are journalized directly by the company from its bank statement. The only evidence of these electronic cash receipts will be a line on the company's bank statement showing the amount, a reference number, and the name or account number of the person paying.

Other customers pay their accounts using EFT and automatic pre-authorized monthly payments. In this case, the company will begin the transaction and electronically request that the funds be transferred from the customer's bank to the company's bank account. Because the company is initiating the transaction, it knows that the transaction is happening and can therefore journalize the transaction before it receives its bank statement.

According to the Canadian Payments Association, the increase in payment options—debit cards, credit cards, on-line banking, telephone banking, automated teller machines (also called automated banking machines), and automatic pre-authorized monthly bill payments—has resulted in a significant decline in customer payments by cheque. Meanwhile, electronic transactions in Canada grew by approximately 1,454% between 1990 and 2007.

Electronic funds transfers normally result in better internal control since no cash or cheques are handled by company employees.

ACCOUNTING IN ACTION: ACROSS THE ORGANIZATION

Canada's Parliament has been examining the fees merchants must pay to accept credit cards, a practice protested by hundreds of thousands of Canadian businesses. Canada's two major credit card companies, Visa and Master-Card, increased merchant charges in 2008, so retailers asked Parliament to examine this escalation in fees, as well as the impact these credit card companies' planned introduction of debit products will have on the current debit card system. As well, merchants have been alarmed by the explosion of premium cards in the Canadian market—cards that carry an increased cost to them. In less than a year, premium cards had grown from a small percentage of credit card transactions to more than 30% for many merchants. Many Canadians aren't aware of these hidden costs, which inevitably get passed onto them whether they pay with credit cards, cash, or debit cards, most likely in the form of higher prices.

Source: Retail Council of Canada news release, May 11, 2009.

Why would businesses continue to accept all credit cards in spite of rapidly increasing credit card fees?

BEFORE YOU GO ON . . .

→ Review It

1. What control activities should be applied to over-the-counter cash receipts?
2. What control activities should be applied to mail-in cash receipts?
3. What is a benefit of using EFT for cash receipts?

→ Do It

Prepare journal entries to record the following selected debit and credit card transactions for Bulk Department Store:

July 18 A customer used her debit card to pay for a $650 purchase. Bulk Department Store was charged a $2 service fee.

22 A customer paid for a $1,200 purchase with her Visa credit card. The bank charges Bulk Department Store a service fee of 3.0%.

25 A customer paid for a $500 purchase with his Bulk Department Store credit card.

Action Plan

- Debit cards are recorded as cash sales, less the service charge.
- Bank credit cards are recorded as cash sales, less the service charge.
- Nonbank credit cards are recorded as receivables. There is no bank service charge when a customer uses a company credit card.

Solution

July	18	Cash	648	
		Debit Card Expense	2	
		Sales		650
		To record debit card sale.		
	22	Cash	1,164	
		Credit Card Expense ($1,200 × 3.0%)	36	
		Sales		1,200
		To record Visa credit card sale.		
	25	Accounts Receivable	500	
		Sales		500
		To record company credit card sale.		

The Navigator

Related exercise material: BE7–2, BE7–3, and E7–5.

Internal Control over Cash Disbursements

STUDY OBJECTIVE 3

Apply control activities to cash disbursements, including petty cash.

Cash is disbursed for a variety of reasons, such as to pay expenses and liabilities, or to purchase assets. Generally, internal control over cash disbursements is better when payments are made by cheque or EFT, rather than in cash. Payment by cheque should occur only after specified control procedures have been followed. The paid cheque gives proof of payment. Illustration 7-3 shows how the control activities explained earlier apply to cash disbursements.

Illustration 7-3 ➡

Application of control activities over cash disbursements

Control Activities over Cash Disbursements

Establishment of Responsibility

Only designated personnel are authorized to sign cheques.

Physical and IT Controls

Store blank cheques in safes with limited access; print cheque amounts electronically

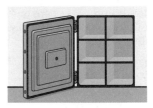

Segregation of Duties

Different individuals approve and make payments; cheque signers do not record disbursements.

Independant Checks of Performance

Compare cheques to invoices; reconcile bank statement monthly.

Documentation Procedures

Use prenumbered cheques and account for them in sequence; each cheque must have an approved invoice.

Human Resources

Hire bonded personnel to perform the cash-related activities.

Cheques

As outlined in Illustration 7-3, the internal controls over cheques include having cheques signed by an authorized person or persons—cheques often require two signatures. The cheque signer(s) should carefully review the supporting documentation for the payment before signing the cheque. There should be a clear segregation of duties between the cheque signing function and the accounts payable function. Cheques should be prenumbered, and all cheque numbers must be accounted for in the payment and recording process. Cheques should never be pre-signed, and blank (unissued) cheques should be physically controlled.

Many large companies use purchase orders to improve their internal control over cash disbursements. A purchase order is an authorization form prepared for each expenditure, or for expenditures larger than a specified amount. The purchase order is usually prepared by the purchasing department.

When the good or service is received, the receiving report is matched with the purchase order. When the seller's invoice is later received, it is matched to the purchase order and receiving report. An authorized person in the accounts payable department then approves the invoice for payment. A cheque is sent on the due date, and the invoice is stamped "Paid."

The accounting department records the payment of the invoice. Companies that have a lot of cash disbursements often use a special journal, called a **cash payments journal**, to record all disbursements of cash. As mentioned earlier, Appendix C at the end of this textbook illustrates the use of special journals.

Electronic Payments

Many companies use electronic funds transfer systems to make payments to suppliers and employees. For example, when a company pays its employees' salaries using a direct deposit option, the cash is instantly transferred from the company's bank account to each employee's bank account. No cheques are issued.

In addition, pre-authorized payments, for things like loans and interest paid on a recurring basis, are often made electronically. As with electronic cash receipts, the only evidence of this payment will be a line on the bank statement showing the amount, reference, and usually the name of the company that was paid.

Internal controls over electronic payments must ensure that all such payments are properly authorized. A person who is independent of the accounts payable department should check that the payments agree with a list of authorized electronic payments. These payments are then journalized from the supporting accounts payable documentation.

EFT payments reduce the extra costs of making payments by cheque, such as postage and envelope costs. They also reduce the risk of lost, stolen, or forged cheques.

BEFORE YOU GO ON . . .

→ Review It

1. What control activities apply to cash disbursements made by cheque?
2. What control activities apply to electronic cash disbursements?

→ Do It

Benett Clothing has the following internal control procedures over cash disbursements:

(a) Blank cheques are stored in an unmarked envelope on a shelf behind the cash register.
(b) The store manager personally approves all payments before signing and issuing cheques.
(c) When the store manager has to go away for an extended period of time, she pre-signs a number of cheques to be used in her absence.
(d) The company cheques are not prenumbered.
(e) The company accountant prepares the bank reconciliation and reports any discrepancies to the store manager.

For each procedure, explain the weakness in internal control and identify the control activity that is violated.

Action Plan

- Identify control activities appropriate for a small business.
- Understand risk exposures.
- Match control activities with risks, based on which control activity will be most effective in reducing the related risk.

Solution

Weakness	Control Activity
(a) Cheques are not stored in a secure area.	Physical and IT controls
(b) The approval and payment of bills is done by the same individual.	Segregation of duties
(c) Blank cheques are signed.	Establishment of responsibility
(d) Cheques are not prenumbered.	Documentation procedures
(e) The bank reconciliation is not independently prepared.	Independent checks of performance.

The Navigator

Related exercise material: BE7–4 and E7–6.

Petty Cash Fund

As you just learned, a company has better internal control over cash disbursements when it makes its payments by cheque or pre-authorized electronic payments. However, using cheques or EFT to pay for small amounts is both impractical and a nuisance. For example, a company may not want to write cheques to pay for postage, couriers, or parking. A common way to handle such payments is to use a petty cash fund. A **petty cash fund** is used to pay relatively small amounts, while still maintaining satisfactory control. The operation of a petty cash fund, also called an imprest system, involves three steps: (1) establishing the fund, (2) making payments from the fund, and (3) replenishing the fund.

Establishing the Fund. Two essential steps are required to establish a petty cash fund: (1) appoint a petty cash custodian to be responsible for the fund, and (2) determine the size of the fund. Ordinarily, the amount is expected to be enough for likely payments in a three- to four-week period. To establish the fund, a cheque payable to the petty cash custodian is issued for the determined amount. If Lee Company decides to establish a $100 petty cash fund on March 1, the entry recorded in the general journal is as follows:

A	=	L	+	OE
+100				
−100				

Cash flows: no effect

Mar. 1	Petty Cash	100	
	Cash		100
	To establish a petty cash fund.		

There is no effect on cash flows because the company's total cash has not changed. There is $100 less in the bank account but $100 more cash on hand. The custodian cashes the cheque and places the proceeds in a locked petty cash box or drawer. No other entries are made to the Petty Cash account unless the size of the fund is increased or decreased. For example, if Lee Company decides on March 15 to increase the size of the fund to $125, it will debit Petty Cash and credit Cash $25 ($125 − $100).

Making Payments from the Fund. The petty cash custodian has the authority to make payments from the fund in accordance with management policies. Usually, management limits the size of expenditures that may be made. Likewise, it may not allow the fund to be used for certain types of transactions (such as making short-term loans to employees). Each payment from the fund should be documented on a prenumbered petty cash receipt, signed by both the custodian and the person who receives the payment. If other supporting documents, such as a freight bill or invoice, are available, they should be attached to the petty cash receipt.

No accounting entry is made to record a payment at the time it is made from petty cash. The receipts are kept in the petty cash box until the fund runs low and the cash needs to be replenished. The sum of the petty cash receipts and money in the fund should equal the established total at all times. Surprise counts can be made by an independent person, such as a supervisor or internal auditor, to determine whether the fund is being properly administered.

Helpful hint For internal control, the receipt satisfies two principles: (1) establishment of responsibility (signature of the custodian), and (2) documentation procedures.

Replenishing the Fund. When the money in the petty cash fund reaches a minimum level, the fund is replenished. The request for reimbursement is made by the petty cash custodian. This individual prepares a schedule (or summary) of the payments that have been made and sends the schedule, supported by petty cash receipts and other documentation, to the controller's office. The receipts and supporting documents are examined in the controller's office to verify that they were proper payments from the fund. The request is approved and a cheque is issued to restore the fund to its established amount. At the same time, all supporting documentation is stamped "Paid" so that it cannot be submitted again for payment.

Helpful hint Replenishing involves three internal control procedures: segregation of duties, documentation procedures, and independent checks of performance.

To illustrate, assume that on March 15 the petty cash fund has $13 cash and petty cash receipts for postage $44, freight in $38 (assume a perpetual inventory system is used), and miscellaneous expenses $5. The petty cash custodian will request a cheque for $87 ($100 − $13). The entry to record the cheque is as follows:

Mar. 15	Postage Expense	44	
	Merchandise Inventory	38	
	Miscellaneous Expense	5	
	Cash		87
	To replenish petty cash.		

A	=	L	+	OE
+38				−44
−87				−5

↓ Cash flows: −87

Note that the Petty Cash account is not affected by the reimbursement entry. Replenishment changes what's in the fund by replacing the petty cash receipts with cash. It does not change the balance in the fund.

Occasionally, when replenishing a petty cash fund, the company may need to recognize a cash shortage or overage. This results when the receipts plus cash in the petty cash box do not equal the established amount of the petty cash fund. To illustrate, assume in the example above that the custodian had only $12 in cash in the fund, plus the receipts as listed. The request for reimbursement would, therefore, have been for $88 ($100 − $12). The following entry would be made:

Mar. 15	Postage Expense	44	
	Merchandise Inventory	38	
	Miscellaneous Expense	5	
	Cash Over and Short	1	
	Cash		88
	To replenish petty cash.		

A	=	L	+	OE
+38				−44
−88				−5
				−1

↓ Cash flows: −88

Conversely, if the custodian had $14 in cash, the reimbursement request would have been for $86 ($100 − $14) and Cash Over and Short would have been credited for $1. A debit balance in Cash Over and Short is reported in the income statement as miscellaneous expense. A credit balance in the account is reported as miscellaneous revenue.

If the petty cash fund is not big enough, it is often increased (or decreased if the amount is too large) when the fund is replenished. Assume that Lee Company decides to increase the size of its petty cash fund from $100 to $125 on March 15 when it replenishes the fund. The entry to record the reimbursement and change in fund size is as follows:

A	=	L	+	OE
+25				−44
+38				−5
−113				−1

Cash flows: −113

Mar. 15	Petty Cash	25	
	Postage Expense	44	
	Merchandise Inventory	38	
	Miscellaneous Expense	5	
	Cash Over and Short	1	
	Cash		113
	To replenish petty cash and increase the fund size by $25.		

In this entry, the Petty Cash account is affected because of the change in size of the fund. After this entry, the general ledger account shows a balance of $125 and the custodian must ensure that cash and paid-out receipts now total $125.

A petty cash fund should be replenished at the end of the accounting period regardless of how much cash is in the fund. Replenishment at this time is necessary in order to recognize the effects of the petty cash payments on the financial statements.

BEFORE YOU GO ON . . .

→ Review It

1. How does using a petty cash system strengthen internal control?
2. When are entries required in a petty cash system?
3. What entries are required in a petty cash system to (1) establish the fund and (2) replenish the fund?

→ Do It

Bateer Company established a $50 petty cash fund on July 1. On July 30, the fund had $12 cash remaining and petty cash receipts for postage $14, office supplies $10, and delivery expense $15. Prepare the journal entries to establish the fund on July 1 and replenish the fund on July 30.

Action Plan

- Set up a separate general ledger account when the fund is established.
- Determine how much cash is needed to replenish the fund—subtract the cash remaining from the petty cash fund balance.
- Total the petty cash receipts. Determine any cash over or short—the difference between the cash needed to replenish the fund and the total of the petty cash receipts.
- Record the expenses incurred according to the petty cash receipts when replenishing the fund.

Solution

July 1	Petty Cash	50	
	Cash		50
	To establish a petty cash fund.		
30	Postage Expense	14	
	Office Supplies	10	
	Delivery Expense	15	
	Cash Over and Short		1
	Cash ($50 − $12)		38
	To replenish petty cash.		

The Navigator

Related exercise material: BE7–5, BE7–6, and E7–7.

Bank Accounts

Use of a Bank Account

STUDY OBJECTIVE 4

Describe the control features of a bank account.

Using a bank makes internal control over cash much stronger. A company can safeguard its cash by using a bank as a depository and reduce the amount of currency that must be kept on hand. In addition, using a bank increases internal control, because it creates a double record of all bank transactions—one by the business and the other by the bank. The asset account Cash, maintained by the company (called the depositor), is the opposite of the bank's liability account for each depositor. It should be possible to reconcile (balance) these accounts at any time.

Many companies have more than one bank account. For efficiency of operations and better control, national retailers like Sears may have local bank accounts. Similarly, a company may have a payroll bank account, as well as one or more general bank accounts. A company may also have accounts with different banks in order to have more than one source for short-term loans when needed.

Bank Deposits and Cheques

Bank deposits should be made by an authorized employee, such as the head cashier. Each deposit must be documented by a deposit slip, as shown in Illustration 7-4.

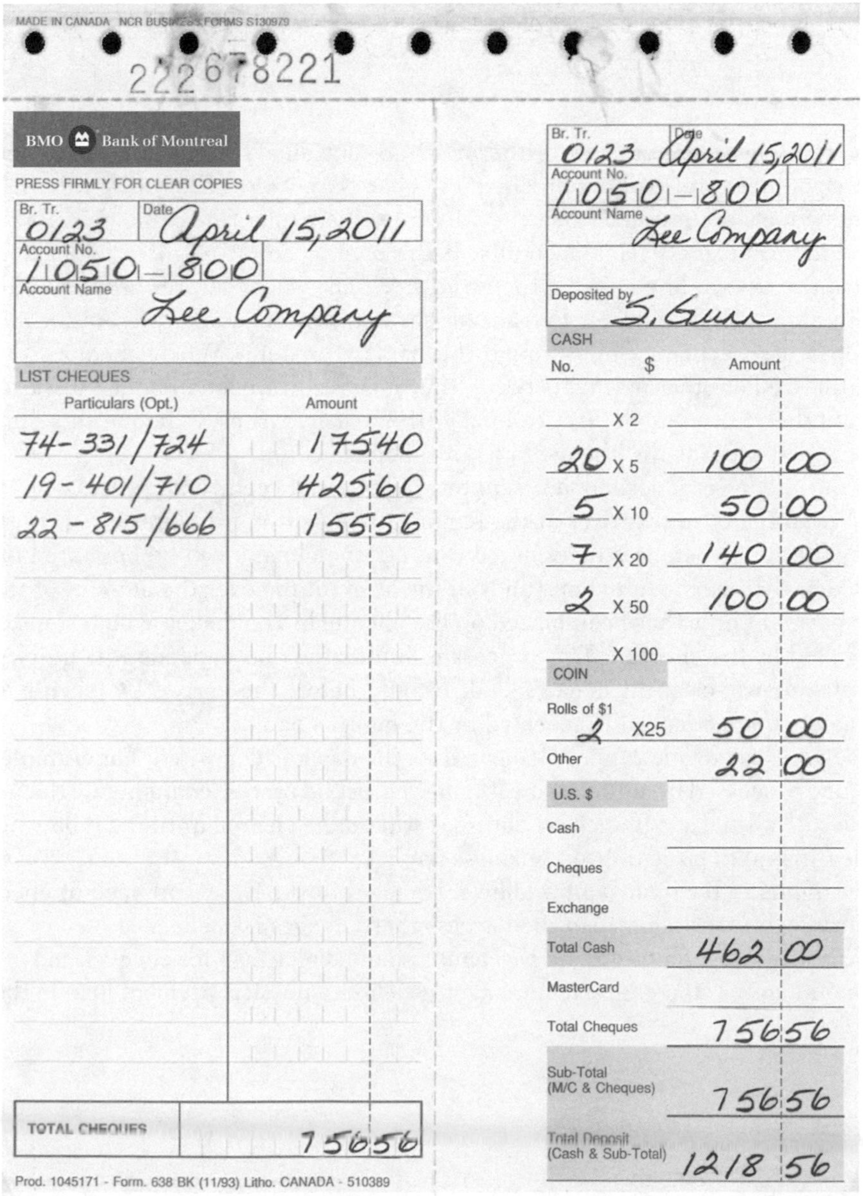
MADE IN CANADA NCR BUSINESS FORMS S130979

222678221

BMO Bank of Montreal

PRESS FIRMLY FOR CLEAR COPIES

Br. Tr. 0123 Date April 15, 2011

Account No. 1050-800

Account Name Lee Company

LIST CHEQUES

Particulars (Opt.)	Amount
74-331/724	175 40
19-401/710	425 60
22-815/666	155 56
TOTAL CHEQUES	756 56

Br. Tr. 0123 Date April 15, 2011

Account No. 1050-800

Account Name Lee Company

Deposited by S. Gunn

CASH No.	$	Amount
	X 2	
20	X 5	100 00
5	X 10	50 00
7	X 20	140 00
2	X 50	100 00
	X 100	
COIN Rolls of $1 2	X25	50 00
Other		22 00
U.S. $ Cash		
Cheques		
Exchange		
Total Cash		462 00
MasterCard		
Total Cheques		756 56
Sub-Total (M/C & Cheques)		756 56
Total Deposit (Cash & Sub-Total)		1218 56

Prod. 1045171 - Form. 638 BK (11/93) Litho. CANADA - 510389

Illustration 7-4

Deposit slip (reproduced with permission of BMO Bank of Montreal)

Both the company and the bank will need a copy of the deposit slip.

While bank deposits increase the bank account balance, cheques decrease it. A cheque is a written order signed by the depositor instructing the bank to pay a specific sum of money to a designated recipient. There are three parties to a cheque: (1) the maker (or drawer) who issues the cheque, (2) the bank (or payer) on which the cheque is drawn, and (3) the payee to whom the cheque is payable. A cheque is a negotiable instrument that can be transferred to another party by endorsement.

Each cheque should clearly explain its purpose. For many businesses, the purpose of a cheque is detailed on the cheque stub, as shown in Illustration 7-5. The purpose of the cheque should also be clear for the payee, either by referencing the invoice directly on the cheque— see the reference to invoice #27622 on the "For" line of the cheque in the illustration—or by attaching a copy of the invoice to the cheque.

Illustration 7-5 ➜

Cheque (reproduced with permission of BMO Bank of Montreal)

Automated teller machine cash withdrawals are not allowed on a business bank account where two signatures are required on cheques. There is no way of knowing if both of the authorized individuals are present when the withdrawal is made. The same principle applies to EFT payments on business bank accounts. If the bank account requires two signatures, the company cannot use on-line banking to pay bills. When two signatures are required, the only way to maintain internal control is to make all payments by cheque or pre-authorized EFT.

How does cash actually flow through the banking system? When cheques, debit cards, and pre-authorized or other payments occur, they may result in one financial institution owing money to another. For example, if a company (the maker) writes a cheque to a supplier (the payee), the payee deposits the cheque in its own bank account.

When the cheque is deposited, it is sent to a regional data centre for processing, usually the same day. When the cheque arrives at the regional data centre, it is "presented" to the payee's financial institution, where it is determined whether the cheque will be honoured or returned (for example, if there are insufficient funds in the account to cover the amount of the cheque, or if a stop payment order has been placed on the cheque by the maker, which stops the money from being paid by the cheque). This process is automated and happens very quickly. In most cases, the cheque will clear the maker's bank account before the next day. **Clearing** is the term used when a cheque or deposit is accepted by the maker's bank.

In some cases, a cheque cannot be cleared on the day it is deposited. For example, cheques that cannot be processed by automated equipment must be processed manually the next day. As well, cheques deposited at a branch on Saturday will not be cleared until the following Monday, because clearing takes place only on business days.

Improvements in technology now allow for images of the front and back of cheques to be taken electronically. Customers can then access these images if needed.

The clearing process for electronic payments is more direct than for cheques and other paper-based payment items, as there is no requirement to deliver a physical payment item in these cases.

Bank Statements

Each month, the bank sends the company a **bank statement** that shows the company's bank transactions and balance. A typical statement is presented in Illustration 7-6. It shows (1) cheques paid and other debits that reduce the balance in the bank account, (2) deposits and other credits that increase the balance in the bank account, and (3) the account balance after each day's transactions.

← Illustration 7-6

Bank statement (reproduced with permission of BMO Bank of Montreal)

Everyday Banking

BMO 🔺 Bank of Montreal

A member of BMO Financial Group

LEE COMPANY
500 QUEEN STREET
FREDERICTON, NB E3B 5C2

Chequing Account# 0123 4567-890
---------------------------------LEE

Fredericton Main Office
505 King Street
FREDERICTON, NB E3B 1E7
Transit number: 0123

Your Everyday Banking statement

For the period ending April 30, 2011

Here's what happened in your account

Date	Description	Amounts deducted from account (debits)	Amounts added to account (credits)	Balance ($)
	Interest Chequing Account # 0123 4567-890			
Owner:				
---------------------------------LEE				
Apr 1	Opening balance			13,256.90
1	Cheque, No. 435	644.95		12,611.95
1	Deposit at BR. 0123		4,276.85	16,888.80
4	Deposit at BR. 0123		2,137.50	19,026.30
4	Cheque, No. 438	776.65		18,249.65
5	Cheque, No. 437	1,185.79		17,063.86
5	Cheque, No. 436	3,260.00		13,803.86
6	Deposit at BR. 0123		1,350.47	15,154.33
7	Deposit at BR. 0249		982.46	16,136.79
7	Cheque, No. 440	1,487.90		14,648.89
8	Cheque, No. 439	1,781.70		12,867.19
8	Cheque, No. 442	2,420.00		10,447.19
11	Deposit at BR. 0123		2,355.28	12,802.47
11	Cheque, No. 441	1,585.60		11,216.87
12	Deposit at BR. 0123		2,720.00	13,936.87
12	Cheque, No. 443	1,226.00		12,710.87
14	Deposit at BR. 0123		757.41	13,468.28
15	Deposit at BR. 0123		1,218.56	14,686.84
15	Deposit at BR. 0123		715.42	15,402.26
18	Returned cheque—NSF	425.60		14,976.66
18	NSF fee	10.00		14,966.66
22	Cheque, No. 444	3,467.11		11,499.55
25	Deposit at BR. 0249		1,578.90	13,078.45
27	EFT, collection from Gillco		1,350.55	14,429.00
28	Service Charge	30.00		14,399.00
29	Deposit at BR. 0123		2,128.60	16,527.60
29	Cheque, No. 447	659.91		15,867.69
29	Interest		39.76	15,907.45

Helpful hint Every deposit received by the bank is credited to the customer's account. The reverse happens when the bank "pays" a cheque issued by a company on the company's chequing account balance. Because payment reduces the bank's liability, the amount is debited to the customer's account with the bank.

At first glance, it may appear that the debits and credits reported on the bank statement are backward. How can amounts that decrease the balance, like a cheque, be a debit? And how can amounts that increase the balance, like a deposit, be a credit? Debits and credits are not really backward. To the company, Cash is an asset account. Assets are increased by debits (e.g., for cash receipts) and decreased by credits (e.g., for cash payments). To the bank, on the other hand, the bank account is a liability account—an amount it must repay to you upon request. Liabilities are increased by credits and decreased by debits. When you deposit money in your bank account, the bank's liability to you increases. That is why the bank shows deposits as credits. When you write a cheque on your account, the bank pays out this amount and decreases (debits) its liability to you.

Note that the cheque for $2,420 shown in Illustration 7-5 is the bank statement's April 8 transaction. Although the cheque was written on April 7, it did not clear the bank until April 8. You can also find the deposit slip for $1,218.56 shown in Illustration 7-4 on the bank statement's April 15 transaction. Other deposits and cheques could be found in the same way by examining the supporting documentation kept on file by the company.

All paid cheques are listed in chronological order on the bank statement, indicating the date the cheque was paid and its amount. A paid cheque is sometimes referred to as a cleared or cancelled cheque. The shift to image-based cheque processing is allowing banks to offer depositors new services that give faster and more convenient access to cancelled cheque images than the common practice of enclosing these cheques with their bank statements once a month. For example, customers can view cancelled cheque images on-line.

Debit Memoranda. Banks charge a monthly fee for using their services, called a **bank service charge**. A **debit memorandum** that explains the charge is usually noted on the bank statement. The symbol DM (debit memo) is often used for such charges. Separate debit memoranda may also be issued for other bank services such as the cost of printing cheques, certifying cheques, and transferring funds to other locations.

A debit memorandum is also used by the bank when a deposited cheque from a customer does not clear because of insufficient funds in the customer's account. In such a case, the cheque is marked **NSF (not sufficient funds)** or RT (returned item) by the customer's bank, and is returned to the depositor's bank (NSF cheques are sometimes referred to as "bounced" cheques). The bank then debits the depositor's account, as shown by the entry "Returned cheque—NSF" on the bank statement in Illustration 7-6. Note that this cheque for $425.60 was originally included in the deposit made on April 15, detailed in Illustration 7-4. Because the deposit was credited (added) to the bank account on April 15 and the cheque was not honoured, it must be debited (deducted) by the bank on April 18.

The company's bank may also charge the company a service charge of $10 or more for processing the returned cheque. In Illustration 7-6 we can see that BMO writes the entry "NSF fee" on the customer's statement for these charges. The company (depositor) then advises the customer who wrote the NSF cheque that their cheque was returned NSF and that a payment is still owed on the account. The company also usually passes the bank charges on to the customer by adding them to the customer's account balance. In summary, the overall effect of an NSF cheque to the depositor is to create an account receivable, and to reduce cash in the bank account. The customer's own bank will also charge the customer an NSF fee of $35 or more for writing an NSF cheque.

Recording an account receivable assumes that the customer will honour the account due by replacing the bounced cheque with a valid cheque, or with cash. This happens in most cases. In the next chapter, we will discuss how to account for uncollectible accounts receivable when customers are unable to pay their accounts.

Credit Memoranda. **Credit memoranda (CM)** identify miscellaneous amounts added to the bank account for items such as interest earned on the bank account, and electronic funds transfers into the depositor's account. For example, as explained earlier in the chapter, some retailers accept electronic payments for merchandise sold on account. Funds are electronically transferred from the customer's account to the retailer's account in payment of the bill. In Illustration 7-6, Lee Company collected an electronic payment from a customer for $1,350.55 on April 27, as indicated by the symbol EFT.

Also note that in Illustration 7-6, interest of $39.76 has been added to Lee Company's bank balance. A bank does not pay interest by sending a cheque to a company. Rather, it deposits the interest earned directly into the company's bank account.

ACCOUNTING IN ACTION: BUSINESS INSIGHT

In addition to being your phone, your cellular device is a mini-computer, an agenda, a camera, and soon it could also be an electronic wallet. UK analysts Juniper Research estimate the value of mobile transactions, or m-payments, will reach US$22 billion worldwide by 2011. Half of this will come from remote payments; for example, using a cell phone to bill a credit card for things like a cab ride. The other half will be from phones with an embedded computer chip, allowing consumers to wave their phones in front of a reader to buy a concert ticket, subway ride, or cup of coffee. Turning cell phones into electronic wallets requires cooperation among all the players: wireless operators, financial institutions, credit card companies, retailers, and handset manufacturers. Still, several players are coming on board. In 2009, cell phone manufacturer Nokia Canada anticipated introducing chip-enabled phones and Visa planned to launch a mobile payment platform in Canada.

Sources: Paul Jay, "Dialing for dollars," CBC News In Depth, CBCNews.ca, November 20, 2007; Visa news release, www.visa.ca/en/merchant/products/mobile.cfm (accessed on May 15, 2009).

What are the benefits of m-payments to consumers? To businesses?

BEFORE YOU GO ON . . .

➔ Review It

1. How does using a bank account contribute to internal control over cash?
2. What is a cleared or cancelled cheque?
3. What are debit memoranda and why do they decrease the balance in a bank account?
4. What are credit memoranda and why do they increase the balance in a bank account?

Related exercise material: BE7–7.

The Navigator

Reconciling the Bank Account

You might assume that the balances you and the bank have for your account will always agree. In fact, the two balances are almost never the same at any specific time. It is necessary to make the balance per books (the balance recorded in a company's general ledger cash account) agree with the balance per bank (the balance recorded on the bank statement)—a process called reconciling the bank account.

> STUDY OBJECTIVE 5
> Prepare a bank reconciliation.

The lack of agreement between the two balances is due to the following:

1. Time lags that prevent one of the parties from recording a transaction in the same period as the other
2. Errors by either party in recording transactions

Except in electronic banking applications, time lags happen often. For example, several days pass between the time a cheque is mailed to a payee and the date the cheque is presented to, and cleared (paid) by, the bank. Cheques recorded by a company that have not yet cleared the bank are called **outstanding cheques**.

Similarly, when the depositor uses the bank's night depository to make deposits, there will be a difference of one day (or more if it's the weekend or a holiday) between the day the receipts are recorded by the depositor and the day they are recorded by the bank. Deposits recorded by the company that have not yet been recorded by the bank are called **deposits in transit**.

Errors also occur. How often errors happen depends on the effectiveness of the internal controls of the depositor and the bank. Bank errors are rare. However, either party could unintentionally record a $450 cheque as $45 or $540. In addition, the bank might mistakenly charge a cheque to the wrong account if the code is missing or if the cheque cannot be scanned.

Reconciliation Procedure

To get the most benefit from a bank reconciliation, it should be prepared by an employee who has no other responsibilities related to cash, or by the owner of the company. In the feature story about Beanz Espresso Bar, the owner prepares the bank reconciliation. If the control activities of segregation of duties and independent checks of performance are not followed when the reconciliation is prepared, cash embezzlements may go unnoticed. For example, a cashier who prepares the reconciliation can steal cash and conceal the theft by misstating the reconciliation. In this way, the bank accounts would appear to reconcile with the company account and the theft would not be discovered.

In reconciling the bank account, it is customary to reconcile the balance per books (found in the Cash account in the general ledger) and the balance per bank (found on the bank statement provided by the bank) to their adjusted (correct) cash balances. The starting point when preparing the reconciliation is to enter the balance per bank statement and balance per books on the schedule. Adjustments are then made to each section, as shown in Illustration 7-7.

Illustration 7-7 →

Bank reconciliation procedures

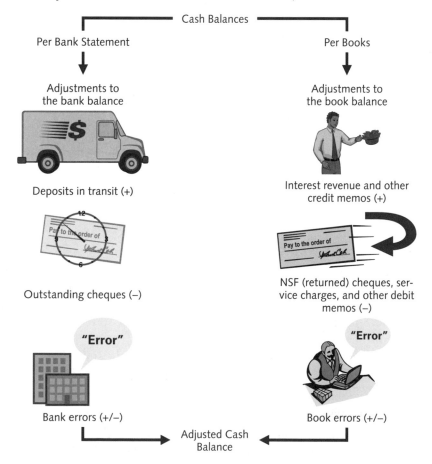

Reconciling Items per Bank. On the bank side of the reconciliation, the items to include are deposits in transit, outstanding cheques, and bank errors.

1. *Deposits in transit.* Compare the individual deposits on the bank statement with (1) the deposits in transit from the preceding bank reconciliation, and (2) the deposits recorded in the company's books. Deposits in transit have been recorded on the company's books but have not yet

been recorded by the bank. They are added to the balance per bank on the bank reconciliation.

Before determining deposits in transit for the current period, you must check whether all deposits in transit that are outstanding from a previous period have cleared. For example, Lee Company used a night deposit slot to deposit $2,201.40 on April 30. The bank did not receive or record this deposit until the next day, May 1. This amount would be treated as a deposit in transit at the end of April and would be added to the balance per bank on the bank reconciliation. However, this outstanding deposit would clear the bank in May and would no longer be a deposit in transit at the end of May. As at the end of May, this amount has been recorded by both the company and the bank.

2. *Outstanding cheques.* Compare the paid cheques shown on the bank statement or returned with the bank statement to (1) cheques that are outstanding from the preceding bank reconciliation, and (2) cheques that have been issued by the company. Outstanding cheques have been recorded on the company's books but have not cleared the bank account yet. They are deducted from the balance per bank on the bank reconciliation.

Note that an outstanding cheque from a previous period means that the cheque was deducted from the books in the previous period but not paid by the bank by the end of that period. If the cheque was paid by the bank in the current month, both sides (book and bank) are now reconciled, the cheque is no longer outstanding, and no further reconciling item is required. If the cheque has still not been presented to the bank for payment, it will continue to be outstanding and needs to be included with the outstanding cheques and deducted from the bank balance on the current month's bank reconciliation.

3. *Bank errors.* Note any errors that are discovered in the previous steps. Errors can be made by either the bank or the company and can be in both directions (increases or decreases). Make sure you include only errors made by the bank as reconciling items when calculating the adjusted cash balance per bank. For example, if the bank processed a deposit of $1,693 as $1,639 in error, the difference of $54 is added to the balance per bank on the bank reconciliation.

Reconciling Items per Books. Reconciling items on the book side include adjustments from any unrecorded credit memoranda (amounts added) and debit memoranda (amounts deducted), and company errors.

1. *Credit memoranda and other deposits.* Compare the credit memoranda and other deposits on the bank statement with the company records. Any amounts on the bank statement but not recorded in the company's records should be added to the balance per books. For example, if the bank statement shows electronic funds transfers from customers paying their accounts online, these amounts will be added to the balance per books on the bank reconciliation, unless they had been previously recorded by the company. This makes the company's records agree with the bank's records.

2. *Debit memoranda and other payments.* Similarly, any unrecorded debit memoranda should be deducted from the balance per books. If the bank statement shows a debit memorandum for bank service charges, this amount is deducted from the balance per books on the bank reconciliation to make the company's records agree with the bank's records. Normally electronic payments have already been recorded by the company. If not, they must also be deducted from the balance per books on the bank reconciliation.

3. *Company errors.* Errors discovered in the company's records must also be included in the bank reconciliation. For example, we will see below that Lee Company wrote a cheque for $1,226 and mistakenly recorded it as $1,262. The error of $36 is added to the balance per books because Lee Company reduced the balance per books by $36 too much when it recorded the cheque as $1,262 instead of $1,226. Make sure you include only errors made by the company as reconciling items when calculating the adjusted cash balance per books.

Bank Reconciliation Illustrated

The bank statement for Lee Company was shown in Illustration 7-6. It shows a balance per bank of $15,907.45 on April 30, 2011. On this date, the balance of cash per books is $11,244.14. Using the above steps, the following reconciling items are determined:

Reconciling items per bank:

1. *Deposits in transit:* After comparing the deposits recorded in the books with the deposits listed in the bank statement, it was determined that the April 30 deposit was not recorded by the bank until May 1. $2,201.40
2. *Outstanding cheques:* After comparing the cheques recorded in the books with the cheques listed on the bank statement, it was determined that three cheques were outstanding:

No. 445	$3,000.00	
No. 446	1,401.30	
No. 448	1,502.70	5,904.00

3. *Bank errors:* None

Reconciling items per books:

1. *Credit memoranda and other deposits:*
   Electronic payment by customer on account $1,350.55
   Interest earned   39.76
2. *Debit memoranda and other payments:*
   NSF cheque from J. R. Baron   425.60
   Bank service charge for NSF cheque   10.00
   Bank service charge   30.00
3. *Company errors:* Cheque No. 443 was correctly written by Lee for $1,226.00 and was correctly paid by the bank. However, it was recorded as $1,262.00 by Lee.   36.00

The bank reconciliation is as follows:

LEE COMPANY Bank Reconciliation April 30, 2011		
Cash balance per bank statement		$15,907.45
Add: Deposit in transit		2,201.40
		18,108.85
Less: Outstanding cheques		
No. 445	$3,000.00	
No. 446	1,401.30	
No. 448	1,502.70	5,904.00
Adjusted cash balance per bank		$12,204.85
Cash balance per books		$11,244.14
Add: Electronic payment by customer on account	$1,350.55	
Interest earned	39.76	
Error in recording cheque No. 443 ($1,262.00 − $1,226.00)	36.00	1,426.31
		12,670.45
Less: NSF cheque and bank charge ($425.60 + $10.00)	$ 435.60	
Bank service charge	30.00	465.60
Adjusted cash balance per books		$12,204.85

Entries from Bank Reconciliation

When determining the adjusted cash balance per books, each reconciling item should be recorded by the depositor. If these items are not journalized and posted, the Cash account will not show the correct balance. The entries for Lee Company on April 30 are as follows:

Apr. 30	Cash	1,350.55	
	Accounts Receivable		1,350.55
	To record electronic collection of account.		
30	Cash	39.76	
	Interest Revenue		39.76
	To record interest earned.		
30	Cash	36.00	
	Accounts Payable		36.00
	To correct error in recording cheque No. 443.		
30	Accounts Receivable ($425.60 + $10.00)	435.60	
	Cash		435.60
	To record NSF cheque plus bank charge from J. R. Baron.		
30	Bank Charges Expense	30.00	
	Cash		30.00
	To record bank service charge expense for April.		

A	=	L	+	OE
+1,350.55				
−1,350.55				

↑ Cash flows: +1,350.55

A	=	L	+	OE
+39.76				+39.76

↑ Cash flows: +39.76

A	=	L	+	OE
+36.00		+36.00		

↑ Cash flows: +36.00

A	=	L	+	OE
+435.60				
−435.60				

↓ Cash flows: −435.60

A	=	L	+	OE
−30.00				−30.00

↓ Cash flows: −30.00

Bank service charges are normally debited to Bank Charges Expense. Some companies use the account Miscellaneous Expense because the charges are often very small in amount. If the bank service charge relates to processing a customer NSF cheque—as in the case of J. R. Baron's NSF cheque—this charge is passed on to the customer and debited to Accounts Receivable.

The five journal entries shown above could also be combined into one compound entry.

Note that in previous chapters Cash was treated as an account that did not require adjustment. This was done to make learning easier, because the bank reconciliation process had not been explained.

After the entries above are posted, the Cash account will show the following:

		Cash		
Apr. 30 Bal.	11,244.14	Apr. 30	435.60	
30	1,350.55	30	30.00	
30	36.00			
30	39.76			
Apr. 30 Bal.	12,204.85			

The adjusted cash balance in the general ledger should agree with the adjusted cash balance per books in the bank reconciliation shown on page 388.

What entries does the bank make? The bank does not make any entries for deposits in transit or outstanding cheques. The bank will record these items when they reach the bank. If any bank errors are discovered in preparing the reconciliation, the bank should be notified. The bank can then make the necessary corrections on its records. The bank does not correct your errors on its books, and you do not correct the bank's errors on your books.

BEFORE YOU GO ON . . .

→ Review It

1. What is the purpose of reconciling a bank account?
2. Give some examples of reconciling items per bank and per book.
3. How are errors treated in the reconciliation process?
4. How are deposits in transit and outstanding cheques from the previous period treated in the reconciling process?

➜ Do It

The Cash account of Zhizhi Company showed a balance of $16,333 on December 31, 2011. The bank statement as of that date showed a balance of $18,084. After comparing the bank statement with the cash records, the following information was determined:

1. The bank returned an NSF cheque in the amount of $239 that Zhizhi had deposited on December 20. The cheque was a payment on a customer's account.
2. Electronic receipts from customers on the last day of the month to pay their accounts totalled $2,300. These receipts have not yet been recorded by the company.
3. The bank issued a credit memo for $9 of interest earned on Zhizhi's account.
4. The bank issued a debit memo for bank service charges of $37. This amount included $10 for processing the NSF cheque (see #1 above).
5. The company made an error in recording a customer's deposit. The company recorded the payment on account as $209 when it should have been $290. The bank correctly recorded the deposit as $290.
6. Deposits in transit as at December 31 amounted to $3,643.
7. Outstanding cheques written in the month of December amounted to $3,000. Cheques still outstanding from the month of November totalled $280.

Prepare a bank reconciliation and any required journal entries for Zhizhi Company at December 31, 2011.

Action Plan

- Prepare the bank reconciliation in two sections: one for the bank and one for the company.
- Determine which reconciling items each side has already recorded and adjust the other side accordingly.
- Be careful when you determine the direction of an error correction; think about how the error has affected the bank balance or the cash account balance.
- Prepare journal entries only for reconciling items to the book side; not the bank side.
- The adjusted cash balances must agree with each other when complete, and with the general ledger account after the journal entries are posted.

Solution

ZHIZHI COMPANY Bank Reconciliation December 31, 2011		
Cash balance per bank statement		$18,084
Add: Deposits in transit		3,643
		21,727
Less: Outstanding cheques ($3,000 + $280)		3,280
Adjusted cash balance per bank		$18,447
Cash balance per books		$16,333
Add: Electronic receipts from customers on account	$2,300	
Interest earned	9	
Deposit error correction ($290 − $209)	81	2,390
		18,723
Less: NSF cheque	$239	
Bank service charges	37	276
Adjusted cash balance per books		$18,447

Dec. 31	Cash	2,300	
	Accounts Receivable		2,300
	To record electronic receipts on account.		
31	Cash	9	
	Interest Revenue		9
	To record interest earned on bank account.		
31	Cash	81	
	Accounts Receivable ($290 − $209)		81
	To correct deposit error.		
31	Accounts Receivable ($239 + $10)	249	
	Cash		249
	To re-establish accounts receivable for NSF		
	cheque and related service charge.		
31	Bank Charges Expense ($37 − $10)	27	
	Cash		27
	To record bank service charges.		

	Cash			
Dec. 31 Bal.	16,333	Dec. 31	249
31	2,300	31	27
31	9		
31	81		
Dec. 31 Bal.	18,447		

Related exercise material: BE7–8, BE7–9, BE7–10, BE7–11, BE7–12, E7–8, E7–9, E7–10, E7–11, and E7–12.

The Navigator

Reporting Cash

STUDY OBJECTIVE 6

Report cash on the balance sheet.

Cash consists of coins, currency (paper money), cheques, money orders, travellers' cheques, and money on deposit in a bank or similar depository. The general rule is that if the bank will accept it for deposit, it is cash. Transactions by debit card and bank credit card—such as Visa and MasterCard—are cash, but transactions by nonbank credit card are not.

Cash does not include cheques that are postdated (payable in the future), staledated (more than six months old), or returned (NSF—not sufficient funds). Postage stamps and employee promises to pay back money (or IOUs) are not cash either, because they cannot be deposited in a bank account. Postage stamps are office supplies and IOUs from employees are receivables.

Cash on hand, cash in banks, and petty cash are normally combined and reported simply as Cash in the balance sheet. Because it is the most liquid asset owned by a company, Canadian companies list cash first in the current assets section of the balance sheet. As explained and illustrated in Chapter 4, international companies frequently follow the practice of listing current assets in *increasing* order of liquidity and thus present cash as the last item in current assets. In this textbook, we will continue to follow the rule of listing current assets in *decreasing* order of liquidity as it is expected that this will continue to be the practice of Canadian companies for many years to come.

Many companies combine cash with cash equivalents. **Cash equivalents** are short-term, highly liquid (easily sold) investments. They typically have maturities of three months or less from the date they are purchased. These investments include short-term deposits and short-term investments such as treasury bills and money-market funds. However, as mentioned in Chapter 4, standard setters have recommended that in the future, cash equivalents not be combined with cash in the balance sheet, but rather reported with other short-term investments. While no decision has been reached to date on this issue, this is a change that we may very well see in the near future.

Illustration 7-8 shows how Sears combines cash and cash equivalents (called short-term investments by Sears) on its balance sheet:

Illustration 7-8 ➜

Presentation of cash

SEARS CANADA INC. Balance Sheet (partial) January 31, 2009 (in millions)	**Sears·**
Assets	
Current assets	
Cash and short-term investments	$819.8

In the notes to its financial statements, Sears reports that its cash and short-term investments include all highly liquid investments with maturities of three months or less at the date of purchase.

Some companies may be in a cash deficit or negative position at year end. This can happen when the company is in an overdraft position at the bank. A **bank overdraft** occurs when withdrawals or payments are more than the amount in the bank account. This becomes a short-term loan from the bank, assuming that the bank does not reject the withdrawal or payment. Most companies have overdraft protection up to a certain amount with their banks. In an overdraft situation, the Cash account shows a credit balance in the general ledger and is reported as a current liability called bank indebtedness.

A company may have cash that is not available for general use because it is restricted for a special purpose. An example is funds held on deposit until completion of an offer to buy real estate. Cash that has a restricted use—and is in a significant amount—should be reported separately on the balance sheet as **restricted cash**. If the restricted cash is expected to be used within the next year, the amount should be reported as a current asset. When restricted funds will not be used in that time, they should be reported as a non-current asset. In the notes to its financial statements, Sears reported a restricted cash balance of $5.2 million related to advance ticket sales from Sears Travel.

In making loans to depositors, banks may require borrowers to keep minimum cash balances. These minimum balances, called **compensating balances**, give the bank support for the loans. They are a form of restriction on the use of cash. Similar to other restricted cash, a compensating balance should be reported as a non-current asset.

BEFORE YOU GO ON . . .

➜ Review It

1. What is included as cash on a company's balance sheet?
2. What is the difference between restricted cash and compensating balances?
3. What was Forzani's cash balance at February 1, 2009? Did the company report any restricted cash? The answer to this question is at the end of the chapter.

The Navigator

Related exercise material: BE7–13, BE7–14, and E7–13.

Demonstration Problem

Demonstration Problems

Trillo Company reports the following condensed information from its general ledger Cash account and bank statement at June 30, 2011:

Cash				
June 1	Bal.	17,540		
June deposits		17,000	June cheques written	19,760
June 30	Bal.	14,780		

TRILLO COMPANY
Bank Statement
June 30, 2011

	Cheques and Other Debits	Deposits and Other Credits	Balance
Balance, June 1			17,690
Deposits		15,248	32,938
Cheques cleared	18,100		14,838
EFT insurance payment	500		14,338
NSF cheque ($165 + $10 service charge)	175		14,163
Service charge	12		14,151
Interest earned		35	14,186

Additional information:
1. There was a deposit in transit of $600 at May 31, the preceding month, which cleared the bank in June.
2. There were $750 of outstanding cheques at the end of May.
3. The EFT payment for insurance has not yet been recorded by the company.
4. The NSF cheque was for $165 from Massif Co., a customer, in payment of its account. The bank added a $10 processing fee.

Instructions

(a) Prepare a bank reconciliation at June 30.
(b) Record the entries required by the reconciliation.

Solution to Demonstration Problem

(a)

TRILLO COMPANY
Bank Reconciliation
June 30, 2011

Cash balance per bank statement		$14,186
Add: Deposits in transit [($17,000 + $600) − $15,248]		2,352
		16,538
Less: Outstanding cheques [($19,760 + $750) − $18,100]		2,410
Adjusted cash balance per bank		$14,128
Cash balance per books		$14,780
Add: Interest earned		35
		14,815
Less: EFT insurance payment	$500	
NSF cheque ($165 + $10)	175	
Bank service charge	12	687
Adjusted cash balance per books		$14,128

Action Plan

- Compare the deposits in transit at the end of May plus the deposits recorded in the books with the deposits on the bank statement to determine the deposits in transit at the end of June.
- Compare the outstanding cheques at the end of May plus the cheques recorded in the books with the cheques that cleared the bank statement to determine the outstanding cheques at the end of June.
- Identify any items recorded by the bank but not by the company as reconciling items per books.
- All the journal entries should be based on the reconciling items per books.
- Make sure the Cash ledger account balance, after posting the reconciling items, agrees with the adjusted cash balance per books.

(b)

June 30	Cash		35	
	Interest Revenue			35
	To record bank interest earned.			
30	Insurance Expense		500	
	Cash			500
	To record monthly insurance payment.			
30	Accounts Receivable		175	
	Cash			175
	To re-establish accounts receivable for Massif Co. for $165 NSF cheque and related $10 service charge.			
30	Bank Charges Expense		12	
	Cash			12
	To record bank service charges.			

Check:

Cash

June	30	Bal.	14,780	June	30		500
	30		35		30		175
					30		12
June	30	Bal.	14,128				

The Navigator

Summary of Study Objectives

1. *Explain the activities that help achieve internal control.* Control activities, as part of a larger control framework, are the policies and procedures that management implements in order to control the risks that threaten the company's ability to achieve reliable financial reporting, effective and efficient operations, and compliance with relevant laws and regulations. They include establishment of responsibility, segregation of duties, documentation procedures, physical and IT controls, independent checks of performance, and human resource controls.

2. *Apply control activities to cash receipts.* Internal controls over cash receipts include (a) designating only personnel such as cashiers to handle cash; (b) assigning the duties of receiving cash, recording cash, and maintaining custody of cash to different individuals; (c) using remittance advices for mail receipts, cash register tapes for over-the-counter receipts, and deposit slips for bank deposits; (d) using company safes and bank vaults to store cash, with only authorized personnel having access, and using cash registers to issue over-the-counter receipts; (e) depositing all cash intact daily; (f) making independent daily counts of register receipts and daily comparisons of total receipts with total deposits; and (g) bonding personnel who handle cash.

3. *Apply control activities to cash disbursements including petty cash.* Internal controls over cash disbursements include (a) authorizing only specified individuals such as the controller to sign cheques; (b) assigning the duties of approving items for payment, paying for the items, and recording the payment to different individuals; (c) using prenumbered cheques and accounting for all cheques, with each cheque supported by an approved invoice; (d) storing blank cheques in a safe or vault, with access restricted to authorized personnel, and printing cheque amounts electronically; (e) comparing each cheque with the approved invoice before issuing the cheque, and making monthly reconciliations of bank and book balances; and (f) stamping each approved invoice "Paid" after payment. To operate a petty cash fund, it is necessary to establish the fund, make payments from the fund, and replenish the fund. Journal entries are only made when the fund is established and replenished.

4. *Describe the control features of a bank account.* A bank account contributes to good internal control by giving physical and IT controls for the storage of cash, reducing the amount of currency that must be kept on hand, and creating a double record of a depositor's bank transactions.

5. *Prepare a bank reconciliation.* In reconciling the bank account, the balance per books and balance per bank are reconciled to their adjusted balances. Reconciling items include deposits in transit, outstanding cheques, errors by the bank, unrecorded bank memoranda, and errors by the company. Adjusting entries must be made for any errors made by the company and unrecorded bank memoranda (e.g., interest).

6. *Report cash on the balance sheet.* Cash is listed usually first in the current assets section of the balance sheet. Cash that is restricted for a special purpose is reported separately as a current asset or a non-current asset, depending on when the cash is expected to be used.

The Navigator

Glossary

Glossary
Key Term Matching Activity

Bank overdraft The situation when withdrawals are more than the amount available in the bank account. (p. 400)

Bank service charge A fee charged by a bank for using its services. (p. 392)

Bank statement A statement received monthly from the bank that shows the depositor's bank transactions and balances. (p. 391)

Cash Resources such as coins, currency, cheques, and money orders that are accepted at face value when they are deposited in a bank or similar depository. (p. 399)

Cash equivalents Highly liquid, short-term investments with maturities of three months or less that are subject to an insignificant risk of changes in value. (p. 400)

Cash payments journal A special journal used to record all cash paid. (p. 385)

Cash receipts journal A special journal used to record all cash received. (p. 381)

Clearing The process of exchanging and settling payment items that results in a transfer of funds from one financial institution to another. (p. 390)

Compensating balances Minimum cash balances required by a bank as support for bank loans. (p. 400)

Credit memoranda (CM) Supporting documentation for increases to a bank account that appear on a bank statement. (p. 392)

Debit memoranda (DM) Supporting documentation for decreases to a bank account that appear on a bank statement. (p. 392)

Deposits in transit Deposits recorded by the depositor that have not been recorded by the bank. (p. 394)

Electronic funds transfer (EFT) A disbursement system that uses telephone, computer, or wireless means to transfer cash from one location to another. (p. 383)

Encryption A procedure used to scramble plain text to prevent anyone except authorized users from reading the data. (p. 337)

External auditors Auditors who are independent of the organization. They examine internal control and report how reasonable the financial statements or other financial information is. (p. 378)

Fidelity insurance An insurance policy where the insurance company will compensate the employer for losses incurred as a result of an employee's dishonesty. (p. 378)

Firewall A system designed to prevent unauthorized access to a private network connected to the Internet. (p. 337)

Internal auditors Company employees who evaluate the effectiveness of the company's system of internal control. (p. 378)

Internal control The processes designed and implemented by management that help an organization to achieve reliable financial reporting, effective and efficient operations, and compliance with relevant laws and regulations. (p. 374)

NSF (not sufficient funds) cheque A cheque that is not paid by the customer's bank and is returned to the depositor's bank because of insufficient funds in the customer's account. (p. 392)

Outstanding cheques Cheques issued and recorded by a company that have not been paid by the bank. (p. 393)

Petty cash fund A cash fund that is used for paying relatively small amounts. (p. 386)

Restricted cash Cash that is not available for general use, but instead is restricted for a particular purpose. (p. 400)

Special journal A journal that is used to record similar types of transactions, such as all cash receipts or all cash payments. (p. 381)

Self-Study Questions

Answers are at the end of the chapter.

(SO 1) K 1. Which of the following factors could limit a company's system of internal control?
(a) Collusion by two or more employees
(b) The cost of internal control being greater than the benefit
(c) Difficulty in segregating duties in small businesses
(d) All of the above

(SO 1) K 2. A well-designed control framework contains which of the following as a key component?
(a) Segregation of duties
(b) Risk assessment
(c) Optimizing the use of resources
(d) Safety and security department

(SO 2) C 3. Permitting only designated personnel to handle cash receipts is an application of the concept of:
(a) segregation of duties.
(b) establishment of responsibility.
(c) independent checks of performance.
(d) human resource controls.

(SO 2) AP 4. Franks Jewellers accepted $12,000 of TD Bank Visa credit card charges for merchandise sold on July 1. TD Bank charges Franks 5.0% for its credit card use. The entry to record this transaction by Franks Jewellers will include a credit to Sales of $12,000 and:
(a) a debit to Accounts Receivable of $12,000.
(b) a debit to Cash of $12,000.
(c) a debit to Accounts Receivable of $11,400 and a debit to Credit Card Expense of $600.
(d) a debit to Cash of $11,400 and a debit to Credit Card Expense of $600.

(SO 3) C 5. The use of prenumbered cheques in disbursing cash is an application of the principle of:
(a) establishment of responsibility.
(b) segregation of duties.
(c) physical and IT controls.
(d) documentation procedures.

(SO 3) AP 6. A cheque is written to replenish a $150 petty cash fund when the fund has receipts of $148 and $7 in cash. In recording the cheque:
(a) Cash Over and Short should be debited for $5.
(b) Cash Over and Short should be credited for $5.
(c) Petty Cash should be debited for $148.
(d) Cash should be credited for $148.

(SO 4) K 7. Bank accounts improve control over cash by:
(a) safeguarding cash by using a bank as a depository.
(b) minimizing the amount of cash that must be kept on hand.
(c) giving a double record of all bank transactions.
(d) all of the above.

(SO 5) AP 8. Suzanne Terriault reports an ending cash balance of $410 in her cheque book at the end of the month and $500 in her bank statement. Reconciling items include deposits in transit of $250, outstanding cheques of $350, and service charges of $10. What is Suzanne's adjusted cash balance?
(a) $390
(b) $400
(c) $410
(d) $500

(SO 5) AP 9. A company mistakenly recorded a $459 cheque written in payment of an account as $495. The journal entry required to correct this would be:
(a) debit Accounts Payable $36; credit Cash $36.
(b) debit Cash $36; credit Accounts Payable $36.
(c) debit Cash $36; credit Accounts Receivable $36.
(d) No journal entry is required.

(SO 6) K 10. Which of the following correctly describes the reporting of cash?
(a) Cash cannot be combined with petty cash.
(b) Restricted cash funds are always reported as a current asset.
(c) Compensating balances are reported as a current asset.
(d) Postdated cheques from customers are not included in the Cash account balance.

Questions

(SO 1) C 1. The first component of an effective control framework is Control Environment. Explain why it is important for management to take responsibility for internal control in order to strengthen this component.

(SO 1) C 2. What must be true about employees who are involved in the monitoring role regarding a company's control framework?

(SO 1) C 3. "Internal control can help organizations achieve efficiency of operations." Do you agree? Explain.

(SO 1) K 4. In the ice cream shop, all employees make change out of the same cash register drawer. Is this a violation of internal control? Why?

(SO 1) C 5. Trushi Miyamura is questioning why independent checks of performance are important if the company also segregates duties. Respond to Trushi's question.

(SO 1) C 6. How do documentation procedures contribute to good internal control?

(SO 1) C 7. Joan Trainer is trying to design internal control activities so that there is no possibility of errors or theft. Explain to Joan why this may be impractical, and may even be impossible.

(SO 2) C 8. What is the difference between a debit card sale and a bank credit card sale to a retailer? To the customer?

(SO 2) C 9. Over-the-counter cash receipts require special care. Explain the procedures that should be followed at the end of the day (or shift) to ensure proper internal control.

(SO 2) C 10. Best Books has just installed electronic cash registers with scanners in its stores. How do cash registers such as these improve internal control over cash receipts?

(SO 2) C 11. Describe appropriate internal control procedures for handling cash received by mail.

(SO 2) C 12. From a company's point of view, what are the similarities and differences between a customer making a payment using EFT and on-line banking or using EFT and automatic pre-authorized monthly payments?

(SO 3) C 13. "Use of cash for disbursements should be avoided. Effective internal control over cash disbursements can only be achieved by the use of cheques or electronic funds transfer." Is this true? Explain.

(SO 3) C 14. Identify potential internal control weaknesses a company may be exposed to if a decision is made to pay fewer suppliers by cheque and to make greater use of an EFT payment method.

(SO 3) C 15. Walter's Watches is a small retail store. Walter, the owner of the company, has recently hired a new employee, Wanda, who will be responsible for ordering merchandise, receiving the goods, and authorizing the merchandise invoices for payment. Describe the various ways Wanda could commit a fraud with this arrangement.

(SO 3) C 16. Chang Company has a petty cash fund that is used to pay for a variety of low-value items. Su Mai, the petty cash custodian, regularly borrows cash from the fund to pay for personal expenses. Su Mai has always repaid these amounts. Is this a problem for Chang Company? If it is, explain what the company could do to strengthen internal control.

(SO 4) K 17. Opening a bank account is a simple procedure. Give four examples of how a bank account improves a company's internal controls.

(SO 5) C 18. The responsibility for preparing a bank reconciliation should be assigned to whom? Why?

(SO 5) C 19. Diablo Company wrote cheque #2375 for $1,325 on March 16. As at March 31, the cheque had not cleared the company's bank account and was correctly listed as an outstanding cheque on the March 31 bank reconciliation. The cheque has still not cleared the bank account on April 30. Anah is doing the bank reconciliation for Diablo and thinks it is not necessary to include the cheque in the April bank reconciliation, because it was already listed as an outstanding cheque on March 31. Is she correct? Explain.

(SO 5) C 20. Paul Reimer does not keep a personal record of his bank account and does not see the need to do a bank reconciliation. He says he can always use on-line banking to look up the balance in his bank account before writing a cheque. Explain why Paul should keep his own records and do regular bank reconciliations.

(SO 5) C 21. Jane Henner is reviewing her June 30 bank statement in advance of completing a bank reconciliation and notices an entry for $26 regarding monthly interest. Jane is comfortable that the interest income is not a reconciling item so she does not include it in her reconciliation. Has Jane handled this situation correctly? Explain.

(SO 6) C 22. "The cash balance is intended to report the amount of funds a company has available to meet short-term liquidity needs." Do you agree? Explain.

(SO 6) C 23. What is restricted cash? What are compensating balances? How should these be reported on the balance sheet?

Brief Exercises

Identify and explain components of a control framework.
(SO 1) C

BE7-1 Frank Hensal, the Chief Risk Officer at Tri-City Rentals, has been asked by the company owner to develop internal controls for the company. Identify each of the components of an effective control framework for Frank.

Identify control activities applicable to cash receipts.
(SO 2) AP

BE7-2 True North Company has the following internal controls over cash receipts. Identify the control activity that is applicable to each of the following:

1. All over-the-counter receipts are recorded on cash registers.
2. All cashiers are bonded.
3. Daily cash counts are made by cashier department supervisors.
4. The duties of receiving cash, recording cash, and maintaining custody of cash are assigned to different individuals.
5. Only cashiers may operate cash registers.
6. All cash is deposited intact in the bank account daily.

Record debit and credit card transactions.
(SO 2) AP

BE7-3 Kopper Kettle Restaurant accepts the Visa card. On April 9, a customer paid for a $125 dinner using his Visa card. The bank charges a 3.5% fee for each transaction. Prepare the entry the Kopper Kettle must make to record this transaction. Assuming the purchase is made using a Kepper Kettle–issued credit card, would the entry change? Prepare the entry to record the purchase assuming a debit card is used for payment and that the bank charges a $1.50 fee for each transaction.

Identify control activities applicable to cash disbursements.
(SO 3) K

BE7-4 Marydale Company has the following internal controls over cash disbursements. Identify the control activity that is applicable to each of the following:

1. Company cheques are prenumbered.
2. The bank statement is reconciled monthly by an internal auditor.
3. Blank cheques are stored in a safe in the controller's office.
4. Only the controller or assistant controller may sign cheques.
5. Cheque signers are not allowed to record cash disbursement transactions.
6. All payments, except for petty cash transactions, are made by cheque.

Record entry to establish a petty cash fund and identify appropriate controls.
(SO 3) AP

BE7-5 Fran Howard noticed that staff at her flower shop were taking money out of the cash register to pay for small items. Fran decided to establish a petty cash fund of $50. Prepare the journal entries to establish the petty cash fund and advise Fran on the procedures she should implement to establish appropriate internal controls for the fund.

Record entry to replenish a petty cash fund.
(SO 3) AP

BE7-6 On June 30, Jon Glinz replenishes his company's petty cash fund, which was originally established with a $100 balance. The fund contains receipts of $25 for office supplies, $64 for delivery charges, and $14 for a cab fare. Make the journal entry to replenish the fund.

Identify bank account operating features.
(SO 4) C

BE7-7 Here are some statements about bank accounts. Next to each statement, record the letter T if the statement is true, and F if the statement is false.

1. ___ Blank cheques cannot be used and therefore do not need to be carefully stored and controlled.
2. ___ Banks issue debit memoranda to record decreases to customers' bank accounts.
3. ___ Banks do not require signature cards for business bank accounts, because the company employees who have signing authority may change.
4. ___ The primary purpose for prenumbering cheques is to help the person receiving the cheque keep track of receipts.
5. ___ Clearing is the term used for when a cheque is accepted by the payee's bank.

BE7–8 Next to each of the following items, record the correct letter from this list: (a) increase to bank balance, (b) decrease to bank balance, (c) increase to company cash balance, (d) decrease to company cash balance, or (e) not included in the bank reconciliation.

1. ___ EFT payment made by a customer
2. ___ Bank debit memorandum for service charges
3. ___ Outstanding cheques from the current month
4. ___ Bank error in recording a $1,676 deposit as $1,766
5. ___ Outstanding cheques from the previous month that are still outstanding
6. ___ Outstanding cheques from the previous month that are no longer outstanding
7. ___ Bank error in recording a company cheque made out for $160 as $610
8. ___ Bank credit memorandum for interest revenue
9. ___ Company error in recording a deposit of $1,140 as $1,410.
10. ___ Bank debit memorandum for an NSF cheque
11. ___ Deposit in transit from the current month
12. ___ Company error in recording a cheque made out for $450 as $540
13. ___ Bank error in recording a $1,676 deposit as $1,766

Indicate location of items in bank reconciliation.
(SO 5) AP

BE7–9 Referring to BE7–8, indicate (a) the items that will result in an adjustment to the company's records, and (b) why the other items do not require an adjustment.

Identify reconciling items that require journal entries.
(SO 5) C

BE7–10 In the month of September, Westshore Hotel Company wrote and recorded cheques in the amount of $8,440. In October, it wrote and recorded cheques in the amount of $11,716. Of these cheques, $7,505 of them were paid by the bank in September, and $10,712 in October. What is the amount for outstanding cheques at the end of September? At the end of October?

Analyze outstanding cheques.
(SO 5) AP

BE7–11 On August 31, Howel Company had an unadjusted cash balance of $8,850. An examination of the August bank statement shows a balance of $7,770 on August 31; bank service charges $30; deposits in transit $2,405; interest earned $12; outstanding cheques $2,240; and an NSF cheque of $180. Prepare a bank reconciliation at August 31.

Prepare bank reconciliation.
(SO 5) AP

BE7–12 Refer to the bank reconciliation prepared in BE7–11. Prepare the adjusting journal entries for Howel Company on August 31.

Prepare entries from bank reconciliation.
(SO 5) AP

BE7–13 Sirois Company owns the following assets at the balance sheet date:

Calculate cash.
(SO 6) AP

Cash in bank—savings account	$ 6,000
Cash on hand	850
Cash refund due from the Canada Revenue Agency	1,000
Cash in bank—chequing account	12,000
Postage stamps	250
Postdated cheques from customers	500
Treasury bill	2,500

What amount should be reported as cash in the balance sheet?

BE7–14 Dupré Company has the following items: cash in bank $17,500; payroll bank account $6,000; store cash floats $1,500; short-term, highly liquid investments with maturity dates of less than 90 days $15,000; and Plant Expansion Fund Cash $25,000. Dupré maintains a $5,000 compensating bank balance in a separate account. Explain how each balance should be reported on the balance sheet.

Explain statement presentation of cash balances.
(SO 6) C

Exercises

Identify control framework components and explain importance.
(SO 1) C

E7–1 The following components of a control framework are in place at Pentium Supplies:

1. The company maintains an up-to-date code of conduct document and holds annual employee training sessions to ensure employee awareness of the code's contents.
2. A new software package is purchased that tracks travel expenditures by employees, and immediately reports when an amount spent is greater than the employee's authorized amount.
3. The company hired a Chief Risk Officer whose primary responsibility is to conduct risk surveys to identify potential business risks.
4. Supervisors receive daily tracking reports on employee travel expenses, and follow up with employees when they exceed their authorized spending limits.
5. The newly hired Chief Risk Officer has appointed a Compliance Officer whose job includes designing operating procedures to help reduce employee theft.

Instructions

(a) For each of the above, identify which of the five components of an effective internal control framework is represented.
(b) Describe how each component contributes to improved internal control at Pentium Supplies.

Identify internal control strengths and weaknesses.
(SO 1) C

E7–2 Discount Toys advertises a customer-friendly return policy. The store allows returns within 30 days for any reason. The store uses a periodic inventory system. When merchandise is returned, store policy instructs employees to:
- Complete a prenumbered return form and refund cash from the cash register.
- Provide a copy of the return form to the supervisor for approval.
- Immediately return goods to the shelf.

Instructions

(a) How is it possible for a dishonest store employee to steal from Discount Toys and avoid getting caught?
(b) What changes to the policy would you recommend to the company to reduce the possibility of employee theft?

Identify internal control strengths and weaknesses.
(SO 1) C

E7–3 The following situations suggest either a strength or a weakness in internal control:

1. At Frederico's, Amanda and Long work alternate lunch hours. Normally Amanda works the cash register at the checkout counter, but during her lunch hour Long takes her place. They both use the same cash drawer and count cash together at the end of the day.
2. Sandeep is a very hard-working employee at Stan's Hardware. Sandeep does such a good job that he is responsible for most of the company's office and accounting tasks. The only thing the owner has to do is sign cheques.
3. At Half Pipe Skate, they are very concerned about running an efficient, low-cost business. Consequently, the manager has eliminated the need to prepare purchase orders and receiving reports.
4. At Traction Tires, most of the tires are stored in a fenced outdoor storage area. One of the employees noticed a place where the fence needed to be repaired and reported this to the manager. The fence was fixed before the close of business that night.
5. The internal auditors at Humber Manufacturing regularly report their findings to senior management, who get the accounting department to investigate and resolve any problems.
6. All employees at Vincent Travel take vacation every year, and during that time their duties are assigned to another individual.

Instructions

(a) State whether each situation above is a strength or a weakness in internal control.
(b) For each weakness, suggest an improvement.

E7–4   The following are four independent situations:

Identify control framework component weaknesses and suggest improvements. (SO 1) AP

(a) Cycle Sports developed and printed employee handbooks that detail company expectations of all employees. However, to save costs, only supervisors receive a copy of the handbook.

(b) Company management at Technology Car Supply believe that company success depends only on successfully managing inventory levels, and that worrying about what's happening outside the company will only distract them from that goal.

(c) Francesca Foods' Chief Financial Officer agreed with the sales manager to stop checking customer credit limits before shipping products, because it sometimes results in late shipments.

(d) Lowe's Window Manufacturing's accounting software tracks and compares actual spending with budgeted amounts. However, company management have not been trained on the computer system and are unable to retrieve the data.

Instructions

(a) Identify weaknesses in each of the above scenarios.

(b) Suggest how each weakness could be corrected.

E7–5   Presented below are three independent situations:

Prepare entries for debit and credit card sales. (SO 2) AP

(a) On March 15, 38 customers used debit cards to purchase merchandise for a total of $8,124 from Hockey Town. Hockey Town pays a $1.25 debit card fee for each transaction. Prepare Hockey Town's journal entries for these transactions.

(b) On June 21, Connie Harrow uses her TD Gold Elite Visa bank credit card to purchase craft supplies for $2,200 from Point Clark Creations gallery. TD Canada Trust charges the gallery a 4.0% credit card transaction fee. On July 12, Connie receives her Visa bill and pays for this purchase. Prepare Point Clark Creations' journal entries for these transactions.

(c) On May 26, A. Ramos uses his Zellers Hbc credit card to purchase merchandise from Zellers for $629. On June 10, Ramos receives his Hbc credit card bill and pays for this purchase. Prepare Zellers' journal entries for these transactions.

E7–6 ━━━▶   At Wiarton Bay Cottages, cheques are not prenumbered. Cheques can be signed by either the purchasing agent or the controller. Each signer has access to unissued cheques kept in an unlocked file cabinet. The purchasing agent pays all bills for goods purchased for resale. Before making a payment, the purchasing agent determines that the goods have been received and verifies the mathematical accuracy of the vendor's invoice. After payment, the invoice is filed by the vendor, and the purchasing agent records the payment in the cash payments journal. The controller pays all other bills after receiving approval from authorized employees. After payment, the controller stamps all bills PAID, files them by payment date, and records the cheques in the cash payments journal. Wiarton Bay Cottages maintains one chequing account that is reconciled by the controller.

Identify weaknesses in internal control over cash disbursements, and suggest improvements. (SO 3) S

Instructions

(a) List the weaknesses in internal control over cash disbursements.

(b) Write a memo to the company controller that recommends improvements.

E7–7   Bolton Bolts uses a petty cash imprest system. The fund was established on April 9 with a balance of $150. On April 30, there were $5 cash and the following petty cash receipts in the petty cash box:

Record petty cash transactions. (SO 3) AP

Date	Receipt No.	For	Amount
Apr. 12	1	Miscellaneous expense	$16
14	2	Office supplies	32
17	3	Freight in (assume perpetual inventory system)	43
20	4	Miscellaneous expense	19
22	5	Delivery charges on outgoing freight	32
28	6	Miscellaneous expense	5

Instructions

(a) Record the journal entry on April 9 to establish the petty cash fund.

(b) Record the journal entry on April 30 to reimburse the fund and increase the balance to $175.

(c) Assume that instead of increasing the petty cash fund balance to $175 on April 30, the company decided to decrease it to $125. Record the April 30 journal entry using this assumption.

Prepare bank reconciliation and related entries.
(SO 5) AP

E7–8   The following information is for Tindall Company in September:

1. Cash balance per bank, September 30, $8,285
2. Cash balance per books, September 30, $6,781
3. Outstanding cheques, $3,175
4. Bank service charge, $24
5. NSF cheque from customer, $230
6. Deposits in transit, $1,554
7. EFT receipts from customers in payment of their accounts, $74
8. Cheque #212 was correctly written and posted by the bank as $518. Tindall Company had recorded the cheque as $581 in error. The cheque was written for the purchase of office supplies.

Instructions

(a) Prepare a bank reconciliation at September 30, 2011.

(b) Journalize the adjusting entries at September 30, 2011, on Tindall Company's books.

Determine deposits in transit and other reconciling items.
(SO 5) AP

E7–9   On April 30, the bank reconciliation of Hidden Valley Company shows a deposit in transit of $1,437. The May bank statement and the general ledger Cash account in May show the following:

HIDDEN VALLEY COMPANY Bank Statement (partial) Deposits/Credits				HIDDEN VALLEY COMPANY Cash Account (partial) Deposits Made	
Date	Description	Amount		Date	Amount
May 2	Deposit	$1,437		May 6	$2,255
10	Deposit	2,255		13	3,218
16	Deposit	3,218		20	954
20	Deposit	945		23	1,298
24	Deposit	1,298		31	1,353
30	EFT	849			
31	Interest Earned	32			

Additional information:

1. The bank did not make any errors in May.
2. EFT is an electronic on-line payment from a customer.

Instructions

(a) List the deposits in transit at May 31.

(b) List any other items that must be included in the bank reconciliation. Describe the impact of each item on the bank reconciliation.

Determine outstanding cheques and other reconciling items.
(SO 6) AP

E7–10   On April 30, the bank reconciliation of Hidden Valley Company shows three outstanding cheques: No. 254 for $560; No. 255 for $262; and No. 257 for $410. The May bank statement and the general ledger Cash account in May show the following:

HIDDEN VALLEY COMPANY Bank Statement (partial) Cheques Paid/Debits			HIDDEN VALLEY COMPANY Cash Account (partial) Cheques Written		
Date	Cheque No.	Amount	Date	Cheque No.	Amount
May 2	254	$560	May 2	258	$159
4	258	159	5	259	275
12	257	410	10	260	500
17	259	275	15	261	867
20	260	50	22	262	750
26	NSF	395	24	263	440
29	263	440	29	264	650
30	262	750			
31	SC	54			

Additional information:

1. The bank did not make any errors in May.
2. NSF is a customer's cheque that is returned because the customer did not have sufficient funds.
3. SC stands for service charge.

Instructions

(a) List the outstanding cheques at May 31.
(b) List any other items that must be included in the bank reconciliation. Describe the impact of each item on the bank reconciliation.

E7–11   The cash records of Matrix Company show the following:

Deposits in transit

1. The March 31 bank reconciliation indicated that deposits in transit totalled $1,200. In April, the general ledger Cash account showed deposits of $14,400, but the bank statement indicated that $15,200 of deposits were received in the month.
2. In May, deposits per bank statement totalled $22,600 and deposits per books totalled $23,750.

Outstanding cheques

1. The March 31 bank reconciliation reported outstanding cheques of $880. In the month of April, Matrix Company's books showed that cheques worth $16,700 were issued. The bank statement also showed that $15,900 of cheques cleared the bank in April.
2. In May, cash disbursements per books were $24,600 and cheques clearing the bank totalled 23,750.

Instructions

(a) What was the amount of deposits in transit at April 30? At May 31?
(b) What was the amount of outstanding cheques at April 30? At May 31?

E7–12   The following information relates to Claymore Company:

Determine deposits in transit and outstanding cheques.
(SO 5) AP

Calculate amounts for bank reconciliation.
(SO 5) AP

CLAYMORE COMPANY Bank Reconciliation July 31, 2011	
Cash balance per bank	$19,420
Add: Deposits in transit	4,280
	23,700
Less: Outstanding cheques	5,780
Adjusted cash balance per bank	$17,920

Additional information:

1. The August bank statement shows the following memoranda:

Debit Memoranda		Credit Memoranda	
NSF cheque: N. Khan	$485	EFT collections	$2,210
Bank service charge	25	Interest earned	46

2. In August, $59,424 of cheques cleared the bank.
3. In August, the company wrote and recorded cheques totalling $60,198.
4. In August, deposits per bank statement (excluding credit memoranda) were $55,905.
5. In August, the company recorded deposits totalling $68,752.

Instructions

(a) Calculate the unadjusted balance in the Cash account on August 31.
(b) Calculate the unadjusted balance in the bank account on August 31.
(c) Calculate the deposits in transit at August 31.
(d) Calculate the outstanding cheques at August 31.
(e) Calculate the adjusted bank balance at August 31.
(f) Calculate the adjusted cash balance at August 31.

Calculate cash balance and report other items.
(SO 6) AP

E7–13 A new accountant at Magnotta is trying to identify which of the following amounts should be reported as the current asset cash in the year-end balance sheet, as at June 30, 2011:

1. Currency and coins totalling $79 in a locked box used for petty cash transactions
2. A $12,000 guaranteed investment certificate, due July 31, 2011
3. June-dated cheques worth $300 that Magnotta has received from customers but not yet deposited
4. A $92 cheque received from a customer in payment of her June account, but postdated July 1
5. A balance of $2,500 in the Royal Bank chequing account
6. A balance of $4,250 in the Royal Bank savings account
7. Prepaid postage of $70 in the postage meter
8. A $100 IOU from the company receptionist
9. Cash register floats of $300
10. Over-the-counter cash receipts for June 30 consisting of $570 of currency and coin, $130 of cheques from customers, $580 of debit card slips, and $750 of bank credit card slips. These amounts were processed by the bank and posted to the bank account on July 1.

Instructions

(a) What amount should Magnotta report as its cash balance at June 30, 2011?
(b) In which financial statement and in which account should the items not included as cash be reported?

Problems: Set A

Identify components of internal control framework.
(SO 1) AP

P7–1A Liam Taylor has been hired by Wang Manufacturing into a newly created Compliance Officer position. Liam's first assignment is to design internal controls for Wang Manufacturing. Liam knows that an effective internal control program has five important components.

Liam gets started by working with company management to write an employee handbook for personnel working at all levels of the organization. Liam also convinces company management to include a statement in the handbook stressing their views on the importance of all company employees' adhering to the highest ethical standards. A company "hotline" is also established, allowing employees to call Liam directly if anyone observes a violation of company policies.

Next, Liam reviews the activities of the company's accounting personnel. Liam is an expert on control activities. Using his knowledge and experience, Liam ensures that all accounting personnel are practising the most effective control procedures. For example, Liam noticed that accounts payable was paying invoices with only a manager's approval signature. Liam has changed the procedure so that invoices will be paid only after the invoice is matched with an authorized purchase order and a valid receiving report.

Finally, using the company's existing information systems, the company IT expert developed reports such as a daily listing of cheque disbursements, accounts receivable balances versus credit limits, and other reports to communicate whether control procedures are being properly followed. These reports are viewed by Liam only.

Instructions

Identify where Liam has successfully designed any of the five components of an internal control framework. Identify any missing components.

Taking It Further   Can you suggest any improvements to Liam's design?

P7–2A   Strivent Theatre's cashier's booth is located near the entrance to the theatre. Two cashiers are employed. One works from 3:00 p.m. to 7:00 p.m., the other from 7:00 p.m. to 11:00 p.m. Each cashier is bonded. The cashiers receive cash from customers and operate a machine that ejects serially numbered tickets. The rolls of tickets are inserted and locked into the machine by the theatre manager at the beginning of each cashier's shift.

Identify internal control activities related to cash receipts.
(SO 1, 2) C

After purchasing a ticket, which may cost different prices depending on the customer's age group, the customer takes the ticket to an usher stationed at the entrance of the theatre lobby, about 10 metres from the cashier's booth. The usher tears the ticket in half, admits the customer, and returns the ticket stub to the customer. The other half of the ticket is dropped into a locked box by the usher.

At the end of each cashier's shift, the theatre manager removes the ticket rolls from the machine and makes a cash count. The cash count sheet is initialled by the cashier. At the end of the day, the manager deposits the receipts in total in a bank night deposit vault located in the mall. The manager also sends copies of the deposit slip and the initialled cash count sheets to the theatre company controller for verification, and to the company's accounting department. Receipts from the first shift are stored in a safe located in the manager's office.

Instructions

Identify the internal control activities and how they apply to the cash receipts transactions of Strivent Theatre.

Taking It Further   If the usher and the cashier decide to collaborate to steal cash, how might they do this?

P7–3A   Each of the following independent situations has one or more internal control weaknesses:

Identify internal controls for cash receipts and cash disbursements.
(SO 1, 2, 3) C

1. Board Riders is a small snowboarding club that offers specialized coaching for teenagers who want to improve their skills. Group lessons are offered every day. Members who want a lesson pay a $15 fee directly to the teacher at the start of the lesson that day. Most members pay cash. At the end of the lesson, the teacher reports the number of students and turns over the cash to the office manager.
2. Coloroso Agency offers parenting advice to young single mothers. Most of the agency's revenues are from government grants. The general manager is responsible for all of the accounting work, including approving invoices for payment, preparing and posting all entries into the accounting system, and preparing bank reconciliations.

3. At Nexus Company, each salesperson is responsible for deciding on the correct credit policies for his or her customers. For example, the salesperson decides if Nexus should sell to the customer on credit and how high the credit limit should be. Salespeople receive a commission based on their sales.

4. Algorithm Company is a software company that employs many computer programmers. The company uses accounting software that was created by one of the employees. In order to be more flexible and share the workload, all of the programmers have access to the accounting software program in case changes are needed.

5. The warehouse manager at Orange Wing distributors is well known for running an efficient, cost-saving operation. He has eliminated the requirement for staff to create receiving reports and purchase orders because it was taking staff too long to prepare them.

Instructions

(a) Identify the internal control weaknesses in each situation.

(b) Explain the problems that could occur as a result of these weaknesses.

Taking It Further Make recommendations for correcting each situation.

Record debit and bank credit card and petty cash transactions, and identify internal controls.
(SO 2, 3) AP

P7–4A Malik & Partners recently made some changes to its operating procedures. As of July 1, 2011, the company started allowing customers to use debit and bank credit cards for purchases of merchandise. Previously, it accepted only cash or personal cheques from customers. Malik's bank charges $1.25 for every debit card transaction and 4.0% for bank credit card transactions.

On July 1, the company also established a petty cash fund. Before creating the petty cash fund, cash was taken from the cash register whenever someone needed cash to pay for a small expense.

The following transactions happened in the first two weeks of July:

July 1 Established the petty cash fund by cashing a cheque for $250.

8 Total sales for the week were $33,750. Customers paid for these purchases as follows: $12,450 in cash and personal cheques; $9,200 on debit cards (134 transactions); and the balance using bank credit cards.

8 Replenished the petty cash fund. On this date, the fund consisted of $72 in cash and the following petty cash receipts:

Freight out	$59
Office supplies	37
Advertising in local paper	45
Personal withdrawal by owner	42

15 Total sales for the week were $37,405. Customers paid for these purchases as follows: $9,435 in cash and personal cheques; $11,668 on debit cards (156 transactions); and the balance using bank credit cards.

15 Replenished the petty cash fund and decreased the balance to $200. On this date, the fund consisted of $70 in cash and the following petty cash receipts:

Postage	$45
Advertising in local newspaper	69
Cleaning supplies	60

Instructions

(a) Record the transactions.

(b) What are the benefits of having a petty cash fund instead of paying small expenses from the cash register receipts? What policies and procedures should Malik follow to ensure there is good internal control over its petty cash fund?

Taking It Further   What are the advantages and disadvantages of accepting debit and bank credit card transactions as opposed to accepting only cash and personal cheques from customers? Consider both the internal control and business reasons.

P7–5A   You are the accountant for Reliable Snow Removal Services. The company established a petty cash fund of $100 for small expenditures on November 1. Your responsibility is to oversee the fund, which includes disbursing cash and prenumbered petty cash fund receipts, collecting supporting documentation, and replenishing the fund.

Record and post petty cash transactions and identify internal controls and petty cash procedures.
(SO 3) AP

It is November 30 and you are about to replenish the fund. The table below shows the petty cash fund receipts currently in the fund. The fund also holds $2.27 in cash.

Prenumbered Receipt	Description	Amount
24	Parking	$12
25	Windshield fluid	3
26	Parking	16
27	Wiper blades	22
28	Flat tire repair	39

Note: The accounts affected are Parking and Vehicle Maintenance.

Instructions

(a) Calculate the amount of cash the fund should hold on November 30.

(b) Record the establishment and replenishment of the fund.

(c) Assuming instead that management decides the fund should be increased to $150, journalize the entry to record the increase.

(d) Describe the steps you must take as the custodian of the fund to replenish it and increase its size to $150.

Taking It Further   Explain control procedures you would put in place to prevent theft.

P7–6A   On October 31, 2011, Lisik Company had a cash balance per books of $9,693. The bank statement on that date showed a balance of $10,973. A comparison of the statement with the Cash account revealed the following:

Prepare bank reconciliation and related entries.
(SO 5) AP

1. The statement included debit memos of $40 for the printing of additional company cheques and $35 for bank service charges.

2. Cash sales of $836 on October 12 were deposited in the bank. The cash receipts journal entry and the deposit slip were incorrectly made out and recorded by Lisik as $856. The bank detected the error on the deposit slip and credited Lisik Company for the correct amount.

3. The September 30 deposit of $990 was included on the October bank statement. The deposit had been placed in the bank's night deposit vault on September 30.

4. The October 31 deposit of $963 was not included on the October bank statement. The deposit had been placed in the bank's night deposit vault on October 31.

5. Cheques #1006 for $330 and #1072 for $1,120 were outstanding on September 30. Of these, #1072 cleared the bank in October. All the cheques written in October except for #1278 for $466, #1284 for $587, and #1285 for $293 had cleared the bank by October 31.

6. On October 18, the company issued cheque #1181 for $685 to Helms & Co., on account. The cheque, which cleared the bank in October, was incorrectly journalized and posted by Lisik Company for $568.

7. A review of the bank statement revealed that Lisik Company received electronic payments from customers on account of $2,055 in October. The bank had also credited the account with $39 of interest revenue on October 31. Lisik had no previous notice of these amounts.

8. Included with the cancelled cheques was a cheque issued by Lasik Company for $600 that was incorrectly charged to Lisik Company by the bank.

9. On October 31, the bank statement showed an NSF charge of $715 for a cheque issued by W. Hoad, a customer, to Lisik Company on account. This amount included a $15 service charge by the bank.

Instructions

(a) Prepare the bank reconciliation at October 31.

(b) Prepare the necessary adjusting entries at October 31.

Taking It Further What are the risks of not performing bank reconciliations? Why not just rely on the bank records?

Prepare bank reconciliation and related entries.

(SO 5) AP

P7–7A The March bank statement showed the following for Yap Co.:

	YAP CO. Bank Statement March 31, 2011				
	Cheques and Other Debits			Deposits	
Date	Number	Amount		Number	Amount
Feb. 28					$14,368
Mar. 3	3451	$2,260		$2,530	14,638
4	3471	845			13,793
6	3472	1,427		1,221	13,587
7	3473	1,461			12,126
10	NSF	550			11,576
11	3475	487		1,745	12,834
15	3477	915			11,919
17	3476	838		2,283	13,364
20				1,823	15,187
21	3474	2,130			13,057
26	3478	357		2,567	15,267
31	LN	1,062			14,205
31	3480	1,679			12,526
31	SC	49		IN 23	12,500

Additional information:

1. The bank statement contained three debit memoranda:
   - An NSF cheque of $550 that Yap had deposited was returned due to insufficient funds in the maker's bank account. This cheque was originally given to Yap by Mr. Jordan, a customer, in payment of his account. Yap believes it will be able to collect this amount from Mr. Jordan.
   - A bank loan payment (LN), which included $62 of interest and a $1,000 payment on the principal.
   - A service charge (SC) of $49 for bank services provided throughout the month.
2. The bank statement contained one credit memorandum for $23 of interest (IN) earned on the account for the month.
3. The bank made an error processing cheque #3474. No other errors were made by the bank.

Yap's list of cash receipts and cash payments showed the following for March:

Cash Receipts			Cash Payments		
Date	Amount		Date	Cheque No.	Amount
Mar. 5	$ 1,221		Mar. 3	3472	$ 1,427
10	1,745		4	3473	1,641
14	2,283		6	3474	2,330
20	1,832		7	3475	487
25	2,567		13	3476	838
31	1,025		14	3477	915
Total	$10,673		19	3478	357
			21	3479	159
			28	3480	1,679
			31	3481	862
			31	3482	1,126
			Total		$11,821

The bank portion of the previous month's bank reconciliation for Yap Co. at February 28, 2011, was as follows:

YAP CO. Bank Reconciliation February 28, 2011		
Cash balance per bank		$14,368
Add: Deposits in transit		2,530
		16,898
Less: Outstanding cheques		
#3451	$2,260	
#3470	1,535	
#3471	845	4,640
Adjusted cash balance per bank		$12,258

Instructions

(a) What is Yap Co.'s unadjusted cash balance in its general ledger on March 31?
(b) Prepare a bank reconciliation at March 31.
(c) Prepare the necessary adjusting entries at March 31. (*Note*: The correction of any errors in the recording of cheques should be made to Accounts Payable. The correction of any errors in the recording of cash receipts should be made to Accounts Receivable.)

Taking It Further   The company will prepare entries to record items found in the above bank reconciliation (see part (c) in the instructions). Describe any other follow-up actions required regarding the other reconciling items in Yap Co's bank reconciliation.

P7–8A   The bank portion of the bank reconciliation for Maloney Company at October 31, 2011, was as follows:

Prepare bank reconciliation and related entries.
(SO 5) AP

MALONEY COMPANY Bank Reconciliation October 31, 2011		
Cash balance per bank		$11,545
Add: Deposits in transit		1,530
		13,075
Less: Outstanding cheques		
#2451	$1,260	
#2470	920	
#2471	845	
#2472	504	
#2474	1,050	4,579
Adjusted cash balance per bank		$ 8,496

The adjusted cash balance per bank agreed with the cash balance per books at October 31. The November bank statement showed the following:

MALONEY COMPANY Bank Statement November 30, 2011				
	Cheques and Other Debits		Deposits	
Date	Number	Amount	Amount	Balance
Oct. 31				$11,545
Nov. 1	2470	$ 920	$1,530	12,155
2	2471	845		11,310
4	2475	1,641	1,212	10,881
5	2474	1,050		9,831
8	2476	2,830	990	7,991
10	2477	600		7,391
13			2,575	9,966
15	2479	1,750		8,216
18	2480	1,330	1,473	8,359
21			2,966	11,325
25	NSF	260	2,567	13,632
27	2481	695		12,937
28			1,650	14,587
29	2486	900	EFT 2,479	16,166
30	2483	575	1,186	16,777
30	LN	2,250		14,527

Additional information from the bank statement:

1. The EFT of $2,479 is an electronic transfer from a customer in payment of its account. The amount includes $49 of interest that Maloney Company had not previously accrued.
2. The NSF for $260 is a $245 cheque from a customer, Pendray Holdings, in payment of its account, plus a $15 processing fee.
3. The LN is a payment of a note payable with the bank and consists of $250 interest and $2,000 principal.
4. The bank did not make any errors.

The cash records per books for November follow. Two errors were made by Maloney Company.

Cash Payments						Cash Receipts	
Date	Number	Amount	Date	Number	Amount	Date	Amount
Nov. 1	2475	$1,641	Nov. 18	2482	$ 612	Nov. 3	$ 1,212
2	2476	2,380	20	2483	575	7	990
2	2477	600	22	2484	830	12	2,575
4	2478	538	23	2485	975	17	1,473
8	2479	1,750	24	2486	900	20	2,699
10	2480	1,330	30	2487	1,200	24	2,567
15	2481	695	Total		$14,026	27	1,650
						29	1,186
						30	1,338
						Total	$15,690

Instructions

(a) Determine the unadjusted cash balance per books as at November 30, before reconciliation.
(b) Prepare a bank reconciliation at November 30.
(c) Prepare the necessary adjusting entries at November 30. (*Note*: The correction of any errors in the recording of cheques should be made to Accounts Payable. The correction of any errors in the recording of cash receipts should be made to Accounts Receivable.)

Taking It Further   When there is an error, how does a company determine if it was a bank error or a company error? How would you know if the bank has made an error in your account?

P7–9A When the accountant of Gurjot Imports prepared the bank reconciliation on April 30, 2011, there were three outstanding cheques: #286 for $217, #289 for $326, and #290 for $105. There were no deposits in transit as at April 30, 2011. The bank balance at April 30 was $4,261. The following is selected information from the May bank statement:

Prepare bank reconciliation and related entries.
(SO 5) AP

Cheques Cleared				Other Bank Account Transactions		
Date	Cheque No.	Amount		Date	Amount	Transaction
May 1	286	$ 217		May 8	$2,620 +	Deposit
8	305	402		12	4,718 +	Deposit
20	306	105		24	3,190 +	Deposit
22	308	1,648		25	280 –	NSF cheque
22	289	326		28	28 –	Service charge
23	304	2,735		31	12 +	Interest
31	309	175				

The NSF cheque was originally received from a customer, R. Siddiqi, in payment of his account of $265. The bank included a $15 service charge for a total of $280. Information from the company's accounting records follows:

Cash Receipts			Cash Payments		
Date	Amount		Date	Cheque No.	Amount
May 5	$2,260		May 5	304	$2,735
12	4,718		5	305	402
23	3,190		19	306	150
31	1,004		19	307	3,266
			31	309	175
			31	310	2,400

Investigation reveals that cheque #306 was issued to pay the telephone bill and cheque #308 was issued to pay rent. All deposits are for collections of accounts receivable. The bank made no errors.

Instructions

(a) Calculate the balance per bank statement at May 31 and the unadjusted Cash balance per company records at May 31.
(b) Prepare a bank reconciliation at May 31.
(c) Prepare the necessary adjusting entries at May 31.
(d) What balance would Gurjot Imports report as cash in the current assets section of its balance sheet on May 31, 2011?

Taking It Further Will the bank be concerned if it looks at Gurjot Imports' balance sheet and sees a different number than the one on the bank statement? Why or why not?

P7–10A Sally's Sweet Shop is a very profitable small business. It has not, however, thought much about internal control. For example, in an attempt to keep clerical and office expenses to a minimum, the company has combined the jobs of cashier and bookkeeper. As a result, Jennifer Espinola handles all cash receipts, keeps the accounting records, and prepares the monthly bank reconciliations.

Prepare bank reconciliation and identify errors.
(SO 2, 3, 5) AN

The balance per bank statement on November 30, 2011, was $21,580. Outstanding cheques were #361 for $514, #484 for $160, #485 for $267, #492 for $175, #493 for $321, and #494 for $173. Included with the statement was an EFT deposit for $750 on November 25 in payment of an account receivable. This EFT has not been recorded by the company.

The company's ledger showed one cash account, with a balance of $20,761. The balance included undeposited cash on hand. Because of the lack of internal controls, Jennifer was able to take all of the undeposited receipts for personal use. She then prepared the following bank reconciliation to try to hide her theft of cash:

Cash balance per books, November 30		$21,761
Add: Outstanding cheques		
#492	$175	
#493	321	
#494	173	669
		20,210
Less: Bank credit memorandum		750
Cash balance per bank statement, November 30		$21,580

Instructions

(a) Prepare a correct bank reconciliation. (*Hint*: The theft is the difference between the adjusted balance per books and per bank.)

(b) Indicate the ways that Jennifer tried to hide the theft and the dollar amount for each method.

Taking It Further   What internal control activities were violated in this case?

P7–11A   A first year co-op student is trying to determine the amount of cash that should be reported on a company's balance sheet. The following information was given to the student at year end:

1. Cash on hand in the cash registers totals $5,000.
2. The balance in the Petty Cash account is $500. At year end, the fund had $125 cash and receipts totalling $375.
3. The balance in the Commercial Bank savings account is $100,000. In the chequing account, the balance is $25,000. The company also has a U.S. bank account, which contained the equivalent of $48,000 Canadian at year end.
4. A special bank account holds $150,000 that is restricted for capital asset replacement.
5. A line of credit of $50,000 is available at the bank on demand.
6. The amount due from employees (for travel advances) totals $14,000.
7. Short-term investments held by the company include $32,000 in a money-market fund, $75,000 in treasury bills, and $40,000 in shares of The Forzani Group Ltd. The money-market fund and treasury bills had maturity dates of less than 90 days.
8. The company has a supply of unused postage stamps totalling $150.
9. The company has NSF cheques from customers totalling $1,750 that were returned by the bank.
10. In a special account, the company has $9,250 of cash deposits (advances) paid by customers.

Instructions

(a) Calculate the Cash balance that should be reported on the year-end balance sheet as a current asset.

(b) Identify where any items that were not reported in the Cash balance in (a) should be reported.

Taking It Further   Why is it important to present restricted cash balances separately from cash?

Problems: Set B

P7–1B   Owners of the Patel Construction Company are concerned about internal control at their company. The owners believe they have an effective control program in place. For example, policies regarding vacation, overtime, breaks, employee purchases, and terminations are written in a 15-page document and posted on a bulletin board in the company's conference room.

The company buys insurance to put the owners' minds at rest regarding any potential unforeseen risks. The company relies on the insurance broker to recommend appropriate policies. To be sure there is sufficient coverage, the broker is told to find the best policies with the lowest deductibles offered, and that cost is not an issue. Given such great insurance coverage, the owners see no reason to impose any special procedures on employees regarding internal control. For example, employee timesheets are completed by employees, and supervisor review and approval is not required. Timesheets are submitted directly to payroll for processing.

Finally, the owners take great pride in having the best, most up-to-date accounting technology. The company has powerful laptops loaded with recently purchased accounting software. The software is very flexible and is capable of tracking and reporting company spending in great detail. The owners have hired an experienced accountant to design internal reports that will keep them updated on company performance on a weekly basis. For example, employee costs can be measured and compared every week with prior-year spending and budgeted amounts.

Instructions

Based on the above information, identify as many components of an effective control framework as you can, and note if any components are missing.

Taking It Further Comment on how each of the components could be better designed.

P7–2B The board of trustees of a local church is concerned about the internal controls of its offering collections made at weekly services and has asked for your help. At a board meeting, you learn the following:

Identify internal control weaknesses over cash receipts. (SO 1, 2) C

1. The board has made the finance committee responsible for the financial management and audit of the financial records. This group prepares the annual budget and approves major disbursements but is not involved in collections or record keeping. No audit has been done in recent years, because the same trusted employee has kept church records and served as financial secretary for 15 years. The church does not carry any fidelity insurance.
2. The collection at the weekly service is taken by a team of ushers who volunteer to serve for one month. The ushers take the collection plates to a basement office at the rear of the church. They hand their plates to the head usher and return to the church service. After all plates have been turned in, the head usher counts the cash collected in them. The head usher then places the cash in the unlocked church safe and includes a note that states the amount counted. The head usher volunteers to serve for three months.
3. The next morning, the financial secretary opens the safe and recounts the collection. The secretary withholds from $150 to $200 in cash, depending on the cash expenditures expected for the week, and deposits the remainder of the collections in the bank. To make the deposit easier, church members who contribute by cheque are asked to make their cheques payable to Cash.
4. Each month, the financial secretary reconciles the bank statement and submits a copy of the reconciliation to the board of trustees. The reconciliations have rarely contained any bank errors and have never shown any errors per books.

Instructions

(a) Indicate the weaknesses in internal control in the handling of collections.
(b) List the improvements in internal control procedures that you plan to recommend at the next meeting of the audit team for (1) the ushers, (2) the head usher, and (3) the financial secretary.

Taking It Further What improvements in internal control do you recommend for the finance committee?

Identify internal controls for cash receipts and cash disbursements.

(SO 1, 2, 3) C

P7–3B Each of the following independent situations has an internal control weakness:

1. Henry's Lawn Care Service provides residential grass cutting services for a large number of clients who all pay cash. Henry collects the cash and keeps it in the glove compartment of his car until the end of the week, when he has time to count it and prepare a bank deposit.
2. Tasty Treats sells a variety of items including ice cream, pop, and other snack foods. A long-term employee is responsible for ordering all merchandise, checking all deliveries, and approving invoices for payment.
3. At Pop's Pizza, there are three sales clerks on duty during busy times. All three of them use the same cash drawer.
4. Most customers at Ultimate Definition TVs use the option to pay for their televisions in 24 equal payments over two years. These customers send the company cheques or cash each month. The office manager opens the mail each day, makes a bank deposit with the cheques received in the mail that day, and prepares and posts an entry in the accounting records.
5. Trends Incorporated manufactures celebrity posters for teenagers. Naimiti Mann is the custodian of the company's $500 petty cash fund. The fund is replenished every week. Frequently people do not have a receipt for their expenses because of things like parking meter expenses. In this case, Naimiti just creates a receipt for that person and gives them their cash. Naimiti has been with the company for 15 years and is good friends with many of the employees. Naimiti is very hard-working and never takes a vacation.

Instructions

(a) Identify the internal control weaknesses in each situation.
(b) Explain the problems that could occur as a result of these weaknesses.

Taking It Further Make recommendations for correcting each situation.

Record debit and bank credit card and petty cash transactions and identify internal controls.

(SO 2, 3, 5) AP

P7–4B Ramesh & Company recently made some changes to its operating procedures. As of May 1, 2011, the company started allowing customers to use debit and bank credit cards for purchases of merchandise. Previously, it had accepted only cash or personal cheques from customers. Ramesh's bank charges $0.75 for every debit card transaction and 3.25% for credit card transactions.

On May 1, the company also established a petty cash fund. Before creating the petty cash fund, cash was taken from the cash register whenever someone needed cash to pay for a small expense.

The following transactions happened in the first two weeks of June:

May	1	Established the petty cash fund by cashing a cheque for $150.
	8	Total sales for the week were $15,750. Customers paid for these purchases as follows: $5,075 in cash and personal cheques; $4,275 on debit cards (52 transactions); and the balance using bank credit cards.
	8	Replenished the petty cash fund. On this date, the fund consisted of $9 in cash and the following petty cash receipts:

Delivery of merchandise to a customer	$42
Postage	28
Advertising in local paper	57
Miscellaneous expense	10

	15	Total sales for the week were $18,200. Customers paid for these purchases as follows: $4,267 in cash and personal cheques; $5,933 on debit cards (80 transactions); and the balance using bank credit cards.
	15	Replenished the petty cash fund and increased the balance to $250. On this date, the fund consisted of $4 in cash and the following petty cash receipts:

B. Ramesh's personal withdrawal	$50
Office supplies	77
Coffee supplies	20

Instructions

(a) Record the transactions.

(b) What are the advantages and disadvantages of accepting debit and bank credit card transactions as opposed to accepting only cash and personal cheques from customers? Consider both the internal control and business reasons.

Taking It Further What are the benefits of having a petty cash fund instead of paying small expenses from the cash register receipts? What policies and procedures should Ramesh & Company follow to ensure there is good internal control over its petty cash fund?

P7–5B Lakeside Sweetshop maintains a petty cash fund for small expenditures. The following transactions happened over a two-month period:

Record and post petty cash transactions.
(SO 3) AP

June 8 Established the petty cash fund by writing a cheque on First Bank for $200.

 21 Replenished the petty cash fund. On this date, the fund consisted of $13 in cash and the following petty cash receipts: freight out $84, postage expense $42, office supplies expense $47, and miscellaneous expense $12.

 30 Replenished the petty cash fund. On this date, the fund consisted of $5 in cash and the following petty cash receipts: freight out $86, charitable contributions expense $40, postage expense $28, and miscellaneous expense $44.

July 1 Increased the amount of the petty cash fund to $300.

 23 Replenished the petty cash fund. On this date, the fund consisted of $58 in cash and the following petty cash receipts: freight out $36, entertainment expense $53, postage expense $33, freight in $60 (assume perpetual inventory system), and miscellaneous expense $54.

 31 Replenished the petty cash fund and reduced the balance to $250. On this date, the fund consisted of $63 in cash and the following petty cash receipts: postage expense $95, travel expense $46, freight out $44, and office supplies expense $57.

Instructions

(a) Journalize the petty cash transactions.

(b) Post them to the Petty Cash account.

Taking It Further It was stated in the chapter that "internal control over cash disbursements is better when payments are made by cheque." Why, then, are some payments made from petty cash rather than by cheque? Does this mean that there is no internal control over payments from petty cash? Explain.

P7–6B The Agricultural Genetics Company's Cash account in its general ledger reported a balance of $9,448 on May 31, 2011. The company's bank statement from Western Bank reported a balance of $11,689 on the same date.

Prepare bank reconciliation and related entries.
(SO 5) AP

A comparison of the details in the bank statement to the details in the Cash account revealed the following facts:

1. The bank statement included a debit memo of $50 for bank service charges.

2. Cash sales of $638 on May 12 were deposited in the bank. The journal entry to record the cash sales and the deposit slip to deposit the cash were correctly made out for $638. The bank credited Agricultural Genetics Company for $386.

3. The April 30 deposit of $2,190 was included on the May bank statement. The deposit had been placed in the bank's night deposit vault on April 30.

4. The May 31 deposit of $1,141 was not included on the May bank statement. The deposit had been placed in the bank's night deposit vault on May 31.

5. Cheques #928 for $233 and #1014 for $689 were outstanding on April 30. Of these, #1014 cleared the bank in May. All of the cheques written in May except for #1127 for $732, #1195 for $813, and #1196 for $401 had cleared the bank by May 31.

6. On May 18, the company issued cheque #1151 for $585 to L. Kingston, on account. The cheque, which cleared the bank in May, was incorrectly journalized and posted by Agricultural Genetics Company for $855.

7. On May 28, the company issued cheque #1192 for $1,738 to Bow Graphics for computer equipment. The cheque was incorrectly recorded by Agricultural Genetics as $1,387. The cheque cleared the bank on May 30.

8. A review of the bank statement revealed that Agricultural Genetics Company received $2,382 of electronic payments from customers on account in May. The bank had also credited the company's account with $24 of interest revenue on May 31. Agricultural Genetics Company had no previous notice of these amounts.

9. On May 31, the bank statement showed an NSF charge of $820 for a cheque issued by Pete Dell, a customer, to Agricultural Genetics Company on account. This amount included a $15 service charge by the bank.

Instructions

(a) Prepare the bank reconciliation at May 31.
(b) Prepare the necessary adjusting entries at May 31.

Taking It Further   What would you say to the Agricultural Genetics Company's bank manager, who is concerned that the company's May 31 Cash account balance shows a different amount than the May 31 bank statement?

Prepare bank reconciliation and related entries.
(SO 5) AP

P7–7B   The bank portion of the bank reconciliation for Katsaris Company at August 31, 2011, was as follows:

KATSARIS COMPANY
Bank Reconciliation
August 31, 2011

Cash balance per bank		$14,368
Add: Deposits in transit		2,530
		16,898
Less: Outstanding cheques		
#3451	$2,260	
#3470	1,100	
#3471	845	
#3472	1,427	
#3474	1,050	6,682
Adjusted cash balance per bank		$10,216

The adjusted cash balance per bank agreed with the cash balance per books at August 31. The September bank statement showed the following:

KATSARIS COMPANY
Bank Statement
September 30, 2011

Date	Cheques and Other Debits Number	Amount	Deposits Amount	Balance
Aug. 31				$14,368
Sept. 1	3451	$2,260	$2,530	14,638
2	3471	845		13,793
5	3475	1,641	1,212	13,364
7	3472	1,427		11,937
8	3476	1,300	2,365	13,002
9	3477	2,130		10,872
15	3479	3,080	3,145	10,937
16			2,673	13,610
20			2,945	16,555
23	NSF	1,027	2,567	18,095
26	3480	600		17,495
27	3483	1,140	2,836	19,191
27	3482	475	1,025	19,741
30	3485	541		19,200
30	SC	45		19,155

Additional information:

1. The deposit of $3,145 on September 15 is an electronic transfer from a customer in payment of its account. The amount includes $65 of interest, which Katsaris Company had not previously accrued.
2. The NSF for $1,027 is for a $1,012 cheque from a customer, Hopper Holdings, in payment of its account, plus a $15 processing fee.
3. SC represents bank service charges for the month.

The bank did not make any errors, but errors were made by Katsaris Company. The cash records per the company's books for September showed the following:

Cash Payments						Cash Receipts	
Date	Number	Amount	Date	Number	Amount	Date	Amount
Sept. 1	3475	$1,641	23	3484	$ 1,274	Sept. 2	$ 1,212
2	3476	1,300	24	3485	441	7	2,365
2	3477	2,130	30	3486	1,390	15	2,673
5	3478	538	Total		$14,816	20	2,954
8	3479	3,080				26	2,567
12	3480	600				28	2,836
17	3481	807				30	1,025
20	3482	475				30	1,198
22	3483	1,140				Total	$16,830

Instructions

(a) Determine the unadjusted cash balance per books as at September 30 before reconciliation.
(b) Prepare a bank reconciliation at September 30.
(c) Prepare the necessary adjusting entries at September 30. (*Note*: The correction of any errors in the recording of cheques should be made to Accounts Payable. The correction of any errors in the recording of cash receipts should be made to Accounts Receivable.)

Taking It Further   The company will prepare entries to record items found in the above bank reconciliation (see part (c) in the instructions). Describe any other follow-up actions required regarding the other reconciling items in Katsaris Company's bank reconciliation.

P7–8B   You are given the following information for River Adventures Company:

Prepare bank reconciliation and related entries.
(SO 5) AP

RIVER ADVENTURES COMPANY
Bank Reconciliation
April 30, 2011

Cash balance per bank		$9,009
Add: Deposits in transit		846
		9,855
Less: Outstanding cheques		
#526	$1,358	
#533	279	
#541	363	
#555	79	2,079
Adjusted cash balance per bank		$7,776

The adjusted cash balance per bank agreed with the cash balance per books at April 30, 2011. The May bank statement showed the following:

RIVER ADVENTURES COMPANY Bank Statement May 31, 2011				
	Cheques and Other Debits		Deposits	
Date	Number	Amount	Amount	Balance
Apr. 30				$9,009
May 3	526	$1,358	$ 846	8,497
4	541	363		8,134
6	556	223		7,911
6	557	1,800	1,250	7,361
10			980	8,341
10	559	1,650		6,691
13			426	7,117
13			1,650	8,767
14	561	799		7,968
18	562	2,045		5,923
18			222	6,145
19	563	2,487		3,658
21	564	603		3,055
25	565	1,033		2,022
26			980	3,002
28	NSF	440	1,771	4,333
31	SC	25		4,308

Additional information from the bank statement:

1. The deposit of $1,650 on May 13 is an electronic transfer from a customer in payment of its account. The amount includes $35 of interest, which River Adventures Company had not previously accrued.
2. The NSF for $440 is for a $425 cheque from a customer, Ralph King, in payment of his account, plus a $15 processing fee.
3. SC represents bank service charges for the month.
4. The bank made an error when processing cheque #564. The company also made two errors in the month. All cheques were written to pay accounts payable; all cash receipts were collections of accounts receivable.

The company's recorded cash payments and cash receipts for the month were as follows:

Cash Receipts			Cash Payments		
Date	Amount		Date	Cheque No.	Amount
May 5	$1,250		May 4	556	$ 223
8	980		5	557	1,800
12	426		7	558	943
18	222		7	559	1,650
25	890		8	560	890
28	1,771		10	561	799
31	1,286		15	526	2,045
Total	$6,825		18	563	2,887
			20	564	306
			25	565	1,033
			31	566	950
			Total		$13,526

Instructions

(a) Calculate the unadjusted cash balance in River Adventures' general ledger at May 31.

(b) Prepare a bank reconciliation and the necessary adjusting journal entries at May 31.

Taking It Further When there is an error, how does a company determine if it was a bank error or a company error? How would you know if the bank has made an error in your account?

P7–9B In the November 30, 2011, bank reconciliation at Kiran's Kayaks, there were two outstanding cheques: #165 for $612 and 169 for $178. There was a $1,128 deposit in transit as at November 30, 2011. The bank balance at November 30 was $7,211. The December bank statement had the following selected information:

Prepare bank reconciliation and related entries.
(SO 5) AP

Cheques Cleared				Other Bank Account Transactions		
Date	Cheque No.	Amount		Date	Amount	Transaction
Dec. 1	165	$ 612		Dec. 1	$1,128 +	Deposit
6	184	592		7	2,321 +	Deposit
20	185	1,165		13	3,691 +	Deposit
22	187	833		19	4,511 +	Deposit
23	183	2,955		22	730 –	NSF cheque
31	188	341		31	88 –	Service charge
				31	12 +	Interest

The NSF cheque was originally received from a customer, M. Sevigny, in payment of her account of $710. The bank included a $20 service charge for a total of $730.

Information from the company's accounting records follows:

Cash Receipts			Cash Payments		
Date	Amount		Date	Cheque No.	Amount
Dec. 4	$2,321		6	183	$2,955
13	2,991		6	184	592
18	4,511		12	185	1,165
31	2,218		12	186	3,491
			13	187	633
			31	188	341
			31	189	1,721

Investigation reveals that cheque #187 was issued to buy office supplies. All deposits are for collections of accounts receivable. The bank made no errors.

Instructions

(a) Calculate the balance per bank statement at December 31 and the unadjusted cash balance per company records at December 31.

(b) Prepare a bank reconciliation for Kiran's Kayaks at December 31.

(c) Prepare the necessary adjusting entries at December 31.

(d) What balance would Kiran's Kayaks report as cash in the current assets section of its balance sheet on December 31, 2011?

Taking It Further Explain why it is important for Kiran's Kayaks to complete the above bank reconciliation before preparing closing entries.

Prepare bank reconciliation
and related entries.
(SO 2, 3, 5) AN

P7–10B   Your newly hired assistant prepared the following bank reconciliation:

CAREFREE COMPANY
Bank Reconciliation[1]
March 31, 2011

Book Balance		$3,125	Bank Balance		$7,350
Add: Deposit in transit	$ 750		Add: Error re: cheque #173		45[4]
EFT receipt from customer	2,645				7,395
Interest earned	15	3,410	Deduct: Pre-authorized payments		
		6,535	Hydro[5]	$ 120	
Deduct: Error re: Careless Company's			Telephone[5]	85	
deposit to our account	$1,100[2]		NSF cheque	220	
Bank service charge	55[3]	1,155	Outstanding cheques	1,650	2,075
Adjusted book balance		$5,380	Adjusted bank balance		$5,320

Notes:

[1] Your assistant did not know why there is a $60 difference between the adjusted book balance and the adjusted bank balance.

[2] The bank credited Carefree's account for a deposit made by Careless Company. Carefree and Careless are unrelated parties.

[3] Of the bank service charge, $15 was due to the NSF cheque.

[4] Carefree's cheque #173 was made for the proper amount of $249 in payment of an account payable; however, it was entered in the cash payments journal as $294.

[5] Carefree authorized the bank to automatically pay its hydro and telephone bills as they are directly submitted to the bank by the hydro and telephone companies. These amounts have not yet been recorded by Carefree.

Instructions

(a) Prepare a correct bank reconciliation at March 31.

(b) Prepare the necessary adjusting entries at March 31.

Taking It Further   Explain how the bank reconciliation process can strengthen internal control.

Calculate cash balance and
report other items.
(SO 6) AP

P7–11B   Sunil's Office Supplies has hired a new junior accountant and has given her the task of identifying what should be reported as cash as at February 28, 2011, on the company's balance sheet. The following information is available:

1. Cash on hand in the cash registers on February 28 totals $1,494. Of this amount, $300 is kept on hand as a cash float.

2. The petty cash fund has an imprest amount of $150. Actual petty cash on hand at February 28 is $32. Paid-out receipts total $115. Of these receipts, $75 is in IOUs from company employees.

3. The balance in the bank chequing account at February 28 is $7,460.

4. Short-term investments include $4,000 in a BMO money-market fund and an investment of $2,000 in a six-month term deposit.

5. The company sold $310 of merchandise to a customer late in the day on February 28. The customer had forgotten her wallet and promised to pay the amount on March 1.

6. The company had a U.S. dollar bank account. At February 28, its U.S. funds were worth the equivalent of $1,995 Canadian.

7. At February 28, the company has American Express credit card slips totalling $650. American Express charges the company a credit card fee of 3.0%. It normally takes two days for American Express charges to clear the banking system and be deposited in the company's bank account.

8. The company received $1,500 of cash on February 28 as an advance deposit in trust on a property sale.

9. In order to hook up utilities, the company is required to deposit $800 in trust with Ontario Hydro. This amount must remain on deposit until a satisfactory credit history has been established. The company expects to have this deposit back within the year.

Instructions

(a) Calculate the balance for cash that should be reported on the year-end balance sheet as a current asset.

(b) Identify where any items that were not reported in the balance for cash in (a) should be reported.

Taking It Further Under certain circumstances, cash may have to be presented as non-current. Why is this important information for users of the financial statements?

Continuing Cookie Chronicle

(*Note:* This is a continuation of the Cookie Chronicle from Chapters 1 through 6.)

Natalie is struggling to keep up with the recording of her accounting transactions. She is spending a lot of time marketing and selling mixers and giving her cookie classes. Her friend John is an accounting student who runs his own accounting service. He has asked Natalie if she would like to have him do her accounting.

John and Natalie meet and discuss her business. John suggests that he do the following for Natalie:

1. Hold onto cash until there is enough to be deposited. (He would keep Cookie Creations' cash locked up in his vehicle.) He would also take all of the deposits to the bank at least twice a month.
2. Write and sign all of the cheques. He would review the invoices and send out cheques as soon as the invoices are received.
3. Record all of the deposits in the accounting records.
4. Record all of the cheques in the accounting records.
5. Prepare the monthly bank reconciliation.
6. Transfer Natalie's manual accounting records to his computer accounting program. John maintains the accounting information that he keeps for his clients on his computer.
7. Prepare monthly financial statements for Natalie to review.
8. Write himself a cheque every month for the work he has done for Natalie.

Instructions

(a) Identify the weaknesses in internal control that you see in the system that John is recommending. For each weakness identified, describe the control activity that is violated.
(b) For each weakness identified in (a), suggest an improvement.
(c) Are there any other components of an effective control framework that Natalie could implement to improve operations, prevent theft, or reduce the chance of errors in financial reporting?

BROADENING YOUR PERSPECTIVE

Financial Reporting and Analysis

Financial Reporting Problem

BYP7–1 Two reports are attached to The Forzani Group Ltd.'s consolidated financial statements presented in Appendix A of this book: (1) Management's Responsibilities for Financial Reporting and (2) the Auditors' Report.

Instructions

(a) What comments, if any, about the company's system of internal control are included in Management's Responsibilities for Financial Reporting? In the Auditors' Report?

(b) Who is mainly responsible for the financial statements? Explain.

(c) What is the name of Forzani's external auditing firm and how has the firm's role changed regarding internal control since the introduction of related legislation in Canada?

(d) What is an audit committee and how does it help the external auditors with their responsibilities?

(e) By how much did cash decrease during the current fiscal year?

(f) Can you identify some things that may have caused the decrease in cash? Remember that in accounting, there are always two impacts of any transaction. For example, if you purchase inventory for cash, cash will go down and inventory will go up. Consider what other items changed significantly on the balance sheet and why and how cash may have been affected.

(g) How large was the balance of cash at the end of the current fiscal year? Express it (1) in dollars, (2) as a percentage of total assets, (3) as a percentage of current assets, and (4) as a percentage of current liabilities.

Interpreting Financial Statements

BYP7–2   Selected information from TELUS Corporation's comparative balance sheet follows:

TELUS CORPORATION Balance Sheet (partial) December 31, 2008 (in millions)		
	2008	2007
Current assets		
Cash and cash equivalents	$ 4	$ 20
Short-term investments	-	42
Accounts receivable	966	711
Income and other taxes receivable	25	121
Inventories	333	243
Prepaid expenses	220	200
Derivative assets	10	4
Total current assets	1,558	1,341
Capital assets, net (note 15)	12,483	11,122
Other assets (notes 16 and 21)	5,119	4,525
Total assets	$19,160	$16,988
Total current liabilities	$3,057	$2,686

Instructions

(a) What is a cash equivalent?

(b) Accounting standard setters have recommended that in the future, cash equivalents not be combined with cash in the balance sheet, but rather reported with other short-term investments. Will this provide financial statement users with better information about TELUS Corporation's financial position and liquidity than how it is currently reported in balance sheet?

(c) Calculate (1) the working capital, (2) the current ratio, and (3) the acid test ratio for each year. The industry averages for the current ratio were 0.64:1 in 2008 and 0.76:1 in 2007 and for the acid test, 0.43:1 in 2008 and 0.52:1 in 2007. Comment on your results.

(d) Is it possible to have too much cash? Explain why or why not.

Critical Thinking

Collaborative Learning Activity

Note to instructor: Additional instructions and material for this group activity can be found on the Instructor Resource Site.

BYP7–3 In this group activity, you will review internal controls. The Enron Coffee Co. has three restaurants and over 100 employees. The firm has three areas of cash.

WILEY PLUS
Working in Groups

Stores → The servers sell coffee and muffins. Customers can pay with cash or debit card. The servers make a nightly bank deposit.

Purchases → The head office pays the suppliers once a month

Payroll → The employees are paid bi-weekly based on their time cards.

The firm has instructed its internal audit group to construct an internal control system to minimize errors and theft of cash.

Instructions

(a) Your instructor will divide the class into pairs. In each pair, one partner will be the internal auditor, and the other will be the consultant.

(b) The internal auditors will form groups of four or five and each group will list controls that will minimize losses from theft or error. Group the controls into the following categories:

- Establishment of responsibility
- Segregation of duties
- Documentation procedures
- Physical and IT controls
- Independent checks of performance
- Human resource controls

(c) The consultants will form groups of four or five and each group will list the potential errors or thefts that could happen if controls are missing.

(d) Return to your original pair and compare the internal auditors' list of controls with the consultants' groups' list of potential error/fraud.

Communication Activity

BYP7–4 Tenacity Corporation is a medium-sized private company that sells auto parts. Blake Pike has been with the company from the beginning, ordering the auto parts, taking delivery of the parts, and authorizing payments for them. Blake often signs cheques and prepares the bank reconciliation if the controller is on vacation. The company has grown in size from five employees to 25. Annual sales have increased tenfold. Blake is still performing the same tasks as he was when the company was small and he says that he does not need any help.

WILEY PLUS
Writing Handbook

Instructions

Using the control framework outlined in the chapter, write a letter to L.S. Osman, owner of Tenacity Corporation, which outlines a plan to improve internal control within the organization given its recent increase in size. Highlight in your letter any weaknesses you are currently aware of and suggest specific recommendations.

Ethics Case

Ethics in Accounting

BYP7–5   Banks charge customers fees of up to $35 per cheque for writing "bounced" cheques; that is, cheques that exceed the balance in the account. It has been estimated that processing bounced cheques costs a bank roughly $1.50 per cheque. Thus, the profit margin on a bounced cheque is very high. Realizing this, some banks process cheques from largest amount to smallest. By doing this, they maximize the number of cheques that bounce if a customer overdraws an account.

Instructions

(a) Who are the stakeholders in this situation?
(b) Antonio Freeman had a balance of $1,200 in his chequing account on a day when the bank received the following five cheques for processing against his account:

Cheque Number	Amount	Cheque Number	Amount
3150	$ 35	3165	$550
3158	1,175	3169	180
3162	400		

Assuming a $35 fee per cheque is assessed by the bank, how much fee revenue would the bank generate if it processed cheques (1) from largest to smallest, (2) from smallest to largest, and (3) in the order of the cheque numbers?
(c) Do you think that processing cheques from largest to smallest is an ethical business practice?
(d) Besides ethical issues, what else should a bank consider when it decides if it should process cheques from largest to smallest?
(e) If you were managing a bank, what would be your policy on bounced cheques?

"All About You" Activity

BYP7–6   In the "All About You" feature, you learned about the dangers of identity theft. To protect yourself from identity theft, you should understand how it can happen and learn what you can do to prevent it.

Instructions

(a) Go to the Ontario Ministry of Consumer Services, Consumer Protection website at http://www.sse.gov.on.ca/mcs/en/pages/default.aspx and click on Identity Theft and select "What is Identity Theft?". Identify how identity thieves can get your personal information.
(b) On the same website, click on "How Do I Know if My Identity Has Been Stolen?" What are some of the signs that may indicate that your identity has been stolen?
(c) Just as a business should implement internal control systems to protect its assets, an individual should also implement controls to prevent and recognize identity theft. On the same website, click on "How to Reduce Your Risk in the Marketplace and Online."

   1. Identify the physical and IT controls that can be implemented to safeguard your identity.
   2. Identify the checks that you can do to recognize identity theft and prevent it from continuing.

ANSWERS TO CHAPTER QUESTIONS

Answers to Accounting in Action Insight Questions

All About You, p. 379

Q: Whose responsibility is it for losses due to unauthorized credit card use?

A: Most major credit card companies offer zero liability for credit card fraud, which protects the cardholder from losses due to fraud. You should find out if your cardholder agreement for any credit cards that you have offers protection from credit card fraud so that you can avoid taking on the identity thief's debts.

Across the Organization, p. 383

Q: Why would businesses continue to accept all credit cards in spite of rapidly increasing credit card fees?

A: The decision about which credit cards to accept has more than just cost implications. A decision to no longer accept a credit card may result in lost sales to competitors who continue to accept all cards. The lost sales and related profits may have a larger negative impact on the business than the additional costs associated with a particular card.

Business Insight, p. 393

Q: What are the benefits of m-payments to consumers? To businesses?

A: Consumers can reduce the number of cards they carry with them. Similarly, no longer having to issue or maintain cards, businesses should experience a reduction in costs. Having this capability on phones will also offer advantages to consumers and businesses to more easily conduct business online. For example, airline tickets could be booked or changed by travellers while in transit.

Answer to Forzani Review It Question 3, p. 400

Forzani's reported cash amount at the end of January 31, 2009, is $3,474,000. Forzani did not report any restricted cash amounts.

Answers to Self-Study Questions

1. d   2. b   3. b   4. d   5. d   6. b   7. d   8. b   9. b   10. d

Remember to go back to the beginning of the chapter to check off your completed work!

←

CHAPTER 8
ACCOUNTING FOR RECEIVABLES

bell aliant.ca

THE NAVIGATOR

- Understand *Concepts for Review*
- Read *Feature Story*
- Scan *Study Objectives*
- Read *Chapter Preview*
- Read text and answer *Before You Go On*
- Work *Demonstration Problem*
- Review *Summary of Study Objectives*
- Answer *Self-Study Questions*
- Complete assignments

CONCEPTS FOR REVIEW:

Before studying this chapter, you should understand or, if necessary, review:

a. How to record revenue. (Ch. 3, pp. 119–121 and Ch. 5, pp. 247–248)

b. Why adjusting entries are made. (Ch. 3, pp. 122–123)

c. How to calculate interest. (Ch.3, pp. 130–131)

Communications Company Makes an Effort to Collect from Incommunicado Clients

Bell Aliant is the product of the 1999 merger of four Atlantic telephone service providers: New Brunswick Telephone, Maritime Tel, Island Tel, and Newfoundland Tel. The history of these four companies goes back 100 years in providing telephone service to Atlantic Canadians. In 2009, the company expanded westward with the purchase of Bell Canada's rural telephone lines in Ontario and Quebec; at the same time, it sold Bell its wireless business. Today, Bell Aliant is predominantly a land-line provider with approximately 3 million access lines across six provinces serving 5.3 million customers. With a staff of approximately 9,000, the company earns $3.2 billion a year under the brands Bell Aliant in Atlantic Canada and Bell in Ontario and Quebec, as well as Télébec, Northern Tel, and Kenora Municipal Telephone Services.

Bell Aliant's main sources of revenue are fees for local and long-distance phone services and high-speed and dial-up Internet services. In most areas, the company's services are bundled with wireless services from Bell Mobility. It also receives revenue from equipment rentals and some information technology products and services provided to large enterprises.

"Our total receivables balance is around $450 million at any one month end," says Eleanor Marshall, Vice-President and Treasurer at Bell Aliant. On the balance sheet, this amount would be netted with amounts of accounts receivable the company has sold as part of its securitization program.

Bell Aliant's billing terms are regulated by the Canadian Radio-television and Telecommunications Commission (CRTC). The company bills monthly for services in arrears, and payments are due within 30 days of the billing date. This results in receivables being about 43 to 45 days outstanding, Marshall explains.

"The vast majority of our consumer customers pay on or slightly before the due date," she says. "We have very few accounts outstanding beyond 30 days." In contrast, businesses take longer to pay, usually 50 to 60 days.

The company allows a three-day grace period beyond a bill's due date, after which late-payment charges will begin to accrue. "The amount of those late-payment charges is also dictated by the CRTC," Marshall explains. "Ours is now approximately one percent per month." Bell Aliant classifies customers as low risk, high risk, or unknown, and this classification will determine how large and how far in arrears the company will allow the bill to get before taking action. It will send a reminder letter to these late customers with a new due date.

If the bill does not get paid, Bell Aliant will start making calls and perhaps negotiate new payment terms. If there is still no payment, the company will suspend the account for 21 days, then reconnect for one day, and contact the client again. If the bill still isn't paid, it will permanently disconnect the customer. The company then sends two notices to the client, and finally the bill goes to a collection agency.

"We establish provisions for bad debts long before it gets to this point," Marshall adds. Receivables are assigned aging categories and certain percentages, which are based on experience, apply to each to estimate the amount of bad debt. The company recognizes bad debt expense, which is typically about 1% of revenue, each month.

The Navigator

STUDY OBJECTIVES:

After studying this chapter, you should be able to:

1. Record accounts receivable transactions.
2. Calculate the net realizable value of accounts receivable and account for bad debts.
3. Account for notes receivable.
4. Demonstrate the presentation, analysis, and management of receivables.

The Navigator

As indicated in our feature story, management of receivables is important for any company that sells on credit, as Bell Aliant does. In this chapter, we will first review the journal entries that companies make when goods and services are sold on account and when cash is collected from those sales. Next, we will learn how companies estimate, record, and then, in some cases, collect their uncollectible accounts. We will also learn about notes receivable, and the statement presentation and management of receivables.

The chapter is organized as follows:

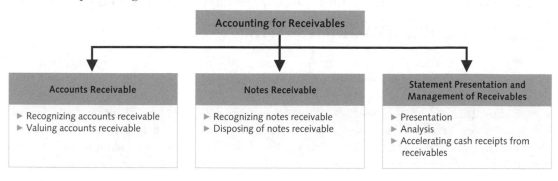

Accounts Receivable

The term "receivables" refers to amounts due from individuals and other companies. They are claims that are expected to be collected in cash. The two most common types of receivables are accounts receivable and notes receivable.

Accounts receivable are amounts owed by customers on account. They result from the sale of goods and services. These receivables are generally expected to be collected within 30 days or so, and are classified as current assets. **Notes receivable** are claims for which formal instruments of credit are issued as proof of the debt. A note normally requires the debtor to pay interest and extends for longer than the company's normal credit terms. Accounts and notes receivable that result from sale transactions are often called **trade receivables**. In this section, we will learn about accounts receivable. Notes receivable will be covered later in the chapter.

Accounts receivable are usually the most significant type of claim held by a company. Two important accounting issues—recognizing accounts receivable and valuing accounts receivable—will be discussed in this section. A third issue—accelerating cash receipts from receivables—is discussed later in the chapter.

Recognizing Accounts Receivable

STUDY OBJECTIVE 1

Record accounts receivable transactions.

Recognizing accounts receivable is relatively straightforward. For a service company, a receivable is recorded when the service is provided on account. For a merchandising company, a receivable is recorded at the point of sale of merchandise on account. Recall that in Chapter 5 we also saw how accounts receivable are reduced by sales returns and allowances and sales discounts.

To review, assume that Adorable Junior Garment sells merchandise on account to Zellers on July 1 for $1,000 with payment terms of 2/10, n/30. On July 4, Zellers returns merchandise worth $100 to Adorable Junior Garment. On July 10, Adorable Junior Garment receives payment from Zellers for the balance due. Assume Adorable Junior Garment uses a periodic inventory system. The journal entries to record these transactions on the books of Adorable Junior Garment are as follows:

Jan. 1	Accounts Receivable—Zellers		1,000	
	Sales			1,000
	To record sale of merchandise on account.			
4	Sales Returns and Allowances		100	
	Accounts Receivable—Zellers			100
	To record merchandise returned.			
10	Cash [($1,000 – $100) × 98%]		882	
	Sales Discounts [($1,000 – $100) × 2%]		18	
	Accounts Receivable—Zellers ($1,000 - $100)			900
	To record collection of accounts receivable.			

A	=	L	+	OE
+1,000				+1,000

Cash flows: no effect

A	=	L	+	OE
−100				−100

Cash flows: no effect

A	=	L	+	OE
+882				−18
−900				

⬆ Cash flows: +882

If Adorable Junior Garment used a perpetual inventory system, a second journal entry to record the cost of the goods sold (and the cost of the goods returned) would be required for the July 1 and July 4 transactions.

Subsidiary Accounts Receivable Ledger

Adorable Junior Garment does not have only Zellers as a customer. It has hundreds of customers. If it recorded the accounts receivable for each of these customers in only one general ledger account, as we did above in Accounts Receivable, it would be hard to determine the balance owed by a specific customer, such as Zellers, at a specific point in time.

Instead, most companies that sell on account use a subsidiary ledger to keep track of individual customer accounts. As we learned in Chapter 5, a subsidiary ledger gives supporting detail to the general ledger. Illustration 8-1 shows an accounts receivable control account and subsidiary ledger, using assumed data.

← Illustration 8-1

Accounts receivable general ledger control account and subsidiary ledger

GENERAL LEDGER

Accounts Receivable is a control account.

Accounts Receivable — No. 112

Date	Explanation	Ref.	Debit	Credit	Balance
2010					
July 4				100	(100)
31			10,000		9,900
31				5,900	4,000

ACCOUNTS RECEIVABLE SUBSIDIARY LEDGER

The subsidiary ledger is separate from the general ledger.

Kids Online — No. 112-203

Date	Explanation	Ref.	Debit	Credit	Balance
2010					
July 11	Invoice 1310		6,000		6,000
19	Payment			4,000	2,000

Snazzy Kids Co. — No. 112-413

Date	Explanation	Ref.	Debit	Credit	Balance
2010					
July 12	Invoice 1318		3,000		3,000
21	Payment			1,000	2,000

Zellers Inc. — No. 112-581

Date	Explanation	Ref.	Debit	Credit	Balance
2010					
July 1	Invoice 1215		1,000		1,000
4	Credit Memo 1222			100	900
10	Payment			900	0

Each entry that affects accounts receivable is basically posted twice: once to the subsidiary ledger and once to the general ledger. Normally entries to the subsidiary ledger are posted daily, while entries to the general ledger are summarized and posted monthly. For example, the $1,000 sale to Zellers was posted to Zellers' account in the subsidiary ledger on July 1. It was also summarized with other sales entries (Kids Online $6,000 + Snazzy Kids $3,000 + Zellers $1,000 = $10,000) in a special sales journal and posted to the accounts receivable control account in the general ledger at the end of the month, on July 31.

Collections on account (Kids Online $4,000 + Snazzy Kids $1,000 + Zellers $900 = $5,900) were also posted individually to the subsidiary ledger accounts and summarized and posted in total to the general ledger account. Non-recurring entries, such as the sales return of $100, are posted to both the subsidiary and general ledgers individually.

Note that the balance of $4,000 in the control account agrees with the total of the balances in the individual accounts receivable accounts in the subsidiary ledger (Kids Online $2,000 + Snazzy Kids $2,000 + Zellers $0). There is more information about how subsidiary ledgers work in Appendix C at the end of this textbook.

Interest Revenue

At the end of each month, the company can use the subsidiary ledger to easily determine the transactions that occurred in each customer's account during the month and then send the customer a statement of transactions for the month. If the customer does not pay in full within a specified period (usually 30 days), most retailers add an interest (financing) charge to the balance due.

When financing charges are added, the seller recognizes interest revenue. If Kids Online still owes $2,000 at the end of the next month, August 31, and Adorable Junior Garment charges 18% on the balance due, the entry that Adorable Junior Garment will make to record interest revenue of $30 ($2,000 × 18% × $1/_{12}$) is as follows:

A	=	L	+	OE
+30				+30

Cash flows: no effect

Aug. 31	Accounts Receivable—Kids Online	30	
	Interest Revenue		30
	To record interest on amount due.		

Bell Aliant in our feature story allows a three-day grace period beyond a bill's due date, after which it starts charging for late payments. The amount the company can charge—currently approximately 1% per month—is dictated by the CRTC. As discussed in Chapter 5, interest revenue is included in other revenues in the non-operating section of the income statement.

Nonbank Credit Card Sales

In Chapter 7, we learned that debit and bank credit card sales are cash sales. Sales on credit cards that are not directly associated with a bank are reported as credit sales, not cash sales. Nonbank credit card sales result in an account receivable until the credit card company pays the amount owing to the seller.

To illustrate, assume that Kerr Music accepts a nonbank credit card on October 24 for a $500 bill. The entry for the sale by Kerr Music (assuming a 4% service fee) is:

A	=	L	+	OE
+480				−20
				+500

Cash flows: no effect

Oct. 24	Accounts Receivable—Credit Card Company	480	
	Credit Card Expense ($500 × 4%)	20	
	Sales		500
	To record nonbank credit card sale.		

When Cash is received from the credit card company, Kerr Music will record this entry:

A	=	L	+	OE
+480				
−480				

⬆ Cash flows: +480

Nov. 7	Cash	480	
	Accounts Receivable—Credit Card Company		480
	To record nonbank credit card sale.		

Advances in technology have created a rapidly changing credit card environment. Transactions and payments can be processed much more quickly, and often electronically, which reduces the time to collect cash from the credit card company. As collection time becomes shorter, credit card transactions are becoming more like cash transactions to the business.

How does a business know if it should debit Cash or Accounts Receivable when it processes a credit card transaction? Basically, it should consider how long it takes to collect the cash. If it takes longer than a few days to process the transaction and collect the cash, it should be treated as a credit sale, as shown above.

Companies that issue their own credit cards, such as Canadian Tire, always record sales paid by their cards as credit sales. When the credit card transaction results in an account receivable from the customer—as opposed to from the credit card company, as shown above—the accounting treatment is the same as we have previously seen for accounts receivable.

As discussed in Chapter 7, credit card expenses, along with debit card expenses, are reported as operating expenses in the income statement.

 ## ACCOUNTING IN ACTION: ALL ABOUT YOU INSIGHT

Interest rates on bank credit cards can vary depending on the card's various features, however, the interest rates on regular Canadian bank credit cards range from 18.5% to 19.9%. Nonbank cards can charge significantly higher interest rates, such as retailer HBC's interest rate of 28.8%. At the same time, the Bank of Canada's prime lending interest rate was .25% and most of the Canadian banks' prime lending rate was 2.25%. The prime lending rate changes depending on the supply and demand for money. Credit card interest rates, on the other hand, hardly budge at all. Why are credit card rates so much higher than other interest rates?

The higher rate is due to the risk involved. A bank loan, such as a mortgage, is a secured loan because the loan is backed by a tangible asset: a house. Using a credit card is essentially taking out an unsecured loan because nothing physical is used as security for the lender. In addition, credit cards are much more susceptible to fraud, and thus require a consistently high interest rate.

Should you use credit cards or not?

BEFORE YOU GO ON . . .

→ Review It

1. The stores that form the Forzani Group do not have their own company credit cards. Customers use cash, debit cards, or bank credit cards to pay for merchandise. Why, then, does the company report accounts receivable on its balance sheet? (See Note 2(h) on Revenue Recognition.) The answer to this question is at the end of the chapter.
2. What are the similarities and differences between a general ledger and a subsidiary ledger?
3. How is interest revenue calculated and recorded on late accounts receivable?
4. What are the differences between bank credit cards and nonbank credit cards?

→ Do It

Information for Kinholm Company follows for its first month of operations:

Credit Sales			Cash Collections		
Jan. 5	Sych Co.	$12,000	Jan.16	Sych Co.	$9,000
9	Downey Inc.	5,000	22	Downey Inc.	3,500
13	Pawlak Co.	6,000	28	Pawlak Co.	6,000

Calculate (a) the balances that appear in the accounts receivable subsidiary ledger for each customer, and (b) the accounts receivable balance that appears in the general ledger at the end of January.

Action Plan

- Use T accounts as a simple method of calculating account balances.
- Create separate accounts for each customer and post their transactions to their accounts.
- Create one account for the Accounts Receivable control account.
- Post the total credit sales and the total cash collections to the general ledger.

Solution

ACCOUNTS RECEIVABLE SUBSIDIARY LEDGER

Sych Co.

Jan. 5	12,000	Jan. 16	9,000
Bal.	3,000		

Downey Inc.

Jan. 9	5,000	Jan. 22	3,500
Bal.	1,500		

Pawlak Co.

Jan. 13	6,000	Jan. 28	6,000
Bal.	0		

GENERAL LEDGER

Accounts Receivable

Jan. 31	23,000[a]	Jan. 31	18,500[b]
Bal.	4,500		

[a] $12,000 + $5,000 + $6,000 = $23,000

[b] $9,000 + $3,500 + $6,000 = $18,500

The Navigator

Related exercise material: BE8–1, BE8–2, BE8–3, BE8–4, E8–1, and E8–2.

Valuing Accounts Receivable

After receivables are recorded in the accounts, the next question is how these receivables should be reported on the balance sheet. Receivables are assets, but determining the amount to report as an asset is sometimes difficult because some receivables will become uncollectible. A receivable can only be reported as an asset if it will give a future benefit. This means that only collectible receivables can be reported as assets in the financial statements. This collectible amount is called the receivables' **net realizable value.**

In order to minimize the risk of uncollectible accounts, companies assess the credit worthiness of potential credit customers. But even if a customer satisfies the company's credit requirements before the credit sale was approved, inevitably, some accounts receivable still become uncollectible. For example, a usually reliable customer may suddenly not be able to pay because of an unexpected decrease in its revenues or because it is faced with unexpected bills.

Why do companies still decide to sell goods or services on credit if there is always a risk of not collecting the receivable? Because they are expecting that the increase in revenues and profit from selling on credit will be greater than any uncollectible accounts or credit losses. Such losses are considered a normal and necessary risk of doing business on a credit basis.

Alternative terminology
Bad debts expense is also sometimes called *uncollectible account expense.*

When receivables are written down to their net realizable value because of expected credit losses, owner's equity must also be reduced. This is done by recording an expense, known as **bad debts expense,** for the credit losses. The key issue in valuing accounts receivable is when to record these credit losses. If the company waits until it knows for sure that the specific account will not be collected, it could end up recording the bad debts expense in a different period than when the revenue is recorded.

Consider the following example. Assume that in 2010, Quick Buck Computer Company decides it could increase its revenues by offering computers to students without requiring any money down and with no credit approval process. On campuses across the country, it sells 100,000 computers with a selling price of $700 each. This increases Quick Buck's receivables and revenues by $70 million. The promotion is a huge success! The 2010 balance sheet and income statement look great. Unfortunately, in 2011, nearly 40% of the student customers default on their accounts. This makes the 2011 balance sheet and income statement look terrible. Illustration 8-2 shows that the promotion in 2010 was not such a great success after all.

Year 2010

AR and Profit

Huge sales promotion. Accounts receivable increase dramatically. Profit increases dramatically.

Year 2011

AR and Profit

Customers default on amounts owed. Accounts receivable drop dramatically. Bad debts expense increases and profit decreases dramatically.

← **Illustration 8-2**

Effects of mismatching bad debts

If credit losses are not recorded until they occur, the accounts receivable in the balance sheet are not reported at the amount that is actually expected to be received. Quick Buck Computer's receivables were overstated at the end of 2010, which misrepresented the amount that should have been reported as an asset.

In addition, bad debts expense will not be matched to sales revenues in the income statement. Recall from Chapter 3 that expenses that are directly related to revenue must be recorded in the same period as the sales they helped generate. Consequently, Quick Buck Computer Company's profit was overstated in 2010 and understated in 2011 because it did not match the bad debts expense with sales revenue.

To avoid overstating assets and profit, we cannot wait until we know exactly which receivables are uncollectible. Instead, in the accounting period where the sales occur, we must estimate the uncollectible accounts receivable. Because we do not know which specific accounts receivable will need to be written off, we use what is known as the allowance method.

The **allowance method** of accounting for bad debts estimates uncollectible accounts at the end of each accounting period. This ensures that receivables are reduced to their net realizable value on the balance sheet. It also gives better matching of expenses with revenues on the income statement because credit losses that are expected to happen from sales or service revenue in that accounting period are recorded in the same accounting period as when the revenue was earned.

The allowance method is required for financial reporting purposes when uncollectible accounts are material (significant) in amount. The allowance method has three essential features:

1. Recording estimated uncollectibles: The amount of uncollectible accounts receivable is estimated at the end of the accounting period. This estimate is treated as bad debts expense and is matched against revenues in the accounting period where the revenues are recorded.
2. Writing off uncollectible accounts: Actual uncollectibles are written off when the specific account is determined to be uncollectible.
3. Recovery of an uncollectible account: If an account that was previously written off is later collected, the original write off is reversed and the collection is recorded.

We will see that neither the write off nor the later recovery affect the income statement.

1. Recording Estimated Uncollectibles

To illustrate the allowance method, assume that Adorable Junior Garment has net credit sales of $1.2 million in 2010. Of this amount, $200,000 remains uncollected at December 31. The credit manager estimates (using techniques we will discuss in the next section) that $24,000 of these receivables will be uncollectible. The adjusting entry to record the estimated uncollectible accounts is:

A	=	L	+	OE
−24,000				−24,000

Cash flows: no effect

Dec. 31	Bad Debts Expense	24,000	
	Allowance for Doubtful Accounts		24,000
	To record estimate of uncollectible accounts.		

Note that Allowance for Doubtful Accounts—a contra asset account—is used instead of a direct credit to Accounts Receivable. Because we do not know which individual customers will not pay, we do not know which specific accounts to credit in the subsidiary ledger. Recall that subsidiary ledger accounts must balance with Accounts Receivable, the control account. This would not happen if the control account was credited and the subsidiary ledger accounts were not.

Assume that Adorable Junior Garment has an unadjusted balance of $1,000 in Allowance for Doubtful Accounts. After recording the estimate of its uncollectibles, the ending balance in the Allowance for Doubtful Accounts is $25,000 ($1,000 + $24,000). This is the amount of receivables that is expected to become uncollectible in the future.

The Allowance for Doubtful Accounts is deducted from Accounts Receivable to calculate the net realizable value of the accounts receivable, as presented by the formula shown in Illustration 8-3.

Illustration 8-3 ➡

Formula for calculating net realizable value

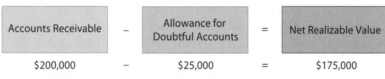

Accounts Receivable	−	Allowance for Doubtful Accounts	=	Net Realizable Value
$200,000	−	$25,000	=	$175,000

In the current assets section of the balance sheet, Accounts Receivable, the Allowance for Doubtful Accounts, and the net realizable value are reported as follows (using assumed data for the other current asset accounts):

ADORABLE JUNIOR GARMENT		
Balance Sheet (partial)		
December 31, 2010		
Current assets		
Cash		$ 14,800
Accounts receivable	$200,000	
Less: Allowance for doubtful accounts	25,000	175,000
Merchandise inventory		310,000
Prepaid expenses		25,000
Total current assets		$524,800

Notice that the net realizable value of the accounts receivable—$175,000—is the amount added to cash, merchandise inventory, and prepaid expenses to calculate total current assets, not the total accounts receivable.

Approaches Used in Estimating the Allowance. To simplify the Adorable Junior Garment example, the amount of the expected bad debts expense in the journal entry above ($24,000) was given. But how was this estimate calculated? There are two approaches that most companies use to determine this amount: (1) percentage of receivables, and (2) percentage of sales.

Percentage of Receivables Approach. Under the **percentage of receivables approach**, management uses experience to estimate the percentage of receivables that will become uncollectible accounts. The easiest way to do this is to multiply the total amount of accounts receivable by a percentage based on an overall estimate of the total uncollectible accounts. However, the more common practice is to estimate uncollectible accounts using different percentages depending on how long the accounts receivable have been outstanding. This is more sensitive to the actual status of the accounts receivable. The longer a receivable is past due or outstanding, the less likely it is to be collected. Bell Aliant in our feature story uses this approach.

A schedule must be prepared, called an **aging schedule**, that shows the age of each account receivable. After the age of each account receivable is determined, the loss from uncollectible accounts is estimated. This is done by applying percentages, based on experience, to the totals in each category. The estimated percentage of uncollectible accounts increases as the number of days outstanding increases. Bell Aliant, in our feature story, follows this process. An aging schedule for Adorable Junior Garment is shown in Illustration 8-4.

Customer	Total	Number of Days Outstanding				
		0–30	31–60	61–90	91–120	Over 120
Bansal Garments	$ 6,000		$ 3,000	$ 3,000		
Bortz Clothing	3,000	$ 3,000				
Kids Online	4,500				$ 2,000	$ 2,500
Snazzy Kids Co.	17,000	2,000	5,000	5,000	5,000	
Tykes n' Tots	26,500	10,000	10,000	6,000	500	
Zellers	42,000	32,000	10,000			
Walmart	61,000	48,000	12,000	1,000		
Others	40,000	5,000	10,000	10,000	5,000	10,000
	$200,000	$100,000	$50,000	$25,000	$12,500	$12,500
Estimated percentage uncollectible		5%	10%	20%	30%	50%
Estimated uncollectible accounts	$ 25,000	$ 5,000	$ 5,000	$ 5,000	$ 3,750	$ 6,250

◀ **Illustration 8-4**

Aging schedule

The $25,000 total for estimated uncollectible accounts is the amount of existing receivables that are expected to become uncollectible in the future. This amount represents the required balance in Allowance for Doubtful Accounts at the balance sheet date. The amount of the bad debts expense adjusting entry is the difference between the required balance and the existing balance in the allowance account.

Recall that we assumed the trial balance shows a credit balance of $1,000 in the Allowance for Doubtful Accounts. Therefore, an adjusting entry for $24,000 ($25,000 − $1,000) is necessary, as follows:

Helpful hint Because the balance sheet is emphasized in the percentage of receivables approach, the existing balance in the allowance account must be considered when calculating the bad debts expenses in the adjusting entry.

Dec. 31	Bad Debts Expense	24,000	
	Allowance for Doubtful Accounts		24,000
	To record estimate of uncollectible accounts.		

A	=	L	+	OE
−24,000				−24,000

Cash flows: no effect

After the adjusting entry is posted, the balance in the Allowance for Doubtful Accounts should be equal to the estimated uncollectible accounts calculated in Illustration 8-4. This is shown in Adorable Junior Garment's accounts:

Bad Debts Expense	Allowance for Doubtful Accounts
Dec. 31 Adj. 24,000	Dec. 31 Bal. 1,000
	31 Adj. 24,000
	Dec. 31 Bal. 25,000

Occasionally, the allowance account will have a debit balance before recording the adjusting entry. This happens when write offs in the year are higher than the previous estimates for bad debts (we will discuss write offs in the next section). If there is a debit balance, prior to recording the adjusting entry, the debit balance is added to the required balance when the adjusting entry is made. For example, if there had been a $500 debit balance in the Adorable Junior Garment allowance account before adjustment, the adjusting entry would have been for $25,500 ($25,000 + $500) to arrive at a credit balance in the allowance account of $25,000.

Because a balance sheet account (Accounts Receivable) is used to calculate the required balance in another balance sheet account (Allowance for Doubtful Accounts), the percentage of receivables approach is also often called the **balance sheet approach**. The percentage of receivables approach is an excellent method of estimating the net realizable value of the accounts receivable.

Percentage of Sales Approach The **percentage of sales approach** calculates bad debts expense as a percentage of net credit sales. Management determines the percentage based on experience and the company's credit policy.

To illustrate, assume that Adorable Junior Garment concludes that 2% of net credit sales will become uncollectible. Recall that net credit sales for the calendar year 2010 are $1.2 million. The estimated bad debts expense is $24,000 (2% × $1,200,000). The adjusting entry is:

A	=	L	+	OE
−24,000				−24,000

Cash flows: no effect

Dec. 31	Bad Debts Expense	24,000	
	Allowance for Doubtful Accounts		24,000
	To record estimate of bad debts expense.		

Recall that Allowance for Doubtful Accounts had a credit balance of $1,000 before the adjustment. After the adjusting entry is posted, the accounts will show the following:

Bad Debts Expense		Allowance for Doubtful Accounts	
Dec. 31 Adj. 24,000			Dec. 31 Bal. 1,000
			31 Adj. 24,000
			Dec. 31 Bal. 25,000

Helpful hint Because the income statement is emphasized in the percentage of sales approach, the balance in the allowance account is not involved in calculating the bad debts expense in the adjusting entry.

When calculating the amount in the adjusting entry ($24,000), the existing balance in Allowance for Doubtful Accounts is ignored. This approach to estimating uncollectibles results in an excellent matching of expenses with revenues because the bad debts expense is related to the sales recorded in the same period. Because an income statement account (Sales) is used to calculate another income statement account (Bad Debts Expense), and because any balance in the balance sheet account (Allowance for Doubtful Accounts) is ignored, this approach is often called the **income statement approach**. Illustration 8-5 compares the balance sheet approach with the income statement approach.

Illustration 8-5 ➡

Comparison of approaches for estimating uncollectibles

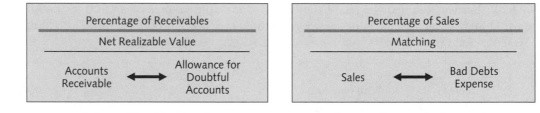

| Balance Sheet Approach | Income Statement Approach |

Both the percentage of receivables and the percentage of sales approaches are generally accepted. The choice is a management decision. The percentage of sales approach is quick and easy to use and it is aimed at achieving the most accurate matching of expenses to revenues. On the other hand, the percentage of receivables approach is focused on presenting the correct net realizable value of accounts receivable in the balance sheet. As accounting standards increasingly emphasize the balance sheet, it has been argued that the percentage of receivables approach is the most appropriate method to use. While most companies prefer using the percentage of receivables approach, the percentage of sales method is still allowed.

Under both approaches, it is necessary to review the company's experience with credit losses. You should also note that, unlike in our example with Adorable Junior Garment, the two approaches normally result in different amounts in the adjusting entry.

2. Writing Off Uncollectible Accounts

Companies use various methods for collecting past-due accounts, including letters, calls, and legal actions. Bell Aliant, in our feature story, classifies customers by risk levels, which it uses to determine how large and how far in arrears it will allow the bill to get before taking action. Bell Aliant follows up on late accounts with letters and calls, and will cut back or suspend service if the customer does not negotiate new payment terms. If there is still no payment from the customer, service is permanently cut off. The final step involves sending the account to a collection agency.

When all the ways of collecting a past-due account have been tried and collection appears impossible, the account should be written off. To prevent premature write offs, each write off should be approved in writing by management. To keep good internal control, the authorization to write off accounts should not be given to someone who also has responsibilities related to cash or receivables.

To illustrate a receivables write off, assume that the vice-president of finance of Adorable Junior Garment authorizes the write off of a $4,500 balance owed by a delinquent customer, Kids Online, on March 1, 2011. The entry to record the write off is as follows:

Mar. 1	Allowance for Doubtful Accounts	4,500	
	Accounts Receivable—Kids Online		4,500
	Write off of uncollectible account.		

A = L + OE
+4,500
−4,500
Cash flows: no effect

Bad Debts Expense is not increased (debited) when the write off occurs. Under the allowance method, every account write off is debited to the allowance account rather than to Bad Debts Expense. A debit to Bad Debts Expense would be incorrect because the expense was already recognized when the adjusting entry was made for estimated bad debts last year.

Instead, the entry to record the write off of an uncollectible account reduces both Accounts Receivable and Allowance for Doubtful Accounts. After posting, using an assumed balance of $230,000 in Accounts Receivable on February 28, 2011, the general ledger accounts will appear as follows:

Accounts Receivable				Allowance for Doubtful Accounts			
Feb. 28 Bal. 230,000	Mar. 1	4,500		Mar. 1	4,500	Jan. 1	Bal. 25,000
Mar. 1 Bal. 225,500						Mar. 1	Bal. 20,500

A write off affects only balance sheet accounts. The write off of the account reduces both Accounts Receivable and Allowance for Doubtful Accounts. Net realizable value in the balance sheet remains the same, as shown below:

	Before Write Off	After Write Off
Accounts receivable	$230,000	$225,500
Less: Allowance for doubtful accounts	25,000	20,500
Net realizable value	$205,000	$205,000

As mentioned earlier, the allowance account can sometimes end up in a debit balance position after the write off of an uncollectible account. This can happen if the write offs in the period are more than the opening balance. It means the actual credit losses were greater than the estimated credit losses. The balance in Allowance for Doubtful Accounts will be corrected when the adjusting entry for estimated uncollectible accounts is made at the end of the period.

3. Recovery of an Uncollectible Account

Occasionally, a company collects cash from a customer after its account has been written off. Two entries are required to record the recovery of a bad debt: (1) the entry previously made when the account was written off is reversed to restore the customer's account; and (2) the collection is recorded in the usual way.

To illustrate, assume that on July 1, 2011, Kids Online pays the $4,500 amount that had been written off on March 1. The entries are as follows:

		(1)		
July 1	Accounts Receivable—Kids Online		4,500	
	Allowance for Doubtful Accounts			4,500
	To reverse write off of Kids Online account.			

A = L + OE
+4,500
−4,500
Cash flows: no effect

		(2)		
July 1	Cash		4,500	
	Accounts Receivable—Kids Online			4,500
	To record collection from Kids Online.			

A = L + OE
+4,500
−4,500
⬆ Cash flows: +4,500

Note that the recovery of a bad debt, like the write off of a bad debt, affects only balance sheet accounts. The net effect of the two entries is a debit to Cash and a credit to Allowance for Doubtful Accounts for $4,500. Accounts Receivable is debited and later credited for two reasons. First, the company must reverse the write off. Second, Kids Online did pay, so the accounts receivable account in the general ledger and Kids Online's account in the subsidiary ledger, if a subsidiary ledger is used, should show this payment as it will need to be considered in deciding what credit to give to Kids Online in the future.

Summary of Allowance Method

In summary, there are three types of transactions that you may need to record when valuing accounts receivable using the allowance method:

1. Estimates of uncollectible accounts receivable are recorded as adjusting entries at the end of the period by debiting Bad Debts Expense and crediting Allowance for Doubtful Accounts. The amount to record can be calculated using either the percentage of sales approach or the percentage of receivables approach.
2. Write offs of actual uncollectible accounts are recorded in the next accounting period by debiting Allowance for Doubtful Accounts and crediting Accounts Receivable.
3. Later recoveries, if any, are recorded in two separate entries. The first reverses the write off by debiting Accounts Receivable and crediting Allowance for Doubtful Accounts. The second records the normal collection of the account by debiting Cash and crediting Accounts Receivable.

These entries are summarized in the following T accounts:

Accounts Receivable		Allowance for Doubtful Accounts	
Beginning balance	Cash collections	Write offs	Beginning balance
Credit sales	Write offs		Later recoveries
Later recoveries			Bad debt adjusting entry
Ending balance			Ending balance

ACCOUNTING IN ACTION: ACROSS THE ORGANIZATION INSIGHT

More and more businesses are turning to collection agencies to pursue their bad debts. And these agencies are using tougher and more creative tactics to extract payment. They scour websites like Facebook and Craigslist to track down people who haven't paid their bills. Collection agencies are generally not allowed to make threats, call clients repeatedly, or be overly aggressive. If people have no means to pay and can't negotiate with the collection agency, the biggest problem they will likely face is damage to their credit report. Still, unless consumers pay their debts, the calls from collection agents are unlikely to stop. Agencies are becoming more effective, with the development of statistical models that use historical information from debt collection records, combined with socioeconomic and other demographic information, to predict which indebted consumers are more likely to pay and thus focus their efforts on these people.

Source: Carly Weeks, "Collection Agencies: The New Big Brother?" *The Globe and Mail*, May 11, 2009.

Why would a business choose to use a collection agency to follow up on late accounts instead of pursuing them internally?

BEFORE YOU GO ON . . .

→ Review It

1. How does the allowance method ensure that expenses are properly matched with revenues?
2. Explain the differences between the percentage of receivables and percentage of sales approaches.
3. How do write offs and subsequent recoveries affect profit and the net realizable value of the accounts receivable when they are recorded?

→ Do It

The unadjusted trial balance at December 31 for Woo Wholesalers Co. shows the following selected information:

	Debit	Credit
Accounts receivable	$120,000	
Allowance for doubtful accounts		$ 2,000
Net credit sales		820,000

(a) Prepare the adjusting journal entry to record bad debts expense for each of the following *independent* situations:

1. Using the percentage of receivables approach, Woo estimates uncollectible accounts to be as follows: 0–30 days, $85,000, 5% uncollectible; 31–60 days, $25,000, 15% uncollectible; and over 60 days, $10,000, 25% uncollectible.
2. Using the percentage of sales approach, Woo estimates uncollectible accounts to be 1% of net credit sales.

(b) Calculate the net realizable value of Woo's accounts receivable for each of the above situations.

Action Plan

- Percentage of receivables: Apply percentages to the receivables in each age category to determine total estimated uncollectible accounts. The total amount determined in the aging schedule is the ending balance required in the allowance account, not the amount of the adjustment. Use the existing balance in the allowance account to determine the required adjusting entry.
- Percentage of sales: Apply the percentage to net credit sales to determine estimated bad debts expense—the adjusting entry amount. Ignore the balance in the allowance for doubtful accounts.
- Net realizable value is equal to the balance in Accounts Receivable minus the balance in Allowance for Doubtful Accounts after the journal entry to record bad debts expense has been recorded.

Solution

(a) 1. Bad Debts Expense ($10,500[1] – $2,000) | 8,500 |
      Allowance for Doubtful Accounts | | 8,500
        To record estimate of uncollectible accounts.
        [1]($85,000 × 5%) + ($25,000 × 15%) + ($10,000 × 25%) = $10,500

  2. Bad Debts Expense ($820,000 × 1%) | 8,200 |
      Allowance for Doubtful Accounts | | 8,200
        To record estimate of uncollectible accounts.

(b) 1. Net Realizable Value = Accounts Receivable – Allowance for Doubtful Accounts
                      = [$120,000 – ($2,000 + $8,500)]
                      = $109,500

  2. Net Realizable Value = Accounts Receivable – Allowance for Doubtful Accounts
                      = [$120,000 – ($2,000 + $8,200)]
                      = $109,800

Related exercise material: BE8–5, BE8–6, BE8–7, BE8–8, BE8–9, E8–4, E8–5, E8–6, and E8–7.

The Navigator

Notes Receivable

Credit may also be granted in exchange for a formal credit instrument known as a promissory note. A **promissory note** is a written promise to pay a specified amount of money on demand or at a definite time. Promissory notes may be used (1) when individuals and companies lend or borrow money, (2) when the amount of the transaction and the credit period are longer than normal limits, or (3) in the settlement of accounts receivable.

In a promissory note, the party making the promise to pay is called the maker. The party to whom payment is to be made is called the payee. In the note shown in Illustration 8-6, Higly Inc. is the maker and Wolder Company is the payee. To Wolder Company, the promissory note is a note receivable. To Higly Inc. it is a note payable.

Illustration 8-6 ➤

Promissory note

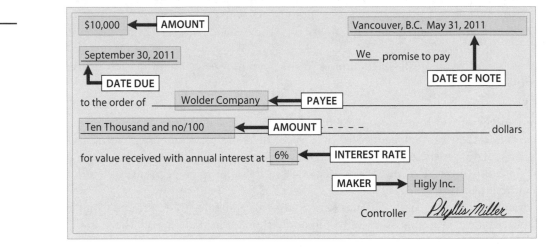

A promissory note might also contain other details such as whether any security is pledged as collateral for the loan and what happens if the maker defaults (does not pay).

A note receivable is a formal promise to pay an amount that bears interest from the time it is issued until it is due. An account receivable is an informal promise to pay that bears interest only after its due date. Because it is less formal, it does not have as strong a legal claim as a note receivable. Most accounts receivable are due within a short period of time, usually 30 days, while a note can extend over longer periods of time.

There are also similarities between notes and accounts receivable. Both are credit instruments. Both can be sold to another party. Both are valued at their net realizable values. The basic issues in accounting for notes receivable are the same as those for accounts receivable, as follows:

1. Recognizing notes receivable
2. Disposing of notes receivable

Recognizing Notes Receivable

To illustrate the basic entries for notes receivable, we will use the $10,000, four-month, 6% promissory note shown in Illustration 8-6. Assuming that Higly Inc. wrote the note in settlement of an account receivable, Wolder Company makes the following entry for the receipt of the note:

A	=	L	+	OE
+10,000				
−10,000				

Cash flows: no effect

May 31	Notes Receivable—Higly	10,000	
	Accounts Receivable—Higly		10,000
	To record acceptance of Higly note.		

If a note is exchanged for cash instead of an account receivable, the entry is a debit to Notes Receivable and a credit to Cash for the amount of the loan.

The note receivable is recorded at its principal value (the value shown on the face of the note). No interest revenue is reported when the note is accepted because, according to the revenue recognition principle, revenue is not recognized until it is earned. Interest is earned (accrued) as time passes.

Recording Interest

As we learned in Chapter 3, the basic formula for calculating interest on an interest-bearing note is the following:

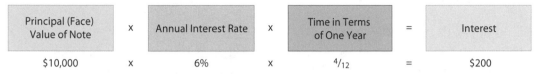

Principal (Face) Value of Note	x	Annual Interest Rate	x	Time in Terms of One Year	=	Interest
$10,000	x	6%	x	$^{4}/_{12}$	=	$200

◄ Illustration 8-7
Formula for calculating interest

The interest rate specified in a note is an annual rate of interest. There are many factors that affect the interest rate. You will learn more about that in a finance course. Interest rates may also be fixed for the term of the note or may change over the term. In this textbook, we will always assume that the rate remains fixed for the term.

The time factor in the above formula gives the fraction of the year that the note has been outstanding. As we did in past chapters, to keep it simple we will assume that interest is calculated in months rather than days. Illustration 8-7 shows the calculation of interest revenue for Wolder Company and interest expense for Higly Inc. for the term of the note.

If Wolder Company's year end was June 30, the following adjusting journal entry would be required to accrue interest for the month of June:

June 30	Interest Receivable	50	
	Interest Revenue ($10,000 × 6% × $^{1}/_{12}$)		50
	To accrue interest on Higly note receivable.		

A	=	L	+	OE
+50				+50

Cash flows: no effect

Notice that interest on a note receivable is not debited to the Notes Receivable account. Instead, a separate account for the interest receivable is used. Since the note is a formal credit instrument, its recorded value stays the same as its face value.

Valuing Notes Receivable

Like accounts receivable, notes receivable are reported at their net realizable value. Each note must be analyzed to determine how likely it is to be collected. If eventual collection is doubtful, bad debts expense and an allowance for doubtful notes must be recorded in the same way as for accounts receivable. Some companies use only one allowance account for both accounts and notes, and call it Allowance for Doubtful Accounts.

Disposing of Notes Receivable

Notes are normally held to their maturity date, at which time the principal plus any unpaid interest is collected. This is known as honouring (paying) the note. Sometimes, the maker of the note defaults and an adjustment to the accounts must be made. This is known as dishonouring (not paying) the note.

Honouring of Notes Receivable

A note is honoured when it is paid in full at its maturity date. The amount due at maturity is the principal of the note plus interest for the length of time the note is outstanding (assuming interest is due at maturity rather than monthly). If Higly Inc. honours the note when it is due on September 30—the maturity date—the entry by Wolder Company to record the collection is:

A	=	L	+	OE
+10,200				+150
−10,000				
−50				

↑ Cash flows: +10,200

Sep. 30	Cash	10,200	
	Notes Receivable—Higly		10,000
	Interest Revenue		150
	Interest Receivable		50
	To record collection of Higly note.		

Recall that one month of interest revenue, $50 ($10,000 × 6% × $1/_{12}$), was accrued on June 30, Wolder's year end. Consequently, only three months of interest revenue, $150 ($10,000 × 6% × $3/_{12}$), is recorded in this period.

Dishonouring of Notes Receivable

A **dishonoured note** is a note that is not paid in full at maturity. Since a dishonoured note receivable is no longer negotiable, the Notes Receivable account must be reduced by the principal of the note. The payee still has a claim against the maker of the note for both the principal and any unpaid interest and will transfer the amount owing to an Accounts Receivable account if there is hope that the amount will eventually be collected.

To illustrate, assume that on September 30 Higly Inc. says that it cannot pay at the present time but Wolder Company expects eventual collection. Wolder would make the following entry at the time the note is dishonoured:

A	=	L	+	OE
+10,200				+150
−10,000				
−50				

Cash flows: no effect

Sep. 30	Accounts Receivable—Higly	10,200	
	Notes Receivable—Higly		10,000
	Interest Revenue		150
	Interest Receivable		50
	To record dishonouring of Higly note where collection is expected.		

Wolder will continue to follow up with Higly. If the amount owing is eventually collected, Wolder will simply debit Cash and credit Accounts Receivable. If Wolder decides at a later date that it will never collect this amount from Higly, Wolder will write off the account receivable in the same way we learned earlier in the chapter—debit Allowance for Doubtful Accounts, and credit Accounts Receivable.

On the other hand, Wolder could directly write the note off on September 30 if it decided there was no hope of collection. Assuming Wolder uses one allowance account for both accounts and notes, it would record the following:

A	=	L	+	OE
+10,050				
−10,000				
−50				

Cash flows: no effect

Sep. 30	Allowance for Doubtful Accounts	10,050	
	Notes Receivable—Higly		10,000
	Interest Receivable		50
	To record dishonouring of Higly note where collection is not expected.		

No interest revenue is recorded, because collection will not occur. The interest receivable that previously had been accrued is also written off.

BEFORE YOU GO ON . . .

➡ Review It

1. Explain the differences between an account receivable and a note receivable.
2. How is interest calculated for a note receivable?
3. At what value are notes receivable reported on the balance sheet?
4. Explain the difference between honouring and dishonouring a note receivable.

→ Do It

On May 1, Gambit Stores accepts from J. Nyznyk a $3,400, three-month, 5% note in settlement of Nyznyk's overdue account. Interest is due at maturity. Gambit has a June 30 year end. (a) What are the entries made by Gambit on May 1, June 30, and on the maturity date of August 1, assuming Nyznyk pays the note at that time? (b) What is the entry on August 1 if Nyznyk does not pay the note and collection is not expected in the future?

Action Plan

- Calculate the accrued interest. The formula is: Principal (face) value × annual interest rate × time in terms of one year.
- Record the interest accrued on June 30 to follow revenue recognition criteria. Use Interest Receivable, not Notes Receivable, for accrued interest.
- If the note is honoured, calculate the interest accrued after June 30 and the total interest on the note. Record the interest accrued and the collection of the note and the total interest.
- If the note is dishonoured, record the transfer of the note and any interest earned to an accounts receivable account if eventual collection is expected or to an allowance account if collection is not expected.

Solution

(a) May 1	Notes Receivable—J. Nyznyk	3,400	
	Accounts Receivable—J. Nyznyk		3,400
	To replace account receivable with 5% note receivable, due August 1.		
Jun. 30	Interest Receivable	28	
	Interest Revenue ($3,400 × 5% × $^2/_{12}$)		28
	To record interest earned to June 30.		
Aug. 1	Cash	3,442	
	Interest Receivable		28
	Notes Receivable—J. Nyznyk		3,400
	Interest Revenue ($3,400 × 5% × $^2/_{12}$)		14
	To record collection of Nyznyk note plus interest.		
(b) Aug. 1	Allowance for Doubtful Accounts	3,428	
	Interest Receivable		28
	Notes Receivable—J. Nyznyk		3,400
	To record dishonouring of Nyznyk note as collection is not expected.		

Related exercise material: BE8–10, BE8–11, BE8–12, E8–8, and E8–9.

The Navigator

Statement Presentation and Management of Receivables

The way receivables are presented in the financial statements is important because receivables are directly affected by how a company recognizes its revenue and bad debts expense. In addition, these reported numbers are critical for analyzing a company's liquidity and how well it manages its receivables. In the next sections, we will discuss the presentation, analysis, and management of receivables.

STUDY OBJECTIVE 4

Demonstrate the presentation, analysis, and management of receivables.

Presentation

Each of the major types of receivables should be identified in the balance sheet or in the notes to the financial statements. Other receivables include interest receivable, loans or advances to employees, and recoverable sales and income taxes. These receivables are generally classified and reported as separate items in the current or noncurrent sections of the balance sheet, according to their due dates. Notes receivable may also be either current assets or long-term assets, depending on their due dates.

If the balance sheet is presented in order of decreasing liquidity, current receivables are reported following cash and short-term investments, as shown in Research In Motion's balance sheet. Research In Motion (RIM) uses the term "trade receivables." Recall from the beginning of the chapter that trade receivables includes both accounts and notes receivable resulting from sales transactions. If current notes receivable are shown separately, they are often listed before accounts receivable because notes are more easily converted to cash.

The presentation of receivables in current assets for Research In Motion Limited is shown below:

RESEARCH IN MOTION LIMITED Balance Sheet (partial) February 28, 2009 (in U.S. thousands)	
Current assets	
Cash and cash equivalents	$ 835,546
Short-term investments	682,666
Trade receivables	2,112,117
Other receivables	157,728
Inventory	682,400
Other current assets	187,257
Deferred income tax asset	183,872
	$4,841,586

In Note 1 to its financial statements, RIM states that its trade receivables include invoiced and accrued revenue and are presented net of an allowance for doubtful accounts of $2,100 thousand. The company also tells us that the allowance for doubtful accounts reflects estimates of probable losses in trade receivables. RIM explains that when it becomes aware of a specific customer's inability to meet its financial obligations, it records a specific bad debt provision to reduce the customer's related trade receivable to its estimated net realizable value. If the circumstances of specific customers change, RIM could then adjust its estimates of the recoverability of its trade receivables balances.

Traditionally, only the net amount of receivables had to be disclosed. It was not required to report both the gross amount of receivables and the allowance for doubtful accounts, either in the statement or in the notes to the financial statements. But if a company had a significant risk of uncollectible accounts or other problems with receivables, it was required to disclose this possibility in the notes to the financial statements. RIM discloses that for the majority of its products, its sales depend on several significant customers and on large, complex contracts. With the introduction of International Financial Reporting Standards, additional disclosures will be required. Companies will have to disclose a reconciliation of changes to the allowance account during the period, which will include items such as the beginning and ending balances of the allowance as well as the amount of write offs and recoveries.

In the income statement, bad debts expense is reported in the operating expenses section. RIM reports that in fiscal 2009, bad debt expense was $24,000 thousand. In fiscal 2008, it had a bad debt recovery (the opposite of an expense) of $26,000 thousand. A recovery of bad debt expenses in 2008 would mean that RIM overestimated its bad debts expense in fiscal 2007 and thus it reversed the expense in fiscal 2008. This shows just how difficult it can be to accurately estimate uncollectible accounts.

Analysis

Managers need to carefully watch the relationships between sales, accounts receivable, and cash collections. If sales increase, then accounts receivable are also expected to increase. But an unusually high increase in accounts receivable might signal trouble. Perhaps the company increased its sales by loosening its credit policy, and these receivables may be difficult or impossible to collect. The company could also end up with higher costs because of the increase in sales since it may need more cash to pay for inventory and salaries.

Recall that the ability to pay obligations as they come due is measured by a company's liquidity. How can we tell if a company's management of its receivables is helping or hurting the company's liquidity? One way of doing this is to calculate a ratio called the **receivables turnover ratio**. This ratio measures the number of times, on average, that receivables are collected during the period. It is calculated by dividing net credit sales by average gross receivables during the year.

Unfortunately, companies rarely report the amount of net sales made on credit in their financial statements. As a result, net sales (including both cash and credit sales) is used as a substitute. In addition, because some companies do not publicly report their gross accounts receivable, net accounts receivable must be used. As long as the components that are used to calculate a ratio are the same for all companies being compared, however, the comparison is fair.

In Illustration 8-8, the substitute figures of total revenue and net accounts receivable were used to calculate the 2009 receivables turnover for Forzani (dollars in thousands). We have calculated this ratio using Forzani's net accounts receivable, even though Forzani reported its gross receivables in note 16(h), because information on 2008 gross accounts receivable was not available.

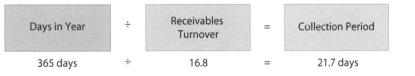

Illustration 8-8

Receivables turnover

The result indicates an accounts receivable turnover ratio of 16.8 times per year for Forzani. The higher the turnover ratio, the more liquid the company's receivables are.

A popular variation of the receivables turnover ratio is to convert it into the number of days it takes the company to collect its receivables. This ratio, called the **collection period**, is calculated by dividing 365 days by the receivables turnover, as shown for Forzani in Illustration 8-9.

Illustration 8-9

Collection period

This means that in fiscal 2009, Forzani collected its receivables, on average, in approximately 21.7 days. Bell Aliant, in our feature story, states that the vast majority of its consumer customers pay on or before the due date but that it takes about 50 to 60 days to collect from businesses. The result is an overall average of between 43 and 45 days.

The collection period is often used to judge how effective a company's credit and collection policies are. The general rule is that the collection period should not be much longer than the credit term period (i.e., the time allowed for payment). Accounts receivable are basically an interest-free loan to the customer, so the faster they are collected, the better.

Both the receivables turnover and the collection period are useful for judging how efficiently a company converts its credit sales to cash. Remember that these measures should also be compared with industry averages, and with previous years.

In addition, these measures should also be analyzed along with other information about a company's liquidity, including the current ratio and inventory turnover. For example, low receivables may result in a low current ratio, which might make the company look like it has poor liquidity. But the receivables may be low because they are turning over quickly. In general, the faster the turnover, the more reliable the current ratio is for assessing liquidity.

The collection period can also be used to assess the length of a company's operating cycle. Recall from Chapter 4 that the operating cycle is the time it takes to go from cash to cash in producing revenues. In a merchandising company the operating cycle may be measured by determining the average time that it takes to purchase inventory, sell it on account, and then collect cash from customers. In Chapter 6, we learned how to calculate days sales in inventory, which is the average age of the inventory on hand. The combination of the collection period and days sales in inventory is a useful way to measure the length of a company's operating cycle. Using the number of days sales in inventory calculated in Chapter 6, this calculation is shown in Illustration 8-10 for Forzani.

Illustration 8-10 ➜

Operating cycle

Days Sales in Inventory	+	Collection Period	=	Operating Cycle in Days
130 days	+	21.7 days	=	151.7 days

This means that in fiscal 2009 it took 151.7 days on average from the time Forzani purchased its inventory until it collected cash.

Accelerating Cash Receipts from Receivables

If a company sells on credit, it has to wait until the customer pays the receivable before it has cash available to pay for such items as inventory and operating expenses. As credit sales and receivables increase in size and significance, waiting for receivables to be collected increases costs because the company cannot use the revenue from the sale until cash is collected. If a company can collect cash more quickly from its receivables, it can shorten the cash-to-cash operating cycle discussed in the previous section.

There are two typical ways to collect cash more quickly from receivables: using the receivables to secure a loan and selling the receivables.

Loans Secured by Receivables

One of the most common ways to speed up cash flow from accounts receivable is to go to a bank and borrow money using accounts receivable as collateral. While this does have a cost (interest has to be paid to the bank on the loan), the cash is available for the company to use earlier. The loan can then be repaid as the receivables are collected. Generally, banks are willing to give financing of up to 75% of receivables that are less than 90 days old. Quite often, these arrangements occur through an operating line of credit, which is discussed in Chapter 10.

Sale of Receivables

Companies also frequently sell their receivables to another company for cash. There are three reasons for the sale of receivables. The first is their size. To be competitive, sellers often give financing to purchasers of their goods to encourage the sale of the product. But the companies may not want to hold large amounts of receivables. As a result, many major companies in the automobile, truck, equipment, computer, and appliance industries have created wholly owned captive finance companies that accept responsibility for accounts receivable financing. An example is Ford Credit Canada, owned by the Ford Motor Company of Canada.

Second, receivables may be sold because they are the only reasonable source of cash. When money is tight, companies may not be able to borrow money in the usual credit markets. Even if credit is available, the cost of borrowing may be too high.

A final reason for selling receivables is that billing and collection are often time-consuming and costly. It is often easier for a retailer to sell its receivables to another party with expertise in billing and collection matters. Credit card companies, such as Visa and MasterCard, specialize in billing and collecting accounts receivable.

Factoring. One way to accelerate receivables collection is by sale to a factor. A **factor** is a finance company or bank that buys receivables from businesses and then collects the cash directly from the customer. If the customer does not pay, the business is usually responsible for reimbursing the factor for the uncollected amounts. This is known as selling receivables on a recourse basis.

Securitization of Receivables. An increasingly common transaction is to sell receivables to investors in return for cash through a process called **securitization**. Receivables are sold to an independent trust that holds them as an investment. This converts the receivables into securities of the trust, which is why the term "securitization of receivables" is used. In some cases, the transfer is treated as a sale of receivables; in other cases, it is treated as a secured loan.

The differences between factoring and securitization are that securitization involves many investors and the cost is lower, the receivables are of higher quality, and the seller usually continues to be involved with collecting the receivables. In factoring, the sale is usually to only one company, the cost is higher, the receivables quality is lower, and the seller does not normally have any involvement with collecting the receivables.

For such companies as **Canadian National Railway** and **Bell Aliant**, securitization of receivables is one method of using their receivables to obtain cash. Each of these companies reports details of the securitization of its receivables in the notes to its financial statements.

 ACCOUNTING IN ACTION: BUSINESS INSIGHT

During the financial crisis in the fall of 2008, Canada's federal government introduced a program to buy up to $125 billion in mortgages from banks. The Insured Mortgage Purchase Program worked well; the country's banks weathered the crisis with few problems. But some analysts think the banks may have sold too many loans to the government. After all, securitization is considered a reason for the decline in lending standards that led to the U.S. subprime mortgage crisis. Canadian banks have securitized about $275 billion worth of mortgages through government programs, including the IMPP—one-quarter of the total outstanding mortgages. The programs have kept mortgage rates low and the housing market active, and have been a source of big gains for the banks. However, as banks securitize more of their insured mortgages, are they weakening their balance sheets? By the summer of 2009, insured mortgages made up just 6% of total assets held by Canadian banks, down from 10% a decade earlier. However, the pace of mortgage securitization was expected to slow as the cost of bank borrowing dropped and banks kept more mortgage loans on their books.

Source: Tara Perkins, "Ottawa Mortgage Aid May cost Banks," *The Globe and Mail Report on Business*, July 10, 2009.

What was the benefit to the banks of securitizing their mortgage receivables?

BEFORE YOU GO ON . . .

→ Review It

1. Explain where and how accounts and notes receivable are reported on the balance sheet.
2. Where is bad debts expense reported on the income statement?
3. What do the receivables turnover and collection period reveal?
4. Why do companies want to accelerate cash receipts from receivables?

Related exercise material: BE8–13, BE8–14, BE8–15, E8–3, E8–10, E8–11, E8–12, and E8–13.

The Navigator

Demonstration Problem

On February 28, Dylan Co. had the following balances in select accounts:

Accounts Receivable	$200,000
Allowance for Doubtful Accounts (credit)	12,500

Selected transactions for Dylan Co. follow. Dylan's year end is June 30.

Mar. 1	Sold $20,000 of merchandise to Potter Company, terms n/30.
1	Accepted Juno Company's $16,500, six-month, 6% note for the balance due on account.
11	Potter Company returned $600 worth of goods.
13	Made Dylan Co. credit card sales for $13,200.
30	Received payment in full from Potter Company.
Apr. 13	Received collections of $8,200 on Dylan Co. credit card sales. Added interest charges of 18% to the remaining balance.
May 10	Wrote off as uncollectible $15,000 of accounts receivable.
June 30	Dylan uses the percentage of receivables approach to estimate uncollectible accounts. Estimated uncollectible accounts are determined to be $20,000 at June 30.
30	Recorded the interest accrued on the Juno Company note.
July 16	One of the accounts receivable written off in May pays the amount due, $4,000, in full.
Sept. 1	Collected cash from Juno Company in payment of the March 1 note receivable.

Instructions

(a) Prepare the journal entries for the transactions. Dylan Co. uses a periodic inventory system.

(b) Open T accounts for Accounts Receivable and the Allowance for Doubtful Accounts, and post the relevant journal entries to these accounts. Calculate the balance in these accounts at June 30 and at September 1.

(c) Calculate the net realizable value of the accounts receivable at June 30 and September 1.

Solution to Demonstration Problem

Action Plan

- Record receivables at the invoice price.
- Recognize that sales returns and allowances reduce the amount received on accounts receivable.
- Calculate interest by multiplying the interest rate by the face value by the part of the year that has passed.
- Record write offs of accounts and recoveries of accounts written off only in balance sheet accounts.
- Consider any existing balance in the allowance account when making the adjustment for uncollectible accounts.
- Recognize any remaining interest on notes receivable when recording the collection of a note.

(a)

Mar. 1	Accounts Receivable—Potter	20,000	
	Sales		20,000
	To record sale on account.		
1	Notes Receivable—Juno	16,500	
	Accounts Receivable—Juno		16,500
	To record acceptance of Juno Company note.		
11	Sales Returns and Allowances	600	
	Accounts Receivable—Potter		600
	To record return of goods.		
13	Accounts Receivable	13,200	
	Sales		13,200
	To record company credit card sales.		
30	Cash ($20,000 – $600)	19,400	
	Accounts Receivable—Potter		19,400
	To record collection of account receivable.		
Apr. 13	Cash	8,200	
	Accounts Receivable		8,200
	To record collection of credit card accounts receivable.		

13	Accounts Receivable [($13,200 − $8,200) × 18% × $1/12$]		75	
	Interest Revenue			75
	To record interest on amount due.			
May 10	Allowance for Doubtful Accounts		15,000	
	Accounts Receivable			15,000
	To record write off of accounts receivable.			
June 30	Bad Debts Expense ($20,000 + $2,500)		22,500	
	Allowance for Doubtful Accounts			22,500
	To record estimate of uncollectible accounts.			
30	Interest Receivable ($16,500 × 6% × $4/12$)		330	
	Interest Revenue			330
	To record interest earned.			
July 16	Accounts Receivable		4,000	
	Allowance for Doubtful Accounts			4,000
	To reverse write off of account receivable.			
16	Cash		4,000	
	Accounts Receivable			4,000
	To record collection of account receivable.			
Sept. 1	Cash [$16,500 + ($16,500 × 6% × $6/12$)]		16,995	
	Interest Revenue ($16,500 × 6% × $2/12$)			165
	Interest Receivable			330
	Note Receivable			16,500
	To record collection of note receivable plus interest.			

(b)

Accounts Receivable

Feb. 28	Bal.	200,000		16,500
		20,000		600
		13,200		19,400
		75		8,200
				15,000
June 30	Bal.	173,575		
		4,000		4,000
Sept. 1	Bal.	173,575		

Allowance for Doubtful Accounts

		15,000	Feb. 28	Bal.	12,500
June 30	Bal.	2,500			
			June 30	Adj.	22,500
			June 30	Bal.	20,000
					4,000
			Sept. 1	Bal.	24,000

(c)

	June 30	Sept. 1
Accounts receivable	$173,575	$173,575
Less: Allowance for doubtful accounts	20,000	24,000
Net realizable value	$153,575	$149,575

The Navigator

Summary of Study Objectives

1. *Record accounts receivable transactions.* Accounts receivable are recorded at the invoice price. They are reduced by sales returns and allowances, and sales discounts. Accounts receivable subsidiary ledgers are used to keep track of individual account balances. When interest is charged on a past-due receivable, this interest is added to the accounts receivable balance and is recognized as interest revenue. Sales using non-bank credit cards result in a receivable, net of the credit card charges, from the credit card company; sales using company credit cards result in a receivable from the customer.

2. *Calculate the net realizable value of accounts receivable and account for bad debts.* The allowance method is used to match expected bad debts expense against sales revenue in the period when the sales occur. There are two approaches that can be used to estimate the bad debts: (a) percentage of receivables, or (b) percentage of sales. The percentage of receivables approach emphasizes determining the correct net realizable value of the accounts receivable. An aging schedule is usually used with the percentage of receivables approach where percentages are applied to different categories of accounts receivable to determine the allowance for doubtful accounts. The percentage of sales approach emphasizes achieving the most accurate matching of expenses to revenues. A percentage is applied to credit sales to determine the bad debt expense. The allowance is deducted from gross accounts receivable to report accounts receivable at their net realizable value in the balance sheet.

3. *Account for notes receivable.* Notes receivable are recorded at their principal, or face, value. Interest is earned from the date the note is issued until it matures and must be recorded in the correct accounting period. Interest receivable is recorded in a separate account from the note. Like accounts receivable, notes receivable are reported at their net realizable value.

Notes are normally held to maturity. At that time, the principal plus any unpaid interest is due and the note is removed from the accounts. If a note is not paid at maturity, it is said to be dishonoured. If eventual collection is still expected, an account receivable replaces the note receivable and any unpaid interest. Otherwise, the note must be written off.

4. *Demonstrate the presentation, analysis, and management of receivables.* Each major type of receivable should be identified in the balance sheet or in the notes to the financial statements. It is desirable to report the gross amount of receivables and the allowance for doubtful accounts/notes. Bad debts expense is reported in the income statement as an operating expense.

The liquidity of receivables can be evaluated by calculating the receivables turnover and collection period ratios. The receivables turnover is calculated by dividing net credit sales by average gross accounts receivable. This ratio measures how efficiently the company is converting its receivables into sales. The collection period converts the receivables turnover into days, dividing 365 days by the receivables turnover ratio. It shows the number of days, on average, it takes a company to collect its accounts receivable. The combination of the collection period and days sales in inventory is a useful way to measure the length of a company's operating cycle.

There are two additional ways to obtain cash from receivables: using the receivables to secure a loan and selling the receivables either to a factor or by securitizing them.

Glossary

WILEY **PLUS** Glossary
Key Term Matching Activity

Accounts receivable Amounts owed by customers on account. (p. 436)

Aging schedule A list of accounts receivable organized by the length of time they have been unpaid. (p. 443)

Allowance method A method of accounting for bad debts that involves estimating uncollectible accounts at the end of each period. (p. 441)

Bad debts expense An expense account to record uncollectible receivables. (p. 440)

Balance sheet approach Another name for the percentage of receivables approach. (p. 443)

Collection period The average number of days that receivables are outstanding. It is calculated by dividing 365 days by the receivables turnover. (p. 453)

Dishonoured note A note that is not paid in full at maturity. (p. 450)

Factor A finance company or bank that buys receivables from businesses and then collects the payments directly from the customers. (p. 455)

Income statement approach Another name for the percentage of sales approach. (p. 444)

Net realizable value The net amount of receivables expected to be received in cash; calculated by deducting the allowance for doubtful accounts from gross receivables. (p. 440)

Notes receivable Claims for which formal instruments of credit are issued as evidence of the debt. (p. 436)

Percentage of receivables approach An approach to estimating uncollectible accounts where the allowance for doubtful accounts is calculated as a percentage of receivables. (p. 442)

Percentage of sales approach An approach to estimating uncollectible accounts where bad debts expense is calculated as a percentage of net credit sales. (p. 444)

Promissory note A written promise to pay a specified amount of money on demand or at a definite time. (p. 448)

Receivables turnover ratio A measure of the liquidity of receivables, calculated by dividing net credit sales by average gross accounts receivable. (p. 453)

Securitization The conversion of assets such as receivables into securities that are then sold to investors in return for cash. (p. 455)

Trade receivables Accounts and notes receivable that result from sales transactions. (p. 436)

Self-Study Questions

Answers are at the end of the chapter.

(SO 1) AP 1. On June 15, Patel Company sells merchandise on account to Bullock Co. for $1,000, terms 2/10, n/30. On June 20, Bullock returns merchandise worth $300 to Patel. On June 24, payment is received from Bullock for the balance due. What is the amount of cash received?
(a) $680
(b) $686
(c) $700
(d) $980

(SO 2) AP 2. Sanderson Company has a debit balance of $5,000 in Allowance for Doubtful Accounts before any adjustments are made. Based on an aging of its accounts receivable at the end of the period, the company estimates that $60,000 of its receivables are uncollectible. The amount of bad debts expense that should be reported for this accounting period is:
(a) $5,000.
(b) $55,000.
(c) $60,000.
(d) $65,000.

(SO 2) AP 3. On January 1, 2011, the Allowance for Doubtful Accounts has a credit balance of $18,000. During 2011, $30,000 of uncollectible accounts receivable were written off. An aging schedule indicates that uncollectible accounts are $20,000 at the end of 2011. What is the required adjustment to Bad Debt Expense at December 31, 2011?
(a) $2,000
(b) $8,000
(c) $20,000
(d) $32,000

(SO 2) AP 4. Net sales for the month are $800,000 and bad debts are expected to be 1.5% of net sales. The company uses the percentage of sales approach. If Allowance for Doubtful Accounts has a credit balance of $15,000 before adjustment, what is the balance in the allowance account after adjustment?
(a) $15,000
(b) $23,000
(c) $27,000
(d) $12,000

(SO 2) AP 5. On January 1, 2011, Allowance for Doubtful Accounts had a credit balance of $35,000. In 2011, $30,000 of uncollectible accounts receivable were written off. On December 31, 2011, the company had accounts receivable of $850,000. Experience indicates that 3% of total receivables will become uncollectible. The adjusting journal entry that would be recorded for bad debts expense on December 31, 2011, would be:

(a) Allowance for Doubtful Accounts	20,500	
Accounts Receivable		20,500
(b) Bad Debt Expense	30,000	
Accounts Receivable		30,000
(c) Bad Debt Expense	25,500	
Allowance for Doubtful Accounts		25,500
(d) Bad Debt Expense	20,500	
Allowance for Doubtful Accounts		20,500

(SO 3) AP 6. On July 1, Sorenson Co. accepts a $1,000, four-month, 8% promissory note in settlement of an account with Parton Co. Sorenson has a September 30 fiscal year end. The adjusting entry to record interest on August 31 is:

(a)	Interest Receivable	20	
	Interest Revenue		20
(b)	Interest Receivable	80	
	Interest Revenue		80
(c)	Notes Receivable	80	
	Unearned Interest Revenue		80
(d)	Interest Receivable	60	
	Interest Revenue		60

(SO 3) AP 7. Schlicht Co. holds Osgrove Inc.'s $10,000, four-month, 9% note. If no interest has been accrued when the note is collected, the entry made by Schlicht Co. is:

(a)	Cash	10,300	
	Notes Receivable		10,300
(b)	Cash	10,900	
	Interest Revenue		900
	Notes Receivable		10,000
(c)	Accounts Receivable	10,300	
	Notes Receivable		10,000
	Interest Revenue		300
(d)	Cash	10,300	
	Notes Receivable		10,000
	Interest Revenue		300

(SO 4) K 8. Accounts and notes receivable are reported in the current assets section of the balance sheet at:
(a) net realizable value.
(b) carrying amount.
(c) lower of cost and net realizable value.
(d) full value.

9. Moore Company had net credit sales of $800,000 (SO 4) AP in the year and a cost of goods sold of $500,000. The balance in Accounts Receivable at the beginning of the year was $100,000 and at the end of the year it was $150,000. What were the receivables turnover and collection period ratios, respectively?
(a) 4.0 and 91 days
(b) 5.3 and 69 days
(c) 6.4 and 57 days
(d) 8.0 and 46 days

10. Which statement about International Financial (SO 4) K Reporting Standards is correct?
(a) Accounts receivable must be presented before Cash on the Balance Sheet.
(b) Companies will be required to disclose the beginning and ending balances in the Allowance for Doubtful Accounts as well as the write offs during the year.
(c) Companies must use the percentage of receivables approach to estimate uncollectible accounts.
(d) All trade receivables must be included in current assets.

Questions

(SO 1) K 1. Why are accounts receivable and notes receivable sometimes called trade receivables?

(SO 1) C 2. (a) What are the advantages of using an accounts receivable subsidiary ledger? (b) Describe the relationship between the general ledger control account and the subsidiary ledger.

(SO 1) K 3. Under what circumstances is interest normally recorded for an account receivable?

(SO 1) C 4. Ashley Dreher is confused about how a retail company should record a credit card sale. She thinks it does not matter if the customer used a bank credit card, a nonbank credit card, or a company credit card—the retail company should always debit Accounts Receivable because the customer is not paying in cash. Is Ashley correct? Explain.

(SO 2) C 5. Rod Ponach is the new credit manager for ACCT Company. He has told management there will be no bad debts in the future because he will do a complete credit check on each customer before the company makes a sale on credit to the customer. Do you think Rod can completely eliminate bad debts for the company? Discuss.

6. Explain the allowance method of accounting for (SO 2) K bad debts. How does this method result in the matching of expenses with revenues?

7. (a) What is the purpose of the account Allowance for (SO 2) C Doubtful Accounts? (b) Although the normal balance of this account is a credit balance, it sometimes has a debit balance. Explain how this can happen.

8. Why is the bad debts expense that is reported in (SO 2) K the income statement usually not the same amount as the allowance for doubtful accounts amount reported in the balance sheet?

9. Explain the difference between the percentage of (SO 2) C receivables and the percentage of sales approaches in estimating uncollectible accounts.

10. Explain why the percentage of receivables approach (SO 2) K is also called the balance sheet approach and the percentage of sales approach is also called the income statement approach.

(SO 2) C **11.** Which approach is a preferable method to estimate uncollectible accounts—percentage of receivables or percentage of sales?

(SO 2) C **12.** Soo Eng cannot understand why net realizable value does not decrease when an uncollectible account is written off under the allowance method. Clarify this for Soo Eng.

(SO 2) C **13.** When an account receivable that was written off is later collected, two journal entries are usually made. Explain why.

(SO 3) K **14.** Explain how notes receivable and accounts receivable are the same and how they are different.

(SO 3) C **15.** Why might a company prefer to have a note receivable instead of an account receivable?

(SO 3) C **16.** Danielle does not understand why a note receivable is not immediately recorded at its maturity value (principal plus interest). After all, you know you are going to collect both the principal and the interest and you know how much each will be. Explain to Danielle why notes are not recorded at their maturity value.

(SO 3) C **17.** Explain how recording interest revenue differs for accounts receivable and notes receivable.

(SO 3) C **18.** What does it mean if a note is dishonoured? What are the alternatives for the payee in accounting for a dishonoured note?

(SO 4) C **19.** Saucier Company has accounts receivable, notes receivable due in three months, notes receivable due in two years, an allowance for doubtful accounts, sales taxes recoverable, and income tax receivable. How should the receivables be reported on the balance sheet?

(SO 4) C **20.** The president proudly announces that her company's liquidity has improved. Its acid-test ratio increased substantially this year. Does an increase in the acid-test ratio always indicate improved liquidity? What other ratio(s) might you review to determine whether or not the increase in the acid-test ratio is an improvement in the company's financial health?

(SO 4) C **21.** Canadian Worldwide Communications Co. receivables turnover was 5.8 times in 2010 and 6.3 times in 2011. Has the company's receivables management improved or worsened?

(SO 4) K **22.** Why do companies sometimes sell their receivables?

(SO 4) C **23.** What is the difference between factoring and securitizing receivables?

Brief Exercises

BE8–1 Seven transactions follow. For each transaction, indicate if the transaction increases, decreases, or has no effect on (a) accounts receivable, (b) notes receivable, (c) total assets, and (d) owner's equity. Use the following format, in which the first transaction is given as an example:

Identify impact of transaction on receivables, total assets, and owner's equity.
(SO 1) K

Transaction:	(a) Accounts Receivable	(b) Notes Receivable	(c) Total Assets	(d) Owner's Equity
1. Performed services on account for a customer.	Increase	No effect	Increase	Increase
2. A customer paid cash for services to be provided next month.				
3. Performed services for a customer in exchange for a note.				
4. Collected cash from the customer in 1 above.				
5. Performed services for a customer for cash.				
6. Extended a customer's account for three months by accepting a note in exchange for it.				
7. Performed services for a customer who had paid in advance.				

Record accounts receivable transactions.
(SO 1) AP

BE8–2   Record the following transactions on the books of Essex Co.:

(a) On July 1, Essex Co. sold merchandise on account to Cambridge Inc. for $15,000, terms 2/10, n/30. The cost of the merchandise sold was $9,500. Essex uses a perpetual inventory system.

(b) On July 3, Cambridge Inc. returned merchandise worth $2,500 to Essex Co. The original cost of the merchandise was $1,580. The merchandise was returned to inventory.

(c) On July 10, Cambridge Inc. paid for the merchandise.

Record accounts receivable transactions.
(SO 1) AP

BE8–3   Record the following transactions on the books of Low Co:

(a) On August 1, Low Co. sold merchandise on account to High Inc. for $25,000, terms 2/10, n/30. Low uses a periodic inventory system.

(b) On August 5, High Inc. returned merchandise worth $4,500 to Low Co.

(c) On September 30, Low Co. charged High Inc. one month's interest for the overdue account. Low charges 12% on overdue accounts. (Round calculation to the nearest dollar.)

(d) On October 4, High Inc. paid the amount owing to Low Co.

Record credit card transactions.
(SO 1) AP

BE8–4   Stewart Department Store accepted a nonbank card in payment of a $400 purchase of merchandise on July 11. The credit card company charges a 3% fee. (a) What entry should Stewart Department Store make? (b) What if the customer had used a Visa credit card instead of a nonbank credit card? Assume Visa also charges a 3% fee. (c) What entry should Stewart Department Store record if the customer had used a Stewart Department Store credit card instead of a nonbank credit card?

Record bad debts using percentage of receivables approach.
(SO 2) AP

BE8–5   Groleskey Co. uses the percentage of receivables approach to record bad debts expense. It estimates that 4% of total accounts receivable will become uncollectible. Accounts receivable are $300,000 at the end of the year. The allowance for doubtful accounts has a credit balance of $2,500.

(a) Prepare the adjusting entry to record bad debts expense for the year ended December 31.

(b) If the allowance for doubtful accounts had a debit balance of $1,500 instead of a credit balance of $2,500, what amount would be reported for bad debts expense?

Complete aging schedule and record bad debts expense.
(SO 2) AP

BE8–6   Refer to BE8–5. Groleskey Co. decides to refine its estimate of uncollectible accounts by preparing an aging schedule. Complete the following schedule and prepare the adjusting journal entry using this estimate. Assume Allowance for Doubtful Accounts has a credit balance of $2,500.

Number of Days Outstanding	Accounts Receivable	Estimated % Uncollectible	Estimated Uncollectible Accounts
0–30 days	$184,000	1%	
31–60 days	60,000	4%	
61–90 days	36,000	10%	
Over 90 days	20,000	20%	
Total	$300,000		

Record bad debts using percentage of sales approach.
(SO 2) AP

BE8–7   Qinshan Co. uses the percentage of sales approach to record bad debts expense. It estimates that 1.5% of net credit sales will become uncollectible. Credit sales are $950,000 for the year ended April 30, 2011; sales returns and allowances are $60,000; sales discounts are $20,000; and the allowance for doubtful accounts has a credit balance of $6,000. Prepare the adjusting entry to record bad debts expense in 2011.

Record write off and compare net realizable value.
(SO 2) AP

BE8–8   At the end of 2010, Searcy Co. has an allowance for doubtful accounts of $36,000. On January 24, 2011, when it has accounts receivable of $650,000, Searcy Co. learns that its $8,000 receivable from Hutley Inc. is not collectible. Management authorizes a write off.

(a) Record the write off.

(b) What is the net realizable value of the accounts receivable (1) before the write off, and (2) after the write off?

BE8–9 Assume the same information as in BE8–8. Hutley's financial difficulties are over. On June 4, 2011, Searcy Co. receives a payment in full of $8,000 from Hutley Inc. Record this transaction.

Record recovery of account written off.
(SO 2) AP

BE8–10 Rocky Ridge Co. has three outstanding notes receivable at its December 31, 2010, fiscal year end. For each note, calculate (a) total interest revenue, (b) interest revenue to be recorded in 2010, and (c) interest revenue to be recorded in 2011.

Calculate interest on notes receivable.
(SO 3) AP

Issue Date	Term	Principal	Interest Rate
1. July 31, 2010	9 months	$15,000	7%
2. September 1, 2010	6 months	44,000	8%
3. November 1, 2010	15 months	30,000	6%

BE8–11 On March 31, 2011, Raja Co. sold merchandise on account to Opal Co. for $24,000, terms n/30. Raja uses a perpetual inventory system and the merchandise had a cost of $14,500. On May 1, 2011, Opal gave Raja a five-month, 7% promissory note in settlement of the account. Interest is to be paid at maturity. On October 1, Opal paid the note and accrued interest. Record the above transactions for Raja Co. Raja Co. has a May 31 fiscal year end and adjusts its accounts annually.

Record notes receivable transactions.
(SO 3) AP

BE8–12 Lee Company accepts a $27,000, three-month, 7% note receivable in settlement of an account receivable on June 1, 2011. Interest is to be paid at maturity. Lee Company has a December 31 year end and adjusts its accounts annually.

Record notes receivable transactions.
(SO 3) AP

(a) Record (1) the issue of the note on June 1 and (2) the settlement of the note on September 1, assuming the note is honoured.
(b) Repeat part (a) assuming that the note is dishonoured but eventual collection is expected.
(c) Repeat part (a) assuming that the note is dishonoured and eventual collection is not expected.

BE8–13 Chant Co. lent Sharp Inc. $100,000 cash in exchange for a five-year, 4% note on July 1, 2010. Interest is payable quarterly on January 1, April 1, July 1, and October 1 each year. Chant Co. has a December 31 year end.

Record notes receivable transactions and indicate statement presentation.
(SO 3, 4) AP

(a) Record Chant's entries related to the note to January 1, 2011.
(b) What amounts related to this note will be reported on Chant's December 31, 2010, financial statements?

BE8–14 WAF Company's general ledger included the following accounts at November 30, 2011:

Prepare current assets section.
(SO 4) AP

Accounts payable	$145,500
Accounts receivable	109,000
Allowance for doubtful accounts	6,950
Bad debts expense	35,970
Cash	74,000
GST recoverable	21,850
Interest receivable	2,500
Interest revenue	10,000
Merchandise inventory	110,800
Note receivable—due April 23, 2012	50,000
Note receivable—due May 21, 2015	150,000
Prepaid expenses	15,300
Short-term investments	80,500

Prepare the current assets section of the balance sheet.

Calculate and interpret ratios.
(SO 4) AN

BE8–15 The financial statements of Maple Leaf Foods Inc. report sales of $5,242,602 thousand for the year ended December 31, 2008. Accounts receivable are $139,144 thousand at the end of the year, and $202,285 thousand at the beginning of the year. Calculate Maple Leaf's receivables turnover and collection period. If the company's receivables turnover and collection period in the previous year were 25.8 and 14.1 days, respectively, has the company's liquidity improved or weakened?

Exercises

Identify impact and
record accounts receivable
transactions.
(SO 1) AP

E8–1 Links Costumes uses a perpetual inventory system. Selected transactions for April and June follow:

Apr. 6 Sold merchandise costing $3,000 to Pumphill Theatre for $6,500, terms 2/10, n/30.

8 Pumphill returned $500 of the merchandise. This merchandise had originally cost Links $235 and was returned to inventory.

16 Pumphill paid Links the amount owing.

17 Sold merchandise costing $2,525 to EastCo Productions for $5,500, terms 1/10, n/30.

18 EastCo returned $400 of the merchandise because it was damaged. The merchandise had originally cost Links $185. Links scrapped the merchandise.

June 17 Added interest charges for one month to the amount owing by EastCo. Links charges 18% on outstanding receivables.

20 EastCo paid the amount owing.

Instructions

(a) For each of these transactions indicate if the transaction has increased (+) or decreased (−) cash, accounts receivable, inventory, and owner's equity and by how much. If the item is not changed, write NE to indicate there is no effect. Use the following format, in which the first one has been done for you as an example.

Transaction Date	Cash	Accounts Receivable	Inventory	Owner's Equity
April 6	NE	+ $6,500	− $3,000	+ $3,500

(b) Prepare journal entries to record the above transactions.

Record accounts receivable
transactions. Post to subsidiary
and general ledgers.
(SO 1) AP

E8–2 Transactions follow for the Adventure Sports Co. store and three of its customers in the company's first month of business:

Mar. 2 Andrew Noren used his Adventure Sports credit card to purchase $575 of merchandise.

4 Andrew returned $75 of merchandise for credit.

5 Elaine Davidson used her Adventure Sports credit card to purchase $380 of merchandise.

8 Erik Smistad purchased $421 of merchandise and paid for it in cash.

17 Andrew Noren used his Adventure Sports credit card to purchase an additional $348 of merchandise.

19 Elaine Davidson made a $100 payment on her credit card account.

22 Erik Smistad used his Adventure Sports credit card to purchase $299 of merchandise.

27 Andrew Noren paid the amount owing on his March 2 purchase.

29 Elaine Davidson used her Adventure Sports credit card to purchase $310 of merchandise.

Instructions

(a) Record the above transactions. Adventure Sports uses a periodic inventory system.
(b) Set up general ledger accounts for the Accounts Receivable control account and for the Accounts Receivable subsidiary ledger accounts. Post the journal entries to these accounts.
(c) Prepare a list of customers and the balances of their accounts from the subsidiary ledger. Prove that the total of the subsidiary ledger is equal to the control account balance.

E8–3   Krazy Hair Salon accepts its own credit card, as well as debit cards, and bank and nonbank credit cards. Krazy is charged 3.5% for all bank credit card transactions, 4.25% for all nonbank credit card transactions, and $0.50 per transaction for all debit card transactions. In October and November 2011, the following summary transactions occurred:

Record credit card transactions and indicate statement presentation.
(SO 1, 4) AP

Oct. 15		Performed services totalling $15,000 for customers who used Krazy credit cards.
	20	Performed services totalling $7,500 for customers who used Visa credit cards.
	30	Performed services totalling $2,000 for customers who used nonbank credit cards.
	31	Performed services totalling $5,000 for customers who used debit cards (100 transactions).
Nov. 15		Collected $9,000 on Krazy credit cards.
	14	Collected the amount owing from the nonbank credit card companies for the October 30 transactions.
	30	Added interest charges of 24% to outstanding Krazy credit card balances.

Instructions

(a) Record the above transactions for Krazy Hair Salon.
(b) Using these transactions, prepare a multi-step income statement for Krazy Hair Salon for the two months ended November 30.

E8–4   The ledger of Assen Company at December 31, 2011, the end of the current year, shows Accounts Receivable $180,000; Allowance for Doubtful Accounts $2,200 (credit); Sales $1,420,000; Sales Returns and Allowances $50,000; and Sales Discounts $20,000.

Record bad debts using two approaches; calculate net realizable value.
(SO 2) AP

Instructions

(a) Record the adjusting entry at December 31, 2011, assuming bad debts are estimated to be (1) 10% of accounts receivable, and (2) 1.5% of net sales.
(b) Calculate the net realizable value of the accounts receivable for each approach to estimating uncollectible accounts in (a) above.
(c) Assume instead that the Allowance for Doubtful Accounts had a debit balance of $2,600 at December 31, 2011. What is bad debt expense for 2011, and what is the net realizable value of the accounts receivable December 31, 2011, assuming bad debts are estimated to be (1) 10% of accounts receivable, and (2) 1.5% of net sales?

E8–5   Grevina Company has accounts receivable of $185,000 at March 31, 2011. An analysis of the accounts shows the following:

Prepare aging schedule and record bad debts.
(SO 2) AP

Month of Sale	Balance
March	$130,000
February	25,200
January	17,000
October, November, and December	12,800
	$185,000

Credit terms are 2/10, n/30. On April 1, 2010, the Allowance for Doubtful Accounts had a credit balance of $16,700. During the year, the company wrote off accounts receivable of $20,000 as uncollectible. The company uses the percentage of receivables approach and an aging schedule to estimate uncollectible accounts. The company's percentage estimates of bad debts are as follows:

Number of Days Outstanding	Estimated % Uncollectible
0–30	2%
31–60	10%
61–90	30%
Over 90	50%

Instructions

(a) Prepare an aging schedule to determine the total estimated uncollectible accounts at March 31, 2011.
(b) Prepare the adjusting entry at March 31 to record bad debts expense.
(c) What is the net realizable value of the accounts receivable at March 31, 2011?

Determine missing amounts.
(SO 1, 2) AP

E8–6 Wilton Corporation reported the following information in its general ledger at December 31:

Accounts Receivable				Sales	
Beg.	bal.	9,000	28,000		30,000
		(a)	(b)		
End.	bal.	(c)			

Allowance for Doubtful Accounts				Bad Debts Expense	
		Beg.	bal.	900	(d)
	500			(d)	
		End.	bal.	(e)	

All sales were on account. At the end of the year, uncollectible accounts were estimated to total $1,000 based on an aging schedule.

Instructions

Using your knowledge of receivables transactions, determine the missing amounts. (*Hint:* You may find it helpful to reconstruct the journal entries.)

Record bad debts, write off, and recovery; calculate net realizable value.
(SO 2) AP

E8–7 On December 31, 2010, Jacey Co. estimated that 4% of its $550,000 of accounts receivable would become uncollectible. Prior to the recording of the bad debts adjusting entry, the Allowance for Doubtful Accounts had a debit balance of $1,200. On May 21, 2011, the company determined that Robert Worthy's $1,850 account and Samir Dusaki's $3,450 account were uncollectible and wrote off the two accounts. Jacey's accounts receivable were $575,000 prior to recording the write offs. On July 11, 2011, Dusaki paid his account that had been written off on May 21. On July 11, 2011, Jacey's accounts receivable were $521,000 prior to recording the cash receipt from Dusaki.

Instructions

(a) Prepare the journal entries on December 31, 2010, May 21, 2011, and July 11, 2011.
(b) Post the journal entries to Allowance for Doubtful Accounts and calculate the new balance after each entry.
(c) Calculate the net realizable value of accounts receivable both before and after writing off the two accounts on May 21, 2011.
(d) Calculate the net realizable value of the accounts receivable both before and after recording the cash receipt from Dusaki on July 11, 2011.

E8–8 Passera Supply Co. has the following transactions:

Record notes receivable transactions.
(SO 3) AP

Nov. 1   Loaned $48,000 cash to A. Morgan on a one-year, 8% note.

    15   Sold goods to H. Giorgi on account for $9,000, terms n/30. The goods cost Passera $5,500. Passera uses the perpetual inventory system.

Dec. 1   Sold goods to Wright, Inc., receiving an $18,000, three-month, 6% note. The goods cost Passera $11,000.

    15   H. Giorgi was unable to pay her account. Giorgi gave Passera a six-month, 7% note in settlement of her account.

    31   Accrued interest revenue on all notes receivable. Interest is due at maturity.

Mar. 1   Collected the amount owing on the Wright note.

Jun. 15   H. Giorgi defaults on the note. Future payment is not expected.

Instructions

Record the transactions for Passera Supply Co. (Round calculations to the nearest dollar.)

E8–9 The following are notes receivable transactions for Rather Co.:

Record notes receivable transactions.
(SO 3) AP

May 1   Received a $10,500, six-month, 5% note from Jioux Company in settlement of an accounts receivable. Interest is due at maturity.

June 30   Accrued interest on the Jioux note, at Rather's year end. Adjustments are recorded annually.

July 31   Lent $3,000 cash to an employee, Noreen Irvine, receiving a three-month, 6% note. Interest is due at the end of each month.

Aug. 31   Received the interest due from Ms. Irvine.

Sep. 30   Received the interest due from Ms. Irvine.

Oct. 31   Received payment in full for the employee note from Ms. Irvine.

Nov. 1   Jioux Company defaults on its note. Rather expects to collect the amount owing in January.

Instructions

Record the transactions for Rather Co. (Round calculations to the nearest dollar.)

E8–10 Ni Co. has the following notes receivable outstanding at December 31, 2011:

Record notes receivable transactions and indicate statement presentation.
(SO 3, 4) AP

Issue Date	Term	Principal	Interest Rate
1. August 31, 2010	2 years	$15,000	4%
2. October 1, 2010	18 months	46,000	5%
3. February 1, 2011	1 year	32,000	4%
4. May 31, 2011	5 years	22,000	6%
5. October 31, 2011	7 months	9,000	5%

For notes with terms of one year or longer, interest is payable on the first day of each month, for interest earned the previous month. For notes with terms less than one year, interest is payable at maturity.

Instructions

(a) Calculate the interest revenue that Ni Co. will report on its income statement for the year ended December 31, 2011. Indicate where this will be presented on the income statement. (Round calculations to the nearest dollar.)

(b) Calculate the amounts related to these notes that will be reported on Ni Co.'s balance sheet at December 31, 2011. Indicate where they will be presented. Assume all required interest payments have been received on time. (Round calculations to the nearest dollar.)

Record bad debts, prepare
partial balance sheet, and
calculate ratios.
(SO 2, 4) AP

E8–11   In its first year of operations, AJS Company had sales of $3 million (all on credit) and cost of goods sold of $1,750,000. Sales allowances of $100,000 were given on substandard merchandise. During the year the company collected $2.4 million cash on account. At year end, December 31, 2011, the credit manager estimates that 5% of the accounts receivables will become uncollectible.

At December 31, 2011, the balances in selected other accounts were:

Accounts payable	$350,000
Cash	85,000
Interest receivable	1,125
Interest revenue	2,250
Merchandise inventory	325,000
Notes receivable, due April 10, 2014	45,000
Short-term investments	50,000
Supplies	10,000
Unearned sales revenue	25,000

Instructions

(a) Prepare the journal entry to record the estimated uncollectibles.
(b) Prepare the current assets section of the balance sheet for AJS Company at December 31, 2011.
(c) Calculate the receivables turnover and collection period. (Remember that this is the end of the first year of business.)

Calculate ratios and comment.
(SO 4) AN

E8–12   The following information (in millions) was taken from the December 31 financial statements of Canadian National Railway Company:

	2008	2007	2006
Accounts receivable, gross	$ 939	$ 397	$ 711
Allowance for doubtful accounts	26	27	19
Accounts receivable, net	913	370	692
Revenues	8,482	7,897	7,929
Total current assets	1,756	1,048	1,336
Total current liabilities	1,892	1,590	2,114

Instructions

(a) Calculate the 2008 and 2007 current ratios.
(b) Calculate the receivables turnover and average collection period for 2008 and 2007.
(c) Are accounts receivable a material component of the company's current assets?
(d) Comment on any improvement or weakening in CN's liquidity and its management of accounts receivable.

Discuss sale of receivables.
(SO 4) C

E8–13   Refer to E8–12. In the notes to its financial statements, Canadian National Railway Company reports that it has a revolving agreement to sell eligible freight trade and other receivables up to a maximum of $600 million of receivables outstanding at any point in time. At December 31, 2008, the company had sold $71 million of these receivables, compared with $588 million at December 31, 2007, and $393 million at December 31, 2006. CN has retained the responsibility for servicing, administering, and collecting the freight receivables sold.

Instructions

Explain why CN, a financially stable company, securitizes (sells) a portion of its receivables. Explain the impact of amounts securitized on the accounts receivable shown on the balance sheet.

Problems: Set A

P8–1A At December 31, 2010, Bordeaux Co. reported the following information on its balance sheet:

Accounts receivable	$480,000
Less: Allowance for doubtful accounts	33,600

Record accounts receivable and bad debts transactions; show balance sheet presentation.
(SO 1, 2) AP

During 2011, the company had the following transactions related to receivables:

1. Sales on account, $1,700,000
2. Sales returns and allowances, $250,000
3. Collections of accounts receivable, $1,500,000
4. Write offs of accounts considered uncollectible, $55,000
5. Recovery of accounts previously written off as uncollectible, $6,750

Instructions

(a) Prepare the summary journal entries to record each of these five transactions.
(b) Enter the January 1, 2011, balances in the Accounts Receivable and Allowance for Doubtful Accounts general ledger accounts, post the entries to the two accounts, and determine the balances.
(c) Prepare the journal entry to record bad debts expense for 2011. Uncollectible accounts are estimated at 7% of accounts receivable.
(d) Calculate the net realizable value of accounts receivable at December 31, 2011.
(e) Show the balance sheet presentation of the receivables as at December 31, 2011.

Taking It Further For several years, Bordeaux Co. has estimated uncollectible accounts at 7% of accounts receivable. Discuss whether or not the company should continue to do this at December 31, 2011.

P8–2A At the beginning of the current period, Huang Co. had a balance of $100,000 in Accounts Receivable and a $7,000 credit balance in Allowance for Doubtful Accounts. In the period, it had net credit sales of $400,000 and collections of $361,500. It wrote off accounts receivable of $10,500 as uncollectible. However, a $1,750 account written off as uncollectible was recovered before the end of the current period. Based on an aging schedule, uncollectible accounts are estimated to be $8,000 at the end of the period.

Record accounts receivable and bad debts transactions; show financial statement presentation.
(SO 1, 2) AP

Instructions

(a) Record sales and collections in the period.
(b) Record the write off of uncollectible accounts in the period.
(c) Record the recovery of the account written off as uncollectible in the period.
(d) Record the bad debts expense adjusting entry for the period.
(e) Show the balance sheet presentation of the receivables at the end of the period.
(f) What is the amount of bad debts expense on the income statement for the period?
(g) Now assume that Huang Co. uses the percentage of sales approach instead of the percentage of receivables approach to estimate uncollectible accounts. Repeat (d) through (f) assuming Huang estimates 2.25% of net credit sales will become uncollectible.

Taking It Further Should Huang Co. use the percentage of receivables approach or the percentage of sales approach to estimating uncollectible accounts? Explain.

P8–3A Information on Hohenberger Company for 2011 follows:

Total credit sales	$1,000,000
Accounts receivable at December 31	400,000
Uncollectible accounts written off	17,500
Uncollectible accounts later recovered (after write off but before year end)	2,500

Calculate bad debt amounts and answer questions.
(SO 2) AP

Instructions

(a) What amount of bad debts expense will Hohenberger Company report if it does not use the allowance method?

(b) Assume that Hohenberger Company decides to estimate its uncollectible accounts using the allowance method and an aging schedule. Uncollectible accounts are estimated to be $24,000. What amount of bad debts expense will Hohenberger Company record if Allowance for Doubtful Accounts had an opening balance of $20,000 on January 1, 2011?

(c) Assume that Hohenberger Company decides to estimate its uncollectible accounts using the allowance method and estimates its bad debts expense at 2.25% of credit sales. What amount of bad debts expense will Hohenberger Company record if Allowance for Doubtful Accounts had an opening balance of $20,000 on January 1, 2011?

(d) Assume the same facts as in (b) except that the Allowance for Doubtful Accounts had a $12,000 balance on January 1, 2011. What amount of bad debts expense will Hohenberger record?

(e) How does the amount of accounts written off during the period affect the amount of bad debts expense recorded at the end of the period if a company is using the allowance method?

(f) How does the collection of an account that had previously been written off affect the net realizable value of accounts receivable?

Taking It Further What are the advantages of using the allowance method of accounting for bad debts?

Prepare aging schedule and record bad debts and explain method.
(SO 2) AP

P8–4A NewWest uses the allowance method to estimate uncollectible accounts receivable. The company produced the following information from aging its accounts receivable at year end:

| | Total | Number of Days Outstanding | | | |
		0–30	31–60	61–90	91–120
Accounts receivable	$520,000	$240,000	$120,000	$100,000	$60,000
Estimated % uncollectible		1.5%	7%	10%	30%
Estimated uncollectible accounts					

The unadjusted balance in Allowance for Doubtful Accounts is a credit of $14,000.

Instructions

(a) Complete the aging schedule and calculate the total estimated uncollectible accounts.

(b) Record the bad debts adjusting entry using the information determined in (a).

(c) In the following year, $21,000 of the outstanding accounts receivable is determined to be uncollectible. Record the write off of the uncollectible accounts.

(d) The company collects $3,900 of the $21,000 of accounts that were determined to be uncollectible in (c). The company also expects to collect an additional $500. Record the journal entry (or entries) to restore the accounts receivable and the cash collected. Collection of the $500 is expected in the near future.

(e) Explain how using the allowance method matches expenses with revenues.

Taking It Further What are the advantages and disadvantages to the company of using an aging schedule to estimate uncollectible accounts, as compared with estimating uncollectible accounts as 10% of total accounts receivable?

Prepare aging schedule and record bad debts.
(SO 2) AP

P8–5A An aging analysis of Hagiwara Company's accounts receivable at December 31, 2010 and 2011, showed the following:

| Number of Days Outstanding | Estimated % Uncollectible | December 31 | |
		2011	2010
0–30 days	2.5%	$115,000	$145,000
31–60 days	6.0%	35,000	63,000
61–90 days	18.0%	45,000	38,000
Over 90 days	35.0%	80,000	24,000
Total		$275,000	$270,000

Additional information:

1. At December 31, 2010, the unadjusted balance in Allowance for Doubtful Accounts was a credit of $4,800.
2. In 2011, $26,500 of accounts were written off as uncollectible and $1,500 of accounts previously written off were recovered.

Instructions

(a) Prepare an aging schedule to calculate the estimated uncollectible accounts at December 31, 2010, and at December 31, 2011.
(b) Record the following transactions:

    1. The adjusting entry on December 31, 2010
    2. The write off of uncollectible accounts in 2011
    3. The collection of accounts previously written off
    4. The adjusting entry on December 31, 2011

(c) Calculate the net realizable value of Hagiwara's accounts receivable at December 31, 2010, and December 31, 2011.

Taking It Further   What are the implications of the changes in the age of the receivables from 2010 to 2011?

P8–6A   Sucha Company operates in an industry that has a high rate of bad debts. On August 31, 2011, before any year-end adjustments, the balance in Sucha's Accounts Receivable account was $312,500 and Allowance for Doubtful Accounts had a debit balance of $7,500. The credit manager closely watches the collection of the accounts receivable and has prepared the following information at August 31, 2011:

Calculate allowance for doubtful accounts and bad debts; show financial statement presentation.
(SO 2) AP

Days Account Outstanding	Amount	Probability of Collection
Less than 16 days	$177,500	97%
Between 16 and 30 days	57,500	92%
Between 31 and 45 days	40,000	80%
Between 46 and 60 days	20,000	75%
Between 61 and 75 days	10,000	40%
Over 75 days	7,500	10%

Instructions

(a) Using the aging method of estimating the percentage of receivables that are uncollectible, what is the appropriate balance for Allowance for Doubtful Accounts at August 31, 2011?
(b) Show how accounts receivable will be presented on the August 31, 2011, balance sheet.
(c) What is the bad debt expense that will be reported in the income statement for the year?

Taking It Further   On December 15, 2011, Sucha writes off all of the $7,500 amount that had been over 75 days old at August 31, 2011. Should the company go back and adjust the Allowance for Doubtful Accounts and the Bad Debt Expense reported on the August 31, 2011, financial statements? Explain.

P8–7A   Kadakus and Company reported the following information in its general ledger at August 31:

Determine missing amounts.
(SO 2) AN

	Accounts Receivable				Sales	
Beg. bal.	854,000	(b)				(f)
	(a)	(c)				
	4,200	(d)				
End. bal.	927,500					

	Allowance for Doubtful Accounts			Bad Debts Expense	
		Beg. bal.	73,300	52,500	
(c)		(e)			
		(b)			
		End. bal.	79,600		

All sales were made on account. Bad debts expense was estimated as 1% of sales.

Instructions

Determine the missing amounts in Kadakus and Company's accounts. State what each of these amounts represents. You will not be able to determine the missing items in alphabetical order. (To solve this problem, it might help if you reconstruct the journal entries.)

Taking It Further   Explain the differences between bad debt expense and the allowance for doubtful accounts.

P8–8A   Bassano Company uses the percentage of sales approach to record bad debts expense for its monthly financial statements and the percentage of receivables approach for its year-end financial statements. Bassano Company has an October 31 fiscal year end, closes temporary accounts annually, and uses a perpetual inventory system.

Identify impact of accounts receivable and bad debts transactions; determine statement presentation.
(SO 1, 2, 4) AP

On August 31, 2011, after completing its month-end adjustments, it had accounts receivable of $74,500, a credit balance of $2,980 in Allowance for Doubtful Accounts, and bad debts expense of $9,860. In September and October, the following occurred:

September

1. Sold $56,300 of merchandise on account; the cost of the merchandise was $25,335.
2. A total of $900 of the merchandise sold on account was returned. These customers were issued credit memos. The cost of the merchandise was $400 and it was returned to inventory.
3. Collected $59,200 cash on account from customers.
4. Interest charges of $745 were charged to outstanding accounts receivable.
5. As part of the month-end adjusting entries, recorded bad debts expense of 2% of net credit sales for the month.

October

1. Credit sales in the month were $63,900; the cost of the merchandise was $28,700.
2. Received $350 cash from a customer whose account had been written off in July.
3. Collected $58,500 cash, in addition to the cash collected in (2) above, from customers on account.
4. Wrote off $7,500 of accounts receivable as uncollectible.
5. Interest charges of $710 were charged to outstanding accounts receivable.
6. Recorded the year-end adjustment for bad debts. Uncollectible accounts were estimated to be 4% of accounts receivable.

Instructions

(a) For each of these transactions, indicate if the transaction has increased (+) or decreased (–) Cash, Accounts Receivable, Allowance for Doubtful Accounts, Inventory, Total Assets, and Owner's Equity and by how much. If the item is not changed, write NE to indicate there is no effect. Use the following format, in which the first one has been done for you as an example.

Transaction	Cash	Accounts Receivable	Allowance for Doubtful Accounts	Inventory	Total Assets	Owner's Equity
September:						
1.	NE	+ $56,300	NE	– $25,335	+ $30,965	+ $30,965

(b) Show how accounts receivable will appear on the October 31, 2011, balance sheet.
(c) What amount will be reported as bad debts expense on the income statement for the year ended October 31, 2011?

Taking It Further   Discuss the appropriateness of Bassano using the percentage of sales approach to estimating uncollectible accounts for its monthly financial statements and the percentage of receivables approach for its year-end financial statements. The monthly financial statements are used by Bassano's management and are not distributed to anyone outside of the company.

P8–9A Bleumortier Company has a March 31 fiscal year end and adjusts accounts annually. Selected transactions in the year included the following:

Record receivables transactions.
(SO 1, 3) AP

Jan. 2	Sold $18,000 of merchandise to Brooks Company, terms n/30. The cost of the goods sold was $12,000. Bleumortier uses the perpetual inventory system.
Feb. 1	Accepted an $18,000, four-month, 6% promissory note from Brooks Company for the balance due. (See January 2 transaction.) Interest is payable at maturity.
15	Sold $13,400 of merchandise costing $8,800 to Gage Company and accepted Gage's two-month, 6% note in payment. Interest is payable at maturity.
26	Sold $8,000 of merchandise to Mathias Co., terms n/30. The cost of the merchandise sold was $5,400.
Mar. 31	Accepted a $8,000, two-month, 7% note from Mathias Co. for its balance due. Interest is payable at maturity. (See February 26 transaction.)
31	Accrued interest at year end.
Apr. 15	Collected the Gage note in full. (See February 15 transaction.)
May 31	Mathias Co. dishonours its note of March 31. It is expected that Mathias will eventually pay the amount owed.
June 1	Collected Brooks Company note in full. (See February 1 transaction.)
July 13	Sold $5,000 merchandise costing $3,300 to Tritt Inc. and accepted Tritt's $5,000, three-month, 7% note for the amount due, with interest payable at maturity.
Oct. 13	The Tritt Inc. note was dishonoured. (See July 13 transaction.) Tritt Inc. is bankrupt and there is no hope of future settlement.

Instructions

Record the above transactions. (Round calculations to the nearest dollar.)

Taking It Further What are the advantages and disadvantages of Bleumortier Company accepting notes receivable from its customers?

P8–10A Tardif Company adjusts its books monthly. On September 30, 2011, notes receivable include the following:

Record note receivable transactions; show balance sheet presentation.
(SO 1, 3, 4) AP

Issue Date	Maker	Principal	Interest	Term
Aug. 1, 2010	RJF Inc.	$19,000	4.5%	2.5 years
Mar. 31, 2011	RES Co.	17,000	5.0%	7 months
May 31, 2011	IMG Ltd.	17,500	5.5%	18 months
Aug. 31, 2011	DRA Co.	6,000	8.5%	2 months
Sept. 30, 2011	MGH Corp.	20,500	6.0%	16 months

Interest is payable on the first day of each month for notes with terms of one year or longer. Interest is payable at maturity for notes with terms less than one year. In October, the following transactions were completed:

Oct. 1	Received payment of the interest due from RJF Inc.
1	Received payment of the interest due from IMG Ltd.
31	Received notice that the DRA note had been dishonoured. (Assume that DRA is expected to pay in the future.)
31	Collected the amount owing from RES Co.

Instructions

(a) Calculate the balance in the Interest Receivable and Notes Receivable accounts at September 30, 2011.

(b) Record the October transactions and the October 31 adjusting entry for accrued interest receivable.

(c) Enter the balances at October 1 in the receivables accounts, and post the entries to the receivables accounts.

(d) Show the balance sheet presentation of the interest and notes receivables accounts at October 31.

(e) How would the journal entry on October 31 be different if DRA were not expected to pay in the future?

Taking It Further   The interest rate for the DRA note is higher than the other notes. Why might that have been the case?

Prepare assets section of balance sheet; calculate and interpret ratios.
(SO 4) AN

P8–11A   Tocksfor Company's general ledger included the following selected accounts (in thousands) at September 30, 2011:

Accounts payable	$1,077.3
Accounts receivable	590.4
Accumulated depreciation—equipment	858.7
Allowance for doubtful accounts	35.4
Bad debts expense	91.3
Cash	395.6
Cost of goods sold	660.4
Equipment	1,732.8
Interest revenue	19.7
Merchandise inventory	630.9
Notes receivable—due May 15, 2012	96.0
Notes receivable—due in 2015	191.1
Prepaid expenses and deposits	20.1
Sales	4,565.5
Sales discounts	31.3
Short-term investments	194.9
Supplies	21.7
Unearned sales revenue	56.3

Additional information:

1. On September 30, 2010, Accounts Receivable was $611.1 thousand and the Allowance for Doubtful Accounts was $36.6 thousand.
2. The receivables turnover was 8.3 the previous year.

Instructions

(a) Prepare the assets section of the balance sheet.
(b) Calculate the receivables turnover and average collection period. Compare these results with the previous year's results and comment on any trends.

Taking It Further   What other information should Tocksfor consider when analyzing its receivables turnover and average collection period?

Comment on approach; calculate and interpret ratios.
(SO 4) AN

P8–12A   Presented here is selected financial information (in millions) from the 2008 financial statements of Rogers Communications Inc. and Shaw Communications Inc.:

	Rogers	Shaw
Sales	$11,335	$3,104.9
Allowance for doubtful accounts, beginning of year	151	15.2
Allowance for doubtful accounts, end of year	163	15.4
Accounts receivable balance (net), beginning of year	1,245	155.5
Accounts receivable balance (net), end of year	1,403	188.1

Instructions

(a) In Shaw's notes to its financial statements, it states that the company considers factors such as the number of days the subscriber account is past due, the company's past collection history, and changes in business circumstances when estimating its bad debts. Is Shaw using the percentage of receivables or sales approach to determining uncollectible accounts? Explain.

(b) Calculate the receivables turnover and average collection period for both companies. Comment on the difference in their collection experiences.

Taking It Further Shaw has an August 31 fiscal year end; Rogers has a December 31 fiscal year end. Does this affect our ability to compare the receivables turnover and average collection period between the two companies? Explain.

P8–13A The following ratios are available for Satellite Mechanical:

Evaluate liquidity.
(SO 4) AN

	2011	2010	2009
Current ratio	2.0 to 1	1.6 to 1	1.4 to 1
Acid-test ratio	1.1 to 1	0.8 to 1	0.7 to 1
Receivables turnover	7.3 times	10.1 times	10.3 times
Inventory turnover	6.3 times	6.1 times	6.4 times

Instructions

(a) Calculate the collection period, days sales in inventory, and operating cycle in days for each year.

(b) Has Satellite Mechanical's liquidity improved or weakened over the three-year period? Explain.

Taking It Further At the beginning of 2011, the owner of Satellite Mechanical decided to eliminate sales discounts because she thought it was costing the company too much money. The terms of credit sales were changed from 2/10, n/30 to n/30. Evaluate this decision.

Problems: Set B

P8–1B At December 31, 2010, Underwood Imports reported the following information on its balance sheet:

Record accounts receivable and bad debts transactions; show balance sheet presentation.
(SO 1, 2) AP

Accounts receivable	$1,990,000
Less: Allowance for doubtful accounts	119,400

During 2011, the company had the following transactions related to receivables:

1. Sales on account, $5,200,000
2. Sales returns and allowances, $80,000
3. Collections of accounts receivable, $5,400,000
4. Interest added to overdue accounts, $400,000
5. Write offs of accounts deemed uncollectible, $130,000
6. Recovery of bad debts previously written off as uncollectible, $50,400

Instructions

(a) Prepare the summary journal entries to record each of these six transactions.

(b) Enter the January 1, 2011, balances in the Accounts Receivable and Allowance for Doubtful Accounts general ledger accounts, post the entries to the two accounts, and determine the balances.

(c) Record bad debts expense for 2011. Uncollectible accounts are estimated at 6% of accounts receivable.

(d) Calculate the net realizable value of accounts receivable at December 31, 2011.

(e) Show the balance sheet presentation of accounts receivable at December 31, 2011.

Taking It Further For several years, Underwood Imports has estimated uncollectible accounts at 6% of accounts receivable. Discuss whether or not the company should continue to do this at December 31, 2011.

Record accounts receivable
and bad debts transactions;
show financial statement
presentation.
(SO 1, 2) AP

P8–2B At the beginning of the current period, Fassi Co. had a balance of $800,000 in Accounts Receivable and a $44,000 credit balance in Allowance for Doubtful Accounts. In the period, it had net credit sales of $1,900,000 and collections of $2,042,000. It wrote off accounts receivable of $58,000. However, a $4,000 account written off as uncollectible was recovered before the end of the current period. Based on an aging schedule, uncollectible accounts are estimated to be $36,000 at the end of the period.

Instructions

(a) Record sales and collections in the period.
(b) Record the write off of uncollectible accounts in the period.
(c) Record the recovery of the uncollectible account in the period.
(d) Record the bad debts expense adjusting entry for the period.
(e) Show the balance sheet presentation of the accounts receivable at the end of the period.
(f) What is the bad debts expense on the income statement for the period?
(g) Now assume that Fassi Co. uses the percentage of sales approach instead of the percentage of receivables approach to estimate uncollectible accounts. Repeat (d) through (f) assuming Fassi estimates 1.25% of the credit sales will become uncollectible.

Taking It Further Should Fassi Co. use the percentage of receivables approach or the percentage of sales approach to estimating uncollectible accounts? Explain.

Calculate bad debt amounts
and answer questions.
(SO 2) AP

P8–3B Information for Tisipai Company in 2011 follows:

Total net credit sales	$3,300,000
Accounts receivable at December 31	1,250,000
Accounts receivable written off	48,000
Accounts receivable later recovered	8,000

Instructions

(a) What amount will Tisipai Company report for bad debts expense if it does not use the allowance method of accounting for uncollectible accounts?
(b) Assume instead that Tisipai Company decides to use the allowance method and estimates its uncollectible accounts to be $52,000 based on an aging schedule. What amount of bad debts expense will Tisipai record if Allowance for Doubtful Accounts had an opening balance of $30,000 on January 1, 2011?
(c) Assume instead that Tisipai Company decides to estimate its uncollectible accounts using 1.5% of net credit sales. What amount of bad debts expense will Tisipai record if Allowance for Doubtful Accounts had an opening balance of $30,000 on January 1, 2011?
(d) Assume the same facts as in (b), except that there is a $2,250 credit balance in Allowance for Doubtful Accounts before recording the adjustment. What amount of bad debts expense will the company record?
(e) How does the write off of an uncollectible account affect the net realizable value of accounts receivable?
(f) Why use an Allowance for Doubtful Accounts instead of directly reducing Accounts Receivable when recording bad debts expense?

Taking It Further Why should companies use the allowance method of accounting for uncollectible accounts?

Prepare aging schedule
and record bad debts
and comment.
(SO 2) AP

P8–4B Imagine Co. uses the allowance method to estimate uncollectible accounts receivable. The computer produced the following aging of the accounts receivable at year end:

		Number of Days Outstanding			
	Total	0–30	31–60	61–90	91–120
Accounts receivable	$192,500	$110,000	$50,000	$20,000	$12,500
Estimated % uncollectible		1.5%	5%	15%	20%
Estimated uncollectible accounts					

The unadjusted balance in Allowance for Doubtful Accounts is a debit of $5,000.

Instructions

(a) Complete the aging schedule and calculate the total estimated uncollectible accounts from the above information.

(b) Record the bad debts adjusting entry using the above information.

(c) In the following year, $11,900 of the outstanding accounts receivable is determined to be uncollectible. Record the write off of the uncollectible accounts.

(d) The company collects $2,100 of the $11,900 of accounts receivable that were determined to be uncollectible in (c). No further amounts are expected to be collected. Prepare the journal entry (or entries) to record the recovery of this amount.

(e) Comment on how your answers to parts (a) to (d) would change if Imagine Co. used a percentage of total accounts receivable of 8% instead of aging the accounts receivable.

Taking It Further   What are the advantages for the company of aging the accounts receivable rather than applying a percentage to total accounts receivable?

P8–5B   An aging analysis of Hake Company's accounts receivable at December 31, 2010 and 2011, showed the following:

Prepare aging schedule and record bad debts.
(SO 2) AP

Number of Days Outstanding	Estimated % Uncollectible	December 31 2011	December 31 2010
0–30 days	3%	$190,000	$220,000
31–60 days	6%	40,000	105,000
61–90 days	12%	65,000	40,000
Over 90 days	24%	75,000	25,000
Total		$370,000	$390,000

Additional information:

1. At December 31, 2010, the unadjusted balance in Allowance for Doubtful Accounts was a debit of $4,200.

2. In 2011, $25,500 of accounts were written off as uncollectible and $2,500 of accounts previously written off were recovered.

Instructions

(a) Prepare an aging schedule to calculate the estimated uncollectible accounts at December 31, 2010, and at December 31, 2011.

(b) Record the following transactions:

1. The adjusting entry on December 31, 2010
2. The write off of uncollectible accounts in 2011
3. The collection of accounts previously written off
4. The adjusting entry on December 31, 2011

(c) Calculate the net realizable value of Hake's accounts receivable at December 31, 2010, and December 31, 2011.

Taking It Further   What are the implications of the changes in the age of accounts receivable from 2010 to 2011?

Calculate allowance for doubtful accounts and bad debts; show financial statement presentation.
(SO 2) AP

P8–6B Paderewski Company operates in an industry that has a high rate of bad debts. On October 31, 2011, before any year-end adjustments, the balance in Paderewski's Accounts Receivable account was $625,000 and Allowance for Doubtful Accounts had a credit balance of $35,000. The credit manager closely watches the collection of the accounts receivable and has prepared the following information at October 31, 2011:

Days Account Outstanding	Amount	Probability of Collection
Less than 16 days	$355,000	97%
Between 16 and 30 days	115,000	92%
Between 31 and 45 days	80,000	80%
Between 46 and 60 days	40,000	75%
Between 61 and 75 days	20,000	40%
Over 75 days	15,000	10%

Instructions

(a) Using the aging method of estimating the percentage of receivables that are uncollectible, what is the appropriate balance for Allowance for Doubtful Accounts at October 31, 2011?

(b) Show how accounts receivable will be presented on the October 31, 2011, balance sheet.

(c) What is the bad debt expense that will be reported in the income statement for the year?

Taking It Further On December 15, 2011, Paderewski collects the $15,000 amount that had been over 75 days old at October 31, 2011. Should the company go back and adjust the Allowance for Doubtful Accounts and the Bad Debt Expense reported on the October 31, 2011, financial statements? Explain.

Determine missing amounts.
(SO 2) AN

P8–7B Armadillo and Company reported the following information in its general ledger at July 31:

Accounts Receivable			Sales		
Beg. bal. 320,000		2,442,450			(a)
(a)		(d)			
(b)		2,250			
End. bal. (c)					

Allowance for Doubtful Accounts			Bad Debts Expense	
	Beg. bal.	(e)	(f)	
25,450		(b)		
		(f)		
	End. bal. 30,400			

All sales were made on account. At the beginning of the year, uncollectible accounts were estimated to be 7% of accounts receivable. At the end of the year, uncollectible accounts were estimated to be 8% of accounts receivable.

Instructions

Determine the missing amounts in Armadillo and Company's accounts. State what each of these amounts represents. You will not be able to determine the missing items in alphabetical order. (To solve this problem, it might help if you reconstruct the journal entries.)

Taking It Further Explain the difference between bad debt expense and the allowance for doubtful accounts.

Identify impact of accounts receivable and bad debts transactions; determine statement presentation.
(SO 1, 2, 4) AP

P8–8B Assiniboia Co. uses the percentage of sales approach to record bad debts expense for its monthly financial statements and the percentage of receivables approach for its year-end financial statements. Assiniboia Co. has a May 31 fiscal year end, closes temporary accounts annually, and uses the perpetual inventory system.

On March 31, 2011, after completing its month-end adjustments, it had accounts receivable of $89,200, a credit balance of $4,930 in Allowance for Doubtful Accounts, and a debit balance in Bad Debts Expense of $19,880. In April and May, the following occurred:

April

1. Sold $64,600 of merchandise on credit. The cost of the merchandise was $35,530.
2. Accepted $800 of returns on the merchandise sold on credit. These customers were issued credit memos. The merchandise had a cost of $440 and was discarded because it was damaged.
3. Collected $69,200 cash on account from customers.
4. Interest charges of $1,645 were charged to outstanding accounts receivable.
5. As part of the month-end adjusting entries, recorded bad debts expense of 3% of net credit sales for the month.

May

1. Credit sales were $76,600. The cost of the merchandise was $42,130.
2. Received $450 cash from a customer whose account had been written off in March.
3. Collected $78,500 cash, in addition to the cash collected in (2) above, from customers on account.
4. Wrote off $9,580 of accounts receivable as uncollectible.
5. Interest charges of $1,570 were charged to outstanding accounts receivable.
6. Recorded the year-end adjustment for bad debts. Uncollectible accounts were estimated to be 6% of accounts receivable.

Instructions

(a) For each of these transactions, indicate if the transaction has increased (+) or decreased (−) Cash, Accounts Receivable, Allowance for Doubtful Accounts, Inventory, Total Assets, and Owner's Equity and by how much. If the item is not changed, write NE to indicate there is no effect. Use the following format, in which the first one has been done for you as an example.

Transaction	Cash	Accounts Receivable	Allowance for Doubtful Accounts	Inventory	Total Assets	Owner's Equity
April:						
1.	NE	+ $64,600	NE	− $35,530	+ $29,070	+ $29,070

(b) Show how accounts receivable will appear on the May 31, 2011, balance sheet.

(c) What amount will be reported as bad debts expense on the income statement for the year ended May 31, 2011?

Taking It Further   Discuss the appropriateness of Assiniboia using the percentage of sales approach to estimating uncollectible accounts for its monthly financial statements and the percentage of receivables approach for its year-end financial statements. The monthly financial statements are used by Assiniboia's management and are not distributed to anyone outside of the company.

P8–9B   On January 1, 2010, Vu Co. had an $18,000, five-month, 5% notes receivable from Annabelle Company dated October 31, 2009. Interest receivable of $150 was accrued on the note on December 31, 2009. Vu Co. has a December 31 fiscal year end and adjusts its accounts annually. In 2010, the following selected transactions occurred:

Record receivables transactions.
(SO 1, 2, 3) AP

Jan. 2   Sold $15,000 of merchandise costing $8,200 to George Company, terms 2/10, n/30. Vu Co. uses the perpetual inventory system.

Feb. 1   Accepted George Company's $15,000, three-month, 6% note for the balance due. (See January 2 transaction.) Interest is due at maturity.

Mar. 31   Received payment in full from Annabelle Company for the amount due.

May 1   Collected George Company note in full. (See February 1 transaction.)

25   Accepted Avery Inc.'s $9,000, two-month, 6% note in settlement of a past-due balance on account. Interest is payable monthly.

June 25   Received one month's interest from Avery Inc. on its note. (See May 25 transaction.)

July 25   The Avery Inc. note was dishonoured. (See May 25 transaction.) Avery Inc. is bankrupt and future payment is not expected.

Oct. 1   Loaned Emily Haworth, an employee, $6,000 on a four-month, 8% note. Interest is due at maturity.

Nov. 30   Gave MRC Corp a $5,000 cash loan and accepted MRC's four-month, 4.5% note.

Dec. 1   Emily Haworth left for a job at another company. Vu Co. asked her to immediately pay the note receivable. (See October 1 transaction.) Emily told the company that she does not have the money to do so.

31   Accrued interest is recorded on any outstanding notes at year end.

Instructions

Record the above transactions.

Taking It Further   Do you think the note receivable from Emily Haworth should be written off as at the year end? If not, do you think interest should be accrued on this note receivable at year end?

Record note receivable transactions; show balance sheet presentation.
(SO 3, 4) AP

P8–10B   Ouellette Co. adjusts its books monthly. On June 30, 2011, notes receivable include the following:

Issue Date	Maker	Principal	Term	Interest
May 1, 2010	ALD Inc.	$ 6,000	3 years	4.0%
October 31, 2010	KAB Ltd.	10,000	15 months	5.0%
January 31, 2011	BFF Co.	15,000	6 months	5.5%
May 31, 2011	DNR Co.	4,800	2 months	8.75%
June 30, 2011	MJH Corp.	9,000	8 months	5.0%

Interest is payable on the first day of each month for notes with terms of one year or longer. Interest is payable at maturity for notes with terms less than one year. In July, the following transactions were completed:

July 1   Received payment of the interest due from ALD Inc.

2   Received payment of the interest due from KAB Ltd.

31   Collected the full amount on the BFF Co. note.

31   Received notice that the DNR Co. note has been dishonoured. Assume that DNR Co. is expected to pay in the future.

Instructions

(a) Calculate the balance in the Interest Receivable and Notes Receivable accounts at June 30, 2011.

(b) Record the July transactions and the July 31 adjusting entry for accrued interest receivable.

(c) Enter the balances at July 1 in the receivables accounts. Post the entries to the receivables accounts.

(d) Show the balance sheet presentation of the receivables accounts at July 31, 2011.

(e) How would the journal entry on July 31 be different if DNR Co. were not expected to pay in the future?

Taking It Further   The interest rate for the DNR note is higher than the other notes. Why might that be the case?

Prepare assets section of balance sheet; calculate and interpret ratios.
(SO 4) AN

P8–11B   Norlandia Saga Company's general ledger included the following selected accounts (in thousands) at November 30, 2011:

Accounts payable	$ 546.2
Accounts receivable	311.4
Accumulated depreciation—equipment	471.7
Allowance for doubtful accounts	14.8
Bad debts expense	43.6
Cash	417.1
Cost of goods sold	353.0
Equipment	924.2

Interest revenue	10.7
Merchandise inventory	336.5
Notes receivable—due in 2012	51.2
Notes receivable—due in 2015	101.9
Prepaid expenses and deposits	19.3
Sales	2,823.8
Sales discounts	18.5
Short-term investments	224.6
Supplies	15.9
Unearned sales revenue	40.2

Additional information:

1. On November 30, 2010, Accounts Receivable was $271.7 thousand and the Allowance for Doubtful Accounts was $13.6 thousand.
2. The receivables turnover was 9.1 the previous year.

Instructions

(a) Prepare the assets section of the balance sheet.
(b) Calculate the receivables turnover and average collection period. Compare these results with the previous year's results and comment on any trends.

Taking It Further What other information should Norlandia Saga consider when analyzing its receivables turnover and average collection period?

P8–12B Presented here is selected financial information from the 2008 financial statements of Nike (in U.S. millions) and Adidas (in Euro millions):

Calculate and interpret ratios. (SO 4) AN

	Nike	Adidas
Sales	$18,627.0	€10,794
Allowance for doubtful accounts, Jan. 1	71.5	111
Allowance for doubtful accounts, Dec. 31	78.4	119
Accounts receivable balance (net), Jan. 1	2,494.7	1,459
Accounts receivable balance (net), Dec. 31	2,795.3	1,624

Instructions

Calculate the receivables turnover and average collection period for both companies and compare the two companies. Comment on the difference in the two companies' collection experiences.

Taking It Further Adidas' financial statements are prepared using Euros, while Nike uses U.S. dollars. How does this affect our ability to compare sales between the two companies? Receivables turnover and collection period?

P8–13B The following ratios are available for Western Roofing:

Evaluate liquidity. (SO 4) AN

	2011	2010	2009
Current ratio	1.6 to 1	2.0 to 1	1.9 to 1
Acid-test ratio	0.8 to 1	1.3 to 1	1.2 to 1
Receivables turnover	10.6 times	8.9 times	9.0 times
Inventory turnover	7.3 times	7.6 times	7.5 times

Instructions

(a) Calculate the collection period, days sales in inventory, and operating cycle for each year.
(b) Has Western Roofing's liquidity improved or weakened over the three-year period? Explain.

Taking It Further At the beginning of 2011, the owner of Western Roofing decided to start offering customers a sales discount for early payment. The terms of credit sales were changed from n/30 to 2/10, n/30. Evaluate this decision.

Continuing Cookie Chronicle

(*Note:* This is a continuation of the Cookie Chronicle from Chapters 1 through 7.)

Natalie has been approached by one of her friends, Curtis Lesperance. Curtis runs a coffee shop where he sells specialty coffees, and prepares and sells muffins and cookies. He is very anxious to buy one of Natalie's fine European mixers because he would then be able to prepare larger batches of muffins and cookies. Curtis, however, cannot afford to pay for the mixer for at least 30 days. He has asked Natalie if she would be willing to sell him the mixer on credit.

Natalie comes to you for advice and asks the following questions:

1. Curtis has given me a set of his most recent financial statements. What calculations should I do with the data from these statements and what questions should I ask him after I have analyzed the statements? How will this information help me decide if I should extend credit to Curtis?
2. Is there another alternative than extending credit to Curtis for 30 days?
3. If, instead of extending credit to Curtis for 30 days, I have Curtis sign a promissory note and he is unable to pay at the end of the agreement term, will having that signed promissory note really make any difference?
4. I am thinking seriously about being able to have my customers use credit cards. What are some of the advantages and disadvantages of letting my customers pay by credit card? Are there differences in the types of credit cards that my customers can use?

The following transactions occur in June and July 2011:

June 1   After much thought, Natalie sells a mixer to Curtis for $1,050 (the cost of the mixer is $551). Curtis signs a two-month, 8.5% promissory note. Curtis can repay the note at any time before the due date with interest accruing to the date of payment.

   30   Curtis calls Natalie. He expects to pay the amount outstanding in the next week or so.

July 15   Natalie receives a cheque from Curtis in payment of his balance owing plus interest that has accrued.

Instructions

(a) Answer Natalie's questions.
(b) Prepare journal entries for the transactions that occurred in June and July.

BROADENING YOUR PERSPECTIVE

Financial Reporting and Analysis

Financial Reporting Problem

BYP8–1   The receivables turnover, collection period, and operating cycle for The Forzani Group Ltd. were calculated in this chapter, based on the company's financial statements for the 2009 fiscal year. These consolidated financial statements are presented in Appendix A.

Instructions

(a) Calculate Forzani's receivables turnover, collection period, and operating cycle for the 2008 fiscal year. At the end of the company's 2007 fiscal year, it reported accounts receivable of $65,543 thousand and inventory of $302,207 thousand. You will have to use the net realizable value reported for accounts receivable for 2007 and 2008 because the company did not disclose the allowance amount prior to 2009 (see note 16 (c) to the 2009 financial statements).

(b) Comment on any significant differences you observe between the ratios for 2009 (as calculated in the chapter) and 2008 (as calculated by you above).

(c) In Note 1 to the 2009 financial statements, Forzani describes itself as "Canada's largest retailer of sporting goods." Large retailers sell goods to the general public and would not normally allow you to negotiate credit terms with them when you buy a pair of running shoes. How do you think their receivables arise? Would they be from Visa or MasterCard sales? Could they be from Forzani's own credit card (if it issues its own)? How can you find this out? Which types of sales described in note 2 (h) and note 16 (c) are most likely to be transacted "on account"?

(d) Note 16 (c) to the 2009 financial statements discusses credit risks associated with receivables. Why do you think they include a breakdown of the aging of overdue accounts and the balance of the allowance for doubtful accounts?

(e) A substantial portion of receivables is shown to be overdue, by even more than 60 days. This seems inconsistent with the textbook's calculation of the average collection period as much less than 60 days. The figures provided by management on page 46 of the "Management's Discussion and Analysis" section in the 2009 Annual Report show an average collection period of 121 days—much more than 60 days. The difference appears to be due to the text using all sales and not just "credit" sales (sales "on account"). Given management's figure for average receivables days outstanding for 2009, what percentage of "wholesale" revenues reported in the statement of operations appear to have been transacted "on account"?

Interpreting Financial Statements

BYP8–2 Suncor Energy Inc. reported the following information (in millions) in its financial statements for the fiscal years 2006 through 2008:

	2008	2007	2006
Operating revenues (assume all credit)	$18,336	$15,020	$13,798
Cash and cash equivalents	660	569	521
Accounts receivable (gross)	1,584	1,441	1,054
Allowance for doubtful accounts	4	3	4
Inventories	909	1012	589
Other current assets	88	141	142
Total current liabilities	3,529	3,156	2,158

Additional detail about Suncor's receivables includes the following:

The company had a securitization program in place to sell to a third party, on a revolving, fully serviced, and limited recourse basis, up to $170 million of accounts receivable having a maturity of 45 days or less. As at December 31, 2008, no outstanding accounts receivable had been sold under the program and the program had been allowed to expire.

Industry averages are as follows: current ratio, 1.3:1; acid-test ratio, 0.8:1; receivables turnover, 10.6 times; and average collection period, 34 days.

Instructions

(a) Calculate the current ratios, acid-test ratios, receivables turnover ratios, and average collection periods for fiscal 2008 and 2007. Comment on Suncor's liquidity for each of the years and compare it with that of the industry.

(b) In 2008, Suncor's dollar amount of its allowance for doubtful accounts was the same as it was in 2006. Comment on the relevance of this as a percentage of accounts receivable.

(c) What are the advantages of having a securitization program to sell accounts receivable? Why might Suncor have allowed its securitization program to expire?

Critical Thinking

Collaborative Learning Activity

Working in Groups

Note to instructor: Additional instructions and material for this group activity can be found on the Instructor Resource Site.

BYP8–3   In this group activity, you will work in pairs to review the following two approaches to estimate bad debts:

1. Percentage of sales
2. Percentage of receivables

Instructions

(a) In your pair, each select one of the above approaches. Temporarily leave your partner and join the "expert" group for that approach.

(b) In the "expert" group, use the handout given to you by your instructor and discuss your approach. Ensure that each group member thoroughly understands it.

(c) Return to your partner and explain your approach.

(d) You may be asked by your instructor to write a short quiz on this topic.

Communication Activity

Writing Handbook

BYP8–4   Toys for Big Boys sells snowmobiles, personal watercraft, ATVs, and the like. Recently, the credit manager of Toys for Big Boys retired. The sales staff threw him a big retirement party—they were glad to see him go because they felt his credit policies restricted their selling ability. The sales staff convinced management that there was no need to replace the credit manager since they could handle this responsibility in addition to their sales positions.

Management was thrilled at year end when sales doubled. However, accounts receivable quadrupled and cash flow halved. The company's average collection period increased from 30 days to 120 days.

Instructions

In a memo to management, explain the financial impact of allowing the sales staff to manage the credit function. Has the business assumed any additional credit risk? What would you recommend the company do to better manage its increasing accounts receivable?

Ethics Case

BYP8–5 The controller of Proust Company has completed draft financial statements for the year just ended and is reviewing them with the president. As part of the review, he has summarized an aging schedule showing the basis of estimating uncollectible accounts using the following percentages: 0–30 days, 5%; 31–60 days, 10%; 61–90 days, 30%; 91–120 days, 50%; and over 120 days, 80%. The president of the company, Suzanne Bros, is nervous because the bank expects the company to sustain a growth rate for profit of at least 5% each year over the next two years—the remaining term of its bank loan. The profit growth for the past year was much more than 5% because of certain special orders with high margins, but those orders will not be repeated next year, so it will be very hard to achieve even the same profit next year, and even more difficult to grow it another 5%. It would be easier to show an increase next year if the past year's reported profit had been a little lower. President Bros recalls from her college accounting course that bad debts expense is based on certain estimates subject to judgement. She suggests that the controller increase the estimate percentages, which will increase the amount of the required bad debts expense adjustment and therefore lower profit for last year so that it will be easier to show a better growth rate next year.

Instructions

(a) Who are the stakeholders in this case?
(b) Does the president's request create an ethical dilemma for the controller?
(c) Should the controller be concerned with Proust Company's reported profit growth rate in estimating the allowance? Explain your answer.

"All About You" Activity

BYP8–6 In the "All About You" feature, you learned about interest rates charged on credit cards and some of the advantages and disadvantages of credit cards. To get the most from your credit card and to save money, you need to understand the features of your credit card and how interest is charged on credit cards.

Instructions

Go to the Financial Consumer Agency of Canada's publication "Credit Cards and You: Getting the Most from Your Credit Card" at **http://www.fcac-acfc.gc.ca/eng/publications/ CreditCardsYou/PDFs/GetMost-eng.pdf** and answer the following questions:

(a) Identify any benefits and risks of credit cards that were not previously identified in the answer to the feature's question.
(b) Credit cards provide interest-free loans on the purchase of goods, as long as you pay your bill in full by the end of the grace period. What is the grace period? The Canadian government brought in regulations that require a minimum grace period of 21 days. Assuming you used a credit card to purchase your textbooks on September 15, your statement date is October 7 and the grace period is 21 days. How many days is the interest-free period?
(c) There is no interest-free period on cash advances or balance transfers on credit cards. What is a cash advance? What is a balance transfer?
(d) Suppose you have one month left in the semester and you take a $1,000 cash advance on your credit card on April 1 to cover your living expenses until you get your first paycheque from your summer job on May 15. The interest rate on your credit card is 19%. Assuming that is the only charge on your credit card, calculate the interest you will be charged assuming you pay your bill in full on May 15. (*Hint:* Go to page 12 of the above publication on the website to see how interest is calculated.)

(e) Go to the Financial Consumer Agency of Canada's interactive tool "Credit Card Payment Calculator." (*Hint:* To find the Credit Card Payment Calculator, go to http://www.fcac-acfc.gc.ca/ and click on "For Consumers," then click on "Interactive Tools," and then click on the credit card icon.)

1. For option A, assume you have a credit card balance of $1,000, the interest rate is 19%, and the minimum monthly payment is $10 or 3%, whichever is greater.
2. For option B, assume the same information as in part 1, but you make an additional monthly payment of $10.
3. For option C assume the same information as in part 1, but you make a monthly payment of $100.

For each of the options a, b, and c, calculate how long it will take to pay off the credit card, assuming there are no additional purchases made, and calculate the total amount of interest paid.

ANSWERS TO CHAPTER QUESTIONS

Answers to Accounting in Action Insight Questions

All About You Insight, p. 439

Q: Should you use credit cards or not?

A: Credit cards can make your life easier, as long as they are used properly. They certainly have advantages: (1) they provide interest-free loans on the purchase of goods, as long as you pay your bill in full by the end of the grace period; (2) monthly credit card statements provide detailed records of all transactions, payments, and returned merchandise; and (3) many transactions, such as Internet purchases, are difficult or impossible to carry out without a credit card.

However, credit cards also have disadvantages: (1) if you do not pay your bill in full every month, expect to pay a very high interest rate on the unpaid balance; (2) they are so easy to use that you might start buying items without thinking about whether you really need them—and can afford them; and (3) credit cards can be stolen, which might damage your credit rating.

Across the Organization Insight, p. 446

Q: Why would a business choose to use a collection agency to follow up on late accounts instead of pursuing them internally?

A: Managers need to make decisions about the best way to use their staff. Many companies, particularly small ones, do not have enough staff to pursue uncollectible accounts. Collection agencies are specialists at following up on late accounts. They use methods that many companies do not have the expertise or the time to use and thus often collect accounts that a company wasn't able to collect. Even though the collection agency may keep a substantial portion of the accounts it collects, for companies that lack the expertise and staff to do so, it is better to receive part of the account than none of it.

Business Insight, p. 455

Q: What was the benefit to the banks of securitizing their mortgage receivables?

A: By securitizing their mortgages receivable, banks were able to raise cash at a time when credit was very tight. This allowed banks to keep their lending rates low and to continue to extend credit to people who were interested in purchasing houses at a time when prices were depressed.

Answer to Forzani Review It Question 1, p. 439

In Note 2 (h) on revenue recognition, The Forzani Group Ltd. states that it earns revenue on both sales to customers in stores and sales to, and service fees from, franchise stores and others. Forzani also states that revenue is recognized on sales to franchise stores at the time of shipment. These sales to franchise stores are probably on credit. Forzani would therefore record a receivable from the franchise store when the merchandise is shipped.

Answers to Self-Study Questions

1. b   2. d   3. d   4. c   5. d   6. a   7. d   8. a   9. c   10. b

Remember to go back to the beginning of the chapter to check off your completed work!

←

CHAPTER 9
LONG-LIVED ASSETS

dawsoncollege.qc.ca

 ## THE NAVIGATOR

- ☐ Understand *Concepts for Review*
- ☐ Read *Feature Story*
- ☐ Scan *Study Objectives*
- ☐ Read *Chapter Preview*
- ☐ Read text and answer *Before You Go On*
- ☐ Work *Demonstration Problems*
- ☐ Review *Summary of Study Objectives*
- ☐ Answer *Self-Study Questions*
- ☐ Complete assignments

CONCEPTS FOR REVIEW:

Before studying this chapter, you should understand or, if necessary, review:

a. Expense recognition criteria (Ch. 3, pp. 120–121).

b. What depreciation is, and how to make adjustments for it. (Ch. 3, pp. 125–126).

c. Non-current assets and the classified balance sheet (Ch. 4, pp. 194–195).

MEASURING VALUE: WHAT'S A HISTORIC BUILDING WORTH?

Montreal, Que.—For a college or university, the buildings where classes and other activities take place are some of its most important assets. Look around the campus of your own school. Where did the money for these buildings come from and what was their cost? Who pays to maintain them and how is the cost of repairs and maintenance recorded? How did the college choose its method of depreciation? And how much are the buildings worth?

For Dawson College in Montreal, the first of these questions is easy. The provincial government financed the 1982 purchase of its current building, the historic former Mother House of the Congrégation de Notre-Dame, at a cost of $12.2 million. With this purchase and subsequent renovations and expansions, Dawson's facilities included the former Mother House and the college's Selby pavilion from 1988 until 1997, when they were consolidated under one roof at the former Mother House.

As for the second question, again, the provincial government pays for most of Dawson's expenses. Established in 1969 as the first English-language institution in Quebec's network of CEGEPs (which are the equivalents of Grades 12 and 13), Dawson receives an annual allocation of about $1.5 million to cover any needed repairs or renovations, explains controller Guy Veilleux. It has also received lump sums from the government for specific projects, such as the $37-million renovations done after the building was purchased, a $10-million expansion in 1990–91, another $23-million expansion that took place from 1995 to 1997, and yet another costing $10 million in 2006–07. In addition, the government allocates specific funds for equipment purchases and renovations required when it revises programs.

How the cost of the buildings should be allocated or depreciated has been a complicated problem. "For years, there was no depreciation of buildings or equipment in our books," says Mr. Veilleux. Until the early 2000s, special accounting principles for government entities did not require accrual accounting. When the public sector accounting principles changed to require accrual accounting, the government and other public institutions began recognizing the depreciation of their physical assets.

In 2000–01, the government instructed its CEGEPs to calculate depreciation retroactively from 1995–96 using the diminishing-balance method. By 2011, Dawson's building will have been depreciated to about 33% of its book value, using a 3% depreciation rate.

How much the buildings are worth now is the trickiest question. "The value of the building is not the cost. The value of the building that we show on the financial statements is the municipal value for 1996 plus the cost of the acquisitions since then, and less the accumulated depreciation over the years," says Mr. Veilleux. However, since the former Mother House is a designated heritage site, some would deem it to be priceless.

The Navigator

STUDY OBJECTIVES:

After studying this chapter, you should be able to:

1. Determine the cost of property, plant, and equipment.
2. Explain and calculate depreciation.
3. Explain the factors that cause changes in periodic depreciation and calculate revisions.
4. Account for the disposal of property, plant, and equipment.
5. Calculate and record depreciation of natural resources.
6. Identify the basic accounting issues for intangible assets and goodwill.
7. Illustrate the reporting and analysis of long-lived assets.

The Navigator

For organizations such as Dawson College, making the right decisions about long-lived assets is critical because these assets represent huge investments. Organizations must make decisions about what assets to acquire, how to account for them, and when to dispose of them.

In this chapter, we address these and other issues surrounding long-lived assets. Our discussions will focus on three types of long-lived assets: (1) property, plant, and equipment; (2) natural resources; and (3) intangible assets.

The chapter is organized as follows:

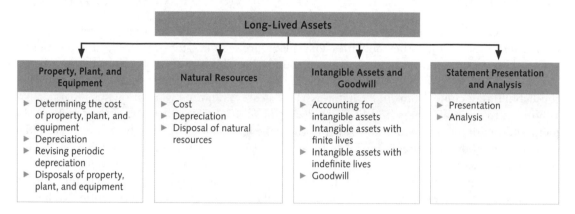

Property, Plant, and Equipment

Alternative terminology
Property, plant, and equipment are also commonly known as *fixed assets*; *land, building, and equipment*; or *capital assets*.

Property, plant, and equipment are long-lived assets that the company owns and uses for the production and sale of goods or services to consumers. They have three characteristics. They (1) have a physical substance (a definite size and shape), (2) are used in the operations of the business, and (3) are not intended for sale to customers. An item of property, plant, and equipment is recognized (recorded) as an asset if it is probable that the company will receive future economic benefits from the item.

In the following sections, we will learn about determining the cost of property, plant, and equipment; the depreciation of property, plant, and equipment; and the accounting for disposals of property, plant, and equipment.

Determining the Cost of Property, Plant, and Equipment

STUDY OBJECTIVE 1

Determine the cost of property, plant, and equipment.

The cost of an item of property, plant, and equipment includes the following:

1. The purchase price, plus any non-refundable taxes, less any discounts or rebates
2. The expenditures necessary to bring the asset to the location and condition necessary to make it ready for its intended use

If there are obligations to dismantle, remove, or restore the asset when it is retired, an initial estimate of these costs is also included in the cost of the long-lived asset. These are known as **asset retirement costs**. Accounting for these costs can be complex and we will leave that discussion to a future accounting course. But you should be aware that the cost of some property, plant, and equipment items includes the cost of retiring the asset. For simplicity, we will assume asset retirement costs are equal to zero in the examples in this text.

Alternative terminology
Asset retirement costs are also called *decommissioning costs*.

All of these costs are capitalized (recorded as property, plant, and equipment), rather than expensed, if it is probable that the company will receive an economic benefit in the future from the asset. Determining which costs to include in a long-lived asset account and which costs not to include is very important. Costs that benefit only the current period are expensed. Such costs are called **operating expenditures**. Costs that benefit future periods are included in a long-lived asset account. These costs are called **capital expenditures**.

For example, the cost to purchase an asset is recorded as a capital expenditure, because the asset will benefit future periods. In addition, the insurance paid on the same asset as it is shipped to the company should also be capitalized because the insurance during transit benefits more than just the current period. It is considered a necessary expenditure to get the asset to its required location and ready for use.

Subsequent to acquisition, the same distinction exists between capital and operating expenditures. For example, once the asset is in use, insurance benefits only the current period and is treated as an expense. But major expenditures that are incurred once the asset is in use that increase the life of the asset or its productivity are capitalized. We will discuss expenditures subsequent to acquisition in more depth later in the chapter.

Property, plant, and equipment are often subdivided into four classes:

1. Land, such as a building site
2. Land improvements, such as driveways, parking lots, fences, and underground sprinkler systems
3. Buildings, such as stores, offices, factories, and warehouses
4. Equipment, such as store checkout counters, cash registers, coolers, office furniture, factory machinery, and delivery equipment

Determining the cost of each of the major classes of property, plant, and equipment is explained in the following sections.

Land

The cost of land includes (1) the purchase price, (2) closing costs such as surveying and legal fees, and (3) the costs of preparing the land for its intended use, such as the removal of old buildings, clearing, draining, filling, and grading. All of these costs (less any proceeds from salvaged materials) are debited to the Land account.

To illustrate, assume that the Budovitch Manufacturing Company purchases real estate for $100,000 cash. The property contained an old warehouse that is removed at a net cost of $6,000 ($7,500 to remove it less $1,500 received for materials from the warehouse that were salvaged and later sold). Additional expenditures include the legal fee of $3,000. The cost of the land is $109,000, calculated as follows:

Land	
Cash price of property	$100,000
Net cost of removing warehouse ($7,500 – $1,500)	6,000
Legal fee	3,000
Cost of land	$109,000

When recording the acquisition, Land is debited for $109,000 and Cash is credited for $109,000 (assuming the costs were paid in cash). Land is a unique long-lived asset. Its cost is not depreciated—allocated over its useful life—because land has an unlimited useful life.

Land Improvements

Land improvements are structural additions made to land, such as driveways, sidewalks, fences, and parking lots. Land improvements, unlike land, decline in service potential over time, and require maintenance and replacement. Because of this, land improvements are recorded separately from land and are depreciated over their useful lives.

Many students confuse the cost to get land ready for its intended use with land improvements. They think, for example, that removing an old building or grading the land is "improving" the land, and thus incorrectly reason that these costs should be considered land improvements. When classifying costs, it is important to remember that one-time costs required for getting the land ready to use are always charged to the Land account, not the Land Improvement account.

Buildings

All costs that are directly related to the purchase or construction of a building are debited to the Buildings account. When a building is purchased, these costs include the purchase price and closing costs (e.g., legal fees). The costs of making a building ready to be used as intended can include expenditures for remodelling, and for replacing or repairing the roof, floors, electrical wiring, and plumbing. These costs are also debited to Buildings.

When a new building is built, cost includes the contract price plus payments for architects' fees, building permits, and excavation costs. The interest costs of financing the construction project are also included in the asset's cost when a significant amount of time is needed to get the building ready to be used. In these circumstances, interest costs are considered to be as necessary as materials and labour are. Only the interest costs that occur during the construction period are included, however. After construction is finished, future interest payments on funds that were borrowed to finance the cost of the constructed building are debited to Interest Expense.

Equipment

The "equipment" classification is a broad one that can include delivery equipment, office equipment, machinery, vehicles, furniture and fixtures, and other similar assets. The cost of these assets includes the purchase price; freight charges and insurance during transit that are paid by the purchaser; and the costs of assembling, installing, and testing the equipment. These costs are treated as capital expenditures because they benefit future periods.

Such annual costs as motor vehicle licences and insurance on company trucks and cars are treated as operating expenditures because they are recurring expenditures that do not benefit future periods.

To illustrate, assume that 1 Stop Florists purchases a used delivery truck on January 1, 2011, for $24,500 cash. Related expenditures include painting and lettering, $500; a motor vehicle licence, $80; and a one-year insurance policy, $2,600. The cost of the delivery truck is $25,000, calculated as follows:

Delivery Truck	
Cash price	$24,500
Painting and lettering	500
Cost of delivery truck	$25,000

The cost of the motor vehicle licence is recorded as an expense and the cost of the insurance policy is recorded as a prepaid asset. The entry to record the purchase of the truck and related expenditures, assuming they were all paid for in cash, is as follows:

		A	=	L	+	OE
		+25,000				−80
		+2,600				
		−27,680				

↓ Cash flows: −27,680

Jan. 1	Delivery Truck	25,000	
	Licence Expense	80	
	Prepaid Insurance	2,600	
	Cash		27,680
	To record purchase of delivery truck and related expenditures.		

Allocating Cost to Multiple Assets and Significant Components

Multiple Assets. Property, plant, and equipment are often purchased together for a single price. This is known as a **basket purchase**. We need to know the cost of each individual asset in order to journalize the purchase, and later calculate the depreciation of each asset. When a basket purchase occurs, we determine individual costs by allocating the total price paid for the group of assets to each individual asset based on its relative fair value.

Alternative terminology
A basket purchase is also known as a *lump sum purchase.*

To illustrate, assume Sega Company acquired a building and a parcel of land on July 31 for $300,000, paying $50,000 cash and incurring a mortgage payable for the balance. The land was recently appraised at $120,000. The building was appraised at $200,000. The $300,000 cost should be allocated based on fair values (i.e., appraised values), as shown in Illustration 9-1.

	Fair value	Allocated Percentage	Allocated Cost
Land	$120,000	37.5% ($120,000 ÷ $320,000)	$112,500 ($300,000 × 37.5%)
Building	200,000	62.5% ($200,000 ÷ $320,000)	187,500 ($300,000 × 62.5%)
Totals	$320,000	100.0%	$300,000

◀ Illustration 9-1

Allocating cost in a basket purchase

The journal entry to record this purchase is as follows:

July 31	Land	112,500	
	Building	187,500	
	Cash		50,000
	Mortgage Payable		250,000
	To record purchase of land and building, with costs allocated based on appraised values of $120,000 and $200,000, respectively.		

A	=	L	+	OE
+112,500		+250,000		
+187,500				
−50,000				

↓ Cash flows: −50,000

Significant Components. When an item of property, plant, and equipment includes components with a cost that is significant relative to its total cost, the cost of the item must be allocated to its different components. This is necessary so that each component can be depreciated separately over the different useful lives or possibly by using different depreciation methods. For example, it may be appropriate to depreciate elements such as aircraft engines separately from the rest of the aircraft instead of doing one depreciation calculation for the entire aircraft. The SAS Group, an airline in Europe, depreciates its aircraft over an estimated useful life of 20 years and its engine components over an estimated useful life of 8 years. This is known as **component depreciation**.

Separating the cost of the entire asset into its significant components can be accomplished using the same process to allocate cost illustrated above for a basket purchase. The asset's total cost would be allocated to the significant components based on the components' relative fair values. The calculations would be similar to those in Illustration 9-1.

Component accounting is a new requirement for Canadian companies, resulting from the change to International Financial Reporting Standards (IFRS). Implementing it will likely require more detailed accounting records than many Canadian companies may have maintained under Canadian accounting standards. For simplicity, we will assume in this text that all of the components of the depreciable asset have the same useful life, and we will depreciate assets as a whole.

BEFORE YOU GO ON . . .

➡ Review It

1. What are the three characteristics of property, plant, and equipment?
2. What types of costs are capitalized for property, plant, and equipment?
3. Explain the difference between operating and capital expenditures.
4. Under what circumstances is it necessary to divide up the cost among different assets or components of an asset?
5. What is the cost of each type of capital asset that The Forzani Group Ltd. reports in Note 5 to its balance sheet? The answer to this question is at the end of the chapter.

➡ Do It

Assume that factory machinery is purchased on November 6 for $10,000 cash and a $40,000 note payable. Related cash expenditures include insurance during shipping, $500; the annual insurance policy, $750; and installation and testing, $1,000. Prepare the journal entry to record these expenditures.

Action Plan

- Capitalize expenditures that are made to get the machinery ready for its intended use.
- Expense operating expenditures that benefit only the current period, or are recurring costs.

Solution

Factory Machinery

Purchase price	$50,000
Insurance during shipping	500
Installation and testing	1,000
Cost of machinery	$51,500

The entry to record the purchase and related expenditures is:

Nov. 6	Factory Machinery	51,500	
	Prepaid Insurance	750	
	Cash ($10,000 + $500 + $750 + $1,000)		12,250
	Note Payable		40,000
	To record purchase of factory machinery and		
	related expenditures.		

The Navigator

Related exercise material: BE9–1, BE9–2, BE9–3, BE9–4, and E9–1.

Depreciation

STUDY OBJECTIVE 2

Explain and calculate depreciation.

Under IFRS, companies have two models they can choose between to account for their property, plant, and equipment: the cost model or the revaluation model. The cost model is by far the more commonly used method, and is the method Canadian companies used prior to IFRS. The cost model is also required under Canadian GAAP for Private Enterprises.

The **cost model** records property, plant, and equipment at cost of acquisition. After acquisition, depreciation is recorded each period and the assets are carried at cost less accumulated depreciation. We will cover the cost model in the following sections of the chapter and refer briefly to the revaluation model in a later section.

As we learned in Chapter 3, depreciation is the systematic allocation of the cost of a long-lived asset, such as property, plant, and equipment, over the asset's useful life. The cost is allocated to expense over the asset's useful life because the asset is used to help generate revenue over that period of time. Assets are depreciated over their useful lives even if the use of the asset is not directly related to earning revenue.

You will recall that depreciation is recorded through an adjusting journal entry that debits Depreciation Expense and credits Accumulated Depreciation. Depreciation expense is an operating expense on the income statement. Accumulated depreciation appears on the balance sheet as a contra account to the related asset account. This contra asset account is similar in purpose to the one used in Chapter 8 for the allowance for doubtful accounts. Both contra accounts reduce assets to their carrying values: *net realizable value* for accounts receivable, and *carrying amount* for property, plant, and equipment.

It is important to understand that depreciation is a process of cost allocation, not a process of determining an asset's real value. Illustration 9-2 shows this. Under the cost model, an increase in an asset's fair value is not relevant because property, plant, and equipment are not for resale. (Fair values are only relevant if an impairment loss has occurred, which we will discuss later in the chapter.) As a result, the carrying amount of property, plant, or equipment (cost less accumulated depreciation) may be very different from its fair value. We saw this in our feature story, where Dawson College's former Mother House building has a carrying amount much lower than its fair value.

Illustration 9-2 ➜

Depreciation as an allocation concept

Depreciation allocation

It is also important to understand that depreciation does not result in the accumulation of cash to replace the asset. The balance in Accumulated Depreciation only represents the total amount of the asset's cost that has been allocated to expense so far. It is not a cash fund. Cash is neither increased nor decreased by the adjusting entry to record depreciation.

During a depreciable asset's useful life, its revenue-producing ability declines because of physical factors such as wear and tear, and economic factors such as obsolescence. For example, a company may replace a truck because it is physically worn out. On the other hand, companies replace computers long before they are physically worn out because improvements in hardware and software have made the old computer obsolete.

You will recall from Chapter 4 that we can expect to see companies using a variety of terms as Canadian public companies start following IFRS. Under IFRS, it is typical to use the term "depreciation" for property, plant, and equipment, and "amortization" for intangible assets. Under Canadian GAAP for Private Enterprises it is acceptable to use either "amortization" or "depreciation" when allocating the cost of property, plant, and equipment. We have followed the IFRS practice in this textbook. We have also adopted the IFRS practice of using the term "carrying amount" instead of "book value." Both of these terms are acceptable under Canadian accounting standards. We will point out a number of other terminology choices related to long-lived assets in this chapter.

Factors in Calculating Depreciation

In Chapter 3, we learned that depreciation expense was calculated by dividing the cost of a depreciable asset by its useful life. At that time, we assumed the asset's residual value was zero. In this chapter, we will now include a residual value when calculating depreciation. Consequently, there are now three factors that affect the calculation of depreciation:

1. Cost. The factors that affect the cost of a depreciable asset were explained earlier in this chapter. Remember that the cost of property, plant, and equipment includes the purchase price plus all costs necessary to get the asset ready for use. We also saw that cost includes an initial estimate of the retirement costs, if there are any.
2. Useful life. **Useful life** is (a) the period of time over which an asset is expected to be available for use or (b) the number of units of production (such as machine hours) or units of output that are expected to be obtained from an asset. Useful life is an estimate based on such factors as the asset's intended use, its expected need for repair and maintenance, and how vulnerable it is to wearing out or becoming obsolete. The company's past experience with similar assets often helps in estimating the expected useful life.
3. Residual value. **Residual value** is the estimated amount that a company would currently obtain from disposing of the asset if the asset were already as old as it will be, and in the condition it is expected to be in, at the end of its useful life. Residual value is not depreciated, since the amount is expected to be recovered at the end of the asset's useful life.

Alternative terminology
Residual value is sometimes called *salvage value*.

Illustration 9-3 summarizes these three factors.

Illustration 9-3

Three factors in calculating depreciation

Cost: Purchase price plus all necessary costs to make the asset ready for its intended use

Useful life: Estimate of the period over which an asset is expected to be available for use

Residual value: Current estimate of the amount that will be received from the disposal of the asset

Depreciation Methods

Depreciation is generally calculated using one of the following methods:

1. Straight-line
2. Diminishing-balance
3. Units-of-production

How do companies choose which of the three depreciation methods to use? Management must choose the method that best matches the estimated pattern in which the asset's future economic benefits are expected to be consumed. The depreciation method must be reviewed at least once a year. If the expected pattern of consumption of the future economic benefits has changed, the depreciation method must be changed. The estimated useful life and residual values must also be reviewed each year.

However, changing methods makes it more difficult to compare the results of one year with another, and so the change must be justifiable. We will discuss how to account for changes in depreciation methods later in the chapter.

To learn how to calculate the three depreciation methods and to compare them, we will use the following data for the small delivery truck bought by 1 Stop Florists on January 1, 2011:

Cost (as shown on page 492)	$ 25,000
Estimated residual value	$2,000
Estimated useful life (in years)	5
Estimated useful life (in kilometres)	200,000

Straight-Line. The straight-line method was first defined in Chapter 3. We will define it again here, this time including the impact of a residual value on the calculation. The **straight-line method** of calculating depreciation has two steps. First, residual value is deducted from the asset's cost to determine an asset's **depreciable amount**—the total amount that can be depreciated. Second, the depreciable amount is divided by the asset's useful life to calculate the annual depreciation expense.

The depreciation expense will be the same for each year of the asset's useful life if the cost, the useful life, and the residual value do not change. The calculation of depreciation expense in the first year for 1 Stop Florists' delivery truck is shown in Illustration 9-4.

Illustration 9-4 ➡

Formula for straight-line method

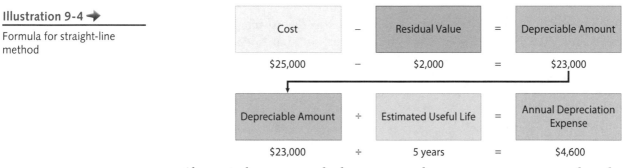

Alternatively, we can calculate an annual percentage rate to use when determining the delivery truck's straight-line depreciation expense. First, the depreciation rate is calculated by dividing 100% by the useful life in years. In this case, the straight-line depreciation rate is 20% (100% ÷ 5 years). Second, the depreciation expense is calculated by multiplying the asset's depreciable amount by the straight-line depreciation rate shown in the depreciation schedule in Illustration 9-5.

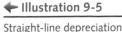

| | | | | | End of Year | |
Year	Depreciable Amount	× Depreciation Rate	= Depreciation Expense	Accumulated Depreciation	Carrying Amount
					$25,000
2011	$23,000	20%	$ 4,600	$ 4,600	20,400
2012	23,000	20%	4,600	9,200	15,800
2013	23,000	20%	4,600	13,800	11,200
2014	23,000	20%	4,600	18,400	6,600
2015	23,000	20%	4,600	23,000	2,000
			$23,000		

1 STOP FLORISTS
Straight-Line Depreciation Schedule

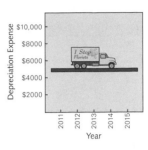

Note that the depreciation expense of $4,600 is the same each year. Also note that the column total for depreciation expense is equal to the asset's depreciable amount, and that the carrying amount at the end of the useful life is equal to the estimated $2,000 residual value.

What happens when an asset is purchased during the year, rather than on January 1 as in our example? In that case, it is necessary to pro-rate the annual depreciation for the part of the year that the asset was used. If 1 Stop Florists' delivery truck was ready to be used on April 1, 2011, the truck would be depreciated for nine months in 2011 (April through December). The depreciation for 2011 would be $3,450 ($23,000 × 20% × $\frac{9}{12}$). Note that depreciation is normally rounded to the nearest month. Since depreciation is an estimate, calculating it to the nearest day gives a false sense of accuracy.

To keep things simple, some companies establish a policy for partial-period depreciation, rather than calculating depreciation monthly. Companies may choose to record a full year's depreciation in the year of acquisition and none in the year of disposal. Others may record a half year's depreciation in the year of acquisition and a half year's depreciation in the year of disposal. Whatever policy is chosen for partial-year depreciation, the impact is not significant in the long run if the policy is used consistently.

The straight-line method of depreciation has been the most popular method for Canadian companies, in part because it is simple to apply. But with the change to IFRS, the depreciation method used must be consistent with the pattern in which the economic benefits from owning the asset are expected to be consumed. Therefore, it is appropriate to use the straight-line method when the asset is used quite uniformly throughout its useful life. Examples of assets that deliver their benefit primarily as a function of time include office furniture and fixtures, buildings, warehouses, and garages for motor vehicles.

Diminishing-Balance. The **diminishing-balance method** produces a decreasing annual depreciation expense over the asset's useful life. It is called the "diminishing-balance" method because the periodic depreciation is calculated based on the asset's carrying amount, which diminishes each year because accumulated depreciation increases. Annual depreciation expense is calculated by multiplying the carrying amount at the beginning of the year by the depreciation rate. The depreciation rate remains constant from year to year, but the rate is applied to a carrying amount that declines each year.

The carrying amount for the first year is the asset's cost, because the balance in Accumulated Depreciation at the beginning of the asset's useful life is zero. In the following years, the carrying amount is the difference between cost and the accumulated depreciation at the beginning of the year. Unlike the other depreciation methods, the diminishing-balance method does not use depreciable amount. Residual value is not used in determining the amount that the diminishing-balance depreciation rate is applied to. Residual value does, however, limit the total depreciation that can be taken. Depreciation stops when the asset's carrying amount equals its estimated residual value.

The diminishing-balance method can be applied using different rates, which results in varying speeds of depreciation. You will find rates such as one time (single), two times (double), and even three times (triple) the straight-line rate of depreciation. A depreciation rate that is often used is double the straight-line rate. This method is referred to as the double diminishing balance method

Alternative terminology
The diminishing-balance method is also sometimes called the *declining-balance* method.

Helpful Hint The straight-line rate is determined by dividing 100% by the estimated useful life. In 1 Stop Florist's case, it is 100% ÷ 5 = 20%.

Illustration 9-6 ➡

Formula for double diminishing-balance method

Illustration 9-7 ➡

Double diminishing-balance depreciation schedule

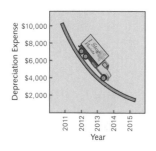

If 1 Stop Florists uses the double diminishing-balance method, the depreciation rate is 40% (2 × the straight-line rate of 20%). Illustration 9-6 shows the calculation of depreciation on the delivery truck for the first year.

Carrying Amount at Beginning of Year	×	Straight-Line Rate × 2	=	Annual Depreciation Expense
$25,000	×	40%	=	$10,000

The depreciation schedule under this method is given in Illustration 9-7.

1 STOP FLORISTS
Double Diminishing-Balance Depreciation Schedule

					End of Year	
Year	Carrying Amount Beginning of Year	×	Depreciation Rate	=	Depreciation Expense	Accumulated Depreciation	Carrying Amount
							$25,000
2011	$25,000		40%		$10,000	$10,000	15,000
2012	15,000		40%		6,000	16,000	9,000
2013	9,000		40%		3,600	19,600	5,400
2014	5,400		40%		2,160	21,760	3,240
2015	3,240		40%		1,240*	23,000	2,000
					$23,000		

* The calculation of $1,296 ($3,240 × 40%) is adjusted to $1,240 so that the carrying amount will equal the residual value.

When an asset is purchased during the year, it is necessary to pro-rate the diminishing-balance depreciation in the first year, based on time. For example, if 1 Stop Florists had purchased the delivery truck on April 1, 2011, the depreciation for 2011 would be $7,500 ($25,000 × 40% × $\frac{9}{12}$) if depreciation is calculated monthly. The carrying amount for calculating depreciation in 2012 would then become $17,500 ($25,000 − $7,500). The depreciation for 2012 would be $7,000 ($17,500 × 40%). Future calculations would follow from these amounts until the carrying amount equalled the residual value.

Returning to Illustration 9-7, which assumes the asset was bought at the start of the year, you can see that the delivery truck is 70% depreciated ($16,000 ÷ $23,000) at the end of the second year. Under the straight-line method, it would be 40% depreciated ($9,200 ÷ $23,000) at that time.

Regardless of the method that is used, the total amount of depreciation over the life of the delivery truck is $23,000—the depreciable amount. In early years, however, diminishing-balance depreciation expense will be higher than the straight-line depreciation expense, and in later years it will be less than the straight-line expense. Methods such as the diminishing-balance method that produce higher depreciation expense in the early years than in the later years are known as *accelerated* depreciation methods.

Managers must choose the diminishing-balance, or another accelerated method, if the company receives more economic benefit in the early years of the asset's useful life than in the later years. That is, this method is used if the asset, for example, has higher revenue-producing ability in its early years, or if the asset is expected to become less useful over time. Dawson College, in the feature story, uses the diminishing-balance method of depreciation for its buildings. It uses a depreciation rate of 3%, which means that its buildings are depreciated over an average useful life of 33 $\frac{1}{3}$ years.

Alternative terminology The units-of-production method is often called the *units-of-activity method*.

Units-of-Production. As indicated earlier, useful life can be expressed in ways other than time. In the **units-of-production method**, useful life is either the estimated total units of production or total expected use from the asset, not the number of years that the asset is expected to be used. The units-of-production method is ideal for equipment whose activity can be measured in units of output, such as kilometres driven or hours in use. The units-of-production method is generally not suitable for buildings or furniture, because depreciation of these assets is more a result of time than of use.

In this method, the total units of production for the entire useful life are estimated. This amount is divided into the depreciable amount (cost – residual value) to determine the depreciable amount per unit. The depreciable amount per unit is then multiplied by the actual units of production during the year to calculate the annual depreciation expense.

To illustrate, assume that the 1 Stop Florists' delivery truck is driven 30,000 kilometres in the first year of a total estimated life of 200,000 kilometres. Illustration 9-8 shows the calculation of depreciation expense in the first year.

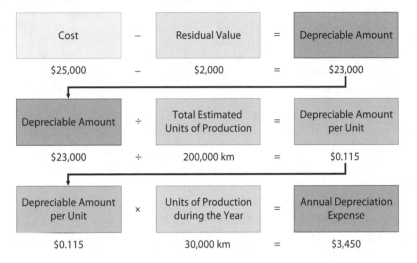

◄ Illustration 9-8

Formula for units-of-production method

Illustration 9-9 shows the units-of-production depreciation schedule, using assumed units of production (kilometres driven) for the later years.

◄ Illustration 9-9

Units-of-production depreciation schedule

| | | | | End of Year | |
Year	Units of Production ×	Depreciable Cost/Unit =	Depreciation Expense	Accumulated Depreciation	Carrying Amount
					$25,000
2011	30,000	$0.115	$ 3,450	$ 3,450	21,550
2012	60,000	$0.115	6,900	10,350	14,650
2013	40,000	$0.115	4,600	14,950	10,050
2014	50,000	$0.115	5,750	20,700	4,300
2015	20,000	$0.115	2,300	23,000	2,000
	200,000		$23,000		

1 STOP FLORISTS — Units-of-Production Depreciation Schedule

In the example in Illustration 9-9, the total actual units of production equal the original estimated total units of production of 200,000 kilometres. But in most real-life situations, the total actual units of production do not exactly equal the total estimated units of production. This means that the final year's depreciation will have to be adjusted—as we saw in the diminishing-balance method in Illustration 9-7—so that the ending carrying amount is equal to the estimated residual value.

This method is easy to apply when assets are purchased during the year. The actual units of production already show how much the asset was used during the year. Therefore, the depreciation calculations do not need to be adjusted for partial periods as is done in the straight-line and diminishing-balance methods.

The units-of-production method is used for assets whose activity can be measured in units of output. But it can only be used if it is possible to make a reasonable estimate of total activity. Later in this chapter, we will see that this method is widely used to depreciate natural resources. The units-of-production method results in the best matching of expenses with revenues when the asset's productivity varies significantly from one period to another.

Comparison of Depreciation Methods

Illustration 9-10 presents a comparison of annual and total depreciation expense for 1 Stop Florists under each of the three depreciation methods. In addition, if we assume for simplicity that profit before deducting depreciation expense is $50,000 for each of the five years, we can clearly see the impact that the choice of method has on profit.

Illustration 9-10 ➡

Comparison of depreciation methods

Year	Straight-Line Depreciation Expense	Profit	Double Diminishing-Balance Depreciation Expense	Profit	Units-of-Production Depreciation Expense	Profit
2011	$ 4,600	$ 45,400	$ 10,000	$ 40,000	$ 3,450	$ 46,550
2012	4,600	45,400	6,000	44,000	6,900	43,100
2013	4,600	45,400	3,600	46,400	4,600	45,400
2014	4,600	45,400	2,160	47,840	5,750	44,250
2015	4,600	45,400	1,240	48,760	2,300	47,700
	$23,000	$227,000	$23,000	$227,000	$23,000	$227,000

Recall that straight-line depreciation results in the same amount of depreciation expense and therefore profit each year. Diminishing-balance depreciation results in a higher depreciation expense in early years, and therefore lower profit, and a lower depreciation expense and higher profit in later years. Results with the units-of-production method vary, depending on how much the asset is used each year. While the depreciation expense and profit will be different each year for each method, *total* depreciation expense and *total* profit after the five-year period are the same for all three methods.

The balance sheet is also affected by the choice of depreciation method because accumulated depreciation is increased by depreciation expense and owner's equity is increased by profit. There is no impact on cash flow because depreciation does not involve cash.

As explained earlier, management should choose the method that best matches the estimated pattern in which the asset's economic benefits are expected to be consumed. If the economic benefit of owning an asset is fairly consistent over time, the straight-line method is appropriate. The diminishing-balance method is appropriate if the company receives more economic benefit in the early years of the asset's useful life than in the later years. The units-of-production method is appropriate for assets whose usage varies over time. Because companies have more than one type of asset, they often use more than one depreciation method.

🔍 ACCOUNTING IN ACTION: BUSINESS INSIGHT

Why does Morris Formal Wear use the units-of-production method for its tuxedos? The reason is that the Ottawa-based family business wants to track wear and tear on each of its 5,200 tuxedos individually. Each tuxedo has its own bar code. When a tux is rented, a clerk runs its code across an electronic scanner. At year end, the computer adds up the total rentals for each of the tuxedos, then divides this number by expected total use to calculate the rate. For instance, on a two-button black tux, Morris expects a life of 30 rentals. In one year, the tux was rented 13 times. The depreciation rate for that period was 43% (13 ÷ 30) of the depreciable cost.

Is the units-of-production method the best depreciation method for Morris Formal Wear to use for its tuxedos or would you recommend another method?

Depreciation and Income Tax

The Canada Revenue Agency (CRA) allows companies to deduct a specified amount of depreciation expense when they calculate their taxable income. As we have just learned, for accounting purposes, a company must choose the depreciation method that best reflects the pattern in which the asset's future economic benefits are consumed. The CRA does not permit a choice among the three depreciation methods. Instead, the CRA requires taxpayers to use the single diminishing-balance method on the tax return, regardless of what method is used in the financial statements.

In addition, the CRA does not allow taxpayers to estimate the useful lives of assets or depreciation rates. Assets are grouped into various classes and maximum depreciation rates for each class are specified. Depreciation allowed for income tax purposes is calculated on a class (group) basis and is called **capital cost allowance (CCA)**. Capital cost allowance is an optional deduction from taxable income, but depreciation expense is not optional in calculating profit. Consequently, you may see a company deduct depreciation on its income statement, which is required by generally accepted accounting principles, but not deduct CCA for income tax purposes.

Helpful Hint Depreciation for accounting purposes is usually different from depreciation for income tax purposes.

BEFORE YOU GO ON . . .

→ Review It

1. What is the relationship, if any, between depreciation and (a) cost allocation, (b) asset valuation, and (c) cash accumulation?
2. Explain the factors that are used to calculate depreciation.
3. How are annual depreciation and profit different each year over the useful life of an asset, and in total after the entire life of an asset, under each of the three depreciation methods?
4. When a company chooses a depreciation method, what should it base its decision on?

→ Do It

On October 1, 2011, Iron Mountain Ski Company purchases a new snow grooming machine for $52,000. The machine is estimated to have a five-year useful life and a $4,000 residual value. It is also estimated to have a total useful life of 6,000 hours. It is used 1,000 hours in the year ended December 31, 2011, and 1,300 hours in the year ended December 31, 2012. How much depreciation expense should Iron Mountain Ski record in each of 2011 and 2012 under each depreciation method: (a) straight-line, (b) double diminishing-balance, and (c) units-of-production?

Action Plan

- Under straight-line depreciation, annual depreciation expense is equal to the depreciable amount (cost less residual value) divided by the estimated useful life.
- Under double diminishing-balance depreciation, annual depreciation expense is equal to double the straight-line rate of depreciation times the asset's carrying amount at the beginning of the year. Residual values are ignored in this method.
- Under the straight-line and diminishing-balance methods, the annual depreciation expense must be pro-rated if the asset is purchased during the year.
- Under units-of-production depreciation, the depreciable amount per unit is equal to the total depreciable amount divided by the total estimated units of production. The annual depreciation expense is equal to the depreciable amount per unit times the actual usage in each year.

Solution

	2011	2012
Straight-line	$2,400	$ 9,600
Double diminishing-balance	5,200	18,720
Units-of-production	8,000	10,400

    (a) Straight-line: ($52,000 − $4,000) ÷ 5 years = $9,600 per year
        2011: $9,600 × $\frac{3}{12}$ = $2,400
    (b) Double diminishing-balance: 100% ÷ 5 years = 20% straight-line rate
        20% × 2 = 40% double diminishing-balance rate
        2011: $52,000 × 40% × $\frac{3}{12}$ = $5,200
        2012: ($52,000 − $5,200) × 40% = $18,720
    (c) Units-of-production: ($52,000 − $4,000) ÷ 6,000 hours = $8.00 per hour
        2011: 1,000 × $8.00 = $8,000
        2012: 1,300 × $8.00 = $10,400

Related exercise material: BE9–5, BE9–6, BE9–7, BE9–8, BE9–9, E9–2, E9–3, E9–4, and E9–5.

The Navigator

Revising Periodic Depreciation

Recall that the three factors that affect the calculation of depreciation are the asset's cost, useful life, and residual value. During the useful life of a long-lived asset, the annual depreciation expense needs to be revised if there are changes to any of these factors. Depreciation therefore needs to be revised if there are (1) capital expenditures during the asset's useful life, (2) impairments in the asset's fair value, (3) changes in the asset's fair value when using the revaluation model, and/or (4) changes in the appropriate depreciation method, or in the asset's estimated useful life or residual value. In the following sections, we discuss each of these items and then show how to revise depreciation calculations.

Capital Expenditures during Useful Life

Earlier in the chapter, we learned that companies can have both operating and capital expenditures when a long-lived asset is purchased. Similarly, during the useful life of a long-lived asset, a company may incur costs for ordinary repairs, or for additions or improvements.

Ordinary repairs are costs to *maintain* the asset's operating efficiency and expected productive life. Motor tune-ups and oil changes, repainting a building, or replacing worn-out gears on machinery are examples of ordinary repairs. These costs are frequently fairly small amounts that occur regularly. They may also be larger, infrequent amounts, but if they simply restore an asset to its prior condition, they are considered an ordinary repair. Such repairs are debited to Repair (or Maintenance) Expense as they occur. Ordinary repairs are operating expenditures.

Additions and improvements are costs that are incurred to *increase* the asset's operating efficiency, productive capacity, or expected useful life. These costs are usually large and happen less often. Additions and improvements that add to the future cash flows associated with that asset are not expensed as they occur—they are capitalized. As capital expenditures, they are generally debited to the appropriate property, plant, or equipment account, or to the specific component of that asset. The capital expenditure will be depreciated over the remaining life of the original structure or the useful life of the addition, if the capital expenditure's useful life does not depend on the original asset's useful life. Additions and improvements can therefore change an asset's annual depreciation, compared with the original depreciation estimate.

In our feature story, Dawson College spent $37 million on renovations and $43 million on three expansions. According to the explanation just given, these would be treated as capital expenditures and would have resulted in revisions to the college's depreciation of its buildings.

Impairments

As noted earlier in the chapter, under the cost model, the carrying amount of property, plant, and equipment is cost less any accumulated depreciation since its acquisition. And, as already discussed, the carrying amount of property, plant, and equipment is rarely the same as its fair value. Remember that the fair value is normally not relevant since property, plant, and equipment are not purchased for resale, but rather for use in operations over the long term.

While it is accepted that long-lived assets such as property, plant, and equipment may be undervalued on the balance sheet, it is not appropriate if property, plant, and equipment are overvalued. Property, plant, and equipment are considered impaired if the asset's carrying amount exceeds its **recoverable amount** (the higher of the asset's fair value less costs to sell, or its value in use). If this is the case, an impairment loss must be recorded. An **impairment loss** is the amount by which the asset's carrying amount exceeds its recoverable amount.

Companies are required to review their assets regularly for possible impairment or do so whenever a change in circumstances affects an asset's recoverable amount. For example, if a machine has become obsolete, or if the market for a product made by a machine has dried up or has become very competitive, there is a strong possibility that an impairment loss exists. Management is then required to estimate the machine's recoverable amount.

To illustrate the writedown of a long-lived asset, assume that on December 31, Piniwa Company reviews its equipment for possible impairment. The equipment has a cost of $800,000 and accumulated depreciation of $200,000. The equipment's recoverable amount is currently $500,000. The amount of the impairment loss is determined by comparing the asset's carrying amount with its recoverable amount as follows:

Carrying amount ($800,000 − $200,000)	$600,000
Recoverable amount	500,000
Impairment loss	$100,000

The journal entry to record the impairment is:

Dec. 31	Impairment Loss	100,000	
	Accumulated Depreciation—Equipment		100,000
	To record impairment loss on equipment.		

A	=	L	+	OE
−100,000				−100,000

Cash flows: no effect

Assuming that the asset will continue to be used in operations, the impairment loss is reported on the income statement as part of operating profit rather than as "other expense." Often the loss is combined with depreciation expense on the income statement. An accumulated depreciation account is credited for the impairment loss, not the asset account; recording the loss this way keeps a record of the asset's original cost.

We had previously defined an asset's carrying amount as its cost less accumulated depreciation. This is still the case, but the Accumulated Depreciation account can now include more than just the depreciation recorded on the asset to date. It will also include impairment losses, if there have been any. Future depreciation calculations will need to be revised because of the reduction in the asset's carrying amount.

International Financial Reporting Standards allow the reversal of a previously recorded impairment loss. Under IFRS, at each year end, the company must determine whether or not an impairment loss still exists by measuring the asset's recoverable amount. If this recoverable amount exceeds the current carrying amount, then a reversal is recorded. The reversal for an asset is limited to the amount required to increase the asset's carrying amount to what it would have been if the impairment loss had not been recorded. The reversal will result in additional revisions to depreciation calculations. Canadian GAAP for Private Enterprises does not permit companies to reverse a previously recorded impairment.

Cost Model versus Revaluation Model

As previously mentioned, under IFRS, companies can choose to account for their property, plant, and equipment under either the cost model or the revaluation model. We have used the cost model in this chapter because it is used by almost all companies. Only about 3% of companies reporting under IFRS use the revaluation model. The revaluation model is allowed under IFRS mainly because it is particularly useful in countries that experience high rates of inflation or for companies in certain industries, such as investment or real estate companies, where fair values are more relevant than cost.

Under the **revaluation model**, the carrying amount of property, plant, and equipment is its fair value less any accumulated depreciation less any subsequent impairment losses. This model can be applied only to assets whose fair value can be reliably measured, and revaluations must be carried out often enough that the carrying amount is not materially different from the asset's fair value at the balance sheet date. As the accounting in the revaluation model is relatively complex, and because so few companies use this model, we will not cover this model in this textbook and leave further discussion of it to a later accounting course.

Changes in Depreciation Method, Estimated Useful Life, or Residual Value

As previously explained, the depreciation method used should be consistent with the pattern in which the asset's future economic benefits are expected to be consumed by the company. The appropriateness of the method should be reviewed at least annually in case there has been a change in the expected pattern. Management must also review its estimates of the useful life and residual value of the company's depreciable assets at least at each year end. If wear and tear or obsolescence indicates that the estimates are too low or too high, estimates should be changed. If the depreciation method, estimated useful life, or residual values are changed, this will cause a revision to the depreciation calculations.

Revised Depreciation Calculations

All of the above discussed factors will result in a revision to the depreciation calculation. In each case, the revision is made for current and future years only. The revision is not made retroactively for past periods. Thus, when a change in depreciation is made, (1) there is no correction of previously recorded depreciation expense, and (2) depreciation expense for current and future years is revised. The rationale for this treatment is that the original calculation made in the past was based on the best information available at that time. The revision is based on new information that should affect only future periods. In addition, if past periods were often restated, users would feel less confident about financial statements.

To calculate the new annual depreciation expense, we must first calculate the asset's carrying amount at the time of the change. This is equal to the asset's original cost minus the accumulated depreciation to date, plus any capital expenditures, minus any impairment in value. We must also determine if the original depreciation method, residual value, and useful life are still appropriate. If not, we must determine which method is now appropriate, and the revised residual value and useful life.

To illustrate how to revise depreciation, assume that 1 Stop Florists decides on December 31, 2014—before recording its depreciation for 2014—to extend the estimated useful life of its truck by one more year (to December 31, 2016) because of its good condition. As a result of using the truck an extra year, the estimated residual value is expected to decline from its original estimate of $2,000 to $700. Assume that the company has been using straight-line depreciation and determines this is still the appropriate method. Recall that the truck was purchased on January 1, 2011, for $25,000 and originally had an estimated useful life of five years.

The carrying amount at December 31, 2014—before recording depreciation for 2014—is $11,200 [$25,000 − (3 × $4,600)]. This is also the amount shown in Illustration 9-5 as the carrying amount at December 31, 2013. The remaining useful life of three years is calculated by taking the original useful life of five years, subtracting the three years where depreciation has already been recorded, and adding the additional estimated years of useful life—in this case one year. The new annual depreciation is $3,500, calculated as in Illustration 9-11.

Illustration 9-11 ➜

Formula for revised straight-line depreciation

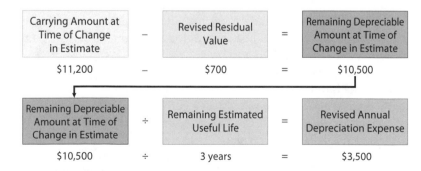

As a result of the revision to the truck's estimated useful life and residual value, 1 Stop Florists will record depreciation expense of $3,500 on December 31 of 2014, 2015, and 2016. The company will not go back and change the depreciation for 2011, 2012, and 2013. Accumulated depreciation will now equal $24,300 [($4,600 × 3) + ($3,500 × 3)] at the end of the six-year useful life instead of the $23,000 that was originally calculated. The $1,300 increase in accumulated depreciation is because the estimated residual value was revised and decreased by $1,300 ($2,000 − $700).

If the units-of-production depreciation method is used, the calculation is the same as we just saw except that the remaining useful life is expressed as units rather than years. If the diminishing-balance method is used, the revised rate would be applied to the carrying amount at the time of the change in estimate. The rate must be revised because the useful life has changed.

In our feature story, we are told that in 2000–01, Dawson College retroactively calculated depreciation from 1995–96. Based on what you have just learned, this retroactive change would appear to be incorrect. However, the retroactive change in 2000–01 was the result of recording depreciation for the first time. Before this, Dawson had not recorded depreciation. This type of change is known as a change in accounting policy. Changes in accounting policy usually apply to past periods.

 ### ACCOUNTING IN ACTION: ACROSS THE ORGANIZATION INSIGHT

The 2008 global financial crisis had a significant impact on the forest industry, a 2009 PricewaterhouseCoopers study found. Canadian producers described 2008 as the worst economic downturn in recent history. The onset of the global financial crisis and reduction in demand resulted in inventory increases and reductions in sales volumes for the last half of the year. Nearly every segment of the industry experienced significant drops in demand, which led to a buildup in inventory and shrinking prices for the products. This resulted in many companies recording writedowns and asset impairments as they looked to restructure and clean up their balance sheets. The total loss for the 11 Canadian companies included in the global survey rose 355% to $4.04 billion, compared with a loss of $889 million in 2007. The top 100 forest, paper, and packaging companies worldwide recorded total losses of US$8 billion in 2008, compared with profits of US$13.8 billion in 2007.

Source: Brenda Bouw, "Global forest earnings slide into red," *The Globe and Mail*, June 25, 2009.

What parts of an organization are responsible for determining if an impairment loss should be recorded?

BEFORE YOU GO ON . . .

➡ Review It

1. Under what circumstances will depreciation need to be revised?
2. What are the differences between operating and capital expenditures?
3. What is an impairment loss? How is it calculated?
4. What are the differences between the cost and revaluation models?
5. Are revisions of depreciation made to prior periods, future periods, or both? Explain.

➡ Do It

On August 1, 1996, just after its year end, Fine Furniture Company purchased a building for $500,000. The company used straight-line depreciation to allocate the cost of this building, estimating a residual value of $50,000 and a useful life of 30 years. After 15 years of use, on August 1, 2011, the company was forced to replace the roof at a cost of $25,000 cash. The residual value was expected to remain at $50,000 but the total useful life was now expected to increase to 40 years. Prepare journal entries to record (a) depreciation for the year ended July 31, 2011; (b) the cost of the addition on August 1, 2011; and (c) depreciation for the year ended July 31, 2012.

Action Plan

• Understand the difference between an operating expenditure (benefits only the current period) and a capital expenditure (benefits future periods).
• To revise annual depreciation, calculate the carrying amount (cost less accumulated depreciation) at the revision date. Note that the cost of any capital expenditure will increase the carrying amount of the asset to be depreciated.

- Subtract any revised residual value from the carrying amount at the time of the change in estimate (plus the capital expenditure in this case) to determine the depreciable amount.
- Allocate the revised depreciable amount over the remaining (not total) useful life.

Solution

(a)

July 31, 2011	Depreciation Expense [($500,000 – $50,000) ÷ 30]	15,000	
	Accumulated Depreciation—Building		15,000
	To record annual depreciation expense.		

(b)

Aug. 1, 2011	Building	25,000	
	Cash		25,000
	To record replacement of roof.		

(c)

Cost:	$500,000
Less: Accumulated depreciation $15,000 per year × 15 years	225,000
Carrying amount before replacement of roof, August 1, 2011	275,000
Add: Capital expenditure (roof)	25,000
Carrying amount after replacement of roof, August 1, 2011	300,000
Less: Revised residual value	50,000
Revised depreciable amount	250,000
Divide by: Remaining useful life (40 – 15)	÷25 years
Revised annual depreciation	$ 10,000

July 31, 2012	Depreciation Expense	10,000	
	Accumulated Depreciation—Building		10,000
	To record revised annual depreciation expense.		

The Navigator

Related exercise material: BE9–10, BE9–11, E9–6, E9–7, and E9–8.

Disposals of Property, Plant, and Equipment

STUDY OBJECTIVE 4

Account for the disposal of property, plant, and equipment.

Companies dispose of property, plant, or equipment that is no longer useful to them. Illustration 9-12 shows three methods of disposal.

Illustration 9-12 →

Methods of property, plant, and equipment disposal

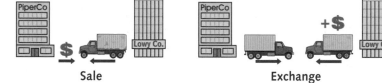

Retirement
Equipment is scrapped or discarded.

Sale
Equipment is sold.

Exchange
Existing equipment is traded for new equipment.

Steps in Recording Disposals of Property, Plant, and Equipment

Whatever the disposal method, a company must take the following four steps to record the retirement, sale, or exchange of the property, plant, or equipment:

Step 1: Update Depreciation.

Depreciation must be recorded over the entire period of time an asset is available for use. Therefore, if the disposal occurs in the middle of an accounting period, depreciation must be updated for the fraction of the year since the last time adjusting entries were recorded up to the date of disposal. Depreciation is recorded even if the asset is not in use, unless it is fully depreciated.

Step 2: Calculate the Carrying Amount.

Calculate the carrying amount at the date of disposal after updating the accumulated depreciation for any partial year depreciation calculated in Step 1 above:

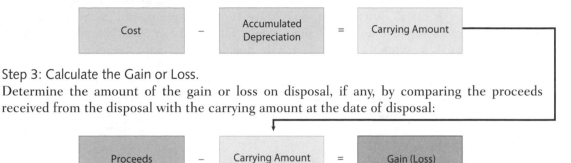

Step 3: Calculate the Gain or Loss.

Determine the amount of the gain or loss on disposal, if any, by comparing the proceeds received from the disposal with the carrying amount at the date of disposal:

If the proceeds of the sale are more than the carrying amount of the property, plant, or equipment, there is a gain on disposal. If the proceeds of the sale are less than the carrying amount of the asset sold, there is a loss on disposal.

Step 4: Record the Disposal.

Record the disposal, removing the asset's cost and the accumulated depreciation from the accounts. The Accumulated Depreciation account is decreased by the balance in the account, which is the total amount of depreciation and any impairment losses that have been recorded for the asset up to its disposal date. This is the same amount that was used to calculate the carrying amount in Step 2 above. Record the proceeds (if any) and the gain or loss on disposal (if any). Gains on disposal are recorded as credits because credits increase owner's equity; losses on disposal are recorded as debits because debits decrease owner's equity.

> Dr. Cash (or other account)
> Dr. Accumulated Depreciation
> Dr. Loss on Disposal OR Cr. Gain on Disposal
> Cr. Property, plant, or equipment account

Gains and losses are reported in the operating section of a multiple-step income statement. Why? Recall that depreciation expense is an estimate. Loss results when the annual depreciation expense has not been sufficient so that the carrying amount at the date of disposal is equal to the proceeds. Gains are caused because annual depreciation expense has been too high, so the carrying amount at the date of disposal is less than the proceeds. Thus gains and losses are basically just adjustments to depreciation expense and should be recorded in the same section of the income statement.

Retirement of Property, Plant, and Equipment

Instead of being sold or exchanged, some assets are simply retired at the end of their useful lives. For example, some productive assets used in manufacturing may have highly specialized uses and consequently have no market when the company no longer needs the asset. In this case, the asset is simply retired.

When an asset is retired, there are no proceeds on disposal. The Accumulated Depreciation account is decreased (debited) for the full amount of depreciation taken over the life of the asset. The asset account is reduced (credited) for the asset's original cost. Even if the carrying amount equals zero, a journal entry is still required to remove the asset and its related depreciation account from the books, as shown in the following example.

To illustrate the retirement of a piece of property, plant, and equipment, assume that on August 1, 2011, Baseyev Enterprises retires its printing equipment, which cost $31,200. At the time of purchase, on August 1, 2007, the printing equipment was expected to have a four-year useful life and no residual value. Baseyev used straight-line depreciation and the annual depreciation expense was $7,800 per year ($31,200 ÷ 4) or $650 per month ($7,800 ÷ 12). The balance in the account Accumulated Depreciation at Baseyev's year end, December 31, 2010, was $26,650 ($650/month × 41 months). Straight-line depreciation for the seven months from December 31, 2010, to August 1, 2011, is $4,550 ($650/month × 7 months).

To update the depreciation since the last time that adjusting journal entries were made, which would have been at Baseyev's year end, December 31, 2010, a journal entry to record the seven months of depreciation is made, as follows:

A	=	L	+	OE						
−4,550				−4,550						

Cash flows: no effect

Aug. 1	Depreciation Expense	4,550	
	Accumulated Depreciation—Printing Equipment		4,550
	To record depreciation expense for the first 7 months of 2011.		

After this journal entry is posted, the balance in Accumulated Depreciation is $31,200 ($26,650 + $4,550). The printing equipment is now fully depreciated with a carrying amount of zero (cost of $31,200 − accumulated depreciation of $31,200).

The entry to record the retirement of the printing equipment is:

A	=	L	+	OE
+31,200				
−31,200				

Cash flows: no effect

Aug. 1	Accumulated Depreciation—Printing Equipment	31,200	
	Printing Equipment		31,200
	To record retirement of fully depreciated printing equipment.		

What happens if a company is still using a fully depreciated asset? In this case, the asset and its accumulated depreciation continue to be reported on the balance sheet, without further depreciation, until the asset is retired. Reporting the asset and related depreciation on the balance sheet informs the reader of the financial statements that the asset is still being used by the company. Once an asset is fully depreciated, even if it is still being used, no additional depreciation should be taken. Accumulated depreciation on a piece of property, plant, and equipment can never be more than the asset's cost.

If a piece of property, plant, and equipment is retired before it is fully depreciated and no residual value is received, a loss on disposal occurs. Assume that Baseyev Enterprises retires its printing equipment on January 1, 2011. The loss on disposal is calculated by subtracting the asset's carrying amount from the proceeds that are received. In this case, there are no proceeds and the carrying amount is $4,550 (cost of $31,200 − accumulated depreciation of $26,650), resulting in a loss of $4,550:

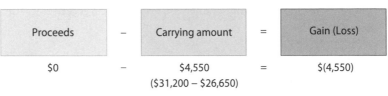

	Proceeds	−	Carrying amount	=	Gain (Loss)
	$0	−	$4,550	=	$(4,550)
			($31,200 − $26,650)		

The entry to record the retirement of equipment is as follows:

A	=	L	+	OE
+26,650				−4,550
−31,200				

Cash flows: no effect

Jan. 1	Accumulated Depreciation—Printing Equipment	26,650	
	Loss on Disposal	4,550	
	Printing Equipment		31,200
	To record retirement of printing equipment at a loss.		

You should also note that there will never be a gain when an asset is retired. The proceeds are always zero and therefore can never be greater than the carrying amount of the retired asset.

Sale of Property, Plant, and Equipment

In a disposal by sale, the four steps listed earlier are followed. Both gains and losses on disposal are common when an asset is sold. Only by coincidence will the asset's carrying amount and fair value (the proceeds) be the same when the asset is sold. We will illustrate the sale of office furniture at both a gain and a loss in the following sections.

Gain on Disposal. To illustrate a gain, assume that on April 1, 2011, Baseyev Enterprises sells office furniture for $15,000 cash. The office furniture had originally been purchased on January 1, 2007, at a cost of $60,200. At that time, it was estimated that the office furniture would have a residual value of $5,000 and a useful life of five years.

The first step is to update any unrecorded depreciation. Annual depreciation using the straight-line method is $11,040 [($60,200 – $5,000) ÷ 5]. The entry to record the depreciation expense and update accumulated depreciation for the first three months of 2011 is as follows:

Apr. 1	Depreciation Expense ($11,040 × ³⁄₁₂)	2,760	
	Accumulated Depreciation—Office Furniture		2,760
	To record depreciation expense for the first 3 months of 2011.		

A = L + OE
−2,760   −2,760
Cash flows: no effect

The second step is to calculate the carrying amount on April 1, 2011. Accumulated depreciation of $46,920 is calculated using four years (January 1, 2007 to December 31, 2010) at $11,040/year plus $2,760 for 2011.

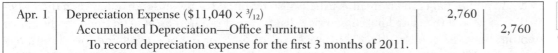

Cost	–	Accumulated Depreciation	=	Carrying Amount
$60,200	–	$46,920	=	$13,280
		[($11,040 × 4) + $2,760]		

The third step is to calculate the gain or loss on disposal. A $1,720 gain on disposal is determined as follows:

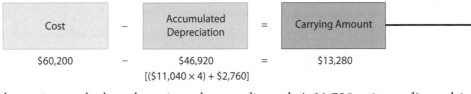

Proceeds	–	Carrying Amount	=	Gain (Loss)
$15,000	–	$13,280	=	$1,720

The fourth step is the entry to record the sale of the office furniture as follows:

Apr. 1	Cash	15,000	
	Accumulated Depreciation—Office Furniture	46,920	
	Gain on Disposal		1,720
	Office Furniture		60,200
	To record the sale of office furniture at a gain.		

A = L + OE
+15,000   +1,720
+46,920
−60,200
⬆ Cash flows: +15,000

Notice that the carrying amount of $13,280 does not appear in the journal entry. Instead, the asset's cost ($60,200) and the total accumulated depreciation ($46,920) are used. Remember the carrying amount is simply a number calculated to determine the gain or loss. It is not an account and cannot be debited or credited.

Loss on Disposal. Assume that instead of selling the office furniture for $15,000, Baseyev sells it for $9,000. In this case, a loss of $4,280 is calculated as follows:

Proceeds	–	Carrying Amount	=	Gain (Loss)
$9,000	–	$13,280	=	$(4,280)

The entry to record the sale of the office furniture is as follows:

A	=	L	+	OE
+9,000				−4,280
+46,920				
−60,200				

↑ Cash flows: +9,000

Apr. 1	Cash	9,000	
	Accumulated Depreciation—Office Furniture	46,920	
	Loss on Disposal	4,280	
	Office Furniture		60,200
	To record the sale of office furniture at a loss.		

As previously explained, the loss on disposal is the result of not recording enough depreciation expense prior to selling the asset.

Exchanges of Property, Plant, and Equipment

An exchange of assets is recorded as the purchase of a new asset and the sale of an old asset. Typically a **trade-in allowance** on the old asset is given toward the purchase price of the new asset. An additional cash payment is usually also required for the difference between the trade-in allowance and the stated purchase price (list price) of the new asset. The trade-in allowance amount, however, is often affected by price concessions for the new asset and therefore rarely reflects the fair value of the asset that is given up. Consequently, as fair value is what matters, trade-in allowances are ignored for accounting purposes.

Instead of using the stated purchase price, the new asset is recorded at the fair value of the asset given up plus any cash paid (or less any cash received). Instead of using the trade-in allowance, the fair value of the asset given up is used to calculate the gain or loss on the asset being given up. A loss results if the carrying amount of the asset being given up is more than its fair value. A gain results if the carrying amount is less than its fair value.

Thus, the procedure to account for exchanges of assets is as follows:

Step 1: Update any unrecorded depreciation expense on the asset being given up to the date of the exchange.
Step 2: Calculate the carrying amount of the asset being given up (cost − accumulated depreciation).
Step 3: Calculate any gain or loss on disposal [fair value − carrying amount = gain (loss)].
Step 4: Record the exchange as follows:
  • Remove the cost and the accumulated depreciation of the asset that is given up.
  • Record any gain or loss on disposal.
  • Record the new asset at the fair value of the old asset plus any cash paid (or less any cash received).
  • Record the cash paid or received.

To illustrate an exchange of long-lived assets, assume that Chilko Company exchanged old computers for new computers on October 1, 2011. The original cost of the old computers was $61,000 on January 1, 2009. Depreciation was calculated using the straight-line method, over a three-year useful life, with an estimated residual value of $1,000. The fair value of the old computers on October 1, 2011, is $5,000.

The list price of the new computers was $51,000. Chilko received an $8,000 trade-in allowance from the computer retailer for the old computers and paid $43,000 cash ($51,000 − $8,000) for the new computers. Chilko's year end is December 31.

The first step is to update the depreciation on the old computers for the nine months ended October 1, 2011. Annual depreciation expense is $20,000 [($61,000 − $1,000) ÷ 3], so depreciation for nine months is $15,000 ($20,000 × $9/12$).

A	=	L	+	OE
−15,000				−15,000

Cash flows: no effect

Oct. 1	Depreciation Expense	15,000	
	Accumulated Depreciation—Computers		15,000
	To record depreciation expense for the first 9 months of 2011.		

After this entry is posted, the balance in Accumulated Depreciation on October 1, 2011, is $55,000 [$20,000 (in 2009) + $20,000 (in 2010) + $15,000 (in 2011)]. The accumulated depreciation can also be calculated as follows: $20,000 × 2.75 years = $55,000. Be sure to watch the dates and time periods carefully when calculating partial period depreciation: thus, the ".75" is for the nine months of depreciation in the current year.

On October 1, 2011, the carrying amount is $6,000 (cost of $61,000 – accumulated depreciation of $55,000). The loss on disposal on the old computers is determined by comparing the carrying amount with the fair value, which represents the proceeds in this situation:

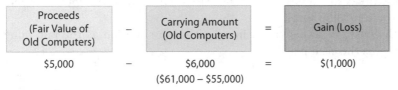

Proceeds (Fair Value of Old Computers)	–	Carrying Amount (Old Computers)	=	Gain (Loss)
$5,000	–	$6,000	=	$(1,000)
		($61,000 – $55,000)		

The entry to record the exchange of computers is as follows:

Oct. 1	Computers (new)	48,000	
	Accumulated Depreciation—Computers (old)	55,000	
	Loss on Disposal	1,000	
	Computers (old)		61,000
	Cash		43,000
	To record exchange of computers, plus cash.		

A	=	L	+	OE
+48,000				−1,000
+55,000				
−61,000				
−43,000				

↓ Cash flows: −43,000

Note that the exchange of computers is not netted. That is, it is shown as a separate increase and decrease to the general ledger account Computers. The cost of the new computers ($48,000) is determined by the fair value of the old computers ($5,000) plus the cash paid ($43,000). The list price of $51,000 and the trade-in allowance of $8,000 are ignored in determining the real cost of the new computers.

In some situations, the exchange lacks commercial substance or else the fair values of the asset acquired, or the asset given up, cannot be determined. In such cases, the new long-lived asset is recorded at the carrying amount of the old asset that was given up, plus any cash paid (or less any cash received). Carrying amount is used in these circumstances because the new asset is basically substituted or swapped for the old asset. As the carrying amount of the old asset is used for the carrying amount of the new asset, and the exchange has therefore not changed the operations of the business significantly, no gain or loss is recorded.

BEFORE YOU GO ON . . .

➡ Review It

1. What is the proper way to account for the retirement, sale, or exchange of a piece of property, plant, and equipment?
2. What is the formula to calculate a gain or loss on disposal?
3. What is the procedure to account for an exchange of assets?

➡ Do It

Overland Trucking has a truck that was purchased on January 1, 2007, for $80,000. The truck had been depreciated on a straight-line basis with an estimated residual value of $5,000 and an estimated useful life of five years. Overland has a December 31 year end. Assume each of the following four independent situations:

1. On January 1, 2012, Overland retires the truck.
2. On May 1, 2011, Overland sells the truck for $9,500 cash.
3. On October 1, 2011, Overland sells the truck for $9,500 cash.
4. On November 1, 2011, Overland exchanges the old truck, plus $60,000 cash, for a new truck. The old truck has a fair value of $9,500. The new truck has a list price of $70,000, but the dealer will give Overland a $10,000 trade-in allowance on the old truck.

Prepare the journal entry to record each of these situations.

Action Plan

- Update any unrecorded depreciation for dispositions during the fiscal year.
- Compare the proceeds with the asset's carrying amount to determine if there has been a gain or loss.
- Record any proceeds received and any gain or loss. Remove both the asset and any related accumulated depreciation from the accounts.
- Determine the cash paid in an exchange situation as the difference between the list price and the trade-in allowance.
- Record the cost of the new asset in an exchange situation as the fair value of the asset given up, plus the cash paid.

Solution

$$\frac{\$80,000 - \$5,000}{5 \text{ years}} = \$15,000 \text{ annual depreciation exspence}$$

$$\$15,000 \div 12 = \$1,250 \text{ per month}$$

1. Retirement of truck:

Jan. 1, 2012	Accumulated Depreciation ($1,250 × 60 months)	75,000	
	Loss on Disposal [$0 – ($80,000 – $75,000)]	5,000	
	Truck		80,000
	To record retirement of truck.		

2. Sale of truck for $9,500 on May 1, 2011:

May 1, 2011	Depreciation Expense ($1,250 × 4 months)	5,000	
	Accumulated Depreciation		5,000
	To record depreciation for 4 months.		
	Cash	9,500	
	Accumulated Depreciation—Truck ($1,250 × 52 months)	65,000	
	Loss on Disposal [$9,500 – ($80,000 – $65,000)]	5,500	
	Truck		80,000
	To record sale of truck at a loss.		

3. Sale of truck for $9,500 on Oct. 1, 2011:

Oct. 1, 2011	Depreciation Expense ($1,250 × 9 months)	11,250	
	Accumulated Depreciation		11,250
	To record depreciation for 9 months.		
	Cash	9,500	
	Accumulated Depreciation—Truck ($1,250 × 57 months)	71,250	
	Gain on Disposal [$9,500 – ($80,000 – $71,250)]		750
	Truck		80,000
	To record sale of truck at a gain.		

4. Exchange of truck on Nov. 1, 2011:

Nov. 1, 2011	Depreciation Expense ($1,250 × 10 months)	12,500	
	Accumulated Depreciation		12,500
	To record depreciation for 10 months.		
	Truck (new) ($9,500 + $60,000)	69,500	
	Accumulated Depreciation—Truck ($1,250 × 58 months)	72,500	
	Gain on Disposal [$9,500 – ($80,000 – $72,500)]		2,000
	Truck (old)		80,000
	Cash ($70,000 – $10,000)		60,000
	To record exchange of trucks, plus cash.		

The Navigator

Related exercise material: BE9–12, BE9–13, BE9–14, E9–9, and E9–10.

Natural Resources

Natural resources consist of standing timber and underground deposits of oil, gas, and minerals. Canada is rich in natural resources, ranging from the towering rainforests in coastal British Columbia to one of the world's largest nickel deposits in Voisey's Bay, Labrador. These long-lived assets have two characteristics that make them different from other long-lived assets: (1) they are physically extracted in operations such as mining, cutting, or pumping; and (2) only an act of nature can replace them. Because of these characteristics, natural resources are sometimes called *wasting assets*.

Natural resources are tangible assets, similar to property, plant, and equipment. A key distinction between natural resources and property, plant, and equipment is that natural resources physically lose substance, or deplete, as they are used. For example, there is less of a tract of timberland (a natural resource) as the timber is cut and sold. When we use equipment, its physical substance remains the same regardless of the product it produces.

Cost

The cost of a natural resource is determined in the same way as the cost of property, plant, and equipment and includes all expenditures necessary in acquiring the resource and preparing it for its intended use. These costs are often referred to as acquisition, exploration, and development costs. The cost of a natural resource also includes the estimated future removal and site restoration cleanup costs, which are often large. Restoration costs are usually required in order to return the resource as closely as possible to its natural state at the end of its useful life.

As discussed earlier in the chapter, accounting for asset retirement costs and the allocation of these costs over the useful life of the natural resource is complicated. Further discussion of these concepts is left to an intermediate accounting course. Accounting for exploration and development costs is also very complex. We will, however, look at how the acquisition cost of a natural resource is allocated over its useful life in the next section.

Depreciation

The units-of-production method (learned earlier in the chapter) is generally used to calculate the depreciation of wasting assets. Under the units-of-production method, the total cost of the natural resource minus its residual value is divided by the number of units estimated to be in the resource. The result is a depreciable amount per unit of product. The depreciable amount per unit is then multiplied by the number of units extracted, to determine the annual depreciation expense.

Alternative terminology
Depreciation for natural resources is frequently called *depletion* because the assets physically deplete as the resource is extracted.

To illustrate, assume that Rabbit Lake Company invests $5.5 million in a mine that is estimated to have 10 million tonnes of uranium and a $200,000 residual value. In the first year, 800,000 tonnes of uranium are extracted. Illustration 9-13 shows the formulas and calculations.

Cost	−	Residual Value	=	Depreciable Amount
$5,500,000	−	$200,000	=	$5,300,000

Depreciable Amount	÷	Total Estimated Units of Production	=	Depreciable Amount per Unit
$5,300,000	÷	10,000,000 t	=	$0.53

Depreciable Amount per Unit	×	Number of Units Extracted and Sold during the Year	=	Annual Depreciation Expense
$0.53	×	800,000 t	=	$424,000

← Illustration 9-13

Formula for units-of-production method for natural resources

The depreciation expense for the amount of the resource that has been extracted is initially charged (debited) to an inventory account, a current asset. Note that this is not the same as depreciation for property, plant, and equipment, which is recorded as an expense. Depreciation on natural resources is accounted for in this way because the resource extracted is available for sale—similar to merchandise that has been purchased or manufactured for sale, as we learned in Chapter 5.

The entry to record depreciation of the uranium mine for Rabbit Lake Company's first year of operation, ended December 31, 2011, is as follows:

A	=	L	+	OE
+424,000				
–424,000				

Cash flows: no effect

Dec. 31	Inventory ($0.53 × 800,000 t)	424,000	
	Accumulated Depreciation—Uranium Mine		424,000
	To record depreciation expense on uranium mine.		

All costs of extracting the natural resource—both current production costs such as labour and depreciation of the natural resource—are recorded as inventory. When sold, the inventory costs are transferred to cost of goods sold and matched with the period's revenue. In other words, the depreciation is charged to the income statement only in the period in which the related goods are sold. Depreciation related to goods not yet sold remains in inventory and is reported as a current asset.

For example, assume that Rabbit Lake Company does not sell all of the 800,000 tonnes of uranium extracted in 2011. It sells 700,000 tonnes and stores 100,000 tonnes for later sale. In this situation, Rabbit Lake Company would include $371,000 (700,000 × $0.53) in the cost of the resource sold on its income statement. As mentioned before, the cost of labour and other production costs related to the goods sold would also be included in the cost of the resource sold on the income statement. The remaining depreciation of $53,000 ($424,000 – $371,000) is for the 100,000 tonnes kept for later sale and will be included in inventory in the current assets section of the company's balance sheet.

Like depreciation for property, plant, and equipment, the depreciation of a natural resource needs to be revised if there are capital expenditures during the useful life. Also, the depreciable amount per unit of a natural resource needs to be revised whenever the estimated total units of the resource have changed as a result of new information. Natural resources such as oil and gas deposits and some metals have provided the greatest challenges. Estimates of the total units (also called reserves) of these natural resources are mostly knowledgeable guesses and may be revised whenever more information becomes available.

Natural resources must also be reviewed and tested for impairment annually or more frequently whenever circumstances make this appropriate. For example, Rabbit Lake Company would need to test the uranium mine for impairment if there was a significant and permanent decline in the selling price of uranium. If there is impairment, the uranium mine must be written down to its fair value, an impairment loss must be recorded, and current and future depreciation needs to be revised accordingly.

Disposal of Natural Resources

At disposal, just as with property, plant, and equipment, any unrecorded depreciation must be updated for the portion of the year up to the date of the disposal. Then proceeds are recorded, the cost and the accumulated depreciation of the natural resource are removed, and a gain or loss, if any, is recorded. As mentioned earlier, there may also be site restoration costs at this time, but we leave the accounting for these costs to a future accounting course.

BEFORE YOU GO ON . . .

→ **Review It**

1. How is depreciation expense calculated for natural resources?
2. Explain how depreciation expense can be both an asset (inventory) and an expense (cost of goods sold).
3. Why might a company need to revise the depreciation of a natural resource?

→ **Do It**

High Timber Company invests $14 million in a tract of timber land. It is estimated to have 10 million cunits (1 cunit = 100 cubic feet) of timber and a $500,000 residual value. In the first year, 40,000 cunits of timber are cut, and 30,000 of these cunits are sold. Calculate depreciation for High Timber's first year of operations and allocate it between inventory and cost of goods sold.

Action Plan

- Use units-of-production depreciation for natural resources.
- Calculate the depreciable amount per unit by dividing the total cost minus the estimated residual value by the total estimated units.
- Multiply the depreciable amount per unit by the number of units cut to determine the total depreciation.
- Allocate the depreciation related to the units that have been cut but not yet sold to inventory.
- Allocate the depreciation related to the units that have been cut and sold to expense.

Solution

1. Depreciable amount per unit: ($14,000,000 – $500,000) ÷ 10,000,000 cunits = $1.35 per cunit
2. Total depreciation for the year: $1.35 per cunit × 40,000 cunits cut = $54,000
3. Depreciation allocated to inventory: $1.35 per cunit × 10,000 cunits on hand = $13,500
4. Depreciation allocated to expense: $1.35 per cunit × 30,000 cunits sold = $40,500

Related exercise material: BE9–15 and E9–11.

The Navigator

Intangible Assets and Goodwill

Similar to property, plant, and equipment, and natural resources, intangible assets provide economic benefits in future periods. They are used to produce products or provide services over these periods and are not intended for sale to customers. However, unlike property, plant, and equipment, and natural resources, which are **tangible assets** because they have a physical substance, **intangible assets** involve rights, privileges, and competitive advantages that have no physical substance. In other words, they are not physical things. Many companies' most valuable assets are intangible. Some widely known intangibles are Alexander Graham Bell's patent on the telephone, the franchises of Tim Hortons, the trade name of President's Choice, and the trademark CBC.

An intangible asset must be identifiable, which means it must meet one of the two following criteria: (1) it can be separated from the company and sold, whether or not the company intends to do so, or (2) it is based on contractual or legal rights, regardless of whether or not it can be separated from the company. Since goodwill cannot be separated from a company and sold, there are differences in the accounting for goodwill versus other intangible assets.

STUDY OBJECTIVE 6

Identify the basic accounting issues for intangible assets and goodwill.

Accounting for Intangible Assets

Like tangible assets (property, plant, and equipment, and natural resources), intangible assets are recorded at cost. Cost includes all the costs of acquisition and other costs that are needed to make the intangible asset ready for its intended use—including legal fees and similar charges.

As with tangible assets, companies have a choice of following the cost model or the revaluation model when accounting for intangible assets subsequent to acquisition. The majority of companies use the cost model for all long-lived assets. So we will leave further study of the revaluation model, as it applies to intangible assets, for a later accounting course.

Under the cost model, if an intangible asset has a finite (limited) life, its cost must be systematically allocated over its useful life. We called this "depreciation" when discussing tangible assets. With intangible assets, we use the term **amortization**.

For an intangible asset with a finite life, its **amortizable amount** (cost less residual value) should be allocated over the shorter of the (1) estimated useful life and (2) legal life. Intangible assets, by their nature, rarely have any residual value, so the amortizable amount is normally equal to the cost. In addition, the useful life of an intangible asset is usually shorter than its legal life, so useful life is most often used as the amortization period.

When a company estimates the useful life of an intangible asset, it must consider factors such as how long the company expects to use the asset, obsolescence, demand, and other factors that can make the intangible asset ineffective at helping to earn revenue. For example, a patent on a computer chip may have a legal life of 20 years, but with technology changing as rapidly as it does, the chip's useful life may be only four or five years maximum.

Amortization begins as soon as the asset is ready to be used as intended by management. Similar to depreciation, the company must use the amortization method that best matches the pattern with which the asset's future economic benefits are expected to be consumed. If that pattern cannot be determined reliably, the straight-line method should be used.

Just as land is considered to have an indefinite life, there are also intangible assets with indefinite life. An intangible asset is considered to have an indefinite (unlimited) life when, based on an analysis of all of the relevant factors, there is no foreseeable limit to the period over which the intangible asset is expected to generate net cash inflows for the company. If an intangible has an indefinite life, it is not amortized.

As with tangible assets, all intangible assets must be reviewed and tested for impairment. Intangible assets with indefinite lives are tested more frequently for impairments than are intangible assets with finite lives. Indefinite-life intangible assets should be tested for impairment at least once a year.

Recall from earlier in this chapter that there is impairment if the asset's recoverable amount falls below its carrying amount. If any impairment is evident, the intangible asset is written down to its recoverable amount and an impairment loss recorded. Under IFRS, an impairment loss cannot be reversed for goodwill, but it can be for other intangible assets.

Similar to tangible assets, the amortization is revised if there are changes in cost, or useful life, or an impairment loss. The revision is accounted for in the current and future periods; retroactive adjustments are not recorded.

At disposal, just as with tangible assets, the carrying amount of the intangible asset is removed, and a gain or loss, if any, is recorded.

Intangible Assets with Finite Lives

Examples of intangible assets with finite lives include patents and copyrights. We also include research and development costs in this section because these costs often lead to the creation of patents and copyrights.

Patents

A **patent** is an exclusive right issued by the Canadian Intellectual Property Office of Industry Canada that allows the patent holder to manufacture, sell, or otherwise control an invention for a period of 20 years from the date of the application. A patent cannot be renewed. But the legal life of a patent may be extended if the patent holder obtains new patents for improvements or other changes in the basic design.

The initial cost of a patent is the price paid to acquire it. After it has been acquired, legal costs are often incurred. There is a saying that "A patent is only as good as the money you're prepared to spend defending it," which is very true. Companies such as Microsoft, Verizon, Dell, and Hewlett Packard are frequently sued for patent infringement. About 80% of patent suits are against large technology and financial companies.

Legal costs to successfully defend a patent in an infringement suit are considered necessary to prove the patent's validity. They are added to the Patent account and amortized over the patent's remaining life.

The cost of a patent should be amortized over its 20-year legal life or its useful life, whichever is shorter. As mentioned earlier, the useful life should be carefully assessed by considering whether the patent is likely to become ineffective at contributing to revenue before the end of its legal life.

Copyrights

A **copyright** is granted by the Canadian Intellectual Property Office, giving the owner an exclusive right to reproduce and sell an artistic or published work. Copyrights extend for the life of the creator plus 50 years. Generally, a copyright's useful life is significantly shorter than its legal life.

The cost of a copyright consists of the cost of acquiring and defending it. The cost may only be the fee paid to register the copyright, or it may amount to a great deal more if a copyright infringement suit is involved.

ACCOUNTING IN ACTION: ALL ABOUT YOU

Canadian copyright laws have not undergone a major reform for over 10 years. The Internet and other new technologies have changed the way in which we produce and access copyright material. In 1998, the first MP3 player, which could store up to one hour of music, was introduced in the market. Today a device that is smaller than a credit card can hold thousands of songs, videos, and photographs. It has been argued that Canadian copyright law needs to be updated to give Canadian creators and consumers the tools they need to participate in the digital marketplace and to foster innovation. On July 20, 2009, the federal government launched nationwide consultations to solicit Canadians' opinions on the issue of copyright following two failed attempts by the Canadian government to change the copyright law. Proposed amendments included a $500 fine for downloading copyrighted material from the Internet for personal use and a fine of up to $20,000 for breaking digital locks on DVDs or uploading copyrighted material for file-sharing.

Source: Government of Canada's Copyright Consultations website, available at: http://copyright.econsultation.ca; Kate Kennedy and Chris Selley, "A users guide to the copyright bill," *Maclean's* magazine, June 16, 2008.

Is it important that the copyrights of artists, writers, musicians, and the entertainment industry be protected?

Research and Development Costs

Research and development (R&D) costs are not intangible assets by themselves. But they may lead to patents and copyrights, new processes, and new products. Many companies spend large sums of money on research and development in an ongoing effort to develop new products or processes. Microsoft spends almost $10 billion a year on R&D—significantly more than any other company in the world.

Research and development costs present two accounting problems: (1) it is sometimes difficult to determine the costs related to specific projects; (2) it is also hard to know the extent and timing of future benefits. As a result, accounting distinguishes between research costs and development costs. **Research** is original, planned investigation that is done to gain new knowledge and understanding. All research costs should be expensed when they are incurred.

Development is the use of research findings and knowledge for a plan or design before the start of commercial production. Development costs with probable future benefits should be capitalized. In addition, all of the following conditions must be met for development costs to be capitalized:

- Management must have the technical feasibility, intention, and ability to complete the intangible asset and use or sell it.
- A future market must be defined.
- Adequate resources must exist to complete the project.
- Management must be able to measure the costs related to the development of the intangible asset.

If any of these conditions are not met, the development costs must be expensed. Illustration 9-14 shows the distinction between research and development.

Illustration 9-14 ➔

Distinction between research and development

Research	Development

Examples	Examples
• Laboratory research aimed at the discovery of new knowledge	• Testing in search or evaluation of product or process alternatives
• Searching for ways to use new research findings or other knowledge	• Design, construction, and testing of pre-production prototypes and models
• Forming concepts and designs of possible product or process alternatives	• Design of tools, jigs, moulds, and dies involving new technology

Intangible Assets with Indefinite Lives

An intangible asset is considered to have an indefinite life when there is no foreseeable limit to the length of time over which the asset is expected to generate cash. Examples of intangible assets with indefinite lives include trademarks and trade names, franchises, and licences. Intangible assets do not always fit perfectly in a specific category. Sometimes trademarks, trade names, franchises, or licences do have finite lives. In such cases, they would be amortized over the shorter of their legal or useful lives. It is more usual, however, for these intangible assets, along with goodwill, to have indefinite lives.

Trademarks, Trade Names, and Brands

A **trademark** or **trade name** is a word, phrase, jingle, or symbol that identifies a particular enterprise or product. Trade names like President's Choice, KFC, Nike, Big Mac, the Blue Jays, and TSN create immediate brand recognition and generally help the sale of a product or service. Each year, Interbrands ranks the world's best brands. In 2008, it ranked Coca-Cola as the most successful brand in the world. There were only two Canadian companies included in the list of the 100 most successful global brands in 2008: Thomson Reuters, ranked 44th, and BlackBerry (from Research In Motion Ltd.), ranked 73rd.

The creator can get an exclusive legal right to the trademark or trade name by registering it with the Canadian Intellectual Property Office. This registration gives continuous protection. It may be renewed every 15 years, as long as the trademark or trade name is in use. In most cases, companies continuously renew their trademarks or trade names. In such cases, as long as the trademark or trade name continues to be marketable, it will have an indefinite useful life.

If the trademark or trade name is purchased, the cost is the purchase price. If the trademark or trade name is developed internally rather than purchased, it cannot be recognized as an intangible asset on the balance sheet. The reason is that expenditures on internally developed trademarks or brands cannot be distinguished from the cost of developing the business as a whole. The cost cannot be separately measured.

Franchises and Licences

When you purchase a Civic from a Honda dealer, fill up your gas tank at the corner Mohawk station, or buy coffee from Tim Hortons, you are dealing with franchises. The Forzani Group also uses franchises to sell its products, including Sports Experts, Intersport, Atmosphere, Econosports, RnR, Tech Shop/Pegasus, Nevada Bob's Golf, and Hockey Experts.

A **franchise** is a contractual arrangement under which the franchisor grants the franchisee the right to sell certain products, to provide specific services, or to use certain trademarks or trade names, usually inside a specific geographic area. Another type of franchise is granted by a government body that allows a company to use public property in performing its services. Examples are the use of city streets for a bus line or taxi service; the use of public land for telephone, power, and cable lines; and the use of airwaves for radio or TV broadcasting. Such operating rights are called **licences**.

When costs can be identified with the acquisition of the franchise or licence, an intangible asset should be recognized. These rights have indefinite lives and are not amortized.

Annual payments, which are often in proportion to the franchise's total sales, are sometimes required under a franchise agreement. These payments are called **royalties** and are recorded as operating expenses in the period in which they are incurred.

Goodwill

Goodwill represents the value of all the favourable attributes that relate to a company. These include exceptional management, a desirable location, good customer relations, skilled employees, high-quality products, fair pricing policies, and harmonious relations with labour unions. Unlike other assets, which can be sold individually in the marketplace, goodwill cannot be sold individually as it is part of the business as a whole. It cannot be separated from the company, nor is it based on legal rights.

If goodwill can be identified only with the business as a whole, how can it be determined? An accountant could try to put a dollar value on the attributes (exceptional management, a desirable location, and so on), but the results would be very subjective. Subjective valuations would not contribute to the reliability of financial statements. For this reason, internally generated goodwill is not recognized as an asset.

Goodwill is recorded only when there is a purchase of an entire business, at which time an independent valuation can be determined. The cost of goodwill is measured by comparing the cost paid to purchase the entire business with the fair value of its net assets (assets less liabilities). If the cost is greater than these net identifiable assets, then the purchaser has paid for something that is not identifiable, that cannot be separated and sold—goodwill. In this situation, because a transaction has occurred, the cost of the purchased goodwill can be measured and therefore recorded as an asset.

Because goodwill has an indefinite life, just as the company has an indefinite life, it is not amortized. Since goodwill is measured using the company's fair value—a value that can easily change—it must be tested regularly for impairment just like other intangible assets with indefinite lives. Both goodwill and indefinite life intangible assets must be tested annually for impairment regardless of whether there is any indication of impairment. This is different than finite-life intangible assets, which are assessed for indications of impairment at the end of each year, and are tested only if the assessment shows that an impairment may exist.

Impairment losses on goodwill are never reversed, even if the value of the company increases after the impairment loss has been recognized. But IFRS does allow for reversals of impairment losses on both finite-life and other indefinite-life intangible assets if their value increases in the future.

BEFORE YOU GO ON . . .

→ Review It

1. What are the similarities and differences between accounting for intangible and tangible assets?
2. Give some examples of intangible assets in your everyday surroundings.
3. What are the differences between the amortization policy for intangible assets with finite lives and the policy for those with indefinite lives?
4. What are the differences between the treatment of impairment losses for (a) intangible assets with finite lives, (b) intangible assets with indefinite lives, and (c) goodwill?

→ Do It

Dummies 'R' Us Company purchased a copyright to a new book series for $15,000 cash on August 1, 2010. The books are expected to have a saleable life of three years. One year later, the company spends an additional $6,000 cash to successfully defend this copyright in court. The company's year end is July 31. Record (a) the purchase of the copyright on August 1, 2010; (b) the year-end amortization at July 31, 2011; (c) the legal costs incurred on August 1, 2011; and (d) the year-end amortization at July 31, 2012.

Action Plan

- Amortize intangible assets with finite lives over the shorter of their useful life and legal life (the legal life of a copyright is the life of the author plus 50 years).
- Treat costs to successfully defend an intangible asset as a capital expenditure because they benefit future periods.
- Revise amortization for additions to the cost of the asset, using the carrying amount at the time of the addition and the remaining useful life.

Solution

(a)

Aug. 1, 2010	Copyright	15,000	
	Cash		15,000
	To record purchase of copyright.		

(b)

July 31, 2011	Amortization Expense ($15,000 ÷ 3)	5,000	
	Accumulated Amortization—Copyright		5,000
	To record amortization expense.		

(c)

Aug. 1, 2011	Copyright	6,000	
	Cash		6,000
	To record costs incurred to defend copyright.		

(d)

July 31, 2012	Amortization Expense	8,000[1]	
	Accumulated Amortization—Copyright		8,000
	To record revised amortization expense.		

[1] $15,000 – $5,000 + $6,000 = $16,000 carrying amount; $16,000 carrying amount ÷ 2 years remaining = $8,000

Related exercise material: BE9–16, E9–12, E9–13, and E9–14.

The Navigator

Statement Presentation and Analysis

STUDY OBJECTIVE 7

Illustrate the reporting and analysis of long-lived assets.

Presentation

Property, plant, and equipment, and natural resources are often combined and reported in the balance sheet as "property, plant, and equipment" or "capital assets." Intangible assets are listed separately, after property, plant, and equipment. Goodwill must be disclosed separately. Other intangibles can be grouped under the caption "intangible assets" for reporting purposes.

For assets that are depreciated or amortized, the balances and accumulated depreciation and/or amortization should be disclosed in the balance sheet or notes. In addition, the depreciation and amortization methods that are used must be described. The amount of depreciation and amortization expense for the period should also be disclosed. For assets that are not depreciated or amortized, the carrying amount of each major type of asset should be disclosed in the balance sheet or notes.

Companies must also disclose their impairment policy in the notes to the financial statements. Impairment losses, if any, should be shown on a separate line on the income statement, with the details disclosed in a note.

The following is an excerpt from Enerflex Systems' 2008 balance sheet:

ENERFLEX SYSTEMS LTD. Balance Sheet (partial) December 31, 2008 (in thousands)	**ENERFLEX**
Assets	
Rental equipment (note 3)	$ 88,641
Property, plant, and equipment (note 3)	70,130
Intangible assets	7,812
Goodwill	126,146

Enerflex provides additional details on the long-lived assets in the notes to its financial statements. For example, note 3 discloses the cost, accumulated depreciation, and carrying amount of Enerflex Systems' property, plant, and equipment, which include land, buildings, equipment, assets under construction, and assets held for sale, and its rental equipment.

Another note, Enerflex Systems' summary of significant accounting policies, further discloses the depreciation methods that are used and the estimated useful lives of the company's long-lived assets. This note also states that major renewals and improvements in rental equipment and property, plant, and equipment are capitalized. It also includes information on Enerflex Systems' policies on testing its long-lived assets for impairment. Rental equipment and property, plant, and equipment are assessed for impairment whenever changes in events or changes in circumstances indicate that the asset's carrying amount may not be recovered. Intangible assets and goodwill are assessed for impairment at least annually. The company did not record any impairment losses in 2008.

Under IFRS, companies such as Enerflex will also have to disclose if they are using the cost or the revaluation model for each class of assets, and include a reconciliation of the carrying amount at the beginning and end of the period for each class of long-lived assets in the notes to the financial statements. This means they must show all of the following for each class of long-lived assets: (1) additions, (2) disposals, (3) depreciation or amortization, (4) impairment losses, and (5) reversals of impairment losses. If a company uses the revaluation model, it must also disclose any increases or decreases from revaluations as well as other information about the revaluation.

Analysis

Typically, long-lived assets are a substantial portion of a company's total assets. We will use two ratios to assess the profitability of total assets: asset turnover and return on assets.

Asset Turnover

The **asset turnover** ratio indicates how efficiently a company uses its assets; that is, how many dollars of sales are generated by each dollar that is invested in assets. It is calculated by dividing net sales by average total assets. If a company is using its assets efficiently, each dollar of assets will create a high amount of sales. When we compare two companies in the same industry, the one with the higher asset turnover is operating more efficiently. The asset turnover ratio for fiscal 2009 for The Forzani Group ($ in thousands) is calculated in Illustration 9-15.

Illustration 9-15 →

Asset turnover

Net Sales	÷	Average Total Assets	=	Asset Turnover
$1,346,758	÷	($689,460 + $754,964) ÷ 2	=	1.9 times

The asset turnover ratio shows that each dollar invested in assets produced $1.90 in sales for Forzani. This ratio varies greatly among different industries—from those that have a large investment in assets (e.g., utility companies) to those that have much less invested in assets (e.g., service companies). Asset turnover ratios, therefore, should only be compared for companies that are in the same industry.

Return on Assets

The **return on assets** ratio measures overall profitability. This ratio is calculated by dividing profit by average total assets. The return on assets ratio indicates the amount of earnings that is generated by each dollar invested in assets. A high return on assets indicates a profitable company. Illustration 9-16 shows the return on assets for Forzani ($ in thousands).

Illustration 9-16 →

Return on assets

Profit	÷	Average Total Assets	=	Return on Assets
$29,325	÷	($689,460 + $754,964) ÷ 2	=	4.1%

Forzani's return on assets was 4.1% for 2009. As with other ratios, the return on assets should be compared with previous years, with other companies in the same industry, and with industry averages, to determine how well the company has performed.

BEFORE YOU GO ON . . .

→ Review It

1. How are long-lived assets reported on the financial statements?
2. What information related to long-lived assets is disclosed in the notes to the financial statements?
3. What is the purpose of the asset turnover and return on assets ratios?

The Navigator   *Related exercise material:* BE9–17, BE9–18, BE9–19, E9–15, and E9–16.

Demonstration Problem 1

Demonstration Problems

DuPage Company purchases a factory machine at a cost of $17,500 on June 1, 2011. The machine is expected to have a residual value of $1,500 at the end of its four-year useful life on May 31, 2015. DuPage has a December 31 year end.

During its useful life, the machine is expected to be used for 10,000 hours. Actual annual use was as follows: 1,300 hours in 2011; 2,800 hours in 2012; 3,300 hours in 2013; 1,900 hours in 2014; and 700 hours in 2015.

Instructions

Prepare depreciation schedules for the following methods: (a) straight-line, (b) units-of-production, and (c) diminishing-balance using double the straight-line rate.

Solution to Demonstration Problem 1

(a) Straight-Line Method

Year	Depreciable Amount	×	Depreciation Rate	=	Depreciation Expense	Accumulated Depreciation	Carrying Amount
							$17,500
2011	$16,000[a]		25%[b] × 7/12		$2,333	$ 2,333	15,167
2012	16,000		25%		4,000	6,333	11,167
2013	16,000		25%		4,000	10,333	7,167
2014	16,000		25%		4,000	14,333	3,167
2015	16,000		25% × 5/12		1,667	16,000	1,500

<small>End of Year (spanning Accumulated Depreciation and Carrying Amount columns)</small>

[a] $17,500 − $1,500 = $16,000
[b] 100% ÷ 4 years = 25%

(b) Units-of-Production Method

Year	Units of Production	×	Depreciable Amount/Unit	=	Depreciation Expense	Accumulated Depreciation	Carrying Amount
							$17,500
2011	1,300		$1.60[a]		$2,080	$ 2,080	15,420
2012	2,800		1.60		4,480	6,560	10,940
2013	3,300		1.60		5,280	11,840	5,660
2014	1,900		1.60		3,040	14,880	2,620
2015	700		1.60		1,120	16,000	1,500

[a] $17,500 − $1,500 = $16,000 depreciable amount ÷ 10,000 total units = $1.60/unit

(c) Diminishing-Balance Method

Year	Carrying Amount Beginning of Year	×	Depreciation Rate (25% × 2)	=	Depreciation Expense	Accumulated Depreciation	Carrying Amount End of Year
							$17,500
2011	$17,500		50% × 7/12		$5,104	$ 5,104	12,396
2012	12,396		50%		6,198	11,302	6,198
2013	6,198		50%		3,099	14,401	3,099
2014	3,099		50%		1,549	15,950	1,550
2015	1,550		50%		50[a]	16,000	1,500

[a] Adjusted to $50 so that the carrying amount at the end of the year is not less than the residual value.

The Navigator

Action Plan

- Deduct the residual value in the straight-line and units-of-production methods, but not in the diminishing-balance method.
- In the diminishing-balance method, the depreciation rate is applied to the carrying amount (cost − accumulated depreciation). The residual value is not used in the calculations except to make sure the carrying amount is not reduced below the residual value.
- When the asset is purchased during the year, the first year's depreciation for the straight-line and diminishing-balance methods must be adjusted for the part of the year that the asset is owned. No adjustment is required for the units-of-production method. In the straight-line method, the final year must also be adjusted.
- Depreciation should never reduce the asset's carrying amount below its estimated residual value.

Demonstration Problem 2

On January 1, 2008, Skyline Limousine Co. purchased a specialty limo for $78,000. The vehicle is being amortized by the straight-line method using a four-year service life and a $4,000 residual value. The company's fiscal year ends on December 31.

Instructions

Prepare the journal entry or entries to record the disposal of the limo, assuming that it is:

(a) retired on January 1, 2012.
(b) sold for $15,000 on July 1, 2011.
(c) traded in on a new limousine on January 1, 2011, for a trade-in allowance of $25,000 and cash of $52,000. The fair value of the old vehicle on January 1, 2011, was $20,000.

Demonstration Problems

Action Plan

- Update the depreciation to the date of the disposal for any partial period.
- Determine the asset's carrying amount at the time of disposal.
- Calculate any gain or loss by comparing proceeds with the carrying amount.
- Remove the asset's carrying amount by debiting accumulated depreciation (for the total depreciation to the date of disposal) and crediting the asset account for the cost of the asset. Record proceeds and any gain or loss.
- Ignore trade-in allowances.
- Record the new asset in an exchange situation at the fair value of the asset given up, plus the cash paid.

The Navigator

Solution to Demonstration Problem 2

$$\frac{\$78,000 - \$4,000}{4 \text{ years}} = \$18,500 \text{ annual depreciation expense}$$

(a)

Jan. 1, 2012	Accumulated Depreciation ($18,500 × 4 years)	74,000	
	Loss on Disposal [$0 − ($78,000 − $74,000)]	4,000	
	Limo		78,000
	To record retirement of limo.		

(b)

July 1, 2011	Depreciation Expense ($18,500 × ⁶⁄₁₂)	9,250	
	Accumulated Depreciation		9,250
	To record depreciation for 6 months.		
	Cash	15,000	
	Accumulated Depreciation ($18,500 × 3.5 years)	64,750	
	Gain on Disposal [$15,000 − ($78,000 − $64,750)]		1,750
	Limo		78,000
	To record sale of limo.		

(c)

Jan. 1, 2011	Limo (new) ($20,000 + $52,000)	72,000	
	Accumulated Depreciation ($18,500 × 3 years)	55,500	
	Loss on Disposal [$20,000 − ($78,000 − $55,500)]	2,500	
	Limo (old)		78,000
	Cash		52,000
	To record exchange of limousines, plus cash.		

Summary of Study Objectives

1. Determine the cost of property, plant, and equipment. The cost of property, plant, and equipment includes all costs that are necessary to acquire the asset and make it ready for its intended use. All costs that benefit future periods (i.e., capital expenditures) are included in the cost of the asset. When applicable, cost also includes asset retirement costs. When multiple assets are purchased in one transaction, or when an asset has significant components, the cost is allocated to each individual asset or component using their relative fair values.

2. Explain and calculate depreciation. After acquisition, assets are accounted for using the cost model or the revaluation model. Depreciation is recorded and assets are carried at cost less accumulated depreciation. Depreciation is the allocation of the cost of a long-lived asset to expense over its useful life (i.e., service life) in a rational and systematic way. Depreciation is not a process of valuation and it does not result in an accumulation of cash. There are three commonly used depreciation methods:

Method	Effect on Annual Depreciation	Calculation
Straight-line	Constant amount	(Cost − residual value) ÷ estimated useful life (in years)
Diminishing-balance	Diminishing amount	Carrying amount at beginning of year × diminishing-balance rate
Units-of-production	Varying amount	(Cost − residual value) ÷ total estimated units of production × actual activity during the year

Each method results in the same amount of depreciation over the asset's useful life. Depreciation expense for income tax purposes is called capital cost allowance (CCA). The single diminishing-balance method is required and depreciation rates are prescribed.

3. *Explain the factors that cause changes in periodic depreciation and calculate revisions.* A revision to depreciation will be required if there are (1) capital expenditures during the asset's useful life, (2) impairments in the asset's fair value, (3) changes in the asset's fair value when using the revaluation model, and/or (4) changes in the appropriate depreciation method, estimated useful life, or residual value. An impairment loss must be recorded if the recoverable amount is less than the carrying amount. Impairment losses can be reversed in future periods if the recoverable amount increases. Revisions of periodic depreciation are made in present and future periods, not retroactively. The new annual depreciation is determined by using the depreciable amount (carrying amount less the revised residual value), and the remaining useful life, at the time of the revision.

4. *Account for the disposal of property, plant, and equipment.* The accounting for the disposal of a piece of property, plant, or equipment through retirement or sale is as follows:

(a) Update any unrecorded depreciation.
(b) Calculate the carrying amount.
(c) Calculate any gain (proceeds > carrying amount) or loss (proceeds < carrying amount) on disposal.
(d) Remove the asset and accumulated depreciation accounts at the date of disposal. Record the proceeds received and the gain or loss, if any.

An exchange of assets is recorded as the purchase of a new asset and the sale of an old asset. The new asset is recorded at the fair value of the asset given up plus any cash paid (or less any cash received). The fair value of the asset given up is compared with its carrying amount to calculate the gain or loss. If the fair value of the new asset or the asset given up cannot be determined, the new long-lived asset is recorded at the carrying amount of the old asset that was given up, plus any cash paid (or less any cash received).

5. *Calculate and record depreciation of natural resources.* The units-of-production method of depreciation is generally used for natural resources. The depreciable amount per unit is calculated by dividing the total depreciable amount by the number of units estimated to be in the resource. The depreciable amount per unit is multiplied by the number of units that have been extracted to determine the annual depreciation. The depreciation and any other costs to extract the resource are recorded as inventory until the resource is sold. At that time, the costs are transferred to cost of resource sold on the income statement. Revisions to depreciation will be required for capital expenditures during the asset's useful life, for impairments, and for changes in the total estimated units of the resource.

6. *Identify the basic accounting issues for intangible assets and goodwill.* The accounting for tangible and intangible assets is much the same. Intangible assets are reported at cost, which includes all expenditures necessary to prepare the asset for its intended use. An intangible asset with a finite life is amortized over the shorter of its useful life or legal life, usually on a straight-line basis, and must be assessed for impairment annually. Intangible assets with indefinite lives and goodwill are not amortized and are tested at least annually for impairment. Impairment losses on goodwill are never reversed.

7. *Illustrate the reporting and analysis of long-lived assets.* It is common for property, plant, and equipment, and natural resources to be combined under the heading "Property, Plant, and Equipment." Intangible assets with finite and indefinite lives are sometimes combined under the heading "Intangible Assets" or are listed separately. Goodwill must be presented separately. Either on the balance sheet or in the notes, the cost of the major classes of long-lived assets is presented. Accumulated depreciation (if the asset is depreciable) and carrying amount must be disclosed either in the balance sheet or in the notes. The depreciation and amortization methods and rates, as well as the annual depreciation expense, must also be indicated. The company's impairment policy and any impairment losses should be described and reported. Under IFRS, companies must include a reconciliation of the carrying amount at the beginning and end of the period for each class of long-lived assets and whether the cost or revaluation model is used.

The asset turnover ratio (net sales ÷ average total assets) is one measure that is used by companies to show how efficiently they are using their assets to generate sales revenue. A second ratio, return on assets (profit ÷ average total assets), calculates how profitable the company is in terms of using its assets to generate profit.

Glossary

WILEY PLUS
Glossary
Key Term Matching Activity

Additions and improvements Costs that are incurred to increase the operating efficiency, productive capac- ity, or expected useful life of property, plant, or equipment. (p. 502)

Amortizable amount The cost of a finite-life intangible asset to be amortized less its residual value. (p. 516)

Amortization The systemic allocation of the amortizable amount of a finite-life intangible asset over its useful life. (p. 515)

Asset retirement costs The cost to dismantle, remove, or restore an asset when it is retired. (p. 490)

Asset turnover A measure of how efficiently a company uses its total assets to generate sales. It is calculated by dividing net sales by average total assets. (p. 521)

Basket purchase The acquisition of a group of assets for a single price. Individual asset costs are determined by allocating relative fair values. (p. 492)

Capital cost allowance (CCA) The depreciation of long-lived assets that is allowed by the *Income Tax Act* for income tax purposes. It is calculated on a class (group) basis and mainly uses the diminishing-balance method with maximum rates specified for each class of assets. (p. 501)

Capital expenditures Expenditures related to long-lived assets that benefit the company over several accounting periods. (p. 490)

Component depreciation Calculating depreciation separately for the different significant components of an item of property, plant, and equipment. Used when the useful life of the component is different from the useful life of the other components or the asset as a whole. (p. 493)

Copyright An exclusive right granted by the federal government allowing the owner to reproduce and sell an artistic or published work. (p. 517)

Cost model A model of accounting for a long-lived asset that carries the asset at its cost less accumulated depreciation or amortization and any impairment losses. (p. 494)

Depreciable amount The cost of a depreciable asset (property, plant, and equipment, or natural resources) less its residual value. (p. 496)

Diminishing-balance method A depreciation method that applies a constant rate to the asset's diminishing carrying amount. This method produces a decreasing annual depreciation expense over the useful life of the asset. (p. 498)

Franchise A contractual arrangement under which the franchisor grants the franchisee the right to sell certain products, offer specific services, or use certain trademarks or trade names, usually inside a specific geographical area. (p. 519)

Goodwill The amount paid to purchase another company that is more than the fair value of the company's net identifiable assets. (p. 519)

Impairment loss The amount by which an asset's carrying amount exceeds its recoverable amount. (p. 503)

Intangible assets Rights, privileges, and competitive advantages that result from owning long-lived assets that have no physical substance. (p. 515)

Land improvements Structural additions to land that have limited useful lives, such as paving, fencing, and lighting. (p. 491)

Licences Operating rights to use public property, granted by a government agency to a company. (p. 519)

Natural resources Long-lived tangible assets, such as standing timber and underground deposits of oil, gas, and minerals, that are physically extracted and are only replaceable by an act of nature. (p. 513)

Operating expenditures Expenditures that benefit only the current period. They are immediately charged against revenues as expenses. (p. 490)

Ordinary repairs Expenditures to maintain the operating efficiency and productive life of the unit. (p. 502)

Patent An exclusive right issued by the federal government that enables the recipient to manufacture, sell, or otherwise control an invention for a period of 20 years from the date of the application. (p. 517)

Property, plant, and equipment Identifiable, long-lived tangible assets, such as land, land improvements, buildings, and equipment, that the company owns and uses for the production and sale of goods or services. (p. 490)

Recoverable amount The higher of the asset's fair value, less costs to sell, and its value in use. (p. 503)

Research and development (R&D) costs Expenditures that may lead to patents, copyrights, new processes, and new products. (p. 517)

Residual value The estimated amount that a company would currently obtain from disposing of the asset if the asset were already as old as it will be, and in the condition it is expected to be in, at the end of its useful life. (p. 496)

Return on assets An overall measure of profitability that indicates the amount of profit that is earned from each dollar invested in assets. It is calculated by dividing profit by average total assets. (p. 522)

Revaluation model A long-lived asset is carried at its fair value less accumulated depreciation or amortization and any impairment losses. (p. 504)

Royalties Recurring payments that may be required under a franchise agreement and are paid by the franchisee to the franchisor for services provided (e.g., advertising, purchasing), and are often proportionate to sales. (p. 519)

Straight-line method A depreciation method in which an asset's depreciable amount is divided by its estimated useful life. This method produces the same periodic depreciation for each year of the asset's useful life. (p. 496)

Tangible assets Long-lived resources that have physical substance, are used in the operations of the business, and are not intended for sale to customers. Tangible assets include property, plant, and equipment and natural resources. (p. 515)

Trade-in allowance A price reduction offered by the seller when a used asset is exchanged for a new asset as part of the deal. (p. 510)

Trademark (trade name) A word, phrase, jingle, or symbol that distinguishes or identifies a particular enterprise or product. (p. 518)

Units-of-production method A depreciation method in which useful life is expressed in terms of the total estimated units of production or use expected from the asset. Depreciation expense is calculated by multiplying the depreciable amount per unit (cost less residual value divided by total estimated activity) by the actual activity that occurs during the year. (p. 499)

Useful life The period of time over which an asset is expected to be available for use, or the number of units of production (such as machine hours) or units of output that are expected to be obtained from an asset. (p. 495)

Self-Study Questions

Answers are at the end of the chapter.

(SO 1) AP 1. Asura Company purchased land, a building, and equipment for a package price of $200,000. The land's fair value at the time of acquisition was $75,000. The building's fair value was $80,000. The equipment's fair value was $50,000. What costs should be debited to the three accounts Land, Building, and Equipment, respectively?
(a) $66,667, $66,667, and $66,666
(b) $73,171, $78,049, and $48,780
(c) $75,000, $80,000, and $50,000
(d) $200,000, $0, and $0

(SO 2) AP 2. Cuso Company purchased equipment on January 1, 2010, at a total cost of $40,000. The equipment has an estimated residual value of $10,000 and an estimated useful life of five years. If the straight-line method of depreciation is used, what is the amount of accumulated depreciation at December 31, 2011, the end of the second year of the asset's life?
(a) $6,000
(b) $12,000
(c) $18,000
(d) $24,000

(SO 2) AP 3. Kant Enterprises purchases a truck for $33,000 on July 1, 2011. The truck has an estimated residual value of $3,000, and an estimated useful life of five years, or a total distance of 300,000 kilometres. If 50,000 kilometres are driven in 2011, what amount of depreciation expense would Kant record at December 31, 2011, assuming it uses the units-of-production method?
(a) $2,500
(b) $3,000
(c) $5,000
(d) $5,333

(SO 2) AP 4. Refer to the data for Kant Enterprises in question 3. If Kant uses the double diminishing-balance method of depreciation, what amount of depreciation expense would it record at December 31, 2011?
(a) $6,000
(b) $6,600
(c) $12,000
(d) $13,200

(SO 3) K 5. Which of the following is true? When there is a change in estimated useful life and/or residual value:
(a) the depreciation of past years should be corrected.
(b) the depreciation of current and future years should be revised.
(c) only the depreciation of future years should be revised.
(d) depreciation does not need to be changed because it is an estimate.

(SO 4) AP 6. Oviatt Company sold equipment for $10,000. At that time, the equipment had a cost of $45,000 and accumulated depreciation of $30,000. Oviatt should record a:
(a) $5,000 loss on disposal.
(b) $5,000 gain on disposal.
(c) $15,000 loss on disposal.
(d) $15,000 gain on disposal.

(SO 4) AP 7. St. Laurent Company exchanged an old machine with a carrying amount of $39,000 and a fair value of $35,000 for a new machine. The new machine had a list price of $47,500. St. Laurent was offered a trade-in allowance of $37,500, and paid $10,000 cash in the exchange. At what amount should the new machine be recorded on St. Laurent's books?
(a) $35,000

(b) $45,000
(c) $47,000
(d) $49,000

(SO 5) AP   8. On April 1, 2010, Shady Tree Farm Company purchased a Christmas tree farm that has an estimated
100,000 harvestable Christmas trees. The purchase
price was $500,000 and the tree farm is expected to
have an estimated residual value of $50,000. Dur-
ing the first year of operations, ended January 31,
2011, Shady Tree Farm cut and sold 10,000 trees.
What amount of depreciation should be included in
cost of goods sold for the year ended January 31?
(a) $37,500
(b) $40,500
(c) $45,000
(d) $50,000

9. Pierce Company had $150,000 of development   (SO 9) AP
costs in its laboratory that were related to a patent granted on January 2, 2011. On July 31, 2011,
Pierce paid $35,000 for legal fees in a successful
defence of the patent. The total amount debited to
Patents through July 31, 2011, should be:
(a) $35,500.
(b) $150,000.
(c) $185,000.
(d) None of the above.

10. WestJet Airlines Ltd. reported net sales of $2,550   (SO 7) AP
million, profit of $178 million, and average total as-
sets of $3,132 million in 2008. What are WestJet's
return on assets and asset turnover?
(a) 0. 81% and 5.7 times
(b) 5.7% and 1.2 times
(c) 7.0% and 5.7 times
(d) 5.7% and 0.81 times

The Navigato

Questions

(SO 1) C   1. What are the three characteristics of property, plant,
and equipment? When are they recorded as assets?

(SO 1) C   2. What are the three components of the cost of property, plant, and equipment?

(SO 1) C   3. Deer Fern Company purchases equipment and incurs a number of expenditures before it is ready to
use the equipment. Give two examples of operating
expenditures and two examples of capital expenditures that the company might incur on new equipment and explain how these expenditures would be
recorded and why.

(SO 1) C   4. What are land improvements? Should the cost of
clearing and grading land be recorded as a land improvement cost or not? Explain.

(SO 1) C   5. Jacques asks why the total cost in a basket purchase has to be allocated to the individual assets.
For example, if we purchase land and a building
for $250,000, why can we not just debit an account
called Land and Building for $250,000? Answer his
questions.

(SO 2) C   6. Some people believe that the fair values of property, plant, and equipment are more relevant than
the asset's cost for decisions made by such users as
creditors, investors, and managers. Why then is the
cost model acceptable and more widely used than
the revaluation model?

(SO 2) C   7. What is the purpose of depreciation? What are some
common misunderstandings about depreciation?

8. Cecile is studying for her next accounting exam.   (SO 2) K
She asks for your help on two questions: (a) What
is residual value? (b) How is residual value used in
calculating depreciation in each of the depreciation
methods? Answer her questions.

9. Contrast the effects of the three depreciation meth-   (SO 2) C
ods on (1) depreciation expense, (2) profit, (3) accumulated depreciation, and (4) carrying amount in
each of the following: (a) in the early years of an
asset's life, and (b) over the total life of the asset.

10. What factors should be considered when choosing   (SO 2, 3) C
a depreciation method? When revising a deprecia-
tion method?

11. Ralph has a plan to reduce the amount of income   (SO 2) C
taxes that will have to be paid on his company's profit. He has decided to calculate depreciation expense
using very low estimated useful lives on his property,
plant, and equipment. Will Ralph's plan work?

12. Explain the difference between operating expen-   (SO 3) C
ditures and capital expenditures during an asset's
useful life and describe the accounting treatment
of each.

13. What factors restrict the ability of companies to use   (SO 3) C
the revaluation model and in what circumstances is
it significantly more useful than the cost model?

14. What factors contribute to an impairment loss? In   (SO 3) C
what circumstances, if any, is a company allowed to
write up its property, plant, and equipment?

(SO 3) C 15. In the third year of an asset's four-year useful life, the company decides that the asset will have a six-year service life. Should prior periods be restated because of the revised depreciation? Explain why or why not.

(SO 4) C 16. If equipment is sold in the middle of a fiscal year, why does depreciation have to be updated for the partial period? Doesn't the subsequent journal entry to record the sale remove the accumulated depreciation from the books anyway?

(SO 4) C 17. Ewing Company owns a machine that is fully depreciated but is still being used. How should Ewing account for this asset and report it in the financial statements?

(SO 4) K 18. How is a gain or loss on the sale of an item of property, plant, or equipment calculated? Is the calculation the same for an exchange of a piece of property, plant, or equipment?

(SO 5) K 19. Describe the similarities and differences between natural resources and property, plant, and equipment.

(SO 5) C 20. Why is the units-of-production method used frequently to calculate depreciation for natural resources? Why is the term "depletion" often used instead of "depreciation?"

(SO 5) C 21. Under what circumstances is the depreciation of natural resources recorded as a current asset under inventory rather than as an expense?

22. What are the characteristics of an intangible asset? (SO 6) C

23. Heflin Company has been amortizing its finite-life (SO 6) C intangible assets over their legal life. The company's accountant argues this is appropriate because an intangible asset's legal life is known with certainty, but its useful life is subjective. Why is this not correct, and what impact might it have on the company's financial statements?

24. Bob Leno, a business student, is working on a case (SO 6) C problem for one of his classes. In this problem, the company needs to raise cash to market a new product it has developed. Saul Cain, an engineering student, takes one look at the company's balance sheet and says, "This company has an awful lot of goodwill. Why don't you recommend that they sell some of it to raise cash?" How should Bob respond to Saul's suggestion?

25. How should long-lived assets be reported on the (SO 7) K balance sheet and income statement? What information should be disclosed in the notes to the financial statements?

26. What information do the asset turnover and return (SO 7) C on assets ratios show about a company?

Brief Exercises

BE9–1 The following costs were incurred by Shumway Company in purchasing land: cash price, $75,000; removal of old building, $5,000; legal fees, $2,500; clearing and grading, $3,500; installation of fence, $3,000. (a) What is the cost of the land? (b) What is the cost of the land improvements?

Determine cost of land and land improvements.
(SO 1) AP

BE9–2 Mabasa Company incurs the following costs in purchasing equipment: invoice price, $31,350; installation, $650; testing, $1,000; one-year insurance policy, $2,000. What is the cost of the equipment?

Determine cost of equipment.
(SO 1) AP

BE9–3 In the space provided, indicate whether each of the following items is an operating expenditure (O) or a capital expenditure (C):

Identify operating and capital expenditures.
(SO 1) K

(a) ___ Repaired building roof, $1,500
(b) ___ Replaced building roof, $27,500
(c) ___ Purchased building, $480,000
(d) ___ Purchased supplies, $350
(e) ___ Purchased truck, $55,000
(f) ___ Purchased oil and gas for truck, $125
(g) ___ Rebuilt engine on truck, $5,000

(h) ___ Replaced tires on truck, $600
(i) ___ Estimated retirement cost of plant, $1,000,000
(j) ___ Added new wing to building, $250,000
(k) ___ Painted interior of building, $1,500
(l) ___ Paid insurance on equipment in transit, $550

Record basket purchase.
(SO 1) AP

BE9–4 Rainbow Company purchased land, a building, and equipment on January 2, 2011, for $800,000. The company paid $200,000 cash and signed a mortgage note payable for the remainder. Management's best estimate of the value of the land was $255,000, of the building, $510,000, and of the equipment, $85,000. Record the purchase.

Calculate straight-line depreciation.
(SO 2) AP

BE9–5 On January 2, 2011, Mabasa Company acquires equipment at a cost of $33,000. The equipment is expected to have a residual value of $3,000 at the end of its three-year useful life. Calculate the depreciation using the straight-line method (a) for each year of the equipment's life, and (b) in total over the equipment's life. Mabasa has a December 31 fiscal year end.

Calculate diminishing-balance depreciation.
(SO 2) AP

BE9–6 Depreciation information for Mabasa Company is given in BE9–5. Use the diminishing-balance method and assume the diminishing-balance depreciation rate is double the straight-line rate. Calculate the depreciation expense (a) for each year of the equipment's life, and (b) in total over the equipment's life.

Calculate units-of-production depreciation.
(SO 2) AP

BE9–7 Speedy Taxi Service uses the units-of-production method in calculating depreciation on its taxicabs. Each cab is expected to be driven 525,000 kilometres. Taxi 10 cost $35,000 and is expected to have a residual value of $350. Taxi 10 is driven 110,000 kilometres in 2010, and 155,000 kilometres in 2011. Calculate the depreciation expense for each year.

Calculate partial-year straight-line depreciation.
(SO 2) AP

BE9–8 Depreciation information for Mabasa Company is given in BE9–5. Assuming the equipment was purchased on March 5, 2011, calculate the depreciation using the straight-line method (a) for each year of the truck's life, and (b) in total over the truck's life. The company pro-rates depreciation to the nearest month.

Calculate partial-year diminishing-balance depreciation.
(SO 2) AP

BE9–9 Depreciation information for Mabasa Company is given in BE9–5. Assuming the equipment was purchased on March 5, 2011, calculate the depreciation using the double diminishing-balance method (a) for each year of the truck's life, and (b) in total over the truck's life. Assume the company has a policy of recording a half year's depreciation in the year of acquisition and a half year's depreciation in the year of disposal.

Record impairment loss.
(SO 3) AP

BE9–10 AMMA Phone Company owns machinery that cost $90,000 and has accumulated depreciation of $54,000. The machinery's recoverable amount is $30,000. Record the impairment loss.

Calculate revised depreciation.
(SO 3) AP

BE9–11 On January 2, 2008, Lapointe Company purchased equipment for $60,000. At that time, the equipment was estimated to have a useful life of seven years and a residual value of $4,000. On January 3, 2011, Lapointe upgrades the equipment at a cost of $9,000. Lapointe estimates that the equipment will now have a total useful life of nine years and a residual value of $3,000. The company uses straight-line depreciation and has a December 31 fiscal year end. Calculate the 2011 depreciation expense.

Record disposal by retirement.
(SO 4) AP

BE9–12 On January 3, 2011, Ruiz Company retires its delivery equipment, which cost $37,000. No residual value is received. Prepare journal entries to record the transaction if (a) accumulated depreciation is also $37,000 on this delivery equipment, and (b) the accumulated depreciation is $33,500 instead of $37,000. Ruiz has a December 31 fiscal year end.

Record disposal by sale.
(SO 4) AP

BE9–13 Wiley Company sells office equipment on September 30, 2011, for $21,000 cash. The office equipment was purchased on January 5, 2008, at a cost of $72,000, and had an estimated useful life of five years and an estimated residual value of $2,000. Adjusting journal entries are made annually at the company's year end, December 31. Prepare the journal entries to (a) update depreciation to September 30, 2011, (b) record the sale of the equipment, and (c) record the sale of the equipment if Wiley Company received $15,000 cash for it.

BE9–14 Subramanian Company has machinery with an original cost of $95,000 and, as at December 31, 2010, accumulated depreciation of $78,000. On January 7, 2011, Subramanian exchanges the machinery, plus $62,000 cash, for new machinery. The old machinery has a fair value of $14,000. The dealer gave Subramanian an $18,000 trade-in allowance on the old machinery. Record the January 7, 2011, journal entry for the machinery exchange.

Record disposal by exchange of machinery.
(SO 4) AP

BE9–15 Cuono Mining Co. purchased a mine for $8 million that is estimated to have 25 million tonnes of ore and a residual value of $500,000. In the first year, 7 million tonnes of ore are extracted and 6.5 million tonnes are sold.

Record depreciation and show balance sheet presentation for natural resources.
(SO 5) AP

(a) Record the depreciation and the cost of the ore extracted for the first year, ended August 31, 2011.
(b) Show how the mine and the ore on hand are reported on the balance sheet on August 31, 2011.

BE9–16 Surkis Company purchases a patent for $180,000 cash on January 2, 2011. Its legal life is 20 years and its estimated useful life is 9 years. On January 5, 2012, Surkis paid $25,000 cash to successfully defend the patent in court.

Record acquisition, legal expenditure, and amortization for patent.
(SO 6) AP

(a) Record the purchase of the patent on January 2, 2011.
(b) Record amortization expense for the year ended December 31, 2011.
(c) Record the legal costs on January 5, 2012.
(d) Calculate amortization expense for 2012.

BE9–17 Indicate whether each of the following items is property, plant, and equipment (write "PPE"), a natural resource ("NR"), or an intangible asset ("I"). If the item does not fit any of these categories, write "NA" (not applicable) in the space provided.

Identify and classify long-lived assets.
(SO 7) K

(a) ___ Building
(b) ___ Cost of goods sold
(c) ___ Franchise
(d) ___ Goodwill
(e) ___ Inventory
(f) ___ Land
(g) ___ Licence right
(h) ___ Mining machinery
(i) ___ Natural gas deposit
(j) ___ Note receivable, due in 3 months
(k) ___ Parking lot
(l) ___ Patent
(m) ___ Supplies
(n) ___ Trademark

BE9–18 Canadian Tire Corporation, Limited reports the following selected information about long-lived assets at December 31, 2008 (in millions):

Prepare partial balance sheet.
(SO 7) AP

Accumulated depreciation—buildings	$ 787.1
Accumulated depreciation—fixtures and equipment	434.5
Accumulated depreciation—leasehold improvements	143.5
Buildings	2,347.2
Fixtures and equipment	645.3
Goodwill	70.7
Land	727.9
Leasehold improvements	460.5
Mark's Work Wearhouse store brands and banners	50.4
Mark's Work Wearhouse franchise agreements and locations	8.0
Other property, plant, and equipment	574.0

Mark's Work Wearhouse store brands, banners, and franchises are considered to have indefinite lives. Prepare a partial balance sheet for Canadian Tire.

Calculate ratios.
(SO 7) AP

BE9–19 Agrium Inc., a global agricultural nutrients producer that is headquartered in Calgary, Alberta, reports the following in its 2008 financial statements (in US millions):

Net sales	$10,268	Total assets, December 31, 2008	$9,818
Profit	1,322	Total assets, December 31, 2007	5,832

Calculate Agrium's return on assets and asset turnover for 2008.

Exercises

Classify expenditures.
(SO 1) AP

E9–1 The following expenditures related to property, plant, and equipment were made by Pascal Company:

1. Paid $45,000 for a new delivery truck.
2. Paid $450 to have the company name and advertising slogan painted on the new truck.
3. Paid the $75 motor vehicle licence fee on the new truck.
4. Paid $900 for a one-year accident insurance policy on the new delivery truck.
5. Paid $300,000 for a new plant site.
6. Paid $4,000 in legal fees on the purchase of the plant site.
7. Paid $6,600 to demolish an old building on the plant site; residual materials were sold for $1,700.
8. Paid $4,700 for grading the plant site.
9. Paid $17,500 in architect fees for work on the new plant.
10. Paid $5,600 interest during the construction of the new plant.
11. Paid $17,500 for paving the parking lots and driveways on the plant site.
12. Paid $18,000 for the installation of new factory machinery.
13. Paid $200 for insurance to cover potential damage to the new factory machinery while it was in transit.
14. Estimated it would cost $25,000 for restoration when the company is finished using the plant site.

Instructions

(a) Explain what types of costs should be included in determining the cost of property, plant, and equipment.
(b) List the numbers of the preceding transactions, and beside each number write the account title that the expenditure should be debited to.

Record basket purchase and calculate depreciation.
(SO 1, 2) AP

E9–2 Hohenberger Farms purchased real estate for $1,150,000. It paid $350,000 cash and incurred a mortgage payable for the balance. Legal fees of $10,000 were paid in cash. The real estate included land that was appraised at $720,000, buildings appraised at $420,000, and fences and other land improvements appraised at $60,000. The buildings have an estimated useful life of 40 years and a $20,000 residual value. Land improvements have an estimated 15-year useful life and no residual value.

Instructions
(a) Calculate the cost that should be allocated to each asset purchased.
(b) Record the purchase of the real estate.
(c) Calculate the annual depreciation expense for the buildings and land improvements assuming Hohenberger Farms uses straight-line depreciation.

Calculate cost and depreciation; recommend method.
(SO 1, 2) AP

E9–3 Randell Equipment Repair purchased machinery on March 15, 2011, for $75,000. The company also paid the following amounts: $1,000 for delivery charges; $200 for insurance while the machine was in transit; $1,800 for a one-year insurance policy; and $2,800 for testing and installation. The machine was ready for use on April 1, 2011, but the company did not start using it until May 1, 2011.

Randell will depreciate the machinery over 10 years with no residual value. It expects to consume the machinery's future economic benefits evenly over the useful life. The company has a December 31 fiscal year end.

Instructions

(a) Calculate the cost of the machinery.
(b) When should the company begin depreciating the machinery: March 15, April 1, or May 1? Why?
(c) Which depreciation method should the company use? Why?
(d) Calculate the depreciation on the machinery for 2011 and 2012.

E9–4 Intercity Bus Lines purchases a bus on January 2, 2010, at a cost of $410,000. Over its five-year useful life, the bus is expected to be driven 500,000 kilometres and to have a residual value of $10,000. The company has a December 31 fiscal year end.

Calculate depreciation using three methods; recommend method.
(SO 2) AP

Instructions

(a) Calculate depreciation under the straight-line method for 2010 and 2011.
(b) Calculate the depreciation expense under the diminishing-balance method using double the straight-line rate, for 2010 and 2011.
(c) Calculate the depreciation expense under the units-of-production method, assuming the actual distance driven was 44,800 kilometres in 2010 and 60,300 kilometres in 2011.
(d) Based on this information, which depreciation method should the company use? Why?

E9–5 Sitrus Company purchased a new machine on October 4, 2010, at a cost of $86,000. The company estimated that the machine will have a residual value of $12,000. The machine is expected to be used for 10,000 working hours during its four-year life. Sitrus Company has a December 31 year end and pro-rates depreciation to the nearest month. The actual machine usage was: 500 hours in 2010; 2,800 hours in 2011; 2,900 hours in 2012; 2,600 hours in 2013; and 1,300 hours in 2014.

Prepare depreciation schedules and answer questions.
(SO 2) AP

Instructions

(a) Prepare a depreciation schedule for the life of the asset under each of the following methods:
 1. straight-line,
 2. diminishing-balance using double the straight-line rate, and
 3. units-of-production.
(b) Which method results in the highest depreciation expense over the life of the asset?
(c) Which method results in the highest cash flow over the life of the asset?

E9–6 Bisor Company has a December 31 year end and uses straight-line depreciation for all property, plant, and equipment. On July 1, 2007, the company purchased equipment for $500,000. The equipment had an expected useful life of 10 years and no residual value.

Record depreciation and impairment.
(SO 3) AP

 On December 31, 2010, after recording annual depreciation, Bisor reviewed its equipment for possible impairment. Bisor determined that the equipment has a recoverable amount of $225,000. It is not known if the recoverable amount will increase or decrease in the future.

Instructions

(a) Prepare journal entries to record the purchase of the asset on July 1, 2007, and to record depreciation expense on December 31, 2007, and December 31, 2010.
(b) Determine if there is an impairment loss at December 31, 2010, and if any, prepare a journal entry to record it.
(c) Calculate depreciation expense for 2011 and the carrying amount of the equipment at December 31, 2011.
(d) Assume that the equipment is assessed again for impairment at December 31, 2011, and that the company determines the recoverable amount is $240,000. Should Bisor make an adjustment to reflect the increase in the recoverable amount? Explain why or why not.

Calculate and record revised depreciation.
(SO 3) AP

E9–7 Lindy Weink, the new controller of Lafrenière Company, has reviewed the expected useful lives and residual values of selected depreciable assets at December 31, 2010 (depreciation for 2010 has not been recorded yet). Her findings are as follows:

Type of Asset	Date Acquired	Cost	Total Useful Life in Years		Residual Value	
			Current	Proposed	Current	Proposed
Building	Jan. 1, 1999	$800,000	20	25	$40,000	$65,000
Equipment	Jan. 1, 2009	120,000	5	4	5,000	3,500

After discussion, management agrees to accept Lindy's proposed changes. All assets are depreciated by the straight-line method. Lafrenière Company has a December 31 year end.

Instructions

(a) For each asset, calculate the annual depreciation expense for 2009 and the carrying amount at December 31, 2009.
(b) For each asset, calculate the annual depreciation expense for 2010 and the carrying amount at December 31, 2010.
(c) For each asset, calculate the annual depreciation expense for 2011 and the carrying amount at December 31, 2011.

Record asset addition and depreciation.
(SO 3) AP

E9–8 Mactaquac Company purchased a piece of high-tech equipment on July 1, 2009, for $60,000 cash. The equipment was expected to last four years and have a residual value of $8,000. Mactaquac uses straight-line depreciation and its fiscal year end is June 30.

On July 1, 2010, Mactaquac purchased and installed a new part on the equipment that is expected to significantly increase the equipment's productivity. Mactaquac paid $10,000 cash for the part. It paid an additional $1,000 for the installation and testing of this part. The equipment is expected to last six years in total now and to have a revised residual value of $6,000.

Instructions

(a) Record the annual depreciation of the equipment on June 30, 2010.
(b) Record the purchase of the part, and its installation and testing, on July 1, 2010.
(c) Record the annual depreciation of the equipment on June 30, 2011.
(d) Calculate the carrying amount of the equipment on June 30, 2011, after recording the annual depreciation.

Record disposal of property, plant, and equipment.
(SO 4) AP

E9–9 Here are some transactions of Surendal Company for 2011. Surendal Company uses straight-line depreciation and has a December 31 year end.

Jan. 2 Scrapped a piece of equipment that originally cost $8,000 and was fully depreciated.

Feb. 28 Retired a piece of machinery that was purchased on January 1, 2002, for $54,000. The machinery had an expected useful life of 10 years with no residual value.

Aug. 1 Received $2,000 cash from the sale of office equipment that was purchased on January 1, 2009. The equipment cost $10,980 and was amortized over an expected useful life of three years with no residual value.

Dec. 1 Traded in an old delivery truck for a new delivery truck, receiving a $10,000 trade-in allowance and paying $35,000 cash. The old delivery truck had been purchased on December 1, 2004, at a cost of $30,000. The estimated useful life was eight years and the estimated residual value was $6,000. The fair value of the old delivery truck was $7,000 on December 1, 2011.

Instructions

(a) For each of these disposals, prepare a journal entry to record depreciation from January 1, 2011, to the date of disposal, if required.
(b) For each these disposals, indicate if the disposal has increased (+) or decreased (–) Cash, Equipment, Accumulated Depreciation, total property, plant, and equipment (PP&E), and profit, and by how much. If the item is not changed, write "NE" to indicate there is no effect. Use the following format, in which the first one has been done for you as an example.

Transaction	Cash	Equipment	Accumulated Depreciation	Total PP&E	Total Assets	Owner's Equity	Profit
Jan. 2	NE	−$8,000	−$8,000	NE	NE	NE	NE

(c) Prepare the journal entry to record each of the disposals.

E9–10   On January 3, 2008, Hamir Company purchased computer equipment for $32,000. Hamir planned to keep the equipment for four years, and expected the equipment would then be sold for $2,000. On January 5, 2011, Hamir sold the computer equipment for $6,500.

Calculate gain or loss on disposal under different depreciation methods and comment.
(SO 4) AP

Instructions

(a) Calculate the depreciation expense for 2008, 2009, and 2010 under (1) the straight-line method and (2) the double diminishing-balance method.
(b) Calculate the gain or loss on disposal if Hamir had used (1) the straight-line method and (2) the double diminishing-balance method.
(c) Explain why the gain or loss on disposal is not the same under the two depreciation methods.
(d) Calculate the total depreciation expense plus the loss or minus the gain under (1) the straight-line method and (2) the double diminishing-balance method. Comment on your findings.

E9–11   On July 1, 2011, Phillips Inc. invests $1.3 million in a mine that is estimated to have 800,000 tonnes of ore. The company estimates that the property will be sold for $100,000 when production at the mine has ended. During the last six months of 2011, 100,000 tonnes of ore are mined and sold. Phillips has a December 31 fiscal year end.

Record depreciation for natural resources; show financial statement presentation; comment on potential impairment.
(SO 5) AP

Instructions

(a) Explain why the units-of-production method is often used for depreciating natural resources.
(b) Record the 2011 depreciation.
(c) Show how the mine and any related accounts are reported on the December 31, 2011, income statement and balance sheet.
(d) Assume that the selling price of ore has dropped significantly after December 31, 2011. By June 30, 2012, it is $1.40 per tonne. Does this indicate that the mine may be impaired? Why?

E9–12   An accounting co-op student encountered the following situations at Chin Company:
1. During the year, Chin Company purchased land and paid legal fees on the purchase. The land had an old building, which was demolished. The land was then cleared and graded. Construction of a new building will start next year. All of these costs were included in the cost of land. The student decided that this was incorrect, and prepared a journal entry to put the cost of removing the building and clearing and grading the land in land improvements and the legal fees in legal fee expense.
2. The student learned that Chin is depreciating its buildings and equipment, but not its land. The student could not understand why land was not included, so she prepared journal entries to depreciate all of the company's property, plant, and equipment for the current year end.
3. The student decided that Chin's amortization policy on its intangible assets is wrong. The company is currently amortizing its patents but not its trademarks. The student fixed that for the current year end by adding trademarks to her adjusting entry for amortization. She told a fellow student that she felt she had improved the consistency of the company's accounting policies by making these changes.
4. One of the buildings that Chin uses has a zero carrying amount but a substantial fair value. The co-op student felt that leaving the carrying amount at zero did not benefit the financial information's users—especially the bank—and wrote the building up to its fair value. After all, she reasoned, you write down assets if fair values are lower. She feels that writing them up if their fair value is higher is yet another example of the improved consistency that her employment has brought to the company's accounting practices.

Apply accounting concepts.
(SO 1, 2, 6) AP

Instructions

Explain whether or not the co-op student's accounting treatment in each of the above situations follows generally accepted accounting principles. If it does not, explain why and what the appropriate accounting treatment should be.

Record acquisition, amortization, and impairment of intangible assets.
(SO 6) AP

E9–13   On December 31, 2010, Erhart Company owned the following intangible assets:

1. Goodwill purchased on August 21, 2003, for $360,000.
2. A patent purchased on January 1, 2009, for $225,000. When the patent was purchased, it had an estimated useful life of five years and a legal life of 20 years.

In 2011, Erhart had the following transactions related to intangible assets:

Jan. 2   Incurred legal fees of $22,500 to successfully defend the patent.
Apr. 1   Purchased a 10-year franchise, which expires on April 1, 2021, for $250,000.
July 1   Purchased a trademark with an indefinite expected life for $335,000.
Nov. 1   Incurred research costs of $185,000.
Dec. 31   Reviewed each intangible asset for impairments. Determined that the recoverable amount of the goodwill had declined to $300,000.

Instructions

(a) Record these transactions. All incurred costs were for cash.
(b) Record any necessary amortization and impairment losses on December 31, 2011. Erhart has not previously recorded any impairment losses on its intangible assets.

Determine balance sheet and income statement presentation for intangible assets and goodwill.
(SO 6) AP

E9–14   Whiteway Company has a December 31 fiscal year end. Selected information follows for Whiteway Company for three independent situations as at December 3, 2011:

1. Whiteway purchased a patent from Hopkins Inc. for $400,000 on January 1, 2008. The patent expires on January 1, 2018. Whiteway has been amortizing it over its legal life. During 2011, Whiteway determined that the patent's economic benefits would not last longer than six years from the date of acquisition.
2. Whiteway has a trademark that had been purchased in 2007 for $250,000. During 2010, the company spent $50,000 on a lawsuit that successfully defended the trademark. On December 31, 2011, it was assessed for impairment and the recoverable amount was determined to be $275,000.
3. In 2009, Whiteway purchased another business and paid $70,000 in excess of the fair value of the net identifiable assets of that business. This goodwill was assessed for impairment as at December 31, 2010, and December 31, 2011. The recoverable amount was determined to be $55,000 at December 31, 2010, and $80,000 at December 31, 2011.

Instructions

(a) For each of these assets, determine the amount that will be reported on Whiteway's December 31, 2010 and 2011, balance sheets.
(b) For each of these assets, determine what, if anything, will be recorded on Whiteway's 2011 income statement. Be specific about the account name and the amount.

Classify long-lived assets; prepare partial balance sheet.
(SO 7) AP

E9–15   BCE Inc. reported the following selected information as at December 31, 2008 (in millions):

Accumulated amortization—finite-life intangible assets	$ 3,050
Accumulated depreciation—buildings	1,570
Accumulated depreciation—machinery and equipment	4,567
Accumulated depreciation—other property, plant, and equipment	133
Accumulated depreciation—satellites	562
Accumulated depreciation—telecommunications assets	28,264
Depreciation and amortization expense	3,269
Buildings	3,459

Cash and cash equivalents	$ 363
Common shares	13,525
Finite-life intangible assets	5,747
Goodwill	5,659
Indefinite-life intangible assets	3,697
Land	77
Machinery and equipment	7,009
Other long-term assets	2,625
Other property, plant, and equipment	333
Plant under construction	1,099
Satellites	1,395
Telecommunications assets	41,131

Instructions

(a) Identify in which financial statement (balance sheet or income statement) and which section (e.g., current assets) each of the above items should be reported.

(b) Prepare the tangible and intangible assets sections of the balance sheet as at December 31, 2008.

E9–16 Suncor Energy Inc. reported the following information for the fiscal years ended December 31, 2008, and December 31, 2007 (in millions):

Calculate asset turnover and return on assets.
(SO 7) AN

	Dec. 31, 2008	Dec. 31, 2007
Net revenues	$30,089	$18,565
Profit	2,137	2,983
Total assets, end of year	32,528	24,509
Total assets, beginning of year	24,509	18,759

Instructions

(a) Calculate Suncor's asset turnover and return on assets for the two years.

(b) Comment on what the ratios reveal about Suncor Energy Inc.'s effectiveness in using its assets to generate revenues and produce profit.

Problems: Set A

P9–1A In 2011, Kadlec Company had the following transactions related to the purchase of a property. All transactions were for cash unless otherwise stated.

Record property transactions.
(SO 1) AP

Jan. 12 Purchased real estate for a future plant site for $220,000, paying $55,000 cash and signing a note payable for the balance. On the site, there was an old building and the fair values of the land and building were $210,000 and $30,000, respectively. The old building will be demolished and a new one built.

16 Paid $4,500 for legal fees on the real estate purchase.

31 Paid $25,000 to demolish the old building to make room for the new plant.

Feb. 13 Received $7,500 for residual materials from the demolished building.

28 Graded and filled the land in preparation for the construction for $8,000.

Mar. 14 Paid $35,000 in architect fees for the building plans.

31 Paid the local municipality $15,000 for building permits.

Apr. 22 Excavation costs for the new building were $17,000.

May 1 Construction on the new building began.

June 15 Received a bill for $300,000 from the building contractor for half of the cost of the new building. Paid $75,000 in cash and signed a note payable for the balance.

Sept. 14 Received a bill for the remaining $300,000 owed to the building contractor for the construction of the new building. Paid $100,000 cash and signed a note payable for the balance.

Oct. 12 Paved the parking lots, driveways, and sidewalks for $42,000.

15 Installed a fence for $8,000.

20 Building was ready for use. Interest costs while the building was under construction amounted to $6,700.

Nov. 30 Kadlec moved in and began using the building.

Dec. 31 Interest costs after the building was in use amounted to $2,800.

Instructions

(a) Record the above transactions.

(b) Determine the cost of the land, land improvements, and building that will appear on Kadlec's December 31, 2011, balance sheet.

Taking It Further Should Kadlec record depreciation on this property in 2011? If yes, on which assets and as of when should it start recording depreciation?

Calculate partial period depreciation. (SO 2) AP

P9–2A In recent years, Flatboard Company purchased two machines. Various depreciation methods were selected. Information on the machines is summarized here:

Machine	Acquired	Cost	Residual Value	Useful Life in Years	Depreciation Method
1	Mar. 2, 2008	$392,000	$ 8,000	10	Straight-line
2	Oct. 25, 2010	120,000	20,000	8	Single diminishing-balance

Instructions

(a) If Flatboard has a policy of recording depreciation to the nearest month, calculate the amount of accumulated depreciation on each machine at December 31, 2011. Round your answers to the nearest dollar.

(b) If Flatboard has a policy of recording a half year's depreciation in the year of acquisition and disposal, calculate the amount of accumulated depreciation on each machine at December 31, 2011. Round your answers to the nearest dollar.

(c) Which policy should Flatboard follow in the year of acquisition: recording depreciation to the nearest whole month or recording a half year of depreciation?

Taking It Further Should Flatboard consider recording depreciation to the nearest day? Why or why not?

Determine cost; calculate and compare depreciation under different methods. (SO 1, 2) AP

P9–3A Whiteline Company purchased a machine on account on September 3, 2009, at an invoice price of $204,000. On September 4, 2009, it paid $10,400 for delivery of the machine. A one-year, $1,975 insurance policy on the machine was purchased on September 6, 2009. On September 20, 2009, Whiteline paid $8,600 for installation and testing of the machine. The machine was ready for use on October 1, 2009.

Whiteline estimates that the machine's useful life will be four years, with a residual value of $13,000. It also estimates that, in terms of activity, the machine's useful life will be 90,000 units. Whiteline has a December 31 fiscal year end and records depreciation to the nearest month. Assume that actual usage is as follows: 6,000 units in 2009; 27,450 units in 2010; 22,950 units in 2011; 20,100 units in 2012; and 13,500 units in 2013.

Instructions

(a) Determine the cost of the machine.

(b) Prepare depreciation schedules for the life of the asset under the following assumptions:

1. Whiteline uses the straight-line method of depreciation.
2. Whiteline uses the diminishing-balance method at double the straight-line rate.
3. Whiteline uses the units-of-production method.

(c) Which method would result in the highest profit in 2009? Over the life of the asset?

(d) Which method would result in the highest cash flow in 2009? Over the life of the asset?

Taking It Further   Assume instead that, when Whiteline purchased the machine, it had a legal obligation to ensure that the machine was recycled at the end of its useful life. Assume the cost of doing this is significant. Would this have had an impact on the answers to (a) and (b) above? Explain.

P9–4A   Arnison Company had the following selected transactions related to property, plant, and equipment in 2011:

Account for operating and capital expenditures, and asset impairments.
(SO 1, 3) AP

Jan. 12   All of the company's light bulbs were converted to energy-efficient bulbs for $2,200. Arnison expects that this will save money on its utility bills in the future.

Feb. 24   An air conditioning system in the factory was installed for $75,000.

Mar.   6   A fee of $5,400 was paid to paint machinery that had started to rust.

May 17   Safety training was given to factory employees on using the machinery at a cost of $3,100.

July 19   Windows broken in a labour dispute (not covered by insurance) were replaced for $5,900.

Aug. 21   Paid $26,000 to convert the company's trucks from gasoline to propane. Arnison expects this will substantially reduce the trucks' future operating costs, but it will not extend the trucks' useful lives.

Sept. 20   The exhaust system in a delivery vehicle was repaired for $2,700.

Oct. 25   New parts were added to a machine for $20,000. Arnison expects this will increase the machine's useful life by four years.

Nov.   9   The tires on two delivery vehicles were replaced for $1,200.

Dec. 31   After recording annual depreciation, Arnison reviewed its property, plant, and equipment for possible impairment. Arnison determined the following:

1. Land that originally cost $200,000 had previously been written down to $125,000 in 2008 as a result of a decline in the recoverable amount. The current recoverable amount of the land is $220,000.
2. The recoverable amount of equipment that originally cost $150,000 and has accumulated depreciation of $62,500 is $50,000.

Instructions

(a) For each of these transactions, indicate if the transaction has increased (+) or decreased (−) Land, Buildings, Equipment, Accumulated Depreciation, total property, plant, and equipment (PP&E), and profit, and by how much. If the item is not changed, write "NE" to indicate there is no effect. Use the following format, in which the first one has been done for you as an example.

Transaction	Land	Buildings	Equipment	Accumulated Depreciation	Total PP&E	Profit
Jan. 12	NE	NE	NE	NE	NE	−$2,200

(b) Prepare journal entries to record the above transactions. All transactions are paid in cash.

Taking It Further   Assume that Arnison also purchases a new machine with an expected useful life of 12 years. Assume also that the machine's engine will need to be replaced every four years. Which useful life should Arnison use when calculating depreciation on the machine? Explain.

P9–5A   At the beginning of 2006, Bérubé Company acquired equipment costing $1.2 million. It was estimated at that time that this equipment would have a useful life of 10 years and a residual value of $100,000. Bérubé uses the straight-line method of depreciation and has a December 31 year end.

Record impairment and calculate revised depreciation.
(SO 3) AP

On December 31, 2010, after recording the annual depreciation expense, Bérubé determined that the equipment's recoverable amount was $400,000. In 2011, Bérubé determined that the equipment's useful life will remain as originally estimated but that the equipment would have no residual value at the end of its useful life.

Instructions

(a) Calculate the depreciation expense for the years 2006 to 2010 and accumulated depreciation at December 31, 2010.

(b) Record the impairment loss on December 31, 2010.

(c) Would you expect Bérubé's depreciation expense to increase or decrease in 2011 after recording the impairment loss? Explain why.

(d) Calculate depreciation expense for the years 2011 to 2015. Assume no further impairments or recoveries.

(e) What will accumulated depreciation and the equipment's carrying amount be at the end of its useful life?

Taking It Further   What factors could cause a decline in the recoverable amount of equipment?

Record acquisition,
depreciation, impairment, and
disposal of land and building.
(SO 2, 3, 4) AP

P9–6A NW Tool Supply Company purchased land and a building on May 1, 2009, for $385,000. The company paid $115,000 in cash and signed a 5% note payable for the balance. At that time, it was estimated that the land was worth $150,000 and the building, $235,000. The building was estimated to have a 25-year useful life with a $35,000 residual value. The company has a December 31 year end and uses the single diminishing-balance depreciation method for buildings. The following are related transactions and adjustments during the next three years.

2009

Dec. 31 Recorded annual depreciation.
     31 Paid the interest owing on the note payable.

2010

Feb. 17 Paid $225 to have the furnace cleaned and serviced.
Dec. 31 Recorded annual depreciation.
     31 Paid the interest owing on the note payable.
     31 The land and building were tested for impairment. The land had a recoverable amount of $120,000 and the building, $240,000.

2011

Jan. 31 Sold the land and building for $320,000 cash: $110,000 for the land and $210,000 for the building.
Feb. 1 Paid the note payable and interest owing.

Instructions

(a) Record the above transactions and adjustments, including the purchase on May 6, 2009.

(b) What factors may have been responsible for the impairment?

(c) Assume instead that the company sold the land and building on October 31, 2011, for $400,000 cash: $160,000 for the land and $240,000 for the building. Record the journal entries to record the sale.

Taking It Further   How might management determine what is the recoverable amount of the land and buildings at each year end? Would the company need to test the assets for impairment every year?

Calculate and compare
depreciation and gain or loss
on disposal under straight-
line and diminishing-balance
methods.
(SO 1, 2, 4) AP

P9–7A Forristal Farms purchased a piece of equipment on December 28, 2008, for $91,500. The equipment had an estimated useful life of five years and a residual value of $7,500. Management is considering the merits of using the double diminishing-balance method of depreciation versus the straight-line method. Management feels that the straight-line method will have a more favourable impact on the income statement.

Instructions

(a) Calculate depreciation for the equipment for 2009 to 2013 under (1) the straight-line method, and (2) the diminishing-balance method, using double the straight-line rate.

(b) Assume that the equipment is sold on January 3, 2013, for $15,000.

1. Calculate the gain or loss on the sale of the equipment, under (a) the straight-line method, and (b) the diminishing-balance method.

2. Prepare a schedule to show the overall impact of the total depreciation expense combined with the gain or loss on sale over the life of the asset under each method of depreciation. (Consider the total effect on profit over the asset's life.) Compare this with the difference between the asset's purchase price and the proceeds received from its sale. Comment on your results.

Taking It Further What factors should influence management's choice of depreciation method?

P9–8A Express Co. purchased delivery equipment on March 1, 2009, for $65,000 on account. The equipment had an estimated useful life of five years, with a residual value of $5,000. The equipment is disposed of on September 30, 2011. Express Co. uses the straight-line method of depreciation and calculates depreciation for partial periods to the nearest month. The company has an August 31 year end.

Record acquisition, depreciation, and disposal of equipment.
(SO 2, 4) AP

Instructions

(a) Record the acquisition of the delivery equipment on March 1, 2009.

(b) Record depreciation at August 31, 2009, 2010, and 2011.

(c) Record the disposal on September 30, 2011, under the following assumptions:

1. It was scrapped with no residual value.

2. It was sold for $30,000.

3. It was sold for $40,000.

4. It was traded for new delivery equipment with a list price of $87,000. Express was given a trade-in allowance of $32,000 on the old delivery equipment and paid the balance in cash. Express determined the old equipment's fair value to be $28,000 at the date of the exchange.

Taking It Further What are the arguments in favour of recording gains and losses on disposals of property, plant, and equipment as part of profit from operations? What are the arguments in favour of recording them as non-operating items?

P9–9A At January 1, 2011, Hamsmith Corporation reported the following property, plant, and equipment accounts:

Record property, plant, and equipment transactions; prepare partial financial statements.
(SO 2, 4, 7) AP

Accumulated depreciation—buildings	$31,100,000
Accumulated depreciation—equipment	27,000,000
Buildings	48,700,000
Equipment	75,000,000
Land	10,000,000

Hamsmith uses straight-line depreciation for buildings and equipment and its fiscal year end is December 31. The buildings are estimated to have a 50-year useful life and no residual value; the equipment is estimated to have a 10-year useful life and no residual value. Interest on the notes is payable or collectible annually on the anniversary date of the issue.

During 2011, the following selected transactions occurred:

Apr. 1 Purchased land for $2.2 million. Paid $550,000 cash and issued a three-year, 6% note for the balance.

May 1 Sold equipment for $150,000 cash. The equipment cost $1.4 million when originally purchased on January 1, 2003.

June 1 Sold land for $1.8 million. Received $450,000 cash and accepted a three-year, 5% note for the balance. The land cost $700,000.

July 1 Purchased equipment for $1.1 million cash.

Dec. 31 Retired equipment that cost $500,000 when purchased on December 31, 2001.

Instructions

(a) Record the above transactions.

(b) Record any adjusting entries required at December 31, 2011.

(c) Prepare the property, plant, and equipment section of Hamsmith's balance sheet at December 31, 2011.

Taking It Further   The owner of Hamsmith suggests the company should start using the revaluation model, not the cost model, for property, plant, and equipment now that it is following International Financial Reporting Standards. Comment on this suggestion.

Correct errors in recording intangible asset transactions. (SO 6) AP

P9–10A   Due to rapid turnover in the accounting department, several transactions involving intangible assets were improperly recorded by Riley Co. in the year ended December 31, 2011:

1. Riley developed a new manufacturing process early in the year, incurring research and development costs of $160,000. Of this amount, 45% was considered to be development costs that could be capitalized. Riley recorded the entire $160,000 in the Patents account and amortized it using a 15-year estimated useful life.

2. On July 1, 2011, Riley purchased a small company and, as a result of the purchase, recorded goodwill of $400,000. Riley recorded a half year's amortization on the goodwill in 2011 based on a 40-year useful life.

3. The company purchased a trademark for $47,500. Shortly thereafter, it was sued for trademark infringement. At the end of the year, Riley determined that the recoverable amount of the trademark was $35,000. Riley did not record an impairment loss because it is hopeful that the recoverable amount will rebound next year after the conclusion of a legal case defending the company's right to use this trademark.

4. Several years ago, Riley paid $70,000 for a licence to be the exclusive Canadian distributor of a Danish beer. In 2008, Riley determined there was an impairment of $40,000 in the value of the licence and recorded the loss. In 2011, because of a change in consumer tastes, the value of the licence increased to $80,000. Riley recorded the $50,000 increase in the licence's value by crediting Gain on Licence Fair Value and debiting the licence account. Management felt the company should consistently record increases and decreases in value.

5. The company made an $8,000 charitable donation on December 31, 2011, which it debited to goodwill.

Instructions

Prepare the journal entries that are needed to correct the errors made during 2011.

Taking It Further   The majority of the intangible assets reported on a balance sheet have been purchased as opposed to being internally generated. Why? What happens to the cost of an internally generated intangible asset if it is not recorded as an asset?

Record intangible asset transactions; prepare partial balance sheet. (SO 6, 7) AP

P9–11A   The intangible assets reported by Ip Company at December 31, 2010, follow:

Patent #1	$70,000	
Less: Accumulated amortization	14,000	$ 56,000
Copyright #1	$48,000	
Less: Accumulated amortization	28,800	19,200
Goodwill		210,000
Total		$285,200

Patent #1 was acquired in January 2009 and has an estimated useful life of 10 years. Copyright #1 was acquired in January 2006 and also has an estimated useful life of 10 years. The following cash transactions may have affected intangible assets during the year 2011:

Jan.   2   Paid $22,400 of legal costs to successfully defend Patent #1 against infringement by another company.

June 30   Developed a new product, incurring $220,000 in research costs and $60,000 in development costs, which were paid in cash. Patent #2 was granted for the product on July 1. Its estimated useful life is equal to its legal life of 20 years.

Sept. 1   Paid $21,000 to an Olympic athlete to appear in commercials advertising the company's products. The commercials will air in September.

Oct.   1   Acquired a second copyright for $16,000 cash. Copyright #2 has an estimated useful life of eight years.

Dec. 31   Determined the recoverable amount of the goodwill to be $245,000. The company had originally paid $250,000 for the goodwill in 2008. In 2009, the company had recorded a $40,000 impairment loss on the goodwill. There is no indication that the patents and copyrights were impaired.

Instructions

(a) Record the above transactions.
(b) Prepare any adjusting journal entries required at December 31, 2011.
(c) Prepare the intangible assets section of the balance sheet at December 31, 2011.

Taking It Further Since intangible assets do not have physical substance, why are they considered to be assets?

P9–12A Yount Mining Company has a December 31 fiscal year end. The following information related to its Gough Alexander mine is available:

Record natural resource transactions; prepare partial financial statements.
(SO 3, 5, 7) AP

1. Yount purchased the Gough Alexander mine on March 31, 2010, for $2.6 million cash. On the same day, modernization of the mine was completed at a cash cost of $260,000. It is estimated that this mine will yield 560,000 tonnes of ore. The mine's estimated residual value is $200,000. Yount expects it will extract all the ore, and then close and sell the mine site in four years.
2. During 2010, Yount extracted and sold 120,000 tonnes of ore from the mine.
3. At the beginning of 2011, Yount reassessed its estimate of the remaining ore in the mine. Yount estimates that there is still 550,000 tonnes of ore in the mine at January 1, 2011. The estimated residual value remains at $200,000.
4. During 2011, Yount extracted and sold 100,000 tonnes of ore from the mine.

Instructions

(a) Prepare the 2010 and 2011 journal entries for the above, including any year-end adjustments.
(b) Show how the Gough Alexander mine will be reported on Yount's December 31, 2011, income statement and balance sheet.

Taking It Further If the total estimated amount of units that will be produced (extracted) changes during the life of the natural resource, is it still appropriate to use the units-of-production method? Explain.

P9–13A Andruski Company and Brar Company both manufacture in-line skates. They reported the following information at December 31, 2011 (in thousands):

Calculate ratios and comment.
(SO 7) AN

	Andruski Company	Brar Company
Net sales	$449.0	$1,464.1
Profit	15.5	84.8
Total assets, start of year	589.6	1,288.5
Total assets, end of year	561.9	1,324.4

Instructions

(a) For each company, calculate the asset turnover and return on assets ratios. Round your answers to two decimal points.

(b) Based on your results in part (a), compare the two companies by commenting on how effective they are at using their assets to generate sales and produce profit.

Taking It Further   What other information would be useful in comparing these two companies?

Problems: Set B

Record property transactions.
(SO 1) AP

P9–1B   In 2011, Weisman Company had the following transactions related to the purchase of a property. All transactions are for cash unless otherwise stated.

Feb.   7   Purchased real estate for $275,000, paying $75,000 cash and signing a note payable for the balance. The site had an old building on it and the fair value of the land and building were $270,000 and $30,000, respectively. Weisman intends to demolish the old building and construct a new building on the site.

9   Paid legal fees of $5,500 on the real estate purchase on February 7.

15   Paid $11,000 to demolish the old building and make the land ready for the construction of the apartment building.

17   Received $4,000 from the sale of material from the demolished building.

25   Graded and filled the land in preparation for the building construction at a cost of $9,000.

Mar.   2   Architect's fees on the apartment building were $18,000.

15   Excavation costs were $15,000. Construction began on March 20.

Aug. 31   The full cost for construction of the apartment building was $650,000. Paid $170,000 cash and signed a note payable for the balance.

Sept.   3   Paid $12,000 for sidewalks and a parking lot for the building.

10   Building was ready for use. Purchased a one-year insurance policy on the finished building for $2,500.

11   Interest costs while the building was under construction amounted to $6,500.

Oct. 31   Moved into the building and began using it.

Dec. 31   Interest costs after the building was completed and rented to tenants amounted to $17,500.

Instructions

(a) Record the above transactions.

(b) Determine the cost of the land, land improvements, and building that will appear on Weisman's December 31, 2011, balance sheet.

Taking It Further   Should Weisman record depreciation on this property in 2011? If yes, on which assets and as of when should it start calculating depreciation?

Calculate partial period depreciation.
(SO 2) AP

P9–2B   In recent years, Tarcher Company purchased two machines and uses a different method of depreciation for each. Information on the machines is as follows:

Machine	Acquired	Cost	Residual Value	Useful Life in Years	Depreciation Method
1	Feb. 5, 2009	$ 97,880	$8,000	7	Straight-line
2	Sept. 25, 2010	168,000	9,000	10	Diminishing-balance

The company uses double the straight-line rate for the diminishing-balance method.

Instructions

(a) If Tarcher has a policy of recording depreciation to the nearest month, calculate the amount of accumulated depreciation on each machine at December 31, 2011. Round your answers to the nearest dollar.

(b) If Tarcher has a policy of recording a half year of depreciation in the year of acquisition and disposal, calculate the amount of accumulated depreciation on each machine at December 31, 2011. Round your answers to the nearest dollar.

(c) Which policy should Tarcher follow: recording depreciation to the nearest month in the year of acquisition or recording a half year of depreciation in the year of acquisition?

Taking It Further   How would Tarcher's choice of how to record depreciation in the year of acquisition affect depreciation calculations if Tarcher used the units-of-production method to amortize the machines?

P9–3B   Orange-Circle Company purchased a machine on account on April 6, 2009, at an invoice price of $360,000. On April 7, 2009, it paid $2,000 for delivery of the machine. A one-year, $3,175 insurance policy on the machine was purchased on April 9, 2009. On April 22, 2009, Orange-Circle paid $6,400 for installation and testing of the machine. The machine was ready for use on April 30, 2009.

Determine cost; calculate and compare depreciation under different methods.
(SO 1, 2) AP

Orange-Circle estimates that the machine's useful life will be five years, with a residual value of $23,000. Orange-Circle estimates that the machine's useful life, in terms of activity, will be 165,000 units. Orange-Circle has a December 31 fiscal year end and records depreciation to the nearest month. Assume actual usage is as follows: 25,500 units in 2009; 36,000 units in 2010; 34,500 units in 2011; 31,500 units in 2012; 28,500 units in 2013; and 9,000 units in 2014.

Instructions

(a) Determine the cost of the machine.

(b) Prepare a depreciation schedule for the life of the asset under each of the following assumptions:
1. Orange-Circle uses the straight-line method of depreciation.
2. Orange-Circle uses the diminishing-balance method at double the straight-line rate.
3. Orange-Circle uses the units-of-production method.

(c) Which method would result in the lowest profit in 2009? Over the life of the asset?

(d) Which method would result in the lowest cash flow in 2009? Over the life of the asset?

Taking It Further   Assume instead that at the time Orange-Circle purchased the machine, it had a legal obligation to ensure that the machine was recycled at the end of its useful life. Assume the cost of doing this is significant. Would this have had an impact on the answers to (a) and (b) above? Explain.

P9–4B   Sugden Company had the following selected transactions related to property, plant, and equipment in 2011:

Account for operating and capital expenditures and asset impairments.
(SO 1, 3) AP

Jan. 22 Performed an annual safety inspection on the equipment for $4,600.

Apr. 10 Installed a conveyor belt system in the factory for $95,000, which is expected to increase efficiency and allow the company to produce more products each year.

May 6 Replaced carpets in the main reception area and hallways for $15,500.

July 20 Repaired a machine for $10,000. An employee had used incorrect material in the machine, which resulted in a complete breakdown.

Aug. 7 Overhauled machinery that originally cost $100,000 for $35,000. This increased the machinery's expected useful life by three years.

15 Trained several new employees to operate the company's machinery at a cost of $1,900.

Nov. 6 Added an elevator and ramps to a building owned by the company to make it wheelchair accessible for $120,000.

28 Replaced the tires on several company vehicles for $5,000.

Dec. 31 After recording annual depreciation, Sugden reviewed its property, plant, and equipment for possible impairment. Sugden determined the following:

1. The recoverable amount on equipment that originally cost $200,000 and has accumulated depreciation of $75,000 is $90,000.

2. Land that originally cost $575,000 had previously been written down to $480,000 as a result of an impairment in 2008. Circumstances have changed, and the land's recoverable amount is $620,000.

Instructions

(a) For each of these transactions, indicate if the transaction has increased (+) or decreased (–) Land, Buildings, Equipment, Accumulated Depreciation, total property, plant, and equipment (PP&E), and profit, and by how much. If the item is not changed, write "NE" to indicate there is no effect. Use the following format, in which the first one has been done for you as an example.

Transaction	Land	Buildings	Equipment	Accumulated Depreciation	Total PP&E	Profit
Jan. 22	NE	NE	NE	NE	NE	–$4,600

(b) Prepare journal entries to record the above transactions. All transactions are on account.

Taking It Further Assume that Sugden also purchased a new machine with an expected useful life of 15 years and that the machine's engine will need to be replaced every five years. Which useful life should Sugden use when calculating depreciation on the machine? Explain.

Record impairment and calculate revised depreciation. (SO 3) AP

P9–5B On January 4, 2007, Harrington Company acquired equipment costing $375,000. It was estimated at that time that this equipment would have a useful life of 10 years and a residual value of $15,000. Harrington uses the straight-line method of depreciation and has a December 31 year end.

On December 31, 2010, after recording the annual depreciation expense, Harrington determined that the equipment's recoverable amount was $155,000. In 2011, Harrington also determined that the equipment's useful life would be 7 years in total, instead of the previously estimated 10. The residual value is still expected to be $15,000 at the end of the equipment's useful life.

Instructions

(a) Calculate the depreciation expense for the years 2007 to 2010 and accumulated depreciation at December 31, 2010.

(b) Record the impairment loss on December 31, 2010.

(c) Would you expect Harrington's depreciation expense to increase or decrease in 2011 after recording the impairment loss? Explain why.

(d) Calculate depreciation expense for each of 2011, 2012, and 2013.

(e) What should the equipment's accumulated depreciation and carrying amount be at the end of its useful life?

Taking It Further What factors could cause a decline in the recoverable amount on equipment? Why might this also reduce the equipment's estimated useful life?

Record acquisition, depreciation, impairment, and disposal of land and buildings. (SO 1, 2, 3, 4) AP

P9–6B SE Parts Supply Company purchased land and a building on August 1, 2009, for $595,000. It paid $200,000 in cash and signed a 5% note payable for the balance. The company estimated the land was worth $340,000 and building, $255,000. The building was estimated to have a 40-year useful life with a $15,000 residual value. The company has a December 31 year end and uses the straight-line depreciation method for buildings. The following are related transactions and adjustments during the next three years.

<u>2009</u>
Dec. 31 Recorded annual depreciation.
31 Paid the interest owing on the note payable.

2010

May 21   Paid $2,000 to fix the roof.
    31   Recorded annual depreciation.
    31   Paid the interest owing on the note payable.
    31   The land and building were tested for impairment. The land had a recoverable amount of $280,000 and the building, $249,000.

2011

Mar. 31   Sold the land and building for $480,000 cash: $250,000 for the land and $230,000 for the building.
Apr. 1   Paid the note payable and interest owing.

Instructions

(a) Record the above transactions and adjustments, including the acquisition on August 1, 2009.
(b) What factors may have been responsible for the impairment?
(c) Assume instead that the company sold the land and building on November 30, 2011, for $650,000 cash: $390,000 for the land and $260,000 for the building. Record the journal entries to record the sale.

Taking It Further   How might management determine the recoverable amount of the land and buildings at each year end? Does the company need to test the assets for impairment every year?

P9–7B   Rapid Transportation Ltd. purchased a new bus on January 5, 2010, at a cost of $254,000. The bus has an estimated useful life of three years with a residual value of $40,000. Management is contemplating the merits of using the units-of-production method of depreciation instead of the straight-line method, which it currently uses.

Under the units-of-production method, management estimates a total estimated useful life of 450,000 kilometres: 175,000 kilometres driven in 2010; 152,000 kilometres in 2011; and 123,000 kilometres in 2012.

Calculate and compare depreciation and gain or loss on disposal under straight-line and units-of-production methods.
(SO 2, 4) AP

Instructions

(a) Calculate depreciation for the life of the bus using (1) the straight-line method and (2) the units-of-production method. Rapid Transportation has a December 31 fiscal year end.
(b) Assume that the bus is sold on December 30, 2011, for $100,000.
  1. Calculate the gain or loss on the sale of the bus under (a) the straight-line method and (b) the units-of-production method. (*Hint*: Round the depreciable cost per unit to four decimals.)
  2. Prepare a schedule to show the overall impact of the total depreciation expense combined with the gain or loss on sale for the two-year period under each method of depreciation. (Consider the total effect on profit over the two-year period.) Compare this with the difference between the asset's purchase price and the proceeds received from its sale. Comment on your results.

Taking It Further   What factors should influence management's choice of depreciation method?

P9–8B   Walker Co. purchased office furniture on February 1, 2009, for $85,000 on account. At that time, it was expected to have a useful life of five years and a $1,000 residual value. The furniture was disposed of on October 26, 2011, when the company moved to new premises. Walker Co. uses the straight-line method of depreciation and calculates depreciation for partial periods to the nearest month. The company has a September 30 year end.

Record acquisition, depreciation, and disposal of furniture.
(SO 2, 4) AP

Instructions

(a) Record the acquisition of the office furniture on February 1, 2009.
(b) Record depreciation for each of 2009, 2010, and 2011.
(c) Record the disposal on October 26, 2011, under the following assumptions:

1. It was scrapped and has no residual value.
2. It was sold for $50,000.
3. It was sold for $40,000.
4. It was traded for new office furniture with a catalogue price of $113,000. Walker Co. was given a trade-in allowance of $45,000 on the old office furniture and paid the balance in cash. Walker Co. determined that the old office furniture's fair value was $38,000 at the date of the exchange.

Taking It Further What are the arguments in favour of recording gains and losses on disposals of property, plant, and equipment as part of profit from operations? What are the arguments in favour of recording them as non-operating items?

Record property, plant, and equipment transactions; prepare partial financial statements.
(SO 2, 4, 7) AP

P9–9B At January 1, 2011, Jaina Company reported the following property, plant, and equipment accounts:

Accumulated depreciation—buildings	$12,100,000
Accumulated depreciation—equipment	15,000,000
Buildings	28,500,000
Equipment	48,000,000
Land	4,000,000

Jaina uses straight-line depreciation for buildings and equipment, and its fiscal year end is December 31. The buildings are estimated to have a 50-year life and no residual value; the equipment is estimated to have a 10-year useful life and no residual value. Interest on all notes is payable or collectible at maturity on the anniversary date of the issue.

During 2011, the following selected transactions occurred:

Apr. 1 Purchased land for $1.9 million. Paid $475,000 cash and issued a 10-year, 6% note for the balance.

May 1 Sold equipment that cost $750,000 when purchased on January 1, 2004. The equipment was sold for $350,000 cash.

June 1 Sold land purchased on June 1, 1993, for $1.2 million. Received $380,000 cash and accepted a 6% note for the balance. The land cost $300,000.

July 1 Purchased equipment for $1 million on account, terms n/60.

Dec. 31 Retired equipment that cost $470,000 when purchased on December 31, 2001.

Instructions

(a) Record the above transactions.
(b) Record any adjusting entries required at December 31, 2011.
(c) Prepare the property, plant, and equipment section of Jaina's balance sheet at December 31, 2011.

Taking It Further The owner of Jaina Company suggests the company should start using the revaluation model, not the cost model, for property, plant, and equipment now that it is following International Financial Reporting Standards. Comment on this suggestion.

Correct errors in recording intangible asset transactions.
(SO 6) AP

P9–10B Due to rapid employee turnover in the accounting department, the following transactions involving intangible assets were recorded in a questionable way by Hahn Company in the year ended August 31, 2011:

1. Hahn developed an electronic monitoring device for running shoes. It incurred research costs of $70,000 and development costs with probable future benefits of $45,000. It recorded all of these costs in the Patent account.
2. The company registered the patent for the monitoring device developed in transaction 1. Legal fees and registration costs totalled $21,000. These costs were recorded in the Legal Fees Expense account.
3. The company successfully fought a competitor in court, defending its patent. It incurred $38,000 of legal fees. These costs were recorded in the Legal Fees Expense account.

4. The company recorded $5,750 of annual amortization on the patent over its legal life of 20 years [($70,000 + $45,000 = $115,000) ÷ 20 years]. The patent's expected economic life is five years. Assume that for amortization purposes, all costs occurred at the beginning of the year.

5. At the end of the year, Hahn tested the patent for impairment and found that its recoverable amount of $110,000 exceeded its carrying amount of $109,250 ($115,000 − $5,750). Since Hahn follows the cost model, it did not record an entry.

Instructions

Prepare the journal entries that are needed to correct the errors made during 2011.

Taking It Further   The majority of the intangible assets reported on a balance sheet have been purchased as opposed to being internally generated. Why? What happens to the cost of an internally generated intangible asset if it is not recorded as an asset?

P9–11B   The intangible assets section of Ghani Corporation's balance sheet at December 31, 2010, is as follows:

Record intangible asset transactions; prepare partial balance sheet.
(SO 6, 7) AP

Copyright #1	$36,000	
Less: Accumulated amortization	24,000	$ 12,000
Trademark		54,000
Goodwill		125,000
Total		$191,000

The copyright was acquired in January 2009 and has an estimated useful life of three years. The trademark was acquired in January 2007 and is expected to have an indefinite useful life. The following cash transactions may have affected intangible assets during 2011:

Jan. 2   Paid $7,000 in legal costs to successfully defend the trademark against infringement by another company.

July 1   Developed a new product, incurring $210,000 in research costs and $50,000 in development costs. A patent was granted for the product on July 1, and its useful life is equal to its legal life.

Aug. 1   Paid $60,000 to a popular hockey player to appear in commercials advertising the company's products. The commercials will air in September and October.

Oct. 1   Acquired a second copyright for $180,000. The new copyright has an estimated useful life of three years.

Dec. 31   The company determined the recoverable amount of the trademark and goodwill to be $65,000, and $90,000, respectively. There was no indication that any of the patents or copyrights were impaired.

Instructions

(a) Prepare journal entries to record the transactions.
(b) Prepare any adjusting journal entries required at December 31, 2011.
(c) Prepare the intangible assets section of the balance sheet at December 31, 2011.

Taking It Further   Since intangible assets do not have physical substance, why are they considered to be assets?

P9–12B   Cypress Timber Company has a December 31 fiscal year end. The following information related to its Westerlund tract of timber land is available:

Record equipment, note payable, and natural resource transactions; prepare partial financial statements.
(SO 2, 5, 7) AP

1. Cypress purchased a 50,000-hectare tract of timber land at Westerlund on June 7, 2010, for $50 million, paying $10 million cash and signing a 7% mortgage payable for the balance. Principal payments of $8 million and the annual interest on the mortgage are due each December 31. It is estimated that this tract will yield 1 million tonnes of timber. The timber tract's estimated residual value is $2 million. Cypress expects it will cut all the trees and then sell the Westerlund site in five years.

2. On June 26, 2010, Cypress purchased and installed weighing equipment at the West-erlund timber site for $196,000 cash. The weighing equipment will be amortized on a straight-line basis over an estimated useful life of seven years with no residual value. Cypress has a policy of recording depreciation for partial periods to the nearest month. The weighing equipment will be scrapped after the Westerlund site is harvested.
3. In 2010, Cypress cut and sold 110,000 tonnes of timber.
4. In 2011, Cypress cut and sold 240,000 tonnes of timber.

Instructions

(a) Prepare the 2010 and 2011 journal entries for the above, including any year-end adjustments.
(b) Show how property, plant, and equipment, natural resources, and related accounts will be reported on Cypress's December 31, 2011, income statement and balance sheet.

Taking It Further   If the total estimated amount of units that will be produced (extracted) changes during the life of the natural resource, is it still appropriate to use the units-of-production method? Explain.

Calculate ratios and comment. (SO 7) AN

P9–13B   STAD Company and STHN Company, two companies that manufacture sea kayaks, reported the following information in 2011 (in millions):

	STAD Company	STHN Company
Net sales	$341.7	$9,411.5
Profit	12.8	672.6
Total assets, January 1, 2011	264.5	4,429.9
Total assets, December 31, 2011	234.0	5,343.9

Instructions

(a) For each company, calculate the asset turnover and return on assets ratios. Round your answer to two decimals.
(b) Based on your results in part (a), compare the two companies by commenting on how effective they are at using their assets to generate sales and produce profit.

Taking It Further   What, if anything, complicates your ability to compare the two companies?

Continuing Cookie Chronicle

(*Note:* This is a continuation of the Cookie Chronicle from Chapters 1 through 8.)

Natalie is thinking of buying a van that will only be used for business. The cost of the van is estimated at $27,200. Natalie would spend an additional $2,500 to have the van painted. As well, she wants the back seat of the van removed so that she will have lots of room to transport her mixer inventory and baking supplies. The cost of taking out the back seat and installing shelving units is estimated at $1,500. She expects the van to last about five years and to be driven for 200,000 km. The annual cost of vehicle insurance will be $1,440. Natalie estimates that at the end of the five-year useful life, the van will sell for $6,600. Assume that she will buy the van on August 15, 2011, and it will be ready for use on September 1, 2011.

Natalie is concerned about the impact of the van's cost on her income statement and balance sheet. She has come to you for advice on calculating the van's depreciation.

Instructions

(a) Determine the cost of the van.

(b) Prepare schedules for each method of depreciation: (1) straight-line (similar to the one in Illustration 9-5), (2) double diminishing-balance (Illustration 9-7), and (3) units-of-production (Illustration 9-9). For units of production, it is estimated that the van will be driven as follows: 15,000 km in 2011, 45,000 km in 2012, 50,000 km in 2013, 45,000 km in 2014, 35,000 km in 2015, and 10,000 km in 2016. Recall that Cookie Creations has a December 31 year end.

(c) What impact will each method of depreciation have on Natalie's balance sheet at December 31, 2011? What impact will each method have on Natalie's income statement in 2011?

(d) What impact will each method of depreciation have on Natalie's income statement in total over the van's five-year useful life?

(e) Which method of depreciation would you recommend that Natalie use? Why?

BROADENING YOUR PERSPECTIVE

Financial Reporting and Analysis

Financial Reporting Problem

BYP9–1 Refer to the financial statements and the Notes to Consolidated Statements for The Forzani Group Ltd., which are reproduced in Appendix A.

Instructions

(a) Identify the following amounts for the company's long-lived assets (capital assets, goodwill and other intangibles, and other assets) at February 1, 2009: (1) cost, (2) accumulated depreciation (amortization), and (3) carrying amount (net book value).

(b) What was the amount of cash used to buy capital assets during the 2009 fiscal year? (*Hint*: Look at the statement of cash flows to determine this amount.)

(c) What depreciation methods are used by Forzani for financial reporting purposes (see note 2 to the financial statements)? What was the amount of depreciation (amortization) expense reported in the statement of operations for fiscal 2009?

(d) What expected useful life does the company use to calculate the depreciation (amortization) on the "furniture, fixtures, equipment, software and automotive" grouping of capital assets?

(e) What types of intangible assets does Forzani have?

(f) Did the company report any impairment losses in 2009 related to capital assets? How does Forzani determine if an impairment loss needs to be recorded?

Interpreting Financial Statements

BYP9–2   Maple Leaf Foods is Canada's largest food processor, serving customers across North America and internationally. Near the end of 2006, the company announced that it was going to restructure its meat processing business. In management's discussion and analysis in the 2008 annual report, it identifies expansion of capacity at the Brandon, Manitoba, pork processing plant as a major milestone achieved in 2008. The cash flow statement identifies "additions to property and equipment" of $206 million in 2008, some of which was for the Brandon expansion. However, some of the "expansion of capacity" involved only adding an extra shift (i.e., running the equipment and staffing the operations for 16 hours per day instead of just 8 hours per day).

Instructions

(a) How should Maple Leaf account for additions to property and equipment at the Brandon, Manitoba, pork processing plant?

(b) Identify and discuss advantages and disadvantages of three different possible depreciation methods for Maple Leaf Foods' pork processing facilities. Which method would you recommend that Maple Leaf use to depreciate the Brandon plant? Which method would you recommend for the equipment? Explain your reason for choosing the method(s) you did.

(c) Would you still choose the same depreciation method(s) in (b) if the plant moved to a three-shift operation (24 hours per day)? If you do choose the same depreciation method, how would the amount of annual depreciation expense be affected by the change to a three-shift operation compared with a double-shift operation?

Critical Thinking

Collaborative Learning Activity

Note to instructor: Additional instructions and material for this group activity can be found on the Instructor Resource Site.

Working in Groups

BYP9–3   In this group activity, you will review the following three depreciation methods:

1. Straight-line
2. Diminishing-balance
3. Units-of-production.

Instructions

(a) Your instructor will divide the class into "home" groups with three members in each "home" group. Each member of your "home" group will choose one of the above methods and then move to the "expert" group for that method.

(b) In the "expert" group, you will be given a handout explaining your method of depreciation. As a group, discuss the handout and ensure that each group member thoroughly understands that method.

(c) Return to your "home" group and explain your method to the other students in the group.

(d) You may be asked by your instructor to write a short quiz on this topic

Communication Activity

BYP9–4 Long Trucking Corporation is a medium-sized publicly owned trucking company with trucks that are driven across North America. The company owns large garages and equipment to repair and maintain the trucks. Ken Bond, the controller, knows that long-lived assets are reviewed annually for impairment. Ken records an impairment loss of $100,000 and the loss appears on the income statement for the current fiscal year. Jason Long, the company president, reviews the financial statements and wants more information from Ken about the impairment loss.

WILEY
PLUS
Writing Handbook

Instructions

Write a memo to Jason Long that explains (1) what might have caused the impairment loss, (2) the journal entry required for the impairment loss, and (3) how this writedown will affect Long Trucking's balance sheet and income statement in future years.

Ethics Case

BYP9–5 Finney Container Company has been seeing sales go down for its main product, non-biodegradable plastic cartons. Although some expenses have also reduced in line with the reduced revenues, there has been a decrease in profit because some expenses, such as depreciation, have not reduced. The company uses the straight-line depreciation method.

WILEY
PLUS
Ethics in Accounting

The president, Philip Shapiro, recalling his college accounting classes, instructs his controller to lengthen the estimated asset lives used for depreciation calculations in order to reduce annual depreciation expense and increase profit. The president's compensation includes an annual bonus based on the amount of net profit reported in the income statement.

A processing line of automated plastic extruding equipment that was purchased for $2.9 million in January 2009 was originally estimated to have a useful life between five and nine years. Therefore, the company used the middle of that estimate, or seven years, as the useful life, and a residual value of $100,000, to calculate the annual straight-line depreciation for the first two years. However, the president now wants the equipment's estimated useful life to be changed to nine years (total), and to continue using the straight-line method.

The controller is hesitant to make the change, believing it is unethical to increase profit in this way. The president says, "Hey, the useful life is only an estimate. Besides, I've heard that our competition uses a nine-year estimated life on its production equipment. You want the company results to be competitive, don't you? So maybe we were wrong the first time and now we are getting it right. Or you can tell the auditors that we think maybe the equipment will last longer now that we are not using it as much."

Instructions

(a) Who are the stakeholders in this situation?
(b) Is the suggested change in asset life unethical, or simply a shrewd business practice by a sharp president?
(c) What would be the impact of the president's proposed change on profit in the year of the change?

"All About You" Activity

BYP9–6 In the "All About You" feature, you learned about actions that have been taken to toughen Canada's copyright law and the radical changes in technology that are driving the need to update the law. You have recently graduated from a music program and have composed two songs that you believe a recording artist may produce. You are wondering how you can best get copyright protection for your songs.

Instructions

Go to the Canadian Intellectual Property Office website at http://www.cipo.ic.gc.ca and search for its publication "A Guide to Copyrights."

Answer the following questions:

(a) What is a copyright and to what does copyright apply?
(b) How can you obtain a copyright for your songs and what do you have to do to be protected?
(c) What are the benefits to you of getting copyright registration for your songs?
(d) How and where do you register a copyright?
(e) Section 55 of the *Copyright Act* is the section that applies to registering the copyrights for the songs that you have written. How much is the registration fee if you file the application on-line?
(f) Should the registration fee for the copyright be recorded as an asset?
(g) What is infringement of copyright? Provide a specific example of infringement.
(h) Whose responsibility is it for policing the use of your songs once you have registered the copyright?

ANSWERS TO CHAPTER QUESTIONS

Answers to Accounting in Action Insight Questions

Business Insight, p. 500

Q: Is the units-of-production method the best depreciation method for Morris Formal Wear to use for its tuxedos or would you recommend another method?

A: Since Morris Formal Wear wants to track wear and tear on each of its tuxedos, the units-of-production depreciation method is the best choice. Rental tuxedos are the type of long-lived asset that will physically wear out with use much faster than they would become obsolete due to changing tuxedo styles. By keeping track of how many times each tuxedo has been used, instead of just how old they are, the company can make better decisions about when to replace the tuxedos.

Across the Organization, p. 505

Q: What parts of an organization are responsible for determining if an impairment loss should be recorded?

A: The accounting department would work closely with the operations department to determine if there might be an impairment. In many companies, the operations department is responsible for forecasting demand and then monitoring sales to determine if its forecasts are accurate and if it needs to adjust production plans. Thus the operations department would be a valuable source of information to the accounting department in determining if an impairment exists.

All About You Insight, p. 517

Q: Is it important that the copyrights of artists, writers, musicians, and the entertainment industry be protected?

A: Just as it is important that you as an individual be compensated in your career, it is important that individuals in artistic, music, entertainment, and literary careers be compensated fairly for their creativity. Without fair compensation, Canada's creativity and innovation will be discouraged. Without copyright protection, it may be difficult to ensure that appropriate individuals are fairly compensated and companies may not be willing to invest in creative ventures if the work is not protected.

Answer to Forzani Review It Question 5, p. 493

Forzani reports (in thousands) land, $3,173; buildings, $20,928; building on leased land, $4,583; furniture, fixtures, equipment, software, and automotive, $243,564; leasehold improvements, $260,030; and construction in progress, $14,029.

Answers to Self-Study Questions

1. b 2. b 3. c 4. b 5. b 6. a 7. b 8. c 9. c 10. d

Remember to go
back to the beginning
of the chapter to
check off your
completed work!

←

CHAPTER 11
FINANCIAL REPORTING CONCEPTS

THE NAVIGATOR

- ☐ Understand *Concepts for Review*
- ☐ Read *Feature Story*
- ☐ Scan *Study Objectives*
- ☐ Read *Chapter Preview*
- ☐ Read text and answer *Before You Go On*
- ☐ Work *Demonstration Problem*
- ☐ Review *Summary of Study Objectives*
- ☐ Answer *Self-Study Questions*
- ☐ Complete assignments

CONCEPTS FOR REVIEW:

Before studying this chapter, you should understand or, if necessary, review:

a. The external users of accounting information. (Ch. 1, pp. 3–4)

b. How accounting standards are set in Canada and internationally. (Ch. 1, p. 7)

c. The definition of generally accepted accounting principles (GAAP) (Ch. 1, p. 7)

d. The accrual accounting and going concern assumptions. (Ch. 1, p. 8 and Ch. 3, pp. 119–120)

e. The revenue recognition and expense recognition criteria. (Ch. 1, p. 12 and Ch. 3, p. 120)

Canadian Accounting Goes Global

As of January 2011, Canadian generally accepted accounting principles (GAAP) will no longer exist as a distinct set of accounting standards for publicly accountable enterprises. Instead, Canadian publicly accountable enterprises must follow International Financial Reporting Standards (IFRS), a set of global accounting standards developed by the International Accounting Standards Board (IASB).

There are a number of reasons why it is important for Canadian companies to adopt IFRS, says Ian Hague, principal in accounting standards at the Accounting Standards Board of Canada (AcSB). "It was very clear to us from the consultations we did with companies and others across the country that it was no longer going to be sustainable to have a unique set of Canadian GAAP for publicly accountable enterprises in what was becoming a global market." Canadian companies wanting access to foreign markets must follow international standards. As well, the recent financial crisis increased support for a single set of high-quality global accounting standards.

The AcSB had two options: adopting U.S. GAAP or IFRS. It chose IFRS because, among other reasons, the standards are more similar to Canadian standards in their style, length, and complexity, Hague explains. "They are written in a similar kind of way, they require a similar degree of judgement, and they don't have all the extra detailed guidance the U.S. standards often have in them." The United States may be following suit. Its Securities and Exchange Commission has proposed a "roadmap" to converging U.S. GAAP with IFRS from 2014 to 2016. The United States already allows foreign companies to file according to IFRS. So, following the move to IFRS, Canadian companies that list on U.S. markets will no longer have to reconcile their financial statements to U.S. GAAP.

While all Canadian publicly accountable companies must adopt IFRS, the AcSB anticipates that others will voluntarily do so as well. "We do expect quite a number of private companies to adopt: those that are subsidiaries of foreign operations that report in accordance with IFRS, those thinking of going public in the near future, and those that want to access international markets. So while there's one group of companies that must adopt, there's another group that probably will adopt," says Hague.

The IASB is also reviewing the conceptual framework underlying the accounting standards. This is a multi-stage project still in the early stages. "Our conceptual framework in Section 1000 [of the *CICA Handbook*] is quite similar to the IASB conceptual framework anyway," says Hague. "So as they update their conceptual framework, we will, for publicly accountable enterprises, update it at the same time because we will be onto IFRS by then, and for private enterprises and not-for-profits, we will also take into account those updates."

"The framework doesn't override accounting standards," Hague continues. "The fact that the framework has changed won't immediately change accounting policies." The changes will have an impact in two ways: if an accounting standard changes, it would need to reflect the new thinking in the framework; and when there's no accounting standard in place, the framework would need to be referred to in developing the new accounting policy. "I don't think there is going to be a pervasive effect of immediate change to accounting just because the framework has changed," says Hague. "What companies are going to see is the new thinking in the framework applied as new standards are developed."

The Navigator

STUDY OBJECTIVES:

After studying this chapter, you should be able to:

1. Explain the importance of having a conceptual framework of accounting, and list the components.

2. Identify and apply the objective of financial reporting and the underlying assumptions used by accountants.

3. Describe the fundamental and enhancing qualitative characteristics of financial reporting.

4. Identify and apply the constraints on financial reporting.

5. Identify and apply the basic recognition and measurement concepts of accounting.

The Navigator

In the first 10 chapters, in Parts 1 and 2, you learned the process that leads to the preparation of a company's financial statements. You also learned that users make decisions based on financial statements, and that to be useful, these statements must communicate financial information to users in an effective way. This means that generally accepted accounting principles must be used. Otherwise, we would have to be familiar with each company's particular accounting and reporting practices in order to understand its financial statements. It would be difficult, if not impossible, to compare the financial results of different companies.

This chapter explores the conceptual framework that is used to develop generally accepted accounting principles. The chapter is organized as follows:

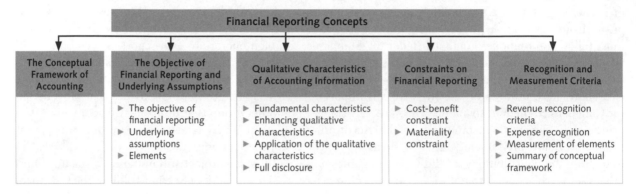

Financial Reporting Concepts				
The Conceptual Framework of Accounting	**The Objective of Financial Reporting and Underlying Assumptions**	**Qualitative Characteristics of Accounting Information**	**Constraints on Financial Reporting**	**Recognition and Measurement Criteria**
	▶ The objective of financial reporting ▶ Underlying assumptions ▶ Elements	▶ Fundamental characteristics ▶ Enhancing qualitative characteristics ▶ Application of the qualitative characteristics ▶ Full disclosure	▶ Cost-benefit constraint ▶ Materiality constraint	▶ Revenue recognition criteria ▶ Expense recognition ▶ Measurement of elements ▶ Summary of conceptual framework

The Conceptual Framework of Accounting

According to standard setters, the **conceptual framework of accounting** is "a coherent system of interrelated objectives and fundamentals that can lead to consistent standards and that prescribes the nature, function, and limits of financial accounting statements." In other words, the conceptual framework of accounting guides choices about what to present in financial statements, decisions about alternative ways of reporting economic events, and the selection of appropriate ways of communicating such information.

A conceptual framework ensures that we have a coherent set of standards. New standards are easier to understand and are more consistent when they are built on the same foundation as existing standards. By relying on an existing framework of basic theory, it should be possible to solve new and emerging problems more quickly.

As a foundation for accounting, the conceptual framework:

1. Ensures that existing standards and practices are clear and consistent.
2. Makes it possible to respond quickly to new issues.
3. Increases the usefulness of the financial information presented in financial reports.

Alternative terminology
Recall that, as we saw in Chapter 1, the words "standards" and "principles" mean the same thing in accounting.

However, it is impossible to create a rule for every situation. Canadian and international standards are therefore based mostly on general principles rather than specific rules. With the help of a conceptual framework and their professional judgement, it is hoped that accountants will be able to quickly determine an appropriate accounting treatment for each situation.

Accounting standards can differ significantly from country to country. This lack of uniformity has arisen over time because of differences in legal systems, in processes for developing standards, in government requirements, and in economic environments. The International Accounting Standards Board (IASB) was formed to try to reduce these areas of difference and unify global standard setting.

In Canada, accounting standards have been developed by the Accounting Standards Board (AcSB), an independent standard-setting body created by the Canadian Institute of Chartered Accountants (CICA). However, as noted in the opening story, the AcSB recognized the need to have globally uniform financial reporting and decided that, starting in 2011, publicly traded companies must follow International Financial Reporting Standards (IFRS).

As indicated in the feature story, the IASB and its U.S. counterpart, the Financial Accounting Standards Board (FASB), are also working on a joint project to improve and bring about convergence of their conceptual frameworks. Canada is participating in the project and the AcSB plans to adopt the improved IASB conceptual framework and to incorporate it into the *CICA Handbook*.

The six major components of the IASB conceptual framework are:

1. The objective of financial reporting
2. The underlying assumptions
3. The elements of financial statements
4. The qualitative characteristics of accounting information
5. The constraints on financial reporting
6. Recognition and measurement criteria

In 2008, the IASB issued an exposure draft recommending changes to two components of the conceptual framework: the objective of financial reporting and the qualitative characteristics of accounting information. These recommendations are expected to be approved and adopted. The IASB is continuing to improve the other components of the conceptual framework and we can expect to see further changes in the future.

This chapter includes the proposed changes to the objective of financial reporting and qualitative characteristics of accounting information, along with the other components of the IASB's current conceptual framework.

We will discuss the six components of the conceptual framework in the following sections.

> **Helpful hint** Accounting principles are affected by economic and political conditions, which change over time. As a result, accounting principles can and do change.

BEFORE YOU GO ON . . .

→ Review It

1. Describe the conceptual framework of accounting.
2. Why do we need a conceptual framework of accounting?
3. Why was the IASB formed?
4. What are the components of the IASB conceptual framework?

Related exercise material: BE11–1.

The Navigator

The Objective of Financial Reporting and Underlying Assumptions

The first step in establishing accounting standards is to decide on the purpose or objective of financial reporting. Once this is established, then the underlying assumptions can be determined.

> **STUDY OBJECTIVE 2**
>
> Identify and apply the objective of financial reporting and the underlying assumptions used by accountants.

The Objective of Financial Reporting

To decide what the objective of financial reporting should be, some basic questions need to be answered first: Who uses financial statements? Why? What information do the users need? How much do they know about business and accounting? How should financial information be reported so that it is best understood?

The main **objective of financial reporting** is to provide useful information for decision-making. More specifically, in the revised conceptual framework, accounting standard setters have decided that the objective for general purpose financial reporting is to provide financial information that is useful to present and potential investors, lenders, and other creditors in making decisions about a business. You will recall from earlier chapters that financial statements are prepared for an economic or business unit that is separate and distinct from its owners. This is referred to as the economic entity assumption. An economic (reporting) entity could be one company or a collection of companies consolidated under common ownership. We will learn more about consolidated companies in Chapter 16.

Although a wide variety of users rely on financial reporting, capital providers (investors and lenders) are identified as the main users of financial reporting. Capital providers play a fundamental role in the efficient functioning of the economy by providing capital (cash) to businesses. Businesses require cash to start up, to maintain operations, and to grow. Cash or capital comes from investors, lenders, and the company's revenue-generating activities.

To make decisions about allocating capital (e.g., about investing or lending), users look for information in the financial statements about a company's ability to earn a profit and generate future cash flows. To assess this ability, users read the financial statements to determine whether or not management acquired and used the company's resources in the best way possible. Consequently, financial statements must give information about the following:

1. Economic resources (assets), and claims on the economic resources (liabilities and equity)
2. Changes in economic resources and claims on the economic resources
3. Economic performance

Underlying Assumptions

Assumptions create a foundation for the accounting process. You already know the two major assumptions from earlier chapters: accrual accounting and going concern. We will review them here briefly.

Accrual Accounting Assumption

You learned in earlier chapters that the **accrual basis of accounting** is widely recognized as being significantly more useful for decision-making than the cash basis of accounting. Under accrual accounting, transactions are recorded in the period when the transaction occurs and not when cash is received or paid. For example, a law firm would record revenue in the accounting period when the legal services are provided to the client and not necessarily in the accounting period when the client pays for the services. Financial statements prepared on an accrual basis provide users with information on what cash will be received in the future and what cash will be paid out in the future.

As a result of the usefulness of the accrual basis in decision-making, it has become an underlying assumption that all financial statements are prepared using the accrual basis of accounting. Because of this **accrual accounting assumption**, there is no need to report that the accrual basis has been used. The basis of accounting (cash or accrual) will need to be explicitly stated only in the rare cases where the cash basis is used.

Going Concern Assumption

The **going concern assumption** is the assumption that the company will continue operating for the foreseeable future; that is, long enough to achieve its goals and respect its commitments. Although there are many business failures, most companies continue operating for a long time.

This assumption has important implications for accounting. If a company is assumed to be a going concern, then financial statement users will find it useful for the company to report assets, such as buildings and equipment, at their carrying amount (cost minus accumulated depreciation). If the company was not a going concern, then the carrying amount would not be relevant; instead the financial statement user would want to know what the assets can be sold for or their net realizable value. Furthermore, if the company is not a going concern, the classification of assets and liabilities as current or non-current would not matter. Labelling anything as long-term would be difficult to justify.

It is an underlying assumption that financial statements are prepared as if the company is a going concern. This means there is no need to report that the going concern assumption has been used. The only time the going concern assumption should not be used is when liquidation is likely. In that case, it will be explicitly stated that the going concern assumption is not being followed. Assets and liabilities should be revalued and stated at their net realizable value rather than at cost, and the current/non-current classifications will not be used. Accounting for liquidations is discussed in advanced accounting courses.

ACCOUNTING IN ACTION: BUSINESS INSIGHT

Nortel is a global leader in delivering communications capabilities. On January 14, 2009, Nortel filed for bankruptcy protection in the United States, Canada, and other countries where Nortel has subsidiaries. Bankruptcy protection gives companies time to reorganize their operations and financial conditions and to develop a comprehensive restructuring plan. While bankruptcy protection is in place, creditors are prevented from taking any action against the company. While Nortel was operating under bankruptcy protection, its 2008 audited consolidated financial statements issued March 2, 2009, were prepared using the going concern basis, not a liquidation basis. In Nortel's notes to its financial statements, the company acknowledged that "it is not possible to predict whether the actions taken in any restructuring will result in improvements to Nortel's financial condition sufficient to allow it to continue as a going concern."

Source: Nortel Networks Corporation, audited consolidated financial statements for the year ended December 31, 2008

How did Nortel justify using the going concern assumption when it was so uncertain that the company would continue operating?

Elements of Financial Statements

Elements of financial statements are the basic categories used in the financial statements to meet the objective of financial reporting. These elements include assets, liabilities, equity, revenues, expenses, and other comprehensive income.

Because these elements are so important, they must be precisely defined and applied in the same way by all reporting entities. Currently the definitions are being reviewed by FASB and the IASB in their joint project to improve the conceptual framework. Finding the appropriate definition for many of these elements is not easy. For example, should the value of a company's employees be reported as an asset on a balance sheet? Should the death of the company's president be reported as a loss? A good set of definitions of financial statement elements should give answers to these types of questions. Because you have already read the current definitions for assets, liabilities, equity, revenues, and expenses in earlier chapters, they are not repeated here. Other comprehensive income is discussed in Chapters 13 and 14.

BEFORE YOU GO ON . . .

→ **Review It**

1. What is the basic objective of financial information?
2. Identify the elements of the financial statements.
3. What are the accrual accounting assumption and going concern assumption?
4. When might the going concern assumption not be appropriate to use?

→ **Do It**

Presented below are the underlying assumptions of accounting standards:

1. Going concern
2. Accrual accounting

Match the assumptions to the following statements:

(a) __ Sales revenue is recorded when the sale occurs, not when cash is collected.
(b) __ It is relevant to classify assets and liabilities as current and long-term.

Action Plan

• Review descriptions of the assumptions underlying accounting standards.

Solution

(a) 2 (b) 1

The Navigator

Related exercise material: BE11–2, BE11–3, and E11–1.

Qualitative Characteristics of Accounting Information

STUDY OBJECTIVE 3

Describe the fundamental and enhancing qualitative characteristics of financial reporting.

How does a company like The Forzani Group Ltd. decide how much financial information to disclose? In what format should its financial information be presented? How should assets, liabilities, revenues, and expenses be measured? Remember that the objective of financial reporting is to provide useful information for decision-making. Thus the main criterion for judging accounting choices is decision usefulness.

What makes information useful in decision-making? Accounting standard setters have decided that there are two fundamental characteristics that accounting information *must* have in order to be useful. In addition, there are other characteristics, complementary to the fundamental characteristics, that enhance the usefulness of accounting information. We discuss the qualitative characteristics in the following sections.

Fundamental Characteristics

In order for information to be useful in decision-making, accounting standard setters have agreed that the information should have two fundamental qualitative characteristics: relevance and faithful representation.

Relevance

Accounting information has **relevance** if it makes a difference in a decision. Relevant information has either predictive value or confirmatory value, or both. Predictive value helps users forecast future events. For example, when Forzani issues financial statements, the information in them is considered relevant because it gives a basis for predicting future profits or earnings. Confirmatory value confirms or corrects prior expectations. When Forzani issues financial statements, the company also confirms or corrects expectations about its financial health.

Faithful Representation

Once it is determined which information is relevant to financial statement users, then how the information is reported must be determined. To be useful, information must be a **faithful representation** of the economic reality of the events that it is reporting and not just the legal form. For example, a company may sign a lease agreement that requires periodic rental payments to be made over the life of the lease. If a company follows the legal form of the transaction, the periodic rental payments will be recorded as rent expense. However, for certain leases the economic reality is that an asset is purchased and the periodic payments are loan payments. For these leases, it is necessary to record an asset and a liability to show the economic reality. You will learn more about the accounting for lease agreements in Chapter 15.

Faithful representation is achieved when the information is (1) complete, (2) neutral, and (3) free from material error, as explained below.

1. Accounting information is **complete** if it includes all information necessary to show the economic reality of the transaction. If information is omitted, users will not be able to make appropriate resource allocation decisions. If Forzani did not disclose when payments are due on its long-term debt, users would not have the necessary information to predict future cash flows. The concept of completeness is discussed later in this chapter in the section on full disclosure.

2. Accounting information is **neutral** if it is free from bias that is intended to attain a predetermined result or to encourage a particular behaviour. For example, accounting information would be biased if the income statement was prepared so that it resulted in a high enough level of profit that the management team receives their bonuses.

3. An error is considered to be a **material error** if the error in the accounting information could have an impact on an investor's or creditor's decision. Accounting information includes estimates. If accounting information is to be free from material error, estimates must be based on the best available information and be reasonably accurate. Accountants must use professional judgement and caution when using estimates in financial reporting.

The fundamental qualitative characteristics of accounting information are summarized in Illustration 11-1.

← **Illustration 11-1**

Fundamental qualitative characteristics of accounting information

Relevance
1. Provides a basis for forecasts
2. Confirms or corrects prior expectations

Faithful Representation
1. Is complete
2. Is neutral
3. Is free from material error

Enhancing Qualitative Characteristics

Enhancing qualitative characteristics complement the two primary qualitative characteristics: relevance and faithful representation. The enhancing characteristics are said to help users distinguish more useful information from less useful information. Comparability, verifiability, timeliness, and understandability are enhancing characteristics.

Comparability

Accounting information about a company is most useful when it can be compared with accounting information about other companies. There is **comparability** when companies with similar circumstances use the same accounting principles. Comparability enables users to identify the similarities and differences between companies.

Comparability is reduced when companies use different methods of accounting for specific items. For example, there are different methods of determining the cost of inventory, which can result in different amounts of profit. But if each company states which cost determination method it uses, the external user can determine whether the financial information for two companies is comparable. This is known as the full disclosure concept, which we will learn about later in this chapter.

Comparability is easier when accounting policies are used consistently. **Consistency** means that a company uses the same accounting principles and methods from year to year. For example, if a company selects FIFO as its inventory cost formula in the first year of operations, it is expected to use FIFO in subsequent years. When financial information has been reported consistently, the financial statements make it possible to do a meaningful analysis of company trends.

This does not mean, however, that a company can never change its accounting policies. Sometimes changes in accounting policies are required by the CICA. For example, companies are required to change some accounting policies in 2011 when they adopt IFRS. At other times, management may decide that it would be better to change to a new accounting policy. To do this, management must prove that the new policy will result in more relevant information in the statements.

In the year of a change in an accounting policy, the change and its impact must be disclosed in the notes to the financial statements. This disclosure makes users of the financial statements aware of the lack of consistency. In addition, the financial statements for past years must be restated as if the new accounting policy had been used in those years. We will learn more about accounting for, and reporting, changes in accounting policies in Chapter 14.

Verifiability

Verifiability helps assure users that the financial information shows the economic reality of the transaction. Information is verifiable if two knowledgeable and independent people would generally agree that it faithfully represents the economic reality. In other words, there must be proof that the information is complete, an appropriate basis of measurement has been used, and there are no material errors and bias. Information must be verifiable for external professional accountants to audit financial statements and ensure that the financial statements reflect the financial reality of the company rather than the legal form of the transactions and events that underlie them.

Timeliness

Timeliness means that accounting information is provided when it is still highly useful for decision-making. In other words, it must be available to decision-makers before it loses its ability to influence decisions. Many people believe that by the time annual financial statements are issued—sometimes up to six months after a company's year end—the information has limited usefulness for decision-making. Timely *interim* financial reporting is essential to decision-making.

Understandability

For the information in financial statements to be useful, users must be able to understand it. **Understandability** enables users to gain insights into the company's financial position and results of operations. But users are expected to have a reasonable knowledge of business, economic, and financial activities, and of financial reporting. Users who do not have this level of understanding are expected to rely on professionals who do have an appropriate level of expertise. In making decisions, users should review and analyze the information carefully.

One of the benefits of Canada moving to a common set of international accounting standards is that Canadian companies' financial statements will be understood by global users.

Understandability is greater when the information is classified, characterized, and presented clearly and concisely.

The enhancing qualitative characteristics of accounting information are summarized in Illustration 11-2.

Illustration 11-2 ➡

Enhancing qualitative characteristics of accounting information

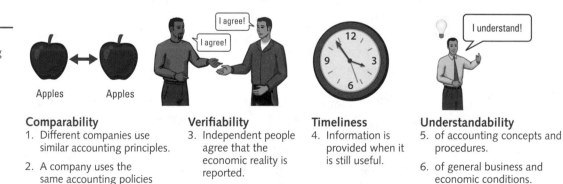

Comparability
1. Different companies use similar accounting principles.
2. A company uses the same accounting policies consistently from year to year.

Verifiability
3. Independent people agree that the economic reality is reported.

Timeliness
4. Information is provided when it is still useful.

Understandability
5. of accounting concepts and procedures.
6. of general business and economic conditions.

Application of the Qualitative Characteristics

The qualitative characteristics are complementary concepts; that is, they work together. Nonetheless, they must be applied in a certain order. The qualitative characteristic of relevance should be applied first because it will identify the specific information that would affect the decisions of investors and creditors and that should be included in the financial report.

Once relevance is applied, faithful representation should be applied to ensure that the economic information faithfully represents the economic events being described. Taken together, relevance and faithful representation make financial reporting information decision useful.

Then the enhancing qualitative characteristics—comparability, verifiability, timeliness, and understandability—are applied. They add to the decision usefulness of financial reporting information that is relevant and representationally faithful. They must be applied after the first two characteristics because they cannot, either individually or together, make information useful if it is irrelevant or not faithfully represented.

Full Disclosure

We have identified the characteristics that financial information must have to provide information that is useful for decisions. But companies must also provide **full disclosure** of circumstances and events that make a difference to financial statement users. It is important that investors be made aware of events that can affect the financial health of a company.

Full disclosure is respected through two elements in the financial statements: the data they contain and the accompanying notes. In most cases, the first note in the statements is a summary of significant accounting policies. The summary includes the methods used by the company when there are alternatives in acceptable accounting principles. For example, The Forzani Group's note on its significant accounting policies (see Note 2 in Appendix A at the end of this textbook) discloses that the company uses the weighted average cost method to determine the cost of its inventory and the declining-balance method to depreciate (or amortize, as Forzani calls it) its building.

The information that is disclosed in the notes to the financial statements generally falls into three additional categories. The information can:

1. Give supplementary detail or explanation (for example, a schedule of property, plant, and equipment)
2. Explain unrecorded transactions (for example, contingencies, commitments, and subsequent events)
3. Supply new information (for example, information about related party transactions)

Deciding how much disclosure is enough can be difficult. Accountants could disclose every financial event that occurs and every contingency that exists. But the benefits of giving this additional information may be less than the cost of making it available. We will discuss this problem in the following section.

BEFORE YOU GO ON . . .

→ Review It

1. Describe the fundamental qualitative characteristics that make accounting information useful.
2. Describe the enhancing qualitative characteristics that make accounting information useful.
3. In what order are the qualitative characteristics to be applied?
4. What is meant by the concept of full disclosure?

→ Do It

Presented below are some of the qualitative characteristics of financial information.

1. Relevance	6. Verifiability
2. Faithful representation	7. Timeliness
3. Complete	8. Understandability
4. Neutral	9. Consistency
5. Comparability	

Match the qualitative characteristics to the following statements:

(a) ___ Information is available to decision-makers before the information loses its ability to influence decisions.

(b) ___ Information is free from bias that is intended to attain a predetermined result.

(c) ___ Information makes a difference in a decision.

(d) ___ Users are assured that the financial information shows the economic reality of the transaction.

(e) ___ The same accounting principles are used from year to year.

(f) ___ All of the information necessary to show the economic reality of transactions is provided.

(g) ___ Accounting information about one company can be evaluated in relation to accounting information from another company.

(h) ___ Accounting information reports the economic reality of a transaction, not its legal form.

(i) ___ Accounting information is prepared on the assumption that users have a general understanding of general business and economic conditions and are able to read a financial report.

Action Plan

* Review the two fundamental qualitative characteristics.
* Review the enhancing qualitative characteristics.

Solution

(a) 7   (b) 4   (c) 1   (d) 6   (e) 9   (f) 3   (g) 5   (h) 2   (i) 8

The Navigator

Related exercise material: BE11–4, E11–2, and E11–3.

Constraints on Financial Reporting

STUDY OBJECTIVE 4

Identify and apply the constraints on financial reporting.

Two pervasive constraints limit the necessary information in financial statements and allow a company to modify GAAP without reducing the usefulness of the information it reports. These two constraints are cost-benefit and materiality.

Cost-Benefit Constraint

The **cost-benefit constraint** exists to ensure that the value of the information is more than the cost of providing it. As we discussed earlier in this chapter, when accountants apply the full disclosure principle, they could disclose every financial event that occurs and every contingency. However, giving more information increases reporting costs, and the benefits of giving this information may be less than the costs in some cases.

As there have been more and more changes to disclosure and reporting requirements, the costs of giving this information have increased. Because of these increasing costs, some critics have argued that the costs of applying GAAP to smaller or non-publicly traded companies are too high compared with the benefits. To respond to this problem, the CICA has developed Canadian GAAP for Private Enterprises for private companies, which is a simplified version of GAAP. As Paul Cherry, the chairman of the Accounting Standards Board, concluded, "One size does not necessarily fit all."

Materiality Constraint

The **materiality constraint** relates to an item's impact on a company's overall financial condition and operations. An item is material when it is likely to influence the decision of a reasonably careful investor or creditor. It is immaterial if including it or leaving it out has no impact on a decision-maker. In short, if the item does not make a difference in decision-making, GAAP does not have to be followed. To determine the materiality of an amount, the accountant usually compares it with such items as total assets, total liabilities, gross revenues, and cash and/or net profit.

To illustrate how the materiality constraint works, assume that Yanik Co. purchases several inexpensive pieces of office equipment, such as wastepaper baskets. Although it would appear that the proper accounting is to depreciate these wastepaper baskets over their useful lives, they would usually be expensed immediately instead. Doing this is justified because these costs are immaterial. Making depreciation schedules for these assets is costly and time-consuming. It will not make a material difference to total assets and profit. The materiality constraint is also applied in the non-disclosure of minor contingencies, and in the expensing of any long-lived assets under a certain dollar amount.

BEFORE YOU GO ON . . .

→ Review It

1. What is the cost-benefit constraint?
2. Why is it necessary to have a simpler GAAP for private enterprises?
3. Describe the materiality constraint. Give an example.

→ Do It

Presented below are the constraints on financial reporting.

1. Materiality
2. Cost-benefit

Match these constraints to the following accounting practices:

(a) ___ Private companies can follow a simplified version of GAAP.
(b) ___ Inexpensive repair tools that the company will use for several years are expensed when purchased.
(c) ___ The financial statements are not restated when a $100 error is found after the statements have been issued.
(d) ___ The company implements a perpetual inventory system that costs $50,000 and the expected cost savings is $20,000 annually in the current year and future years.

Action Plan
• Recall that an item is immaterial if leaving it out will have no impact on the financial statements.
• Recall that the value of the information should be more than the cost of providing it.

Solution
(a) 2   (b) 1   (c) 1   (d) 2

The Navigator

Recognition and Measurement Criteria

STUDY OBJECTIVE 5

Identify and apply the basic recognition and measurement concepts of accounting.

The objective of financial reporting, the elements of financial statements, and the qualitative characteristics of accounting information are very broad. Because accountants must solve practical problems, they need more detailed standards or criteria to help them decide when items should be included in the financial statements and how they should be measured. Recognition is the process of including an item in the financial statements. Recognition criteria help determine when items should be included or recognized in the financial statements. Measurement criteria outline how to measure or assign an amount to those items.

Generally an item will be included in the financial statements if it meets the definition of an asset, liability, equity, revenue, or expense; if it can be measured; and if a reasonable estimate of the amount can be made. The item is reported in the financial statements in a monetary amount. In Canada, the monetary unit used for financial reporting is generally the Canadian dollar.

There are two important concepts underlying the general criteria. The first concept is that if an asset is going to be recorded, then it must be probable that there will be a future economic benefit, and for a liability to be recognized, it is probable that economic resources will be given up. For example, a company does not have to be 100% certain that it will collect an account receivable to record the receivable; it just has to be probable that cash will be collected. The second concept is that estimates may be used to record the dollar amounts if the precise dollar amount is not known.

It would be easy to determine when to recognize revenues or expenses if the only determining factor was when the cash is received or paid. But since accounting standards require the use of accrual accounting, it is necessary to have criteria to determine when to record revenues and expenses. Should the revenue be recorded when the customer places an order with the company, or when the goods are delivered? How should the transaction be recorded if cash collection is uncertain? The revenue recognition criteria discussed in the next section provide guidance in answering these questions. Expense recognition will be discussed later in the chapter.

Revenue Recognition Criteria

In the opinion of many people, when to recognize revenue is the most difficult issue in accounting. And it is an issue that has been responsible for many of the accounting scandals of the past decade. There have been many high-profile cases that highlight improper use of the revenue recognition criteria. For example, when Alexa Life Sciences, the manufacturer of ColdFx, first started selling its products in the United States in 2006, it failed to recognize that there was considerable risk that a significant amount of the product would be returned by retailers. As a result, the company overstated its 2006 revenues (net sales) by $5.6 million because it recorded sales returns in 2007 that should have been recorded in 2006. As a result, Alexa Life Sciences was required to restate its 2006 financial statements.

Why is revenue recognition such a difficult concept to apply? In a few cases, revenue recognition has been intentionally abused in order to manage profits in a way that favours management or the shareholders. However, in most cases, revenue recognition is just a difficult concept because the activities that generate revenues have become a lot more innovative and complex than in the past. These include "swap" transactions, "bill and hold" sales arrangements, risk-sharing agreements, complex rights of return, price-protection guarantees, and post-sale maintenance contracts—all topics that go beyond an introductory accounting course. In these situations, professional judgement is required to determine if the criteria have been met before revenue can be recognized.

International Financial Reporting Standards provide the fundamental criteria to help accountants decide when revenue should be recognized. Basically, the **revenue recognition criteria** state that, revenue is recognized at the same time that an increase in an asset is recognized or a decrease in a liability is recognized for profit-generating activities. The question that needs to be answered is when assets have actually increased or liabilities decreased. We will see that professional judgement is often required to apply the basic criteria.

In the following sections, we will discuss revenue recognition criteria for the most common revenue-generating activities:

1. The sale of goods, and
2. Service contracts and construction contracts.

The Sale of Goods

Revenue from the sale of goods is recognized when all of the following conditions have been met:

1. The seller has transferred to the buyer the significant risks and rewards of ownership.
2. The seller does not have control over the goods or continuing managerial involvement.
3. The amount of the revenue can be reliably measured.
4. It is probable there will be an increase in economic resources (that is, cash will be collected).
5. Costs relating to the sale of the goods can be reliably measured.

For sales in a retail establishment, these conditions are generally met at the point of sale. Consider a sale by Forzani. At the point of sale, the customer pays the cash and takes the merchandise. The company records the sale by debiting Cash and crediting Sales Revenue. If the sale were on account rather than for cash (assuming the company accepts credit sales, and the customer has a good credit rating), the company would record the sale by debiting Accounts Receivable and crediting Sales Revenue. The cost of goods sold can be measured and directly matched to the sales revenue at the point of sale.

Typically the risks and rewards of ownership are transferred when legal title passes and the customer is in possession of the goods. For goods that are shipped, the shipping terms determine when the legal title passes. If the customer pays for the shipping (FOB shipping point), then revenue is recognized when the goods are shipped. If the company (the seller) pays for the shipping (FOB destination), then revenue is recognized when the goods are delivered.

When merchandise is sold on credit, revenue is recognized at the point of sale as long as it is reasonably sure that the cash will be collected. Of course, not all accounts are actually collected. However, as we learned in Chapter 8, revenue can be recognized as long as an estimate can be made of any possible uncollectible accounts and bad debts matched against revenue in the appropriate period.

Similarly, if a company provides refunds to customers for goods returned, revenue is recognized at point of sale if the company is able to reliably estimate future returns and recognizes a liability for the estimated returns.

Revenues and costs that relate to the sales transaction are recognized in the same accounting period. If a company provides free warranty service on its merchandise, revenue is recognized at point of sale if the company is able to reliably estimate the future warranty costs and it recognizes a warranty liability. If costs relating to the sale cannot be reliably measured, then the revenue cannot be recognized.

Service Contracts and Construction Contracts

Generally, in businesses that provide services, revenue is recognized when the service has been fully provided and it is probable that the cash will be collected. For example, when you visit your doctor for a routine checkup, the doctor will bill your provincial health care plan and recognize revenue when your checkup is completed.

In certain cases, revenue can be recognized before the service has been fully provided. Consider a law or accounting firm that provides services for a client over several months. Companies that provide services like this are different from retail companies, as the client is identified and the work is agreed upon (usually with an engagement letter) before the services are performed. In such cases, the client is usually billed every month for the hours of service provided during the particular month. These situations result in a continuing earnings process where revenue can be recognized as chunks of services are provided at a predetermined price (as long as it probable that cash will be collected).

Revenue recognition becomes even more difficult when the earnings process lasts years. This happens in the case of long-term service contracts and construction contracts for large projects, such as building bridges, roads, and aircraft. For example, the construction for the Richmond Olympic Oval, the venue for the speed skating events at the Vancouver 2010 Olympics, began in September 2005 and was completed in the fall of 2008.

Assume that Warrior Construction Co. has a contract to build a dam for the Province of British Columbia for $400 million. Construction is estimated to take three years (starting early in 2009) at a cost of $360 million. If Warrior recognizes revenue only when the construction is complete, it will report no revenues and no profit in the first two years. When completion and sale take place, at the end of 2011, Warrior will report $400 million in revenues, costs of $360 million, and the entire profit of $40 million. Did Warrior really produce no revenues and earn no profit in 2009 and 2010? Obviously not. The earnings process can be considered completed at various stages.

In situations like this, revenue can be partially recognized before the contract is completed if the following conditions are met:

1. The amount of revenue can be measured (an agreed price on the contract).
2. It is probable the company will receive the economic benefits (probable that cash will be collected).
3. The stage of completion of the contract can be reliably measured.
4. The costs to complete the contract can be reliably measured.

This is known as the percentage-of-completion method.

The **percentage-of-completion method** recognizes revenue on a long-term project based on reasonable estimates of the progress toward completion. Note that long-term construction and service contracts usually specify that the contractor (builder) may bill the purchaser at certain times throughout the contract period. However, revenue recognition should not be based on billings (this would be more similar to the cash basis of accounting). Rather, revenue should be recognized based on how much of the work has been performed to date.

There are three steps in the percentage-of-completion method. (1) Progress toward completion is measured by comparing the costs incurred in a period with the total estimated costs for the entire project. This results in a percentage that indicates the percentage of the work that is complete. (2) That percentage is multiplied by the total revenue for the current project, and the result is recognized as the revenue for the period. (3) The costs incurred are then subtracted from the revenue recognized to arrive at the gross profit for the current period. These three steps are presented in Illustration 11-3.

Illustration 11-3 ➜

Percentage-of-completion method

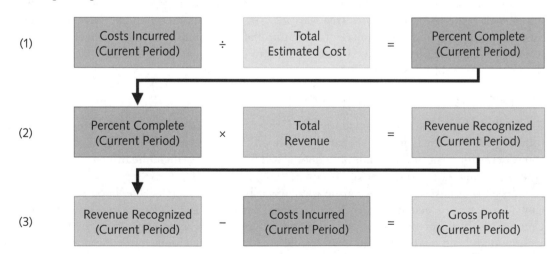

Let's look at an illustration of the percentage-of-completion method. Assume that Warrior Construction has costs of $54 million in 2009, $180 million in 2010, and $126 million in 2011 on the dam project mentioned earlier. The portion of the $400 million of revenue and gross profit that is recognized in each of the three years is shown below (all amounts are in millions):

Year	Costs Incurred (Current Period) ÷	Total Estimated Cost	Percentage Complete = (Current Period) ×	Total Revenue	Revenue Recognized = (Current Period) −	Costs Incurred (Current Period) =	Gross Profit (Current Period)
2009	$ 54	$360	15%	$400	$ 60	$ 54	$ 6
2010	180	360	50%	400	200	180	20
2011	126	360	35%	400	140	126	14
Total	$360				$400	$360	$40

In this example, the company's cost estimates were completely accurate. The costs incurred in the third year brought the total cost to $360 million—exactly what had been estimated. In reality, this does not always happen. As additional information becomes available, it may be necessary to revise estimates for what remains to be done in a project.

When an estimate is revised, the amounts incurred for the current period are changed so they include amounts incurred to date. Another step is added to the formulas shown in Illustration 11-3 to adjust for the revenue that has already been recognized. Illustration 11-4 shows this new step (now step 3), and it also shows, in red, minor adjustments to the wording of the formula.

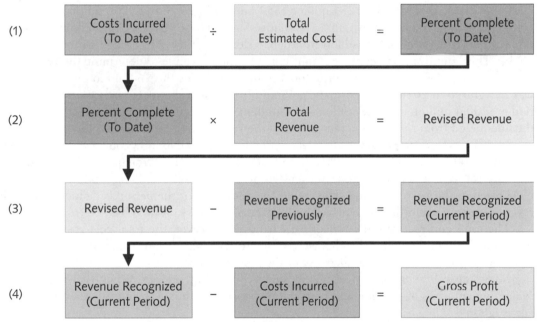

◀ **Illustration 11-4**

Percentage-of-completion method—revision of estimate

As when estimates are changed for useful lives or residual values for depreciation, the data for the percentage-of-completion method are only changed for current and future years, rather than for past years also. The percentage that is complete is revised according to the new total estimated costs. A **cumulative percentage** is used. It is calculated by dividing the costs incurred to date by the revised total estimated cost. This formula is similar to the one shown in step 1 of Illustration 11-3, except that the costs incurred are cumulative (to date) rather than just for the current period.

Similar to step 2 of Illustration 11-3, this cumulative percentage is then multiplied by total revenue to determine the revised revenue amount. In a new step—which is not used when actual costs equal estimated costs—the revenue that was recognized previously is now deducted from the revised revenue. This has to be done in order to account for previously recorded amounts and to "catch up" the difference in the estimate.

The remaining step (now step 4) is the same as step 3 demonstrated in Illustration 11-3, where actual costs are deducted from revenue to determine the amount of gross profit to recognize, as shown below.

To apply this formula for a change in estimate, assume the costs estimated to complete the dam project change partway through the three-year contract period for Warrior Construction. In 2010, the estimated total cost rises to $390 million, from its earlier estimate of $360 million. Actual costs incurred are $200 million in 2010 and $136 million in 2011.

The revised calculations for revenue, cost, and gross profit are as follows (all amounts in millions):

Year	Costs Incurred (To Date)	÷	Total Estimated Cost	=	Percentage Complete (To Date)	×	Total Revenue	=	Revised Revenue	−	Revenue Recognized (Previously)	−	Revenue Recognized (Current Period)	−	Costs Incurred (Current Period)	=	Gross Profit (Current Period)
2009	$ 54		$360		15.0%		$400		$ 60.0		$ 0.0		$ 60.0		$ 54		$ 6.0
2010	254		390		65.1%		400		260.4		60.0		200.4		200		0.4
2011	390		390		100.0%		400		400.0		260.4		139.6		136		3.6
Totals													$400.0		$390		$10.0

The calculations for 2009 are unchanged from the ones in the shaded table above. However, because of the change in estimate in 2010, the revenue, cost, and gross profit change in 2010 and 2011. In 2010, the $254 million ($54 million in 2009 and $200 million in 2010) of actual costs incurred are shown on a cumulative basis. These costs are divided by the revised total estimated cost of $390 million in order to determine the percentage complete to date, 65.1%. This cumulative percentage is multiplied by total revenue to determine the revised revenue amount. This revenue amount, $260.4 million, includes the $60 million of revenue that was recognized in 2010. Therefore, the amount of revenue to be recognized in the current period is $200.4 million ($260.4 million − $60 million). The actual cost incurred for the period is then deducted from the revenue recognized in the same period to determine the gross profit.

In 2011, when the project is complete, costs incurred to date now total $390 million ($54 million in 2009, $200 million in 2010, and $136 million in 2011). One hundred percent of the contract revenue less any amounts recognized previously ($400 million − $260.4 million) is recognized in the current period. The actual cost incurred for the period is deducted from the revenue recognized in the same period to determine the gross profit.

The total contract revenue remains unchanged. However, the total cost rose from $360 million to $390 million after the change in estimate. This also means that total gross profit fell from $40 million to $10 million because of the increased costs.

Sometimes there are cost overruns in the last year of a contract. When that happens, the remaining amounts of revenue and costs are recognized in that year and the relevant percentage is ignored.

In the percentage-of-completion method, it is necessary to be subjective to some extent. As a result, errors are possible in determining the amount of revenue to be recognized and gross profit to be reported. But to wait until completion would seriously distort each period's financial statements. Naturally, if it is not possible to get dependable estimates of costs and progress, then the percentage-of-completion method cannot be used. In this situation, revenue is recognized to the extent of the contract costs that have been incurred; no gross profit is recognized until reliable estimates can be made or the contract has been completed.

If we assume that Warrior Construction is a public company and it was not able to estimate its costs reliably, it would recognize revenue equal to the costs incurred for the first two years. In the third year, it would recognize the remaining revenue of $146 ($400 − $200 − $54). Gross profit would be zero in the first two years (because revenue equals expenses) and the full gross profit earned would be recognized in 2011, the final year of the project. This method is often referred to as the zero profit method.

If we compare the **zero profit method** and the percentage-of-completion method for the same contract data, Warrior Construction would have recognized the following amounts for revenue and gross profit.

	Zero Profit Method		Percentage-of-Completion Method	
	Revenue	Gross Profit	Revenue	Gross Profit
2009	$ 54	$ 0	$ 60.0	$ 6.0
2010	200	0	200.4	0.4
2011	146	10	139.6	3.6
Totals	$400	$10	$400.0	$10.0

For Canadian private companies that are not reporting under IFRS, if the revenues and costs on a long-term project cannot be reliably measured, the completed contract method would be used to recognize revenue and gross profit. Under the **completed contract method**, revenues and gross profit are recognized only when the contract is completed.

We have reviewed the timing of revenue recognition for common revenue-generating activities including the sale of goods, provision of services, and long-term service and construction contracts. Revenue recognition is a complex topic with many more dimensions than we have explored here.

Currently, revenue recognition is the topic of a substantial joint project between IASB and FASB. The boards want to eliminate weaknesses in the current approach, which is commonly referred to as the earnings approach and which emphasizes the income statement. At the time of writing this textbook, a discussion paper had been issued. It is proposed that a contract-based approach be adopted for recognizing revenue which emphasizes the balance sheet. However, it is not anticipated that new criteria will be established for several years.

ACCOUNTING IN ACTION: ACROSS THE ORGANIZATION INSIGHT

"Revenue recognition accounting remains one of the most troublesome reporting issues for many companies," according to *CAmagazine*. "In fact, more than 40% of respondents to a recent survey rated revenue as being more vulnerable to errors and inaccuracies than any other key finance and accounting process." Why is revenue recognition so troublesome? Well, many departments and individuals in a company may be involved in the revenue-generating activities. In large companies, these activities occur every day in many departments: sales, production, customer service, shipping, and billing. Revenue recognition is also affected when the customer accepts the product or agrees that the service is complete. All of these activities mean that the revenue reporting risk remains high.

Source: Gerry Murray, "Revenue reporting risk remains high," *CAmagazine.com*, December 2008, http://www.camagazine.com/ archives/print-edition/2008/dec/upfront/value-added/camagazine4221.aspx [accessed March 29, 2009]

What is the manager of the shipping department's role in making sure revenue is recognized in the appropriate period?

Expense Recognition

The basic **expense recognition criteria** state that expenses are recognized when there is a decrease in an asset or increase in a liability, excluding transactions with owners. This is not necessarily when cash is paid. For example, as supplies are used, the asset Supplies is decreased and an expense is recognized. Alternatively, when a liability for wages payable is recorded, wage expense is recognized.

Expense recognition is tied to revenue recognition when there is a direct association between costs incurred and the earning of revenue. For example, there is a direct association between cost of goods sold and sales revenue. As we learned in Chapter 3, this process is commonly referred to as matching. Under matching, revenues and expenses that relate to the same transaction are recorded in the same accounting period.

Sometimes, however, there is no direct relationship between expenses and revenue. When it is hard to find a direct relationship, and assets are expected to benefit several accounting periods, a rational and systematic allocation policy can sometimes be developed instead.

To develop an allocation policy, assumptions have to be made about the benefits that will be received. Assumptions must also be made about the costs associated with those benefits. For example, the cost of a long-lived asset can be allocated to depreciation expense over the life of the asset because it can be determined that the asset contributes in some way to revenue generation during the asset's entire useful life.

In other cases, when expenditures are made that do not qualify for the recognition of an asset, an expense is recognized immediately. For example, expenditures for research do not qualify for recognition of an asset as it is impossible to determine the future benefits arising from the research, so the research costs are expensed immediately.

Sometimes a previously recognized asset ceases to have future benefit, and the asset must be expensed. For example, inventory that is obsolete and cannot be sold is expensed when it becomes apparent it cannot be sold.

In summary, costs need to be analyzed to determine whether it is probable there is a future benefit to the company or not. If there is a direct relationship between the revenues recognized and costs, the costs are recognized as expenses (matched against the revenue) in the period when the revenue is recognized. If it is hard to determine a direct relationship, but the costs are expected to benefit several periods, then it might be appropriate to systematically and rationally allocate the cost to expense over the periods that are expected to benefit. If there is no future benefit, or if the benefit is uncertain, the costs should simply be expensed in the current period.

Measurement of Elements

So far, we have looked at when items should be recognized or recorded in the accounting records. Now we will look at what dollar amounts should be used to record the items. There are a number of different measurements used in accounting. They include the following:

1. Cost
2. Fair value
3. Amortized cost

Assets are recorded at cost when they are acquired. Cost is used because it is both relevant and provides a faithful representation of the transaction. Cost represents the price paid, the assets sacrificed, or the commitment made at the date of acquisition. Cost is objectively measurable, factual, and verifiable. It is the result of an exchange transaction. Cost is relevant for reporting certain assets in the balance sheet because the assets are intended for use in the business and are not going to be sold.

Alternative terminology
Other common terms for fair value are market and realizable value.

However, for some assets it is more relevant to provide the assets' fair value: the amount of cash that is expected to be collected if the asset is sold. Users of financial information are better able to assess the impact of changes in fair value on the company's liquidity and solvency. For example, trading securities that are purchased for the purpose of resale are reported at their fair value in the financial statements. We will learn more about fair values used to report trading securities and some strategic long-term equity investments in Chapter 16.

Certain assets and liabilities, such as investments in bonds and bonds payable, are measured at amortized cost. We will learn more about amortized cost and investments in bonds and bonds payable in Chapters 15 and 16.

Cost is the most common basis used by companies in preparing their financial statements. Cost may be combined with other measurement bases. For example, you will recall from Chapter 6 that inventory is reported at the lower of cost and net realizable value.

ACCOUNTING IN ACTION: ALL ABOUT YOU

Before you started your post-secondary education, your parents may have invested cash in a Registered Education Savings Plan (RESP). An RESP is a special savings account registered with the Canadian government that helps families to save for students' education after high school. The plan allows the savings to grow tax-free and the government provides additional funds to the savings account through the Canada Education Savings Grant. The funds in the RESP may be invested in a simple cash savings account, a guaranteed investment certificate, or an equity investment fund. If the funds are invested in an equity investment fund, the value of the RESP will fluctuate with the market values of the equities in the investment fund.

The cost to your parents is the amount they have put into the RESP. However, combined with the contributions from your parents, the Canadian government grants, and the income earned on the amount invested in the RESP, the account's value may be significantly higher than the cost to your parents. On the other hand, if there is a significant portion in equity and the market fluctuates, it might be worth a lot less. An RESP is a valuable asset for you as a student as you pursue your education.

If you were preparing your personal financial report, what information about your RESP would be relevant: the cost of the RESP contributions or the fair value of the RESP?

Summary of Conceptual Framework

As we have seen, the conceptual framework for developing sound reporting practices starts with the objective of financial reporting. It then describes the underlying assumptions, the elements of the financial statements, the qualitative (fundamental and enhancing) characteristics of accounting information, and the constraints on financial reporting. Finally, more detailed recognition and measurement criteria are provided. The conceptual framework is summarized in Illustration 11-5.

The IASB and FASB are working on a joint project to improve the conceptual framework. At the time of writing this book, a discussion paper had been issued proposing new definitions for the financial statement elements. The standard-setting bodies are also working on a joint project to eliminate weaknesses in the current revenue recognition criteria. It is anticipated that there will be significant changes to GAAP in the next few years.

← Illustration 11-5

Conceptual framework

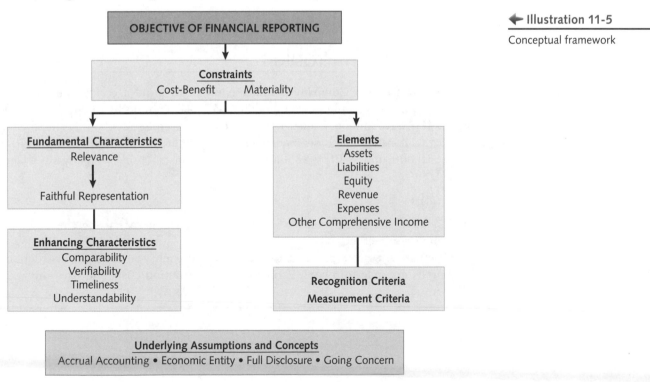

BEFORE YOU GO ON . . .

→ Review It

1. What is the basic criterion for revenue recognition under the current International Financial Reporting Standards?
2. What are the revenue recognition criteria for the sale of goods?
3. Describe when expenses are recognized.
4. What is stated about revenue recognition in Note 2 Significant Accounting Policies found in the financial statements of The Forzani Group Ltd.? The answer to this question is at the end of the chapter.

→ Do It

For each of the following independent situations, indicate if the revenue should be recognized in 2010 or 2011.

(a) Customer orders widgets on December 15, 2010; widgets are shipped FOB destination December 24, 2010; customer receives the goods January 15, 2011.
(b) Customer orders widgets on December 15, 2010; widgets are shipped FOB shipping point December 14, 2010; customer receives the goods January 15, 2011.

Action Plan

• Determine when all the significant risks and rewards of ownership have been transferred to the customer.

Solution

(a) Revenue should be recognized in 2011 as the seller retains ownership until the customer receives the goods.
(b) Revenue should be recognized in 2010 as ownership of the widgets is transferred to the customer when the goods are shipped.

The Navigator

Related exercise material: BE11–5, BE11–6, BE11–7, BE11–8, BE11–9, BE11–10, BE11–11, BE11–12, BE11–13, E11–4, E11–5, E11–6, E11–7, E11–8, E11–9, E11–10, and E11–11.

WILEY PLUS

Demonstration Problems

Demonstration Problem

The Wu Construction Company is under contract to build a condominium building at a contract price of $2 million. The building will take 18 months to complete, at an estimated cost of $1.4 million. Construction begins in November 2009 and is finished in April 2011. Actual construction costs incurred in each year are as follows: in 2009, $140,000; in 2010, $910,000; and in 2011, $350,000. The Wu Construction Company has a December year end.

Instructions

(a) Calculate the gross profit to be recognized in each year using the percentage-of-completion method.
(b) Calculate the gross profit to be recognized in each year if Wu Construction Company is not able to reliably estimate the construction costs and uses the zero profit method.

Solution to Demonstration Problem

($ in thousands)

(a) Percentage-of-completion method

Year	Costs Incurred (Current Period)	÷	Total Estimated Cost	=	Percentage Complete (Current Period)	×	Total Revenue	=	Revenue Recognized (Current Period)	−	Costs Incurred (Current Period)	=	Gross Profit (Current Period)
2009	$ 140		$1,400		10%		$2,000		$ 200		$ 140		$ 60
2010	910		1,400		65%		2,000		1,300		910		390
2011	350		1,400		25%		2,000		500		350		150
Totals	$1,400								$2,000		$1,400		$600

(b) Zero profit method

Year	Revenue Recognized in Current Period	Costs Incurred in Current Period	Gross Profit Recognized in Current Period
2009	$ 140	$ 140	$ 0
2010	910	910	0
2011	950	350	600
Totals	$2,000	$1,400	$600

Action Plan

- The percentage-of-completion method recognizes revenue as construction occurs. The ongoing construction is viewed as a series of sales.
- Determine the percentage complete by dividing the costs incurred by total estimated costs.
- Multiply the percentage complete by the contract price to find the revenue to be recognized in the current period.
- Calculate gross profit: revenue recognized less actual costs incurred.
- If costs cannot be reliably estimated, no gross profit is recognized until the remaining costs can be reliably estimated.
- Record revenues equal to costs incurred each year until the year the contract is completed or cost can be reliably estimated.

The Navigator

Summary of Study Objectives

1. Explain the importance of having a conceptual framework of accounting, and list the components. The conceptual framework ensures that there is a consistent and coherent set of accounting standards. The key components of the conceptual framework are: (1) the objective of financial reporting, (2) the underlying assumptions, (3) the elements of financial statements, (4) the qualitative characteristics of accounting information, (5) the constraints on financial reporting, and (6) recognition and measurement criteria.

2. Identify and apply the objective of financial reporting and the underlying assumptions used by accountants. The objective of financial reporting is to provide useful information for investors and creditors in making decisions in their capacity as capital providers. The underlying assumptions are that, unless otherwise stated, the financial statements have been prepared using accrual accounting and the going concern assumption.

3. Describe the fundamental and enhancing qualitative characteristics of financial reporting. The fundamental qualitative characteristics are relevance and faithful representation. Accounting information has relevance if it makes a difference in a decision. Information is faithfully represented when it shows the economic reality.

The enhancing qualitative characteristics are comparability, verifiability, timeliness, and understandability.

Comparability enables users to identify the similarities and differences between companies. The consistent use of accounting policies from year to year is part of the comparability characteristic. Information is verifiable if two knowledgeable and independent people would generally agree that it faithfully represents the economic reality. Timeliness means that accounting information is provided when it is still highly useful for decision-making. Understandability enables users to gain insights into the company's financial position and results of operations.

4. Identify and apply the constraints on financial reporting. The major constraints are the cost-benefit and materiality constraints. The cost-benefit constraint exists to ensure the value of the information is more than the cost of providing it. If an item does not make a difference in decision-making, it is immaterial and GAAP does not have to be followed.

5. Identify and apply the basic recognition and measurement concepts of accounting. The revenue recognition criteria require that revenue be recognized when assets have increased or liabilities have decreased as a result of a transaction with a customer. Expenses are recognized when there is a decrease in an asset or increase in a liability, excluding transactions with owners. Three measurements used in accounting are cost, fair value, and amortized cost.

The Navigator

Glossary

Accrual accounting assumption The assumption that the accrual basis of accounting has been used. (p. 618)

Accrual basis of accounting The method of accounting where revenues are recorded in the period when the transaction occurs and not when cash is received or paid. (p. 618)

Comparability An enhancing qualitative characteristic that accounting information has if it can be compared with the accounting information of other companies because the companies all use the same accounting principles. (p. 621)

Completed contract method A method of recognizing revenue and gross profit on a project where they are recognized when the project is completed. (p. 631)

Complete The characteristic of accounting information when it provides all information necessary to show the economic reality of the transactions. Completeness is part of the faithful representation fundamental qualitative characteristic of accounting information. (p. 620)

Conceptual framework of accounting A coherent system of interrelated elements that guides the development and application of accounting principles: it includes the objective of financial reporting, underlying assumptions, elements of financial statements, qualitative characteristics of accounting information, constraints, and recognition and measurement criteria. (p. 616)

Consistency The use of the same accounting policies from year to year. Consistency is part of the comparability enhancing qualitative characteristic of accounting information. (p. 621)

Cost-benefit constraint The constraint that the costs of obtaining and providing information should not be more than the benefits that are gained. (p. 624)

Elements of financial statements The basic categories in financial statements: assets, liabilities, equity, revenue, expenses, and other comprehensive income. (p. 619)

Expense recognition criteria The criteria that state that expenses should be recognized when there is a decrease in an asset or increase in a liability, excluding transactions with owners. (p. 631)

Faithful representation A fundamental qualitative characteristic of accounting information that shows the economic reality of a transaction and not just its legal form. (p. 620)

Full disclosure The accounting concept that requires the disclosure of circumstances and events that make a difference to financial statement users. (p. 623)

Going concern assumption The assumption that the company will continue operating for the foreseeable future; that is, long enough to achieve its goals and respect its commitments. (p. 618)

Material error An error in the accounting information that could impact an investor's or creditor's decision. (p. 621)

Materiality constraint The constraint of determining whether an item is important enough to influence the decision of a reasonably careful investor or creditor. (p. 625)

Neutral The characteristic of accounting information when it is free from bias that is intended to attain a predetermined result or to encourage a particular behaviour. Neutrality is part of the faithful representation fundamental qualitative characteristic of accounting information. (p. 621)

Objective of financial reporting The goal of providing useful information for investors and creditors in making decisions in their capacity as capital providers. (p. 617)

Percentage-of-completion method A method of recognizing revenue on a long-term construction or service contract. When costs can be reliably estimated, a portion of the total revenue can be recognized in each period by applying a percentage of completion. This percentage is determined by dividing the actual costs incurred by the estimated costs for the entire project. (p. 628)

Relevance A fundamental qualitative characteristic that accounting information has if it makes a difference in a decision. (p. 620)

Revenue recognition criteria The criteria that state that revenue should be recognized when there is an increase in assets or decrease in liabilities from profit-generating activities. (p. 626)

Timeliness An enhancing qualitative characteristic that accounting information has if it is provided when it is still highly useful to decision-makers. (p. 622)

Understandability An enhancing qualitative characteristic of accounting information that enables users to gain insights into the company's financial position and results of operations. (p. 622)

Verifiability An enhancing qualitative characteristic of accounting information that assures users that the information shows the economic reality of the transaction. (p. 622)

Zero profit method A method of recognizing revenue where revenue is recognized to the extent of costs incurred and no gross profit is recognized until the contract is complete or costs can be estimated, (p. 630)

Self-Study Questions

Answers are at the end of the chapter.

(SO 1) K 1. Which of the following is *not* one of the components of the conceptual framework?
(a) Underlying assumptions
(b) Qualitative characteristics
(c) The dimensions of the financial statements
(d) Recognition and measurement criteria

(SO 1) K 2. Which of the following is *not* a reason for having a conceptual framework for financial reporting?
(a) To provide specific rules for every situation in accounting
(b) To ensure that existing standards and practices are clear and consistent
(c) To make it possible to respond quickly to new issues
(d) To increase the usefulness of the financial information presented in financial reports

(SO 2) K 3. Which of the following is *not* information that is required to meet the objective of financial reporting?
(a) Information about the economic resources and claims on the economic resources
(b) Information about the company management's personal economic resources
(c) Information about the changes in economic resources and claims on the economic resources
(d) Information about the economic performance of the reporting entity

(SO 2) C 4. Which of the following is *not* an example of accrual accounting?
(a) Sales revenue for goods sold on credit is recorded when the goods are shipped.
(b) Interest expense is debited and interest payable is credited on December 31.
(c) The utility expense for December is recorded in January when the bill is paid.
(d) Prepaid insurance is debited and cash is credited when the annual insurance bill is paid.

(SO 3) K 5. The qualitative characteristics that must be applied first to ensure that information is useful are:
(a) relevance and comparability.
(b) relevance and faithful representation.
(c) faithful representation and verifiability.
(d) faithful representation and comparability.

(SO 3) K 6. The full disclosure concept says that financial statements:
(a) should disclose all assets at their cost.
(b) should disclose only those events that can be measured in dollars.
(c) should disclose all events and circumstances that would matter to users of financial statements.
(d) should not be relied on unless an auditor has expressed an unqualified opinion on them.

(SO 4) C 7. An item is considered material when:
(a) it is more than $500.
(b) it affects profits.
(c) not reporting it would influence or change a decision.
(d) it occurs infrequently.

(SO 5) K 8. Which of the following is *not* a condition that must be met for revenue recognition on the sale of goods?
(a) The seller does not have control over the goods or continuing managerial involvement.
(b) The amount of the revenue can be reliably measured.
(c) Cash is collected.
(d) The seller has transferred to the buyer the significant risks and rewards of ownership.

(SO 5) C 9. It is not appropriate to use the percentage-of-completion method for long-term construction contracts when:
(a) it is not possible to get reliable estimates of costs and progress.
(b) it is estimated that the project will take seven years to construct.
(c) cash is collected from the customer every month during construction.
(d) you are not 100% certain as to what the total costs to complete the project will be.

(SO 5) C 10. Which of the following is *not* an appropriate time to recognize an expense?
(a) When cash is paid for the purchase of computer equipment
(b) When an expenditure is made that does not qualify for the recognition of an asset
(c) When the cost of computer equipment is allocated over its useful life
(d) When a previously recorded asset no longer has any future benefit

The Navigator

Questions

(SO 1) C   1. Describe the conceptual framework of accounting and explain how it helps financial reporting.

(SO 1) C   2. Why are principles-based standards better than rules-based standards?

(SO 2) K   3. What is the basic objective of financial reporting?

(SO 2) C   4. Explain the underlying assumptions of: (a) accrual accounting and (b) going concern.

(SO 2) C   5. (a) Why does it matter whether accountants assume an economic entity will remain a going concern? (b) How does the going concern assumption support reporting the cost of an asset instead of its fair value?

(SO 3) K   6. Identify and explain the two fundamental qualitative characteristics of accounting information.

(SO 3) K   7. Identify and explain the four enhancing qualitative characteristics of accounting information.

(SO 3) C   8. What is the difference between comparability and consistency?

(SO 3) K   9. The qualitative characteristics should be applied in a certain order. Identify the order and explain why it matters.

(SO 3) C 10. Explain the accounting concept of full disclosure.

(SO 4) C 11. Describe the two constraints that affect the accounting information reported in financial statements.

(SO 3, 4) C 12. Explain how the full disclosure concept relates to the cost-benefit constraint.

(SO 4) C 13. The controller of Mustafa Corporation rounded all dollar figures in the company's financial statements to the nearest thousand dollars. "It's not important for our users to know how many pennies we spend," she said. Do you believe rounded financial figures can provide useful information for decision-making? Explain why or why not.

(SO 4) C 14. Isabelle believes that the same GAAP should be used by every company, whether large or small and whether public or private. Do you agree? Explain your answer by referring to the appropriate accounting constraint.

(SO 5) C 15. Why is revenue recognition a difficult concept to apply in practice?

(SO 5) K 16. Describe the general criteria for revenue recognition under International Financial Reporting Standards.

(SO 5) K 17. What are the five conditions that must be met for revenue to be recognized from the sale of goods?

(SO 5) K 18. What are the four conditions that must be met for revenue and gross profit from long-term service and construction contracts to be recognized using the percentage-of-completion method?

(SO 5) C 19. What are the advantages of using the percentage-of-completion method to recognize revenue?

(SO 5) C 20. Explain how the percentage-of-completion method should be adjusted when a company's cost estimates change during the contract period.

(SO 5) AP 21. (a) Under what circumstances is it not appropriate to recognize revenue and gross profit using the percentage-of-completion method for long-term service and construction contracts? (b) Describe how revenue and gross profit would be recognized under these circumstances.

(SO 5) K 22. Describe when expenses should be recognized.

(SO 5) C 23. Explain why certain assets are reported at fair value not cost.

Brief Exercises

Identify items included in the conceptual framework.
(SO 1) K

BE11–1 Indicate which of the following items are included in the conceptual framework. (Write "Yes" or "No" beside each item.)

(a) The analysis of financial statement ratios
(b) The objective of financial reporting
(c) The qualitative characteristics of accounting information
(d) The elements of financial statements
(e) The rules for calculating taxable income
(f) The constraints on applying generally accepted accounting principles
(g) The measurement of the market value of a business

BE11–2 Presented below are the underlying assumptions of accounting standards.

Identify assumptions in the conceptual framework.
(SO 2) C

1. Accrual accounting
2. Going concern

For each of the following, indicate the assumption that has been violated.

(a) ___ All of the company's assets are reported in the balance sheet at the amount expected to be collected if the assets were sold.

(b) ___ The sale of goods received by the customer in December was recorded as revenue in January when the cash was collected from the customer.

BE11–3 Here are the basic elements of financial statements that we learned about in earlier chapters:

Identify elements of financial statements.
(SO 2) K

1. Assets	4. Revenues
2. Liabilities	5. Expenses
3. Owner's equity	6. Drawings

Instructions

Each statement that follows is an important aspect of an element's definition. Match the elements with the definitions. *Note*: More than one number can be placed in a blank. Each number may be used more than once or not at all.

(a) ___ Increases in assets or decreases in liabilities resulting from the main business activities of the organization

(b) ___ Existing debts and obligations from past transactions

(c) ___ Resources owned by a business

(d) ___ Goods or services used in the process of earning revenue

(e) ___ A residual claim on total assets after deducting liabilities

(f) ___ The capacity to provide future benefits to the organization

BE11–4 Presented below is a set of qualitative characteristics of accounting information:

Identify qualitative characteristics.
(SO 3) K

1. Predictive value	6. Comparability
2. Neutral	7. Feedback value
3. Verifiability	8. Consistency
4. Timeliness	9. Understandability
5. Faithful representation	

Instructions

Match these qualitative characteristics to the following statements, using numbers 1 to 9.

(a) ___ Accounting information must be available to decision-makers before the information loses its ability to influence their decisions.

(b) ___ Accounting information provides a basis to evaluate decisions made in the past.

(c) ___ Accounting information cannot be selected, prepared, or presented to favour one set of interested users over another.

(d) ___ Accounting information reports the economic substance of a transaction, not its legal form.

(e) ___ Accounting information helps reduce uncertainty about the future.

(f) ___ Accounting information must be provided in a way that knowledgeable and independent people agree that it faithfully represents the economic reality of the transaction or event.

(g) ___ Accounting information about one company can be evaluated in relation to accounting information from another company.

(h) ___ Accounting information is prepared based on the assumption that users have a reasonable understanding of accounting concepts and procedures, and of general business and economic conditions.

(i) ___ Accounting information in a company is prepared using the same principles and methods year after year.

Identify violation of concept or constraint.
(SO 4, 5) AP

BE11–5 For each of the following, indicate the accounting concept or constraint that has been violated, if any:

(a) The company currently records its accounting transactions and prepares its financial reports manually. The cost of using a new computerized accounting system to do these tasks is estimated at $25,000. Annual savings are expected to be $10,000.

(b) Inventory is reported at cost when market value is higher.

(c) Paper clips expense appears on the income statement, at $10.

(d) Bad debt expense is recorded in the period when the account receivable is written off.

(e) Small tools are recorded as long-lived assets and depreciated.

Identify concept, assumption, or constraint.
(SO 2, 3, 4, 5) C

BE11–6 Here are some of the accounting concepts, assumptions, and constraints discussed in this chapter:

1. Going concern	5. Cost
2. Economic entity	6. Cost-benefit
3. Matching	7. Materiality
4. Full disclosure	

Instructions

Identify by number the accounting assumption, concept, or constraint that describes each situation below. Do not use a number more than once.

(a) ___ is why land is not reported at its liquidation value. (Do not use item 5, cost.)

(b) ___ indicates that personal and business record-keeping should be kept separate.

(c) ___ ensures that all relevant financial information is reported.

(d) ___ requires that GAAP be followed for all significant items.

(e) ___ requires expenses to be recognized in the same period as related revenues.

(f) ___ indicates the value at which an asset is recorded when acquired.

Identify concepts.
(SO 4, 5) C

BE11–7 A list of accounting concepts follows:

1. Revenue recognition	4. Cost
2. Matching	5. Expense recognition
3. Full disclosure	6. Fair value

Instructions

Match these concepts to the following statements, using numbers 1 to 6.

(a) ___ The Hirjikaka Company reports information about pending lawsuits in the notes to its financial statements.

(b) ___ The Sudin Company reduces prepaid insurance to reflect the insurance that has expired.

(c) ___ The Joss Company recognizes revenue at the point of sale, not when the cash is collected.

(d) ___ The Rich Bank reports its short-term investments that are held for resale at market.

(e) ___ The Hilal Company reports its land at the price it paid for it, not at what it is now worth.

(f) ___ The law firm Thériault, Lévesque, and Picard records interim billings and costs for its clients at the end of each month.

(g) ___ The Nickel Company depreciates its mining equipment using the units-of-production method.

Determine point of revenue and expense recognition.
(SO 5) AP

BE11–8 Howie, Price, and Whynot operate an accounting firm. In March, their staff worked a total of 2,000 hours at an average billing rate of $200 per hour. They sent bills to clients in the month of March that totalled $150,000. They expect to bill the balance of their time in April, when the work is complete. The firm's salary costs total $100,000 each month. How much revenue should the firm recognize in the month of March? How much salaries expense?

BE11–9 Mullen Manufacturing Ltd. sold $350,000 of merchandise on credit in the month of September to customers. All of the merchandise was sold FOB shipping point. At September 30, $25,000 of the merchandise was in transit. During September, the company collected $250,000 of cash from its customers. The company estimates that about 1% of the sales will become uncollectible and that about 2% of the sales will be returned by customers. How much revenue should the company recognize for the month of September? Describe how the uncollectible sales and returns by the customers should be accounted for.

Determine revenue to be recognized.
(SO 5) AP

BE11–10 Abbotsford Ltd., a sports equipment wholesaler, sold $275,000 of merchandise during November to customers. The cost of the merchandise shipped was $150,000. All of the merchandise was shipped FOB destination. At November 30, $35,000 of the merchandise was in transit. The cost of the merchandise in transit was $19,000. During November, Abbotsford purchased $100,000 of merchandise inventory and made cash payments for merchandise inventory of $125,000. How much revenue should the company recognize for the month of November? What is the gross profit recognized in November?

Determine revenue and expenses to be recognized.
(SO 5) AP

BE11–11 Flin Flon Construction Company is under contract to build a commercial building at a price of $4.2 million. Construction begins in January 2009 and finishes in December 2011. Total estimated construction costs are $2.8 million. Actual construction costs incurred in each year are as follows: in 2009, $840,000; in 2010, $1,120,000; and in 2011, $840,000. Calculate the revenue and gross profit to be recognized in each year, using the percentage-of-completion method.

Calculate revenue and gross profit—percentage-of-completion method.
(SO 5) AP

BE11–12 Refer to the data presented in BE11–11. Assume that the estimated total costs rose from $2.8 million to $3.1 million in 2010. Actual costs incurred are $840,000 in 2009, $1,260,000 in 2010, and $1 million in 2011. Calculate the revenue and gross profit that should be recognized each year, using the percentage-of-completion method.

Calculate revenue and gross profit with change in estimate—percentage-of-completion method.
(SO 5) AP

BE11–13 Refer to the data presented in BE11–11. Calculate the revenue and gross profit to be recognized in each year, assuming that Flin Flon is not able to reliably estimate the construction costs and uses the zero profit method.

Calculate revenue and gross profit—zero profit method.
(SO5) AP

Exercises

E11–1 The Skate Stop is owned by Marc Bélanger. It sells in-line skates and accessories. It shares space with another company, Ride Snowboards. Ride Snowboards is owned by Marc's wife, Dominique Maltais, who was an Olympic bronze medallist in snowboarding. Ride Snowboards sells snowboards and related accessories. The following transactions occurred during a recent year:

Apply the economic entity assumption.
(SO 2) AP

(a) In January, Marc purchased fire and theft insurance for the year to cover the rented space and inventory. He paid for all the insurance since he had more cash than Dominique.
(b) Dominique paid the rent for the month of July since she had more cash that month than Marc.
(c) Marc recorded skate sales for the month of September.
(d) Dominique purchased and paid for her winter inventory of snowboards in September.
(e) Marc and Dominique had such a successful year that they went out to a fancy restaurant to celebrate. They charged the bill to Marc's company.
(f) Dominique paid her annual membership fee to the local ski hill from company funds.
(g) Marc paid his annual membership fee to the curling club from company funds.

Instructions

Identify which of the above transactions should be recorded by Skate Stop, and which should be recorded by Ride Snowboards. State also if the transaction cost is a personal one or if it relates to both companies and should be allocated to each of them.

E11–2 When they have to choose among generally accepted accounting principles, some managers may try to adopt policies that allow them to influence the company's profit.

Instructions

(a) Explain why a manager might be motivated to try to influence profit.
(b) Give an example of an accounting policy choice that management could use to (1) improve the company's profit, and (2) reduce the company's profit.
(c) How would this type of behaviour meet, or not meet, the objective of financial reporting?
(d) Explain how likely it is that a manager would be able to change accounting principles to manage profits as you describe in (b).

E11–3 Presented below is a set of qualitative characteristics of accounting information.

1. Relevance	5. Faithful representation
2. Neutrality	6. Comparability
3. Verifiability	7. Consistency
4. Timeliness	8. Understandability

Instructions

For each of the following, indicate which qualitative characteristic was violated.

(a) ___ Allen Ltd. reported its merchandise inventory at a net realizable value of $25,000. The company's auditors disagree with this value and estimated the net realizable value to be $20,000.
(b) ___ Owens Corporation does not issue its annual financial statements for the year ended December 31, 2009, until November 2010.
(c) ___ Silver Mining Ltd. is the only company in the mining industry that uses the straight-line method to depreciate its mining equipment.
(d) ___ Chapman Ltd. switches inventory cost formulas from average to FIFO and back to average in a three-year period.
(e) ___ Enco Ltd. intentionally recorded revenue in 2009, for sales made in 2010, to ensure that management would receive their bonuses, which were based on profits.
(f) ___ World Talk Corporation used terminology in its financial statements and notes to the financial statements that is not commonly used in financial reporting and did not provide explanations of the terminology.
(g) ___ Precision R Us Ltd., a multinational drilling company, reported separately its paper, paper clips, and pens in the balance sheet rather than reporting a single line item for office supplies. Total office supplies were $5,000.
(h) ___ Community Health Foods Ltd. signed a legal agreement to finance the purchase of equipment. The agreement required annual payments of $15,000 for five years. The agreement referred to the payments as rental payments. The company records rent expense when the annual payments are made.

E11–4 Here are some assumptions, constraints, and concepts discussed in this chapter:

1. Going concern	5. Cost
2. Economic entity	6. Cost-benefit
3. Matching	7. Materiality
4. Full disclosure	

Instructions

Identify by number the accounting assumption, principle, or constraint that describes each situation below. Do not use a number more than once.

(a) ___ Barb Denton runs her accounting practice out of her home. She separates her business records from her household accounts.

(b) ___ The cost should not be more than the benefits.

(c) ___ Significant accounting policies are reported in the notes to the financial statements.

(d) ___ Assets are not stated at their liquidation value.

(e) ___ Dollar amounts on financial statements are often rounded to the nearest thousand.

(f) ___ Bad debts expense is recorded using the allowance method of accounting.

(g) ___ Land is recorded at its cost of $100,000 rather than at its market value of $150,000.

E11–5 Several reporting situations follow:

1. Tercek Company recognizes revenue during the production cycle. The price of the product and how many items will be sold are not certain.
2. In preparing its financial statements, Seco Company left out information about its cost flow assumption for inventories.
3. Martinez Company amortizes patents over their legal life of 20 years instead of their economic life, which is usually about five years.
4. Ravine Hospital Supply Corporation reports only current assets and current liabilities on its balance sheet. Long-term assets and liabilities are reported as current. The company is unlikely to be liquidated.
5. Barton Company reports inventory on its balance sheet at its current market value of $100,000. The inventory has an original cost of $110,000.
6. Bonilla Company is in its third year of operations and has not yet issued financial statements.
7. Watts Company has inventory on hand that cost $400,000. Watts reports inventory on its balance sheet at its current market value of $425,000.
8. Steph Wolfson, president of the Download Music Company, bought a computer for her personal use. She paid for the computer with company funds and debited the computer account.
9. Smith Company decided not to implement a perpetual inventory system that would save $40,000 annually. The cost of the system was $100,000 and was estimated to have a 10-year life.

Identify qualitative characteristic, assumption, constraint, or concept violated.
(SO 2, 3, 4, 5) AP

Instructions

For each of the above, list the qualitative characteristic, assumption, constraint, or concept that has been violated, if any.

E11–6 Business transactions for Ellis Co. follow:

1. Equipment worth $100,000 is acquired at a cost of $85,000 from a company going out of business. The following entry is made:

Equipment	100,000	
Cash		85,000
Gain		15,000

2. The president of Ellis Co., Evan Ellis, purchases a truck for personal use and charges it to his expense account. The following entry is made:

Travel Expense	42,000	
Cash		42,000

Identify assumption, concept, or constraint violated and correct entries.
(SO 2, 4, 5) AN

3. An account receivable becomes a bad debt. The following entry is made:

Bad Debts Expense	5,000	
Accounts Receivable		5,000

4. Merchandise inventory with a cost of $255,000 is reported at its fair value of $280,000. The following entry is made:

Merchandise Inventory	25,000	
Gain		25,000

5. An electric pencil sharpener costing $40 is being depreciated over five years. The following entry is made:

Depreciation Expense	8	
Accumulated Depreciation—Pencil Sharpener		8

6. East Air sells an airline ticket for $650 in February for a trip scheduled in April. The following entry is made:

Cash	650	
Flight Revenue		650

Instructions

In each of the situations above, identify the assumption, concept, or constraint that has been violated, if any. If a journal entry is incorrect, give the correct entry.

Identify point of revenue recognition.
(SO 5) C

E11–7 The following situations require professional judgement to determine when to recognize revenue from the transactions:

(a) Air Canada sells you a nonrefundable Tango fare airline ticket in September for your flight home at Christmas.

(b) Leon's Furniture sells you a home theatre on a "no money down, no interest, and no payments for one year" promotional deal.

(c) The Toronto Blue Jays sell season tickets to games in the Rogers Centre on-line. Fans can purchase the tickets at any time, although the season doesn't officially begin until April. It runs from April through October.

(d) Babineau Company sells merchandise with terms of 2/10, n/30, FOB destination.

(e) In September, Centennial College collects tuition revenue for the term from students. The term runs from September through December.

(f) The College Bookstore has the following return policy for textbook sales: "Textbooks (new and used) may be returned for seven calendar days from the start of classes. After that time, textbooks (new and used) may be returned within 48 hours of purchase."

Instructions

Identify when revenue should be recognized in each of the above situations.

Identify point of revenue recognition.
(SO 5) C

E11–8 Over the winter months, the Green-Lawn Company pre-sells fertilizing and weed control lawn services to be performed from May through September, inclusive. If payment is made in full by April 1, a 10% discount is allowed. In March, 250 customers took advantage of the discount and purchased the summer lawn service package for $540 each. In June, 300 customers purchased the package for $600, and in July, 150 purchased it for the same price. For customers who pay after May 1 service starts in the month payment is made by the customer.

Instructions

How much revenue should be recognized by the Green-Lawn Company in each of the months of March, April, May, June, July, August, and September? Explain.

E11–9 Consider the following transactions of the Mitrovica Company, a diversified manufacturing and construction company, for the year ended December 31, 2009:

Determine amount of revenue to be recognized.
(SO 5) AP

(a) Leased office space for a one-year period beginning September 1. Three months of rent at $2,000 per month was received in advance.

(b) Received a sales order for merchandise that cost $9,000. It was sold for $16,000 on December 28 to Warfield Company. The goods were shipped FOB destination on December 31. Warfield received them on January 3, 2010.

(c) Signed a long-term contract to construct a building at a total price of $1.6 million. The total estimated cost of construction is $1.2 million. During 2009, the company incurred $300,000 of costs and collected $400,000 in cash.

(d) Mitrovica introduced a new product into the market. The company shipped product costing $25,000 to its regular customers. The customers were billed $50,000 for the product. To promote the product, Mitrovica does not require payment until June 2010 and if Mitrovica's customers do not sell all of the product by June 2010 they can return the unsold product to Mitrovica. The product is new and Mitrovica is uncertain if it will sell.

(e) Issued a $6,000, six-month, 5% note receivable on August 1, with interest payable at maturity.

(f) Received a sales order for $20,000 of merchandise that cost $10,000 from a new customer. The customer was required to prepay the invoice. On December 29, 2009, a cheque for $20,000 was received from the customer. The merchandise was shipped on January 4, 2010.

Instructions

For each item above, indicate the amount of revenue Mitrovica should recognize in 2009. Explain.

E11–10 Shen Construction Company had a long-term construction project that lasted three years. The project had a contract price of $150 million with total estimated costs of $100 million. Shen used the percentage-of-completion method. At the end of construction, the following actual costs had been incurred:

Calculate gross profit—percentage-of-completion method.
(SO 5) AP

	2009	2010	2011
Actual cost	$25 million	$55 million	$20 million

Instructions

(a) Calculate the gross profit that was recognized for each year of the construction contract.

(b) Assume instead that at the beginning of 2010, Shen revised the total estimated cost remaining for the last year of the contract to $25 million instead of $20 million. Actual costs incurred in 2011 were later determined to be $25 million. Calculate the gross profit that was recognized for each year of the construction contract.

E11–11 Refer to the data in E11–10(a) for Shen Construction Company. Assume that Shen was not able to reliably estimate the cost of the construction project.

Calculate gross profit—zero profit method.
(SO 5) AP

Instructions

Calculate the gross profit that should be recognized for each year of the construction contract if the zero profit method is used.

Problems: Set A

Comment on the objective of financial reporting, relevance, and faithful representation.
(SO 2, 3) C

P11–1A "Note 13. Commitments" in The Forzani Group Ltd.'s consolidated financial statements provides the following information on the future cash payments under lease agreements: "The Company is committed, at February 1, 2009, to minimum payments under long-term real property and data processing hardware and software equipment leases, for future years, as follows:

Year	Gross
2010	$87,523
2011	$77,283
2012	$65,083
2013	$52,753
2014	$40,403
Thereafter	$86,471"

Instructions

Explain why Forzani is required to disclose the future cash payments under its lease agreements. Support your answer with reference to the objective of financial reporting and the qualitative characteristics.

Taking It Further Refer to the Notes to Consolidated Financial Statements for The Forzani Group Ltd. in Appendix A and provide another example for which the company discloses required future cash payments.

Assumptions and concepts—going concern, full disclosure.
(SO 2, 3) AP

P11–2A General Motors Corporation reported significant losses from 2005 to 2008. General Motors acknowledged in its 2008 financial statements that with these losses, combined with the economic crisis in 2008 and the first part of 2009, it would not be able to meet its financial obligations. As a result, General Motors entered into an agreement with the United States government in which the government agreed to lend General Motors funds and the company made a commitment to restructure its operations. However, General Motors acknowledged that, due to the many uncertainties it faced, there was substantial doubt as to the company's ability to continue as a going concern.

Instructions

(a) What is the potential effect on a company's financial statements if the company files for bankruptcy?
(b) General Motors' 2008 consolidated financial statements were prepared under the assumption the company was a going concern. How did General Motors justify using the going concern assumption when it was so uncertain that the company would continue operating?

Taking It Further Describe the dilemma that a company's management faces in disclosing that a company may not be able to continue as a going concern.

Comment on objective of financial reporting, qualitative characteristics, and constraints.
(SO 1, 3, 4) C

P11–3A Starting in January 2011, Canadian public companies are required to follow International Financial Reporting Standards. The Canadian Accounting Standards Board recognized that a simpler approach to financial reporting was required for Canadian private enterprises and issued new Canadian GAAP specifically for private enterprises. Under the Canadian GAAP for Private Enterprises, there will be significantly less information required to be disclosed in the financial statements.

Instructions

Explain why it is appropriate that there are different reporting and disclosure standards for public and private companies. Support your answer with reference to the objective of financial reporting, qualitative characteristics, and the accounting constraints.

Taking It Further Regardless of the new GAAP for Canadian private enterprises, a Canadian private company may choose to prepare its financial statements using International Financial Reporting Standards. In what circumstances might a Canadian private company choose to report under IFRS rather than under the simpler GAAP for private enterprises?

P11–4A Czyz and Ng are accountants at Kwick Kopy Printers. Kwick Kopy has not adopted the revaluation model for accounting for its property, plant, and equipment. The accountants are having disagreements over the following transactions from the calendar year 2010:

Identify concept or assumption violated and prepare entries.
(SO 2, 4, 5) AN

1. Kwick Kopy bought equipment on January 1, 2010, for $80,000, including installation costs. The equipment has a useful life of five years. Kwick Kopy depreciates equipment using the double declining-balance method. "Since the equipment as installed in our system cannot be removed without considerable damage, it will have no resale value. It should not be depreciated but, instead, expensed immediately," Czyz argues.
2. Depreciation for the year was $43,000. Since the company's profit is expected to be low this year, Czyz suggests deferring depreciation to a year when there is higher profits.
3. Kwick Kopy purchased equipment at a fire sale for $36,000. The equipment would normally have cost $50,000. Czyz believes that the following entry should be made:

Equipment	50,000	
Cash		36,000
Gain		14,000

4. Czyz says that Kwick Kopy should carry its furnishings on the balance sheet at their liquidation value, which is $30,000 less than cost.
5. Kwick Kopy rented office space for one year, effective September 1, 2010. Six months of rent at $3,000 per month was paid in advance. Czyz believes that the following entry should be made on September 1:

Rent Expense	18,000	
Cash		18,000

6. Land that cost $41,000 was appraised at $59,000. Czyz suggests the following journal entry:

Land	18,000	
Gain on Appreciation of Land		18,000

7. On December 15, Kwick Kopy signed a contract with a customer to provide copying services for a six-month period at a rate of $1,500 per month starting January 1, 2011. The customer will pay on a monthly basis. Czyz argues that the contract should be recorded in December because the customer has always paid its bills on time in the past. The customer is legally obligated to pay the monthly amount because a contract has been signed. Czyz believes the following entry should be recorded:

Accounts Receivable	9,000	
Service Revenue		9,000

Ng disagrees with Czyz on each of the situations.

Instructions

(a) For each transaction, indicate why Ng disagrees. Support your answer with reference to the conceptual framework—definition of elements, characteristics, assumptions, constraints, recognition, and measurement criteria.
(b) Prepare the correct journal entry to record each transaction.

Taking It Further Discuss the circumstances in which it is appropriate to record property, plant, and equipment at its liquidation value.

Identify assumption or
concepts and correct entries.
(SO 2, 5) AN

P11–5A Business transactions for Durkovitch Company from the current year follow. The company has not adopted the revaluation model of accounting for its property, plant, and equipment.

1. An order for $90,000 was received from a customer for products on hand. The customer paid a $10,000 deposit when the order was placed. The order is to be shipped on January 9 next year. The following entry was made:

Cash	10,000	
Accounts Receivable	80,000	
Sales		90,000

2. Because of a "flood sale," equipment worth $350,000 was acquired at a cost of $285,000. The following entry was made:

Equipment	350,000	
Cash		285,000
Gain on Acquisition of Equipment		65,000

3. Because the general level of prices decreased during the current year, Durkovitch determined that there was a $60,000 overstatement of depreciation expense on its equipment. The following entry was made:

Accumulated Depreciation	60,000	
Depreciation Expense		60,000

4. On December 31, merchandise purchased for resale was received. The following entry was made:

Cost of Goods Sold	78,000	
Accounts Payable		78,000

5. Land was purchased on April 30 for $230,000. The company plans to build a warehouse on the land. On December 31, the land would have cost $200,000. The following entry was made:

Loss on Decline in Value of Land	30,000	
Land		30,000

Instructions

(a) In each of the situations above, identify the assumption or concept that has been violated, if any.

(b) Prepare the journal entry to correct each incorrect transaction identified in (a).

Taking It Further Would your answer for 5 have been different if the Durkovitch company was a real estate company and the land had been purchased for resale? Explain.

Identify point of revenue and
expense recognition.
(SO 5) C

P11–6A Santa's Christmas Tree Farm grows pine, fir, and spruce trees. The company cuts and sells the trees for cash during the Christmas season. Most of the trees are exported to the United States. The remaining trees are sold to local tree lot operators.

It normally takes about 12 years for a tree to grow to a good size. The average selling price for a mature tree is $48. The owner of Santa's Christmas Tree Farm believes that the company should recognize revenue at the rate of $4 a year ($48 ÷ 12 years) for each tree that it cuts. The biggest cost of this business is the cost of fertilizing, pruning, and maintaining the trees over the 12-year period. These costs average $40 a tree and the owner believes they should also be spread over the 12-year period.

Instructions

Do you agree with the proposed revenue recognition policy for Santa's Christmas Tree Farms? Explain why or why not. Use the revenue recognition criteria to explain your argument for when the revenue should be recognized for this tree-farming business.

Taking It Further   Explain how the costs of fertilizing, pruning, and maintaining the trees should be recorded.

P11–7A   On February 11, 2010, Security Equipment was awarded a $6-million contract to develop a new security system for a nuclear plant. Work began on April 1 and estimated costs of completion at the contract date are $4.5 million over a two-year period. By December 31, 2010, Security Equipment's year end, costs of $1.8 million have been incurred. Contract payments totalling $2 million have been collected so far.

Calculate revenue at various points of recognition. (SO 5) AP

Instructions

(a) Describe the two methods that may be used to recognize revenue for construction projects.
(b) Calculate the amount of revenue that would be recognized in fiscal 2010 for Security Equipment under each of the revenue recognition methods described in your response to (a).

Taking It Further   Which method would you recommend that Security Equipment use? Explain why.

P11–8A   Cosky Construction Company is involved in a long-term construction contract to build an office building. The estimated cost is $40 million and the contract price is $56 million. Additional information follows:

Calculate revenue, expense, and gross profit—percentage-of-completion and zero profit methods. (SO 5) AP

Year	Cash Collections	Actual Costs Incurred
2009	$ 9,000,000	$ 6,000,000
2010	20,000,000	18,000,000
2011	14,000,000	10,000,000
2012	13,000,000	6,000,000
	$56,000,000	$40,000,000

The project is completed in 2012 as scheduled and all cash collections related to the contract have been received.

Instructions

(a) Prepare a schedule to determine the revenue, expense, and gross profit for each year of the contract, using the percentage-of-completion method.
(b) How would your answer in (a) change if Cosky Construction used the zero profit method?

Taking It Further   Assume that Cosky can estimate costs reliably and that partway through the contract the customer encountered financial difficulty and fell behind in its cash payments, and Cosky is unsure if the customer will be able to pay the full amount owing. Would it still be appropriate to recognize revenue using the percentage-of-completion method? Explain.

P11–9A   Refer to the data in P11–8A for Cosky Construction. Assume instead that the actual costs were $14 million in 2011. Because costs were higher than expected, Cosky revised its total estimated costs from $40 million to $48 million at the end of 2011. Actual costs incurred in 2012 were $10 million. All other data are unchanged.

Revise revenue, expense, and gross profit—percentage-of-completion. (SO 5) AP

Instructions

Assuming Cosky Construction uses the percentage-of-completion method, prepare a revised schedule to determine the revenue, expense, and gross profit for each year of the long-term construction contract.

Taking It Further   Assume that during 2010, Cosky Construction encountered difficulty in the construction of the office building as it discovered that the foundation was leaking and it was not able to estimate the costs to fix the foundation and complete the building reliably. Would it still be appropriate to use the percentage-of-completion method for the remaining years of the contract? Explain.

Calculate revenue, expense, and gross profit—percentage-of-completion method.
(SO 5) AP

P11–10A Kamloops Construction Company has a contract for the construction of a new health and fitness centre. It is accounting for this project using the percentage-of-completion method. The contract amount is $5.0 million and the cost of construction is expected to total $2.8 million. The actual costs incurred are as follows for the three-year life of the project:

Year	Actual Costs Incurred
2009	$1,120,000
2010	980,000
2011	700,000
	$2,800,000

Instructions

Calculate the amount of revenue, expense, and gross profit to be recognized in each year.

Taking It Further What if Kamloops Construction receives more cash in each of the first two years than the amount it has recognized as revenue? Is it still appropriate to recognize the amount of revenue as calculated? Explain.

Revenue recognition criteria—sale of goods.
(SO 5) AP

P11–11A Dave's Deep Discount Furniture Store opened for business October 1, 2009. To promote the store and develop a loyal customer base, customers could buy furniture with no money down and no payments for 12 months. Customers wishing to take advantage of the special promotion were required to pass a thorough credit check. Of the customers from October 1 to December 31, 2009, 75% took advantage of the special promotion; the other customers paid for the furniture in full when it was delivered. Total sales from October 1 to December 31, 2009, were $325,000, of which $250,000 was for customers who chose to delay payment for 12 months. Of the remaining $75,000 of sales, $60,000 worth had been delivered to the customers by December 31, 2009, and the remaining $15,000 would be delivered in January 2010. The accountant for the store made the following entry to record the sales.

Accounts Receivable	15,000	
Cash	60,000	
Sales Revenue		75,000

Dave disagreed with the accountant and argued that sales revenue of $325,000 should be recorded in 2009.

Instructions

(a) Identify the revenue recognition criteria that must be met before revenue is recorded for the sale of goods.

(b) Identify the critical factors relating to the Dave's Deep Discount Furniture Store's sales transactions that should be considered in determining how much revenue should be recognized.

(c) Indicate the amount of revenue that should be recognized for the period October 1 to December 31, 2009.

Taking It Further Would your response to (c) be different if the customers were not required to pass a thorough credit check? Explain why or why not.

Problems: Set B

Comment on relevance and faithful representation.
(SO 2, 3) C

P11–1B "Note 2. Significant Accounting Policies" in The Forzani Group Ltd.'s consolidated financial statements states: "The preparation of the financial statements in conformity with Canadian Generally Accepted Accounting Principles ('GAAP') requires management to make estimates and assumptions that affect the reported amounts of assets and liabilities and disclosures of contingent assets and liabilities at the date of the consolidated financial statements and the reported amounts of revenue and expenses during the reporting period. Actual results could differ materially from these estimates."

Instructions

Explain why Forzani's management is required to use estimates in the company's financial statements. Support your answer with reference to the objective of financial reporting and the qualitative characteristics.

Taking It Further Which qualitative characteristics may be sacrificed when management is required to make estimates in the financial statements that may differ materially from actual results?

P11–2B Air Canada reported a $1-billion loss for the year ended December 31, 2008. This loss, combined with increasing debt and pension obligations and reduced passenger travel during the first quarter of 2009, raised speculation by the financial markets that Air Canada's future is uncertain. If Air Canada is not able to meet its financial obligations, it may be forced into bankruptcy.

Comment on application of accounting assumptions and concepts.
(SO 2, 3) AP

Instructions

(a) What is the potential effect on a company's financial statements if the company files for bankruptcy?
(b) With the uncertainty facing Air Canada's future, should the company's financial statements be prepared under the assumption that it will continue to operate for the foreseeable future? Explain.

Taking It Further Explain the implications of the full disclosure concept on Air Canada's financial statements in these circumstances.

P11–3B Under Canadian GAAP prior to January 2008, Canadian companies were not required to separately disclose cost of goods sold in their financial statements. Because this disclosure was not specifically required, less than half of the Canadian companies that produced reports disclosed their cost of goods sold separately in their income statements. For fiscal years beginning after January 1, 2008, companies are required to disclose separately in their financial statements the amount of inventories recognized as an expense (cost of goods sold).

Comment on objective of financial reporting, qualitative characteristics, and constraints.
(SO 1, 3, 4) C

Instructions

In your opinion, will this new requirement improve financial statements? Include references to the objective of financial reporting and qualitative characteristics in your explanation.

Taking It Further Why do you think companies have been reluctant to separately disclose cost of goods sold in their financial statements?

P11–4B Jivraj and Juma are accountants at Desktop Computers. Desktop Computers has not adopted the revaluation model for accounting for its property, plant, and equipment. They disagree over the following transactions that occurred during the calendar year 2010:

Identify elements, assumptions, constraints, and recognition and measurement criteria.
(SO 2, 4, 5) AN

1. Desktop purchased equipment for $60,000 at a going-out-of-business sale. The equipment was worth $75,000. Jivraj believes that the following entry should be made:

Equipment	75,000	
Cash		60,000
Gain		15,000

2. Land costing $90,000 was appraised at $215,000. Jivraj suggests the following journal entry.

Land	125,000	
Gain on Appreciation of land		125,000

3. Depreciation for the year was $18,000. Since the company's profit is expected to be lower this year, Jivraj suggests deferring depreciation to a year when there is higher profit.

4. Desktop bought a custom-made piece of equipment for $54,000. This equipment has a useful life of six years. Desktop depreciates equipment using the straight-line method. "Since the equipment is custom-made, it will have no resale value," Jivraj argues. "So, instead of depreciating it, it should be expensed immediately." Jivraj suggests the following entry:

Equipment Expense	54,000	
Cash		54,000

5. Jivraj suggests that the company building should be reported on the balance sheet at the lower of cost and fair value. Fair value is $15,000 less than cost, although it is expected to recover its value in the future.

6. On December 20, 2010, Desktop hired a marketing consultant to design and implement a marketing plan in 2011. The plan will be designed and implemented in three stages. The contract amount is $60,000, payable in three instalments in 2011 as each stage of the plan is completed. Jivraj argues that the contract must be recorded in 2010 because there is a signed contract. Jivraj suggests the following:

Marketing Expense	60,000	
Accounts Payable		60,000

7. On December 23, Desktop received a written sales order for 10 computers. The computers will be shipped in January when the required software is installed. Jivraj suggests the following entries:

Accounts Receivable	103,000	
Sales Revenue		103,000
Cost of Goods Sold	53,000	
Inventory		53,000

* Juma disagrees with Jivraj on each of the situations.

Instructions

(a) For each transaction, indicate why Juma disagrees. Support your answer with reference to the conceptual framework (definition of elements, characteristics, assumptions, constraints, and recognition and measurement criteria).

(b) Prepare the correct journal entry to record each transaction.

Taking It Further   How would your response in (a) differ if Desktop adopted the revaluation model of accounting for its property, plant, and equipment?

Identify assumptions and concepts and correct entries.
(SO 2, 5) AN

P11–5B   Business transactions for SGI Company in the current year follow:

1. The company used the average cost formula to determine that the cost of the merchandise inventory at December 31 was $65,000. On December 31, it would have cost $80,000 to replace the merchandise inventory, so the following entry was made:

Merchandise Inventory	15,000	
Gain on Inventory		15,000

2. An order for $35,000 of goods on hand was received from a customer on December 27. The customer paid a $5,000 deposit when the order was placed. This order is to be shipped on January 9 next year. The following entry was made on December 27:

Cash	5,000	
Accounts Receivable	30,000	
Sales		35,000

3. On December 31, SGI Company's fiscal year end, a 12-month insurance policy for the following year was purchased. The following entry was made:

| Insurance Expense | 24,000 | |
| Cash | | 24,000 |

4. At a fire sale, equipment worth $300,000 was acquired at a cost of $225,000. It had soot and smoke damage, but was otherwise in good condition. The following entry was made:

Equipment	300,000	
Cash		225,000
Gain on Acquisition of Equipment		75,000

5. The cost of utilities used during December was $4,200. No entry was made for the utilities in December as the bill was not received until January and was paid in February.

Instructions

(a) In each of the situations, identify the assumption or concept that has been violated, if any.
(b) Prepare the journal entry to correct each incorrect transaction identified in (a).

Taking It Further Would your response to item 5 be different if you did not know the cost of the December utilities?

P11–6B Superior Salmon Farm raises salmon that it sells to supermarket chains and restaurants. The average selling price for a mature salmon is $6. Many people believe that the selling price will increase in the future, because the demand for salmon is increasing as more people become aware of the health benefits of the omega-3 fatty acids in this fish.

Identify point of revenue and expense recognition. (SO 5) C

It normally takes three years for the fish to grow to a saleable size. During that period, the fish must be fed and closely monitored to ensure they are healthy and free of disease. Their habitat must also be maintained. These costs average $4.50 per fish over the three-year growing period. The owner of Superior Salmon Farm believes the company should recognize revenue at a rate of $2 a year ($6 ÷ 3 years) for each fish that it harvests.

Instructions

Do you agree with the proposed revenue recognition policy for Superior Salmon Farm? Explain why or why not. Use the revenue recognition criteria to explain when you believe the revenue should be recognized for this salmon-farming business.

Taking It Further Explain how the costs of feeding, monitoring, and maintaining healthy fish and a proper habitat should be recorded.

P11–7B Devany Construction was awarded a $60-million contract on June 19, 2010, to build a civic centre. Construction began on August 1 and estimated costs of completion at the contract date are $50 million over a two-year period. By November 30, 2010, Devany's year end, construction costs of $13.5 million had been incurred. Contract payments totalling $20 million had been collected so far.

Calculate revenue at various points of recognition. (SO 5) AP

Instructions

(a) Describe the two methods that may be used to recognize revenue for construction contracts.
(b) Calculate the amount of revenue and gross profit that would be recognized in fiscal 2010 for Devany Construction under each of the revenue recognition methods described in your response to (a).

Taking It Further Which method would you recommend that Devany Construction use? Explain why.

P11–8B MacNeil Construction Company has a long-term construction contract to build a shopping centre. The centre has a total estimated cost of $60 million, and a contract price of $76 million. Additional information follows:

Calculate revenue, expense, and gross profit—percentage-of-completion and zero profit methods. (SO 5) AP

Year	Cash Collections	Actual Costs Incurred
2009	$12,000,000	$ 9,000,000
2010	16,000,000	12,000,000
2011	$25,000,000	$24,000,000
2012	23,000,000	15,000,000
	$76,000,000	$60,000,000

The shopping centre is completed in 2012 as scheduled. All cash collections for the contract have been received.

Instructions

(a) Prepare a schedule to determine the revenue, expense, and gross profit for each year of the long-term construction contract, using the percentage-of-completion method.

(b) How would your answer in (a) change if MacNeil Construction used the zero profit method?

Taking It Further Which of the revenue recognition methods used in (a) and (b) provides the most relevant information? Explain.

Revise revenue, expense, and gross profit—percentage-of-completion method.
(SO 5) AP

P11–9B Refer to the data in P11–8B for MacNeil Construction. Assume instead that the actual costs were $28 million in 2011. Because costs were higher than expected, MacNeil revised its total estimated costs from $60 million to $68 million at the end of 2011. Actual costs incurred in 2012 were $19 million. All other data are unchanged.

Instructions

Using the percentage-of-completion method, prepare a revised schedule to determine the revenue, expense, and gross profit for MacNeil Construction for each year of the long-term construction contract.

Taking It Further Explain why it is appropriate to use the percentage-of-completion method if actual costs differ from the estimated costs.

Calculate revenue, expense, and gross profit—percentage-of-completion method.
(SO 5) AP

P11–10B Hamilton Construction Company has a contract to build a new recreation centre. It accounts for this project using the percentage-of-completion method. The contract amount is $9 million and the cost of construction is expected to total $6.6 million. The actual costs incurred are shown below for the three-year life of the project:

Year	Actual Costs Incurred
2009	$1,980,000
2010	2,970,000
2011	1,650,000
	$6,600,000

Instructions

Calculate the amount of revenue, expense, and gross profit to be recognized in each year.

Taking It Further What if Hamilton Construction was uncertain about whether or not it would collect the full purchase price in cash from the customer: Is it still appropriate to recognize the amount of revenue calculated? Explain.

Determine when to recognize revenue when revenues are uncertain.
(SO 5) AP

P11–11B Vitamins R Us developed a new 100% organic multivitamin, Vita X, which is more easily absorbed by the body. Vita X is significantly more expensive than other vitamins on the market. In order to promote the product, Vitamins R Us shipped 50,000 bottles of Vita X, FOB destination, to retailers during December 2010. Retailers can return any Vita X not sold by March 31, 2011. As an added incentive, the retailers do not have to pay Vitamins R Us for any bottles of Vita X that they do not return to Vitamins R Us until March 31, 2011.

The selling price of the vitamins to the retailers is $45 per bottle. Vitamins R Us has not had previous promotions of this nature. Vitamins R Us has a December 31 fiscal year end.

The company's bookkeeper recognized the revenue on the vitamins when the vitamins were shipped to the retailers and made the following entry:

DR. Accounts Receivable	2,250,000	
CR. Sales Revenues		2,250,000

Instructions

(a) Indicate whether you agree or disagree with the bookkeeper's decision to recognize revenue when the vitamins were shipped. Support your answer with reference to the revenue recognition criteria.

(b) Indicate when the revenue for Vita X should be recognized.

Taking It Further Would your answers to (a) and (b) be different if Vitamins R Us had previously used the same promotion for Vita X and only 10% of the product was returned to Vitamins R Us? Explain your answer.

Continuing Cookie Chronicle

(*Note:* This is a continuation of the Cookie Chronicle from Chapters 1 through 10.)

Natalie's high school friend, Katy Peterson, has been operating a bakery for approximately 10 months, which she calls The Baker's Nook. Natalie and Katy usually meet once a month to catch up and discuss problems they have encountered while operating their respective businesses. Katy wishes to borrow from her bank so she can purchase a new state-of-the-art oven. She recognizes that the bank will be evaluating her income statement and wants to ensure that her profit is maximized. Katy thinks that she has found the solution to her problem.

Katy has recently negotiated a one-year contract with Coffee to Go to provide 1,500 cinnamon buns every week. Coffee to Go, upon receipt of a monthly invoice, will send Katy a cheque by the 15th of the following month. Katy has decided that, because she has signed this contract, she is able to record as revenue in her financial statements the contracted revenue that she is about to earn over the next 12 months. Katy assures Natalie that this is the right way to account for this revenue and is delighted because she is now sure that the bank will lend her the money that she needs to purchase this new oven.

Natalie is confused and comes to you with the following questions:

1. Is Katy accounting for this revenue correctly?
2. What other information will the bank be considering when deciding whether or not to extend the loan to Katy?
3. Do you think that Katy is being honest when she identifies this revenue as being earned on her income statement?

Instructions

(a) Answer Natalie's questions.

(b) How should Katy be recording this revenue?

(c) How could Katy ensure that the bank is aware of this contractual arrangement with Coffee to Go when it reads her financial statements?

Cumulative Coverage—Chapters 6 to 11

Johan Company and Nordlund Company are competing businesses. Both began operations six years ago and they are quite similar. The current balance sheet data for the two companies are as follows:

	Johan Company	Nordlund Company
Cash	$ 70,300	$ 48,400
Accounts receivable	309,700	312,500
Allowance for doubtful accounts	(13,600)	0
Merchandise inventory	463,900	520,200
Property, plant, and equipment	255,300	257,300
Accumulated depreciation	(112,650)	(189,850)
Total assets	$972,950	$948,550
Current liabilities	$440,200	$436,500
Long-term liabilities	78,000	80,000
Total liabilities	518,200	516,500
Owner's equity	454,750	432,050
Total liabilities and owner's equity	$972,950	$948,550

You have been hired as a consultant to do a review of the two companies. Your goal is to determine which one is in a stronger financial position. Your review of their financial statements quickly reveals that the two companies have not followed the same accounting policies. The differences, and your conclusions, are summarized below:

1. Johan Company has had good experience in estimating its uncollectible accounts. A review shows that the amount of its write offs each year has been quite close to the allowances the company provided.

    Nordlund Company has been somewhat slow to recognize its uncollectible accounts. Based on an aging analysis and review of its accounts receivable, it is estimated that $20,000 of its existing accounts will become uncollectible.

2. Johan Company has determined the cost of its merchandise inventory using the average inventory cost formula. The result is that its inventory appears on the balance sheet at an amount that is slightly below its current replacement cost. Based on a detailed physical examination of its merchandise on hand, the current replacement cost of its inventory is estimated at $477,000.

    Nordlund Company has used the FIFO inventory cost formula. The result is that its ending inventory appears on the balance sheet at an amount that is close to its current replacement cost.

3. Johan Company estimated a useful life of 12 years and a residual value of $30,000 for its property, plant, and equipment, and has been depreciating them on a straight-line basis. Nordlund Company has the same type of property, plant, and equipment. However, it estimated a useful life of 10 years and a residual value of $10,000. It has been depreciating its property, plant, and equipment using the double declining-balance method.

    Based on engineering studies of these types of property, plant, and equipment, you conclude that Nordlund's estimates and method for calculating depreciation are more appropriate.

Instructions

(a) Where would you find the above information on the two companies' accounting policies? Be specific about what information would be available and where you would find it.

(b) Using similar accounting policies for both companies, revise the balance sheets presented above.

(c) Has preparing the revised statements in (b) improved the quality of the accounting information for the two companies? How?

Financial Reporting and Analysis

Financial Reporting Problem

BYP11–1   Refer to the Notes to Consolidated Financial Statements for The Forzani Group Ltd. in Appendix A.

Instructions

(a) Note 2, Significant Accounting Policies, states that the preparation of the financial statements in conformity with Canadian generally accepted accounting principles requires management to make estimates. Indicate for which items reported in the financial statements estimates were made. Why are estimates required?

(b) Subsection (h) of Note 2, Significant Accounting Policies, describes Forzani's revenue recognition policy. Does this policy sound reasonable to you, given the types of goods Forzani sells?

(c) Subsection (i) of Note 2, Significant Accounting Policies, describes Forzani's treatment of its store opening expenses. Explain how the company's treatment of these expenses relates to the timing of recognition of revenue from new stores. Some costs are more directly associated with specific revenues than others. Would you consider there to be a direct association between these costs and the revenues to come in future accounting periods from the new stores? What alternative treatment for these expenses might you recommend according to the basic expense recognition criteria?

(d) Note 15, Contingencies and Guarantees, discloses several commitments by the company that are not recorded in the financial statements. Do you think this additional disclosure was necessary? Explain why or why not, referring to the appropriate concepts or items from the Conceptual Framework of accounting in your answer.

(e) Forzani's independent auditors' report is provided in Appendix A with the company's financial statements. What is the purpose of an independent audit? What did Forzani's auditors say about the company's financial statements?

Interpreting Financial Statements

BYP11–2   Today, companies must compete in a global economy. For example, Canada's oldest candy company, Ganong Bros., Limited, which has been making chocolates since 1873, must compete with Nestlé S.A., among others. Although Nestlé is best known for its chocolates and confections, this Swiss company is one of the largest food companies in the world.

Comparing companies such as Ganong and Nestlé can be challenging not only because of their size differences, but also because Ganong uses Canadian accounting principles and Nestlé uses international accounting principles. Consider the following excerpt from the notes to Nestlé's financial statements:

> NESTLÉ S.A.
> Notes to the Financial Statements (partial)
> December 31, 2008
>
> **Nestlé**
> Good Food, Good Life
>
> **1. Accounting policies**
>
> **Accounting convention and accounting standards**
>
> The Consolidated Financial Statements comply with International Financial Reporting Standards (IFRS) issued by the International Accounting Standards Board (IASB) and with the Interpretations issued by the International Financial Reporting Interpretations Committee (IFRIC).
>
> The consolidated accounts have been prepared on an accruals basis and under the historical cost convention, unless stated otherwise.

Instructions

(a) Discuss the implications that Nestlé's (1) larger size with a more diversified product line, and (2) use of international financial reporting standards might have (positively or negatively) on your ability to compare Ganong with Nestlé.

(b) Ganong is a private corporation. Generally, Canadian private corporations will have the option of reporting under Canadian GAAP for Private Enterprises or reporting under IFRS starting January 1, 2011. What may be the benefits to Ganong of reporting under Canadian GAAP for Private Enterprises? What may be the benefits to Ganong of reporting under IFRS?

Critical Thinking

Collaborative Learning Activity

Note to instructor: Additional instructions and material for this group activity can be found on the Instructor Resource Site.

BYP11–3 Recognition and Measurement elements are major components of the conceptual framework of accounting. In this group activity, you will apply your knowledge by choosing the assumption, constraint, or recognition and measurement elements that applies in a situation and then explain your choice to your classmates.

Instructions

(a) Your instructor will divide the class into groups.

(b) Look around the classroom at the signs taped on the wall by your instructor. After reviewing the accounting situation presented by your instructor, choose one representative from your group to move to the sign that applies. Once each representative from each group has chosen a place, discuss with those in your group why you believe your choice is correct. The instructor will randomly select a student in each group to explain to everyone in the class why the members of the group selected their position. You may move to another sign if you are convinced by another group's explanation.

(c) Repeat the above activity for each situation presented by the instructor.

(d) You may be asked by your instructor to write a short quiz on this topic.

Communication Activity

BYP11–4 Junk R Us (Junk) is a wholesale distributor of goods. Junk purchases goods that are not selling from manufacturers and other wholesalers and sells them to discount retail outlets. You are a professional accountant and are preparing Junk's financial statements for the year ended September 30, 2010. The company had $110,000 of mini-disc players in inventory that were not selling. Junk has not had an order for mini-disc players for over a year. The president is reluctant to write off the inventory so the president signed an agreement with Cheap But Good, a retailer, to sell the mini-disc players to it for $150,000, with the understanding that Cheap But Good could return any mini-disc players not sold by December 31, 2010, to Junk and that Cheap But Good was not required to pay for any of the mini-disc players it sold to customers until December 31, 2010. The mini-disc players were shipped to Cheap But Good on September 29, 2010.

WILEY PLUS

Writing Handbook

Instructions

Write a memo to the president of Junk R Us answering the following questions:

(a) When should revenue be recognized on the mini-disc players sold to Cheap But Good? Explain.

(b) How should the mini-disc players be reported in Junk R Us's financial statements for the year ended September 30, 2010? Explain.

Ethics Case

BYP11–5 When the IASB and ACSB issue new accounting recommendations, the required implementation date (the date when a company has to start applying the recommendations) is usually 12 months or more after the date of publication. For example, in November 2009, the IASB issued new recommendations for classifying and reporting investments: companies are required to implement the new recommendations for fiscal years starting January 1, 2013. This allows companies some time to change their accounting procedures. Nevertheless, early implementation is usually encouraged for those who are able to do so, because new rules are intended to provide better representation of the company's financial performance and position.

WILEY PLUS

Ethics in Accounting

Carol DesChenes, an accountant at Grocery Online, discusses with her vice-president of finance the need for early implementation of a recently issued recommendation. She says it will result in a much more faithful representation of the company's financial position. When the vice-president of finance determines that early implementation will have a negative impact on the profits reported for the year, he strongly discourages Carol from implementing the recommendation until it is required.

Instructions

(a) Who are the stakeholders in this situation?

(b) What, if any, are the ethical considerations in this situation?

(c) What could Carol gain by supporting early implementation? Who might be affected by the decision against early implementation?

"All About You" Activity

BYP11–6 In the "All About You" feature, you learned about Registered Education Savings Plans (RESPs) and that the fair value of the RESP may be the most relevant information for some decisions and that cost may be the most relevant for other purposes.

To apply this concept further, assume that you are applying for a car loan. The loan application requires that you prepare two reports: (1) a projected cash budget and (2) information about your assets and liabilities. The information in the loan application will be used to determine if the bank manager will approve the loan or not.

Instructions

(a) Why would a bank manager ask you to complete a projected cash budget and provide information about your assets and liabilities in order to decide whether or not to approve your loan? What is the bank manager trying to determine about you?

(b) Recall from the chapter that there are different measurement bases used for different decisions. Two measurement bases we learned about in the chapter are cost (historical value), and fair value. Another measurement basis that is useful for some decisions is future replacement cost. For each item listed below, indicate (1) which of the two reports to the bank the item would be included in; (2) the measurement basis (cost, fair value, or future replacement cost) that is relevant to the bank manager's decision to approve or not approve your loan; and (3) the rationale for your specific choice of measurement basis.

1. Rent
2. Groceries
3. Cash in savings account
4. Tuition fees
5. RESP—equity fund
6. Textbooks
7. Clothes
8. Student loan
9. Summer earnings
10. Two-year-old mountain bike
11. Three-year-old furniture

ANSWERS TO CHAPTER QUESTIONS

Answers to Accounting in Action Insight Questions

Business Insight, p. 619

Q: How did Nortel justify using the going concern assumption when it was so uncertain that the company would continue operating?

A: Nortel used the going concern assumption because it was in the process of developing a plan to restructure its operations. It expected that the company would continue to operate in the foreseeable future.

Across the Organization, p. 631

Q: What is the manager of the shipping department's role in making sure revenue is recognized in the appropriate period?

A: The manager of the shipping department should ensure that the appropriate documentation is prepared for goods shipped and that it is sent to the accounting department. When the goods are shipped to the customer, the shipping department can prepare a shipping document that indicates what was shipped, the shipment date, and the terms of the shipping. A copy of the shipping document will be forwarded to the accounting department. The accounting department can review the shipping documents to determine what revenue should be recognized and when.

All About You, p. 633

Q: If you were preparing your personal financial report, what information about your RESP would be relevant: the cost of the RESP contributions or the fair value of the RESP?

A: The answer to the question depends on what the information is being used for. In the years that your parents were contributing to the RESP, the cost of the contributions may be the most relevant if they were deciding how much they could afford to contribute to the plan, and keeping track of how much they needed to contribute to collect the full Canada Education Savings Grant. Now that you have started your post-secondary education, the fair value of the RESP is probably more relevant because that is the amount that is available for you to use to pay for your education.

Answer to Forzani Review It Question 4, p. 634

Note 2 (h) Significant Accounting Policies, Revenue Recognition, states: "Revenue includes sales to customers through corporate stores operated by the Company and sales to, and service fees from, franchise stores and others. Sales to customers through corporate stores operated by the Company are recognized at the point of sale, net of an estimated allowance for sales returns. Sales of merchandise to franchise stores and others are recognized at the time of shipment. Royalties and administration fees are recognized when earned, in accordance with the terms of the franchise/license agreements."

Answers to Self-Study Questions

1. c 2. a 3. b 4. c 5. b 6. c 7. c 8. c 9. a 10. a

Remember to go back to the beginning of the chapter to check off your completed work!

←

The Forzani Group Ltd.

In this appendix we illustrate current financial reporting with a comprehensive set of corporate financial statements that are prepared in accordance with generally accepted accounting principles. We are grateful for permission to use the actual financial statements of The Forzani Group Ltd.—Canada's largest sporting goods retailer.

Forzani's financial statement package features a balance sheet, statement of operations (or income statement as we know it), statements of retained earnings, comprehensive earnings and accumulated other comprehensive earnings (loss), cash flow statement, and notes to the financial statements. The financial statements are preceded by two reports: a statement of management's responsibilities for financial reporting and the auditors' report.

We encourage students to use these financial statements in conjunction with relevant material in the textbook. As well, these statements can be used to solve the Review It questions in the Before You Go On section within the chapter and the Financial Reporting Problem in the Broadening Your Perspective section of the end-of-chapter material.

Annual reports, including the financial statements, are reviewed in detail on the companion website to this textbook.

Management's Responsibilities For Financial Reporting

The Annual Report, including the consolidated financial statements, is the responsibility of the management of the Company. The consolidated financial statements were prepared by management in accordance with generally accepted accounting principles. The significant accounting policies used are described in Note 2 to the consolidated financial statements. The integrity of the information presented in the financial statements, including estimates and judgments relating to matters not concluded by year-end, is the responsibility of management. Financial information presented elsewhere in this Annual Report has been prepared by management and is consistent with the information in the consolidated financial statements.

Management is responsible for the development and maintenance of systems of internal accounting and administrative controls. Such systems are designed to provide reasonable assurance that the financial information is accurate, relevant and reliable, and that the Company's assets are appropriately accounted for and adequately safeguarded (refer also to page 55 under "internal control over financial reporting"). The Board of Directors is responsible for ensuring that management fulfils its responsibilities for final approval of the annual consolidated financial statements. The Board appoints an Audit Committee consisting of three directors, none of whom is an officer or employee of the Company or its subsidiaries. The Audit Committee meets at least four times each year to discharge its responsibilities under a written mandate from the Board of Directors. The Audit Committee meets with management and with the independent auditors to satisfy itself that they are properly discharging their responsibilities, reviews the consolidated financial statements and the Auditors' Report, and examines other auditing, accounting and financial reporting matters. The consolidated financial statements have been reviewed by the Audit Committee and approved by the Board of Directors of The Forzani Group Ltd. The consolidated financial statements have been examined by the shareholders' auditors, Ernst & Young, LLP, Chartered Accountants. The Auditors' Report outlines the nature of their examination and their opinion on the consolidated financial statements of the Company. The independent auditors have full and unrestricted access to the Audit Committee, with and without management present.

Robert Sartor
Chief Executive Officer

Micheal R. Lambert, CA
Chief Financial Officer

Auditor's Report

To the Shareholders of
The Forzani Group Ltd.

We have audited the consolidated balance sheets of The Forzani Group Ltd. as at February 1, 2009 and February 3, 2008 and the consolidated statements of operations, retained earnings, comprehensive earnings, accumulated other comprehensive earnings (loss) and cash flows for the 52 week period ended February 1, 2009 and the 53 week period ended February 3, 2008. These financial statements are the responsibility of the Company's management. Our responsibility is to express an opinion on these financial statements based on our audits.

We conducted our audits in accordance with Canadian generally accepted auditing standards. Those standards require that we plan and perform an audit to obtain reasonable assurance whether the financial statements are free of material misstatement. An audit includes examining, on a test basis, evidence supporting the amounts and disclosures in the financial statements. An audit also includes assessing the accounting principles used and significant estimates made by management, as well as evaluating the overall financial statement presentation.

In our opinion, these consolidated financial statements present fairly, in all material respects, the financial position of the Company as at February 1, 2009 and February 3, 2008 and the results of its operations and its cash flows for the 52 week period ended February 1, 2009 and the 53 week period ended February 3, 2008 in accordance with Canadian generally accepted accounting principles.

Ernst & Young LLP

Calgary, Canada
April 7, 2009

Ernst & Young LLP
Chartered Accountants

The Forzani Group Ltd.
Consolidated Balance Sheets
(in thousands)

As at		February 1, 2009		February 3, 2008
ASSETS				
Current				
Cash	$	3,474	$	47,484
Accounts receivable		84,455		75,506
Inventory (Note 3)		291,497		319,445
Prepaid expenses (Note 4)		2,827		14,501
		382,253		456,936
Capital assets (Note 5)		196,765		188,621
Goodwill and other intangibles (Note 6)		91,481		89,335
Other assets (Note 7)		9,280		3,863
Future income tax asset (Note 12)		9,681		16,209
	$	689,460	$	754,964
LIABILITIES				
Current				
Indebtedness under revolving credit facility (Note 8)	$	17,130	$	-
Accounts payable and accrued liabilities		277,820		279,910
Current portion of long-term debt (Note 8)		7,501		51,863
		302,451		331,773
Long-term debt (Note 8)		126		6,586
Deferred lease inducements		47,811		55,089
Deferred rent liability		5,893		6,033
		356,281		399,481
SHAREHOLDERS' EQUITY				
Share capital (Note 11)		147,161		157,105
Contributed surplus		6,401		7,210
Accumulated other comprehensive earnings (loss)		863		(8)
Retained earnings		178,754		191,176
		333,179		355,483
	$	689,460	$	754,964

See accompanying notes to the consolidated financial statements
Approved on behalf of the Board:

Roman Doroniuk, CA

John M. Forzani

The Forzani Group Ltd.
Consolidated Statements of Operations
(in thousands, except per share data)

	For the 52 weeks ended February 1, 2009	For the 53 weeks ended February 3, 2008
Revenue		
Retail	$ 994,043	$ 969,256
Wholesale	352,715	361,753
	1,346,758	1,331,009
Cost of sales	863,239	852,608
Gross margin	483,519	478,401
Operating and administrative expenses		
Store operating	277,089	251,630
General and administrative	109,328	103,801
	386,417	355,431
Operating earnings before undernoted items	97,102	122,970
Amortization of capital assets	47,613	44,468
Interest	5,175	5,797
Loss on sale of investment (Note 21)	-	864
	52,788	51,129
Earnings before income taxes	44,314	71,841
Income tax expense (recovery) (Note 12)		
Current	6,273	27,439
Future	8,716	(3,049)
	14,989	24,390
Net earnings	$ 29,325	$ 47,451
Earnings per share (Note 11(c))	$ 0.94	$ 1.40
Diluted earnings per share (Note 11(c))	$ 0.93	$ 1.39

See accompanying notes to the consolidated financial statements

59

The Forzani Group Ltd.
Consolidated Statements of Retained Earnings, Comprehensive Earnings and Accumulated Other Comprehensive Earnings (Loss)
(in thousands)

Consolidated Statements of Retained Earnings	For the 52 weeks ended February 1, 2009	For the 53 weeks ended February 3, 2008
Retained earnings, beginning of period	$ 191,176	$ 171,095
Adjustment arising from adoption of new accounting policy (Note 2)	(1,357)	-
Adjusted Retained earnings, beginning of period	$ 189,819	$ 171,095
Net earnings	29,325	47,451
Dividends paid (Note 11(f))	(9,327)	(2,472)
Adjustment arising from shares purchased under a normal course issuer bid (Note 11(e))	(31,063)	(24,898)
Retained earnings, end of period	$ 178,754	$ 191,176

Consolidated Statements of Comprehensive Earnings

	For the 52 weeks ended February 1, 2009	For the 53 weeks ended February 3, 2008
Net earnings	$ 29,325	$ 47,451
Other comprehensive earnings (loss):		
Unrealized foreign currency gains and (losses) on cash flow hedges	1,340	(138)
Tax impact	(469)	51
Other comprehensive earnings (loss)	871	(87)
Comprehensive earnings	$ 30,196	$ 47,364

Consolidated Statements of Accumulated Other Comprehensive Earnings (Loss) ("AOCE")

	For the 52 weeks ended February 1, 2009	For the 53 weeks ended February 3, 2008
Accumulated other comprehensive earnings (loss), beginning of period	$ (8)	$ -
Transitional adjustment upon adoption of new financial instruments standard	-	79
Accumulated other comprehensive earnings (loss), beginning of period, as restated	(8)	79
Other comprehensive earnings (loss)	871	(87)
Accumulated other comprehensive earnings (loss), end of period	$ 863	$ (8)

See accompanying notes to the consolidated financial statements

60

The Forzani Group Ltd.
Consolidated Statements of Cash Flows
(in thousands)

	For the 52 weeks ended February 1, 2009	For the 53 weeks ended February 3, 2008
Cash provided by (used in) operating activities		
Net earnings	$ 29,325	$ 47,451
Items not involving cash:		
Amortization of capital assets	47,613	44,468
Amortization of deferred finance charges	377	738
Amortization of deferred lease inducements	(11,500)	(11,109)
Rent expense (Note 9)	152	524
Stock-based compensation (Note 11(d))	(174)	2,756
Future income tax expense (recovery)	8,716	(3,049)
Loss on sale of investment (Note 21)	-	864
Unrealized loss on ineffective hedges	321	44
	74,830	82,687
Changes in non-cash elements of working capital related to operating activities (Note 9)	20,913	23,737
	95,743	106,424
Cash provided by (used in) financing activities		
Net proceeds from issuance of share capital (Note 11(b))	2,384	13,273
Share repurchase via normal course issuer bid (Note 11(e))	(44,027)	(33,331)
Long-term debt	(51,199)	(19,198)
Revolving credit facility	17,130	-
Lease inducements received	4,221	7,648
Dividends paid (Note 11(f))	(9,327)	(2,472)
	(80,818)	(34,080)
Changes in non-cash elements of financing activities (Note 9)	(1,121)	(1,698)
	(81,939)	(35,778)
Cash provided by (used in) investing activities		
Capital assets	(52,139)	(40,660)
Other assets	(2,998)	2,151
Acquisition of wholly-owned subsidiaries (Note 17)	-	(8,774)
	(55,137)	(47,283)
Changes in non-cash elements of investing activities (Note 9)	(2,677)	1,363
	(57,814)	(45,920)
Increase (decrease) in cash	(44,010)	24,726
Net cash position, opening	47,484	22,758
Net cash position, closing	$ 3,474	$ 47,484

See accompanying notes to the consolidated financial statements

The Forzani Group Ltd.
Notes to Consolidated Financial Statements (tabular amounts in thousands)

1.   Nature of Operations

The Forzani Group Ltd. ("FGL" or "the Company") is Canada's largest national retailer of sporting goods, offering a comprehensive assortment of brand-name and private-brand products, operating stores from coast to coast, under the following corporate and franchise banners: Sport Chek, Coast Mountain Sports, Sport Mart, National Sports, Athletes World, Sports Experts, Intersport, Econosports, Atmosphere, RnR, Tech Shop, Pegasus, Nevada Bob's Golf, Hockey Experts, S3 and The Fitness Source.

2.   Significant Accounting Policies

The preparation of the financial statements in conformity with Canadian generally accepted accounting principles ("GAAP") requires management to make estimates and assumptions that affect the reported amounts of assets and liabilities and disclosures of contingent assets and liabilities at the date of the consolidated financial statements and the reported amounts of revenue and expenses during the reporting period. Actual results could differ materially from these estimates. Estimates are used when accounting for items such as employee benefits, product warranties, inventory provisions, amortization and assessment for impairment, uncollectible receivables and the liability for the Company's loyalty program. The financial statements have, in management's opinion, been prepared within reasonable limits of materiality and within the framework of the accounting policies summarized below:

(a)   Organization

The consolidated financial statements include the accounts of The Forzani Group Ltd. and its subsidiaries, all of which are wholly owned.

(b)   Inventory valuation

Inventory is valued at the lower of laid-down cost and net realizable value. Laid-down cost is determined using the weighted average cost method and includes invoice cost, duties, freight, and distribution costs. Net realizable value is defined as the expected selling price.

Volume rebates and other supplier discounts are included in income when earned. Volume rebates are accounted for as a reduction of the cost of the related inventory and are "earned" when the inventory is sold. All other rebates and discounts are "earned" when the related expense is incurred.

(c)   Capital assets

Capital assets are recorded at cost and are amortized using the following methods and rates:

Asset	Basis	Rate
Building	Declining balance	4%
Building and leased land	Straight-line	Lesser of the term of the lease or estimated useful life, not exceeding 20 years
Furniture, fixtures, equipment, software and automotive	Straight-line	3-8 years
Leasehold improvements	Straight-line	Lesser of the term of the lease and estimated useful life, not exceeding 10 years

The carrying value of long-lived assets is reviewed at least annually or whenever events indicate a potential impairment has occurred. An impairment loss is recorded if and when a long-lived asset's carrying value exceeds the sum of the undiscounted cash flows expected from its use and eventual disposition. The impairment loss is measured as the amount by which the carrying value exceeds its fair value.

(d)   Variable interest entities

Variable interest entities ("VIE") are consolidated by the Company if and when the Company is the primary beneficiary of the VIE, as described in Canadian Institute of Chartered Accountants ("CICA") Accounting Guideline 15, *Consolidation of Variable Interest Entities*.

(e)   Goodwill and other intangibles

Goodwill represents the excess of the purchase price of entities acquired over the fair market value of the identifiable net assets acquired.

Goodwill and other intangible assets with indefinite lives are not amortized, but tested for impairment at year end or more frequently if events or changes in circumstances indicate the asset might be impaired and, if required, asset values reduced accordingly. The method used to assess impairment is a review of the fair value of the asset based on expected present value of future cash flows.

Non-competition agreement costs are amortized, on a straight-line basis, over the life of the agreements, not exceeding five years.

(f)   Other assets

Other assets include system and interactive development costs, long-term receivables and other deferred charges.

System development costs relate to the implementation of computer software. Upon activation, costs are amortized over the estimated useful lives of the systems (3 – 8 years).

Long-term receivables are carried at cost less a valuation allowance, if applicable.

(g)   Deferred lease inducements and property leases

Deferred lease inducements represent cash and non-cash benefits that the Company has received from landlords pursuant to store lease agreements. These lease inducements are amortized against rent expense over the term of the lease.

The Company capitalizes any rent expense during a related fixturing period as a cost of leasehold improvements. Such expense is recognized on a straight-line basis over the life of the lease.

(h)   Revenue recognition

Revenue includes sales to customers through corporate stores operated by the Company and sales to, and service fees from, franchise stores and others. Sales to customers through corporate stores operated by the Company are recognized at the point of sale, net of an estimated allowance for sales returns. Sales of merchandise to franchise stores and others are recognized at the time of shipment. Royalties and administration fees are recognized when earned, in accordance with the terms of the franchise/license agreements.

(i)   Store opening expenses

Operating costs incurred prior to the opening of new stores, other than rent incurred during the fixturing period, are expensed as incurred.

(j)   Fiscal year

The Company's fiscal year follows a retail calendar. The fiscal years for the consolidated financial statements presented are the 52-week period ended February 1, 2009 and the 53-week period ended February 3, 2008.

(k)   Foreign currency translation

Foreign currency accounts are translated to Canadian dollars. At the transaction date, each asset, liability, revenue or expense is translated into Canadian dollars using the exchange rate in effect at that date. At the year-end date, monetary assets and liabilities are translated into Canadian dollars using the exchange rate in effect at that date, and the resulting foreign exchange gains and losses are included in income.

(l)   Stock-based compensation

The Company accounts for stock-based compensation using the fair value method. The fair value of the options granted are estimated at the date of grant using the Black-Scholes valuation model and recognized as an expense over the option-vesting period.

(m)   Income taxes

The Company follows the liability method under which future income tax assets and liabilities are determined based on differences between the financial reporting and tax basis of assets and liabilities, measured using tax rates substantively enacted at the balance sheet dates.

Changes in tax rates are reflected in the consolidated statements of operations in the period in which they are substantively enacted.

(n)   Asset retirement obligations

The Company recognizes asset retirement obligations in the period in which a reasonable estimate of the fair value can be determined. The liability is measured at fair value and is adjusted to its present value in subsequent periods through accretion expense. The associated asset retirement costs are capitalized as part of the carrying value of the related asset and amortized over its useful life.

(o)   Financial Instruments - Recognition and Measurement – CICA Section 3855

Section 3855 establishes standards for recognizing and measuring financial assets, financial liabilities, and non-financial derivatives. It requires that financial assets and financial liabilities, including derivatives, be recognized on the consolidated balance sheet when the Company becomes a party to the contractual provisions of the financial instrument or non-financial derivative contract. It also requires that all financial assets and liabilities are to be classified as either a) Held for Trading, b) Available for Sale, c) Held to Maturity, d) Loans/ Receivables, or e) Other Financial Liabilities, depending on the Company's stated intention and/or historical practice. Under this standard, all financial instruments are required to be measured at fair value (or amortized cost) upon initial recognition, except for certain related party transactions. Treatment of the fair value of each financial instrument is determined by its classification.

In accordance with the standard, the Company's financial assets and liabilities are generally classified as follows:

Asset/Liability	Category	Measurement
Assets		
Cash	Held for trading	Fair value
Accounts receivable	Loans/Receivables	Amortized cost
Long-term receivables	Loans/Receivables	Amortized cost
Liabilities		
Indebtedness under revolving credit facility	Other financial liabilities	Amortized cost
Accounts payable and accrued liabilities	Other financial liabilities	Amortized cost
Long-term debt	Other financial liabilities	Amortized cost

Foreign currency options and forward exchange contracts, which are included in accounts receivable, have been classified as held for trading and measured at fair value. Fair value is determined by reference to published price quotations.

New Accounting Policies

Effective February 4, 2008 the Company adopted the following accounting standards issued by the CICA:

Capital Disclosures – CICA Section 1535

The standard establishes disclosure requirements about an entity's capital and how it is managed. The new standard requires disclosure of an entity's objectives, policies and processes for managing capital, quantitative data about what an entity regards as capital and whether the entity has complied with any externally imposed capital requirements and the consequences of any non-compliance. Additional disclosure required as a result of the adoption of this standard is contained in Note 10.

Financial Instruments - Disclosures (CICA Section 3862) and Financial Instruments – Presentation (CICA Section 3863)

The standards replace Section 3861, *Financial Instruments - Disclosure and Presentation*, revising and enhancing disclosure requirements while carrying forward, substantially unchanged, its presentation requirements. These new sections place increased emphasis on disclosure about the nature and extent of risks arising from financial instruments and how the entity manages those risks. Additional disclosure required as a result of the adoption of this standard is contained in Note 16.

Inventory - CICA Section 3031

The standard introduces significant changes to the measurement and disclosure of inventories, including the allocation of overhead based on normal capacity, the use of the specific cost method for inventories that are not ordinarily interchangeable for goods and services produced for specific purposes, and the reversal of previous write-downs to net realizable value when there is a subsequent increase in the value of inventories. Inventory policies, carrying amounts, amounts recognized as an expense, write-downs and the reversals of write-downs are required to be disclosed.

Under the prior guidance, the Company included storage costs in the cost of inventory. This is no longer permitted, resulting in a $1,357,000 adjustment to opening inventory for the year and a corresponding adjustment to opening retained earnings. Prior periods have not been restated.

Future Accounting Pronouncements

The following are new standards that have been issued by the CICA that are not yet effective but may impact the Company:

Goodwill and Intangible Assets

In November 2007, the CICA issued Section 3064, *Goodwill and Intangible Assets* ("Section 3064"). Section 3064, which replaces Section 3062, *Goodwill and Intangible Assets*, and Section 3450, *Research and Development Costs*, establishes standards for the recognition, measurement and disclosure of goodwill and intangible assets. This standard is effective for the Company for interim and annual consolidated financial statements relating to fiscal years beginning on or after October 1, 2008. The Company is currently assessing the impact that this section will have on its financial position and results of operations. Any adjustment required will be recorded through opening retained earnings in the first quarter of the Company's fiscal 2010 year.

Business Combinations and Consolidated Financial Statements – CICA Section 1582 and 1601

As of January 30, 2011, the Company will be required to adopt new CICA standards with respect to business combinations and consolidated financial statements. The new CICA Section 1582 will replace CICA Section 1581 and is meant to align the accounting for business combinations under Canadian GAAP with the requirements of International Financial Reporting Standards. Likewise, CICA Section 1601 will replace CICA Section 1600 with respect to consolidated financial statements.

Under sections 1582 and 1601 the definition of a business is expanded and is described as an integrated set of activities and assets that are capable of being managed to provide a return to investors or economic benefits to owners, members or participants. In addition, acquisition costs are not part of the purchase consideration and are to be expensed when incurred. With the adoption of these standards, the Company expects that all acquisition related costs will be expensed through the statement of operations. These standards will be applied on a prospective basis.

International Financial Reporting Standards ("IFRS")

In February 2008, the CICA announced that GAAP for publicly accountable enterprises will be replaced by IFRS for fiscal years beginning on or after January 1, 2011. Companies will be required to provide IFRS comparative information for the previous fiscal year. Accordingly, the conversion from GAAP to IFRS will be applicable to the Company's reporting for the first quarter of fiscal 2012 for which the current and comparative information will be prepared under IFRS.

The Company is in the process of completing the scoping and assessment phase of the transition. This phase identified a number of topics possibly impacting either the Company's financial results and/or the Company's effort necessary to changeover to IFRS. This phase is ongoing, as the Company will continue to assess future International Accounting Standards Board ("IASB") pronouncements for transitional impacts.

The Company has started the key elements phase of implementation which includes the identification, evaluation and selection of accounting policies necessary for the Company to transition to IFRS. Consideration of impacts on operational elements such as information technology and internal control over financial reporting are integral to this process.

Although the Company's impact assessment activities are underway and progressing according to plan, continued progress is necessary before the Company can prudently increase the specificity of the disclosure of pre- and post-IFRS changeover accounting policy differences.

3.   Inventory

Included within cost of sales for the period ended February 1, 2009, are normal course charges to inventory made throughout the year, of $12,265,000 (2008 – $12,514,000). These charges include the disposal of obsolete and damaged product, inventory shrinkage and permanent markdowns to net realizable values.

4.   Prepaid Expenses

	2009	2008
Prepaid rent	$ -	$ 10,200
Advertising	1,348	1,720
Service contracts	785	773
Other	694	1,808
	$ 2,827	$ 14,501

5.   Capital Assets

	2009			2008		
	Cost	Accumulated Amortization	Net Book Value	Cost	Accumulated Amortization	Net Book Value
Land	$ 3,173	$ -	$ 3,173	$ 3,173	$ -	$ 3,173
Buildings	20,928	5,382	15,546	20,928	4,680	16,248
Building on leased land	4,583	3,114	1,469	4,583	2,852	1,731
Furniture, fixtures, equipment, software and automotive	243,564	173,611	69,953	217,365	149,386	67,979
Leasehold improvements	260,030	167,435	92,595	239,439	146,003	93,436
Construction in progress	14,029	-	14,029	6,054	-	6,054
	$ 546,307	$ 349,542	$ 196,765	$ 491,542	$ 302,921	$ 188,621

6.   Goodwill and Other Intangibles

	2009			2008		
	Cost	Accumulated Amortization	Net Book Value	Cost	Accumulated Amortization	Net Book Value
Goodwill	$ 61,162	$ 1,178	$ 59,984	$ 61,162	$ 1,178	$ 59,984
Trademarks/Trade names	32,359	934	31,425	30,140	934	29,206
Non-competition agreements	4,000	3,928	72	4,000	3,855	145
	$ 97,521	$ 6,040	$ 91,481	$ 95,302	$ 5,967	$ 89,335

7.   Other Assets

	2009			2008		
	Cost	Accumulated Amortization	Net Book Value	Cost	Accumulated Amortization	Net Book Value
Interactive development	$ 2,649	$ 2,649	$ -	$ 2,649	$ 2,649	$ -
System development	1,641	1,641	-	1,641	1,641	-
Other deferred charges	6,967	3,153	3,814	4,176	2,094	2,082
	$ 11,257	$ 7,443	$ 3,814	$ 8,466	$ 6,384	$ 2,082

	2009	2008
Depreciable other assets net book value (see above)	$ 3,814	$ 2,082
Deferred advertising charges	2,566	-
Long-term receivables (at interest rates of prime plus 1% and expiring between September 2010 and July 2011)	2,900	1,781
	$ 9,280	$ 3,863

8. Long Term Debt

	2009	2008
G.E. term loan	$ -	$ 49,744
Mortgage with monthly payments of $58,000 and an interest rate of 6.2% compounded semi-annually, secured by land and building, expiring October 2009.	5,458	5,782
Vendor take-back, unsecured with implied interest rate of 4.8% and payments due March 2009	2,043	2,792
Asset retirement obligation	126	113
Other	-	18
	7,627	58,449
Less current portion	7,501	51,863
	$ 126	$ 6,586

Principal payments on the above, due in the next five years, are as follows:

2010	$ 7,501
2011	$ -
2012	$ -
2013	$ -
2014	$ -

Effective June 11, 2008, the Company renewed its credit agreement with GE Canada Finance Holding Company. The renewed agreement increased the $235 million credit facility, which was comprised of a $185 million revolving loan and a $50 million term loan, to a $250 million facility, comprised entirely of a revolving loan and having a June 11, 2013 expiry date. Under the terms of the credit agreement, the interest rate payable on the revolving loan is based on the Company's financial performance as determined by its interest coverage ratio. As at February 1, 2009, the interest rate paid was bank prime less 0.45%. The facility is collateralized by general security agreements against all existing and future acquired assets of the Company. As at February 1, 2009, the Company is in compliance with its financial covenant.

Based on estimated interest rates currently available to the Company for mortgages with similar terms and maturities, the fair value of the mortgage at February 1, 2009 amounted to approximately $6,119,000 (2008 - $5,274,000). Interest costs incurred for the 52-week period ended February 1, 2009 on long-term debt amounted to $851,000 (2008 - $3,178,000). The fair value of the other long-term debt components above approximates book value given their short terms to maturity and floating interest rates.

9.   Supplementary Cash Flow Information

	For the 52 weeks ended February 1, 2009	For the 53 weeks ended February 3, 2008
Rent expense		
Straight-line rent expense	$ (140)	$ 228
Non-cash free rent	292	296
	$ 152	$ 524
Change in non-cash elements of working capital related to operating activities		
Accounts receivable	$ (11,137)	$ (9,963)
Inventory	21,753	13,772
Prepaid expenses	11,674	(11,813)
Financial Instruments	764	-
Accounts payable and accrued liabilities	(2,141)	31,741
	$ 20,913	$ 23,737
Change in non-cash elements of financing activities		
Lease inducements	$ (907)	$ (1,115)
Long-term debt	-	(568)
Change in fair value of cash flow hedge	871	-
Net financial assets	(1,085)	(15)
	$ (1,121)	$ (1,698)
Change in non-cash elements of investing activities		
Capital assets	$ 668	$ 795
Other assets	(3,345)	568
	$ (2,677)	$ 1,363
Net cash interest paid	$ 4,648	$ 5,017
Net cash taxes paid	$ 26,109	$ 29,509

10. Capital Disclosures

The Company's objectives in managing capital are to ensure sufficient liquidity to pursue its strategy of organic growth combined with strategic acquisitions and to deploy capital to provide an appropriate return on investment to its shareholders. The Company's overall strategy remains unchanged from the prior year. The capital structure of the Company consists of cash, short and long-term debt and shareholders' equity comprised of retained earnings and share capital. The Company manages its capital structure and makes adjustments to it in light of economic conditions and the risk characteristics of the underlying assets. The Company's primary uses of capital are to finance non-cash working capital requirements, capital expenditures and acquisitions, which are currently funded from its internally-generated cash flows. The Company is in compliance with all externally imposed capital requirements, including its debt covenant.

11. Share Capital

(a) *Authorized*

An unlimited number of Class A shares (no par value)

An unlimited number of Preferred shares, issuable in series

(b) *Issued*

Class A shares	Number	Consideration
Balance, January 28, 2007	33,696	$ 148,424
Shares issued upon employees exercising stock options	1,077	13,273
Stock-based compensation related to options exercised	-	3,841
Shares repurchased via normal course issuer bid	(1,803)	(8,433)
Balance, February 3, 2008	32,970	157,105
Shares issued upon employees exercising stock options	192	2,384
Stock-based compensation related to options exercised	-	636
Shares repurchased via normal course issuer bid	(2,694)	(12,964)
Balance, February 1, 2009	30,468	$ 147,161

(c) *Earnings Per Share*

	2009	2008
Basic	$ 0.94	$ 1.40
Diluted	$ 0.93	$ 1.39

The Company uses the treasury stock method to calculate diluted earnings per share. Under the treasury stock method, the numerator remains unchanged from the basic earnings per share calculation, as the assumed exercise of the Company's stock options does not result in an adjustment to earnings. Diluted calculations assume that options under the stock option plan have been exercised at the later of the beginning of the year or date of issuance, and that the funds derived therefrom would have been used to repurchase shares at the average market value of the Company's stock, 2009 – $13.11 (2008 - $19.91). Anti-dilutive options, 2009 – 1,264,000 (2008 – 26,000) are excluded from the effect of dilutive securities. The reconciliation of the denominator in calculating diluted earnings per share is as follows:

	2009	2008
Weighted average number of Class A shares outstanding (basic)	31,298	33,787
Effect of dilutive options	67	370
Weighted average number of common shares outstanding (diluted)	31,365	34,157

(d)   Stock Option and Unit Plans

The Company has granted stock options to directors, officers and employees to purchase Class A shares at prices between $7.70 and $23.00 per share. These options expire on dates between February 2009 and June 2013.

The Company has three stock option plans. The first plan has the following general terms: options vest over a period ranging from 2 to 5 years and the maximum term of the options granted is 5 years. During the year, no options (2008 – Nil) were issued under this plan. The related stock-based compensation expense was $25,000 (2008 - $323,000).

The second plan has the following general terms: options vest over a period ranging from 2 to 5 years dependent on the Company achieving certain performance targets (in 2007 these targets were met thereby causing the options to become fully vested by the first quarter of fiscal 2008), and the maximum term of the options granted is 5 years. During the year, 120,000 (2008 – 200,000 options) were issued under this plan. The related stock-based compensation expense of $383,000 was recognized immediately (2008 - $1,886,000) as the Company met the targets in fiscal 2007.

The third plan, which forms part of a Long Term Incentive Plan ("LTIP"), has the following general terms: option grants are made annually and options vest over 3 years with a maximum term of 5 years. Under the terms of the plan, options issued carry a tandem share appreciation right ("TSAR") which allows holders to exercise vested options in either the traditional fashion, where shares are issued from treasury, or surrender their option in exchange for an amount of cash equaling the difference between the market price for a common share on the date of surrender and the strike price of the option. The final details of this plan were approved by the Company in the third quarter of fiscal 2008. During the year, as a result of the TSAR exercise history being predominantly for cash, the Company deemed the plan to be cash-settled and accounted for it as a liability-classified award with TSARs measured at their fair value on the date of issuance, and re-measured at each reporting period, until settlement. During the year ended February 1, 2009, 309,590 options (2008 – 388,710) were issued under this plan and a credit of $582,000 to stock-based compensation expense was recognized (2008 - $547,000 expensed).

The total number of shares authorized for option grants under all option plans is 3,406,622.

During the 52-weeks ended February 1, 2009, the following options were granted:

Options issued	Weighted average fair value per option	Weighted average risk-free rate	Weighted average expected option life	Weighted average expected volatility	Weighted average expected dividend yield
429,590	$2.99	2.93%	3.00	27.41%	2.01%

A summary of the status of the Company's stock option plans as of February 1, 2009 and February 3, 2008, and any changes during the period ending on those dates is presented below:

	2009		2008	
Stock Options	Options	Weighted Average Exercise Price	Options	Weighted Average Exercise Price
Outstanding, beginning of year	1,658	$15.04	2,157	$12.85
Granted	430	$15.85	589	$18.08
Exercised	(204)	$12.39	(1,077)	$12.33
Forfeited	(189)	$14.93	(11)	$13.32
Outstanding, end of year	1,695	$15.56	1,658	$15.04
Options exercisable at year end	1,174		1,254	

The following table summarizes information about stock options outstanding at February 1, 2009:

	Options Outstanding			Options Exercisable	
Range of Exercise Prices	Number Outstanding	Weighted Average Remaining Contractual Life	Weighted Average Exercise Price	Number of Shares Exercisable	Weighted Average Exercise Price
$7.70 - $15.98	769	1.80	$13.01	718	$13.33
$16.00 - $23.00	926	3.55	$17.57	456	$18.07
	1,695	2.76	$15.56	1,174	$15.17

The Company issues director stock units ("DSU"), restricted stock units ("RSU") and performance stock units ("PSU") from time to time. These units are accounted for as liability-classified awards and are measured at their intrinsic value on the date of issuance, and re-measured at each reporting period, until settlement.

During the year, 166,865 (2008 – 168,390) PSUs were issued and an expense of $1,710,000 (2008 – $2,428,000) was charged to compensation expense.

During the year, 46,622 (2008 – 49,520) RSUs were issued and an expense of $580,000 (2008 - $137,000) was charged to compensation expense.

During the year, 20,327 (2008 – 16,049) DSUs were issued and $630,000 (2008 - $154,000 expense) was credited to compensation expense due to a reduction in the fair value of units.

As at February 1, 2009, the Company has recorded a total amount payable for all units outstanding of $2,149,000 (2008 - $2,172,000) of which $1,346,000 (2008 - $1,976,000) relates to DSUs, paid when a director leaves the Board of Directors.

(e) *Normal Course Issuer Bid*

For the year ended February 1, 2009, 2,694,376 (2008 – 1,802,900) Class A shares were repurchased pursuant to the Company's Normal Course Issuer Bid for a total expenditure of $44,027,000 (2008 - $33,331,000) or $16.34 (2008 - $18.49) per share. The consideration in excess of the stated value of $31,063,000 (2008 – $24,898,000) was changed to retained earnings.

(f) *Dividends*

On April 7, 2009 the Company declared a dividend of $0.075 per Class A common share, payable on May 4, 2009 to shareholders of record on April 20, 2009. The Company's stated intention is to declare annual dividends of $0.30 per share, payable quarterly, subject to the Board of Directors discretion.

The Company has declared quarterly dividends of $0.075 per Class A common share, payable to shareholders of record as follows:

Date Declared	For Shareholders of Record Dated
December 7, 2007	January 21, 2008
April 9, 2008	April 21, 2008
June 10, 2008	July 21, 2008
September 2, 2008	October 20, 2008
December 12, 2008	January 19, 2008
April 7, 2009	April 20, 2009

All dividends paid by the Company are, pursuant to subsection 89 (14) of the Income Tax Act (Canada), designated as eligible dividends. An eligible dividend paid to a Canadian resident is entitled to the enhanced dividend tax credit.

12. Income Taxes

The components of the future income tax asset amounts as at February 1, 2009 and February 3, 2008 are as follows:

	2009	2008
Current assets	$ (1,286)	$ (2,401)
Capital and other assets	(10,885)	(14,957)
Tax benefit of share issuance and financing costs	87	167
Deferred lease inducements	14,198	16,863
Non-capital loss carry forward	3,156	13,345
Accruals and deferred liabilities	4,411	3,192
Future income tax asset	$ 9,681	$ 16,209

A reconciliation of income taxes, at the combined statutory federal and provincial tax rate to the actual income tax rate, is as follows:

	2009		2008	
Federal and provincial income taxes	$ 13,471	30.4%	$ 24,354	33.9%
Increase (decrease) resulting from:				
Non deductible expenses	615	1.4%	1,796	2.5%
Effect of substantively enacted tax rate changes	-	-	(2,155)	(3.0%)
Other, net	903	2.0%	395	0.5%
Provision for income taxes	$ 14,989	33.8%	$ 24,390	33.9%

The Company has non-capital losses available to be carried forward of $9,804,000 expiring in 2028.

For the period ending February 1, 2009, the Company has recorded a tax receivable balance of $11,125,000 (2008 - ($3,944,000)) which is included within accounts receivable.

13. Commitments

(a)   The Company is committed, at February 1, 2009, to minimum payments under long-term real property and data processing hardware and software equipment leases, for future years, as follows:

Year	Gross
2010	$ 87,523
2011	$ 77,283
2012	$ 65,083
2013	$ 52,753
2014	$ 40,403
Thereafter	$ 86,471

In addition, the Company may be obligated to pay percentage rent under certain of the leases.

(b)   As at February 1, 2009, the Company has open letters of credit for purchases of inventory of approximately
        $1,961,000 (2008 - $1,890,000).

14.   Employee Benefit Plans

The Company has a defined contribution plan and an employee profit sharing plan (replaces the previous deferred profit sharing plan).
Defined contributions are paid to employee retirement savings plans and are expensed when incurred.

Under the employee profit sharing plan, the Company creates a pool of funds to distribute to participating employees on a predetermined
basis. Distributions are tied to the value of the Company's common shares and the employees' achievement of individual financial and
operational targets. Payouts under the employee profit sharing plan are made annually. The deferred profit sharing plan contributions were
previously paid to a Trustee for the purchase of shares of the Company and then distributed to participating employees on a predetermined
basis, upon retirement from the Company. Contributions to both the employee profit sharing plan and previously to the deferred profit
sharing plan are recognized as an expense when incurred.

For the period ended February 1, 2009, the Company has expensed $1,090,000 (2008 - $1,095,000) to the defined contribution plan
and has accrued $504,000 for the employee profit sharing plan (2008 - $150,000).

15.   Contingencies and Guarantees

In the normal course of business, the Company enters into numerous agreements that may contain features that meet the Accounting
Guideline ("AcG") 14 definition of a guarantee. AcG-14 defines a guarantee to be a contract (including an indemnity) that contingently
requires the Company to make payments to the guaranteed party based on (i) failure of another party to perform under an obligating
agreement or (ii) failure of a third party to pay its indebtedness when due.

The Company has provided the following guarantees to third parties:

(a)   The Company has provided guarantees to franchisees' banks pursuant to which it has agreed to buy back inventory from
        the franchisee in the event that the bank realizes on the related security. The Company has provided securitization guarantees
        for certain franchisees to repay equity loans in the event of franchisee default. The terms of the guarantees range from less than
        a year to the lifetime of the particular underlying franchise agreement, with an average guarantee term of 4 years. Should a
        franchisee default on its bank loan, the Company would be required to purchase between 50% – 100%, with a weighted average
        of 65%, of the franchisee's inventory up to the value of the franchisee's bank indebtedness. As at February 1, 2009, the
        Company's maximum exposure is $43,707,000 (2008 - $37,174,000). Should the Company be required to purchase the
        inventory of a specific franchisee, it is expected that the full value of the inventory would be recovered. Historically, the Company
        has not had to repurchase significant inventory from franchisees pursuant to these guarantees. The Company has not recognized
        the guarantee in its consolidated financial statements.

(b) In the ordinary course of business, the Company has agreed to indemnify its lenders under its credit facilities against certain costs or losses resulting from changes in laws and regulations and from any legal action brought against the lenders related to the use, by the Company, of the loan proceeds, or to the lenders having extended credit thereunder. These indemnifications extend for the term of the credit facilities and do not provide any limit on the maximum potential liability. Historically, the Company has not made any indemnification payments under such agreements and no amount has been accrued in the consolidated financial statements with respect to these indemnification agreements.

(c) In the ordinary course of business, the Company has provided indemnification commitments to certain counterparties in matters such as real estate leasing transactions, securitization agreements, director and officer indemnification agreements and certain purchases of assets (not inventory in the normal course). These indemnification agreements generally require the Company to compensate the counterparties for costs or losses resulting from any legal action brought against the counterparties related to the actions of the Company or any of the obligors under any of the aforementioned matters or failure of the obligors under any of the aforementioned matters to fulfill contractual obligations thereunder. The terms of these indemnification agreements will vary based on the contract and generally do not provide any limit on the maximum potential liability. Historically, the Company has not made any payments under such indemnifications and no amount has been accrued in the consolidated financial statements with respect to these indemnification commitments.

(d) Claims and suits have been brought against the Company in the ordinary course of business. In the opinion of management, all such claims and suits are adequately covered by insurance, or if not so covered, the results are not expected to materially affect the Company's financial position.

16. Financial Instruments and Hedges

(a) **Fair Value of Financial Assets and Liabilities**

The following table details carrying values and fair values of financial assets and liabilities by financial instrument classification:

	As at February 1, 2009	
	Carrying Value	Fair Value
Loans and Receivables:		
Trade and accrued receivables	$ 84,455	$ 84,455
Long-term receivables	$ 2,900	$ 2,900
Other Financial Liabilities:		
Revolving credit facility	$ 17,130	$ 17,130
Trade payables and accrued liabilities	$ 277,820	$ 277,820
Current and long-term debt	$ 7,627	$ 8,288

The fair value of a financial instrument is the estimated amount that the Company would receive or pay to settle the financial assets and financial liabilities as at the reporting date. The fair values of cash, trade and accrued receivables, revolving credit facilities, trade payables and accrued liabilities, approximate their carrying values given their short-term maturities. The fair values of long-term receivables and long-term debt approximate their carrying values given the current market rates associated with these instruments. The fair value of the interest rates is determined based on current market rates and on information received from the Company's counterparties to these agreements.

b)   **Interest Income and Expense, and Gains or Losses by Class of Financial Asset and Financial Liability**

All interest income and expense, regardless of the class of financial asset or financial liability, is recorded in the consolidated statement of operations as interest.

All foreign exchange gains and losses, regardless of the class of financial asset or financial liability, are recorded in the consolidated statement of operations in cost of sales (realized) or general and administrative expense (unrealized).

c)   **Risks**

Exposure to credit risk and interest rate risk arises in the normal course of the Company's business. The Company does not currently enter into derivative financial instruments to reduce exposure to fluctuations in any credit or interest risks impacting the operations of the Company.

i. Credit risk

The Company is exposed to credit risk on its accounts receivable from franchisees. The accounts receivable are net of applicable allowances for doubtful accounts, which are established based on the specific credit risks associated with individual franchisees and other relevant information. Concentration of credit risk with respect to receivables is limited, due to the large number of franchisees.

As at February 1, 2009, the aging of the Accounts receivable is as follows:

Current	$	74,924
Past due 0 - 60 days		4,190
Past due over 61 days		6,102
Accounts receivable		85,216
Less: allowance for doubtful accounts		(761)
	$	84,455

ii. Interest rate risk

The Company is exposed to interest rate risk on the credit facility as the rate is based on an index rate and on the Company's financial performance as determined by its interest coverage ratio. As at February 1, 2009, the interest rate paid was bank prime less 0.45%.

On February 1, 2009, a 25 basis point increase or decrease in interest rates, assuming that all other variables are constant, would have resulted in a $157,000 decrease or increase in the Company's net earnings for the period ended February 1, 2009.

The Company is not exposed to interest rate risk on long-term receivables, mortgages and vendor take-back loans as the rates are fixed.

iii. Asset-backed exposures

The Company has no exposure to asset-backed securities.

iv. Exchange risk

The Company currently uses forward currency contracts and options to hedge anticipated transactions whose terms do not exceed one year.

The Company has recorded an unrealized gain in the consolidated statement of comprehensive earnings for the fiscal year ended February 1, 2009 of $1,340,000 (net of tax - $871,000) (2008 - ($138,000), net of tax -($87,000)) relating to forward foreign currency contracts that qualify for hedge accounting.

The outstanding forward foreign exchange contracts to which hedge accounting was applied at February 1, 2009 have notional amounts of $3,629,000 (2008 - $6,208,000) and terms ranging from February 6, 2009 to August 21, 2009 at forward rates ranging from $1.021 to $1.2695.

Items currently reported in AOCE will be reclassified to net earnings when the hedged item is settled and the related non-financial asset is expensed or when a hedge is deemed ineffective and the hedged item has settled.

On February 1, 2009, a 1% increase or decrease in the exchange rate of the Canadian dollar compared to the U.S dollar, assuming that all other variables are constant, would have resulted in a $85,000 decrease or increase in the Company's net earnings for the period ended February 1, 2009.

v. Liquidity Risk

Liquidity risk is the risk the Company will encounter difficulties in meeting it's financial liability obligations. The Company manages its liquidity risk through cash and debt management. See Note 10 for a more detailed discussion.

17. Acquisitions

(a)   Effective September 9, 2007, the Company acquired select net assets of Al DiMarco's Custom Golf Shop Ltd. and various other related entities ("DiMarco"). The acquisition was accounted for using the purchase method as net assets acquired encompass the necessary inputs, processes and outputs to sustain the business, thereby meeting the definition of a business and accordingly the consolidated financial statements include the results of operations since the date of the acquisition.

The consideration for the transaction was $1,039,000 in cash and the settlement of an outstanding account receivable by the Company from DiMarco of $3,095,000.

The assigned fair values of the underlying assets and liabilities acquired by the Company as at September 9, 2007 are summarized as follows:

Cash	$	3
Inventory		3,755
Prepaid expenses		39
Capital assets		425
Total assets acquired		4,222
Less: amounts due to others		(88)
Net assets acquired	$	4,134

(b)   Effective November 26, 2007, the Company acquired 100% of the outstanding shares of Athletes World Limited ("AWL") which was operating under Companies' Creditors Arrangement Act ("CCAA") protection. While under CCAA protection, FGL maintained its usual role in the management of the day-to-day operation of Athletes World under the supervision of a court-appointed monitor who was responsible for reviewing Athletes World's ongoing operations, assisting with the development and filing of the Court documents, liaising with creditors and other stakeholders and reporting to the Court. On June 30, 2008 AWL successfully exited from CCAA protection.

The acquisition was accounted for using the purchase method and accordingly the consolidated financial statements include the results of operations since the date of acquisition.

The assigned fair values of the underlying assets and liabilities acquired by the Company as at November 26, 2007, are summarized as follows:

Inventory	$	26,171
Capital assets		2,626
Intangible asset - trademark		2,212
Future income tax asset		13,215
Total assets acquired		44,224
Bank indebtedness		108
Accounts payable		17,254
Long-term debt		18,196
Total liabilities acquired		35,558
Net assets acquired	$	8,666
Consideration given:		
Cash	$	1,500
Acquisition costs		7,166
Total Consideration	$	8,666

18. Segmented Financial Information

The Company operates principally in two business segments: corporately-owned and operated retail stores and as a wholesale business selling to franchisees and others. Amortization and interest expense are not disclosed by segment as they are substantially retail in nature.

In determining the reportable segments, the Company considered the distinct business models of the retail and wholesale operations, the division of responsibilities, and the reporting to the CEO and Board of Directors.

	For the 52 weeks ended February 1, 2009	For the 53 weeks ended February 3, 2008
Revenues:		
Retail	$ 994,043	$ 969,256
Wholesale	352,715	361,753
	1,346,758	1,331,009
Operating Profit:		
Retail	115,431	143,517
Wholesale	37,229	35,296
	152,660	178,813
Non-segment specific administrative expenses	55,558	55,843
Operating profit before under noted items	97,102	122,970
Amortization of capital assets	47,613	44,468
Interest expense	5,175	5,797
Loss on sale of investment	-	864
	52,788	51,129
Earnings before income taxes	44,314	71,841
Income tax expense	14,989	24,390
Net earnings	$ 29,325	$ 47,451

As at		February 1, 2009		February 3, 2008
Accounts receivable				
Retail	$	617	$	2,796
Wholesale		74,031		71,036
Non-segment specific		9,807		1,674
	$	84,455	$	75,506
Capital assets				
Retail	$	172,146	$	164,740
Wholesale		21,262		20,596
Non-segment specific		3,357		3,285
	$	196,765	$	188,621
Goodwill and other intangibles/Other assets				
Retail	$	73,162	$	63,291
Wholesale		23,263		20,336
Non-segment specific		4,336		9,571
	$	100,761	$	93,198
Total assets				
Retail	$	476,711	$	515,739
Wholesale		169,915		164,541
Non-segment specific		42,834		74,684
	$	689,460	$	754,964

19. Related Party Transaction

An officer of the Company holds an interest in franchise store operations. During the year, the franchise operations transacted business, in the normal course and at fair market value, with the Company, purchasing product in the amount of $11,438,000 (2008 - $7,660,000). At the year end, accounts receivable from the franchise operation were $4,404,000 (2008 – $1,821,000).

20. Variable Interest Entities

At February 1, 2009, the Company had a long-term receivable due from an entity which is considered a variable interest entity VIE under CICA AcG 15. The entity operates several franchise stores. The Company has received guarantees for the full amount of the receivable from the shareholders of the entity. The Company has concluded that it is not the primary beneficiary of the VIE and that it is not required to consolidate this VIE in its consolidated financial statements. The Company has no exposure to loss related to the long-term receivable.

21. Sale of Investment

During fiscal 2008, the Company sold its investment in a trademark licensing company. The investment had a cost of $3,088,000 and was sold for $2,224,000 with a one-time loss of $864,000 recognized during the period ended February 3, 2008.

22. Subsequent Events

Effective February 18, 2009, the Company completed an asset purchase from Access Distribution Inc., for total expected consideration of $4,000,000, payable over 5 years on the completion of certain performance measures.

23. Comparative Figures

Certain comparative figures have been reclassified to conform to the presentation adopted for the current period.

APPENDIX B ▶ SALES TAXES

All businesses operating in Canada need to understand how sales taxes apply to their particular business in their particular province or territory. Sales taxes may take the form of the Goods and Services Tax (GST), Provincial Sales Tax (PST), or Harmonized Sales Tax (HST). GST is levied by the federal government. PST is levied by the provinces and territories, with the exception of Alberta, the Northwest Territories, Nunavut, and Yukon, where no Provincial Sales Tax is charged. Nova Scotia, New Brunswick, and Newfoundland and Labrador, and recently British Columbia and Ontario (effective July 1, 2010) have combined the GST and PST into one Harmonized Sales Tax.

A business is considered an agent of the federal and provincial governments and is therefore required to collect sales taxes on the sale of certain goods and services. In addition, businesses pay sales taxes on most disbursements. We will discuss the collection, payment, recording, and remittance of each of these types of sales taxes in the following sections.

Types of Sales Taxes

Goods and Services Tax

The GST is a federal sales tax on most goods and services provided in Canada. A business must register for the GST if it provides taxable goods or services in Canada and if it has revenues of more than $30,000 in any year. Businesses that have to or decide to voluntarily register for the GST are called registrants. Registrants can claim a credit—called an input tax credit (ITC)—for the amount of GST they pay or owe on purchases of goods or services against the GST they collect or are owed. GST returns are submitted quarterly for most registrants (monthly for large registrants) to the Canada Revenue Agency. The taxes are payable to the Receiver General, who is the collection agent for the federal government.

For those provinces that have adopted the Harmonized Sales Tax, where the PST and GST have been combined into one tax, the Receiver General is the collection agent for both the federal and provincial governments.

The GST applies at a rate of 5% on most transactions (13% in the case of HST). Transactions subject to GST/HST are called taxable supplies. There are two other categories of goods and services with respect to the GST/HST:

- zero-rated supplies, such as basic groceries and prescription drugs
- exempt supplies, such as educational services, health-care services, and financial services

No GST/HST applies to zero-rated or exempt supplies. However, zero-rated suppliers can claim input tax credits.

Illustration B-1 provides the GST/HST status of some typical goods and services.

Taxable Supplies	Zero-Rated Supplies	Exempt Supplies
Building materials	Prescription drugs	Used house
Ready-to-eat pizza	Uncooked pizza	Dental services
Two doughnuts	Six or more doughnuts	Insurance policy

◀ Illustration B-1

Examples of GST/HST status

The reason ready-to-eat pizza and two doughnuts have GST/HST added to the purchase price is because they are considered convenience items, which are taxable, and not basic groceries, which are not taxable.

Provincial Sales Tax

Provincial sales taxes are charged on retail sales of certain goods and services. As of July 1, 2010, there are only four provinces that charge a separate Provincial Sales Tax: Saskatchewan, Manitoba, Quebec, and Prince Edward Island. In Saskatchewan and Manitoba, this tax is applied to the selling price of the item before GST is applied. Similarly, GST is charged on the selling price of the item before PST is applied, thus avoiding GST being charged on PST. In Quebec and Prince Edward Island, however, the Provincial Sales Tax is cascaded; that is, it is applied to the total of the selling price plus GST. Quebec's sales tax is also known as the QST (Quebec Sales Tax).

The following example shows the calculation of cascaded sales tax, using a taxable item sold in Quebec for $100 (at the rate applicable in 2011):

Selling price	$100.00
GST ($100 × 5%)	5.00
QST [($100 + $5) × 8.5%]	8.93
Total	$113.93

Provincial sales taxes are remitted periodically to the Minister of Finance or Provincial Treasurer in each province.

PST rates vary by province and can change with each provincial budget. Certain goods are exempt, such as children's clothing, textbooks, and residential rent, and may be purchased with no PST. Examples of exempt services that are not taxable include personal services such as dental and medical services. Because rates and exemptions vary by province, it is important, when starting a business, to check with provincial officials for details on how to calculate the provincial tax that must be applied to sales.

Harmonized Sales Tax

The provinces of Newfoundland and Labrador, Nova Scotia, New Brunswick, and most recently British Columbia and Ontario charge Harmonized Sales Tax, or HST. Instead of charging GST and PST separately, only the HST is charged at a combined rate of 13%, or 12% in British Columbia. Similar to GST, HST returns are submitted quarterly for most registrants (monthly for large registrants) to the Receiver General for Canada. The federal government then gives the provincial portion of the tax to the province.

To summarize, two provinces—Manitoba and Saskatchewan—apply PST and GST to the selling price of a taxable good or service. Two provinces—Prince Edward Island and Quebec—apply PST to the total of the purchase price and the GST. Five provinces—New Brunswick, Newfoundland and Labrador, Nova Scotia, British Columbia, and Ontario—charge a combined GST and PST (harmonized) rate of 13% (12% in British Columbia) on the selling price. Four provinces and territories do not charge PST: Alberta, the Northwest Territories, Nunavut, and Yukon. In addition to the different ways of applying sales taxes, the rates of sales tax differ in each province and territory, as shown in Illustration B-2.

← Illustration B-2

Province/Territory	GST (HST) Rate	PST Rate	Combined Rate[1]
Alberta	5.0%	0.0%	5.0%
British Columbia	12.0%	N/A	12.0%
Manitoba	5.0%	7.0%	12.0%
New Brunswick	13.0%	N/A	13.0%
Newfoundland and Labrador	13.0%	N/A	13.0%
Northwest Territories	5.0%	0.0%	5.0%
Nova Scotia	13.0%	N/A	13.0%
Nunavut	5.0%	0.0%	5.0%
Ontario	13.0%	N/A	13.0%
Prince Edward Island	5.0%	10.0%	15.5%[2]
Quebec	5.0%	8.5%	13.925%[2]
Saskatchewan	5.0%	5.0%	10.0%
Yukon	5.0%	0.0%	5.0%

[1] These rates are in effect as of August 31, 2009, and are subject to change. Quebec rates are effective January 1, 2011, and Ontario and British Columbia rates are effective July 1, 2010.
[2] In Prince Edward Island and Quebec only, the GST is included in the Provincial Sales Tax base.

Sales tax rates

Sales Taxes Collected on Receipts

Sales taxes are collected by businesses from consumers on taxable goods and services. It is important to understand that sales taxes are not a source of revenue for a company. They are collected by a company on behalf of the federal and provincial governments. Consequently, collected sales tax is a current liability to the company until remitted to the respective government at regular intervals.

Services

Now let's look at how service companies record sales taxes on the services they provide.

Services with PST

Assume that $250 of cleaning services were provided by a company in Manitoba for cash on July 24. These services are subject to both PST (7%) and GST (5%), and would be recorded as follows:

July 24	Cash	280.00	
	Cleaning Service Revenue		250.00
	PST Payable ($250 × 7%)		17.50
	GST Payable ($250 × 5%)		12.50
	To record cleaning service revenue.		

A	=	L	+	OE
+280.00		+17.50		+250.00
		+12.50		

↑ Cash flows: +280.00

Note that the revenue recorded is $250, and not $280. The cleaning service revenue is exclusive of the GST and PST amount collected, which are recorded as current liabilities.

Services with HST

Assume now that these same services were provided by a company in New Brunswick, where HST is 13%. The entry would be as follows:

July 24	Cash	282.50	
	Cleaning Service Revenue		250.00
	HST Payable ($250 × 13%)		32.50
	To record cleaning service revenue.		

A	=	L	+	OE
+282.50		+32.50		+250.00

↑ Cash flows: +282.50

Merchandise

Entries are needed to record the sales taxes owed when merchandise inventory (goods) is sold, or to reduce sales taxes payable when merchandise inventory is returned.

Sales with PST

Assume that Staples sells $1,000 of office furniture, on account, in the province of Manitoba, where PST is 7%. GST is 5%. Staples uses a perpetual inventory system and the cost of the furniture to Staples was $800. Staples will make the following two entries to record the sale and the cost of the sale on May 20:

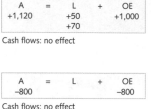

A	=	L	+	OE
+1,120		+50		+1,000
		+70		

Cash flows: no effect

A	=	L	+	OE
−800				−800

Cash flows: no effect

May 20	Accounts Receivable	1,120	
	Sales		1,000
	GST Payable ($1,000 × 5%)		50
	PST Payable ($1,000 × 7%)		70
	To record sale of merchandise on account.		
20	Cost of Goods Sold	800	
	Merchandise Inventory		800
	To record cost of merchandise sold.		

The merchandise inventory does not include any sales taxes that may have been paid when the company purchased the merchandise. We will learn more about that in the next section of this appendix.

Under a periodic inventory system, the second entry would not be recorded.

Sales Returns and Allowances with PST

If a $300 sales return and allowance were granted by Staples on May 25 for returned merchandise from the above sale, Staples' entries to record the sales return would appear as follows:

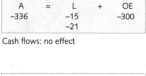

A	=	L	+	OE
−336		−15		−300
		−21		

Cash flows: no effect

A	=	L	+	OE
+240				+240

Cash flows: no effect

May 25	Sales Returns and Allowances	300	
	GST Payable ($300 × 5%)	15	
	PST Payable ($300 × 7%)	21	
	Accounts Receivable		336
	To record credit for returned merchandise.		
25	Merchandise Inventory ($300 ÷ $1,000 × $800)	240	
	Cost of Goods Sold		240
	To record cost of merchandise returned.		

Note that the GST and PST payable accounts, rather than a receivable account, are debited, to indicate that this is a return of previously collected sales tax. This entry assumes that the merchandise was in good condition and returned to inventory. Note also that, as GST and PST are not included in the original cost of the merchandise, they are therefore not considered in restoring the cost of the merchandise to the inventory account.

Under a periodic inventory system, the second entry would not be recorded.

Sales with HST

Assume now that Staples sells the same $1,000 of office furniture, on account, in the province of Nova Scotia, where there is no PST and where HST is 13%. Staples uses a perpetual inventory system and the cost of the furniture to Staples was $800. Staples will record the following two entries to record the sale and the cost of the sale on May 20:

A	=	L	+	OE
+1,130		+130		+1,000

Cash flows: no effect

A	=	L	+	OE
−800				−800

Cash flows: no effect

May 20	Accounts Receivable	1,130	
	Sales		1,000
	HST Payable ($1,000 × 13%)		130
	To record sale of merchandise on account.		
20	Cost of Goods Sold	800	
	Merchandise Inventory		800
	To record cost of merchandise sold.		

Under a periodic inventory system, the second entry would not be recorded.

Sales Returns and Allowances with HST

Assume the same $300 sales return and allowance were granted by Staples on May 25 for returned merchandise from the above sale. Staples' entries to record the sales return would appear as follows:

May 25	Sales Returns and Allowances	300	
	HST Payable ($300 × 13%)	39	
	Accounts Receivable		339
	To record credit for returned merchandise.		
25	Merchandise Inventory ($300 ÷ $1,000 × $800)	240	
	Cost of Goods Sold		240
	To record cost of merchandise returned.		

A	=	L	+	OE
−339		−39		−300

Cash flows: no effect

A	=	L	+	OE
+240				+240

Cash flows: no effect

Under a periodic inventory system, the second entry would not be recorded.

Sales Taxes Paid on Disbursements

As a consumer of goods and services, a business must pay the applicable PST and GST or HST charged by its suppliers on taxable goods and services.

Purchase of Merchandise for Resale

When purchasing merchandise for resale, the treatment of the PST is different than that of the GST. PST is a single-stage tax collected from the final consumers of taxable goods and services. Consequently, wholesalers do not charge the tax to the retailer, who will in turn resell the merchandise, at a higher price, to the final consumer. By presenting a vendor registration number, retailers are able to buy merchandise for resale, exempt of the PST.

    Businesses must pay GST/HST on the purchase of merchandise but can then offset the GST/HST paid against any GST/HST collected. Consequently, when merchandise is purchased, the GST/HST paid by a business is *not* part of the inventory cost. The GST/HST paid on purchases is debited to an account called GST or HST Recoverable and is called an input tax credit.

    In Quebec, the QST works somewhat like the GST. Businesses can offset QST paid against any QST collected. The QST paid on purchases is debited to an account called QST Recoverable and is called an input tax refund. Other differences also exist in the treatment of QST. This appendix will focus on PST and does not discuss the QST in any detail.

Purchases with GST

The following is an entry to record the purchase of merchandise, for resale in the province of Manitoba, on May 4 at a price of $4,000, on account, using a perpetual inventory system:

May 4	Merchandise Inventory	4,000	
	GST Recoverable ($4,000 × 5%)	200	
	Accounts Payable		4,200
	To record merchandise purchased on account.		

A	=	L	+	OE
+4,000		+4,200		
+200				

Cash flows: no effect

As previously discussed, the cost of the merchandise, $4,000, is not affected by the GST, which is recorded as a receivable.

    Under a periodic inventory system, the $4,000 debit would have been recorded to the Purchases account.

Purchase Returns and Allowances with GST

The entry to record a $300 return of merchandise on May 8 is as follows:

A	=	L	+	OE
−15		−315		
−300				

Cash flows: no effect

May 8	Accounts Payable	315	
	GST Recoverable ($300 × 5%)		15
	Merchandise Inventory		300
	To record the return of merchandise.		

Note that the GST Recoverable account is credited instead of the GST Payable account because this is a return of previously recorded GST.

Under a periodic inventory system, the credit of $300 would have been recorded to the Purchase Returns and Allowances account.

To summarize, PST is not paid on purchases of merchandise for resale. GST paid on purchases is recoverable and recorded as a current asset in the GST Recoverable account. Purchase returns and allowances require an adjustment of GST only, since PST was not paid on the original purchase.

Purchases with HST

The following is an entry to record the purchase of merchandise for resale in the province of British Columbia, where the HST rate is 12%, on May 4 at a price of $4,000, on account, using a perpetual inventory system:

A	=	L	+	OE
+4,000		+4,480		
+480				

Cash flows: no effect

May 4	Merchandise Inventory	4,000	
	HST Recoverable ($4,000 × 12%)	480	
	Accounts Payable		4,480
	To record merchandise purchased on account.		

The cost of the merchandise, $4,000, is not affected by the HST, which is recorded as a receivable.

Under a periodic inventory system, the $4,000 debit would have been recorded to the Purchases account.

Purchase Returns and Allowances with GST

The entry to record a $300 return of merchandise in the province of British Columbia, where the HST rate is 12%, on May 8 is as follows:

A	=	L	+	OE
−36		−336		
−300				

Cash flows: no effect

May 8	Accounts Payable	336	
	HST Recoverable ($300 × 12%)		36
	Merchandise Inventory		300
	To record the return of merchandise.		

Note that the HST Recoverable account is credited instead of the HST Payable account because this is a return of previously recorded HST.

Under a periodic inventory system, the credit of $300 would have been recorded to the Purchase Returns and Allowances account.

To summarize, HST paid on purchases is recoverable and recorded as a current asset in the HST Recoverable account.

Operating Expenses

The accounting treatment of sales taxes incurred on operating expenses depends on the type of sales taxes that the company is charged.

Operating Expenses with PST

Although PST is not charged on goods purchased for resale, it is charged to businesses that use taxable goods and services in their operations. For example, a business must pay GST and PST when it buys office supplies. As with all purchases made by a registered business, the GST is recoverable (can be offset as an input tax credit against GST collected). Because the PST is not recoverable, the PST forms part of the cost of the asset or expense that is being acquired.

The following is the entry for a cash purchase of office supplies on May 18 in the amount of $200 in the province of Saskatchewan, where PST is 5% and GST is 5%:

May 18	Office Supplies ($200 + $10* PST)	210	
	GST Recoverable ($200 × 5%)	10	
	Cash		220
	To record purchase of office supplies.		
*$200 × 5% = $10			

A = L + OE
+210
+10
−220

↓ Cash flows: −220

In this situation, the cost of the supplies includes both the supplies and the PST. Because GST is recoverable, it does not form part of the asset cost.

This same purchase would be recorded as follows if it occurred in the province of Prince Edward Island, where GST is 5% and PST is charged on GST at 10%:

May 18	Office Supplies ($200 + $21* PST)	221	
	GST Recoverable ($200 × 5%)	10	
	Cash		231
	To record purchase of office supplies.		
*$200 + $10 = $210 × 10% = $21			

A = L + OE
+221
+10
−231

↓ Cash flows: −231

Remember that in Prince Edward Island, the Provincial Sales Tax base includes both the cost of the item and the GST. That is, the PST of $21 is determined by multiplying 10% by $210 ($200 + $10).

Operating Expenses with HST

When HST is applied, it is treated in the same manner as GST. HST is recoverable and does not form part of the cost of the item purchased. The purchase of office supplies would be recorded as follows if it had occurred in the province of Ontario, where HST is 13%:

May 18	Office Supplies	200	
	HST Recoverable ($200 × 13%)	26	
	Cash		226
	To record purchase of office supplies.		

A = L + OE
+200
+26
−226

↓ Cash flows: −226

Note that the type and amount of sales tax paid changes the amount recorded as the cost of office supplies in each province: $210 in Saskatchewan, $221 in Prince Edward Island, and $200 in Ontario.

Property, Plant, and Equipment

Businesses incur costs other than those for merchandise and operating expenses, such as for the purchase of property, plant, and equipment. The PST and GST or HST apply to these purchases in the same manner as described in the operating expenses section above. All GST (or HST) paid is recoverable and is not part of the cost of the asset. The PST, however, is part of the cost of the asset being purchased as it is not recoverable.

Property, Plant, and Equipment with PST

The following is the entry for the purchase of office furniture on May 20 from Staples, on account, for $1,000 plus applicable sales taxes in Manitoba, where PST is 7% and GST is 5%.

A = L + OE		
+1,070 +1,120		
+50		

Cash flows: no effect

May 20	Office Furniture ($1,000 + $70* PST)	1,070	
	GST Recoverable ($1,000 × 5%)	50	
	Accounts Payable		1,120
	To record purchase of office furniture.		
*$1,000 × 7% = $70			

Because the PST is not recoverable, the cost of the furniture is $1,070, inclusive of the PST.

Compare this entry made by the buyer to record the purchase with the entry made by the seller (Staples) to record the sale on page B4. Both companies record accounts payable and accounts receivable in the same amount, $1,120. However, the seller records both GST and PST payable while the buyer records only GST recoverable. The PST paid by the buyer is not recoverable, so it becomes part of the cost of the office furniture, $1,070.

In Prince Edward Island, where GST is 5% and PST is charged on GST at 10%, the same entry would be recorded as follows:

A = L + OE		
+1,105 +1,155		
+50		

Cash flows: no effect

May 20	Office Furniture ($1,000 + $105* PST)	1,105	
	GST Recoverable ($1,000 × 5%)	50	
	Accounts Payable		1,155
	To record purchase of office furniture.		
*$1,000 + $50 = $1,050 × 10% = $105			

In P.E.I., PST is calculated on a cost base that includes the GST. Therefore, the PST of $105 is calculated on $1,050 ($1,000 + $50). Because PST is not recoverable, the cost of the furniture is $1,105.

Property, Plant, and Equipment with HST

In Nova Scotia, where HST is 13%, the entry would be recorded as follows:

A = L + OE		
+1,000 +1,130		
+130		

Cash flows: no effect

May 20	Office Furniture	1,000	
	HST Recoverable ($1,000 × 13%)	130	
	Accounts Payable		1,130
	To record purchase of office furniture.		

As we have noted before, the type and amount of sales taxes paid changes the amount recorded as the cost of the office furniture in each province: $1,070 in Manitoba, $1,105 in Prince Edward Island, and $1,000 in Nova Scotia.

Remittance of Sales Taxes

As mentioned in the introduction, businesses act as agents of the federal and provincial governments in charging and later remitting taxes charged on sales and services. For example, Staples, the seller of office furniture illustrated on page B4, must remit GST or HST to the Receiver General for Canada and PST to the Minister of Revenue, where applicable. Notice that even if Staples has not received payment from a customer buying on account before the due date for the remittance, the tax must still be paid to the government authorities. As a registrant, however, Staples will also benefit from claiming input tax credits and recording a reduction in amounts payable from applying GST/HST on sales.

GST (HST)

When remitting the amount owed to the federal government at the end of a reporting period for GST (or HST), the amount of GST (or HST) payable is reduced by any amount in the GST/HST Recoverable account. Any difference is remitted, as shown in the following journal entry, using assumed amounts payable and recoverable:

June 30	GST (or HST) Payable	6,250	
	GST (or HST) Recoverable		2,500
	Cash		3,750
	To record remittance of GST (or HST).		

A	=	L	+	OE
−2,500		−6,250		
−3,750				

↓ Cash flows: −3,750

The GST (HST) remittance form requires the registrant to report at specified dates, depending on the business's volume of sales. The amount of the sales and other revenue as well as the amount of GST/HST charged on these sales, whether collected or not, is reported on the remittance form. The amount of the input tax credits claimed is also entered on the form to reduce the amount owing to the Receiver General. If the GST/HST recoverable exceeds the GST/HST payable, the remittance form should be sent as soon as possible in order to ask for a refund. The entry to record the cash receipt from a GST/HST refund will be similar to the entry shown above, except that there will be a debit to Cash, instead of a credit.

The above discussion of the remittance of GST/HST explains why all registrants need two general ledger accounts. One account, GST Payable or HST Payable, is used to keep track of all GST or HST charged on sales and revenues. The second account, GST Recoverable or HST Recoverable, is used to keep track of the GST/HST input tax credits that have been paid on all of the business's purchases. Failure by a business to capture the proper amounts of input tax credits has a significant impact on income and on cash flows.

PST

The remittance of PST to the Treasurer or Minister of Finance of the applicable province is similar to that of GST/HST except that, since no credit can be claimed, the amount paid at the end of each reporting period is the amount of the balance in the PST Payable account.

Consequently, the entry to record a remittance of PST, using an assumed amount payable, would appear as follows:

June 30	PST Payable	7,400	
	Cash		7,400
	To record remittance of PST.		

A	=	L	+	OE
−7,400		−7,400		

↓ Cash flows: −7,400

Conclusion

Be careful when you record the amounts of taxes charged or claimed in the business accounts. Numbers must be rounded carefully. If the amount of the tax calculated is less than half a cent, the amount should be rounded down. If the amount of the tax as calculated comes to more than half a cent, the amount should be rounded up. For example, applying 13% HST on an amount of $49.20 would give you $6.396. The tax amount to be recorded can be rounded up to $6.40. Rounding might seem insignificant, but when a business has many transactions, the amounts can add up and the registrant is responsible to the government authorities for any shortfall created in error.

Sales tax law is intricate. It has added a lot of complexity to the accounting for most transactions flowing through today's businesses. Fortunately, computers that are programmed to automatically determine and record the correct sales tax rate for each good or service provided have simplified matters somewhat. Before recording sales tax transactions, however, it is important to understand all of the relevant sales tax regulations. Check the federal and provincial laws in your jurisdiction.

Brief Exercises

Record inventory purchase—perpetual inventory system.

BEB–1   Record the purchase on account of $4,500 of merchandise for resale in the province of Manitoba. The company uses a perpetual inventory system and the purchase is PST exempt.

Record purchase return—perpetual inventory system.

BEB–2   Record the return of $1,000 of the merchandise purchased in BEB–1.

Record inventory purchase—perpetual inventory system.

BEB–3   Record the purchase on account of $4,500 of merchandise for resale in the province of Ontario, where HST is 13%. The company uses a perpetual inventory system.

Record purchase return—perpetual inventory system.

BEB–4   Record the return of $1,000 of the merchandise purchased in BEB–3.

Record purchase of supplies.

BEB–5   Record the cash purchase of $600 of office supplies in the province of Saskatchewan, where PST is 5%.

Record purchase of supplies.

BEB–6   Record the cash purchase of $600 of office supplies in the province of British Columbia, where HST is 12%.

Record purchase of capital item.

BEB–7   Record the purchase on account of a $25,000 delivery truck in the province of Ontario, where HST is 13%.

Record purchase of capital item.

BEB–8   Record the purchase on account of a $25,000 delivery truck in the province of Saskatchewan, where the PST is 5% and the GST is 5%.

Record purchase of supplies and inventory—perpetual inventory system.

BEB–9   Record the purchase on account of $200 of office supplies and $4,000 of merchandise for resale in the province of Manitoba. The company uses a perpetual inventory system and the purchase of merchandise is PST exempt. The PST rate is 7%.

Record sales—perpetual inventory system.

BEB–10   Record the sale on account, for $1,800, of merchandise costing $1,100 in the province of Quebec. Assume the company uses a perpetual inventory system. The QST is 8.5% and the GST is included in the Quebec Sales Tax base.

Record sales return—perpetual inventory system.

BEB–11   Half of the shipment described in BEB–10 is returned as the incorrect sizes have been shipped. Record the return of merchandise on the seller's books.

Record sales and sales return—periodic inventory system.

BEB–12   Record the sale in BEB–10 and the sales return in BEB–11 assuming the business uses a periodic inventory system.

Record exempt services.

BEB–13   Record the billing for $250 of services by D. R. Wong, dentist, in the province of British Columbia. Dental services are exempt from GST and PST.

Record fees.

BEB–14   Record the billing of accounting fee revenue of $400 for the preparation of personal income tax returns in the province of Alberta. GST is applicable on this service. Alberta does not charge PST.

Record remittance of GST and PST.

BEB–15   Record two payments: one cheque to the Receiver General for GST and one to the Minister of Finance of Saskatchewan for PST. The balances in the accounts are as follows: GST Payable $4,450, GST Recoverable $900, and PST Payable $4,870.

Record HST refund.

BEB–16   Record the deposit of a cheque from the Receiver General for a refund of $1,690 following the filing of an HST return. The balances in the accounts are as follows: HST Payable $2,920 and HST Recoverable $4,610.

Exercises

EB–1 Stratton Company is a merchant operating in the province of Manitoba, where the PST rate is 7%. Stratton uses a perpetual inventory system. Transactions for the business are shown below:

Record sales transactions—perpetual inventory system.

Mar. 1 Paid March rent to the landlord for the rental of a warehouse. The lease calls for monthly payments of $5,500 plus 5% GST.

     3 Sold merchandise on account and shipped merchandise to Marvin Ltd. for $20,000, terms n/30, FOB shipping point. This merchandise cost Stratton $10,600.

     5 Granted Marvin a sales allowance of $700 for defective merchandise purchased on March 3. No merchandise was returned.

     7 Purchased on account from Xu Ltd. merchandise for resale at a list price of $14,000, plus applicable tax.

   12 Made a cash purchase at Home Depot of a desk for the shipping clerk. The price of the desk was $600 before applicable taxes.

   31 Paid the quarterly remittance of GST to the Receiver General. The balances in the accounts were as follows: GST Payable $5,280 and GST Recoverable $1,917.

Instructions

(a) Prepare the journal entries to record these transactions on the books of Stratton Company.

(b) Assume instead that Stratton operates in the province of Alberta, where PST is not applicable. Prepare the journal entries to record these transactions on the books of Stratton.

(c) Assume instead that Stratton operates in the province of Prince Edward Island, where PST is charged on GST at 10%. Prepare the journal entries to record these transactions on the books of Stratton.

(d) Assume instead that Stratton operates in the province of Ontario, where HST is 13%. Prepare the journal entries to record these transactions on the books of Stratton. Assume that the GST balances on March 31 are the balances in the HST accounts.

EB–2 Using the information for the transactions of Stratton Company in EB–1, assume now that Stratton uses a periodic inventory system.

Record sales transactions—periodic inventory system.

Instructions

(a) Prepare the journal entries to record these transactions on the books of Stratton Company.

(b) Assume now that Stratton operates in the province of Alberta, where PST is not applicable. Prepare the journal entries to record these transactions on the books of Stratton.

(c) Assume now that Stratton operates in the province of Prince Edward Island, where PST is charged on GST at 10%. Prepare the journal entries to record these transactions on the books of Stratton.

(d) Assume now that Stratton operates in the province of Ontario, where HST is 13%. Prepare the journal entries to record these transactions on the books of Stratton. Assume that the GST balances on March 31 provided in EB–1 are the balances in the HST accounts.

EB–3 Otto Cheng is a sole proprietor providing accounting services in the province of Manitoba, where PST is charged at the rate of 7% and GST is at the rate of 5%. Transactions for the business are shown below:

Record service transactions.

June 8 Purchased a printer on account at a cost of $1,500. The appropriate sales taxes were added to this purchase price.

   10 Purchased toner for the printer for $50 cash from a local stationery store. The store added the appropriate sales taxes to the purchase price.

   12 Billed a client for accounting services provided. The fee charged was $950 and the appropriate sales taxes were added to the fee billed.

15 Collected $112 on account. The original fee was $100, the GST charged was $5 and the PST charged was $7.

30 Paid the quarterly remittance of GST to the Receiver General. The balances in the accounts were as follows: GST Payable $1,520.60 and GST Recoverable $820.45.

30 Paid the quarterly remittance of PST to the Minister of Revenue for the province of Manitoba. The balance in the PST Payable account was $2,128.84.

Instructions

Prepare the journal entries to record these transactions on the books of Otto Cheng's accounting business.

Record service transactions.

EB–4 Baole Chen is a sole proprietor providing legal services in the province of Ontario, where the HST rate is 13%. Transactions for the business are shown below:

June 8 Purchased a printer on account at a cost of $1,500. The appropriate taxes were added to this purchase price.

10 Purchased toner for the printer for $50 cash from a local stationery store. The store added the appropriate taxes to the purchase price.

12 Billed a client for accounting services provided. The fee charged was $950 plus appropriate taxes.

15 Collected $113 on account. The original fee was $100; the HST charged was $13.

30 Paid the quarterly remittance of HST to the Receiver General. The balances in the accounts were as follows: HST Payable $1,520.60 and HST Recoverable $820.45.

Instructions

Prepare the journal entries to record these transactions on the books of Baole Chen's legal practice.

Problems

Record purchase and sales transactions—perpetual inventory system.

PB–1 Mark's Music is a store that buys and sells musical instruments in Ontario, where the HST rate is 13%. Mark's Music uses a perpetual inventory system. Transactions for the business are shown below:

Nov. 2 Purchased two electric guitars from Fender Supply Limited, on account, at a cost of $700 each.

4 Made a cash sale of two keyboards for a total invoice price of $2,200, plus applicable taxes. The cost of each keyboard was $950.

5 Received a credit memorandum from Western Acoustic Inc. for the return of an acoustic guitar that was defective. The original invoice price before taxes was $400 and the guitar had been purchased on account.

7 One of the keyboards from the cash sale of November 4 was returned to the store for a full cash refund because the customer was not satisfied with the instrument.

8 Purchased store supplies from a stationery store. The price of the supplies is $100 before all applicable taxes.

10 Sold one Omega trumpet to the Toronto Regional Band, on account, for an invoice price of $2,700 before applicable taxes. The trumpet had cost Mark's Music $1,420.

13 Purchased two saxophones from Yamaha Canada Inc. on account. The invoice price was $2,100 for each saxophone, excluding applicable taxes.

14 Collected $3,990 on account. The payment included all applicable taxes.

16 Returned to Yamaha Canada Inc. one of the saxophones purchased on November 13, as it was the wrong model. Received a credit memorandum from Yamaha for the full purchase price.

20 Made a payment on account for the amount owing to Fender Supply Limited for the purchase of November 2.

Instructions

(a) Prepare the journal entries to record the Mark's Music transactions.
(b) Assume now that Mark's Music operates in the province of Manitoba, where the PST rate is 7% and the GST rate is 5%. Prepare the journal entries to record these transactions on the books of Mark's Music.

PB–2 Transaction data for Mark's Music are available in PB–1. Assume Mark's Music uses a periodic inventory system instead of a perpetual inventory system.

Record purchase and sales transactions—periodic inventory system.

Instructions

(a) Prepare the journal entries to record the Mark's Music transactions.
(b) Assume now that Mark's Music operates in the province of Manitoba, where the PST rate is 7% and the GST rate is 5%. Prepare the journal entries to record these transactions on the books of Mark's Music.

PB–3 David Simmons, L.L.B., is a lawyer operating as a sole proprietor in Nunavut. Nunavut does not charge provincial sales taxes and the GST rate is 5%. Transactions for the business are shown below:

Record service transactions.

May	1	Signed a two-year lease for the office space and immediately paid the first and last months' rent. The lease calls for the monthly rent of $1,800 plus applicable taxes.
	4	Purchased an office suite of furniture, on account, from George's Furniture at a cost of $3,100. The appropriate sales taxes were added to this purchase price.
	5	Returned one chair to George's due to a defect. The cost of the chair before taxes was $400.
	6	Billed a client for the preparation of a will. The client was very pleased with the product and immediately paid David's invoice for fees of $1,000 plus taxes.
	10	Purchased paper for the photocopier for $300 cash from a local stationery store. The store added the appropriate sales taxes to the purchase price.
	13	Billed Manson Ltd. for legal services rendered connected with the purchase of land. The fee charged is $900 plus applicable taxes.
	18	Paid George's for the furniture purchase of May 4, net of returned items.
	19	Paid $15 cash to a local grocery store for coffee for the office coffee machine. Groceries are GST exempt.
	21	In accordance with the lease agreement with the landlord, David must pay for water supplied by the municipality. The water invoice was received and the services amounted to $100. No GST is charged for municipal water.
	25	Collected a full payment from Manson Ltd. for the May 13 bill.
	27	Completed the preparation of a purchase and sale agreement for Edwards Inc. and billed fees of $1,200.

Instructions

(a) Prepare the journal entries to record these transactions on the books of David Simmons' law practice.
(b) Determine the balances GST Payable and GST Recoverable accounts. Determine if the company must make a payment to the Receiver General or if it will apply for a refund. Record the appropriate journal entry.
(c) Assume now that David Simmons operates in the province of Ontario, where the HST rate is 13%. Prepare the journal entries to record these transactions on the books of David Simmons' law practice.
(d) Determine the balances HST Payable and HST Recoverable accounts. Determine if the company must make a payment to the Receiver General or if it will apply for a refund. Record the appropriate journal entry.

In the textbook, we learned how to record accounting transactions in a general journal. Each journal entry was then individually posted to its respective general ledger account. However, such a practice is only useful in a company where the volume of transactions is low. In most companies, it is necessary to use additional journals (called special journals) and ledgers (called subsidiary ledgers) to record transaction data.

We will look at subsidiary ledgers and special journals in the next sections. Both subsidiary ledgers and special journals can be used in either a manual accounting system or a computerized accounting system.

Subsidiary Ledgers

Imagine a business that has several thousand customers who purchase merchandise from it on account. It records the transactions with these customers in only one general ledger account—Accounts Receivable. It would be virtually impossible to determine the balance owed by an individual customer at any specific time. Similarly, the amount payable to one creditor would be difficult to locate quickly from a single accounts payable account in the general ledger.

Instead, companies use subsidiary ledgers to keep track of individual balances. A subsidiary ledger is a group of accounts that share a common characteristic (for example, all accounts receivable). The subsidiary ledger frees the general ledger from the details of individual balances. A subsidiary ledger is an addition to, and an expansion of, the general ledger.

Two common subsidiary ledgers are:

1. The accounts receivable (or customers') ledger, which collects transaction data for individual customers
2. The accounts payable (or creditors') ledger, which collects transaction data for individual creditors

Other subsidiary ledgers include an inventory ledger, which collects transaction data for each inventory item purchased and sold, as was described in Chapter 5. Some companies also use a payroll ledger, detailing individual employee pay records. In each of these subsidiary ledgers, individual accounts are arranged in alphabetical, numerical, or alphanumerical order.

The detailed data from a subsidiary ledger are summarized in a general ledger account. For exaple, the detailed data from the accounts receivable subsidiary ledger are summarized in Accounts Receivable in the general ledger. The general ledger account that summarizes subsidiary ledger data is called a control account.

Each general ledger control account balance must equal the total balance of the individual accounts in the related subsidiary ledger. This is an important internal control function.

Example

An example of an accounts receivable control account and subsidiary ledger is shown in Illustration C-1 for Mercier Enterprises.

Illustration C-1 ➔

Accounts receivable general ledger control account and subsidiary ledger

GENERAL LEDGER					
Accounts Receivable					**No. 112**
Date	Explanation	Ref.	Debit	Credit	Balance
2011 Jan. 31			12,000		12,000
31				8,000	4,000 ◄

ACCOUNTS RECEIVABLE SUBSIDIARY LEDGER					
Aaron Co.					**No. 112-172**
Date	Explanation	Ref.	Debit	Credit	Balance
2011 Jan. 11	Invoice 336		6,000		6,000
19	Payment			4,000	2,000 ◄

Branden Inc.					**No. 112-173**
Date	Explanation	Ref.	Debit	Credit	Balance
2011 Jan. 12	Invoice 337		3,000		3,000
21	Payment			3,000	0 ◄

Caron Co.					**No. 112-174**
Date	Explanation	Ref.	Debit	Credit	Balance
2011 Jan. 20	Invoice 339		3,000		3,000
29	Payment			1,000	2,000 ◄

The example is based on the following transactions:

Credit Sales			Collections on Account		
Jan. 11	Aaron Co.	$ 6,000	Jan. 19	Aaron Co.	$4,000
12	Branden Inc.	3,000	21	Branden Inc.	3,000
20	Caron Co.	3,000	29	Caron Co.	1,000
		$12,000			$8,000

The total debits ($12,000) and credits ($8,000) in Accounts Receivable in the general ledger match the detailed debits and credits in the subsidiary accounts. The balance of $4,000 in the control account agrees with the total of the balances in the individual accounts receivable accounts (Aaron $2,000 + Branden $0 + Caron $2,000) in the subsidiary ledger.

Rather than relying on customer or creditor names in a subsidiary ledger, a computer system expands the account number of the control account. For example, if the general ledger control account Accounts Receivable was numbered 112, the first customer account in the accounts receivable subsidiary ledger might be numbered 112-001, the second 112-002, and so on. Most systems allow inquiries about specific customer accounts in the subsidiary ledger (by account number) or about the control account.

As shown, postings are made monthly to the control account in the general ledger. We will learn, in the next section, how special journals facilitate monthly postings. We will also learn how to fill in the posting references (in the Ref. column) in both the general ledger and subsidiary ledger accounts. Postings to the individual accounts in the subsidiary ledger are made daily. The rationale for posting daily is to ensure that account information is current. This enables Mercier Enterprises to monitor credit limits, send statements to customers, and answer inquiries from customers about their account balances. In a computerized accounting system, transactions are simultaneously recorded in journals and posted to both the general and subsidiary ledgers.

Advantages of Subsidiary Ledgers

Subsidiary ledgers have several advantages:

1. They show transactions that affect one customer or one creditor in a single account. They provide up-to-date information on specific account balances.
2. They free the general ledger of excessive details. A trial balance of the general ledger does not contain vast numbers of individual customer account balances.
3. They help locate errors in individual accounts. The potential for errors is minimized by reducing the number of accounts in one ledger and by using control accounts.
4. They make possible a division of labour in posting. One employee can post to the general ledger while different employees post to the subsidiary ledgers. This strengthens internal control, since one employee verifies the work of the other.

In a computerized accounting system, the last advantage doesn't apply. Computerized accounting systems do not make errors such as calculation errors and posting errors. Other errors, such as entry errors, can and do still occur. Internal control must be done using different means in computerized systems since account transactions are posted automatically.

Special Journals

As mentioned earlier, journalizing transactions in a two-column (debit and credit) general journal is satisfactory only when there are few transactions. To help with the journalizing and posting of multiple transactions, most companies use special journals in addition to the general journal.

If a company has large numbers of similar transactions, it is useful to create a special journal for only those transactions. Examples of similar transactions that occur frequently include all sales of merchandise on account, or all cash receipts. The types of special journals a company will use depend largely on the types of transactions that occur frequently for that company.

While the form, type, and number of special journals used will vary among organizations, many merchandising companies use the journals shown in Illustration C-2 to record daily transactions. The letters that appear in parentheses following the journal name represent the posting reference used for each journal.

Sales Journal (S)	Cash Receipts Journal (CR)	Purchases Journal (P)	Cash Payments Journal (CP)	General Journal (J)
All sales of merchandise on account	All cash received (including cash sales)	All purchases of merchandise on account	All cash paid (including cash purchases of merchandise)	Transactions that cannot be entered in a special journal, including correcting, adjusting, and closing entries

← **Illustration C-2**

Use of special journals and the general journal

If a transaction cannot be recorded in a special journal, it is recorded in the general journal. For example, if you have four special journals, as listed in Illustration C-2, sales returns and allowances are recorded in the general journal. Similarly, correcting, adjusting, and closing entries are recorded in the general journal. Other types of special journals may sometimes be used in certain situations. For example, when sales returns and allowances are frequent, an additional special journal may be used to record these transactions. A payroll journal is another example of a special journal. It organizes and summarizes payroll details for companies with many employees.

The use of special journals reduces the time needed for the recording and posting process. In addition, special journals permit a greater division of labour. For example, one employee may journalize all cash receipts. Another may journalize credit sales. The division of responsibilities ensures that one person does not have control over all aspects of a transaction. In this instance, recording the sale has been separated from recording the collection of cash from that sale. This may reduce the opportunity for intentional or unintentional error, and is one aspect of good internal control.

For a merchandising company, the same special journals are used whether a company uses the periodic or perpetual system to account for its inventory. The only distinction is the number of, and title for, the columns each journal uses. We will use Karns Wholesale Supply to show the use of special journals in the following sections. Karns uses a perpetual inventory system. The variations between the periodic and perpetual inventory systems are highlighted in helpful hints for your information. In addition, special journals under a periodic inventory system are shown more fully at the end of this appendix.

Sales Journal

The sales journal is used to record sales of merchandise on account. Cash sales of merchandise are entered in the cash receipts journal. Credit sales of assets other than merchandise are entered in the general journal.

Journalizing Credit Sales

Under the perpetual inventory system, each entry in the sales journal results in one entry at selling price and another entry at cost. The entry at selling price is a debit to Accounts Receivable (a control account supported by a subsidiary ledger) and a credit of an equal amount to Sales. The entry at cost is a debit to Cost of Goods Sold and a credit of an equal amount to Merchandise Inventory. Some companies also set up Merchandise Inventory as a control account supported by a subsidiary ledger.

A sales journal with two amount columns can show a sales transaction recognized at both selling price and cost on only one line. The two-column sales journal of Karns Wholesale Supply is shown in Illustration C-3, using assumed credit sales transactions.

← Illustration C-3

Sales journal—perpetual
inventory system

				Accounts Receivable Dr. Sales Cr.	Cost of Goods Sold Dr. Merchandise Inventory Cr.
Date	Account Debited	Invoice No.	Ref.		
2011					
May 3	Abbot Sisters	101		10,600	6,360
7	Babson Co.	102		11,350	7,370
14	Carson Bros.	103		7,800	5,070
19	Deli Co.	104		9,300	6,510
21	Abbot Sisters	105		15,400	10,780
24	Deli Co.	106		21,210	15,900
27	Babson Co.	107		14,570	10,200
				90,230	62,190

KARNS WHOLESALE SUPPLY
Sales Journal   S1

Helpful hint In a periodic inventory system, the sales journal would have only one column to record the sale at selling price (Accounts Receivable Dr., Sales Cr.). The cost of goods sold is not recorded. It is calculated at the end of the period.

The reference (Ref.) column is not used in journalizing. It is used in posting the sales journal, as explained in the next section. Also, note that, unlike in the general journal, an explanation is not required for each entry in a special journal. Finally, note that each invoice is prenumbered to ensure that all invoices are journalized.

If management wishes to record its sales by department, additional columns may be provided in the sales journal. For example, a department store may have columns for home furnishings, sporting goods, shoes, etc. In addition, the federal government, and practically all provinces, require that sales taxes be charged on items sold. If sales taxes are collected, it is necessary to add more credit columns to the sales journal for GST Payable and PST Payable (or HST Payable).

Posting the Sales Journal

Postings from the sales journal are made daily to the individual accounts receivable accounts in the subsidiary ledger. Posting to the general ledger is done monthly. Illustration C-4 shows both the daily postings to the accounts receivable subsidiary ledger and the monthly postings to the general ledger accounts. We have assumed that Karns Wholesale Supply does not maintain an inventory subsidiary ledger. However, if it did, the procedure is similar to that illustrated for the accounts receivable subsidiary ledger.

A check mark (√) is inserted in the reference posting column to indicate that the daily posting to the customer's account has been made. A check mark is used when the subsidiary ledger accounts are not individually numbered. If the subsidiary ledger accounts are numbered, the account number is used instead of the check mark in the reference posting column. At the end of the month, the column totals of the sales journal are posted to the general ledger. Here, the column totals are posted as a debit of $90,230 to Accounts Receivable (account no. 112), a credit of $90,230 to Sales (account no. 401), a debit of $62,190 to Cost of Goods Sold (account no. 505), and a credit of $62,190 to Merchandise Inventory (account no. 120). Inserting the account numbers below the column totals indicates that the postings have been made. In both the general ledger and subsidiary ledger accounts, the reference S1 indicates that the posting came from page 1 of the sales journal.

Illustration C-4 ➔

Sales journal—perpetual
inventory system

KARNS WHOLESALE SUPPLY
Sales Journal   S1

Date	Account Debited	Invoice No.	Ref.	Accts. Receivable Dr. Sales Cr.	Cost of Goods Sold Dr. Merchandise Inventory Cr.
2011					
May 3	Abbot Sisters	101	√	10,600	6,360
7	Babson Co.	102	√	11,350	7,370
14	Carson Bros.	103	√	7,800	5,070
19	Deli Co.	104	√	9,300	6,510
21	Abbot Sisters	105	√	15,400	10,780
24	Deli Co.	106	√	21,210	15,900
27	Babson Co.	107	√	14,570	10,200
				90,230	62,190
				(112)/(401)	(505)/(120)

Individual amounts are posted daily to the subsidiary ledger.

ACCOUNTS RECEIVABLE SUBSIDIARY LEDGER

Abbot Sisters

Date	Ref.	Debit	Credit	Balance
2011				
May 3	S1	10,600		10,600
21	S1	15,400		26,000

Babson Co.

Date	Ref.	Debit	Credit	Balance
2011				
May 7	S1	11,350		11,350
27	S1	14,570		25,920

Carson Bros.

Date	Ref.	Debit	Credit	Balance
2011				
May 14	S1	7,800		7,800

Deli Co.

Date	Ref.	Debit	Credit	Balance
2011				
May 19	S1	9,300		9,300
24	S1	21,210		30,510

Totals are posted at the end of the accounting period to the general ledger.

GENERAL LEDGER

Accounts Receivable   No. 112

Date	Ref.	Debit	Credit	Balance
2011				
May 31	S1	90,230		90,230

Merchandise Inventory   No. 120

Date	Ref.	Debit	Credit	Balance
2011				
May 31	S1		62,190	62,190cr[1]

Sales   No. 401

Date	Ref.	Debit	Credit	Balance
2011				
May 31	S1		90,230	90,230

Cost of Goods Sold   No. 505

Date	Ref.	Debit	Credit	Balance
2011				
May 31	S1	62,190		62,190

The subsidiary ledger is separate from the general ledger.

Accounts Receivable is a control account.

[1] The normal balance for Merchandise Inventory is a debit. But, because of the sequence in which we have posted the special journals, with the sales journal first, the credits to Merchandise Inventory are posted before the debits. This posting sequence explains the credit balance in Merchandise Inventory, which exists only until the other journals are posted.

Proving the Ledgers

The next step is to "prove" the ledgers. To do so, we must determine two things: (1) The sum of the subsidiary ledger balances must equal the balance in the control account. (2) The total of the general ledger debit balances must equal the total of the general ledger credit balances. The proof of the postings from the sales journal to the general and subsidiary ledgers follows:

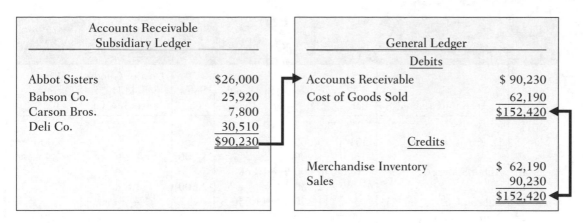

Advantages of the Sales Journal

The use of a special journal to record sales on account has a number of advantages. First, the one-line–two-column entry for each sales transaction saves time. In the sales journal, it is not necessary to write out the four account titles for the two transactions. Second, only totals, rather than individual entries, are posted to the general ledger. This saves posting time and reduces the possibility of errors in posting. Third, the prenumbering of sales invoices helps to ensure that all sales are recorded and that no sale is recorded more than once. Finally, a division of labour results, because the individual responsible for the sales journal does not have to take responsibility for other journals, such as cash receipts. These last two advantages help internal control.

Cash Receipts Journal

All receipts of cash are recorded in the cash receipts journal. The most common types of cash receipts are cash sales of merchandise and collections of accounts receivable. Many other possibilities exist, such as a receipt of money from a bank loan and cash proceeds from disposals of equipment. A one- or two-column cash receipts journal would not have enough space for all possible cash receipt transactions. A multiple-column cash receipts journal is therefore used.

Generally, a cash receipts journal includes the following columns: a debit column for cash, and credit columns for accounts receivable, sales, and other accounts. The Other Accounts column is used when the cash receipt does not involve a cash sale or a collection of accounts receivable. Under a perpetual inventory system, each sales entry is accompanied by another entry that debits Cost of Goods Sold and credits Merchandise Inventory. A separate column is added for this purpose. A five-column cash receipts journal is shown in Illustration C-5.

Additional credit columns may be used if they significantly reduce postings to a specific account. For example, cash receipts from cash sales normally include the collection of sales taxes, which are later remitted to the federal and provincial governments. Most cash receipts journals have a separate credit column for sales tax collections. Other examples include the cash receipts of a loan company, such as Household Financial Centre, which cover thousands of collections from customers. These collections are credited to Loans Receivable and Interest Revenue. A significant saving in posting time would result from using separate credit columns for Loans Receivable and Interest Revenue, rather than using the Other Accounts credit column. In contrast, a retailer that has only one interest collection a month would not find it useful to have a separate column for Interest Revenue.

Illustration C-5 →

Cash receipts journal—
perpetual inventory system

Helpful hint In a periodic inventory system, the Cash Receipts journal would have one column fewer. The Cost of Goods Sold Dr. and Merchandise Inventory Cr. would not be recorded.

KARNS WHOLESALE SUPPLY
Cash Receipts Journal

CR1

Date	Account Credited	Ref.	Cash Dr.	Accounts Receivable Cr.	Sales Cr.	Cost of Goods Sold Dr. Mdse. Inv. Cr.	Other Accounts Cr.
2011							
May 1	D. Karns, Capital	301	5,000				5,000
7			1,900		1,900	1,240	
10	Abbot Sisters	√	10,600	10,600			
12			2,600		2,600	1,690	
17	Babson Co.	√	11,350	11,350			
22	Notes Payable	200	6,000				6,000
23	Carson Bros.	√	7,800	7,800			
28	Deli Co.	√	9,300	9,300			
			54,550	39,050	4,500	2,930	11,000
			(101)	(112)	(401)	(505)/(120)	(X)

Individual amounts are posted daily to the subsidiary ledger.

Totals are posted at the end of the accounting period to the general ledger.

ACCOUNTS RECEIVABLE SUBSIDIARY LEDGER

Abbot Sisters

Date	Ref.	Debit	Credit	Balance
2011				
May 3	S1	10,600		10,600
10	CR1		10,600	0
21	S1	15,400		15,400

Babson Co.

Date	Ref.	Debit	Credit	Balance
2011				
May 7	S1	11,350		11,350
17	CR1		11,350	0
27	S1	14,570		14,570

Carson Bros.

Date	Ref.	Debit	Credit	Balance
2011				
May 14	S1	7,800		7,800
23	CR1		7,800	0

Deli Co.

Date	Ref.	Debit	Credit	Balance
2011				
May 19	S1	9,300		9,300
24	S1	21,210		30,510
28	CR1		9,300	21,210

The subsidiary ledger is separate from the general ledger.

Accounts Receivable is a control account.

GENERAL LEDGER

Cash   No. 101

Date	Ref.	Debit	Credit	Balance
2011				
May 31	CR1	54,550		54,550

Accounts Receivable   No. 112

Date	Ref.	Debit	Credit	Balance
2011				
May 31	S1	90,230		90,230
31	CR1		39,050	51,180

Merchandise Inventory   No. 120

Date	Ref.	Debit	Credit	Balance
2011				
May 31	S1		62,190	62,190Cr.
31	CR1		2,930	65,120Cr.

Notes Payable   No. 200

Date	Ref.	Debit	Credit	Balance
2011				
May 22	CR1		6,000	6,000

D. Karns, Capital   No. 301

Date	Ref.	Debit	Credit	Balance
2011				
May 1	CR1		5,000	5,000

Sales   No. 401

Date	Ref.	Debit	Credit	Balance
2011				
May 31	S1		90,230	90,230
31	CR1		4,500	94,730

Cost of Goods Sold   No. 505

Date	Ref.	Debit	Credit	Balance
2011				
May 31	S1	62,190		62,190
31	CR1	2,930		65,120

Journalizing Cash Receipt Transactions

To illustrate the journalizing of cash receipts transactions, we will continue with the May transactions of Karns Wholesale Supply. Collections from customers are for the entries recorded in the sales journal in Illustration C-3. The entries in the cash receipts journal are based on the following cash receipts:

May 1 D. Karns makes an investment of $5,000 in the business.
     7 Cash receipts for merchandise sales total $1,900. The cost of goods sold is $1,240.
    10 A cheque for $10,600 is received from Abbot Sisters in full payment of invoice No. 101.
    12 Cash receipts for merchandise sales total $2,600. The cost of goods sold is $1,690.
    17 A cheque for $11,350 is received from Babson Co. in full payment of invoice No. 102.
    22 Cash is received by signing a 4% note for $6,000, payable September 22 to the National Bank.
    23 A cheque for $7,800 is received from Carson Bros. in full payment of invoice No. 103.
    28 A cheque for $9,300 is received from Deli Co. in full payment of invoice No. 104.

Further information about the columns in the cash receipts journal follows:

Debit Columns:

1. Cash. The amount of cash actually received in each transaction is entered in this column. The column total indicates the total cash receipts for the month. The total of this column is posted to the cash account in the general ledger.
2. Cost of Goods Sold. The Cost of Goods Sold Dr./Merchandise Inventory Cr. column is used to record the cost of the merchandise sold. (The sales column records the selling price of the merchandise.) The cost of goods sold column is similar to the one found in the sales journal. The amount debited to Cost of Goods Sold is the same amount credited to Merchandise Inventory. One column total is posted to both accounts at the end of the month.

Credit Columns:

3. Accounts Receivable. The Accounts Receivable column is used to record cash collections on account. The amount entered here is the amount to be credited to the individual customer's account.
4. Sales. The Sales column is used to record all cash sales of merchandise. Cash sales of other assets (property, plant, and equipment, for example) are not reported in this column. The total of this column is posted to the account Sales.
5. Merchandise Inventory. As noted above, the Cost of Goods Sold Dr./Merchandise Inventory Cr. column is used to record the reduction in the merchandise available for future sale. The amount credited to Merchandise Inventory is the same amount debited to Cost of Goods Sold. One column total is posted to both accounts at the end of the month.
6. Other Accounts. The Other Accounts column is used whenever the credit is not to Accounts Receivable, Sales, or Merchandise Inventory. For example, in the first entry, $5,000 is entered as a credit to D. Karns, Capital. This column is often referred to as the sundry accounts column.

In a multi-column journal, only one line is generally needed for each entry. In some cases, it is useful to add explanatory information, such as the details of the note payable, or to reference supporting documentation, such as invoice numbers if cash sales are invoiced. Note also that the Account Credited column is used to identify both general ledger and subsidiary ledger account titles. The former is shown in the May 1 entry for Karns' investment. The latter is shown in the May 10 entry for the collection from Abbot Sisters.

Debit and credit amounts for each line must be equal. When the journalizing has been completed, the amount columns are totalled. The totals are then compared to prove the equality of debits and credits in the cash receipts journal. Don't forget that the Cost of Goods Sold Dr./Merchandise Inventory Cr. column total represents both a debit and a credit amount. Totalling the columns of a journal and proving the equality of the totals is called footing (adding down) and cross-footing (adding across) a journal.

The proof of the equality of Karns' cash receipts journal is on the following page:

Debit		Credits	
Cash	$54,550	Accounts Receivable	$39,050
Cost of Goods Sold	2,930	Merchandise Inventory	2,930
	$57,480	Sales	4,500
		Other Accounts	11,000
			$57,480

Posting the Cash Receipts Journal

Posting a multi-column journal involves the following steps:

1. All column totals, except for the Other Accounts total, are posted once at the end of the month to the account title specified in the column heading, such as Cash, Accounts Receivable, Sales, Cost of Goods Sold, and Merchandise Inventory. Account numbers are entered below the column totals to show that the amounts have been posted.
2. The total of the Other Accounts column is not posted. Individual amounts that make up the Other Accounts total are posted separately to the general ledger accounts specified in the Account Credited column. See, for example, the credit posting to D. Karns, Capital. The symbol X is inserted below the total for this column to indicate that the amount has not been posted.
3. The individual amounts in a column (Accounts Receivable, in this case) are posted daily to the subsidiary ledger account name specified in the Account Credited column. See, for example, the credit posting of $10,600 to Abbot Sisters.

The abbreviation CR is used in both the subsidiary and general ledgers to identify postings from the cash receipts journal.

Proving the Ledgers

After the posting of the cash receipts journal is completed, it is necessary to prove the ledgers. As shown below, the sum of the subsidiary ledger account balances equals the control account balance. The general ledger totals are also in agreement.

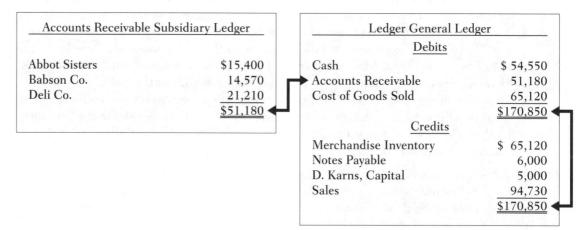

Accounts Receivable Subsidiary Ledger		Ledger General Ledger	
		Debits	
Abbot Sisters	$15,400	Cash	$ 54,550
Babson Co.	14,570	Accounts Receivable	51,180
Deli Co.	21,210	Cost of Goods Sold	65,120
	$51,180		$170,850
		Credits	
		Merchandise Inventory	$ 65,120
		Notes Payable	6,000
		D. Karns, Capital	5,000
		Sales	94,730
			$170,850

Purchases Journal

All purchases of merchandise on account are recorded in the purchases journal. Each entry in this journal results in a debit to Merchandise Inventory and a credit to Accounts Payable. When a one-column purchases journal is used, other types of purchases on account and cash purchases cannot be journalized in it. For example, credit purchases of equipment or supplies must be recorded in the general journal. Likewise, all cash purchases are entered in the cash payments journal. If there are many credit purchases for items other than merchandise, the purchases journal can be expanded to a multi-column format.

The purchases journal for Karns Wholesale Supply is shown in Illustration C-6, with assumed credit purchases.

← Illustration C-6

Purchases journal— perpetual inventory system

KARNS WHOLESALE SUPPLY
Purchases Journal   P1

Date	Account Credited	Terms	Ref.	Merchandise Inventory Dr. Accounts Payable Cr.
2011				
May 6	Jasper Manufacturing Inc.	n/20	√	11,000
10	Eaton and Howe, Inc.	n/20	√	7,200
14	Fabor and Son	n/20	√	6,900
19	Jasper Manufacturing Inc.	n/20	√	17,500
26	Fabor and Son	n/20	√	8,700
28	Eaton and Howe, Inc.	n/20	√	12,600
				63,900
				(120)/(201)

Helpful hint When a periodic inventory system is used, this journal is still known as a purchases journal. The debit to the Merchandise Inventory account is replaced by a debit to the Purchases account.

Individual amounts are posted daily to the subsidiary ledger.

Totals are posted at the end of the accounting period to the general ledger.

ACCOUNTS PAYABLE SUBSIDIARY LEDGER

Eaton and Howe, Inc.

Date	Ref.	Debit	Credit	Balance
2011				
May 10	P1		7,200	7,200
28	P1		12,600	19,800

Fabor and Son

Date	Ref.	Debit	Credit	Balance
2011				
May 14	P1		6,900	6,900
26	P1		8,700	15,600

Jasper Manufacturing Inc.

Date	Ref.	Debit	Credit	Balance
2011				
May 6	P1		11,000	11,000
19	P1		17,500	28,500

GENERAL LEDGER

Merchandise Inventory   No. 120

Date	Ref.	Debit	Credit	Balance
2011				
May 31	S1		62,190	62,190Cr.
31	CR1		2,930	65,120Cr.
31	P1	63,900		1,220Cr.

Accounts Payable   No. 201

Date	Ref.	Debit	Credit	Balance
2011				
May 30	P1		63,900	63,900

Accounts Payable is a control account.

The subsidiary ledger is separate from the general ledger.

Journalizing Credit Purchases of Merchandise

Entries in the purchases journal are made from purchase invoices. The journalizing procedure for the purchases journal is similar to that for the sales journal. In contrast to the sales journal, the purchases journal may not have an invoice number column, because invoices received from different suppliers would not be in numerical sequence.

Posting the Purchases Journal

The procedures for posting the purchases journal are similar to those for the sales journal. In this case, postings are made daily to the accounts payable subsidiary ledger accounts and monthly to the Merchandise Inventory and Accounts Payable accounts in the general ledger. In both ledgers, P1 is used in the reference column to show that the postings are from page 1 of the purchases journal.

Proof of the equality of the postings from the purchases journal to both ledgers is shown by the following:

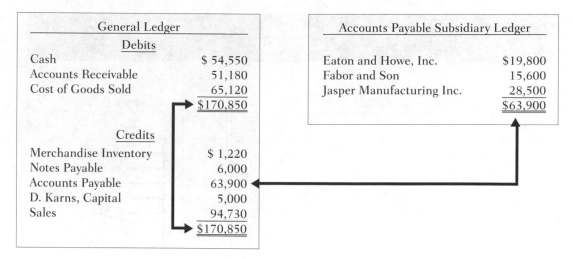

General Ledger		Accounts Payable Subsidiary Ledger	
Debits			
Cash	$ 54,550	Eaton and Howe, Inc.	$19,800
Accounts Receivable	51,180	Fabor and Son	15,600
Cost of Goods Sold	65,120	Jasper Manufacturing Inc.	28,500
	$170,850		$63,900
Credits			
Merchandise Inventory	$ 1,220		
Notes Payable	6,000		
Accounts Payable	63,900		
D. Karns, Capital	5,000		
Sales	94,730		
	$170,850		

Note that not all the general ledger accounts listed above have been included in Illustration C-6. You will have to refer to Illustration C-5 to determine the balances for the accounts Cash, Accounts Receivable, Cost of Goods Sold, Notes Payable, Capital, and Sales.

Cash Payments Journal

Alternative terminology
The cash payments journal is also called the *cash disbursements journal.*

All disbursements of cash are entered in a cash payments journal. Entries are made from pre-numbered cheques. Because cash payments are made for various purposes, the cash payments journal has multiple columns. A four-column journal is shown in Illustration C-7.

Journalizing Cash Payments Transactions

The procedures for journalizing transactions in this journal are similar to those described earlier for the cash receipts journal. Each transaction is entered on one line, and for each line there must be equal debit and credit amounts. It is common practice in the cash payments journal to record the name of the company or individual receiving the cheque (the payee), so that later reference to the cheque is possible by name in addition to cheque number. The entries in the cash payments journal shown in Illustration C-7 are based on the following transactions for Karns Wholesale Supply:

May 3	Cheque No. 101 for $1,200 issued for the annual premium on a fire insurance policy from Corporate General Insurance.	
3	Cheque No. 102 for $100 issued to CANPAR in payment of freight charges on goods purchased.	
7	Cheque No. 103 for $4,400 issued for the cash purchase of merchandise from Zwicker Corp.	
10	Cheque No. 104 for $11,000 sent to Jasper Manufacturing Inc. in full payment of the May 6 invoice.	
19	Cheque No. 105 for $7,200 mailed to Eaton and Howe, Inc., in full payment of the May 10 invoice.	
24	Cheque No. 106 for $6,900 sent to Fabor and Son in full payment of the May 14 invoice.	
28	Cheque No. 107 for $17,500 sent to Jasper Manufacturing Inc. in full payment of the May 19 invoice.	
31	Cheque No. 108 for $500 issued to D. Karns as a cash withdrawal for personal use.	

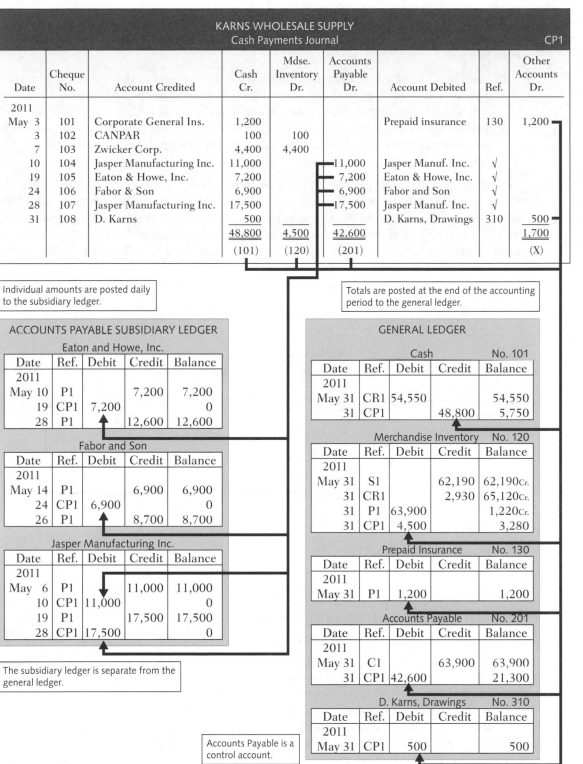

Cash payments journal—perpetual inventory system

Helpful hint In a periodic inventory system, the debits to Merchandise Inventory would be recorded to the accounts Purchases and Freight In.

Note that whenever an amount is entered in the Other Accounts column, a specific general ledger account must be identified in the Account Debited column. The entries for cheque numbers 101 and 108 show this situation. Similarly, a subsidiary account must be identified in the Account Debited column whenever an amount is entered in the Accounts Payable column (as, for example, the entry for cheque no. 104).

After the cash payments journal has been journalized, the columns are totalled. The totals are then balanced to prove the equality of debits and credits. Debits ($4,500 + $42,600 + $1,700 = $48,800) do equal credits ($48,800) in this case.

Posting the Cash Payments Journal

Helpful hint If a company has a subsidiary ledger for merchandise inventory, amounts in the merchandise inventory column would be posted daily in the cash payments journal, as well as in the sales, cash receipts, and purchases journals.

The procedures for posting the cash payments journal are similar to those for the cash receipts journal:

1. Cash and Merchandise Inventory are posted only as a total at the end of the month.
2. The amounts recorded in the Accounts Payable column are posted individually to the subsidiary ledger and in total to the general ledger control account.
3. Transactions in the Other Accounts column are posted individually to the appropriate account(s) noted in the Account Debited column. No totals are posted for the Other Accounts column.

The posting of the cash payments journal is shown in Illustration C-7. Note that the abbreviation CP is used as the posting reference. After postings are completed, the equality of the debit and credit balances in the general ledger should be determined. The control account balance should also agree with the subsidiary ledger total balance. The agreement of these balances is shown below. Note that not all the general ledger accounts have been included in Illustration C-7. You will also have to refer to Illustration C-5 to determine the balances for the Accounts Receivable, Cost of Goods Sold, Notes Payable, Capital, and Sales accounts.

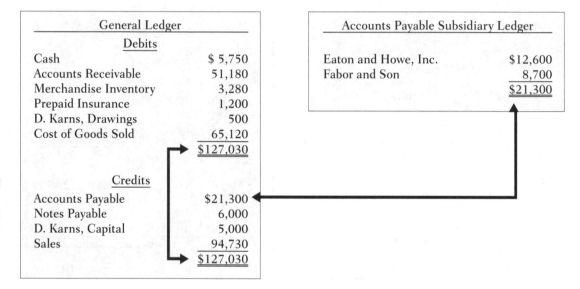

General Ledger		Accounts Payable Subsidiary Ledger	
Debits			
Cash	$ 5,750	Eaton and Howe, Inc.	$12,600
Accounts Receivable	51,180	Fabor and Son	8,700
Merchandise Inventory	3,280		$21,300
Prepaid Insurance	1,200		
D. Karns, Drawings	500		
Cost of Goods Sold	65,120		
	$127,030		
Credits			
Accounts Payable	$21,300		
Notes Payable	6,000		
D. Karns, Capital	5,000		
Sales	94,730		
	$127,030		

Effects of Special Journals on the General Journal

Special journals for sales, purchases, and cash greatly reduce the number of entries that are made in the general journal. Only transactions that cannot be entered in a special journal are recorded in the general journal. For example, the general journal may be used to record a transaction granting credit to a customer for a sales return or allowance. It may also be used to record the receipt of a credit from a supplier for purchases returned, the acceptance of a note receivable from a customer, and the purchase of equipment by issuing a note payable. Correcting, adjusting, and closing entries are also made in the general journal.

When control and subsidiary accounts are not used, the procedures for journalizing and posting transactions in the general journal are the same as those described in earlier chapters. When control and subsidiary accounts are used, two modifications of earlier procedures are required:

1. In journalizing, both the control and the subsidiary account must be identified.
2. In posting, there must be a dual posting: once to the control account and once to the subsidiary account.

To illustrate, assume that on May 31 Karns Wholesale Supply returns $500 of merchandise for credit to Fabor and Son. The entry in the general journal and the posting of the entry are shown in Illustration C-8. Note that if cash had been received instead of the credit granted on this return, then the transaction would have been recorded in the cash receipts journal.

◀ Illustration C-8

General journal

Helpful hint In a periodic inventory system, the credit would be to the Purchase Returns and Allowances account rather than to Merchandise Inventory.

KARNS WHOLESALE SUPPLY
General Journal J1

Date	Account Title and Explanation	Ref.	Debit	Credit
2011				
May 31	Accounts Payable—Fabor and Son	201/ √	500	
	Merchandise Inventory	120		500
	Received credit for returned goods.			

ACCOUNTS PAYABLE SUBSIDIARY LEDGER
Faber and Son

Date	Ref.	Debit	Credit	Balance
2011				
May 14	P1		6,900	6,900
21	CP1	6,900		0
26	P1		8,700	8,700
31	J1	500		8,200

GENERAL LEDGER

Merchandise Inventory   No. 120

Date	Ref.	Debit	Credit	Balance
2011				
May 31	S1		62,190	62,190Cr.
31	CR1		2,930	65,120Cr.
31	P1	63,900		1,220Cr.
31	CP1	4,500		3,280
31	J1		500	2,780

Accounts Payable   No. 201

Date	Ref.	Debit	Credit	Balance
2011				
May 31	C1		63,900	63,900
31	CP1	42,600		21,300
31	J1	500		20,800

Notice that in the general journal two accounts are indicated for the debit (the Accounts Payable control account and the Fabor and Son subsidiary account). Two postings (201/√) are indicated in the reference column. One amount is posted to the control account in the general ledger (no. 201) and the other to the creditor's account in the subsidiary ledger (Fabor and Son).

Special Journals in a Periodic Inventory System

Recording and posting transactions in special journals is essentially the same whether a perpetual or a periodic inventory system is used. But there are two differences. The first difference relates to the accounts Merchandise Inventory and Cost of Goods Sold in a perpetual inventory system. In this system, an additional column is required to record the cost of each sale in the sales and cash receipts journals, something which is not required in a periodic inventory system.

The second difference concerns the account titles used. In a perpetual inventory system, Merchandise Inventory and Cost of Goods Sold are used to record purchases and the cost of the merchandise sold. In a periodic inventory system, the accounts Purchases and Freight In accumulate the cost of the merchandise purchased until the end of the period. No cost of goods sold is recorded during the period. Cost of goods sold is calculated at the end of the period in a periodic inventory system.

Each of the special journals illustrated in this appendix is shown again here. Using the same transactions, we assume that Karns Wholesale Supply uses a periodic inventory system instead of a perpetual inventory system.

Illustration C-9 →

Sales journal—periodic inventory system

Helpful hint Compare this sales journal to the one presented in Illustration C-4.

							KARNS WHOLESALE SUPPLY — Sales Journal	S1

KARNS WHOLESALE SUPPLY
Sales Journal S1

Date	Account Debited	Invoice No.	Ref.	Accts Receivable Dr. Sales Cr.
2011				
May 3	Abbot Sisters	101	√	10,600
7	Babson Co.	102	√	11,350
14	Carson Bros.	103	√	7,800
19	Deli Co.	104	√	9,300
21	Abbot Sisters	105	√	15,400
24	Deli Co.	106	√	21,210
27	Babson Co.	107	√	14,570
				90,230

Illustration C-10 →

Cash receipts journal— periodic inventory system

Helpful hint Compare this cash receipts journal to the one presented in Illustration C-5.

KARNS WHOLESALE SUPPLY
Cash Receipts Journal CR1

Date	Account Credited	Ref.	Cash Dr.	Accounts Receivable Cr.	Sales Cr.	Other Accounts Cr.
2011						
May 1	D. Karns, Capital	301	5,000			5,000
7			1,900		1,900	
10	Abbot Sisters	√	10,600	10,600		
12			2,600		2,600	
17	Babson Co.	√	11,350	11,350		
22	Notes Payable	200	6,000			6,000
23	Carson Bros.	√	7,800	7,800		
28	Deli Co.	√	9,300	9,300		
			54,550	39,050	4,500	11,000

Illustration C-11 →

Purchases journal—periodic inventory system

Helpful hint Compare this purchases journal to the one presented in Illustration C-6.

KARNS WHOLESALE SUPPLY
Purchases Journal P1

Date	Account Credited	Terms	Ref.	Purchases Dr. Accounts Payable Cr.
2011				
May 6	Jasper Manufacturing Inc.	n/20	√	11,000
10	Eaton and Howe, Inc.	n/20	√	7,200
14	Fabor and Son	n/20	√	6,900
19	Jasper Manufacturing Inc.	n/20	√	17,500
26	Fabor and Son	n/20	√	8,700
28	Eaton and Howe, Inc.	n/20	√	12,600
				63,900

Illustration C-12 →

Cash payments journal— periodic inventory system

Helpful hint Compare this cash payments journal to the one presented in Illustration C-7.

KARNS WHOLESALE SUPPLY
Cash Payments Journal CP1

Date	Cheque No.	Payee	Cash Cr.	Accounts Payable Dr.	Account Debited	Ref.	Other Accounts Dr.
2011							
May 3	101	Corporate General Ins.	1,200		Prepaid Insurance	130	1,200
3	102	CANPAR	100		Freight In	516	100
7	103	Zwicker Corp.	4,400		Purchases	510	4,400
10	104	Jasper Manufacturing Inc.	11,000	11,000	Jasper Manuf. Inc.	√	
19	105	Eaton & Howe, Inc.	7,200	7,200	Eaton & Howe, Inc.	√	
24	106	Fabor and Son	6.900	6,900	Fabor and Son	√	
28	107	Jasper Manufacturing Inc.	17,500	17,500	Jasper Manuf. Inc.	√	
31	108	D. Karns	500		D. Karns, Drawings	310	500
			48,800	42,600			6,200

Brief Exercises

BEC–1 Information related to Bryan Company is presented below for its first month of operations. Calculate (a) the balances that appear in the accounts receivable subsidiary ledger for each customer, and (b) the accounts receivable balance that appears in the general ledger at the end of January.

Calculate subsidiary ledger and control account balances.

Credit Sales			Cash Collections		
Jan. 7	McNeil Co.	$800	Jan. 17	McNeil Co.	$700
15	Hanson Inc.	6,000	24	Hanson Inc.	5,000
23	Lewis Co.	9,500	29	Lewis Co.	9,500

BEC–2 Identify in which ledger (general or subsidiary) each of the following accounts is shown:

Identify general and subsidiary ledger accounts.

1. Rent Expense
2. Accounts Receivable—Chen
3. Notes Payable
4. Service Revenue
5. Wages Payable
6. Accounts Payable—Kerns
7. Merchandise Inventory
8. Sales

BEC–3 Chiasson Co. uses special journals and a general journal. Identify the journal in which each of the following transactions is recorded:

Identify special journals.

1. Paid cash for equipment purchased on account.
2. Purchased merchandise on credit.
3. Paid utility expense in cash.
4. Sold merchandise on account.
5. Granted a cash refund for a sales return.
6. Received a credit on account for a purchase return.
7. Sold merchandise for cash.
8. Purchased merchandise for cash.
9. Received a collection on account.
10. Recorded depreciation on vehicles

BEC–4 Swirsky Company uses the cash receipts and cash payments journals illustrated in this appendix for a perpetual inventory system. In October, the following selected cash transactions occurred:

Identify special journals—perpetual inventory system.

1. Made a refund to a customer for the return of damaged goods that had been purchased on credit.
2. Received payment from a customer.
3. Purchased merchandise for cash.
4. Paid a creditor.
5. Paid freight on merchandise purchased.
6. Paid cash for office equipment.
7. Received a cash refund from a supplier for merchandise returned.
8. Withdrew cash for personal use of owner.
9. Made cash sales.

Instructions

Indicate (a) the journal, and (b) the columns in the journal that should be used in recording each transaction.

BEC–5 Identify the journal and the specific column title(s) in which each of the following transactions is recorded. Assume the company uses a periodic inventory system.

Identify special journals—periodic inventory system.

1. Cash sale
2. Credit sale
3. Sales return on account
4. Cash purchase of merchandise

5. Credit purchase of merchandise
6. Payment of freight on merchandise purchased from a supplier
7. Return of merchandise purchased for cash refund
8. Payment of freight on merchandise delivered to a customer

Use general journal for closing entries.

BEC–6 Willis Company has the following year-end account balances on September 30, 2011: Service Revenue $53,800; Salaries Expense $15,400; Rent Expense $12,000; Supplies Expense $3,500; B. Willis, Capital $67,000; and B. Willis, Drawings $22,000.

Instructions

Prepare the closing entries for Willis Company.

Use general journal for adjusting entry.

BEC–7 As part of the year-end procedures, depreciation for furniture was recorded in the amount of $2,500 for Leelantna Company. Prepare the adjusting entry dated October 31, 2011, using the appropriate journal.

Exercises

Identify special journals.

EC–1 Below are some transactions for Dartmouth Company:
1. Credit received for merchandise returned to a supplier
2. Payment of employee wages
3. Revenues and expenses closed to income summary
4. Depreciation on building
5. Purchase of office supplies for cash
6. Purchase of merchandise on account
7. Purchase of equipment for cash
8. Payment on account
9. Return of merchandise sold for credit
10. Collection on account from customers
11. Sale of land for cash
12. Sale of merchandise on account
13. Sale of merchandise for cash

Instructions

For each transaction, indicate whether it would normally be recorded in a cash receipts journal, cash payments journal, sales journal, purchases journal, or general journal.

Record transactions in sales and purchases journals—perpetual inventory system.

EC–2 Sing Tao Company uses special journals and a general journal. The company uses a perpetual inventory system and had the following transactions:

Sept. 2 Sold merchandise on account to T. Lu, $1,520, invoice #101, terms n/30. The cost of the merchandise sold was $960.
3 Purchased office supplies on account from Berko Co., $350.
10 Purchased merchandise on account from Lavigne Co., $800, FOB shipping point, terms n/30. Paid freight of $50 to Apex Shippers.
11 Returned unsatisfactory merchandise to Lavigne Co., $200, for credit on account.
12 Purchased office equipment on account from Wells Co., $8,000.
16 Sold merchandise for cash to L. Maille, for $800. The cost of the merchandise sold was $480.
18 Purchased merchandise for cash from Lavigne Co., $450, FOB destination.
20 Accepted returned merchandise from customer L. Maille, $800 (see Sept. 16 transaction). Gave full cash refund. Restored the merchandise to inventory.

Sept. 24 Paid the correct amount owing for the merchandise purchased from Lavigne earlier in the month.

25 Received payment from T. Lu for Sept. 2 sale.

26 Sold merchandise on account to M. Christie, $890, invoice #102, terms n/30, FOB destination. The cost of the merchandise was $520. The appropriate party paid $75 to Freight Co. for shipping charges.

30 Paid September salaries, $2,800.

30 Withdrew cash for owner's personal use, $800.

30 Paid for office supplies purchased on September 3.

Instructions

(a) Draw a sales journal and a purchases journal (see Illustrations C-3 and C-6). Use page 1 for each journal.

(b) Record the transaction(s) for September that should be recorded in the sales journal.

(c) Record the transaction(s) for September that should be recorded in the purchases journal.

EC–3   Refer to the information provided for Sing Tao Company in EC–2.

Record transactions in cash receipts, cash payments, and general journals—perpetual inventory system.

Instructions

(a) Draw cash receipts and cash payments journals (see Illustrations C-5 and C-7) and a general journal. Use page 1 for each journal.

(b) Record the transaction(s) provided in EC–2 that should be recorded in the cash receipts journal.

(c) Record the transaction(s) provided in EC–2 that should be recorded in the cash payments journal.

(d) Record the transaction(s) provided in EC–2 that should be recorded in the general journal.

EC–4   Narang Company has the following selected transactions during March:

Record transactions in general journal and explain posting.

Mar. 2 Purchased equipment on account, costing $7,400, from Lifetime Inc.

5 Received credit memorandum for $300 from Lyden Company for merchandise returned that had been damaged in shipment to Narang.

7 Issued a credit memorandum for $400 to Marco Presti for merchandise the customer returned. The returned merchandise has a cost of $275 and was restored to inventory.

Narang Company uses a purchases journal, a sales journal, two cash journals (receipts and payments), and a general journal. Narang also uses a perpetual inventory system.

Instructions

(a) Record the appropriate transactions in the general journal.

(b) In a brief memo to the president of Narang Company, explain the postings to the control and subsidiary accounts.

EC–5   Maureen Company uses both special journals and a general journal. On April 30, after all monthly postings had been completed, the Accounts Receivable control account in the general ledger had a debit balance of $320,000, and the Accounts Payable control account had a credit balance of $87,000.

Determine control account balances and explain posting.

The May transactions recorded in the special journals are summarized below. Maureen Company maintains a perpetual inventory system. No entries that affected accounts receivable and accounts payable were recorded in the general journal for May.

Sales journal: total sales, $161,400; cost of goods sold, $112,800
Purchases journal: total purchases, $56,400
Cash receipts journal: accounts receivable column total, $141,000
Cash payments journal: accounts payable column total, $47,500

Instructions

(a) What is the balance of the Accounts Receivable control account after the monthly postings on May 31?

(b) What is the balance of the Accounts Payable control account after the monthly postings on May 31?

(c) To what accounts are the column totals for total sales of $161,400 and cost of goods sold of $112,800 in the sales journal posted?

(d) To what account(s) is the accounts receivable column total of $141,000 in the cash receipts journal posted?

Record transactions in sales and purchases journals—periodic inventory system.

EC–6 Refer to the information provided for Sing Tao Company in EC–2. Complete instructions (a), (b), and (c), assuming that the company uses a periodic inventory system instead of a perpetual inventory system.

Post journals to control and subsidiary accounts.

EC–7 On September 1, the balance of the Accounts Receivable control account in the general ledger of Pirie Company was $10,960. The customers' subsidiary ledger contained account balances as follows: Jana, $2,440; Kingston, $2,640; Cavanaugh, $2,060; Zhang, $3,820. At the end of September, the various journals contained the following information:

Sales journal: Sales to Zhang, $800; to Jana, $1,260; to Iman, $1,030; to Cavanaugh, $1,100. The cost of each sale, respectively, was $480, $810, $620, and $660.

Cash receipts journal: Cash received from Cavanaugh, $1,310; from Zhang, $2,300; from Iman, $380; from Kingston, $1,800; from Jana, $1,240.

General journal: A $190 sales allowance is granted to Zhang, on September 30.

Instructions

(a) Set up control and subsidiary accounts, and enter the beginning balances.

(b) Post the various journals to the control and subsidiary accounts. Post the items as individual items or as totals, whichever would be the appropriate procedure. Use page 1 for each journal.

(c) Prepare a list of customers and prove the agreement of the control account with the subsidiary ledger at September 30.

Record transactions in cash receipts, cash payments, and general journals—periodic inventory system.

EC–8 Refer to the information provided for Sing Tao Company in EC–3. Complete instructions (a) to (d), assuming that the company uses a periodic inventory system instead of a perpetual inventory system.

Problems

Record transactions in special and general journals—perpetual inventory system.

PC–1 Selected accounts from the chart of accounts of Genstar Company are shown below:

101	Cash	201	Accounts payable
112	Accounts receivable	401	Sales
120	Merchandise inventory	412	Sales returns and allowances
126	Supplies	505	Cost of goods sold
157	Equipment	726	Salaries expense

The company uses a perpetual inventory system. The cost of all merchandise sold is 60% of the sales price. During January, Genstar completed the following transactions:

Jan. 3 Purchased merchandise on account from Sun Distributors, $9,800.

4 Purchased supplies for cash, $280.

4 Sold merchandise on account to R. Hu, $6,500, invoice no. 371.

5 Returned $450 of damaged goods to Sun Distributors.

6 Made cash sales for the week totalling $4,650.

8 Purchased merchandise on account from Irvine Co., $5,400.

Jan. 9 Sold merchandise on account to Mays Corp., $5,600, invoice no. 372.
11 Purchased merchandise on account from Chaparal Co., $4,300.
13 Paid Sun Distributors account in full.
13 Made cash sales for the week totalling $5,290.
15 Received payment from Mays Corp. for invoice no. 372.
15 Paid semi-monthly salaries of $14,300 to employees.
17 Received payment from R. Hu for invoice no. 371.
17 Sold merchandise on account to AMB Co., $1,500, invoice no. 373.
19 Purchased equipment on account from Johnson Corp., $4,800.
20 Cash sales for the week totalled $3,400.
20 Paid Irvine Co. account in full.
23 Purchased merchandise on account from Sun Distributors, $7,800.
24 Purchased merchandise on account from Levine Corp., $4,690.
27 Made cash sales for the week totalling $3,370.
30 Received payment from AMB Co. for invoice no. 373.
31 Paid semi-monthly salaries of $13,200 to employees.
31 Sold merchandise on account to R. Hu, $9,330, invoice no. 374.

Genstar Company uses a sales journal, a purchases journal, a cash receipts journal, a cash payments journal, and a general journal.

Instructions

(a) Record the January transactions in the appropriate journal.
(b) Foot and cross-foot all special journals.
(c) Show how postings would be made by placing ledger account numbers and check marks as needed in the journals. (Actual posting to ledger accounts is not required.)

PC–2 Selected accounts from the chart of accounts of Tigau Company are shown below:

Record transactions in special and general journals— perpetual inventory system.

101 Cash	145 Buildings
112 Accounts receivable	201 Accounts payable
120 Merchandise inventory	401 Sales
126 Supplies	505 Cost of goods sold
140 Land	610 Advertising expense

The company uses a perpetual inventory system. The cost of all merchandise sold was 65% of the sales price. During October, Tigau Company completed the following transactions:

Oct. 2 Purchased merchandise on account from Madison Co., $5,800.
4 Sold merchandise on account to Petro Corp., $8,600, invoice no. 204.
5 Purchased supplies for cash, $315.
7 Made cash sales for the week that totalled $9,610.
9 Paid the Madison Co. account in full.
10 Purchased merchandise on account from Quinn Corp., $4,900.
12 Received payment from Petro Corp. for invoice no. 204.
13 Issued a debit memorandum to Quinn Corp. and returned $260 of damaged goods.
14 Made cash sales for the week that totalled $8,810.
16 Sold a parcel of land for $45,000 cash, the land's book value.
17 Sold merchandise on account to Martin Co., $5,530, invoice no. 205.
18 Purchased merchandise for cash, $2,215.
21 Made cash sales for the week that totalled $8,640.
23 Paid in full the Quinn Corp. account for the goods kept.
25 Purchased supplies on account from Frey Co., $260.
25 Sold merchandise on account to Golden Corp., $5,520, invoice no. 206.
25 Received payment from Martin Co. for invoice no. 205.
26 Purchased for cash a small parcel of land and a building on the land to use as a storage facility. The total cost of $45,000 was allocated $26,000 to the land and $19,000 to the building.

Oct. 27 Purchased merchandise on account from Schmid Co., $9,000.
    28 Made cash sales for the week that totalled $9,320.
    30 Purchased merchandise on account from Madison Co., $16,200.
    30 Paid advertising bill for the month from The Gazette, $600.
    30 Sold merchandise on account to Martin Co., $5,200, invoice no. 207.

Tigau Company uses a sales journal, purchases journal, cash receipts journal, cash payments journal, and general journal.

Instructions

(a) Record the October transactions in the appropriate journals.
(b) Foot and cross-foot all special journals.
(c) Show how postings would be made by placing ledger account numbers and check marks as needed in the journals. (Actual posting to ledger accounts is not required.)

Record transactions in special and general journals—perpetual inventory system.

PC–3 The post-closing trial balance for Gibbs Music Co. follows:

GIBBS MUSIC CO. Post-Closing Trial Balance December 31, 2010		
	Debit	Credit
101 Cash	$ 49,500	
112 Accounts receivable	15,000	
115 Notes receivable	45,000	
120 Merchandise inventory	22,000	
140 Land	25,000	
145 Building	75,000	
146 Accumulated depreciation—building		$ 18,000
157 Equipment	6,450	
158 Accumulated depreciation—equipment		1,500
200 Notes payable		–
201 Accounts payable		42,000
275 Mortgage payable		82,000
301 M. Gibbs, capital		94,450
310 M. Gibbs, drawings	–	
401 Sales	–	
410 Sales returns and allowances	–	
505 Cost of goods sold	–	
725 Salaries expense	–	
920 Loss—damaged inventory	–	
	$237,950	$237,950

The subsidiary ledgers contain the following information:
1. Accounts Receivable—R. Goge, $3,000; B. Zerrs, $7,500; S. Armstrong, $4,500
2. Accounts Payable—Fieldstone Corp., $9,000; Watson & Co., $17,000; Harms Distributors, $16,000

Gibbs Music Co. uses a perpetual inventory system. The transactions for January 2011 are as follows:
Jan. 3 Sold merchandise to B. Rohl, $1,000. The cost of goods sold was $550.
     5 Purchased merchandise from Warren Parts, $2,400.
     7 Received a cheque from S. Armstrong, $3,000, in partial payment of its account.
    11 Paid freight on merchandise purchased, $350.
    13 Received payment of account in full from B. Rohl.
    14 Issued a credit memo to acknowledge receipt of $600 of damaged merchandise returned by R. Goge. The cost of the returned merchandise was $250. (*Hint:* Debit Loss—Damaged Inventory instead of Merchandise Inventory.)

Jan. 15 Sent Harms Distributors a cheque in full payment of account.
     17 Purchased merchandise from Lapeska Co., $1,900.
     18 Paid salaries of $3,700.
     20 Gave Watson & Co. a 60-day note for $17,000 in full payment of account payable.
     23 Total cash sales amounted to $8,200. The cost of goods sold was $3,840.
     24 Sold merchandise on account to B. Zerrs, $7,800. The cost of goods sold was $3,300.
     27 Sent Warren Parts a cheque for $950 in partial payment of the account.
     29 Received payment on a note of $35,000 from S. Lava.
     30 Returned merchandise costing $600 to Lapeska Co. for credit.
     31 Withdrew $1,800 cash for personal use.

Instructions

(a) Open general and subsidiary ledger accounts and record December 31, 2010, balances.
(b) Record the January transactions in a sales journal, a purchases journal, a cash receipts journal, a cash payments journal, and a general journal, as illustrated in this appendix.
(c) Post the appropriate amounts to the subsidiary and general ledger accounts.
(d) Prepare a trial balance at January 31, 2011.
(e) Determine whether the subsidiary ledgers agree with control accounts in the general ledger.

PC–4 The post-closing trial balance for Lee Co. follows:

Record transactions in special and general journals, post, and prepare trial balance—perpetual inventory system.

LEE CO.
Post-Closing Trial Balance
April 30, 2011

		Debit	Credit
101	Cash	$ 36,700	
112	Accounts receivable	15,400	
115	Notes receivable—Cole Company	48,000	
120	Merchandise inventory	22,000	
157	Equipment	8,200	
158	Accumulated depreciation—equipment		$ 1,800
200	Notes payable	–	
201	Accounts payable		43,400
301	C. Lee, capital		85,100
310	C. Lee, drawings	–	
401	Sales		–
410	Sales returns and allowances	–	
505	Cost of goods sold	–	
725	Salaries expense	–	
730	Rent expense	–	
		$130,300	$130,300

The subsidiary ledgers contain the following information:

1. Accounts Receivable—W. Karasch, $3,250; L. Cellars, $7,400; G. Parrish, $4,750
2. Accounts Payable—Winterware Corp., $10,500; Cobalt Sports, $15,500; Buttercup Distributors, $17,400

Lee uses a perpetual inventory system. The transactions for May 2011 are as follows:

May 3 Sold merchandise to B. Simone, $2,400. The cost of the goods sold was $1,050.
      5 Purchased merchandise from WN Widgit, $2,600, on account.
      7 Received a cheque from G. Parrish, $2,800, in partial payment of account.
     11 Paid freight on merchandise purchased, $318.
     12 Paid rent of $1,500 for May.
     13 Received payment in full from B. Simone.
     14 Issued a credit memo to acknowledge $750 of merchandise returned by W. Karasch. The merchandise (original cost, $325) was restored to inventory.

May 15 Sent Buttercup Distributors a cheque in full payment of account.
 17 Purchased merchandise from Lancio Co., $2,100, on account.
 18 Paid salaries of $4,700.
 20 Gave Cobalt Sports a two-month, 10% note for $15,500 in full payment of account payable.
 20 Returned merchandise costing $510 to Lancio for credit.
 23 Total cash sales amounted to $9,500. The cost of goods sold was $4,450.
 27 Sent WN Widgit a cheque for $1,000, in partial payment of account.
 29 Received payment on a note of $40,000 from Cole Company.
 31 C. Lee withdrew $1,000 cash for personal use.

Instructions

(a) Open general and subsidiary ledger accounts and record April 30, 2011, balances.
(b) Record the May transactions in a sales journal, a purchases journal, a cash receipts journal, a cash payments journal, and a general journal, as illustrated in this chapter.
(c) Post the appropriate amounts to the subsidiary and general ledger accounts.
(d) Prepare a trial balance at May 31, 2011.
(e) Determine whether the subsidiary ledgers agree with the control accounts in the general ledger.

Record transactions in special and general journals—periodic inventory system.

PC–5 Selected accounts from the chart of accounts on Weir Company are shown below:

101	Cash	401	Sales
112	Accounts receivable	412	Sales returns and allowances
126	Supplies	510	Purchases
157	Equipment	512	Purchase returns and allowances
201	Accounts payable	726	Salaries expense

During February, Weir completed the following transactions:

Feb. 3 Purchased merchandise on account from Zears Co., $9,200.
 4 Purchased supplies for cash, $290.
 4 Sold merchandise on account to Gilles Co., $7,220, invoice no. 371.
 5 Issued a debit memorandum to Zears Co. and returned $450 worth of goods.
 6 Made cash sales for the week totalling $3,950.
 8 Purchased merchandise on account from Fell Electronics, $5,200,
 9 Sold merchandise on account to Mawani Corp., $7,050, invoice no. 372.
 11 Purchased merchandise on account from Thomas Co., $3,100.
 13 Paid Zears Co. account in full.
 13 Made cash sales for the week totalling $4,850.
 15 Received payment from Mawani Corp. for invoice no. 372.
 15 Paid semi-monthly salaries of $14,700 to employees.
 17 Received payment from Gilles Co. for invoice no. 371.
 17 Sold merchandise on account to Lumber Co., $1,600, invoice no. 373.
 19 Purchased equipment on account from Brown Corp., $6,400.
 20 Cash sales for the week totalled $4,900.
 20 Paid Fell Electronics account in full.
 23 Purchased merchandise on account from Zears Co., $8,800.
 24 Purchased merchandise on account from Lewis Co., $5,130.
 27 Made cash sales for the week totalling $3,560.
 28 Received payment from Lumber Co. for invoice no. 373.
 28 Paid semi-monthly salaries of $14,900 to employees.
 28 Sold merchandise on account to Gilles Co., $9,810, invoice no. 374.

Weir Company uses a sales journal, purchases journal, cash receipts journal, cash payments journal, and general journal. Weir uses a periodic inventory system.

Instructions

(a) Record the February transactions in the appropriate journal.

(b) Foot and cross-foot all special journals.

(c) Show how postings would be made by placing ledger account numbers and check marks as needed in the journals. (Actual posting to ledger accounts is not required.)

Cumulative Coverage—
Chapters 2 to 6 and Appendix C

LeBrun Company has the following opening account balances in its general and subsidiary ledgers on January 1. All accounts have normal debit and credit balances. LeBrun uses a perpetual inventory system. The cost of all merchandise sold was 40% of the sales price.

GENERAL LEDGER

Account No.	Account Title	January 1 Opening Balance
101	Cash	$ 35,050
112	Accounts receivable	14,000
115	Notes receivable	39,000
120	Merchandise inventory	20,000
125	Office supplies	1,000
130	Prepaid insurance	2,000
140	Land	50,000
145	Building	100,000
146	Accumulated depreciation—building	25,000
157	Equipment	6,450
158	Accumulated depreciation—equipment	1,500
201	Accounts payable	36,000
275	Mortgage payable	125,000
301	A. LeBrun, capital	80,000

Accounts Receivable Subsidiary Ledger			Accounts Payable Subsidiary Ledger	
Customer	January 1 Opening Balance		Creditor	January 1 Opening Balance
R. Draves	$1,500		Liazuk Co.	$10,000
B. Jacovetti	7,500		Mikush Bros.	15,000
S. Kysely	5,000		Nguyen & Son	11,000

LeBrun's January transactions follow:

Jan. 3 Sold merchandise on credit to B. Sota $3,100, invoice no. 510, and J. Ebel $1,800, invoice no. 511.

     5 Purchased merchandise on account from Welz Wares for $3,000 and Laux Supplies for $2,700.

     7 Received cheques for $5,000 from S. Kysely and $2,000 from B. Jacovetti on accounts.

     8 Paid freight on merchandise purchased, $180.

     9 Sent cheques to Liazuk Co. for $10,000 and Nguyen & Son for $11,000 in full payment of accounts.

     9 Issued credit memo for $400 to J. Ebel for merchandise returned. The merchandise was restored to inventory.

    10 Summary cash sales totalled $16,500.

Jan. 11 Sold merchandise on credit to R. Draves for $1,900, invoice no. 512, and to S. Kysely for $900, invoice no. 513.

15 Withdrew $2,000 cash for A. LeBrun's personal use.

16 Purchased merchandise on account from Nguyen & Son for $15,000, from Liazuk Co. for $13,900, and from Welz Wares for $1,500.

17 Paid $400 cash for office supplies.

18 Returned $500 of merchandise to Liazuk and received credit.

20 Summary cash sales totalled $17,500.

21 Issued $15,000 note to Mikush Bros. in payment of balance due. The note bears an interest rate of 10% and is due in three months.

21 Received payment in full from S. Kysely.

22 Sold merchandise on credit to B. Soto for $1,700, invoice no. 514, and to R. Draves for $800, invoice no. 515.

23 Sent cheques to Nguyen & Son and Liazuk Co. in full payment of accounts.

25 Sold merchandise on credit to B. Jacovetti for $3,500, invoice no. 516, and to J. Ebel for $6,100, invoice no. 517.

27 Purchased merchandise on account from Nguyen & Son for $14,500, from Laux Supplies for $1,200, and from Welz Wares for $2,800.

28 Paid $800 cash for office supplies.

31 Summary cash sales totalled $19,920.

31 Paid sales salaries of $4,300 and office salaries of $2,600.

31 Received payment in full from B. Soto and J. Ebel on account.

In addition to the accounts identified in the trial balance, the chart of accounts shows the following: No. 200 Notes Payable, No. 230 Interest Payable, No. 300 Income Summary, No. 310 A. LeBrun, Drawings, No. 401 Sales, No. 410 Sales Returns and Allowances, No. 505 Cost of Goods Sold, No. 711 Depreciation Expense, No. 718 Interest Expense, No. 722 Insurance Expense, No. 725 Salaries Expense, and No. 728 Office Supplies Expense.

Instructions

(a) Record the January transactions in the appropriate journal—sales, purchases, cash receipts, cash payments, and general.

(b) Post the journals to the general and subsidiary ledgers. New accounts should be added and numbered in an orderly fashion as needed.

(c) Prepare an unadjusted trial balance at January 31, 2011. Determine whether the subsidiary ledgers agree with the control accounts in the general ledger.

(d) Prepare adjusting journal entries. Prepare an adjusted trial balance, using the following additional information:

1. Office supplies at January 31 total $700.
2. Insurance coverage expires on September 30, 2011.
3. Annual depreciation on the building is $6,000 and on the equipment is $1,500.
4. Interest of $45 has accrued on the note payable.
5. A physical count of merchandise inventory has found $44,850 of goods on hand.

(e) Prepare a multiple-step income statement and a statement of owner's equity for January, and a classified balance sheet at the end of January.

(f) Prepare and post the closing entries.

(g) Prepare a post-closing trial balance.

Company Index

Subject Index

Photo Credits

All images are copyright © iStockphoto unless otherwise noted.

Logos are registered trademarks of the respective companies and are reprinted with permission.

Chapter 1 Opener: Courtesy The Forzani Group Ltd.; Page 4: Courtesy Great Little Box Company. **Chapter 2** Opener: Courtesy Prestige Dance Academy; Page 69: Courtesy Goodyear Tire and Rubber Company. **Chapter 3** Opener: Courtesy Seneca College of Applied Arts and Technology; Page 124: PhotoDisc/Getty Images. **Chapter 4** Opener: Courtesy Moulé. Page 190: The Canadian Press/Adrian Wyld. **Chapter 5** Opener: Courtesy The Forzani Group Ltd.; Page 257: Courtesy Liquidation World. **Chapter 6** Opener: Courtesy The Forzani Group Ltd. **Chapter 7** Opener: Courtesy Barrett & Mackay Photography. **Chapter 8** Opener: Cindy Wilson/Telegraph-Journal. **Chapter 9** Opener: Courtesy Dawson College. **Chapter 10** Page 569: The Canadian Press/Marcos Townsend. Pages 582-583: Reproduced with permission of the Minister of Public Works and Government Services Canada, 2009. **Chapter 11** Page 619: The Canadian Press/Frank Gunn. **Chapter 12** Opener: Courtesy Bailey Altrogge Matchett LLP; Page 667: Courtesy Assiniboia Capital Corporation. Page 691: The Canadian Press/Ben Margot. **Chapter 13** Opener: Courtesy ZENN Motor Inc.; Page 721: PhotoDisc, Inc. **Chapter 14** Opener: Courtesy Sun Life Financial; Page 789: Courtesy WestJet. **Chapter 15** Opener: Courtesy Hydro-Québec; Page 834: The Canadian Press/John Woods. **Chapter 16** Opener: Courtesy Scotiabank; Page 880: Courtesy Suncor Energy Inc. **Chapter 17** Opener: Courtesy Clearwater Foods; Page 963: The Canadian Press/Elaine Thompson. **Chapter 18** Opener: Courtesy The Canadian Institute of Chartered Accountants; Page 1015: Reproduced with Permission from Wyeth Consumer Healthcare.